Strategy:

Analysis and practice

SECOND EDITION

Strategy:

Analysis and practice

SECOND EDITION

WITHDRAWN

John McGee, Howard Thomas and David Wilson

McGraw-Hill
Higher Education

London Boston Burr Ridge, IL Dubuque, IA Madison, WI New York San Francisco
St. Louis Bangkok Bogotá Caracas Kuala Lumpur Lisbon Madrid Mexico City
Milan Montreal New Delhi Santiago Seoul Singapore Sydney Taipei Toronto

Strategy: Analysis and Practice, 2nd Edition
John McGee, Howard Thomas and David Wilson
ISBN-13 978-0-07-712691-9
ISBN-10 0-07-712691-2

**McGraw-Hill
Higher Education**

Published by McGraw-Hill Education
Shoppenhangers Road
Maidenhead
Berkshire
SL6 2QL
Telephone: 44 (0) 1628 502 500
Fax: 44 (0) 1628 770 224
Website: www.mcgraw-hill.co.uk

British Library Cataloguing in Publication Data
A catalogue record for this book is available from the British Library

Library of Congress Cataloguing in Publication Data
The Library of Congress data for this book has been applied for from the Library of Congress

Acquisitions Editor: Leiah Batchelor
Development Editor: Tom Hill
Marketing Manager: Alice Duijser
Senior Production Editor: James Bishop

Cover design by Adam Renvoize
Printed and bound in Spain by Grafo

Dedication

To our colleagues and students, past and present, who have shaped our thinking and to Jenny, Lynne and Jo, who have always inspired us.

Brief Table of Contents

Detailed Table of Contents

Preface

The first edition of this book in 2005 deliberately took a broad and eclectic approach to strategy. We tried to avoid sharp critique of particular perspectives and, instead, attempted to be more holistic, looking for complementarities between paradigms; integration of perspectives where possible; a general avoidance of schools of thought and assumptions of paradigm incommensurability. In this second edition, we have tried to continue and develop this approach but with greater and hopefully a sharper focus than previously. As a result, there have been some significant changes along the way. Changes which, we hope, will have resulted in a more focused and accessible text and one which will usefully support and inform teachers, students and practitioners of strategy alike.

The book has been reduced in length from 21 chapters in the first edition to 16. We have, however, retained the overall logic of the various sections of the book which were laid out in the first edition. The Introduction provides the reader with the basic concepts of strategy and introduces the systemic model to convey both the complexity of strategy as well as how analysis and practice are interrelated and linked. The model may look complex at first sight, but the rest of the book is largely guided by the model, so readers can dip into various parts of the text and, at the same time, refer back to the model to see where their focus fits in the grand scheme of things. Feedback from the first edition indicated that the model was seen as useful by some readers and as unduly complex by others. On balance, we decided to keep the model as an orientating device. In this way, readers can emphasise as much, or as little, as they feel appropriate in the ways they interrogate and teach the subject. A major simplification of this second edition has been to reduce the sections of the book into two main parts.

Part One introduces the concepts and tools of strategy analysis. Here we introduce some of the basic economic and positioning concepts and models of strategy analysis. The overriding concern of each chapter is to help readers see how to apply the various models introduced (e.g. the value chain, or macroeconomic theory). Part One also emphasises that one of the key differences between economics and strategy lies in the assumption of perfect knowledge by the economist and having to deal with often very imperfect knowledge in the domain of the strategist. In the latter case, exploiting advantage and gaining position are key for organizations to become and remain successful. We recognise, however, that many educational institutions have parallel courses to strategy (such as economics and global business). While we have included two separate chapters in this part of the book to cover macroeconomics and global strategies, they can easily be omitted from any strategy course where economics and globalization are taught separately. A further feature of the book (and in particular Part One) is not only to introduce the many models of strategy analysis so that students can become familiar with them and their use, but also to highlight the limitations of such models and thus avoid oversimplistic thinking.

Part Two comprises chapters which focus on strategy implementation and practice. From this perspective, questions of organizational structures, cultures and processes become the focus of attention. To help the transition from analytical models to organizational thinking, there is a brand new chapter (Chapter 10) which deals with organization and strategy. The point here is to emphasize that strategy can be seen both as a behavioural set of processes and as a function of organizational structures and cultures. We hope this new, linking, chapter helps the transition of the argument from analysis to practice. We have retained and expanded the chapter on risk which we view as an inherent part of practice and which is an area skimmed over, or often missing completely, from many strategy texts. This section also retains chapters from the first edition on governance and performance but both are substantially rewritten. In particular, the chapter on governance has substantially greater coverage of international aspects of governance (as opposed to the first edition's focus primarily on UK governance models and processes). The chapter on performance now is an amalgamation of two previous chapters from the first edition and is, we hope, an appropriate and accessible finale for any strategy text. Taking the balanced scorecard as its central leitmotiv, this chapter completes the circle around the systemic model introduced in the first chapters of the book. More behavioural approaches are contained in chapters on decision making, strategic change and innovation and learning. We feel these are an integral part of strategy and we try to maintain the perspective of introducing the models (and the jargon) as well as turning a critical eye towards their limitations. This sometimes means introducing the reader to complex perspectives, such as seeing innovation as effectively growth in a multi-dimensional space, consisting of products/services, their features and user needs for example. Hence innovation becomes a trade-off activity with competitors often blind-sided by rivals who innovate on other combinations of these factors. Decision making and change are introduced as two of the key issues any strategist (as a manager) has to face and deal with successfully. There is many a slip between cup and lip and impeccable strategic analysis can easily founder on the rocks of poor decision making, implementation and the management of change necessary during implementation.

Many end of chapter cases and in-chapter vignettes have been updated and changed to fit the substantial revisions contained in this second edition. We hope you find them useful aids and exemplars for your teaching and understanding of strategy. Although our eclectic approach to strategy may not suit all readers, we have consistently tried to avoid fads and fashions as well as schools of thought which, in our view, limit the field of inquiry. We feel this second edition is a significant improvement on the first, but we have stayed true to what we feel are the defining characteristics of the first edition:

- Strong emphasis on strategy in practice: An innovative approach which is informed by academic research but remains highly practical and 'hands on'. Dedicated chapters on risk management, managing strategic change, strategy and the learning organization, and corporate governance.

- An analytical approach to strategy: A thorough study of competitive advantage provides students with the level of analysis fundamental to understanding business and corporate level strategy.

- An understanding of the link between strategy, knowledge and technological change, and value and performance. Value and value-based management is shown as central to strategic management. Three themes are treated explicitly because they are particularly close to the core of strategic management thinking. These are (i) performance assessment; (ii) organizational knowledge, learning and value innovation; and (iii) total quality management and customer value.

- A range of contemporary and relevant cases throughout: Illustrative case examples and end of chapter cases offer insights into a variety of globally recognized companies such as Google, Yahoo!, eBay, Amazon, Fiat, Tesco, Gillette and more.

- A section of longer cases places strategy into a variety of contemporary international contexts and offers students the opportunity to analyse strategic decisions across an array of international businesses including Renault, Apple, Honda, Citigroup and Canon.

- Clear and well-developed pedagogy: An introduction to each part orients the student to the landscape of the chapters that follow. To aid learning, each chapter introduces its themes and concepts, and leads the student through the topic with key terms highlighted in bold for easy reference. Case examples contained within the chapters provide illustrations of strategy in practice within real organizations, and at the end of each chapter, a summary and assignments draw together the overarching themes and test understanding. A concluding chapter-end case study encourages the student to analyze how some of the concepts raised in the chapter can be applied within an organization. See the Guided Tour for more information.

■ An unparalleled range of supporting resources: The book is accompanied by an Online Learning Centre website, www.mcgraw-hill.co.uk/textbooks/mcgee, which provides a range of resources for lecturers and students. Lecturers will find PowerPoint presentations, lecture guides and case study notes to assist them in teaching with the textbook. The student area contains a wealth of extra resources including test questions, help with studying cases, guide answers to the end of chapter assignments questions and more. For more information see our guide to technology to enhance teaching and learning on the following pages.

Cases

Strategically placed throughout chapters you will find case boxes that explore the themes and concepts covered on the preceding pages. At the end of most chapters there is a case study which is slightly longer and draws on a key concept covered in that chapter. Where appropriate, the case boxes and case studies have questions at the end. Below is a list of all the cases.

Chapter	Case Title	Questions
1 – What is strategy? Concepts and practices	Case box 1.1: Magazines take on Amazon	✓
	Case box 1.2: How Honda became successful	✓
	Case study 1.1: Building the 'Centrica model'	✓
2 – A systemic analysis of strategy and practice	Case box 2.1: The legacy of Russ Ackoff	✓
Part 1 – Strategy Analysis		
3 – Industry analysis and competitive advantage	Case box 3.1: Profitability of UK retailers	✓
	Case box 3.2: Wal-Mart's British accent needs polish	✓
	Case box 3.3: Capital intensity in retailing	✓
	Case box 3.4: The scale economy brander	✓
	Case box 3.5: World of dealcraft – video games	✗
4 – The macroeconomics of strategy	Case box 4.1: The Swedish banking crisis 1992	✗
	Case box 4.2: Lessons from the global banking crisis 2008	✗
	Case study 4.1: The Big Mac Index	✓
5 – Competitive strategy: the analysis of strategic position	Case box 5.1: The Germans are coming	✗
	Case box 5.2: The end of the free lunch – again	✗
	Case study 5.1: The Novotel value chain	✓
	Case study 5.2: Molecular weight: BASF and the chemical industry	✓
6 – Competitive strategy: the analysis of strategic capability	Case box 6.1: The game of chess	✗
	Case box 6.2: Out of Africa	✓
	Case study 6.1: Google: fuzzy maths	✓
7 – Strategy for the digital economy	Case box 7.1: Many-to-many networks	✗
	Case box 7.2: Facebook	✗
	Case box 7.3: Standards versioning	✗
	Case box 7.4: Market power and interoperability	✗
	Case box 7.5: The rise of co-evolution and cooperation	✗
	Case box 7.6: Lock-in and switching costs	✗
	Case box 7.7: Expectations management	✗
	Case study 7.1: Surviving the net: Yahoo!, eBay and Amazon	✓
	Case study 7.2: Browser wars are back	✓
8 – Corporate strategy: adding value in multi-business firms	Case box 8.1: Conglomerates in the FTSE 100	✗
	Case box 8.2: Mars buys Wrigley	✓
	Case box 8.3: The case for conglomerates	✗
	Case box 8.4: Merck's manoeuvres	✗
	Case box 8.5: Marauding maharajahs: India's acquisitive companies	✓
	Case study 8.1: Fiat's ambitions: the Italian solution	✓

Guided Tour

Part Openers

At the beginning of each part, the authors introduce the topics and themes covered throughout the proceeding chapters.

Chapter Introduction

Each introduction section indicates the key areas that will be discussed within each chapter and helps to put the chapter content into a wider perspective.

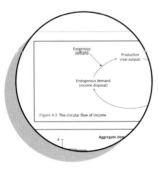

Figures and Tables

Each chapter has a number of tables and figures to help you visualise the various economic models and to illustrate and summarise important concepts.

Case Boxes/Case Studies

Case Boxes appear throughout the chapters and help relate the theory learnt to real life situations. Longer Case Studies are at the back of most chapters and they provide a more in-depth discussion of organisations through which to explore the ideas from the chapter.

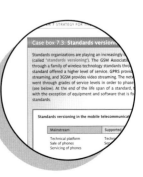

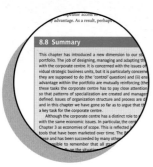

End of Chapter Summary

This briefly reviews and reinforces the main topics you will have covered in the chapter.

Key Terms

These are highlighted throughout each chapter and a list is compiled at the end for reference.

Recap Questions and Assignments

These questions encourage you to review and apply the knowledge you have acquired from the chapter and can be undertaken to test your understanding.

References and Further Reading

A comprehensive list of references is provided at the end of each chapter along with suggested further reading for further exploration into the topic.

Case Study Section

At the back of the text there are cases from various industries and organizations, offering real business situations around which to explore, analyse and critique strategy in action.

Visit www.mcgraw-hill.co.uk/textbooks/mcgee today

Online Learning Centre (OLC)

After completing each chapter, log on to the supporting Online Learning Centre website. Take advantage of the study tools offered to reinforce the material you have read in the text, and to develop your knowledge of strategy in a fun and effective way.

Resources for students include:
- Multiple Choice Questions
- A guide to how to interpret case studies
- Glossary of key terms
- Learning objectives
- Suggested answers to end of chapter recap questions and assignments
- Web links

Also available for lecturers:
- Case study teaching notes
- PowerPoint presentations
- Course outlines
- Figures and tables from the book
- A guide on how to teach using case studies
- Essay questions and solutions

Custom Publishing Solutions: Let us help make our **content** your **solution**

At McGraw-Hill Education our aim is to help lecturers to find the most suitable content for their needs delivered to their students in the most appropriate way. Our **custom publishing solutions** offer the ideal combination of content delivered in the way which best suits lecturer and students.

Our custom publishing programme offers lecturers the opportunity to select just the chapters or sections of material they wish to deliver to their students from a database called CREATE™ at
www.mcgrawhillcreate.com

CREATE™ contains over two million pages of content from:

- Textbooks
- Professional books
- Case books – Harvard Articles, Insead, Ivey, Darden, Thunderbird and BusinessWeek
- Taking Sides – debate materials

across the following imprints:

- McGraw-Hill Education
- Open University Press
- Harvard Business Publishing
- US and European material

There is also the option to include additional material authored by lecturers in the custom product – this does not necessarily have to be in English.

We will take care of everything from start to finish in the process of developing and delivering a custom product to ensure that lecturers and students receive exactly the material needed in the most suitable way.

With a Custom Publishing Solution, students enjoy the best selection of material deemed to be the most suitable for learning everything they need for their courses – something of real value to support their learning. Teachers are able to use exactly the material they want, in the way they want, to support their teaching on the course.

Please contact your local McGraw-Hill representative with any questions or alternatively contact Warren Eels e: warren_eels@mcgraw-hill.com.

Acknowledgements

Our thanks go to the following reviewers for their comments at various stages in the text's development:

John Anchor, Huddersfield University
Lynne Butel, Plymouth University
Charlie Carroll, University of Groningen
Romano Dyerson, University of London, Royal Holloway
Beverly Jones, Keele University
Dr de Jong, University of Groningen
Pikay Richardson, University of Manchester
Dr Van Wijk, Erasmus University

We would also like to thank the following individuals and organisations that granted permission for material to be reproduced within the textbook:

The Economist Newspaper Limited
INSEAD
John Wiley and Sons, Inc.
Palgrave Macmillan
IMD
The Telegraph Group Limited
Kogan Page Publishers
Blackwell Publishing
Harvard Business School Publishing
Bloomberg BusinessWeek
Fortune Magazine
The Financial Times Limited
Warwick Business School
Thunderbird School of Global Management

Every effort has been made to trace and acknowledge ownership of copyright and to clear permission for material reproduced in this book. The publishers will be pleased to make suitable arrangements to clear permission with any copyright holders whom it has not been possible to contact.

About the Authors

John McGee is Professor of Strategic Management at Warwick Business School, University of Warwick, UK.

Howard Thomas is Distinguished Chair of Strategic Management, Dean of the Lee Kong Chain School of Business, Singapore Management University. He is also Emeritus Professor at Warwick Business School, University of Warwick, UK.

David Wilson is Professor of Strategy and Organization at Warwick Business School, University of Warwick, UK.

What is strategy?
Concepts and practices

Introduction

Strategy remains one of the most contested and ill-defined concepts in management theory. As Magretta (2003) states:

> *. . . of all the concepts in management, strategy is the one that attracts the most attention and generates the most controversy. Almost everyone agrees that it is important. Almost no-one agrees on what it is.*

This book acknowledges some of the key debates concerning how scholars and practitioners have viewed and practised strategy. But it does not dwell in great detail on either the historical development of the field or the intense debates which have emerged from five or so decades of theoretical and empirical work. This has already been achieved in many textbooks on strategy (see, for example, Hussey, 1998 for a conventional history of strategy, Pettigrew et al., 2002 (for an extensive background) and Cummings and Wilson, 2003 for a less conventional mapping of the field). This book analyses the meaning of strategy by breaking it down into its component parts, namely, *its external logic* – how the organization positions itself relative to its external context, *its internal logic* – the levels of the organization at which strategy has different meanings and what distinctive resources and competences it must acquire, *its performance over time* – distinguishing between achievement of long-term objectives, meeting milestones along the way, and preserving short-term stability and, finally, *its managerial requirements* – the role of general managers and how strategy is planned, managed, monitored and maintained.

As managers you will also need to be able to *describe strategy* and *assess progress* – these ideas are introduced in this opening chapter and are further developed in Chapter 4.

Our intention in this opening chapter is to review briefly some of the key frameworks and characteristics of the field and then to see to what extent it is possible both to acknowledge and combine competing perspectives to create a more systematic yet practical approach to understanding strategy.

1.1 The nature of strategy

Strategy has always dealt with the future, usually a long-term, rather uncertain future, for which preparations have to be made, plans established and actions taken, together with provision for alternative actions should the future turn out to have unexpected characteristics. Orientation to the future is an essential ingredient in the idea of strategy and we can best explore this by looking at the key characteristics of strategic decisions.

First, strategy is essentially about *the future* but primarily about that part of the future about which there is uncertainty. We don't plan for tomorrow because tomorrow is either essentially known and surprises are likely to be few and/or there is little that can be done in preparation for tomorrow's surprise. What is important to us is how we might cope with an uncertain future by making preparations against future possibilities today.

Second, it follows that strategy is essentially about *taking risk*. We make preparations today against expected futures knowing that these futures might never materialize. For example, we plan to defend the country against floods and storms not knowing when, if ever, storms and floods of critical magnitude might occur.

Third, strategic decisions are typically *complex*. The expected futures arise from complex social, technical and other interactions as well as often being a joint product of many smaller but more frequent events. Typically the preparations and plans envisaged require the construction of complex assets (such as flood barriers or early-warning weather-forecasting systems in planning for storms or floods) which themselves have a distinct risk of not working as required. These custom-built assets may require complex interactions between several human agencies and extensive research and development may be required.

Fourth, strategic decisions take *time* to bring to fruition and are *irreversible*. Strategy is typically delivered through capital investment that can take decades to complete. Investment is the process of creating assets customized for a specific purpose – once the process has begun the assets cannot be disassembled back to their raw material form.

Fifth, there is an internal logic attached to strategic decisions that requires the *organization and coordination* of large numbers of people within organizations. The top-management task of organization and coordination is itself complex and difficult. It is often referred to as the need to create a *strategic fit* between the resources and capabilities of the organization and the requirements asked of it.

Sixth, the future is uncertain, with unknowable consequences, but strategies as bets against this uncertainty do have immediate implications for *change* that have at least some knowable (and often unpleasant) consequences. Thus strategy makes demands that are often alarming and unpleasant, with further consequences none of which are conducive to the quiet life.

Finally, strategic decisions have significant *scale and importance*. They typically concern expenditures of significant amounts of money in relation to total resources. Thus a house purchase for a family is strategic in terms of the commitments out of income required to service the loan whereas the purchase of a computer is much less strategic (but note that the control of multiple minor amounts of expenditure has strategic consequences if that control is ineffective). Strategic decisions are also important in that they are intended to make a big difference.

1.2 Characteristics of strategic problems

Strategy as a subject has a body of knowledge and captures the accumulated experience and wisdom of practitioners and theorists in a set of general propositions about the nature of strategy and how it works in practice. Unlike many 'academic' disciplines, strategy is essentially a practice-driven subject – i.e. its general propositions are highly contingent on particular circumstances. This is reflected in the way managers think about strategy. There are formal occasions at which strategy is reviewed and restated, and strategic planning takes place. However, in reality, strategy is posed by issues and questions that arise in many different parts and at many different levels in an organization. Therefore, strategy manifests itself in the form of strategic questions and strategic problems. The responses to these problems mean that strategy is often developed dynamically or, as Mintzberg and Waters (1985) put it, strategy is very often *emergent* rather than *planned*.[1]

We discussed strategy as a phenomenon in the previous section, but how would we recognize a strategic problem? They differ from the ordinary run of problems in the following ways:

1 Strategic problems have many stakeholders within the organization. For example, marketing will have a view on a new product development idea but so will the production team and so will the R&D team. Top management may see the new product as a natural addition to its competitive arsenal but lower-level managers may see it as disruptive change.

2 These problems will have multiple and imprecise **objectives** because of the many stakeholders. These objectives may be conflicting as well as ambiguous, unclear as well as aggressive, and challenging as well as desirable.

3 They will also be 'important' in their significance to the organization's prosperity, survival, values and culture. They will be typically of long duration both in gestation and in terms of their effects.

4 But, despite their importance, strategic problems will have no obvious right answer because of the many uncertainties surrounding their future impacts.

5 Because these problems are so important there is a significant opportunity cost in taking no decision or leaving the outcome to chance.

6 Strategic problems are typically complex, requiring analytically difficult interplay between many variables and organizationally much internal coordination.

---

[1] A stunning example of this is provided by the following quotation: 'The internet has taken shape with startlingly little planning ... The most universal and indispensable network on the planet somehow burgeoned without so much as board of directors, never mind a mergers & acquisitions department. There is a paradoxical lesson here for strategists. In economic terms, the great corporations are acting like socialist planners, while old-fashioned free-market capitalism blossoms at their feet.' (James Gleick, *New York Times Magazine*, 1 May 1994)

1.2.1 Examples of strategic problems and questions

You should look through the end-of-chapter cases in Part 1 for good illustrations of strategic problems.

In this chapter Centrica is faced with building a new business, defining new objectives and finding essentially a new identity. *Problem: who are we?*

In Chapter 5 we see how a hotel value chain can be identified. *Problem: what is the cost structure and what are the sources of differentiation advantage?*

Also in Chapter 5 there is a picture of how BASF sets out to be an industry leader. *Problem: is its cost advantage substantial and defensible?*

In Chapter 6 we debate whether 'fuzzy maths' is the core competence for Google. *Problem: how do we define a core competence, and then build and defend it within a company?*

In Chapter 7 we discuss the survival of the three internet heavyweights, Yahoo, eBay and Amazon. We also look at the latest round in the battle of the browsers. *Problem: what are network externalities and how can they be deployed by rivals?*

In Chapter 8 we look at Fiat's ambitious plans to take over Chrysler and GM Europe. *Problem: what is the parenting advantage that enables a company to run a portfolio of businesses successfully?*

In Chapter 9 Terry Leahy explains his global expansion vision for Tesco. *Problem: what is international advantage and what extra core competences does it require?*

How should strategic problems, such as these above, be addressed? This is not an easy question to answer. Practitioners can give guidance as to how they did it in their specific circumstances. Alternatively, academics can describe a body of knowledge that gives general guidance. The essence of strategy making in practice is how to combine these two perspectives (often complementary but sometimes conflicting) with concepts and practices that can be applied in your own situation.

1.3 Key definitions of strategy

In a conference at Harvard Business School in 1963 Cook (reported in Bower, 1982) argued that strategy is made up of 'messy, unsolved and perhaps undefined problems of importance characterizing business management'. Bower (1986) argued that 'the charter of business policy is to focus on the life and death issues of central interest to top management . . . to help top management to deal with these issues effectively, profitably and morally'. In general, if you ask someone to define strategy, you will likely be told that *strategy is a plan* or something equivalent – a direction, a guide, a course of action into the future, a path to get from here to there (Legge, 2003). Mintzberg et al. (1998) made the celebrated argument that the idea of strategy as plan fails to recognize *strategy as an emergent process*, which is best seen as a pattern in a stream of decisions. Strategy, for Mintzberg, is what emerges from actions rather than something planned in advance or in anticipation of future contexts. We explore this planned versus emergent aspect of strategy in later sections of this chapter.

Prahalad and Hamel (1990) have also been very influential in influencing how we view strategy. They conceptualized strategy in terms of *strategic intent*, which they define as providing an overarching strategic direction. Strategic intent is, in essence, about winning in a competitive game. This leads to a focus on strategy as a process for reinforcing intent by developing the core competencies of a corporation, and leading and managing change. They also propose the viewpoint of *strategy as stretch and leverage*, in which the strategist sees the advantage of breaking conventional frames of reference by deploying (*leveraging*) the organization's critical core competences in an innovative and distinctive manner. Indeed, the concept of *strategy as innovation* is dominant in their thinking and they stress the need for strategists to embrace radical innovation and innovate to stay ahead in the competitive game. Their thinking in this respect mirrors that of Christensen (1997) who has discussed the role of *disruptive technologies* in the shaping of new competitive landscapes.

Perhaps the definition of strategy that is most common in the field is that attributed to the renowned Harvard business historian Alfred D. Chandler in his landmark book *Strategy and Structure*. The Chandler (1962) definition characterizes strategy as

> *the determination of the basic long-term goals and objectives of an enterprise and the adoption of courses of action and the allocation of resources necessary for carrying out these goals.*

This is the classical view of strategy, very much rational in analysis and following militaristic traditions, including those specified in the Japanese strategy book by Sun Tzu entitled *The Art of War*. Quinn (1980), in an equally famous book entitled *Strategies for Change: Logical Incrementalism*, follows Chandler's case study tradition and talks about strategy in a more process-oriented way. Quinn's definition is

> *the pattern or plan that integrates an organization's major goals, policies and action sequences into a cohesive whole. A well-formulated strategy helps to marshal and allocate an organization's resources into a unique and viable posture based on its relative internal competencies and shortcomings, anticipated changes in the environment and contingent moves by intelligent opponents.*

Porter (1980), the Harvard Business School strategy professor, who has also had a tremendous influence on the field of strategic management and competitive strategy, highlights and emphasizes the themes of being different and achieving strategic coherence in organizational strategy. He argues that **competitive strategy** is essentially about *being different* (using the language of strategic positioning). This means deliberately choosing a different set of activities to deliver a unique mix of value. However, a **strategic position** is not sustainable unless there are trade-offs with other positions. Trade-offs create the need for choice (making strategic decisions) and protect against competitive attack. Strategy is about combining activities that are complementary and reinforcing. This strategic *coherence* among many activities is fundamental, not only to achieving competitive advantage but also to the **sustainability** of that advantage. It is harder for a rival to match an array of interlocked activities than it is merely to match a particular sales force approach, match a single process technology or replicate a specific set of product features. Positions built on a series of coherent activities are far more sustainable than those built on individual activities.

Although the previous definitions might seem at odds with one another (even mutually exclusive in some cases, for example between planned and emergent strategies), there are some common elements which we can identify to help us clarify the analysis. Common elements in these viewpoints include the following and Figure 1.1 summarizes them:

- Strategy as a means of establishing organizational purpose.
- Strategy as a definition of the competitive domains of the firm and the external context of the organization.
- Strategy as a response to the conjunction of external opportunities and threats with internal strengths and weaknesses in order to achieve sustainable competitive advantage.

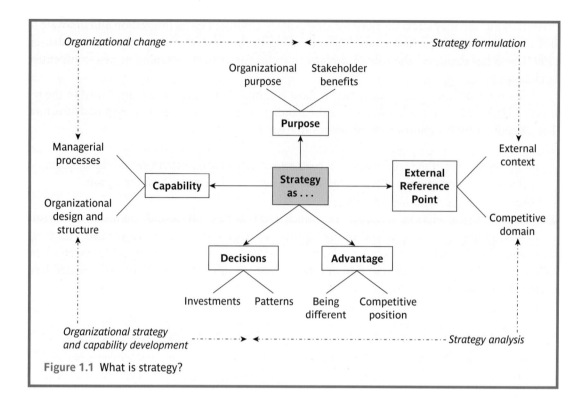

Figure 1.1 What is strategy?

- Strategy as the focus required to define managerial tasks and processes and to integrate corporate, business and functional perspectives.
- Strategy as a coherent, unifying and integrative systematic pattern of decisions.
- Strategy as a definition of the economic and non-economic contributions which the firm intends to make to its stakeholders.
- Strategy as an architectural design for developing the distinctive competences of an organization.
- Strategy as the criterion for determining investments in tangible and intangible resources to develop the core capabilities which lead to sustainable advantages.
- Strategy as an expression of strategic intent, stretching the organization to innovate, leverage resources and develop new skills.
- Strategy as being different.

These common elements form the backbone of this book. They include the economic analysis of strategy to help plan and inform strategic decisions (in Part 1); the analysis of strategy as a feature of both organizational positioning and capabilities, especially in a changing context of globalization and the new economy (also in Part 1); the analysis of strategy as a series of processes in which decisions have to be implemented and put into practice and which require an understanding of how organizations and individuals change and develop; and a view of strategy as monitoring, improving and developing, helping data feed back into the next wave of strategy formulation (Part 2). Complex though all these factors are, the basics of strategy are relatively easily summarized and described. We examine these in the next section.

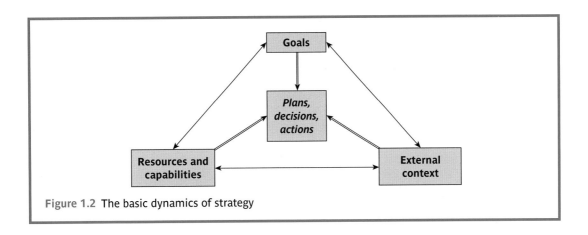

Figure 1.2 The basic dynamics of strategy

1.4 Basic strategy analysis

Figure 1.2 outlines the main basic dynamics and key factors of strategy. It takes the elements of Figure 1.1 and condenses the elements of this figure into a framework focused on managerial action. Thus, Figure 1.2 has Plans, Decisions and Actions as its centrepiece, showing the dynamic interplay with Goals, External Context and Resources and Capabilities. We examine each of these key factors in more detail in the following sections.

1.4.1 Plans, decisions and actions

The notion of planning heralds the beginnings of strategy. Many authors such as Quinn (1980) and Cummings and Wilson (2003) have traced the military genesis of the term strategy from the Greeks and the Macedonians.

The word *strategos* began as a term describing the commanding role in the army (a general, for example) and by the time of Alexander the Great (330BC) had become the word which described the successful deployment of troops to overcome the enemy and the system of governance which facilitated this planning. It is this combined notion of planned deployment and governance that pervades the planning schools of strategy. Authors such as Ansoff (1965, 1972), building on the earlier work of the Stanford Research Institute, epitomize the translation of this planning orientation to the strategic conduct of business and the view of the general manager as a 'strategist' (coining the phrase **'strategic management'** in 1972).

Most of today's organizations have some form of corporate plan or strategic plan and some form of planning process. In terms of Figure 1.2, **strategic planning** is the process by which the firm organizes its *resources* and *actions* in relation to an *external environment* in order to achieve its *goals* or objectives. This is usually a formal rather than an informal process, the key elements of which are outlined in Figure 1.3.

Planning is conducted in a very hierarchical and formal manner. It is typically top down, with the direction and energy being supplied by top management. The process is iterative and the cycle is repeated (typically) on an annual basis. Planning horizons are in practice about three to five years in Western companies but this does depend on the length of product life cycles and the life of capital equipment.

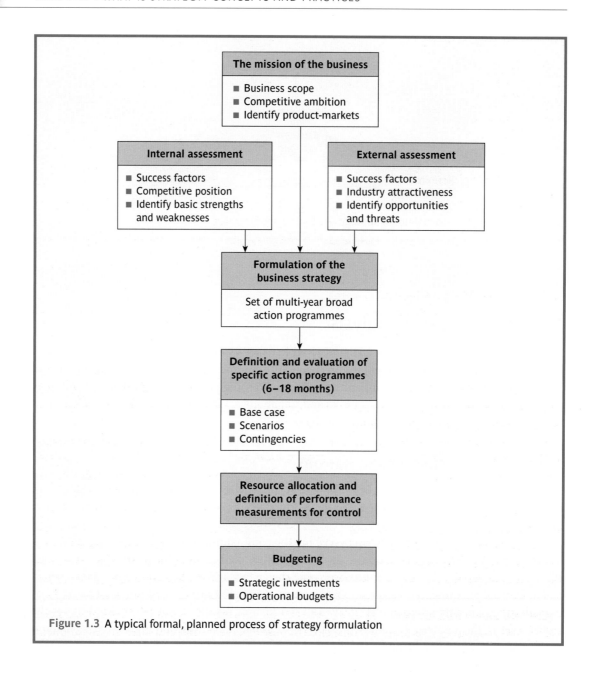

Figure 1.3 A typical formal, planned process of strategy formulation

Formal analysis would go through a number of stages in sequence. The first is typically the statement of the *mission* of the business. This would then be followed by a review of the *external environment* in which, for example, the economics of the industry would be assessed, the nature of markets and customers analysed, and broader political and social trends identified. In parallel there would be a review of the *internal environment* of the organization. This covers basic strengths and weaknesses, core competences and capability assessments. Based on these, views of the strengths and weaknesses and opportunities and threats (the well-known SWOT analysis covering the reviews of the internal and external environments) are used as a starting point for *formulating the strategy*. From the basic business strategy will come a definition of the specific action *programmes* required to put the strategy into practice. This is what is usually called the business plan, although the way

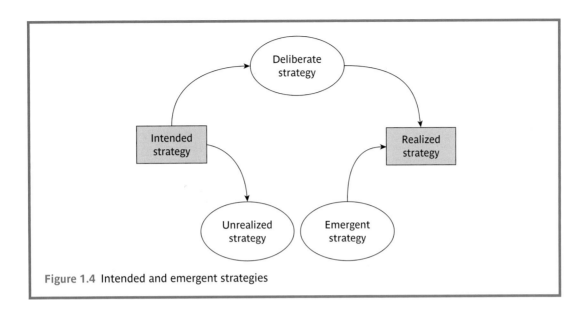

Figure 1.4 Intended and emergent strategies

in which this term is used varies widely between firms. This business plan is then submitted to an investment committee (this also goes under a variety of names) for *resource allocation* along with definition of performance milestones. After the investment expenditures are agreed, *budgets* are specified and agreed throughout the organization.

However, any person who has had experience of this process in action in any organization may well have a wry smile on their face as they read the above seemingly rational and militaristic procedure. 'Great in theory, but never happens in practice' might summarize their feelings. According to Mintzberg and Waters (1985), some strategies may be planned, at least in their first stages, but many more just simply *emerge* in an organization without being consciously intended or being deliberate acts. We might make sense of the *pattern* of these actions later and call them a strategy, but we do so with the luxury of hindsight. We construct a logic which was never intended in the first place. Emergent strategies can be seen as responses to unexpected opportunities and problems and are usually developed from the locations at which business-level strategies are usually implemented, i.e. within business units and not at corporate headquarters. The pure definition of emergence requires the absence of any intentions. This is too strong for most occasions but, as Mintzberg and Waters (1985) observe, organizations come close to pure emergent strategies when an environment directly imposes a pattern of actions on them.

Quinn (1980) developed logical incrementalism as a way of explaining the combination of longer-term plans and targets with evolutionary, learning-based patterns of movement on the way (patterns of decisions which emerge). This is an attractive explanation because it seems to combine rational resource-allocation thinking with practical learning by doing. Quinn argues that, 'properly managed, it is a conscious, purposeful, pro-active, executive practice'.

The twin lenses of intentions and emergence are useful tools by which to analyse strategy of intentions and emergence. Indeed, there is a continuum on which different blends can be identified (Figure 1.4). In this figure we see **intended strategies** being formulated as deliberate strategies, some of which come to fruition. But we also see a simultaneous pressure from circumstances producing a stream of emergent (but purposeful) thinking. *Realized strategy* is a blend of intentions and emergence which can be interpreted by reference to the strength of pressure from the external environment – a kind of environmental determinism.

Case box 1.1: **Magazines take on Amazon**

Magazines attempt to win back control of their digital editions

LET it never again be said that old-media firms are slow to deal with new technology. On December 8th Condé Nast, Hearst, Meredith, News Corporation and Time Inc invested in an as-yet-unnamed venture that will create and sell digital magazines and newspapers for the new generation of e-readers that is likely to succeed Amazon's monochrome Kindle in the next year or so. It was as if a group of explorers had announced plans to settle a country that had not yet been discovered.

Consumers can already get hold of many publications on smart-phones and e-readers. But smart-phones have small screens, and e-readers render magazines as crudely illustrated black-and-white books. They cannot reproduce magazines' distinctive fonts or elegant graphics. Worse, they are un-suited to advertising, on which most magazines depend. In the year to June, Meredith's publishing arm, which produces *Better Homes and Gardens* among dozens of other titles, made almost twice as much from advertising as it did from newsstand sales and subscriptions.

Publishers are irked at the prospect of formatting content for multiple devices with slightly different requirements – a problem that will worsen. They are even more irked at the current market leader, Amazon, which returns as little as 30% of the sale price of a digital magazine to publishers and provides less detail about customers' reading habits than they would like. Publishers who want to go digital currently have a choice between the open internet, which generally provides revenue from advertising (but not much) and no subscriptions, and e-readers, which provide revenue from subscriptions (but not much) and no advertising.

The consortium plans to develop software that can be used to create digital publications for a wide range of devices. It will also set up a storefront similar to iTunes, Apple's online music outlet. This will not be restricted to the consortium's publications, nor will it be the only way to get hold of them. Condé Nast is already working with Adobe to develop software of its own for advanced e-readers. Hearst, another member of the consortium, has a start-up called Skiff. How the new venture's efforts will mesh with these other projects is not yet certain. Yet the destination is clear, says John Squires of Time Inc, who will manage the consortium at first. His company has produced a mock-up of an edition of *Sports Illustrated*, complete with video and interactive ads, which provides a compelling, if hypothetical, glimpse into the future of magazines.

In important ways the consortium resembles Hulu, an outfit Mr Squires praises as 'artful'. Hulu's website streams television programmes from three of America's four big English-language broadcasters, as well as a few pay-television shows. It has no sneezing pandas, tedious home-made tirades or any of the other detritus with which YouTube is filled. Hulu is popular with both consumers and companies, which pay stiff rates to place advertisements in its programmes (it helps that Hulu does not yet run many ads). As with the magazine consortium, media companies own equity stakes in Hulu.

This model is spreading. On the very day the publishers agreed to set up their venture, record companies launched a Hulu of sorts for music videos in America. Vevo is partly owned by Universal and Sony and licenses other content from EMI. Although it is run in conjunction with YouTube, it is intended to be a separate, cleaner world. Such is the evolving wisdom for traditional media firms that want to engage with digital technology: put some distance between your content and the dross, and make sure you have a stake in any new outfit that appears.

Source: 'A Hulu for Print', *The Economist*, 10 December 2009

Questions

1 Is the decision of magazines to take on Amazon in this way a planned strategic decision or a defensive opportunistic act?

2 Is this decision based on strategic strengths or weaknesses? How do Amazon's strengths and weaknesses compare?

3 Amazon is said to have spare infrastructure capacity: would this be a strength or a weakness?

4 Will the old-media firms be competing primarily with each other or with Amazon?

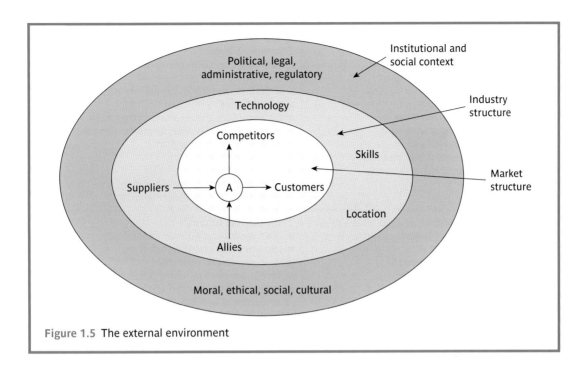

Figure 1.5 The external environment

1.4.2 External assessment

The external context of strategic decisions is very broad ranging. In principle, it can include anything and everything that might have an effect on decisions. We could include governments, international trade organizations, buyer and supplier markets, competitors, trade associations, civil servants, and the impersonal progression of science and technology. In order to provide some structure to this variety of influences, we can think of three regions of impact upon firm A (see Figure 1.5). These are market structure, industry structure, and the institutional/social context.

Market structure (often called the *competitive domain*) includes the intimate competition for the customers' attention between rivals in the marketplace. This is the competitive battleground within which the firm's long-term objectives are gained or lost and which provides the basis for assessing the distinctiveness of rival offerings to customers. It is here that competitive advantage (which we will define in Part 2) is won or lost.

The broader **industry structure** provides inputs of traded goods, knowledge, technical rules and procedures that condition the conduct of firms. Thus pharmaceutical firms will hire scientists trained at universities. Car assemblers like Ford and GM buy from components manufacturers like GKN and Valeo. Industry trade associations stipulate rules of conduct and may conduct joint research. Distribution channels act across the board as intermediate customers and sometimes as powerful buyers in their own right. This industry structure has a deep impact on the underlying economic possibilities open to the participants in the market structure.

The broader institutional and social structure sets out the rules of the game in terms of what is morally, legally and ethically possible as well as setting the political terms of reference within which firms are obliged to operate.

These regions represent zones of influence for firms. Most influence is exercised within the market structure and least within the broad institutional context – at least as a general rule. However, firms see it as at least possible that they might shape the rules of the game by seeking to promote changes at various levels. But firms might also see their sphere of influence as tightly focused with

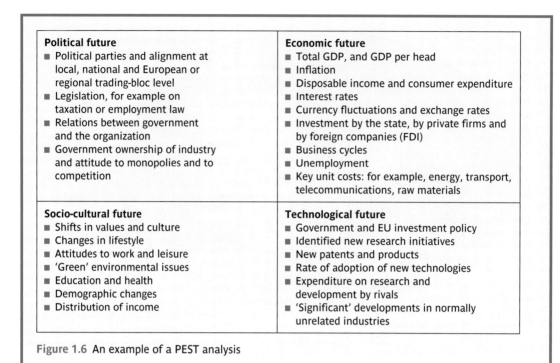

Political future
- Political parties and alignment at local, national and European or regional trading-bloc level
- Legislation, for example on taxation or employment law
- Relations between government and the organization
- Government ownership of industry and attitude to monopolies and to competition

Economic future
- Total GDP, and GDP per head
- Inflation
- Disposable income and consumer expenditure
- Interest rates
- Currency fluctuations and exchange rates
- Investment by the state, by private firms and by foreign companies (FDI)
- Business cycles
- Unemployment
- Key unit costs: for example, energy, transport, telecommunications, raw materials

Socio-cultural future
- Shifts in values and culture
- Changes in lifestyle
- Attitudes to work and leisure
- 'Green' environmental issues
- Education and health
- Demographic changes
- Distribution of income

Technological future
- Government and EU investment policy
- Identified new research initiatives
- New patents and products
- Rate of adoption of new technologies
- Expenditure on research and development by rivals
- 'Significant' developments in normally unrelated industries

Figure 1.6 An example of a PEST analysis

their market environment and subject, without any recourse to powerful forces from elsewhere. One way for firms to assess exposure to forces within this broad context is through a **PEST** analysis. This is an analysis of Political, Economic, Social and Technological forces. Occasionally, specific legal aspects of dealing in particular national legal systems (for example) can be added to this analysis, but for simplicity they are excluded in the description below. Figure 1.6 provides an illustration of the variety of forces that can be identified via a PEST analysis.

In order to make sense of this broad 'shopping list' some analysis is needed to identify the really significant influences. This involves assigning probabilities and possible outcomes to each event and calculating an 'expected value' (technically the probability multiplied by the outcome). In practice this requires considerable judgement because many of the events can only be described in qualitative terms and because managers may have little, or very partial, information on each factor. We need also to identify ways in which the probabilities of the events and the outcomes of the events might be moderated by management action.

1.4.3 Internal assessment

The **SWOT** (Strengths, Weaknesses, Opportunities, Threats) is a method of analysing both the internal and the external factors that can affect a firm, and as such has always been accepted as useful when assessing the current circumstances of a firm. SWOT is a tool of the 'design school' (Mintzberg et al., 1998, p. 24) where firms set strategy by matching their internal capabilities with the external environment (Figure 1.7). Strengths and Weaknesses relate to the internal ('resources and capabilities' in Figure 1.2) aspects of a firm, while Opportunities and Threats relate to the external aspects that affect a firm's environment (the 'external context' in Figure 1.2). While Porter's (1980) **Five Forces** analysis relates to an industry as its unit of analysis, a SWOT analysis relates to the business level. There are, however, criticisms of the technique: Hill and Westbrook (1997) note the descriptive

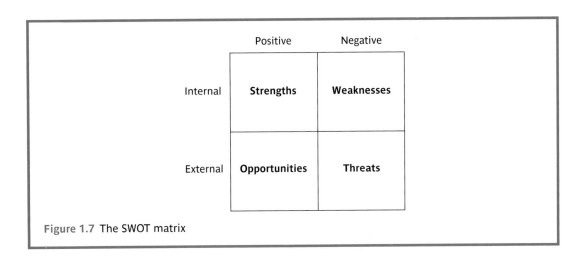

Figure 1.7 The SWOT matrix

nature of a SWOT analysis. It is therefore important to go beyond merely undertaking the analysis – which, after all, merely generates lists – towards formulating and implementing strategy. However, appraising strengths and weaknesses taking into account the firm's external opportunities and threats proves to be a popular, fast method of analysing the external and internal factors that can influence a firm's subsequent strategy.

Strengths and weaknesses

The first part of a SWOT analysis concerns the identification of an organization's strengths and weaknesses in relation to the competition. Strengths for an organization may include a significant market share, robust financial resources, innovative products or a strong customer base. Weaknesses may include lack of managerial skills, a poor distribution network, falling behind in research and development, or obsolete facilities (Morris, 2005). According to Weihrich (1982), despite the fact that internal strengths and weaknesses vary greatly for different enterprises, they can be categorized into (1) management and organization, (2) operations, (3) finance and (4) other factors important for a particular organization.

Management and organization

Weihrich (1982) classifies in this category not only managerial talent but also labour relations, personnel policies, the appraisal, selection, training and development of employees, and the reward system. Under 'organization' he proposes analysing the planning and control system as well as the organizational structure and climate.

Operations

Operations are assessed in terms of research and development capabilities and the adequacy and productivity of the manufacturing facilities available to meet the expected growth, while marketing is analysed in terms of product distribution channels, brand name protection, competitive pricing, appropriate customer identification, service and company image (Weihrich, 1982).

Finance

The specific areas for evaluation include capital structure, financing, profitability, the tax situation, financial planning and the accounting system. Weihrich (1982) also suggests conducting short- and long-term financial planning according to the firm's objectives and strategy.

Ahmed et al. (2006) provide a SWOT analysis of Air China, the largest air carrier in China in terms of traffic volume and company assets and employing over 20,000 employees, including more than 2,300 pilots and 4,520 flight attendants.

According to these authors, Air China's strengths include: well-trained flight crew who are experienced in international operations and services; updated fleet and competent repair and maintenance expertise; advanced information systems; good reputation in both international and domestic markets; quality service; and a number of rapidly increasing loyal frequent flyers.

On the other side, Air China's weaknesses are: the unclear strategic direction largely diluting its capabilities and seriously confusing its brands; the fact that many quality service initiatives and practices are easily copied by its competitors; and finally, the fact that the majority of resources, organizational concentration and management time are consumed on the domestic operation, resulting in weak offerings for the international market.

Opportunities and threats

Whether a particular factor is an opportunity or a threat depends on the specific environmental factor. For instance, the introduction of new legislation can either pose an opportunity for a firm or reduce its ability to compete. Unlike Porter's Five Forces, the analysis is specific to the business, rather than specific to a particular market independent of the firm we are considering. Mintzberg et al. (1998, p. 29, after Power et al., 1986) cite six environmental variables that can be used when undertaking the 'OT' of the SWOT analysis. Examples of such changes are shown below, with indications of whether they are a strength or a weakness, and you should note that their magnitude is dependent upon the firm that is being analysed.

Societal changes

An ageing population may mean that products or services for elderly people may become more attractive; changes in immigration/emigration may lead to a threat of having too few qualified employees.

Governmental changes

Deregulation may provide opportunities for the firm entering new markets; introduction of new laws may outlaw certain products or services.

Economic changes

Recession may reduce buyers' demand for products; changes in taxation policy may increase demand for services.

Competitive changes

Anti-trust laws being invoked may lead to a threat to current operations; incumbents exiting the market may lead to opportunities for growth.

Supplier changes

Closure of a key supplier may threaten the current operations of the firm; sourcing a new supplier may present opportunities.

Market changes

New markets may emerge that constitute an opportunity; commodities may be used for other purposes (e.g. bio-fuels), leading to market shocks.

There are links between Porter's Five Forces framework and the environmental factors considered by a SWOT analysis. In fact, all five forces (bargaining power of suppliers, bargaining power of buyers, threat of new entrants, competitor rivalry, and threat of substitutes) can feature in a SWOT analysis. There is a difference, however: the Five Forces analysis tends to be static in nature, taking a snapshot of a particular industry structure at one time, while the environmental part of the SWOT analysis focuses on changes in environmental features that may give rise to opportunities or threats. Furthermore, the unit of analysis from a SWOT analysis is that of the focal firm, rather than the industry as a whole.

Case box 1.2: How Honda became successful

During the 1960s, when it was a small manufacturer, Honda broke out of the Japanese motorcycle market and began exporting to the US. Taking Honda's story as an archetype of the smaller manufacturer entering a new market already occupied by highly dominant competitors, the story of their market entry, and their subsequent huge success in the US and around the world, has been the subject of some academic controversy. Competing explanations have been advanced to explain Honda's strategy and the reasons for their success.

The first of these explanations was put forward when, in 1975, Boston Consulting Group (BCG) was commissioned by the UK government to write a report explaining why and how the British motorcycle industry had been out-competed by its Japanese competitors. The report concluded that the Japanese firms, including Honda, had sought a very high scale of production (they had made a large number of motorbikes) in order to benefit from economies of scale and learning curve effects. It blamed the decline of the British motorcycle industry on the failure of British managers to invest enough in their businesses to profit from economies of scale and scope.

The second explanation was offered in 1984 by Richard Pascale, who had interviewed the Honda executives responsible for the firm's entry into the US market. As opposed to the tightly focused strategy of low cost and high scale that BCG accredited to Honda, Pascale found that their entry into the US market was a story of 'miscalculation, serendipity, and organizational learning' – in other words, Honda's success was due to the adaptability and hard work of its staff, rather than any long-term strategy. For example, Honda's initial plan on entering the US was to compete in large motorcycles, around 300 cc. It was only when the team found that the scooters they were using to get themselves around their US base of San Francisco attracted positive interest from consumers that they came up with the idea of selling the Supercub.

The most recent school of thought on Honda's strategy was put forward by Gary Hamel and C.K. Prahalad in 1989. Creating the concept of core competencies with Honda as an example, they argued that Honda's success was due to its focus on leadership in the technology of internal combustion engines. For example, the high power-to-weight ratio engines Honda produced for its racing bikes provided technology and expertise which was transferable into mopeds.

Source: Compiled by the authors from various sources including *Wikipedia*: Honda, 9 March 2009

Questions

1 How many different explanations for success are evident here? Can you think of any more possibilities?

2 How might you judge between the validity of these rival explanations?

3 Does a company ever know whether its planned strategy is ever responsible for success?

Further conceptual developments

The SWOT analysis has been criticized for being composed largely of broad guidelines lacking explicit underpinnings, thus leading to misleading results and even harming performance (Hill and Westbrook, 1997; Menon et al., 1999).

Valentin (2001) suggested incorporating contemporary strategic management theory into SWOT analysis to gain more penetrating strategic insights. Weihrich (1982) has further developed the SWOT analysis into the TOWS matrix (see Figure 1.8). He argues that the TOWS matrix enables the strategist to relate external conditions to internal characteristics so that potential strategic responses and requirements can be identified – see below for further elaboration.

There have also been a number of efforts to combine the SWOT analysis with other strategy tools. For example, scholars have suggested combining the balanced scorecard (see Chapter 16), SWOT analysis and quality function deployment (QFD) into one single strategic tool (Ip and Koo, 2004; Koo, 1998). Proctor (2000) suggests combining the cross-impact analysis, the TOWS matrix and brainstorming towards generating sustainable strategies and for specifying objectives.

1.4.4 Applying SWOT in practice

The acronym of Strengths, Weaknesses, Opportunities and Threats, SWOT analysis provides a simple but powerful tool for evaluating the strategic position of the firm. It is especially useful for senior executives undertaking a fundamental reappraisal of a business, in that it permits a free-thinking environment, unencumbered by the constraints often imposed by a finance-driven budgetary planning system. It also allows a test of perceived common purpose within an organization when carried out at various levels within the firm. The requirements for undertaking such an analysis are relatively simple and, at the end of the exercise, key information needs can usually be identified which might prove to be the subject of further research.

A list of common strengths, weaknesses, opportunities and threats is shown in Figure 1.9. This list is not comprehensive and other critical factors may be identified. In terms of usage, executives may be divided into groups to initially identify – first as individuals and second as groups – their views as to the firm's SWOT. It may well be useful to focus on only a prioritized list of these and also to assess the cross-impacts of strengths and weaknesses on threats and opportunities, utilizing a form such as that shown in Figure 1.8 (the TOWS matrix).

For strategy formulation, the firm attempts to build upon its strengths and eliminate its weaknesses. When the firm does not possess the skills required to take advantage of opportunities or avoid threats, the necessary resources needed may be identified from the SWOT analysis and steps taken to procure the strengths or to reduce any weaknesses.

SWOT analysis is most often undertaken as a stand-alone analysis. However, it is our view that it is best used as a way of pulling together the various strands in a resources/competences audit and a positioning/competitive analysis (read Chapter 6 for an explanation of core competences). Opportunities and threats require a close analysis of the environment. The tools provided from macroeconomics and also from marketing are essential here. You may wish to extend the analysis in the form of scenarios so as to get a longer-run and more dynamic picture. The article by Paul Schoemaker is particularly helpful in relating scenarios to core competences (see Chapter 6).

The typical problem with the SWOT style of analysis is the production of long 'laundry lists' that have no capacity to provide insight into the critical issues. One way of differentiating between elements in a long list is to apply a form of A-B-C analysis. The A category refers to issues which are critical to competitive advantage. The B category can represent those issues that are relevant to best practice. The C category refers to threshold-level issues below which neither strengths nor weaknesses show up on the radar screen.

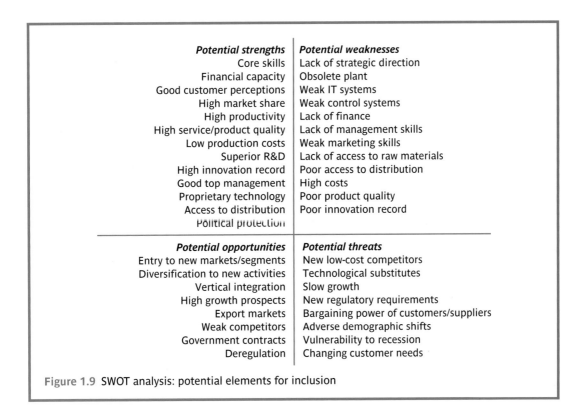

Figure 1.8 SWOT analysis: the TOWS cross-impact matrix

	Potential strengths	Potential weaknesses
	Core skills	Lack of strategic direction
	Financial capacity	Obsolete plant
	Good customer perceptions	Weak IT systems
	High market share	Weak control systems
	High productivity	Lack of finance
	High service/product quality	Lack of management skills
	Low production costs	Weak marketing skills
	Superior R&D	Lack of access to raw materials
	High innovation record	Poor access to distribution
	Good top management	High costs
	Proprietary technology	Poor product quality
	Access to distribution	Poor innovation record
	Political protection	
	Potential opportunities	**Potential threats**
	Entry to new markets/segments	New low-cost competitors
	Diversification to new activities	Technological substitutes
	Vertical integration	Slow growth
	High growth prospects	New regulatory requirements
	Export markets	Bargaining power of customers/suppliers
	Weak competitors	Adverse demographic shifts
	Government contracts	Vulnerability to recession
	Deregulation	Changing customer needs

Figure 1.9 SWOT analysis: potential elements for inclusion

The use of a **cross-impact matrix** gives much depth and subtlety to a SWOT analysis. This is what Weihrich (1982) referred to as the TOWS matrix. The interaction of Strengths and Weaknesses with Opportunities and Threats is an obvious springboard for developing and growing a business – Figure 1.8 illustrates the idea. It helps you ask and answer some key questions:

- How to make the most of your strengths?
- How to avoid the consequences of your weaknesses?
- How to capitalize on your opportunities?
- How to manage the threats to your business?

It then goes on to address the more complicated questions:

- Are my strengths sufficient for the opportunities available?
- Can my strengths cope with the threats?
- Are my weaknesses going to inhibit exploitation of the available opportunities?
- Are my weaknesses going to be critical in the face of the anticipated threats?

For example, you might have strengths in new product development and in low costs/high productivity coupled with growth opportunities in new industrializing markets (such as the Asian Tigers). Conversely, the conjunction of significant threats with weaknesses can pose a significant threat to the survival of your business. For example, a high cost base as a weakness coupled with a direct threat of low cost/price competition from Asian competitors is a familiar story for Western businesses. The conjunction of weaknesses with opportunities tells a story of investments that must be made. The conjunction of strengths with threats tells of defensive strength and sustainability of the business.

This kind of analysis helps you to understand the strategic choices you face and to frame the key decisions you will need to address. By itself this analysis does not answer these questions – the following chapters use the logic of competitive advantage to give you the concepts and the approaches you need to develop appropriate answers and thus to define successful strategies.

A mini case study of a company, Centrica, facing a turbulent environment is presented at the end of the chapter. A PEST and SWOT analysis can be used to assist the management of this company in developing appropriate strategies for the future.

1.5 Summary

This chapter has set out some basic ideas about strategy. We have looked at the way in which strategy is different from other areas of study – *the nature of strategy*. We then explored some of the many definitions of strategy (*key definitions*) and developed a simple diagram (Figure 1.1) that expressed strategy as comprising five main elements – *strategy as . . . purpose, external reference point, advantage, decisions, and capability*. We then presented a simple, basic analysis routine (see Figure 1.2) as consisting of a simultaneous interplay between *plans, decisions and outcomes* as a kind of dependent variable that is influenced by the three main drivers of *Goals, External context,* and *Resources and capabilities*.

We then examined three main tools and processes. The first was strategic planning as typically practised, PEST analysis which is a way of systematically canvassing the external context, and SWOT analysis which is used as a way to assess current position and potential future position. We concluded with an elaboration of SWOT, sometimes called TOWS but often referred to as a cross-impact matrix by virtue of the way in which it relates strengths and weaknesses to opportunities and threats. We noted throughout this discussion that these ad hoc methods of strategy analysis have many benefits, including their simplicity and their ease of communication. But the downside of all these methods is that they do not systematically address or define a body of empirical data or theoretical knowledge that can be applied more broadly rather than on a situational basis. The purpose of this book is to develop the body of knowledge about strategy that can be used both by practitioners and by researchers to attack strategy problems.

Chapter 2 starts this process by developing a systemic model of strategy which we then use as the background framework by which each chapter of the book is related to each other.

Key terms

competitive domain	11	mission	8
competitive strategy	5	objectives	3
cross-impact matrix	17	PEST	12
disruptive technology	5	realized strategy	9
emergent strategy	3	strategic intent	4
external environment	7	strategic management	7
Five Forces	12	strategic plan/planning	7
goals	7	strategic position	5
industry structure	11	stretch and leverage	4
intended strategy	9	sustainability	5
internal environment	8	SWOT	12
market structure	11	TOWS	16

Recap questions and assignments

1 For your own organization (or any other company or case study that you know well), use the following figures in the core text:

   i   Figure 1.3 to assess how much top-down strategic planning takes place.

   ii   Figure 1.5 to assess the nature of the external environment.

   iii   Figure 1.6 for a PEST analysis of your organization.

   iv   Use Figure 1.3 to critique your own mission statement.

   v   How much of Figure 1.1 can you identify within your organization?

2 Identify from your own organization a strategic problem that did not emerge through the top-down strategic planning process. Using the criteria in this chapter, assess how 'strategic' was this problem. How was the problem handled? Outline how the strategic tools shown in Section 4 of this chapter could have been applied.

3 Draw a mind map to illustrate your study and learning plan for this module.

Case study 1.1: **Building the 'Centrica model'**

Centrica was originally formed as part of the restructuring programme for British Gas, when British Gas was demerged into two separate companies, BG and Centrica. The process began the previous decade, in 1986, with the privatization of the state-held gas monopoly, British Gas. British Gas was the sole natural gas supplier until 1990, when deregulation provided the opportunity for commercial competition. It was a vertically integrated firm and it was a classic example of the utility that extracted the gas out of the ground and then supplied it to homes and businesses.

The first challenge for Centrica was survival. The speed of the deregulation in the industry drove forward competition in supply. At the same time the drop in the wholesale cost of gas rendered all of the take-or-pay contracts that British Gas had negotiated economically unsound. By the end of 1998 Centrica had successfully renegotiated most of its take-or-pay contracts, with its Chevron contract being terminated in October 1998 and compensation paid to end the deal. The contracts with Conoco, Elf, Total, Phillips, Total Oil Marine, Fina and Agip were renegotiated, with lower volumes supplied and compensation paid accordingly. As a result, Centrica's exposure to the higher prices fixed in previous contracts was significantly reduced. Another important decision was to turn round or shut down the loss-making businesses. Hence 240 British Gas showrooms were closed.

With resolution of the British Gas legacy problems in sight, the focus of the Centrica management shifted towards implementing a *'new business model and getting in shape for the future'* (Sir Roy Gardner, CEO). During the early 1980s, vertical integration characterized most energy markets around the world. This enabled countries to build an infrastructure, to protect government strategic assets and also to provide incentives for people to invest. In most situations, vertically integrated businesses existed and gas, electricity and water were separate under state control and boundaries set by strict regulations. Over the past 20 years, these vertically integrated businesses have been privatized and their markets liberalized. The value chains have been fragmented as those parts of the value chain which could be subject to competition have been opened up.

Overall, the main contextual changes in the broad UK electricity and gas industry concerned its regulatory status and the introduction of new technologies. The deregulation and liberalization process broke up the main segments that make up the electricity value chain (generation–transmission/distribution–supply). Hence utilities have been forced by the regulator to separate their businesses and the traditional model of vertically integrated monolithic utilities seems no longer to be justified since there is no room for considerable economies of scale any more. Alongside deregulation, new-generation technologies have consistently reduced the minimum thresholds of efficient entry into a market, because of their lower costs compared to old-style nuclear or fossil-fuelled generation. Therefore, investment on a massive scale is no longer needed to enter the electricity market. As a result, many utilities have moved from being nationalized and vertically integrated to a situation where their management is making choices about the elements of the value chain on which they should concentrate. At the same time the lifting of public protection has made utilities more sensitive to competition and customer-related issues.

In these new conditions, Centrica's CEO and other key executives sought to replace the old utility model that they inherited from British Gas. At the same time, it was widely accepted that customer acquisition and retention was gradually becoming very expensive, cutting margins to almost nothing. One way to deal with this issue was to sell a wide range of products and services to each customer, increasing individual customer value. To achieve this, the top management decided to develop a new business model where customer satisfaction and retention would be central. The new design would be powered by the drive to gain as much value from each customer as possible but at the same time reward loyal customers. However, this bold decision not to build Centrica around the established utility model where assets were a central priority raised a number of doubts regarding the future financial stability of the company. Investors and analysts were among those who expressed their worries.

Despite these initial doubts, Centrica's management saw the demerger as a prime chance to build a new business model where the customer would have a prime position together with a strong asset base and retailing/supply capabilities. In contrast to the other business models dominating the utilities sector, namely the 'pure independent power producer', 'integrated independent power producer', 'pure retail reseller' and 'traditional utility' models, the new model would focus on gaining the maximum value per customer by exploiting synergies across multiple areas of expertise (namely: customers, assets, energy and retailing).

It is noteworthy that the energy customer was already high on the list of priorities for the Centrica management team, since the demerger effectively made Centrica responsible for the customer-oriented British Gas businesses: providing gas, electricity and energy-related products and services to homes and businesses in the UK. Further than that, the demerger enabled the top management team to focus on the customer service issue in a way that was considered almost impossible under the old British Gas structure. Hence, Centrica became the first utility to make customer satisfaction an integral part of executive pay packages and the management team invested heavily in improving the company's customer support systems and training its staff.

Source: Paroutis and Pettigrew (2003) The Challenges of Making and Executing Strategy in a Multibusiness Firm, Case Study for the WBS Full Time MBA; http://www.centrica.co.uk; 'Pan-European Utilities' report by HSBC, May 2002; Centrica Annual Reports 1997–2002.

Questions

1 Use the PEST and SWOT tools to analyse the environment that Centrica is facing after its demerger from British Gas.

2 What do you think would be the principal challenges in implementing the new Centrica business model?

3 Conduct another PEST and SWOT analysis for Centrica in 2015. In your analysis, consider the trends to aim towards more environmentally friendly production, supply and consumption of energy.

References

Ahmed, A.M., Zairi, M. and Alwabel S.A. (2006) Global benchmarking for internet and e-commerce applications. *Benchmarking: An International Journal*, **13**, **1/2**, 68–80.

Ansoff, H.I. (1965) *Corporate Strategy*, Penguin, Harmondsworth.

Ansoff, H.I. (1972) The concept of strategic management. *Journal of Business Policy*, **2**, **4**, Summer.

Bower, J.L. (1982) Business policy in the 1980s. *Academy of Management Review*, **7**, **4**, 630–8.

Bower, J.L. (1986) *Managing the Resource Allocation Process*, Harvard Business School Press, Boston, MA.

Chandler, A.D. (1962) *Strategy and Structure: Chapters in the History of the Industrial Enterprise*, MIT Press, Cambridge, MA.

Christensen, C. (1997) *The Innovator's Dilemma: When New Technologies Cause Great Firms to Fail*, Harvard Business School Press, Cambridge, MA.

Cummings, S. and Wilson D.C. (2003) *Images of Strategy*, Blackwell, Oxford.

Hill, T. and Westbrook, R. (1997) SWOT analysis: it's time for a product recall. *Long Range Planning*, **30**, **1**, 46–52.

Hussey, D. (1998) *Strategic Management: From Theory to Implementation*, 4th edn, Butterworth-Heinemann, Oxford.

Ip, Y.K. and Koo, L.C. (2004) BSQ strategic formulation framework: a hybrid of balanced scorecard, SWOT analysis and quality function deployment. *Managerial Auditing Journal*, **19**, **4**, 533–43.

Koo, L.C. (1998) Building balanced scorecard on the house of quality. The 1st Industrial Engineering and Management (IEM) Symposium, *Transformational Strategy towards the 21st Century*, Hong Kong, 20–21 November.

Legge, K. (2003) Strategy as organising. In S. Cummings and D.C. Wilson (eds) *Images of Strategy*, Blackwell, Oxford.

Magretta, J. (2003) *What Management is*, Profile Books, London.

Menon, A., Bharadwaj, S.G., Phani Tej Adidam, P.T. and Edison, S.W. (1999), Antecedents and consequences of marketing strategy making. *Journal of Marketing*, **63**, 18–40.

Mintzberg, H., Ahlstrand, B. and Lampel, J. (1998) *Strategy Safari*, FT Prentice Hall, Harlow.

Mintzberg, H. and Waters, J. (1985) Of strategies, deliberate and emergent. *Strategic Management Journal*, **6**, 257–72.

Morris, D. (2005) A new tool for strategy analysis: the opportunity model. *Journal of Business Strategy*, **26**, **3**, 50–6.

Pettigrew, A.M., Thomas, H. and Whittington, R. (eds) (2002) *Handbook of Strategy and Management*, Sage, London.

Porter, M. (1980) *Competitive Strategy*, Free Press, New York.

Power, D.J., Gannon, M.J., McGinnis, M.A. and Schweiger, D.M. (1986) *Strategic Management Skills*, Addison-Wesley, Reading, MA.

Prahalad, C.K. and Hamel, G. (1990) The core competence of the organization. *Harvard Business Review*, May–June.

Proctor, T. (2000) Strategic marketing management for health management: cross impact matrix and TOWS. *Journal of Management in Medicine*, **14**, **1**, 47–56.

Quinn, J.B. (1980) *Strategies for Change: Logical Incrementalism*, Irwin, Homewood, IL.

Valentin, E.K. (2001) SWOT analysis from a resource-based view. *Journal of Marketing*, **9**, **6**, 54–69.

Weihrich, H. (1982), The TOWS matrix: a tool for situational analysis. *Journal of Long Range Planning*, **15**, **2**, 54–66.

Further reading

Cova, B. (1996) The postmodern explained to managers; implications for marketing. *Business Horizons*, **39**, **6**, 15–23.

D'Aveni, R. (1994) *Hypercompetition*, Free Press, New York.

McGee, J. (2005) *The Blackwell Encyclopedia of Management 2nd edition, Strategic Management*, Blackwell, Oxford.

Mintzberg, H., Ahlstrand, B. and Lampel, J. (1998) *Strategy Safari*, FT Prentice Hall, Harlow.

Porter, M.E. (1986) What is strategy? *Harvard Business Review*, Nov–Dec, 61–78.

Chapter 2

A systemic analysis of strategy and practice

Introduction

Chapter 1 introduced the concept of strategy. It explained its significance for an organization and why it is distinctive compared to other activities in the organization. It also described the intuitive and ad hoc strategy tools such as SWOT, commonly used by organizations, particularly but not exclusively business organizations, in planning for the future. These strategy tools help organizations to systematically structure their thoughts, to identify key areas such as market data for research and discovery and key decisions that need to be taken. Websites and popular strategy texts describe many such strategy tools with detailed instructions on how to put them to good use. However, none of these approaches sets out to define or make any decision, let alone a 'correct' decision. What this chapter does is to set out how academics and other serious business researchers have provided a more formal structure by which strategy and strategic decisions can be analysed, made and implemented. This calls for a body of knowledge which this formal analysis uses to illuminate the strategic choices faced by firms. There are three figures that are central to the point of view in this chapter. The first is a *systems model* of an organization in which the world external to the organization and its internal organizational world are linked together through a process of analysis, decision, and implementation over time to generate organizational performance (see Figure 2.1). The next two focus more directly on the internal workings of the organization to consider (i) the basic systems and structures through which the organization manages itself (Figure 2.3) and (ii) the processes of managerial action that lie behind the elements of the system (Figure 2.4).

De Wit and Meyer (1999) provide some useful language to help us distinguish between the three major elements of our system, namely the environment, the nature of strategy, and the organizational processes involved. Their definitions are:

- *Strategy Context*: the 'where' of strategy. This is the set of factors which comprise the setting for a strategy. This includes the internal context of the organization as well as the characteristics of the external context in the operating environment (such as the nature of inter-organizational relations or the influence of government agencies).

- *Strategy Content*: basically the 'what' of strategy. This means defining what strategic decisions are about (for example, new product or service) and what their intention is (for example, cost reduction or profit maximization). The content perspective also addresses such questions as where are we going (what are the long-term goals?) and what is the scope of the business (what are we going to do?).

- *Strategy Process*: the 'how' of strategy. This details who is involved in the process and when and where activities take place. It is the story, the drama and the cast of players in the strategy as well as the characteristics of the process itself (for example, continuous or discontinuous, short or drawn out over time).

In our overall model, which we call the *strategy map*, we use content, context and process as key ingredients of the business model and strategy system. Using these ideas we develop further the concept of strategy which guides the rest of this book.

2.1 Thinking about strategy: schools of thought

Strategy, as a topic of study, concentrates very much on the situational problems of the general manager (or top management team or CEO). Strategy is different, then, from a more general theory of organizations – it is more specific and more focused. The general manager's job is to diagnose what is critical in complex business situations and to find realistic solutions to strategic and organizational problems. To solve problems, the general manager must be capable of understanding and using the knowledge from each of the organization's functional areas to provide a holistic 'total business' (systems) perspective on issues pertaining to strategic management. For example, the general manager must be able to analyse competitive situations within industries in order to understand the sources of the firm's competitive advantage.

In consequence, we believe that a strategist (or the strategic team) must focus on understanding the specific context of the strategic problem. He or she must have an intuitive as well as a rational feel for defining the boundaries of the problem and the issues to include in any analysis. A strategist must also recognize the interrelationships between all the organizational functions, activities and processes, and be able to frame the problem by recognizing the influence, not only of history but also of the future, on the problem context. The strategist must be willing to act, must have a bias for action and be equally willing to accept the consequences – be they success or failure – of the strategies he or she chooses. Therefore, unashamedly, we present in this book a conception of strategy which focuses on the role and the perspective of the general manager.

While this essentially practical approach is generally uncontroversial, it says little about how strategies develop, evolve and change. For example, are managers in complete control of their strategic futures? Or, alternatively, are companies and top managers simply pawns in the movement of larger industrial and economic futures?

Therefore, it is important to develop a discussion about strategy around an appreciation of some of the theories which contribute to current strategic thinking and which help to outline how managers can frame and interpret strategy. It is important to understand how these theories develop, how they have evolved and what problems they either seek to solve or begin to explain. What follows, therefore, is a very brief review of the main theories in the strategy field as a basis for showing how they are reflected in the development of the strategic framework and strategic systems model which is the basis for this book.

As noted and defined in the previous chapter, Chandler's definition of strategy (1962) is the guiding principle underlying the so-called *classical or rational view* of strategy. A range of other eminent academics, including March and Simon (1958), Cyert and March (1963), Mintzberg (1994), Alchian (1950), Henderson (1973), Williamson (1975) and Pascale (1984), have provided the main alternative viewpoints. The *evolutionary view* emphasizes the competitive processes of natural selection and environmental determinism; survival is everything and nature is the optimizer. In this world, strategy can be a delusion and *economy* (minimizing costs) is the best strategy. On the other hand, the *processual or organizational process view* of strategy expresses a more agnostic view about a market's ability to produce satisfactory outcomes. In this view, both organizations and markets are sticky and messy, and strategies emerge slowly with much confusion and in small steps. Strategic behaviour is embedded and entrenched in internal cultures, routines and standard operating procedures. In this view, strategy is programmed by the DNA of organizations. An alternative and more recent viewpoint, focusing on the *strategy as systems view*, has room for managers and organizations to look forward and make effective plans, in contrast with the agnostic and even nihilistic stance of the evolutionary and organizational process perspectives. The systemic view is drawn principally from the work of organizational sociologists such as Granovetter (1985) and rests on notions of social embeddedness. Embeddedness maintains that people's economic behaviour is embedded in a network of social relations that may involve their families, the state, their professional and educational backgrounds, even their religion and ethnicity. Such influences are largely absent from the restricted environment of the classical and processual approaches but find some expression in the evolutionary view.

There is a new approach which has gained recent significant support. This is the *resource-based view* attributed to economist Edith Penrose (1959). In this view, the emphasis is on those resources and competences that are distinctive to the organization and are the fundamental underpinning of their marketplace positioning. In this world, competition is a contest for the acquisition of skills and competences and other intangible assets. This has been termed a theory of *core competences* (to use the words popularized by gurus CK Prahalad and Gary Hamel[1]) that provides linkages between the classical, processual and systemic views. By virtue of its focus on tacit and intangible resources, it links directly with new theories of knowledge management and is the basis for a new knowledge-based view of strategy advanced by Nelson and Winter (1982) and others, in which superior knowledge is put forward as the most valuable resource of all.

Our observation of many of these writers as well as business consultants and other advisers is that they err on the side of conventional rationality, the classical model, and provide the reader with little guidance about how to interpret the changing world of technology and globalization in which we live and the way in which organizations form strategic positions in this world. Strategizing in the real world is something of a caricature in these conventional writings, with little attention

---

[1] Expressed in 'The core competence of the organization', *Harvard Business Review* (1990).

paid to providing realistic appreciations of the forces at work. It is obvious that the drivers of change have been new structures of scientific knowledge, the internationalization of experience in a time of rapid media access to diverse cultures, and the acceleration of technological change in post-industrial society. Thus, we see strategy as marked increasingly by an eclectic and multi-cultural nature and a post-industrial, high-tech, internationalist context. For example, the US and the UK are essentially post-industrial, service economies; Asia is entering the industrial stage with specialized industries but markets that are almost entirely international. Structural change is endemic in the world economy and even the largest corporations are caught up in the ebb and flow of outsourcing, refocusing new technologies and intangible, human capital. This is in sharp contrast to the world of the rationalist, where strategy is the preserve of top management and the approach is strategy-as-planning, where organizations are efficient, rational resource-allocation mechanisms designed to achieve competitive advantage and economic rents.

What we propose in our conceptual strategic model is a much more blended, balanced and systemic view of the world. It is a treatment of strategy that builds on the roots provided by the classical model (after all, there is still virtue in rationality) and reflects the modern resource-based and knowledge-based view but uses all the available lenses and viewpoints of strategy and strategic thinking to interpret, make sense of and provide a basis for strategic decisions.

2.1.1 The Honda debate

As a motivating example to illustrate the use of multiple viewpoints in framing strategy, we as teaching professors attempt to make sense of Honda's strategic behaviour in the celebrated case of its entry into the US motorcycle market. This has been extensively discussed in the strategy literature but its very familiarity enables us to make the point convincingly. The classical view held that Honda's successful entry was a masterpiece of rational economic calculation, so much so that Boston Consulting Group, in a celebrated report (1975), laid out their view about the importance of market share objectives and economies of scale and experience in the motorcycle industry. They used this argument as a benchmark in providing advice to the British government for its own attempts to revitalize the failing British motorcycle industry in the mid-1970s. The opposing explanation of Honda's success was the processual view advanced powerfully by Richard Pascale. He maintained that Honda's successful entry was, indeed, a masterpiece of strategic thinking but rather of flexible, quick incremental adjustment to the marketplace realities and emergent thinking in framing its ongoing strategy. Honda management did not know what they were taking on but learned very quickly. There is a still broader, all-encompassing systemic view that holds that it is not the Japanese management of Honda that determines the strategy, nor is it simply a version of 'muddling through', but it is the local US management of Honda that works out how the game has to be played. Indeed, Honda USA becomes embedded in the network of American social and business relationships, albeit with a very distinctive Japanese flavour. In particular, Honda, like all auto/motorcycle companies, worked out that it faces the same industry conditions of scale economies, access, capacity, persistent entry by newly industrializing countries and trends towards commoditization. Although Honda may have found short-term distinctiveness in the US market, in the end it will find that this will erode and the only strategy available to it over the long term will be to keep its costs low and its options open.

This commentary on Honda exemplifies the need for contemporary strategic thinking to move away from the purely rational or planned view towards a more eclectic view that embraces the emergent, incremental or processual approaches with a stronger respect for the power or markets and institutions – primarily governments – to shape the behaviour of corporations. Corporate behaviour is neither simply rational nor simply determined by its various environments. Any strategic model has to capture the increasing complexity of modern corporate life, first by providing alternative lenses (perspectives, theories and rules of thumb) through which to see the world and, second, by articulating a way of telling the strategy story so that the reader can see how organizations frame their strategic positioning in their drive for long-term strategic successes. Thus, the centrepiece – our strategy story – is the juxtaposition of intangible resources at the firm level with imperfectly competitive markets in the context of ever more dynamic and intrusive environments involving globalization and rapid, disruptive technological change. We now move on to a discussion of the strategy systems framework which defines the structure and context of this book.

2.2 The strategy systems framework

Figure 2.1 shows the *systemic model* of strategy and the logic underlying our approach to understanding strategy. It argues that the various models, definitions of strategy and frameworks provided in the book are vehicles for thinking about strategy and policy and carrying out a dialogue about strategic options. In essence, our vignettes of strategy in the following chapters should be interpreted as elements on the strategy map of Figure 2.1.

This model (or map) is a system in that it portrays how the individual elements of the larger system are interconnected by causality and through time. A systems model requires feedback between elements so that system behaviour changes dynamically through either self-adaptation or intentional adaptation (by managers). Feedback would normally be negative, so that extreme behaviours will be forced back towards normality. But it can be positive feedback, so that system behaviour gets driven further and further away from the norm. The role of management, especially the top management team, is to manage the whole system so as to achieve desired objectives without undue perturbations or risks. Effective management of each element is not by itself sufficient to change the behaviour of the whole system towards desirable objectives – it is the whole system that has to be the target for attention. From this systems perspective, top management is attempting to manage the intersections and inter-connections between multiple external systems (the strategy *context*) and the organization itself.

Seen from a systems perspective, the task of management is to keep the organization in a controlled balance against the multiple and diverse forces in the broader strategic context. We use the terms *alignment* and *strategic fit* to indicate how a strategy needs to be fitted ('aligned') with its external context and how the internal organization needs to be properly meshed ('aligned') with the strategy. Thus the strategic fit of strategy with the external context and of strategy with internal organization is the prime task of the general management team.

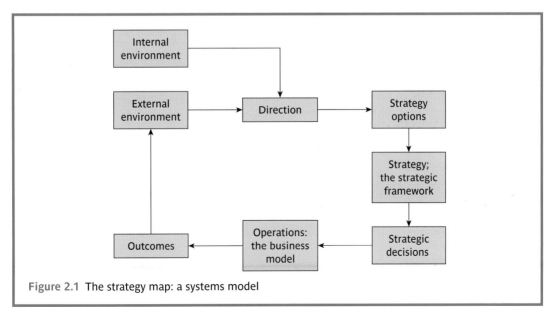

Figure 2.1 The strategy map: a systems model

Case box 2.1: **The legacy of Russ Ackoff**

In the study of management our ideas about systems (or *systemic*) thinking are largely due to Russ Ackoff who died on 29 October 2009. He wrote over 30 books on management and became one of the most influential management gurus of the 20th century, known primarily for his ideas about systemic thinking.

Ackoff contrasted systemic thinking with the reductionist, atomistic thinking that, according to him, had long dominated management's approach to problem solving. Put simply, systems thinking (see Ackoff, *Redesigning the Future: A Systems Approach to Societal Problems*, 1974) focuses on the performance of a system as a whole. This is in contrast to an approach that breaks the system into parts and then focuses on the performance of individual parts on the assumption that if each individual part is improved then the sum of the parts will not only be better but will be the best possible outcome. This assumption often proves wrong in practice, according to Ackoff.

The only profession that he believed had truly embraced systems thinking is architecture, where the design process starts by asking what sort of building is required and then works backwards to focus on what individual parts are required. An architect never starts by saying 'Here are the parts, what can I build from them?' Thus an architect will often choose a part that is not by itself the best performing as long as it is fit for purpose, no better than it need be.

In business, flawed analytical thinking, a focus on parts rather than the whole, manifests itself almost everywhere. For example, firms often focus on growth over development, or bigger over better. Mergers and acquisitions frequently make firms bigger but arguably no better (see Chapter 8). Businesses also adopt partial approaches such as concentrating on pricing and neglecting other elements of the marketing mix. In terms of strategy one frequently sees an over-emphasis on analysis at the expense of implementation and evaluation. For example, see the widely documented failure of the American administration to prepare for post-war planning in Iraq.

According to *The Economist* (3 November 2009), the meltdown of the financial system during 2007–8 was a classic example of the dangers of putting atomized thinking ahead of systems thinking. The conventional wisdom judges the efficiency of markets by the accuracy of their individual prices rather than on their robustness in the event of shocks or their vulnerability when liquidity dries up. The performance of individual financial institutions was judged by their profits, their capital cushions and their risk management systems, which were supposedly becoming ever more sophisticated but failed to detect the approaching systemic collapse (see Chapter 4 for an extended discussion of this). The challenge, therefore, is to design a regulator for the finance industry that actually measures and focuses on systemic risks rather than on individual parts of the system.

Source: Compiled by the authors from 'How to Change the System', The Economist Online, 3 November 2009, and other sources

Questions

1 Identify more examples of partial rather than systemic thinking approaches in business. Try also to identify examples of effective systems thinking.

2 Is it fair to compare architecture with management? After all, architects spend most of their time on new buildings whereas the time of managers is dominated by legacies from the past, i.e. refurbishing existing buildings.

3 To optimize a whole system is obviously not on the cards for every decision. In other words, some degree of sub-optimization is inevitable because of the costs of decision making. So where does systems thinking break down and at what point does partial thinking become defensible?

In the following chapters the many, diverse elements of the system, the strategy map, are examined and various sub-systems are discussed. What follows in the next section is a brief description of each of the elements within the system.

2.2.1 The environment

The environment was discussed extensively in Chapter 1. Figure 1.5 provides a picture of the different layers in the **external environment**. A more analytical approach would differentiate the inner layers relating to the market and the industry context from a middle layer of domestic government macroeconomic and other policies, and also from an outer layer of international trade and international institutions. The aim here is to build a multi-layered portrayal of the drivers of demand for the company's products. While the inner layer of market drivers is important, of more long-term significance is the *deep structure* of the market containing the fundamental forces that shape and drive the large economic trends (such as the continuing credit crunch of 2009).

The *internal environment* was also discussed in Chapter 1. There we used the language of SWOT analysis which we criticized for its laundry list mentality. We need to go rather deeper than this. Economists see the firm as a bundle of productive resources where resources are defined as inputs into the firm's operations so as to produce goods and services. In this view resources are generic and specific categories are not suggested. But typical examples include patents, capital equipment, and skilled and unskilled human resources. Strategists go further and distinguish *capabilities* from *resources*. A capability is the ability to perform a task or activity that involves complex patterns of coordination and cooperation between people and other resources. Capabilities would include research and development expertise, customer service and high-quality manufacturing. Skills, by contrast, are more specific, relating to narrowly defined activities such as typing, machine maintenance and bookkeeping.

Strategists are interested in those resources and capabilities that can earn rents (a surplus of revenue over cost). These collectively are known as ***strategic assets*** or *core competences*[2] and are a sub-set of, but distinct from, those other resources and capabilities that do not distinctively support competitive advantage. The strategic task for the firm is to sustain these rent streams over time by creating and protecting the competitive advantage and the strategic assets that together underpin them. The inherent value of the strategic assets for the firm depends on the ways in which the firm combines, coordinates and deploys these assets in concert with the other firm-specific and more generic resources and capabilities.

The internal economy of the firm can be seen as sets of discrete activities (e.g. a product line), each of which leads to market positions and each of which is supported by assets which we later describe as (in Chapters 3 and 5) resources and capabilities. Similar activities (for example, the Ford Mondeo and Ford Focus product lines) share some common strategic assets and some common generic assets. This sharing can lead to economies of scale (if different components share the same production line), to economies of scope (where products might go through common distribution channels), and experience effects. Complementary activities require dissimilar sets of strategic assets which would then require degrees of coordination (for example, marketing activities and production activities). The skills of coordination and internal cooperation are in fact high-level capabilities with considerable strategic significance.

This means that strategic management cannot be captured in the form of a strategic theory of the firm in a way that enables equations to be identified, data collected and analysed and simple

---

[2] But note that there are many other labels, such as distinctive capabilities from Selznick (1957), and many other terms are and have been current.

rules inferred. Strategic management is much more eclectic and diverse. Contexts both external and internal to the firm are highly idiosyncratic. This places a premium on the ability to diagnose situations and formulate options. The specific routes to high performance are many and varied and not readily susceptible to simple generalizations.

2.2.2 Direction and strategy options

Understanding the firm's *overarching direction* is critical. The general question being asked here is 'What does the organization want to be?'. The language commonly used is *vision*, *mission* and *values*. None of these terms has an unambiguous definition and, indeed, academic research does not pay much attention to them as academic entities. However, the popular business press and the very many websites that discuss strategy offer definitions and much advice about writing effective vision and mission statements. Generally accepted and succinct definitions are the following:

- Vision describes where the organization wants to be in the future: '*an image of the future we seek to create*'.
- Mission defines where the organization is and what its purpose is: '*who we are and what we do*'.
- Values are beliefs that are shared among the stakeholders: '*what we believe in*'.

The organization is usually encouraged to develop a long-term *vision* of what it wants to be and it takes into account the company's culture, reputation, competences and resources in addressing that question. The vision is the core ideology of the organization, which provides the glue that binds the organization together. It encompasses a set of core *values* that address questions such as why the company exists and what it believes in. The core values may include such things as honesty and integrity, hard work and continuous self-improvement, strong customer service, creativity, and imagination. On the other hand, the *mission* is to do with the company's reason for being – in Walt Disney's case, it is simply stated as being to make people happy or, in Hewlett-Packard's case, to make a technological contribution to the advancement and welfare of humanity. Purpose, in this sense, is very close to the mission of the organization and, as stated earlier, the vision is the core ideology which binds the organization together. Collins and Porras (2000) argue that what they describe as 'big, hairy, audacious goals' improve long-term vision – for example, Stanford University's statement in the 1940s that it wanted to become 'the Harvard of the West' or Boeing's vision in the 1950s of becoming the 'dominant player in aviation and bringing the world into the jet age'. It is simplistic but powerful to think of the Vision as built upon the Values and the Mission – what currently exists and what are the fundamental values that constitute the foundation for seeking an image of the future to which the organization can aspire.

A term also used to indicate long-term purpose is *strategic intent*. It has been argued that Western firms seeking strategic fit have often found themselves overtaken by firms, especially the Asian conglomerates, driven by long-term visions of the future, which are then relentlessly and ruthlessly pursued with strategic intent. Companies like Honda, NEC and Sony have succeeded (according to this argument) because of their sustained obsession with achieving global dominance in their industries. Strategic intent is the label that has been given to this obsession (Hamel and Prahalad, 1989). The significance of this is that the intent of these companies was out of proportion to their existing resources and capabilities. This gap between ambition and resources is known as *strategic stretch*. These companies had to expand and adapt their current stock of resources and create new ones. They were more concerned with 'leveraging' resources than with achieving strategic fit between their current resources and their industry environments.

2.2.3 Strategies: the strategic framework

The *strategic framework* is the design of the business that follows from creative strategic thinking. We saw from Chapter 1 that strategy is the exercise of choice and the making of trade-offs between alternative courses of action for the deployment of scarce resources. The practical anatomy of strategy can be seen as follows:

1 Where are we going?   – clear set of long-term goals
2 What businesses are we in and why?   – the scope of the business
3 How are we going to succeed?   – competitive advantage(s)
4 How do we know it will work?   – the business model

Step 1 requires a description of the underlying vision, mission and values of the organization and the strategic intent and long-term objectives (including financial performance) that it wants to achieve over a defined time horizon.

Step 2 describes the scope of the organization – in which product-markets does it choose to compete? Firms obviously cannot compete in any and every market. They must make some choices. However, the logic for making choices is not obvious in itself. Firms might choose to compete in closely related markets where, for example, the technologies and production methods are similar, where distribution channels are common, or where there are common customers for a range of products. But such *relatedness* or *synergy* can be difficult to define or achieve and some firms have preferred to adopt more conglomerate-style approaches where the chosen businesses are apparently very diverse. Another facet of scope is geographic markets. Should one restrict the focus to the home market? Or are there arguments for adopting a more multinational posture? Ansoff's (1965) famous *product-market diversification matrix* shows the different types of diversification.

Step 3 articulates the benefits that the firm can bring to its customers and to itself by its positioning within its chosen product-markets. Why should the customer buy this product? Why should he or she buy from us? What value can we gain from making this proposition to the customer? These are all ways of describing the nature of the *competitive advantage* that the firm can achieve.

This has implications for positioning choices in product-markets. This takes us into **Step 4**, the practical strategic logic behind competitive advantage. This has three parts. The first is the positioning logic – the market-based logic which underpins our competitive advantage ambitions. The second part is the resource-based logic that states why we think our intentions and actions about resources and capabilities will lead to the products and services that can be positioned in markets in the desired way. Finally, it is important that these be converted into actions that result in the desired pattern of cash flows – the business model.

2.2.4 Strategic decisions

Strategic decisions (or strategy content) are the substance of a firm's strategy. The strategic content is developed within the confines of the strategic context with the view of taking advantage of the opportunities and minimizing the threats that are afforded to the firm. There are numerous perspectives on how strategies should be, and are, developed (see later in this chapter) and the concept of strategic content does not prescribe how the content should be developed.

Researchers have distinguished between three levels of strategy – *single business*, *multi-business* and *multinational* – and have offered a typology for each. The dimensions used reflect the tensions of strategic choice. At the level of business strategy the dimension runs from cost based to differentiation based (e.g. Porter's generic strategies, 1980, 1985). At the multi-business level (*corporate*

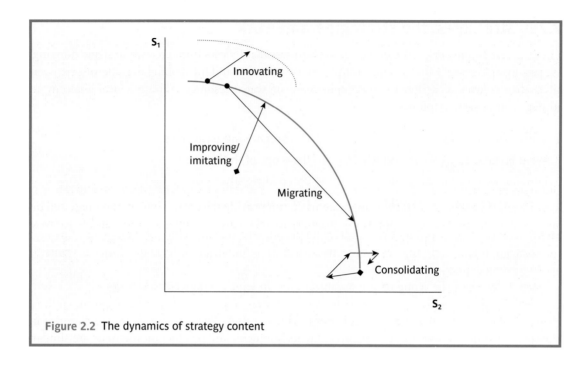

Figure 2.2 The dynamics of strategy content

strategy) there is tension between scale and scope, i.e. between *vertical and horizontal specialization* (in a way that Adam Smith would have recognized and George Stigler, 1951 would have analysed), and *vertical and horizontal integration* (a process that Chandler, 1990 described so vividly. At the multinational level scholars such as Prahalad and Doz (1986) and Bartlett and Ghoshal (1989) distinguish between global integration and national responsiveness. This is an analogue of cost-based standardization versus differentiation at the business level.

Figure 2.2 presents a two-dimensional strategy space (S_1 and S_2) that can be used to represent these strategy tensions or trade-offs. The curved solid line represents a strategy frontier (in economics this would be an efficiency frontier) on which those firms with best current practice are situated. Using this framework we can think of four different types of strategy with their own dynamic characteristics. *Improving and imitating* involves a move from within the frontier to a best-practice position on the frontier. *Innovating* represents an attempt to move beyond the existing frontier to create a new best practice. *Migrating* is a shift of position from one strategy emphasis to another, such as moving from a cost-based strategy to a differentiation-based strategy. *Consolidating* is the shoring up and improving of an existing position, e.g. investing more in capital equipment to gain further economies of scale.

2.2.5 Operations: the business model

We describe *operations* as the **business model**. There is a complete literature on operations and operations management which we do not need to replicate or summarize. From a strategy perspective, what we are really interested in is how the strategy decisions turn into a sustainable business model. This is a widely used term intended to provide the link between an intended strategy, its functional and operation requirements, and the performance (typically cash flows and profits) that is expected. It usually applies to single businesses where a specific competitive strategy can be identified but it can also apply to those multi-business portfolios that are linked by strong synergies and therefore have common or similar strategies.

What the business model does is to articulate the logic of the intended strategy in terms of the specific operations that have to take place. With this detailed plan the consequences for cash flows can be determined and the link between (intended) strategy and (expected) performance can be established. In practice, a business model would be articulated in terms of detailed plans and budgets that provide guidance to managers relating to their operational responsibilities. The logic that drives plans and budgets lies within the business model.

The business model is explained and discussed in more detail in Chapter 5.

2.2.6 Outcomes

Outcomes are surprising difficult to define. A critical element in successful strategy implementation is an appropriate scoring system. Many systems do not provide the critical information required by management to assess the corporation's progress to achieving its strategic vision and objectives. The *balanced scorecard* is a performance measurement system developed by Kaplan and Norton (1992) which, although including financial measures of performance, also contains operational measures of customer satisfaction, internal processes, and the corporation's innovation and improvement activities, which are seen as the key drivers of future financial performance. The approach provides a mechanism for management to examine a business from the four important perspectives of:

1 How do customers see the firm? (*customer perspective*)
2 What does the firm excel at? (*internal perspective*)
3 Can the firm continue to improve and create value? (*innovation and learning perspective*)
4 How does the firm look to shareholders? (*financial perspective*)

The system also avoids information overload by restricting the number of measures used so as to focus only on those seen to be essential. The balanced scorecard presents this information in a single management report and brings together often disparately reported elements of the firm's strategic position, such as short-term customer response times, product quality, teamwork capability, new product launch times and the like. Second, the approach guards against sub-optimization by forcing management to examine operational measures comprehensively.

The balanced scorecard is developed in more detail in Chapters 5 and 16.

2.3 Linking organization and strategy

The positioning and analytical models of strategy introduced in Chapter 1 are often logical and simple in structural terms. In turn, they can be made sense of by managers in an equally simple way, ignoring the nuances which may lie in the way of thinking and acting strategically. As Michaud and Thoenig (2003) point out, a good strategy model such as Figure 1.2 (the basic dynamics of strategy) in Chapter 1 is one which is easily readable, can be understood quickly by managers and is transparent to organizational members and outsiders. The philosophy here is that logically simple is best. The best performances come from adopting and implementing simple models which can be easily understood throughout the organization. Thus, multiple views on strategy and nuances of interpretation are to be avoided as far as possible.

Yet with this view comes a paradox. If all organizations have access to the same models of strategy and to the same external consultants who prescribe best practices which they distribute in the manner of a cure-all, then what is to differentiate them? Where is the source of competitive advantage, since most organizations will follow similar routes based upon models of best practice and effective strategic positioning?

Part of the answer lies in the difficult choices made between uncertain futures and the risks involved in these. But a deeper answer seems to lie in how managers and organizations interpret such models and also in how they put strategies into practice in organizations. In short, when strategy meets organization, the actions and processes which ensue have a large impact upon the extent to which strategy is effective, competitive and ultimately successful. How managers think and act, as well as the distinctive organizational routines which they develop, matters as much as the models which may have informed strategy in the first place.

2.3.1 Thinking and acting strategically

Strategic management, like many other management sub-disciplines, favours dualisms to make conceptual distinctions in the models it uses. These can take many forms, such as competition versus cooperation, or strategy versus structure. While they are useful thinking devices, such contrasts tend to mask the extent to which they are really not polar extremes at all, but are closely interrelated. Structure is as much a part of process as process is a part of structure. And certainly, competition and cooperation both inform one another and are part of one another, rather than existing as separate entities. In the same way, the terms thinking and acting strategically are also interrelated and blend together in the strategy process.

The primary reason for focusing on *strategic thinking and acting* is that simply focusing on strategy content (strategic positioning) is insufficient to guarantee desired outcomes, for example securing a competitive advantage. This explains why we regard the strategy concepts in Figure 2.1 as a business systems model, which links all elements of the strategy formulation and implementation processes together. Consider Porter's Five Forces model, for example (Porter 1980).[3] This is accepted as the most famous and well-described tool for assessing a firm's competitive position. Informed largely by economic models of the firm, the Five Forces model assesses a firm's position in regard to such factors as the power of suppliers and customers, the ease with which substitution can take place and the barriers to entry for new competitors. The compelling argument from this analysis is that strategy should be guided by the nature of the industry structure and the interrelationships amongst the forces and the firm (allowing, for example, a choice of generic versus specialist strategies or quality and customer service strategies). As in many economic models, however, the assumptions that have to be made in order for the analysis to work are fairly restrictive. For example, the Five Forces model assumes:

- independence amongst all the factors;
- that organizations can formulate strategies 'at arm's length' in relation to rivals, customers and suppliers;
- that structural advantage is the sole key to competitive success (the more a firm has relative power over customers, suppliers etc. the greater is its competitive advantage);
- that, even where such structural advantages occur, firms can always act to exercise such power without any constraints;
- that the industry is the key unit of analysis.

Even at a common-sense level of analysis, not all of the above assumptions can hold true. Even within the same organization, chief executives report severe difficulties in gathering enough information to assess and to mobilize their own operating companies. Looking outside their own organizations to try to implement a Five Forces model is even harder and less realistic.

---

[3] See Chapter 3 for a full discussion.

So what really goes on when managers run with the strategic baton and think about how the analytic models can be applied in handling competition with other firms and rivals? This chapter begins to unpack this question – the *practice of strategy* in organizations.

2.4 The role of management systems

Many authors have called for a view of strategic management which is strongly anchored on the individual and focused on an activity-based view of what managers do (see, for example, Johnson et al., 2003). The intention is to try to relate what happens in the day-to-day activities of individuals in organizations and link these events to strategy processes and outcomes. Some authors go further and argue that the analysis of dialogue and conversations of all individuals in organizations (not just managers) is relevant for the study of how strategies are formulated, supported and implemented (see, for example, Samra-Fredericks, 2003). While we agree that some micro-activities in organizations may reveal information previously overlooked by 'traditional' strategic management, such a perspective is nevertheless highly reductionist. As Balogun et al. (2003) argue, while micro-perspectives may reveal more about the deeply rooted nature of individual activity (and routines) in organizations, there is a simultaneous need to understand breadth and macro levels of analysis. They argue that if we are to understand any possible relationships between changing forms (structures) of organizations and the characteristics of strategy, we must adopt a broad and more systems-based view of the interactions between context, organization and individual action.

Such a systems perspective is a guiding principle of this chapter. Micro-perspectives allow us to see the detail. They allow us to observe, follow and dissect the activities of individuals as they go about their day-to-day activities and we can learn a great deal about human behaviour in organizations this way, but this prevents us seeing the overall picture. Such a micro-level view, however, can never provide a complete explanation of the strategy process. A more systemic view allows us to move across levels of analysis and across the patterns of organization which any organism adopts in relation to its wider environment (Capra, 1982). In this way we can emphasize the relational aspects of management practice and organizational context.

All organizations are essentially complex systems which interact with their environments. In the case of living systems (such as a species of animal) the relationships between the system and its environment can be characterized by the term *structural coupling* – a series of interactions between the living system and its environment trigger a set of responses in the living system resulting in structural and processual changes. These changes can be viewed as the way in which the organism learns, develops and adapts. The same process holds true for complex social organizations. Figures 2.3 and 2.4 show the main systems and strategy processes which help keep the organization aligned with its environment.

Against a backdrop of the system map shown in Figure 2.1, Figure 2.3 shows typical formal systems that operate within an organization. Those of principal interest to us are the *strategic planning process*, the *business planning process*, *budgeting and control systems* and *performance measurement systems*.

2.4.1 Strategic planning

Most corporations today have some form of corporate plan. However, it is often said that very few are successfully implemented. In theory, strategic planning is the mechanism whereby the corporation organizes its resources and actions to achieve its objectives. It is a formal rather than an informal process, the usual contents of which were discussed in Chapter 1. Planning is conducted at hierarchical levels within the corporation, dependent upon its complexity. For the multi-business firm, plans will be established at the corporate, business unit, and departmental or market segment levels.

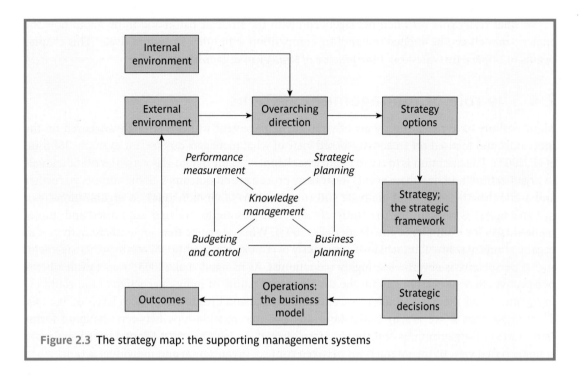

Figure 2.3 The strategy map: the supporting management systems

At the corporate level, the overall mission is established consistent with internal resources and external opportunities and threats. The direction in which the corporation will go is determined in large part by a corporate vision of where it would like to be. The CEO plays a disproportionate role in the establishment of such a vision.

At the business unit level (often described as a strategic business unit or SBU), the concept of mission translates into the markets and activities that the business unit would like to address, subject to corporate-level constraints such as resource allocation. At the market segment level, mission is less ambitious and more constrained, being based on the scope of activities assigned to that segment. Similar cascades apply to the other elements of a plan.

The system is an iterative process, involving a repetitive sequence of strategic developments, strategic planning, plan implementation, and strategic performance measurement. The cycle is normally repeated on an annual basis, with plan horizons presently tending to be around three years in Western companies. Normally, the procedures are standardized, with schedules also phased throughout the planning cycle.

The main steps often consist of the following elements, although the precise timing and content vary from company to company:

Executive briefing

The starting point of the plan commences with a senior management review which includes:
– assumptions about the external environment;
– changes from previous assumptions;
– alternative futures/scenarios;[4]
– a review of progress against the existing plan and an update of performance against goals;
– a possible theme for the forthcoming plan cycle.

---

[4] See scenario planning, Chapter 11.

General management meeting

This establishes the mission, goals and objectives of the corporation, and decisions reached are then broadly communicated to operating managers at business unit level and to other operating managers.

Strategy assessment meeting

Follow-up meetings are held between corporate and SBU executives to discuss issues and options, and policies and guidelines.

Plan overview

Plan submissions from SBUs are consolidated and reviewed with corporate management.

Strategy review meetings

The corporate centre and SBU management negotiate to develop shared views on SBU plans by selecting strategic options, plan modifications, resource allocations and performance targets.

Plan resubmission

Resubmitted plans by SBUs are then consolidated with any corporate-level adjustments and given a final review by corporate management.

Board presentation

The final plan is then summarized in strategic terms, formally submitted to the board of directors for discussion, and usually approved.

The plan and planning cycle are never fully finalized in the sense that both internal and external events may cause them to change. Nevertheless, the plan should provide a blueprint for the development of the corporation over the next period of time. One major consideration is the relationship between the plan and the budget. Theoretically, the two systems should coincide at the point where plans become activities. However, many line executives tend to focus their attention more on the budget than the longer-term plan, and as a consequence there is often some cynicism about the plan unless it is clearly taken seriously by top management.

Interestingly, perhaps, the literature on strategic management in the 1990s and in the new millennium pays little attention to the practicalities of the mechanics of strategic planning, unlike in the 1970s, when formal systems were emphasized. Moreover, while during the 1980s many corporations built up substantial central planning units, these have lost considerable credibility, as the growth and volatility of markets were seen to outpace the ability of central strategists to keep up. In addition, many managers believe that top management in the West has become relatively obsessed with short-term rather than long-term performance.

Interestingly, Japanese corporations have built significant planning departments. Employees in these departments, however, have rarely been trained as specialist planners; rather, they are assigned to planning departments as a regular element in their development, based on job rotation, and many come to such departments from anywhere in the company. While plans themselves tend to have a three-year time horizon, they are not seriously changed each year. Furthermore, such plans, all of which have a formal name, usually form elements in much longer-term 'visions' established by the president of the corporation. These visions may have time horizons spanning 20 years or more and, rather than being driven by financial objectives, have broader technical and social goals.

2.4.2 Business planning

Business planning is typically used to describe both strategic and operational planning. We use it here as a complement to strategic planning to describe the process by which organizations get the individual businesses to express the various strategic objectives in specific targets and objectives together with action plans and supporting funding lines. The business plan is thus the detailed operational expression of the strategic plan and is the main ingredient of the business model (see earlier).

2.4.3 Budgeting and control

The essence of budgeting and control systems is captured by this quotation from the Chartered Institute of Public Finance and Accountancy (CIPFA):

> *All organizations need to manage performance so that their financial and strategic objectives are achieved and management and financial stakeholders can be confident in the associated control processes. The proper construction and control of budgets is central to this, to safeguard the organization's viability and the effective delivery of its objectives. This requires a comprehensive financial planning and approval framework; consistent and rigorous processes for constructing budgets, both capital and revenue; sound methodologies for assessing the financial impact of proposed expenditure; compatibility with other management and performance data; and a control system that sets clear responsibilities and produces prompt and accurate monitoring information on performance against budgets.*[5]

In our system model it is important, even critical, to note that budgets are derived from plans, which in turn are derived from strategies, and so on. Thus budgets are *smart*, being driven by a well-designed systems model. However, using budgets as a device for transmitting cost-cutting measures is commonly experienced but is generally not the smartest or most sensible strategic use of a powerful management control system.

2.4.4 Performance measurement

Performance measurement systems go beyond management control systems. They are important because 'you measure what you value and you get what you measure'. In any organization, there must be a linkage to performance. The feedback that is necessary for any organization in reframing its strategy in a sensible way is the answer to the question: 'How do we do a check of performance against targets and cost?' Performance metrics are extremely important – they highlight issues such as progress towards goals and, more importantly, how certain tasks and certain strategies can be adjusted better and faster and how change can be incorporated most effectively within the context of the organization.

Michael Hammer, a well-known author on lean-management and business process redesign, captures our intent very well:

> *A contemporary approach to measurement recognizes that modern businesses are complex systems, for which intuition no longer suffices. Today any action that a manager takes can have myriad and unpredictable consequences throughout the organization. Therefore measurement*

---

[5] http://www.cipfa.org.uk/conduct/download/budgetarySOPP.pdf, 25 July 2008.

must be based on a careful (end-to-end) analysis of the business, one that links the objectives of the business to the things over which managers and front-line personnel have control. Only then can the recognition of a problematic measure lead to the right actions that will correct it and to improved performance of the business a whole.[6]

Obviously, changing the organization through performance monitoring and strategy adjustment is but one process in a series of feedbacks and feedback loops which are absolutely necessary in analysing information about both internal and external environments. In the external environment, we have to question 'what is happening around us'; there must be a process of data gathering and development of insight and knowledge about such issues as new technology and its impact on the business, and the potential impact of regulation and legislation on the activities of the company. The underlying national economic and macroeconomic conditions are also important in setting the global economic context for the organization and, at a more micro level, framing intelligence and analysis about competition, the nature and changing shape of markets and customer needs and opinions. Key success factors in this external environment enable the firm to focus on appropriate product renewal and generate knowledge and insight about new products and ideas. In the context of the internal environment, the firm needs to analyse and identify the firm's key resources and capabilities and evaluate their impact on competitive advantage. For example, a company's culture and the history of its development can provide a source of competitive strength as in the case of Johnson and Johnson (J&J), regarded by many as an extremely ethical and well-run pharmaceutical company. That perception is a result of J&J's strong culture, its history and the strength of its financial resources over a long period of time. Internal analysis also requires a process of continual investigation, discovery and criticism leading to new ideas, new product concepts, updated financial results and updated metrics. Information about organizational strengths and weaknesses can, in turn, lead to the continual renewal of the strategy process.

2.5 The role of management thought processes

The ways in which managers interpret the environment and instigate changes in their organizations is a fundamental part of the strategy process. Getting this interpretation wrong will increase the risk of demise for the organization and getting it right will increase the chances of growth and success.

A common conception of strategy is that it is the 'brain' of an organism, telling the rest of the body what to do. But 'strategy' also comprises controls, monitoring, measurement and procedures. For an organization to be viable (coexist with and adapt to its environment), the understanding of strategy needs to go beyond a simple understanding of senior management control and direction setting and embrace a broader organizational perspective of tactics, control and execution. The systemic approach facilitates such a broad perspective.

In Figure 2.4 we show how management (thought) processes shape and guide the systems of the organization. In this figure we select seven different (but related) management processes, namely, *strategic thinking*, *strategy formulation*, *strategic decision making*, *implementation*, *measurement*, *interpretation*, and *learning*. These are shown for convenience as sequential processes but some, such as interpretation and learning, are conducted simultaneously with the others.

2.5.1 Strategic thinking

Strategic thinking is the intellectual, analytical activity that makes sense of the triad of forces – external context, resources and capabilities, and goals (in Figure 1.2 in Chapter 1) – to visualize and

---
[6] Hammer (2003).

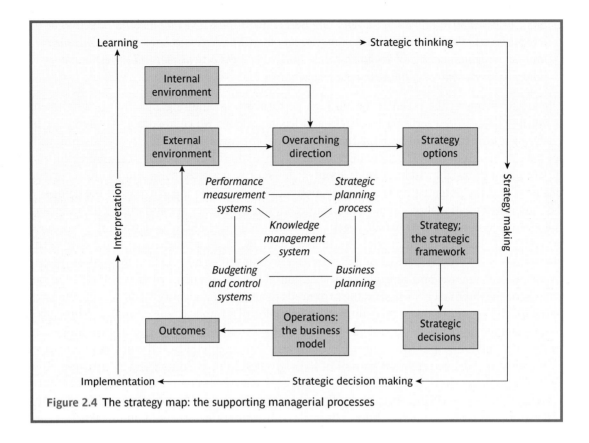

Figure 2.4 The strategy map: the supporting managerial processes

define the strategies that are to be at the heart of the organization. Strategic thinking aims to ensure that the firm's strategy is such that the elements complement and reinforce each other, i.e. the strategies are cohesive. In other words, a coordinated framework of high-level enterprise strategies is developed to achieve the vision.

Strategic thinking as an intellectual activity has many characteristics. First, it is usually free of organization and is not located in any particular part of the organization. Second, it deals with the future, not the present. Third, it is usually marked by creativity in trying to construct strategies that are different and distinctive and that also fit the unknown future. Fourth, it can and usually does use a range of analytical models such as Porter's Five Forces in order to make sense of the current situation. Fifth, it can and often does use data-structuring methods such as scenario analysis in order to make sense of vast amounts of data. Finally, it is not uniquely located in any one individual, or in any one group. Without the benefit of strategic thinking, particularly its creative element, the strategies of the organization would not be different, distinctive or appropriate. It is the engine room of the strategy effort within an organization.

2.5.2 Strategy making

Strategy making concerns how strategies come about in practice. Strategy is essentially a practical subject and strategic decisions can be very individual in character. But we have also seen that the direction and purpose of the organization are very much the province of the general management team. However, general managers cannot know everything. It is evident that strategy requires some form of directional input. This input might be to maintain continuity or momentum in strategy making. It might be to create organizational frameworks within which strategy can be addressed.

The kind of attention required by general managers can be understood through the simple distinction between *intended* and *emergent* strategies. As we saw in Chapter 1, intended strategy refers to desired strategic direction deliberately planned or formulated, whereas emergent strategy is the strategy or sequence of strategic decisions actually followed in practice. Mintzberg's notion of strategy is 'a pattern in the stream of decisions'. This idea enables us to see intentions as one source of patterning and (successful) emergence as another but equally valid source.

Intended strategies rest on systematic, comprehensive approaches to managing the whole business and are articulated through formal strategic planning processes. This view of managerial intent includes the planning view, the command view and the logical incremental view. The planning view (which we have dubbed the rational, classical school) contains a logical sequence of activities, setting of objectives, the analysis of the environment and the resources of the organization, the generation of the strategic alternatives, and their evaluation. This has been codified in practice as SWOT analysis: analysis of strengths, weaknesses, opportunities and threats in which the former two are matched against the latter two in order to obtain an appropriate strategic fit. The command view is simply that of an autocratic leader, while logical incrementalism offers a view of strategy making built up of **incremental** steps.

Emergent strategies are effective responses to unexpected opportunities and problems and are developed from the locations at which business-level strategies are usually implemented, i.e. within business units and not at corporate headquarters. The pure definition of emergence requires the absence of any intentions. This is too strong for most occasions but, as Mintzberg and Waters (1985) observe, organizations come close to pure emergent strategies when an environment directly imposes a pattern of actions on them.

Again as we saw in Chapter 1, the twin lenses of intentions and emergence do come together in the form of *realized strategy* – a blend of intentions and emergence.

Strategy making raises issues of intended and planned strategies (typically top down), versus emergent strategies that arise from experience and learning where the emphasis is on knowledge that is distributed throughout the organization, versus accidents, serendipity and *muddling through* within which strategy is very much the junior partner to flexibility, operations expertise and tactical acumen, and speed of response.

The next question of how to choose between options focuses on the nature of data and information required, the analytical processes used, and how trade-offs are made. It confronts the logic approach of economic and quantitative models with the uncertainty and risk endemic in long-term decisions and raises questions about criteria for decision making and the nature and role of organizational influences.

2.5.3 Strategic decision making

Strategic decision making lies at the heart of strategy. Having analysed the environment, assessed organizational capabilities and investigated technological shifts, managers have to take preferred courses of action. They have to examine possible alternatives and choose amongst them. As Coyne and Subramaniam (1996) observe, strategic decisions are the handful of decisions that drive or shape most of an organization's actions, are not easily changed once made and have the greatest impact upon organizational performance. Strategy may be a grand concept, but it is the individual strategic decisions that matter.

At its simplest, decision making may be considered an instantaneous action, a choice between two or more known alternatives, made by individuals or groups. However, this 'point of decision' approach is unable to capture the richness and complexity of the processes which lead up to the point of decision, the influences on putting the decision into action and the ultimate performance of that decision. It also assumes that managers have full agency and control over decisions. Sometimes they may have very limited discretion to make decisions or choose amongst alternatives. This could be the case, for example, where strategic decisions in organizations are heavily constrained by interventionist government policies (such as privatization or deregulation) where all strategic decisions are framed and shaped by this wider context. Nevertheless, managers still have some degree of strategic choice (Child, 1972) even if the wider context (e.g. privatization) is firmly set in place. Managers can still make strategic decisions, for example, concerning such key topics as organizational design, choice of suppliers, choice and sophistication of information systems and general product or service portfolios.

Of course, most people are aware that much of decision making is not a simple process which happens in a linear sequence – a period of thinking followed by a period of acting. Decision making, and the development of alternative courses of action, are fashioned in their doing. Therefore, factors such as previous experience or whether things 'feel' right are likely to have as much influence over strategic choices (and what follows) as analysis and planning. Yet, these decisions are what will influence the fortunes or otherwise of any organization (from a sports club to a multinational enterprise) and understanding strategic decision-making processes therefore represents a key aspect of examining how strategies are put into practice. Our discussions of *strategy* and *strategic management* enable us to see how strategy, as an overall direction an organization might take, can be formulated by analytical and rational thinking. In this view, strategy is a positioning process by which organizations chart their way through the seas of competition, internationalization and changing markets and technologies. Positioning alone, however, leaves open the question of how particular choices are made amongst a set of alternatives – however incomplete those alternatives might be. In short, to understand strategy fully we need to understand the processes of strategic decision making.

The processes of making decisions can appear deceptively simple. Actions are formulated towards the solution of a particular problem. The problem with this approach is that there may be discernible actions and there may be observable outcomes, but they need not necessarily be wholly related to one another. Problems may be solved by factors other than strategic decisions and, sometimes, taking a strategic decision can create a whole new set of problems (without solving the initial problem the decision was supposed to address).

These polar views can be represented as the *planning* versus the *chaotic* processes of strategic decision making. They are extremes and, although most decisions lie somewhere between the planned and the chaotic, both perspectives are useful for understanding the processes of strategic decision making. Planning facilitates decision makers in analysing and codifying what appear initially as complex problems. Planning simplifies complexity and helps reduce uncertainty. Because of this, planning can also help decision makers examine current planning practices in their organization and assess their utility in the light of current problems. From a behavioural perspective, planning can ensure that others in the organization are involved and are communicated with as fully as possible. Note that although involvement and communication can be explicit parts of the plan, this may not endow those participants with any influence over the process or its eventual outcome. Finally, planning processes help decision makers identify key performance indicators by which progress of the decision can be monitored and judged.

Chaotic processes (Cohen et al., 1972; Stacey, 1993) argue that organizations can be viewed as *anarchy* or as a system with chaotic tendencies. Hence decision makers can neither understand fully nor control decision processes. Means and ends are unlikely to be coupled (Weick, 1987, 1995), which implies that actions do not lead to expected outcomes and are swayed one way and another by other decisions, other actions and unforeseen circumstances. The main components of a strategic decision-making process (problems, solutions, participants and choice situations) interact in an apparently haphazard way, a stream of demands for the fluid attention and energies of managers.

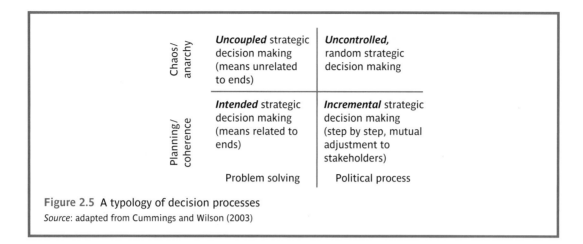

Figure 2.5 A typology of decision processes
Source: adapted from Cummings and Wilson (2003)

Participants move in and out of the decision-making process (every entrance is an exit elsewhere) and this can create discontinuity. At other times, participants fight for the right to become involved and then never exercise any influence they may have.

Viewing decision-making processes as chaotic also has some advantages for decision makers. Unlike the planning approach, the chaos perspective does not seek to simplify and to reduce uncertainty. It avoids any over-simplification of the process and allows decision makers to appreciate and expect the role of politics and influence to be a natural part of the decision-making process. In theory, the chaos perspective should encourage decision makers to think creatively around complex problems and help them to avoid thinking solely in linear sequences. Creativity and innovation may be enhanced by decision makers being encouraged to take actions which seem unrelated to the decision under consideration. On the other hand, we should bear in mind that the distinction between creativity and madness is a rather fine line (March, 1999)! From a decision-making perspective, this means that no one will know whether the tangential explorations were useful or folly until a long way down the track of the decision process. Figure 2.5 summarizes four polar types of decision process which can arise from counter-posing planned versus chaotic and political versus planned perspectives.

2.5.4 Implementing

Implementing is the practical heartland of delivering strategies that work. In a recent survey barely 40% of executives surveyed rated their organization as being successful at strategy implementation.[7] This element of the strategy map demonstrates how strategic plans are turned into concrete actions. The agenda for implementation typically includes the development of action plans, consideration of appropriate organization structure, taking a close look at human resource needs, provision of funding for the strategies through the annual business plan, and the development of a plan to monitor and control their strategies and tactics. And yet they still fail to successfully implement those strategies and tactics. These matters are the subject of many other parts of a business studies curriculum. But often the most troublesome is the lack of appropriate coordination or linking of the multiple activities required to implement a strategy.

Strategies require linkage both vertically and horizontally. Vertical linkages establish control, support and coordination between corporate, divisional and departmental plans. For example, a divisional strategy calling for development of a new product should be driven by a corporate objective – calling for growth, perhaps – and on a knowledge of available resources – capital

---

[7] http://www.strategy-execution.co.uk/expertise/strategy_execution_overview.htm, 24 July 2008.

resources available from corporate as well as human and technological resources in the R&D department. Linkages which are horizontal – across departments, across regional offices, across manufacturing plants or divisions – require coordination and cooperation to get the organizational units 'all playing in harmony'. For example, a strategy calling for introduction of a new product requires the combined efforts of – and thus coordination and cooperation among – the R&D, marketing and manufacturing departments.[8]

2.5.5 Interpreting

Managers in organizations interpret the environment and they interpret their organizational performance against their targets. They then have to communicate this interpretation amongst others in the organization. They may have to build a strategic vision (an ideal goal to aim for) and they may also have to create a new language which can be shared by all organizational members in order to close any gaps between ambition and action. Interpretation and communication allow *strategic options* to be outlined. These are the key choices amongst a number of possible courses of action which managers might take. Having decided upon a course of action, a number of decisions have to be taken in order to *implement* the chosen strategy. In turn, the actions taken by an organization may have an impact upon the environment and perhaps modify it slightly. The process then recycles.

Strategy is reflected in asset choices and investments made by firms (recall Figure 1.1 in Chapter 1). The majority of strategy research is based on the outcomes of these investment decisions, these being naturally subject to observation and measurement. However, outcomes are not necessarily the same as intentions, whether because of mistakes in translating intent into action, changes in the environment, or competitor behaviour. Thus strategy as observed might be an imperfect measure of strategic positioning as originally intended. This observation leads to the question of how 'management cognition' should be included in the strategic management process.

The theoretical background of this approach is in cognitive science. Stubbart and Ramaprasad describe the nature and scope of cognitive analysis in the following way:

> *Cognitive science characterizes minds . . . as intentional, representational, and computational. In addition, it stresses the significance of tracking the overt manifestations of intelligent behaviour: intelligent strategic behaviour in strategic management – that is, observing what strategists do. These four themes span philosophy, cognitive psychology, artificial intelligence, and anthropology, respectively. A cognitive science approach . . . uses these four themes to comprehend managerial minds: fathoming managers' strategic intentions, deciphering their representational knowledge about strategy, studying their reasoning processes and recording a description of managerial behaviour in strategic management settings. In short, cognitive science applied to strategic management means that scholars must research, model, understand and extend the mind(s) of strategic managers.* (1990, pp. 251–2)

Research on *cognitive communities* (groups of like-minded individuals) was developed by researchers' interests in how management of different firms perceive the competitive environment and act on the basis of their perception. The argument is that there is a difference between what has traditionally been defined as an objective environment and what top management perceives. Top management takes decisions on the basis of how it perceives the environment and the way it sees that the activities of the firms and its competitors might have tangible effects on strategy reformulation and subsequent industry structure:

---

[8] http://www.birnbaumassociates.com/strategy-implementation.htm for a succinct statement of the linkage problem, 24 July 2008.

Material decisions ultimately reflect the intuition and cognitive constructions of decision makers. At a cognitive level, business competition must be analyzed in terms of the mental models of decision makers and how such mental models lead to a particular interpretation of the competitive milieu. (Porac et al., 1989, p. 398)

Thomas and Carroll (1994) argue that two definitions of cognitive communities can be identified. A weak definition limits the analysis to similarity of cognitive community. It is argued that individuals sharing similar beliefs about a given transaction will be more likely to interact among themselves. Furthermore, they may influence each other through the diffusion of information. A strong definition requires further active interactions, mutual influence, and evidence of collective efforts. These have also been defined as *cognitive oligopolies* (Porac et al., 1989) to indicate the importance of interaction between firms. A cognitive community could therefore extend the boundaries of individual rationality by pooling existing information and cognitions.

2.5.6 Learning

Writers such as Senge (1990) stress and emphasize the role of processes of learning and adaptability in organizations not only with regard to understanding the pace of strategic change but also in providing new ways of conceptualizing the business environment. Thus, strategists can frame strategic issues in terms of the web of customers, stakeholders etc. in order to manage the business better (create more value).

Senge emphasizes the importance of what he calls 'adaptive learning' and 'generative learning' in organizations. Adaptive learning is similar to what Argyris and Schön (1978) call 'single-loop' learning in which individuals, groups and organizations adjust their behaviour according to fixed organizational goals, norms and assumptions. Generative learning, on the other hand, is akin to 'double-loop' learning, in which organizational goals, norms and assumptions as well as behaviour arc all open to change. In Senge's terms (Senge, 1990):

... Increasing adaptiveness is only the first stage in moving towards learning organisations. The impulse to learn in children goes deeper than desires to respond and adapt more effectively to environmental change. The impulse to learn, at its heart, is an impulse to be generative, to expand our capability. This is why leading corporations are focusing on generative learning, which is about creating, as well as adaptive learning, which is about coping.

Nevertheless, the systems view also cannot tell the whole story. While it can show how each level of analysis is important in its own right and that, combined, the levels provide an understanding of complex systems, it makes inadequate allowances for such issues as the role of managers, the availability of information and managers' abilities to interpret correctly and communicate effectively under sub-optimal conditions of uncertainty. We explore these issues in the next section.

2.6 Managerial agency and practice

The previous sections of this chapter do more than simply suggest that managers are important and pivotal agents of practice and change. The overt assumption is that strategy comes down to managers correctly interpreting an environment 'out there' and taking actions to align their organizations in an optimal interrelationship with that environment. Such a view is quite consistent with micro-perspectives on the strategy process, since they also give very strong legitimacy to the key role of *managerial agency*, i.e. the ability of managers to make effective decisions. However, the simple view that merely to understand micro-practices is decisive in revealing the pieces in the strategy jigsaw is flawed.

Indeed, many authors have suggested that, especially in recent years, the operating environment of organizations has become increasingly deterministic and less open to managerial discretion. However skilfully managers interpret their environments, ultimately strategy is determined by conditions and events external to the organization and outside the direct control of managers or their organizations (see authors such as Bettis and Hitt, 1995; Hamel and Prahalad, 1996; Hitt et al., 1998). They argue that the simple feedback loops in systems theory, or the assumptions of perfect knowledge on the part of managers, have been surpassed by changes in what they term the *competitive landscape* facing organizations. There are two principal drivers of this new landscape – information technology and globalization. Key features are:

- hypercompetition;
- blurring of traditional industry boundaries;
- greater knowledge intensity;
- greater reliance on knowledge as a strategic asset;
- discontinuous change.

The result is to make traditional, somewhat static models of competitive advantage questionable (such as Porter's Five Forces) and to render anachronistic traditional efficiency-oriented vertical organizational structures. It also brings into question to what extent managers can act as 'perfect' interpreters of environmental signals and as 'perfect' communicators of strategy within their organizations. Cummings and Wilson (2003) argue that there has been a shift of strategic emphasis towards flexibility and dynamics and an increased focus on contexts and processes. Figure 2.6 summarizes some of these changes of emphasis.

Following this line of thinking, strategy is firmly rooted in processes where flexibility, knowledge creation and retention, and collaboration within and between organizations are critical elements of strategy formulation (Cummings and Wilson, 2003). Performance benefits are likely to be the result of effective combinations of strategy content, process and context and from interlinked systems and practices. Performance benefits are less likely from an organization becoming 'distinctively

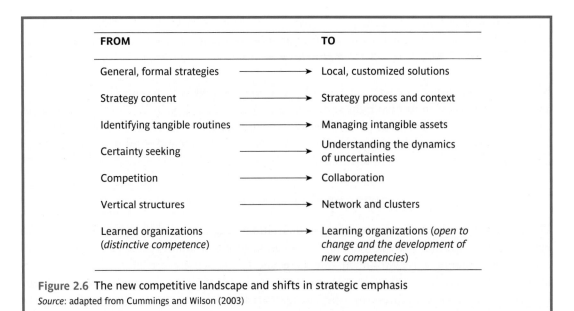

FROM	TO
General, formal strategies →	Local, customized solutions
Strategy content →	Strategy process and context
Identifying tangible routines →	Managing intangible assets
Certainty seeking →	Understanding the dynamics of uncertainties
Competition →	Collaboration
Vertical structures →	Network and clusters
Learned organizations (*distinctive competence*) →	Learning organizations (*open to change and the development of new competencies*)

Figure 2.6 The new competitive landscape and shifts in strategic emphasis
Source: adapted from Cummings and Wilson (2003)

competent' – in other words, excellent at what it currently does (see Figure 2.2), since such distinctiveness will soon be eroded in the new competitive landscape.

The majority of the abundant literature on strategy and strategic management tends to emphasize the positioning of organizations in relation to their competitive and operating environment but from a rather static view of the competitive landscape. While this is certainly an important part of understanding strategic management, it tells only part of the story. The other parts of the story concern the strategy process in relation to the context in which such processes take place.

The view that managerial agency is the sole influence upon strategy is certainly questionable in a number of other respects. Much of the work on strategic decision-making processes by Henry Mintzberg and his colleagues sheds light on the middle ground between strategy resulting from environmental determinism and managerial choice. As Mintzberg and Waters (1985) argue, strategies do not always come about as a direct result of managerial action. Nor do they come about as a direct result of environmental determinism. Instead, they emerge as a pattern that can be detected in a number of strategic decisions made over time in any organization. This emergent *pattern in a stream of decisions* – taken under conditions of uncertainty – is what they call strategy. It is the interplay between environmental determinism and managerial agency.

Obviously, many strategies fall in between these polar extremes of planned versus emergent. Andrews (1987) suggests that, in practice, the only fully planned strategies that can be observed in organizations amount to little more than financial planning statements. Figure 2.7 illustrates a range of planned versus externally determined strategies.

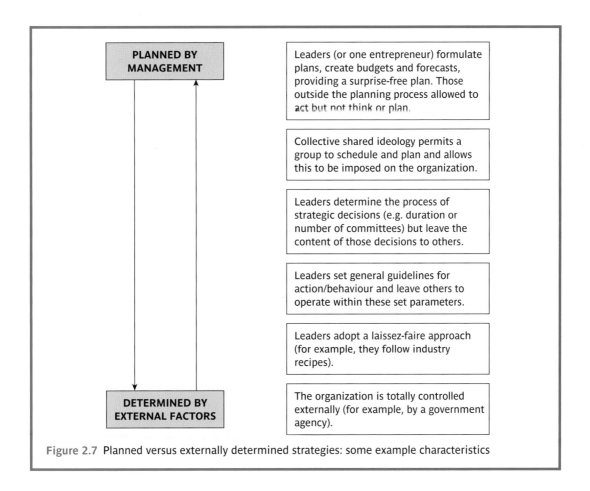

Figure 2.7 Planned versus externally determined strategies: some example characteristics

	Short-term	Long-term
External pressure perceived as strong	The mercenary organization	The organic organization
External pressure perceived as weak	The fragmented organization	The self-sufficient organization

Figure 2.8 Strategic orientation
Source: adapted from Michaud and Thoenig (2003)

One of the key features of these debates about the critical role of managerial agency is that managers do have a degree of choice in the strategies they formulate and pursue. As Child (1972) recognized, managers are rarely so constrained by external conditions that they have no discretion to act at all. They simply have varying limits to the autonomy of their actions. Michaud and Thoenig (2003) have characterized how organizational types might emerge over time depending upon how strong external pressures are and to what extent they try to formulate strategies for long-term effectiveness or for short-term gain. Their theoretical arguments owe much to Vincent's (1996) book *La Chair et le Diable*[9] which has not been translated from the original French. The basic argument is that organizational typologies and styles of managing emerge over time depending upon how managers think and act strategically. These typologies and styles of managing can be represented for illustrative purposes in a simple matrix (see Figure 2.8).

2.6.1 The fragmented organization

Here, managers have been typically exposed to quite benign and calm external contexts. Over time, their strategic thinking and acting have led to the embedding of relatively bureaucratic organizational features. Specialized sub-units have built up, each with its own short-term perspective and each pitched against the other sub-units for resources and senior management attention. Such an organization is fragmented in the sense that there is little incentive to think longer term or to engage in innovation or renewal. In many ways, the organization distances itself from the immediacy of the competitive marketplace. Internal cooperation amongst sub-units is very restricted, and formalized and standardized procedures take the place of individual or cooperative initiatives. Referring to Figure 2.6, such an organization has become learned (very good at what it presently does) but is one which has difficulties in learning (changing and developing what the organization does and how it does it). Individuals in the organization have no incentive to change. Examples of such organizations would include many public sector organizations prior to privatization and financial services organizations, especially banks, which had a long history of such strategic thinking.

---

[9] Meat and the Devil.

2.6.2 The self-sufficient organization

Here, we have an organization typified by perhaps years of managers facing a benign environment, but also characterized by managers who think strategically in a particular way – they assume they can find the resources needed for innovation and renewal within their organization and can change incrementally towards more longer-term goals. Such an organization may be equally as bureaucratic as the fragmented stereotype. However, the key difference is that managers get around specialization and fragmentation by ad hoc and informal processes. Improvisation and informal processes drive strategic thinking. There is strong emotional attachment by individuals to the organization, although strategy may still be imposed from the top rather than be fostered at other levels in the hierarchy. This is an organization characterized by 'in' groups and 'out' groups. Those who are members of the 'in' groups (often informal groups) are those who can influence strategy longer term and can bestow upon themselves privileges which are invisible to the 'out' groups. Examples would include many professional organizations, including universities and further education establishments.

2.6.3 The mercenary organization

Typified by a threatening and turbulent external context, managers in these organizations permanently seek short-term changes by exploiting the current situation. There are no assumptions that the required skills and knowledge reside within the organization's boundaries, with a readiness to recruit and employ individuals who can bring such needed skills within the organization. In this way, the structure of this organization permanently changes as sections are closed and abandoned in favour of new ones which suit the market more closely. Strategic thinking in these kinds of organizations is very much like that of the mercenary soldier. Temporary clusterings of skilled individuals make policy 'on the hoof' as market conditions demand and individual managers (mercenaries) can join or leave the organization at any time. The key to innovation and change is to be found in the engagement of these professionals and the skills they bring with them from outside the organization. Such an organization attracts weak loyalty and, therefore, strategy is inevitably short term in its focus. Nevertheless, such an organization demands strong bonds of cooperation to get the job done. It is likely also to operate in a context where there may be common standards or benchmarks for performance. Examples of such organizations would include many management or professional consulting firms as well as many project-based organizations.

2.6.4 The organic organization

The environment is unstable and perhaps threatening. Competition, regulation and technological changes are all around. Yet, this organization is populated by managers who think and act strategically in very different ways from the mercenaries described above. In this organization, socialization and loyalty to the organization are extremely high. Cooperation between people is high and is perhaps seen as something of a normative process (e.g. a moral duty). While there may be differentiated sub-units in the organization, there is mutual loyalty between them. There is also a prevailing assumption that the required skills and knowledge reside inside the organizational boundaries rather than outside them (as in the mercenary organization). As Michaud and Thoenig (2003, p. 32) note, there is a sense of a shared adventure in such organizations where cognitive channels spread rapidly across the sub-units to provide a strong and relatively unified organizational culture. Such features allow senior managers to capture ideas and embryonic suggestions made at lower levels in the organization. Internal networks and communities are strongly in evidence and provide a sound platform for longer-term thinking. In more extreme cases, managers may have developed, over time, a community of language and expression unique to the organization in which to express and to short-cut complex ideas and suggestions. In the terminology of organizational cultures, these organizations exhibit strong, cohesive cultures which allow longer-term strategic thinking even in the face of highly turbulent environments.

2.7 Summary

This chapter has laid out the elements of a systems model of strategy that forms the framework around which all the chapters of this book have been written and against which each of the chapters should be interpreted. The systems model – colloquially we call it the strategy map – has three levels. The first level (Figure 2.1) describes the main elements of strategy, namely Internal and External Environments, Direction, Strategy Options, Strategy or the strategic framework, Strategic Decisions, the Business Model, and Outcomes. These are displayed as flowing from one to the other in conventional linear form, although the pattern of causation and the time line is in practice more complex. The second level (Figure 2.3) describes the principal business systems and formal processes, namely the strategic planning process, business planning, budgeting and control systems, and performance measurement systems. The third level (Figure 2.4) describes the key supporting managerial processes. These may or may not be formal processes but nevertheless are key activities through which the business of strategy takes place. These processes are strategic thinking, strategy making, strategic decision making, implementing strategy, interpreting, and learning. These processes are essentially cognitive processes, that is, processes of intelligence, understanding and deliberation. By contrast, the systems variables in the second level are organized formal activities which absorb and process data and deliver it in standard formats to managers. The elements of the first strategy map are what we normally take as the subject matter of strategy. The systems components at the second level are how we process data in a regular and routine fashion. The managerial processes at the third level are where the thinking and deliberation take place.

The chapter concludes with an important message that managers do, most often, fall between the two extremes of god-like effectiveness and being the creatures of a larger environment. In fact, managers do have a degree of choice in the strategies they pursue given the degree of strength of external pressures. Given these pressures taking alternately short and long views over which decisions are pursued, we reported some simple typologies of organizations to indicate the vast differences that can exist between the conditions facing organizations and managers in pursuing coherent strategies. Thus organizations are inherently different and, as we shall see in later chapters, strategies will also be very different.

Key terms

alignment	27	organic organization	49
balanced scorecard	33	performance measurement	35
budgeting and control systems	35	processual/organizational process view	25
business model	32	realized strategy	41
business planning	35	self-sufficient organization	49
capabilities	29	strategic assets	29
classical view	25	strategic decision making	39
cognitive communities	44	strategic decisions	31
emergent	41	strategic fit	27
evolutionary view	25	strategic framework	31
external environment	29	strategic intent	30
fragmented organization	48	strategic planning	35
implementation	39	strategic thinking	34,39
incremental	26,41	strategy as systems view	25
innovating, innovation	32	strategy content	24
intended	41	strategy context	24
internal environment	29	strategy formulation	39
interpretation	39	strategy map	24
learning	39	strategy process	24
mercenary organization	49	structural coupling	35
mission	30	systems (systemic) model	24
multi-business	31	values	30
multinational	31	vision	30

Recap questions and assignments

1 Draw up a list of the benefits for a large organization of adopting a systemic view of strategy.
2 What do you think the implementation difficulties would be?
3 Does traditional (or normal) strategic planning contain elements of the systemic view? What are the main omissions?

References

Alchian, A.A. (1950) Uncertainty, evolution and economic theory. *Journal of Political Economy*, **58**, 211–21.

Andrews, K.R. (1987) *The Concept of Corporate Strategy*, 3rd edn, Irwin, Homewood, IL.

Ansoff, H.I. (1965) *Corporate Strategy*, Penguin, Harmondsworth.

Argyris, C. and Schön, D.A. (1978) *Organizational Learning: Theory of Action Perspective*, Addison-Wesley, Reading, MA.

Balogun, J., Huff, A.S. and Johnson, P. (2003) Three responses to the methodological challenges of studying strategizing. *Journal of Management Studies*, **40**, **1**, 197–224.

Bartlett, C. and Ghoshal, S. (1989) *Managing Across Borders: the Transnational Solution*, Harvard Business School Press, Boston, MA.

Bettis, R. and Hitt, M. (1995) The new competitive landscape. *Strategic Management Journal*, **16**, 7–19.

Boston Consulting Group (1975) *Strategy Alternatives for the British Motorcycle Industry*, HMSO, London.

Capra, F. (1982) *The Turning Point: Science, Society and the Rising Culture*, Bantam Books, New York.

Chandler, A.D. (1962) *Strategy and Structure: Chapters in the History of the Industrial Enterprise*, MIT Press, Cambridge, MA.

Chandler, A.D. (1990) The enduring logic of industrial success. *Harvard Business Review*, March/April, 130–40.

Child, J. (1972) Organizational structure, environment and performance: the role of strategic choice. *Sociology*, **6**, 1–22.

Cohen, M., March, J. and Olsen, J. (1972) A garbage can model of organizational choice. *Administrative Science Quarterly*, **17**, 1–25.

Collins, J.C. and Porras, J.I. (2000) *Built to Last: Successful Habits of Visionary Companies*, Random House, New York.

Coyne, K.P. and Subramaniam, S. (1996) Bringing discipline to strategy. *The McKinsey Quarterly*, 14–25.

Cummings, S. and Wilson, D.C. (2003) *Images of Strategy*, Blackwell, Oxford.

Cyert, R.M. and March, J.G. (1963) *A Behavioral Theory of the Firm*, Blackwell, Oxford.

De Wit, B. and Meyer, R.J.H. (1999) *A Strategy Synthesis: Resolving Strategy Paradoxes to Create Competitive Advantage*, International Thompson Press, London.

Granovetter, M. (1985) Economic action and social culture: the problem of embeddedness. *American Journal of Sociology*, **91**, **3**, 481–510.

Hamel, G. and Prahalad, C.K. (1989) Strategic intent. *Harvard Business Review*, **89**, May–June, 63–76.

Hamel, G. and Prahalad, H. (1996) Competing in the new economy. *Strategic Management Journal*, **17**, 237–42.

Hammer, M. (2003) *The Agenda: What every business must do to dominate the decade*, Three Rivers Press, New York.

Henderson, B.D. (1973) *The Experience Curve Reviewed*, Boston Consulting Group, Boston, MA.

Hitt, M., Keats, B. and de Marie, S. (1998) Navigating in the new competitive landscape: building strategic flexibility and competitive advantage in the 21st century. *Academy of Management Executive*, **12**, **4**, 22–42.

Johnson, G., Melin, L. and Whittington, R. (2003) Micro strategy and strategizing: towards an activity-based view. *Journal of Management Studies*, **40**, **1**, 2–22.

Kaplan, R.S. and Norton, D.P. (1992) The balanced scorecard: measures that drive performance. *Harvard Business Review*, Jan–Feb.

March, J.G. (1999) *The Pursuit of Organisational Intelligence*, Blackwell, Oxford.

March, J.G. and Simon, H.A. (1958) *Organizations*, Blackwell, Cambridge, MA.

Michaud, C. and Thoenig, J-C. (2003) *Making Strategy and Organization Compatible*, Palgrave Macmillan, Basingstoke.

Mintzberg, H. (1994) *The Rise and Fall of Strategic Planning*, Prentice Hall, Englefield Cliffs, NJ.

Mintzberg, H. and Waters, J.A. (1985) Of strategies deliberate and emergent. *Strategic Management Journal*, July/Sept, 257–72.

Nelson, R.R. and Winter, S.G. (1982) *An Evolutionary Theory of Economic Change*, Harvard University Press, Cambridge, MA.

Pascale, R. (1984) Perspectives on strategy: the real story behind Honda's success. *California Management Review*, **14**, **3**, 47–72.

Penrose, E. (1959) *The Theory of the Growth of the Firm*, Blackwell, Oxford.

Porac, J.F., Thomas, H. and Baden-Fuller, C. (1989) Competitive groups as cognitive communities: the case of Scottish knitwear manufacturers. *Journal of Management Studies*, **26**, 397–416.

Porter, M. (1980) *Competitive Strategy: Techniques for Analysing Industries and Competitors*, Free Press, New York.

Porter, M.E. (1985) *Competitive Advantage*, Free Press, New York.

Prahalad, C.K. and Doz, Y.L. (1986) The dynamics of global competition. In C.K. Prahalad and Y.L. Doz (eds) *The Multinational Mission: Balancing Local Demands and Global Vision*, Free Press, New York.

Prahalad, C.K. and Hamel, G. (1990) The core competence of the organization. *Harvard Business Review*, May–June.

Samra-Fredericks, D. (2003) Strategizing as lived experience and strategists: everyday efforts to shape strategic direction. *Journal of Management Studies*, **40**, **1**, 141–74.

Selznick, P. (1957) *Leadership and Administration*, University of California Press, Berkeley, CA.

Senge, P.M. (1990) *The Fifth Discipline*, Century Books, London.

Stacey, R.D. (1993) *Strategic Management and Organizational Dynamics*, Pitman, London.

Stigler, G.J. (1951) *The Theory of Price*, 2nd edn, MacMillan New York.

Stubbart, C.I. and Ramaprasad, A. (1990) Comments on the empirical articles and recommendations for future research. In A.S. Huff (ed.) *Mapping Strategic Thought*, John Wiley & Sons, Chichester.

Thomas, H. and Carroll, C. (1994) Theoretical and empirical links between strategic groups, cognitive communities and networks of interacting firms. In H. Daems and H. Thomas (eds) *Strategic Groups, Strategic Moves and Performance*, Pergamon, New York.

Vincent, J.D. (1996) *La Chair et le Diable*, Odile Jacob, Paris.

Weick, K. (1987) Substitutes for strategy. In J. Teece (ed.) *The Competitive Challenge*, Ballinger, Cambridge, MA.

Weick, K.E. (1995) *Sensemaking in Organizations*, Sage, London.

Williamson, O.E. (1975) *Markets and Hierarchies: Analysis and Antitrust Implications*, Free Press, New York.

Further reading

Chandler, A.D. (1962) *Strategy and Structure: Chapters in the History of the Industrial Enterprise*, MIT Press, Cambridge, MA.

Lave, C. and March, J. (1993) *An Introduction to Models in the Social Sciences*, University Press of America, New York.

McGee, J. (2005) *The Blackwell Encyclopedia of Management 2nd edition: Strategic Management*, Blackwell, Oxford.

Pettigrew, A.M., Thomas, H. and Whittington, R. (2002) *Handbook of Strategy and Management*, Sage, London.

Weick, K.E. (1995) *Sensemaking in Organizations*, Sage, London.

PART 1
Strategy Analysis

The logic of Part 1 is the logic of the strategy analyst. In terms of the systemic model in Chapter 2 (shown in full in Figure 2.3), the analyst concentrates on the basic elements of the strategy map – as shown in Figure 2.1. This is where the analyst makes a massive contribution. The analyst assesses the nature of the economic, market and competitive environment, identifies and assesses major strategy options, and is a prime contributor to the basic thinking behind the 'theory of the business' which is captured in the strategy statements and the business model. The analyst's role is cast around the central ideas of *competitive advantage* – how to be different and yet be successful. The analyst is obsessed with data, with calculations about trade-offs and with testing out alternative ideas and hypotheses. But the analyst also has to be concerned with qualitative data because not everything can be captured by numbers. Alternatives are measured in terms of returns versus risk and many of the judgements to be made have to incorporate shrewd assessment alongside objective data. Both the data and the judgements are informed by strong theoretical frameworks and these are the subject of this part of the book.

Chapters 3 and 4 taken together present an outline of the basic economic principles that are required in order to understand the detail of strategic management. Economics is a very broad subject, ranging from microeconomics (the organization of markets and the behaviour of firms and individuals) through macroeconomics (the study of whole economies and the determinants of national income, growth etc.) to international trade (the exchange of goods and services by people in different economies). The basic economics in these chapters represent a bare minimum of economics sufficient to gain an understanding of strategic management. For readers who really want to read further in economics we recommend reading one of the many excellent economics textbooks.

At this stage in the book we construct the fundamental notion that what underpins all strategy analysis is *competitive advantage*. This is the keystone in the architecture of strategy analysis that holds together all the data, discussion and supporting analyses. It is a powerful intellectual construct that is used universally. The idea of competitive advantage is gained through the denial of perfect competition, the economist's competitive ideal explained in **Chapter 3**. Whereas perfect competition leaves no room for individual firms and their strategies, the whole idea of strategy is built on the presence of imperfections in markets.

This starting point for strategy is explained in **Chapter 3**. The first two parts concentrate on the economic underpinnings of strategy and on the analysis of industries and competition. This takes us through territory familiar to the economist, namely the analysis of costs structure, of demand and of markets and competition. We then turn this into a focus on industries and competition in which we develop the crucial idea of strategy depending on (firm-specific) market imperfections. These basic economic principles are then developed into a discussion of the sources of competitive advantage, or – to put it another way – what kinds of imperfections form the basis of strategy. The chapter concludes by showing how we move from the ideas of competitive advantage to a fuller expression of competitive strategy. Here we have a deeper discussion of the details of cost and differentiation-based advantages and how through strategic positioning these are articulated and shaped. Positioning is about the deployment of cost and differentiation-based advantages. It is about the identification of distinctive cost strategies and distinctive differentiation strategies. In practice we see the need for detailed analysis of markets and industries, first to see what the 'rules' are and how to play them but second to see how we might innovate with our strategies so as to break the rules and get ahead. In industry terms this means understanding how we can be better than our competitors. In market terms it means understanding what the customer wants. Strategy is about value creation and value analysis is an important element of this chapter.

The immediate operating environment usually refers to markets for goods and services and to industries – those elements in the supply chain that combine to deliver products and services into final markets. Often overlooked, however, are the more distant influences of an organization's context, such as the impact of government policies or the actions of a regulator. These influences are evident in the deeper context that comprises the infrastructure of government, civil administration, the law, and social custom and practice that shapes the behaviour of businesses and consumers. The fit of an organization with its environment goes beyond its understanding of the market context of business. All firms and organizations are sensitive in some degree to events in the wider economy. Even with no change in the strategy of the firm, major changes in its performance and prospects will occur for macroeconomic reasons beyond its control. Whereas the firm might reasonably hope to condition and control its markets, the macroeconomy is typically beyond control but has to be factored into the firm's plans and expectations for the future.

This deeper context is covered in **Chapter 4**. This covers the fundamentals of aggregate demand and supply and the implications for GDP, inflation and unemployment. It also examines the causes and effects of business cycles and what in a global economy causes booms and slumps to come to an end. It pays special attention to the financial and economic crises of 1997 in Asia and the credit crunch and financial crisis in 2008. It goes on to consider issues concerning the sustainability of strong economic growth, especially in emerging markets, and the issues of forecasting in such a disturbed financial climate. The basic proposition of the chapter is that businesses that don't understand their economic environment make strategic errors, sometimes catastrophic ones, especially if they do not know that booms and slumps are both bound to end.

Moving from these micro- and macro-economic foundations for strategy analysis we introduce a more practitioner-oriented flavour in **Chapter 5**. If we understand the idea of competitive advantage as a key attribute that is specific to the firm, then we have the beginnings of a description of strategy. We lay out a template for describing and identifying a strategy – how would you recognize a strategy if you saw one? Whereas competitive advantage is an external positioning concept, strategy also needs to say something about the internal disposition of resources and assets as well. The internal logic of strategy is shown in the *strategy cycle* and cost analysis is reflected in the *value chain*. The latter is extremely well known, being another product of Porter analysis (1985). The strategy cycle illustrates the significance of the balance between internal resources, external market positioning and financial performance. The value chain builds directly on cost analysis ideas to enable us to identify a picture of the internal asset structure and activity structure of the firm. We also look at two powerful grouping concepts – market segments and strategic groups. These capture the idea of segments that can be targeted and industry clusters of similar competitors. The chapter concludes with a template for a practical overview of strategy – a self-testing of your firm's strategy IQ. This can be turned into a simple questionnaire for assessing the strategy of your own firm or of any firms of which you have some knowledge. By the end of this chapter we will see the significance of competitive advantage for the study of strategy and for strategy making in firms.

Chapter 6 steps back into the firm to ask what capabilities are needed for the desired positioning to be achieved. This has become known as the resource-based view often captured in the term *core competence*. This approach to strategy has become very widespread but suffers from a high degree of subjectivity and lack of agreement about terminology and definitions. This chapter sets out to review some of the main contributions and to indicate a basic language to which we might all subscribe. Core competence, like competitive advantage, is an intellectual construct that is useful because it can be deployed to gain understanding and insight in a wide range of situations. The chapter goes on to examine how competence-based competition can be conducted in practice and suggests some practical ways of relating these ideas to value creation.

Following Chapters 5 and 6 we should now have the ability to develop our own strategic theory of the firm comprising both a view of competitive advantage and core competence *and* the way in which they support and complement each other.

Chapter 7 is concerned with the emerging structure of the new economy that is being generated by the digital economy, namely the world of microelectronics, technology networks and knowledge intensity. Information technology and knowledge intensity, driven by highly successful R&D programmes over the past 40 years, have transformed the cost conditions and demand conditions to which we became accustomed in the familiar manufacturing-based economy. Cost structures have become predominantly fixed cost in nature, with vanishingly small variable costs. Markets have been transformed by the flood of new products that have redefined the elements of consumer leisure time and the patterns of consumer expenditure. Also significant (but quite how much is not yet known) is the emergence of a consumer phenomenon based on standardisation and complementarity.[1] Customers increasingly and consciously buy products that conform to known standards and that technically complement their existing products and the products that other people have (you buy a new 'Wintel' computer because your Windows-based software and that of your friends will run on it). This means that we are increasingly buying products because other people have them.[2] It also results in very large, quasi-monopolistic market positions for some companies (like Microsoft), dependency positions for others so that, for example, one is obliged to buy Microsoft's operating systems, and expensive market failures for others (On-Digital versus BSkyB). Business risk has risen markedly in these conditions. Strategies have to be adapted to these specific conditions. Maybe, also, these industries are becoming a bigger proportion of the whole economy. Chapter 7 and some of the case studies at the end of the book discuss the reasons why these new economy characteristics have taken hold and indicate how strategies in the new digital economy represent significant adaptations to the strategies common in the traditional manufacturing economy.

Chapter 8 shifts the focus from the single business to the multi-business portfolio. This is the arena of corporate strategy where the task of the corporate centre is to choose what portfolio it wants and to design and manage the organization structure and its management processes. There are other key tasks: the mission statement and the choice of strategic objectives are discussed in Chapter 1. Managing performance is mentioned in many places but Chapter 16 is devoted to the analysis and measurement of performance. In Chapter 8 the key issue is the way in which the

[1] Strictly speaking it is a re-emergence: it was well known back in the 19th century as a characteristic of utilities (e.g. railways and the telegraph), but in a sense was forgotten as manufacturing-style cost conditions became pervasive in the 20th century.

[2] This is characteristic of fashion products as well where the benefit is psychological rather than practical.

portfolio creates value. This revolves around the economies of scope that we introduced and discussed in Chapter 3, often called synergy by practitioners and relatedness by analysts and academics. Depending on how synergies arise, there are implications for the fit of strategy and structure and for the styles by which the organisation is managed. These are discussed in Chapter 8 and also recur throughout Part 2. The final part of this chapter continues the corporate-level theme with mergers and acquisitions (M&A). These are the biggest and riskiest decisions that most companies make. Mistakes can destroy a company but companies can also grow and prosper very quickly. This chapter lays out the context for M&A decisions and alliances where the risks are very high, the rewards are enticing, but the track record of companies is very varied, with perhaps more glaring failures than conspicuous successes. But remember that we said strategy is about risk – a theme we return to in Chapter 11.

Chapter 9 introduces the international domain. This again is controversial and risky (you should be getting used to the idea that these are defining characteristics of strategy) because of the difficulties inherent in moving out of one's home base to international markets and to international suppliers. Globalization is presented in its specialized meaning as global standardization (e.g. the 'world car'). This forms the basis for discussion of the two contrasting strategies of global standardization versus local differentiation. These are a replay of our old friends cost and efficiency on the one hand, and differentiation on the other. Not surprisingly, therefore, there is the possibility of combining globalization and localization into a joint approach characterized as 'transnational'. Some think this is just a theoretical possibility but it has led to widespread discussion about the nature of the multinational firm. The chapter concludes with a profile of the 'flagship firm', a concept originated by Alan Rugman in which he portrays how some international firms can sit at the nexus of opposing forces – international versus local forces, global customers versus global suppliers, and different host governments. Overall the theme for the international company is how to blend and balance host-country-specific advantages (CSAs) with firm-specific advantages (FSAs).

Chapter 3

Industry analysis and competitive advantage

Chapter contents

Introduction

In this chapter we outline and explain the main ideas of industry analysis and show how these lead us to an understanding of **competitive advantage** and how, in turn, competitive advantage leads to an understanding of competitive strategy. In Chapter 5, after the macroeconomic analysis in Chapter 4, we go on to paint a broader picture of competitive strategy showing how it can be defined, understood and applied. Industry analysis is essentially a set of microeconomic concepts drawn from the research and writings of many distinguished economists.[1] So we start with concise review

---

[1] The seminal works of Richard Caves and F.M. Scherer were direct antecedents of Porter's well-known book on analysis of industries and competition (1980).

of the essential microeconomic concepts of cost and demand analysis and of market structure. We then show how these have been brought together to form the subject of industry analysis and its iconic manifestation in the form of Porter's Five Forces analysis. Alongside this development of industry analysis we show how the notion of profitable success is bound up with the differences between the ideal of perfect ('profitless') competition and the more normal reality of imperfections in markets. The reader should be aware at this point that this is a controversial subject about which economists and others can take very different views. The idea of 'generic strategies' emerges from this debate about imperfections. It was developed by Porter to show a typology of strategies which we can use to label and characterize different ways of competing. These different ways of competing are encapsulated in the idea of 'competitive advantage' – this is a critical concept in this chapter which indicates ways in which success in markets might be found and forms the link between analysis of markets and industries and the formation of competitive strategy. The final part of the chapter shows how different competitive advantages can be melded together as the basis for a wide variety of competitive strategies.

3.1 The economic underpinnings of strategy

It is well known that firms can vary greatly in their performance. One explanation for these differences is variation in managerial competence and in particular in strategic capability. Anticipating the discussion in Chapter 5, we set out here the definition of competitive advantage:

> *Delivering superior value to customers and in doing so earning an above average return for the company and its stakeholders.*

One measure of the existence of competitive advantage is the ability of a company to outperform its sector rivals systematically over time. But how, then, do we explain the substantive causes of such sustainable advantage? Economic analysis suggests that we should first look at four key features of the market 'context' in which these rivals sell their products:

1 The supply side of the market which tells us how costs arise and which we will label *cost analysis* and from which we can observe the phenomenon of *cost advantage*.

2 The demand side of the market which tells us how value is perceived and paid for by customers and which we will label *demand analysis* and from which we can observe the nature of *differentiation advantage*.

3 Market rivalry which tells us how competition takes place and the effects on prices and costs and which we will label *analysis of markets and competition*.

4 Industry analysis which tells us the economic configuration of firms and the impact on the strategic choices that they make and which we will label *analysis of industry and competition*.

The first three of these key features are discussed at length in microeconomics and managerial economics textbooks (and also the Study Guide for this textbook), but we summarize the key concepts in this section. Section 3.2 is devoted to the fourth key feature, industry analysis.

Consider the following simple profits equation:

Profits = total revenue − total costs

The supply side mostly focuses on the cost element of the profits equation while the other two key features mainly deal with revenue issues like price, sales volume and market share. However, costs are also influenced by sales volume and hence demand and rivalry issues. Analysis of industry and competition assesses the combination of forces that leads to greater or lesser profitability. Note how in our approach to understanding the economic concepts we indicate how the nature of markets affects the way competition works through the interaction of buyers/consumers in the marketplace. But we also show that the economic configuration of the firms in the industry also affects competition by virtue of the cost structures and the nature of their resources and capabilities that condition the competitive offerings that they wish to make.

3.1.1 Cost analysis

The microeconomics of strategy is built initially on an understanding of the nature of costs. Cost for economists is essentially opportunity cost, the sacrifice of the alternatives forgone in producing a product or service. Thus, the cost of a factory building is the set of houses or shops that might have been built instead. The cost of capital is the interest that could have been earned on the capital invested, had it been invested elsewhere. In practice, money prices may not reflect opportunity costs, because of uncertainty, imperfect knowledge, natural and contrived barriers to movements of resources, taxes and subsidies, and the existence of externalities (spillover effects of private activities onto other parties; for example, pollution imposes costs on more than just the producer of pollution). Opportunity cost provides the basis for assessing costs of managerial actions, such as in 'make or buy' decisions, and in all those situations where alternative courses of action are being considered.

Economies of scale

Costs are also collected and reported routinely both for purposes of stewardship and for control. The behaviour of these costs in relation to the scale of output is of much importance. We see, for example, that break-even analysis is based on the extent to which costs vary in relation to output (in the short term) or are fixed in relation to output. The distinction between fixed and variable costs has implications for the flexibility a firm has in pricing to meet competitive conditions. Thus, one would always wish to price above variable cost per unit, in order to maintain positive cash flow. Fixed costs in this example are *sunk* costs; they are paid and inescapable, and the only relevant costs are those that are affected by the decision under consideration. It is the behaviour of costs in the long term that has strategic implications for firms and for the structure of industries. The long term is the time horizon under consideration and affects what is considered to be 'fixed'. In the very long term, all economic factors are variable, whereas in the very short term, nearly all economic conditions are fixed and immutable. An economy of scale refers to the extent to which unit costs (costs per unit of output) fall as the scale of the operation (for example, a factory) increases (in other words, as more capital-intensive methods of operation can be employed).

In Figure 3.1 we can see that Plant 1 exhibits increasing returns to scale or, simply, economies of scale. By contrast, Plant 2 shows decreasing returns to scale or diseconomies of scale. The strategic significance of economies of scale depends on the minimum efficient plant size (MEPS). This means that economies of scale are important in relation to market size. The higher the ratio of MEPS to market size, the larger the share of the market taken by one plant, and the more market power that can be exercised by the firm owning the plant.

The major sources of economies of scale are usually described as:

- indivisibilities and the spreading of fixed costs;
- the engineering characteristics of production.

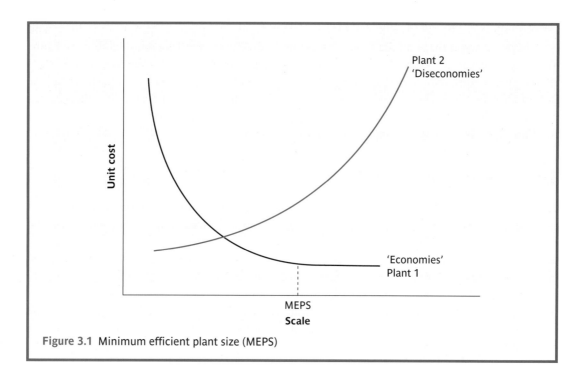

Figure 3.1 Minimum efficient plant size (MEPS)

Indivisibility means that an input cannot be scaled down from a certain minimum size and can only be scaled up in further minimum size units. Thus, costs per unit diminish after the initial investment until a further new block of investment is required. The original examples of 'special-ization' (the term coined by Adam Smith) were often engineering in nature. As volumes go up, it is usually cheaper to make work tasks more specialized – as exemplified dramatically in Henry Ford's mass-production assembly-line operations in the first decade of the last century. Economies of scale also arise because of the physical properties of processing units. This is exemplified by the well-known cube-square rule. Production capacity is usually determined by the volume of the pro-cessing unit (the cube of its linear dimensions), whereas cost more often arises from the surface area (the cost of the materials involved). As capacity increases, the average cost decreases, because the ratio of surface area to cube diminishes.[2]

These general principles apply to functional areas other than production. In marketing, there are important indivisibilities that arise out of branding and the creation of reputation effects. There are important scale effects in advertising, as the costs of campaign preparation can be spread over larger (for example, global) markets. Research and development requires substantial minimum in-vestments – another indivisibility – in advance of production, and the costs of R&D therefore fall as sales volumes increase. Purchasing in bulk exhibits economies of scale, in that the price per unit falls as the number of purchased items goes up. Sometimes this is because of monopolistic buying power (for example, supermarkets in the UK). But each purchase does have a certain element of fixed costs attached to it (writing contracts, negotiation time, setting up production runs) and these may be significant.

The experience curve, sometimes called the **learning curve**, has similar strategic implications. The experience curve is an empirical estimate of the proportion by which unit costs fall as experience of production increases. An 80% experience curve arises when costs fall to 80% of their previous level after production has doubled (see Figure 3.2). Strategically, this means that a firm which establishes

---

[2] For a full discussion of economies of scale see Besanko et al. (2000, chapter 5).

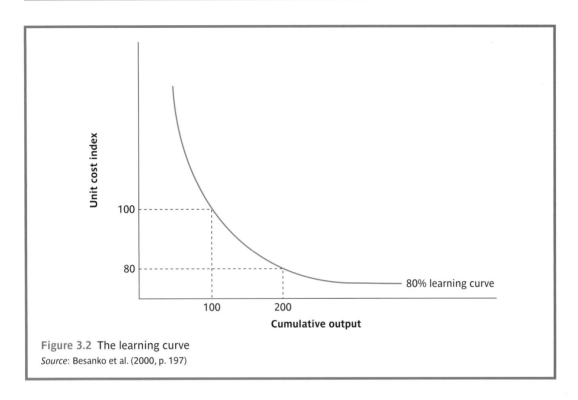

Figure 3.2 The learning curve
Source: Besanko et al. (2000, p. 197)

itself first in the market and manages to build a cost advantage by being twice the size of its nearest competitor would have a 20% production cost advantage over this competitor if an 80% experience curve existed. Experience and learning effects arise where there are complex, labour-intensive tasks. The firm can facilitate learning through management and supervisory activities and coaching. It can also use incentives to reward learning.

In general, economies of scale and experience effects provide the basis in terms of cost advantage for those strategies that depend on cost leadership. The objective of cost leadership strategies is to realize a margin premium reflecting the size of the cost advantage which can be applied to create a price discount for customers and/or an increase in margins and profitability. Cost advantages are also available through vertical **integration** and the exercise of buying power.

Economies of scope

A source of superior financial performance is the ability of a firm to exploit *economies of scope*. These arise when the average cost of a single product is lowered by its joint production with other products in a multi-product firm. This is due to the use of one or more common resources in the production of both outputs. If a common resource (or input) is available only in units of a certain minimum size, then a single firm producing both outputs is able to spread the common resource costs over both outputs. A study (Pratten, 1988) of the cost effects of halving the number of products made by each producer in a selection of EU industries shows impacts that range from +3% in carpet manufacture to +8% in motor vehicles.

In contrast to economies of scale, economies of scope refer to increased variety in operations, not higher volume of output. Economies of scope therefore emerge where unit costs fall because of the occurrence of common resources and/or knowledge being applied to the production of more than one product. Such common resources could be, for example, the result of shared distribution, advertising, purchasing, and similar activities. Together with cross-subsidization, economies of scope could allow the monopolization of a perfectly competitive industry.

These scope economies may arise from the opportunity to leverage a core *capability* arising from knowledge and learning, organization or management skill, so as to reduce the average total cost of all products produced in a multi-product firm. A good example is the expertise that arises from technical and scientific knowledge within the firm. Exploiting this distinctive expertise by innovation and product diversification lowers the average total cost of all products. Pharmaceutical manufacture and steel production are both sectors where this kind of cost economy is important. Scope economies can also arise from efficient use of *resources*, for example, where a number of related goods are produced using a common process. Car manufacture of a range of models is an example and part of the reason for the significant scope economies found in Pratten's study. Another source of scope economies arises from spreading the fixed cost of a network over a wider range of products. Commercial banks, for example, incur a large fixed cost from their branch networks. If they spread this cost over a large range of related corporate and retail financial products, the average total cost of each product is reduced. Economies of scope can therefore be an active component of strategy development when the application of centralized management leads to lower costs. Ironically, some financially oriented acquisitive conglomerates may be relatively more successful in achieving such economies than many related diversified concerns. Indeed, diseconomies of scope can also readily occur when endless diversification adds to managerial bureaucracy or when a failure occurs in strategy implementation, such as when like concerns fail to integrate. This is especially common when moves aimed at achieving strategic fit fall down, usually on cultural and/or organizational grounds.

One of the main dimensions of strategic choice (see Section 3.3.1) revolves around the notion of *scope* and its application to diversification of the portfolio of businesses within the firm. We have described economies of scope as arising when the average cost of a single product is lowered by its joint production with other products in a multi-product firm based on the indivisibility of certain resources. For example, knowledge is indivisible in the sense that it cannot be divided into pieces some of which you choose to have and some of which you choose not to have. Knowing about aluminium means that you will have knowledge relevant to airframe manufacture and to pots and pans. Economies of scope arise when your knowledge or other indivisible resource can be applied in multiple directions without using up that resource. Thus the overall scope becomes interesting strategically. A firm may choose to operate with broad scope (such as Ford in the automobile assembly industry covering a very wide product range and covering also the whole globe). Conversely a firm may choose to operate on a very narrow scope (such as Morgan Cars which covers only a particular part of the sports car market). The choice of broad scope suggests a calculation about available economies of scope in such a fashion that once chosen it is a commitment that cannot readily be reversed. The choice of narrow scope suggests an alternative calculation that the benefits of assets and other resources and capabilities focused and handled in specific ways creates differentiation and/or cost advantages of a different sort.

3.1.2 Demand analysis

Demand analysis is important in two ways: (i) it provides a framework for analysing price and other influences on the sales of the firm's products, and (ii) it provides a baseline for pricing products, and marketing generally, and for forecasting and manipulating demand.

Demand analysis is built around the price–quantity relationship and the many ways in which this relationship is manifested. It is easy to see how important price and volume are to the firm. Price and quantity together determine sales revenue. Sales volume dictates production volume and the scale of production operations together with the capital required for production and for working capital. Thus, volume and price fundamentally drive cash flow, profits and return on capital

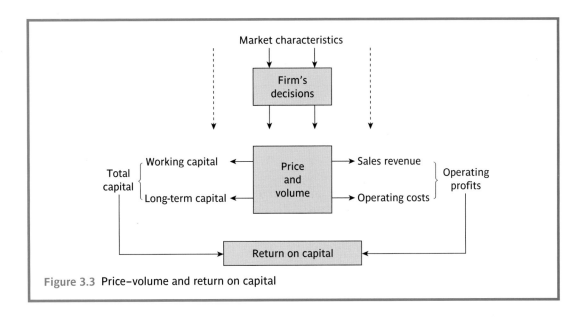

Figure 3.3 **Price–volume and return on capital**

(see Figure 3.3). Consequently the extent to which price can influence volume is of great importance to the firm.

In understanding how return on capital is driven it is helpful to consider those characteristics that shape demand (market characteristics in the figure) and how the firm's decisions can affect the outcome. One of the enduring problems for a firm is how to avoid its activities being totally dictated by market conditions and for its own decisions to provide it with some distinctiveness in markets and therefore some ability to earn profits beyond the minimum rate of return required merely to stay in business. The following characteristics of demand are particularly important:

- price elasticities and their implications for revenues;
- individual versus market demand;
- final demand versus derived demand;
- producer versus consumer goods;
- durable versus perishable (non-durable) goods.

These are described in some detail in texts such as McAleese (2004).

3.1.3 The analysis of markets and competition

The critical market-level influence on firm performance is the form and intensity of rivalry between the existing firms in a market. The economist's approach to market structure and the form and extent of rivalry is to use a taxonomy based on the number of firms in each industry. Figure 3.4 illustrates this.

At one extreme, we have *perfect competition*, in which products are not differentiable, rivalry is intense and no firm has the power to alter market prices. In such a market the price is determined at the market level by the forces of supply and demand, so from the firm's point of view the price of their product is given. The forces of competition limit strategic discretion and drive profits down to the 'normal' level, i.e. a level insufficient to attract new entrants to the market. Markets for agricultural products like wheat are often viewed as perfectly competitive, because no single producer can alter

Market structure	Number of firms	Degree of differentiation	Comments
Perfect competition	Many	Zero	Fragmented, commodity-like
Monopolistic or imperfect competition	Many	Some	Multiple niches, localized competition
Oligopoly – undifferentiated	Some to very few	Low	Commodity-like with scale economies, e.g. steel
Oligopoly – differentiated	Some to very few	High	Strategic interdependence, large segments
Dominant firm	One to very few	High	Price leadership, high entry barriers, competitive fringe
Monopoly	Single	Not applicable	Natural monopoly due to very high scale economies

Figure 3.4 Market structure: the broad spectrum for competition

the market price. Perfect markets are not common. Firms have a huge incentive to adopt strategies which avoid the 'strategic hell' of perfect competition.

At the other extreme, we have a *monopoly* in which one firm supplies the whole market. The firm is able to fix prices and hence enjoys control over its market environment and as such enjoys significant market power. Patents like those secured by the UK pharmaceutical company, Glaxo, in the market for ulcer drugs confer this kind of market power. A high level of market power enables the monopolistic firm to earn higher profits than the competitive firm, as Glaxo did with Zantac in the 1980s and until 1997.

In between these two extremes, we have *oligopolistic* markets, in which a few firms compete against each other, and *monopolistic competition*. Most economists would regard these intermediate cases as the norm. In the monopolistic competition case, there are many firms each with small market shares, but each is able to differentiate its product to some degree and to obtain modest control over its prices and other aspects of its strategy, to build competitive advantage over other players. The restaurant business in a big city like London or Singapore is a good example of monopolistic competition.

In oligopolistic markets, there are fewer players, each able to gain competitive advantage by exploiting scale economies, by product differentiation and so on. There are numerous examples of this kind of market, including, for example, the global car market and the EU steel market. In both of these cases, a handful of firms compete against each other. This competition could be muted because of collusion between firms aimed at reducing rivalry. Although this collusion is possible and gives market control to all colluding producers, improving the financial performance of both individual firms and the sector as a whole, it is sometimes difficult to create and to sustain, and is usually illegal.

Intense competition could also occur in oligopolistic markets. Each firm knows that in this case, effective strategic management may create competitive advantage, but also each needs to be aware that its rivals may strive to copy any strategic move.

As well as the rivalry from existing players, it is important to take account of the threat of new entrants. This is technically known as 'contestable markets'. Sometimes the threat of new entrants is very low, because of the huge entry costs. These arise from the large fixed costs of installing plant, as well as the costs of acquiring the key competencies of these businesses. The existence of static and dynamic scale economies arising from learning curve effects also creates market barriers for incumbent firms. In other sectors, this may not be the case.

3.2 Industry analysis

Perfect competition is presented as the benchmark by which economists and others such as government departments and regulators judge the efficiency of markets. In general, markets are seen as efficient if they are perfect in their principal characteristics demonstrating price competition, ease of entry and exit, and wide distribution of relevant knowledge. Conversely, individual firms see it as in their own interest to have specific knowledge that enables them to build unique assets and offer distinctive products for which they can charge a price premium. In other words, firms have an interest in constructing imperfections that favour them in the marketplace. Firms may also have a joint interest in colluding together to create collective imperfections by which they can artificially limit competition and charge higher prices than otherwise. This is not the subject of this book, but there is a very considerable literature on these monopolistic practices and the ways in which governments pursue pro-competitive policies in order to make industries more efficient and markets more competitive. Firms actually compete on two levels. One level is in the marketplace where customers compare rival offerings, make choices and in doing so prices emerge from these market processes. Firms also compete through their plans and investments for the future and in doing so they construct assets that they hope will be sufficiently distinctive for them to offer distinctive products. Thus, the R&D activities of pharmaceutical firms are intended to create new and unique products that can be protected by patents and which can then be sold as unique high-priced products in the market. Industry analysis is the analysis of assets, resources and capabilities that set out the basic economic conditions under which firms collectively operate (the 'industry context') and which condition their individual abilities to create distinctive individual positions in their industries.

For example, Ford and Toyota operate in the automobile industry. They share some common operating characteristics such as significant economies of scale in assembly operations, a largely common knowledge basis and technology characteristics, and a set of competing products that compete more on price than on product differences. To some extent they share common economic characteristics. However, they each conduct R&D and other development activities in order to gain points of difference versus each other. Toyota might claim a distinctive way of organizing its manufacturing activities with beneficial effects on quality and reliability. Ford might claim a better organization of distribution and servicing activities with beneficial consequences for the way in which consumers experience the service process. This mixture of common economic characteristics coupled with attempts at individual differentiation comprises the content of industry analysis. As we have seen in the section on cost analysis, the nature of economies of scale in an industry (such as automobile assembly) affects the number of potential competitors in an industry (the greater the minimum efficient scale the fewer competitors that can survive). Thus the economic characteristics of the industry shape the nature of competition in the market by affecting the number of players (in this example). More generally, the economic characteristics of an industry are shaped by the investment and planning decisions of firms, and the extent to which firms can sustain uniqueness affects the way in which competition then plays out in the marketplace.

3.2.1 Porter's Five Forces

Industry analysis is best known as Porter's Five Forces (introduced initially in Chapter 1). This was first popularized by Michael Porter in his path-breaking *Analysis of Industry and Competition* first published in 1980. Figure 3.5 shows the celebrated diagram of the five forces of competition, namely rivalry, threat of entry, supplier power, buyer power, and threat of substitutes. These are the five fundamental forces that determine the 'attractiveness' of the industry, a term which is a surrogate for industry profitability. Thus the weaker/stronger are these forces then the more/less attractive will be the industry taken as a whole and the larger/smaller will be its overall profitability. On the whole, the more attractive the industry then the more likely it is that participants will enjoy 'good' profits.

The supply chain

The heart of the Five Forces diagram is the horizontal line. Porter draws this as a force diagram with all the arrows pointing towards the central box which represents the industry in question measured in terms of the competitors present. Alternatively this can be shown as a supply chain representing the build-up and flow of goods to the final customer. Thus for the food industry, goods flow from the farm, to food ingredients companies (such as flour milling), to food manufacturers (such as cake and bread manufacturers), to wholesalers, to supermarkets, and then to final consumers. At each stage of the supply chain there is an industry that invests in assets, that accumulates fixed and variable costs and then prices its goods to the next stage of the chain. The difference between its revenues and its material costs is its added value, i.e. the value it adds to its material input costs.[3] This added value can be partitioned into three parts: labour costs, capital costs, and profits. The more attractive the industry the greater is likely to be the value added, including also the profits, and vice versa. Where perfect competition is the norm, then prices will tend to converge

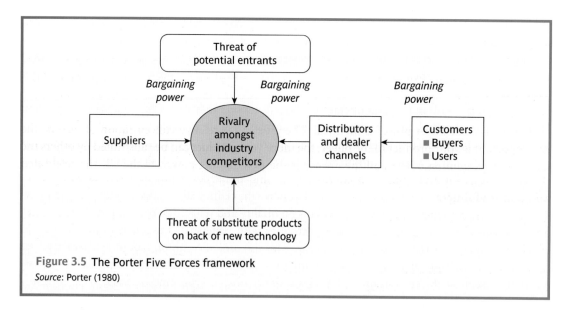

Figure 3.5 The Porter Five Forces framework
Source: Porter (1980)

---

[3] Economists use the difference between revenue and materials costs as the definition of value added being the value added to materials by the actions of the firm. However, many business analysts use 'value added' in a much more intuitive sense to mean profitability.

downwards and profits will fall to a level that is the minimum rate of return on capital that will enable the capital to be retained in the industry. If profits fall below this, there will be pressure to withdraw capital and place it in more profitable employment. If profits are higher then there will be an incentive for more capital to enter the industry. This is the basic mechanism behind the threat of entry in Figure 3.5.

The threat of entry

At each stage of the supply chain there is an industry that can be analysed in terms of the five forces. Firms considering investment in an attractive industry will make an entry calculation. This takes the form of a conventional capital investment decision with three components. The revenue stream depends on prices that can be charged (taking account of the price elasticity of demand) and the volumes attainable. The costs depend on the unit costs of production and access to available economies of scale, scope and learning, and on the level of marketing and other costs of getting the product to markets. Finally, the capital cost of the investment needs to be reckoned. If any of the cost elements (expressed in cost per unit of output form) are higher than those of the incumbents and if the prices relative to incumbents are lower, then the potential entrant faces 'entry barriers', i.e. its profit margins are lower than those of the incumbents and it faces a cost disadvantage or barrier. If the cost disadvantages are high in relation to the profit margins then they serve as an effective barrier to entry. If, for other reasons, such as access to technology or to distribution systems, the entrant is effectively barred from entry, we say that entry is *blockaded*.

The power of suppliers and buyers

Suppliers have a natural interest in raising their prices at your expense. To the extent that they succeed they enhance their margins at your expense. Under what conditions might this happen? Where there are relatively few suppliers you may not have many alternatives to an aggressive supplier. Where the supplier is providing a product that is very important to the eventual performance of your own product, then he might be able to charge a 'premium' price. Where you are accustomed to using a particular product there may be costs of *switching* from this product to an alternative. This provides a price umbrella for the supplier in his negotiations with you. If there are no substitution possibilities then price can go up. For example, if as an electricity generator your power stations are configured around coal supplies and conversion to other supplies such as gas or oil are only longer-term possibilities, then coal suppliers have bargaining power. OPEC in pricing oil has to be aware that an over-aggressive pricing policy provides incentives for its customers to convert to other fuels and/or to invest in energy saving.

The analysis of buyer power is identical. The greater the relative concentration of buyers, the less important is your product to the buyer; the more your product can be substituted by others the less is your bargaining power and the greater is their bargaining power. In the UK the celebrated example of this is the power of supermarket chains over food manufacturers. The larger and more powerful the chain, the more it can force down its input prices. However, the principal defence of the manufacturer vis-à-vis the supermarket is its ability to differentiate its products. Thus, the more distinctive is Nestlé's Nescafé brand then the less will Tesco be able to force its price down. Nestlé's calculation could be that customers will come into the store having already decided to buy the Nescafé brand regardless of any price differentials between Nescafé and other brands, including the supermarket's own brand. However, if Tesco could legitimately conclude that customers respond principally to Tesco's own branding and will therefore buy whatever Tesco put on the shelves (especially its own brand), then Tesco's buying power is strong and it will be more able to treat Nestlé and its other suppliers as providers of commodity products. The threat of vertical integration can be very effective in disciplining suppliers. Some retailers such as Marks and Spencer have an own brand policy that is a form of quasi-vertical integration that leaves strategic power effectively with the retailer. Conversely, the distinctiveness of luxury brand purveyors such as Louis Vuitton and Gucci has enabled many of these players to invest in their own captive distribution and retailing systems so that they can extract every drop of the product differentiation premium for themselves.

The balance between supplier power and buyer power is a key issue in business. Very often the biggest threat to your margins comes not simply from your competitors but from the adjacent (and sometimes even the more remote) parts of the supply chain. The biggest threat to food manufacturers probably comes from retailers. In the personal computer business the power in the supply chain lies upstream with the suppliers of components, that is, with Microsoft's operating systems and other software, and with Intel and its microprocessors. Estimates in Harvard Business School's case studies on Apple in the 1980s suggested that more than half of all the profits made in the personal computer (PC) industry supply chain were earned by Microsoft and Intel (Yotte, 1992). Thus, the location of power along the supply chain is a key issue in understanding how profits can be earned. The history of Dell shows how a strategic innovation downstream, close to the customer, has been able to create a defensible and profitable position in spite of the power of Microsoft and Intel.

The threat of substitutes

The pressure from substitutes tends to be longer-term pressure. If you conceive your product in this industry as having a certain benefit–cost ratio to the immediate customer, then pressure from substitutes can be calibrated in terms of alternative benefit–cost ratios. A simple but powerful example concerns the substitution of fibre optic cable for coaxial cable in telecommunications in the 1980s. Fibre optic cable offered so many more benefits at relatively low **marginal cost** that the costs of investing in entirely new cabling systems could very quickly be earned back. Most technological changes can be assessed in the same way, trading off the added benefits, the added costs, and the required investments. Complications arise when the products involved are components within larger systems. The increased use of modularity of electronic components and the standardization of electronic interfaces has increased the incentives for substitution. Another problem arises when the scale and scope of substitution is so large as to effectively disrupt the existing supply chains. The advent of photocopying, the laser printer and the personal computer demonstrate that there can be system-level substitutions that cause industries and supply chains to transform.

Note the similarity and the difference between **threat of entry** and **threat of substitutes**. Both are about the entry of new capacity into the industry and into the set of competitors. However, entry is essentially about imitation and the entry of new competitors to take advantage of the existing attractiveness of the industry. Substitution, however, is about new dimensions of competition and the ability of new ways of competing to displace existing ways. New entrants reckon to be able to exploit the existing value proposition to customers whereas substitute products expect to be able to change the value proposition.

Competitive rivalry

The intensity of competition is the fifth force on our diagram. This is regarded by economists as the first force in that it is the essence of the competitive forces present in all economic textbooks. The propositions follow from our earlier discussion of perfect competition. Thus, competition will be the stronger (and profits the lower) the more competitors there are and the more commodity-like the products are. In addition, the supply–demand balance directly affects the market price. In declining markets prices fall as excess supply chases decreasing levels of demand. The more the cost structure is fixed rather than variable and marginal costs are therefore low, the more room there is to cut prices before contribution margins become negative. This explains why capital-intensive industries with low marginal costs suffer so much in a recession. Prices can keep falling as long as cash flows remain positive (remembering that the capital costs are sunk, for example Eurotunnel) and fixed costs are programmed over a time period, so the only discretionary policy is to place price somewhere above marginal cost. In extreme cases cash flows might remain positive and sufficient to pay cash costs including interest payments on capital) while accounting losses could be very high.

3.3 Strategy as imperfections

Many writers have emphasized that strategy is, in the end, a practical matter, as are management studies in general. However, the long-run nature of strategic decisions and their inherent complexity, coupled with the uncertainty attached to futurity, means that there can be a substantial pay-off to strategic thinking. Strategic thinking places a premium on good understanding and use of concepts. Strategy was always recognized to centre on resource allocation decisions that determine the long-term capability of organizations in relation to choices about how and where the organization intends to compete. The foundation for strategic thinking requires an understanding of the nature of markets. Perfectly competitive markets are characterized by free entry, perfect information and identical commodity-like products. The consequence of such 'perfect' competition is that price is the only competitive variable, that firms are essentially identical and, therefore, that there are no super-normal profits to be had. Profit is sufficient to provide a normal return on capital and any profits above this will be transitory, either through random shocks or because competition erodes the profit benefits of new initiatives. Thus, the perfectly competitive world is not conducive to super profits ('rents') and does not provide much incentive to entrepreneurial behaviour.

However, imperfections in markets do provide the possibility for rents and rent-seeking activities. Imperfections could be, for example, differences in information about production possibilities, or consumer ignorance about product benefits. Some imperfections are market-wide, in that monopoly might prevail, perhaps because of government edict, or because of natural economies of scale, or perhaps through cartels. These imperfections are associated with rents, because prices can be held artificially high without (much) fear of competition. The worldwide wave of privatization and deregulation is usually marked by lower prices and greater competition. Figure 3.6 portrays the

Figure 3.6 Perfect competition versus competitive advantage

differences between the conditions under which perfect competition obtains and competitive advantage exists.

Imperfections can be firm-specific. Thus, a pharmaceutical company may, through its R&D activity, develop specific proprietary knowledge that results in new products, which cannot be imitated without a significant time lag. An office equipment company might establish a worldwide service system that allows it to give 24-hour service response to clients. Competitors can imitate only after substantial delay. **Firm-specific imperfections** enable firms to be different from their competitors and to expect this difference to be sustainable over a non-trivial time span. If firms can be different, and if customers value such differences, then these firms can earn super-normal profits, at least for a time. In economic terms, this is the essence of strategy. Firms create advantage by creating assets and positions that are distinctively different from those of their competitors. The essence of these firm-specific imperfections lies first in the creation of different assets (either tangible or intangible), and second in the creation of distinctive, defensible positions in their chosen product-markets. The '**positioning**' school (which could be known as the '**market-based view**') focuses primarily on the latter, with analysis of the nature and dynamics of competitive advantage. The **resource-based view** is concerned with the former.

What industry analysis does is to create a framework within which all the possible ways in which imperfections arise can be identified, assessed and analysed. The next section looks at how these firm-specific imperfections can be described as generic types of strategy.

Case box 3.1: Profitability of UK retailers

It is a commonplace to observe that British supermarket groups are much more profitable than their counterparts elsewhere in Europe or north America – isn't it? The companies themselves do not agree, and claims and counter-claims fly around like confetti … Several factors make comparisons inherently difficult. One factor is that the UK groups are all publicly owned, while many of the continental firms are still private. Definitions of profit, and the motivation to opt to declare a higher or lower figure, are different. If you want to please the stock exchange, you tend to declare high profits; if you and your family will be paying income tax on the sum, you may want to minimize it.

Another factor is that accounting conventions vary, in particular in relation to the treatment of goodwill, and amortization of property costs. Sums arising from the purchase of goodwill are amortized against the profit and loss account over 20 years in France; in the UK they will usually be written off immediately to reserves. In France, store assets (land and buildings) are depreciated over a 20-year period, while in the UK this has not until recently been true. The argument in Britain was that because of the high quality of the buildings, they would not decline very quickly in value over time, and the re- sidual asset would have a high resale value. This was clearly not true after the collapse of the property market in the early 1990s, and increasing criticism from analysts eventually led some retailers to ac- knowledge the validity of the argument. First, Morrison and Asda, then later all the others, agreed from the mid-1990s to depreciate their freehold and long-lease buildings. This reduced profits in the first few years. … With these preliminaries, we can look at some actual figures. There are (at least) two ways of analyzing profitability: margin on sales, and return on capital employed (ROCE). It turns out that they produce different patterns. With return on sales, which critics most often quote, it is clear that UK supermarkets appear to have an advantage. The profit margins on sales in Britain rose steadily over the decades until the early 1990s, and have consistently been above those for continental and US oper- ators. Over the period 1988–93, the average operating margin for six French supermarket groups was 2 per cent. For six British groups, the average was over 6 per cent (Burt and Sparks, 1997). Adjustment of the British figures to take account of the differences in accounting treatment mentioned above (and certain other factors) will bring the UK figures down to around 4 to 5 per cent, but the French figures will still be significantly lower at 1–2 per cent. Almost all the US supermarket chains have been nearer the French than the British levels (though in general, US and continental margins have been rising through the 1990s, while UK rates have been falling).

These comparisons have aroused most attacks from critics. They claim that the UK margins are the result of massive buying power exerted by the supermarket groups and the use of oligopoly power to impose on consumers a higher-than-normal price level. It is virtually impossible to compare price levels across countries, and it is also the case that there are large and powerful buying groups in many other countries. The British firms tend to be more centralized than some continental competitors, and to use a single fascia; this should help in reducing costs. It may also be that British firms are more experienced and more skilful in using their buying power to extract better terms from suppliers.

Other possible explanations for higher British margins flow from lower costs:

■ British companies have a lead in applying IT to logistics. Their distribution systems are centralized, with deliveries to a small number of company warehouses. Such efficiencies are reflected, for example, in fewer days' stockholding: an average of 20 days in the period 1988–93 for British firms, compared with 35 for French (Burt and Sparks, 1997).

■ Labour costs are lower in the UK, both because of lower social costs borne by employers, and because in Britain the proportion of part-time labour in supermarkets is higher than elsewhere.

■ The significantly higher level of own-label penetration in British supermarkets means that the average cost of goods sold is lower than in the rest of Europe, and the gross margin higher.

On the other hand, the costs of buying sites and of building superstores are considerably higher than in other countries; not all cost comparisons favour the British. Another element in the difference between British margins and those of continental and US operators is the nature of competition in the different markets. Price plays a much more important role in both the USA and continental Europe than in Britain, for whatever reason.

When we turn to ROCE, we see a different picture. A study of the years 1988–93 showed an average ROCE for six French companies of 19 per cent, and for six British of 21 per cent. A later analysis (Deutsche Morgan Grenfell, 1998) compared store groups in Britain, France, Belgium and the United States. The results from 1991–7 were consistent, and 1997 showed.

ROCE per cent	
Six British companies	16
Nine US companies	21
Eight French companies	20
Three Belgian companies	24

Any comparison of ROCE across countries shows that even the best British supermarket groups are at best similar to their rivals, but certainly not more profitable. The higher capital investment needs servicing by higher margins.

Source: pp. 215–16 from *The Grocers* by Seth and Randall, 1999, Kogan Page Publishers

Questions

1 Are the British supermarkets more profitable than their European and US counterparts?

2 Using the industry analysis framework, why might you expect the profitability of retailers to be different on average in different countries?

When you have read Chapter 5 and the section on the business model, you can answer these questions:

1 Do British supermarkets operate on a different business model from their rivals?

2 On what basis would you judge whether a different business model was sustainable or not?

3.3.1 Generic strategies

Porter's **Five Forces** and the various sources of imperfections are summarized in Figure 3.7. These powerful economic forces on industries, supply chains and markets suggest that firms can have substantial problems in identifying and responding to the competitive pressures that surround them. However, we have seen some examples where firms very deliberately set out to countervail these forces and create space within which they can earn profits at a higher rate than their competitors. This is the essence of strategy, the creation of space within which discrete and distinctive actions can secure improved positioning within markets and greater performance. Using the basic economic models popularized by Porter, we can see that competitive position can be improved in two basic ways. A firm might enjoy cost advantages, or alternatively create a differentiated product. In either case, its rivals will find difficulty imitating the firm's strategies. The essence of perfect competition is that imitation will be easy, not too costly, and speedy. Any differences that emerge will be competed away very quickly. The introduction of an extra feature on a car (such as rear parking sensors) is generally easy to copy. However, to offer hybrid motors (electric plus gasoline such as in the Toyota Prius) is much more difficult to copy in terms of quality, of cost and in speed of imitation. Firms with distinctive cost advantages will typically have built up economies of scale and scope over a long period of time and rivals may find it difficult to attain the same low costs. The very well-known report on the British motorcycle industry (Boston Consulting Group, 1975) identified huge scale economies in Japanese motorcycle factories leading, for example, to labour productivity figures of c.500 bikes per man year compared to the traditional craft-based production processes of European and US producers whose labour productivity was around 18 bikes per man year. This kind of cost advantage is inherently difficult to replicate and would take a very long time even if it were judged sensible to try to emulate it.

The other main dimension of strategic choice revolves around the notion of *scope*. The choice of broad scope suggests a calculation about available economies of scope in such a fashion that once chosen it is a commitment that cannot readily be reversed. The choice of narrow scope suggests an alternative calculation that the benefits of assets and other resources and capabilities

---

Supplier/buyer power
- Relative concentration
- Relative importance of product to the provider and the user
- Credible threat of vertical integration
- Substitution possibilities
- Control of information
- Switching costs

Barriers to entry
- Scale economics and experience
- Product differentiation

- Capital requirements
- Switching requirements
- Access to distribution
- Scale-independent cost advantages
- Level of expected retaliation

Intensity of rivalry *High if . . .*
- Several equally strong players
- Low/no growth in market
- High fixed costs and cyclical demand
- Few changes for differentiation
- Large-scale capacity increments
- Different 'culture' of players
- High strategic stakes
- Major exit barriers

Pressure from substitutes
- Benefits not product features
- Sideways competition
- Comparative price/performance
- Comparative technology life cycle
- What business are you in?
- Backing by rich competitor

Figure 3.7 Behind the competitive forces

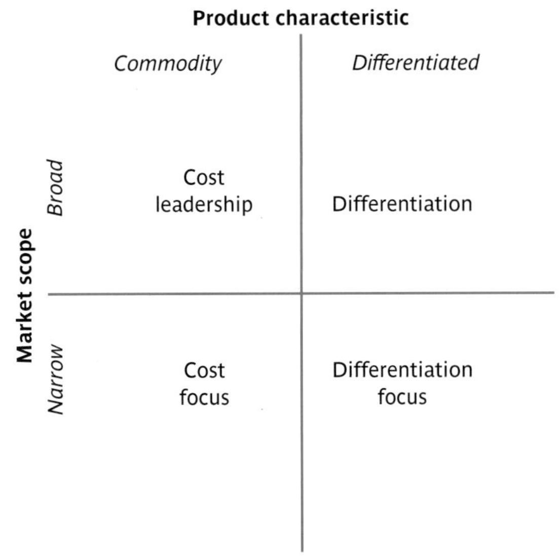

Figure 3.8 Porter's generic strategies
Source: Porter (1980)

focused and dedicated to specific ways creates differentiation and/or cost advantages of a different sort. Figure 3.8 illustrates these generic strategies.

Generic strategies represent typologies that illustrate the type and range of strategic options that in principle are available. Thus within the brewing industry over time it is possible to see some brewing companies as low-cost players relying on size of brewing plants to reduce costs to the lowest possible levels. Other brewers would see themselves as offering a wide range of differentiated products (e.g. cask-conditioned beer). Many well-known breweries are comparatively quite small but offer only a small range of 'real ale' products. Historically, most brewers were small local operations producing cheap and cheerful low-cost products. These typologies are useful in understanding the nature of the strategic options that face firms but they do not in themselves provide prescriptions for strategic choice. Choice depends on the ways in which an individual firm can deploy advantages from cost, differentiation and scope – the key dimensions of the generic strategies box.

Case box 3.2: Wal-Mart's British accent needs polish

Its ASDA discount chain is struggling to hold its own against the ubiquitous Tesco
Six years after it entered the British market with its bold $10.8 billion purchase of ASDA Group Ltd., Wal-Mart Stores Inc. is suddenly struggling. Following five solid years, sales and profits at the discount chain have stagnated in 2005. 'We're not where we used to be, and we're not where we want to be,' ASDA President and Chief Executive Andy Bond told a retail conference in London on Oct. 18. 'I'm not saying it's bad. But it's not good enough.'

Britain's retail scene has become increasingly competitive since Wal-Mart made landfall in 1999, intensifying the nation's price wars (page 40). Tesco, the No. 1 player, with $51.3 billion in sales in Britain, has nabbed more than 30% of the grocery market, according to London researcher TNS Superpanel. ASDA's share, meanwhile, has held steady at just below 17% for the past two years. And while ASDA and Tesco log the same sales per square foot, ASDA's operating margins of 4.8% are lower than Tesco's 6.2%. Although Wal-Mart is famed in the US for wresting deep discounts from suppliers, Tesco is the champ in Britain because of its size. 'Tesco has a much bigger stick to beat local suppliers with,' says Bryan Roberts, retail analyst at London consultancy Planet Retail.

Another issue ASDA must contend with is Tesco's broad appeal. ASDA attracts mostly lower-income shoppers, while Tesco ranks No. 1 among both blue- and white-collar workers. It seems that no matter what shoppers want – be it portobello mushrooms or plain white ones – Tesco has it. 'I love Tesco's,' says Lubna Khan, a 32-year-old Pakistani stay-at-home mom in London. 'Even the smallest shop has everything I need.'

With outlets as small as 300 square meters to as large as 5,500 square meters, Tesco has a presence on both the High Street and the out-of-town areas. By contrast, ASDA's reliance on the megastore format has hampered it, since local zoning laws do not favor big-box stores – or their shoppers. Nicola Hall, a 24-year-old British nurse who resides in central London, is a case in point: 'I do prefer ASDA as it's cheaper, but there aren't any near me.' So where does she shop? Tesco.

HEAD WINDS

To tackle this issue, ASDA has opened 10 small stand-alone stores since 2003 that sell its popular George clothing line, as well as five ASDA Living stores that carry household furnishings, toys, and jewelry. 'There's no refuting the fact that it's a tough property market,' says Bond, who was promoted to CEO in March. 'That's one of the reasons we are looking at new formats. All of those are trying to bring ASDA to a broader customer base.' Analysts say the new formats look promising.

Still, Bond faces strong head winds. Britain's economy is slowing down, with retail sales in the third quarter rising by just 1% over last year's level. Plus, there are signs that ASDA, which accounted for 45% of Wal-Mart's $56 billion in international sales in the 12 months through Jan. 31, is losing business. Wal-Mart's trademark 'everyday low prices' formula is no match for the endless promotions run by rivals Tesco and No. 3 J. Sainsbury. According to a TNS survey, ASDA lost $17 million in sales to other retailers in the 13 weeks through Oct. 9, vs. the same period last year. During the same time frame, Tesco gained $414 million in sales.

Most analysts are optimistic that Bond will turn ASDA around. He's adding healthier food sourced from local producers, and selling new products online, such as contact lenses and airline tickets. In July he announced about 1,400 job cuts. But what about beating out its archrival? 'Tesco is too far ahead,' says Gavin Rothwell, senior analyst at Verdict Research in London.

ASDA's Challenges

REAL ESTATE	Space for big-box stores is limited in Britain
THE ECONOMY	Consumer spending is slowing down
STORE FORMAT	ASDA has largely restricted itself to the megastore format
SHORT ON QUALITY	ASDA's products are seen as offering value, as opposed to quality
COMPETITION	Britain's No. 1, Tesco, keeps gaining market share, while No. 3 J. Sainsbury is turning itself around

Source: Business Week, by Laura Cohn, 21 November 2005
© Bloomberg BusinessWeek

Questions for discussion

1 Outline the different ways in which ASDA and Tesco compete in the same industry (UK food retailing).

2 What differences might you expect to see in other countries?

3 Are there any new sources of competitive advantage available to retailers in the UK?

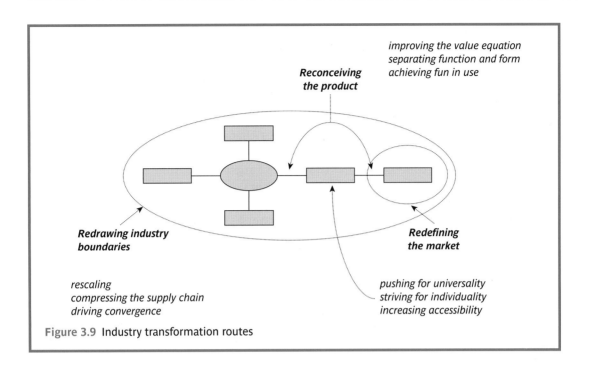

improving the value equation
separating function and form
achieving fun in use

Reconceiving
the product

Redrawing industry
boundaries

Redefining
the market

rescaling
compressing the supply chain
driving convergence

pushing for universality
striving for individuality
increasing accessibility

Figure 3.9 Industry transformation routes

3.3.2 Industry transformation

It is common to observe that change is endemic and many consulting firms have been very successful in promoting programmes of strategic change. However, many also note that strategies by their nature are not things that one changes readily or frequently. Strategies involve investment in lumpy and sticky assets without the comfort of knowing that mistakes can be easily undone. Nevertheless, markets and industries do evolve and grow. Growth very often is continuous and cumulative, especially when research and development follows cumulative trajectories. The experience of the last quarter of a century shows that new knowledge has very often moved sideways into adjacent industries and done an excellent job of unsettling long-held beliefs and strategies. Thus new materials such as plastics have undermined the steel industry and the coming of the internet has caused major changes in distribution industries. So are there any patterns in the way in which industries are transformed? In what ways does Porter's famous picture of the Five Forces change systematically? Figure 3.9 suggests the major possibilities.

The principal routes as a result of which the five forces are reconfigured are:

1 redefining the market;
2 reconceiving the product;
3 redrawing the industry boundaries.

Market redefinitions involve changing the relationship with the customer. At one level firms may seek universality, that is, striving to get a wider take-up of their products across hitherto distinct market segments. This is the approach typically taken in internationalization and we could say that Coca-Cola has succeeded in achieving a universal market. The opposite approach is individualization, with segments of size one person – an approach typical in modern electronic and internet-based industries. Most redefinition strategies have some element of higher accessibility involving major changes in logistics and distribution.

Rethinking the role of the product is also an attempt to capture changes that are taking place in the psychology of consumers. There have been fundamental and controversial changes in the nature of drinks on offer to young people (alco-pops for example) where the producers have been trying to tap into the rapid changes that are taking place. Similarly, sports cars are being redefined as toys for the retired. Product changes typically involve changing the value equation (benefit–cost ratio to the customer).

Redrawing industry boundaries stems from major changes in the underlying economics of production and of the supply chain in general. The drivers of change are usually rescaling to obtain economies, and driving convergence and eliminating variety to the same end. A simple way of reducing costs has been to outsource more and more, but this in itself is not strategic – it is more a rebalancing of the location of costs along the chain. More significant is the compressing of the supply chain where new technology raises the possibility of changing the nature of the operations in the chain with the effect of changing the product and its cost characteristics.

3.4 Sources of competitive advantage

The idea of a generic strategy is a powerful foundation for understanding how competitive strategies are in practice articulated and implemented. A generic strategy is a simple typology that captures the essential economic forces at work in a market (the demand side) and in an industry (the supply side). Porter suggested that there are three generic strategies to choose from, and each business unit can have its own strategy. According to Porter, a business can strive to supply a product or service more cost-effectively than its competitors (**cost leadership**), it can strive to add value to the product or service through differentiation and command higher prices (**differentiation**), or it can narrow its focus to a special product market segment which it can monopolize (focus). Not following any of these strategies characterizes a firm as being 'stuck in the middle'. The choice of generic strategy should be based on the firm's business unit's strengths and weaknesses, and a comparison of those with the strengths and weaknesses of competitors.

If a firm can become the lowest-cost producer in the industry, then *cost leadership* may be the most appropriate strategy to pursue. Cost reduction should be continuous, so that the cost differential with competitors is maintained, and should involve all stages of the **value chain**. It can be achieved by means of methods such as proprietary access to cheaper inputs or technologies, or by positioning to exploit any experience effects (see Figure 3.2). Typically, these come with market share, so the control of a large share of the market is likely to be necessary. Where there are limited opportunities to build efficient plant, the second, third, or other low-cost producers may also be able to achieve above-average performance. Moreover, because of the reliance on economies of scale and the like, cost leadership is likely to be more sustainable in the **long run** if relatively stable, no-frills products of reasonable quality are involved. For the same reason, cost leadership strategies are more appropriate in relatively stable environments. The typical staffing and administrative requirements of a cost leader are also distinct. Unskilled personnel can undertake much of the workload, and technocrats such as scientists and engineers are not required on any large scale, particularly where commodity products are involved. Similarly, cost control is of the utmost importance, and very developed formal systems are often encountered.

If cost leadership is not a feasible option, but the firm is able to differentiate its products along some attributes which customers value, and the cost of doing so is lower than the extra revenue envisaged, then *differentiation* may be the appropriate strategy to pursue. Porter defines differentiation in terms of the ability to charge higher prices, and not on the basis of the product's attributes per se. It can be based, therefore, on either product innovation or marketing. In order to pursue a differentiation (value added) strategy, an accurate picture of the target market will have to be obtained to ensure that there are sufficient ways in which to differentiate the product, and that the marketplace can be subdivided – and is willing to pay for the differentiation. An effort will then have to be made to avoid imitation, and this typically involves a regular redefinition of the basis of differentiation. For the same reason, it would be desirable for the differentiation to be based on a mix of features and activities rather than a simple product feature or service, and for it to involve many parts of the value chain. Added protection from imitation may also be possible by linking into the value chains of suppliers and buyers. Differentiation, whether innovation or marketing based, is more appropriate in dynamic industry environments, in which it can help to avoid, at least in the **short run**, potentially more costly forms of competition such as price cuts. However, as it often involves new technologies and unforeseen customer and competitor reactions, it also contributes, in turn, to environmental unpredictability. As far as staffing and administrative requirements are concerned, differentiation typically requires the employment of experts, and the establishment of mechanisms to facilitate the coordination of these experts, who may work in different functional departments.

If it is not possible to access the entire market on the basis of either low cost or differentiation, a defensible niche may still be available to provide above-average performance. Marketing to such a niche would again involve a choice between low cost or differentiation but, this time, if the niche is well chosen, the scope of the market would enable the firm to advance on more limited cost and differentiation capabilities. In principle, a *focus* strategy exploits the differences in cost behaviour in some segments, or the special needs of the buyers in those segments, so it is available only where such segments are poorly served by the broadly targeted competitors and, of course, sustainable only for as long as the niche can be defended. The difficult point for the focuser is reached when the niche has been exhausted, at which time he may be tempted, out of a false sense of security derived from his success within the narrow scope of the niche, to target the broader market. This can have catastrophic consequences.

From the above discussion, it should be evident that each generic strategy makes its own demands on the organization in terms of skills and administrative structure, and is more appropriate in different sets of circumstances. Nevertheless, a firm pursuing one strategy would act foolishly if it did not act to gain from elements of the other strategies too, as long as this did not detract from its chosen strategy. A differentiator, for example, should pursue all cost reduction which does not sacrifice differentiation, and a cost leader could differentiate until this started to cost too much. However, when a firm confuses its primary goal and source of competitive advantage, and pursues both cost reduction and differentiation indiscriminately (or not at all), then it is said by Porter to be 'stuck in the middle'. This, he said, is an unenviable strategy because, in general, cost leadership and differentiation are inconsistent in principle, and there will typically be a cost leader, differentiator or focuser that will be able to compete better than the firm stuck in the middle in any one segment of the market. Firms with such a (lack of) strategy, Porter said, typically end up stuck in the middle because they find it difficult to make the necessary choices.

There are a few cases, however, in which cost leadership and differentiation are not mutually inconsistent, at least in the short run. This may occur, for example, when the firm pioneers a proprietary innovation (whether a product, service or process), which enables it to reduce cost and at the same time differentiate successfully. With the appropriate barriers erected, it may be possible to exploit such an innovation for a considerable period of time. Similarly, cost leadership and differentiation may also be pursued together when costs are largely determined by market share, and control of a considerable share enables the firm to use the extra margin to differentiate, and still remain the cost leader. The same may be possible if there are interrelationships between industries that a competitor may be able to exploit while others are not. In any case, the profitability of a 'stuck in the middle' company may remain adequate in the medium term in a high-growth environment (as this sustains inefficiencies), in a particularly attractive industry, or if the firm faces similarly 'stuck in the middle' competitors.

Porter's claim that *no* firm should be stuck in the middle has, however, received critical attention and a lot of effort has gone into interpreting and questioning this advice. J. Sainsbury, the retailer ('Good food costs less at Sainsbury's'), is often cited as proof that a stuck in the middle strategy can be viable and successful (Cronshaw et al., 1990) because Sainsbury's exhibits both low cost and differentiation. Gilbert and Strebel (1991) distinguished between one-dimensional and outpacing strategies, and suggested that the latter are designed for being stuck in the middle. The crux of this debate is that there exists no reason to imply that a low-cost base should necessarily be coupled with lower prices, or that a differentiated product should be coupled with premium prices. The low-cost base could simply be used to earn higher margins or, indeed, a differentiated product could be priced low enough to achieve a higher volume of sales (pricing differentiated products low enough to gain entry into a new market is only a temporary strategy which can lead to no competitive advantage, so it is of no relevance here). The underlying cause that leads to the overlap has been identified by Mathur (1988), who observed that whereas differentiation is an output concept, cost leadership is relevant to both inputs and outputs. Finally, some of the most common dangers to sustainability that are inherent in each of the strategies are shown in the tables in Chapter 5.[4]

It is common to hear protests that generic strategies are too simple. But this is to miss the point. Generic strategies are intended to capture and portray the essential underlying economic forces. What firms do is to interpret these in the context of their own circumstances and formulate more or less complex strategies accordingly. Criticism has also focused on the lack of market orientation in the generic strategies matrix (Figure 3.8). Also missing is government and its frequently very significant role in the operation of markets. However, typologies and generics are not intended to be an accurate portrayal of the world – that is the role of the strategist in practice. The well-known Ansoff diversification matrix is another generic strategies matrix. This sets out to define appropriate types of strategy for the marketing of new or existing products to new or existing markets. This attracted much attention because it drew the distinction between horizontal and vertical integration and conglomerate styles. These are pure types of strategy (like cost, differentiation and focus) that are applied in specific ways according to circumstances. Porter's generic strategy approach enables us to focus on the essence of strategy, which is to seek out and defend competitive advantage, a unique **strategic position**. This chapter and the one that follows go behind the three generic strategies to examine the nature of strategic positioning so as to capture a sustainable competitive advantage.

Case box 3.3 is included here for you to look at a specific characteristic of retailing, namely capital intensity, and ask: 'How does this affect the way we look at a business and how, therefore does it affect the way in which we judge progress over time?'

---

[4] Tables 5.1 and 5.2 in Chapter 5.

Case box 3.3: **Capital intensity in retailing**

A distinctive feature of the UK supermarket industry has been that it is far more capital intensive than in other countries. This stems, firstly, from certain aspects of the property market in the UK. Britain is a small country, and land for development is scarce and therefore expensive. During a long period of rising prosperity and therefore of increased demand it has become more scarce (as Mark Twain noted, 'They've stopped making it'). In these circumstances leases always contain regular, upward-only rent reviews. Ownership of commercial sites is concentrated among institutional investors, who are interested only in their capital gains and revenue streams. British leasehold law allows the lessor to recover all rent due from the head lessee, even though the lease may have been assigned, often many times. The original lessee may thus find that – when the latest tenant has defaulted, and even if the premises are shuttered – the owner will pursue him for all rent owing. British supermarket companies have therefore concentrated almost entirely on freehold properties.

Furthermore, the planning authorities have insisted on high building standards, so the cheap, large sheds of continental or US hypermarkets are not an option for UK grocers. One estimate suggests that a US supermarket can be built for half the cost of its UK equivalent.

High investment is also needed for the IT systems on which a modern retail chain depends. It would be impossible to run a group of several hundred stores, each with 20,000 or more SKUs (stocking units), without a formidably effective IT system. All the UK chains have invested hundreds of millions of pounds over the years on IT.

Finally, compared with France at least, UK retailers have to fund more of their own working capital. In France, the large food retailers take at least 90 days' credit from their suppliers; in Britain, the figure is nearer 30 days. UK food manufacturers may feel that they are supplying their retail customers with much of their working capital along with their products, but the situation is much worse in continental Europe.

High capital investment has been forced on the UK chains, and has dictated much of their strategy; they *have* to achieve higher margins. Their drive for efficiency has led them inexorably to the superstore format (seemingly unique to Britain, because of the market size and population density), and to take over much of the distribution chain themselves. Return on capital, the ultimate measure of profitability, shows that they achieve results similar to their rivals elsewhere but the route is different – higher margins and higher capital intensity.

Source: pp. 226–7 from *The Grocers* by Seth and Randall, 1999, Kogan Page Publishers

Questions

1 How does capital intensity affect the way in which profits are earned?

2 What does this imply for strategic decisions such as store expansion and pricing?

3.5 From competitive advantage to competitive strategy: the market positioning view

In this section we develop the market positioning view in some more detail. We look at cost analysis, especially the nature of economies of scale and learning effects, as the basis for cost leadership strategies. We consider further the nature of advantage and the different forms in which it can be seen. Finally, we look at some practical advice when formulating competitive strategy.

3.5.1 Cost advantage

This chapter emphasizes the way in which the microeconomics of strategy is built on an understanding of the nature of costs. Economic analysis is built on an understanding of the operation of markets in which markets are assumed to be perfect (an assumption that we challenge later in this chapter) and therefore the driving logic behind competition is the achievement of low costs. Where there are no economies of scale or scope that can be claimed by individual competitors then competition is truly perfect, with similar/same prices and costs facing everyone. This leads to a situation of no competitive advantage accruing anywhere and, in general, a level of sustainable profitability that is capable only of paying the opportunity cost of capital. Where, however, there are scale, experience or scope effects that can be appropriated by individual competitors (or a group of competitors) then there is the opportunity for a competitive advantage based in distinctively and sustainably low relative costs. This is the essence of *cost advantage* as originally described by Porter in his generic strategies matrix.

At this point we outline the various ways in which scale and experience economies arise and the online study guide enables you to examine in more detail the various drivers of scale and experience effects. Scale is recognized as a key characteristic that determines cost advantage and industry structure. Table 3.1 contains estimates from the work of Scherer and Ross (1990). The final two columns show the ratio of minimum efficient scale to market size (MES) for various industries in the US and the UK. It is evident, for example, that industry x will be much more *concentrated* than industry y (it will have many fewer players), because economies of scale are so much bigger in relation to the market size.

So, we can see that the existence of sufficiently large-scale economies directly determines the number of players that can enjoy these scale benefits in a market of any given size. This gives rise to the old saying that the size of the market determines the degree of specialization (another term for scale intensity) – a big enough market gives rise to the discovery of scale effects.

Scale effects can sometimes be deliberately claimed by an individual competitor. The example in Table 3.2 is taken from a case study on Du Pont's attempt in the 1970s to dominate the market for titanium dioxide in the USA by virtue of its superior cost position. The cost advantage is based on economies of scale, on experience effects, on vertical integration, and on lower raw material prices.

Table 3.1 Minimum efficient scale for selected industries in the UK and the USA

Industry	% Increase in average costs at $^1/_2$ MES[5]	MES as % of market in	
		UK	USA
Cement	26.0	6.1	1.7
Steel	11.0	15.4	2.6
Glass bottles	11.0	9.0	1.5
Bearings	8.0	4.4	1.4
Fabrics	7.6	1.8	0.2
Refrigerators	6.5	83.3	14.1
Petroleum refining	4.8	11.6	1.9
Paints	4.4	10.2	1.4
Cigarettes	2.2	30.3	6.5
Shoes	1.5	0.6	0.2

Source: Scherer and Ross (1990) *The Economics of Multiplant Operations,* Tables 3.11 and 3.15

---

[5] This gives a measure of the sensitivity of costs across the range of plant sizes.

Table 3.2 Du Pont's calculation of its cost advantage

	Limenite Chloride	Rutile Chloride 1972 cents/lb	Difference
From exhibit 3	18.80	21.50	−2.70
Less depreciation	−3.00	−2.50	−0.50
Capital charge	6.80	5.60	1.20
	22.60	24.60	−2.00
Learning effect	−4.75	0.00	−4.75
Scale effect	−3.75	0.00	−3.75
Integration effect	−1.30	0.00	−1.30
Capacity effect	1.30	1.00	0.30
Cost per lb	14.10	25.60	−11.50

capital charge = investment requirements per lb multiplied by hurdle rate (say 15%)
learning effect = 79% learning curve and double the experience
scale effect   = 85% doubling effect and twice the scale
capacity effect = differences in capacity utilization
Source: Ghemawat (1994a) *Du Pont in Titanium Dioxide (A)*, Harvard Business School case 9-385-140 (1984) exhibits 2 and 3, also Ghemawat (1989, 1994b)

In total, the cost advantage over typical competitors is around 40%. As a result, the competitors were unable to stop Du Pont building scale-efficient new plant to take advantage of market growth – a classic example of a pre-emptive strategy. Similar arguments lay behind the analysis of the rapid growth of Japanese companies in the 1970s. Significant economies of scale gave the opportunity for lower prices, the building of market share, even lower costs, and the gradual dominance of markets. In general, the analysis of *first-mover advantage* relies on the existence of significant scale and experience effects, a price-sensitive market, and the willingness to commit capital ahead of competition.

Here we see also reference to learning (experience) effects. They are technically known as *dynamic economies of scale* and usually exist in tandem with conventional scale (or *static*) economies of scale. The most celebrated and discussed example of these is contained in the BCG analysis of the Japanese motor cycle industry (1975). Not only did the main Japanese manufacturers (Honda, Kawasaki, Suzuki and Yamaha) produce at several times the scale of their European and American manufacturers, but by virtue of their volumes produced per period were able to learn more quickly about how to design, manufacture and market. This is captured in the phrases *learning by doing* and the *experience effect*. Thus competitors such as these are advantaged by both static and dynamic scale effects where sustainability of the original scale advantage is buttressed by the barrier to entry embedded in the learning effects. This happy combination has been particularly evident in assembly line operations in consumer durable good industries.

3.5.2 Differentiation advantage

Product differentiation is a characteristic of imperfect markets where non-price strategies are important. Product differentiation is the act of making products different from one another. This might involve tangible differences such as quality, reliability, performance or design. Alternatively (or in addition) it might be based on intangible elements such as reputation and branding. Thus Subaru's cars might be differentiated on the basis of their performance characteristics as attested

Table 3.3 Comparison of cost and differentiation strategies

	Cost leadership	Differentiation
Cost advantage	Scale and scope	None required
Differentiation advantage	Low (price strategies)	High (non-price strategies)
Market segmentation	Low (mass market)	High (many markets)
Distinctive competences	Manufacturing and buying	Marketing, R&D

by their success in motor sport. But Mercedes would rely heavily on accumulated reputation in addition to other tangible differentiators such as build quality.

Differentiation[6] requires the investment of resources – typically time, capital cost and higher variable costs – in a risky bet that the customer will respond to the differentiated product by buying it at a premium price and/or more frequently. The bet is risky because the attempt to differentiate might fail:

1 Product quality might fail to improve as a result of the product development activity.

2 A competitor does it better (for example, Jaguar cars is involved in an attempt to catch up with the differentiation power of the German brands BMW and Mercedes).

3 Customers fail to respond to the new proposition (see, for example, the failure of laser disks in the consumer electronics market).

4 The costs of differentiation might be in excess of the gains from differentiation – the capital costs and any higher variable costs might not be offset by the new price–volume combination. The classic case of this is IBM's attempts to differentiate its personal computers from the stream of IBM-compatible new entrants in the 1980s. IBM offered a new operating system, OS/2, but the benefits of this were not apparent to customers who preferred to stay with the Microsoft DOS system that had become the industry standard.

Successful differentiation makes the market less perfect because the firm that has created the differentiation has in fact created a firm-specific imperfection. Product differentiation is therefore the process of creating a competitive advantage by making the product (or service) different from those of rivals to the extent that superior performance results.

In Table 3.3 we can see that there are different bases for cost advantage and differentiation advantage. Cost leadership typically requires large (mass) markets in which minimum efficient plant sizes can be reached. Differentiation by contrast prospers in market segments in which different customer needs can be identified and products designed for those needs. The approaches to the market are distinctive. Cost leadership is accompanied by price (low price) strategies whereas differentiation is based in non-price strategies. Different competences are also indicated. Cost leadership is usually manufacturing and procurement based whereas differentiation activity is marketing based and R&D intensive. Michael Porter argued, controversially, that firms could not do both and if they tried they would get 'stuck in the middle'. However, his position clearly depends on a particular view of the competences that support cost and differentiation positions. Case box 3.4 describes the emergence of the 'scale economy brander' in the food processing industry.

---

[6] It is important to distinguish product differentiation from differentiation as applied to organization structure. The building blocks of organization structure are differentiation and integration. In this context differentiation is the way in which a company allocates people and resources to different organization tasks – the greater the number of functions and activities, the higher is the level of differentiation.

Case box 3.4: **The scale economy brander**

The consumer packaged goods industries (including the food processing industry) enjoyed halcyon days in the 1960s when manufacturers were dominant. This was a period when mass markets in processed foods were growing quickly, retail distribution was highly fragmented, economies of scale were available, and processing technologies were proprietary. These substantial economic advantages were buttressed by the creation of mass marketing systems comprising national media advertising, national sales forces, and increasingly sophisticated marketing support services. The visible output of this business system was the brand, the repository of guarantees to the customer of product qualities arising from proprietary technology. The creation of the brand was subject to many economies of marketing scale, and fostered scale economies available elsewhere in the system. The brand was the visible symbol of the manufacturers' strength, and was the visible barrier to entry behind which grew a series of oligopolies earning monopoly rents. There were seven entry barriers around these brand positions:

1 National sales force and distribution: 'filling up the backroom and stealing shelf space';

2 Listing muscle: fragmented retailers felt they had to stock the leading brands on manufacturers' terms;

3 Intensive media advertising bought at preferential rates and defrayed across large volumes;

4 Superior product quality arising from proprietary processing technology and/or from consumer perceptions;

5 Low-cost processing either from superior technology or from scale economies;

6 Sophisticated support services, e.g. market research, product management support structure, advertising skills;

7 Discounts on raw material purchases based on volume.

Branding economics was all about premium prices, consumer pull, and economies of scale. The association of market share and profitability was well attested in this regime of the scale economy brander. Behind the brand lay a technology edge and a new management structure and style – the style of the marketing company.

   These marketing companies came in two forms. The first was the Multinational Major Branders (e.g. Unilever, BSN, and Heinz). These were multinational companies operating multiple, related consumer goods businesses across the world, with strong perceived product differentiation accompanied by strong branding.[7]

   The second were the National Major Branders (e.g. St Ivel). These were nationally based and focused companies with very high levels of marketing support for a product range, which, by the standards of the multinationals, was more limited.

Source: McGee and Segal-Horn, 1992

Questions

1 Why was it possible for scale and differentiation effects to be simultaneously present?

2 What effect do you think this could have on the pattern of competition?

Sources of differentiation advantage

Product differentiation opportunities arise from the physical characteristics of the product, from the technological foundations of the product, and from the nature of customers and markets.

---

[7] These companies have been traditionally multi-domestic in character as opposed to global (Porter, 1986) or transnational (Bartlett and Ghoshal, 1989). See the discussion in Chapter 9 on the nature of international advantage.

Table 3.4 Dimensions of differentiation

Dimensions of differentiation	Tangible	Intangible
Quality	Performance Reliability	Reputation
Innovation	New functional attributes New usage patterns	Modernity
Customer responsiveness	New distribution system	Brand Relationship management

As shorthand, we can observe that 'quality' reflects the physical characteristics of the product; 'innovation' captures the technological dimension; and 'customer responsiveness' reflects market and customer factors. If we correlate these with the tangibility/intangibility dimension, we can see Table 3.4 describing the arena in which product differentiation works.

Table 3.4 is a simple representation of the complexity of differentiation. However, you can see the elements that can make up differentiation. Performance and reliability of products (such as **durable goods**, computers, cars and washing machines) are obvious characteristics but ones which can be imitated. However, reputation is less easily gained and less easily lost. So a Rolls-Royce reputation for automobile quality may linger for a long time even if the objective data on tangible characteristics might suggest that others have long since caught up.[8] Innovation allows for a reshaping of the way in which the product works and the way in which customers use the product. Thus laptop computers are an innovation sitting alongside the desktop alternatives but operating in different ways and places and requiring different technical solutions. Sometimes innovation captures a style which we have called modernity that reflects lifestyle choices. Thus architectural innovation may have tangible effects on the nature of buildings but much of the benefit may be felt in the feel, style, and texture of the space. The (high) fashion industry is one where intangibles are predominant and functionality unimportant. Customer responsiveness captures the extent to which products have value because of the degree and style of interaction between buyer and seller. Dell Computers offers the lesson that product features are not all-important. Michael Dell's innovation was to identify that customers valued close interaction between buyer and seller through the distribution system. Dell's competitive advantage rests on the closeness of links to the customer and the entire business is about creating the logistics that give the customer maximum choice and timeliness of choice.

Dell Computers is a good example of how differentiation advantages can be built in self-reinforcing pyramids. Dell innovated, created a new tangible marketing and distribution process, and has created also an enviable reputation and brand name. The more diverse the bases and dimensions of differentiation, the more powerful will be the differentiation effect. As a result, companies that are successful at this (see Case box 3.4 above) become infused with the differentiation culture. See, for example, how the scale economy branders such as Procter & Gamble, General Foods, Unilever and others are known as marketing companies despite their very considerable talents in manufacturing and other non-marketing functions. The prime source of advantage is differentiation secured through **core competences** (see Chapter 6) in marketing.

Differentiation covers many approaches to the customer. It might rest on a broad market appeal or it might rely on narrow market niches in which it offers highly specific solutions for customers.

---

[8] This is *not* true of the Rolls-Royce reputation for aero engines which continues to be high on both tangible and intangible dimensions.

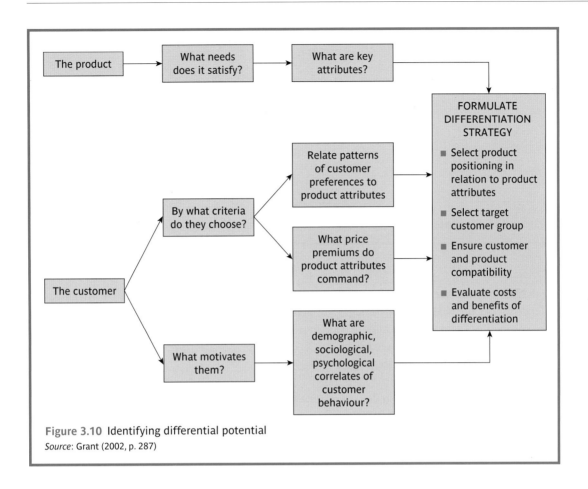

Figure 3.10 Identifying differential potential
Source: Grant (2002, p. 287)

Figure 3.10 suggests a methodology by which you can begin an assessment of the market and the potential for differentiation. In looking at the product and customer dimensions in this figure you are trying to work out whether this is a market in which common needs prevail or whether there is a diversity of needs. Where you might identify commonality and make your differentiation investments accordingly, you are open to the niche player who might target a niche in your market to which a more specific and valuable customer proposition can be made. In mature markets this process of continuous segmentation allows smaller firms to chip away at the bigger but broader positions of the market leaders. Conversely, a niche play is susceptible to innovation by large players such that the niche offer is swept up in a bigger and better offer that covers many segments. The decline of small and medium-sized retailers is testament to the ability of large retailers to provide an unmatchable price proposition together with different differentiation propositions.

3.5.3 Competitive advantage

In earlier chapters we asserted the connection between strategy choices and profitability. We argued that strategy choices are resource allocation decisions that enable the firm to create distinctive assets and capabilities (this is the language of core competences, as we shall see below). These enable the firm to create imperfections in markets that are specific to it and therefore the firm can capture the benefits of this positioning in terms of higher prices or lower costs or both. Figure 3.11 illustrates the point. A successful strategy can earn superior financial returns because it has an *unfair advantage*, that is, it creates, exploits and defends firm-specific imperfections in the market vis-à-vis competitors.

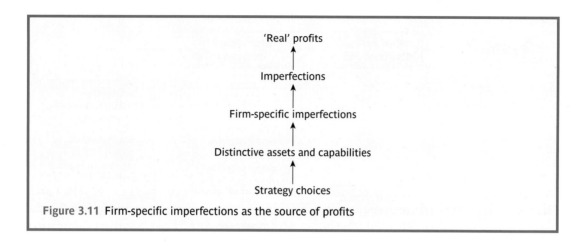

Figure 3.11 Firm-specific imperfections as the source of profits

We deliberately use the term unfair advantage as a colloquial simile for competitive advantage in order to underline that such advantages are achieved in the teeth of organized opposition both from competitors who wish to emulate your success and from customers who would like to exercise bargaining power to achieve lower prices.

In theory, competitive advantage is

> *the delivering of superior value to customers and in doing so, earning an above-average return for the company and its stakeholders.*

These twin criteria impose a difficult hurdle for companies, because competitive advantage cannot be bought by simply cutting prices, or by simply adding quality without reflecting the cost premium in higher prices. Competitive advantage requires the firm to be sustainably different from its competitors in such a way that customers are prepared to purchase at a suitably high price. Classic perfect competition works on the basis that all products are so alike as to be commodities, and that competition takes place solely on the basis of price. The search for competitive advantage is the search for differences from competitors, and for purchase on the basis of value (that is, the offer of an attractive performance-to-price ratio). Competitive advantage is a statement of positioning in the market and consists of the following elements:

■ a statement of competitive *intent*;

■ outward evidence of *advantage* to the customer;

■ some combination of:
  – superior delivered cost position
  – a differentiated product
  – protected niches;

■ evidence of *direct benefits*, which:
  – are perceived by a sizeable customer group
  – these customers value and are willing to pay for
  – cannot be readily obtained elsewhere, both now and in the foreseeable relevant future.

The sustainability of competitive advantage depends on the following:

- *power* – maintaining the levels of commitments in resource terms relative to competitors;
- *catching-up* – ease of copying and nullifying the advantages;
- *keeping ahead* – productivity of one's own continuous search for enhanced or new advantages;
- *the changing game* – rate of change of customer requirements;
- *the virtuous circle* – the self-sustainability and mutual reinforcing of existing advantages.

Economists argue that competitive advantages are by their nature temporary in character and therefore decay quickly. This is to argue that product markets and the market for underlying resources are reasonably competitive. Indeed, much of the analysis of competitive advantage is concerned with assessing just how defensible, durable and large the advantages can be. The Porter Five Forces framework (Porter, 1980) provides a useful basis for categorizing and understanding the industry economics that lie behind competitive advantage. Figure 3.7 (shown earlier) summarizes the competitive forces. Notice that the barriers to entry are in essence the competitive advantages that are available in the industry. They represent the cost premiums that entrants would have to pay in order to enter the industry and compete on equal terms. In other words, these are the imperfections that the incumbents have created (or are the beneficiaries of). It is important to note that the barriers to entry may be generic, meaning that the incumbents do not have advantages over each other, but have a shared advantage with a shared rent. Or the barriers may be firm-specific, implying that different incumbents are protected by different advantages and are themselves different from one another. Barriers are also entrant-specific in that different potential entrants have different assets and therefore different ways in which they might compete.

Figures 3.12 and 3.13 show a reworking of Porter's generic strategy matrix (Figure 3.8) to emphasize that the three routes to advantage are potentially reinforcing. Figure 3.13 outlines the arguments for and against more than one generic strategy. The argument rests on the point that the different strategies require different resources and capabilities and, therefore, different organizational forms and cultures. The alternative argument suggests that new technologies are leading to more similarities in the strategies. Figures 3.14, 3.15 and 3.16 summarize the generic strategies in terms of the essence of the strategy, the nature of its advantages, the competences required, and the risks

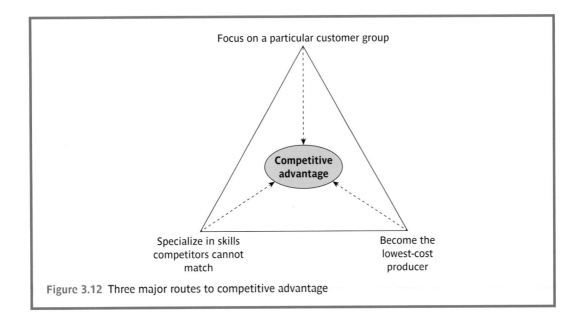

Figure 3.12 Three major routes to competitive advantage

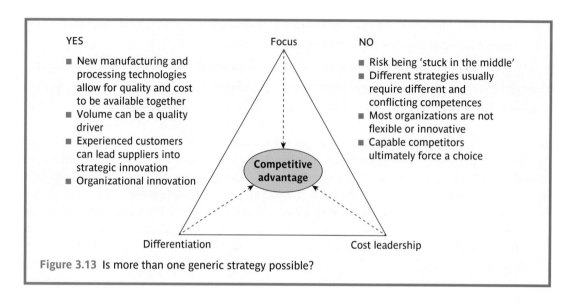

Figure 3.13 Is more than one generic strategy possible?

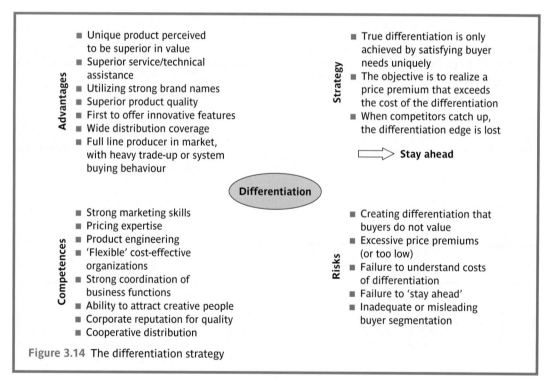

Figure 3.14 The differentiation strategy

that it has to face. This should reinforce the idea that strategy is about making a commitment and about the deliberate calculation and taking of risk.

Figure 3.13 shows the implications of composite differentiation and cost strategies. The figure arrays cost advantage against a composite differentiation and focus dimension. For example, where there are high cost advantages and high differentiation advantages, the risk for the company is that the supporting skills might become mass-produced or that technological change will outmode the skills. Conversely, where the advantages from both sources are small, then there might be entry from other industries where the skills are similar. The point of the figure is to demonstrate how patterns

Advantages
- Creation of uniquely low cost to the customer
- Usually through economies of scale, often in manufacturing, but also in other functions, e.g. in marketing and logistics
- Also through 'learning' and/or 'experience' effects
- Also through vertical integration and exercise of buying power

Strategy
- True cost leadership is only achieved by the possession of undisputed cost advantage
- The objective is to realize a margin premium that reflects the size of the cost advantage
- If competitors catch up, the differentiation edge is lost

⟹ **Stay ahead**

Cost leadership

Competences
- Size and scale of operation
- Operating and overhead cost controls
- (Out)sourcing
- Products/service design (de-frilling)
- Management focus
- Focus fixed asset turnover
- Tactical pricing expertise

Risks
- New forms of product differentiation, so that cost is not the major purchase criterion
- New focus strategies
- Technical change
- Changes in consumer buying behaviour towards new products and/or in taste and style
- Overcommitment to specific capital intensity

Figure 3.15 The cost leadership strategy

Bases for focus
- Product features
- Buyer type
- Channels
- Geographical area
- Pre-sale service level
- Post-sale service level
- Volume
- Payment method
- Quality

Strategy
- The ability to serve the needs of a specific buyer group better than any other competitor
- Establish a cost or differentiation advantage for the target
- Isolate the target group from other offers, especially from your own
- If competitors catch up, the focus advantage is lost

⟹ **Stay ahead**

Focus

Competences
- Cost and/or differentiation competences, as before
- Real understanding of the nature of the market, its niches, and customer buying behaviour
- Ability to construct protected niches, through patents and other IPRs, and through regulatory, taxation and other government action

Risks
- Target segment becomes unattractive
- Broad scope competitors create offers that overwhelm the target segment
- New focuses and focusers re-segment the market
- The strategy is imitated

Figure 3.16 The focus strategy

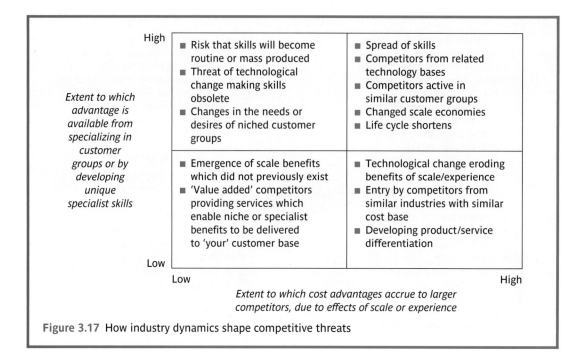

Figure 3.17 How industry dynamics shape competitive threats

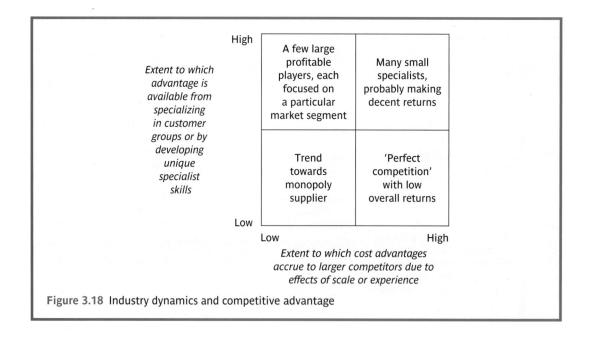

Figure 3.18 Industry dynamics and competitive advantage

of advantage (and the supporting patterns of skill and capability) can be eroded by shifts in the competitive environment. Nothing is safe from competitive threat in the long term – the variables of concern to the firm are (i) how large is my advantage, and (ii) for how long can I retain it?

Figure 3.18 takes the same dimensions and draws out the implications for industry structure. The combination of low advantages from both sides leads eventually to a perfectly competitive market.

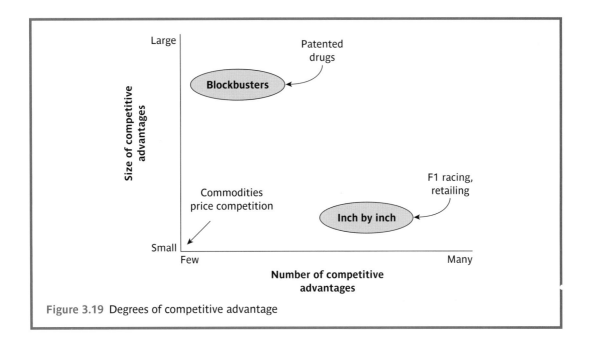

Figure 3.19 Degrees of competitive advantage

By contrast, the combination of large advantages from both sides yields a kind of **specialization**, where each large player dominates a large segment. Where there are low cost advantages but high differentiation/focus advantages, we often see a variety of small or medium-sized speciality firms with protectable niche positions. The position of high-cost advantage and no differentiation effects is typically the profile of a monopoly supplier, such as a water or power utility.

Industries and firms differ markedly in the size and shape of the advantages that are available. In Figure 3.19 we array the number of advantages against the size of the advantages. The point of origin is the perfectly competitive solution, where there are no advantages and/or the advantages are extremely small. The typical comparison is between the 'blockbusters' and the 'inch by inch' polar alternatives. The blockbuster situation arises where there are very few, usually one or two, sources of advantage, but these are very large in size. The prescription pharmaceuticals industry is like this. Its sources of advantage are research and development (including product registration) and sales force. But products are protected by patent and are typically price insensitive in the markets, so the advantages are huge. Perhaps more typical in most situations is the pattern of multiple sources, but each being of small consequence. This would be typical of much of retailing, where there are a great many ways to compete through choice of product ranges, locations, sourcing policy, staff training and skills, and so on. A more dramatic example is Formula One racing, where the racing teams are very close to each other in terms of performance, but performance does depend on a myriad of different dimensions. What Formula One does demonstrate is that it is possible for the compounding of many different sources of small advantage to result in predictable and sustainable differences between teams. The source of performance differences here lies in the way in which the resources and capabilities are systematically managed – another resource-based argument.

Read Case box 3.5 on the video gaming industry and interpret the rules of the game in terms of Porter's Five Forces analysis. Do this for the original rules of the game and for the new rules that Vivendi is trying to establish. What benefit is Vivendi expecting to gain? How would you expect its competitors to react?

Case box 3.5: **World of dealcraft – video games**

The biggest-ever video-game deal shows how the industry is changing

THE bride and groom, a guitar-wielding rock vixen and a muscle-rippling dragon-slayer, make an odd couple – so it is hardly surprising that nobody expected their marriage. But on December 2nd the video-game companies behind 'Guitar Hero' and 'World of Warcraft', Activision and Vivendi Games respectively, announced plans for an elaborate merger. Vivendi, a French media group, will pool its games unit, plus $1.7 billion in cash, with Activision; the combined entity will then offer to buy back shares from Activision shareholders, raising Vivendi's stake in the resulting firm to as much as 68%.

Activision's boss, Bobby Kotick, will remain at the helm of the new company, to be known as Activision Blizzard in recognition of Vivendi's main gaming asset: its subsidiary Blizzard Entertainment, the firm behind 'World of Warcraft', an online swords-and-sorcery game with 9.3m subscribers. The deal was unexpected, but makes excellent strategic sense, says Piers Harding-Rolls of Screen Digest, a consultancy. Activision has long coveted 'World of Warcraft', and Vivendi gets a bigger games division and Activision's talented management team to run it. As well as making sense for both parties, the $18.9 billion deal – the biggest ever in the video-games industry – says a lot about the trends now shaping the business.

The first is a push into new markets, especially online multiplayer games, which are particularly popular in Asia, and 'casual' games that appeal to people who do not regard themselves as gamers. 'World of Warcraft' is the world's most popular online subscription-based game and is hugely lucrative. Blizzard will have revenues of $1.1 billion this year and operating profits of $520m. 'World of Warcraft' is really 'a social network with many entertainment components,' says Mr Kotick.

Similarly, he argues, 'Guitar Hero' and other games that use new kinds of controller, rather than the usual buttons and joysticks, are broadening the appeal of gaming by emphasising its social aspects, since they are easy to pick up and can be played with friends. Social gaming, says Mr Kotick, is 'the most powerful trend' building new audiences for the industry. He is clearly excited at the prospect of using Blizzard's expertise to launch an online version of 'Guitar Hero' for Asian markets. Online music games such as 'Audition Online', which started in South Korea, are 'massive in Asia,' says Mr Harding-Rolls.

A second trend is media groups' increasing interest in gaming. Vivendi owns Universal Music, one of the 'big four' record labels. As the record industry's sales decline, it makes sense to move into gaming, a younger, faster-growing medium with plenty of cross-marketing opportunities. (Activision might raid Universal's back catalogue for material for its music games, for example, which might in turn boost music sales.) Other media groups are going the same way. Last year Viacom, an American media giant, acquired Harmonix, the company that originally created 'Guitar Hero'. It has been promoting its new game, 'Rock Band', using its MTV music channel. Viacom has also created online virtual worlds that tie in with several of its television programmes, such as 'Laguna Beach' and 'Pimp My Ride'. Disney bought Club Penguin, a virtual world for children, in August. And Time Warner is involved in gaming via its Warner Bros Home Entertainment division, which publishes its own titles and last month bought TT Games, the British firm behind the 'Lego Star Wars' games.

Time to level up

The third trend is consolidation, to plug gaps, address new markets and achieve economies of scale. Electronic Arts, for example, until this week the largest independent games-publisher (Activision Blizzard will be bigger), recently bought two studios, BioWare and Pandemic, to strengthen its position in role-playing and action games. Greater scale can help to spread costs and risk as new games become costlier to develop. A new title for Microsoft's Xbox 360 console or Sony's PlayStation 3 (PS3), both of which have high-definition graphics, can cost as much as $30m, says Mr Harding-Rolls. Bigger firms can afford to develop tools that make it easy to produce different versions of the same game for different platforms, says Robbie Bach, the head of Microsoft's entertainment and devices division. They can also make savings on distribution.

This week's deal shows how the software business is changing; and things are happening in hardware too. Microsoft's Xbox 360, Sony's PS3 and Nintendo's Wii are fighting for supremacy. In September the Xbox 360, which was launched in late 2005, a year ahead of its two rivals, was overtaken by the Wii as the most popular of the present generation of consoles (see chart). Mr Bach says he is unfazed. 'It's not even a statistic I track all that closely,' he says. The Wii's popularity stems from its low price and its innovative motion-sensitive controller, which can be pointed and waved to control the on-screen action and encourages novices to give gaming a try. But the Wii lacks the high-definition graphics of its two rivals, so it could soon start to look dated. The real battle is between the Xbox 360 and the PS3, Mr Bach suggests.

Sales of the PS3, which have been sluggish, seem to have taken off after Sony removed some features and dropped the price. In Japan the PS3 even outsold the Wii in November, according to Enterbrain, a market-research firm. As more games become available for the PS3 next year, sales are expected to rise even further, says Mr Harding-Rolls, so that by 2011 the PS3 will have caught up with the Wii. In short, each of the consoles will be in front at various points in the 'console cycle'.

In the previous cycle, dominated by Sony, programmers could address most of the market simply by writing games for the PlayStation 2. But if all the consoles matter, games companies have to produce games that run on all of them. That strengthens the case for consolidation. In other words, expect more deals.

Source: 'Video Games', *The Economist*, 8 December 2007

3.6 Summary

This chapter provides a foundation for the strategy analysis that continues in Part 2. In this chapter we have introduced the idea of competitive advantage as a firm-specific imperfection that is the foundation and cornerstone of all strategy analysis. Strategy cannot be understood without this concept and it cannot exist without it existing in practice. Without competitive advantage we are consigned to the 'strategic hell' of perfect competition in which profits are elusive, products are commodities, and firms are creatures of their environments. With competitive advantage, firms can be different, managers and managements can exercise choice and discretion, and entrepreneurial profits are possible. With competitive advantage we can have strategic choice. We can observe industries in which the participants can pursue similar or different strategies. Above all, with diverse and changing consumers firms can be entrepreneurial in constructing new value propositions. The ways in which competitive advantage can be deployed in different strategic clothes is the subject of the later chapters in this part of the book. The way the practice of strategy is carried on in the pursuit of competitive advantage is the subject of Chapters 5–9.

Key terms

Recap questions and assignments

1 Undertake a strategy audit of a business with which you are familiar. How attractive is the industry in which it competes? What strategies seem to be available in this industry? How would you describe the strategy of your selected business?

2 Choose two companies in the same industry – preferably direct competitors – and compare the configuration of their value chains. Explain how these configurations relate to their competitive positioning.

3 Do a SWOT analysis for your chosen businesses. Explain why you have chosen each of the key entries.

4 Using Figure 3.16 and the case examples on Tesco and Retailing, try to create a balanced scorecard for Tesco (or any other major retailer).

References

Bartlett, C. and Ghoshal, S. (1989) *Managing Across Borders*, Hutchinson, London.

Besanko, D., Dranove, D. and Shanley, M. (2000) *Economics of Strategy*, 2nd edn, John Wiley & Sons, New York.

Boston Consulting Group (1975) *Strategy Alternatives for the British Motorcycle Industry*, HMSO, London.

Burt, S. and Sparks, L. (1997) Performance in food retailing: a cross national consideration and comparison of retail margins. *British Journal of Management*, **8**, 133–50.

Cronshaw, M.J., Davis, E. and Kay, J. (1990) On being stuck in the middle – good food costs less at Sainsbury's. *Proceedings of the British Academy of Management Annual Conference, Glasgow*.

Deutsche Morgan Grenfell (1998) *Analysis of Food Retailer Results in Britain, France, Belgium and the USA*, London.

Ghemawhat, P. (1989) *Du Pont's Titanium Business (A)*. Harvard Business School Case Study 9–390–112.

Ghemawat, P. (1994a) *Du Pont in Titanium Dioxide (A)*. Harvard Business School Case Study 9–385–140.

Ghemawat, P. (1994b) Capacity expansion in the titanium dioxide industry. *Journal of Industrial Economics*, **XXXIII**, December, 145–63.

Gilbert, X. and Strebel, P. (1991) Developing competitive advantage. In H. Mintzberg and J.B. Quinn (eds) *The Strategy Process: Concepts, Contexts, Cases*, Prentice-Hall, Englewood Cliffs, NJ, pp. 82–93.

Grant, R.M. (2002) *Contemporary Strategic Analysis: Concepts, Techniques and Applications*, 4th edn, Blackwell Business, Oxford.

Mathur, S. (1988) How firms compete: a new classification of generic strategies. *Journal of General Management*, **14**, **1**, 30–57.

McAleese, D. (2004) *Economics for Business*, 3rd edn, Prentice Hall, London.

McGee, J. and Segal-Horn, S. (1992) Will there be a European food processing industry? In S. Young and J. Hamill (eds) *Europe and the Multinationals: Issues and Responses for the 1990s*, Edward Elgar Cheltenham.

Porter, M. (1980) *Competitive Strategy*, Free Press, New York.

Porter, M.E. (1986) What is strategy? *Harvard Business Review*, Nov/Dec, 61–78.

Pratten, C. (1988) A survey of the economies of scale. In *Research on the Costs of Europe*, **Vol. 2**, Office for Official Publications of the European Communities, Luxembourg.

Scherer, F.M. and Ross, D. (1990) *The Economics of Multiplant Operations*, Harvard University Press, Boston, MA.

Seth, A. and Randall, G. (1999) *The Grocers: The Rise and Fall of the Supermarket Chains*, Kogan Page, London.

Yotte, D.B. (1992) *Apple Computer 1992*, Harvard Business School Case Study, revised August 1994, 9–792–081.

Further reading

Chandler, A.D. (1990) The enduring logic of industrial success. *Harvard Business Review*, March/April, 130–40.

Chandler, A.D. (1962) *Strategy and Structure: Chapters in the History of the Industrial Enterprise*, MIT Press, Cambridge, MA.

Chandler, A.D. (1977) *The Visible Hand: The Managerial Revolution in American Business*, Harvard University Press, Cambridge, MA.

Ghemawat, P. (1991) *Commitment: The Dynamic of Strategy*, Free Press, New York.

Haldi, J. and Whitcomb, D. (1967) Economies of scale in industrial plants. *Journal of Political Economy*, **75, 4**, August, 373–85.

McGee, J. and Channon, D.F. (eds) *Encyclopedic Dictionary of Management*, 2nd edn, Blackwell Business, Oxford.

Moore, F.T. (1959) Economies of scale: some statistical evidence. *Quarterly Journal of Economics*, May, 232–45.

Panzer, J.C. and Willig, N.D. (1981) Economies of scope. *American Economic Review*, **71**, 268–77.

Porter, M.E. (1985) *Competitive Advantage*, Free Press, New York.

Porter, M.E. (1986) *Competition in Global Industries*, Harvard Business School Press, Boston, MA.

Scherer, F.M. (1970) *Industrial Market Structure and Economic Performance*, Rand McNally, Chicago, IL.

Teece, D.J. (1980) Economies of scope and the scope of the enterprise. *Journal of Economic Behavior and Organisation*, **1**, 223–47.

Chapter 4

The macroeconomics of strategy

Chapter contents

Introduction

This chapter[1] focuses on the influence on businesses of changes taking place in the external context, especially in the macroeconomy. This involves not just the systemic impact of external forces but also, in particular, the way these forces are augmented and mediated by public policy. The chapter covers the fundamentals of aggregate demand and supply and the implications for GDP, inflation and unemployment. It also examines the causes and effects of business cycles and what causes booms and slumps in a global economy to come to an end. It goes on to consider issues concerning the sustainability of strong economic growth, especially in emerging markets. It also explores issues of uncertainty and risk, and some of the forward-looking strategies business might adopt to limit the effects of exposure to risk. How might uncertain and volatile economic factors (for example, exchange or interest rates) be incorporated into strategic thinking?

---

[1] This chapter was written by K.G. Ben Knight.

4.1 The basics of macroeconomics

All firms and industries are exposed to the wider macroeconomy. This is true in any economy irrespective of its geographical location or stage of development. The extent of macroeconomic exposure for each industry varies greatly across industries but differs little across countries. Booms and slumps in national and global output measured by changes in gross domestic product (GDP) lead to changes in the rate of growth of sales and output at both the market sector and at the individual firm levels. Figure 4.1 shows the impact of changes in GDP on the volume of sales (real sales) in various sectors of the OECD (Organisation for Economic Co-operation and Development; www.oecd.org). The metal-making sector (principally steel and aluminium) has the greatest exposure to changes in GDP. Each 1% fall (rise) in the GDP growth rate leads to a fall (rise) in industry output of 2.6%. In early 2009 OECD GDP fell by around 4% and on average the demand for metals fell 10.4%. This is a significant reduction to which firms and their managers must respond. In contrast, in the food, drink and tobacco sector the response to a macroeconomic 'shock' is a lot more muted. Each 1% fall (rise) in the GDP growth rate leads to a fall (rise) in industry output of just 0.2%. The macroeconomy is a lot less important for managers in firms producing necessities like food.

These fluctuations in demand feed through to financial performance and, although they have to be managed, are totally outside of the control of the individual firm or its managers. Figure 4.2 shows the experience of Nippon Steel which is a major Japanese producer in the most exposed metal-producing sector. Nippon enjoys a high reputation for the quality of its products, which are sold, among many others, to Toyota. The downturn in Nippon's financial performance coincides with the slowdowns in global growth and in Japanese performance in 2001 and 2008 and is driven by it. Similarly, the upturns in the period 2004–8 reflect strong GDP growth in both Japan and the global economy.

Hence, even with no change in the strategy of the individual firm, major changes in its performance and prospects will occur for reasons outside of its direct control. If the threat of adverse

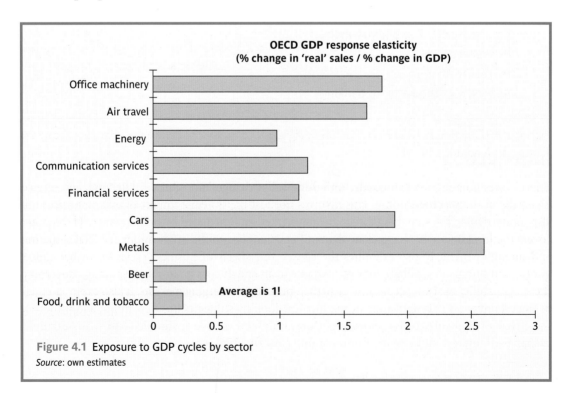

Figure 4.1 Exposure to GDP cycles by sector
Source: own estimates

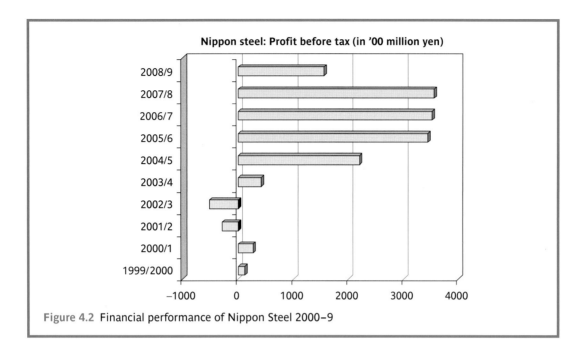

Figure 4.2 Financial performance of Nippon Steel 2000–9

developments is to be minimized and the benefit of the opportunity afforded by favourable conditions is to be maximized, these macroeconomic factors need to be understood and be taken into account by managers. The first critical question to be considered is what causes the short-run fluctuations in GDP growth which have such a significant impact on firm-level performance.

4.1.1 Short-run fluctuations in GDP

Initially we will focus on national economies. Goods and services in any national macroeconomy, as a whole, are produced to meet demand not necessarily immediately but eventually. Hence the normal cause of booms and slumps in GDP is fluctuations in the volume of demand for goods and services in the economy as a whole (aggregate demand). If aggregate demand goes up, so does GDP and if it goes down, GDP again follows suit.

What is *aggregate demand*? It is the total demand for goods and services from all sources in the national economy. Where does the demand originate? Economists identify the following sources of aggregate demand.

1 The demand for consumer goods, both durable like cars and non-durable like food, and services by all households resident in the national economy. In most economies this constitutes the biggest source of demand. In the UK, for example, just over 50% of aggregate demand originates from this source and this is very typical of the OECD economies, although in the US the share is nearly two-thirds of total demand.[2]

2 Demand for investment goods (buildings, plant and machinery) and services by private companies. This varies in importance across industries but is rarely less than 10% of the total aggregate demand for goods and services and in some countries (like the economies of East Asia) can be as high as 25%. In China in 2007 it was even higher at 32%.[3]

---

[2] Source: OECD.

[3] Source: UN.

3 Demand for goods and services by the government. This arises from public spending on defence, education, health and so on. It does not include 'transfer payments' (like state pensions), i.e. payments made to individuals by the government using funds raised from other citizens. These funds are used by other households and hence are included in consumer demand. The share of the government in aggregate demand for goods and services also varies a lot but the 15% level found in the UK is very typical of the industrial economies as a whole.

4 Demand for 'net' exports. Net exports are the difference between gross exports and imports of goods like cars and services like tourism. This is also known as the balance of trade. Gross exports are a source of demand for home-produced goods and services. Gross imports reduce the home demand for home-produced goods and services. This element of demand is satisfied by overseas producers. Net exports are the addition to the aggregate demand of an economy arising from overseas trade. This can be positive where exports exceed imports, which is the normal situation in Japan and China, or negative as it is normally in the US and the UK. In these economies imports normally exceed exports.

Aggregate demand for goods and services in any economy is therefore the sum of each of these sources of demand:

$C + I + G + (X - F)$ where

C = consumer demand by households

I = investment demand by firms

G = public sector demand

X = exports to other economies

F = imports from other economies

$X - F$ = net exports

What determines the level of aggregate demand for goods and services in any national economy? The first and most important answer is the level of aggregate income (wages and salaries plus profits) received by all firms and all households in the economy. The government's income is derived from the same source via taxation. In the case of exports, what counts is the income of firms and households in the overseas economies where exports are sold.

Where does this income come from? The most important source is from the proceeds of producing goods and services in the national economy as a whole, i.e. from GDP! We started by wanting to explain GDP and the explanation ends up with GDP! Not surprisingly, economists refer to this as the *circular flow of income* and this is shown in Figure 4.3.

Figure 4.3 shows the interaction between the three fundamental macroeconomic processes described above, namely:

1 the national production of goods and services;

2 the income generated by this production of goods and services; and

3 the disposal of income to create the aggregate demand for goods and services which completes the circle.

Each of these processes feeds back on the others. Production in an *open economy* (i.e. one that engages in international trade) would not occur without demand, which in its turn would not happen without income which itself depends on the production of goods and services. The demand which arises from the circular flow of income is called *endogenous* by economists. It refers to the demand (spending) which arises in the home economy from income earned from the home

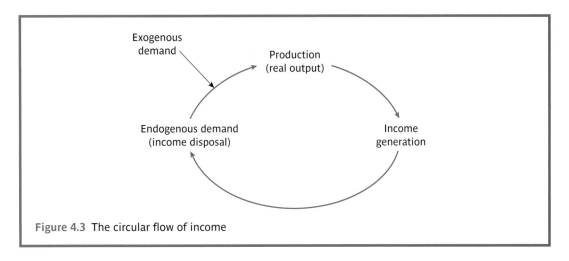

Figure 4.3 The circular flow of income

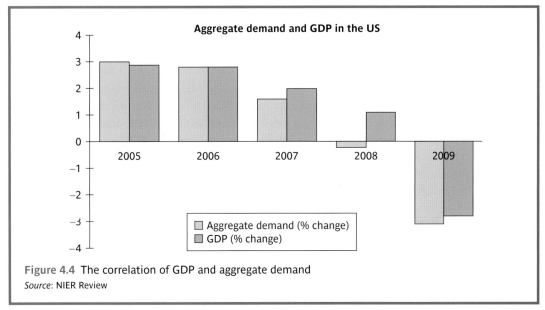

Figure 4.4 The correlation of GDP and aggregate demand
Source: NIER Review

production of goods and services. Note that some of this income is lost to the home economy because it is spent on imports produced in other economies. Economists call this loss of income a *leakage* from the circular flow of income of any national economy.

Demand, however, can also arise from other sources and this offsets the leakage which arises from imports. This type of demand is called *exogenous* because it does not arise from **within** the circular flow of income but rather from **outside** it. It can come from outside the home economy, i.e. from exports of goods and services to the outside world, or from within the domestic economy as a result of spending changes driven by forces other than changes in current income, especially the important spending changes which result from changes in wealth and/or in the level of borrowing.

Figure 4.4 shows the close correspondence of aggregate demand and GDP growth in the US and it confirms the predictions of the circular flow of income analysis. Notice that after the strong growth in aggregate demand in 2005 there is a steady downturn culminating in the fall in both demand and GDP in 2009. Note also that despite always moving in the same direction, the growth rates of the two variables are equal only in 2006. In 2007 and 2008 the growth in output exceeded the growth in demand so stocks of finished products grew. In 2009 the same thing happened because the fall in demand outstripped the fall in output. Only in 2005 were stock levels reducing. In 2009 the need to reverse the accumulation of stocks over the previous three years is likely to slow down the recovery of output growth in 2010.

Changes in any component of aggregate demand can cause fluctuations in GDP. History has taught us that the key drivers of the circular flow of income and the changes observed in GDP are shocks to aggregate exogenous demand. There are many exogenous shocks to aggregate demand which can lead to changes in GDP. In all cases, demand originating in the private sector (consumer demand and investment) and in exports plays a crucial role, not least because, in most economies, this is at least 80% of the total demand for goods and services. However, there is also a role for government in stimulating exogenous demand. Note this in the examples set out below.

4.1.2 Factors driving aggregate demand

Among the many examples of potent causes of change in the volume of exogenous demand are changes in the following.

i The cost and availability of credit

Easy, cheap credit increases consumer spending at any income level. This causes an increase in exogenous demand. The result of this is an increase in output. If, on the other hand, credit becomes more expensive, aggregate demand would fall (or increase by less) and this would cause output to fall (or increase by less). In 1999 US interest rates were raised in order to slow down the US economy. The problem is that this slowdown happened rather more quickly and dramatically than the monetary authorities thought in 2000, so a correction was required. In 2001 onwards, US interest rates fell several times to stop the slowdown turning into a severe slump. As it turned out, the fall in rates and easy credit conditions led to a significant boom in private sector spending, especially in the US housing market, and in 2006 the US Central Bank increased base rates to slow down a boom that they feared was too intense. The authorities succeeded but at the cost of a severe financial crisis which led, as you see later in this chapter, to a major US and global recession starting in 2008. Sometimes interest rate increases are also used to reduce capital outflows and stabilize exchange rates which are under pressure. In November 1998 interest rates in Brazil were 49% as the government and the central bank attempted to maintain the real/$ parity! Unsuccessfully, it turned out, so rates fell in 1999 but remained high for some time thereafter. Changes in the interest rate also change the cost of finance as well as the opportunities for gain from financial investment. This has an important effect on investment in physical capital. When the interest rate rises, firms cut back their fixed investment because borrowing is dearer and financial investment is a more attractive alternative. This response is not, however, immediate.

ii Changes in wealth

Changes in wealth affect the take-up of credit opportunities by consumers. Increases in wealth increase consumer confidence and encourage consumers to borrow, especially when interest rates are falling. The most important source of wealth for many consumers is equity in houses. When house prices rise, as they did in the UK in the mid-1980s and again in 1999/2008, households experience an increase in wealth enabling them to increase debt without increasing their debt/wealth ratio. Since additional wealth also encourages greater consumer confidence, increased consumer demand results and output rises. The whole chain of events is reversed when house prices stabilize and then fall as they did in the period 1989–95 and 2008 onwards. This both causes and lengthens a recession because it makes consumers reluctant to increase their spending even when interest rates fall. This was a persistent feature of the UK until mid-1996 and 1997 when house prices and hence household wealth started to rise. Similar effects can occur through changes in the value of non-housing wealth. A repetition of these events has led to some UK commentators predicting a long slow recovery from the large fall in GDP in 2009. Rising share prices also generate these positive *wealth effects* and were profoundly important in explaining the strong growth of private sector demand and GDP in the US from 1992 until 2000. In the opposite direction, falls in the value of shares in Japan, for example, contributed to the slump in consumer demand in 1993 and the subsequent 15-year record of poor and volatile performance of the Nikkei share price index which has held back consumer demand and contributed to the difficulty experienced by Japan in getting a strong recovery under way even when base interest rates fell to 0.5%. Falls in world stock markets in 2001 and 2002 and 2008/9 also triggered these kinds of negative wealth effects and contributed to reduced confidence, lower demand and global slowdown, despite lower interest rates in these periods.

iii Changes in government spending and changes in tax rates

Increases in government spending (current or capital) increase aggregate demand and output. This is an important means through which the government can influence the economy. The Japanese government adopted this approach to ending recession in 1993/4 and 1996 and also in 2000/2001. It is an important reason for the relatively (compared to other G7 economies) strong performance of the UK in the years 2000−4.

Cuts in income taxes increase consumer spending because they increase net household income, and if government spending is not cut aggregate demand rises as well. Cuts in the US tax rates in 2001 were intended to boost consumer spending to stop a prolonged recession. Further cuts in both personal and corporate tax rates had the same effect. In contrast, increases in personal or corporate tax rates have the opposite effect, reducing consumer and investment demand. To combat the emerging global recession in 2008/9 many governments used the fiscal stimulus of spending increases and cuts in taxes on both income and spending. The UK government reduced the VAT rate in 2008 and 2009, after which it returned to its previous level. The scale of fiscal stimulus (expressed as a % of GDP) in the biggest 20 economies is shown in Table 4.1.

Table 4.1 G20 countries: discretionary measures, 2008−10 (% of GDP, relative to 2007 baseline)

	2008	2009	2010
G20 PPP-GDP weighted average	0.5	1.8	1.3
Advanced countries *of which*	0.6	1.6	1.2
US	1.1	2.0	1.8
EU G20	0.1	1.0	0.8
Japan	0.4	1.4	0.4
Emerging and developing G20 *of which*	0.4	2.0	1.4
China	0.4	3.2	2.7
G20 discretionary impulse	0.5	1.2	−0.5

1 Figures reflect the budgetary cost of crisis-related discretionary measures in each year compared to 2007 (baseline), based on measures announced through early March. They do not include (i) 'below-the-line' operations that involve acquisition of assets (including financial sector support) or (ii) measures that were already planned for. Some figures represent staff's preliminary analysis.
2 Change from the previous year.
Source: IMF staff estimates

Note that the data in Table 4.1 does not include the direct cost of *bail-outs* for distressed financial institutions. The fiscal stimulus starts in 2008 and peaks in 2009 and reduces in 2010 on the basis of 2009 policy announcements. Reliance on fiscal stimulus is much higher in China, the US and Japan than in the EU members of the G20. This reflects the different views of policy makers on the scale of the stimulus that is needed and possible. Overall, however, the data reveals a widespread belief in the efficacy of these measures in stimulating aggregate demand.

iv Changes in the exchange rate

One critical driver of exogenous aggregate demand is the exchange rate. The exchange rate sets the price of one currency in terms of another: e.g. if the £/$ rate is 1.50 it tells us the US dollars needed to buy a £ – i.e. 1.50. The exchange rate is fixed daily in foreign exchange markets across the world. Changes in the exchange rate have a big effect on cross-border spending on exports, which are a component of exogenous demand. They also affect imports, which are leakages from the circular flow of income so exchange rate changes also impact on the endogenous demand arising from the circular flow of income. The effect is shown in Table 4.2. $P_£^x$ is the price of exports in the home currency (£ in this example) and $P_\$^x$ is the price in export markets. What is the effect of a change in the exchange rate when the home price remains the same (£100 in Table 4.2)? When the exchange rate is £1 = $2 the price in the export market is $200 but when the exchange rate depreciates to £1 = $1 the price in the export market falls to $100. This fall in price increases export sales and leads to faster export volume growth. In the home market $P_\$^f$ is the price of imports in the overseas currency and $P_£^f$ the price charged in the home market. When the exchange rate falls the price paid in the home market goes up, benefiting the domestic producer who sells more at the expense of the now dearer imported product so leakages from the circular flow of income fall. As a result GDP also goes up.

If the exchange rate goes up (appreciates), exactly the opposite happens. Table 4.2 shows that prices in export markets rise when the £ is stronger. This rise will reduce export volume and hence exogenous demand will fall. Note also the fall in import prices, which increases both import volume and the level of leakages from the circular flow of income.

There are many examples of the effect of exchange rates on exogenous demand and GDP. An increase in the exchange rate, like that which occurred in the UK 1996–2000 and in the euro area after 2004, reduced trade competitiveness and exports. It also increased import leakages from the circular flow of income. This reduced the demand for domestically produced goods and as a result output growth fell.

If the exchange rate falls, the opposite happens. The strong growth of the euro area economies in 2000 was a direct result of the fall in the € after its introduction in 1999. The depreciation of the Korean won and other Asian currencies in 1997/8 had the same effect on those economies in 1999/2000. In the 1930s the Scandinavian economies experienced large falls in their exchange rate, and output growth between 1929 and 1935 was very much higher than in Germany, France and Italy.

Table 4.2 Exchange rate arithmetic

	$P_£^x$	$P_\$^x$	$P_\$^f$	$P_£^f$	
£1 = $2	100	200	300	150	strong £ (weak $)
£1 = $1	100	100	300	300	weak £ (strong $)

4.1.3 Implications for business

Some businesses are highly exposed to exchange rate movements and these can have a big impact. Exposure is especially high in businesses that are heavily engaged in exports or importing raw materials or components. Exchange rate fluctuations can cause unwanted fluctuations in financial performance and can even lead to closure of factories. To illustrate this dependence, consider the case of Jaguar Land Rover, the UK-based and now Indian-owned producer of luxury motor cars. In July 2005 Jaguar closed one of its main UK production facilities in Coventry. One reason was the impact of changes in the £/$ in Jaguar's main export market (US). Examine the arithmetic shown in Table 4.3. Remember the dollar was strong and sterling was weak in 2001, but despite its recovery in 2005, the dollar was still a lot weaker at the end of the year. The first thing to note from Table 4.3 is that if Jaguar held the UK price constant, the US price increased by nearly a third between 2001 and the end of 2005. As a result, sales volume fell. The reduced rate of production worsened asset utilization and this increased average (unit) cost, thereby squeezing Jaguar's profit margins.

Jaguar could, alternatively, have maintained its US price. In this case the UK revenue per unit is reduced by about a quarter which, again, squeezes margins (price – average unit costs). Whatever the strategy the outcome was the same: UK production suffered an exchange-rate-induced *margin squeeze*, which required a drastic remedy – closing a historic site of vehicle production in the British Midlands. After 2005 this was reversed but the advantage to Jaguar Land Rover in 2008/9 was undermined by the collapse of the US car market. Airbus has suffered in a similar way as a result of the strength of the euro against the dollar after 2004. Airbus's main global competitor in the large airframe market is Boeing. Boeing is a US company that incurs almost all of its costs in dollars. The world's airlines buy airplanes at prices fixed in dollars so the appreciation of the euro put significant pressure on Airbus. Either it raised the price of its planes in US dollars and lost orders or it cut its price in euros and accepted a large squeeze on its profit margins. Not surprisingly, it chose the latter but this was painful and required it to exert significant downward pressure on its cost base.

Other EU-based companies bemoan a weak dollar. Several experienced the significant effect of the fall in the dollar in 2006/7. The UK-based GlaxoSmithKline pharmaceutical company reported in April 2007 that the weaker dollar reduced the sterling value of its worldwide sales, contributing to a £21 million fall in first quarter pre-tax profit. Toyota has a large production presence in the US. Profits made in US dollars are worth less in Japanese yen when the dollar depreciates and this is bad news for the parent company. Other Japanese companies have similar issues with the exchange rate. Not surprisingly, the Bank of Japan has a track record of intervention in foreign exchange markets to weaken the yen in order to relieve the pressure on Japan's global exporters.

Why does the exchange rate change? The exchange rate is determined in the foreign exchange market and reflects the forces of both supply and demand in that market. The drivers of supply and demand in the foreign exchange (FOREX) market are set out in Table 4.4.

Table 4.3 Jaguar prices in the UK and US	
Price of Jaguar car in UK	£30k
Price of Jaguar car in US in 2001	$43.2k
Price of Jaguar car in US end 2005	$53.1k
If the price of Jaguar car in US is maintained at $43.2k this generates: revenue in 2001	£30k

---

Table 4.4 The exchange rate in the FOREX market

Demand for home currency rises (falls) if . . .
- Exports rise (fall)
- Demand for home assets from overseas investors rises (falls)

Supply of home currency rises (falls) if . . .
- Imports rise (fall)
- Demand for overseas assets from home investors rises (falls)

Table 4.5 Exchange rates in the FOREX market

	Demand for £ by overseas residents	Supply of £ by UK residents	£/Euro (price of pounds in euros)
Increase in government spending			
Home interest rate down			
Foreign interest rate down			
Balance of trade (Exports – Imports) worsens			
Home inflation rate up			

If the demand for home currency rises, the exchange rate also rises (appreciates). What causes this to happen? An increase in the demand for home assets is a common driver. This will happen if home interest rates rise, increasing the desire for overseas investors or home-based investors to deposit their money in the home economy. Similarly, if foreign interest rates fall, the impact on investor behaviour will lead to a rise in the exchange rate of the home economy. An increase in exports from the home economy will lead to increased demand for the home currency by foreign buyers and this causes the exchange rate to appreciate. A decrease in imports has the same effect because home residents who want less foreign currency to pay for the imports decrease the supply of home currency in the FOREX market. Test your understanding of these ideas by filling in the blank boxes in Table 4.5. Use arrows to indicate the direction of change. Note that this table focuses on the rate of exchange between sterling and the euro. The euro was introduced in 1999 and after a very difficult start its long-run trend is to appreciate against sterling.

Knowledge of these relationships helps a business to anticipate government and central bank policy, especially with respect to interest rates. Rises in interest rates will take place if a government wants to stabilize exchange rates which are under downward pressure. The idea is to increase the demand for home assets from international investors by increasing the interest rate for them. This is the experience of many Asian and Latin American economies. For example, in November 1998 interest rates in Rio were 49% as the Brazilian government attempted to maintain the real/$ parity! This turned out to be unsuccessful so rates were allowed to fall in 1999. There are countless other examples of this kind. Despite significant improvements in economic performance since 2000, Turkey has to maintain high interest rates to hold back pressure on the Turkish lira.

In summary, booms can occur only if there is an increase in the aggregate demand for goods and services. Similarly, slumps would not happen if the aggregate demand for products did not fall.

The global recession which started in 2008 is no exception. From a business strategy point of view it is important to keep track of both the movements in aggregate demand and the key determinants of these movements, and also to relate this to knowledge of the macroeconomic exposure of the business and its markets. It is also important to understand why booms end and what enables recovery. This is the subject of the next section.

4.2 Aggregate supply and the end of booms

It is evident from Figure 4.5 that booms end. After five years of strong growth in the world economy and especially in the emerging economies, the end is dramatic. Why do booms end?

To answer this question we need, initially, to examine the supply side of the macroeconomy. In a prolonged boom all economies experience pressure on their capacity to supply goods and services. This happens despite the increases in capacity that arise from the high levels of investment in physical capacity and human capital (i.e. skills and knowledge) that occur in boom periods.

When this happens there will be two main consequences:

1 Excess demand for both goods and services causes prices to rise directly. The ensuing derived demand for labour lowers unemployment and increases labour shortages, and these impact directly on wages, increasing labour costs and, indirectly, prices. Employers experiencing recruitment difficulties, especially of skilled workers, will bid up their wage offers. To prevent a loss of workers, others will follow suit. Workers will be in a stronger bargaining position to drive up wages. In short, an acceleration of the rate of wage inflation will occur. Since labour costs are a very significant part of the average costs of production incurred by firms, any increase in the rate of wage inflation will have a quick positive effect on the rate of price inflation. There may also be other, more direct routes which lead to higher prices. Shortages are likely to extend to other input markets for raw materials and energy. Also, profit margins will increase as firms raise prices in what they see to be favourable times in their markets. However, the evidence from upturns in Europe and North America is that even in historically inflation-prone economies like the UK, France and Italy the growth in inflation is much more muted after the 1980s, so that there is now much less inflation at all stages of the business cycle, but it still occurs and may still play a role in the ending of a boom.

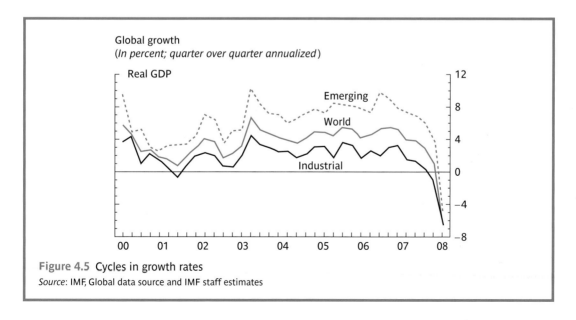

Figure 4.5 Cycles in growth rates

Source: IMF, Global data source and IMF staff estimates

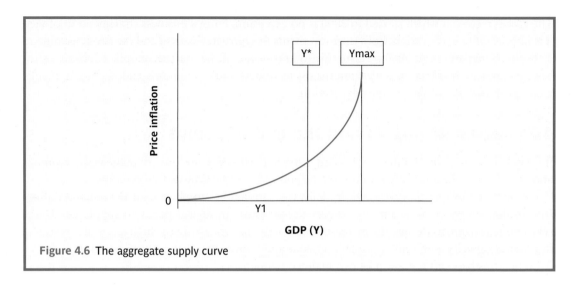

Figure 4.6 The aggregate supply curve

2 The shortage of home economy capacity will cause an increase in imports of goods and services to satisfy the excess demand. This will worsen the balance of trade. In addition, as economies approach full capacity, domestic producers tend to shift output to the local economy to satisfy the demand of local customers. This happens because home sales are generally more profitable than overseas sales. The effect of this behaviour will decrease exports and worsen the balance of trade (exports – imports) even further.

Initially, let us focus on the impact on prices and price inflation. This issue is explored with the aid of an aggregate supply (AS) curve, shown in Figure 4.6, which shows the positive relation of GDP growth and price inflation. If GDP is less than Y1, the economy experiences negative inflation or deflation. Increases in GDP reduce price deflation. If GDP is greater than Y1, this leads to increases in price inflation. Note that the AS curve has an increasing slope, the implication of which is that each successive increment to GDP produces a greater increase in price inflation. This is particularly noticeable when GDP approaches and then exceeds Y* which is *economic full capacity*. Beyond Y* and until Ymax it is possible to produce even more but only at the expense of decreasing efficiencies arising from fatigue, machine breakdown, bottlenecks and so on. At Ymax the economy reaches the absolute limit of its ability to produce.

The difference between actual GDP and economic full capacity (Y − Y*) is called the *output gap*. Above Y* it is positive and below Y* it is negative. As the output gap changes, the rate of price inflation will change in the same direction but (probably) at an increasing rate. This means that inflation increases (falls) disproportionately as the output gap rises (falls). Figure 4.7 illustrates these ideas with data on China.

The link between GDP growth and price inflation in the early 1990s is particularly strong following the beginning of the market reform period in the late 1980s. The growth in GDP was very rapid and 'unbalanced' in its demand/supply relationship so the output gap was positive and growing. The result was a major rise in price inflation, reaching a peak of just under 25% per annum in 1994. This was a serious inflationary event which the Central Bank has been anxious not to repeat in the 2000s. As you can see from Figure 4.7, the big boom of 1994 was followed by a significant recession where the output gap was strongly negative, reaching the bottom of this large amplitude cycle in 1999. GDP growth was less than Y1 so deflation occurred.

In the 2000s growth in GDP has been strong but, in general, has been a lot more 'balanced', so the output gap has, on average, been comfortably close to zero. In 2002 deflation occurred, but since

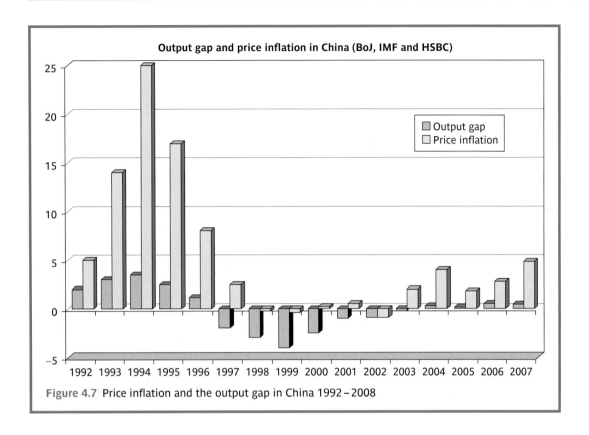

Figure 4.7 Price inflation and the output gap in China 1992–2008

then China has experienced modest inflation and nothing like the unbalanced growth experience of the early 1990s. Inflation did pick up in 2004 and 2008, but quantitative restrictions on credit and interest rate rises contained the growth in demand to more or less match the growth in supply so the output gap was consistently close to zero and, as a result, inflation fell back in 2005 and late 2008.

As you can see from the China example, the acceleration of inflation as the economy runs out of spare capacity brings the boom to an end. Partly this is because of the impact of public policy aimed at cutting aggregate demand. This might involve use of the instruments outlined in Section 4.1, namely, higher interest rates, cutbacks in public spending and so on. In addition, increases in inflation have a direct impact on private sector demand in home and overseas markets. In early 2008 global inflation accelerated because of large increases in oil, food and other commodity prices. Central banks (except in the US) were reluctant to lower interest rates, which would have impacted adversely on aggregate demand.

There are three main reasons why aggregate demand is reduced by inflation:

1 The real value of the wealth (including cash deposits) of asset holders falls as price inflation rises. This encourages increased savings as asset holders attempt to rebuild the purchasing power of their wealth, especially if it has been accumulated to finance retirement from work. This is a very powerful force bearing on those approaching retirement. The increased savings implies that there is less consumer demand for output.

2 Large increases in price inflation when the output gap is positive create uncertainty, and this leads to reductions in consumer and business confidence which also reduces private sector demand.

3 A rise in inflation causes an appreciation in the *real exchange rate*, and this reduces the international competitiveness of both exports and home-produced substitutes for imports. In both cases this will reduce net export demand, reducing the home economy's total aggregate demand for goods and services. What is the real exchange rate? The real exchange rate is the nominal rate corrected for changes in the aggregate price of one country compared to the rest of the world, that is:

Real exchange rate = ε (Ph ÷ Pw)

where:
ε = nominal exchange rate
Ph = home aggregate price of a common basket of goods
Pw = world aggregate price of a common basket of goods.

How do we define the home and world aggregate price levels? To calculate this we need to define a basket of goods sold across the world. Because of differences in national tastes this is not always easy. One simple solution is to select a global product (for example, a Big Mac) and use the price of this common product in the home economy and the rest of the world. You can see from the equation above that if the home price level (Ph) increases and price inflation increases, the real exchange rate appreciates. Its effect is the same as an appreciation of the exchange rate discussed earlier in this chapter. Home-produced goods and services become relatively more expensive and hence less competitive in both world and home markets, so there is a fall in demand for home-produced goods and services – that is, in aggregate demand. If the world price (Pw) increases the logic is reversed. This causes a depreciation of the real exchange rate, boosting the competitiveness of home products and also aggregate demand.

The combination of these automatic and discretionary effects will help to end a boom in which the output gap is positive. This is not the only mechanism and in 2008 is not the most potent reason for the end of the boom.

At this point you should read the end of chapter case study on the Big Mac Index, *The Economist* newspaper's 'light-hearted' guide to whether currencies are at their 'correct' level. This makes the obvious point that to convert national GDPs into dollars at current market exchange rates is misleading and a better method is to use purchasing power parities (PPP) which take account of price differences between economies.

4.2.1 The Asian economic crisis 1997

A further factor that sometimes brings a boom to an end arises from its effects on the overseas balance of payments, especially the balance of trade (exports – imports). Rapid growth in output increases income through the circular flow mechanism and this causes an increase in a country's imports to take place. At the same time, strong pressure of demand can lead to a reduction in exports as home producers seek to meet burgeoning home demand. Hence the balance of trade (exports – imports) worsens.

In fact, this is key to understanding the end of the boom in the East Asian economies in 1997. The countries in this region of the world, almost without exception, grew unusually quickly throughout the 1990s. So successful were these economies that the World Bank promoted the idea of an 'East Asian Miracle' and urged other emerging economies to look to East Asia to find the ingredients for successful long-run performance.

Figure 4.8 shows GDP growth across the world and indicates just how successful East Asia was in the period up until 1997 (note that the only OECD country that compared with East Asia was

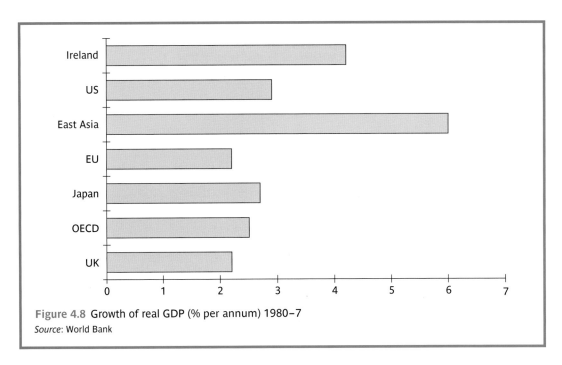

Figure 4.8 Growth of real GDP (% per annum) 1980–7
Source: World Bank

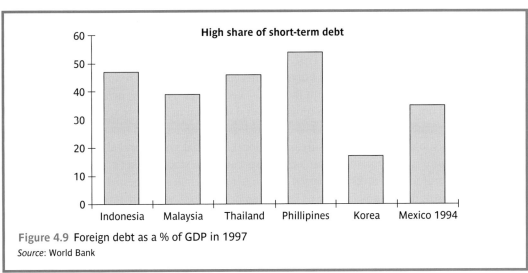

Figure 4.9 Foreign debt as a % of GDP in 1997
Source: World Bank

Ireland). However, this rapid growth in GDP led to strong growth in imports and a slowdown in exports, especially in Thailand. The effect on the current account (i.e. where trade flows are recorded) of the balance of payments was substantial deficits. Normally, as you can see from the analysis of exchange rate movements above, this deficit should lead to a fall in the demand for Asian currencies and an increase in their supply in FOREX markets. As a result the exchange rate should have fallen, but most of the region's economies had fixed their exchange rates against the US dollar, partly to encourage foreign investors to believe that their money was safe. The only way left to 'pay' for the deficit on the current account was to borrow from overseas investors. Only modest incentives to achieve this were necessary since the international financial community also believed that a 'miracle' was happening and lending to East Asian economies was thought to be a good bet. You can see in Figure 4.9 (which also shows the position of Mexico in 1994 when similar events occurred as a

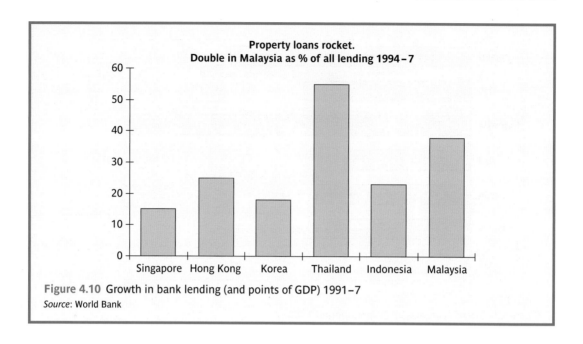

Figure 4.10 Growth in bank lending (and points of GDP) 1991–7
Source: World Bank

result of the same rapid GDP growth) the impact on the overseas debt position of various Asian economies. Much of the debt was short-term lending to East Asian banks which, in turn, had borrowed money from OECD financial institutions in order to fuel the boom (see Figure 4.10).

Problems started (in Thailand) in 1997 when a GDP-boom-driven 'bubble' in the property market burst. Property developers had borrowed heavily, drawing upon funds provided by local Thai banks that used capital inflows from the OECD economies. They overinvested in projects on which they could not secure a short-run return. Several went out of business, with an adverse effect on the poorly regulated banking sector. The ensuing loss of confidence led to a flight of foreign investors and irresistible downward pressure on the local financial system and also on the exchange rate. This contagion spread to other Asian economies causing a stock market crash throughout the region. The flight of foreign investors caused exchange rates to fall, as suggested by your answers in Table 4.5. As a result the US dollar value of East Asian debt soared, which, combined with the stock market crash, led to dramatic falls in GDP growth in 1998 (see Figure 4.11) as reductions in wealth and increasing debt hit exogenous aggregate demand growth. Hong Kong was one exception to these events where the monetary authorities were able to resist the downward pressure on the HK dollar by using some of Hong Kong's huge reserves of foreign currencies, including US dollars.

However, the fall in the exchange rate also brought relief to most of the East Asian economies, so that by mid-1999 the boost to international competitiveness led to significant increases in GDP being reported in several economies in the region. This emphasizes the important role often played by the exchange rate as a 'shock absorber'. It also showed the importance of the OECD which provided a market for East Asian products at this time. The end of this slump was facilitated by the fact that a) it was restricted to emerging economies in a particular global region and b) the advanced economies were in a position to provide a bail-out to East Asian (Mexican) exporters. In 1998 OECD interest rates were cut at a time when most commentators expected them to rise. The effect was to create the much-needed OECD markets for goods and services produced in the OECD but also in the non-OECD world, especially in East Asia.

The Asian experience illustrates the importance of *balanced growth* in the emerging economies. Balanced growth implies a growth in the aggregate demand for goods and services which is in line with the growth in aggregate supply not only of physical assets like machines and labour (i.e. 'resources')

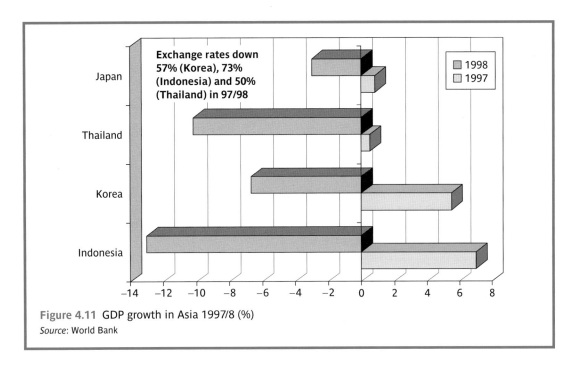

Figure 4.11 GDP growth in Asia 1997/8 (%)
Source: World Bank

but also in capabilities like skill and knowledge, some of which arises from the large learning-curve effects evident in emerging economies. More rapid growth in demand is a characteristic of emerging economies where there are few slow-growing mature markets, but if this proceeds at a pace which is faster than aggregate supply, the impact on imports, especially of the capital goods necessary for sustained development, creates financial pressures which are difficult to manage.

The Asian crisis also reflects the development and interdependence of the global economy in the 1990s. Rapid growth in the region would not have been possible without the huge inflows of both long-term (i.e. investment in fixed assets) and short-term (i.e. investment in financial assets) capital from the OECD economies. The growth in global financial markets and the global strategies of large transnational and largely OECD-based businesses are crucial here. Also important is the issue of interdependence. Crisis in Asia carried an important threat for the OECD economies. It had obvious implications for global financial stability but also impacted on global trade and hence global GDP growth. It required the governments of the OECD economies to take an increasingly global view and to take on board the global implications of their domestic policies.

At this point you should read Case box 4.1 on the Swedish banking crisis of 1992. Ask yourself about the points of similarity with the Asian banking crisis of 1997 and, looking ahead to Case box 4.2, ask also about the similarities with 2008.

Case box 4.1: **The Swedish banking crisis 1992**

This is an extract from a speech by the former governor of the Central Bank of Sweden. Scandinavia experienced a major financial crisis in the early 1990s and many commentators have been searching for lessons from this experience. It has a lot to say about financial crises in general but note that what happened in 1992 in northern Europe was a 'local difficulty' which few people in the rest of the world noticed at the time. It was not a major transnational crisis originating in the world's biggest economy.

Allow me now to summarize what I consider to be the most important lessons from Sweden's financial crisis:

1 Prevent the conditions for a financial crisis

The primary conclusion from our experience of Sweden's financial crisis is that various steps should be taken to ensure that the conditions for a financial crisis do not arise.

1 Fundamentally it is a matter of conducting a credible *economic policy focused on price stability.* This provides the prerequisites for a monetary policy reaction to excessive increases in asset prices and credit stocks that would be liable to boost inflation and create the type of speculative climate that paves the way to a financial crisis.

2 Looking back, it can be said that if *various indicators* that commonly form the background to a financial crisis had been followed systematically, then incipient problems could have been detected early on. That in turn could have influenced the conduct of fiscal and monetary policy so that Sweden's financial crisis was contained or even prevented. In spite of the evident signs, few if any in the public discussion warned of what might happen. . . .

3 In Sweden's case the *supervisory authority* was not prepared for the new environment that emerged after credit market deregulation. This meant that during the 1980s the banks were able to grant loans on doubtful and sometimes even directly unsound grounds without any supervisory intervention. In addition, in many cases the loans were poorly documented. The lesson from this is that much must be required of a supervisor operating in an environment characterized by deregulated markets.

2 If a financial crisis does occur

In a sense all major financial crises are unique and therefore difficult to prepare for and avoid. Once a crisis is about to develop there are some important lessons concerning its handling that can be learnt.

1 If an economy is hit by a financial crisis, the first important step is to *maintain liquidity in the banking system* and *prevent the banking system from collapsing.* For the management of Sweden's banking crisis the political consensus was of major importance for the payment system's credibility among the Swedish public as well as among the banking system's creditors throughout the world. The transparent approach to the banking problems and the various projects for spreading information no doubt had a positive effect, too.

2 The prompt and transparent handling of the banking sector problems is also important. The terms for recapitalization should be such as to avoid moral hazard problems.

3 *Automatic stabilizers in the government budget* and *stimulatory monetary conditions* can help to mitigate the economy's depressive tendencies but they also entail risks. Economic policy has to strike a fine balance so that inflation expectations do not rise, the exchange rate weakens and interest rates move up, which could do more harm than good. In this respect a small, open economy has less freedom of action than a larger economy.

4 It is important both to avoid a widespread failure of banks and to bring about a macroeconomic stabilization. *The two are interdependent.* The collapse of much of the banking system would aggravate the macroeconomic weaknesses, just as failure to stabilize the economy would accentuate the banking crisis.

Source: What Lessons Can be Learned from Recent Financial Crises? The Swedish Experience

Remarks by Mr Urban Bäckström, Governor of Sveriges Riksbank, at the Federal Reserve Symposium 'Maintaining Financial Stability in a Global Economy', Jackson Hole, Wyoming, USA, 29 August 1997

4.2.2 The credit crunch and financial crisis in 2008

The global recession that gathered pace in 2008 has some similarities with the Asia crisis but also many significant differences. To understand what happened in 2008 and 2009 it is necessary to go back to 2004–6 when the effects of rapid US GDP growth and an increasing output gap in the US was not serious inflation but a mounting trade deficit. Almost all of the deterioration is in US trade with the rest of the world, especially with China and Japan. On the other side of this unbalanced equation, China and Japan had a large and growing surplus reaching a peak in 2006. This US/China and Japan disparity in trade performance suggests that there was a serious global trade imbalance.

You saw in the discussion of the Asia crisis that unless a country with a deficit attracts a capital inflow its exchange rate will fall – and the US is no exception. A strong capital inflow in 2003–6 kept the dollar strong despite the trade deficit, but weaker capital inflows in 2006/7 caused the dollar to fall. Much of the capital inflow came from the economies with big surpluses (China and Japan plus the big oil producers whose surpluses rose as the oil price increased). It fed on the global trade imbalance!

A capital inflow has other effects. It lowers the interest rate in deficit-country capital markets. It can trigger a 'bubble' with overvalued assets like it did in Asia in 1997. In the US there was a big increase in overseas acquisition of government debt which resulted in a fall in the long-term interest rate on the debt and on long-term debt in general. It fell from an average value of 6% in 2000 to 4% in 2003.

As a result, it became very much cheaper for US banks, mortgage companies and other financial intermediaries to borrow on wholesale capital markets and then lend to the private sector at a higher, but still low from the borrower's perspective, rate of interest. This led to a much higher level of corporate and residential investment plus general consumer borrowing. Of particular importance to subsequent events was mortgage lending. The availability of low-cost debt in the housing market led to a large increase in house prices starting in 2003, as you can see from Figure 4.12.

This happened elsewhere, notably in Spain, the UK and Ireland, but its consequences proved much more serious for the US and eventually the global economy. The asset 'bubble' was made a lot worse by 'financial innovation', initially in the corporate loan sector but, particularly important for house prices, later in the house mortgage sector. To raise more cash which would expand their

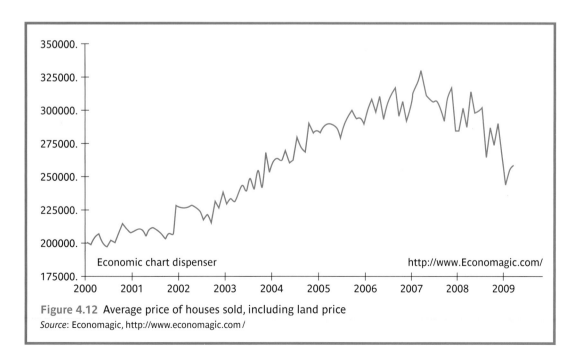

Figure 4.12 Average price of houses sold, including land price
Source: Economagic, http://www.economagic.com/

lending, mortgage companies and banks securitized their assets by selling mortgage books (*asset securitization*) to companies (*Special Purpose Vehicles* (SPVs), or *Special Investment Vehicles* (SIVs)), many of which were 'owned' by OECD banks. The SPVs/SIVs thought the loan books were low-risk assets from which they would earn a steady and secure income. They issued bonds (asset-backed securities) to finance the purchase of the mortgage book and a credit mountain started to grow as a result. Note that the value of these bonds was ultimately derived from the underlying value in the asset (a house in this case) which backed the original debt. The bonds became known as *asset-backed securities*, also known as *derivatives*. The SPVs/SIVs were sometimes *off bank balance sheet* entities and effectively unregulated by the financial authorities. Because of the risk of default on these assets, new obligations were also created (*credit default swaps*). These insured the holder of the asset against default. Insurance companies like AIG were keen to provide this insurance because they believed (or were led to believe) that the default risk was miniscule.

Securitization of mortgage loan books broke the link between lender and borrower. It weakened the monitoring of loans and the regulation and supervision of debtor risk. This encouraged lending to sub-prime borrowers and, in the housing market, led to the use of risky practices like 'self-certification'. The growth of the 'debt mountain' was encouraged by the incentives in the financial system which boosted the short-run performance of financial intermediaries but, as it turned out, profoundly damaged long-run performance. Each instrument in the creation of the debt mountain earned a commission, so some bankers and other financial managers got very, very rich!

The fragility of the debt mountain was exposed when the Federal Reserve increased short interest rates from 1.6% in 2004 to 5.3% in 2006. This move hit the US housing market at the moment when many fixed low-cost mortgages were expiring and the new mortgage payments incorporated the effect of this large rise in short rates. Many US home owners, especially those categorized as sub-prime, could not meet the new, much higher mortgage payments and, as a result, defaults and repossessions increased (by 93% in 2007/8) on a scale that far exceeded the expectation when these mortgages were advanced. It turned out that the income stream from the asset-backed security was a lot less secure than originally thought. It was made worse in October 2007 when Moody's rating agency cuts its estimate of what lenders could recoup in the event of default on these securities from 70% to 40%. At the same time, Moody's also cut its rating of $32bn of the mortgage-backed bonds. Moody's was followed by other rating agencies and the downgrades started to extend to the most highly rated AAA mortgage-backed bonds, the price of which fell to 90% of face value in late 2007. Mortgage defaults and the higher cost of new mortgages impacted on the housing market where prices started to fall, as can be seen from Figure 4.12. This reduced the value of the assets which backed the asset-backed securities whose prices collapsed even further. Banks and other financial intermediaries experienced dramatic erosion in their asset base.

> *To understand these forces read the Appendix to this chapter which sets out some basic analysis of bank balance sheets, how they can be compromised by 'toxic assets', and how banking regulation takes place.*

At the same time conditions in the corporate loan market worsened and banks and other financial intermediaries were forced to write down the value of both these and the mortgage-backed assets on their books. Remember that these were the assets which were required by banks so that they could match their liabilities to their customers. They were forced to draw on their *tier 1*[4]

---

[4] Tier 1 capital is the core measure of a bank's financial strength from a regulator's point of view. It is composed of *core capital* which consists primarily of common stock and *disclosed reserves* (or retained earnings), but may also include non-redeemable non-cumulative preferred stock.

capital reserves to plug the gap in their net assets. Some banks also raised capital from the *sovereign wealth funds*[5] of countries which had accumulated large trade surpluses. In late 2007 and early 2008 Citi raised $7.5bn from the Abu Dhabi Investment Fund and Merrill Lynch raised $5bn from a Chinese government fund. It was an unwelcome turn of events, with the pillars of US capitalism forced to turn to countries which, in the past, they were more accustomed to bailing out.

The financial malaise had also spread outside the US to banks which had acquired the increasingly toxic mortgage-backed assets. For example, between 2005 and 2007 the Swiss bank, UBS, acquired $50bn of these assets. Banks in the UK and the rest of the EU had also become exposed to the collapse in asset value of both the US and their own asset-backed derivatives, especially those based on housing market debt.

In 2008 banks continued to write down the value of their asset base and depleted their capital reserves to stabilize their balance sheets. It didn't work and bank shares fell dramatically. In September 2008 there was a major fan-collision incident with the collapse of Lehman Brothers. The global financial system was clearly in crisis and financial meltdown was believed to be imminent. The world's central banks responded quickly and started to bail out the banks, although they were worried about the *moral hazard* attached to the bail-outs. Moral hazard arises when an individual or a business believes that there is always a rescue package available when they get into trouble, so they become more careless as a result. This is endemic for large insurance companies. In this context the central banks were worried that if the banks were bailed out there would be no incentive for their managers to behave more prudently in the future. A variety of bail-out strategies were employed and Table 4.6 provides some of the details. The strategies adopted by central banks had three key ingredients. The first was to recapitalize the banks that survived. The second was to deal with the distressed or toxic assets which compromised balance sheets. The third was to make sure the banks had access to the liquidity they needed to honour their liabilities. It is evident from Table 4.6 that dealing with these issues was a huge and burdensome task, especially in the advanced economies of the world and notably in the US.

At the time of writing (May 2009) and as a result of these draconian measures, the global financial system has stabilized but serious anxieties remain.

History is littered with financial crises but most are localized and eventually contained. Few of these episodes are as serious as 2007–9 which is the most widespread since the 1930s. Almost invariably, financial crises impact of GDP, price inflation, unemployment, public finances and corporate profits. Often the impact is dramatic. The 2008/9 downturn is no exception. The origins of this global and synchronized recession were in the financial crisis that preceded it. Early on in late 2007 and early 2008 banks became increasingly anxious about the risks of interbank lending so they demanded higher rates of interest in return for this lending. In the UK the interbank lending rate rose above 6% in September 2007 and for the rest of the year and again in September 2008. It had been 4% at the beginning of 2003. This increase in lending rates was a clear precursor of a 'credit crunch' in which banks become very risk-averse, being reluctant to take almost any risk at all. In such circumstances, banks also reduce the availability of credit, and the adverse impact of that on demand and GDP is examined earlier in this chapter. According to the IMF, the US private sector reported a significant tightening of lending conditions in 2008, with 90% of respondents reporting

---

[5] A sovereign wealth fund (SWF) is a state-owned investment fund composed of financial assets such as stocks, bonds, property, precious metals or other financial instruments. Sovereign wealth funds invest globally. Some of them have grabbed attention by making bad investments in several Wall Street financial firms, including Citigroup, Morgan Stanley, and Merrill Lynch. These firms needed a cash infusion due to losses resulting from mismanagement and the sub-prime mortgage crisis. Some sovereign wealth funds are held solely by a central bank, which accumulates the funds in the course of their management of a nation's banking system; this type of fund is usually of major economic and fiscal importance. Other sovereign wealth funds are simply the state savings which are invested by various entities for the purposes of investment return, and which may not have a significant role in fiscal management (*source*: Wikipedia).

Table 4.6 Headline support for the financial sector and upfront financing need (as of 18 February 2009; in % of GDP)

Average (iv)	Capital injection	Purchase of assets and lending by Treasury	Central bank support provided with Treasury backing	Liquidity provision and other support by central bank (i)	Guarantees (ii)	Total	Upfront government financing (iii)
	(A)	(B)	(C)	(D)	(E)	A+B+C+D+E	
All members of G20	1.90	3.29	0.96	9.34	12.39	27.88	3.31
Advanced economies	2.90	5.20	1.34	13.93	19.74	43.11	5.22
EU members of G20	2.57	3.83	3.15	0.51	13.71	23.77	6.65
Emerging economies	0.22	0.09	0.32	1.64	0.06	2.33	0.11

(i) This table includes operations of new special facilities designed to address the current crisis and does not include the operations of the regular liquidity facilities provided by the central banks. Outstanding amounts under the latter have increased substantially and their maturity has been lengthened in recent months in many cases including the ECB.

(ii) Excludes deposit insurance provided by deposit insurance agencies.

(iii) This includes components of A, B and C that require upfront government outlays.

(iv) Weighted average using PPP GDP weights.

Source: FAD-MCM database on public interventions

reduced credit availability. Similar tightening happened in the UK where the Northern Rock bank was close to collapse in late 2007 because it had financed a large share of its new lending to households through borrowing from wholesale capital markets. Northern Rock's strategy unravelled when the cost of this borrowing rose and its availability also became more problematic.

More generally, credit to businesses and householders became both more expensive and less readily available from late 2007 onwards, though its impact became most severe in the last quarter of 2008. This impacted adversely on private sector demand and therefore GDP fell. This fall in GDP across the world has also increased unemployment in its train, with further damaging effects on consumer confidence.

Led by bank shares, equity markets also fell in 2008 and early 2009. Just like the early 2000s, this contributed to a further, almost catastrophic, fall in private sector confidence. This added to the downward pressures on aggregate demand (and the AD curve) that led to large falls in GDP in 2009.

The GDP fall in the US and in the OECD as a whole has led to a marked fall in world trade in 2009, with major impacts on the big exporting countries like China, Japan and Germany. It was thought by some commentators that they would escape the worst of the world recession, but their dependence on export markets to drive GDP and income growth meant that almost no economy has escaped the 2008/9 downturn.

The future evolution of the global economy is uncertain in June 2009. After you have read this brief introduction to recent events you should get into the habit of keeping abreast of expert opinion, especially in the important international institutions like the IMF, the OECD and the World Bank. Their regular updates are accessible via the websites included in the Further Reading for this chapter.

4.3 Long-run macroeconomic performance

The data in Figure 4.13 shows the long-run GDP growth rates in 1996–2007 for a selection of economies. The first point to note is the higher growth rates experienced in the developing and the 'transition' economies, namely Russia and Central and Eastern Europe (CEE). In the EU only Spain appears among the growth leaders shown in Figure 4.13.

What explains these differences in the long-run performance of these economies?

Growth accounting is one way economists address this issue. This starts with the following relationship:

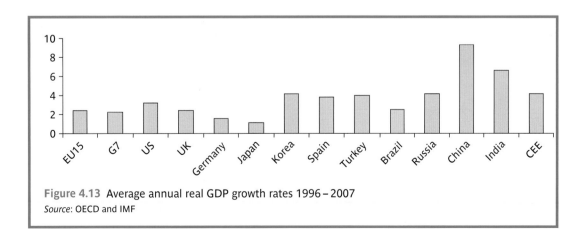

Figure 4.13 Average annual real GDP growth rates 1996–2007
Source: OECD and IMF

$\dot{Y} = \alpha\dot{K} + \beta\dot{L} + TFP$ where

$\dot{Y}$ = rate of growth of output (GDP) $\dot{K}$ = rate of growth of physical capital

$\dot{L}$ = rate of growth of labour input   TFP = rate of growth of total factor (input) productivity

α = elasticity of output with respect to K[6]

β = elasticity of output with respect to labour

The intuition underpinning this equation is that the growth of output is the result of two factors, firstly, the growth in inputs (factors of production) of physical capital and labour measured in working hours, and secondly, increases in the productivity of those inputs arising from technical and organizational change and investment in human capital. There have been many attempts to analyse rates of growth in GDP using this framework. Englander and Gurney (1994) carried out an influential study of long-run average annual GDP growth rates in the biggest five economies (G5) between 1960 and 1990. Their results are shown in Table 4.7. The EU economies are very similar, with the larger part of their growth resulting from improvements in input productivity. Almost none of the growth is the result of increases in labour growth. In Japan and the US the growth in the quantity of inputs is more important. Labour force growth makes a huge contribution to explaining long-run growth in the US. This mainly reflects the high rate of inward migration into the US. A recent study by economists at the ECB (2006) attributes 17% of euro area growth 1993–2003 to the more rapid growth in the labour input caused by higher levels of inward migration in the later period covered by this study.[7]

Growth accounting research offers a globally expanding business some clues to the factors that determine long-run macroeconomic performance in any national economy. Most important is evidence of a sustained increase in aggregate supply. High long-run rates of capital accumulation are clearly critical, but increasing input productivity, technical progress and human capital accumulation are also important. Of particular importance is investment in human capital. The World Bank (1993) calculates that between 26% and 56% of the growth of GDP experienced in the East Asia region (the 56% figure refers to Hong Kong) is the product of high levels of human capital investment.

Another issue is the long-run rate of savings. One of the features of East Asia is the very high rates of personal savings. This is shown in a recent paper by Qin and Ren (2008). They carefully calculate household savings rates in China and the US for the years 1992–2004. This shows a 22.9% rate of household saving in China compared with 5.4% in the US. Does this explain the rapid GDP growth rate of China? The neo-classical growth theory from which the growth accounting model is derived says no. The effect of high savings is to encourage investment, which raises the capital

Table 4.7 Contributions to long-run growth (% share of each factor)

	Capital growth	Labour growth	TFP growth
UK	38	0	61
Germany	45	0	55
France	33	4	63
Japan	44	11	45
US	37	42	20

---

[6] This means the proportion that output grows as the proportion of capital (or labour) grows.

[7] Musso, A and Westermann, T (2005).

intensity of production but does not increase the long-run rate of growth in the economy. A key element in this theory is that technical progress is *disembodied*, so it does not depend on the rate of capital accumulation. Note that in the growth accounting approach total factor (input) productivity is an 'add-on' unconnected with the rate of growth of physical capital. If, alternatively, technical progress is partly embodied in human and/or physical capital investment the answer is different. Higher savings encourages higher investment and this leads to high rates of total factor productivity growth because each piece of investment embodies the latest ideas and methods.

One central feature of the fast-growing economies in Asia is that the high rates of saving, capital accumulation and innovation result in a high level of national competitive advantage, especially in international trade. As a result, many of the Asian economies have achieved strong trade performance and this is reflected in the big increase in their share of world trade, notably in manufacturing goods, which represents 60% of world exports and which is the fastest-growing global product market.

Of course, no nation actually engages in international trade itself. This is done by the individual businesses operating in a nation state and competing in the global markets for their products. A competitive economy is, hence, one in which the average business located in the economy enjoys global competitive advantage. Note the emphasis on *average*. Even in the most uncompetitive economies, there are still firms with competitive advantage. There just aren't many of them. Similarly, there are laggards in the most competitive nation states, but not many. What follows from this link is that competitive advantage is not simply to do with a 'natural' endowment of resources, but can be created by policy at *both* company and national level. Company-level global competitive advantage can be facilitated by a favourable political-economic context, but there is still a role for company-level strategic 'actions' in building both *company and national competitive advantage*.

Porter's 'diamond' analysis explores this further by identifying the importance to national competitive advantage of firm strategy and structure, and in particular, the organizational frameworks which facilitate the development of firm-level competitive advantage.[8] He also emphasizes that no single managerial system is universally appropriate, so that, '*competitiveness in a particular industry results from the convergence of the management practices and organisational modes favoured in the country'*. A key issue here is the way management practices encourage commitment and effort from the entire labour force.

Porter also emphasizes the importance of a supportive home market:

> *Nations gain competitive advantage in industries where the home market gives their companies a clearer or earlier picture of emerging buyer needs, and where demanding buyers pressure companies to innovate faster and achieve more sophisticated competitive advantages than their foreign rivals.* (Porter, 1990)

A good example is Denmark's global expertise in windmills for electricity generation. In part, this reflects the 'green' preferences of Danish consumers, but it also reflects local rural community preference for small-scale, local electricity generation. Another example is the competitive advantage of Italian textile and footwear manufacturers. The home market preference for well-designed, innovative and well-crafted clothes and shoes has put pressure on Italian manufacturers to meet the demanding home consumer market and this has contributed to their global competitive advantage. Other examples can be found in Porter (1990).

Another key ingredient in building a competitive economy noted by Michael Porter (1990) is the responsibility of government for maintaining high levels of domestic competition and, hence,

---

[8] See Chapter 9 for a full discussion of globalization.

low levels of *horizontal integration*. Horizontal integration is the process of merger in which firms producing the same products come together, thus reducing the degree of competition in the market, which enables firms to charge higher prices than would prevail under competitive conditions. Porter draws attention to the large number of rivals producing the same product in Japan in the period of greatest economic success. Similarly, McAleese (2004) shows that the dominance of large firms in the UK is over 3 times the rate found in Japan. In Sweden it is nearly 7 times the Japanese rate. Domestic rivalry also pressurizes companies to innovate and improve, and hones the skills necessary for successful international competition, and this helps explain, in part, the international competitive success of Japanese business.

In apparent contradiction to this presumption that horizontal integration is socially undesirable, Porter also emphasizes the need to maximize those business synergies which require a high degree of inter-firm cooperation. These synergies, or *agglomeration economies* as economists call them, arise from the location of firms in *clusters*. These clusters create benefits for all the firms in the cluster which lower their costs and increase their competitive advantage. Porter uses the success of the Italian footwear industry as an example to support his argument. Italian designers and manufacturers of shoes, of leather and leather-working machinery have formed 'clustering' relationships which involve a high degree of cooperative interaction along vertical supply chains. Porter remarks that '*Close and ongoing interchange with suppliers and buyers is integral to the process of creating and sustaining competitive advantage in international competition.*'

Knowledge of these requirements for the creation of national competitive advantage is helpful to globalizing businesses, which need to take a long view of the markets in which they plan to locate. When the markets of interest are in the emerging economies, statistical forecasting of the future development of the macroeconomy is difficult, if not impossible. Therefore, in order to make useful judgements about long-run prospects, it makes sense to identify the key determinants of long-run economic success and to benchmark the markets of interest, in terms of their local performance against these determinants.

Next, we explore in more detail the way in which business can use other economic information as part of a strategy to build competitive advantage over its rivals.

At this point, read Case box 4.2 and compare the crises of 1992 in Sweden and 1997 in Asia with the global crisis of 2008.

Not by banks alone

Although banks' own efforts will be sufficient and successful in many areas, intervention by standard-setting bodies and authorities will be needed in others. On valuation issues, for example, reforms must recognize that this is more than merely an accounting issue. Mark-to-market accounting imposes stricter discipline on banks' risk management and increases market discipline, because it acts as an early-warning system, where losses show up in banks' P&L accounts before they materialize in the real economy. Any changes must respect these benefits of fair-value accounting, but must at the same time address the issues of illiquid markets, pro-cyclicality and consistency between accounting standards.

International coordination is essential for these efforts and for any state action aimed at stabilizing financial markets and banks. For sure, state action needs to be attuned to individual circumstances. But uncoordinated action using a plethora of diverging instruments will only create yet more uncertainty, spread the virus and distort competition.

History will record 2009 as the year that reshaped the global financial system. This holds particularly true for the European Union, where member states will be faced with a stark choice. They can either act jointly and at last create a supervisory system that is commensurate with a truly integrated financial market, or relapse into a system of essentially separate national markets.

Case box 4.2: **Lessons from the global banking crisis 2008**

How to restore the financial markets to health? Josef Ackermann, chief executive of Deutsche Bank, gives his answer

The crisis that engulfed first the financial industry and then entire economies is a watershed event. Broad segments of global financial markets stopped working. Structures and institutions that had been the bedrock of the system for decades disappeared literally overnight. And in response central banks and governments deployed counter-measures on an unprecedented scale.

Three issues stand out. First, *liquidity*. This is at the heart of the stability of any financial system. Yet the crisis revealed that the assumption of continuously available liquidity can no longer be upheld, and our understanding of market dynamics in times of illiquidity is poor. The repercussions for the valuation of illiquid assets in a mark-to-market accounting regime need to be addressed with urgency.

Second, *transparency*. It would be wrong if the focus of this issue were limited to greater transparency about banks' exposures. Rather, it must extend to better disclosure of a bank's institutional arrangements for risk management, risk models and techniques. Moreover, greater transparency must be achieved for financial products, especially the complex structured credit products at the heart of this crisis. Investors will return to these markets only if originators disclose sufficient data in the underlying assets so as to enable investors to make their own due diligence rather than rely passively on the judgment of originators and rating agencies. Even this will not save these markets from shrinking dramatically as investors' preferences shift to simpler products.

Third, we need to strengthen the *infrastructure* of financial markets, the 'plumbing'. In order to increase price transparency, transaction data should be pooled and made available. To reduce settlement risk and enable netting in over-the-counter markets, central counterparties will be established. Greater automation in these markets will also reduce settlement risk, but will obviously require a higher degree of standardisation.

Source: 'Lessons From a Crisis', *The Economist*, 19 November 2008. From *The World in 2009* print edition

More calls for tighter regulation will be heard in 2009. This is understandable. The financial crisis will cost us dearly and the financial industry bears as much responsibility for this as past mistakes in both macroeconomic and regulatory policies. But it must not result in the dissolution of financial-market integration and the stifling of financial innovation.

Though it seems hard to believe these days, the market-based financial system has made a big contribution to global growth. Reverting to fragmented, nation-based and over-regulated banking markets is not the answer. What we need is greater resilience via sophisticated market participants, as well as stronger market infrastructure and supranational structures for the regulation and supervision of the global financial system.

4.4 Macroeconometric forecasting and business

In this part of this chapter we will examine further the link between business and macroeconomic performance and explore the implications for business strategy. As we have seen, effective strategy requires an insightful understanding of the macroeconomic environment. In part, this is needed to evaluate and explain past and current performance and this is what we have emphasized so far. However, strategy is about future actions, so a forward-looking view of the macroeconomic environment is also needed. One simple way to do this is to access one of the many published macroeconomic forecasts and use that. A number of websites are available which contain the kind of forecasts that businesses need. Some of these websites are listed below:

- www.imf.org
- www.worldbank.org
- www.oecd.org
- www.niesr.ac.uk

How are these forecasts prepared? A starting point for most forecasters is to look at past experience and use this as a guide to the future. One simple approach would be to collect past information on a particular economic variable (for example, exchange rates), explore its statistical properties and forecast the future time path from this information. The problem with this approach is that it fails to use all the available information, since no attempt is made to link the behaviour of one economic variable with other variables. For example, we know from earlier in this chapter that the link between a nation's interest rates and its exchange rate is critical.

The solution adopted by most forecasters, including the forecasts that can be found in the websites listed above, is to build a macroeconometric model capable of use for forecasting purposes. A macroeconometric model consists of a set of equations that identify the links between macroeconomic variables. It will use all the macroeconomic links discussed earlier in this chapter and many others as well. One of the basic relationships in a macroeconometric model is that between aggregate demand and GDP. It assumes GDP growth is driven by growth in aggregate demand. It will be accompanied by a set of relationships, which set down the variables that cause aggregate demand to change. The interest rate, for example, will feature as a determinant of both consumer demand and investment demand. Share prices and wealth will figure as drivers of consumer demand. Past experience is used to measure the impact of variables on each other. The objective of the model builder is to construct a set of relationships capable of explaining past history.

How do forecasts derived from macroeconometric models of this type perform? The answer is 'not very well'. In an article in the *Financial Times* in 1995, Professor John Kay reviewed the performance of 34 UK forecasts of GDP growth in the years after 1987. He found that the forecasts tended to cluster around an average value, but the average seldom forecasted accurately. He found that all the forecasts in 1993 and 1994 were significantly below the actual growth rate, while the opposite was true in 1991 and 1992. A more recent OECD study of forecasts of both GDP growth and inflation for seven countries after 1974 found the same. Detailed results of this exercise can be found in McAleese (2004, chapter 16).

Why are the published forecasts so notoriously inaccurate? The most important reason is that the models are constructed using past experience. They have to make a number of strong assumptions:

- *Links observed in the past continue in the future.* For example, assuming that interest rates will continue to influence investment as they have done in the past may not be correct. Cuts in interest rates may not stimulate investment if there is a crisis of business confidence.

- *The strength of the relationships embodied in the links in the model stays the same.* This may not be true. Increases in wages tend to follow increases in prices, but the size of the effect is a lot less nowadays than in the 1970s and 1980s, so 21st century inflation of prices will tend to be overestimated in a macroeconometric model which uses 1970s and 1980s data for its estimate of the strength of the link. Analysis of the impact of the oil price increases of early 2008 was hampered by significant changes in the strength of the links between oil prices, GDP and price inflation.

- *There are no events for which there is no historical experience.* This is clearly not true. When the price of oil quadrupled in the 1990s, forecasts of both inflation and GDP growth across the world were in error, because none incorporated an historical experience of a change of this magnitude.

■ *Historical data exists and is a good representation of what has happened in the past.* This is especially problematic in emerging markets, where historical data is scarce and where the collection of statistics is at a rudimentary stage. Macroeconometric forecasts are unlikely to be accurate.

What can be done when uncertainty about the macroeconomic future cannot be eliminated by the use of a forecasting model? One solution is simply to accept that the risk is endemic and has to be managed as far as possible by shifting the risk to another party (at a price). This is what is done when businesses are exposed to exchange rate risk. This may happen because they have a contract to buy a product (for example, raw materials) from an overseas supplier who wants to be paid at some time in the future in an overseas currency. Given the volatility of exchange rates and the notorious difficulty of forecasting movements in the rate, the business cannot predict what the cost of the purchase in the home currency will be at the date of payment. The simplest solution is to 'buy forward' – to enter into a contract with a bank to supply overseas currency at an agreed rate on the date of the payment to the overseas supplier. There will be a cost associated with this forward contract, but it eliminates risk and obviates the need to forecast the exchange rate between the home and the overseas currency. The problem is that forward markets of the kind we see for exchange rate dealings do not exist in many other areas where macroeconomic risk is critical to strategy.

Another solution is to adopt a signalling approach, that is, to use signals that past experience has said are good predictors of the future. This is a good solution to the problem for OECD-based businesses (for example, retailers like Wal-Mart and Carrefour) seeking to pursue a global strategy. How do they select suitable emerging markets in which to build a presence? There are no reliable long-run forecasts of future macroeconomic performance to guide their decision. What could they do? One solution is to search in the national economies they wish to target for some of the favourable signals set out earlier in this chapter.

The failure of macroeconometric forecasting models to provide a single accurate view of the future has led to the introduction of new methodologies for the presentation of forward-looking macroeconomic scenarios in a different form. Extensive use is made of the 'fan' method. This involves a best-guess central scenario presented alongside a wide range of less likely alternatives both more optimistic and more pessimistic than the central scenario. This has implications for business strategy. Planning models using a single deterministic approach to the future are no longer the only option for strategic 'actions' that need to be informed by some kind of forward-looking assessment. The first stage in the solution is to assess the historical impact of exogenous macroeconomic changes on the individual firm and its market(s). This assessment needs to be built upon the same econometric foundations, using the same statistical methodology, as embodied in the macro model.

Using this extended macroeconometric model enables the creation of a variety of 'what if' scenarios of market prices, volumes and so on. These scenarios set out the impact of a wide variety of uncontrollable shocks from the macroeconomic environment on the business and show both a central scenario and the range of alternatives using the 'fan' methodology. Macroeconomic shocks need to be managed by business so this methodology helps to establish some of the limits of strategic action. These scenarios could explore, for example, the impact of different home exchange rates or different rates of growth of world trade over a five-year period. This is no longer difficult. Twenty years ago, economists needed up to six weeks to run a full five-year scenario on a mainframe computer. Now relatively inexperienced users can do this in seconds on a PC. It is a simple matter, once the model is built, to use it to think about the future state of the macroeconomy.

4.5 Summary

A useful proposition with which to end this chapter is:

Businesses that don't understand their economic environment make strategic errors, sometimes catastrophic ones, especially if they do not know that booms and slumps are bound to end!

This chapter is not intended to turn you into an economist. On the other hand, it is critical for managers to be sensible, practical economists because macroeconomics plays such a significant role and has such a direct impact on firms. The argument in this chapter directs attention to the uncontrollable nature of macroeconomic forces and the contextual constraints that it imposes on managerial discretion. This chapter has detailed some of the major forces in the macroeconomy so that managers can, through analysis, understanding and preparation, be able at least to anticipate the pressures on the firm. There are two main themes here. The first considers the nature of the business cycle and the demand and supply characteristics of boom and bust. A well-informed and prepared firm might be able to take strategic decisions contra-cyclically so as to avoid herd behaviour in merely following the economy. The second theme is the nature of national competitiveness and the relation of firms to this. Much of the infrastructure of the economy falls within the range of government spending. Thus the fortunes of firms in any economy are going to be dependent in part on the ability of governments to foster national competitiveness and to achieve sustainable long-run economic growth. But firms also need to respond to these pressures themselves in forming their own strategies so as to mitigate the undesirable effects of economic misfortunes.

All businesses are sensitive to macroeconomic shocks outside of their control and have to find ways in which to manage them. Strategic 'actions' need an understanding of the contextual links between an individual company, its markets and GDP growth in both the home and export markets. Exchange rates play a particularly important role for the company that trades outside of its own home market but also for those who face competition from imports and whose business is sensitive to GDP fluctuations in their own home economy. It also requires an understanding both of how economies, in general, work and also of the particular economies in which the business's markets are located.

Recap questions and assignments

To check your understanding of the ideas set out in this chapter, answer the following question.

1 What are the main effects on GDP growth, the rate of price inflation and unemployment in an economy of:
   i   a fall in the home rate of interest?
   ii   a decrease in the rate of income tax or social security contribution rates?
   iii an increase in the rate of indirect (e.g. VAT) tax?
   iv   a rise in government spending on a) health, b) defence?

Case study 4.1: **The Big Mac Index**

The world economy looks very different once countries' output is adjusted for differences in prices
How fast is the world economy growing? How important is China as an engine of growth? How much richer is the average person in America than in China? The answers to these huge questions depend crucially on how you convert the value of output in different countries into a common currency. Converting national GDPs into dollars at market exchange rates is misleading. Prices tend to be lower in poor economies, so a dollar of spending in China, say, is worth a lot more than a dollar in America. A better method is to use purchasing-power parities (PPP), which take account of price differences.

The theory of purchasing-power parity says that in the long run exchange rates should move towards rates that would equalise the prices of an identical basket of goods and services in any two countries. This is the thinking behind *The Economist*'s Big Mac Index. Invented in 1986 as a light-hearted guide to whether currencies are at their 'correct' level, our 'basket' is a McDonald's Big Mac, which is produced locally in almost 120 countries.

The Big Mac PPP is the exchange rate that would leave a burger in any country costing the same as in America. The first column of our table converts the local price of a Big Mac into dollars at current exchange rates. The average price of a Big Mac in four American cities is $2.90 (including tax). The cheapest shown in the table is in the Philippines ($1.23), the most expensive in Switzerland ($4.90). In other words, the Philippine peso is the world's most undervalued currency, the Swiss franc its most overvalued.

The second column calculates Big Mac PPPs by dividing the local currency price by the American price. For instance, in Japan a Big Mac costs ¥262. Dividing this by the American price of $2.90 produces a dollar PPP against the yen of ¥90, compared with its current rate of ¥113, suggesting that the yen is 20% undervalued. In contrast, the euro (based on a weighted average of Big Mac prices in the euro area) is 13% overvalued. But perhaps the most interesting finding is that all emerging-market currencies are undervalued against the dollar. The Chinese yuan, on which much ink has been spilled in recent months, looks 57% too cheap.

The Big Mac Index was never intended as a precise forecasting tool. Burgers are not traded across borders as the PPP theory demands; prices are distorted by differences in the cost of non-tradable goods and services, such as rents.

Yet these very failings make the Big Mac Index useful, since looked at another way it can help to measure countries' differing costs of living. That a Big Mac is cheap in China does not in fact prove that the yuan is being held massively below its fair value, as many American politicians claim. It is quite natural for average prices to be lower in poorer countries and therefore for their currencies to appear cheap.

The prices of traded goods will tend to be similar to those in developed economies. But the prices of non-tradable products, such as housing and labour-intensive services, are generally much lower. A haircut is, for instance, much cheaper in Beijing than in New York.

One big implication of lower prices is that converting a poor country's GDP into dollars at market exchange rates will significantly understate the true size of its economy and its living standards. If China's GDP is converted into dollars using the Big Mac PPP, it is almost two-and-a-half-times bigger than if converted at the market exchange rate. Meatier and more sophisticated estimates of PPP, such as those used by the IMF, suggest that the required adjustment is even bigger.

Weight watchers

The global economic picture thus looks hugely different when examined through a PPP lens. Take the pace of global growth. Anyone wanting to calculate this needs to bundle together countries' growth rates, with each one weighted according to its share of world GDP. Using weights based on market exchange rates, the world has grown by an annual average of only 1.9% over the past three years. Using PPP, as the IMF does, global growth jumps to a far more robust 3.1% a year.

The main reason for this difference is that using PPP conversion factors almost doubles the weight of the emerging economies, which have been growing much faster. Measured at market exchange rates, emerging economies account for less than a quarter of global output. But measured using PPP they account for almost half.

Small wonder, then, that global economic rankings are dramatically transformed when they are done on a PPP basis rather than market exchange rates. America remains number one, but China leaps from seventh place to second, accounting for 13% of world output. India jumps into fourth place ahead of Germany, and both Brazil and Russia are bigger than Canada. Similarly, market exchange rates also exaggerate inequality. Using market rates, the average American is 33 times richer than the average Chinese; on a PPP basis, he is 'only' seven times richer.

The way in which economies are measured also has a huge impact on which country has contributed most to global growth in recent years. Using GDP converted at market rates, China has accounted for only 7% of the total increase in the dollar value of global GDP over the past three years, compared with America's 25%. But on PPP figures, China has accounted for almost one-third of global real GDP growth and America only 13%.

This helps to explain why commodity prices in general and oil prices in particular have been surging, even though growth has been relatively subdued in the rich world since 2000. Emerging economies are not only growing much faster than rich economies and are more intensive in their use of raw materials and energy, but they also account for a bigger chunk of global output if measured correctly. As Charles Dumas, an economist at Lombard Street Research, neatly puts it, even if a Chinese loaf is a quarter of the cost of a loaf in America, it uses the same amount of flour.

All measures of PPP are admittedly imperfect. But most economists agree that they give a more accurate measure of the relative size of economies than market exchange rates – and a better understanding of some of the dramatic movements in world markets. The humble burger should be part of every economist's diet.

After the credit crunch

Ever since the credit storms first broke last August, the prices of stocks, bonds, gold and other investment assets have been blown this way and that. Currencies have been pushed around too. Did this buffeting bring them any closer to their underlying fair value? Not according to the Big Mac Index, our lighthearted guide to exchange rates. Many currencies look more out of whack than in July 2007, when we last compared burger prices.

Only a handful of currencies are close to their Big Mac PPP. Of the seven currencies that make up the Federal Reserve's major-currency index, only one (the Australian dollar) is within 10% of its fair value. Most of the rest look expensive. The euro is overvalued by a massive 50%. The British pound, Swedish krona, Swiss franc and Canadian dollar are also trading well above their burger benchmark. All are more overvalued against the dollar than a year ago. Only the Japanese yen, undervalued by 27%, could be considered a snip.

The dollar still buys a lot of burger in the rest of Asia too. The Singapore dollar is undervalued by 18% and the South Korean won by 12%. The currencies of less well-off Asian countries, such as Indonesia, Malaysia and Thailand, look even cheaper. China's currency is among the most undervalued, though a bit less so than a year ago.

The angrier type of China-basher might conclude that the yuan should revalue so that it is much closer to its burger standard. But care needs to be taken when drawing hard conclusions from fast-food prices. PPP measures show where currencies should end up in the long run. Prices vary with local costs, such as rents and wages, which are lower in poor countries, as well as with the price of ingredients that trade across borders. For this reason, PPP is a more reliable comparison for the currencies of economies with similar levels of income.

For all these caveats, more sophisticated analyses come to broadly similar conclusions to our own. John Lipsky, number two at the IMF, said this week that the euro is above the fund's medium-term valuation benchmark. China's currency is 'substantially undervalued' in the IMF's view. The dollar is

The hamburger standard

	Big Mac prices		Implied PPP* of the dollar	Actual exchange rate: Jan 30th	Under (−)/over (+) valuation against the dollar, %
	in local currency	in dollars			
United States†	$3.54	3.54	–	–	
Argentina	Peso 11.50	3.30	3.25	3.49	−7
Australia	A$3.45	2.19	0.97	1.57	−38
Brazil	Real 8.02	3.45	2.27	2.32	−2
Britain	£2.29	3.30	1.55‡	1.44‡	−7
Canada	C$4.16	3.36	1.18	1.24	−5
Chile	Peso 1,550	2.51	438	617	−29
China	Yuan 12.5	1.83	3.53	6.84	−48
Czech Republic	Koruna 65.94	3.02	18.6	21.9	−15
Denmark	DK 29.5	5.07	8.33	5.82	43
Egypt	Pound 13.0	2.34	3.67	5.57	−34
Euro area§	€3.42	4.38	1.04**	1.28**	24
Hong Kong	HK$13.3	1.72	3.76	7.75	−52
Hungary	Forint 680	2.92	192	233	−18
Indonesia	Rupiah 19,800	1.74	5,593	11,380	−51
Israel	Shekel 15.0	3.69	4.24	4.07	4
Japan	¥290	3.23	81.9	89.8	−9
Malaysia	Ringgit 5.50	1.52	1.55	3.61	−57
Mexico	Peso 33.0	2.30	9.32	14.4	−35
New Zealand	NZ$4.90	2.48	1.38	1.97	−30
Norway	Kroner 40.0	5.79	11.3	6.91	63
Peru	Sol 8.06	2.54	2.28	3.18	−28
Philippines	Peso 98.0	2.07	27.7	47.4	−42
Poland	Zloty 7.00	2.01	1.98	3.48	−43
Russia	Ruble 62.0	1.73	17.5	35.7	−51
Saudi Arabia	Riyal 10.0	2.66	2.82	3.75	−25
Singapore	S$3.95	2.61	1.12	1.51	−26
South Africa	Rand 16.95	1.66	4.79	10.2	−53
South Korea	Won 3,300	2.39	932	1,380	−32
Sweden	SKR 38.0	4.58	10.7	8.30	29
Switzerland	CHF 6.50	5.60	1.84	1.16	58
Taiwan	NT$75.0	2.23	21.2	33.6	−37
Thailand	Baht 62.0	1.77	17.5	35.0	−50
Turkey	Lire 5.15	3.13	1.45	1.64	−12

*Purchasing-power parity; local price divided by price in the United States

†Average of New York, Chicago, Atlanta and San Francisco ‡Dollars per pound §Weighted average of prices in euro area **Dollars per euro

Sources: McDonald's; The Economist

▶ sandwiched in between. The big drop in the greenback's value since 2002 has left it 'close to its medium-term equilibrium level', said Mr Lipsky.

If that judgment is right, the squalls stirred up by the credit crises have moved at least one currency – the world's reserve money – closer to fair value. Curiously, the crunch has not shaken faith in two currencies favoured by yield-hungry investors: the Brazilian real and Turkish lira. These two stand out as emerging-market currencies that trade well above their Big Mac PPPs. Both countries have high interest rates. Turkey's central bank recently raised its benchmark rate to 16.75%; Brazil's pushed its key rate up to 13% on 23 July. These rates offer juicy returns for those willing to bear the risks. Those searching for a value meal should look elsewhere.

Questions

1 Draw up a list of strengths and weaknesses of market exchange rates versus purchasing-power parity for assessing the relative size of different national economies.

2 In assessing a foreign country as a place in which to make investments in plant and machinery, what specific advantages would you get from the use of a PPP approach?

3 The PPP approach suggests that one country (such as Britain) has its currency overvalued against the dollar whereas another country (such as Brazil) has its currency quite heavily undervalued. What does this imply about the relative strength of these two economies and their competitiveness on world markets?

Source: Compiled by the authors from 'Big Mac Index', *The Economist*, 29 May 2004, 24 July 2008 and 4 February 2009

References

Englander, A.S. and Gurney, A. (1994) *OECD Productivity Trends*, OECD Economic Studies No. 22, www.oecd.org/dataoecd/49/11/33937707.pdf

Begg, D. and Ward, D. (2009) *Economics for Business*, 3rd edn, McGraw-Hill, London.

McAleese, D. (2004) *Economics for Business*, 3rd edn, Financial Times/Prentice Hall, Harlow.

Musso, A. and Westermann, T. (2005) Assessing potential output growth in the euro area – a growth accounting perspective. *ECB Occasional Paper 22*, European Central Bank, Frankfurt.

Porter, M.E. (1990) *Competitive Advantage of Nations*, Macmillan, London.

Qin, X. and Ren, R. (2008) Comparable household saving rates for China and the United States. *Review of Income and Wealth*, **54**, **4**, 656–70.

World Bank (1993) *East Asian Miracle*, Oxford University Press, New York.

Further reading

A more complete analysis of the macroeconomic environment than could be provided in this chapter can be found in Begg and Ward (2009). You should use it as a source of reference to further explore the ideas presented in the chapter. Of particular importance are chapters 9–13. They will help you to think through the effect of factors referred to in this lesson but not fully developed. The chapter also deals with policies to control inflation and the role of central banks in this regard. Chapter 14 deals with the economic analysis of globalization.

You will also find excellent supporting material on www.bized.co.uk. This includes a glossary of economic terms as well as many other useful features, including the 'Virtual Economy' which is a computer-based model of a real-life macroeconomy. You can carry out a variety of experiments to build your understanding of the concepts developed in this chapter, including the self-assessed exercise at the end. Its problem is that it's very much in need of an update.

The macroeconomic environment changes rapidly so it is important to keep up to date with events. There are many websites which provide up-to-date information on the macroeconomic context of strategy and which employ many of the concepts developed in this lesson. Examples of the best are:

www.imf.org
www.oecd.org
www.worldbank.org
www.niesr.ac.uk

Appendix A: The basics of banking
Bank lending and money creation

Commercial banks create money and increase the availability of credit to the non-bank sector of the economy. They are regulated by the central bank precisely because of this feature of their activity. In order to see how this works, consider Table 4.1a. This shows what happens if a business or an individual located in the € area makes a cash deposit of €100k in Bank A. The motivation for the deposit will be to take advantage of the bank's superior security systems and also to use its money management services, for both of which the commercial bank will charge a fee. The table shows this transaction in a simple balance sheet. The cash becomes the bank's asset and also its liability (to the depositor).

Table 4.1a Bank A: balance sheet

Assets	Liabilities
€100k	€100k

The bank knows that the depositor is unlikely to withdraw its cash at a single point in time but in smaller tranches spread over time. It will need to keep a reserve of cash to meet the depositor's cash needs but realizes that it can use the rest of the cash to make loans to other customers and make extra profits by charging interest on the loan. Suppose it makes a loan of €80k to another business and keeps the rest as the cash reserve it needs. The reserves are either kept in its vaults or deposited in the Central Bank (the ECB in the € area). Its new balance sheet is shown in Table 4.2a.

Table 4.2a Bank A: balance sheet

	Assets	Liabilities
Cash reserves	€20k	€100k
Loans	€80k	
Total	€100k	€100k

Bank A has created credit/money. The business or household that receives the loan will deposit this either in Bank A or in another bank, B, which also keeps 20% of the deposit in cash and lends out the remainder. This is shown in Table 4.3a.

Table 4.3a Bank B: balance sheet		
	Assets	**Liabilities**
Cash reserves	€160k	€800k
Loans	€640k	
Total	€800k	€800k

The process of credit creation does not stop here, because those who receive the loans from Bank B will deposit them in, say, another bank, C, that behaves in the same way as Banks A and B – this is shown in Table 4.4a.

Table 4.4a Bank C: balance sheet		
	Assets	**Liabilities**
Cash reserves	€128k	€640k
Loans	€512k	
Total	€640k	€640k

Note, therefore, that the original deposit of €100k has grown through successive bank lending. This is shown in Table 4.5a.

Table 4.5a The Growth of Money Supply (in €k)

Initial deposit = 1000
Bank A lending = 800 = $(1 - \rho) \times 1000$
Bank B lending = 640 = $(1 - \rho)^2 \times 1000$
Bank C lending = 512 = $(1 - \rho)^3 \times 1000$

Where ρ = reserve ratio = .2 in the example above

The process of credit creation does not stop with Bank C. It continues until the lending capacity of the banking system is exhausted, which happens when there is no loanable surplus in excess of the target level of reserves. Mathematically, the total money supply created is

Equation 4.1a: $[1 + (1 - \rho) + (1 - \rho)^2 + (1 - \rho)^3 + \ldots] \, 1000 = (1/\rho) \times 1000$

In the example above $\rho = .2$ so the total money supply is $(1/.2) \times 1000 = 5000$. Banks create this money! The initial deposit has been multiplied by the actions of the commercial banks. The *money multiplier* in the example above is 5.

You can probably see that this system has some significant risks attached to it. The risks grow if the reserve ratio is lower than 20%, as it normally is in practice. It enables the commercial banks to lend more but raises the chance that they will be exposed to a demand for cash from their depositors which they do not have. There is also the further risk that their loans do not perform. Borrowers may default on the capital sum or on the interest that is due. Banks have to be good at evaluating the risk attached to each loan they make and if they aren't, the banks (and the overall financial system) are under pressure, as shown by the experience since 2000.

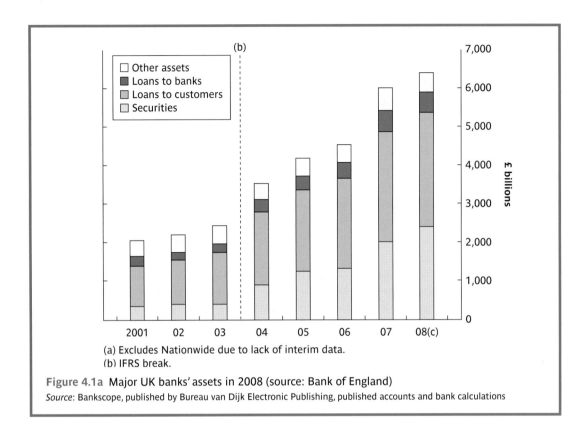

(a) Excludes Nationwide due to lack of interim data.
(b) IFRS break.

Figure 4.1a Major UK banks' assets in 2008 (source: Bank of England)

Source: Bankscope, published by Bureau van Dijk Electronic Publishing, published accounts and bank calculations

In practice, banks have a much wider range of assets than simple loans to the private sector to match their liabilities. They lend to government, they also acquire securities and hold a wide variety of derivatives.[9] Figure 4.1a shows this range for UK banks in 2008. This wider range exposes the banks to further risks of asset failure and consequential difficulty in managing their liabilities, especially to their customers. This is exactly what has happened from 2007.

Regulation of banks

As a result of these various risks, which are potentially damaging to the whole financial and economic system, banks are regulated by central banks which, in their turn, are regulated by the Bank of International Settlements (BIS). Central banks will set upper limits on the reserve ratio. In practice, they also require joint stock banks to meet rules on *Tier 1 capital*.[10] Banking regulators also subject

---

[9] In simple terms a derivative is an asset that derives its value from a claim on an underlying asset. The underlying value on which a derivative is based can be an asset such as a residential property or indexes like stock market indices. *Credit derivatives* are based on loans and other forms of credit.

[10] Tier 1 capital is the highest form of capital of the bank and is regarded by the Financial Services Authority (FSA) as broadly equivalent to equity. This means it must be capable of absorbing losses so that the bank can continue trading even if it makes losses up to the value of that capital. The majority of this capital is made up of:

- fully paid-up ordinary shares,
- perpetual non-cumulative preference shares,
- retained earnings (profits taken to reserves after payment of dividends and tax).

The capital must be permanent, which means it is undated. The capital must be fully paid so that the bank has the funds. There are further requirements designed to ensure that the holder of the instrument can't take priority over the depositors of the bank. For example, dividends must be discretionary, so that they cannot be paid in the absence of distributable profits. This capital is known as core Tier 1 capital.

commercial banks to *stress tests*. As a result, in May 2009 US regulators directed several large commercial banks to add $75bn in capital to enhance their ability to withstand further macroeconomic pressures.

From a macroeconomic policy perspective, central banks want to control the money supply and the availability of credit. If the economy is in a recession they will want to increase the availability of credit and in a boom period they will want to reduce the money supply. One way this can be done is by imposing a required reserve ratio and increasing it when credit restriction is needed and reducing it when credit expansion is deemed to be necessary. This adjustment in the required reserve ratio changes the size of the money multiplier. In practice, this is not an instrument favoured by central bankers, who prefer alternative ways of changing the size of the monetary base, which is the sum of currency in the hands of the private non-bank sector plus the reserves of the banks which are kept in accounts held at the central bank which is the 'bankers' bank'. One widely used mechanism is open market operations in which the bank buys (sells) various forms of government debt, including bonds (government debt) and 'repos' or other forms of short-term government debt (bills). Repos are repurchase agreements by which the sale of *government debt* is tied to an agreement to buy the securities back later. These deals are, effectively, short-term loans to the government with an effective interest rate which is called the *repo rate*. When the central bank sells government debt the purchaser pays with money which reduces the monetary base and restricts the money supply. If it buys existing government debt the central bank pays with money (a cheque drawn on the bank) and the monetary base increases and the money supply expands. This will also impact on the long-run rate of interest in the economy. This is explored in Section 4.3.

The central bank can also change the monetary base and the money supply by altering the base rate (also called the *official* rate or the *discount rate*). In general, there is usually a shortage of cash in the market each day. The central bank supplies the cash to the banking system and charges it the base rate. If the base rate is lowered, banks are inclined to borrow more, which increases their reserves, expands the monetary base and enables an increase in the money supply. This also affects interest rates in the wider economy.

It is important to note that the central bank cannot and does not fix the money supply on a daily basis. It has substantial influence, but it is sometimes constrained by the behaviour of the commercial banks. For example, in times of financial turmoil and crisis (like 2008/9) commercial banks are inclined to become cautious and raise their reserve ratios above the minimum level in order to ensure they can satisfy the cash needs of their customers. This reduces the size of the money multiplier and, hence, the money supply to levels below the policy targets set by the central bank. The commercial banks may also reduce their borrowing from the central bank even when the base rate is very low. This also reduces the money multiplier, the money supply and the availability of credit to the non-bank sector of the economy. This credit-restricting behaviour helps to drive down spending and GDP despite the best efforts of the monetary authorities.

Chapter 5

Competitive strategy: the analysis of strategic position

Introduction

Chapter 3 set out the essence of strategy as the denial of perfect competition and the search for firm-specific advantages that we call competitive advantage. There we developed the economic concepts that underpin the operation of markets and the analysis of industry structure. These concepts give us the frameworks and the language for analysing markets and costs. Chapter 4 sets out the large-scale macro forces that can shape the fortunes of firms. In this chapter we set out the basic framework of **competitive strategy** itself and how it enables us to analyse the *market positioning view*, which is, as its name suggests, the **positioning** of the firm in its markets versus competitors. The central pillar of this is *competitive advantage*. Chapter 6 presents the *resource-based view*. This focuses on the distinctive nature of the resources and capabilities that are required to produce competitive advantage. The central pillar of this is *core competence*. Chapter 7 considers how new technologies have impacted the way we think about our now traditional ideas of competitive advantage.

This chapter takes the ideas of cost advantage and **differentiation** advantage beyond the introduction given in Chapter 3 to offer a description of the internal logic of competitive strategy.

This internal logic looks at the overall disposition of assets within the firm and their relation to competitive advantage and to financial performance. Essentially there are two important lags within the internal economy. The first and best known is the way in which financial performance comes after competitive advantage. Thus company accounts show a history and not the present or even the recent present. But the more endemic and powerful lag in the system is the gap between the creation of critical assets (core competences – the subject of Chapter 6) and the achievement of competitive advantage. The other element in the internal logic is the pattern of investment and cost behaviour. This is captured in the idea of the value chain, another Porterian concept but one which has not been as fully appreciated as the idea of competitive advantage. The internal logic of strategy concerns the way in which the pattern of investments and costs leads to competitive advantage.

This chapter then goes on to look at two powerful grouping concepts – market segments and strategic groups. The former is well developed in marketing and is explored here for its basis for differentiation strategies and for pricing and value capture. Strategic groups capture the idea of industries within industries and are useful in trying to understand complex industry structures. But they are also valuable in looking ahead to ways in which industries might evolve. Industry transformation looks at bigger, more revolutionary changes in structure. We then go on to ask some questions about how in practice you can assess strategy and evaluate its success. Finally we look at business models. This phrase has become current since the advent of the internet and was used there to show how the internet creates new rules and new ways of making profits – hence the ideas of new business models.

All of the ideas in Chapters 3 and 5 contribute to the way in which the firm positions itself in markets to gain competitive advantage. The concepts and frameworks can be deceptively simple, even generic. But the applications require care with data and with interpretation. Above all, application requires a strong grasp of what are the competitive strategy concepts and how to think through their implications. This chapter should be powerful in helping you turn concepts and frameworks into tools for strategic thinking.

5.1 Describing strategy

We are now in a position to set out the key headings under which we can describe an organization's strategy. The basic paradigm is set out in the strategy map developed in Chapter 2 and is further developed in Figure 5.1.

Step 1 requires a description of the underlying mission of the organization and the objectives (including financial performance) that it wants to achieve over a defined time horizon. This includes coverage of mission and vision statements, the notion of strategic intent, and an assessment of stakeholders and shareholders (as discussed in Chapter 2).

Step 2 describes the **scope** of the organization – in which product-markets does it choose to compete? Firms obviously cannot compete in any and every market. They must make some choices.

1 A clear set of long-term goals
   'Where are we going?'

2 The scope of the business
   'What are we going to do?'

3 Competitive advantage
   'How are we going to do it?'

4 The strategic logic
   'How do we know it will work?'

Figure 5.1 Describing strategy

However, the logic for making choices is not obvious in itself. Firms might choose to compete in closely related markets where, for example, the technologies and production methods are similar, where distribution channels are common, or where there are common customers for a range of products. But such 'relatedness' or 'synergy' can be difficult to define or achieve and some firms have preferred to adopt more conglomerate-style approaches where the chosen businesses are apparently very diverse. (See, for example, Hanson plc and Tomkins in the UK.) Another facet of scope is geographic markets. Should one restrict the focus to the home market? Or are there arguments for adopting a more multinational posture? Ansoff's (1965) famous diversification matrix shows the different types of diversification. The grounds for making diversification (that is, scope) decisions are treated more formally in Chapter 8 on corporate strategy, in which business portfolio choices are analysed.

Step 3 articulates the benefits that the firm can bring to its customers and to itself by its positioning within its chosen product-markets. Why should the customer buy this product? Why should he or she buy from us? What value can we gain from making this proposition to the customer? These are all ways of describing the nature of the competitive advantage that the firm can achieve.

Our definition of competitive advantage is:

Delivering superior value to customers and in doing so earning an above-average return for the company and its stakeholders.

This has implications for positioning choices in product-markets. This takes us into Step 4, the strategic logic behind competitive advantage. This has two parts. The first is the positioning logic – the market-based logic which underpins our competitive advantage ambitions. The second part is the resource-based logic that states why we think our intentions and actions about resources and capabilities will lead to the products and services that can be positioned in markets in the desired way – see Figures 5.2 and 5.3.

Listing the sources of advantage in this way gives us one way of focusing on the resources and capabilities that are needed. In this language we use resources to refer to tangible assets, and capabilities to refer to intangibles such as knowledge, organization, and management skills. More recently there has been much attention paid to the notion of '*core competence*' – an amalgam of the languages of resources and capabilities. We define core competence as the underlying capability that is the distinguishing characteristic of the organization. We explore these ideas further in Chapter 6. Putting together the market-based logic of positioning and the resource-based logic we should be able to make a simple statement of the underlying strategic logic – see Figure 5.4 for an example.

- Statement of competitive intent.

- The outward evidence of competitive advantage.

- Combination of:
  - superior delivered cost position
  - differentiation advantage
  - protected niches.

- Differences in positional advantage cannot be exploited profitably unless they can be seen to provide *direct benefits* which:
  - are perceived by a sizeable customer group
  - their customers value and are willing to pay for
  - cannot be readily obtained elsewhere both now and in the foreseeable future.

Figure 5.2 Positional advantage

Resources	Capabilities
Distribution coverage	Specialized knowledge
Financial capacity	Customer service orientation
Shared expertise with related businesses	Design expertise
Low cost manufacturing and distribution	Application experience
Production capacity	Trade relations
Ownership of raw material sources	Technology application expertise
Long-term supply contracts	Systems design capability
	Fast, flexible response capability

Figure 5.3 Resources and capabilities as sources of advantage

'Our strategy is to dominate the UK market for inexpensive widgets by being the low-priced manufacturer selling through mass market channels. Our low price in these channels will generate high volume and, because there are economies of scale in the production of widgets, will make us the low-cost producer enabling us to achieve favourable margins even with a low price.'

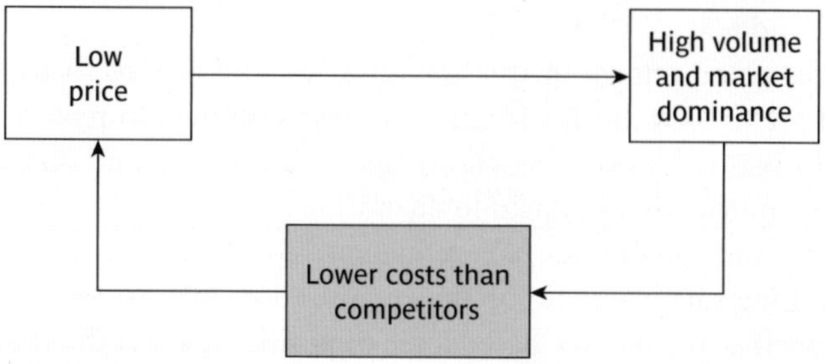

Figure 5.4 A simple strategic logic

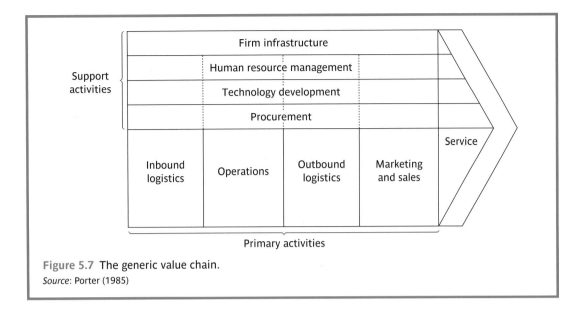

Figure 5.7 The generic value chain.
Source: Porter (1985)

firm has its own *value chain*, a sub-set of the supply chain. Figure 5.7 is Porter's classic picture of the value chain. It has two parts. The lower part contains those activities (labelled primary activities) that are organized in sequence just like a production line. Thus, inbound logistics is the first step, leading to manufacturing operations, then outbound logistics, marketing and sales, and eventually service. This is a caricature of each firm's value chain and will contain different headings according to the nature of the operations. These categories can be described as follows:

- *Inbound logistics.* Activities associated with receiving, storing, and disseminating rights to the product, such as material handling, warehousing, stock management, and the like.
- *Operations.* All of the activities required to transform inputs into outputs and the critical functions which add value, such as machining, packaging, assembly, service, testing, and the like.
- *Outbound logistics.* All of the activities required to collect, store, and physically distribute the output. This activity can prove to be extremely important both in generating value and in improving differentiation, as in many industries control over distribution strategies is proving to be a major source of competitive advantage – especially as it is realized that up to 50% of the value created in many industry chains occurs close to the ultimate buyer.
- *Marketing and sales.* Activities associated with informing potential buyers about the firm's products and services, and inducing them to do so by personal selling, advertising and promotion, and the like.
- *Service.* The means of enhancing the physical product features through after-sales service, installation, repair, and the like.

The second part of the value chain is the upper section which contains all the overhead service elements (labelled support activities) required by the firm. In Porter's picture he named four elements, firm infrastructure, human resource management, technology development, and procurement:

1 *Procurement.* This concerns the acquisition of inputs or resources. Although technically this is the responsibility of the purchasing department, almost everyone in the firm is responsible for purchasing something. While the cost of procurement itself is relatively low, the impact can be very high.

2 *Human resource management.* This consists of all activities involved in recruiting, hiring, train-ing, developing, rewarding, and sanctioning the people in the organization.

3 *Technology development.* This is concerned with the equipment, hardware, software, technical skills, and the like used by the firm in transforming inputs to outputs. Some such skills can be classified as scientific, while others – such as food preparation in a restaurant – are 'artistic'. Such skills are not always recognized. They may also support limited activities of the business, such as accounting, order procurement, and the like, and in this sense may be likened to the value added component of the experience effect (see Section 5.5).

4 *Firm infrastructure.* This consists of the many activities, including general management, plan-ning, finance, legal, external affairs, and the like, which support the operational aspect of the value chain. This may be self-contained in the case of an undiversified firm or divided between the parent and the firm's constituent business units.

Within each category of primary and support activities, Porter identifies three types of activity which play different roles in achieving competitive advantage:

1 *Direct.* These are activities directly involved in creating value for buyers, such as assembly, sales, and advertising.

2 *Indirect.* These are activities that facilitate the performance of the direct activities on a continu-ing basis, such as maintenance, scheduling, and administration.

3 *Quality assurance.* These are activities that ensure the quality of other activities, such as monitor-ing, inspecting, testing, and checking.

The value chain is another generic framework that permits a range of applications and analyses. It permits the analyst to divide the firm's activities into broad categories (as above) and increasingly into more specific categories. Thus operations might be refined into sub-components and assembly: marketing and sales into market research, product development, sales force and so on. The usefulness of this is to be able to identify those activities that are the source of the competitive advantage and to be able to locate them within the value chain. For example, if Intel's competitive advantage is product performance and this is derived (at least in large part) from R&D activities, then this can be isolated within the value chain and measured, compared to competitors, and provided with support.

Competitive advantage is often quite subtle in its manifestation and in its sources. Cost advan-tage might arise from the way in which every single activity in the value chain is linked to the others and managed for efficiency. The story of the low-cost airlines such as easyJet, Ryanair and Southwest Airlines is about system management of the costs as well as focus on driving down each cost com-ponent. Differentiation may be delivered as a service quality perception driven by the way in which each element of service delivery is managed systematically along with all other elements in order to differentiate the product. One of the case studies at the end of the chapter illustrates this for the hotel chain Novotel.

The Novotel example shows how the value chain can be a powerful tool in diagnosing and explain-ing how the management of competitive advantage takes place within the firm. The interrelation-ships between the elements of the value chain provide an important explanation of the nature of competitive advantage in large, complex organizations. Such organizations typically are rich in tacit knowledge. This is the kind of knowledge that you call upon to describe how you ride a bicycle. We all know how to do this – but it is impossible to explain it. Similarly, large corporations are used to making links between complex and far-flung activities, and between related and unrelated technologies. This 'glue' binds these companies together and makes it impossible for others to imitate quickly. The 'hidden' part of the value chain is these linkages that contain the tacit knowledge. In the Novotel example we can see how the authors use Novotel's own management processes to describe how the elements of the chain are linked together. The way this 'glue' works determines the level of vertical integration, i.e. those elements of the supply chain that can be brought within the value chain and within the firm, and those that should remain outside the firm. The guiding principle is that when the costs of internal transactions (making the glue work properly) exceed the costs of buying outside, then the firm should source outside its boundaries. This glue is part of the core competence that we will be discussing in Chapter 6. We turn now to the issues of cost analysis and outsourcing.

5.2.3 The value chain and cost analysis

The value chain provides a good basis on which to conduct a cost analysis. Its principal advantage is that the elements of the value chain are already organized around those issues that are important in driving competitive advantage and profitability. Porter was therefore able in his 1985 book to make very strong links with the array of literature and practice on cost cutting that was already available. A criticism of the cost analysis literature was the difficulty of defining the correct units of analysis, an issue which the value chain solved brilliantly.

Therefore a normal cost analysis procedure can take place with the following stages.[2]

1 Define the value chain in terms of those elements that relate to the sources of competitive advantage. Key considerations are:
   - the separateness and independence of one activity from another;
   - the importance of an activity in relation to competitive advantage and to the margin;
   - the dissimilarity of activities in terms of requiring different cost drivers;
   - the extent to which there are differences in the way competitors perform activities (i.e. where there are differences there are potential advantages to be gained).

2 Establish the relative importance of different activities in the total cost of the product. This means assigning costs to each activity based on management accounts or other customized analysis procedures. The distinctions made earlier about fixed and variable costs, sunk costs and cost allocations are really significant issues at this stage. Errors in cost analysis can lead to significant misunderstanding of what contributes to profits and how valuable is a competitive advantage.

3 Compare costs by activity and benchmark against competitors. The comparison is not in terms of how big are the costs but how different are they from efficiency benchmarks and from competitor standards.

4 Identify cost drivers. These are the forces that move costs up or down. Planned scale of activities is a driver of overall plant cost and so also is degree of capacity utilisation. A driver of sales force costs might be product range – if the range is too small costs will be high. Another driver will be geographical concentration of customers and another might be sales communication methods (face to face or remote teleconferencing). For labour-intensive activities critical drivers might be wage rates, speed of production line, and defect rates. It is the understanding of cost drivers that signifies how well you understand the nature of your business. One needs to look behind the obvious in order to identify the fundamentals.

---

[2] This section draws on Grant (2002, Ch. 7).

5 Identify linkages between activities. As we see from the Novotel example, interrelationships may be very many in number – the critical cost drivers may seemingly relate to another activity entirely. We will see in later chapters a comparison between Xerox and Canon in the photocopying industry. Xerox found that its service costs were driven by design complexity and manufacturing inefficiencies. Grant observes that:

> . . . the optimisation of activities through the value chain has become a major source of cost reduction, and speed enhancement has become a key challenge for computer integrated manufacturing. (Grant, 2002, p. 271)

6 Identify opportunities for reducing costs. By identifying areas of obvious inefficiency (i.e. deviations from designed machine performance standards) and of deficiencies against competitive benchmarks, opportunities for cost reduction become evident. Very often the option is posed of contracting outside the firm for components or services. Some firms have subcontracted entire IT departments. Currently European firms are outsourcing their call centres to India. The automobile companies are going through an extensive process of outsourcing. The Ford Fiesta plants in Cologne outsource fully made-up doors (as a subsystem) to plants adjacent to the Ford plant.

5.2.4 Identifying the value chain[3]

The value chain concept thus helps to identify cost behaviour in detail. From this analysis, different strategic courses of action should be identifiable in order to develop differentiation and less price-sensitive strategies. Competitive advantage is then achieved by performing strategic activities better or cheaper than competitors.

To diagnose competitive advantage, it is necessary to define the firm's value chain for operating in a particular industry and compare this with those of key competitors. A comparison of the value chains of different competitors often identifies ways of achieving strategic advantage by reconfiguring the value chain of the individual firm. In assigning costs and assets it is important that the analysis be done strategically rather than seeking accounting precision. This should be accomplished using the following principles:

- Operating costs should be assigned to activities where incurred.
- Assets should be assigned to activities where employed, controlled, or influencing usage.
- Accounting systems should be adjusted to fit value analysis.
- Asset valuation may be difficult, but should recognise industry norms – particular care should be taken in evaluating property assets.

The reconfiguration of the value chain has often been used by successful competitors in achieving competitive advantage. When seeking to reconfigure the value chain in an industry, the following questions need to be asked:

- How can an activity be done differently or even eliminated?
- How can linked value activities be reordered or regrouped?
- How could coalitions with other firms reduce or eliminate costs?

---

[3] See Channon (2005).

Case box 5.1 continues with our retailing theme from Chapter 3 and describes the latest strategy to hit the UK retailing scene – the emergence of the volume discounters. You should ask yourself how different is this strategy from that of Tesco and ASDA, what kind of competitive advantage it seeks, and what risks are being taken. Finally, what are the chances of taking a significant market share from Tesco?

Case box 5.1: **The Germans are coming**

Germany's 'hard discount' model of supermarket retailing is spreading in Europe

It is as far from the charming ideal of French farmers' markets and small family-owned shops as you could imagine: strip lights glare down on a narrow range of products in ugly packaging, displayed in cardboard boxes piled on the floor and on low shelves. But sales are booming at the new Lidl discount supermarket in south-west Paris. Previously, the German chain stuck to the suburbs, where poorer folk live, says Fatouh Mourad, the store's manager. But rising food prices and widespread concern about 'pouvoir d'achat', or purchasing power, in France, have given Lidl the confidence to push inside the city's limits.

As economic prospects worsen across Europe, discounters such as Lidl – and Aldi, another German chain – are taking market share. They generally charge some 30–50% less for groceries than ordinary supermarkets. In France, according to TNS, a research firm, discounters increased their market share to 11.2% in the second quarter of this year, up from 10.5% a year ago, whereas the share fell at Carrefour, the world's second-largest retailer. In Belgium a local discounter, Colruyt, is gaining share at the expense of Carrefour and other pricier chains. Dutch shoppers too are trading down to discounters, says TNS, and in Britain, where Aldi and Lidl struggled for years, they are now the fastest-growing grocers.

Discounters affect prices well beyond their own stores. 'There's a massive global price-war in food retailing, much of it provoked by the gains by Aldi and Lidl and other discounters,' says James Amoroso, a food-industry consultant. Tesco, the world's fourth-biggest retailer, is fighting an all-out price war against Lidl in Ireland, and Belgium's Delhaize recently slashed prices in response to discounters. Carrefour, too, is under pressure to cut prices.

But can the discounters hold on to their gains? Tesco's finance director recently suggested that they were merely having a 'moment in the sun'. He was quickly contradicted by the head of buying for Aldi in Britain, who pledged to open a store a week and win a tenth of the market (it has 2.9% now). In Germany, the heartland of discounting, cut-price operators have some 30% of the market[4] . . . and shopping at Aldi and Lidl is the norm for rich and poor alike. The two firms doubtless reckon they have a shot at replicating that position elsewhere.

They may well succeed, at least in some markets. 'It's the best business model for retail in the world,' says Philippe Suchet of Exane BNP Paribas in Paris. Discounters stock a fraction of the goods that a normal supermarket offers, resulting in fewer suppliers, a high volume of purchases and sales, and massive economies of scale. 'You would find 16 brands of tomato ketchup in a normal big supermarket,' says Paul Foley, managing director of Aldi in Britain. 'In my store you will find a choice of one.' Discounters mostly sell their own private-label goods, which are more profitable than branded goods, where the brand owner takes a big cut, and also more efficient – having bar codes in exactly the same place on every product, for instance, says Mr Foley, means faster checkouts.

Aldi and Lidl, which dominate the world of discounting, have annual sales estimated at €43 billion ($64 billion) and €35 billion respectively, compared with €102 billion for Carrefour. They are privately owned and can take a long-term approach to expanding abroad. New stores cost little to open and generate rapid sales, says Jürgen Elfers, retail analyst at Commerzbank in Frankfurt, so the discounters can expand during hard times more rapidly than any other kind of retailer.

---

[4] According to Planet Retail.

The two firms are intensely secretive and say little about their expansion plans, but new stores are opening all the time. They are expected to expand quickly in France now that a law designed to keep discounters out has been changed. Lidl is poised to go into Switzerland, and in a rare interview last year its chief executive said it wanted to tackle America – Aldi is already present in both markets.

Lidl recently caused a fuss in Dublin, when it bid for a site on fashionable Grafton Street: critics complained it would lower the tone. But Lidl may not be so out of place, since middle-class people are changing their shopping habits to buy at least basic items at hard-discount stores. Five years ago in Britain, says Mr Foley, a quarter of his customers were well-off shoppers; now half of them are. Economic worries are part of the reason for that, of course, but Aldi appeals to middle-class shoppers because it manages to produce goods of surprisingly high quality at a low price.

What should perhaps worry conventional supermarkets most, in fact, is that the discounters have proven themselves adept at moving upmarket, even as they retain most of their efficiencies. In many markets, for instance, Lidl now stocks a limited range of branded goods alongside its cheaper own-label items. In Britain Aldi used to be known for tinned and packaged foods, but has introduced fresh and delicatessen products. In Germany Lidl even tried to buy a chain of organic supermarkets until an outcry scared it off. But there is a limit to the range of products discounters can stock while maintaining the efficiency of their model, cautions Mr Amoroso.

In recent years the German discount model has experienced only one big setback. In March Lidl pulled out of Norway after four years of trying to establish itself. Rema 1000, a local discounter, will take over Lidl's stores there. Executives at the posher kind of supermarket must be longing to know how the Norwegians did it.

Source: 'The Germans Are Coming', *The Economist*, 16 August 2008

5.3 Strategic market segments

In Chapter 3 we saw that the basis for market segmentation lies in the existence of different responses to price (and other marketing variables) by individuals or groups of individuals. Earlier in this chapter we saw how differentiation activities are intimately related to the existence of market segments. One of the most creative endeavours in strategy making has been the seeking out of new markets or market niches to which customized products can be directed. In general we can see that a market can be divided into strategic segments based on product range and on associated price differentials. Figure 5.8 illustrates the general case.

Customers are faced by an *offer curve* that summarizes the range of options open to them. This shows what groups of customers exist for each combination of product performance and price. Thus group A is content with a low product specification and a correspondingly low price. Group B is a larger segment where both the product specification and price are higher. Group C is higher still on both counts, the premium market. Given this offer curve, firms would be unwilling, in general, to offer a product at point X for two reasons. First, it does not fall into any of the established segments A, B or C. Secondly, it falls above the offer curve, meaning that for that level of product performance it is overpriced. Another way of putting it is to say that at that price the product is under-specified. The shape of the offer curve depends on customer price sensitivities – how much are they prepared to pay for extra product performance? It also depends on the cost characteristics of the product. Thus, the premium product may require different product development routines, and specialized attention in production and marketing. The existence of only a small market for the premium product is likely, due to the high costs involved and the level of the minimum price that has to be charged in order to make a profit. Innovation in the market can take place by transforming

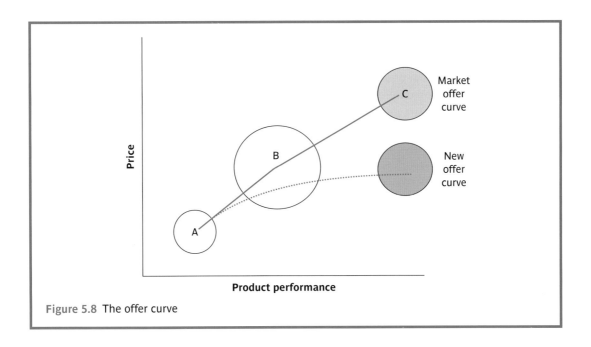

Figure 5.8 The offer curve

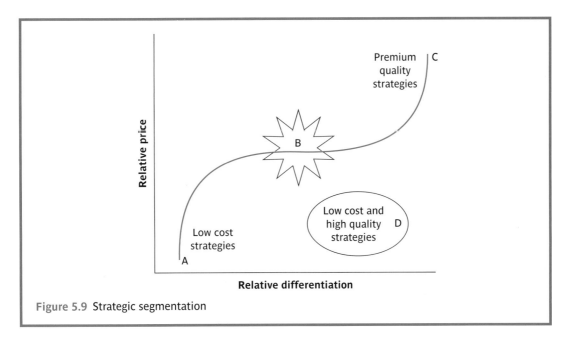

Figure 5.9 Strategic segmentation

the offer curve as shown in Figure 5.8. The innovation, for example, could be due to cost reductions in product development and manufacturing so that lower prices can be charged. A good example is the way the Lexus intruded on the premium car market in Europe and in the US by creating its own version of a premium offer at lower prices than Mercedes. The unfair advantage was the application of the Toyota production system to the Lexus (which is Toyota's premium brand), giving Toyota considerable cost advantage over Mercedes.

Another way of looking at strategic segmentation is to compare price and differentiation patterns across a market (see Figure 5.9). This figure suggests a pattern of locations along which the price differentiation trade-off takes place. Starting from point A you can charge relatively higher prices for modest increases in differentiation. This, however, flattens out so that a plateau is achieved around point B where the price is relatively stable whatever the level of differentiation. This implies a stable price point at which product changes make little difference. Eventually the plateau is broken because differentiation differences are so large as to be able to command higher prices. In this example point C represents a journey through progressively steep trade-offs where customers are prepared to pay disproportionately high prices for modest changes in differentiation. This locus of trade-offs enables us to locate different market positioning strategies. Around point A but below the curve we could see low-cost strategies being deployed. Around point C but above the curve we could see premium quality strategies. Below the curve and to the right of the mass market located at B we could see a combination of low-cost and high-quality strategies in region D. Although strategies around A, B and C are stable and consistent in relation to each other, the offerings in D have the potential to destabilize the market.

5.3.1 Identifying segmentation variables

The bases for segmentation have always been a major issue for companies. The conventional approach is to look at the characteristics of buyers and the characteristics of products as in Figure 5.10. This is a very well-known approach and is probably more useful for identifying existing patterns of segmentation than for discovering new and untested segments. Figure 5.10 should remind you of the earlier section on differentiation because the drivers are very much the same in each case. This is to be expected, but what is difficult to do is to develop new bases for segmentation and differentiation. The better known the segmentation pattern, the more all competitors following the

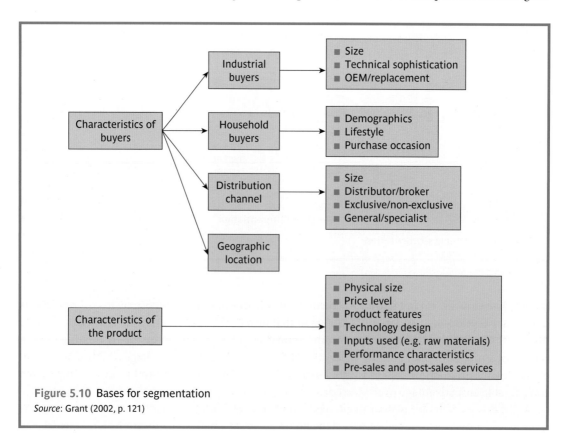

Figure 5.10 Bases for segmentation
Source: Grant (2002, p. 121)

same logic are likely to end up with the same kinds of strategies. By definition these will cancel out and competitive advantage will be elusive.

The analysis of strategic segments leads towards the firm's choice of pricing strategy. In assessing pricing options the firm is essentially concentrating on issues of *value* – how to price in order to gain value to the firm while still delivering value to the customer. The next section addresses this.

5.3.2 Value creation and value analysis

The concept of value is central to economics and to the understanding of competitive advantage. The theory of value in economics deals with the determination of final market prices (as opposed to factor prices which are determined by the theory of distribution).

Perceived benefit and consumer surplus

If you buy a car for $15,000 but it is worth $20,000 to you in terms of the services it renders, then you are better off by $5,000. This is known as *consumer surplus*. Given a choice of cars with identical service values you would (rationally) buy the cheaper car – this would save you money and increase your consumer surplus. The idea of consumer surplus is a profit idea – it is the 'profit' that the consumer makes from a purchase. If the 'consumer' was a firm buying a machine for $15,000 but as a result lowering its costs by $20,000 the value created by the purchase (i.e. the profit) is $5,000.

In tabular form:

    Perceived gross benefit
       less   user costs
       less   transactions costs
  = Perceived net benefit
       less   price paid
  − Consumer Surplus

Value maps

The idea of competitive advantage is that a firm must deliver consumer surplus to compete successfully. **Value maps** illustrate the competitive implications of consumer surplus analysis. The vertical axis shows the price of the product and the horizontal axis shows quality or performance characteristics of the product. Each point corresponds to a particular price–quality combination. At any point in time the series of price–quality combinations available to consumers is shown by an upward-sloping schedule, an indifference curve. The slope shows the trade-off between price and quality; the steeper the slope the higher the extra price to be paid for increased quality. This is an 'indifference' curve because at each point on the curve the consumer surplus is the same. Above the curve is lower consumer surplus, because prices are higher. Below the curve is higher consumer surplus, because prices are lower. Without any innovations in product or process, any firm wishing to price below the indifference curve to gain volume will do so at the expense of profit. Genuine innovation might enable a competitor to make a different 'offer' in the form of a new indifference curve below the original one. This will offer higher consumer surplus, divert volume towards the new competitor and take volume and profit away from the non-innovating competitor.

This is illustrated in Figure 5.11 by the luxury car market in the US (the example is taken from Besanko et al., 2000). When the Japanese luxury automobiles, Lexus, Infiniti and Acura, were introduced in the late 1980s they offered comparable quality to Mercedes but at lower prices. Not surprisingly, they gained market share. Eventually the Japanese firms increased prices and Mercedes lowered price, converging on a new and lower indifference curve. Overall the consumer

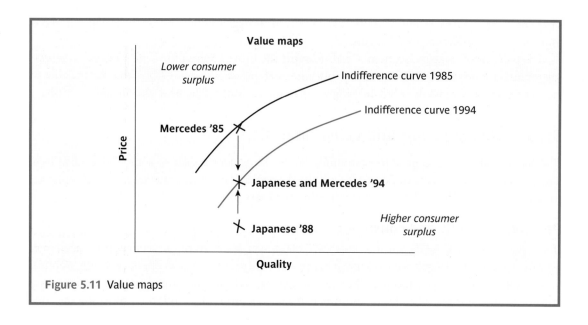

Figure 5.11 Value maps

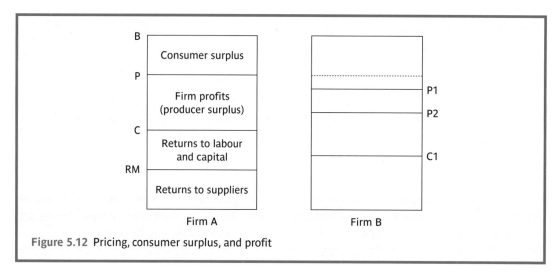

Figure 5.12 Pricing, consumer surplus, and profit

gained – consumer surplus increased. The suppliers would have benefited if their costs had fallen by at least an equivalent amount.

Value creation and pricing

As goods move along the supply chain and into and along the firm's value chain, economic value is created. Firm A in Figure 5.12 illustrates the different **value creation** packages:

■ Consumer Surplus is benefit less price paid: B – P

■ Firm profit (or producer surplus) is price paid by the consumer less costs: P – C

■ Total Value created is consumer surplus and firm profit: B – C

■ Value added (as measured in the national accounts and used as a measure of output of the economy) is technically firm profit less costs of raw materials: P – RM

Table 5.1 Pricing, advantage, and profits		
	Cost advantage	**Differentiation advantage**
High price elasticity	SHARE STRATEGY Under-price competitors to gain share	SHARE STRATEGY Maintain price parity and let differentiation gain share
Low price elasticity	MARGIN STRATEGY Maintain price parity and gain profits through high margins	MARGIN STRATEGY Charge price premium relative to competitors

The firm's pricing decision can be seen as critical in partitioning Total Value between consumers and firms. A high price claims more for the firm, giving less to the consumer and thus running the risk that Firm B, for example, might opt for lower prices and attract volume away from Firm A. With similar costs competitive forces will move the market towards a common price level P. However, if Firm A is innovative and reduces costs to C1, then it has the option of various prices below P such as P1 or P2. The choice of price depends on the price elasticity of demand.

Pricing, price elasticity, costs and profits

Table 5.1 illustrates the interactions between price elasticity for the firm (not the market) and type of advantage – differentiation (benefit) or cost. The four boxes tell different stories:

- With a cost advantage and high price elasticity it pays to under-price competitors to gain share.
- With a differentiation (benefit) advantage and high price elasticity it pays to maintain price parity and let the differentiation advantage increase volume and thereby pull profits through.
- With cost advantage and low price elasticity the best option is a margin strategy whereby prices are maintained and profits are increased through the margin benefit.
- With a differentiation (benefit) advantage and low price elasticity a margin strategy is again indicated where prices can be substantially raised because of the low elasticity and high benefits – profits accrue through increased margins with only small volume offsets.

In setting prices the task is to create a competitive advantage by (i) creating unique value to consumers (best possible consumer surplus) and (ii) creating above-average profits for the firm. If every firm was like Firm A in Figure 5.12 there would be no competitive advantage. If one firm can innovate and create lower costs like Firm B or higher benefits then a competitive advantage is possible for a range of possible prices depending on the price elasticities of demand and the type and scale of advantage available to the innovating firm. In this situation Firm B would wish to identify the *break-even price elasticity*, that elasticity that would enable it to identify the borderline between a share strategy and a margin strategy.

5.4 Strategic groups

In the same way that there are segments on the demand side, there are groups on the supply side. We call these *strategic groups*. From Figure 3.18 in Chapter 3 you can see that we arrayed differentiation characteristics against cost characteristics to show how the forces of industry dynamics operated to create maps of different locations for firms within an industry. In this figure we looked at the consequences for profits for firms in different locations. The dimensions of this figure (or matrix) are strategic choices and thus difficult to change and difficult to imitate. Strategic groups are configurations of this kind. They represent substructures within an industry that enable us to identify groups of firms with similar strategies. Figures 5.13–5.16 (see below) map changes in the strategic groups in the European food processing industry over a 20-year period.

The definition of a strategic group is:

> *A firm within a group makes strategic decisions that cannot readily be imitated by firms outside the group without substantial costs, significant elapsed time, or uncertainty about the outcome of those decisions.* (McGee and Thomas, 1986, p. 150)

The dimensions of the matrix are key strategic decisions faced by firms in this industry, namely geographical coverage of the EC (representing internationalization strategy) and marketing intensity (representing brand focus). The map is good at distinguishing different kinds of brand players, national versus European in scope, and cost-based own-label suppliers.

Strategic groups maps are based on the notion of mobility barriers (Table 5.2):

> *Mobility barriers are a corollary to the existence of strategic groups. They are factors which deter or inhibit the movement of a firm from one strategic position to another and, more generally, the expansion of firms in one group to a position held by another group. Therefore a mobility barrier is essentially a limitation on replicability or imitation. It acts like an entry barrier, but it acts for the group within the industry rather than for the industry as a whole.*
>
> *A group structuring carries no meaning without costs attached to the imitation of strategy by other firms. Mobility barriers thus reflect the decisions of firms and are a way of defining the set of key strategies available to a firm. The essential characteristic is relative cost advantage over all other competitors. The remedy for cost disadvantage of this kind probably involves investment expenditure on tangible or intangible assets with significant elapsed time before the investment comes to fruition. Moreover, the investment expenditures are irreversible . . . and there will typically be considerable uncertainty attached to the outcome of the investment expenditures.* (McGee and Thomas, 1986, p. 153)

Table 5.2 Sources of mobility barriers

Market-related strategies	Supply and cost characteristics	Characteristics of firms
Product line	Economies of scale: production, marketing, administration	Ownership
User technologies	Manufacturing processes	Organization structure
Market segmentation	R&D capability	Control systems
Distribution channels	Marketing and distribution systems	Management skills
Brand names		Boundaries of firms: diversification, vertical integration
Geographic coverage		Firm size
Selling systems		Relationships with influence groups

Source: McGee and Thomas (1986, p. 151)

5.4.1 The implications of strategic groups

Groups may exist for many different reasons. Investments in distinctive assets and therefore in competitive advantage are risky investments and firms may have quite different risk-aversion postures. Thus strategic positions, which are the outcome of patterns of decisions over time, can be seen in terms of return–risk trade-offs calculated ex ante. Corporate structure may also affect the nature of strategic groupings. Business units can vary considerably in their relationship with their corporate parents and may pursue different goal structures in ways that lead to strategy differences (see Sjostrom, 1995). More generally, the historical development of an industry bestows differential advantages on firms depending on their timing of entry (first-mover advantages versus follower advantages), geographical location (country-specific advantages), and sheer luck. Whatever the historical genesis of strategic groups, the essential characteristic is similarity along key strategic dimensions. The patterns of similarity and the extent of variety in an industry will have consequences along three dimensions:

1 the structure of the industry and its evolution over time,
2 the nature of **competition**, and
3 implications for relative performance of firms.

Industry structure analysis is intended to identify the nature and range of profit-earning possibilities for the participants. There are benchmark but simple models of perfect competition and monopoly (see Chapter 3). But the real interest lies in oligopolistic market structures within which different groups of firms may behave in systematically different ways protected (at least for a time) by their mobility barriers. Figure 3.18 (in Chapter 3) illustrates the variety of structural types. Where there are significant opportunities available for both cost and differentiation there will be firms or groups of firms with different strategies and differing expansion paths. This becomes more important as the concept of industry becomes more fluid as entry conditions change, as boundaries become flexible and as 'new' industry groupings are formed (e.g. new media industries, new electronic commerce industries). Industry definition is in itself a form of classification process. Strategic group analysis provides a more fundamental basis for assessing future strategic possibilities and the emergence of new industry boundaries.

Strategic groups affect the nature of competition. Because of their structural similarities, firms in the same group are likely to respond in the same way to disturbances from outside the group and to competitive activities within the group. Here we can see oligopolistic interdependence at work on the basis of ability to imitate the moves of rivals. The interdependence here does not arise from targeting the same customers (although this may be a consequence of similar strategies) but stems solely from the possession of structural similarities.

The ability to explain the relative performance of firms is a central theme in strategic management research. Wide variation in profitability is characteristic of many industries and means that industry structural characteristics are not likely to be a good or stable predictor of profitability. However, mobility barriers (i.e. strategy differences) can explain persistent differences in profit rates between groups in an industry. Porter (1979) argued that the pattern and intensity of inter-group competition and the consequences for profitability in the industry depend on three factors:

1 *The number and size distribution of groups.* Other things held constant, the more numerous and more equal in size are the strategic groups, the higher is **competitive rivalry**. On the other hand, if one strategic group constitutes a small portion of an industry while another is a very large portion, then strategic asymmetry is likely to have little impact on rivalry since the power of the small group to influence the large group is probably low.

2 *The strategic distance between groups.* This is the degree to which strategies in different groups differ in terms of the key strategic decision variables. The greater this distance, the more difficult tacit coordination becomes and the more vigorous rivalry will be in the industry.

3 *The market interdependence between groups.* Diversity of strategies increases rivalry between groups the most, where market interdependence is high. However, those strategic groups that possess high mobility barriers are relatively more insulated from rivalry. On the other hand, when strategic groups are targeting very different segments, their effect on each other is much less severe.

Profits may be differentially affected across strategic groups for other reasons:

1 There may be differences in *bargaining power* that some strategic groups may have towards customers and/or suppliers. These differences may be due to differences in scale, threat of vertical integration or product differentiation following from differing strategies.

2 There may be differences in the degree of exposure of strategic groups to *substitute products* produced by other industries.

3 There may be great differences in the degree to which firms *within* the group compete with each other. While mutual dependence should be fully recognized within groups that contain few firms, it may be difficult to sustain if there are numerous firms in the strategic group or if the risk profiles of the firms differ.

There are also firm-specific factors that influence profitability within a group:

1 *Differences in firms' scale within the strategic group.* Although firms within the same strategic groups are likely to be similar in the scales of their operations, differences in scale *may* exist and may work to the disadvantage of smaller firms in the group where there are aspects of the strategy subject to economies of scale.

2 *Differences in the cost of mobility into a strategic group.* If there are absolute cost advantages of being early in establishing brand names, locating raw materials, etc., a later entrant in a specific strategic group may face some disadvantages with respect to established firms. Timing is in this case a factor that may impact profit differences. This may also be the case if an established firm also possesses assets from its operations in other industries that could be jointly utilized.

3 *Ability of the firm to execute or implement its strategy* in an operational sense. Some firms may be superior in their ability to organize and manage operations, develop creative advertising themes, make technological breakthroughs with given inputs of resources and the like. While these are not structural advantages of the sort created by mobility barriers, they may be relatively stable advantages if the market for managers, scientists and creative personnel is imperfect. Those firms in a group with superior abilities to execute strategies will be more profitable than other firms in the same group.

5.4.2 Strategic mapping

It is convenient and conventional to turn the multidimensional concept of strategic groups into a practical tool by drawing *strategic maps*. These are two-dimensional replications of the larger group structure within which the important strategic dimensions can be seen and through which key opportunities and threats can be depicted. The key steps in this process are (following Fiegenbaum et al., 1990, and Fiegenbaum and Thomas, 1990):

1 choice of the strategy space (industry);

2 choice of organizational levels to be incorporated (corporate, business, or functional);

3 identification of the variables which best capture firms' strategies;

4 identification of stable time periods;

5 clustering of firms into strategic groups.

The main issue concerning choice of strategic space relates to the identification of the boundaries of the 'industry'. The concept of industry is fuzzy in concept but in practice we often over-rely on Standard Industrial Classification (SIC) codes. However, these mirror product variation and are typically bounded by nationality. The term strategic space is used as an alternative to industry to indicate that the relevant criterion for choice is competitive interaction.

When choosing the organizational level at which to analyse firms' strategies one must not simply focus on business-level characteristics such as product and geographical scope, and relative emphasis on cost versus differentiation. Corporate parenting can provide a significant element of the eventual competitive advantage and it would be an oversimplification to exclude corporate effects. Similarly, functional strategies such as advertising intensity and sales force characteristics can be critical investments in support of the business strategy.

On the identification of the variables representing firms' strategies it is common to argue that there are a small number of dimensions that capture the essence of strategy differences between firms and between groups. This suggests that it is entirely possible to adopt a pragmatic approach. Typically an in-depth case study can reflect the views of industry participants, can give peer group judgements on competitors' strategies, and can also give the analyst a database for independent judgement. The alternative is to use clustering and other statistical techniques to determine de facto what groups exist and then to interpret the groupings using independent data on strategy dimensions. This is typically the route taken by academic researchers.[5]

Much research in strategic management has studied industry change over long periods of time. This contrasts with research in economics where the emphasis has been much more on cross-section, relatively short-period studies. When studying strategic groups longitudinally there is a problem about identifying the nature of change and the way it affects the groupings. The typical approach is to think in terms of 'punctuated equilibria'. Periods of stability are punctuated by periods of change within which strategies are changed, new positions taken up, and rivalry adjusts in response. Firms' strategies and industry structure are seen in equilibrium during each strategic time period. When the equilibrium ends (maybe because of exogenous shocks in the environment or alternatively triggered by autonomous firm actions), some firms change their strategies, new strategic groups are formed and others disappear. Statistical techniques can be used to identify the relatively stable sub-periods within which strategic groups are identifiable (see Bogner et al., 1996) and the transition points or periods from one equilibrium position to the next.

---

[5] A number of different methods exist for clustering firms into groups. Analysis of empirical research indicates that most researchers use cluster analysis. Once strategic variables have been identified, researchers generally use clustering techniques to form groups so that homogeneity is at its maximum internally and at its minimum externally. There is considerable debate about the nature of cluster analysis; see Ketchen and Shook (1996) for a review of the way it has been used in strategy research. The advantage of cluster analysis is that it indicates the distance that exists between strategic groups and between companies within the same strategic group. The distance between groups can be considered as approximating the height of mobility barriers, while the distance between firms can be used as a basis to analyse the differences between them. The main difficulty with cluster analysis is that it identifies clusters regardless of the presence or absence of any underlying structure (Ketchen and Shook, op. cit.). Then there remains the question how to describe and empirically validate the dimensions that the analysis reveals.

5.4.3 Strategic groups in practice

We illustrate these points by looking at a study of the food processing industry in Europe at the time of the enactment of the European Single Market Act 1987–1992 (McGee and Segal-Horn, 1990, 1992). This looked across conventional market (national) boundaries and asked how the industry might evolve given the exogenous legislation shocks to the industry.

The practical question concerned the possible emergence of a pan-European food industry from the existing mosaic of separate nationally focused industries, i.e. transnational companies emerging from multidomestic structures. This possibility was mooted in the context of the Single European Act conceived in 1987 for implementation by 1992. This was expected to reduce the costs of access to separate European markets and, along with expectations about increasing homogeneity of consumers across Europe, constituted external triggers for structural change.

The approach to this was to develop a model of 'strategic space' onto which the prospective movements of firms could be mapped. An historical overview enabled the identification of periods of stability and the conditions causing breaks between periods. On the basis of this history, key variables were identified as the basis for strategic group identification. These were market scope (territories covered), marketing intensity and brand strength, manufacturing focus, and R&D intensity (the latter two were not statistically validated). These were used to identify the strategic group configuration in 1990, enabling the identification of at least four distinct groupings. However, the real interpretive power of the configuration lay in the specification of the mobility barriers between the groups. The strategic space idea is the converse of the strategic group, i.e. why there is no group present in a particular location on an n-dimensional map. The first possible answer is that some spaces are currently infeasible and the asset structures implied by that space are competitively dominated by other asset structures. The second possible answer is that some spaces have never been entered because the construction of the implied assets was not thought to be competitively viable. This second insight allowed the analysis of certain empty spaces to suggest that certain assets could technically be constructed (e.g. European marketing systems and brands) and that changing market conditions might yield a pay-off for those new asset structures.

Thus the strategic groups/space analysis allowed the juxtaposition of a changing market situation in Europe with a lowering of mobility barriers between existing groups and the empty spaces. The conclusion drawn is that certain kinds of new asset structures of firms are very likely to be constructed and that these will fall into two or three key new groups. The processes by which this might happen can be identified, including a wave of mergers and acquisitions. The consequences for competition both in the transition period and for a period of subsequent stability can be analysed, although the time period over which the transition will take place could not be identified. The analysis is distinctive in that it is almost entirely prospective in character, laying out a framework for analysing future change in the industry.

Figures 5.13, 5.14, 5.15 and 5.16 summarize the analysis. Figure 5.13 shows the existing strategic group structure in the late 1980s. Figure 5.14 summarizes the mobility barriers that protect each group. Figure 5.15 contains the strategic space analysis and Figure 5.16 shows the authors' conjectures about the group configuration in 2000.

The authors conclude:

> First, two major new strategies are likely to emerge, the pan-European own label supplier and the pan-European brander. Second, the strategic space analysis tells us something about the pathways to achieving these positions. Third, it also tells us something about the nature of competition both en route and in the new structure. This approach does not tell us how long the process of change will take, nor does it say who will be the winners and losers. It does, however, say a great deal about the characteristics of the winners and losers. (ibid, 1990, p. 190)

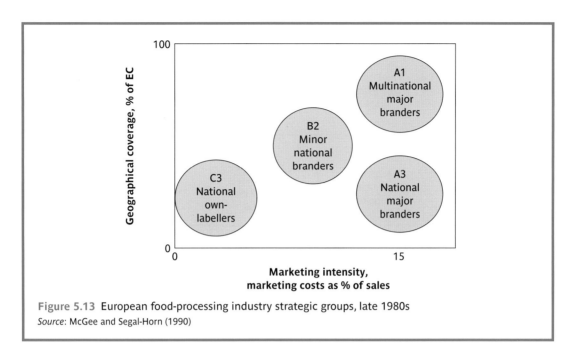

Figure 5.13 European food-processing industry strategic groups, late 1980s
Source: McGee and Segal-Horn (1990)

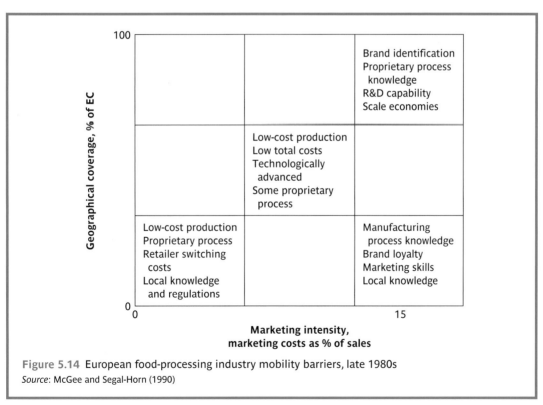

Figure 5.14 European food-processing industry mobility barriers, late 1980s
Source: McGee and Segal-Horn (1990)

After the passage of time since this paper was written, it is interesting to reflect on the extent to which the pan-European brander space has been occupied. At that time it seemed like an attractive space since it offered economies of scale across a European market that was showing signs of converging consumer tastes, developing its logistics networks, and creating fewer larger factories. In

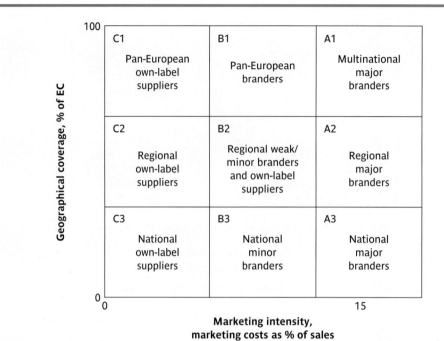

Figure 5.15 European food-processing industry strategic space analysis
Source: McGee and Segal-Horn (1990)

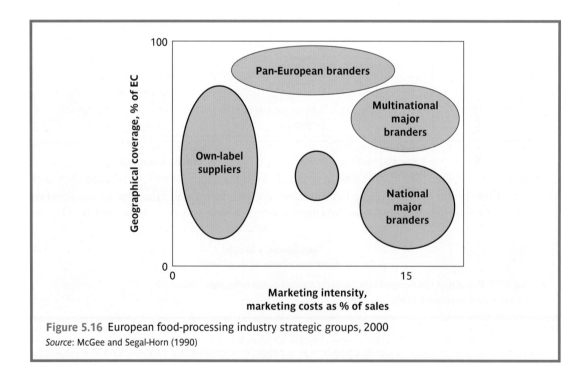

Figure 5.16 European food-processing industry strategic groups, 2000
Source: McGee and Segal-Horn (1990)

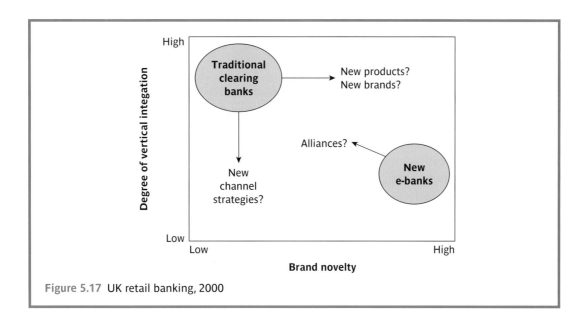

Figure 5.17 UK retail banking, 2000

the 1990s it becomes clear that Unilever, Nestlé and Mars were beginning to focus on just such a strategy (Johnson and Scholes, 1999, p. 129).[6]

Strategic group maps do not have to be historical and therefore 'backward-looking'. History is important in developing an understanding of the nature of mobility barriers and the time and cost involved in investing to overcome them. However, one can assess the present and make forward-looking conjectures. For example, Figure 5.17 is a speculative map constructed in 1996 of retail banking in 2000 in order to assess the implications of new possibilities like banking through the internet. The two strategy dimensions are degree of vertical integration and brand novelty. Traditional banks have a 'complete' value chain and do everything in-house whereas the new e-banks focus for the most part on electronic distribution and subcontract everything else such as cheque processing. The new e-banks have enormous brand novelty, indicated by the plethora of 'cute' names like Egg, Goldfish and Smile. Thus we have two utterly distinct groups. Are these groups highly rivalrous, or is the emergence of the new group merely indicative of a new market segment? This poses a degree of threat to traditional banks who need to ask whether they can remain where they are with some strategic adaptation, such as opening of new electronic channels of distribution in parallel to their existing channels (viz. the High Street). Or should they seek to develop some brand novelty? Or perhaps deconstruct their integrated value chains into separate upstream and downstream businesses? Or is there a different dimension on which they can play, for instance TV banking? For the new e-banks the question is to what extent this strategic group is defensible. Should a highly deconstructed value chain be supported by a series of alliances to secure access to best-in-class highly complementary activities?

These two examples demonstrate some key themes:

1 Strategic group analysis enriches our discussion of the nature of strategic choice.

2 The formation of groups reflects strategy innovations and risky decisions.

3 The stability of group structures over time tells us, through mobility barriers, about sustainability.

---

[6] Note that the Pan-European group emerges with lower marketing sales ratios because transnationals (and trans-regionals) save costs by eliminating duplication of marketing costs across country markets.

4 The nature of mobility barriers forces us to think about the investments that underpin market position and competitive advantage. It points us towards the nature of resources and the idea of core competences.

Any analysis of group structures leads very quickly from history to predictive ability. The essence of strategic decision is investment in distinctive assets against an uncertain future and therefore strategy innovations and industry evolution are closely linked. Innovation disturbs the industry equilibrium and foreshadows the emergence of new ways of competing and new group structures. Ex ante analysis of possible strategy innovations gives an indication of new strategy dimensions and therefore the nature, pattern and intensity of future rivalry. The pay-offs from this approach can be summarized in terms of interpretation, framework, and language:

1 a richer *interpretation* of current industry structures and the interaction of firm asset (tangible and intangible) structures with intra-industry competition;

2 a conceptual *framework* for analysing change over time and across industries;

3 a *language* for interpreting change in terms of asset structures of firms and the ensuing effects on competition in the long run.

5.5 Strategy making in practice

As we saw in Chapter 1, strategic management deals essentially with four questions:

1 How do we develop and formulate strategy?

2 How do we make choices between strategic options?

3 How do we put the strategy into operation and sustain it over time?

4 How do we manage the processes of strategic change and strategy renewal?

The first question raises issues of intended and planned strategies (typically top-down), versus emergent strategies that arise from experience and learning where the emphasis is on knowledge that is distributed throughout the organization, versus accidents, serendipity and 'muddling through' within which strategy is very much the junior partner to flexibility, operations expertise and tactical acumen, and speed of response.

The second question focuses on the nature of data and information required, the analytical processes used, and how trade-offs are made. It confronts the logic approach of economic and quantitative models with the uncertainty and risk endemic in long-term decisions and raises questions about criteria for decision making and the nature and role of organizational influences.

The third question is widely regarded as the key to superior performance. This view is based on the observation that ideas are cheap but action is difficult. However, we argue throughout this book that these questions are linked and, for example, difficulties in implementation are partly (if not largely) to do with over-ambition and error in the first two parts. Nevertheless, implementation is distinctively difficult. It is complex in the range and the depth of detail, making operational planning and control highly complex. It often requires the adoption of path-breaking new knowledge beyond the known best-practice. Thus it is not clear that matters may not proceed as expected and contingencies have to be anticipated. If operational matters are clear-cut and lack complexity it almost always follows that the strategy lacks distinctiveness and competitive advantage will not be attained. The points at which competitive advantage are delivered are generally through specific operations and activities. Where these are unique or at least new to the firm, successful implementation is clearly not assured. The issue of sustainability is to be seen in similar fashion. Keeping ahead of competitors involves continuous reinvestment and reappraisal of key operations. Thus the firm is continually having to prospect into new territory in order to keep ahead, with all the risks and uncertainties that this implies. These issues are all taken up in detail in Part 2 of this book.

The fourth question has provided significant employment and fee income for consultants. Referring back to the strategy cycle diagram (Figure 5.5), we observed that strategies get out of date and performance suffers when markets change faster than organizations can respond. This gives rise to the need for strategic change and renewal. The management of strategic change has been one of the central practical and theoretical issues of the past 25 or 30 years. The era since 1979 has been one of radical external change, resulting in radical changes to the business portfolios and activities of firms and to their traditional ways of doing business. The most common management responses have been to divest businesses and product lines in order to refocus on sustainable core businesses in which competitive advantage can be pursued. The pressures for internationalization have been very strong and companies have used acquisitions, alliances and organic growth in order to enter new markets. This combination of retrenchment plus expansion has obliged firms to undertake major programmes of change in which these changes in strategy have had to be matched by internal changes in organization structure and in habitual ways of doing business (culture), and management processes have also had to be adapted and re-engineered.

5.5.1 Assessing progress

Bearing in mind the complexities arising from the proposition that at least part of your strategy may in practice be emergent or accidental (see Chapter 1), there is nevertheless a need to assess progress against your intentions. This section suggests a number of questions that you can use to judge the underlying logic of a strategy and the validity of the underlying planning process.

Judging a competitive strategy

1 What does the customer really want and is willing to pay for?
2 What is the economic logic of the industry and how is it changing?
3 What are the key forces for change and how are we planning to take advantage of them?
4 What is the company's competitive advantage (business idea) that makes it unique?
5 How can it gain this competitive advantage?
6 How are the competitors likely to react?

You can see that these questions are closely related to our description of strategy in Section 5.2.1.

How good is the strategic thinking?

1 Is strategy clearly articulated:
   - in product-market terms?
   - with measurable objectives?
   - with clear milestones?
   - specific on source of competitive advantage?
2 Is it evident that strategy has been created with reference to the external environment?
3 Does strategy provide a clear guide to resource allocation?
4 Are business unit strategies clearly stated and linked to corporate strategy?
5 Is strategic planning linked to operational decision making?
6 Is the budgeting process subservient to the strategic planning process?

Points 1 to 6 relate directly to the content of the strategy and the way it is linked up and down the organization to its main systems and processes.

7　Is strategy consciously set by senior management?

8　Is the company's culture and value system conducive to strategic thinking?

9　Is strategy widely understood by division and middle-level managers?

10　Is the concept of strategy understood by those providing 'strategy inputs'?

Points 7 to 10 bring in managers and management and provide a basis for asking how strategy processes and the values in the company actually support the production of 'good' strategy content.

Ten questions for judging a strategic plan

1　Will a high-quality business position result?
- At the end of the planning period we should feel good about the character and quality of our achievement, that is, a strong foundation and competitive position, and attractive financial results.

2　Is it clear what we want to have in our value chain?
- What will we invest in, what will we discard? Resource priorities should be focused in order to develop a healthy portfolio and a value chain of activities that can be managed with economies of scale and scope.

3　How are we anticipating and managing change to our advantage?
- The environment is changing rapidly: how will competitors respond and what are we planning to do?

4　Are the assumptions sound?
- Major changes in volume, share or margins should be firmly based on plans that support such changes, taking into account market realities and competitor reactions.

5　Are there specific concrete ideas driving the plan?
- Avoid 'hollow' plans that are superficially attractive but lack a solid idea capable of good execution.

6　Is there a sustainable competitive advantage?
- What is it that is going to result in superior performance over time and will warrant investment?

7　Is the implementation clear and specific?
- The organization must be able to understand, accept, and carry out the key actions involved.

8　Are the financial results achievable?
- Is cash generation evident within an appropriate time frame with clear milestones identified?

9　Are the necessary resources identified?
- The plan must be within the existing capabilities of the company or have identified how these will be obtained.

10　Will the organization be able to adapt to the plan and its implementation?
- How much change in current operations and motivation of key managers will be required for successful achievement?

5.5.2　The balanced scorecard

A critical element in successful strategy implementation is an appropriate performance measurement system and we develop this theme at greater length in Chapter 16 (Analysing and measuring strategic performance). Conventional accounting systems often do not provide the critical information required by management to assess the company's progress to achieving its strategic vision and objectives because of their focus on reporting the past rather than assessing the future consequences of decisions made now. The **balanced scorecard** is a performance measurement system developed by Kaplan and Norton (1992) which, although including financial measures of performance, also contains operational measures of customer satisfaction, internal processes, and the company's innovation and improvement activities. These are seen collectively as the key drivers of future financial performance and individually as key success factors.

The balanced scorecard examines a business from the four important perspectives of:

1 How do customers see the firm? (*Customer perspective*)
2 What does the firm excel at? (*Internal perspective*)
3 Can the firm continue to improve and create value? (*Innovation and learning perspective*)
4 How does the firm look to shareholders? (*Financial perspective*)

This approach avoids information overload by restricting the number of measures used so as to focus only on those seen to be essential – the key success factors.[7] The balanced scorecard presents this information in a single management report and therefore brings together often disparately reported elements of the firm's strategic position such as short-term customer response times, product quality, teamwork capability, new product launch times and the like. As a result, the approach guards against sub-optimization by forcing management to examine individual operational measures systematically and comprehensively.

A typical scoreboard is illustrated in Figure 5.18. From this you can see how management can translate its general mission statements into the four perspectives, each of which contains a series of

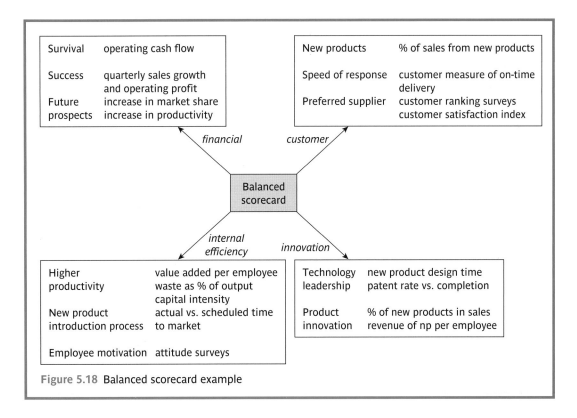

Figure 5.18 Balanced scorecard example

---

[7] The term 'key success factors' is widely used but rarely defined, but just think of it as referring to the range of competitive advantages evident in an industry from which firms can make profits.

specific measures. The precise scorecard design should reflect the vision and strategic objectives of the individual company. The key point is that the scorecard approach puts strategy and corporate vision rather than financial reporting as the key driver of performance management design (see Chapter 1). This is consistent with the development of corporate transformation techniques, cross-functional organizations, and customer–supplier interrelationships and other major corporate programmes that are designed to have major effects on business performance.

5.6 The business model

In Chapter 3 and in this chapter we have been using the idea of an 'economic model' that captures the essential economic characteristics and cash flows of the firm. In assessing strategic position we wish to be able to relate the intended strategic position and the nature of the competitive advantage to the performance of the firm. This leads us to the idea of the *business model*. This is a widely used term intended to provide the link between an intended strategy, its functional and operation requirements, and the performance (typically cash flows and profits) that is expected. It usually applies to single businesses where a specific competitive strategy can be identified but can also apply to those multi-business portfolios that are linked by strong synergies and therefore have common or similar strategies.

Chesbrough and Rosenbloom (2002) cite their experience in turning up 107,000 references to 'business model' on the World Wide Web while finding only three citations in the academic literature. In the usual practitioner sense, a business model is the method of doing business by which a company can sustain itself – that is, generate revenue. The business model spells out how a company makes money by specifying where it is positioned in the value chain. A more precise definition has been offered by the consultants KM Lab (2000): 'business model is a description of how your company intends to create value in the marketplace. It includes that unique combination of products, services, image and distribution that your company carries forward. It also includes the underlying organization of people and operational infrastructure that they use to accomplish their work.'

Chesbrough and Rosenbloom (2002) describe the functions of a business model as:

1 to articulate the value proposition;
2 to identify a market segment;
3 to define the structure of the value chain;
4 to estimate the **cost structure** and profit potential;
5 to describe the position of the firm within the supply chain;
6 to formulate the strategic logic by which the firm will gain and hold advantage.

The simple Du Pont accounting identities are a good starting point for identifying a business model. Thus,

$$\pi = (p - c)Q - F$$

and

$$\mathbf{NA = WC + FA}$$

where
π is profits
p is price
c is variable costs

Q is quantity sold
F is fixed costs
NA is net assets
WC is working capital
FA is fixed assets

An intended strategy should have specific effects on the variables in these equations. For example, a cost leadership strategy would be expected to reduce variable costs, to increase **fixed costs** and to increase fixed assets – according to the economies of scale available. Accordingly, profits and return on investment (π/NA) will be expected to increase because the rise in fixed costs and fixed assets due to the investment will be more than offset by the increase in contribution margin (p – c). A more ambitious business model might also specify a price reduction that will result in a volume increase through the medium of a high price elasticity and no imitation by competitors. The validity of such an assumption about lack of competitor response depends on judgements about competitor cost levels and their willingness to sacrifice margin for volume.

Similarly, a differentiation strategy would be expected to raise both costs and prices. Costs would go up because of the variable costs (such as quality and service levels) and fixed costs (such as advertising and R&D) of differentiation. Prices would be expected to increase disproportionately if the value to customers was sufficiently high to make the product price inelastic. This business model then calls for a higher-margin game, offset to some degree by higher fixed costs. A more ambitious model might also aim for a volume increase on the basis of higher product 'value' stimulating demand (a rising demand curve rather than a negatively sloped one).

What the business model does is to articulate the logic of the intended strategy in terms of the specific operations that have to take place. With this detailed plan the consequences for cash flows can be determined and the link between (intended) strategy and (expected) performance can be established. Beyond the obvious benefit of quantifying the strategic logic of the firm, the business model also enables sensitivity testing and risk analysis. In the case of the cost leadership example, the intention might be to reduce variable costs by a target %. The implications of a shortfall in cost reduction can easily be calculated and expressed in terms of the percentage change in profits in relation to a given percentage shortfall from the target cost reduction. Where the business model calls for price changes, the implications of competitor imitation or non-imitation can also be calculated.

In practice, a business model can be articulated in terms of detailed plans and budgets that provide guidance to managers relating to their operational responsibilities. The logic that drives plans and budgets lies within the business model. The business model itself is the mechanism through which a business intends to generate revenue and profits. Figure 5.19 shows a schematic diagram (Yip, 2004) that describes the process from inputs to customers – in many ways this is simply a re-styled value chain. This should not be surprising – the value chain is an activity map onto which can be placed assets and costs. Figure 5.20 shows an application to a mobile telephony business. The merit of this is the explicit nature of the choices made and from this the implications for cash flows will follow. A different example is shown in Figure 5.21. This describes the leasing operations of a London-located bank. This shows clearly the performance dimensions at the top of the figure. Shareholder value is decomposed into components such as market share, price and costs. The bottom of the figure shows the drivers of the cash flows, starting with characteristics like flexibility and moving upwards to a higher level of aggregation to customer satisfaction and brand strength from which the cash flows stem directly. This is an unusual picture of a business model because it is not faithful to the value chain idea – only selected activities are shown. You should look at this and ask yourself: (i) is this likely to be an accurate model if some variables are excluded? (ii) not all the

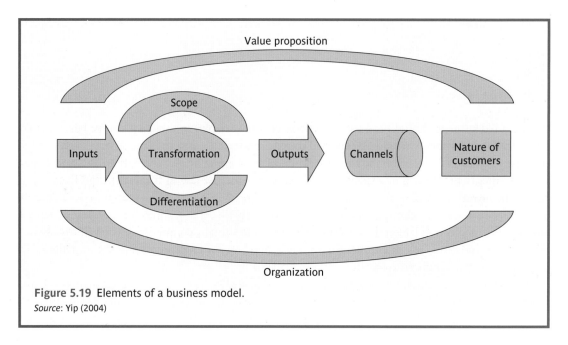

Figure 5.19 Elements of a business model.
Source: Yip (2004)

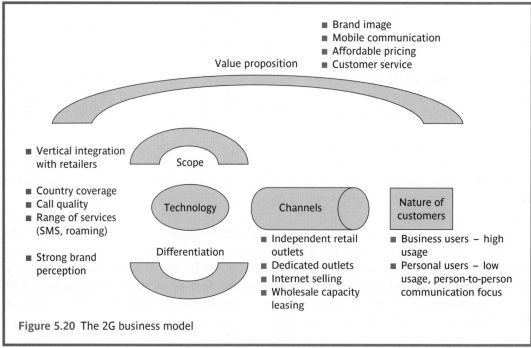

Figure 5.20 The 2G business model

variables are observable and quantifiable – does this matter?, and (iii) what extra information would you require (hint – consider sensitivity analysis)?

5.6.1 Commitment and sustainability

The business model has become a standard part of the business lexicon to indicate the way its cash flows are underpinned by a strategic logic. For the business model to be genuinely useful it needs to reflect the sustainability and defensibility of its strategic position and the nature of the commitment

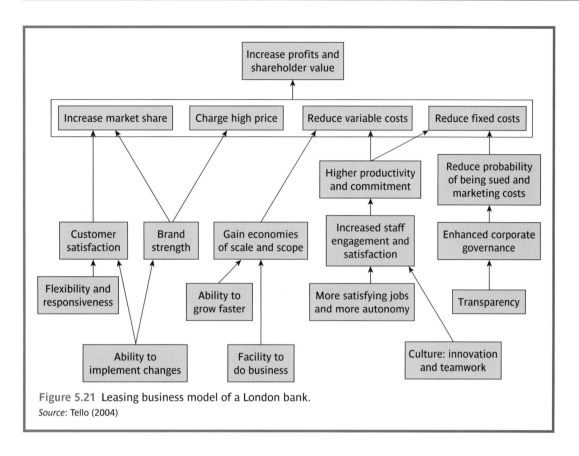

Figure 5.21 Leasing business model of a London bank.
Source: Tello (2004)

that is required in the strategic assets of the firm. Recall the strategy cycle (Figure 5.5) and note that the top line requires a balancing of resources and assets with the market position. The resource and asset component of this is discussed in the next chapter. Sustainability of the strategic position is to do with the imitability (or otherwise) of the competitive advantage. The Five Forces model gives an indication of the overall attractiveness of the industry – attractiveness means the degree to which the profits of the industry players are protected from erosion by the five competitive forces. More specifically, sustainability is to do with the insulation of the net cash flows (and the net present value of the firm) from attack by any individual competitor. A failing of the generic Five Forces model is its inability to move beyond the industry on average or in general. Sustainability analysis involves analysing potential responses by competitors and potential entrants and the impact of those actions on the degree of competition and on the cash flows that are generated by the competitive advantage of the incumbent firm. Richard Rumelt invented the term 'isolating mechanisms' to refer to the economic forces that limit the extent to which a competitive advantage can be neutralized or duplicated. Isolating mechanisms are to the firm what entry barriers are to an industry – they are the forces that inhibit other firms from competing away profits from incumbent firms. There are different approaches to identifying and classifying isolating mechanisms.[8] Besanko et al. (2000) put them in two distinct groups.

Impediments to imitation

These isolating mechanisms prevent firms from imitating and/or surpassing the resources, competences and strategic assets that underpin the incumbent's advantage. Thus, many firms compete

---

[8] See Rumelt (1984), Ghemawat (1991), and Yao (1988)

in the executive car market but few, if any, can match the approach of BMW and Mercedes. Note, however, that there exist concerted efforts of Audi, Jaguar and Lexus to do so. In the soft drinks industry Coca-Cola has been unrivalled in fostering its brand name as a symbol of uniqueness. These impediments include legal restrictions, superior access to inputs or to customers, and intangible barriers (resource-based) to imitating the incumbent's core competences.

Early-mover advantages

Once a firm establishes a competitive advantage then certain economic forces can protect its position. We saw earlier in Chapter 3 the example of Du Pont in titanium dioxide. Its first move pre-empted the market by establishing a requirement for sufficiently large size to attain competitive costs that there was insufficient room in the market for followers. Similarly, Microsoft's position as the effective standard in the personal computer (see Chapter 7 for an analysis of network effects) has meant that no follower has been able to create a value proposition for consumers such that they would be willing to incur the costs of switching to a new (and presumably much improved) standard. These impediments are all related to market size and scale economies, and also to technological change and the creation of legally recognized or de facto standards.

5.6.2 Strategic fit

The essential intangible barrier to strategy imitation is *strategic fit*. In summary, the way in which a firm's activities and capabilities fit together is often achieved by sustained **learning** and experimentation over time and cannot readily be imitated by would-be followers. Thus all car assemblers know that BMW produces its cars to enhance driver appeal, but it is extraordinarily difficult to replicate the way in which BMW has learned how to fit everything together. Strategic fit is the classic riposte to the economic analyst who argues that all profits decay: 'yes, maybe: but look how long it takes!'

Strategic fit[9] occurs usually in related diversified businesses as a result of superior competitive position arising from overall lower cost and the successful transfer of core skills, technology and managerial know-how between businesses. The earlier concepts of synergy and shared experience have similar meanings.

Strategic fit, however, may apply in apparently unrelated businesses where financial synergy may be found. For example, a high cash flow business may financially complement a business that is a high capital user. Examples of this phenomenon include Reo Stakis – a combination of casinos and hotels, the Ladbroke Group and Donald Trump's empire, all of which are engaged in similar sets of activities.

Diversification into businesses in which shared technology, marketing and production skills are required can lead to economies of scope when the costs of operating two or more businesses are less than operating each individually. The key to such cost reductions is therefore diversification into businesses with strategic fit.

Market-related fit occurs when the activity cost chains of different businesses overlap such that they attempt to reach the same consumers via similar distribution channels, or are marketed and promoted in similar ways. In addition to such **economies of scope**, it may also be possible to transfer selling skills, promotion and advertising skills, and product positioning/differentiation skills across businesses. Care must, however, be taken to ensure that market-related fit is possible. Successful examples include Canon's strategic position in cameras and photographic equipment being logically extended into copying and imaging equipment, and Honda's position in motorcycles

---

[9] See D.F. Channon in McGee and Channon (eds.) (2005).

being extended into other activities using engines, including automobiles and lawnmowers. However, not all such moves are successful. Thus BAT found that selling branded cosmetics was different from selling branded tobacco items.

Operating fit is achieved where the potential for cost sharing or skills transfer can occur in procurement, R&D, production, assembly and/or administration. Cost sharing amongst these activities can lead to economies of scale. Again, successes such as the sale of life insurance policies by retail banking branches can be identified. Similarly, failures are frequently due to inabilities to ensure integration between activities from different businesses brought together by acquisition.

Management fit occurs when different business units enjoy comparable types of entrepreneurial administrative or operating problems. This type of gain is very difficult to achieve due to differences in corporate culture. Classic failures in achieving such fit gains occurred in the attempted diversification moves by the oil industry majors after the first oil-price shock in 1973. Redefinitions of their businesses into 'energy' and 'raw materials' encouraged moves into minerals, coal and gas. Most of these moves were serious failures, or the expected strategic fit did not materialize.

Ironically, the only strategic fit which is almost certain to be achieved is the financial one. The operational strategic fits have lower probabilities of success, that for marketing being higher than that for production which, in turn, is higher than that for R&D. The strategic fit concept has also been criticized as being too static and limiting, focusing as it does on existing resources and the existing environment rather than seeking out the future opportunities and threats which are the focus of firms with strategic intent.

Case box 5.2 describes the business model that underlies 'free' internet service. This has been used to justify the mixture of online content and services that is provided free to internet users. Now there is some doubt that this business model is in fact working. If not, who is going to pay for online content and how?[10]

Case box 5.2: **The end of the free lunch – again**

The demise of a popular but unsustainable business model now seems inevitable
'In recent years, consumers have become used to feasting on online freebies of all sorts: news, share quotes, music, e-mail and even speedy internet access. These days, however, dotcoms are not making news with yet more free offerings, but with lay-offs – and with announcements that they are to start charging for their services.' These words appeared in *The Economist* in April 2001, but they're just as applicable today. During the dotcom boom, the idea got about that there could be such a thing as a free lunch, or at least free internet services. Firms sprang up to offer content and services online, in the hope that they would eventually be able to 'monetise' the resulting millions of 'eyeballs' by selling advertising. Things did not work out that way, though, and the result was the dotcom crash. Companies tried other business models, such as charging customers for access, but very few succeeded in getting people to pay up.

Then it happened all over again, starting in 2004 with the listing of Google on the stockmarket, which inflated a new 'Web 2.0' bubble. Google's ability to place small, targeted text advertisements next to internet-search results, and on other websites, meant that many of the business models thought to have been killed by the dotcom bust now rose from the grave. It seemed there was indeed money to be made from internet advertising, provided you could target it accurately – a problem that could be conveniently outsourced to Google. The only reason it had not worked the first time around, it was generally agreed, was a shortage of broadband connections. The pursuit of eyeballs began again, and a series of new internet stars emerged: MySpace, YouTube, Facebook and now Twitter. Each provided a

10 For an extended and informative discussion of this see 'Rupert Murdoch vs. The Internet' by Mark Oakley in *Micromart*, 10–16 December 2009, issue 1085, pp. 24–28.

▶ free service in order to attract a large audience that would then – at some unspecified point in the future – attract large amounts of advertising revenue. It had worked for Google, after all. The free lunch was back.

Now reality is reasserting itself once more, with familiar results. The number of companies that can be sustained by revenues from internet advertising turns out to be much smaller than many people thought, and Silicon Valley seems to be entering another 'nuclear winter'.

Internet companies are again laying people off, scaling back, shutting down, trying to sell themselves to deep-pocketed industry giants, or talking of charging for their content or services. Some Web 2.0 darlings (MySpace, YouTube) managed to find buyers before the bubble burst, thus passing the problem of finding a profitable business model to someone else (News Corporation and Google, respectively). But quite how Facebook or Twitter will be able to make enough money to keep the lights on for their millions of users remains unclear. Facebook has had several stabs at a solution, most recently with a scheme called Facebook Connect. Twitter's founders had planned to forget about revenues until 2010, but the site now seems to be preparing for the inclusion of advertising.

The bill, sir

The idea that you can give things away online, and hope that advertising revenue will somehow materialise later on, undoubtedly appeals to users, who enjoy free services as a result. There is business logic to it, too. The nature of the internet means that the barrier to entry for new companies is very low – indeed, thanks to technological improvements, it is even lower in the Web 2.0 era than it was in the dotcom era. The internet also allows companies to exploit network effects to attract and retain users very quickly and cheaply. So it is not surprising that rival search engines, social networks or video-sharing sites give their services away in order to attract users, and put the difficult question of how to make money to one side. If you worry too much about a revenue model early on, you risk being left behind.

Ultimately, though, every business needs revenues – and advertising, it transpires, is not going to provide enough. Free content and services were a beguiling idea. But the lesson of two internet bubbles is that somebody somewhere is going to have to pick up the tab for lunch.

Source: 'The End of the Free Lunch – Again', *The Economist*, 21 March 2009

5.7 Summary

This chapter has examined competitive strategy as the way of establishing and defending strategic position in the marketplace. This requires a deep understanding of the economic drivers of the firm, its essential cost position, its approach to differentiating itself in the market from its competitors, and its chosen position in the market in terms of ability to exploit natural economies of scale and scope. We have also looked at what competitive advantage means to customers and to firms and the ways firms have of understanding their positions in terms of strategic market segments (on the demand side) and of strategic groups (on the supply side). This leads to an understanding of pricing and value and the sustainability of value over time. Any competitive strategy has to be turned into action – the notion of the business model is the way in which the firm's individual theory of its business (its competitive strategy) is turned into cash flows. A proper understanding of the business model leads to an appreciation of how the various pieces of a business fit together (strategic fit) and how the strategy might be sustained into the future (sustainability).

In the next chapter we turn our attention to the assessment of strategic capability, those core competences that underpin competitive advantage and are the target of the firm's strategic investment programmes.

Key terms

Recap questions and assignments

1 Undertake a strategy audit of a business with which you are familiar. How attractive is the industry in which it competes? What strategies appear to be available in this industry? How would you describe the strategy of your selected business (use Figure 5.1)?

2 Choose two companies in the same industry – preferably direct competitors – and compare the configuration of their value chains. Explain how these configurations relate to the strength of their competitive positions.

3 Do a SWOT analysis (see Chapter 1) for your chosen businesses. Explain why you have chosen each of the key entries. Then explain how their competitive positions relate to the SWOT entries.

4 Explain how the balanced scorecard relates to competitive positioning. Use your companies as an example.

Case study 5.1: **The Novotel value chain**

The figure on the next page captures some of the key elements in the Novotel value chain. Each of the elements of the chain is important in itself for service delivery. But also most of them interact with other elements.

To expand further on the hospitality concept, one would need to describe intangibles such as 'greeting', 'welcome for the traveller' and personal warmth. It lends a relevant insight into the nature of the management task in services to reflect on the robustness of internal systems and processes to deliver these service elements to the customer on a routine basis. Indeed, Novotel uses the layout of its

Novotel value chain

Overlay bands (top to bottom): HIGH EXPERIENCE EFFECTS (e.g. site selection, hotel construction) · EFFECTIVE MANAGEMENT OF LINKAGES · PURCHASING SCALE EFFICIENCIES

	SERVICE DESIGN	MARKETING	DISTRIBUTION	SERVICE DELIVERY	SERVICE MONITORING AND ENHANCEMENT
FIRM INFRASTRUCTURE	■ Central design unit ■ NPD	■ Global branding and positioning ■ Image management	■ Central systems ■ Accor HQ	■ Academie Accor ■ G M autonomy	■ Flat reporting structure ■ WAR ROOM ■ Transfer of best practice
HRM	■ HOSPITALITY CONCEPT ■ Core values ■ Multi-culture	■ Relationship marketing (internal and external) ■ Incentive programmes	■ Relationship-building	■ Superior recruitment and selection ■ TRAINING ■ Superior staff retention	■ Extensive training ■ Skills grading
TECHNOLOGY DEVELOPMENT	■ Customer interface ■ Service needs ■ Rapid roll-out of new specifications	■ Software and systems development	■ Global reservation systems ■ Network linkages ■ Dedicated suppliers (global)	■ Unique service features	■ Process development
PROCUREMENT	■ Standardization ■ Worldwide global best suppliers ■ High quality components and features	■ Media selection placement and negotiation ■ Market research	■ Dedicated software/systems	■ Best available inputs ■ EOS	■ Continuous enhancement and upgrading
(primary activities)	■ Tight design specifications ■ Global coverage ■ 3-star Features: ■ hotels ■ rooms ■ restaurants ■ Layout ■ Locations ■ Image	■ Corporate travel management ■ Partnership programmes ■ Special promotions ■ segmentation ■ Advertising themes for segments ■ Materials ■ brochures ■ give-aways ■ Campaign mgt. ■ Pricing ■ Supplier partnerships ■ Personal relationships with suppliers	■ Geographic network ■ Best locations ■ Centralized systems ■ Corporate agency network ■ Travel agency network ■ Availability ■ Rapid response/ timeliness ■ Capacity utilization ■ Vertical and horizontal integration	■ Staff multi-skilling ■ Staff exchanges ■ Transferability of staff and skills ■ Languages ■ Responsiveness to customer requirements ■ Interface mgt. ■ High service recovery ■ Attractive styles/ appearance (people and hotels)	■ High quality controls ■ High conformance ■ Standard setting/quality measures ■ Skills – testing and banding/grading ■ Extensive supplier training ■ Directors Clubs ■ Progress Groups (all staff levels) ■ 'Progress Novotel' ■ Customer surveys/feedback ■ Staff surveys/feedback ■ Staff empowerment ■ 'Pilot Case' ■ 'Quick' meetings ■ Refurbishment

Source: McGee and Segal-Horn (1997)

hotel (part of service design, the first lower half (primary) activity in column 1) to lead the customer immediately to the 'hospitable' public spaces of bar and restaurant, which are always on the entry floor adjacent to reception.

Marketing (lower half, column 2) is extensive, sophisticated and linked closely to distribution systems. Novotel operates within both the individual and corporate business and leisure markets. Its special promotions and advertising themes (column 2, lower half) address these different segments. For example Dolphi, a baby dolphin, is the marketing and promotional symbol for children's events worldwide. However, although all locations worldwide (column 1, lower half) will use the coordinated symbol and marketing materials for this (or any other) segment, general managers at different locations and in different countries will tailor promotions to local holidays and lifestyles.

Partnership programmes (column 2, lower half) are common nowadays. Novotel links them with deepening relationship marketing (column 2, top half). Particularly noteworthy are the supplier partnership programmes, linked with purchasing and learning efficiencies (see firm infrastructure and procurement in top half of value chain), delivering both scale and scope economies. An example of this would be an agreement to purchase televisions from a sole preferred supplier worldwide (column 1, top half) – a recent innovation at Novotel where local purchasing had been common. The television (or any other) supplier would be expected to develop a reciprocal relationship through utilizing their customer's hotels for corporate travel purposes (column 3). Purchasing efficiencies are thus linked to internal and external relationship marketing (see linkages between columns 1, 2 and 3 in top half).

The hospitality concept is further implemented by other key elements in Service Delivery (column 4). Staff exchanges (column 4, lower half) (between countries, locations and type of customer mix) contributing to multi-culture (column 1, top half) are essential to the philosophy of 'welcome'. They provide a means of motivating staff in an industry where labour-turnover is typically high (column 4, top half – 'staff retention') and service delivery is dependent on the quality of the service encounter, to which staff motivation is crucial (column 4, lower half – 'responsiveness' etc.). It also ensures an international mix of hotel staff to interact sympathetically with an international client mix.

However, the more interesting elements of the Novotel offering for the purposes of this discussion are the management processes which enable the standardized service levels to be delivered at all locations worldwide.

Since hotel design and guest bedrooms are standardized, basic housekeeping and maintenance functions can in turn be standardized (see all Service Design and Firm Infrastructure elements in the figure above). That means that training of staff in all basic functions may be simplified and the procedures for training can be themselves standardized (see all HRM and Service Delivery elements). Indeed, one of the features of the Accor Group (Novotel's parent) is the 'Academie Accor', set up in 1985 as the centre for all staff training within the Group. Its 'campus' is located on the site of Group corporate headquarters just outside Paris. From there, all training is designed and delivered. This standardized approach to the core service concept places special requirements on the staff as the key medium for delivery of consistent service standards wherever the customer is staying. Standardized procedures and centrally designed training programmes are one of the core mechanisms for securing such consistency (columns 4 and 5).

Taking the notion of consistency one stage further, the Novotel senior management developed a new approach to staffing in the hotel sector which is described as 'multi-skilling'. The idea behind multi-skilling is to develop staff as a team able to perform tasks and work as needed in a flexible manner. Obviously, this would have many advantages for hotel management, not least in smoothing the need for certain types of staff at peak bottleneck periods of the day or evening. Pressures on checking-in or checking-out at reception and getting rooms cleaned while guests are at breakfast are common bottlenecks dramatically affecting patterns of staffing. With the Novotel approach to flexible skilling and team working, a new pattern is emerging. Flexible working patterns have broken down some of the staff demarcation normal within the hotel industry. Reception and front-of-house activities (e.g. showing guests to rooms) may be carried out by the same staff as serve in the restaurant at peak mealtimes or perform housekeeping or room-cleaning tasks at other times of the day. The benefits of this to the firm have been enormous, resulting in a reduction of core staff levels and a more resourceful workforce. However, maintaining universal quality standards as the chain grew rapidly over a 25-year period became more and more problematic, especially when many new staff were recruited from other hotel groups with different working practices.

A system to monitor standard procedures was introduced in 1987 which became known as the '95 Bolts'. This system was intended to be, and duly became, a template for learning. It was a hierarchical system, centrally designed and centrally driven. It emphasized structural elements of service and was authoritarian in both concept and style. It was about managerial direction and control. The 'Bolts' were 95 points or regulated systems applied to the 13 main points of staff/customer interaction. These key service encounters or 'moments of truth' included: reservation, arrival/access, parking, check-in, hall, bedroom, bathroom/WC, evening meal, breakfast, shops, bar, outdoor games/swimming-pool and checkout. Each of these key interaction points was divided into a series of compulsory directives for staff, e.g. how to set out a bedroom, lay a place setting in the restaurant or welcome a guest. A booklet containing the 95 Bolts was issued to all staff and was a mainstay in induction for new staff. Monitoring of standards was carried out by an internal team of inspectors who visited each hotel approximately twice each year. They functioned in the same way as 'mystery shoppers' in that they made reservations, arrived, stayed and departed incognito. On completion of their stay they would make themselves known to the General Manager (GM) for review and discussion. Percentage grades were awarded and recommendations made. The 95 Bolts, while helpful to control and consolidate after a period of rapid growth, gradually became over-rigid and procedural in orientation and were replaced by a more adaptive system in 1992.

Source: McGee and Segal-Horn (1997)

Questions

1 Describe Novotel's strategy using the Describing Strategy framework (Section 5.1).

2 What are its competitive advantages?

3 How does the value chain configuration help us to understand how the competitive advantages are managed and delivered?

Case study 5.2: **Molecular weight: BASF and the chemical industry**

By defying industry fashion and exploiting the power of the 'cluster', the world's biggest chemical company keeps growing.

In German, it is called the Verbund. Jürgen Hambrecht, the chief executive of BASF, describes his company's sprawling complex of pipes, towers and storage tanks as the 'ultimate business cluster'. Spread over ten square kilometres…it is the biggest integrated chemical site in the world.

At first glance, BASF's third-quarter results, out on November 2nd (2006), did not look great. Profits plunged because of restructuring costs at Engelhard, an American producer of catalysts (as in catalytic converters) which BASF bought earlier this year. And, on the same day, BASF announced 2,000 job losses.

But the underlying trend at BASF is surprisingly healthy, given that it is an old-fashioned manufacturing company in a part of the world where heavy industry tends not to flourish these days. It more than doubled its profits between 2002 and 2005. One-off charges aside, its third-quarter results suggest the company is in line for a 20% increase in turnover this year to over €50 billion ($64 billion), with pre-tax profits up 11%. Although many industries are fleeing from Europe to less costly countries, the efficiencies of the Verbund show how a traditional business can remain highly competitive, even when it operates in an expensive place like Germany.

The complex at Ludwigshafen, across the Rhine from Mannheim, comprises up to 250 individual chemical factories turning out 8,000 different products. These range from simple petroleum distillates to sophisticated nanomaterials – tiny particles which can be used to change the properties of plastics or other substances. BASF employs about 36,000 people in Ludwigshafen, where it also has its headquarters. Many travel around the site on red works-bicycles, individually numbered.

The site's legendary efficiency comes from extracting the last drop of value from every chemical reaction. It makes use of the numerous by-products from each process. At other places these are often sold or shipped from one factory to another for further processing. At the Verbund, what is left over from one process is used only a few hundred metres away to make something else. This saves BASF a fortune. Compared with having, say, 70 separate factories some 100km apart, BASF calculates its cluster enjoys annual savings of €300m ($380m) in logistics, €150m in energy and €50m in infrastructure.

For Mr Hambrecht, the Verbund represents a huge advantage in an industry in which competition is increasing, especially in Asia. So BASF is trying to replicate the benefits of its cluster, not only in other countries but also at the corporate level. Instead of splitting into lots of firms specialising in one chemical, as many giants have done, BASF is seeking to become an even bigger conglomerate.

Mr Hambrecht, who is 60, has spent half his working life at BASF, which was founded in 1865 as Badische Anilin- & Soda-Fabrik. Anilin was once important in making dyes; soda is used in glass, soaps and textiles. Today the company's products end up in goods ranging from cars to electrical goods, cosmetics, sports equipment and medical devices.

Mr Hambrecht enthuses about 'the industry of industries'. Indeed, chemicals seem to be in Germany's blood. The country accounts for a quarter of the chemical industry's sales in Europe and a similar share of employment there. Germany supplies more than 12% of world exports of chemicals, the biggest single share. And the German industry spends a higher proportion of its revenue on research and development than that of any other country.

In many countries, chemical factories are hardly the subject of civic pride. They are in Germany. In September an 'open day' attracted thousands of visitors. Frankfurters, in particular, are proud of the huge chemical complex straddling the river Main at Hoechst, west of the city. Though Hoechst, once the local chemical giant, was absorbed into Sanofi-Aventis of France in 1999, its Frankfurt site still churns out polymers, pigments and pharmaceuticals. The former Hoechst headquarters, a redbrick relic of the 1920s, is an admired piece of Bauhaus architecture.

Yet few sites are as efficient as the Verbund. A recent study of Germany's chemical industry by A.T. Kearney, a consultancy, found that most other production centres had big gaps in their 'value chain': raw materials and by-products had to be shipped around, at extra cost. The reasons are often historical or political. A complex at Leuna in East Germany, for example, was cleaned up at huge expense after German unification. It has never achieved its potential, even though firms such as Dow Chemical, Linde, Total and BASF have operations there. Other sites are too small or are underused, but cannot be closed for political reasons.

BASF has recently been adding to its product range in a big way. In March it bought Degussa Construction Chemicals, part of a German maker of specialty chemicals, for €2.7 billion; in May it spent $470m to buy America's Johnson Polymers and in June it paid $5 billion for Engelhard, the cause of the profits crash.

Asia starts producing

Although these European and American additions bolster its business, BASF cannot ignore developments elsewhere. Ever bigger petrochemical and other downstream production facilities are being built in the Middle East. And burgeoning demand in Asia, particularly in China, is resulting in more chemicals being produced locally. Moving into developing regions can have benefits beyond lower production costs. It can allow chemical companies to get closer to both suppliers of raw materials and more potential customers.

It nearly always makes sense to produce bulky chemicals, such as washing powder, where they are sold, to keep transport costs low. This puts places like China, which is a long way from the big Western consumer markets, at a disadvantage in exporting some products. But there are plenty of others to be made. Anything that can be conveniently put into a container and shipped cheaply is likely eventually to be made in Asia's low-cost factories.

Hence even BASF is having to shed businesses in which it thinks it is no longer competitive. The next to go may be a factory in Minden, Germany, which among other things makes caffeine. The Chinese now offer caffeine, which is easy to ship, to firms such as Coca-Cola at a third of the price that European factories can.

Nevertheless, demand in China is so great that it will be many years before the country becomes a net exporter of chemicals, Mr Hambrecht believes. Demand across Asia is strong. Around half of future worldwide demand for chemicals is expected to come from the region. BASF already has almost 19% of its turnover in Asia, up from just 9% in 1995.

As it expands overseas, BASF is trying to replicate the Verbund concept. It has built smaller versions of the cluster in Belgium, Texas, Louisiana, Malaysia and China. The foundations of its Chinese factory in Nanjing were laid in 2001. Last year petrochemical production began there in a joint venture with Sinopec, a Chinese oil company. Mr Hambrecht, who fought internal opposition to the investment, believes that such opportunities in Asia offer European chemical companies their only chance to grow faster than at home.

Chemical companies can be highly vulnerable to changes in the price of raw materials. Here too BASF hopes to gain some protection from its cluster effect. As long ago as 1969 it bought Wintershall, an oil producer. It has proved to be a useful hedge against oil-price rises. BASF is now trying to secure its lines of supply from Russia by a joint project with Gazprom to build a gas pipeline across the Baltic. It also has a share in a west Siberian oilfield.

BASF was mining coal until the late 1980s, and today even that might again make sense. The company's expansion into energy seems set to continue: it recently announced plans for a joint-venture bio-diesel plant in Belgium, which will use rapeseed and other organic material to produce fuel. Indeed, oil and gas provided 40% of the group's profits in 2005.

Other giants in the chemical industry have spun off various divisions to narrow the spectrum of their business. For instance, Bayer, Germany's second-largest chemical firm, listed its specialty chemical division, Lanxess, as a separate company in January 2005. Although the trend in the industry is to put new labels on bits of the business, such as 'life sciences', which includes health and food, or 'coatings', which includes paint, BASF still brands itself as 'The Chemical Company'. The one business it has quit is pharmaceuticals, accepting that there is little overlap between drugs and its other products.

The diversity of its operations makes BASF unpopular with some investors because it muddies their view of the firm as a 'pure play' on chemicals. Mr Hambrecht is unrepentant. He argues that conglomerates are better overall long-term performers than specialists. Through diversity, he maintains, companies can weather poor performance in one or two of their divisions. The specialist can also be more vulnerable to disruptive technology and the sudden substitution of one material for another. This is a particular risk for the chemical industry in Germany, which is highly exposed to the car business. Almost 70% of the German industry's innovations, such as smarter or lighter materials, go into vehicles.

But it is harder to apply the Verbund effect in the developing field of biotechnology. A big handicap for BASF is the German government. Despite vowing in its coalition agreement last year to clear the way for genome technology, the government has since dragged its feet. Bayer is developing genetically modified rice, rape and cotton, but in America not Germany. BASF has the majority of its biotech research in Europe and believes Germany to be an excellent place for genome activities. But, says Mr Hambrecht, the government's attitude risks driving it away.

The virtue of virtuality

Perhaps the biggest danger to the Verbund, and the conglomerate-building which it encourages, is that it could lack the flexibility to cope with rapid market changes. But a variation of the concept might overcome this. This is the 'virtual' Verbund; a large chemical site where a number of independent companies could voluntarily work together to achieve the same economies of scale, but use different processes as market conditions change.

A.T. Kearney suggests that something like this might be done at some of the chemical sites in Germany where production capacity is underused. A European Union project supported by seven big companies, including Siemens and Degussa, is trying to get the idea going by streamlining test-production. Called Impulse, the project aims to reduce the cost and time of research and development by miniaturising test equipment. This would primarily benefit smaller, more flexible companies. The political objective is to keep jobs and factories in Europe.

Perhaps such initiatives might one day steal away some of the Verbund's advantages. But not yet. For now Mr Hambrecht, whose contract with BASF runs until 2011, is confident in the future prospects of his firm. As he jogs through the vineyards near his Rhineland home in the early morning he can indulge in thinking up new things to make. One fantasy is that in the future solar energy will be stored and put to work chemically, much as it is in plants through photosynthesis. This will require special ingredients, which no doubt the Verbund could find room to make.

Source: 'Molecular Weight', *The Economist*, 4 November 2006

Questions

1 Why is BASF able to be so profitable in a supposedly difficult industry environment?

2 Identify and explain the elements of BASF's cost-based strategy. Is it a 'pure' cost-play, or does it have extra ingredients?

3 Does BASF operate in a strategic group? – see reference to the Ludwigshafen complex and the 'cluster'. What are the characteristics of this group?

4 Mr Hambrecht argues that conglomerates are better performers than 'pure plays' in chemicals. Outline the arguments for and against this view. You might want to answer this question after reading Chapter 8.

References

Ansoff, H. (1965) *Corporate Strategy*, Penguin, Harmondsworth.

Besanko, D., Dranove, D. and Shanley, M. (2000) *Economics of Strategy*, 2nd edn, John Wiley & Sons, New York.

Bogner, W.C., Thomas, H. and McGee, J. (1996) A longitudinal study of the competitive positions and entry paths of European firms in the US pharmaceutical market. *Strategic Managment Journal*, 17, 2, 85–107.

Channon, D.F. (2005) Value chain analysis. In J. McGee and D.F. Channon (eds) *Encyclopedic Dictionary of Management*, 2nd edn, Blackwell Business, Oxford.

Chesbrough, H. and Rosenbloom, R.S. (2002) The role of the business model in capturing value from innovation: evidence from Xerox Corporation's technology spin-off companies. *Industrial and Corporate Change*, 11, 3, 529–55.

Fiegenbaum, A. and Thomas, H. (1990) Strategic groups and performance: the US insurance industry 1980–84. *Strategic Management Journal*, **11**, 197–215.

Fiegenbaum, A., Tang, M.J. and Thomas, H. (1990) Strategic time periods and strategic group research: concepts and an empirical example. *Journal of Management Studies*, **27**, 133–48.

Ghemawat, P. (1991) *Commitment: The Dynamic of Strategy*, Free Press, New York.

Grant, R.M. (2002) *Contemporary Strategic Analysis: Concepts, Techniques and Applications*, 4th edn, Blackwell Business, Oxford.

Johnson, G. and Scholes, K. (1999) *Exploring Corporate Strategy*, Prentice Hall, Hemel Hempstead.

Kaplan, R.S. and Norton, D.P. (1992) The balanced scorecard: measures that drive performance. *Harvard Business Review*, **1**, Jan/Feb.

Ketchen, D.J. and Shook, C.L. (1996) The application of cluster analysis in strategic management research: an analysis and critique. *Strategic Management Journal*, **17**, 441–58.

KM Lab (2000) www.kmlab.com/46warfare.htm, 20 June.

McGee, J. and Channon, D.F. (eds) (2005) *The Encyclopaedic Dictionary of Strategic Management*, 2nd edn, Blackwell Publishing, Oxford.

McGee, J. and Segal-Horn, S. (1990) Strategic space and industry dynamics. *Journal of Marketing Management*, **6**, **3**, 175–93.

McGee, J. and Segal-Horn, S. (1992) Will there be a European food processing industry? In S. Young and J. Hamill (eds) *Europe and the Multinationals: Issues and Responses for the 1990s*, Edward Elgar, Cheltenham.

McGee, J. and Thomas, H. (1986) Strategic groups: theory, research and taxonomy. *Strategic Management Journal*, **7**, **2**, 141–60.

Porter, M.E. (1979) The structure within industries and company performance. *Review of Economics and Statistics*, **61**, May, 214–27.

Porter, M.E. (1985) *Competitive Advantage*, New York, Free Press.

Rumelt, R. (1984) Towards a strategic theory of the firm. In R. Lamb (ed.) *Competitive Strategic Management*, Prentice-Hall, Englewood Cliffs, NJ, pp. 566–70.

Sjostrom, C. (1995) *Corporate Effects on Industry Competition: A Strategic Groups Analysis*, unpublished doctoral dissertation, University of Oxford.

Tello, M. (2004) *Opportunities in the Leasing Market for London-based Banks*, Warwick Business School.

Yao, D. (1988) Beyond the reach of the invisible hand: impediments to economic activity, market failures, and profitability. *Strategic Management Journal*, Special Issue, **9**, 59–70.

Yip, G. (2004) Using strategy to change your business model. *Business Strategy Review*, **15**, **2**, Summer, 17–24.

Further reading

De Geuss, A. (1988) Planning as learning. *Harvard Business Review*, **66**, **2**, 70–4.

Eccles, R.G. and Nohria, N. (1992) Strategy as a language game. From *Beyond the Hype: Rediscovering the Essence of Management*, Harvard Business School Press, Boston, MA.

Hamel, G. and Prahalad, C.K. (1993) Strategy as stretch and leverage. *Harvard Business Review*, March/April.

Hamel, G. and Prahalad, C.K. (1994) Competing for the future. *Harvard Business Review*, July/Aug, 122–8.

MacMillan, I. and McGrath, R.G. (1997) Discovering new points of differentiation. *Harvard Business Review*, July/August, 3–11.

McGee, J. and Segal-Horn, S. (1997) Global competences in service multinationals. In H. Thomas, D. O'Neal and R. Alvarado (eds) *Strategic Discovery: Competing in New Arenas*, J. Wiley & Sons, Chichester, pp. 49–7.

Miller, D. (1992) The generic strategy trap. *Journal of Business Strategy*, **13**, **1**, 37–42.

Mintzberg, H. (1987) Crafting strategy. *Harvard Business Review*, **65**, **4**, 66–75.

Mintzberg, H. (1993) The fall and rise of strategic planning. *Harvard Business Review*, Jan/Feb, 107–14.

Mintzberg, H. (1994) *The Rise and Fall of Strategic Planning*, Prentice Hall, Englewood Cliffs, NJ.

Mintzberg, H. and Waters, J. (1985) Of strategies, deliberate and emergent. *Strategic Management Journal*, **6**, 257–72.

Porras, J.I. and Collins, J.C. (1996) *Built to Last*, Century Books, New York.

Porter, M.E. (1986) What is strategy? *Harvard Business Review*, Nov/Dec, 61–78.

Quinn, J.B. (1980) *Strategies for Change: Logical Incrementalism*, Irwin, Homewood, IL.

Rumelt, R., Schendel, D. and Teece, D. (eds) (1994) *Fundamental Issues in Strategy*, Harvard Business School Press, Boston, MA.

Seth, A. and Randall, G. (1999) *The Grocers: The Rise and Fall of the Supermarket Chains*, Kogan Page, London.

Sloan, A.P. (1983) *My Years at General Motors*, Doubleday, New York.

Whittington, R. (1993) *What Is Strategy and Does It Matter?* Routledge, London.

Competitive strategy:
the analysis of strategic capability

Introduction

In setting out to understand strategic management we are in effect building our own strategic theory of the firm. The usual starting point of this endeavour was provided in Chapters 3 and 5. These described the behaviour of firms in markets, the nature of competition, and the search for unique and sustainable market positions. To attain **competitive advantage** is to open the door to higher profits, other things being equal. This chapter sets out the internal agenda for the firm seeking to create competitive advantage. What resources and **capabilities** should the firm create and protect that will be the critical underpinning of its desired competitive advantage? In common parlance this is the concern with 'core competences'. In the academic discourse this is the **resource-based view (RBV)** of the firm in which it is recognized that firms are internally heterogeneous and in effect possess unique clusters of resources. Thus firms in the same industries and markets will very likely have different strategies and different performance levels. Critics of the market-based view (MBV) have argued that it is nonsensical to place the MBV at the centre of strategy making, leaving the inside of the firm to operate as a black box. Some, therefore, use the RBV to place the firm rather than the industry or the market at the centre of strategy making. However, the emphasis of this chapter is to emphasize that the RBV and the MBV provide complementary perspectives on how to compete and jointly provide the basis for a strategic theory of the firm.[1]

6.1 The resource-based view in theory

In Chapters 1 and 2 we discussed the firm's internal environment in some detail. We made the point that economists see the firm as a bundle of productive resources, where resources are defined as inputs into the firm's operations so as to produce goods and services. In this view, we said, resources are generic and specific categories are not suggested. We then made the salient point that strategists are interested in only those resources and capabilities that can earn rents (a surplus of revenue over cost), i.e. *strategic assets or core competences*.[2] The strategic task for the firm is to sustain these rent streams over time by creating and protecting the competitive advantage and the strategic assets that together underpin them. The inherent value of the strategic assets for the firm depends on the ways in which the firm combines, coordinates and deploys these assets in concert with the other firm-specific and more generic resources and capabilities.

But in the real competitive world of uncertainty and imperfect information the firm may have (and usually does have) considerable problems in knowing which particular configurations of its strategic assets will maximize profits. Managers do not have perfect knowledge of future states of the world, of alternative actions that could be taken, nor of the pay-offs from adopting various alternatives. Moreover, the way a manager chooses to allocate resources will be a function of past personal experience, the firm's experience, values, biases, and personality. Accordingly, even if two managers were given identical bundles of resources they would use them in different ways. The result is that a firm's set of resources and capabilities will diverge from those of its competitors over time. Managers in competing firms in the same markets do not face the same sets of choices – rather they have different menus with different choices. The future, as firms see it, is to a greater or lesser degree uncertain and unknowable and their capacities for addressing the unknowable are diverse. Further, no amount of information gathering can resolve this fundamental uncertainty of what the future will hold. Thus, strategy making is a long way from the simplistic assumptions of the economic model. Strategies tend to be unique and idiosyncratic and simplistic theories for success are usually 'magic theories', i.e. theories which explain everything but predict nothing.[3] Nor are there simple rules for riches, i.e. there are no automatic rules that provide benefits in the long run. Case box 6.1 uses the game of chess as an analogy.

---

[1] However, this is to ignore important contributions such as the theory of the growth of the firm by Edith Penrose (1954) and the evolutionary theory of Nelson and Winter (1982).

[2] But note that there are many other labels such as distinctive capabilities from Selznick (1957) and many other terms are and have been current.

[3] Lave and March (1993).

Case box 6.1: **The game of chess**

'If the theory of chess were really fully known there would be nothing left to play. The theory would show which of the three possibilities {"white wins", "tie", or "black wins"} actually holds and accordingly the play would be decided before it starts...human difficulty necessitates the use of incomplete, heuristic methods of playing, which constitute "good" Chess; and without it there would be no element of "struggle" and "surprise in the game".'

Rationality and full information would give us the ability to solve well-specified problems like chess. The initial resources (i.e. whether you start with white or black) would fully determine the outcome. Furthermore, no-one would read or write books on how to play chess well, because all the optimal moves would already be known. In practice, people differ widely in their ability to play chess and many find that studying books on chess ('rules' for winning) improves their play. People rely on heuristics, on search, on experience, and on training to aid their decisions. Such individuals can learn better heuristics and search patterns from books and can improve their performance.

If we assume in both chess and in strategy that no-one knows all the 'rules', then there can exist rules for riches that can benefit many participants. Indeed, half the firms in any industry could improve their status by becoming average. Neither in chess nor in strategy is there a fully fledged theory with optimization procedures in place. Participants have therefore to make progress by adopting heuristics (or intellectual constructs) that help them make sense of the possible varieties of moves and counter-moves. There cannot exist simple nostrums or simple rules for riches that apply universally.

This means that strategic management is not captured in the form of a strategic theory of the firm in a way that enables equations to be identified, data collected and analysed, and simple rules inferred. Strategic management is much more eclectic and diverse. Contexts external to the firm and internal to the firm are highly idiosyncratic. This places a premium on the ability to diagnose situations and formulate options. The specific routes to high performance are many and varied and not readily susceptible to simple generalizations. This goes some way to explaining why the RBV is widely seen as lacking specificity and definable concepts, and having no traceable connection to real performance improvements.

6.2 The language of the resource-based view: what is core competence?

In Chapter 5, we introduced the resource-based view with a figure similar to Figure 6.1. The top line of this diagram shows how the firm's investment programmes are directed towards the creation and development of resources and capabilities, and that these underpin the positional advantage from which superior value can be delivered to customers. The bottom line shows the value and financial consequences, in terms of the capacity of the firm to finance its investment programmes. The resource-based view focuses on the resources and capabilities of the firm, asserting that it is the distinctiveness of these that enables **sustainable positional advantages** to be constructed. The added element in this diagram is the presence of core competences as representing those resources and capabilities that are distinctive to the firm. As a result, competitive advantage is seen as the joint product of core competences and positional advantage. What many writers observe is that imperfections in the resource and capability markets are more in number and larger in size than those in product-markets. This places the burden on firms to pay attention to the underpinnings of competitive advantage in resource and capability terms. However, many writers have also observed that

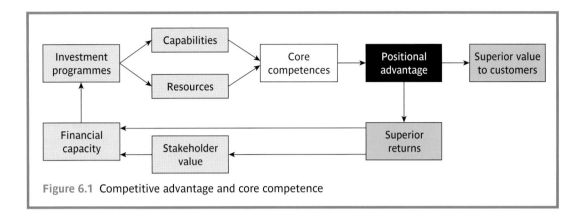

Figure 6.1 Competitive advantage and core competence

Resources
- Distribution coverage
- Financial capacity
- Shared expertise with related businesses
- Low-cost manufacturing and distribution systems
- Production capacity
- Ownership of raw material sources
- Long-term supply contracts

Capabilities
- Specialized knowledge
- Customer service orientation
- Design expertise
- Application experience
- Trade relationships
- Ability to utilize relevant technologies
- Systems design capability
- Fast, flexible response capability

Figure 6.2 Resources and capabilities

markets are changeable and even volatile and it is often quite difficult to get firms to change their internal cultures and processes quickly enough to keep pace with market changes.

Here we follow Grant's (1991, 2002) lead in using 'resources' to describe inputs that can in general be purchased on open markets and customized for use by the purchasers. Thus, production capacity might be generally available, but will be configured for specific use by each purchaser. The activities of individual purchasers may lead to imperfections in supply markets. For example, a company may seek to monopolize certain raw materials through acquisition, or maybe through offering long-term supply contracts. But, on their own, few resources are immediately productive. By contrast, the 'capabilities' described here are firm-specific. They are developed internally against the specific needs and ambitions of each company. They often depend on tacit knowledge, are path dependent in that they emerge and develop over time, and are not in the form of assets that can be traded. These resources and capabilities have individual characteristics, but a large part of their value-in-use to a firm is related to their configuration and their coordination. Figure 6.2 compares typical resources and typical capabilities. The distinctiveness of the firm's specific set of resources and capabilities is a function of which resources to acquire and what capabilities to develop (the *configuration* issue), the way in which each of these is developed (the *firm-specificity* issue), and the way in which they are internally managed to create positional advantage (the *coordination* issue).

6.2.1 Prahalad and Hamel on core competence

The language of assets, resources and capabilities can be confusing. The Grant (2002) distinction between resources and capabilities is as easy a distinction as any to maintain. However, it is laborious to keep referring to strategic resources and capabilities as those that systematically and uniquely underpin the competitive advantage relative to those other resources and capabilities that do not. Thus it is attractive to refer to these as core competences, the language popularized by Prahalad and Hamel in the *Harvard Business Review* (1990). They provided an unusual metaphor:

> *The diversified corporation is a large tree. The trunk and the major limbs are core products, the smaller branches are business units; the leaves, flowers, and fruit are end products. The root system that provides nourishment, sustenance, and stability is the core competence. You can miss the strength of competitors by looking only at their end products, in the same way you miss the strength of a tree if you look only at its leaves . . .*
>
> *Core competences are the collective learning in the organisation, especially how to coordinate diverse production skills and integrate multiple streams of technologies.*

6.2.2 BCG and capabilities-based competition

Prahalad and Hamel's approach is to define core competence as the combination of individual technologies and production skills that underlie a company's product lines. Sony's core competence in miniaturization allows it to make everything from the Sony Walkman to video cameras and digital cameras. Honda's core competence in engines and powertrains allows it to compete with products ranging from lawnmowers to racing cars. But this latter example shows a difficulty in their approach in that Honda's dealer network would be invisible – because of the focus on competences that lead directly to products. A development of their idea is contained in a Boston Consulting Group paper in 1992[4] on 'capabilities-based' competition. This contained four basic principles:

1 The building blocks of strategy are not products and markets but business processes.
2 Competitive success depends on transforming these key processes into strategic capabilities that consistently provide superior value to the customer.
3 Companies create these capabilities by making strategic investments in a support infrastructure that links together and transcends traditional strategic business units.
4 Because capabilities necessarily cross functions, the champion of a capabilities-based strategy is the chief executive officer.

This approach has the real merit of focusing on business processes as the integrative glue that binds together the various lower-level ingredients and on the investments that are required to make this effective. Unfortunately, the continued use of capabilities makes for some confusion. The essence of the idea here is that these business processes should connect to real customer needs. Things are only strategic when they begin and end with the customer because that is where value is sensed and created. Figure 6.3 is an extract from the same paper and summarizes the five dimensions on which a company's strategic resources and capabilities should aim to outperform the competition.

Boston Consulting Group presents this discussion in the language of strategic capabilities in an attempt to avoid an overuse of competences which is a feature of the Prahalad and Hamel approach.

---

[4] Stalk et al. (1992).

- **Speed**: the ability to respond quickly to customer or market demands and to incorporate new ideas and technologies quickly into products
- **Consistency**: the ability to produce a product that unfailingly satisfies customers' expectations
- **Acuity**: the ability to see the competitive environment clearly and thus to anticipate and respond to customers' evolving needs and wants
- **Agility**: the ability to adapt simultaneously to many different business environments
- **Innovativeness**: the ability to generate new ideas and to combine existing elements to create new sources of value

Figure 6.3 The competitive dimensions of resources and capabilities
Source: Stalk et al. (1992)

6.2.3 Amit and Schoemaker on strategic assets

A similar approach can be seen in another classic paper from the same era. Amit and Schoemaker (1993) build on the resource and capability language to create 'strategic assets'. By resources they mean stocks of available factors of production that are owned and controlled by the firm. Capabilities refer to the firm's capacity to deploy resources, usually in combination, using organizational processes to effect a desired end. They are information-based, tangible and intangible processes that are firm-specific and are developed over time through complex interactions with each other and with the firm's resources. Unlike resources, capabilities are based on developing, sharing, and exchanging information through the firm's human capital – as information-based assets they are often called 'invisible assets'. The authors describe 'strategic assets' as

> the set of difficult to trade and imitate, scarce, appropriable and specialised resources and capabilities that (underpin) the firm's competitive advantage.

In practice it is difficult to draw clear distinctions between the core competences of Prahalad and Hamel, the capabilities-based competition of Boston Consulting Group and the strategic assets of Amit and Schoemaker. They all convey the sense of firm-specific assets that are typically process and information based and intangible in character.

There are other assets and activities in the value chain, notable complementary assets that when linked to strategic assets (core competences) are necessary for the existence of the competitive advantage. Thus, a research-based pharmaceuticals company like Merck or SmithKlineGlaxo would identify research expertise as a core competence but management of government regulations as a complementary asset, essential but not unique. Many other assets and activities in the firm can be classified as 'make-or-buy', that is, the firm makes a financial calculation as to make or buy. Figure 6.4 distinguishes 'strategic assets' from 'complementary' assets and 'make-or-buy' assets. Strategic assets are those that are truly distinctive and unique to the firm and provide the underpinning of positional advantage in product markets. Complementary assets are those assets that are jointly required with the strategic assets in order to produce and deliver the product or service. Thus, product development might be a strategic asset, but production capacity is required for product trials and for product adaptations, even though that capacity is not unique to the firm. These assets are sometimes called *co-specialized* assets, in that they are complementary to the specialized assets and (lightly) customized to interface with them. Make-or-buy assets are those that you choose to include in the assets portfolio solely on the basis of financial calculations. For example, the decision to own or lease company cars might be made solely on financial criteria, because there are no strategic implications. In principle, if there are no strategic implications (which means that there is

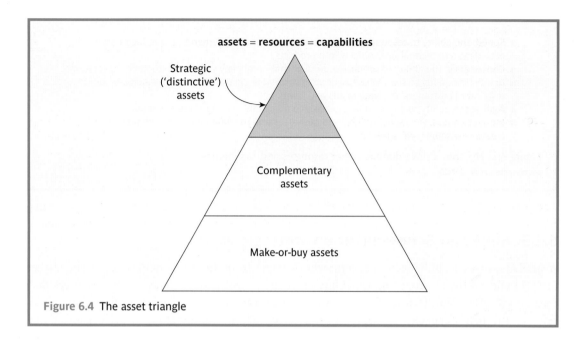

Figure 6.4 The asset triangle

no need to customize the assets for specific purposes), then there will, in general, be a free outside market. This in turn generally means that the market is able to supply more cheaply than is possible internally. You can see from this that the pressure to outsource can be very high and depends critically on the characteristics of supply markets.

6.2.4 Core competence = Distinctive capability = Strategic asset

In this chapter we propose to follow the terminology shown in Figure 6.1. This means that we follow the definition of resources and capabilities as discussed by Grant (2002) and that we use the term 'core competences' to cover the capabilities language of Boston Consulting Group and the strategic assets approach of Amit and Schoemaker. This language of core competences is nevertheless abstract and hard to put into practice. This reflects the idiosyncratic and unique nature of the strategic problems faced by individual firms. But it also reflects the need to have a clear concept upon which to base strategic thinking. The two building blocks of strategy (identified so far in this book) are competitive advantage and core competence. They are both intellectual constructs. Each relies on situational characteristics for their application in practice. Each provides a way of thinking so that strategists can develop a 'theory in use' that applies to their own situation. Gary Hamel (1994) has attempted to codify the idea of core competence further. He offers the following essential characteristics of a core competence:

1 A competence is a bundle of constituent skills and technologies rather than a discrete skill or technology and a core competence is the integration of a variety of individual skills.

2 A core competence is not an asset in the accounting sense of the word. A factory, a distribution channel or brand cannot be a core competence but an aptitude to manage that factory, that channel or that brand may constitute a core competence.

3 A core competence must make a disproportionate contribution to customer-perceived value. The distinction between core and non-core competence thus rests on a distinction between the relative impacts on customer value.

4 A core competence must also be competitively unique. This means either that (i) a competence is held uniquely by one firm in the competitive set or that (ii) a competence that is ubiquitous across an industry must be held at a superior level in the firm (for example, powertrains are ubiquitous in the automobile industry but one could argue that Honda has unique strength in this area and thus it is a core competence for Honda).

5 From the corporate (multi-business) perspective[5] a core competence should provide an entrée into new markets. A particular competence may be core from the perspective of an individual business, but from a corporate perspective it will not be core if there is no way of imagining an array of new product-markets issuing from it.[6]

The language of core competence has become widespread. Core competence and competitive advantage together have become the central conceptual terms in the analysis of competitive strategy. We define core competence quite simply as

> *the underlying capability that is the distinguishing characteristic of the organization.*

- It is the way we do things.
- It is how we organize the way we do things.
- It is how we systematically *communicate* this knowledge and build upon it.
- It is understanding the difference, and building bridges, between tangible and intangible assets, tacit and explicit knowledge, and individual and team knowledge and skill.

More formally, we define core competences as

> *the set of firm-specific skills and cognitive processes directed towards the attainment of competitive advantage.* (McGee and Segal-Horn, 1997)

Core competence is a fundamental concept in our understanding of what strategy making is. It is *only* through core competence that the firm attains competitive advantage and is therefore the mainspring of sustainable distinctiveness. But it is also the lens through which the world is seen and interpreted. Different firms (and people) see different things in their environments and this is a function of the inheritance and their experience. In the same way firms (and people) differ in the way in which they see themselves and therefore in their understanding of what they might achieve. In this way we can see core competences as the link between managerial cognition (Thomas and Porac, 1990) and the economics of the firm (see Figure 6.5). The key tasks of the strategy analyst are interpreting the external environment, understanding the dynamics of markets and of competition, and understanding the internal dynamics of one's own organization. Core competences provides the links to these economic assessments through a clarity of perception about the shared values and beliefs in the firm (often explicit in the mission statement), through tacit knowledge and understandings (that are possibly unique to the firm), and through flexible routines and recipes that enable non-standard challenges to be comprehended.

---

[5] See Chapter 9 for an explanation of the way in which competitive advantage should be deployed across multiple businesses within one company.

[6] For an excellent example see the case study Canon: Competing on Capabilities, Ackenhusen, 1992.

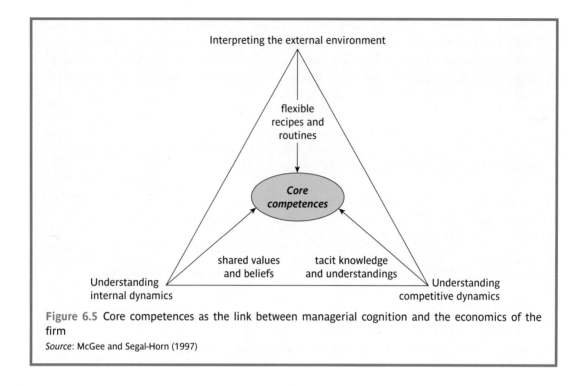

Figure 6.5 Core competences as the link between managerial cognition and the economics of the firm

Source: McGee and Segal-Horn (1997)

6.3 Related issues and the management of core competences

There are some mistakes that managers make very frequently. The first is to assume that acquiring and leveraging generic resources will be a major source of advantage in a new market. Advantage requires some degree of difference between firms and this requires the construction of assets that are unique to the firm. Another common mistake is to overestimate the transferability of specific assets and capabilities to a new product-market. Assets are unique to the firm in relation to the use for which they have been designed. New uses require some degree of further customization or re-adaptation. Even where the firm has constructed unique assets, it is easy to overestimate their capability to compete in highly profitable markets. This is merely to say that strategic choices are highly risky. Even if one can create a distinctive asset base it does not necessarily follow that customers will like the product offering that follows. Through this observation, you can see that competitive advantage is a composite of a resource-based view and a market-based view. Both are necessary: neither is necessary and sufficient on its own.

6.3.1 Resource leverage

Managers often neglect ways of creating advantage from a resource-based perspective. It is common to see firms paying much attention to the detail of product positioning in attempts to create those pieces of unique advantage that can make a difference. However, attention to the resource side can have significant pay-offs. For example, the approach of the Japanese automobile assemblers, especially Toyota,[7] shows the benefits from rearranging the supply chain in such a way that essential customer values such as reliability can be fundamentally changed. There are five ways in which management can **leverage** its resources so as to create the conditions under which a core competence

---

[7] See Fane et al. (2003).

can emerge.[8] The idea of 'leverage' (a much-used word of strategists) is to focus attention and effort on a specific object to the exclusion of rival objects so as to create a desired outcome. The exercise of leverage requires clear strategic intent and the possession of the relevant assets and competences.

1   *Concentrating resources: convergence and focus.* Convergence is the idea of focusing resources on few rather than many objectives and focus itself prevents the dilution of resources being applied to a specific target. The basic principle is the concentration of resources and the avoidance of dissipation of effort.

2   *Accumulating resources: extracting and borrowing.* Extraction is the ability to surface resources and capabilities that exist within the firm but might be lying concealed or dormant. The capacity to draw from the stockpile of resources is a facet of the ability to learn. Borrowing resources is the ability to tap into the resources of other companies. A simple example is the use of one company's basic research as an input to another company's commercialization. Thus Sony commercialized the transistor that was pioneered by Bell Laboratories. As Hamel and Prahalad (1993) point out:

> *Increasingly, technology is stateless. It crosses borders in the form of scientific papers, foreign sponsorship of university research, international licensing, cross border equity stakes in high-tech start-ups and international academic conferences. Tapping into the market for technology is a potentially important source of resource leverage.*

3   *Complementing resources: blending and balancing.* Blending resources is similar to what we called co-specialization (above). How resources fit together in planned and unplanned ways gives the possibility to transform the value of resources while using them. Blending requires integrative skills such as technological integration, functional integration and new product development. The blending of functional skills is a new way of restating the nature of general management. This traditionally has involved the integration of functions such as production, marketing and R&D. Balancing requires the firm's resources and capabilities to be able to support a business model. Unbalanced firms would have gaps such that resources and capabilities would be required from others for a sustainable revenue stream to be achieved. A balanced firm may benefit from tapping into the resources of others but has a defensible position on its own.

4   *Conserving resources: co-opting and shielding.* Conserving resources simply means retaining resources so that they are reusable – the basis for economies of scope. The issue is how to retain knowledge in the memory banks so that it is addressable and recyclable to other activities. Co-option has the same theme as recycling but involves collaborative efforts to work collectively towards new standards or new products. Shielding resources is about not wasting non-renewable resources (such as cash) on difficult targets. Attacking competitors directly in their home markets is an example of a difficult target where the probabilities are more of failure than of success. The example of Canon taking on Xerox in plain paper copying is a classic example. Xerox's R&D budgets were very much higher than those of Canon, but Canon chose to compete in areas where the Xerox business model was weak, e.g. small machines, third-party distribution systems, and machine reliability.[9]

5   *Recovering resources: expediting success.* Pace is a significant dimension of performance. The faster the cycle time from investment through to sales the more quickly that resources can be renewed and redeveloped (see Figure 6.1 where the strategy cycle indicates the process). The speed at which Japanese automakers and motorcycle manufacturers operated gave these companies higher cash flows than their Western counterparts but also more up-to-date products and a greater ability to respond to changing markets.

---

[8] This is taken from Hamel and Prahalad (1993).

[9] See the case study Canon: Competing on Capabilities, Ackenhusen, 1992, on page 550.

6.3.2 Identifying intangibles

The expression 'intangible' is being applied more and more frequently to resources and to capabilities. For our purposes it refers to the following:

- intellectual property rights of patents, trademarks, copyright and registered designs;
- trade secrets;
- contracts and licences;
- databases;
- information in the public domain;
- personal and organizational networks;
- the know-how of employees, advisers, suppliers and distributors;
- the reputation of products and of the company;
- the culture of the organization.

Richard Hall conducted a study of the relative contribution of intangible resources and capabilities to business success.[10] Some of the results are summarized in the next three tables. Table 6.1 summarizes the average weightings for each intangible drawn from the above list. Hall found that the results were common and systematic across a wide sample of companies. Four factors stood out as most important, namely, company reputation, product reputation, employee know-how and organization culture. By contrast, intellectual property rights and trade secrets were by far the least

Table 6.1 Relative importance of intangible resources in overall business success

Ranking (1 = highest, 2 = lowest)	Average Weight (crucial = 10, insignificant = 1)
1. Company reputation	8.6
2. Product reputation	8.4
3. Employee know-how	8.1
4. Organization culture	7.9
5. Networks	7.1
6. Specialist physical resources	6.1
7. Databases	6.0
8. Supplier know-how	5.8
9. Distributor know-how	5.3
10. Public knowledge	5.2
11. Contracts	4.7
12. Intellectual property rights	3.2
13. Trade secrets	2.9

Sample size = 95
Source: Hall (1992)

---

[10] Hall (1992).

significant. Table 6.2 unpacks the employee know-how factor seen in Table 6.1. Here CEOs were asked which business function was the most important contributor to employee know-how. 'Operations' scores highly because of the high tacit content of know-how (learning by experience). In contrast, in finance know-how has a large external knowledge content which means that skills can be formalized and transferred. The importance attached to sales and marketing by both manufacturers and retailers is to be expected, whereas the contribution of technology is quite modest.

Table 6.3 looks at the time it takes to replace an intangible asset. The question posed was 'how many years would it take to replace the *particular resource* if you had to start from scratch?' This gives an indication of protection from new entrants depending on the transferability of existing reputation. Reputational resources dominate this list. Company reputation, in particular, gives strong incumbents a significant advantage. By contrast, much know-how can be replaced or rebuilt over quite a short period (around three years), suggesting that speedy imitation is quite probable in most situations.

The importance of reputation suggests that it should receive constant management attention. The distinction between company and product is interesting, implying, first, that attention to both is probably necessary, and second, that in multi-business companies the corporate name could have a significant halo effect across businesses and product lines. The experience of companies like Sony, Hewlett-Packard and IBM provides good examples of this. The high scores for employee know-how

Table 6.2 Percentage of CEOs quoting the function as the most important area of employee know-how

	Total sample	Manufacturing	Retailing
Operations	43	27	8
Sales and marketing	29	46	46
Technology	17	18	31
Finance	6	0	15
Other	5	9	0
Total	100	100	100

Source: Hall (1992)

Table 6.3 Replacement periods

	Average replacement period (years)
Company reputation	10.8
Product reputation	6.0
Employee know-how	4.6
Networks	3.4
Supplier know-how	3.1
Databases	2.1
Distributor know-how	1.6

Source: Hall (1992)

support the idea of invisible assets that are information and experience rich. This is clearly fertile ground for the development of core competences. In Table 6.1 the term culture has a specific meaning: it refers to ability to manage change, ability to innovate, teamworking ability, participative management style, perception of high quality standards, and perception of high standards of customer service. These also are ingredients that are information and experience rich.

6.3.3 What determines the value of a core competence?

Figure 6.6 summarizes the conditions that determine the value of a core competence (strategic asset). The basic foundations of value are *imitability*, *durability*, *substitutability* and *appropriability*. The ability of competitors to imitate your assets is in part to do with *physical uniqueness*. More subtle issues around inimitability are:

- *path dependency* – cumulative learning and experience over time, which is difficult to replicate over short periods;
- *causal ambiguity* – not really knowing what it is that is the important element in a complex asset;
- *first-mover advantage* – the pre-emption of a market by being the first to create scale-efficient assets.

Substitutability is often an unknown, in that new technologies can emerge which very quickly outdate older solutions. For example, the battle between satellite and cable television systems is still raging – substitutability is high, but it is not clear which standard will prevail. Appropriability is an important but subtle issue. A central question about a strategic asset is: Who can capture the value that is created? Is it the firm? Could it be the skilled technicians? Might it be patent owners? Perhaps there are long-term supply contracts?

Following this discussion of intangibles you should reflect on the issues in Case box 6.2 where PPR, the owner of Gucci is trying to extend the luxury goods brand image into other areas. Is this really a logical extension of the Gucci super luxury brand? Or is it an extension too far?

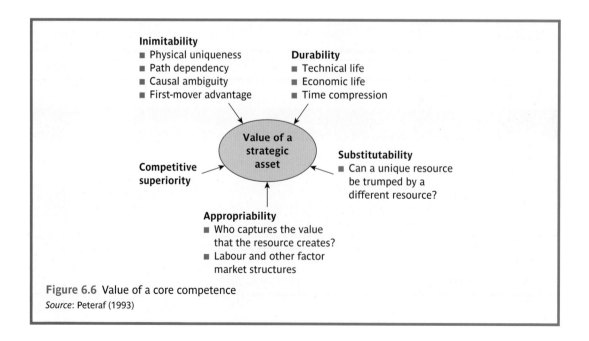

Figure 6.6 Value of a core competence
Source: Peteraf (1993)

Case box 6.2: **Out of Africa**

The family firm that owns Gucci is shedding assets to focus on fashion

Leopard-skin print is in style this winter, but PPR, the French conglomerate that owns Gucci Group, a luxury-goods firm, has decided to sell its African division. Next week the group will conclude the sale of over half of the shares of CFAO, a trading house founded in France's colonial era, on the Euronext stockmarket. PPR plans to use the resulting €900m ($1.3 billion) or so to add more big international fashion brands to its collection.

PPR has long traded in and out of businesses: François Pinault, its founder, started with a sawmill in Brittany and built it into an integrated timber-trading and processing firm before buying CFAO in 1990. He then bought several household names in French retailing: Conforama, a furniture chain, Au Printemps, which owns department stores, and Fnac, a books-and-records chain. In 1999 Mr Pinault moved into luxury goods with the acquisition of 42% of Gucci Group, later taking full control.

Under his son, François-Henri Pinault, who took over as chief executive in 2005, the group bought 69% of Puma, a German sportswear firm, and has made a few disposals. Now François-Henri wants to get out of everyday retailing to focus on luxury and upmarket global brands. As well as listing CFAO, he plans to sell Conforama, Fnac and La Redoute, a catalogue business.

PPR's French retail businesses have far lower profit margins and less promising growth prospects than Gucci Group and Puma. But CFAO is another story. Revenues at the firm, which sells Western cars, pharmaceuticals and other equipment to businesses and middle-class consumers across Africa, have grown strongly, from €1.2 billion in 2000 to €2.9 billion in 2008. For big manufacturers such as Toyota, IBM, Heineken and Peugeot, CFAO provides access to markets which are too small or risky to justify a local operation.

CFAO has had to exit some markets abruptly. But it carefully spreads its risk across 34 countries and has little competition other than small local firms. Eventually CFAO may be disintermediated as markets develop and big firms begin selling directly, but that will probably take generations, says a banker involved in the listing.

Being inside PPR has certainly benefited CFAO. It was Mr Pinault senior who decided to jettison its European operations and focus on Africa. 'CFAO used to reinvest cash from Africa into European distribution, but as part of PPR we concentrate our investment on Africa,' says Alain Viry, chairman of the supervisory board.

Focusing PPR on luxury and global fashion brands will appeal to investors, who dislike conglomerates. But the fashion business is fickle and crowded. Any big acquisition in the field 'had better be a good one to justify giving up most of the value of CFAO,' says Luca Solca of Bernstein Research. CFAO's recent return on assets, of over 20% a year, he points out, far exceeds that of the Gucci Group, at around 7%, mainly because PPR paid so much for the latter. The same problem will surely afflict any future purchases in fashion.

Source: 'Out of Africa', *The Economist*, 26 November 2009

Questions

1 What are the core competences of the typical luxury goods business and fashion brands in particular?

2 Why do you think that Francois-Henri Pinault wants to get out of everyday retailing to focus on luxury and upmarket global brands? What risks does he face?

3 Will any of the core competences in CFAO be applicable in fashion businesses? Does this matter?

4 To what extent is the core competence of PPR dependent on the Pinault family itself?

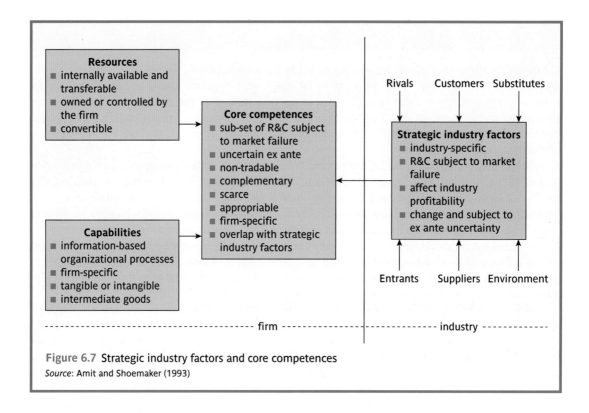

Figure 6.7 Strategic industry factors and core competences
Source: Amit and Shoemaker (1993)

6.4 Linking core competence to competitive advantage

The resource-based view (RBV) is not a theory in its own right. But coupled with the market-based view (MBV) it enables the strategist to link the firm's internal behavioural decisions and organizational choices with the need to secure a defensible positional advantage in the market. RBV and MBV together provide a theory in use for the strategist. Figure 6.1 shows the link between RBV and MBV as a juxtaposition of core competence and competitive advantage. Amit and Schoemaker (1993) went a stage further. Their full model is shown in Figure 6.7, adapted only to use the phrase core competence for strategic asset. The extra dimension (compared to Figure 6.1) provided here is contained in the phrase 'strategic industry factors'. These are the sources of market imperfections that firms can capture as elements in their competitive advantage.[11]

From our earlier discussion of industry analysis and Porter's Five Forces we obtained a general description of the characteristics of an industry. Porter's model (1980) provides five generic characteristics and others have suggested more, such as government and deeper environmental variables. Other ad hoc analyses have developed over the years, particularly the idea of key success factors (KSFs). Later in this chapter we suggest a way of using KSFs in practice, but in general KSFs can be seen as those elements in the industry that are deemed as *important* for customers. Strategic industry factors are a way of articulating KSFs as those elements in the industry and in the market that are subject to market failure and therefore where firms can provide them they will have an advantage. Using our language of advantage, these factors are those firm-specific imperfections that represent competitive advantage. Amit and Schoemaker synthesize contributions from many writers in producing this list of characteristics that apply to strategic industry factors:

---

[11] Economists often refer to these imperfections as market failures, that is, inabilities to trade in these factors in perfect markets. Our view of competitive advantage as firm-specific imperfections in the market rests on this notion of market failure.

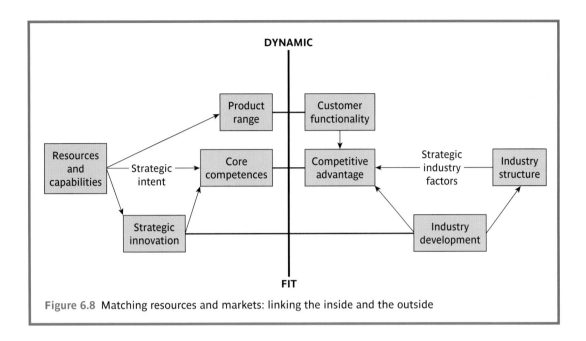

Figure 6.8 Matching resources and markets: linking the inside and the outside

1 They are determined through a complex interaction among industry rivals, new entrants, customers, regulators, innovators, suppliers and other stakeholders.

2 They are strategic in that they are subject to market failures and may be the basis for competition among rivals.

3 They are known ex post but not ex ante; in particular, not all aspects of their development and interactions with other factors in the market will be known or controllable.

4 Their development takes time, skill, and capital: they may be specialized to particular uses.

5 Investments in them are largely irreversible (i.e. sunk costs).

6 Their pace of accumulation is affected by own prior knowledge and experience and that of rivals (i.e. path dependent) and cannot be readily increased (doubling the investment will not usually halve the time).

7 Their value to any particular firm will depend on its control of other factors (the complementarity property).

In examining Figure 6.8 you will see that the list of core competences has similarities to the list of strategic industry factors. This is not an accident, nor is it an error. The difference is that firms seek to design their core competences in anticipation of their usefulness in creating and sustaining an intended competitive advantage. The strategic industry factors are those imperfections in the market that have succeeded. The core competences are ex ante in nature; they are intentions. The strategic industry factors are ex post, those characteristics that have actually worked in the market to produce competitive advantage.

6.4.1 Competence-based competition in practice

In 1977 Dan Bricklin, an MBA student at the Harvard Business School, developed on his Apple computer a type of 'electronic blackboard' that allowed him to display a grid of numbers linked together by formulae. His professor told him (allegedly) that it had no future as a product. Why?

Because software was (and is) easily imitated. There was virtually no entry barrier. There were established firms selling mainframe languages to do pro-forma calculations. Moreover, the Apple was a mere toy! What was wrong with the professor's reasoning?

In 1973 one of the authors wrote a case on the Japanese motorcycle industry. The final discussion question asked 'should Honda enter the emerging global automobile business?' It was a 'give-away' question – anyone who said 'yes' flunked, because markets were saturated, efficient competitors existed in Japan, the US and in Europe. Honda had little or no experience in automobiles and it had neither automobile distribution system nor access to one. In 1985 his wife drove a Honda! What was wrong with this answer?

This was a common fault in the strategy analyses of that period. Why was it that Canon could beat Xerox? How did Komatsu manage to beat Caterpillar? The fault lay in the lack of a proper resource-based perspective. There are three parts to an answer to this question: strategic intent, strategic innovation and core competences.

Strategic intent

Strategic intent has a particular meaning in encouraging people to go beyond 'business as usual'. It appeals to the resource language that we reported above, particularly the sense of concentration, convergence and focus, and to the idea of resource leverage.

It has been argued that US firms seeking strategic fit have often found themselves overtaken by firms, especially the Asian conglomerates, driven by long-term visions of the future, which are then relentlessly and ruthlessly pursued with *strategic intent*. Companies like CNN, Honda, NEC and Sony have succeeded (according to this argument) because of their sustained obsession with achieving global dominance in their industries. This obsession has been labelled strategic intent (Hamel and Prahalad, 1989). The significance of this is that the intent of these companies was out of proportion to their existing resources and capabilities. This gap between ambition and resources is known as *strategic stretch*. These companies had to expand and adapt their current stock of resources and create new ones. They were more concerned with 'leveraging' resources than with achieving *strategic fit* between their current resources and their industry environments.

Strategic intent can thus be used as a psychological target which provides a focus for all members of the organization to adopt. Becoming the industry leader or dominating a specific segment is a frequent missionary goal. The fundamental focus of the firm's strategy commits well beyond its current resource profile. The prophecies can therefore become self-fulfilling, provided that employees have faith in their leadership and that, in many cases, the existing industry leaders fail to recognize that the challenge is on. The logic of expansion coupled with economies of scope provides an economic basis for justifying strategic intent. However, there are limits to economies of scope which arise when industries and markets require more variety than the fixed factors that support scope effects can support.

Strategic intent implies a stretch beyond current resources and capabilities and means. But for those companies that have adopted this style it became a necessity and was not a luxury.

Strategic innovation

Strategic investments are bets against an unknowable future. These bets often require technical progress and substantial investment in R&D and in new products. In 1980 Xerox had a stranglehold on the copier industry. IBM was poised to enter, attracted by Xerox's huge profits. Canon also had an interest in fine optics and precision mechanics on the basis of their existing camera business. On whom would you have bet? Table 6.4 shows the Xerox hand.

The barriers to entry were formidable. In IBM's favour was their own large scale, which meant that it could probably afford to spend as much money as Xerox (but note that Kodak had had the same thoughts earlier without too much success). Canon had no obvious points of superiority

Table 6.4 The Xerox position in 1980

	Xerox
Technology	Leading-edge product technology: 7000 patents
Distribution	Worldwide direct sales (units): 7000 in US, 5000 in Europe, 3000 in Japan
Financing	Leasing
R&D investment	$600 million p.a.
Manufacturing	Worldwide network of plants
Scale	Market share = 90%
Image	Photocopy = Xerox

Source: Ackenhusen (1992)

Table 6.5 How Canon rewrote the rules of the game

	Xerox existing business	Canon's new rules
Customer definition	Medium/large companies	Small companies/individuals
Use pattern	Centralized copying	Decentralized
Product	High copy volume features	Utility, value for money
Distribution	Own sales force	Office products dealers
Service	Own network	By dealers
Financing	Lease	Sale
Technology	Leading-edge dry toner	Low-cost liquid toner

Source: Ackenhusen (1992)

given the nature of the market and the strategic industry factors that were present at that time. The idea of strategic innovation is to rewrite the rules of the game. Table 6.5 catches the essence of what Canon did to outflank Xerox and one can do similar analyses to show how Komatsu outflanked Caterpillar by changing the point of competition from quality to cost and reliability, and how Honda managed to enter the global automobile industry by emphasizing quality.

Strategic innovation leads to a new form of competitive advantage, a different conception of the required core competences, and a different business model through which the cash could be seen to flow. In the case of the Apple computer and Dan Bricklin's spreadsheet invention, the spreadsheet became the killer application that placed the new Apple personal computer on millions of desks by appealing to a similar sense that Canon identified – the customers' wish to have desktop capability.

Core competence

The core competences in each of these examples were created by investments in the operational and organizational infrastructure of the strategic innovators. The new capabilities spawned through this investment were linked across business units and the learning and experience of diverse business units were captured and leveraged across the company. For example, Canon's distinctive management processes (compared to Xerox) were high levels of decentralization, strong internal coordination processes and external cooperation. Canon exemplified the value of external cooperation through importing knowledge from strategic alliance partners and joint ventures. The complex core competences that arose could be described as (i) a high pace of learning and innovation, (ii) a long-term approach to developing capabilities, and (iii) the systematic transfer of competences across businesses and into new businesses.

The risks associated with the Japanese approach – most of the examples have been Japanese companies – is that an overdependence on a resource-based perspective can lock you into your own view of the world away from changing markets and customer preferences.

How do we balance the inside view with the outside view? Figure 6.8 summarizes inside and outside perspectives and the links between them. The firm is driven by the link of resources and capabilities through strategic intent to core competences. This is the crux of the firm's intended strategy, culminating in the match between core competences and competitive advantage. A failed strategy would have empty boxes in the middle of the diagram. The core competences are captured in products which have to match customer functionality. The dynamics of the process are shown by strategic innovation which through 'newgame' strategies match with and/or drive industry development.

The demand side, the outside, is captured by the link between industry structure through strategic industry factors to competitive advantage. Industry structure has multiple industry factors and competitive advantages associated with it. The firm's task is to identify one of the set and match with it – this implies a set of customer functionalities to be satisfied. The dynamics are captured through industry development and other exogenous factors.

The design of the firm's theory in use is shown by the strategic fit between core competences and competitive advantage. The practical present-day fit is shown by the fit between product range and customer functionality. The dynamic fit is between strategic innovation and industry development. Lack of fit in the short term can be a result of (i) the requirements of the outside moving too quickly for the inside to keep pace, or (ii) the strategic drive from the inside missing its targets. There may be a short-term fit that erodes because the dynamic linkages through innovation and industry development do not work properly.

6.4.2 The role of learning

When we compare product-markets and resource-markets, we can see that fundamentally competition is a contest for the acquisition of skills. Moreover, competition in product-markets is a superficial expression of the more fundamental competition over competences. Looked at in this way, the dynamics of markets, of industries and of firms is about 'learning', rather than technical theories of product-market evolution, hence all the current concern with the 'learning organization' and with 'knowledge management'. Core competences arise through the collective learning of the firm, through accumulated experience with the coordination of diverse production skills and the integration of multiple streams of technology. Prahalad and Hamel (1990) take the proposition further. They argue that core competences span across businesses and products within a corporation – they can support several products or businesses. Thus, they argue that the narrow focus of strategic business units is dysfunctional. It is also clear that core competences have temporal dominance over products. They evolve more slowly than the products that they make possible, or core competences support several generations of essentially the same product classes. Figure 6.9 suggests a framework within which all these strands can be seen. The focus of the diagram is on the way in which the resource-based view is becoming accepted as the genesis of advantage in the firm, but also reflects the modern debate about the contribution of learning and knowledge to our understanding of how firms compete.

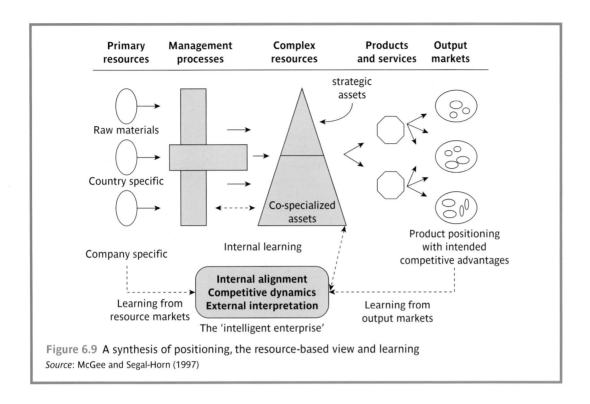

Figure 6.9 A synthesis of positioning, the resource-based view and learning
Source: McGee and Segal-Horn (1997)

6.5 Competitive strategy in practice

We start from the premise that there can be great differences between the abilities of firms to succeed – there are fundamental inequalities between most competitors. This contrasts with the conventional economics textbook view of perfect competition which holds that firms are essentially similar, if not the same, and that over time their performances will converge on a minimum rate of return on capital. Less efficient firms will be obliged to exit and the more efficient firms will be subject to imitation. But the competitive strategy view of the firm is that understanding and manipulating the factors that cause these inequalities, so as to give the firm a sustainable competitive advantage, largely govern long-term business success. These factors vary widely; so different businesses, even within the same industry, often need to be doing different things. Thus, there are many strategies open to firms. The usual starting point is to recognize that strategy is the outcome of the resolution of several different, conflicting forces. These are summarized in Figure 6.10. Society has expectations of its business organizations. Owners, managers and other implementers of strategy have their own personal values and ambitions. The company has strengths and weaknesses, and the industry context offers opportunities and threats. The traditional, top-down view of strategy is encapsulated in the *strategic planning view*. This involves deciding on long-term objectives and strategic direction, eliminating or minimizing weaknesses, avoiding threats, building on and defending strengths, and taking advantage of opportunities. But, from reading this chapter, it should be clear that given the strategic direction, the key strategic decision is product-market selection. This should be based on the existence of long-term viable business opportunities (not merely the existence of growing markets), together with the prospect of creating the relevant core competences. Viable business opportunities depend on:

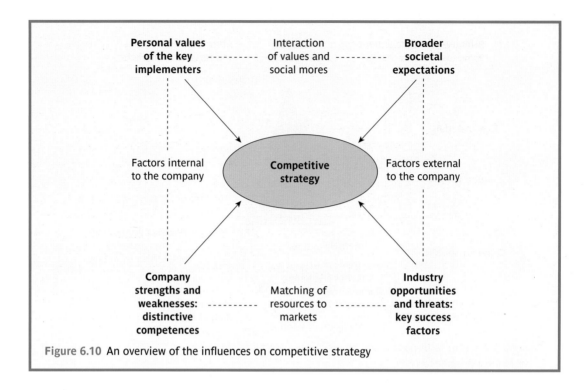

Figure 6.10 An overview of the influences on competitive strategy

Figure 6.11 Identifying key success factors
Source: Grant (2002)

- the existence of valuable market segments;
- the existence of a sustainable positional advantage;
- the creation of the appropriate strategic assets.

In conducting the assessment of viable business opportunity, the term *key success factors* is often used. Intuitively, this means 'What do we have to do to succeed?' We can put some analytical flesh on these bones. Figures 6.11 and 6.12 illustrate the process (see Grant, 1991). There is a set of key questions to ask:

Industry	What do customers want? (analysis of demand)	+ How do firms survive competition? (analysis of competition)	= Key success factors
Steel	Customers include automobiles, engineering, and container industries. Customers acutely price sensitive. Also require product consistency and reliability of supply. Specific technical specifications required for special steels.	Competition primarily on price. Competition intense due to declining demand, high fixed costs and low-cost imports. Strong trade union bargaining power. Transport costs high. Scale economies important.	Cost efficiency through scale-efficient plants, low-cost location, rapid adjustment of capacity to output, low labour costs. In special steels, scope for differentiation through quality.
Fashion clothing	Demand fragmented by garment, style, quality, colour. Customers willing to pay price premium for fashion, exclusivity, and quality. Retailers seek reliability and speed of supply.	Low barriers to entry and exit. Low seller concentration. Few scale economies. Strong retail buying power. Price and non-price competition both strong.	Combine effective differentiation with low-cost operation. Key differentiation variables are speed of response to changing fashions, style, reputation with retailers/ consumers. Low wages and overheads important.
Grocery supermarkets	Customers want low prices, convenient location and wide range of products.	Markets localized, concentration normally high. But customer price sensitivity encourages vigorous price competition. Exercise of bargaining power a key determinant of purchase price. Scale economies in operations and advertising.	Low-cost operation requires operational efficiency, scale-efficient stores, large aggregate purchases to maximize buying power, low wage costs. Differentiation requires large stores to provide wide product range and customer convenience facilities.

Figure 6.12 Identifying key success factors
Source: Grant (2002)

- Is there a market?
- Do we have some advantage?
- Can we survive the competition?

These lead us into two pieces of analysis: the analysis of customers and demand, and the analysis of competition (summarized in Figure 6.11). Figure 6.12 shows how these can be put together to identify key success factors in three different industries. The key success factors represent the strategic logic(s) (there is usually more than one) available. In the steel industry, for example, the key success factors revolve around low cost, cost efficiencies and scale effectiveness, with some scope for speciality steels. On the other hand, in the fashion industry, key success factors are about differentiation, coupled with an element of low cost. Differentiation has speed of response characteristics, but the industry and the market are so broad that there are distinctive segments, some of which are cost driven, while others are differentiation driven. This industry provides a good example of the multiplicity of available strategies.

In formulating competitive strategy, there are some important things to remember:

- *Resources are limited*, opportunities are infinite. The essence of strategy lies in saying 'Yes' to only some of the options and, therefore, 'No' to many others. *Trade-offs* are essential to strategy – they reflect the need for choice and they purposefully limit what a company offers.
- Always factor in *opportunity costs*. A dollar invested 'here' is a dollar not invested 'there', or not given back to shareholders.
- The essence of strategy is choosing to perform activities *differently* from rivals.
- In the long run, what matters is not how fast you are running, but whether you are *running faster than your competitors*.
- A company can only outperform rivals if it can establish a difference that it can sustain. So always test for the *sustainability* of your competitive advantage. Competitors are likely to view relieving you of your competitive advantage as their cardinal duty. Further, not all of them are likely to be stupid.
- The competitive value of individual activities cannot be separated from the whole. So, *fit* locks out imitators by creating a value chain that is stronger than its weakest link.
- The long-run test of any strategy lies not in what it contributes to market share or profit margins but in what it contributes to long-term *return on investment*.
- Strategic positions should have a *time horizon* of a decade or more, not just of a single planning cycle and/or product cycle.

6.5.1 Managing the business for value

Firms are often poor at devising practical procedures for carrying out the strategy analyses of the kind suggested in this chapter. The ideas are frequently expressed only as concepts. Data is often not collected nor organized as evidence to test out alternative possibilities. This section outlines one way of capturing the analysis of competitive advantage.

Competitive advantage is about creating value both for the customer and for the firm. The first task is to define what this means in practice. Thus value to the customer can be defined as

1 firm's ability to position a product better/different than competitors;
2 firm's ability to persuade customers to recognize, purchase and value the difference.

Strategic indicators		Company 1	Benchmark
price: performance segment maps	**Positioning**		
repeats; price premium; share	**Customer persuasion**		
peer ratings; tech benchmarking	**Capability**		
engineering studies cost analysis	**Efficiency**		
Financial indicators	Sales Margins Asset t/o ROI		

Figure 6.13 Managing the business for value

Value to the firm can be defined as

1 firm's ability to create and sustain core competences that underpin the positioning at manageable cost premiums;
2 firm's ability to run (the rest of) the business efficiently and at best-practice levels.

These definitions can be operationalized according to the schema shown in Figure 6.13. The four elements of value are coded as Positioning, Customer Persuasion, Capability, and Efficiency. Note that Efficiency is not enough! Each of these requires strategic indicators by which performance can be measured. The figure suggests some starting points. Then data should be collected to identify the firm's own performance on these measures and then some benchmark comparisons. To complement this, strategic performance analysis financial indicators can also be shown, remembering that these reflect the outcomes of previous strategies whereas the strategic indicators will predict future financial performance.

6.5.2 Positioning the business for growth

Competitive strategy will usually have a limited time scale over which assessments can be made reliably. This is usually related to the tangibility of assets and to the speed with which the product life cycle operates. As a rule of thumb, firms can see to the end of the current product life cycle and are actively engaged in the planning of the next cycle. The cycle beyond that is much less clearly seen. Thus in practice we can expect firms to see one and a half life cycles ahead (subject to the life expectancy of their capital assets). Thus if a car manufacturer has a product life cycle of four years we would expect it to be able to see and forecast about six or seven years ahead. So how do we plan beyond this if the numbers are missing? Figure 6.14 shows the break in our planning horizons.

The shorter period of competitive strategy horizon (shown for example as five years) should not and does not mean that we do not do any strategic thinking beyond that. One way of dealing with this is to compare alternative growth targets (shown in the figure). For each of these identify the

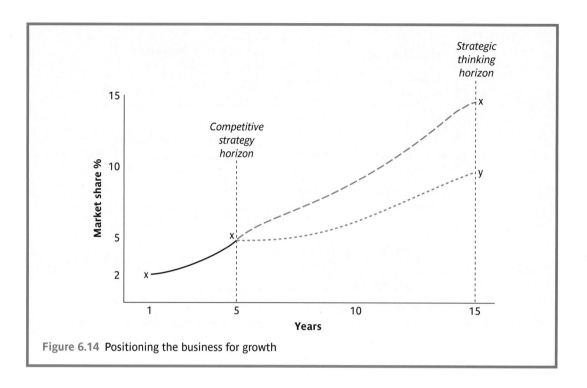

Figure 6.14 Positioning the business for growth

	Technical	Internal	External
Enablers			
Blockers			

Growth target = %

Figure 6.15 Enablers and blockers

enablers and the blockers of success and assess the nature of these as technical, internal or external (see Figure 6.15). An enabler might, for example, be a creative and productive research team and it would be internal in nature. A blocker might be the growth of low-cost manufacturing capability among competitors and it would be external in character. An example of a technical issue might be the development of new technical standards (such as for DVD rewriting) and this might be either an enabler or a blocker depending on the firm's capabilities.

Longer-term strategic thinking requires both enablers and blockers to be managed properly. Thus we would expect a focus on the key enablers to develop measures and information sources, to create an intelligence system to track their progress. The need is to assess and keep assessing the prior probability of these enablers occurring. The blockers are more difficult. The task is to identify the blockers, sort them into groups according to their common factors, discover the underlying forces and dynamics, and develop strategies to shift the blocks or to get round them (note how in the reprographics industry in the 1970s Canon developed an R&D strategy to get around Xerox's

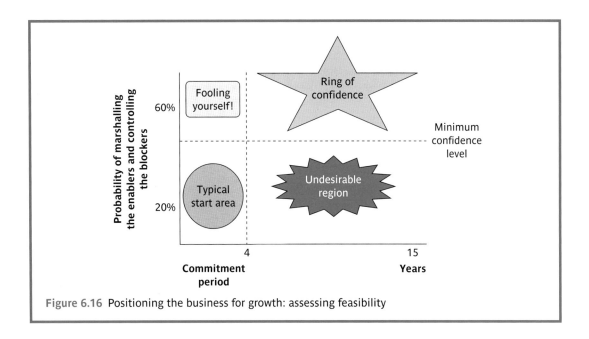

Figure 6.16 Positioning the business for growth: assessing feasibility

network of blocking patents). For blockers we need (as for enablers) to assess and track over time the prior probability of controlling the blockers and moderating their influence. This analysis then should be repeated for different growth targets. The outcomes will of course be quite qualitative and multidimensional but Figure 6.16 suggests a way of summarizing the outputs.

The vertical axis is the prior probabilities of facilitating the enablers and controlling the blockers (a joint probability of achieving a target would be one way of operationalizing this). The horizontal axis is time. The first part of this is a commitment period during which the foundations are being established (typically the first part of a J-curve), shown here for example as four years. Beyond this period we are looking for a confidence that growth can be managed – *the ring of confidence* in the figure, and not *the undesirable region*. More generally you would expect to see a curve showing the prior probabilities rising over time. The key question is whether the probabilities are sufficiently high early enough. The bad position is when the probabilities remain low well beyond the commitment period. Conversely, happiness occurs when they rise quickly.

Approaches such as this one require considerable judgement and they often will defy the objective tests implied by quantification. However, the advantage here is of applying a systematic forecasting or scenario planning procedure (see Chapter 11) that is rooted in the economics of the firm.

6.6 Summary

This chapter asserts that competitive advantage and core competence are two key intellectual constructs that together provide the foundation for understanding strategy. Competitive advantage is the basis for the market-based view (MBV), providing us with a way of assessing the positioning of the firm relative to its competitors. Core competence is one of many phrases that capture the resource-based view. It represents the idea of *'the underlying capability that is the distinguishing characteristic of the organization'* and that underpins competitive advantage.

We have reviewed the various languages of the resource-based view, mentioning resources, capabilities, competences and strategic assets. However, rather than pursue semantic differences between such an array of titles we have chosen to follow the definition of resources and capabilities as discussed by Grant (2002) and to use the term 'core competences' to cover the capabilities language of Boston Consulting Group and the strategic assets approach of Amit and Schoemaker. Further, we suggest Hamel's clarification as both practical and theoretically sound, namely:

1 A competence is a bundle of constituent skills and technologies rather than a discrete skill or technology and a core competence is the integration of a variety of individual skills.

2 A core competence is not an asset in the accounting sense of the word. A factory, a distribution channel or brand cannot be a core competence but an aptitude to manage that factory, that channel or that brand may constitute a core competence.

3 A core competence must make a disproportionate contribution to customer-perceived value. The distinction between core and non-core competence thus rests on a distinction between the relative impacts on customer value.

4 A core competence must also be competitively unique. This means either that (i) a competence is held uniquely by one firm in the competitive set or that (ii) a competence that is ubiquitous across an industry must be held at a superior level in the firm.

5 From the corporate (multi-business) perspective a core competence should provide an entrée into new markets. A particular competence may be core from the perspective of an individual business, but from a corporate perspective it will not be core if there is no way of imagining an array of new product-markets issuing from it.

The language of the resource-based view can be confusing and it is no surprise that the concept of core competence has been difficult to apply. However, it is an intellectual construct in just the same way as is competitive advantage and should be used to clarify thinking. It is not intended as a simple framework or tool (such as SWOT or PEST) that contains within it simple practical guidelines. The second half of the chapter is devoted to practical applications of the core competence concept. Core competence leads directly into issues of resource leverage (for value and profit). We discuss the importance of identifying intangibles. We have emphasized the link to competitive advantage using the language of strategic industry factors and key success factors. We have examined strategic intent, strategic innovation, and the role of learning. What core competence does is to focus attention on the managerial processes, information content and communications that are the intangible heart of the resource-based view. Core competences are hardly ever tangible assets – they reflect intangible, sometimes designed but sometimes informal managerial process. As intangibles it is then not surprising that firms are essentially different from one another (as opposed to the traditional view of economists who hold that firms are essentially similar in the long term). Bringing competitive advantage and core competence together as core elements for competitive strategy in practice we see how managing the business for value and managing the business for growth depend on both concepts.

In the following chapters we explore how strategy (i.e. competitive advantage plus core competence) is developed in a number of different situations. In Chapter 7 we look at competitive strategy in the world of the 'new economy'. Chapter 8 introduces multi-business or corporate strategy and develops this into an examination of mergers and acquisitions. Chapter 9 focuses on international strategy and the importance of the concept of global strategy.

Key terms

capabilities	182	market-based view (MBV)	183
causal ambiguity	194	path dependency	194
competitive advantage	182	resource-based view (RBV)	183
core competences	183	strategic assets	183
co-specialized assets	187	strategic fit	198
first-mover advantage	194	strategic intent	198
intangibles	192	strategic stretch	198
leverage	190	sustainable positional advantage	184

Recap questions and assignments

1 Undertake a resource audit of an organization with which you are familiar, then identify which resources, if any, are unique in the sense that they are difficult to imitate. Has the organization gained competitive advantage as a result of this uniqueness?

2 Refer to question 2 in Chapter 5. For these same two companies, identify the core competences and show where they are located within their value chains.

3 Refer to question 3 in Chapter 5. For the same organization, show how its core competences are contained within the SWOT analysis. Convert your SWOT analysis into a diagram based on Figure 6.8 in this chapter.

Case study 6.1: **Google: fuzzy maths**

In a few short years, Google has turned from a simple and popular company into a complicated and controversial one

Mathematically confident drivers stuck in the usual jam on highway 101 through Silicon Valley were recently able to pass time contemplating a billboard that read: '{first 10-digit prime found in consecutive digits of *e*}.com.' The number in question, 7427466391, is a sequence that starts at the 101st digit of *e*, a constant that is the base of the natural logarithm. The select few who worked this out and made it to the right website then encountered a 'harder' riddle. Solving it led to another web page where they were finally invited to submit their curriculum vitae.

If a billboard can capture the soul of a company, this one did, because the anonymous advertiser was Google, whose main product is the world's most popular internet search engine. With its presumptuous humour, its mathematical obsessions, its easy, arrogant belief that it is the natural home for geniuses, the billboard spoke of a company that thinks it has taken its rightful place as the leader of the technology industry, a position occupied for the past 15 years by Microsoft.

In tone, the billboard was 'googley', as the firm's employees like to say. That adjective, says one spokeswoman, evokes a 'humble, cosmopolitan, different, toned-down' classiness. A good demonstration of googley-ness came in the speeches at a conference in Las Vegas this year. Whereas the bosses of other technology companies welcomed the audience into the auditorium with flashing lights and blasting rock music, Google played Bach's Brandenburg Concerto Number Three and had a thought puzzle waiting on every seat. The billboard was also googley in that, like Google's home page, it had visual simplicity that belied the sophistication of its content. To outsiders, however, googley-ness often implies audacious ambition, a missionary calling to improve the world and the equation of nerdiness with virtue.

The main symptom of this, prominently displayed on the billboard, is a deification of mathematics. Google constantly leaves numerical puns and riddles for those who care to look in the right places. When it filed the regulatory documents for its stockmarket listing in 2004, it said that it planned to raise $2,718,281,828, which is $e billion to the nearest dollar. A year later, it filed again to sell another batch of shares – precisely 14,159,265, which represents the first eight digits after the decimal in the number *pi* (3.14159265).

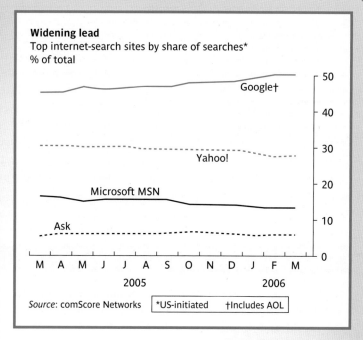

Widening lead
Top internet-search sites by share of searches*
% of total

Source: comScore Networks   *US-initiated   †Includes AOL

The mathematics comes from the founders, Sergey Brin and Larry Page. The Russian-born Mr Brin is the son of a professor of statistics and probability and a mother who works at NASA; Mr Page is the son of two computer-science teachers. The breakthrough that made their search engine so popular was the realisation that the chaos of the internet had an implicit mathematical order. By counting, weighting and calculating the link structures between web pages, Messrs Page and Brin were able to return search results more relevant than those of any other search engine.

So far, they have maintained this superiority. Danny Sullivan, the editor of *Search Engine Watch*, an online industry newsletter, ranks Google as the best search engine, Yahoo! as second-best, Ask (the re-named Ask Jeeves) third, and Microsoft's MSN last among the big four. Google's share of searches has gone up almost every month of the past year. Including those on AOL, an internet portal that uses Google's search technology, Google had half of all searches in March. Excluding AOL, the figure was 43%. This is why people 'google' – rather than, say, 'yahoo' – their driving directions, dates and recipes.

Mathematical prowess is also behind the other half of Google's success: its ability to turn all those searches into money. Unlike software companies such as Microsoft which get most of their revenues from licence fees, Google is primarily an advertising agency. It does not sell the usual sort of advertising, in which an advertiser places a display on a page and pays per thousand visitor 'impressions' (views): it has perfected the more efficient genre of 'pay-per-click' advertising. It places little text advertisements ('sponsored links') on a page in an order determined by auction among the advertisers. But these advertisers pay only once an internet user actually clicks on their links (thereby expressing an interest in buying). This works best on the pages of search results, which account for over half of the firm's revenues, because the users' keywords allow Google to place relevant advertisements on the page. But it also works on other web pages, such as blogs or newspaper articles, that sign up to be part of Google's 'network'.

The world brain

These two interlocking 'engines' – the search algorithms coupled with the advertising algorithms – are the motor that powers Google's growth in revenues ($6.1 billion last year) and profits ($1.5 billion), as well as its $117 billion market capitalisation. Its horsepower is the reason why Andy Bechtolsheim, Google's first investor (as well as a co-founder of Sun Microsystems, a big computer-maker), still holds on to all his shares in the firm. It's all about advertisers 'bidding up the keywords' in Google's auctions, he says. 'How far this thing could go, nobody can say.'

Since its stockmarket debut, however, Google has been adding new and often quite different products to this twin engine. It now owns Picasa, which makes software to edit digital photos on computers; Orkut, a social-networking site popular mainly in Brazil; and Blogger, which lets people start an online journal. It also offers free software for instant-messaging and internet telephony, for searching on the desktop computers of users, for (virtually) flying around the Earth, for keeping computers free of viruses, for uploading and sharing videos, and for creating web pages. It has a free e-mail program and calendar. It recently bought a firm called Writely, which lets people create and save text documents (much as Microsoft's Word does) online rather than on their own computers. Google is also scanning books in several large libraries to make them searchable. It is preparing to offer free wireless internet access in San Francisco and perhaps other cities, and dabbling in radio advertising. And that is only the start of a long list.

Whether these are arbitrary distractions or not depends on one's point of view. For Messrs Brin and Page, they make mathematical sense. Mr Brin ('the strategy guy') has calculated that Google's engineers should spend 70% of their time on core products (ie, the search and advertising engines), 20% on relevant but tangential products, and 10% on wild fun that might or might not lead to a product. The result is that lots of tiny teams are working on all sorts of projects, the most promising ones of which end up on the prestigious 'top 100' list that Mr Page ('the product guy') spends a lot of his time on. Most of the items on that list in theory have something to do with Google's mission, which is 'to organise the world's information'. Scanning and indexing books, for instance, brings offline information online.

The outside world increasingly sees it differently. Among Google fans, the company has come to epitomise the more mature (ie, post-bust) internet generation, which goes by the marketing cliché 'Web 2.0'. In this context, it is assumed to be working on absolutely everything simultaneously, and every new product announcement, no matter how trivial, is greeted as a tiny step toward an eventual world-changing transformation.

At a minimum, this hypothetical transformation would consist of moving computation and data off people's personal computers and on to the network – ie, Google's servers. Other names for this scenario are the 'GDrive' or the 'Google grid' that the company is allegedly working on, meaning free (but ultimately advertising-supported) copious online storage and possibly free internet access. Free storage threatens Microsoft, because its software dominates personal computers rather than the internet; free access threatens other internet-access providers.

At a maximum, the transformation goes quite a bit further. George Dyson, a futurist who has spent time at Google, thinks that the company ultimately intends to link all these digital synapses created by its users into what H.G. Wells, a British science-fiction writer, once called the 'world brain'. Google, Mr Dyson thinks, wants to fulfil the geeks' dream of creating 'artificial intelligence'. Passing the so-called 'Turing test', created by Alan Turing, a British mathematician, to determine whether a machine can be said to be able to think, would be the ultimate reward.

From primes to share prices

But many who deal with Google in their daily lives are getting fed up with such grandiose notions. Google's shares, after nearly quintupling since they began trading, have fallen in recent months. Pip Coburn, an investment strategist, says that 'Google was a simple story at one point: online ads on top of the most popular search mechanism on the planet. Simple. But now it is pretty much a mess and to get the stock going again, the company may need to work on its own simplicity so as to match the simplicity of the Google home page itself.'

Mr Sullivan of *Search Engine Watch* says Google has become distracted. 'Oh, give me a break,' he wrote in his blog after yet another product announcement. 'A break from Google going in yet another direction when there is so much stuff they haven't finished, gotten right or need to fix.' He points to a rule in Google's corporate philosophy that 'it's best to do one thing really, really well,' and suggests that the company is 'doing 100 different things rather than one thing really, really well.'

Google is thus starting to look a bit as Microsoft did a decade ago, with one strength (Windows for Microsoft, search for Google) and a string of mediocre 'me-too' products. Google Video, for instance, was supposed to become an online marketplace for video clips, both personal and business, but has been overtaken by YouTube, a start-up that is a few months old but already has four times as much video traffic. Google News, where the stories are, characteristically, chosen by mathematical algorithms rather than by editors, perennially lags behind Yahoo! News, with its old-fashioned human touch. Google's instant-messaging software is tiny compared with AOL's, Yahoo!'s and MSN's.

Google is beginning to resemble the old Microsoft in another way, too. A decade ago, Microsoft stood accused of stifling innovation, because entrepreneurs would stay away from any area of technology in which it showed any interest. Google, whose slogan is 'Don't be evil', hates this comparison and wants to think of itself as ventilating rather than stifling the ecosystem of developers and entrepreneurs. 'I don't see how they can say that,' says an entrepreneur and competitor who is too afraid of unspecified consequences to speak on the record. Like most of Silicon Valley these days, he finds Google's slogan ridiculous, because 'we're not evil either, we just don't go around saying it.'

Entrepreneurs like him are getting annoyed by Google's seemingly endless 'betas', also known as 'technical previews', when new products are not yet officially launched but available, ostensibly for testing and review. Traditionally, beta reviews were meant to last weeks or months and were targeted at testers who would find and report bugs. Google seems to use betas as dogs sprinkle trees – so that rivals know where it is. Google News recently graduated out of its beta after about four years.

In fairness, Google's role today is more complex than Microsoft's was in the 1990s, when start-ups often hoped to 'exit' by listing their shares on the stockmarket, and were occasionally expunged by Microsoft before they got there. Today, start-ups (such as Writely, Picasa, Orkut and Urchin) often use Google (or the other internet titans) as the exit, selling themselves to the big guy. It works for individuals too. Paul Rademacher is a software engineer who last year came up with a clever way of combining Google's interactive maps with other websites. Google hired him.

To Google's initial surprise and subsequent chagrin (is it not enough to vow never to be evil?), it alienates more groups of people as it enters more areas of modern life. It appeared to be genuinely taken aback that some book publishers oppose its plan to scan their books and make them searchable. Google also seemed surprised when privacy advocates voiced concerns over its practice of placing advertisements in contextually related e-mail messages on its webmail service, and again this year when it announced a Chinese version that censors the search results.

Slowly, the company is realising that it is so important that it may not be able to control the ramifications of its own actions. 'As more and more data builds up in the company's disk farms,' says Edward Felten, an expert on computer privacy at Princeton University, 'the temptation to be evil only increases. Even if the company itself stays non-evil, its data trove will be a massive temptation for others to do evil.' In a world of rogue employees, intruders and accidents, he says, Google could be 'one or two privacy disasters away from becoming just another internet company'.

Such concerns are forcing Messrs Brin and Page, still in their early 30s, and Eric Schmidt, whom they hired as chief executive and who is in his early 50s, to behave increasingly like a 'normal' company. Google recently sent its first lobbyists to Washington, DC. Its decision to build an 'evil scale' to help it devise its China strategy was more unusual, but its hiring of Al Gore, a former American vice-president, to aid the process, was just the kind of thing that old-fashioned empire-building firms do all the time.

Other companies are reacting in traditional ways to Google's dominance. Former rivals, such as eBay, Yahoo! and Microsoft, are exploring alliances to counter its influence. When Microsoft tried to buy AOL from its parent, Time Warner, Google's Mr Schmidt flew in for talks that led to Google taking a defensive stake in AOL, thus keeping it out of Microsoft's and Yahoo!'s reach. In response, Microsoft has contemplated buying all or part of Yahoo!, and has recently announced a vague but large increase in research spending which amounts to an arms race. Google is now alleging that Microsoft is unfairly steering users of its web browser to MSN for searches, and is preparing to dispatch lawyers to keep Microsoft in check.

Google thus finds itself at a defining moment. There are plenty of people within the company who want it to play the power game. 'The folks who are closest to Larry and Sergey are very, very worried about Microsoft, as well they should be,' says John Battelle, the author of a blog and a book on Google. Yet the company's founders themselves may not be prepared to drop their idealism and their faith in their own mathematical genius. They have always wanted to succeed by being good and doing good. 'Never once did we consider buying a big company,' says David Krane, Google's 84th employee, by way of example. It would not be googley. It would, he says, be 'yuck'.

Source: 'Fuzzy Maths', *The Economist*, 11 May 2006

Questions

1 Is 'fuzzy maths' a core competence for Google? What are the arguments for and against this?

2 How does fuzzy maths support the principal positioning of the Google search engine? Can this positioning be imitated without imitating the fuzzy maths core competence?

3 Recent criticism of Google's product portfolio is that it lacks distinctiveness. Comment on this from a core competence perspective.

References

Ackenhusen, M. (1992) Canon: competing on capabilities. INSEAD case study, reprinted in B. de Wit and R. Meyer (1998) *Strategy: Process, Context, and Content*, 2nd edn, International Thomson Business Press, London.

Amit, R. and Schoemaker, P.J. (1993) Strategic assets and organisational rent. *The Strategy Management Journal*, **14**, pp. 33–46, reprinted in S. Segal-Horn (ed.) (1998) *The Strategy Reader*, Blackwell Business, Oxford.

Fane, G., Vagheti, R., Van Deusen, C. and Woods, L. (2003) Competitive advantage the Toyota way. *Business Strategy Review*, **14**, **4**, Winter, 51–60.

Grant, R.M. (1991) The resource-based theory of competitive advantage: implications for strategy formulation. *California Management Review*, Spring, 114–35.

Grant, R.M. (2002) *Contemporary Strategy Analysis*, 4th edn, Basil Blackwell, Oxford.

Hall, R. (1992) The strategic analysis of intangible resources. *Strategic Management Journal*, **13**, 135–44.

Hamel, G. (1994) The concept of core competence. Chapter 1 in G. Hamel and A. Heene (eds) *Competence Based Competition*, in the Strategic Management Series, John Wiley & Sons, Chichester.

Hamel, G. and Prahalad, C.K. (1989) Strategic intent. *Harvard Business Review*, **67**, **3**, 63–76.

Hamel, G. and Prahalad, C.K. (1993) Strategy as stretch and leverage. *Harvard Business Review*, **71**, **2**, 75–84.

Lave, C. and March, J. (1993) *An Introduction to Models in the Social Sciences*, University Press of America, New York.

McGee, J. and Segal-Horn, S. (1997) Global competences in service multinationals. In H. Thomas and D. O'Neal (eds) *Strategic Discovery: Competing in New Arenas*, the Strategic Management Series, John Wiley & Sons, Chichester, pp. 49–77.

Nelson, R.R. and Winter, S.G. (1982) *An Evolutionary Theory of Economic Change*, Harvard University Press, Boston, MA.

Penrose, E. (1995) *The Theory of the Growth of the Firm*, 3rd edn (original edition 1954), Oxford University Press, Oxford.

Peteraf, M.A. (1993) The cornerstones of competitive advantage; a resource-based view. *Strategic Management Journal*, **14**, **2**, 179–91.

Porac, J. and Thomas, H. (1990) Taxonomic mental models in competitor definition. *Academy of Management Review*, **5**, **2**, 224–40.

Porter, M.E. (1980) *Competitive Strategy: Techniques for Analysing Industries and Competitors*, Free Press, New York.

Prahalad, C.K. and Hamel, G. (1990) The core competence of the corporation. *Harvard Business Review*, May/June, pp. 79–91, reprinted in S. Segal-Horn (ed.) (1998) *The Strategy Reader*, Blackwell Business, Oxford.

Selznick, P. (1957) *Leadership and Administration*, University of California Press, Berkeley, CA.

Stalk, G., Evans, P. and Shulman, L.E. (1992) Competing on capabilities: the new rules of corporate strategy. *Harvard Business Review*, **70**, **2**, 57–69.

Further reading

Barney, J.B. (1991) Firm resources and sustained competitive advantage. *Journal of Management*, **17**, 99–120.

Besanko, D., Dranove, D. and Shandley, M. (2000) *The Economics of Strategy*, 2nd edn, John Wiley & Sons, New York.

Collis, D. and Montgomery, C. (1995) Competing on capabilities. *Harvard Business Review*, **73**, **4**, 118–28.

Hamel, G. and Heene, A. (eds.) (1994) *Competence Based Competition*, the Strategic Management Series, John Wiley & Sons, Chichester.

Porter, M.E. (1985) *Competitive Advantage*, Free Press, New York.

Schoemaker, P. (1992) How to link strategic vision to core capabilities. *Sloan Management Review*, Fall, 67–81.

Segal-Horn, S. (ed.) (1998) *The Strategy Reader*, Blackwell Business, Oxford.

Thomas, H. and O'Neal, D. (eds) (1997) *Strategic Discovery: Competing in New Arenas*, the Strategic Management Series, John Wiley & Sons, Chichester.

Chapter 7

Strategy for the digital economy

Chapter contents

Introduction

This chapter[1] is concerned with the emerging structure of the new economy provided, particularly, by the digital economy of technology networks and knowledge intensity. This is a world marked by big investments in R&D, different cost structures and significantly changed demand conditions. You should read this chapter and also review material in Chapter 14, which deals with knowledge, information and innovation. In this chapter we are concerned with how the logic of competitive advantage applies to the conditions in which we find ourselves in an interconnected world dominated by internet and telecommunication networks. To anticipate the conclusions, we will see

---

[1] This chapter was written jointly with Tanya Sammut-Bonnici.

that the strategic context has shifted a great deal. This means that fundamental demand and cost conditions have acquired new dimensions, resulting in different strategies becoming available and being pursued. The new structure of the digital economy does not mean that the old strategic logic is outmoded. Instead we see a significant change in the strategic context that results in the logic of competitive advantage being applied in different ways.

The chapter presents and contrasts the differences between the old world of scale and scope economies and the interconnected world of **network externalities** which we now call the **digital economy**. There is an extensive discussion of what network externalities are and how they arise but the reader should read this in the context of addition, not replacement – scale and scope have not been replaced. There is also an important practical phenomenon to consider. Networks are supported by many layers of infrastructure and we go into some detail to show how the technological infrastructure can be identified and analysed. There are many implications for competition, which we review. Finally, we summarize the implications for strategy, and argue that although it is a new world, the logic of competitive advantage still applies.

7.1 The emergence of a network economy

We examine here how the older industrial economy was characterized by economies of scale and scope, while the contemporary information economy is driven by the economics of **positive feedback** in **network industries**. We will discuss the nature of network industries, such as railroads, telecommunications, and software and hardware networks. We will see how network companies benefit from positive feedback on both the demand side and supply side. On the demand side, the more customers join a network, such as a telecommunications service, the higher the incentive for other customers to join. On the supply side, the larger a network becomes in terms of number of users and also in size of assets deployed, the easier it is for a company to lower costs and prices. The lower the price introduced by a network company, the more subscribers will join the network and positive feedback kicks in. The result is a self-reinforcing spiral. The importance of **critical mass**, competition and **standards** is discussed in the light of these dynamics of positive feedback.

7.1.1 The old world: economies of scale and scope

As we have seen in Chapters 3, 5 and 6, the theory of strategic management was given impetus by the realization that industrial organization as a subject could be turned around to give a perspective on the entrepreneurial profit-seeking activity of firms. This led to the notion of firms seeking market power in which rents could be protected, at least for a time, by barriers to entry. These barriers were derived from the cost functions of firms, the dominant theme being the ability of firms to sustain differential cost positions through economies of scale.[2] In the world of scale economies, where minimum efficient plant sizes are a significant fraction of the market, oligopolistic market structures prevail and are overturned principally by the growth of markets or by the advance of technology enabling the creation of new assets with more advantageous cost positions. The notion of economies of scale is therefore fundamental to strategic management because it provides a rationale for firms to be different in terms of both asset configuration and performance.

However, this is an insufficient argument on its own for the existence of diversified firms. Diversification requires the notion of economies of scope. These are defined as '*the cost savings*

---

[2] Saloner et al. (2001) identify three types of entry barriers: barriers from production or distribution technology barriers, barriers from brand name or reputation, and legal barriers (p. 138). The first two are essentially cost barriers in that replication of the incumbent's assets is inhibited by the costs of so doing. The third type is an absolute barrier that arises from institutional characteristics that are idiosyncratic from a market point of view.

realized when two different products are produced within the same organization rather than at separate organizations' (Saloner et al., 2001, p. 364). They arise because the products may share a common input such as plant or equipment, obtain volume discounts on purchases (exercising monopsony power), or apply common expertise or reputation. The advantages conferred by economies of scope are not, however, inherent in the jointness of production but in the barrier to entry which protects the 'original' asset. There is nothing to prevent two firms enjoying identical economies of scope if there is free competition for the underlying asset. Thus, economies of scale convey the fundamental advantage that underpins superior profitability in single-product and multiple-product firms.

The discussions about competitive advantage in strategic management textbooks are all variations upon this same theme. The simplest articulation of the theme is the cost differential that arises in production. The more complex argument concerns knowledge assets, where the essence of the argument is about the cost to reproduce knowledge and not the possession of knowledge per se. The subtlety in strategy making resides in the variety of ways in which knowledge and expertise are acquired (which is where the cost function of knowledge acquisition is important) and then captured in products and services (the generic differentiation theme). In this almost idyllic world the supply side and the market side are linked through some form of arm's-length market exchange process. Customer desires are conveyed through the pattern of their purchasing decisions and producers respond by adjusting the nature of their offerings. Where competition is monopolistic (or imperfect) producers may attempt to shape customer preferences, and to the extent they succeed, demand functions become downward sloping in the conventional manner and producers can then price according to the nature of their marginal cost curves and the price elasticities in the market. But demand and supply are mediated through a market mechanism in which product demand is independent of other products[3] and demand is not time dependent. This latter point is crucial.

7.1.2 The new digital economy: the world of network industries

However, there is a class of markets and industries that do not conform to these assumptions. These are known as network industries.[4] According to Economides and Flyer (1997):

> *The value of nearly every good is influenced by aggregate consumption levels in its market and in the markets for related goods. In many cases, high aggregate consumption in its own market, and in the markets for complementary goods, affects positively the value of a good. Traditionally such effects have been called network externalities, since they were first identified in network industries. While such effects are salient in some markets, such as for telephones, fax machines and computer operating systems, for most goods these influences are more subtle and tend to be smaller.*

Network industries are common. Many physical networks have been around for a long time, e.g. railroads, telephone, electricity. So-called **virtual networks** have arisen largely through information technology and include facsimile machines and computer operating systems. These are 'virtual' because the key knowledge and information assets are intangible. We can distinguish intuitively between pure networks and indirect or weak networks. Pure networks exist where it is an essential characteristic of the product that it is organized through complementary nodes and links, such as a railway network or the telephone system. A key element is the notion of complementarity, thus the value of a railway station is derived from the existence of other railway stations on the network.

---

[3] This exaggerates the point, as we will see later when we discuss product complementarity.

[4] In this discussion the terms 'industry' and 'market' are used as if interchangeable.

A weaker definition relies also on complementarity between products (or nodes, in network language) but allows the links to be created *by* the customer rather than *for* the customer. Economides and Flyer (1997) have some powerful examples:

> ... the value of a washing machine is affected by the aggregate consumption of washing machines and the consumption level of the particular brand, since this determines the availability of parts, repairmen, detergents, fabric softeners and various other related goods and services. The value of a sporting event is influenced by the aggregate size of the audience, as this enhances the excitement level, analysis, discussion and remembrance of the event. Even a grapefruit is influenced by network externalities, since the variety of accessible complements, such as peeler, slicers, juicers, recipes, nutritional information and specialized spoons, are affected by the aggregate consumption of the fruit.

The essence of this idea is that the demand for a product is influenced by total demand for the product class or by total demand in a complementary product class. Thus demand is conditioned by a consumer externality. Where these consumer externalities are powerful the feedback effect on demand is such that there is a tendency towards a single network (or platform or standard). The value for consumers of being on a common standard outweighs any specific differences between alternative standards. We see this from the Blu-ray–HD-DVD battle. Blu-ray was adopted by default as an industry standard over HD-DVD. At that point Toshiba Corporation announced that it had undertaken a thorough review of its overall strategy for HD-DVD and decided it would no longer develop, manufacture and market HD-DVD players and recorders. This decision has been made following recent major changes in the market, namely the adoption of Blu-ray by PlayStation.

In personal computers the Wintel standard became greatly preferred to the Apple standard in the 1980s. Apple continued to exist in the niche design market, hovering between 7% and 10% of the computer market share for two decades. The situation has changed dramatically in recent years as the Apple brand gained more popularity with the success of iPod and iPhone products. Products such as media players and mobile phones, which have high social visibility, that is, they are used in the open, are therefore likely to have high network effects.

A similar effect is detected in the efforts made to target people in key leadership positions who are therefore likely to be more visible across social groups. For instance, Tucker (2008) suggests that network firms should target those individuals and opinion leaders who derive their informal influence from occupying key boundary-spanning positions in communication networks, in addition to those with sources of formal influence, when launching a new network technology.

Where the externality is smaller and the intrinsic difference between standards is relatively larger then we might observe multiple competing and coexisting 'platforms'.[5] An example of a platform can be seen in the automobile industry where a company might develop a core of components and sub-assemblies that can be used to support alternative body styling to create a product range. Such a platform can coexist with other platforms because the scale efficiencies associated with platforms are modest in relation to market size.

7.2 Networks in a digital economy

A network is a set of connections (links) between nodes. A two-way network allows the links to be operated in both directions, whereas a one-way network has distinct directionality. Two-way networks include railroads and telephone systems. Figure 7.1 shows a simple star network where A can

---

[5] To observe multiple standards defies common sense, hence the term 'platform' which denotes an array of linked complementary products that together are compatible with other products.

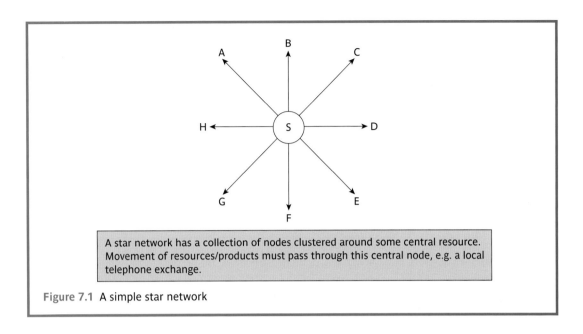

A star network has a collection of nodes clustered around some central resource. Movement of resources/products must pass through this central node, e.g. a local telephone exchange.

Figure 7.1 A simple star network

communicate with B through a switch S. B can also communicate with A by reversing the direction of the link (viz. a telephone call). In Figure 7.1 we have eight nodes (A through H) linked through a switch, S. If this were a two-way network, AB and BA would be distinct products (different telephone calls, different rail journeys). The total number of products in the network is 56, i.e. $n(n-1)$ where n is the number of nodes in the network. If there were to be a ninth member this would increase the total number of products to 72 (n is now 9), a total increase of 16 products available from the expanded network. If the value to each user of being in the network is proportional to the number of users, then the value of this network has just increased by 28.5% (16 as a percentage of 56) even though the size of the network has increased by only 12.5% (one added to eight).[6] This is an algebraic characteristic of network economies of scale: that the value rises disproportionately higher than the increase in network size as long as prices are constant and products are independent. Intuitively we might expect that an increase in network size beyond a certain point has little value.[7] If this network were a one-way network there would be half the number of products but the value of the network would nevertheless increase at the same rate but achieving only half the value.

The analysis of complementarity is equivalent to the analysis of a one-way network. Figure 7.1 can be extended, as in Figure 7.2, to show a typical one-way network. Here we can interpret the Ai as ATMs[8] and the Bj as banks. The network runs only from A to B. The significance of the two switches SA and SB is that they have only one link. This means that there is compatibility between all ATMs and all banks. This maximizes the value of the network but increases the competition between banks for customers through ATMs.[9] It is this compatibility that makes the complementarity actual and the network operational. For complex products actual complementarity has to be achieved through adherence to specific technical standards. Other complementary products can be visualized

---

[6] Assuming for convenience in this example that prices are constant.

[7] Using calculus we would expect the first derivative to be positive but the second derivative to be negative. Therefore total value increases but at a decreasing rate.

[8] Automatic teller machines.

[9] Two complementary components, A and B, are compatible when they can be combined to produce a composite good. A Blu-ray video is compatible with Blu ray disks. Two substitute components A_1 and A_2 are compatible when each of them can be combined with a complementary good B to produce a composite good. Thus two Blu-ray disks are compatible and two Blu-ray DVD players are compatible.

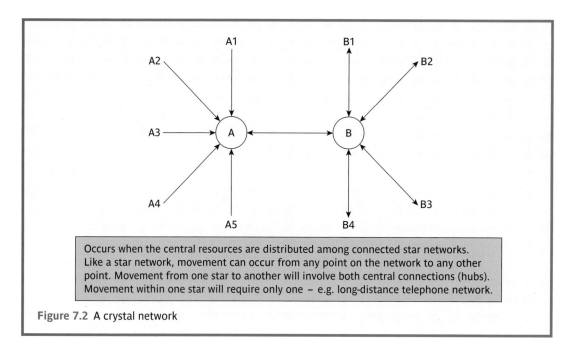

Figure 7.2 A crystal network

in terms of Figure 7.2. VHS tapes could be the Ai and VHS players could be the Bj. Think also of copier paper and copiers, or printer paper and printers, or car accessories and cars, or local and long-distance telephone networks.

7.2.1 Network externalities: an economic force

Earlier in this chapter we looked at the traditional economic model for the 'old world', which was driven by economies of scale and scope. The digital world, characterized by information and communications technology, is governed by a different dynamic. Network externalities are the new drivers of the network economy. It is important to recognize that economies of scale/scope and network externalities represent the extreme ends of a spectrum of effects, and that the presence of one does not imply the exclusion of the other. Companies may experience the effects of both to varying degrees, with a tendency for network externalities to have more strategic relevance in the digitized network economy. The concept of network externalities has attracted the attention of academics and practitioners alike. The extent to which network industries have proliferated in the economy is a recent phenomenon. The effects of network externalities, however, have been recognized for some time with the development of the older network companies such as the railroads and the electricity systems. In 1804 Trevithick constructed the first practical locomotive in England. In 1882 the Edison Electric Lighting Company completed the first commercial generating station at Holborn Viaduct in London. The first commercial telephone line was installed in Boston, Massachusetts, in 1877. Network externalities are defined as the increasing utility that a user derives from consumption of a product as the number of other users who consume the same product increases (Katz and Shapiro, 1985). For example, the more people there are in a telephone network, the more users can be reached on the network, thereby increasing its usability. Fax machines, broadcast industry services, credit card networks, and computer hardware and software are examples of products exhibiting network externalities. Networks were originally analysed on the assumption that each network was owned by a single firm and research concentrated on the efficient use of the network structure and on the appropriate allocation of costs (Economides, 1996; Sharkey and Sharkey, 1993). With the anti-trust cases against AT&T and its later break-up, attention shifted towards economies of scope, the efficiency gains from joint operation of complementary components of networks (Baumol et al., 1982). This led to issues of interconnection and compatibility in parallel with the reduced role of IBM in the 1980s and 1990s in the setting of technical standards in computer hardware and software. As technology has advanced, there have been significant reductions in telecommunications costs and a shift towards fragmented ownership of telecommunications networks. Market structure has shifted from natural monopoly to oligopoly. Similar trends are evident in other IT-intensive industries. Thus, the focus of interest in network economics has shifted from the analysis of natural monopoly towards issues of interconnection, compatibility, **interoperability** and coordination of quality.

The exponential adoption of a network service which is subject to network externalities is evident in the rapid rise of peer-to-peer networks in three main categories: social networks, e-marketplaces, and information services, such as Facebook, eBay and Wikipedia. Case box 7.1 on many-to-many networks, and Case box 7.2 on Facebook, provide some insights into the explosive growth of these services.

Case box 7.1: **Many-to-many networks**

Network externalities that lie behind the exponential adoption rates of a new service have been the driving force behind new many-to-many internet services. The basis of many-to-many networks, or peer-to-peer networks, is that the number of suppliers to the service can potentially be equal to the number of users of the service. Examples of such networks would be Wikipedia, customer-to-customer (C2C) selling on eBay and Amazon, Craigslist, Kijiji classifieds, Facebook, Hi5 and many others.

Less than a decade ago, Jimmy Wales, a wealthy options trader, set out to build a global online encyclopaedia in a novel way, by using a many-to-many model of database building through an 'open collective'. The encyclopaedia is freely available to all and it is produced by voluntary contributors rather than experts and editors. At its inception the framework was, of course, controversial. Assembling academic knowledge has been the job of scholars with authority. Wikipedia pulls in the collective knowledge of thousands of people ranging from professionals to amateur experts.

The many-to-many model of content building on the net has been adopted by several other companies. Amazon started to show a profit when it introduced its C2C model whereby consumers could sell their books to other consumers through the Amazon platform. eBay adopted this model right from the start, introducing the innovation of auctioning for all items to add interest, a pursuit previously reserved for luxury items.

Craigslist and eBay's Kijiji create advertising revenues based on the high site traffic generated by the volume of free content posted by their users. Facebook takes the many-to-many concept of content building to another level, turning the objective of networking from transacting goods to building marketable social groups.

As the internet grew in speed, accessibility and size it created a shift of economic power from the corporations to the masses. Product and content no longer had to be created by organizations with the market power to overcome entry barriers. Internet users were given the power to communicate globally the nature of their services, products or even the entertainment content we see on YouTube. Wikinomics is the term used of the emerging economics of 'collective contribution'. The dynamics has changed the way companies manage innovation and customer relationships, how they market and compete. The power of the new marketplaces is 'mass collaboration'.

The peer-to-peer revolution has raised new challenges for stakeholders, who have had to restructure their business models. Web 2.0 promises network services that create the environment to collect and process 'the Wisdom of the Crowds'. The internet provides a very high level of rapid connectivity which seems to create a market environment of extraordinarily high returns (such as Google's financial success). Information, media, software, new or even used products are easy to communicate, develop and distribute, bringing power to the masses.

Case box 7.2: **Facebook**

Facebook, the leading site for social networking, has catapulted to more than 200 million users. Over 100 million users log in daily, creating a sizeable market for advertising and public relations.

Facebook can give brands and organizations automated information that would otherwise require costly market research. Facebook knows the address, contacts, interests and behaviour patterns of its users. The social network is a fertile ground for psychographic data. From this information, advertising agencies can target customers directly in a more efficient manner than Google. Facebook has introduced advertising with thumbnail icons, while Google is coming up to speed where visual advertising is concerned. Advertising and promoting public relations messages, such as Obama's political campaign, on social networking sites not only raises profile but also creates a direct link between advertising and sales.

The number of Facebook users is equivalent to the fifth most populated nation in the world, behind China, India, the United States and Indonesia. Most of its users come from the United States, with the largest concentration of users in the Eastern US and Western Europe. People aged 26 to 44 make up the fastest-growing segment of the Facebook population.

That Facebook, Twitter and other online social networks[10] will increase the size of human social groups is an obvious hypothesis, given that they reduce a lot of the friction and cost involved in keeping in touch with other people. Once you join and gather your 'friends' online, you can share in their lives as recorded by photographs, 'status updates' and other titbits, and, with your permission, they can share in yours. Additional friends are free, so why not say the more the merrier?

But perhaps additional friends are not free. Primatologists call at least some of the things that happen on social networks 'grooming'. In the wild, grooming is time-consuming and here computerization certainly helps. But keeping track of whom to groom – and why – demands quite a bit of mental computation. You need to remember who is allied with, hostile to, or lusts after whom, and act accordingly. Several years ago, therefore, Robin Dunbar, an anthropologist who now works at Oxford University, concluded that the cognitive power of the brain limits the size of the social network that an individual of any given species can develop. Extrapolating from the brain sizes and social networks of apes, Dr Dunbar suggested that the size of the human brain allows stable networks of about 148. Rounded to 150, this has become famous as the **Dunbar number**.[11]

7.2.2 Network externalities and the battle for critical mass

For normal goods, the demand curve slopes downwards. As price decreases, more of the product is demanded. Other elements in the demand function, such as income or advertising, serve as 'demand shifters' that elevate demand to a higher level. Figure 7.3 illustrates the traditional role of a demand shifter. Higher levels of consumption are derived from higher incomes (positive income elasticities) or from lower prices (negative price elasticities).

This fundamental relationship is greatly distorted in the presence of network externalities. In the presence of network externalities, we specify that sales rise as accumulated sales (the **installed base**) rise. However, there may be a chicken and egg problem. That is, customers may not be interested in purchasing because the installed base is small and/or not expected to grow. For example, imagine the purchase of complex software without internet support, help lines and user groups.

---

[10] Source: Primates on Facebook, 26 February 2009, *The Economist*.

[11] Dunbar's number has been popularized by Malcolm Gladwell's (2000) *The Tipping Point*, where it plays a central role in Gladwell's arguments about the dynamics of social groups.

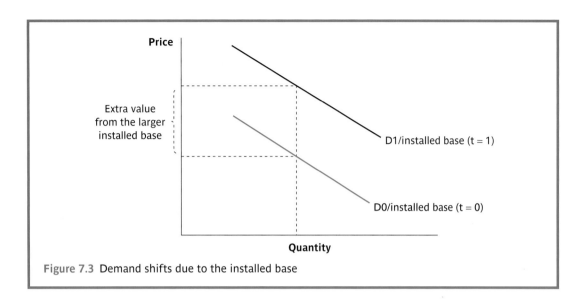

Figure 7.3 Demand shifts due to the installed base

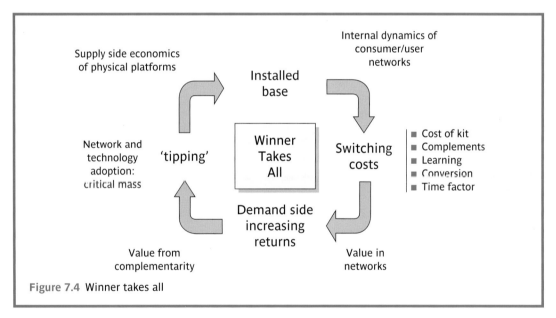

Figure 7.4 Winner takes all

Alternatively, there may be confident expectations that the installed base will grow substantially and therefore consumers will confidently make purchases. The paradox is that consumers will not buy if the installed base is too low. But, the installed base is too low because customers will not buy. The crux of the paradox lies in the management of consumer expectations. In markets for normal goods, equilibrium is explained in terms of a balance between costs and demand, between marginal costs and marginal utility. In network markets, there is also equilibrium to be struck between actual demand and consumer expectations of total demand.

This gives rise to an economic paradox. Almost the first law of economics is that value comes from scarcity. However, in the digital economy value comes from plenty: the more something is demanded and the more it is expected to be demanded then the more valuable it becomes. Expectations are so important in driving demand that a point exists where the momentum is so overwhelming that success becomes a runaway event and we observe a **winner takes all** phenomenon (see Figure 7.4).

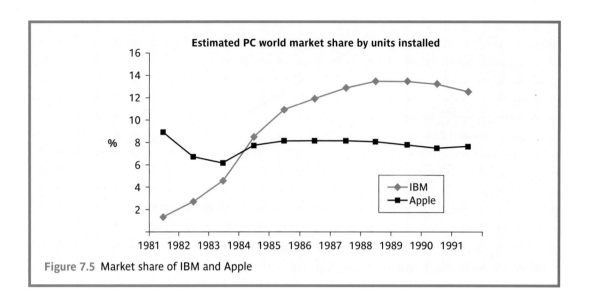

Figure 7.5 Market share of IBM and Apple

The **tipping point** is when the installed base (i.e. the size of the network) tips expectations sharply towards one player (or one network) and away from its rival. We observed this effect when the market moved towards Windows as the prevailing computer operating system, rather than OS_2. We discussed the example of IBM-compatibles versus Apple in section 7.1.2 above. This is also shown in Figure 7.5. The tipping point comes somewhere in 1984–5 when IBM system sales overtake those of Apple. The most recent example is the tipping of the DVD market towards Blu-ray and away from HD-DVD in 2008.

The tipping point mechanism in the computer industry had the effect of determining the pattern of market shares for a long time to come. Apple computer sales continued to remain at a constant level, showing a market share of 7.8% at the end of 2008. The market is showing signs of shifting upwards slightly in 2009 and beyond as Apple's popularity increases with the success of its iPod product.[12]

The exception to the winner takes all phenomenon in the presence of network externalities is a *regulated* network market where the regulation requires strong interconnections between competing platforms. The mobile communications industry is the classic example. The standards are harmonized across the network providers, at least by continental region. The platforms are interlinked and the sales curves of the regulated network providers follow the pattern of the overall subscription curve for the industry and market shares are not only stable but broadly equal in size.

Traditional economic thinking is based on **negative feedback systems** in which the strong get weaker at the margin and the weak get stronger, thus providing a drive towards a competitive equilibrium. This is captured in economics by the concept of diminishing marginal utility as consumption grows. However, in the digital world of networks, feedback rules. In this world the valuation of a product increases the more that others consume the product. Strictly speaking, it arises from the *interdependence* of consumer decisions, whereas diminishing marginal utility dominates when consumer decisions are *independent* – the normal assumption in economics.

The price–quantity relationship is normally held to be downward sloping, but the demand curve for a network product should be drawn differently (Figure 7.6). The value to the consumer of a

---

[12] Apple has shifted its focus from the PC industry to competing in the market for network devices.

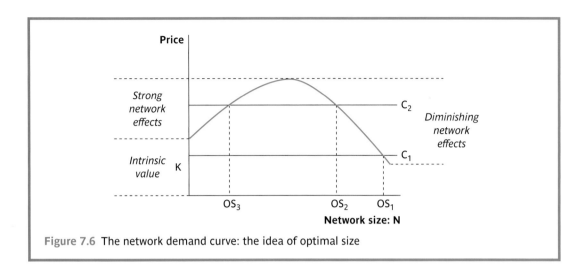

Figure 7.6 The network demand curve: the idea of optimal size

network product is reflected in the price he or she is willing to pay – the vertical axis. The principal driver of value is the size of the network, also referred to as the installed base, and is shown on the horizontal axis. Quantity demanded does still have an effect on price but, for these products, this is secondary to the network effect.

The initial upward slope of the curve reflects a rising valuation at the margin, as consumers perceive that they gain value by virtue of other consumers having the product. Being on the Wintel standard gives value to new users. However, as the network grows, the extra consumers at the margin eventually become less valuable – i.e. this shape assumes that those users with higher potential valuation of the network will join first. As the network gets very large, further growth has less and less value for future customers [13] The intercept on the vertical axis represents the value the network product has as a stand-alone product. Thus a Wintel computer has some stand-alone value, but a telephone has no value on its own and is a **pure network good**.

There is a notion of an optimal size of a network. This can be seen from the interaction of demand and cost so that as less and less valuable customers join the network there may come a time when the costs of acquiring and servicing new customers begins to exceed the price those customers are willing to pay. This determines the optimal size and has significant implications for competition.

The three configurations shown in Figure 7.7 indicate the range of possibilities. The first is a pure network good, such as a telephone system, in which the optimal size of network is a very high proportion of the available market. This implies there is little or no room for rival networks. The second is a product with a significant intrinsic value that attracts a modest size group of users. For example, this could be a corporate software package (e.g. enterprise solutions) that attracts dedicated user support from the supplier through the web. Alternative networks could coexist. The third case is one of very high intrinsic demand but extensive consumer interactions (small in size but very many in numbers) provide a substantial total network value. The obvious example is word processing software where the value from standardizing on MS Word is very high, with the result that alternative standards (such as WordPerfect) are being frozen out of the market even though the intrinsic value of any word processing package is high.

---

[13] In the language of demand curves this is an average revenue curve.

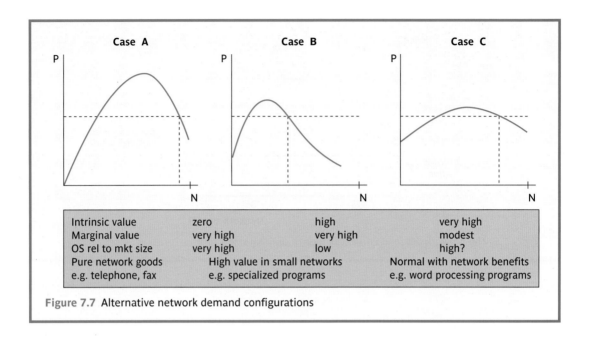

Case A	Case B	Case C

Intrinsic value	zero	high	very high
Marginal value	very high	very high	modest
OS rel to mkt size	very high	low	high?
Pure network goods	High value in small networks		Normal with network benefits
e.g. telephone, fax	e.g. specialized programs		e.g. word processing programs

Figure 7.7 Alternative network demand configurations

7.3 The technological infrastructure of network industries

Much of the popular discussion of technology and its effects makes powerful but general claims for the effect of technology but is less than clear about the underlying mechanisms. We observe four nested levels of infrastructure within network industries. Each of these levels has its own economic dynamics and each makes a contribution to the overall network (increasing returns characteristic).

These levels are (i) technology standards, (ii) the supply chain driven by such standards, (iii) the physical platforms that are the output of the supply chains and are the physical basis from which the company delivers its product (e.g. the digital TV, the decoder, the satellite system, and the telephone lines that are the platform from which Sky TV delivers its programmes), and (iv) the consumer network (Figure 7.8). The economic characteristics of the first three levels are the prevalence of fixed costs and joint products coupled with economies of scale. Networks of interacting and inter-dependent customers provide the increasing returns characteristic of networks. Then the whole can have such a powerful combination of scale, scope and positive feedback characteristics that the winner might be able to take all.

Each level displays distinctive economic characteristics of significance. Technology standards can be achieved either by rule or by emergence and in the latter case early-mover advantages are important. The economics of modularity and the specialization of knowledge shape the structure of supply chains. Physical platforms are a melding of standards and components in which modularity and the economics of substitution also play a significant role. Consumer networks, of course, require positive feedback effects for their full power to be gained. We use the mobile telecommunications business as a running example to show how these technological dimensions and strategy interact.

7.3.1 Technology and standards

The significance of the economics of information is attributed to two key factors: the continuing reduction in cost of information technology hardware products and the scale effect of global standards. Gordon Moore, founder of Intel Corporation, created a corporate empire on his eponymous

Column 1	Broadcasting	Search engines	Online marketplace	Providers of IT solutions	Telecoms
Consumer networks	Personal and commercial marketing. Local, regional, international	Personal, commercial	B2B, B2C and C2C[1] Peer-to-peer networks expanded the customer and supplier base	Commercial corporations	Personal, commercial
Physical platforms	Large-scale networks based on cable, satellite, wireless networks	Internet platforms. Media platforms	Internet broadband. Php scripting language. Security platforms	Telecommunications and internet platforms. Physical distribution of hardware	Broadcasting, telephone, mobile and internet networks
Technology standards	Digital distribution	Digital distribution	Digital distribution	Digital distribution	Digital distribution
R&D, supply chain, innovation	Disintermediation. Revenue collection. Innovation. Product bundling on-demand consumer data	Use-driven strategy. Online documents, calendars, email, data storage. Revenue from partners and offline content	Auction and direct selling. eBanking. Telecommunications on VoIP.[2] Local marketplace sites such as Craigslist, eBay's Kijiji	Customer driven. Provision of business solutions. Customized technology bundling. Open source promotion. Partnership networks and collaboration	Counteract content bottleneck advantage from broadcasting companies through multi-play provisioning and collaborative distribution

[1] B2B is business to business; B2C is business to consumer; C2C is consumer to consumer.
[2] VOIP is voice over internet protocol – e.g. the ability to make telephone calls over the internet.

Figure 7.8 Strategic levels of network industries

Moore's Law, which states that every year and a half processing power doubles while costs hold constant. Moore's foresight proved prophetic and 'Moore's Law' is expected to remain valid for the foreseeable future.[14] Computer memory, storage capacity and telecommunications bandwidth are all going through a similar pattern of cost reduction. This makes it very affordable for individuals and small businesses to be equipped with the electronic means to conduct commerce and transfer information as fast and freely as large corporations can. Hence, the demand for the products of the ICT industries continues to grow.[15]

However, the rapid growth of products from the ICT economy depends on operating technology standards as well as on production costs. For example, automated teller machines across the world must work on an agreed standard to ensure customers can use one card in different countries. A technology standard is the important enabler to create wide reach and to capture a wide network of subscribers. With the globalization of commerce, national and regional boundaries blur and the need for international standards is more urgent and critical.

A new standard can be registered with organizations such as the British Standards Institute, the American National Standards Institute or the International Standards Organization. But the process to determine the prevailing standard does not stop there. The path to achieving a de facto standard stems from three modes of selection process: market-based selection, negotiated selection and a hybrid selection process where both market competition and negotiation operate jointly.

Market-based selection is reflected in standards wars such as that between VHS and Betamax and Blu-ray and HD-DVD where consumers decided on the dominance of the VHS standard. The

[14] See *The Economist*, 26 March 2005, p. 88 for a happy 40th birthday comment on the now famous law and see also Leyden, 1997, for a more cautious view.

[15] The feast and famine evident in the telecommunications industry is reminiscent of the fragility of corporate structures during the railway boom of the 1840s.

Case box 7.3: **Standards versioning**

Standards organizations are playing an increasingly important role in the process of upgrading standards (called 'standards versioning'). The GSM Association guided the evolution of the mobile industry through a family of wireless technology standards through to GPRS, EDGE and 3GSM. Each subsequent standard offered a higher level of service. GPRS provided open internet. EDGE facilitated faster data streaming, and 3GSM provides video streaming. The network of companies supporting the technologies went through grades of service levels in order to phase out older standards and introduce new ones (see below). At the end of the life span of a standard, the technology platform is decommissioned, with the exception of equipment and software that is forward compatible with the next generation of standards.

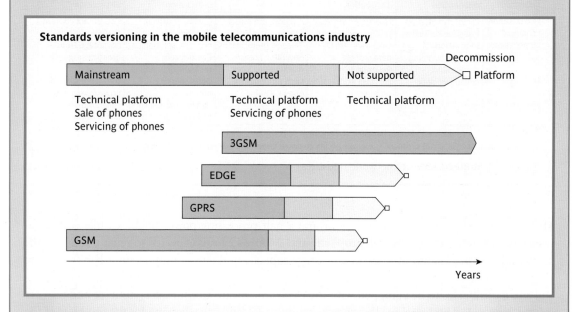

Standards versioning in the mobile telecommunications industry

Software standards follow a similar versioning strategy. Microsoft publishes the *Windows Desktop Product Lifecycle Guidelines* to provide advanced notice of changes in product availability and support. Microsoft makes Windows licenses available for purchase for a minimum of five years and provides assisted support for a further four years. The guidelines are important so that companies can plan their investment through software upgrades of Windows 2003, 2007, XP and the latest version of Windows Vista. Switching costs are minimized when standards are designed to evolve from one another. The introduction of revolutionary standards, however, is costly. The pay-off is superior performance against the high cost of switching standards.

Source: Windows Life-Cycle Policy (April 2008). Available from: www.microsoft.com/windows/lifecycle

marketing strategies of firms are key to which firm and standard is most likely to win. VHS gained a decisive advantage from a strategy of wider distribution channels and a range of complementary products (Hollywood films) as well as longer recording time than Betamax, in spite of other more advanced features available only on Betamax.

Negotiated standardization is becoming more widespread. Organizations that determine prevailing standards are emerging to reduce the cost and the uncertainty associated with adopting new standards. Negotiated standard setting guarantees the smooth interchange of information, technical components and services along different networks. The telecommunications industry was able to keep up with the speed of technological development by opening up the negotiation process to market players (David and Steinmueller, 1994; David and Shurmer, 1996). Groupe Speciale Mobile (GSM), the current mobile technology in Europe, is an association of 600 network operators and suppliers of the mobile phone industry. The UMTS Forum[16] is a similar association, developed to speed convergence between telecommunications, IT, media and content suppliers for the 3G industry. As with GSM, the name of the UMTS association is synonymous with the name for the industry technology standard.

The internet has a different history of standardization. Standards were completely open and established within the research communities of universities. As the internet has become a commodity for the domestic and commercial communities, other players are increasingly influencing its evolution.

Hybrid standard setting emerges as private firms adopt strategies to undercut collaborative decisions taken in negotiated standardization. They introduce new products, which initiate unprecedented developments but also create incompatibilities, lock-in effects and pockets of market power. Internet telephony is a typical example, where companies, standards organizations and governments create a hybrid standard-setting environment (Vercoulen and Wegberg, 1998).

The myriad of standards and versions in network industries necessitates a conscious effort to plan for the migration of the consumer from one standard to the other. The mobile telecoms industry and the software industry have had to initiate international versioning strategies to upgrade millions of customers from one level of technology to the next. Case box 7.3 provides more information on how these strategies are managed on a global scale.

7.3.2 Supply chain

In the past 20 years, the structure of the information economy has evolved through the interaction of three factors: the increase in computational capacity for data mining; the growth of telecommunication networks both fixed and mobile; and the explosion of information sharing via the internet.

Figure 7.9 depicts the modular structure of the ICT industries, which constitute the digital economy. The structure is built on layers of communication network companies, hardware and software manufacturers, internet service providers, e-commerce transaction companies, media and content companies, and myriad service companies.

The *network operators* are infrastructure suppliers such as Alcatel, Nortel Networks, Motorola and Ericsson that provide communications networking equipment. Intel and 3Com form a sub-set of companies in this category, which supply interfacing hardware and software. They provide the physical medium for the exchange of information between companies and their customers. The medium they operate could be any of satellite, telephone, mobile, television or area networks. British Telecom, AT&T, Vodafone and T-Mobile offer landline and mobile telecommunications networks. The operation of these companies is interconnected with other companies. For example, Vodafone uses BT's network. Credit card companies use Vodafone's mobile network for off-site credit verification. Vodafone has sold fixed-line telephone services from Energis and Racal Telecom networks. The interoperability of different telecom networks has become a complex business operation (see Case box 7.4 on market power and interoperability). British Telecom set up BT to develop and manage such relationships. BT Wholesale sells its fixed network product to independent

---

[16] Universal Mobile Telecommunications System (UMTS) is one of the third-generation (3G) mobile telecommunications technologies, which is also being developed into a 4G technology.

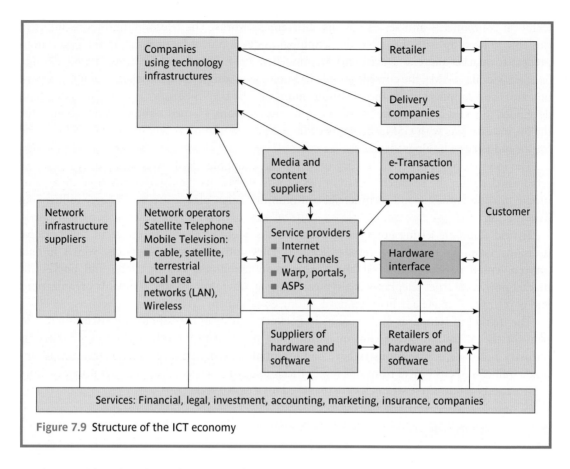

Figure 7.9 Structure of the ICT economy

service providers (ISPs), i.e. businesses that wish to provide telecom services to end consumers without owning their own networks. Specialized network operators include satellite networks and digital television networks.

Satellite networks provide the infrastructure for long-distance television, telephony and data interchange transmission. *Digital television networks* operate on a host of platforms such as satellite, copper or optic fibre cable. Interactive television has opened a host of business opportunities for retailing. The use of two-way cable networks, or a return medium via a normal telephone line, is changing the way consumers use and respond to television content. The business model for this service implies a new form of supply chain, for a new form of retailing.

The *service providers* purchase the network facility from BT and other network operators, adding their own value and service brand. Internet Service Providers are part of a complex web that provides the supply chain of information to the internet user. ISPs such as AOL and Fastnet convey internet content over the infrastructure of the telecommunication companies. At the back-end of the supply web, ISPs receive web pages from various organizations. The owners of the web pages are the *media and content suppliers*, or in many cases, they may have purchased the services of the media and content suppliers to create their web presence. At the front-end, where the supply web touches the customer, ISPs have to collaborate or to conform to consumer *hardware interface* manufacturers (typically computer suppliers). The supply web for the internet is due for another major revolution with third-generation (3G) mobile communication, which carries high speed internet and video streaming. The 3G telephone, which will become the new customer interface, could dictate a change in internet transmission management and the nature of media content all the way down the supply chain.

The supply chain in the information economy shown in Figure 7.9 takes the form of a web-like network where each member may have to collaborate with many other members. Intercollaboration is possible because of software and hardware compatibility, and necessary because of the high degree of knowledge specialization at each point on the supply chain. An example of this web-like structure is the relationship between e-transaction companies, ISPs and media content providers and the companies that own the web pages. The four types of organization have to ensure the compatibility of their services across the supply network.

Case box 7.4: **Market power and interoperability**

Microsoft and the European Competition Commission have been in contention over a number of cases and issues regarding market power.[17]

In February 2008, the European Union fined the company an unprecedented $1.35 billion penalty.[18] The Competition Commission found that Microsoft refrained from making available to competitors the documentation required to develop software that is compatible with the Windows operating system.

In March 2004, the Commission fined Microsoft $613 million and ruled that the company had failed to provide rivals with information for interoperability and for providing Windows on the condition that it is bought with Windows Media Player, limiting the entry of new players.

The 2008 case illustrates how interoperability has important implications for power relationships. The European Competition Commission found that Microsoft had abused its market power by intentionally limiting interoperability between Windows work group servers and non-Microsoft work group servers. In this way, Microsoft defended its dominant market position for server operating systems which make up the infrastructure of corporate IT networks. Microsoft was ordered to disclose complete and accurate interface documentation, which would give competitors the ability to compete on an equal footing. The court termed this the **interoperability remedy**. Microsoft's more recent actions signal a shift in their approach to interoperability. These include the migration of Microsoft Office file formats to ECMA Office Open XML, and several partner interoperability agreements, and interestingly the collaboration agreement with Novell.

Interoperability has also emerged in the software patent discussion in the European Parliament. Patents on techniques used for interoperability are kept under RAND (reasonable and non-discriminatory licensing) conditions, which mean customers will have to pay licence fees twice – once for the product and, in the appropriate case, once for the patent-protected programme the product uses.

The infrastructure of the information economy does not look like a normal, traditional and competitive supply chain in the 'old' industrial economy. Telephony and the internet have made it possible for corporations to have commercial partnerships with many more companies. The notion of 'information is power' is turned on its head. As more companies have access to more information through communication, power is dissipated to more members in the supply chain. This increase in information exchange has become the overriding equalizer of power throughout the supply networks.

The basis of this digital economy is the increase in connectivity among the various players in the chain. The connectivity level itself is rapidly evolving as communication and computational technologies become faster. The whole supply network is in a state of flux. Flexibility and adaptability have

---

[17] Details of the course cases are available at http://ec.europa.eu/competition/antitrust/cases. Other articles: McDougall, P. (2009) Microsoft To Answer EU Antitrust, *InformationWeek*, May. Available at <http://www.informationweek.com/news/government/policy>

[18] This has since then been exceeded by the $1.5bn fine on Intel in 2009.

become essential strategic stances. Faster connectivity within the supply chain not only implies more interconnections between companies, but also creates more volatile and replaceable interrelationships.

The concept of replaceable interrelationships has come about because companies are becoming isomorphic, or similar in nature. DiMaggio and Powell (1983, p. 149) define **isomorphism** as '*a constraining process that forces one unit in a population to resemble other units that face the same set of environmental conditions*'. With the standardization of technology, products are becoming more similar in design and quality. With the standardization of internal operations, through materials resource planning (MRP), enterprise resource planning (ERP) and electronic customer relationship management (eCRM), the service levels of competing companies are becoming similar in content and in construction. The implication is that suppliers are easily replaced with similar companies that have similar products and similar delivery attributes.

The information economy is creating a web of companies that have lower barriers of entry but fewer safety nets for retaining business. Whereas the traditional, hierarchical value chains of the industrial economy reinforced exclusivity, the web structure of the information economy is more inclusive. Case box 7.5 on co-evolution and cooperation provides industry examples of how competitors in the digital economy face the challenge of having to work together to build common network platforms on which their competing products operate.

Case box 7.5: **The rise of co-evolution and cooperation**

The new web-like value chain gives rise to a **self-organizing** system. In nature, flocking is a form of self-organization. The formation of flocking birds is a self-organizing form of collaboration, with simple goals of direction and velocity. Similarly, companies organize and adapt their relationships with vendors and distributors. They select and substitute their partners in the value chain according to changes in the consumer market. Vendors and distributors in turn adapt to new market scenarios. For example, a wave of collaborative buying (when competitors join forces for purchasing) is counteracted by a wave of collaborative vending from vendors. The system eventually normalizes the balance of power.

The self-organizing aspect in the information economy leads to the concept of **co-evolution**.[19] Evolving to meet the needs of other members in the value chain is becoming a more effective strategy than satisfying the company's own needs. Adapting to meet the needs of other companies leads to more business. Riding the new wave of co-evolution, companies are avoiding costly races against each other in favour of a strategy to join forces to gain more customers.

Skype announced the availability of Skype for Intel-based mobile internet devices (MIDs) in January 2009. The new version of Skype software is the result of working with Intel Corporation to develop a new mobile Skype experience for MIDs based on the Intel® Atom™ processor and Moblin-based Linux OS. At the same time, LG Electronics and Intel Corporation today announced a collaboration around mobile internet devices (MIDs) based on Intel's next-generation MID hardware platform, codenamed 'Moorestown,' and Linux-based Moblin v2.0 software platform. The LG device is expected to be one of the first Moorestown designs to market. Collaboration between consumer electronics and luxury goods firms LG and Prada, announced in April 2009, yields products with a 'good combination' of strong technology and style.

Co-evolution and collaboration are even more relevant in industries where network externalities are a vital part of corporate success. The more customers join a network, such as a telecommunications service, the higher is the incentive for other customers to join. This effect is causing companies to collaborate on issues of compatibility.

Source: Austin, T. (2009) Skype to support Android, Java-enabled mobile phones, Intel mobile internet devices. January. Available at http://www.itwire.com/content/view/22571/1127/

---

[19] See Kelly (1994) for an overview of the implications of adaptive behaviour.

7.3.3 Physical platforms

A **physical platform** is the tangible infrastructure (such as computers, telephones, satellites, digital TV and local area networks) that delivers a service to consumers. A simple example of a platform is the PC on your desk. This comprises a set of hardware and software items joined together to provide a computing service. The component items are built according to explicit technology standards and are delivered through separate but parallel supply chains to the PC assembler. Similarly, to obtain Sky's pay-TV service one needs a physical platform consisting of digital TV receiver, set-top decoder, telephone landlines, satellites and ground stations. The physical platform is an assembly of items, each constructed to specific standards and integrated to deliver service to the customer.

Physical platforms have evolved from simple structures, such as regional railway systems, to a complex structure of interconnected sub-platforms. For this reason, the joints between the sub-networks become the strength of the whole structure, or, conversely, they could be its Achilles' heel. It is therefore vital to define standards for joints. The standards that govern how a system and its modules interact is called the network's architecture (Morris and Ferguson, 1993).

Henderson and Clark (1990) review two kinds of dynamic processes in modular systems: **modular innovation** and **architectural innovation**. The former retains the architecture of the network, including its joints, but modifies the modules. By preserving the basic architecture of a system, network providers offer users enough compatibility to shift from one product generation to the next. The changes occur in the innovations and improvements of the modular components. They can be fitted into the system when required, and will be removed when obsolete. The result is a hybrid dynamic of change that preserves the platform's architecture while creating innovations within the module structure. A series of minor incremental modular changes can lead to an overall network platform that is radically new (Vercoulen and Wegberg, 1998).

In architectural innovation, the modules are largely unchanged, but the architecture that connects them (the jointing system) is changed (Henderson and Clark, 1990). The speed of innovation can be fast, as a key part of the system, the modular structure, is retained. New joints between these modules are installed. In some cases, adopting new standards and installing some new modules that embody these standards create an architectural innovation. The development of the internet in the late 1990s is an example of an architectural innovation in a network platform. The main proponents of the internet evolution are standard-setting bodies such as the World Wide Web Consortium and the Internet Engineering Task Force (Vercoulen and Wegberg, 1998).

7.3.4 Consumer networks

A **consumer network** requires interdependencies between consumers. In a consumer market there are two levels of value attached to a product. **Autarky value** (Liebowitz and Margolis, 1999) refers to the value associated with a product irrespective of the number of other users. In marketing terms, this would be the 'core' value of a product. In economics this is the normal assumption and the theory of the firm is based on assumptions about the independence of individual consumer preferences. **Synchronization value** is the augmented value derived from being able to interact with other consumers. The latter fuels the dynamics of the network effect discussed earlier in this chapter and in McGee and Sammut-Bonnici (2002). For example, the relative abilities of Microsoft, Apple or other companies to capture synchronization value will determine who will gain critical mass first and win the race to establish the new operating system for third-generation mobile telephones. The market for Pocket PCs and PDAs is changing rapidly with the introduction of the iPod and the iPhone. This new Apple platform is much more advanced in terms of ease of use and interactivity than Microsoft Mobile and BlackBerry. The market is currently shifting at a rapid rate towards the iPod platform, but we will have to wait and see how the market shares settle. The success of the winning operating system might depend on the psychology of consumer choice, or it could depend on technology characteristics from supply chain strategies and technology standards. For example, Microsoft and Intel cooperated to make Windows 95 exclusively compatible with Intel x86 microprocessor architectures and vice versa. The media coined this the *Wintel advantage*.

Lock-in and switching costs

The Wintel case led to a situation of lock-in for Windows users. The Wintel operating system quickly gained critical mass through rapid adoption and it became the most popular system throughout the world. On top of this, Windows users then invested in complementary software such as the Microsoft Office suite. Lock-in arises whenever users invest in the multiple complementary and durable assets of a physical platform and then find the costs of switching to an alternative to be prohibitive. Lock-in can occur on an individual level, company level and even a societal level. Thus, individuals may face switching costs in adopting a rival to Microsoft software, but so also do companies in having to provide systematic retraining costs, and so might whole communities in having to move from one software product to another. The key is that it would usually be necessary to switch from one dominant product to retain the interdependencies and complementarities between consumers.

Private users were locked into the long-playing record technology because records could not be used on CD players (but were persuaded to switch when the benefit–cost ratio of the new products became sufficiently large). Note that the benefits of tape recording were never large enough to persuade customers to make a wholesale switch from LPs but the extra benefits of tapes (ability to record) were sufficient to persuade customers to invest in parallel systems. Companies became locked into Lotus 1-2-3 spreadsheets because their employees were trained in using the program command structure but later were persuaded to switch to Excel within Microsoft Office because of the extra complementarities. On a societal level, millions of users throughout the world are locked into using Microsoft's Windows desktop operating environment, as it has become the standard software in offices around the world.[20]

On a societal level, economists observe that the practice of using lock-in strategies can have negative welfare effects as new superior technologies are suppressed. Liebowitz and Margolis (1990) discuss the fascinating example of typewriter keyboard layouts. In the 1870s the QWERTY configuration was selected by the creators of the TypeWriter brand in order to slow down typists so as to reduce jamming of the keys. The Dvorak layout patented in 1932 is a more efficient layout and allows faster typing. This would suggest that QWERTY should then give way to the more efficient keyboard layout. The phenomenon of sticking to the slower QWERTY system is explained in terms of high switching costs. The collective switching costs are far higher than the individual switching costs because the coordination for mass switching to Dvorak is so difficult. With the advent of electric typewriters of the 1950s and then computer keyboards the expectation is even stronger but QWERTY still remains. Case box 7.6 explores further the link between lock-in and switching costs.

---

[20] However, we should note the entry of netbooks to this market. They are selling like 'hot cakes': most of them run on a Linux OS rather than Microsoft. Netbooks are being accepted as an option offering 'lower level' computing (internet browsing, emails, and basic typing and spreadsheet work). This may disrupt the comfortable dominance of Microsoft Office.

Case box 7.6: **Lock-in and switching costs**

Telecommunication systems providers have chosen to offer new, superior technologies despite high switching costs. The industry has undergone three generations of technologies – TACS, ETACS and GSM – and is now in the early days of introduction of 3G, incurring significant investment costs. Their calculation is made on the basis that the new systems will provide backward compatibility plus the expected benefits of new services. Switching costs and lock-in at the consumer level can be deliberately used to inhibit or prevent consumers from adopting newer technologies or moving to alternative networks. In mobile communications, users may switch to another network provider with the same technology but with a different price structure. They may choose to switch to another technology when they replace their handsets with higher-level models. The strategies of the mobile telecommunication companies have focused on manipulating the tangible and intangible consumer costs when switching networks. In the introductory phase customers were contractually bound to a network for a year. They had to pay a release fee to end the contract and a connection charge to go to the next network. In the later 1990s switching networks became easier with the introduction of pay-as-you-go cards. But the hidden, intangible costs of switching remain, irrespective of payment structures and Oftel's[21] recent pressure to minimize switching cost in the industry. Customers are deterred from switching by the investment in the time required to get used to a new product and are further inhibited by the uncertainty about the quality of untested products. The influence of brand loyalty is also significant. To the consumer, another very relevant switching cost is the loss of the mobile number when moving to another network (this was also a very big issue in the development of the telephone system in the US over a century ago). Subscribers' reluctance to give up their familiar numbers resulted in the introduction of subsidized phones and more competitive tariffs. The power of switching costs can be observed in the entry strategies against powerful incumbents. Vodafone and Cellnet started to operate in 1984 and had a captive customer base by the time Orange and One2One entered the market in 1993 and 1994 respectively. The new entrants had to generate new customer-winning strategies with stronger branding and lower costs.

7.4 Networks and standards: competition and regulation

Companies that operate in competitive markets dominated by network externalities face distinct trade-offs regarding the choice of a technical standard. Holding on to a primary compatibility standard permits a firm's product to capture the value added by a large network. Conversely, the firm loses direct control over the market supply of the good and faces (direct) intra-platform competition. Alternatively, adhering to a unique standard permits the firm to face less or no intra-platform competition, but it forgoes the added value related to a large network (Economides and Flyer, 1997).

This trade-off is a key strategic decision that depends in part on the control that firms have in making their output compatible with competitors' outputs and complementary products. The ability to conform to a common standard opens the opportunity to make this trade-off. Where standards are proprietary, the decision rests with the owner of the standard. The owner's trade-off is the pay-off associated with developing the existing network and its spillovers versus the introduction of more intra-platform competition. Essentially the trade-off is the same: to adhere to a common standard or to seek uniqueness. This can be expressed as a sequential game: at the outset, one chooses the appropriate technical standard (and, therefore, the network to join), and later one chooses how

---

[21] Oftel was the UK telecommunications systems regulator. It has been superseded by Ofcom.

to compete. Normal markets do not have this choice of network and there are consequences for market structure and competition in the presence of network externalities. The mathematical model in Economides and Flyer (1997) defines networks as coalition structures and analyses the stability of coalitions under different standards regimes and varying levels of network externalities. There are a number of implications for market structure and competition in the presence of network externalities.

First: it is intuitively clear that industry output will be higher when there are network externalities and when standards are open. Firms are free to choose which standard to adopt and are deterred only by the costs of adoption. Second, when standards are incompatible and the owners of standards can exercise proprietary control, incumbents are more strongly protected against the consequences of new entrants. Moreover, there will usually be considerable asymmetries between firms in terms of outputs, prices and profits. (Under incompatibility regimes, firms are equivalent to platforms and constitute one-firm networks.) For pure network goods the asymmetries are particularly marked.

Second: in general, with total incompatibility of standards market concentration, output inequality and price and profit inequality increase with the extent of the network externality. This is an important result because it explains why one or two firms so often dominate network industries. The mechanism is straightforward. The leading network establishes its critical mass, leaving the second network to establish a critical mass across the remaining untapped market coverage. The third network follows in the same fashion and so on. It follows that there will be a tendency to provide large incentives to organize customers into few platforms so as to maximize the added value from the available networks. Firms will be keen to abandon their own weak standards in favour of the higher value obtainable from a leading network.

There is a *third* implication. Where there are proprietary standards and strong network effects, there is no natural equilibrium in terms of network offerings. There are always incentives for at least one firm to move to a stronger network and the consequence of any one move is to shift the incentives for all other firms. However, equilibrium can be reinforced by the refusal of firms to make their proprietary standards available. Again, the mechanism is straightforward. Under strong externalities, the owner of a standard has a considerable incentive to exploit the standard by itself and to exclude other firms with weaker standards. Conversely, where the externality is weak, the owner will find a stronger incentive to admit other firms to its proprietary standard in order to grow the network through collective effort and thus generate more added value. In summary, strong network externalities suggest the following eventualities:

1 larger industry output;
2 very large asymmetries between firms/platforms;
3 likelihood of market dominance;
4 enhancement and protection of proprietary standards;
5 equilibrium market structures that are the reverse of the world without network externalities.

This leads directly to the *fourth* implication. Competition as we know it can be seriously compromised by the size consequences of 'winner takes all'. Microsoft's continuing presence in front of the competition regulators in the US and in the EU is testament to this. The creation of a substantial market share (a de facto monopoly) not only leads to the possibility of monopolistic behaviour in that market but in the potential transfer of that position into adjacent industries. Hence the concern that a company like Microsoft might be able to create similar large market shares in network industries (such as browsers). In addition to the monopoly question there is continuing controversy about intellectual property rights such as patents and access by smaller firms to the knowledge bases of the larger ones. As the ICT industry is inherently global there are also continuing concerns about the ability of the smaller local firms to survive against the global players. Just what is a level playing field is a matter of dispute. Consequently the competition authorities in the US and the EU have paid considerable attention to the ways in which competition in the digital economy should be managed. The following section outlines the more important issues from a European perspective.

7.4.1 Regulatory framework for the digital economy

The convergence of digital services means that an array of different industries begins to merge together because of the digital technologies that are common to all of them. This means that we can no longer treat certain industries as essentially separate and different – they are linked together by a powerful scope economy – a common technology. This then challenges the accepted norms regarding regulation. The traditional regulatory rationale was intended for a period when clear operational distinctions existed between infrastructure and services – this has become outdated for dealing with the new ICT landscape (Sammut-Bonnici, 2009).

In recent years, regulators and policy makers have begun to respond to the challenge of the new digital landscape.[22] Governments are adjusting the management of regulation by establishing a central authoritative body to administer the telecommunications, broadcasting and information technology sectors collectively. Policy makers are preparing and putting into practice new rules to construct a legal framework to enable further development of the digital economy. Different infrastructure platforms, such as cable TV, internet, mobile and fixed telephony, are being given an equal or technology-neutral regulatory treatment.

Hot topics within the regulatory arena are intellectual property, content, data protection, security, country of origin, excess VAT charges on electronic products, open access and the harmonization of enforcement across regions. What are some of the positive outcome's limiting factors and new challenges in the regulatory environment? We give some examples drawn from the EU context, which may also apply in other areas of the world.

Positive outcomes

Regulation is always controversial because it involves constraints on freedom of action in markets. But regulation has not always been a constraining force on the ICT industry. There have been many positive effects of particular EU regulations on the industry and its many markets.

Freedom of provisioning in different EU countries

The freedom of establishment and the freedom to provide services across borders set out by the EU are fundamental enabling mechanisms that are central to the effective functioning of the ICT industry in the EU's internal market. The principle of freedom of establishment allows investors in platform infrastructures to carry on an economic activity in several countries, and consequently such companies are able to enjoy more sound economies of scale. The net result of more profitable operations is the opportunity to reduce consumer prices across Europe.

Level playing field

The ICT industry has benefited from regulation that creates a level playing field at a European level to enhance cross-border business opportunities. Overall principles such as mutual recognition and country of origin principles have been more effective and more appropriate than attempting to enforce maximum harmonization.

---

[22] This is usually referred to as the ICT (information and communication technologies) industries.

Country of origin

The e-Commerce Directive and its use of the Country of Origin principle have encouraged online sellers, particularly independents and micro-firms, to build and consolidate e-shopping services. The directive enhances legal certainty, reduces compliance costs and removes the 'fear factor' of trading online across borders. There are other positive effects in the e-Commerce Directive, such as the liability exemption for intermediaries. However, given that there are conflicting provisions, e.g. between the e-Commerce Directive and IPR (intellectual property rights) regulations, this can lead to negative effects as outlined in the next section.

Broadcasting

The European Union is setting new regulations for broadcasting and on-demand content. The Audiovisual Media Services Directive (AVMS), formerly known as the Television without Frontiers Directive, updates regulations on broadcasting in Europe and brings in new guidelines for content viewed on alternative platforms, like the internet or mobile phones.

The new directive also includes an important reference to the country of origin principle, which means that content will continue to be regulated by the rules of the country from which it originates. Each country within the European Union will have broadly similar rules but there may be subtle differences. Anyone supplying content to users would only have to worry about one set of rules, rather than differing laws across the EU's Member States. The reversal of the country of origin principle could force many ICT players to redesign business strategies and possibly to exit some markets.

It is too early to confirm the positive effects of the AVMS Directive at this stage, as transposition into national law is pending and the AVMS Directive is not yet implemented. There are some issues, such as the exemption of user-generated content (UGC), also known as consumer generated media (CGM), from its scope, which are not clear yet.

Access Directive

The directive stipulates procedures and principles for imposing pro-competitive obligations regarding access to and interconnection of networks on operators with significant market power. The regulation reduced restrictions that prevent undertakings from negotiating access and interconnection arrangements between ICT companies, in particular on cross-border agreements. This has facilitated the industry's expansion and diversification.

Intellectual property rights

The broadcasting and publishing sectors have been assisted by the upholding of IPR in order to protect the creators of media such as film, music and other content. If content is not paid for when downloaded or copied, the pecuniary incentives for content developers would diminish, and new content would become less available as a result.

Media literacy efforts

Regulatory bodies across Europe have set up media literacy objectives that are complementary to the ICT industry's efforts to empower users to navigate the internet safely and knowledgeably. Regulators have helped the ICT industry with education campaigns to empower users to use information technology services and to be able to distinguish between different types of online content. The campaigns have complemented the industry players' efforts in the area.

Prudence in regulation

The ICT markets and their operators have benefited in areas where the regulators exercised prudence and caution when dealing with nascent technology and new business models. When a 'light touch' regulatory regime is applied, it enables the development of small and medium-sized enterprises into larger corporations, depending on the freedom to innovate without regulatory burdens. A case in point is the success story of the proliferation of search engine services.

Limiting factors

Regulation, even light-touch regulation, does not always have the desired or even desirable effects, as we outline in this section.

The uneven application of the EU distance-selling directive hinders online sellers from full exploitation of the potential of the internal market. This problem affects sellers who are selling via auction sites and other e-marketplace sites. The cost of compliance is prohibitive for many of the small sellers, the majority of which are SMEs and micro-firms.

The uneven implementation of the length of the cooling-off period by EU Member States creates complexity and uncertainty for online traders. Different rules in different Member States create ambiguity in the level of protection that they need to provide to their customers in different jurisdictions. Consequently traders only do business in their local markets, thus the potential of the single market is undermined.

The previous section referred to the positive effects of the liability exemption for intermediaries in the e-Commerce Directive. However, given that there are conflicting provisions, for example between the e-Commerce Directive and IPR regulations, this can lead to differences in national regulations and diverging case-law, leading to an uneven playing field at EU level as well as legal uncertainty.

The loading of VAT for electronic delivery is a disincentive to the development of electronic content supply. In the publishing sector, material supplied in print carries either no VAT or a reduced rate of VAT. When it is supplied electronically, it has to be charged the full VAT rate. Exempt suppliers, such as universities and individual consumers, cannot recover VAT, which implies that the real cost of electronically supplied products can be from 18% to 25% higher, depending on the tax rate of the country.

7.4.2 New challenges for regulation strategy

As digital technology continues to develop (remember Moore's Law), the need for continuous and active regulation becomes even more important. You may recall similar sentiments about the need for more proactive regulation of banking following the international banking crises of 2008. In both cases, advances in technology and in managerial sophistication require care to be taken that anti-competitive consequences and system breakdown do not ensue.

The ICT landscape and the EU's regulatory role[23]

Post-convergence and digitization, the new ICT landscape is based on continuous innovation that challenges accepted consumption behaviour and regulatory paradigms. Industry players recommend that for the EU to protect and develop its competitiveness in the ICT industry it must parallel the rapid evolution of the market by seeking to:

- **Increase e-confidence** as the motor of EU ICT competitiveness through the empowerment of the consumer via education campaigns. Confidence in the industry and an increase in usage are encouraged by consumer protection mechanisms that are similar to the offline world.
- **Reflect the global context**. Considering the global characteristics of technology and markets in the ICT sector, regulation is most effective when it offers an international perspective.

---

[23] This section is based on technical reports submitted to industry players by Tanya Sammut-Bonnici, Marco Gatti and John McGee (2009).

- **Adapt to new business models**. The industry is constantly testing new forms of business models in this fast-moving and changing industry. The evidence of extensive business collaboration among new media, internet, telecommunications and publishing companies is the engine room for industry convergence. In this context, regulation should promote new forms of businesses and encourage the evolution of new competition in the market. Regulation can create new opportunities, but also jeopardize old and emerging business models. Regulatory limitations should therefore be carefully deployed.

- **Focus on the next wave of innovation**. To secure an accelerated migration path from analogue to digital and to accelerate the creation of the digital home in Europe, EU policy makers would need to focus on four key areas:
  - Refocus attention from broadband internet to convergence based on digital TV.
  - Ensure a balanced market structure and competition.
  - Balance consumer protection with long-term investment and employment objectives.
  - Balance regulation of infrastructure-based competition.

- **Adopt a technology-neutral approach**. A regulatory framework that is technology neutral, market led and focused on creating a level playing field will increase the scale and scope of the competitive environment in the EU.

- **Promote innovation**. Regulation should be adaptive, clear, flexible and reduced to the minimum intervention necessary in order to promote innovation. Innovation flourishes in an open environment of creativity rather than limiting rules. Innovation should be encouraged in:
  - conceptual design;
  - investment in new service infrastructure;
  - innovation diffusion in consumer markets.

- **Apply a 'light touch'**. To ensure that consumers' preferences are truly reflected, regulation should be applied with a light touch and not try to second-guess the choices that ICT users and businesses make. This principle implies a delicate balance of ex-ante and ex-post regulation. Attempting to implement a regulatory framework before the technology is clear and fully developed would be an obstacle to innovation and risky.

- **Encourage self-regulation**. With specific regard to access to information, ICT players encourage regulators to work with companies in developing a self-regulatory approach to increasing access to information. In the fast-paced environment characterized by convergence and digitization, it is difficult for regulators to anticipate and meet the needs of future changes. Working directly with, and meeting regularly with, industry will allow regulators to increase their understanding of industry issues. Self-regulation is advocated as the primary tool, given the fast-paced changes in the industry, and the difficulty of predicting consumer reaction to new technologies and services. The risk of regulatory failure can be high.

- **React to market failure**. A clear call for regulatory interventions occurs when market failure is present in terms of discrepancies in access to content, consumer pricing and excessive market power.

- **Harmonise the EU regulatory environment**. Harmonization is a one-way method of ensuring a common and clear regulatory environment. However, it should be carefully used and not applied as a panacea at all costs. Maximum harmonization is not always beneficial and some regional customization may be called for.

- **Regulate with clarity and coherence**. The ICT industry within the EU would benefit from a reduction of ambiguity, a decrease in complex bureaucracy and more coherence of regulation across markets and countries.

In addition to the broad thrust of regulation, there are a number of specific issues that have serious implications for the evolution of competition. These are discussed briefly below.

Next-generation networks (NGNs)

Looking into the future, the prospect of infrastructure competition between NGNs providing multi-play offerings is strong. However, significant investments in these NGNs must be based on the notion that there is strategic value in these networks and their relationships with customers. Regulators would be assisting ICT consumer markets and the industry if they could design the next-generation broadband policies to maximize infrastructure growth opportunities. Large-scale commitments to investments in digital cable can only be made long term where the value proposition inherent in the vertically integrated network operator model is preserved. This implies that regulatory and public policy should proceed with caution to avoid a disproportionate shift of value to infrastructure-independent service providers operating over the application layer. Broadcast companies in particular are actively looking to partner strategically with new media and internet companies so as to provide customers with an innovative and compelling broadband service over a 'managed pipe' network.

Open standards

For search engines and other content aggregators to be able to compete with vertically integrated operators on a fair basis, it is vital for regulators to preserve open access to the market across technology platforms and infrastructure networks. The ICT industry calls for a balanced intellectual property rights regime that allows for open solutions, open standards and open source software.

Digital rights management (DRM)

The broadcasting sector contends that the underlying tenet of the development of DRM is to enable the licensing and acquisition of copyright through technology, while avoiding premium content from being used without authorization. The responsibility of making licensing easier can usually be shared by copyright owners and users. However, particular rights or mass usage of copyright material such as music cannot, in practical terms, be authorized or remunerated otherwise than through collective management agreements. DRM policies would make the broadcaster's own management of rights acquisition and licensing significantly easier by allowing for the automatic reporting of the use of digital content (e.g. music, film). Regarding mass piracy of premium content via the internet, broadcasters have interests in controlling illegal copying and redistribution activities.

Intellectual property rights

Copyright laws encourage consumers to make use of content in limited ways, for example for educational purposes or within agreed time frames. Fair use provisions for content are instrumental to encourage ICT investments as it increases the demand for content.

Net neutrality

The net neutrality debate revolves around the issues of content censorship, traffic prioritisation and network architecture. Content censorship caused a public outcry when Cox Interactive customers discovered that they were unable to access Craigslist. The second issue, traffic prioritization or 'traffic shaping', is the hottest issue in the neutrality regulation debate. Net neutrality would imply that file-sharing traffic, which could cause internet congestion, should not be blocked, slowed down or given lower priority. The third issue concerns the internet's network architecture, which allows for 'short lanes' and 'fast lanes' that allow selected files to be transmitted down faster routes. Arguments for network neutrality regulations are based on the tenet that the facility poses discriminatory advantages that are affordable only by the more affluent firms.

Net neutrality is of benefit mainly to innovators and smaller firms that are less likely to spend on traffic prioritization, and to consumers, who would be allowed to continue to determine what content they access. Network operators, broadcasters and search engine sectors have divergent views on the subject. Any regulation in this respect would have to be cautious to achieve net economic gain in the wider ICT market. Light-touch regulation, which is enforceable, is required to allow the internet to continue to evolve.

The underlying theme behind these propositions about future regulatory practice reflects the complexity of an industry where the pace of technical advance is high and not diminishing in pace, where economies of various sorts are endemic and where globalization is intrinsic. The industry landscape in practice is not allowed to evolve organically on its own because the underlying imperfections and distortions are so great. This, therefore, is an industry marked by frequent and sophisticated interaction between the players and the various regulatory authorities.

7.5 Implications for strategy

This chapter argues that there are major differences between the economic and strategic characteristics of the digital economy compared to the traditional industrial order. These major differences can be summarized as follows:

1 The information economy depends on connectivity. Without connectivity, consumer interdependence is indirect. Positive feedback gives an economic law of plenty – more gives more.

2 Upfront costs are very large and revenues can be substantially delayed and are significantly at risk. As a result, the nature of business models is different, with higher degrees of risk embedded in them.

3 It is also a world of immense uncertainty where even the range of potential outcomes is not known, but also where there is a significant probability that future technological change might undermine an apparently winning position.

4 The competition between rival networks/standards can be hard to call in advance.

5 'Tippy markets' substantially raise the level of risk.[24]

In this new world there is much more uncertainty and companies need to take bigger risks in order just to survive. The prospect of entrepreneurial profits is enticingly large but there are probably greater probabilities of failure. The list of failures and near failures in the last decade by large companies is very long. There are some new strategic 'rules' for competing in the digital economy. While these are quite generic in nature, they illustrate that companies need to come to these markets with a different mindset about how to compete:

1 Expectations management is central to the way in which marketing strategy is conceived (see Case box 7.7).

2 Open standards are the key to volume. Protected standards are only viable as small high-priced niche markets. The old preoccupation with protection of intellectual property is giving way to a sharing and cooperating approach.

3 There is a law of inverse pricing. The best (i.e. the most valuable in the future) products are given away, such as web browsers, in order to create a consumer standard and sheer volume causes both marginal costs and prices to fall over time as the product becomes more valuable. The cash

---

[24] 'Tippy' markets are those that display potential network externalities but have not yet tipped to show these externalities at work.

flow machine consists of modest (even small) margins multiplied by gigantic volumes to defray massive investments. The machine is volume driven and protected by very large switching costs.

4   The first strategic choice is which network to join (which standard to adopt). The second, and a long way behind, is how to compete within the network of choice.

5   Networked complementarities and cooperative strategies are replacing the old order of hierarchical business organization and competition.

6   In a world of uncertainty, customers are also uncertain about which standards, technologies and products will prevail. This will increase the power of brands and place upon marketing the need to manage customer expectations so as to speed adoption rates towards tipping points in the market.

7   Post-convergence and digitization, the new ICT landscape is based on continuous innovation that challenges accepted consumption behaviour and regulatory paradigms. Industry players recommend that for the EU to protect and develop its international competitiveness in the ICT industry it must develop a mixture of light-touch regulation complemented by detailed and specific measures (directives) to ensure a properly competitive landscape (Sammut-Bonnici, 2009).

Case box 7.7: **Expectations management**

When consumers choose products in network markets, their expectations play a crucial role in sales of the products or their network components, since consumer utility depends on the number of other consumers purchasing the same products. Therefore, rival firms in a network industry seek to influence consumers' expectations in order to maximize their profits. The process is facilitated by consumers' imperfect information about the size of the installed base in the market. Sales figures are often exaggerated to impress consumers about leadership over rivals in the installed base. The competition between OS/2 and Microsoft Windows in 1992 is a classic example. IBM and Microsoft both announced wider adoption of their operating systems than actual. Later on, each company disputed the estimated numbers of sales of the other (Bensen and Farrell, 1994).

Expectations management is a strategic device that goes beyond the inflation of penetration figures and moves into the realms of brand and corporate image building. In competing to achieve critical mass and to become market leaders in the mobile communications industry, consumer expectations were significant. The mobile company that was expected to grow the fastest would gain most market share. Self-fulfilling expectations are one manifestation of positive feedback economics and bandwagon effects. The mobile communications industry has made consistent use of semiotics in expectations management through its media campaigns. Images, music themes and slogans are used to imply magnitude and leadership.

The model in Figure 1 illustrates the adoption process. Adoption typically follows an S-shaped pattern around the long-term trend growth rate. The early adopters ('anoraks') rush in. There is then a pause while other prospective early adopters make up their minds – marketing is focused on persuading them to move quickly and decisively so as to create a rapid growth that will become self-sustaining (through point B in the diagram). Following this, the push to sustain the market through attracting late adopters is the next marketing focus. This suggests some rules for marketing – these are summarized in Figure 2. Marketing is about creating momentum so as to minimize the risks that are endemic in this new world. Brands and reputation are, if anything, even more important. The emphasis is on volume, so open standards are attractive and low, penetration-style pricing will be common.

Vodafone's corporate image campaign in its early days included images of the Thames Barrier and the cliffs of Dover. Symbols of national interest were used to give the subliminal message that Vodafone will succeed throughout the UK. The musical theme in the Thames Barrier campaign was from *Close Encounters*, implying universal reach. The cliffs of Dover campaign involved the draping of a large section of the cliffs with material by a contemporary artist. Orange has had one of the most famous slogans in UK media history: 'The future is bright, the future is Orange'. One2One has had equally expansionist

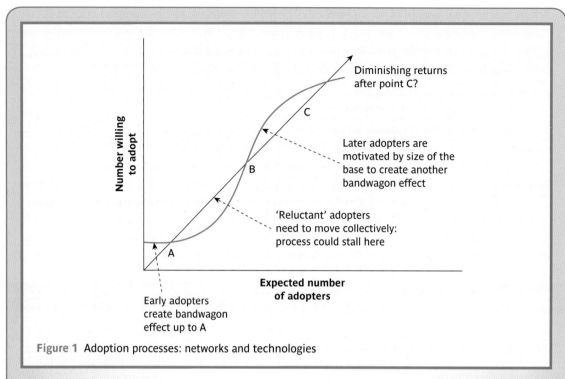

Figure 1 Adoption processes: networks and technologies

media campaigns, particularly with its award-winning 'Welcome to Our World'. All these campaigns imply market leadership and a sense of network growth.

The effects in Figure 1 can be seen in research by Huberman (1988), which shows how consumers' expectations are being linked to critical mass. The stronger the consumers' expectation that a new network will be widely adopted in the future, the faster the market reaches critical mass. Once a critical number of users is achieved, the rate of increase of new users increases exponentially up to the limit of the user population (or to some other natural limit; see Figure 1). The implication for strategists is that the time required to achieve critical mass can be reduced in proportion to the degree of optimism of people's expectations.

Market to create momentum:
create the belief that this technology will be the standard
Leverage reputation:
brands and reputation matter
Commit to 'open' standards:
open standards can give access to volume
proprietary standards can result in small niches
Win over an influential buyer
e.g. supermarkets and UPCs (bar codes)
Advance sign-ups:
prior commitments create confidence
Wink at piracy:
adoption at zero price is better than no adoption
Pricing:
leasing, long-term contracts, give-aways, penetration pricing

Figure 2 Managing the adoption process

Hence, strategic action aimed at increasing consumers' expectations of the success of a new product would have a double effect of inducing more new users, who in turn influence even more users. This effect can be powerful – Huberman's simulations demonstrate that even if there is only a small group of individuals with double the propensity for innovation in relation to the group average, the critical mass can be reached very rapidly. This has been evident in the mobile communications industry. Once the phones were affordable and accessible to the youth market (the early adopters), sales boomed for this particular segment. As a result, even more users from other segments were attracted to the market.

The economic characteristics of network industries are dependent in large part on the interconnectivity that is characteristic of the technologies of information goods. Interconnectivity allows customers to view, use and link products, and fosters the development of networks of customers. In these networks, powerful demand-side increasing returns can operate. Where consumer-based externalities are powerful there are strong pressures towards 'winner takes all' phenomena (e.g. Wintel globally, and Sky TV in the UK). In these circumstances, conventional economic laws are challenged. De facto monopoly can emerge: but uncertainty is high and markets may be intrinsically unstable. Successive waves of technology may outmode old monopolies and serve as the basis for new monopolies.

The rate of growth and now the sheer size of the ICT industry has been the progenitor of major changes in the economy. We have seen major effects on other industries through the new value possibilities that information technology offers and through the substantial fixed costs and minimum scales required for effective deployment of these technologies. When linked to networks of interdependent customers we see the potential emergence of 'winner takes all' strategies and the emergence of new monopolies.

We have decomposed the ICT industry into its component parts in order to see who the players are and how they interact with one another. In doing this, we argue that we are beginning to see a new type of industrial order – one marked by networked complementarities and cooperation in place of the traditional model of hierarchy and competition. We have also decomposed the industry into four horizontal levels – technology, supply chain, platform, and network – to show that these have different economic characteristics and therefore that corporate strategies have different dynamics. The examples quoted indicate the range and extent of the possibilities inherent in the new technologies and in terms of rivalry in the form of pre-emptive strikes and technology races. We note particularly the pervasive changes that are taking place in supply chains generally. The increasing importance of connectivity and modularity is forcing a shift from competitive mode towards cooperative mode. This raises thoughts of self-organizing systems and the notion of co-evolution, rather a long way from the search for, and exercise of, crude bargaining power. The sheer size and cost of physical platforms also create new dynamics. The pervasive use of alliances is an obvious example. Less obvious is how the need for interoperability requires new attitudes towards complexity and requirements for agility.

A new set of strategies is emerging to offset the risks and pressures exerted by these rules. This is visible in the setting up of global standards and their ensuing platforms. For example, Group Speciale Mobile, commonly known as GSM, is an association of 600 network operators and suppliers of the mobile phone industry. Their primary objective is to set a common standard for mobile communications in order to create a homogeneous industry where equipment, software and networks can seamlessly talk to each other. Strategies of standardization are stabilizing the markets and charting the course for research and development policies.

Finally, we remark on the significance of interdependence between consumers. This effect at its strongest completely shifts our thinking from the prevalence of oligopolistic competition (size matters but so do diminishing returns) to the possibility of 'winner takes all' and the monopoly (size matters – full stop). Clearly, such network effects are not always going to be so extreme but there is a real possibility that the combination of high fixed costs, significant economies of scale and high degrees of knowledge specialization will, when taken together with consumer bandwagons, create massive new corporate structures in which the major (and perhaps only) discipline will be further developments in technology. However, the analysis of consumer lock-in suggests the real possibility that switching costs might inhibit the adoption of valuable new technologies.

7.6 Summary

Thus, the brave new world has a sting in the tail. The pervasive development of the ICT industries has promoted, and continues to promote, very substantial consequential changes throughout the economy. In doing so, industry economics and dynamics change and significant adaptations have to take place in order to avoid getting run down by the juggernaut. Changes are needed in the nature of the corporate strategies and in the mindsets required. Where the conjunction of certain technological and consumer circumstances takes place, the strategy game becomes a very direct race to establish a dominant position. Where such games fail to achieve their objectives, the cost of unproductive investment could be enormous. Where they in fact succeed, many will nevertheless have failed and we as a society would also face the difficulties in managing the consequences of de facto monopoly. The data available does not suggest that 'winner takes all' is likely to be a frequent phenomenon. However, all the other indications suggest that various forms of scale-intensive, pre-emptive strategies will become much more common (see, for example, the telecommunications boom and bust). But as a counterpoint we can also see that there are very considerable forces promoting more cooperation and stronger incentives towards a much more subtle blending of cooperative and competitive modes of practice within industries.

Key terms

Recap questions and assignments

1 Explain how network externalities might (or might not) occur in the following situations, paying particular attention to the way in which critical mass is reached:

(a) the mobile telecommunications industry;

(b) BSkyB and the satellite TV market.

2 For the situations in question 1, give examples of co-evolution and/or cooperation. In which case is cooperative behaviour most marked? Why?

3 For any internet-based business with which you are familiar, explain its business model and compare it to any one of the business models discussed in Chapter 5.

Case study 7.1: Surviving the net: Yahoo!, eBay and Amazon

What the diverging fates of Yahoo!, eBay and Amazon say about the internet

Yahoo! has survived. The internet company – which, at the age of 14, is one of the oldest – appears in the end to have rebuffed Microsoft, the software Goliath that wanted to buy it. It has done so, in part, by surrendering to Google, the younger internet company that is its main rival. In a vague deal apparently designed to confuse antitrust regulators, Yahoo! is letting Google, the biggest force in web-search advertising, place text ads next to some of Yahoo!'s own search results. Google thus controls some or all of the ads on all the big search engines except Microsoft's. Yahoo! lives, but on the web's equivalent of life support.

Yahoo!'s descent, first gradual then sudden, during this decade marks a surprising reversal of the fates of the only three big internet firms to have survived since the web's earliest days. Back in 1994 Jerry Yang and David Filo, truant PhD students at Stanford, started to publish a list, eventually named Yahoo!, of links to cool destinations on the nascent web. Around the same time, Jeff Bezos was writing his business plan for a website, soon to be called Amazon, for selling books online. The following year, Pierre Omidyar, a French-born Iranian-American, put an auction site on the web that would become eBay.

Even as hundreds of other dotcoms fell by the wayside at the turn of the century, these three made it through the great internet crisis and have since prospered, to varying degrees and at different times. Their fates have reflected the evolution of the web as a whole, and now suggest its future direction. For many years eBay and Yahoo! made more money than Amazon, which, as a capital-intensive retailer, struggled longer with losses and then made profits at lower margins (see chart). And yet, says Pip Coburn of Coburn Ventures, an investment adviser, Yahoo! is now drifting and eBay is a washed-up quasi-monopoly, whereas Amazon finds itself at the internet's cutting edge.

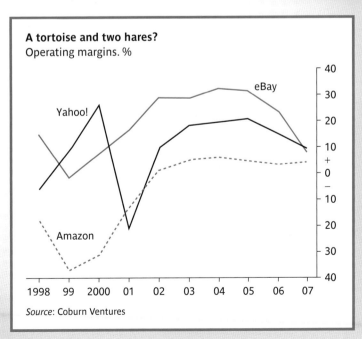

A tortoise and two hares?
Operating margins. %

Source: Coburn Ventures

▶ Yahoo! set out to be a new sort of media company. To that end, it hired a Hollywood mogul, Terry Semel, during the internet depression in 2001. He had a backward-looking idea of the media business. Yahoo!'s site became a tawdry strip mall, with big, flashing advertisements next to users' e-mail inboxes. The firm slipped into a mindset of product silos, with the teams for the home-page, e-mail, finance and sports pages competing with each other and for advertisers, and confusing users.

Yahoo!'s bigger mistake was not to see how the web was changing. Google, also founded by two truant Stanford PhD students, became the leader of a new generation with a vision that web search, rather than Yahoo!'s 'portal' approach, would guide surfers around the internet. Google valued simplicity, interactivity and the collective intelligence gleaned from the web and its users. Yahoo! belatedly tried to keep up and bought sites such as flickr for photo-sharing and del.icio.us for bookmark-sharing, but it 'put them in the curio cabinet' without transforming the company, says Jerry Michalski, a technology consultant. Yahoo! was 'so bent on being the future', he says, that it 'missed the new'. Mr Yang replaced Mr Semel last year, but the crisis was so grave that he has now ended up surrendering to Google.

EBay took a different route, recognising that its business – in effect, online yard sales – had potential network effects: in short, that sellers and buyers would flock to whichever site already did the most trading. The firm became a de facto monopoly, but with that came a culture that left many of its users disenchanted, and growth slowed. Some measures, such as the number of new listings of items for sale, are even in decline. Buyers and sellers increasingly rely on Google's search model, or online social networks, to find things and one another. EBay's new boss, John Donahoe, is not facing a crisis like Yahoo!'s – but neither does he appear to have a big idea for the future.

Amazin'

Amazon, by contrast, has found exactly that. It is the only one of the three that has been led continuously by the same man, its founder Jeff Bezos. A caricaturist's dream, Mr Bezos has an outsized neck, striking pate and an infectious guffaw that spreads enthusiasm. And, unlike his peers at the other two firms, Mr Bezos has stuck to his original vision – while adding two new ideas as they presented themselves.

His original plan, in the 1990s, was to become 'Earth's biggest river' of merchandise, from books and toys to electronics and almost anything else that can be shipped. He tried and failed to become a rival to eBay in auctions. But then Mr Bezos realised that the same online store-front and logistics system that worked for Amazon itself could also work for others. So he added an entirely new category of customers: third-party sellers, who account for 30% of all items sold through Amazon's site today. They range from one-man-bands to huge retailers, such as Target.

Then, about four years ago, another, and potentially bigger, idea struck Mr Bezos. 'We had built this huge infrastructure internally for us,' says Mr Bezos. 'We thought, surely others out there could use the same infrastructure services.' That infrastructure consists of Amazon's prodigious numbers of server computers and storage discs, rivalled in scale by only a few other firms in the world, including Google. So Mr Bezos again added an entire category of customers: firms that wanted to rent computing capacity – from processing to storage to database functionality – from Amazon over the internet, rather than build their own data centres in a warehouse. It has signed up over 370,000 customers, ranging from web start-ups to the New York Times, which used Amazon's infrastructure to digitise much of its archive.

Almost by accident, Amazon has thus 'backed into cloud computing,' as Mr Michalski puts it, using the buzzword for today's next big thing: the trend among both consumers and companies to compute and store data on the internet, rather than on a local computer. If there is a leader in the cloud, it is Google. But Amazon is now right up there. Better yet, although Amazon overlaps with Google in the cloud, it does not rival it directly. Google mostly offers entire applications, such as word processing or spreadsheets, to consumers though their web browsers. Amazon offers services to programmers so they can build and run their own applications.

So there they are. Jerry Yang is still boss of Yahoo!, although angry, restive shareholders may oust him at their annual meeting on August 1st, and his top lieutenants are leaving in droves. John Donahoe is looking hard for a purpose that will enable eBay to survive another decade. And Mr Bezos is right where he wants to be.

Source: The Three Survivors', *The Economist*, 19 June 2008

Questions

1 One of the key underpinnings of network strategy is to capitalize on the network externalities of other networks. Mobile telephone companies used this strategy to grow on the incumbent structure of fixed telephone networks. How can Yahoo!'s survival strategy and its choice to collaborate with its main competitor, Google, be interpreted in terms of network externalities of larger platforms?

2 How have Amazon and eBay exploited the peer 2 peer public networks to expand their customer base? How did this strategy expand its commercial base and secure more revenue for the companies? What are the key differences in how Amazon and eBay have managed suppliers?

Case study 7.2: **Browser wars are back**

The battle is over security rather than features

The good news is that the latest version of Microsoft's web-browser, Internet Explorer version 8, which was finally released to the public on March 20th, is a vast improvement over its predecessor. The bad news is that it is not an automatic upgrade; you have to download and install it yourself.

That is a strange decision. Internet Explorer has 67% of the browser market precisely because it comes ready-installed as the default browser on nine out of ten personal computers. Usually, one of the first things done by those who care about setting up a Windows computer properly is to replace Internet Explorer with a safer and more flexible browser such as Firefox or Opera. Yet most people leave the Microsoft browser in place and suffer the consequences.

The same goes for Macintosh users. Over the past half a dozen years, the default browser on all Macs has been Apple's Safari – a nifty program that uses a rendering engine and tools for running Java scripts borrowed from a venerable Linux browser called Konqueror. Certainly Safari, which is used on 8% of computers, is as light and nimble as Konqueror. Unfortunately, though, it offers an open door for cyber-criminals seeking to hijack computers for dastardly deeds. Both Firefox (22% market share) and Opera (less than 1%) are better bets for Macs, though neither is as secure on Apple's operating system as it is on Windows.

One of the main reasons why a Windows machine is harder to crack than a Mac is because of the way Microsoft randomises the memory locations of code inserted into processes. Even if they can get into the system, hackers then have trouble finding where their nefarious bit of code is lurking. And if they cannot find the malicious code, they cannot get it to do its dirty work.

Apple is not big on randomisation, which is part of the reason why Macintosh computers are so vulnerable to online attack, whether running Safari or even Firefox. Hackers agree the toughest nut to crack is Firefox running on Windows.

The reason why Macs do not suffer as much as Windows machines from break-ins and hijackings is because there are just not enough of them around to make it worthwhile for 'black hat' programmers in the underworld to write software to exploit them for criminal purposes. Equally, there is nowhere near enough reward money to encourage 'white hat' programmers in the security field to find ways of exploiting bugs in Apple's operating system and its Safari browser.

Such vulnerabilities have a market value. In the Apple world, confidential tips about identifying bugs fetch around $5,000 apiece compared with $50,000 or more in the Windows realm. Lots of security firms make a living from selling information to Microsoft and software firms that produce applications for Windows.

That does not mean Macintosh computers are impervious to attack. In fact, Macs running Safari, even with all the latest security patches, are among the easiest to crack. For the second year running, a team led by Charlie Miller of Independent Security Evaluators won a $10,000 prize at the CanSecWest security conference in Vancouver held between March 16th and 20th, with a 'drive-by' attack on a MacBook Air. With judges watching every keystroke, it took him only seconds to break remotely into the fully patched Macintosh laptop running Safari and take control of it. How? Mr Miller would not say. That secret is strictly for Apple's eyes only.

Even so, cracking Safari on a Mac is becoming a bit of a party trick. Another security researcher at the Vancouver meeting cracked both Safari and Firefox on a Mac as bonus while doing something seriously tricky. The researcher in question, known only by his first name, Nils, broke into a Sony Vaio laptop running Internet Explorer 8 on Vista's heavily fortified replacement, Windows 7. For compromising all three browsers – Internet Explorer, Firefox and Safari – Nils walked away with $5,000 in prize money.

The only browser left standing was Google's one-year-old Chrome. The consensus was that even the lightning-fast Chrome would have been toppled if Google made a habit of buying information about bugs – thereby giving researchers an incentive to develop exploits.

At the moment, Google doesn't. Because it has such a minuscule slice of the market (1.2%), hackers have not bothered to attack Chrome. The same goes for Opera, which many professionals rate as the best browser around. The reason why Opera has not secured a bigger share of the market is probably because, although it is free, it is not a piece of 'open-source' software like Firefox. As such, it lacks the fanatical support of the open-source movement.

Apart from having a small share of the market, what makes Chrome seemingly so robust? Although they drew on the same Linux tool box as Apple did for Safari, Google's engineers broke with the traditional architecture adopted by all web browsers. Instead of using a monolithic structure that combines both the user and the web together in a single protected area, Chrome ingeniously separates the main part of the program, the browser kernel, from the various rendering processes that recreate web pages on a computer screen. The browser kernel, which interacts directly with the operating system, is therefore shielded from anything questionable lurking on the web.

Meanwhile, the rendering engine resides in a 'sandbox' that strictly controls what resources can be read or written to. Like a virtual machine, a sandbox creates an artificial environment within the computer that mimics elements of the machine it is running on – and thus prevents guest programs from taking charge of the actual computer.

That, at least, is the theory. In practice, Trojan horses and other nasty bits of malware can leak across from the sandbox to a supposedly protected computer. That is because the operating system needs various browser plug-ins, such as JavaScript and ActiveX controls, to run the web program. It remains to be seen whether Chrome will survive in the real world as well as it did at the Vancouver meeting, especially if it gains in popularity.

Come what may, computer users are going to need browsers that are a good deal more secure than they are today. As computer applications move from the desktop to the web ('cloud' in modern geek-speak), more of people's personal and professional lives will be filtered through their browsers. Keeping such information secure is becoming essential.

Source: 'Browser Wars Are Back', *The Economist*, 27 March 2009

Questions

1 Define each of the following concepts and discuss the implications of each in the 'browser wars' that took place as the internet evolved:
   - network effects;
   - critical mass;
   - tipping point;
   - standards wars.

2 What is the strategic rationale of Google, Apple, Mozilla and Microsoft to run their own branded internet browsers?

References

Baumol, W., Panzar, J. and Willig, R. (1982) Contestable markets and the theory of industry structure. *American Economic Review*, **73**, **3**, 492–6.

Bensen, S.M. and Farrell, J. (1994) Choosing how to compete: strategies and tactics standardization. *Journal of Economic Perspectives*, **8**, Spring, 117–30.

David, P.A. and Shurmer, M. (1996) Formal standards-setting for global telecommunications and information services: towards an institutional regime transformation. *Telecommunications Policy*, **20**, 10.

David, P.A. and Steinmueller, W.E. (1994) Economics of compatibility standards and competition in telecommunication networks. *Information Economics and Policy*, **6**.

DiMaggio, P.J. and Powell, W.W. (1983) The iron cage revisited: institutional isomorphism and collective rationality in organizational fields. *American Sociological Review*, **48**, April, 147–60.

Economides, N. (1996) The economics of networks. *International Journal of Industrial Organization*, **14**, **2**, 675–99.

Economides, N. and Flyer, F. (1997) *Compatibility and Market Structure for Network Goods*. Discussion Paper EC–98–02.

Gladwell, M. (2000). *The Tipping Point – How Little Things Make a Big Difference*. Little, Brown and Company, New York, pp. 177–81, 185–6.

Henderson, R.M. and Clark, K.B. (1990) Architectural innovation: the reconfiguration of existing product technologies and the failure of established firms. *Administrative Science Quarterly*, **35**.

Huberman, B.A. (1988) *The Ecology of Computation*, Elsevier Science Publishers, Amsterdam.

Katz, M. and Shapiro, C. (1985) Network externalities, competition and compatibility. *American Economic Review*, **75**, **3**, 424–40.

Kelly, K. (1994) *Out of Control – The New Biology of Machines*, Addison-Wesley, Reading, MA.

Leyden, P. (1997) Moore's Law repealed, sort of. *Wired*, 5.05, May.

Liebowitz, S.J. and Margolis, S.E. (1990) The fable of the keys. *Journal of Law and Economics*, **XXXIII**, April.

Liebowitz, S.J. and Margolis, S.E. (1999) *Winners, Losers & Microsoft*, The Independent Institute, Oakland, CA.

McGee, J. and Sammut-Bonnici, T. (2002) Network industries in the new economy: the effect of knowledge and the power of positive feedback. *European Business Journal*, **14**, **3**, September, 116–32.

Morris, C.R. and Ferguson, C.H. (1993) How architecture wins technology wars. *Harvard Business Review*, **71**, **2**, 86–96.

Saloner, G., Shepard, A. and Podolny, J. (2001) *Strategic Management*, Wiley, New York.

Sammut-Bonnici, T. (2009) *The Digital Economy: New Industry Structure and Regulation*. Working Paper, Warwick Business School, UK.

Sammut-Bonnici, T., Gatti, M. and McGee, J. (2009) *Convergence and Digitisation in the ICT Economy – Guidelines for Strategists and Policy Makers*. Working Paper, Warwick Business School.

Sharkey, N.E. and Sharkey, A.J.C. (1993) Adaptive generalisation and the transfer of knowledge. *Artificial Intelligence Review*, Special Issue on Connectionism, **7**, 313–28.

Vercoulen, F. and Wegberg, M. (1998) *Standard Selection Modes in Dynamic, Complex Industries: Creating Hybrids between Market Selection and Negotiated Selection of Standards*. NIBOR Working Paper, nib98006, Maastricht.

Tucker, C. (2008) Identifying formal and informal influence in technology adoption with network externalities. *Management Science*, **54**, **12**, 2024–38.

Further reading

Arthur, W.B. (1989) Competing technologies, increasing returns, and lock-in by historical events. *Economic Journal*, **99**, 116–31.

Arthur, W.B. (1990) Positive feedback in the economy. *Scientific American*, **262**, 92–9.

Arthur, W.B. (1996) Increasing returns and the new world of business. *Harvard Business Review*, July/Aug.

Dumont, B. (2000) Book review of Carl Shapiro and Hal R. Varian, 'Information rules: a strategic guide to the network economy'. *Journal of Network Industries*, **1**, **1**, 101–7.

Evans, P. and Wurster, T.S. (2000) *Blown to Bits*, Harvard Business School Press, Boston, MA.

Gottinger, H-W. (2003) *Economics of Network Industries*, Routledge, London.

Langlois, R.N. and Robertson, P.L. (1992) Networks and innovation in a modular system: lessons from the microcomputer and stereo component industries. *Research Policy*, **21**, **4**, 297–313.

Sammut-Bonnici, T. and McGee, J. (2002) Network strategies for the new economy: emerging strategies for new industry structures. *European Business Journal*, **14**, **4**, December, 174–85.

Shapiro, C. and Varian, H. (1999) *Information Rules: A Strategic Guide to the Network Economy*, Harvard Business School Press, Boston, MA.

Shy, O. (2001) *The Economics of Network Industries*, Cambridge University Press, Cambridge, UK.

Chapter 8

Corporate strategy:
adding value in
multi-business firms

Introduction

This chapter[1] concerns the portfolio of businesses held within a common, 'corporate' ownership, and the organization structure and management processes required to manage such portfolios. It covers the economic analysis of portfolios using, for example, BCG and McKinsey models, the

---

[1] This chapter is written in association with Chris Smith and Duncan Angwin.

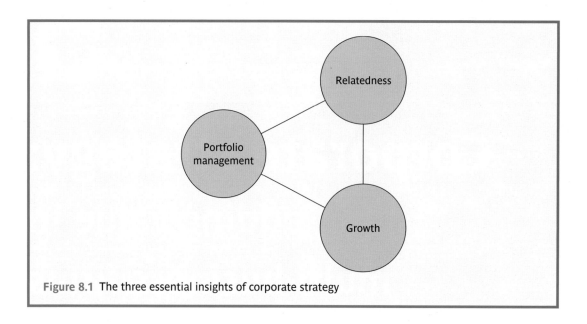

Figure 8.1 The three essential insights of corporate strategy

concept and practice of parenting advantage, and the role of the corporate headquarters. It also covers the elements of the organization design and structure, and methods of resource allocation and control.

The importance of the study of corporate strategy stems from the fact that large businesses are increasingly large *multi-businesses* and networks between businesses (for example, strategic alliances) are becoming more common. This is true across the globe, from the *chaebols* of Korea and the *keiretsus* of Japan to the corporate sweep of America's GE and Europe's ABB. As such, it is not just ongoing competitive strategy – the long-term dynamics of serving customers better than the competition – that occupies the minds of the top managers and investors. It is also ongoing *corporate* strategy – the value gained from the mixture of businesses and how to manage those businesses to optimize that value. Corporate strategy for multi-business firms goes far beyond the traditional ideas of the choices of which industry/markets/products to be in. Figure 8.1 captures the three main ideas or insights that are fundamental to corporate strategy:

1 portfolio management – the businesses that should make up the portfolio;
2 the growth idea – the way in which profitable growth is to be achieved through both internal investment and/or external acquisitions;
3 relatedness – the way in which the synergies between businesses are to be managed and exploited.

8.1 The changing organizational structure

The modern, hierarchical business enterprise arose in the 1850s in the US and Europe, to administer the new railroad and telegraph companies. An organizational structure based on a split into functional responsibilities (the 'U-form' – unitary form) was the norm at this time (see Figure 8.2).

Expanding size, however, particularly where expansion included diversification, compromised the effectiveness of the U-form:

The inherent weakness in the centralised, functionally departmentalised operating company . . . became critical only when the administrative load on the senior executives increased to such an

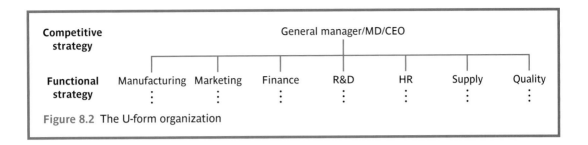

Figure 8.2 The U-form organization

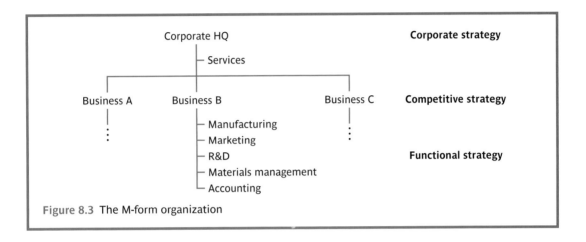

Figure 8.3 The M-form organization

extent that they were unable to handle their entrepreneurial responsibilities efficiently. This situation arose when the operations of the enterprise became too complex and the problems of co-ordination, appraisal and policy formulation too intricate for a small number of top officers to handle both long-run, entrepreneurial, and short-run, operational administrative activities. (Chandler, 1962, p. 299)

To overcome such problems, the large American companies Du Pont, General Motors, Jersey Standard and Sears Roebuck pioneered a movement to an innovative organizational form in the early 1920s. This innovation, which became known as the 'multidivisional' or '**M-form**', divided tasks and responsibilities into semi-autonomous operating units (profit centres) organized on brand, product or regional lines (see Figure 8.3).

After slow early growth, the spread of the M-form increased dramatically following the Second World War. In 1949 less than a quarter of the Fortune 500 were divisionalized. This had risen to just over a half in 1959. By 1969 only one-fifth of companies in the top 500 were not divisionalized (Hill, 1994). Similar trends have been evident in Europe and the UK and today the multidivisional form is the most prevalent organizational structure in large companies in Western economies.

The basic reason for its success was simply that it clearly removed the executives responsible for the destiny of the entire enterprise from the more routine operational activities, and so gave them time, information, and even more psychological commitment for long-term planning and appraisal... Thus the new structure left the broad strategic decisions as to the allocation of existing resources and the acquisitions of new ones in the hands of a top team of generalists. Relieved of operating duties and tactical decisions, a general executive was less likely to reflect the position of just one part of the whole. (Chandler, 1962, pp. 309–310)

The M-form has several positive attributes. It enables business managers to maximize economies of specialization, by allowing them to focus on their products and markets, while freeing corporate managers from the distractions of day-to-day operations. It makes it easy for corporate management to measure and compare the performance of business units through financial statements, and facilitates the addition (acquisition) or deletion (divestment) of businesses. On top of this, the stand-alone business ethos fits well with Western values of individualism and accountability, and encourages the development of autonomous general managers.

Alfred Chandler, the eminent business historian, chronicled the rise of the M-form organizations in the US in his celebrated book *Strategy and Structure* (1962). He also provided a telling and powerful argument for the benefits of size in papers like 'The enduring logic of industrial success' (1990). He argued that economics of scale and scope were the motive power behind large organizations. These enable large plants to produce at much lower costs than small ones (*scale*). Large plants use many of the same raw and semi-finished materials and intermediate production processes to make a variety of different products (*scope*). To capitalize on the new, larger scale of manufacturing investment firms needed to make two further, related sets of investment. The first was to create national, then international marketing and distribution organizations (both scale and scope effects). The second was to develop new management teams. The lower/middle levels were to coordinate the flow of products through production and distribution. The top level was to coordinate and monitor current operations and to plan and allocate resources for future activities. The new levels of investment thus require an integrated and balanced economic and managerial infrastructure to ensure constant flow of product and high capacity utilization. In simple economic terms the scale- and scope-driven savings in operations have to be balanced in part by higher administrative and managerial costs. But these, too, offer scale and scope benefits as long as volumes are maintained.

Chandler took the argument further. He observed that first movers quickly dominated their industries and continued to do so (for decades). Those who failed to make the right scale of investments rarely became competitive at home or in international markets, nor did the home-based industries in which they operated. But success was not simply a matter of cost efficiencies and competing on price. Competition took place through strategic positioning and innovation. The largest organizations were able to compete on quality improvement, innovations in marketing and market development and on systematic R&D. At the same time they made continuous improvements in production and distribution, product and process improvement, and better sources of supply. Competitive strategy was a blend of cost and differentiation. The corporate strategy objectives of the emerging giants were growth by expansion into related products (mostly *scope*-driven), or by moving abroad (mostly *scale* effects). These were based on the organizational capabilities acquired in the process of domestic oligopolistic competition. There were also some horizontal movements (acquisitions) and some vertical integration to control material supplies or distribution outlets.

This is the history of the emergence of international oligopolies founded initially on scale and scope advantages in production and distribution but enhanced and secured by scale and scope effects in marketing, R&D, supply management and organization. However, large is not always logical. The giants can and do stagnate, with Ford Motor Co. providing the leading example in the 1920s. In its case the direct competition between two giants, Ford and GM, was to leave at least one of them injured. In post-war years, particularly the 1960s, the compulsion for growth led companies to much broader-based diversification. This became known as conglomerate style diversification and was, and is, highly controversial.

The economic argument for large size required an organization structure that was capable of managing both scale effects (which require specialization and depth) and scope effects (which need variety and breadth). The divisionalized corporation, M-form in style, was clearly appropriate for

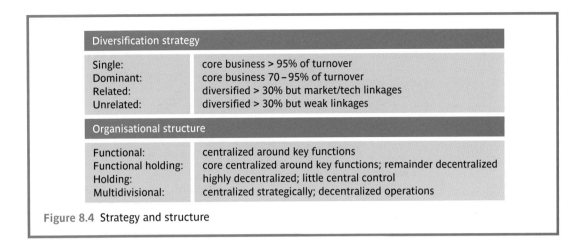

Figure 8.4 Strategy and structure

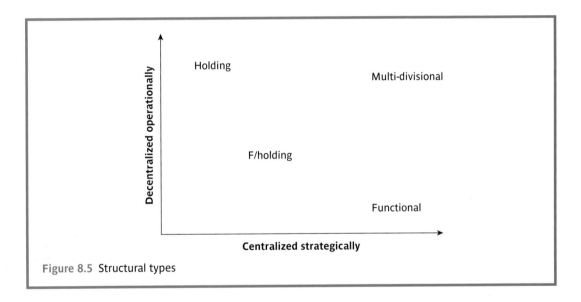

Figure 8.5 Structural types

the task in comparison to the earlier U-form. Figures 8.4 and 8.5 illustrate the strategy-structure choices. The term *U-form* has given way to *Functional*, emphasizing the focus on functional specialization as the source of managerial economies. Figure 8.5 indicates the value of the divisionalized (M-form) structure in that it allows for operational decentralization as well as strategic direction.

The relationship between strategy and structure has been established for a long time. The concept has been broadened to include other variables with a further extension that a successful 'fit' between these elements and corporate strategy is essential for success. McKinsey and Company introduced the 7S model (see Waterman, 1982 and Waterman et al., 1980) with seven broad areas that need to be integrated together. The seven variables are Structure, Systems, Style, Staff, Skills, Shared values, and Strategy. Figure 8.6 shows how the McKinsey 7S model can be applied to the M-form organization, demonstrating the nature of the fit between its different components.

However, there are also manifest drawbacks. Because corporate managers are free from operational distractions, they also tend to get out of touch with business and divisional issues and hence are reliant on the input of their politically aware general managers. The clear structural split does not necessarily mean there is a clear split of responsibilities, and confusion often reigns as to which

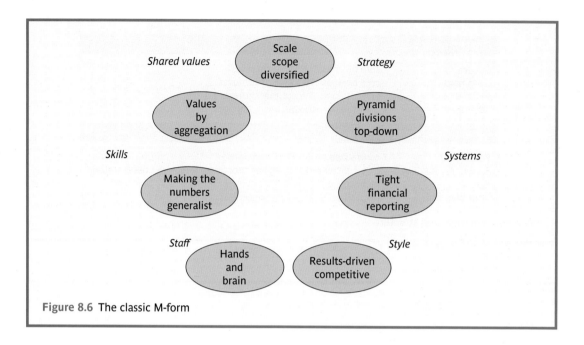

Figure 8.6 The classic M-form

level is accountable for various outcomes or processes. Further complications arise due to the (rational) tendency of business units to compete rather than cooperate with each other for the limited resources available. This leads to general managers 'selling' their business needs to the corporate level, with the resultant blurring of reality that selling frequently entails. As will be discussed in more detail below, perhaps the most significant problem with the M-form is its tendency to impede the development of trans-firm competencies.

Issues

Given these opposing dynamics and their prevalence, the multidivisional firm has attracted the interest of academics and management authors. Two major questions have been the focus of research and writing:

1 *What is the additional value generated by such firms?* This is an economic question, which addresses what value is inherent in having a group of potentially stand-alone businesses under one management. Writings on this question are found mainly in academic journals and focus particularly on the value of groupings of *related* businesses and the associated issue of *synergy*.

2 *How are they best managed?* This is an organizational/strategic question, which addresses how value is optimized and, in particular, what is the role of the corporate head office in all this. This question addresses what is known as 'corporate strategy' in the strategic management literature. While 'corporate strategy' is still used by some in an all-encompassing sense, most authors now identify 'corporate strategy' with multi-business firms. Porter's (1987) view is typical:

> Corporate strategy, **the overall plan for a diversified company** . . . concerns two different questions: what businesses the corporation should be in and how the corporate office should manage the array of business units. (Porter, 1987, p. 43, emphasis added)

Thus, corporate strategy is concerned with the choice of industries to compete in, the setting of an organizational context for the operations of the component business units, and managing the relationships between those businesses.

8.2 Theory and concepts

8.2.1 The inherent value

The M-form originated as a response to the complexity of large U-form organizations. Its continued existence as the dominant structure of large companies, however, suggests that it possesses ongoing 'ecological' advantages over other organizational forms. It has been proposed that its ubiquity is driven by the status, power and material hunger of managers – a bigger company means more benefits for the top people. The ecological argument still suggests that, even if managerial greed were a significant driver, competitive forces in free markets would select out these forms if they were sufficiently inefficient relative to other structures.[2]

Writers in economics and strategic management are agreed that the *economic* logic of multi-business corporations, and hence a potential reason for their proliferation, is that the whole is worth more than the sum of its parts:

$$V_c = A_s + B_s + C_s + M_c$$

where:

V_c	= the value of the corporation
A_s, B_s, C_s	= the respective values of the stand-alone businesses A, B and C
M_c	= the total net[3] value of corporate membership, that is, *membership benefits*
so:	$V_c > A_s + B_s + C_s$ by the value of M_c

In many cases M_c has proven to be negative. When this situation prevails, the break-up of the corporation is a financially attractive strategy, as proved by the corporate raiders – asset strippers – of the 1980s.

M_c has different sources. Organizational gain, derived from the splitting of strategy and operations, has a value-logic grounded in managerial efficiency and focus. This traditional rationale, allied to the benefits of size and scale, seems an adequate explanation of the *reorganization* of growing companies from (inefficient) U-form to (efficient) M-form. However, this argument does not explain why the total value of the component businesses can be higher under a corporate umbrella than if they were stand-alone.[4]

Theorists in the general area of what is known as transaction cost economics (TCE)[5] offer some of the most persuasive ideas about the potential added value of the M-form. They propose two major categories of benefit: *governance* and *scope* advantages:

■ **Governance:** Under this category, the corporate office takes the role of a more informed and involved investor. Unlike arm's-length investors, it is fully knowledgeable about the businesses via direct reporting and auditing mechanisms and can pressure business managers for improved

---

[2] 'Ecologists' might suggest that we should 'watch this space', as the time frame in which the M-form has existed is very short in population ecology terms.

[3] The idea of 'net' value acknowledges that there are a variety of 'costs' of membership. These are more than the financial overheads of corporate staff etc. Examples of other costs include business time and resource invested in corporate or inter-business activities; the potential loss of entrepreneurial drive, as market incentives are replaced by more focused, internal rewards that encourage 'satisficing' behaviour; the containment of business activities to a more narrow product, process or geographic range than might be attainable in stand-alone mode; the sustained cross-subsidisations of businesses that, in a stand-alone capacity, would be bankrupt etc.

[4] This is a very important issue for investors, who are free to invest directly in the stand-alone businesses without the necessity of a corporate layer.

[5] TCE breaks with neo-classical economics by dropping several of the latter's (unreal) assumptions. In particular, it concerns itself with the effects of the costs of interactions (transactions) between businesses, between businesses and customers, etc.

performance, while paying market-rate salaries. In a stand-alone business, a manager can take advantage of the fact that s/he controls the information flow to the investment community and can hide the true nature of any problems. In a multi-business firm, the corporate office has all the necessary information and can sanction or replace managers of under-performing units. The corporate office also has an overview that the business manager lacks, and can thus add further information and insight to his/her decisions. In stand-alone units, business managers can maximize what has been called 'on-the-job consumption', for example making (unnecessary) spouse-accompanied, week-long, visits to desirable locations, flying first class and staying in five-star hotels. The additional corporate layer can police and prevent such dissipation of shareholders' funds.[6]

- **Scope:** As well as potentially dealing with the tensions between owners and managers through governance mechanisms, the multi-business organization is argued to have value-enhancing properties, in that it can facilitate economies of scope. *Related* businesses (those with similar markets/technologies/processes) can share specialized physical capital, knowledge and managerial expertise. The sharing process is overseen and controlled, and disputes resolved, by corporate management. With stand-alone businesses, such sharing is problematic. Potential problems include ongoing haggling, the risk of one partner exploiting the trust of the other, the risk of being let down, and the tendency for partners to try to benefit more than their input would warrant.[7] Under normal circumstances, stand-alone businesses attempt to control these problems through formal contracts and a 'trading relationship'. However, such sharing is not amenable to formal contract, particularly in the case of specialized organizational knowledge embodied in people. Tacit components, team embeddedness and the uncertainty of its value make such learning particularly difficult to trade.

It is through scope economies between related businesses that corporate *synergies* (the total being more than the sum of the parts) are hypothesized to be most attainable. A relatively recent expression of scope economies has been the popularization of the concept of *core competencies* that are 'the collective learning in the organization, especially how to coordinate diverse production skills and integrate multiple streams of technology' (Prahalad and Hamel, 1990, p. 82). The importance of core competencies for multi-business firms is that they can '*span businesses* and products within a corporation. Put differently, powerful core competencies *support several* products or *businesses*.'

Prahalad and Hamel (1990), emphasizing the importance of trans-business capabilities, assert that core competencies are the 'central subject of corporate strategy' (p. 220) and that multi-business companies should see themselves as a 'portfolio of competencies' (p. 221) – as well as a portfolio of products and services, that is. Economies of scope are the nub of corporate strategy and the fundamental rationale for the M-form company.

8.3 Managing the multi-business firm

8.3.1 The strategy – structure balance

At the level of the business, we have seen from earlier chapters that strategy has three key dimensions, competitive advantage (how to compete), the key resource allocation decisions at the business level,

---

[6] This 'advantage' begs the obvious question of who guards the guards. In the light of increasingly spectacular returns to directors of public companies, this is a question worth asking.

[7] This is an example of the 'free-rider' problem and is familiar to students undertaking group work, when one member seems to get out of most of the duties, but shares in the overall assessment.

and the organization of the business. At the corporate level there is a parallel concern with resource allocation decisions, but at the corporate level, and with organization structure and process. But the distinguishing characteristic of the multi-business firm is that at the centre it is concerned with what businesses to be in – the portfolio question. The answer is, of course, contingent on the nature of competitive advantages but decisions about the portfolio are taken at the corporate level whereas the responsibility for securing competitive advantage is at the business level.

The economics of corporate strategy revolve around three issues (see Figure 8.1).

1 The characteristics of the portfolio expressed as its overall return and its overall risk. This allows for gains from the statistical nature of pooled variances that means that imperfectly correlated risks of the individual businesses result in lower overall risk. This is on the basis of avoiding having all one's eggs in the same basket.[8]

2 How synergies between businesses are captured – the idea of relatedness.

3 The growth ambitions of the firm and how these are to be achieved by internal investment and/or expansion.

There are insights and traps attached to each of these. Portfolio analysis arrays the strengths and weaknesses of each business. In particular, the sources of cash and profit can be established and investment needs specified. Thus it is possible to assess for the portfolio what are its cash flow and profit characteristics in relation to its overall risk. However, if taken too literally, portfolio analysis can focus excessively on eliminating unprofitable, low-potential businesses and expanding high-potential businesses without attention to any underlying synergies and complementarities.

Relatedness determines whether interdependencies between businesses can create value and competitive advantage or whether each business should be treated on its own merits. The trap is that poor-performing businesses should not be maintained from 'overall strength' without strong evidence of value potential from relatedness.

Sensible growth objectives and analysis identifies how resources can be deployed to maintain a balance between investment, cash flow and profits over time. Proper analysis prevents misdirected growth that focuses on growth for its own sake, leading to inappropriate timing and falling into cash traps.

Corporate organization has to be consistent with the economics of the strategy. This too can be described in three parts:

1 definition of division and business unit boundaries;

2 the intended lateral integration and coordination between business units;

3 the vertical relationships between corporate tasks and roles and line operations – the corporate–business interface.

Business unit boundaries and groupings of businesses (divisions or sectors) can be the natural and powerful way to exploit relatedness opportunities. Superior performance frequently requires that businesses be properly focused on relevant markets – that the boundaries should be drawn correctly. New boundaries should be drawn[9] when the value of increasing the focus (narrowing the scope) exceeds the cost of lost relatedness benefits, and vice versa.

---

[8] We should note that the gains from diversification may mitigate against disaster but themselves don't promote competitive advantage.

[9] This is often called 'reorganization'.

The corporate–business interface sets out authority and accountability in the firm. Three particular styles are commonly observed (see the discussion below). *Strategic planning* involves corporate executives deeply in defining and monitoring corporate and business strategies. It is most appropriate for capital-intensive operations and highly interrelated businesses. *Strategic control* involves corporate executives in influencing business-level strategies and monitoring financial results. It is a 'loose–tight' approach. *Financial control* decentralizes control of business strategy to the business and relies solely on financial control at the corporate level. It is deemed to be most appropriate for conglomerate-like strategies.

Integration mechanisms are used to balance choices made on boundaries and on the corporate–business interface. The formality of the latter two can be supplemented by less formal arrangements that can pick up on related possibilities not captured within business boundaries and neglected by the corporate-level need to have strong vertical controls. Therefore, self-interested lateral cooperation has a natural place in complementing the formal organizational arrangements. More formal lateral mechanisms include centres of excellence, people transfers, transfer pricing systems, special study teams, lead business arrangements, and internal consulting. Vertical mechanisms are also possible, such as intermediate levels of organization and arrangements of cross-functional authority. Strategic control styles of management typically require more explicit processes for lateral integration than other forms of control.

8.3.2 Corporate strategies

Adding value through buying and selling businesses has been one form of corporate strategy. The corporate centre acts as a funds investor and seeks opportunities to buy companies that are undervalued by the market and then waits until the inherent value is recognized and sells them on at a profit. A more active role than this entails buying companies that are under-performing, and hence are available at a relatively low price, and acting to improve performance and selling price. A variant of this was undertaken by the so-called 'raiders' and 'asset strippers' of the 1980s, who bought conglomerates and then sold off the component parts for a total price far in excess of the overall purchase price. Opportunities to profit from this mode of corporate strategy are now rare, as the general market is more attuned to such opportunities, as are potential targets.[10]

Porter (1987) terms this corporate buy-and-sell approach *portfolio management*. The Ashridge researchers, Goold et al. (1994), call it *corporate development*, and include the reshaping of existing businesses by amalgamation or division and the creation of new businesses by internal venturing. Both sets of authors agree that this is no longer a viable value-generating corporate strategy, as the market now anticipates the potential under-valuation and reflects this in the (speculative) premium in the price paid. Such premiums ensure that profitable acquisitions must now be based on better management of the acquired business, or other forms of synergistic benefits of belonging to the new corporation.

In discussing the aspect of corporate strategy that is to do with the management of the multi-business organization, Porter (1987) identifies three organizational/process concepts of corporate strategy: *restructuring*, *sharing activities* and *transferring skills*.

- *Restructuring* occurs when businesses are acquired with the specific intent of achieving value by active intervention and improvement. The centre needs the capability to effect such transformation and thus it exerts strong direct influence on business performance and processes. In Porter's view, once restructuring has been successful, the business should then be sold to capture the new value, unless it benefits in some way from ongoing membership of the corporation.

---

[10] The trend for conglomerates to become focused on fewer 'core' businesses was a consequence of such threats.

- *Sharing activities* is a value activity that is based on the component businesses using the same facilities, services, processes or systems and thereby reaping utilization, learning curve (scope) scale or differentiation benefits. Management is based on interrelationships, but not necessarily interdependencies between the business units, that is, the shared facility can be a corporate-level activity.

- *Transferring skills* is managing ongoing interrelationships between the businesses. In this case, the corporate centre actively fosters the sharing of expertise or skills among the businesses, even though they might have different value chains. As with 'sharing activities', the centre is actively involved, but this time it develops and promotes linkages and interdependencies between business units.

Goold et al. (1994) have spent a considerable time focusing on the multi-business company and how its corporate strategy adds (or subtracts[11]) value. Consistent with the well-known 'competitive advantage', they coined the intuitively attractive term *parenting advantage* to denote the additional value that an insightful parent company can add to its component businesses through appropriate orientation and management. They suggest three requisites for parenting advantage:

1 the corporate advantage must translate into more competitive advantage in at least one business or membership of each business in the portfolio must create extra value somewhere in the portfolio;

2 must create more value than the cost of the corporate overhead;

3 must add more value than any other possible parent otherwise the market for corporate control might eventually challenge your ownership and parenting credentials.

Goold et al. (1994) also identify three classes of value-adding corporate strategy: *stand-alone influence, functional and services influence*, and *linkage influence*, which parallel Porter's categories. They emphasize that these are not either/or choices but can all be in operation at the same time. Figure 8.7 illustrates the range of sources of value creation.

- *Stand-alone influence* is the value created by the influence on the individual business strategy and performance. The major focus is on vertical linkages, mainly between the CEO and the MDs of the businesses. In this category, successful corporate parents have to overcome the '10% versus 100% paradox' – the idea that part-time, organizationally removed managers can enhance the performance of the business's dedicated management.

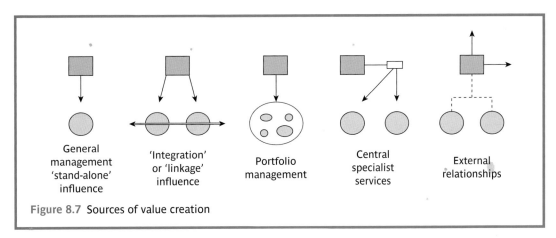

General management 'stand-alone' influence 'Integration' or 'linkage' influence Portfolio management Central specialist services External relationships

Figure 8.7 Sources of value creation

---

[11] This is more than a technical parenthesis, as the general thrust of their findings is that *value destruction* is the norm in multi-business companies.

- *Functional and services influence* is again a vertical process, with the focus on adding value through the influence of a range of centrally controlled staff functions. These may replace or augment those already in place in the businesses. The problem the corporate centre faces here is offering a higher value-added service than specialist outsiders – the 'beating the specialist' paradox.

- *Linkage influence* aims to increase value through the relationships between the businesses. The focus is on horizontal processes and incorporates both the 'shared activities' and 'transfer of skills' categories of Porter. It is difficult to explain, however, why the managers of the businesses would not do this themselves if extra value would accrue as a result, that is, the 'enlightened self-interest' paradox.

The general management influence is generally reckoned to be the key (only) justification for long-term survival of conglomerates. Linkages, portfolio effects and specialist capabilities are all part of the synergy and relatedness themes. The external relationship management theme harks back to much earlier thinking about the role of the top team and the board. This maintains that the specialist skills at the top are about understanding the external environment and finding ways to cope with it and to position against it. Modern thinking has focused very much on the internal management and dynamics of the organization, perhaps to a fault.

In Case box 8.1 you can read a brief description of the incidence of conglomerates in the FTSE 100. You should ask yourself why conglomerates became important and is there a good reason why they should have become unfashionable.

Case box 8.1: **Conglomerates in the FTSE 100**

The FTSE 100 is the leading index on the London Stock Exchange and comprises the 100 fully quoted public companies with the largest market capitalizations. Since its creation in January 1984, membership of the index has changed significantly as companies have entered and left the index for a variety of reasons, including increase/decrease in value, transfers to/from other exchanges, privatizations, bankruptcy, and merger and acquisitions activity. By 2003, only 23 of the original members of the FTSE 100 remained in the index, with famous names including Midland Bank, Dunlop Holdings and Distillers disappearing from the index having been acquired by HSBC, BTR and Guinness respectively.

Composition of the index, in terms of strategies pursued, has also changed significantly through its first 20 years. There has been a broad move, especially since 1993, towards more focused strategies and away from diversification, especially unrelated diversification (conglomeration). Between 1993 and 2003 the percentage of FTSE 100 companies that were conglomerates fell from 16% to 10%, with reductions seen in service and industrial/manufacturing companies. Prime examples of this decline in conglomeration are BTR, Hanson and Williams. BTR, after enduring several years of poor performance, was acquired by Seibe in 1999 forming Invensys; Hanson, after the retirement and death of its driving forces Lords Hanson and White respectively, broke itself up through a series of sales and flotations in 1995 and 1996; and Williams divested its peripheral activities before floating its two core business Kidde and Chubb in 2000 and leaving the index. In each case investors welcomed the break-ups, valuing the newly separated companies more highly than when they were part of a conglomerate, supporting the contention that the markets discounted conglomerate values.

While this suggests that the FTSE 100 conglomerate is in terminal decline, there is a strong argument that conglomerates are still in rude health but less visible, being private rather than public companies. The 'new conglomerates' are private equity companies, e.g. APEX Partners and CinVen, that have acquired diverse portfolios of under-performing businesses with a view to turning them round and selling them within a limited time horizon of, say, three to five years. Private equity companies may be the 21st-century conglomerates.

Source: Paul Simmonds (2009)

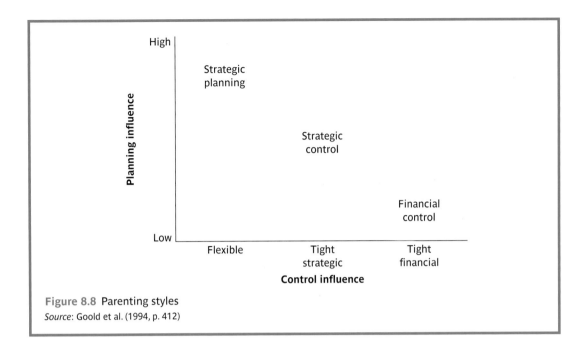

Figure 8.8 Parenting styles
Source: Goold et al. (1994, p. 412)

8.3.3 Corporate styles

In an earlier study, Goold and Campbell (1987) examined high-performing corporations and concluded that the *style* of the parent is an important factor in the level of performance achieved. They examined the extent to which management styles varied along the dimensions of *planning influence* (that is, the extent to which the corporate level became involved in the strategic and operating planning of the business) and *control influence* (that is, the extent to which the businesses were held to budgetary and operational targets) (see Figure 8.8).

Three styles seemed to stand out. In *financial control* companies (for example, BTR), the centre allowed a high degree of strategic and operational autonomy to the businesses (low planning influence). The budget, however, was sacrosanct and any slippage from planned performance needed swift correction, if it were not to mean the curtailment of the career of the responsible GM (high control influence). At the other end of the continuum, *strategic planning* companies (for example, ICI) involved themselves on an ongoing basis in the strategic planning and management of the businesses (high planning control). They were more flexible if strategic contingencies caused operational performance to slip against budgeted targets, that is, the budget was a reflection of the strategy (low control influence). In between these two extremes were the *strategic control* companies.[12]

This work on styles is consistent with the view that optimizing corporate strategy is contingent on the appropriate organizational structures, systems, processes, etc.

> *Corporate strategies which predominantly use one or other of these three roles to realise the value inherent in their resources should, according to contingency theory, align their structure, systems and procedures according to those roles.* (Collis, 1991c, p. 7)

In accordance with this view, corporations do not need large corporate staffs if they are relying on a stand-alone influence role, whereas a coordinated and integrated staff is needed if inter-business

---

[12] In a summary of this work in their 1994 text, the authors conclude that there is a continuing movement away from the *financial control* to the strategic *planning/control styles.*

relationships are to be a major source of value. In a similar way the structure of business manager incentives should vary, with group-based incentives needed for 'inter-business'-oriented corporations and stand-alone incentives appropriate for the more 'managerial' orientations.

As well as the view that organizational structure, processes etc. should be contingent on the corporate role, there is also the view that the optimal corporate role is contingent on the degree of *relatedness* between the business units. To realize economies of scope (synergy) from relatedness, *cooperation* between businesses is required. This leads to increased centralization of functions and systems, and an increase in integrating mechanisms between businesses. The performance ambiguities inherent in sharing facilities and functions are tackled by seeking more information on a broader, less financial, range of indicators, and by business incentives based on group rather than individual performance. A value-enhancing, cooperative form may be a sustainable parenting advantage for a firm, as its unique history and social context make it idiosyncratic to the firm and thus, more difficult to imitate.

Unrelated businesses have no opportunities for increased value from economies of scope and are argued to benefit from M-form membership due to governance benefits (Williamson, 1975). Within such a framework, the corporate office of the M-form takes on the role of informed investor and runs the businesses on a *competitive* basis, as stand-alone entities that are rivals for capital which is allocated on a 'best-use' basis, consistent with external capital markets. Performance incentives are based on unambiguous, financial outputs. A summary of the proposed relationships between inherent value, basic corporate strategy and organizational factors is shown in Table 8.1.

In contrast to the optimism of multiple, coexistent corporate roles expressed by Porter (1987) and Goold et al. (1994), Hill (1994) points out that the 'radical differences' between these two types of M-form are such that:

> ... it may be difficult for diversified firms to simultaneously realise economic benefits from economies of scope and efficient governance ... Competitive and co-operative organisations have different internal configurations with regard to centralisation, integration, control practices and incentive schemes. As a result **the internal management philosophies of co-operative and competitive organisations are incompatible**. (Hill, 1994, pp. 312–313, emphasis added)

Table 8.1 Comparing cooperative and competitive strategic orientations

	Source of inherent (economic) value	
	Economies of scope (related businesses)	Governance (unrelated businesses)
Basic corporate strategy	Cooperative multidivisional	Competitive multidivisional
Operating and business-level strategic decisions	Some centralization of critical functions	Complete decentralization
Inter-business integrating mechanisms	Moderate to extensive	Non-existent
Business performance appraisal	Mix of subjective and objective criteria	Primary reliance on objective financial criteria
Business incentive schemes	Linked to corporate performance	Based on business performance only

Source: adapted from Hoskisson et al. (1993, pp. 269–98).

This means that cooperative and competitive philosophies are different strategies with different organizational and managerial arrangements. Thus, if an M-form firm is comprised of a set of businesses, some of which are related and others not, it is faced with an economic and organizational dilemma. One resolution of this dilemma is to divest units and focus on a *core* business grouping.

Another resolution is through the creation of another organizational level – the *division*, into which all the businesses related in a particular way (for example, all those in the automotive components industry) are placed. In this sense, the division becomes an internal (quasi) corporation and the divisional-level managers can focus on optimizing the relatedness of their component businesses.

8.4 Practical frameworks and applications

The M-form seemed a boon to managers as an apparent answer to the complexities of size, growth and diversity. The intuitive value of divisionalization was further boosted during the 1960s, as diversification became a strategic imperative in its own right and acquisition and merger became a major mechanism for growth. Emboldened by shareholder approval, and armed with increasingly all-encompassing definitions of synergy[13] and faith in the transferability of general management skills, companies embarked on a diversifying buying spree.

In many cases, senior managers had no previous occupational experience of the operations and/or markets of the businesses which they bought and subsequently 'controlled'. Seemingly, however, the corporate office had no need to fully understand operational details, as this was the domain of the general managers of the business units. While demand exceeded supply, industries experienced stable growth and hence, even relatively inefficient firms were able to prosper. By the early 1970s, a more complex and turbulent economic environment highlighted the unwieldy nature of many conglomerates. Senior managers sought different rationales and tools to manage their set of businesses. The new portfolio planning techniques and, most notably, the **growth-share matrix** (Figure 8.9)

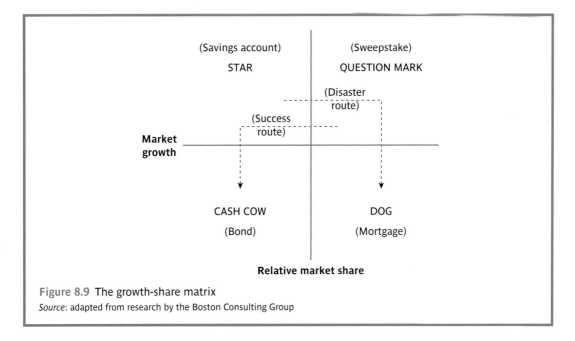

Figure 8.9 The growth-share matrix
Source: adapted from research by the Boston Consulting Group

---

[13] For example, Goold et al. (1994) cite the example of the British Oxygen Company (now BOC) buying a manufacturer of frozen pizza on the synergistic basis that gases were used in the freezing process.

developed by the Boston Consulting Group (BCG), seemingly met their needs. (See Day, 1977 for a critical review.)

Based on the cost-reducing effects of experience curve dynamics,[14] the growth-share matrix gave a cash flow rationale for business linkage, acquisition and divestment. Companies needed a balanced portfolio of investments. The mid-point for relative market share was often 1.0 and for market growth the mid-point was commonly the growth of the economy/GDP as a whole. The route to success implied by 'the boxes' approach was deceptively simple. (Relatively) large businesses in mature markets ('cash cows') generated free cash flow above their reinvestment needs. This cash could then be invested in the high-growth (and hence, cash-consuming) businesses, so that the 'question marks' became 'stars', and the 'stars' maintained their strong positions, until eventually they became 'cash cows'. Relatively small businesses in low-growth industries ('dogs') were targets for divestment, or the basis for acquisition of similar businesses, to achieve the critical mass necessary to have the highest relative market share (a 'kennel of dogs'). The disaster route was equally simple to understand (Figure 8.9).

When it was first used as an analytic aid with the Mead Corporation in the early 1970s, the boxes were described in neutral, investment-oriented terms – that is 'bond', 'savings account', 'sweepstake' (lottery ticket) and 'mortgage'. The commonly known descriptors that came later are more colourful, but also more implicitly prescriptive, particularly in the case of 'dogs'. (On the way to being 'dogs', they were also known as 'pets', which, in the American context, is markedly less negative.)

(*Note*: By definition, most businesses are 'dogs' and the wholesale divestment of such units by all corporations is not logically feasible. See McKiernan (1992) for a good discussion of the 'boxes' in general and the 'dog' box in particular.)

A variety of other portfolio techniques followed, with differences centred on the dimensions along the axes, such as industry attractiveness/competitive position (GE) and stage of product-market evolution/competitive position. The helicopter view offered by such techniques encouraged managers to correct past mistakes, by divesting weak businesses and establishing a seemingly more solid rationale for the corporate mix than some tenuous definition of synergy. By the end of the 1970s, nearly half the Fortune 500 companies were using portfolio planning in some way, to deal with a collection of businesses that were often beyond the scope of senior executives to manage and control other than at arm's length. What started off as an *aid to analysis* became a strategic paradigm in its own right and one that was accepted relatively uncritically by managers.

The over-simplistic assumptions underlying such techniques became apparent with the whole-sale value destruction manifest in acquisition-driven conglomerates in the 1980s and the associated success of corporate raiders, who bought (using very high debt levels) and immediately broke up and sold their acquired conglomerates at vast profits. The era of the boxes was at an end:

> In most countries the days when portfolio management was a valid concept of corporate strategy are past. (Porter, 1987 p. 51)

Although no longer the core of corporate strategy, some of the analytic language and assumptions of portfolio management are still reflected in annual reports today, for example the almost universally accepted idea of the need for a 'balanced' portfolio – 'balance' often being discussed in terms of three-legged stools.

In Case box 8.2 we show the example of Mars, the maker of chocolate bars, persuading Wrigley, the world's biggest chewing gum company, that the two are a perfect match. There appears to be

---

[14] The critical *assumption* being that having a *larger market share* than competitors meant higher volumes of production, leading to swifter progress down the experience curve (each doubling of cumulative volume bringing a known percentage reduction in costs) and hence, the advantage of lower costs.

Case box 8.2: **Mars buys Wrigley**

Mars buys Wrigley with Warren Buffett's help

Of all the possible snacks, the deal was struck over a plate of sandwiches. Paul Michaels, the boss of Mars, a big maker of chocolate bars, invited Bill Wrigley, executive chairman of Wrigley, the world's biggest chewing-gum company, to his house to persuade him that the two firms were a perfect match. After all, both are old, American and dominated by their founding families. They have both focused on creating a few global 'power' brands such as Mars's Twix, M&M's and Snickers and Wrigley's Extra and Orbit. And there is little overlap between them.

A few weeks later, on April 28th, Mars and Berkshire Hathaway, Warren Buffett's investment firm, announced a friendly takeover of Wrigley for about $23 billion. Mr Wrigley, who presented strong results for the first quarter on the same day, says his family did not need a lot of convincing to accept. They could see the advantages of a bigger global distribution network, whereas the Mars family liked the idea of diversifying into gum, which is considered healthier and has higher growth rates than chocolate. Mars is offering a 28% premium over the price of Wrigley's shares before the deal was announced. Mr Wrigley and other senior managers will remain in place. The firm will keep its close association with Chicago – Wrigley Field is the home stadium of the local baseball team, the Cubs. Mars will even move the offices of its non-chocolate division to the Wrigley building, a Chicago landmark.

'The price is high,' admits Olivier Goudet, Mars's finance chief. But Mr Goudet thinks savings in distribution and marketing will outweigh the cost of the merger in the long run. Mars, which is America's third-largest privately owned firm after Cargill, an agricultural company, and Koch Industries, a conglomerate, can afford to take a longer view. 'We have no intention ever to go public,' says Mr Michaels. Mr Buffett, meanwhile, will receive a 20% stake in Wrigley on preferential terms, in exchange for offering a $4.4 billion loan – a huge boon in such credit-starved times.

The deal is a challenge to Cadbury, which is also trying to focus on chocolate and chewing gum. It is about to spin off Dr Pepper Snapple Group, its American drinks business, leaving only confectionery. But a combined Mars and Wrigley will control some 14% of the global market, compared to Cadbury's 10%, giving them greater clout with retailers. And Cadbury is already under intense pressure from shareholders to improve its margins.

Cadbury may start looking for acquisitions of its own. Kraft's confectionery unit is one possible target, although Cadbury would struggle to pay for it. It had originally hoped to sell its drinks unit to a private-equity firm for a higher price than it is likely to raise on the stockmarket, but the credit crunch wrecked that option.

Hershey, with its 43% share of the American chocolate market, the world's biggest, is another candidate. The two are a near-perfect fit, and have discussed a tie-up in the past. But Cadbury cannot buy Hershey without the approval of the Hershey Trust, which owns 78% of the firm and is determined to retain control. What is more, Hershey has been struggling with higher commodity prices, falling margins and flat sales. According to Andrew Wood, of Sanford Bernstein, a research firm, the savings from such a merger would probably be too small to justify the deal.

So Cadbury and Hershey are likely to face the new goliath alone. That may not be the end of the world: as it is, Cadbury is making inroads into the American gum market, while Wrigley's share has dropped from 66% to 60% in two years. It could also swallow a smaller rival, such as Lindt, a Swiss chocolate firm. Its boss is adamant that it's not for sale – but that is what Wrigley used to say, too.

Source: 'A Sugary Mouthful', *The Economist*, 3 May 2008

Questions

1 What is the logic of a friendly takeover for both sets of shareholders?

2 Explain what is meant by a 'near-perfect fit'. What are the risks of such a concept?

3 Do you think Mars is increasing its business risk by absorbing Wrigley?

little product overlap between them. From the information given, identify the potential for synergy between these two venerable consumer goods companies.

8.5 Evidence and experience

The concept of the M-form, and its obvious implications for the conduct of corporate strategy, receives little support from *academic* or practical (*market*) evidence as a value-adding entity. This is surprising, given the longevity of the idea and its near-universal adoption in large companies worldwide.

8.5.1 Academic

It has always been difficult to mount a successful academic defence of the pure conglomerate as a value-adding grouping. *Governance* as a justification per se assumes sufficiently endemic and material opportunism, incompetence, goal displacement, etc. amongst managers of stand-alone businesses that the reduction of these creates corporate value, despite the added corporate overhead and lack of market incentive. It is feasible that in the relatively early days of large businesses, the development of professional management skills in formerly stand-alone units may have added value, but this offers no rationale for ongoing membership.

Academic research has tended to focus on the presumed benefits of groupings of *related* businesses. Related businesses are those where a 'common skill, market or resource applies to each' (Rumelt, 1974, p. 29) and hence, where scope benefits are appealing as a source of potential value. Rumelt produced a landmark study of 246 US firms over the period 1949–69, which supported the performance superiority of the multidivisional form, but questioned the relative value of different forms of diversification. He confirmed the intuitive logic of academics and managers that companies that had undertaken related diversification out-performed those that had undertaken unrelated (that is, conglomerate) diversification.

Following Rumelt's work, the relationship between the make-up of business groupings and their economic performance became a major research focus. While some authors were supportive of Rumelt's main contentions, a significant body of research was in disagreement. Factors such as industry structure and specific firm characteristics played important roles and, once these were controlled, 'relatedness' seemed to have little explanatory power. Using market-based measures of relatedness has produced equivocal evidence on the link between firm performance and the composition of the corporate business portfolio, with few *strong* findings on either side.

The problem with the demonstrated lack of relationship between relatedness and performance is argued to rest primarily with the validity of the traditional market or industry-based relatedness measures, which, while they incorporate surface characteristics of *similarity*, do not capture relatedness of *strategic importance*. The relatedness that is really valuable is that between 'strategic assets', which are important to competitive advantage and cannot be quickly or cheaply gained by non-diversified competitors. The second drawback is that traditional researchers have tended to have a narrow, static view of relatedness, which does not take into account the *dynamic* creation and accumulation of trans-business competencies, so managers must specifically manage for the benefits of relatedness across the businesses, to achieve added (corporate) value.

Hamel and Prahalad (1994) are particularly scathing about the inherent structural bias of the M-form *against* the exploitation of scope economies (core competencies) inherent in relatedness. They decry what they see as a dominant focus on strategic business units (SBUs) in multidivisional firms being defined in *external* terms of markets, products and competitors. The 'tyranny of the SBU', as it promotes its own autonomous functioning, does not facilitate the complex interactions and sharing that are necessary for corporate-wide development and exploitation of core competencies. This ultimately results in the demise of capabilities linking the businesses and thus impairs the exploitation of potentially valuable relatedness.

8.5.2 Market

As mentioned above, value destruction became the norm for multidivisional companies throughout the late 1970s and the 1980s. So much was this the case that the value of the M-form and, in particular, the value-adding capability of its head office became a significant focus of research and discussion. While diversified conglomerates have been seen as the main cause of value loss it has yet to be proven (see above) that corporations of *related* businesses are much better. Perhaps it is true, as some authors contend, that the future of value creation lies in huge one-business companies, although these entities will still have to deal with the complexities of size, growth, and local–global dilemmas that gave rise to the M-form in the first place. Certainly, the mid–late 1990s saw the rise of the mega-merger between businesses in the same industry, as globalization became a driver for senior executives.

(*Note*: Market valuation is not a good guide to the value-creation of businesses. As Collis (1991a, 1991b) points out, a *significant* loss of value is necessary before take-over-break-up-and-sell becomes a viable option. With typical transaction costs of 2% and an acquisition premium of 20%, a corporation 'can be creating only 78% of the value that could be generated … and yet still be immune to the threat of a change in corporate control', p. 6.)

8.5.3 Issues for the future

The past problems of optimizing the management of multi-business corporations continue to challenge managers in the modern world. However, superimposed on the 'traditional' dilemmas of centralization versus decentralization, businesses (vertical) versus pan-corporate (horizontal) focuses, and (internal) cooperation versus competition, are the local versus global issues inherent in globalization. The increasing pace of change, turbulence and complexity of the business environment continue to test the structures, systems, processes and underlying rationale reflecting and underpinning corporate strategy, as managers strive to achieve a material parenting advantage which exceeds the value-generating capability of the stand-alone units. Perhaps the biggest issue facing these managers is to be able to demonstrate to increasingly sceptical stakeholders that there are tangible benefits of corporate membership. If the whole is not demonstrably more valuable than the sum of the parts, then corporate managers will continue to battle against the inexorable economic and market forces for disintegration.

8.6 The role of headquarters: the case of GE in the post Jack Welch era[15]

Among the many works that lionize General Electric (GE) as a model of management excellence is one entitled 'If Harry Potter Ran General Electric', which claims to draw lessons for managers from J.K. Rowling's tales of the boy wizard. The book is unlikely to rival the original Harry in the bestsellers' chart. But its title might just appeal to shareholders of the American industrial giant, who have watched aghast as their company has fallen under a particularly nasty spell. Since the turn of the year GE has slashed its dividend by two-thirds, lost a prized AAA credit rating on its long-term debt and seen its stock battered by speculation about the quality of some loans made by its huge

---

[15] Adapted from *The Economist*, 21 March 2009.

financial-services division, GE Capital. Some analysts have portrayed this business as GE's very own chamber of horrors. On March 19th 2009, after *The Economist* had gone to press, GE was due to reveal more details of the contents of GE Capital's asset portfolio in a bid to quell concerns about problems within.

These setbacks have been deeply painful for a 130-year-old company that has been a member of the Dow Jones Industrial Average since 1896. As well as underlining the importance of swift action to right GE Capital, they also raise big questions about the future of the conglomerate model that GE has long championed. And they have exposed mistakes by the company's senior managers.

How did GE get itself into a mess that has seen $269 billion wiped off its stock market value since the beginning of 2008? The main reason is that the strategy which helped GE gain its reputation for consistently producing bumper profits, year in and year out, has backfired. At its core was GE Capital. Founded in 1932 as General Electric Contracts Corporation to provide financing that supported the group's industrial businesses, the operation gradually expanded into other areas of lending unrelated to GE. Under Jack Welch, GE's chief executive from 1981 to 2001, GE Capital grew rapidly.

Although Mr Welch has recently argued that it is a 'dumb idea' for managers to become obsessed with short-term profit goals, during his reign GE made Herculean efforts to hit its quarterly earnings targets. If GE's industrial businesses fell short of the mark, the company's finance arm would stage a last-minute sale of assets to close the gap. 'GE used GE Capital like a cookie jar' into which it dipped when needed, says James Schrager, a professor at the University of Chicago's Booth School of Business.

Jeffrey Immelt, Mr Welch's successor, sold some of GE's financial operations, including its poorly performing insurance businesses. But he continued to expand GE Capital, which built up large portfolios of property loans, credit-card debt and other assets in increasingly far-flung places, such as Eastern Europe. If GE Capital were a bank, it would rank as one of the biggest in America. Its growth has made the division more and more important to its parent's overall revenues and performance. In 2007 GE Capital's profit made up 55% of the company's total.

GE's managers were delighted with this. But they failed to appreciate the risk of GE Capital's funding model, which left the business dangerously exposed to disruption in financial markets. With few retail deposits to speak of, the firm gorged on long-term debt and commercial paper to fund its lending. While the world was awash with credit, these cheap funds provided GE Capital with a licence to print money. But when the credit markets suddenly seized up, the strains soon began to show. In April 2008 GE shocked investors when it missed its first-quarter earnings target by a mile.

Since then, GE has been battling to shore up confidence in its financial arm. Among other things, GE Capital has tapped cheap funding lines backed by the American government and has greatly reduced its exposure to the short-term commercial-paper market. It has also secured more than 90% of the long-term debt that it needs for the year.

At the same time, GE has been building up cash, some of which has been deployed to prop up the finance business. Last October the firm raised $15 billion from a group of investors including Warren Buffett's Berkshire Hathaway. In February it said it would slash its quarterly dividend by 68% from the second half of 2009 in order to conserve $9 billion of cash on an annual basis. The dividend cut was a bitter blow for small investors who had come to view GE stock as tantamount to an annuity. It was the first time the firm had reduced its dividend since 1938.

Out of the club

Despite all this, GE failed to save its top-notch credit rating. On March 12th Standard & Poor's (S&P) stripped the parent company and GE Capital of their AAA long-term ratings, downgrading them to AA+. A mere five non-financial companies still have the agency's top rating. GE had been in the elite since 1956. Some expect its rating to slide further this year as the economy worsens. GE Capital clocked up $12.2 billion in 2007 and made $8.6 billion in 2008. Analysts, predicting write-downs, have been doubting whether it will make a profit of $5 billion in 2009, as its parent forecast earlier this year.

At this week's meeting GE was due to lay out for analysts the prospects for GE Capital's portfolio under two different economic scenarios. The company was expected to say that, under the less auspicious of these, GE Capital would only break even this year.

Given the unit's difficulties, it would be understandable if Mr Immelt wanted to jettison GE Capital as soon as it has been nursed back to health – which may take a while. But he insists he is committed to the business, which he says has strong franchises in areas such as aviation and energy finance, thanks to its close association with GE's industrial activities. The goal is to shrink the financial-services division so that it represents no more than 30% of GE's profit, to reduce its lever-age and to develop a bigger deposit base, so that it is less reliant on wholesale funding.

There are two risks with this plan. The first is that investors will remain leery of GE's stock for as long as the company owns a sizeable business that is vulnerable to a systemic upset in the financial world. Shrinking it would lessen the threat to GE's cash-pumping industrial operations, but not remove it altogether. The second risk is that tomorrow's finance is going to look very different from today's. GE Capital flourished as a member of the 'shadow banking' system of firms that offered myriad financial products without having to bear the regulatory burdens of banks. In future, firms that perform bank-like activities can expect much stricter oversight, whether or not they have a banking licence. That will impose greater costs on the business. And if GE Capital's credit rating continues to slip, raising its funding costs, it will find it much harder to turn a decent profit. GE reckons that a shrunken finance operation can achieve a 15% return on investment. However, this may be wishful thinking.

Imagine, though, that Mr Immelt changed his mind and decided he would like to be rid of GE Capital. To say so now would be foolhardy, because this would trigger speculation about the unit's longevity as a stand-alone business, possibly unnerving its counterparties and sending more shockwaves through the financial system. There would also be huge legal, tax and other headaches to contend with – assuming Mr Immelt could find a buyer. But if GE's repair job were complete and the credit crunch a distant memory, there would be fewer hurdles to a sale.

Whatever the ultimate fate of GE Capital, a bigger question remains: does GE itself still make sense? The justification for a conglomerate is that in difficult times its broad selection of businesses should enable it to maintain profitability when its more specialized rivals struggle. GE's hybrid industrial-financial model was supposed to be a superior version of the type.

Yet by Mr Immelt's own admission, GE's reputation as a safe port in an economic storm has been 'tarnished'. Although the company made a profit of $18.1 billion in 2008, this was nearly 20% less than in 2007. This year is likely to see another sharp decline. Aside from the problems at GE Capital, several of GE's other businesses, such as media and health care, are having a torrid time. Nicholas Heymann of Sterne Agee, a stockbroking firm, reckons that GE's health-care business could see earnings drop by 25–30% this year as its customers suffer budget cuts.

Under the charismatic Mr Welch, the firm focused on cutting fat and boosting efficiency, and used the cash generated to go on a shopping spree, building leading positions in industries such as energy and transport. He also sold a number of ailing businesses. But by the time Mr Immelt became chief executive on September 7th 2001, just four days before the terrorist attacks on New York and Washington, it was clear that GE needed to change direction. For one thing, its rivals had aped many of the efficiency-boosting management tools that had once given GE an edge. For another, the rise of deep-pocketed private-equity firms had created stiff competition in buying top-notch assets.

Mr Immelt, recognizing that the world has changed, has placed more emphasis on organic growth since taking office. He has built up the company's marketing expertise, whereas in Mr Welch's GE engineers and spreadsheet jockeys were the masters. And he has focused on innovation. Since 2001 GE has invested $330m to expand its research facilities around the world. It spent $4.3 billion on R&D in 2008, up from $2.3 billion in 2002.

In a bold initiative, 'Ecomagination', GE is aiming to dominate the market for clean technologies such as wind and solar power. By lifting its investment in clean-tech R&D to $1.5 billion a year by 2010, the company hopes to produce more ideas like its hybrid diesel-electric locomotive, which stores the energy dissipated during braking in batteries that can be called on to power the engine later. Such ideas have boosted organic growth in GE's industrial businesses to 8% in 2008 from 4% in 2001.

The firm has also dumped a number of its underperforming operations and made acquisitions in promising areas such as Hispanic media and clean technology. Altogether, GE has snapped up about $101 billion of assets since 2001 and disposed of $53 billion of businesses. Now looks like the time to pick up more high-quality targets on the cheap. Given the problems with GE Capital, however, the company is likely to think twice before splashing out. Mr Immelt and his lieutenants have repeatedly stressed in recent weeks that their number one priority is to keep the company 'safe and secure'.

Here lies the rub. One tenet of the conglomerate model is that a judicious mix of businesses should offer insurance against the worst ravages of a recession, leaving enough capital free at the corporate centre to support expansion when rival firms are pulling in their horns. Yet GE Capital's problems are so great that the priority now for its parent seems to be to hoard as much cash as it can. So does this mean that GE should be broken up? Assuming the company can revive GE Capital, there might be a case for hanging on to that business even if its margins are squeezed. By refocusing on its original mission, a stripped-down finance unit could help drive sales at GE's industrial operations by providing finance for large infrastructure projects and other activities. But investors would need cast-iron reassurance that the business would be kept out of the freewheeling activities in which it has come a cropper.

The case for keeping the rest of GE together, at least for the time being, is based on three arguments. For a start, the company's leaders deserve more time to show that their R&D investments can pay off as the economy recovers. Next, in a world in which governments will become bigger customers for GE's wares, thanks partly to huge fiscal stimulus packages, the company's expertise in dealing with public authorities should benefit all of its divisions. Given GE's strength in areas such as clean technology, energy and transport, it stands to benefit from at least some of the public money that will be up for grabs.

The third argument in favour of keeping GE's industrial side intact is that it has learnt how to sell its disparate wares to foreign governments in compelling combinations rather than one by one. Last year, for example, GE signed a wide-ranging partnership with Mubadala, the commercial-investment arm of Abu Dhabi, which included a joint venture in commercial finance, some renewable energy projects and a new GE training centre. The company also struck deals in China, connected to the Beijing Olympic Games, that generated $2 billion of revenue. At a time of rising protectionist sentiment, GE's ability to assemble such packages could ease its path into new markets.

In his annual report to GE's shareholders, which was published last month, Mr Immelt argued that so long as the company could get itself through the recession, it would benefit as global capitalism was 'reset' in some of the ways outlined above. To weather the cycle, GE's management plans to keep cutting billions of dollars from its costs, to generate more revenue from its growing business that services turbines, jet engines and other GE gear, and to keep investing in the development of its employees' capabilities, on which it spends $1 billion a year.

Fallen heroes

GE prides itself on being a breeding ground for exceptionally talented managers. That is likely to remain true. Its industrial businesses are basically well run, even though recession will be a drag on their results. Yet the company's halo has slipped because of the debacle at its finance arm. Given the precarious nature of GE Capital's funding structure, GE should have been alert to the risk of a complete dislocation in financial markets. But it failed to consider such a possibility. The firm says it now plans to give a greater voice to contrarian types within its ranks, who can play devil's advocate in planning meetings.

GE was not the only blue-chip company to be caught out by the speed with which credit markets shut down. But it made matters worse by being slow to reveal details of GE Capital's loan portfolio. Instead it tried to persuade investors that the business could ride out the storm, without giving them enough information on the contents of the finance arm's black box of assets. This sparked wild speculation about the state of GE Capital's balance-sheet, undermining GE's share price. 'As financial services became more volatile, we should have given more transparency and less guidance,' admits Mr Immelt.

The chief executive has paid personally for GE's poor performance. At his own suggestion he is going without a bonus for last year (though he was paid a salary of $3.3m). For 2007 he scooped $5.8m. Mr Immelt has also given up a special, three-year, long-term incentive payment that would have been worth $11.7m. Some critics claim that GE's boss has dented his credibility by making several optimistic predictions that have been quickly proved wrong. For instance, barely a couple of weeks before the company revealed that it had missed its earnings in the first quarter of 2008, Mr Immelt declared that he expected GE to hit its target. In September he denied that the company needed a fresh capital injection. But soon afterwards it announced that it had raised $15 billion from Mr Buffett and others.

Mr Immelt argues that he had to reverse course swiftly in the autumn because financial markets suddenly took a turn for the worse. 'What you don't want to be is a consistent but dumb guy,' he says. He has a point: had GE not moved fast to build up its finances then it would certainly be in a far worse predicament now. Nevertheless the suspicion lingers that GE's boss has a habit of promising too much. The best way for him to rebuild confidence in his leadership will be to demonstrate that GE can bounce back quickly from its woes. It will require a prodigious feat of managerial wizardry to pull that off.

Consider the questions below:

1 Is GE any different from any other large conglomerate-style corporation?

2 Ideally, how should a large M-form diversified corporation deal with massive dislocations in financial markets such as in 2008?

3 Should GE move towards a more focused business portfolio and, if so, how? Or should it remain as a conglomerate and, if so, how should it adapt its operating principles?

You should consider GE's recent experience in the light of the debate on conglomerates (see Case box 8.3 below). Does GE have the management experience and talent to manage such a wide spread of businesses? Alternatively, can you argue that there is a focus and a thread running through the business so that synergies can be achieved? To what extent does a management team depend on its leader – consider again the critical role of Jack Welch – and is a conglomerate more dependent on charismatic leadership than other large corporations? What is the nature of the management talent that can make conglomerates succeed beyond the expectations of the stock market?

Case box 8.3: **The case for conglomerates**

Conglomerates have experienced turbulent times over the last quarter of the 20th century. In the US and UK, conglomerate strategies were adopted by an increasing number of companies in the post-war period through to the 1980s in the US and 1990s in the UK when the rationale for conglomeration was questioned. Peters and Waterman encapsulated the new thinking in *In Search of Excellence* (1980), encouraging companies to '*stick to their knitting*' and do what they're good at rather than create and manage diversity. In the corporate refocusing of the late 20th century, conglomerates have become an endangered species.

Conglomerates were a product of the prevailing economic, political and business environments of the US and UK in the 1960s, 70s and 80s. Key drivers included anti-trust (competition) policies that limited growth in core business activities, effectively encouraging diversification, a desire to spread financial risk and reduce volatility in financial performance by creating a portfolio of counter-cyclical businesses and an increase in management power that resulted from the divorce of ownership and control. The quality of management also improved, not least because of the growth in formal training, including MBA programmes, and management teams became convinced that they could manage any business regardless of its products or services and their experience in those sectors; the perceived risk of diversification had fallen. The relatedness of the target's business activities was often a secondary consideration even though the scope for synergy benefits is minimal between unrelated businesses; acquisitions could be financially justified on efficiency improvements at the target alone. There was also a substantial pool of inefficient and poorly managed companies to acquire.

By the 1990s the pool of targets began to dry up and the quality of incumbent managements improved, as did the financial performance of their companies, making their acquisition more expensive and, therefore, less likely. Conglomerates were forced to look to replace acquisitive with organic growth; a difficult transition for many. There was also a growing belief that the complexity of the conglomerate model added costs which were not negated by synergies across unrelated activities and depressed shareholder returns. Conglomerates were becoming so complex that even City analysts were struggling to understand underlying performance and to value them fairly. Furthermore, institutional investors began to take a more proactive interest in the companies in which they were substantial investors, discouraging unrelated acquisitions, believing that they could, through share trading, create their own balanced portfolios more cheaply than conglomerates who incur acquisition premia when buying companies.

Source: Paul Simmonds (2009)

8.7 Changing the business portfolio: acquisitions and strategic alliances

Corporate portfolios can change quickly through mergers and acquisitions.[16] Both agreed and contested acquisitions became very common, first in the US, then in the UK and latterly in Western Europe. But during the 1990s general dissatisfaction with acquisition performance motivated the search for an alternative form of expansion and strategic alliances became a popular alternative. Subsequently, firms learned that alliances, with their partial control and ownership, also suffer

---

[16] The terms 'merger' and '**acquisition**' are often used interchangeably in the literature. There are differences in so far as mergers are generally the bringing together of businesses of equal size, paid for by the exchange of shares and with no premium. Acquisitions imply a dominant party controlling another, and often there is a premium paid. Where the distinction becomes problematic is in the post-deal phase, where 'mergers' often become 'zero premium acquisitions', and some acquisitions become rather like mergers in having a 'level playing field'.

from high failure rates. But the need for growth strategies in a world of globalizing firms meant that attention stayed focused on both acquisitions and alliances. This section provides, firstly, an introduction to pre-acquisition planning and the issues involved in post-acquisition integration and secondly, a framework for assessing cooperative strategies (alliances).

8.7.1 Acquisitions

General reading of the business press and of academic writings suggests that **acquisitions**, although common, are not so tractable and it is worth pausing to consider why this is so (see Tables 8.2 and 8.3). Acquisitions touch all aspects of corporate life and so can be viewed from a multiplicity of angles. From a strategic perspective, much attention has been devoted to understanding the drivers for acquisition and identifying suitable targets. The underlying assumptions with this planning approach are that if one can correctly identify such targets, then the acquisition will be successful. This exposes us to Mintzberg's criticism of the planning school: does success inevitably follow from

Table 8.2 Consultancy and business press evidence on acquisition failure

Consultancy	Date	Method	Failure rate
Business	1975	400 postal questionnaires	49%
International	1978	150 postal questionnaires	48%–56%
Coopers and Lybrand	1992	Qualitative in-depth interviews with senior executives in the UK's top 100 companies	54%
Coopers and Lybrand	1996	125 companies. Low revenues, cash flow, profitability	66%
Mercer MC	1995	150 companies. Poor returns to shareholders after three years	50%
McKinsey & Co	1995	Examined 58 acquisitions. Success was measured as financial return exceeding the cost of capital	58.6%

Source: KPMG (1998)

Table 8.3 Academic evidence on failure rates

Types of academics	Conclusions	Authors	Date
Financial economists	Target shareholders benefit by c. 20% whereas acquirer shareholders do not, benefiting by c. 0–2%	Jensen and Ruback Jarrell and Poulsen Sudarsanam	1983 1994 1994
Industrial economists ■ Using accounting data ■ Subsequent market share ■ Divestment	■ Bidders suffer an immediate decline in relative profitability ■ Subsequent market share showed dramatic decline ■ 58.5% of 2,021 acquisitions (1950–86) subsequently divested	Hughes Mueller Caves Porter	1993 1985 1988 1987

a good plan? However, CEOs are reputedly heard to remark that if the acquisition failed then it was due to a poor plan! This circular argument is not helpful and indeed, obscures the point that the causal link between plan and performance is weak at best – the relationship being substantially mediated by the way in which acquisitions are integrated into the buying company. As a consequence, strategy research efforts have turned to the post-acquisition phase, where implementation is seen as the bridge between the islands of plan and the realities of performance.

8.7.2 The context

Acquisitions come in waves. The 1960s were characterized by a wave of diversification activity designed to spread financial risk across a portfolio of businesses. Companies such as the tobacco giant BAT Industries spent vast sums trying to establish sound footings in other industries, but with very poor results. The 1980s exposed the fallacy of diversification, as its supposed advantages were more than offset by the difficulties of managing such large, diverse groups. It was realized that shareholders could diversify more effectively themselves, and, with the rise of more aggressive financial techniques, such giants were no longer bid-proof. Break-ups became the new order, as businesses streamlined, downsized and generally 'stuck to the knitting'. The 1990s saw a massive resurgence in acquisition activity, spurred by deregulation, globalization and technological change. Differences from previous waves of activity are the number of mega-mergers to create global giants, such as Travelers/Citicorp forming the world's biggest financial services group, Exxon and Mobil creating an oil behemoth, and the intention of Deutsche Telekom and Telecom Italia, in a $162bn deal, to create Europe's first supranational.

In Europe, the drive towards a single market has encouraged internal, cross-border acquisitions. Free of the political barriers that have fragmented their markets, many European companies have sought to consolidate their efforts as a means of matching the advantages in economic scale of their US and Far East counterparts (Calori and Lubatkin, 1995). At the same time, the initial fears of Fortress Europe, as well as its size and sophistication, have made it an attractive hunting ground for non-European multinationals. This has not only resulted in a sharp increase in acquisitions on the continent, but also resulted in the rise of the almost unheard-of hostile takeover. While almost a thing of the past in the US and UK, where they attract little attention, continental Europe is in the grip of such acrimonious deals which regularly feature in its business press.

Another feature of this recent wave of acquisition activity is the rise in cross-border acquisitions. In 1998 the value[17] of these acquisitions was estimated at about $230bn but then there was a dramatic increase in 1999 to break the $1 trillion level. Industry figures suggest further big increases in the 2000s, from £1.2 trillion in 2002 to $4.2 trillion in 2007. The recession has since taken its toll and the 2008 figure has slipped to a more 'modest' $2.9 trillion.[18]

8.7.3 Motives for acquisition

Most texts on acquisitions cite strategic and financial motives as the main drivers for making acquisitions (see Table 8.4). From a strategic perspective the principal intent is to gain competitive advantage by increasing the firm's power in the marketplace. All the elements cited in the box derive from a Porter framework, especially through reducing costs and reducing rivalry. The main addition to this is a corporate portfolio motive whereby the overall risk return profile of the firm

---

[17] These figures undoubtedly understate the case, as the values of many cross-border deals are not publicly known. The numbers of deals, however, are a more reliable measure of activity.

[18] KPMG data from http://www.reuters.com/article/euMergersNews/idUSL9452330090112

Table 8.4 Motives for acquisition	
Strategic motives	**Financial motives**

■ To restructure the industry
  – remove competitors
■ For access to new markets
  – without start-up costs
■ To gain economies of scale and/or scope
  – improve cost position
■ To acquire new skills
■ To diversify the business portfolio
  – improve risk/return
	■ To obtain a bargain
	  – buy cheap
	■ For tax advantages
	  – e.g. to offset tax liabilities elsewhere
	■ For financing advantages
	  – lower cost of capital
	  – easier access to finance

can be improved. The issues of relatedness and synergy that lie behind this are hotly debated and success is frequently elusive. Strategic motives may easily be overshadowed by apparently simpler and more straightforward financial motives – a bargain may prove irresistible! But also in the complex world of large corporate structures, there may be many tax and cost of capital attractions to an acquisition.

In Case box 8.4, a major new acquisition by Merck of Schering-Plough is announced. These are two of the pharmaceuticals industry's premier companies. Given what we know about the historic record of successes and failures of acquisitions, identify the principal reasons for and against undertaking this sort of major acquisition. What reasons are there for thinking this acquisition may be a value creator?

Case box 8.4: **Merck's manoeuvres**

In an artfully constructed deal, Merck is to pay $41 billion for Schering-Plough
The language was reminiscent of a happier time before the credit crunch and the economic crisis closed the book on most such mergers. Dick Clark, the boss of Merck, an American pharmaceutical giant, called the agreement to acquire Schering-Plough, which was announced on March 9th, a 'transformational event' and went on to expound on the 'strategic sense' and 'exceptional promise' of the deal.

Perhaps Mr Clark can be forgiven his exuberance. The deal is a bright spot amid a corporate landscape of bankruptcy and retrenchment. Merck will pay $41 billion for Schering-Plough, paying with a combination of shares, $9.8 billion from cash reserves and another $8.5 billion prised from the clutches of a bank, JPMorgan.

Although credit has dried up almost everywhere else, drugs companies, with their cash reserves and healthy revenues, can still call on the banks. Last month Pfizer, another American drugs giant, was able to count on bank loans to assist in its $68 billion acquisition of Wyeth. And on March 12th Switzerland's Roche said it had reached an agreement to pay $46.8 billion for the 44% of Genentech, an American biotech firm, that it does not already own. Sanofi-Aventis of France is also said to be on the acquisition trail.

Big drugs companies hope consolidation will solve their various problems: the lack of new blockbuster drugs coming through their research pipelines, looming competition from generic drugs as patents expire, the global economic crisis and an over-dependence on sales in America, where health-care reforms will squeeze margins, at the very least. Alas, the evidence suggests that many of the supposed benefits of pharmaceutical mega-mergers fail to materialise: bigger firms are no better at innovation, and are often worse. But bosses are pressing ahead anyway.

The main attraction of buying Schering-Plough is that Merck will, in one swoop, double (to 18) the number of drugs it has in late-stage development. Merck will also bolster its international and over-the-counter sales, both areas where Schering is strong (70% of its revenues come from outside America). In addition, Mr Clark promises that there will be cost savings of $3.5 billion a year after 2011. But this sounds dubious, given that both companies are already cutting costs heavily. And if the two firms' research teams are so complementary and do not overlap much, as Merck claims, who is going to get sacked?

A bigger worry is that Johnson & Johnson (J&J), another drugs giant, could spoil the party in one of two ways. It could make a bid for Schering itself (and some analysts think it would make a better partner than Merck). Or J&J could jeopardise its co-marketing agreement with Schering for Remicade, a money-spinning anti-inflammatory drug. J&J has the right to terminate the agreement if there is a change of control at Schering. So Mr Clark is cunningly structuring his deal as a reverse takeover in which Merck will be acquired by Schering-Plough – which will then rename itself Merck. J&J may not be impressed.

Such trickery aside, the deal does at least answer critics who complained that Merck was not acting as vigorously as competitors in buying rivals and moving into new markets. But it also represents a change in strategy for Merck, which unlike many of its peers has stayed on the sidelines during the industry's previous waves of mega-mergers. Instead, the company has always preferred to grow by developing new products in its laboratories. The task for Mr Clark, who will become boss of the new company, will be to make the deal go smoothly, despite his lack of experience with big mergers.

Pfizer's acquisition of Wyeth and Roche's takeover of Genentech are also predicated on cost savings and replenishing the acquiring companies' pipelines. The acquisitions in the pharmaceutical industry do have some logic to them, to the extent that they will provide a short-term boost. But there is also a growing herd mentality, as firms rush to do deals in order not to be left out. And none of these tie-ups does much to address the industry's chief problem – its inability to innovate.

Take your partners

Biggest pharmaceutical companies by market capitalisation, 11 March 2009, $bn

*Assuming deal goes ahead

Source: Thomson Datastream

Source: 'Merck's Manoeuvres', *The Economist*, 12 March 2009

8.7.4 Issues in post-acquisition integration

In focusing upon implementation, a new set of strategic issues present themselves. Implementation has opened up the black box of the 'messy' detail of organizations, which pre-acquisition planning frameworks largely overlook. This has implications for our view of strategy and the role of the HQ. Pre-acquisition frameworks tend to assume a top-down approach to strategy, whereas the latter is embedded within the organization, and is multilevel and complex. Focusing internally upon the resources and capabilities of the business echoes a shift in emphasis as noted in Chapter 5, in the field of strategy itself, from the positioning, market-based school to the resource-based school.

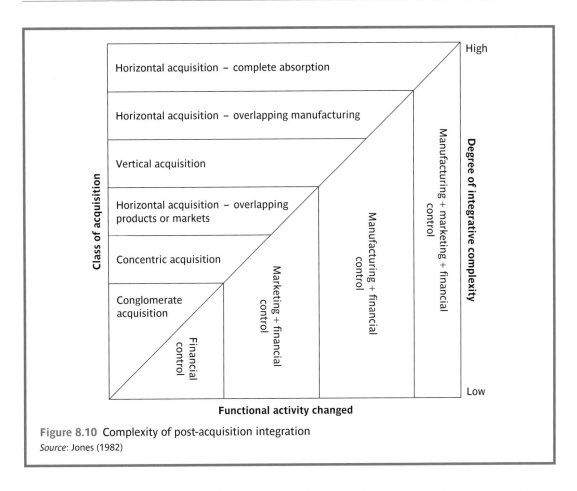

Figure 8.10 Complexity of post-acquisition integration
Source: Jones (1982)

However, rather than being an 'either/or' choice, this is really a question of emphasis, with the recognition that success in the latter is crucial to achieving the former.

It is in the post-acquisition phase that value from the acquisition is created or destroyed. Many attempts have been made to produce simple diagrams that capture the complexities inherent in how the strategic intention behind an acquisition translates into post-acquisition integration actions. One such diagram is shown in Figure 8.10.

This diagram relates the different types of acquisition to their impact on how the functional and operation activities have to be adapted and changed. Thus, conglomerates with little relatedness between the businesses in the portfolio are simple to integrate. By contrast, complete absorption will have complex ramifications right through the firm.

Case box 8.5 recounts the recent history of Indian companies marauding acquisitively across the globe. This tide of acquisitions looks set to continue, albeit with a pause due to current economic conditions. But how successful will these acquisitions be? Assess the general critical factors for success in making these acquisitions. What does this tell you about the inherent difficulties and rewards of such large-scale mergers given the complexities of post-acquisition outlined above?

8.7.5 Managing strategic alliances

The poor performance record of mergers and acquisitions has led to corporate disenchantment, with criticism also coming from financial analysts and from academics. Corporate indigestion meant that acquirers found the immediate advantages of acquisition to be frequently undermined

Case box 8.5: Marauding maharajahs: India's acquisitive companies

The more Indian firms make acquisitions, the more acquisitions they want to make

For proud Indians, nothing – except perhaps victory for their national cricket team – is as sweet as the sight of Indian companies marauding acquisitively across the globe. And marauding they are. So far this year Indian firms have announced 34 foreign takeovers worth more than $10.7 billion in all, according to Dealogic, a market-research outfit. Last year's total was $23 billion, more than five times the previous record and more than the investments made by foreigners in Indian companies. For local industrialists, among the proudest Indians, the buying binge indicates a renaissance, and not only in business. 'There's a new India emerging,' says Kumar Mangalam Birla, chairman of the Aditya Birla Group, a big conglomerate. 'This shows the new-found respect that India commands in the global arena.'

He should know. Last month Hindalco, the group's aluminium company, bought Novelis, an American rival, for $6 billion, making it the world's biggest aluminium-rolling company. This was barely a week after Tata Steel, India's biggest private steelmaker, sealed an even bigger deal that it had embarked upon last October. It agreed to buy Corus, an Anglo-Dutch rival, for $13.2 billion, a sum nine times the size of the previous largest foreign acquisition by an Indian firm.

Both deals partly reflect the conditions that are encouraging many smaller Indian businesses to buy globally, in pharmaceuticals, computing, car parts, energy and so on. With GDP growth averaging 8% and efficiencies wrought in leaner times, Indian firms have been minting money in the past three years. Their average profit margins are around 10% – more than twice the global average. By one estimate, 60% of India's 200 leading companies are looking to invest this loot in foreign purchases.

Financing such deals is easier than ever. After reforms to capital markets, the stockmarket has exploded even as interest rates have remained low. Other bottlenecks have been removed, including rules limiting the debt that companies can accrue. Last year Ranbaxy, a pharmaceuticals company, used a $440m bond issue to help fund eight acquisitions, in America, Romania, Italy, South Africa and elsewhere. Equally important is the bristling confidence that these advances have imbued in Indian companies. Mr Birla says it would have been very hard to imagine buying Novelis five years ago.

The total value of Indian purchases abroad accounted for 1.8% of that of all cross-border deals last year. But they are growing, with the size of the average Indian foreign acquisition rising tenfold, to $315m, in recent years. Indian business looks certain to continue globalising, partly by buying foreign companies. The removal of remaining barriers to foreign direct investment in India will also bring global benefits, of technology and scale, back home. On March 22nd, after much delay, the government approved a proposal to raise the limit on foreign ownership of telecoms firms to 74%.

Indian companies began their spree in around 2000, which saw 50 foreign deals, together worth less than $1 billion. Most of the deals were, as they still are, done by pharmaceutical and computer-services companies. These were notable survivors of a traumatic liberalisation in the 1990s. They emerged sleeker, more competitive and lusting for new markets for their exports. For such firms, foreign acquisitions are a way to connect their cheap and skilled workforce to new markets and established clients. 'For us, India is only one market in the world, though an important one,' says Malvinder Singh, the boss of Ranbaxy, which generates 80% of its business abroad. (That said, Ranbaxy has been more cautious of late. On March 20th it pulled out of the bidding for a subsidiary of Merck, a German drugs giant, which would have made it the world's seventh-biggest maker of generic drugs.)

Another acquisitive urge is for technology, for example in manufacturing. That is one reason behind Hindalco's purchase of Novelis, which makes aluminium cans, a high-value product. To develop a similar facility in India would have taken Hindalco around five years, which it did not have. 'In the next three years we'll be long on aluminium,' said Mr Birla. 'And this aluminium needs to go somewhere to get value added.' Technology is a big concern for Suzlon Energy, the world's fifth-biggest maker of wind turbines. Last year it paid $565m for Hansen, a Belgian gearbox-maker. 'Suzlon understands wind technology and Hansen understands only gearboxes. Now both R&D teams are sitting together, designing products,' says Suzlon's chairman, Tulsi Tanti. Last month Suzlon made a $1.3 billion bid – the third-biggest by an Indian firm – for REpower, a German turbine-maker.

Such deals are typical for companies from emerging economies. Tata Steel's acquisition of Corus was different. The company survived liberalisation, and then prospered, by investing in sophisticated capital-intensive production. As the world's lowest-cost steel producer, it was able to raise the money to buy Corus, its bigger rival, and become the world's fifth-largest steelmaker. It now aims to dominate its market. Only a handful of Indian firms are capable of such vast ambition. And most, being family-owned, may be too reticent to accept the associated risks.

Nonetheless, the tide of foreign acquisitions by Indian companies

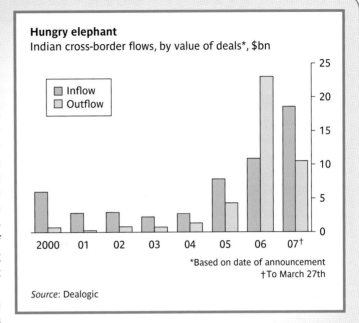

Hungry elephant
Indian cross-border flows, by value of deals*, $bn

*Based on date of announcement
†To March 27th

Source: Dealogic

will continue to rise, with more and bigger deals. How successful they will be is less certain. No big foreign acquisition has failed so far – even though, according to consultants at McKinsey, that is the fate of 60–70% of cross-border takeovers. 'It's important for companies to look at the economic rationale, and not get taken to extremes by emotion and ego,' says Ranbaxy's Mr Singh. Wise words for proud Indians, especially since their cricket team keeps losing.

Source: 'Marauding maharajahs', *The Economist*, 29 March 2007

Questions

1 How can you judge whether these acquisitions by Indian companies are related or unrelated acquisitions? Does it matter?

2 What are the natural limits to the pace of acquisitions? In what ways might the exchange rate be a factor?

3 Does India as the home country and the home base confer advantages in the rate of globalization? (Consult Chapter 9 before answering this question.)

by the trauma of integration. Acquirers often had difficulty in assimilating the expertise of the target company and, where the target company had considerable flexibility and innovative capacity, these characteristics were often lost in the subsequent bureaucracy. Added to this disenchantment and indigestion there has also been a diminishing number of appropriate targets available to purchase. These twin constraints led companies to search for alternative means of rapid, safer expansion, so as to improve their control over the competitive environment.

Strategic alliances appeared to overcome many of the limitations of mergers and acquisitions. They seemed to avoid culture and organizational shock and yet achieve rapid presence in specific areas, for the companies concerned. However, there do appear to be growing concerns here also, with companies recognizing problems of sustainability of strategic alliances, some feeling strongly that acquisitions would have been preferable.

The term *strategic alliance* itself covers a multitude of different arrangements and there is no agreed typology in the literature. However, it is critical to understand the different forms in existence, as they have profound implications for the way in which the alliance is to be managed. In particular, there is an important distinction on the grounds of whether or not the partner is a competitor – note that even if the partner is a competitor, this may not mean collusion.

Strategic alliances between non-competitors

The following provides a useful way of linking alliance types amongst competitors to options for strategic expansion. These growth options may be grouped into three categories:

1 *international expansion*: where a company extends its activities into a new geographic market, often after having established a dominant position in their domestic market;

2 *vertical integration*: where a company extends its activities upstream or downstream to become its own supplier or customer;

3 *diversification*: where a company expands outside its industry of origin.

In Figure 8.11 the implications for these expansion options for types of strategic alliance amongst non-competing firms are shown. There are three main types of strategic alliance amongst non-competing firms:

1 *International expansion joint ventures*: these are formed by companies that originate in different countries. One company often has a product that it seeks to market in another country in which the other firm has privileged access. The mutual benefits are that the local firm gains a product to distribute, while the manufacturer gains a foothold in a new country. Often these alliances are between partners with unequal skills and resources, one coming from the developed world with technical skills and considerable resources and the other from the developing world without the ability to develop such a product on its own but having a profound understanding of the local market.

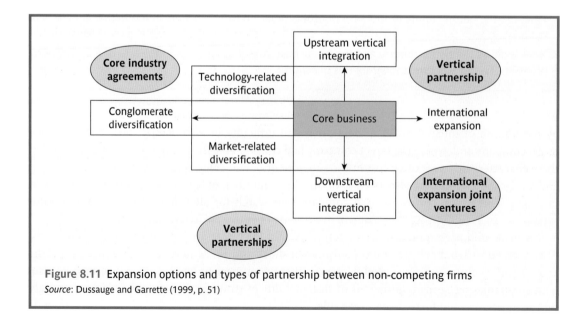

Figure 8.11 Expansion options and types of partnership between non-competing firms
Source: Dussauge and Garrette (1999, p. 51)

2 *Vertical partnerships*: these bring together two companies that operate at two successive stages in the same production process. For instance, fast-food chains are critical customers of soft drinks suppliers, so Coca-Cola has set up an alliance with McDonald's and Domino's Pizza.

3 *Cross-industry agreements*: these are collaborations formed by companies from totally different industries to leverage their complementary capabilities. For instance, BMW forged an alliance with Rolls-Royce in aircraft engines in order to enter that market. Although for Rolls-Royce this meant the emergence of a new competitor, it also provided the opportunity to foster and control its long-term development. This raises the issue of competing agendas, with the newcomer trying to close the expertise gap as rapidly as possible, while the established company attempts the reverse. Such alliances may also occur where there is technical convergence between two industries. For instance, Philips has teamed up with Du Pont de Nemours for the production of surface coatings for data storage applications.

Strategic alliances amongst competitors

Alliances amongst competitors seem rather paradoxical, but according to Morris and Hergert (1987), they account for approximately 70% of all cooperation agreements. Maybe it is in recognition of this that Hamel and Prahalad's (1989) famous article is entitled 'Collaborate with Your Competitors – and Win'. While it is tempting to think of these alliances as collusive, it is a question of degree, with some being more collusive than others. Through the use of cluster analysis techniques on 200 alliances, Dussauge and Garrette (1999) have identified three main alliance types between competitors (see Figure 8.12) in terms of balance of power between the partners (degree of symmetry) and impact upon competition.

The three types of alliance identified may be characterized in the following way:

1 *Pre-competitive* or *shared supply alliance*: this may cover only one stage in the production process, so that while the final product contains inputs from both companies, these are specific to the parents and the alliance is not apparent to the market. These alliances occur when the minimum efficient size at a particular stage in the production process is much greater than for the entire product and when neither firm produces enough volume to achieve this critical size. These sorts of alliances are mainly between firms of similar size, often intra-zonal, and in areas of R&D and manufacturing. Industries with such alliances are automotive, electronics and data processing.

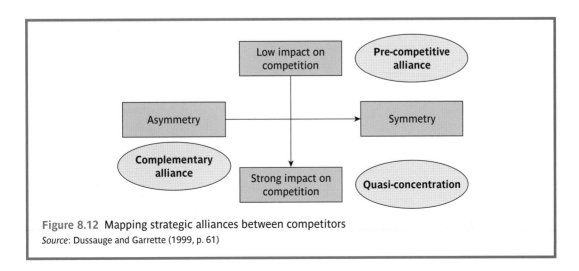

Figure 8.12 Mapping strategic alliances between competitors
Source: Dussauge and Garrette (1999, p. 61)

2 *Quasi-concentration alliance*: this covers the entire production process and results in a common product marketed by all allies. The assets and skills brought by each partner are similar in nature and the goal is to benefit from economies of scale. Such an alliance is clearly visible to the customer, such as in the Airbus consortium or the production of the Tornado fighter aircraft. Clearly, such alliances eliminate competition between competitors, although there can be internal rivalry within the alliance. These sorts of alliances are found mostly in the aerospace and defence industries.

3 *Complementary alliance*: when the assets contributed by the partner firms are different in nature. Most commonly, one may be a manufacturer and the other a distributor. For instance, Matra manufactures the Espace, a mini van, which is marketed in Europe by Renault. For such alliances to work, the product brought in by an ally must not compete directly with the products of the other firm. Complementary alliances are usually between two firms (unlike the other two styles) and the companies may be very different sizes. These alliances are often found in the automotive and telecommunications industries.

Outcomes

Assessing the outcomes of alliances is no easy matter. As we have shown, there are many different types and the partners have very different reasons for pursuing them. Tables 8.5 and 8.6 show the variety of outcomes for both non-competing and competing firms in alliances. For alliances between competitors, the most frequent outcomes overall are either an extension of the alliance or premature termination – it seems it is unusual to have a natural end or be acquired. In most cases, alliances between competitors had significant strategic consequences for the partner firms, with one-way skills appropriation in particular, and such alliances tend to affect the levels of competition in the industry. However, there is considerable variation between the different types of alliance between competitors, as Table 8.6 shows.

With an alliance strategy it has been possible for corporations to swiftly gain access to markets, exchange technologies, form defensive shareholding blocs, enter third markets in combination with

Table 8.5 Outcomes of alliances between non-rival firms

Alliance type	Evolution of the alliance	Strategic consequences for each firm	Impact on competition
International expansion joint ventures	High mortality rate in their first years in existence, followed by stability	Stability in the partners' relative positions	Globalization
Vertical partnerships	Long-term relationship between the partners	New division of the value added within the industry	Concentration of the upstream industry and changes in the relative bargaining power of suppliers and buyers
Cross-industry agreements	Results are frequently disappointing when compared to initial expectations	Joint venture becomes independent or intensification of competition between partners	Creation of new activities and arrival of new competitors

Source: Dussauge and Garrette (1999, p. 209)

Table 8.6 The evolutions and outcomes of strategic alliances between competitors

Alliance type	Evolution of the alliance	Strategic consequences for each firm	Impact on competition
Shared supply	Natural end or premature termination	No consequence	No impact on the intensity of competition
Quasi-concentration	Extension	Mutual specialization	Reduced intensity of competition
Complementary	Extension or continuation by one partner	One-way skill appropriation	Increased intensity of competition

Source: Dussauge and Garrette (1999, p. 220)

other partners, and engage in otherwise prohibitively expensive technologies, production facilities, and the like. They have the advantage of being relatively easily formed and disbanded – more so than joint ventures – and by joining in multiple alliances firms may contain risk and hold down costs.

Despite these apparent advantages, however, their value has been seriously questioned by many corporations; and especially by those with proprietary technology, strategic cost advantage and high market share. For such concerns it has been argued that the potential loss of technical skills, the provision of competitor access to markets, and organizational and cultural clashes may well outweigh any advantage. As a result, perhaps 50% of such alliances are therefore regarded as failures.

8.8 Summary

This chapter has introduced a new dimension to our strategy discussion – the multi-business portfolio. The job of designing, managing and adapting the portfolio of businesses lies generally with the corporate centre. It is concerned with the issues of competitive advantage, just like individual strategic business units, but it is particularly concerned to (i) make sure that SBUs do what they are supposed to do (the 'control' question) and (ii) ensure that the patterns of competitive advantage within the portfolio are mutually reinforcing (the 'synergy' question). In order to fulfil these tasks the corporate centre has to pay close attention to the structure of the organization so that patterns of specialization are created and management responsibilities can be properly defined. Issues of organization structure and process are discussed in more detail in Chapter 10 and in this chapter we have gone so far as to argue that the strategy–structure fit and balance is a key task for the corporate centre.

Although the corporate centre has a distinct role to play compared with the SBUs, it still deals with the same economic issues. In particular, the centre is concerned with synergy, introduced in Chapter 3 as economies of scope. This is reflected in the many practical frameworks and strategy tools that have been marketed over time. The BCG growth-share matrix is the grandfather of all these and has been succeeded by many other portfolio management frameworks. In noting these, it is sensible to remember that all strategy tools and frameworks are highly contextual. They depend critically on the situation of the particular organization. Frameworks in and of themselves do not convey truth or 'good' theory: they are merely ways of presenting data and alternatives. The trick with tools is to note the exclusions or, rather, to be clever with choosing a focus on just a few elements of the strategic context.

▶ The role of the centre is to find a way of managing the whole organization that fits its overall context. This is reflected in the range of strategies available. We discussed restructuring, activity sharing, and skills transfer. These capture different ways of creating value. We also discussed how companies have different styles that also reflect the same point – how to actually create extra value.

We have also noted the academic debate. This has focused on the defensibility of the conglomerate where in general academics are unconvinced that this is a sustainable approach. Also we have noted that this is an area where many big mistakes can be made. Experience suggests that these mistakes are all too common. The final part of this chapter goes on to look at the area in which there is a high degree of controversy – mergers and acquisitions.

The discussion on headquarters organization is illustrated with an extended discussion of GE in the era after Jack Welch stepped down as President/CEO. Welch's period has been highly celebrated but the later period is more controversial. GE ranks as one of the largest and most successful diversified businesses in history. It put together a wide range of businesses under a distinctive management style under a series of charismatic chief executives. This exemplifies the significant role of corporate-level decisions and the high risks attached to them.

The chapter concludes with a discussion of the advantages and disadvantages of mergers and acquisitions as a method of corporate renewal. Disenchantment with the method has spurred businesses to seek alternative avenues to improve their competitive advantage. A whole new set of options has arisen in the form of strategic alliances, although the chapter has pointed out that the term embodies a substantial range of different forms. However, we are now beginning to perceive something of a backlash, as managers become disenchanted with the instability of alliances, the difficulties of realizing anticipated benefits and the risks of knowledge leakage. The irony, then, is that strategic alliances, like mergers and acquisitions, also have considerable implementation difficulties that need to be fully considered before the deal is signed.

Key terms

acquisition	277	post-acquisition integration	280
complementary alliances	286	relatedness	261
cross-industry agreements	285	restructuring	262
decentralization	257	sharing activities	263
financial control	262	strategic alliances	283
growth-share matrix	267	strategic control	262
joint ventures	284	strategic planning	262
M-form	255	transferring skills	263
merger	276	U-form	254
portfolio management	262	vertical partnerships	285

Recap questions and assignments

1 Make a critical appraisal of the importance of the centre–division relationship in the strategic direction and development of large multi-business companies. Illustrate your answer by describing the relationships that you feel would be most important to a chosen company. You may wish to choose one from the text and cases version of this book.

2 Evaluate the nature of the additional value that is being suggested as a rationale for an ongoing merger or acquisition being reported in the current financial press. What actions need to be undertaken to realize this value? How would you classify this value in the terms used in the above chapter and how would you describe the parenting role best suited to the merged corporation?

3 Choose an acquisition/merger or an alliance which has featured prominently in the business press or with which you have been involved.

  i Critically assess the motives behind the making of the deal. In answering this question, you should consider different levels of analysis and specifically address the question of how the deal contributed to the creating and/or sustaining of competitive advantage.

  ii *Either* assess the outcome in terms of subsequent events, *or* comment critically upon what you perceive to be the main difficulties ahead in realizing the intentions of the deal.

4 Why do you think acquisitions and alliances continue to be made, when so many fail?

Case study 8.1 Fiat's ambitions: the Italian solution

Fiat's chief executive, Sergio Marchionne, has gone merger mad

His company is among the smallest of the global volume carmakers. But right now Sergio Marchionne is without question the most talked-about car executive in the world. The chief executive of Fiat Group has been alone in seeing an extraordinary opportunity in the meltdown in Detroit. By seeking to take over the running of both Chrysler and Opel, the European arm of General Motors (GM), Mr Marchionne is attempting not only to transform Fiat into a car group almost of the scale of mighty Toyota and Volkswagen (VW), but also to change the face of a perennially troubled industry.

Last December Mr Marchionne said of his stricken industry: 'What we are seeing is unprecedented. I have never seen the failure of so many systems at once.' Fiat was in a fight for survival. 'We're just going to slam the brakes on, use as many temporary lay-offs as needed, cut everything back to essentials.' He added an apocalyptic forecast. 'By the time we finish with this in the next 24 months, as far as mass producers are concerned, we're going to end up with one American house [Ford or GM, you presume]; one German of size [VW Group]; one French-Japanese, maybe with an extension in the US [the Renault-Nissan alliance]; one in Japan [Toyota], one in China [several possible candidates] and one potential European player [either Fiat or PSA Peugeot Citroën].'

The details of this vision may be wrong. Despite its present travails and imminent bankruptcy, few believe that GM will vanish and leave Ford as the sole American-owned champion. France's PSA Peugeot Citroën, though unwieldy, is not about to disappear either. The strength of Hyundai-Kia in emerging markets and North America should ensure that the South Korean producer makes the cut. And in Japan, however great the cull of smaller outfits such as Mitsubishi and Suzuki, Honda and perhaps Mazda will still be around to challenge the dominance of Toyota in its home market. So will Renault's partner, Nissan.

But if the shake-up is likely to be less dramatic than Mr Marchionne expects, that is only because much of the industry remains addicted to wildly unrealistic market-share forecasts and value-destroying investments. Mr Marchionne thinks it has been living beyond its means for too long. 'Out in front,' he says, 'this business is glamorous like Las Vegas. But behind the scenes, the industrial machine is complex and chaotic. We just look round at what to invest in and it's hard to justify the economics. To sort it out, you have to go back to the industrial machine and fix it.'

Critically, Mr Marchionne says, you need to sell in sufficient volume – about 1m a year on each platform – to drive down costs. Take the platform for the VW Golf, which yields sales of more than 1.5m a year because VW also uses it for the Skoda Octavia, the Seat Leon and the Audi A3. About 75% of the cost of a car is in its architectural underpinnings. The rest goes on giving it a distinctive body and cabin, while

Changing up
Global vehicle sales, 2008, m

Source: News reports; Company reports; *The Economist*

honing the brakes, steering and suspension. Fiat gets sales of about 600,000 from its city-car A platform (the basis of the Panda, the retro-styled 500 and Ford's new Ka). But none of its other platforms comes close to what is required: the whole group sold only 2.15m cars last year (see chart). Mr Marchionne reckons the minimum for a volume maker competing in every sector is about 5.5m – leaving Fiat far from safety.

In the past Fiat has tried to get around this problem with various alliances. A tie-up with GM lasted for five years until 2005, when Mr Marchionne extracted $2 billion from the American firm to extinguish a put option that would have forced it to buy the then-sickly Italian company. Mr Marchionne believes that alliances are all very well, but they react too slowly and require too many compromises. Without speed, he believes, you are doomed.

Over the past year he has been developing a more ambitious strategy, at first constructed around Chrysler, but now including Opel. Cruelly mismanaged by Daimler during its decade of ownership, and too dependent on pickup trucks and an ageing line-up of SUVs, Chrysler was in no condition to withstand the storm. Its increasingly desperate management sought help from a host of other carmakers, including Fiat. It reached a tentative agreement in which Nissan would have made a small car for Chrysler and Chrysler would have built a pickup for Nissan. But that was the limit for Carlos Ghosn, under pressure as boss of the Renault–Nissan alliance.

Mr Marchionne came up with a plan that might win Chrysler the federal loans it needed to stay alive while getting Fiat much of what it wanted. In exchange for an equity stake of around 35%, Fiat would make available to Chrysler its small and medium-sized platforms and advanced, fuel-efficient powertrains. Chrysler would give Fiat some of the scale it was seeking for its platforms, joint purchasing of parts, some expertise in producing large cars, a distribution network in America and manufacturing capacity to build new Alfa Romeos and perhaps the Fiat 500 for the American market. As Mr Marchionne put it: 'They have everything I don't have (including some I will never need) and I have everything they don't have and need.'

But Mr Marchionne's scheme, which won the backing of the Treasury's car-industry task-force, went further. Although Fiat would initially get only a stake of 20% (rising to 35% after fulfilling criteria set by the Treasury) and would have to repay all Chrysler's federal loans before taking majority control, the

Treasury accepted that Fiat should take over the responsibility of managing Chrysler and integrating the two operations as closely as possible.

Having presided over a near-miraculous turnaround at Fiat since being appointed in 2004, Mr Marchionne saw in Chrysler an opportunity to apply the same lessons. At Fiat he saw a sluggish organisation that lacked leadership and had become accustomed to management by committee. But he also saw, buried within the company, a new generation of leaders.

'The single most important thing was to dismantle the organisational structure,' he recalls. 'We tore it apart in 60 days, removing a large number of leaders who had been there a long time and who represented an operating style that lay outside any proper understanding of market dynamics.' In their place he promoted a group of younger executives, many with a background in consumer marketing, who understood and could provide what he wanted: accountability, openness, rapid communication and impatience with hierarchy and internal politics.

Some doubt that Fiat's lean management has the resources to spread itself across Chrysler, let alone Opel too. Mr Marchionne understands the concern, but rejects it. He believes he already knows who the new leaders at Chrysler will be. He is confident that the same will apply to Opel, should that too fall into his lap.

Chrysler is essentially a done deal, although some uncertainty remains, not least because a few senior debtholders chose to push the firm into bankruptcy rather than accept the Treasury's offer of $2.2 billion on the $6.9 billion they are owed. Fortunately for Fiat, the bankruptcy court judge, Arthur Gonzales, this week rejected the lenders' argument that they had been treated illegally and cleared the way for Chrysler to emerge as a going concern within a couple of months. Mr Marchionne is preparing for the day: 'We must act very quickly to cut overheads, lighten everything, speed up new models.'

Nor has Mr Marchionne been twiddling his thumbs in Europe. Having insisted for weeks that he had made no direct approaches about GM Europe, on May 4th he went to Berlin to present the German government with a plan that would give Fiat control of much of Opel (which includes Vauxhall in Britain) and possibly Saab, GM's bankrupt Swedish unit. GM, which can no longer fund the lossmaking operations of its European arm, has been looking for a partner to take a majority stake in Opel since March. If it cannot find one, the German government will be loth to provide bridging finance. Fiat's main rival is a group consisting of Magna, a Canadian car-parts and engineering business, and Oleg Deripaska, a Russian oligarch.

As with Chrysler, Mr Marchionne will have to win over both government and unions. He says that the deal depends on the willingness of European governments, but chiefly Germany's, to stump up €5 billion–7 billion ($6.6 billion–9.3 billion) in bridging loans. In return, Mr Marchionne has promised to keep open Opel's three main assembly plants in Germany, although there are fears for factories in Belgium and Britain. Over time he intends to reduce combined capacity by 22%, but he says he will do so by slimming factories rather than closing them. It is, he says, the preferred way in Europe – but it will mean forgoing savings of about €250m a year.

Even so, combining Opel and Fiat could save at least €1 billion a year. Partly because of Fiat's shared history with GM, Mr Marchionne says that Opel fits perfectly. GM lacks an A platform, which Fiat has. They already share a B platform (for the Corsa and the Grande Punto) and Fiat would be happy to use Opel's excellent new C and D platforms. 'We can achieve convergence on all the big platforms by 2012. Ultimately, I need to do this with Chrysler, but Opel gets me there much faster and with more immediate returns.' Mr Marchionne adds: 'I'm offering the German government a car business that will be effectively debt-free and I will take on Opel's liabilities, including pensions. I told them: if you have a better offer, take it.'

If Mr Marchionne pulls it off, he will create a new company consisting of Fiat Auto (without Ferrari and Maserati or the rest of the Fiat Group), Chrysler and GM Europe. Among the probable stakeholders would be the Agnelli family (which controls Fiat), the United Auto Workers union health-care fund (until it cashes out) and GM. The rest of the equity would be sold in a public offering. In a normal year that combination could expect revenue of $100 billion from the sale of 6m cars – just above Mr Marchionne's viability threshold.

▶ Others think that amalgamating three different cultures and several less-than-stellar brands is beyond even the formidably self-confident Mr Marchionne. The tale of Mr Ghosn is not wholly reassuring. It is now pretty clear that his heroic rescue of Nissan came at the expense of taking his eye off Renault, which in recent years has produced a succession of mediocre cars. This week Martin Winterkorn, the boss of VW, pointed out that his company had been applying its vaunted platform strategy since 1992. 'I wonder if he will be able to succeed,' said Mr Winterkorn, 'because successfully managing several brands and obtaining true synergies is really difficult.'

Some see Mr Marchionne as an empire builder who has come to believe his own publicity. The charge exasperates him. 'It's just nonsense,' he says. 'Fiat Group employs 200,000 people, but I'm going to carve out the car business and let the rest of it go its own sweet way. Look, I really hate the personal issue. It's not about me, let's just fix the industry. I'm only a conduit for change. You can't just have Toyota on its own, we need this to guarantee survival. Now it's up to others.'

Source: 'The Italian Solution', *The Economist*, 7 March 2009.

Questions

1 What was the logic behind Marchionne's plan to take over Chrysler and the European operations of GM?

2 We know now that his plan did not come to fruition, but what at the time were the risks involved and could the benefits have ever been sufficient to warrant these risks?

3 What kinds of major changes, corporate transformations and other restructurings do you expect to take place in the global auto industry? What key principles or criteria guide your thinking?

4 What has FIAT learned from its own restructuring? What new core competences would it deploy in a successful implementation of Marchionne's plan?

References

Calori, R. and Lubatkin, M. (1995) Euro-mergers 1993: viewpoints and predictions. In G. Von Krogh, A. Sinatra and H. Singh (eds) *Perspectives on the Management of Acquisitions*, Macmillan, London.

Caves, R.E. (1988) Effects of mergers and acquisitions on the economy: an industrial organisation perspective. In L.E. Browne and E.S. Rosengren (eds) *The merger boom*, Federal Reserve Bank of Boston, Boston, MA.

Chandler, A.D., Jr (1962) *Strategy and Structure: Chapters in the History of the Industrial Enterprise*, MIT Press, Cambridge, MA.

Chandler, A.D., Jr (1990) The enduring logic of industrial success. *Harvard Business Review*, March/April, 130–40.

Collis, D. (1991a) *Corporate Strategy: A Conceptual Framework*. Harvard Business School Case Study, 9–391–284.

Collis, D. (1991b) *Corporate Strategy: Identifying and Exploiting Resources*. Harvard Business School Case Study, 9–391–285.

Collis, D. (1991c) *Managing the Multibusiness Corporation*. Harvard Business School Case Study, 9–391–286.

Day, G.S. (1977) Diagnosing the product portfolio. *Journal of Marketing*, April, 264–80.

Dussauge, P. and Garrette, B. (1999) *Co-operative Strategy: Competing Successfully through Strategic Alliances*, John Wiley & Sons, Chichester.

Goold, M. and Campbell, A. (1987) *Strategies and Styles*, Blackwell, Oxford.

Goold, M., Campbell, A. and Alexander, M. (1994) *Corporate Level Strategy: Creating Value in the Multibusiness Company*, John Wiley & Sons, New York.

Hamel, G. and Prahalad, C.K. (1989) Collaborate with your competitors – and win. *Harvard Business Review*, **67**, **1**, 133–9.

Hamel, G. and Prahalad, C.K. (1994) *Competing for the Future*, Harvard Business School Press, Boston, MA.

Hill, C.W.L. (1994) Diversification and economic performance: bringing structure and corporate management back into the picture. In R. Rumelt, D. Schendel and D. Teece (eds) *Fundamental Issues in Strategy*, Harvard Business School Press, Boston, MA.

Hoskisson, R.E., Hill, C.W.L. and Kim, H. (1993) The multidivisional structure: organizational fossil or source of value? *Journal of Management*, **19**, **2**, 269–98.

Hughes, A. (1993) Mergers and economic performance in the UK: a survey of the empirical evidence 1950–1990. In M. Bishop and J.A. Kay (eds), *European Mergers & Merger Policy*, Oxford University Press, New York.

Jarrell, G.A. and Poulsen, A.B. (1994) The returns to acquiring firms in tender offers: evidence from three decades. In P.A. Gaughan (ed.) *Readings in Mergers & Acquisitions*, Blackwell, Oxford, chapter 16.

Jensen, M.C. and Ruback, R. (1983) The market for corporate control: the scientific evidence. *Journal of Financial Economics*, **11**, 5–50.

Jones, C.S. (1982) *Successful Management of Acquisitions*, Derek Beattie, London.

KPMG (1998) *KPMG Deal Watch*, KPMG, London.

McKiernan, P. (1992) *Strategies of Growth*, Routledge, London.

Morris, D. and Hergert, M. (1987) Trends in international collaborative agreements. *Columbia Journal of World Business*, **19**, **4**, 319–32.

Mueller, D.C. (1985) Mergers & market share. *The Review of Economics and Statistics*, **67**, May, 259–67.

Porter, M.E. (1987) From competitive advantage to corporate strategy. *Harvard Business Review*, May/June, 2–21.

Prahalad, C.K. and Hamel, G. (1990) The core competence of the corporation. *Harvard Business Review*, May/June, 79–91.

Rumelt, R. (1974) How much does industry matter? *Strategic Management Journal*, **12**, 167–85.

Simmonds, P. (2009) *Conglomerates in the FTSE 100 1983–2003*, unpublished doctoral dissertation, University of Warwick.

Sudarsanam, S. (1994) *The Essence of Mergers and Acquisitions*, Prentice-Hall, London.

Waterman, R. (1982) The seven elements of strategic fit. *Journal of Business Strategy*, **3**, 68–72.

Waterman, R., Peters, T. and Phillips J. (1980) Structure is not organization. *The McKinsey Quarterly*, Summer, 2–20.

Williamson, O.E. (1975) *Markets and Hierarchies: Analysis and Antitrust Implications*, Free Press, New York.

Further reading

Angwin, D.N. (2000) *Implementing Successful Post-Acquisition Management*, Pearson Education, London.

Angwin, D.N. (2001) Mergers and acquisitions across European borders: national perspectives on pre-acquisition due diligence and the use of professional advisers. *Journal of World Business*, Spring.

Angwin, D.N. (2003) Strategy as exploration and interconnection. Chapter 8 in S. Cummings and D. Wilson (eds) *Images of Strategy*, Blackwell, Oxford.

Angwin, D.N., Stern, P. and Bradley, S. (2004) Condemned or redeemed: the target CEO in a hostile takeover. *Long Range Planning*, **37**, 3 June.

Angwin, D.N. and Saville, B. (1997) Strategic perspectives on European cross-border acquisitions: a view from top European executives. *European Management Journal*, **15**, **4**, 423–35.

Bartlett, C.A. (1990) Matrix management not a structure, a frame of mind. *Harvard Business Review*, **68**, **4**, 138–45.

Bartlett, C.A. and Ghoshal, S. (1993) Beyond the M-form: toward a new managerial theory of the firm. *Strategic Management Journal*, **14**, 23–46, reprinted in S. Segal-Horn (ed.) (1998) *The Strategic Reader*, Blackwell Business, Oxford.

Buono, A.F. and Bowditch, J.L. (1989) *The Human Side of Mergers and Acquisitions: Managing Collisions Between People and Organizations*, Jossey-Bass, San Francisco.

Campbell, A. and Goold, M. (1994) Adding value from corporate headquarters. In B. De Wit and R. Meyer (eds) *Strategy: Process, Content, Context*, West Publishing Company, New York.

Campbell, A., Goold, M. and Alexander, M. (1995) Corporate strategy: the quest for parenting advantage. *Harvard Business Review*, March/April, 120–32.

Campbell, A. and Luchs, K. (1992) *Strategic Synergy*, Butterworth-Heinemann, Oxford.

Capron, L. (1999) The long term performance of horizontal acquisitions. *Strategic Management Journal*, **20**, **11**, 987–1018.

Cartwright, S. and Cooper, C. (1996) *Acquisitions – the Human Factor*, Butterworth-Heinemann, Oxford.

Chandler, A.D., Jr (1990) *Scale and Scope: The Dynamics of Industrial Capitalism*, Belknap, Cambridge, MA.

Chandler, A.D., Jr (1994) The functions of the HQ unit in the multibusiness firm. In R. Rumelt, D. Schendel and D. Teece (eds) *Fundamental Issues in Strategy*, Harvard Business School Press, Boston, MA.

Child, J. and Faulkner, D. (1998) *Strategies of Co-operation: Managing Alliances, Networks, and Joint Ventures*, Oxford University Press, Oxford.

Cohen, W.M. and Levinthal, D.A. (1990) Absorptive capacity: a new perspective on learning and innovation. *Administrative Science Quarterly*, **3**, 128–52.

Collis, D.J. (1996) Corporate strategy in multibusiness firms. *Long Range Planning*, **29**, 416–18.

Contractor, F.J. and Lorange, P. (eds) (1988) *Cooperative Strategies in International Business*, Lexington Books, Lexington, MA.

Hamel, G. (1991) Competition for competence and inter-partner learning within international strategic alliances. *Strategic Management Journal*, **23**, special issue, 83–103.

Haspeslagh, P. and Jemison, D. (1991) *Managing Acquisitions*, Free Press, New York.

Johnson, G. and Scholes, K. (2002) *Exploring Corporate Strategy*, 6th edn, Pearson Education, Harlow.

Killing, J.P. (1983) *Strategies for Joint Venture Success*, Croom Helm, London.

Kogut, B. (1988) Joint ventures: theoretical and empirical perspectives. *Strategic Management Journal*, **19**, **4**, 319–32.

Mirvis, P.H. and Marks, M.L. (1992) *Managing the Merger: Making it Work*, Prentice Hall, Englewood Cliffs, NJ.

Mockler, R.J. (1999) *Multinational Strategic Alliances*, Wiley, Chichester.

Ravenscraft, D.J. and Scherer, F.M. (1989) The profitability of mergers. *International Journal of Industrial Organisation*, **7**, 101–16.

Schaan, J.L. and Beamish, P.W. (1988) Joint venture general managers in LDCs. In F.J. Contractor and P. Lorange (eds) *Cooperative Strategies in International Business*, Lexington Books, Lexington, MA.

Segal-Horn, S. (ed.) (1998) *The Strategy Reader*, Blackwell Business, Oxford.

Teece, D.J. (1982) Towards an economic theory of the multiproduct firm. *Journal of Economic Behavior and Organization*, **3**, 39–63.

Weston, F., Chung, K.S. and Siu, J.A. (2003) *Take-overs, Restructuring and Corporate Governance*, 2nd edn, Prentice Hall, Englewood Cliffs, NJ.

Chapter 9

Global strategies and international advantage

Chapter contents

Introduction

This chapter reviews the forces that are shaping the global economy and the responses that are being made by firms. We look at the characteristics of 'global' and 'multidomestic' strategies. We review the evolution of the multinational enterprise (MNE) and examine the contrasts between MNEs, which are multidomestic, global and transnational.

> *Over the past few years the concept of global strategy has taken the world of multinational corporations (MNCs) by storm. Scores of articles in the* Harvard Business Review, Fortune, The Economist, *and other popular journals have urged multinationals to 'go global' in their strategies.*

The topic has clearly captured the attention of MNE managers. Conferences on global strategy, whether organised by the Conference Board in New York, the Financial Times in London, or Nomura Securities in Tokyo, have attracted enthusiastic corporate support and sizeable audiences. Even in the relatively slow-moving world of academe the issue of globalisation of industries and companies has emerged as a new bandwagon, as manifest in the large number of papers on the topic presented at recent meetings of the Academy of Management, the Academy of International Business, and the Strategic Management Society. 'Manage globally' appears to be the latest battle cry in the world of international business. Ghoshal (1987)

9.1 International business: the context for international strategy

9.1.1 Definition of terms

This interaction of world, country, industry and company is inherently far-reaching and complex – never more evident than in the the global economic crisis that began in 2008. In this section we introduce some of the terminology used in international business so that we can distinguish the concepts that we use from the words and phrases that are used in practice. The approach used here follows that of Rugman and Collinson's (2009) excellent introduction to international business.

International business is the study of transactions taking place across national borders for the purposes of satisfying the needs of individuals and organizations. These transactions consist of trade (called *world trade*), which is exporting and importing, and capital transfers – foreign direct investment. Over half of all world trade and about 80% of all foreign direct investment is carried out by the 500 largest firms in the world. These companies are called *multinational enterprises* (MNEs). Typically they are headquartered in one country but have operations in one or more other countries. In 2007 the MNEs that earned over $120 billion annual revenue were:

Wal-Mart (USA)	BP (UK)
Exxon Mobil (USA)	General Motors (USA)
Royal Dutch/Shell Group (UK/Netherlands)	Toyota (Japan)
ChevronTexaco (USA)	Citigroup (USA)
DaimlerChrysler (Germany)	AXA (France)
Conoco Phillips (USA)	Volkswagen (Germany)
Total (France)	Sinopee (China)
General Electric (USA)	Credit Agricole (France)
Ford (USA)	Allianz (Gemany)
ING Group (Netherlands)	Fortis (Belgium/Nethelands)

Each of these comes from one of three geographic locales: the US, Japan, or the EU. This group is called the *triad*. Of these 20 companies seven are from the US, two from Japan/China, and eleven from the EU. It is interesting to note that compared to the equivalent list in 2000 there are four more companies of this very large size, five of the original list of 16 have dropped out (four Japanese and one American), and there have been nine new entrants (seven from the EU). The North American Free Trade Association (NAFTA) is a regional free trade agreement between Canada, the US and Mexico. NAFTA is often used in place of the US as the North American element of the triad. Also, Asia can be used in place of Japan to reflect the size and growth of markets such as China, India, Indonesia etc. Table 9.1 shows the breakdown of world trade by region. World trade is the sum of all export and imports. In 2005 the EU was the biggest 'trader', accounting for more than 37% of world trade, with Asia over 28% and North America at 17.6%.

Table 9.1 World trade 2000–5

$ bn	Imports 2000	Imports 2005	% Increase	Exports 2000	Exports 2005	% Increase	Trade gap 2000	Trade gap 2005	World trade % 2000	World trade % 2005
North America	1692.8 25.60%	2099.9 20.30%	24.0	1213.6 19.20%	1542.9 14.40%	27.1	−479.2	−557	22.4	17.6
EU	2284.9 34.60%	4000.6 38.70%	75.1	2283.0 35.80%	3796.9 35.40%	66.3	−1.9	−203.7	35.2	37.7
Asia	1563.5 23.70%	2614.8 25.30%	67.2	1742.6 27.40%	3249.7 30.30%	86.5	179.1	634.9	25.5	28.4
Others	1067.5 16.20%	1619.4 15.70%	51.7	1129.5 17.17%	2129.1 19.90%	88.5	62	509.7	16.9	18.1
Total	6608.7 100%	10334.7 100%	56.4	6368.7 100%	10718.6 100%	68.3				

Table 9.2 US: inward and outward FDI 2005		
	Into US $bn	**From US $bn**
Total	1635.3	2070.0
Europe	1143.6	1059.4
Asia and Pacific	252.6	376.8
Latin America	82.5	353.0
Middle East	10.0	21.6
Africa	2.6	24.3

Looking more carefully at the changes in world trade between 2000 and 2005, there are some interesting pointers towards a shift in the balance of economic power across the world. World trade (the sum of exports and imports) has increased by 62%. Everyone has benefited from this but the the smallest gainer by far has been the US with an increase of only about 25%. The biggest winners have been the Asian group who have not only shown huge increases in exports (85%) but a very substantial improvement in their surplus of exports over imports (the trade gap). The EU has shifted into a small trade deficit (about 37% of the American deficit). This is indicative of the shift towards Asia, especially in manufactured goods, and a continuing *relative* decline in US trade performance.

However, it is still the case that in absolute terms the US economy is the biggest in the world by some margin. This is evident from the data in Table 9.2, which shows *foreign direct investment* (FDI). FDI is capital invested in other nations by MNEs through their control of their foreign subsidiaries and affiliates. Most of the world's FDI is invested both by and into the triad. This has implications for the pattern of trade and industrial activity and is a highly controversial issue (see, for example, the discussions at the Cancun meeting of the World Trade Organization about access by underdeveloped regions and countries to the rich markets of the OECD countries). The US is an excellent example of a country that is a major target of investment as well as a major investor in other countries. In 2005 about $1635 billion was invested in the US and the US itself (through its MNEs) invested about $2070 billion in all other countries. Table 9.2 shows a breakdown of US inward and outward FDI by region. This demonstrates how the US is the engine room of the world economy but shows also how the EU is getting closer to the US in size and economic strength.

Trade and investment is subject to various rules and procedures. There are many international or supranational bodies that help to set trading rules and resolve trade disputes. For example:

■ *The Organisation for Economic Co-operation and Development* (OECD) is a group of the 30 wealthiest countries that provides a forum for the discussion of economic, social and governance issues across the world.

■ *The World Trade Organization* (WTO) is an international body that deals with the rules of trade among member countries. One of its most important functions is to act as a dispute-settlement mechanism.

■ *The General Agreement on Tariffs and Trade* (GATT) is major trade organization that has been established to negotiate trade concessions among member countries.

The patterns of trade and investment are highly significant and are reflected in the nature of MNEs. The United Nations has identified over 60,000 MNEs but the largest 500 account for 80% of all

FDI. Of these 500, 430 are from triad countries (interpreted narrowly to mean US, EU and Japan); 185 come from the US, 141 from the EU and 104 from Japan. This means that the triad is a basic unit of analysis for international strategy. It also means that for MNEs the actions and policies of a few key countries are highly important for their corporate strategies. However, most countries are concerned and seek to maintain and foster their own economic competitiveness. As we have seen from Chapter 4, countries have significant incentives to invest in physical infrastructure and in human capital. In doing so they hope to provide conditions under which business and trade can prosper and macro-economic goals such as low employment, low inflation and high growth can be sustained.

9.1.2 'National' competitive advantage

Why are some firms able to innovate consistently while others cannot? Michael Porter (1990) provided an intriguing answer to this question. He undertook a comprehensive study of 100 industries in 10 countries. It is not simply due to the strength of individual corporate strategies. He found that the success of nations and their individual firms is determined by four broad attributes – factor (supply) conditions, demand conditions, related and supporting industries, and market (industry) structure. He called this the *diamond* of national advantage (see Figure 9.1).

First, it is not just factor endowments and **factor conditions** that are an index of competitiveness – these are the typical concerns of government policy. Also on the supply side is the supporting, related industry infrastructure, through which various externalities come into play. Thus, an automobile assembly industry is advantaged by a domestic infrastructure of auto component suppliers, who themselves have sustainable competitive advantages. Similarly, domestic rivalry and intensity of competition are seen to have a direct effect on competitiveness.

Finally, Porter points to demand conditions as a determinant of competitiveness. The size, growth and character of demand shape the supplying industries. The sophistication of local demand will be reflected in the developing characteristics of domestic suppliers. The point to take away from Porter's diamond is that the companies are embedded in and influenced by their industries, and these industries are in turn embedded in a wider economic and social structure. However, it is not clear from this analysis, nor is it asserted in this analysis, that competitive advantage is necessarily determined by the broader economic context. It is possible to see that clusters of firms and clusters of industries might have shared benefits from a common location, at the expense of (in terms

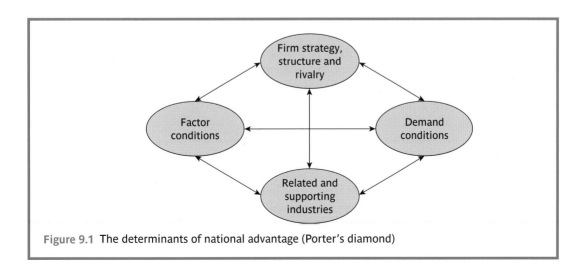

Figure 9.1 The determinants of national advantage (Porter's diamond)

of competitive advantage) firms located elsewhere. Thus, it has been advantageous to be an auto assembler in Japan, a pharmaceutical company in Switzerland and a chemical manufacturer in Germany. It may also be the case that in these circumstances, it might not pay any one local player to attempt to be different[1] from other local players. Strategically, any one firm can choose between shared local benefits ('nationality is destiny') and striving to create a unique and distinctive position.

9.1.3 The internationalization process

From this discussion we can see that the MNE has two areas of concern, its home country and its host country/countries. The linkages across these areas are in the end manifested by the cash flows across country boundaries. These are influenced by home and host government policies and by the actions of supranational bodies in setting trade rules and regulations. Rugman and Collinson (2009, pp. 40–1) identify three main characteristics of MNEs:

1 MNEs have to be responsive to a number of forces across and within countries, some of which are competition related (as per the Five Forces) and some of which are government related (as per the diamond).
2 MNEs draw on a common pool of resources that are typically founded in the home country and which are made available throughout the MNE's affiliates.
3 MNEs link their operations through a common strategic vision and a unified international strategy.

> What is international strategy? According to Hill and Jones (1995):

> *Companies that pursue an international strategy try to create value by transferring valuable skills and products to foreign markets where indigenous competitors lack those skills and products. Most international companies have created value by transferring differentiated product offerings developed at home to new markets overseas. Accordingly they tend to centralise product development functions (for instance, R&D) at home. However, they also tend to establish manufacturing and marketing functions in each major country in which they do business.... Ultimately, in most international companies the head office retains tight control over marketing and product strategy.* (Hill and Jones, 1995, p. 233)

Figure 9.2 illustrates the stages by which companies enter into foreign markets and eventually become full-blown MNEs.

Domestic firms go through a process of learning about foreign markets and minimizing the risks attached to them. Licensing, for example, gives access to the firm's standardized products for distribution by third parties in new markets. Similarly, the process of exporting gains access to markets initially through independent local sales agents. If exports to particular countries become sufficiently large then there is the possibility of setting up one's own sales force. This is an important stage. It marks the arrival of sales in sufficient quantities to gain efficiencies from the fixed costs of own sales activities. It also represents a stage at which direct contact with customers becomes possible, with potential for customization and differentiation. It also results in familiarity at first hand with local conditions and could lead to direct investment in production and marketing and possible other value chain activities. This stage of FDI is what separates an MNE from other domestically rooted companies. At this stage there is a risk investment in a new territory and the MNE has to manifest the three characteristics shown above, namely local responsiveness, distinctive central resources and an overarching strategy.

---

[1] 'Different' in this context meaning different in the strategic sense of different generic strategies or different strategic groups.

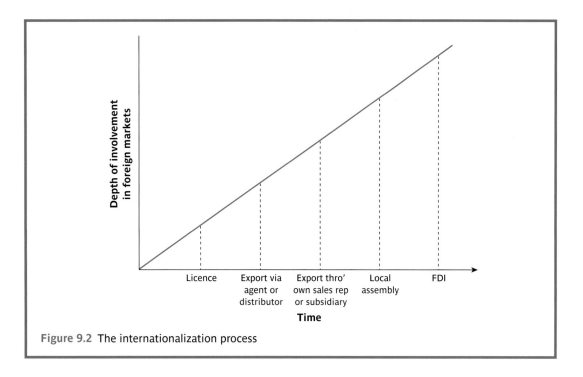

Figure 9.2 The internationalization process

There are many reasons why companies decide to take the plunge and face the new, often unfamiliar risks facing a multinational company. These are usually:

1 to diversify against the risks and uncertainties of the domestic (home country) business cycle;

2 to tap into new and growing markets;

3 to 'follow' competitors;

4 to reduce costs by (i) building larger volumes and gaining scale effects, (ii) gaining access to lower factor costs, and (iii) 'internalizing' control by eliminating middlemen and other transactions costs;

5 to overcome barriers to trade; and

6 to protect intellectual property rights by undertaking value chain activities in-house rather than giving third parties access through licensing and sales agreements.

Case box 9.1 identifies the developing world's most promising multinationals and describes how they are internationalizing so rapidly. Relate the growth of these new multinationals to the internationalization process model shown in Figure 9.2. Assess the ways in which they conform to or deviate from this model. Are they different from the many Japanese firms that came to prominence in the 1960s and the 1970s (e.g. Honda, Komatsu, Sony and NEC)?

Case box 9.1: **Emerging multinationals: they're behind you**

A new report identifies the developing world's most promising multinationals
'We started out abroad as "accidental tourists",' says Anand Mahindra, managing director of Mahindra & Mahindra, an Indian maker of tractors and off-road vehicles. Owed money by a Greek manufacturing plant, it took an equity stake instead, and so Mahindra Hellenic was born in 1984.

Mahindra & Mahindra is now one of 100 companies from the developing world that Boston Consulting Group (BCG) thinks have the clout and ambition to upset the world's multinationals. The consultants sifted over 3,000 companies from 30 countries, picking firms that had revenues approaching or surpassing $1 billion last year and are expanding overseas aggressively (not accidentally). They measure this expansionism by five criteria, including the firms' international sales and assets, and the money they can tap for foreign raids and acquisitions.

The result is a list that cunningly appeals to the pride of the aspirants and the insecurity of rich-world incumbents. According to *Fortune* magazine, Jeff Immelt sent last year's list to his underlings at General Electric, ordering them to identify the companies it could sell to and buy from, and those it would have to compete with.

Like parvenus everywhere, these emerging multinationals often buy their way into the top ranks. Supported by high share valuations, many have rejected organic growth in favour of bold acquisitions. The 100 firms on BCG's list completed about 70 cross-border deals between them in 2006, seven of which were worth more than $1 billion. India's Suzlon Energy, which builds wind farms, bought REpower of Germany in June, for example, thus combining REpower's offshore-turbine technology with its own cheap components. This year, according to Thomson Financial, firms from developing countries have acquired assets in rich countries worth $171 billion, compared with a previous peak of $52 billion in 1999.

Some of these purchases have looked expensive. But, BCG points out, to this new breed of buyers a target company can appear very different from the way it looks to Western or Japanese eyes. A firm burdened with high costs and a declining domestic market may nonetheless have a brand, customers or know-how that emerging multinationals covet. High costs do not deter them. CIMC, a Chinese firm that makes shipping containers, dismantles entire production lines in expensive countries and rebuilds them back home.

The companies on BCG's list have ventured overseas for different reasons. Sixteen of the 41 Chinese companies on the list are owned by an arm of the government dedicated to managing state assets. They break into foreign markets with the state's help and its say-so. Ten companies (half of them from China) have left home in search of natural resources. And another 17 have sought to cash in on the high price of metals and other commodities.

But some companies simply believe they can be the biggest and best in their industries – China's BYD, for example, is the world's largest maker of nickel-cadmium batteries, and India's Reliance Group makes more polyester fibre and yarn than anyone else. Others have brands, nurtured at home, that they think they can milk in foreign markets. Sadia, for example, is a Brazilian frozen-foods company that has become a household name in the Middle East, helped perhaps by its name's similarity to *sa'ada*, the Arabic word for happiness.

How should incumbent multinationals respond? BCG advises them to fight the developing world's multinationals over there, so they do not have to fight them at home. It points out that the aspirants often move upmarket in their own countries as a prelude to expanding abroad. So if the incumbents can woo affluent customers in emerging Asia, Eastern Europe and Latin America, they may be able to slow the emergence of global rivals. They should also consider acquiring the upstarts before they are unseated by them, says BCG. But, the consultants point out, few Western multinationals have a mergers-and-acquisitions team in Delhi or Shanghai that can draw up a shopping list. And up-and-coming firms tend to be pricey.

At least incumbents have no excuse for getting caught on the hop. In addition to BCG's list, Columbia University's Programme on International Investment is carrying out a similar exercise, and released a report on Brazil's multinationals on December 3rd. And the phenomenon of emerging multinationals is not as new as you might think. UNCTAD (the United Nations Conference on Trade and Development) points out that Argentina has been producing multinationals at least since Alpargatas, a textile-maker, set up an affiliate in Uruguay – in 1890.

Source: 'They're Behind You', *The Economist*, 6 December 2007

9.2 Globalization

There is no doubt that globalization and internationalization have, as ideas, inspired our imagination, even though the words themselves are cumbersome and awkward. In this section we intend to give an economic meaning to the term globalization.

9.2.1 Global markets and industries

International trade incorporates many different types of competition, and across industries we can observe marked differences in the patterns of international competition. On the supply side of industries, the dimension of competition and of strategic choice in which we are interested is geographic scope, the extent to which firms' activities extend across national borders. But it is the demand side which is more important. We use the term *multidomestic* (or *multilocal*) to describe industries where the competition in any one country is independent of competition elsewhere. We use the term *global* when competition in one country is influenced by competition elsewhere. Multidomestic is the situation where markets are different in terms of their consumer behaviour patterns. Thus, the market for food can be seen to be very different across the countries of the European Union and even wider across the countries of the world. By contrast, the market for Coca-Cola is broadly similar across the world, with consumers exhibiting similar if not the same utility functions and buying behaviour. Global markets lead to standardized products, whereas multidomestic markets lead to product differences and diversity. Multidomestic industries are, as the name implies, a collection of domestic industries. A global industry leads directly to international rivalry. In a multidomestic industry a firm can and should manage its worldwide activities as a portfolio of independent subsidiaries in each country – this is a country-centred strategy and relatively little coordination is necessary or valuable. In a global industry, to have a global strategy a firm must develop and implement a strategy that integrates its activities in various countries, even though some portion of the firm's activities must take place in each individual country.

Figure 9.3 puts this approach to globalization in a broader context. 'Global' refers broadly speaking to an entwined web of economic forces. The world dimension indicates the extent to which there is economic interdependence between countries, as indicated by the cross-border flows of goods, services, capital and knowledge. At the country level, countries will differ in their degree of

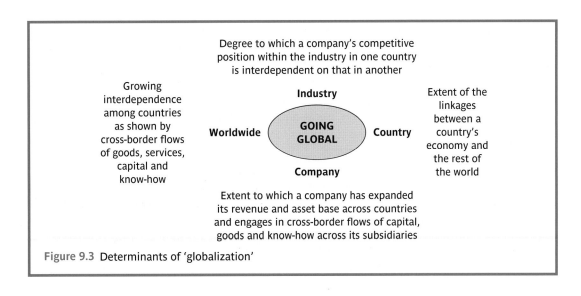

Figure 9.3 Determinants of 'globalization'

Table 9.3 Degree of internationalization of Fortune 100 companies (early 1990s)

- c.40 companies generate >50% of sales abroad
- <20 companies maintain >50% of production capacity abroad
- 13 companies have >10% of shareholdings abroad
- R&D remains firmly domestic
- Executive boards and management styles remain solidly national
- Almost all highly internationalized companies originate from 'small' economies
  - Netherlands: Philips, Royal Dutch/Shell (60% Dutch), Unilever (40% Dutch)
  - Sweden: Volvo, Electrolux, ABB (50% Swedish)
  - Switzerland: Nestlé, Ciba-Geigy, ABB (50% Swiss)

linkage between their economy and the rest of the world, using the same indicators. Our definition of global industry has thus to be seen in the context of the worldwide pattern and the role of individual countries. At the firm level, we are looking at the extent to which its revenue and asset bases are spread across borders.

9.2.2 Global companies

Table 9.3 indicates the degree of internationalization of Fortune 100 companies. Although we have a reasonably clear concept of what constitutes global at the industry level, it is much harder to distinguish a 'global' firm from any other. From Table 9.3 we can see that many firms have a high proportion of sales and production abroad. But there are deeper levels of internationalization. Table 9.3 picks out research and development, management style, and membership of boards of directors as indicators of the extent to which firms can transcend national boundaries.

The nature of globalization is complex and multidimensional, even without bringing in broader issues of culture, behaviour, national tastes and so on. Accordingly, there have been many attempts to capture the term in a single definition. The original proponent of globalization was Theodore Levitt (1983), whose concept was that of *global standardization* – a single global market with standard products and a corporate focus on gaining efficiencies through standardization. Kenichi Ohmae (1985) introduced the idea of the 'triad' – to compete effectively, firms should be present in each of the three major regions of the world. This has become known as *global localization*. Wisse Dekker, a former Chairman of Philips, saw globalization as *assembly abroad* to *circumvent competition*. More recent commentators see *global niches* sitting alongside defensive domestic positions. Toyota in its Annual Report in 1995 said:

> Our global strategy used to centre on 'world cars' which we would modify slightly to accommodate demand in different markets. Today our focus is shifting to models that we develop and manufacture for selected regional markets.

We seem to be moving from a market-based focus on standardization (standard products and centralized production facilities) to a firm-level resource-based view of standardization. This would argue for a common approach to knowledge and learning, and resources and capabilities across the world, but with products adapted to local or regional needs from a common core competence.

Table 9.4 highlights what might be the deeper drivers. There are five forces at work. The first is a *cultural homogenization* – a 'global village' argument that recognizes similar needs and requirements

---

Table 9.4 Why globalization?

- Cultural homogenization ('global village')
- Convergence of markets
- Globalization of customers
- Cost drivers
  - economies of scale and scope
  - increase in levels of fixed cost
- Fundamental changes in industry structure
  - deregulation, privatization
  - technological change

---

across different cultures. Two of the forces are from the demand side, *convergence of markets* and *growing similarity of customers*. Markets in this context are about the infrastructure and the processes by which markets work. This covers legislation, application of competition law, organization of selling and distribution systems, consumer protection laws, local tariffs and so on. The markets for agricultural products are vastly different between Russia and the United States. The markets for packaged groceries are different between European countries, to the extent that the laws governing price promotions and use of television advertising are different and the extent to which superstores are allowed to develop as between France and Italy, for example. One of the aims of the Single Market Acts in the EC in 1992 was to create broadly similar market conditions across Western Europe – the 'level playing field'.

The customer argument is more plainly about the degree of similarity between the utility functions of customers in different locations and the impact this has on buying behaviour. This can be exemplified by considering two buyers of auto components, one for Ford Motor Company's plants in Europe, the other for General Motors. Their buying criteria are likely to be very similar and component companies are very likely to be designing and selling very similar components across Europe. It is less clear that Italian and English shoppers in supermarkets will have the same attitudes and ideas about buying food products. To the extent that these buyers are fundamentally different in their behaviour, the suppliers will be adapting their products to reflect different requirements in Italy and in England.

On the supply side of industries, the cost drivers are very important. We learned in Chapter 3 of the significance of economies of scale and experience. The costs of investment can be so high that single national markets, even those of the US, might be too small to support them. It is difficult to see how the design and development costs of large aeroplanes can be economically supported from even the US. The development costs of automobiles, prescription drugs, many high-technology new products and much military hardware require a large international market. It is in the interests of companies to make the offer of a standardized product across the world in competition with the more locally differentiated, but more expensive, options offered by local companies. From a cost point of view, the presence of significant scale and experience effects drives customers towards the cheaper, more standardized options. This is the basis of Levitt's approach to global standardization.

Finally, fundamental changes in industry structure can result in major changes to the underlying economics of industries (for example, through technological change). Coupled with new management teams (for example, through privatization and deregulation) this can change the terms on which companies approach their marketplaces and their opportunities to move across borders. For example, the worldwide trend towards privatization of telecommunications and utility companies has challenged the presumption that the natural market for utilities is domestic only.

Scale is commonly considered to be a major characteristic of being global. But there are other benefits:

■ exposure to the world's 'best' practice;
■ learning and transfer of opportunities for best practice;
■ access to technology;
■ ability to serve new customer groups;
■ ability to anticipate moves of global competitors;
■ ability to defend national profit sanctuaries through counter-attack.

In looking at global industries and the firms that compete in them, you should be able to examine and test the proposition that industries do not go global by accident. They are global because of innovations in strategy. Global strategies can create advantage only if they:

■ change the economics of the industry;
■ serve local markets better than the local incumbents;
■ are hard to emulate;
■ are sustainable;
■ are capable of further development.

As you gain experience in operating within a global industry, some of the original strategic innovations become embedded into the industry structure and thus, the industry economics will have characteristics like large-scale economies – high and rising R&D costs, extensive interaction with governments, and links with changes in country infrastructures. But there are still many strategy choices open to each firm: for example, how to increase local content without sacrificing global scale, how to increase product homogeneity through design, how to shape demand, how to develop systems to make coordination easier. Some firms will be striving to develop local/domestic niches, others will be focusing on global segments, and still others might be attempting global standardization.

9.2.3 Globalization and the value chain

The key strategic choices in globalization revolve around local differentiation versus global standardization. These might be seen as polar opposites, but more usually the question is how to secure the right blend between the two. What would this mean for how we should conduct our business?

Figure 9.4 enables us to think of the implications of global choices in terms of how we manage the activities in the value chain, where we locate them, and how we coordinate the whole chain. The opportunity for global standardization occurs when:

■ Upstream value chain activities can be decoupled from downstream activities and, in particular, from buyer locations.
■ These activities are a large part of total costs.
■ Scale effects are important in these activities.

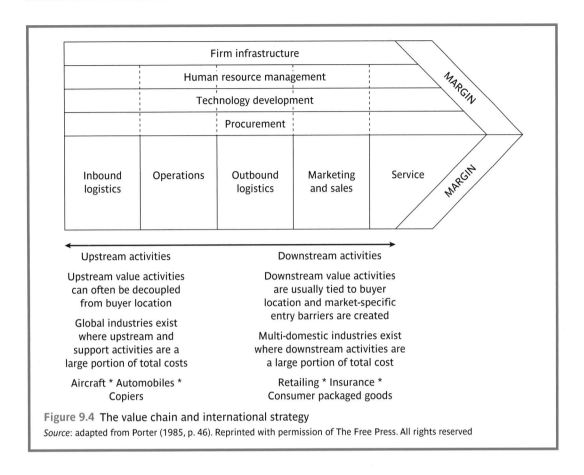

Figure 9.4 The value chain and international strategy
Source: adapted from Porter (1985, p. 46). Reprinted with permission of The Free Press. All rights reserved

We see that these conditions exist in the automobile industry. Production does not need to be close to the customer, nor even to the sales channel. Assembly is a very large part of the cost and there are very big scale economies. Conversely, multidomestic industries exist where:

- Downstream activities are tied to buyer locations and market-specific entry barriers can be created.
- These activities are a large part of total costs.

These are situations where the competitive advantages reside primarily in the downstream activities, and the focus of strategic attention lies with managing its capacity to differentiate the product offering. This is typical of retailing, many service operations like investment banking and consumer packaged goods.

The possibility for gaining globalization advantages usually means that the value chain has to be partitioned in some way. The key strategic dimensions of choice are:

- where to perform each activity in the value chain – the *configuration* question;
- how to link similar activities wherever they are located;
- how to coordinate all the activities in the value chain – the *coordination* question.

The degree of coordination is largely dependent on how globally standardized the product is, or conversely how varied the local market conditions are. Table 9.5 summarizes the kinds of high and

Table 9.5 Coordination across international markets

Reasons for high coordination	Reasons for low coordination
Share know-how and learning	Respond to diverse local conditions
Reinforce brand reputation	– product needs
Supply identical differentiation worldwide	– marketing systems
Differentiate to local buyers by meeting their needs anywhere	– business practices
	– raw material sources
Seek bargaining counters with governments	– infrastructure
Respond to competitors' flexibility	Circumvent government restrictions on flow of goods or information
	Avoid high coordination costs
	Acknowledge organizational difficulties of achieving coordination across subsidiaries

low coordination patterns that might be observed. The contrast between high and low degrees of coordination stems from the balance between the two types of competitive pressure that are evident in global markets: pressures for cost reductions and efficiency, and pressures for local responsiveness. Typically, local differentiation requires low coordination, as each country operation contains much of the value chain that it needs, and those inputs it may require, such as components, will be relatively standardized. Pressures for global efficiency usually mean that there is product standardization and close integration of production and service delivery across all the value chain activities, which themselves will have been located in the lowest cost regions/countries.

For multinational companies, the tension between the pressures for efficiency and for local responsiveness is a constant concern. In essence, the efficiency dimension focuses on pressures for global coordination and integration. This argues that cost and efficiency pressures, together with product standardization, produce simple standardization while taking account of the variety and diversity that takes place at the margin itself. On the other hand, the pressures for national or local responsiveness recognize a wide range of differentiating forces. These include differences in consumer tastes and preferences, differences in local infrastructures and traditional practices, differences in distribution channels and other forms of access to markets, and host government demands.

Digital media and globalization have not heralded an inevitable decline in the paper industry. But they have provoked major shifts in the structure of the industry and the strategy of its biggest players. From Case box 9.2, identify and assess the major changes that have taken place – use the concepts from Chapter 7 to show how new technologies and globalization often go hand-in-hand.

Case box 9.2: **Flat prospects: pulp and paper**

Digital media and globalisation shake up an old industry
Reports of the death of paper, rampant in the 1990s, were evidently greatly exaggerated. The paperless office never materialised; nor, yet, have e-books. People still print letters and flip through pages of magazines. They also eat cereal and drink milk from cartons, and wipe their bottoms with loo roll. Computers have, oddly, failed to do away with such habits.

Even so, the vast pulp-and-paper multinationals have been hard hit by the electronic age, especially in America. Demand for many types of paper there is declining, though mill closures and shrinking capacity buoy prices. Newsprint has been worst hit, as circulation and classified advertising at newspapers fall and the *Wall Street Journal* and other papers grow skinnier. North America's two biggest newsprint-makers, Abitibi of Canada and Bowater of South Carolina, are merging.

'The only grade of paper immune to technological substitution is tissue,' such as bathroom or facial tissue, says Steve Chercover, an analyst at D.A. Davidson. This week SCA, a Swedish firm, announced plans to buy Procter & Gamble's European tissue business (including the Bounty brand) for €512m ($676m), citing growth prospects of 3–4% annually.

Restructuring in the paper industry is proceeding at a furious pace. The first thing some paper companies have jettisoned is ownership of forests. International Paper (IP), one of the world's biggest pulp-and-paper companies which is based in Tennessee, used to be the largest private landowner in America. A year ago the company sold 5.7m acres, or 90%, of its forestland – an area larger than Massachusetts. The $6.6 billion sale was 'probably the hardest decision that I've had to make since I became CEO,' says John Faraci, IP's boss since 2003. Most buyers were financial investors, but 5% of the land went to conservation groups.

IP is shedding entire businesses, as well as land. Gone are the company's interests in lumber and plywood (for home-building); juice and milk cartons; brown-paper grocery bags; and even magazine paper. Last month the company finished selling its North American drinks-packaging business to a New Zealand company. The company's focus is now on uncoated white paper (where growth is flat to negative in North America) and packaging.

Many other paper giants are slimming down too. Weyerhaeuser, an American lumber company in the middle of its own overhaul, just merged its 'fine paper' division (ie, white and copy paper) with a Canadian rival. Smurfit-Stone, an American packaging giant, sold its consumer-goods-packaging business (milk cartons and the like) to focus on containerboard, which goes into large boxes for shipping, and corrugated containers.

As they thrash about for new direction, pulp-and-paper giants in America and Europe must also deal with the forces of globalisation. Cheap imports from South America, Russia and China are starting to arrive. Brazil, where production is dominated by plantations of fast-growing eucalyptus trees, is the cheapest place to make paper, says Edings Thibault of Morgan Stanley. China has recently gone from a net importer to a net exporter of newsprint. (Rising global competition may help persuade antitrust authorities to approve the new wave of North American mergers, notes Mr Chercover.)

At the same time, emerging economies also represent new markets that are not as hooked on e-mail as the developed world is. At IP, Mr Faraci has his eye on Russia for production, as well as on China and Brazil. Last year IP announced a joint venture with Russia's largest forest-products company. It has also become the partner of a huge Chinese firm and did a land-swap in Brazil that 'essentially doubled the size of our paper business' there, says Mr Faraci. For the moment, then, emerging markets offer hope. But BlackBerrys and Dells will not keep a low profile in Brazil forever.

Source: 'Flat Prospects', *The Economist*, 17 March 2007

9.2.4 Sources of competitive advantage

As we have seen in Chapter 8, corporate strategy is about exploiting economies of scope across the business units of the corporation. **Global strategy** requires the exploitation of economies of scale, scope, knowledge and learning across national boundaries. Ghoshal (1987) provides an excellent framework (Table 9.6) for understanding the sources of advantage that can spring from 'globalization' and the strategic objectives that can be pursued. As Segal-Horn puts it:

Table 9.6 Global strategy: sources of competitive advantage

Strategic objectives	National differences	Scale economies	Scope economies
Achieving efficiency in current operations	Benefiting from differences in factor costs – wages and cost of capital	Expanding and exploiting potential scale economies in each activity	Sharing of investments and costs across products and businesses
Managing risks	Managing different kinds of risks arising from market policy-induced changes in comparative advantages of different countries	Balancing scale with strategic and operational flexibility	Portfolio diversification and risks and of options and side bets
Innovation, learning and adaptation	Learning from societal differences in organizational and managerial processes and systems	Benefiting from experience-based cost reduction and innovation	Shared across organizational components in different markets or businesses

Source: Ghoshal (1987)

Ghoshal creates a roadmap to guide managers of multinational companies through their choices for global strategic management. (Segal-Horn, 1998, p. 325)

Ghoshal refers to this framework as a mapping of means and ends. The means are the sources of advantage and the ends are the strategic objectives. The goals are an elegant articulation of three contrasting but complementary themes:

1 *Achieving efficiency* is the dominant perspective in strategic management, where the objective is to maximize the value of the ratio between outputs and inputs. The basic strategies of cost leadership and differentiation are both maximizers in this sense, cost strategies reducing the value of inputs and differentiation strategies increasing the exchange value of the outputs.

2 The notion of *managing risks* gets far too little attention in the academic and in the business literatures. Ghoshal identifies several different categories of risk:

– macroeconomic risks,

– political or policy risks,

– competitive risks, and

– resource risks.

3 *Innovation, learning and adaptation* are an outcome of resource-based thinking. Here Ghoshal makes an interesting argument that increasing geographic scope ('globalization') is in effect an exposure to diversity and variety. The twin pressures of managing for efficiency and for local variety impose a greater need to innovate, to learn and to adapt than is faced by a purely domestic firm.

Ghoshal maintains there are three fundamental tools for building global competitive advantage:

- The first is to exploit the differences in input and output markets in different countries. This is to exploit *comparative advantage* – the economic characteristics that make national economies different.

- The second is to achieve *economies of scale.*

- The third is to exploit *economies of scope.*

The term *national differences* refers to what economists call factor conditions or differences in factor costs between different countries. According to international trade theory, a country will export those goods that make use of the factor conditions with which it is relatively well endowed. Thus a country like China is concentrating on modern assembly plants in which the low cost of Chinese labour plays a significant role in reducing costs. MNEs seek to locate their activities in regions with specific factor advantages. For example, BT along with many UK-based banks are relocating their call centres to India to take advantage of a relatively low-cost but skilful labour force. Rugman and Collinson (2009, p. 19) cite the example of the Netherlands as the world's leading exporter of flowers. It has maintained its position by creating research institutes in the cultivation, packaging and shipping of flowers. Therefore any company wishing to compete in this industry has to have an operation in the Netherlands. Similarly in Formula 1 Racing the central cluster of activity is to be found in Motor Sport Valley in the South of England. Here are to be found skilled labour and craftsmen in engineering, advanced materials, software, and project management. For Ferrari to become successful again in F1 Racing it had to gain access to these skills by first establishing an operation in England and then finding ways to transfer this knowledge throughout their Italian home base.

From this framework Ghoshal is able to articulate the nature of the trade-offs between alternative strategy choices. In other words, the framework is not deterministic, but it does enable the consistencies and contradictions among different moves to be evaluated.

In the next section we will revisit some of the basic concepts that lie behind globalization and will return to Ghoshal's organizing framework at the end of the chapter. But before we move on, it is helpful to read Segal-Horn's (1993) interesting paper on the internationalization of service industries. Service industries have traditionally been seen as domestic or local, but there have been many celebrated attempts to go global, some of which have been seen to fail (for example, Saatchi & Saatchi) and some of which are clearly successes (for example, American Express). Segal-Horn's contribution is to take Chandler's logic of internationalization (and also Ghoshal's later framework – above) as developed for manufacturing firms and show how the basic assumptions are now relevant for service organizations. Thus, we see that scale and scope economies – the roots of strategy analysis – are as relevant for service firms as for any others. With service firms, it is clear that the source of scope economies is rooted for the most part in the way in which knowledge and information can create scope benefits. It is worth noting also that the service element of hitherto traditional manufacturing has increased dramatically and that the role of services in the advanced economies now outweighs that of manufacturing (Quinn, 1992). Thus the consequences of Segal-Horn's approach are significant both in terms of the economy as a whole and for the nature of internationalization as a knowledge-based phenomenon.

In Case box 9.3 the authors argue that the conventional assumption of globalization is misplaced. You should also look again at Table 9.3 which uses the same data sources. Ask yourself: what is the criterion you would use to assess whether a company is 'global'? Ask also what difference this makes to the strategies that companies should follow and the relationships that they should cultivate with their home governments and with their many host governments.

Case box 9.3: **US multinationals are regional not global**

Karl Moore and Alan Rugman argue that globalization is not what it seems
'Go global.' That's what CEOs have been hearing from gurus and academics for a while now. But how global are the US' biggest MNEs? We argue not very global at all. Each year *Fortune* magazine ranks the world's largest MNEs in its annual *Fortune 500*. The US accounts for 185 of the companies: the EU has 141 and Japan 104. Together this 'triad' has 430 of the top 500 companies.

But, if you examine the data on the US' 25 largest multinationals it becomes clear that they are what we would call home-region based. Of the US' 25 largest MNEs 22 have more than 50% of their sales in their home region of North America. None of these US MNEs are 'global'. For example, Wal-Mart has 94.1% of its sales in the North American Free Trade Area (NAFTA); GM has 81% – and so on. Indeed, the average intra-regional sales figure for all the 185 US MNEs is 77.3%. With well over two-thirds of their sales in North America, these are home-based triad MNEs – so much for the globe-girdling US MNE.

Only IBM, ranked at number seven, is a truly 'global' firm, with over 20% of its sales in each region of the triad. Other US global firms (not in the top 25) are Intel and Coca-Cola. Indeed, only eight of the *Fortune 500* firms in the world are global – the others are Sony, Philips, Canon, Flextronics, and LVMH.

'So what?' the hard-nosed CEO may ask. Good question: what this data tells us is that US companies should focus corporate energies and push government policies to secure access to the vital regional NAFTA market. At the same time US companies should continue to increase their involvement in the two other regions of the triad economies, the EU and the small number of critical Asian economies. That is the reality of to-day's global economy.

Source: Extract from Karl Moore and Alan Rugman (2003) *Business Strategy Review*, vol 14, no. 4, p.2. Reproduced with permission of Blackwell Publishing.

9.3 Strategic choices

9.3.1 Strategic positioning

There are four basic strategies that companies use to enter and compete in the international environment. Bartlett and Ghoshal's well-known work (1989) depicts these in Figure 9.5.

Multidomestic strategies are, as we described above, country-centred with extensive customization for local markets and with an almost full set of value chain activities in each major market. They do transfer skills and products developed at the home base, but high degrees of local discretion are given to meet local conditions. Typically, these strategies cannot realize value from centralized, scale-effective, experience-rich production facilities. Bartlett and Ghoshal describe multidomestic companies as decentralized federations (Figure 9.5) and regard them as typically European, being conceived in days of higher transport and communication costs and higher tariffs.

International strategies create value by transferring key skills, capabilities and products to local markets. The degree of differentiation developed in the home base is advanced and the intent is that the differentiation delivered in each local market reflects this. Thus, local differentiation is complementary to that from the centre. However, the organization is usually country-centred and local managers have important degrees of discretion in deciding what product portfolio to offer and how it should be presented locally. Product development and R&D tends to be centralized in the home base, but other value chain activities are usually closer to market. Head office retains close control over marketing strategy and product strategy, and also exercises close financial control. Bartlett and Ghoshal regard this as typically North American – born in the 1950s and 1960s, as US companies began to realize the benefits of the scale and technological achievement of 50 years of

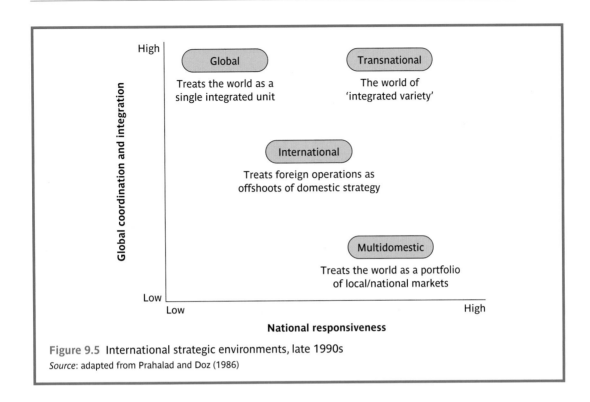

Figure 9.5 International strategic environments, late 1990s

Source: adapted from Prahalad and Doz (1986)

distinctively large, progressive markets. They see this form as a coordinated federation, the degrees of coordination (especially in marketing and finance) being distinctive American contributions to management practice in the post-war years. Many writers are tempted to place international strategies into the bottom left corner of Figure 9.5. This would be to deny the distinctive coordinating power of these companies (for example, Procter & Gamble, IBM, Kellogg, McDonald's, Merck). Moreover, with low coordination and low responsiveness, there would not appear to be a sustainable strategy.

Global strategies focus on increasing profitability through product standardization, and capturing the cost reductions that come from location economies (exploiting comparative advantage in Ghoshal's framework in Table 9.6), economies of scale and experience effects, and the organizational focus on procedures and processes that support low costs. Bartlett and Ghoshal see these strategies as quintessentially Japanese, having emerged in the growth years and tariff reduction years of the 1970s and 1980s. These companies are typically highly centralized, with little attempt to build local differentiation (marketing) activity. They do, however, often pursue global branding and 'quality' positioning, along with or after their initial focus on low cost (for example, Sony). Toyota was a good example of a global strategy in the 1980s – its productivity (cars per employee) was about 37 compared to 20 at Ford, which would be regarded as having an international strategy. Many industries can be seen to be global in character. Thus, the semiconductor industry has global standards with enormous worldwide demands for standardized products. Not surprisingly, the players such as Intel, Texas Instruments and Motorola pursue global strategies. Bartlett and Ghoshal describe global companies as centralized hubs, reflecting the high degree of centralization.

Transnational strategies:

Exploit experience-based cost economies and location economies, transfer distinctive competences within the company, and at the same time pay attention to pressures for local responsiveness. (Bartlett and Ghoshal, 1989)

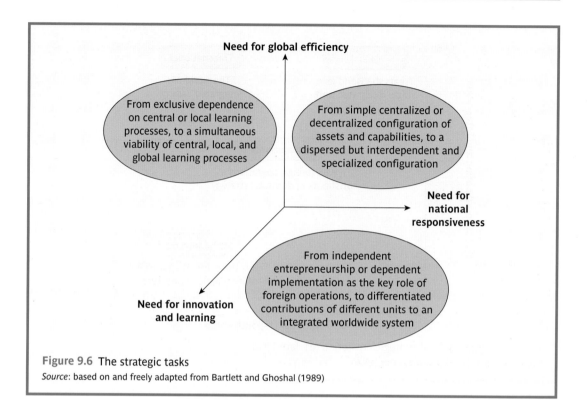

Figure 9.6 The strategic tasks
Source: based on and freely adapted from Bartlett and Ghoshal (1989)

Bartlett and Ghoshal argue that the two dimensions of Figure 9.5 are an incomplete description of the strategic choices. They offer a resource-based addition, suggesting that the need for innovation and learning should be a third dimension (Figure 9.6). With this focus on capabilities, competences (Prahalad and Hamel (1990) language) and strategic assets (Amit and Schoemaker (1993) language), they argue that these characteristics do not simply reside in the home base. On the contrary, by careful investment, they can be developed anywhere appropriate in the company's worldwide operations. This is a locational economy (or comparative advantage), where the advantage is in the form of knowledge and capability, rather than low cost. So the flows of skills and products can be in any direction within the worldwide configuration of activities.

The role of the centre is to provide an organizational and strategic context within which the complex flows and interactions can take place. Toyota is a good example, as are other Japanese auto manufacturers, such as Nissan and Honda. We saw earlier that Toyota has moved from a focus on the 'world car' to something more regional. This initially involved the development of manufacturing capabilities and sites in North America, Europe and elsewhere in the world. Along with this goes a spreading of product development beyond Japan.

Unilever is another example. Once it was a classic multidomestic company in the European tradition. It has moved from 17 different and largely self-contained detergents operations in Europe toward a single European entity with detergents being manufactured in a handful of cost-efficient plants, and with standard packaging and advertising across Europe. Unilever's estimate of the cost savings is over $200 million per year. However, Unilever recognizes that there are major differences in distribution channels and that brand values and brand awareness vary a lot across Europe, and therefore, that local responsiveness must not be sacrificed for simple standardization benefits. In other words, Unilever intends to move from multidomestic to transnational. By contrast, Procter & Gamble have seemingly moved more in the direction of a global strategy from an international

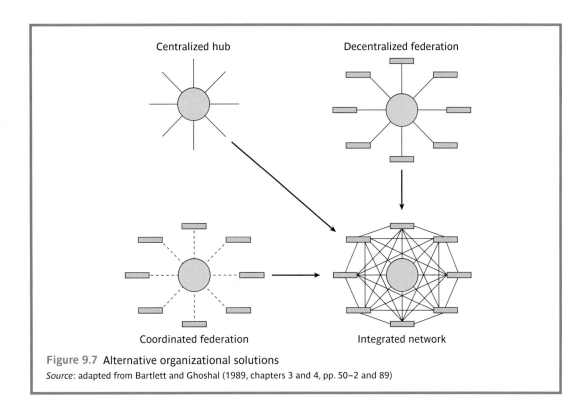

Figure 9.7 Alternative organizational solutions
Source: adapted from Bartlett and Ghoshal (1989, chapters 3 and 4, pp. 50–2 and 89)

position. Bartlett and Ghoshal maintain that the transnational company must have a network organization (Figure 9.7).

Strategic choice involves making trade-offs. It is not always clear what strategies should be followed, because it is rare that one choice will dominate all other possibilities. The advantage of a pure global strategy is the ability to become a low-cost player, but the disadvantage is the lack of local responsiveness (see the Matsushita example in Bartlett and Ghoshal, 1989). The multidomestic has the opposite trade-off. It is able to differentiate to local markets and respond to local conditions, but it cannot manage itself into a distinctive low-cost position. The international company is able to transfer distinctive competences to new markets, but it can be caught between the inability to differentiate enough locally or to be sufficiently low cost. It could be a case of 'stuck-in-the-middle' – this seems to be Procter & Gamble's own diagnosis. The transnational appears to solve all of these conventional trade-offs, but it clearly has major difficulties of implementation, because the network organization is so fundamentally different from more traditional 'command and control' organizations.

9.3.2 Country issues

The double diamond

The balancing of efficiency, responsiveness and innovation is in a sense an elaboration of Porter's classic generic strategies (cost, differentiation and focus), bringing in the dynamics of innovation to his essentially static model. Porter's later model (1990) on the diamond of national advantage and its implications for companies can also be elaborated in this context. According to the diamond model, the MNE takes sustenance from its home markets and these provide the strategic asset base from which advantage can be gained.

First, here is a reminder of the four key variables in the diamond: factor conditions; demand conditions; related and supporting industries; market structure and rivalry. A first elaboration of the diamond introduces two other variables.

1 *The role of chance and uncertainty*. Unforeseen developments are paradoxically normal, namely new knowledge and inventions, interventions of foreign governments, wars and insurrections, financial market crises, discontinuities in costs such as oil shocks, surges in demand, emergence of new competitors or new types of competition. The longer the time scale of strategic thinking the more likely there will be unforeseen events (see Chapter 11 for the discussion on scenario planning that aims to deal directly with these problems).

2 *The role of (home country) government*. Government's task is to influence all four of the major determinants of national advantage summarized in the diamond through actions such as subsidies, education and training policies, regulation of markets, particularly financial markets, establishment of standards, its purchasing policy, tax laws, anti-trust and policies towards competition.

Critique of the diamond

Figure 9.8 illustrates the diamond with these extra variables. Rugman and D'Cruz (1993) have provided a comprehensive critique of Porter's diamond.

Firstly, they observe that the data on which the diamond is based contains only triad-based countries and therefore refers only to firms with strong home bases. MNEs in non-triad countries would not expect such a supportive home base and these must therefore look elsewhere for strategic assets.

Secondly, government is a crucial player but not all governments even in triad regions follow identical policies. Mistakes are possible that might, for example, result in the creation of sheltered domestic industries that cannot compete in international markets. Policy fashions might also result in misdirected investments intended to create national flagships.

Thirdly, the diamond is uncomfortably positioned between the determinism of governments and the discretion of companies. In the end it is companies that make the strategic investments

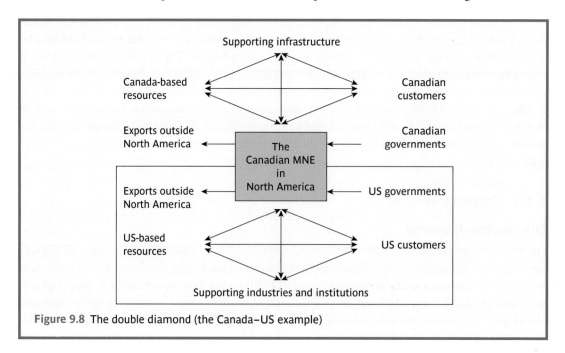

Figure 9.8 The double diamond (the Canada–US example)

and these may often be at odds with the prevailing national orthodoxy. See, for example, the rise of Honda in spite of Japan's MITI (Ministry of International Trade Investment) officially disapproving of its international ambitions.

Fourthly, behind Porter's model is an assumption of a life cycle of evolution of national development. This proceeds in linear fashion through factor driven (e.g. China currently), to investment driven (such as Korea's support of its *chaebol*), to innovation driven (such as Japan), and eventually wealth driven (such as the UK – this is Porter's rather unlikely example). Over a short period of, say, a decade this may have some merit. But over a longer period it is plainly unsatisfactory by leaving no prospect for fundamental reappraisals of national policy. Since the stage of development greatly influences the way in which a company responds, the placement of a country in the cycle is clearly critical.

Fifth, the model is peculiar in crediting only outbound FDI as a source of change and profits. But surely inbound FDI has the same effects and thus the home country's position in the cycle can be changed. The McKinsey study of the world automobile industry (McKinsey & Co., 1993) is explicit in its recognition of the way in which Japanese FDI into the US had a significant impact on Detroit.

Sixth, Porter implicitly states that factor-driven strategies will not promote international competitive advantage for MNEs from such countries. However, Canadian researchers have been quick to criticize this (Safarian, 1968; Rugman and D'Cruz, 1993; Crookell, 1990), observing many Canadian counter-examples. In addition, the growth of Asian MNEs suggests (although the evidence is not yet conclusive) that Korean and Chinese and maybe Indian MNEs will soon be as large and as strategically well founded as their triad counterparts.

Finally, the model does not adequately address the role of the multinational in creating a distinctive position for itself. Dunning has observed:

> there is ample evidence to suggest that MNEs are influenced in their competitiveness by the configuration of the diamond in other than their home countries, and that this in turn may impinge upon the competitiveness of home countries. (Dunning, 1993, p. 11)

For example, Nestlé earns the vast bulk of its revenues outside its home base (Switzerland), as also do virtually all Canada's multinationals. Nearly every country outside the main triad regions and the big industrial countries within these regions has a small home diamond whereupon its MNEs overcome this problem by gaining access elsewhere. Rugman and Collinson conclude (2009, p. 423):

> . . . different diamonds need to be constructed and analysed for different countries.

These criticisms of the original diamond model can be captured under two broad headings. First, there is the neglect of government as a major driving force. Essentially government actions create externalities that can give MNEs (or local firms) firm-specific advantages (FSAs) in terms of location decisions and the emergence and sustenance of regional clusters of economic activity. Second, the diamond has quite different implications for the big as opposed to the small MNEs. The larger the MNE the more capability it has to take advantage of market imperfections, especially government-induced externalities. The MNEs from small home bases gain less advantage from their home locations and are impelled to seek advantages elsewhere. It is the combination of these effects that has led to the formulation of the *double diamond*. The value of this is that it gives a more realistic basis for analysing the international competitiveness of smaller MNEs. But it also captures the complex interactions (and rivalry) between the policies of governments. Figure 9.8 shows the basic figure.

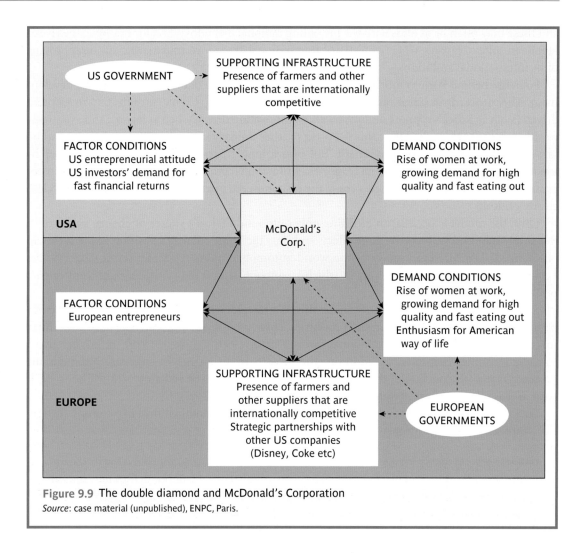

Figure 9.9 The double diamond and McDonald's Corporation
Source: case material (unpublished), ENPC, Paris.

In the double diamond the MNE is at the centre of the diamond but is focused on (at least) two 'home' bases. From each it gains resources and factor characteristics. From each it benefits from the nature of demand conditions. Also, from each it is sustained by the supporting infrastructure. However, it gains by taking a highest common factor approach, that is, it takes advantage of the best infrastructure, it locates in the lowest-cost region, it learns from the most advanced customers and so on. Rugman and D'Cruz (1993, p. 32) use the example of Canadian businesses within the North American Free Trade Area (NAFTA). Thus, Canadian plants gained economies of scale by producing for the North American market as a whole. They argue that the result of North American economic integration has been the development of a Canadian–US double diamond that shows that for strategy purposes in the Canadian companies the two countries have become integrated. This suggests that the double diamond results from government policies, in this case the creation of NAFTA. However, companies themselves can take the initiative. We saw earlier that the emergence of the transnational is a deliberate attempt to be both centralized and localized and the double diamond is a facet of this. Figure 9.9 illustrates a double diamond for McDonald's taking the US and Europe as the two 'home' countries. We can see that any moves from the security and sanctuary of a single home base will involve the MNE in a multiple set of close interactions with its markets. For the MNE from smaller home countries this enables an entry into a larger game (see, for example, the power of Nestlé from its small Swiss base, the restored power of Philips from its Dutch home, and the growth of ABB from its Swedish-Swiss base). But multiple homes are not just the prerogative of the 'small' MNE. We see that companies like Toyota and McDonald's deliberately took the transnational line and effectively work in the context of double/multiple diamonds.

9.3.3 The competitive advantage matrix: CSAs and FSAs

Firm-specific advantage (FSA) is a term used in the international business literature to describe the unique capabilities of an organization and is identical to the concept of *core competence* that we discussed in Chapter 6. **Country-specific advantage** (CSA) arises from the discussion above of the diamond, the double diamond, and the impact of the home base(s) on the MNE. These can be interrelated to produce a competitive advantage matrix (Figure 9.10) that provides a useful framework for discussion.

Quadrant 1 firms rely on strong CSAs and are usually in mature markets that are globally oriented, commodity in style and marked by price competition. Typical CSAs would be low factor costs and low energy costs. Cost leadership would be the desired strategy. Firms in quadrant 2 display no advantages, would typically be inefficient in scale and would be candidates for exit, restructuring and/or absorption. Firms in quadrant 4 are generally differentiated firms with strengths in marketing, product development and customization. Their home base is largely irrelevant and these firms are very self-sufficient. Firms in quadrant 3 can benefit from both low cost and differentiation, with major contributions from the factor costs and supporting infrastructure of the home base.

From quadrant 4 a firm can have ambitions to develop FSAs that will take it into quadrant 3 with an even stronger position. However, firms in quadrant 4 are faced with exogenous CSAs and cannot in general expect to develop new CSAs unless they deliberately undertake to shift location or adopt a double diamond approach. Note, however, that firms may not be homogeneous in their portfolios: individual businesses may be in different quadrants and require different strategic approaches. This raises the questions posed in Chapter 8 about the nature of the portfolio and the dangers of excessive diversification. It is also worth noting that changes in the trading environment can and do affect the CSAs. The foundation of trading areas like NAFTA has affected the positioning

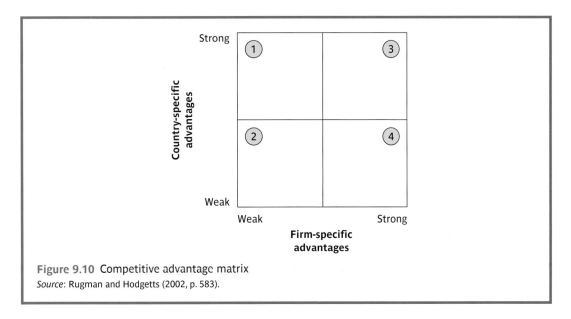

Figure 9.10 Competitive advantage matrix
Source: Rugman and Hodgetts (2002, p. 583).

of Canadian companies (some companies moving from 2 to 1, and better still, some moving from 4 to 3). Similarly, the thinking behind European integration and the creation of the single market in 1992 was to create the conditions under which European-based MNEs might compete more effectively by enjoying stronger CSAs.

9.3.4 The flagship model

Much of the above discussion and indeed discussions within governments has been about the way government policy can affect the success of companies. But the theme of this course is more on the ability of companies to construct their own destiny and not have to be mere respondents to market and institutional change. In international business this has been evident in the ways by which successful MNEs have business networks and relationships that have the effect of creating a favourable context without being dependent on the policy whims of others. The main theme in this is the replacement of the traditional adversarial supply chain structure with cooperative supply networks. This stems from the success of Japanese companies in the 60s and 70s and in particular the Toyota production system. The Japanese recognized that creating additional value by creating close relationships with buyers/suppliers can add more to profitability than simple value extraction strategies (exemplified in the traditional explanation of the Five Forces). These strong cooperative relationships typically require sharing information on costs and manufacturing processes and the coordination of logistics to minimize inventories and waiting times. These characteristics are evident in the successful working of alliances (recall Chapter 8). The implication of this is that there must be a clear recognition of how such coordination takes place. In the world of value extraction this is a simple exercise in economic power. But in the world of value creation there must still be an orchestration of events by the most powerful or influential firms. This is described by Rugman and D'Cruz (2000) as the *flagship model* and is depicted in Figure 9.11.

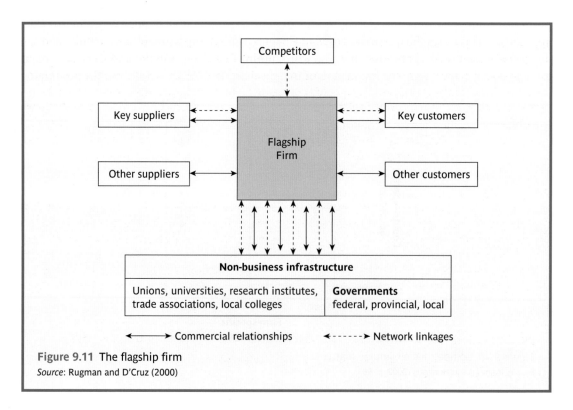

Figure 9.11 The flagship firm
Source: Rugman and D'Cruz (2000)

This is derived from a diamond framework but is distinctive in the way it parallels commercial relationships with network (cooperative) relationships. This extends not just to suppliers and buyers but also to competitors and the non-business infrastructure. The point about conventional supply chain relationships is the observation that cooperation along the chain can result in better outcomes for customers. This is not always easy to prove and can easily be confounded with convenience to the players. More challenging are the emerging sets of relationships with competitors in the form of joint ventures, technology transfers, and market-sharing agreements. Again there is tension between cooperation and competition and economists would argue that such cooperation is only productively possible if markets are not too concentrated with the result that cooperation would shade into monopolization. The international automobile industry provides a dramatic example of multiple linkages in a highly competitive arena. Other elements of the business infrastructure are also being pulled into cooperation. MNEs are now sharing their strategies with the unions (see, for example, the Detroit discussions in the summer of 2003 with the UAW in the face of intense competition). Partnerships are being effected with universities (e.g. by pharmaceutical companies). Above all, governments and MNEs are increasingly cooperating not only around issues of FDI but also about local content and other forms of local reinvestment in infrastructure. Figure 9.12 shows a picture of L'Oréal as a flagship company.

Case box 9.4: The first multinationals: Assyria circa 2000 BC

In an effort to fill an important gap in the history of MNEs, Karl Moore and David Lewis presented evidence suggesting that the first MNEs appeared in the Old Assyrian Kingdom shortly after 2000 BC. Using the eclectic paradigm as a model to analyse ancient international trade, it demonstrates that the major characteristics of MNEs were a part of the Assyrian business organizations of the time. The definition of MNE accepted by the OECD and the UNCTC (the United Nations Centre for Transnational Corporations), 'an enterprise that engages in foreign direct investment (FDI) and owns or controls valueadding activities in more than one country', leads us to conclude that there were MNEs in ancient Assyria around 2000 BC. Characteristics found in modern MNEs, such as hierarchical organization, foreign employees, value-adding activities in multiple regions, common stock ownership, resource- and market-seeking behaviour, were present in these ancient firms. These early MNEs successfully operated considerable business empires in multiple foreign locations from their corporate headquarters in the capital of Ashur. Undoubtedly more will be learned about the commerce of the Old Assyrian Kingdom as records from archaeological finds continue to be translated and new finds uncovered.

Were there early MNEs or proto-MNEs earlier than the Assyrian Empire? There may well have been. The records have yet to be uncovered.

Note

The eclectic paradigm can be readily summarized by the acronym OLI which indicates ownership, location and internalization advantages. Ownership advantages are firm-specific advantages (FSAs) owned or controlled by the firm. Location advantages are country-specific advantages (CSAs) that arise from the location(s) of the MNE. Internalization advantages are those that accrue to a firm when it internalizes or brings inside the hierarchy of the firm activities which could be performed by the market (remember the discussions on make versus buy and the boundaries of the firm).

Question

Would these early MNEs be founded and sustained on the same principles as today's MNEs?

Source: adapted from The First Multinationals: Assyria circa 2000 BC, by Karl Moore and David Lewis, *Management International Review*, vol. 38. 1998/2, 95–107

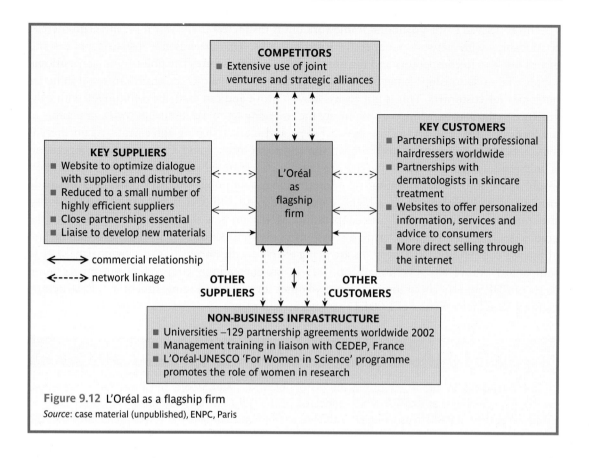

Figure 9.12 L'Oréal as a flagship firm
Source: case material (unpublished), ENPC, Paris

9.4 Managing international organizations

The international company has always had a tendency towards a complex organization structure and difficulties of management control. Stopford and Wells (1972) demonstrated how multinationals tend towards matrix structures (Figure 9.13).

Multinationals historically have moved along the route of increasing product diversity followed by geographic expansion, or geographic expansion followed by product diversity. A multi-product firm with limited overseas commitment will naturally organize around product divisions. A multi-country, single product firm will naturally organize around area or country divisions. The difficulty comes with multi-product, multi-country operations – should it be organized around geography or around products? The pure strategies offer clear advice. A global company should operate product divisions, because of the imperative to standardize and achieve cost efficiencies. The multidomestic company should organize around countries, because the foundation of competitive advantage lies within the countries. Trade-offs have to be made in international firms and in transnational organizations.

Where there is a fine balance to be struck, there has been much experimenting with matrix structures. The matrix attempts to substitute formal, vertically oriented control and planning processes with more direct contact between individuals. It does this by placing line managers in situations where they have two bosses and are required to meet the needs of both. Figure 9.14 illustrates this with reference to a global chocolate company. This example is inspired by the

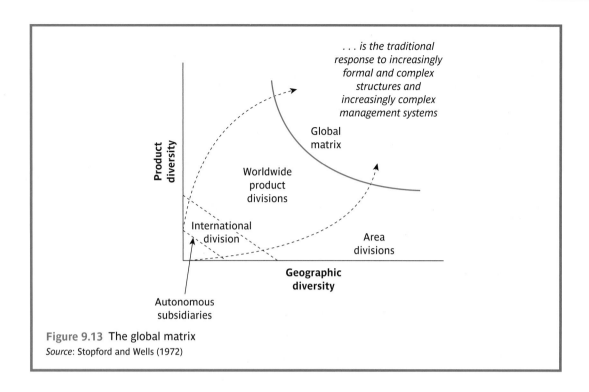

Figure 9.13 The global matrix
Source: Stopford and Wells (1972)

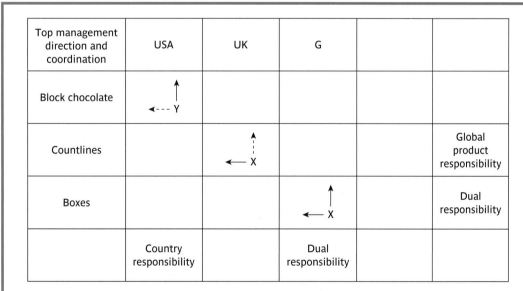

Figure 9.14 Managing the matrix example: global chocolate company

acquisition of Rowntree by Nestlé, when the new parent argued for the continuation of its country-centred structure, and Rowntree managers argued that because the chocolate industry was global (at least it was European), there should be a product division structure. However, many managers have been very uncomfortable with matrix structures:

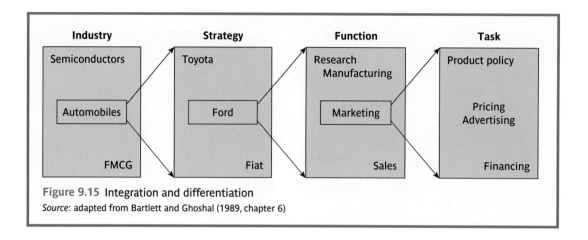

Figure 9.15 Integration and differentiation
Source: adapted from Bartlett and Ghoshal (1989, chapter 6)

- The time taken to make decisions may be too long.
- Priorities may be confused, because equal priorities are implied in the matrix.
- Responsibilities may not be clear, because of dual reporting lines.
- A matrix may engender conflict, because of the lack of vertical control processes.

Many MNEs use matrix structures. Some seem to work quite well but in general they provoke much controversy. The dual-line of reporting is the source of many problems and requires explicit procedures that can resolve the inherent tensions. Bartlett and Ghoshal (1990) suggest three important criteria for making a matrix structure work well. These are clarity, continuity and consistency. *Clarity* refers to how well people understand what they are doing and how well they are doing it. It is built on clear corporate objectives within which relationships in the structure have to be spelt out in simple, direct terms. *Continuity* means that the company remains committed to the same values, objectives and principles of operation. This means that people know what is required and what the company stands for and how it operates. *Consistency* relates to how well all parts of the company work in relation to each other. This means that different parts of the operation should work in the same way without (too many) unnecessary variations and adaptations.

One of the difficulties with organizational design and the management processes that support each design is that they have a 'one size fits all' character. The multi-business company has more complexity than any single organization structure can accommodate. Sometimes a central policy is needed, sometimes local discretion is required, often there needs to be a debate about how something should be done. The need for innovation, learning and adaptation usually requires local discretion within a clear strategic intent (see ABB and Percy Barnevik for an attempt to achieve this (Taylor, 1991)). A useful approach is to seek to build our diagnosis of a company from the bottom up and not from the top down. Figure 9.14 implies that an overall judgement can be made about which type a company belongs to.

Alternatively, consider Figure 9.15. This breaks down the unit of analysis into its constituent parts (rather like a parts explosion diagram). An international-type industry (automobiles) is broken down into its member companies, some of which are global, some international etc. The Ford Motor Company, international in type, is broken down into its major functions. Research is seen to be global and centralized, sales are multidomestic and decentralized, and marketing is international (and it is probably difficult to decide how it should be organized).

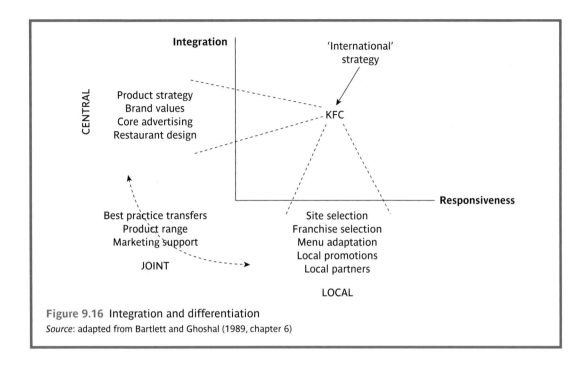

Figure 9.16 Integration and differentiation
Source: adapted from Bartlett and Ghoshal (1989, chapter 6)

Breaking marketing into its constituents, we see that some parts, like product policy, should be centralized, whereas others, like advertising, still have a complex mixture of local and central contributions. In practice, the diagnosis can be built from the bottom as well as from the top. Thus, the bottom-up approach identifies how things are done. The top-down approach can challenge this and ask how things should be done. The result might look like Figure 9.16. In this we show the integration–responsiveness trade-off diagram for KFC (Kentucky Fried Chicken, now part of Tricon Global Restaurants Inc).[2] The company is diagnosed in general as international in type. The vertical axis displays the tasks and functions that are to be done centrally, to gain the integration benefits. The horizontal axis displays those tasks and functions that ought to be carried out locally. Grouped around the origin of the diagram are those activities that require both central and local contributions. It is in these areas that a matrix-style structure would be relevant. Rather than adopting a one-size-fits-all structure, it would be appealing to be able to differentiate the structure according to needs.

In Part 2 we will develop these themes in more detail. We will be looking at the development and history of multinational companies and the way in which they fit within international trade patterns and the scale and significance of their interaction with governments. We will be looking also at the typical entry strategies of companies into new markets, for example through exporting, licensing, franchising, joint ventures and wholly owned subsidiaries. The nature and significance of global strategic alliances and the management challenges that they pose will also be on our agenda.

In Case box 9.5 the recent history of new ties for VW, GM and Peugeot-Citroën in Asia is recounted. This begs the question as to whether these represent global or regional initiatives and to what extent the three companies involved are becoming genuine global organizations. What are the pay-offs for the Asian companies involved and how are their global ambitions being pursued?

---

[2] See the case study on KFC, Harvard Business school (1986).

Case box 9.5: **Asian alliances**

New ties for VW, GM and Peugeot Citroën signal a way forward for the car industry

Having weathered the storm, the thoughts of global carmakers are now focused on the tie-ups they hope will give them an edge in the upturn. Two such deals, the first involving General Motors and its Chinese partner SAIC, the second between Volkswagen and Suzuki, have been concluded in the past few days. Another, linking PSA Peugeot Citroën and Mitsubishi, is still under negotiation. All three are aimed at winning a bigger presence in Asia and tapping into low-cost manufacturing expertise, while sharing components and development budgets.

Of the three, the most significant is Volkswagen's announcement on Wednesday December 9th that it has agreed to pay $2.5 billion for 19.9% of Suzuki, a family-owned Japanese maker of small cars and motorcycles. Along with Fiat, Suzuki is the only international outfit that knows how to make money out of small, inexpensive cars. That is something VW forgot long ago. But it needs to relearn it, argues Max Warburton of Bernstein, an asset-management firm, if it is not to suffer from the worldwide trend towards downsizing, as new emissions laws bite and growth shifts to poorer consumers in emerging markets.

The other thing Suzuki offers is unique exposure to emerging markets. Through its 54% stake in Maruti Suzuki, it has managed to keep more than 40% of the increasingly competitive Indian market. It also has a strong position in Pakistan and Indonesia, two other teeming countries with nascent car markets. VW, which is the market leader in China and has around a quarter of the Brazilian market, was uncharacteristically late setting out its stall in India, where it only began manufacturing this year. If the alliance blossoms, and VW ends up turning Suzuki into its 11th brand, it will have taken a big step towards its long-term goal of overtaking Toyota as the world's biggest car firm.

The deal between GM and SAIC to set up a 50:50 joint venture to produce small cars in India, announced on December 4th, is another sign of the times. GM will contribute the factories and distribution network it already owns in India; SAIC will invest up to $350m in cash and other assets. The plan gives China's biggest carmaker a foothold in the second-fastest-growing car market in the world (after China), while helping cash-strapped GM to mount a more vigorous push into India, where it has struggled for several years to reach its target of a 10% market share. GM and SAIC are also intending to bring to India the ultra-cheap micro-cars, minivans and pickups they make with another Chinese partner, Wuling.

At the same time, GM said that it was ceding control of its successful joint venture with SAIC in China by selling a 1% stake to the Chinese firm for $85m. With a 51% shareholding, SAIC will have the right to approve budgets and all senior appointments. Nick Reilly, the architect of GM's Asian strategy who was recently appointed boss of Opel/Vauxhall, insisted that the sale was merely a technicality to allow SAIC to consolidate its earnings from the venture. Some observers interpret it as the price for getting SAIC's help in India. Others detect the beginning of a trend whereby Chinese car manufacturers will assert greater authority over their Western and Japanese partners. Mr Reilly merely said that GM had agreed in order to get SAIC's 'full co-operation and the full co-operation of the Chinese government in other things.'

PSA's negotiations to buy between 30% and 50% of Mitsubishi, which has several times been close to bankruptcy and is still carrying a heavy burden of debt, have some way to go. The two firms have had ties for several years: Peugeot and Citroën sell a rebranded version of Mitsubishi's Outlander crossover (somewhere between a car and an SUV) and PSA shares a factory with Mitsubishi in Russia. Mitsubishi, with its presence in Asia and its network of factories and dealers in America, could help the French group reduce its reliance on Europe. But cultural clashes have bedevilled such cross-border deals in the past. And PSA, whose automotive business has junk-rated debts of $3 billion, may have difficulty finding the $3.5–4 billion that a 50% stake in the Japanese firm is likely to cost.

Source: *The Economist*, 9 December 2009

9.5 Summary

In this chapter we have positioned international strategy as a significant extension of the logic of competitive advantage. We do not go into a full discussion of how the economics of trade inter-relates with the genesis and nature of multinational firms – this is the province of international business as a subject. However, the subjects do overlap and what we do is reflect on how the fundamental issues of competitive strategy (cost and differentiation) are played out on the international stage.

The chapter opened with a review of international trade and its institutional context and the significance of 'national' competitive advantage. This should be read as an extension of the discussion on macroeconomics in Chapter 4. The core of the chapter revolves around the nature of globalization and the sources of competitive advantage that flow from this. Whereas interna-tionalization of companies (exemplified in the internationalization process) is seen as the general consequence of international trade, globalization is presented here as a particular form of this – the (debatable and controversial) trends towards international standardization.

The second key element of the chapter concerns the application of standardization strategies (crudely speaking, cost based) versus differentiation strategies (differentiation based). Following from this is the tantalizing debate as to whether both are possible (the transnational solution). You will recall from earlier chapters that exactly the same debate has taken place within com-petitive strategy about the possible simultaneity of cost- and differentiation-based strategies.

The importance of these discussions is profound because they affect the balance between country-specific advantages (CSAs) and firm-specific advantages (FSAs). These issues are discussed against the broad backdrop of Porter's diamond and the double diamond extensions popularized by Rugman. They are also discussed specifically in terms of the advent of the 'flagship firm' with its ability to manage its context and secure its position.

Just as in corporate strategy (Chapter 8), the nature of the (international) strategy has to be complemented by appropriate organization structures and processes. The logic of strategy and structure implies that complex strategies seem to require complex organizations such as the matrix form and the double diamond.

Key terms

comparative advantage	311	global strategy	308
country-specific advantage (CSA)	319	globalization	303
diamond of national advantage	299	international strategy	312
double diamond	317	internationalization	303
factor conditions	299	multidomestic	303
firm-specific advantage (FSA)	319	multinational enterprise (MNE)	296
flagship model	320	national differences	311
foreign direct investment (FDI)	298	transnational	313
global markets	303	world Trade	296

Recap questions and assignments

1 Compare the structures of companies like ABB, Diageo, Canon and DaimlerChrysler. To what extent do you think they are in line with current thinking on organizational structures for multinational corporations? What suggestions can you make for any changes in approach?

2 Consider the argument for global standardization as advanced originally by Ted Levitt in the *Harvard Business Review* and as popularized in the business press and in popular journalism.

   ■ Outline the main arguments against this view.

   ■ Identify an alternative to global standardization and explore its implications for multinational corporations.

Case study 9.1: Leahy's global shopping spree: interview with Sir Terry Leahy

The fanatically dedicated boss of the UK's biggest retailer aims to grow around the world, taking on all-comers – as he tells Jenny Davey in an exclusive interview

Sir Terry Leahy may be a softly spoken, unassuming Scouser but, make no mistake, the boss of Tesco, Britain's biggest supermarket chain, is bent on world domination. Next year, this 50-year-old knight of the realm, who grew up on a council estate in Liverpool, will celebrate 10 years at the helm.

As rivals clamour for the Competition Commission to put the brakes on Tesco's increasing dominance in the British market, Leahy is plotting an ambitious international expansion that could keep the company growing at the vertiginous pace it has enjoyed since 1997. He may not look superhuman. In fact he looks like an average bloke in a blue shirt rather than one of Britain's most powerful businessmen. But since Leahy got the top job in 1997, 18 years after he first joined the company as a marketing executive in 1979, Tesco's profits have tripled and it has become the nation's biggest retailer.

Cut Leahy in two and you would probably find Tesco imprinted on his heart. *'Like most Tesco people, I think mainly about...erm...Tesco...oh, and Christmas trade,'* he said in a quip typical of his dry, understated humour. *'I think that most Tesco people have got their brains compartmentalised into two. One half is Tesco and the other is all the rest.'*

His fanatical dedication to the business has already led to Tesco's profits exceeding £2billion. That has been achieved by strengthening its core food business, developing new store formats, expanding into non-food areas and pioneering services such as car insurance and bank accounts.

But if the company is to transform itself from a national champion into a truly global behemoth, it will need to get its international expansion right. There is little doubt that this will be Leahy's biggest challenge yet. Tesco has already begun to build an overseas presence in countries from South Korea to Hungary.

It has not been easy, and the roller-coaster journey it has had so far provides a taster for the challenges that lie ahead. In the past 12 months, a military coup has put the brakes on new store openings in Thailand, its trading in Hungary has been affected by the country's economic crisis, and its South Korean business could have done without a panic over nuclear testing by the regime in Pyongyang. In India, Tesco wanted to go into partnership with Bharti Enterprises but earlier this month lost out to the American giant Wal-Mart. In Poland, it wanted to buy the operations of its Dutch rival Ahold but was beaten by France's Carrefour.

After those setbacks, speculation was rife that the wheels had come off the Tesco expansion train. But just as the failure story was gaining traction, Tesco popped up last week with news that it had paid £180m to raise its stake in Hymall, the Chinese hypermarket chain, from 50% to 90% in a move that will enable it to accelerate its expansion in the Asian superpower.

By Leahy's own admission, pursuing global growth has been a 'huge gamble' for Tesco. New store networks have had to be created as well as new distribution centres. The message is clear, though. *'We haven't even begun to fully exploit the opportunities we have opened up in international markets,'* said Leahy. He believes that in five to ten years the group's fast-expanding international operations – which currently account for about a quarter of profits – could overtake its domestic business.

'Of course, if we buy businesses it could happen sooner,' he said. *'In the past ten years we have gone from a home market of 60m people to 2 billion people worldwide and in those countries we have either market-leading positions or fastest-growing businesses, so actually the future for Tesco is very promising in terms of its ability to access growth.'*

China, India and America are the big three for Leahy. *'If you are looking at the 21st century, these are the places to put your chips. Clearly, China and India are the growing markets, but actually you have to remember that the United States still accounts for a third of the world's GDP. Everyone knows about China and India, but you also have to remember the United States.'*

Tesco is currently the third-biggest grocery retailer by sales – only Wal-Mart and Carrefour are bigger. Leahy points out that in terms of market value Tesco could be regarded as the second biggest. So, will Tesco in ten years be as big as, or even bigger than, Wal-Mart? *'No is the answer,'* said Leahy with a grin. But then he pondered light-heartedly: *'Do you mean as big as they are now? Any company that is successful in the world of international retailing will end up being a very big company.'*

'How big (will Tesco become)? Who knows? The instructive thing is to look back at the growth of Tesco and then look forward and see if there is the same opportunity to grow – well, not in the UK, but as a group. Is there the opportunity to grow in the same way? Absolutely. So Tesco can carry on growing at the same kinds of rates it has been growing at.'

Next year Tesco will launch its convenience-store business on the west coast of America. Leahy said the US has the attractive combination of a growing population and high disposable incomes. In contrast to Europe, the American market is lightly regulated, so if you build a successful business it can be rolled out rapidly. Analysts at Shore Capital are already predicting that the US business will be a success and will rapidly expand to other areas, including New York, Chicago and Florida. *'Tesco hasn't gone to America to open a few convenience stores on the west coast,'* said analyst Clive Black. Shore's working model projects that by 2020 Tesco could have 4,000 stores in America generating sales of £21.5billion and profit of £1.3billion.

Leahy just smiled when asked if Tesco would seek to conquer the whole of America. *'It is a format designed for the American consumer,'* he said pointedly. *'But we are starting on the west coast and there are a lot of people on the west coast.'* America has long proved the stumbling block for ambitious British businesses looking to grow overseas, but Leahy said he was confident that Tesco would not be another casualty.

'You have to judge Tesco by its own record, not the record of other retailers. We have done our home-work. We know that it is a very competitive market. So there is no point going to America and doing the same as every other retailer – that won't be successful, so we haven't done it. We have sat down over the past three or four years and designed a format that is exactly right for the American consumer today. The more we work at it and research it, the more confident we are that we are on to something.'

Leahy said the group's investment in the project was well balanced in terms of risk and reward. *'We could have gone out and bought a supermarket chain for billions of dollars, but we didn't. We invested an amount of money that is significant but survivable if it doesn't go well. But there is no reason why it shouldn't go well. If it is successful we will have a big success on our hands that will transform the prospects of Tesco.'*

▶ Despite the termination of talks with Bharti, Leahy said Tesco was just as keen on developing in India as it ever was, but he is in no hurry. '*We never rush things. Look at the level of disposable income and the infrastructure at this point and you quickly realise that India has lots of potential, but this will not be realised overnight. Speed is not the issue in India. The issue is getting the right partner and putting in the right foundations for a business. One of the strengths of Tesco internationally is that we never rush anywhere.*' Leahy argues that Tesco is well placed to deal with the difficulties and challenges of expanding overseas. He shrugs off the political situation in Thailand. '*There has obviously been a problem in Thailand but that doesn't mean you can't make progress. We have a wonderful business in Thailand. It is all part and parcel of growing an international business. You just have to navigate your way through it. Tesco has shown more than any other company that it has a recipe for successful international expansion. It has had more success than any other retailer, and in a way that comes out of its core philosophies – the business has always been based round customers rather than being wedded to particular business systems or formats, and so it has always been much more adaptable. It's an accident really that this is what you need to be successful in overseas markets.*'

So is international expansion needed to compensate for slowing growth in Britain? Leahy looked aghast at this suggestion. '*Tesco is a fast-growing business,*' he said. He was equally horrified when asked if he would still be at Tesco in five or ten years to see through his growth plans. After all, this is the man nicknamed 'Tesco Terry' for his company loyalty. '*I'm only 50,*' he protested. '*Tesco has been good enough to give me a great career. It's a wonderful business and there's lots of wonderful people in it. I don't really think very much beyond that. I don't want to have a personality or a legacy outside Tesco. I am very happy.*'

There is a close-knit executive team at Tesco, including Tim Mason, who is heading the expansion in America, and Richard Brasher, the company's commercial director. With Leahy apparently so firmly in the saddle, is there a chance that the team could break up if, for example, ambition gets the better of one his colleagues? '*Of course, Tesco has been successful, so headhunters are on the phone all the time. But people don't go,*' said Leahy. '*The remarkable thing about Tesco is not that there's a problem, it's that there's no problem. Tesco is a good company in a highly competitive market. It's a fascinating place to be and people stay around. It's not just about counting the pound notes.*'

Questions

1 What does any company and Tesco in particular have to do to 'dominate the world'?

2 How does the Tesco international expansion journey compare with the profiles discussed in this chapter? Has it been a planned journey designed eventually to reach the US?

3 According to Leahy, global growth has been a 'huge gamble'. How, therefore, is it justified in the face of so many very effective competitors around the world?

4 Tesco's venture in California is directly in the face of Wal-Mart and other US retailers. What new core competences might be needed in California and are these likely to be consistent with the key factors for success in other countries such as India and China?

5 Would you buy Tesco's shares?

Source: Jenny Davey, *The Sunday Times*, 17 December 2006

References

Amit, R. and Schoemaker, P.J.H. (1993) Strategic assets and organizational rent. *Strategic Management Journal*, **14**, 33–46, reprinted in S. Segal-Horn (ed.) (1998) *The Strategy Reader*, Blackwell Business, Oxford.

Bartlett, C. and Ghoshal, S. (1989) *Managing Across Borders: The Transnational Solution*, Harvard Business School Press, Boston, MA.

Bartlett, C. and Ghoshal, S. (1990) Matrix management: not a structure, a frame of mind. *Harvard Business Review*, July/August, 138–45.

Crookell, H. (1990) *Canadian-American Trade and Investment under the Free-Trade Agreement*, Quorum Books, Westport, CT.

Dunning, J.H. (1993) Internationalising Porter's diamond. *Management International Review*, **33**, Special Issue 2, 7–16.

Ghoshal, S. (1987) Global strategy: an organizing framework. *Strategic Management Journal*, **8**, 425–40, reprinted in S. Segal-Horn (ed.) (1998) *The Strategy Reader*, Blackwell Business, Oxford.

Harvard Business School (1986) *Kentucky Fried Chicken (Japan) Ltd*, Case Study 9–987–043, Harvard College, Boston, MA.

Hill, C.W. and Jones, G.R. (1995) *Strategic Management Theory: An Integrated Approach*, 3rd edn, Houghton Mifflin, Boston, MA.

Levitt, T. (1983) The globalization of markets. *Harvard Business Review*, May/June, 92–102.

McKinsey & Co. (1993) *Manufacturing Productivity Units*. McKinsey Global Institute Report, October.

Ohmae, K. (1985) *Triad Power: The Coming Shape of Global Competition*, Free Press, New York.

Porter, M.E. (1985) *Competitive Advantage*, Free Press, New York.

Porter, M.E. (1990) The competitive advantage of nations. *Harvard Business Review*, March/April, 73–93.

Prahalad, C.K. and Doz, Y.L. (1986) The dynamics of global competition. In C.K. Prahalad and Y.L. Doz (eds) *The Multinational Mission: Balancing Local Demands and Global Vision*, Free Press, New York.

Prahalad, C.K. and Hamel, G. (1990) The core competence of the corporation. *Harvard Business Review*, May/June, 79–91, reprinted in S. Segal-Horn (ed.) (1998) *The Strategy Reader*, Blackwell Business, Oxford.

Quinn, J.B. (1992) *Intelligent Enterprise*, Free Press, New York.

Rugman, A.M. and Collinson, S. (2009) *International Business*, 5th edn, FT Prentice Hall, London.

Rugman, A.M. and D'Cruz, J.R. (1993) The 'Double Diamond' model of international competitiveness: the Canadian experience. *Management International Review*, **33**, Special Issue 2, 32.

Rugman, A.M. and D'Cruz, J.R. (2000) *Multinationals as Flagship Firms: Regional Business Networks*, Oxford University Press, Oxford.

Rugman, A.M. and Hodgetts, R.M. (2002) *International Business*, Financial Times/Prentice-Hall, London.

Safarian, A.E. (1968) *Foreign Ownership of Canadian Industry*, McGraw-Hill, Toronto.

Segal-Horn, S. (1993) The internationalisation of service firms. *Advances in Strategic Management*, **9**, 31–55, reprinted in S. Segal-Horn (ed.) (1998) *The Strategy Reader*, Blackwell Business, Oxford.

Segal-Horn, S (ed.) (1998) *The Strategy Reader*, Blackwell Business, Oxford.

Stopford, J. and Wells, L.T. (1972) *Managing the Multinational Enterprise*, Basic Books, New York.

Taylor, W. (1991) The logic of global business: an interview with ABB's Percy Barnevik. *Harvard Business Review*, March/April, 91–104.

Further reading

Bartlett, C. and Ghoshal, S. (1992) What is a global manager? *Harvard Business Review*, **70**, **5**, 124–32.

Bartlett, C.A. and Ghoshal, S. (1993) Beyond the M-form: toward a new managerial theory of the firm. *Strategic Management Journal*, **14**, 23–46, reprinted in S. Segal-Horn (ed.) (1998) *The Strategy Reader*, Blackwell Business, Oxford.

Douglas, S.P. and Wind, Y. (1987) The myth of globalization. *Columbia Journal of World Business*, Winter, 19–29.

Ghemawat, P. (2007) Managing differences. *Harvard Business Review*, **85**, **3**, March.

Ghoshal, S. and Nohria, N. (1993) Horses for courses: organizational forms for multinational corporations. *Sloan Management Review*, Winter, 23–35.

Gupta, A.K. (2001) Converting global presence into global competitive advantage. *The Academy of Management Executive*, **15**, **2**, May.

Jarillo, J.C. (1993) *Creating the Borderless Organization*, Butterworth-Heinemann, Oxford.

Rugman, A.M. and Girod, S. (2003) Retail multinationals and globalization: the evidence is regional. *European Management Journal*, **21**, **1**.

Rugman, A.M. and Verbeke, A. (2004) A perspective on regional and global strategies of multinational enterprises. *Journal of International Business Studies*, **35**, **1**.

Segal-Horn, S. and McGee, J. (1997) Global competences in service multinationals. In H. Thomas and D. O'Neal (eds) *Strategic Discovery: Competing in New Arenas*, the Strategic Management Series, John Wiley & Sons, Chichester, 49–77.

Yip, G. (1995) *Total Global Strategy*, Prentice-Hall, Englefield Cliffs, NJ.

PART 2
Strategy Implementation and Practice

This section of the book deals with a range of topics which are based largely in behavioural economics, a perspective which runs contrary to classical economic theory (which assumes that individuals will always behave rationally to achieve the best possible outcomes). This perspective is important because, while strategies can be planned in advance (often using the assumptions of classical economics), putting them into practice reveals that intention and outcomes can be two very different things.

The objectives of this section are to introduce the reader to the more behaviourally and process-oriented perspectives on strategy. The vagaries of individuals, imperfect markets and organizations all influence strategy, primarily through the processes of strategic decision making (which can be far from ideal in terms of the optimal outcomes sought by the classical economist). This section of the book examines strategy from two important perspectives. One perspective concerns the importance of organization (its structures, cultures and processes) and how these influence strategy and the other is the importance of understanding implementation as well as formulation if we are to understand strategy fully.

Taking strategic decision making as a key perspective (a leitmotiv), this section of the book examines the interactions of external context, organizational context, behaviours and strategy. It is through these interactions that we can fully appreciate how these factors can shape, block, change or radically modify planned strategies.

Chapter 10 introduces the reader to an organizational perspective on strategy. Drawing primarily on the discipline of organization theory, the chapter first of all shows how strategy can be considered to be primarily a behavioural process. Strategies are the result of behavioural interactions between individuals and groups in organizations. Anchored in the work of Cyert and March, these behavioural approaches reveal consistencies which impact strongly on strategy. For example, individuals and groups see the world primarily from their 'local' perspective – if they are marketing managers they will tend to see strategic issues from a marketing perspective and not, for example, from a financial or a production perspective. The chapter also reveals how we can characterize strategy as a process which can change in character as markets demand changes in strategic orientation or as political infighting between many 'local views' gathers force and influences what happens. Finally, the chapter highlights strategy as essentially a practice-based process. From this perspective, strategy is viewed not as a grand, overarching set of executive formulations, but, instead, is seen as something managers 'do' on a daily basis. Understanding strategy is best done by understanding the micro-practices of management.

Chapter 11 examines the concepts of risk and uncertainty in the strategic decision-making process. The chapter first of all distinguishes between risk and uncertainty and provides working definitions of each. The chapter then identifies the sources and the types of risks typically faced by decision makers. The chapter outlines models for risk analysis, including those based on expected utilities, and introduces techniques such as net present value, internal rate of return and the use of decision trees to reduce both uncertainty and risk. The chapter concludes by looking at scenario building, looking forward to plausible futures as a way or reducing risk and uncertainty. The chapter outlines a method for conducting scenario analysis and shows how that can be reflected back on the firm to help guide and inform the strategy process.

Chapter 12 defines strategic decision making as important or key decisions made in organizations of all types. The term organization includes any collective social, economic or political activity involving a plurality of human effort. Strategic decisions emphasize the social practice of decision making as it is carried out among and between groups of such individuals. It is both the organizing of decision activity as a collective phenomenon and the cognitive processes of individual choice makers that take centre stage in analysing decision making. Strategic decisions also can be characterized as processes which transcend the individuals involved. For example, they can be fast, slow, continuous or discontinuous, devolved or centralized, complex and political. This chapter describes these characterizations of process and shows how they are associated with decision performance.

Chapter 13 shows that thinking and acting strategically will, of necessity, involve an organization in some degree of strategic change. Such changes can be to structures, processes, technologies, markets, products and services, ownership and so forth. Change processes themselves can also be characterized, for example, as relatively continuous (that is, piecemeal and evolutionary) or discontinuous (that is, dramatic and revolutionary). The story of strategy implementation is also the story of strategic change. The primary focus of the chapter is on analysing and understanding the characteristics and dimensions of change processes, looking at how these relate to organizational strategies, and concludes by examining what we know about relatively more and less successful change strategies.

Chapter 14 deals with the systemic knowledge which is ingrained in the firm. Namely, its processes and its people are the single most important set of resources for the firm and for strategists to utilize. The chapter shows how this systemic knowledge is slowly developed, is distinctive and unique to the firm, is not easily transferable to others and may be protected by intellectual property regulations or other competitive barriers. The ease with which such knowledge is capitalized upon by the firm and its strategists depends in part on how such knowledge is managed internally in the firm and transferred and replicated easily throughout the organization. The writing on organizational knowledge has shown it as the lynchpin between internal organizational structures and processes and the achievement of competitive advantage. The chapter also deals with the concept of how organizations learn, showing how the process of learning from new knowledge (for example) and strategy are recursive. The one informs the other. Without strategy there is likely to be little learning. Learning from doing is necessary but not sufficient. Organizations and individuals need also to create, sustain and feed learning back into the strategy process so that new decisions can be made, based on the new knowledge created by learning.

Chapter 15 looks at the most senior echelons of organization, the board or the top policy-making team. Drawing on a wide range of literature and research, the chapter shows how the roles and actions of this top team are pivotal in shaping the questions which revolve around the purposes, responsibilities, control, leadership and power of boards. The chapter deals with questions which revolve around the purposes, responsibilities, control, leadership and power of boards and top teams. These include questions such as, how is oversight to be exercised over those delegated to the executive management of the firm and how are owners' interests to be protected? What about the interests of the other stakeholders such as consumers, employees and local communities? How is power over the organization legitimized and to whom is an organization accountable and responsible? The chapter assesses what we know about effective and less effective boards. Drawing on a wide range of literature and research, the chapter emphasizes the pivotal role of these top teams in shaping both the strategy process and its outcomes. The chapter provides details of recent changes in regulations and recommended guidelines for effective governance. Although the majority of these have emanated from the UK, the chapter takes an international perspective towards effective governance.

Chapter 16 examines the concept of strategic performance and its measurement. Performance constructs such as a strategic 'business model', managing a business for value and the 'balanced scorecard' illustrate the fundamental importance of analysing the performance and health of the firm. Firms have a range of targets or goals with profit maximization or shareholder value maximization often stated as one of the key strategic objectives. Performance feedback provides important information to enable organizational renewal and strategic reorientation to take place. The chapter introduces both the idea of multiple measures of performances (such as accounting based or market based) and also discusses the concepts of economic value (such as 'shareholder value' and 'economic value-added'). Finally, the chapter discusses the 'balanced scorecard' approach to performance measurement. Here, the focus is upon key performance indicators which address the multiple goals and foci of the business (these include financial, marketing, internal process and learning goals). Critical success factors (appropriate and robust performance metrics) allow managers to evaluate strategic success and help them adjust the 'business model' if necessary to achieve stated goals and targets.

Chapter 10

Organizational models and strategy

Chapter contents

Introduction

Organizational approaches to strategy have a long history and are usually (but by no means always) focused on the processes of strategic decision making. The key aspects highlighted by organization theorists are that strategic decisions are complex, political and can only be understood over time and not (for example) by taking a snapshot view of an organization in its environment.

The problems which result from strategic decision being complex were well documented in the 1960s. Cyert and March (1963) argued that human beings and organizations have limits to the extent to which they can handle complex decisions and the uncertainty inherent in such decisions. According to Cyert and March (1963), human beings and organizations seek to avoid uncertainty and act in predictable ways toward complex problems. For example, they only search for new alternatives when problems get so bad that existing or 'known' alternatives will not suffice. Decision makers are likely to attend to issues in a sequential way, rather than tackle the complex problem holistically.

Search for alternatives, therefore, tends to be 'simple-minded' (Cyert and March, 1963) because simple or well-known alternatives are unlikely to change the status quo very much (hence reducing uncertainty). Other researchers showed how complex problems were cut down to a size where they could be understood, taking into account only a limited amount of information or advice (Simon, 1960). Braybrooke and Lindblom (1963) showed how examining every possible alternative and trying to understand every aspect of complexity was, in reality, impractical because it would swamp the mental capacities (and working hours) of managers involved. Therefore, in practice (Braybrooke and Lindblom studied what they termed 'real world' strategic decision making), decisions are handled in a piecemeal way, and if marginal steps can be achieved then that is what will be implemented, at least for the time being. This is known as the incremental approach to strategic decision making – a direct result of the complexity of strategic decisions. We explore these aspects in more detail later in this chapter.

Organization theorists also pointed out that strategy was not a politically neutral topic. Allison (1969, 1971) showed how strategic decision making involves many interests (in today's jargon, 'stakeholders') who fight it out between themselves to influence both the process of the decision and its outcome so these fit as far as possible with their 'interests'. Strategy is, therefore, not only complex but is also a political game rooted in both personal interest and functional perspective (sales will want something different than production, for example, from a decision). An organization, therefore, is an arena for decision-making games (Crozier, 1976) in which a range of interests benefit (and a range do not). However, all interests have an overriding stake in the survival of the organization, so political processes are unlikely to become so acute that they fragment or seal the demise of the organization. Such 'schismatic tendencies' (Morgan, 1981) are, therefore, mostly avoided. Who has more power in these games (and how a power base is secured) is a topic in its own right and is outside the scope of this book, but Chapter 12 on strategic decision making goes into more detail about this perspective.

Strategy is also a process which happens and unfolds over time (see, for example, Pettigrew, 1992, 2003). It matters what has happened in the past, since history has a heavy hand which can shape current strategic decisions. And strategic decisions themselves can only be understood as they unfold over time, with different players and interests entering and leaving the arena over often considerable periods of time. Hickson et al. (1986) showed that decision formulation (from first idea to authorization) takes on average 12.4 months and Miller et al. (2004) showed that implementation takes even longer (up to three years and longer). Pettigrew (2003) also emphasized that the strategy process could only be understood as being shaped over time by the context in which strategic decisions take place. Context includes factors such as history (what has happened in the past can influence current decisions) as well as organizational structure and culture, both explored later in this chapter.

Whittington (2001) in his aptly titled book *What is Strategy and Does it Matter?* raises an important point at the outset. Strategy should not be taken for granted as a series of models and matrices all delivered without a jot of doubt or uncertainty. Strategy involves people and organizations and is, therefore, to different degrees uncertain and unpredictable. Up to this point in the book, we have been dealing predominantly (but not exclusively) with a classical approach to strategy, firmly rooted in economics and apparently rational analysis. Organizational approaches to strategy begin to question the classical approach in a number of very different ways. This chapter introduces the reader to the concepts of strategy from the perspectives of organization theory. It also serves as an introduction for the following chapters in this section of the book, which deal with key issues of risk, uncertainty, decision making, innovation and change.

Why is an organizational perspective on strategy important? There is a practical answer to this question and a theoretical answer. Both are fundamental. From a practical perspective, all strategies have to be processed by people through organizational structures which can vary greatly (small to large, centralized to decentralized, for example). Doing strategy in a small decentralized organization is likely to be a very different process from doing strategy in a large multinational firm. In the former case, strategic decisions can be made quickly and put into practice, involving staff (perhaps all of them) in the process. In the latter case of the multinational, strategic decisions once crafted will go through a series of stages and will be handled by a variety of committees, policy teams, project teams and others. Strategy will certainly not involve everyone in the organization and it is unlikely to be speedy or simple.

From a theoretical perspective, organization studies shows us that we cannot necessarily take for granted the seemingly certain and prescriptive vocabulary of strategic management. Organization studies deals for the most part with contested perspectives. In doing so, strategy can be characterized as neither a certain recipe for success nor a normative tool box of charts, matrices and models. To give an example, Sillince (2006) shows that the majority of strategy texts and models use terms without much sensitivity to how they are used and what might be interpreted differently from such terminology. Take the term 'competitive advantage'. Most strategy texts would use the term almost as everyday language, meaning (uncontestably) that advantage (the creation of value) is a direct function of the resources an organization controls and the products or services it produces. However, as Sillince (2006) argues, this omits any consideration of what might constitute value or what comprises a resource. Both are subject to very different interpretations and meanings. Organization studies reveals that much of the vocabulary and terminology of strategy is built upon contestable notions, rather than the seemingly solid and incontrovertible foundations described by the classical economist. Case box 10.1 illustrates the concept of competitive advantage in a retailing context, showing that Tesco understood clearly how to establish a competitive advantage in the minds of consumers.

Case box 10.1: What Tesco knows and what Woolies forgot

The cab driver was bemoaning the closure of the local Woolworths. 'The problem, guv, is Tesco.' That company, he explained, offered better quality and value in the goods people used to buy at Woolworths.

I suggested this was a problem for Woolworths, but not for him. He would only repeat that Tesco was too powerful. I tried to respond that the failure of Woolworths demonstrated the opposite: that the power of a giant retailer lasted only as long as its customers wanted it to. Then we arrived at the station.

The abrupt end to the argument let me feel I was winning. I did not think I was winning when I talked to a group of health and education professionals, upset about recent reforms. They explained that what people wanted from medicine was good treatment, not choice of treatment. Having your appendix out was not like buying a dress, where some people wanted one thing and others another. All parents want to send their child to a good school, and choice just means that the best schools are oversubscribed.

I countered that this did not make choice a bad idea: it was evidence of failure to act on the very obvious signals that choice was giving. If there are queues at Tesco and the Woolworths stores are empty, then Tesco expands and Woolworths closes. But when some schools outperform others, nothing much happens. Choice is not an end in itself, but a means to the good services everyone seeks. Choice is working best when no one wants to exercise it.

But those who defend the market system are often the system's worst enemies. I recently listened to a group of businessmen deploring the anti-capitalist tone of much of what is taught in schools. They had a point. But they spoiled it by promoting a description of capitalism that was at once repulsive and false.

They talked about 'wealth creation', although most of what they described seemed to be a diversion of wealth for the benefit of particular individuals rather than the creation of new wealth. They thought private sector activities – such as securities trading and automobile manufacture – created wealth;

▶ while public sector activities – such as health and education – used wealth up. They stressed that financial rewards were the mainspring of innovation, apparently unaware that material gain was not even at the back of the minds of those who invented computers, discovered antibiotics or created green-revolution crops.

They explained that in addition to the considerable salaries senior managers receive, large financial incentives were needed to persuade them to perform the duties that were attached to their jobs. In contrast, people who worked in the public sector mostly did so because they were too lazy or ineffective to get jobs in large corporations. They professed surprise that teachers did not relay these opinions to their charges. I understood why, and was relieved they did not.

The complacent sense of personal entitlement these corporate politicians expressed was deeply unattractive: as unattractive as the similar sense of personal entitlement displayed by the lazy teacher who knows he will not be fired. I do not think children should be taught that greed is the most powerful human motivation, because it is not, and if children are taught that greed is the most powerful business motivation we should be pleased, not disappointed, when business does not attract them.

Young people looking towards the world of work should understand that the greatest reward from a job is the satisfaction of doing it well. The people who are most successful in business in the long run are people who are passionate about business – whose aspirations are to bring new products and services to market, to serve customers better, to motivate their staff to greater efforts. And, by the way, you can make a lot of money in the process. That is why Tesco is prospering and Woolworths has failed. That is the lesson we should teach our kids, and which our cabbies should have learnt. It is a lesson that is as relevant to the public sector as to the private.

Source: by John Kay, *Financial Times*, 6 January 2009
© The Financial Times Limited

In this chapter, we take a more detailed look at some of these issues. One of the most notable elements in what follows is that the discipline of organization studies has paralleled that of strategic management in its development. Both deal with uncertainty, advantage, ambiguity and the life and death of organizations, for example. But not too often have organization theory and strategic management cross-referenced each other, despite these common concerns. This chapter tries to identify some of the key perspectives in organization studies and show how these relate to strategic management. For readers interested in the detail of organization theory and its development, there are plenty of handbooks and shorter potted histories (see Clegg et al., 2006 and Grey, 2005 for example). Space limitations here mean that we shall deal with some of the major organizational approaches to strategy but by no means all of them.

10.1 Strategy as a behavioural process

10.1.1 The behaviours of individuals

Herbert Simon (1945) was one of the earliest scholars to point out the limitations of assuming that strategy was crafted and implemented by rational actors. Together with Richard Cyert and James March (all then at the Carnegie-Mellon School in North America), he firmly established strategy as a behavioural phenomenon. In particular, these researchers emphasized that strategists were prone to two behavioural traits which took them far away from rational economic action.

First, they are 'boundedly rational' (Cyert and March, 1963). Strategists will accept the first satisfactory option rather than the best (known as satisficing behaviour); they will be unable to consider more than a very limited number of alternatives at any one time (bounded rationality); they will only seek information when there is a problem (problemistic search) and they are biased in their interpretation of data (March and Simon, 1958). Managers operate as intendedly rational, but do so within bounds. It is important to note that their behaviour is reasoned and not irrational (which is entirely different).

Second, as we noted in the introduction to this chapter, strategists will engage in political behaviours. They will fight their corner, particularly from the perspective of their functional role. Organizations are divided into various functions (such as marketing or finance) and each will view strategy predominantly from a functional perspective (Cyert and March, 1963). In the absence of any unitary voice, strategy becomes shaped by a '**dominant coalition**' of these perspectives. Bargaining will take place and compromises will be reached. Essentially, strategy is a political process from this point of view, where profit maximization is replaced by bargaining and eternal compromise between interested parties. Power (the ability of one interest to exert influence over another and, hence, shape decision processes and outcomes) can be viewed in many ways. For the purposes of this book, we have chosen to take the perspective of power as a resource. Power is something groups and individuals have (and can choose to exercise in the strategy process). Many authors have shown how power can accrue to some individuals (and groups). Some of the most well known are summarized below.

French and Raven (1960) were amongst the first to define how power could be gained. They called these the five bases of power:

1 *Reward*: Where an individual has the capacity to reward another and where this is recognized by both parties then there is an imbalance of power. A manager who can promote or otherwise reward has this base of power.

2 *Coercive*: Where individual A has the capacity to impose sanctions or punishments against B then A has a coercive base of power.

3 *Legitimate*: Where B feels it is right that A should demand things of them, then A has legitimate power. This closely fits the concept of managerial authority.

4 *Expert*: If B perceives A to have key knowledge or specialized skills then A will have an expert base of power over B.

5 *Referent*: To the extent that others in the organization wish to identify with A, for example in terms of leadership style or manner of handling difficult situations, then A has referent power.

Looking at these five bases of power, it would be reasonable to assume that the more senior the manager, the greater would be his or her power base, since all five bases are likely to strengthen the higher up the hierarchy one goes. However, Hickson et al. (1971) proposed a theory of power which they termed a **strategic contingencies** theory which did not necessarily correspond to hierarchy. To gain power according to this theory one needs to be indispensable, in the right place at the right time, well networked and considered by others to be doing a critically important job. The three power sources are coping with uncertainty, being non-substitutable and central. Table 10.1 summarizes these factors.

These factors are additive. If an individual or group copes with uncertainty, is the only source of information, product or service and is well networked, then power will be greatest. It is these individuals and groups that will influence and shape strategy. This theory had the advantage of being empirically testable and it revealed that those who were most powerful in organizations were not always at the most senior levels. Hinings et al. (1974), for example, revealed that brewers and not senior management had most power in a large beer-producing company. The crucial aspect of this organization is the quality and quantity of the beer it produces, hence the power of the brewers. Crozier (1964) had earlier revealed that maintenance workers had more power than

Table 10.1 Strategic contingencies: factors which confer power	
Source of power (contingencies)	**Characteristics**
Coping with uncertainty	Functional specialization means some departments or individuals cope with ambiguity and unpredictable events. They absorb uncertainty in the organization, creating more certainty for others in the firm. By doing this, they gain power.
Non-substitutable	If a group or an individual cannot be substituted in an organization, then they will gain power since other parts of the organization will be dependent upon them.
Central	Being well networked confers power. The greater are the number of links in this network with others, the greater is the power base (pervasity) and where stopping work would have an immediate effect on the organization the power base similarly increases (immediacy).

senior managers in a cigarette factory in France. They kept the old and often unreliable machines going and no one else had this knowledge. As a result, they successfully negotiated a substantial pay rise, effectively holding senior management to ransom.

In the present competitive environment, we can see that those with expert knowledge become influential over a range of decisions and outcomes. For example, students who are often greater experts than their teachers in terms of web-based learning technologies can shape the curriculum and how it is taught. Bio-technologists who are experts in recombinant DNA (for example) and other scientists who have the potential for new discoveries to advance human progress have a strong influence over the future economic and social strategies of nations all over the world. In essence, a firm's knowledge can be regarded as a key strategic resource.

An interesting result of this cognitive and political view of strategy is that it is likely to result in predominantly conservative and routine-bound processes. Suggestions of novel changes, or of big leaps forward, will always be tempered either by suspicion (from various different interests) or by standard operating procedures (resulting from earlier compromises between interests) which allow strategists to adapt to conditions as they emerge. The likely result is inherently conservative strategic decision making (Quinn, 1980). Interestingly, firms can survive for long periods by adopting these small adjustments to the environment and making a profit (albeit sub-optimal). This is because those who monitor a firm's performance (such as regulators or shareholders) are themselves trapped in the same satisficing context with insufficient knowledge to know that the firm could perform better and more profitably (Nelson and Winter, 1982).

10.1.2 The behaviours of markets

This perspective assumes that markets (or the wider environment of an organization) will secure profit maximization for the firm (and will seal the demise of others). In effect, the behaviours of these markets render managerial decision making as, at best, an operational activity. Strategy is effectively decided by the behaviours of the market. The prevailing perspective of this approach is one of natural selection amongst organizations. Strategists don't really need to be optimizers since forces in the market (or the wider environment) will ensure that only the best performers remain in business. Essentially this is organizational Darwinism where only the fittest firms survive.

The biological underpinnings of this perspective have a long tradition which can be found in systems theory (see Chapter 2), evolutionary theory and population ecology analyses (Hannan and

Freeman, 1977). Alchian (1950) described an evolutionary view of the firm, emphasizing that an organization's fit with its environment is key. Strategy is a case of assuring best fit and then assuming that competitive markets will do the rest. In essence the market is the strategy of the firm since a lack of environmental fit will seal the demise of the firm over time. As many commentators have noted, entire industries as well as individual organizations can literally disappear in the context of continuous misfit.

Case box 10.2: **The UK car industry: failure to adapt to the external environment**

We see mixed prospects for companies manufacturing passenger cars in this country, and for individual plants. There were particular reasons why Longbridge and Ryton closed and for the loss of the third shift at Ellesmere Port. However, though the combination of problems experienced by these plants may have been especially acute, we heard nothing to make us believe that they were unique to these plants or their parent companies.

At present the automotive industry still seems to be wedded to a regional approach to its markets, expanding or contracting capacity to meet regional demand. Logistical costs and the need to reflect local tastes are important factors in limiting the scope for supplying customers from plants outside the region. While we do not believe that a shift in production from Western Europe to the cheaper Asian economies is imminent, we believe that the closure of car plants in Western Europe and the opening of up-to-date facilities in Eastern Europe, using cheaper labour, will continue. The success of Eastern Europe in attracting inward investment is likely to continue in the short to medium term. There are suggestions that the 'low cost' advantage of producers in this region is beginning to erode as wage inflation takes hold but, in turn, new low-cost regions will emerge elsewhere. Ultimately, the plants that survive will be the ones with a strong focus on cost management and, crucially, with the right products for the market.

Unsurprisingly, the age of plants influences decisions on which factories to run down or close where there is over-production. However, it is not simply the case that if a facility is old, it will close. Some companies have invested large sums of money in developing and upgrading factories – for example, neither BMW's Cowley plant nor Ford's Dagenham one is a new facility on a greenfield site. It is also arguable that, after more than 20 years of operation, Nissan's factory in Sunderland is hardly 'new'.

Of more importance than simple age is the degree to which plants are capable of adaptation to modern manufacturing equipment and practices, and the cost of adapting them relative to building or upgrading facilities elsewhere. Competitiveness depends on a wide range of factors. For instance, manufacturing the right products for which there is a demand is critical to success – without this no amount of investment will render any plant viable, whatever its age. As Ellesmere Port has recently shown, even long-established UK car plants can still win investment against the stiffest of competition and here, the UK's success can be directly attributed to industry's capacity and willingness to adapt to change.

The job losses at Ryton and Ellesmere Port appear to have resulted from a combination of causes. The fundamental one, for volume car producers, is the excess production capacity in areas of the world (including Western Europe) where demand is stagnant or falling. This does not mean that the UK automotive industry is doomed; but it does indicate that individual plants which are old-fashioned and inflexible, are simple assembly plants, are remote from the company's supply chain, produce only one main model, and have productivity or skills problems will be vulnerable. There may be large-scale job losses, such as those seen at Ryton and Ellesmere Port, in the UK automotive industry in future. It is therefore all the more important that lessons are learned from the experiences of dealing with the mass redundancies arising from the collapse of MG Rover.

Source: adapted from 'Success and failure in the UK car manufacturing industry: Government Response to the Committee's Fourth Report of Session 2006–07', Third Special Report of Session 2006–07 Ordered by The House of Commons, printed Tuesday 5 June 2007, ftp://ftp.bls.gov/pub/special.requests/ForeignLabor/ind3361naics.txt

In the above example, it is striking that the role of the manager is largely absent from the reasons the UK car manufacturing industry is in trouble. The blame is laid firmly at two key aspects of changes in the external environment and the failure of organizations to adapt to these changes. Although the full report does go on to talk about the pressing need for re-skilling and re-training in the industry, there is still an almost complete lack of discussion of the 'manager as strategist' or that strategy is anything other than adaptation to environmental and market changes. The behaviours of markets, therefore, and organizational adaptation are viewed as the key drivers of both strategy and competitive success (or failure). Even if we can ascribe some managerial agency to the process of adaptation (calling this strategy), this evolutionary perspective emphasizes the power of markets and their ability to influence performance over strategic decision making by strategists.

A parallel perspective on this kind of Darwinist view comes from organization theory and is one which the field of strategy has also embraced. This is known as the 'population ecology' perspective. There are immediate parallels with the evolutionary perspective described above, which emanated mainly from the discipline of economics. The population ecology perspective emphasizes (not surprisingly) the changing numbers of organizations in a population over time (Aldrich, 1979; Hannan and Freeman, 1977; Lomi and Larsen, 1996). There are predictable behavioural patterns in populations of organizations which (like evolutionary theory) de-emphasize the influence of the strategist over firm performance. This perspective is a combination of environmental determinism (the behaviours of markets is all) and systems theory (see Chapter 2). Therefore, the population ecology view does allow for the influence of strategists as key players in changing the context of the population. Achieving and sustaining a competitive position within the general population of organizations is achieved by a combination of determinism (environmental niches) and strategic choices made by managers (see Carroll, 1985; Harrigan, 1985). So strategy is important here.

Niches are the constellation of resources which constrain or support action. Populations of organizations exist in each niche as 'strategic groups' (see Porter, 1980; McGee and Thomas, 1986). Chapter 5 in this book also discusses strategic groups in detail. From the population ecology perspective these groups are organizations within one industry or one industrial sector which, facing similar niches, adopt strategies based upon the actions of other organizations in the same domain. Niches can be wide or narrow. Width is determined by the combination of general resources and factors specific to a particular industrial sector. These include elements such as business cycles, product life cycles, rates of innovation, the general economy, government policies, regulation and fiscal trends. Broad niches comprise organizations which can transform or reproduce themselves with relative ease since they can adapt to changing conditions quickly and flexibly. Narrow niches comprise specialist organizations in tightly defined markets.

Strategies: In a given population of organizations, the pursuit of particular strategies by some organizations can upset the previous equilibrium of the system. Such strategies include either a more efficient use of the existing resource base, or exploiting new aspects of the niche, usually by exploiting and acting upon information to which other organizations in the niche are not privy. These strategies create a temporary disequilibrium which can lead in turn to competitive advantage for some organizations (Rosenfeld and Wilson, 1999).

Despite the apparently all-deterministic nature of markets and the bounded rationalities (and other cognitive failures) of individuals and organizations, the population ecology perspective reminds us that key choices by strategists matter. Therefore, studying key elements of the choice process becomes important since it should reveal how and why some strategists make the 'right' choices and others do not. The strategist's world is far from being totally deterministic. Hence, this section of the book looks at those elements of choice. It examines how managers assess risk and uncertainty, how they make decisions, implement change, innovate and learn. In this respect, the following sections and chapters reflect the emergence of strategy as an organizational phenomenon (as opposed to being primarily conceived of as a matter of economics).

We have already seen how Jim March, Herbert Simon, Richard Cyert and others argued the case strongly against assuming rationality in either individuals or organizations. These early writings (many of them from the Carnegie-Mellon School in the US) were the beginning of a journey culminating in what we now take for granted as processual and organizational aspects of strategic management (see, for example, Hickson et al., 1986; Miller et al., 2004; Pettigrew, 2003; Mintzberg et al., 1976). Hard on the heels of the Carnegie-Mellon work, scholars all over the world began to show that strategy was an imperfect art, full of negotiation, the assessment of probabilities in extreme uncertainty, the exercise of power and the pursuit of self-interest, and, above all, was a process which needed to be characterized and understood.

10.2 Strategy as a process

Rejecting the rational, planned or deterministic models (or 'design school' as Mintzberg, 1994 termed this approach) meant acknowledging that strategy was a messy process which took place over often considerable periods of time. The main arguments were:

- Strategy was unlikely to be a planned activity with neat periods of formulation followed by implementation.

- Strategy was likely to be a messy mixture of formulation and implementation and one did not necessarily precede the other. They were inextricably interlinked and it made no sense to try to separate out these 'phases'. They were inseparable.

- Strategy was not planned but was emergent. This means that strategy is more about making sense of what has happened in the recent past (such as reconstructing a pattern in important decisions that have been taken) and less about planning in advance.

Mintzberg and his colleagues went on to classify nine alternative ways of looking at strategy away from the design (planning) school assumptions and these can be read at length in the Mintzberg et al. (2002) book *A Strategy Safari*. This work seeks to understand, categorize, and assess the full range of approaches to strategic decision making. The authors identify ten separate schools of strategy (see Table 10.2).

Mintzberg et al. (2002) argue that what they term the 'strategy beast' is not any one of these, but that each school represents a partial picture of what strategy really is. They argue that academics may spend time examining parts of strategy (such as planning or the exercise of power), but practising managers have to work with the whole lot! Table 10.2 summarizes the key characteristics of the ten schools of thought. The following chapters in this section of the book provide more detail on many of these perspectives, particularly those which are more processual in nature (the design, planning, positioning and environmental perspectives have been covered in detail in Chapters 5, 6, 7 and 8). Specifically, we examine the power and cognitive perspectives when we consider strategic decision making (Chapter 12); the cultural and environmental perspectives when we consider strategic change (Chapter 13) and the configuration perspective (Chapter 14) where we examine knowledge and learning in organizations and in Chapter 11 where we consider risk and uncertainty.

10.3 Strategy and organizational structure

Analysts have long emphasized how different structures may be found in organizations (for example, ranging from formal bureaucracies to virtual structures connected only by a web of communications

Table 10.2 Ten schools of thought to characterize strategy

School of thought	Analytical approach	Strategy is...	The key aspect of strategy is...
Design	A process of conception, matching the internal organization to the external environment	About ensuring 'fit' as closely as possible between internal and external environments	Getting the architecture of the firm right
Planning	A formal process of planned steps toward formulating and executing strategy	About being as formal, planned and clear as possible	Getting planning and resource allocation in line
Positioning	A process which tries to see how a firm could improve its position in an industry	Driven by economic analysis and occasionally is characterized by military metaphors	Strategy is a science and benefits from a systematic approach
Entrepreneurial	A visionary process of top leaders	A function of the knowledge, wisdom, intuition and insight of top managers	The crucial role of founders and/or the CEO who must have clear vision and insight
Cognitive	A perceptual process	A series of perceived patterns or is how individuals 'map' strategy processes	Creativity and cognition
Learning	Strategy cannot be planned but emerges over time	A series of lessons learned over time	To achieve both individual and organizational learning over time
Power	A negotiated process between different parts of the organization	Primarily about political negotiation between different and conflicting interests	Politics are inevitable and are the most powerful shaper of strategy
Cultural	Strategy reflects corporate culture	A function of understanding organizational culture	Understanding social processes and the influence of beliefs and values
Environmental	Strategy reflects the reaction of an organization to its external environment	Primarily about contingencies from the environment	Understanding and interpreting correctly key signals from the environment.
Configuration	Strategy is a constant process of transformation	Action, change, regrouping adapting to current contexts	Strategy and organizational change are inherently intertwined

technologies). We have seen earlier in this book how Alfred Chandler (1962) extolled the virtues of organizational size, arguing that larger organizations were more 'futureproof' than smaller ones. However, Chandler was also one of the first analysts to identify links between strategy and organizational structure, a connection still foremost today amongst strategists and researchers alike. Chandler showed that organizations manufacturing and selling differentiated products to different groups of customers adopted the multidivisional structure (and were successful). Figure 10.1 shows a typical divisionalized structure.

Chandler also showed that successful organizations with one major product (or closely related product lines) selling in high volumes adopted a centralized, bureaucratic structure. Many of these

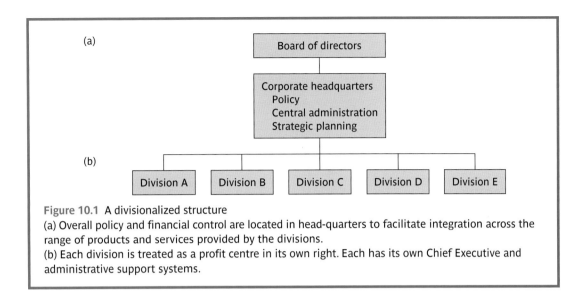

Figure 10.1 A divisionalized structure
(a) Overall policy and financial control are located in head-quarters to facilitate integration across the range of products and services provided by the divisions.
(b) Each division is treated as a profit centre in its own right. Each has its own Chief Executive and administrative support systems.

centralized structures persist in government organizations today. Figure 10.2 shows a typical centralized organizational structure (Canadian Government Ministry of Fisheries and Oceans).

Taking a historical perspective, Chandler traces the evolution of companies such as Du Pont, General Motors and Jersey Standard, showing how (during expansion) communication and authority channels could not cope and that responsibility for expanding market share was impossible to identify in the organizational structure, as tastes and demand began to fluctuate widely in very different markets. He went on to argue that a multidivisional structure would cope far better than centralized structures for such (often international) markets.

This historical work sowed the seeds for a great deal of work examining how **strategy and structure** were interrelated. Chandler had proposed a powerful nostrum, based upon in-depth historical accounts of organizational development, growth and success. It is important to recognize that he did not herald the multidivisional structure (with its autonomous and integrated divisions) as the 'ultimate' structure for success. What Chandler did was to bring to our attention that organizations adapt and shape their structures in line with the strategies they adopt (taking into account all the various constraints and contingencies this implies). So structure 'follows' strategy in the sense that successful organizations appear to adapt their structures to match the strategy they are pursuing. Those organizations that do not adapt in this way tend not to survive. Thompson (1967) later summarized the strategy/structure links in his classic book *Organizations in Action*:

1 Key contingencies for organizational structures arise from their technologies-in-use and their task environments. Because these differ across organizations, there is no one best way to structure complex organizations.

2 Complex organizations try to minimize contingencies and do so by allocating them to local disposition (such as in a multidivisional structure). But again, there are a variety of contingencies and an equal variety of structural responses to them. There is no one best structure.

3 Where there are many contingencies, organizations try to cluster capacities into self-sufficient units where each has the resources necessary for the organization to cope with its contingencies.

(adapted from Thompson, 1967, p. 78)

From a strategic management perspective, what this implies is that strategists will put more effort and resources into handling contingencies they cannot control (or cannot escape). This may

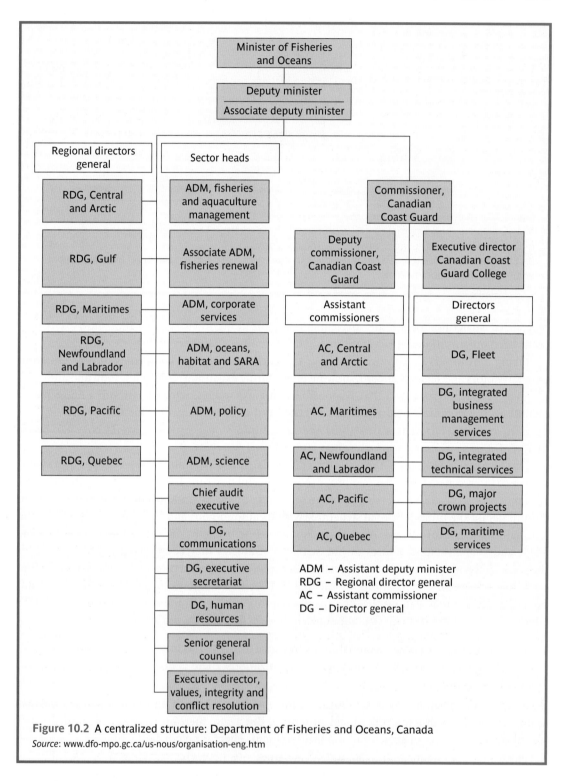

Figure 10.2 A centralized structure: Department of Fisheries and Oceans, Canada
Source: www.dfo-mpo.gc.ca/us-nous/organisation-eng.htm

seem obvious, but it has an important effect. As Thompson notes, we would predict that where strategists face many contingencies, they will try hard to control those contingencies they do control. Giving the example of a hospital, Thompson (1967, p. 78) shows that such organizations 'which operate an intensive technology, which penetrates and is penetrated by the environmental object it seeks to change' are vulnerable to many contingencies. But managers do not seek to create flexible structures to cope. Instead, they (paradoxically) exercise rigorous control over the contingencies they do control and in turn create a highly routinized and inflexible organization which Goffman (1968) referred to as 'total institutions', batch processing patients and patient care in order to remove variation as much as possible.

A great deal of research has subsequently been carried out to investigate the structures of organizations and the factors which shape the choices of appropriate structures. It is beyond the scope of this book to examine this topic in depth. Indeed, books have been written about this subject alone (see, for example, Mintzberg, 1979). However, links between strategy and structure can be summarized as:

- The larger an organization, the greater will be its tendency to be more formalized and specialized in structure. Strategy, in turn, will tend towards being a bureaucratic planning process, experiencing likely difficulties in coordinating a large number of specialized units.

- As organizations get older they tend to become specialized, again creating potential coordination difficulties for strategists.

- Complex technologies mean that organizations need to recruit more professionals who understand the technology and, hence, strategy can easily become shaped and influenced by these professional experts (rather than by other senior managers).

- The more unpredictable and dynamic is the environment of an organization, the greater is the likelihood that it will adopt a decentralized structure. Strategy is likely to be dynamic, with decisions being made quickly and subject to change as environmental conditions alter. The reverse holds true for organizations in unchanging, stable environments, where they will adopt a centralized structure and likely be characterized by slower, more bureaucratic strategic decision making.

10.4 Strategy as an organizational culture

Although cultural studies have a long scholarly tradition, notions of culture did not really enter the world of the strategist until the late 1970s and early 1980s. National and international cultural studies began to permeate the field of the global strategist. Doing business in Japan was different to doing business in India or Scandinavia and researchers such as Geert Hofstede (1980) gave us cultural classifications of different countries in the world so that the strategist might know what to expect when doing business internationally or why values, norms and social customs can vary widely between countries in the world. In the US, Deal and Kennedy (1982) classified **organizational culture** as simply 'the way things are done around here' and argued that the culture of an organization was a large potential barrier to change and innovation and was a cornerstone of corporate success. While this set the stage for the 'softer' side of business, strategy as a discipline was hit with a path-breaking text by two ex-McKinsey consultants (Peters and Waterman) in 1982. This was a bombshell text in many ways. From a pure research point of view it was sloppy and poorly executed, yet its message chimed with the times and it became one of the biggest sellers of all management texts.

Peters and Waterman argued that something called organizational culture was the key influence over the economic performance of a range of organizations. More specifically, these authors argued that Japanese organizations were posing a huge economic threat to North American firms, prompting Pascale and Athos (1982) to argue that North American organizations needed to embrace the 'art of Japanese Management' (Grey, 2005, p. 65). This meant abandoning the emphasis on rational and structural aspects of strategy and, instead, concentrating on a more holistic approach emphasizing softer and more 'human' factors such as management style and generally how it feels to work in an organization. The concept of organizational culture was born. More importantly, organizational culture was deemed by these and many subsequent authors to be the holy grail in ensuring successful and competitive strategies. Schein (1992, p. 12) defined organizational culture as:

> *A set of basic tacit assumptions about how the world is and ought to be that is shared by a set of people and determines their perceptions, thoughts, feelings and, to some extent, their overt behaviour.*

From an organizational perspective culture comprises the basic values, ideas, assumptions and norms which guide individual and business behaviour. These can be found in factors such as stories, organizational legends, ritual, language, dress codes and jargon. Martin (1992) suggests that these cultural factors in an organization can be harnessed at all levels in the organization, but can be particularly effective when the top teams in a firm embrace the 'culture' and try to integrate and socialize the rest of the organization into this perspective. Such cultures can be seen in strategic mission statements designed to unite an organization during strategic decision making. This is what Hamel and Prahalad (2005) termed 'strategic intent'. Examples include:

Yamaha	'Kill Honda'
Avis	'We try harder'
Federal Express	'Absolutely on time'
3M	'Traditional 3M margin'

(adapted from Rosenfeld and Wilson, 1999, p. 271)

If these values became constantly reinforced throughout the organization by formal and informal policies, they would become second nature to all employees, creating greater commitment to the organization and ultimately generating more profits. It is hardly surprising that organizational culture became the hottest topic for any management consultant during the 1980s and early 1990s and, to a great extent, is still seen as a panacea for successful strategic decision making today. Kotter and Heskett (1992) argued that 'strong' (i.e. unitary) organizational cultures are fundamentally associated with excellent performance. Small wonder that 'value engineering' (to try to establish such strong cultures) became the preoccupation of consultants and strategists alike and remains a concern today. However, many authors argue that organizations were likely to be characterized as collections of different sub-cultures rather than as a unitary strong culture (see Rosenfeld and Wilson, 1999; Wilson, 1999). It is unlikely that many organizations will achieve such a degree of integration as to allow them to be called unitary cultures. It is far more likely that differentiation of sub-cultures is the norm, with large organizations comprising many different sub-cultures within their bounds. For example, Bloor and Dawson (1994) revealed that an overall organizational culture in a healthcare service organization was characterized by high professional standards and a commitment to client rehabilitation. Social workers within the organization certainly worked by these 'core values' but also created their own sub-culture by focusing on ethical behaviour and client advocacy. However, the organization did not fragment or fall apart. This was because all parts of the organization agreed that the central values of the organization were important and the sub-culture values they adopted did not interfere with the organization's central culture. Social workers' beliefs did not detract from the strength of the dominant organizational culture. Many organizations which comprise different groups of professionals are likely to exhibit evidence of sub-cultures.

Wolfgang and Ferracuti (1970) suggested that a sub-culture, like a child, could never be entirely different from its parent, the dominant culture. However, some sub-cultural values may conflict with the dominant organizational culture. Wolfgang and Ferracuti (1970) and Zellner (1995) have identified sub-cultures (which align with and tolerate the dominant organizational culture) and counter-cultures (which adopt discordant values and oppose central aspects of the dominant culture). Sometimes this can be destructive, resulting in organizational fragmentation and, sometimes, counter-cultures can result in positive changes in organizations. An example of the latter can be found in the work of Martin and Siehl (1983) who examined how John DeLorean created a counter-culture in General Motors. This was characterized by dissent and a desire for independence and autonomy because he was dissatisfied with General Motors' strong organizational culture which was characterized by loyalty and conformity. By means of his charismatic leadership and his storytelling practices, John DeLorean was able to convince others that his cultural values were superior to those of General Motors. His counter-culture movement gained strong momentum and its values were eventually integrated into the dominant culture.

From a strategy perspective, these debates matter because the links between culture and performance are an almost constant claim in many studies of organizational culture. The following chapters in this part of the book address some of these questions, such as how are strategic decisions made and does organizational culture matter? And what happens when implementing a strategy means changing a culture or sub-culture? And is organizational culture a source of competitive advantage?

Before we investigate these aspects of strategy, there is one final 'organizational' perspective on strategy which has been gaining in influence and importance (its devotees would argue) in recent years. This perspective is known as the '**strategy as practice**' approach to understanding strategy and it was born out of a dissatisfaction by many authors that strategy as a subject was increasingly divorced (and remote) from any discussion about the managers who crafted and implemented strategy. Strategy as practice was, above all, a plea for getting away from abstract models and concepts and instead examining what managers actually do when they engage in strategy. We examine this approach in the next section.

10.5 Strategy as practice

A relatively recent approach to strategy (although it has easily traceable historical roots) is the practice approach, drilling down into what managers actually 'do' when they 'strategize' (a term which seems to have emerged alongside the emerging popularity of this perspective). As Jarzabkowski and Wilson (2006) note, much of 'traditional' strategy theory has been criticized because it is not actionable in practice. Prahalad and Hamel (1994, p. 5) argue that practitioners are 'abandoning traditional approaches to strategy' while academics are 're-examining the relevance of the concepts and tools of the strategy field' and looking instead to see what managers do in practice. This is a deceptively easy question, since it is by no means easy to tell when strategic activity is taking place and when it is not; nor is it easy to identify an appropriate level (or levels) of analysis to these questions. For example, should we examine the cognitive and psychological aspects of individuals when they engage in strategic activities, or should we look at their physical activities or try to describe the processes in which they engage (such as decision making)?

There are no concrete answers to the above question, since all would be legitimate ways of drilling deep into what managers do when they engage in strategy. Jarzabkowski (2005) provides a useful perspective to the practice approach by concentrating on what she terms an 'activity-based' view. By this, she means that managers themselves define what is (and is not) strategic and their actions, discussions and decisions constitute an important part of understanding strategy. A large part of this perspective, viewing managers as agents and examining how they manage strategy, shapes the following chapters in this part of the book. We look at how managers interpret uncertainty, how they make decisions, how they manage implementation and change, how they learn and, finally, how they govern at the highest levels of the organizational hierarchy.

One of the key contributions made by Jarzabkowski's (2005) study is that strategy is what she terms a 'situated' activity. Although there are many arguments about what is meant by the term 'situated', it predominantly describes the relational nature of managers (as actors) with situations (the contexts in which they operate). Any particular action by managers must be seen (and understood) in the context of the situation in which that action occurs. Just to make things even more complicated, managers are both recipients and creators of the situational context in which they carry out the activities which go into creating strategy.

Why is such a micro focus useful? The main answer is that the strategy as practice perspective highlights differences in strategy making that might otherwise be missed. From a more macro perspective, organizations can look fundamentally similar. They face similar social, political and economic contexts in which they are embedded. However, this similarity can be deceptive. Jarzabkowski (2005) shows how three universities, all facing the same often mutually contradictory tensions of increasing revenue from research and from commercial activities, craft and implement very different strategies towards trying to resolve this tension and increase revenue streams. Only a micro focus can reveal these key differences between organizations in the ways in which their managers handle strategy.

Strategy as practice is certainly an organizational approach to strategy (something which will be developed in the following chapters). It shows how face-to face interactions between managers are imbued with the context of administrative and organizational procedures, all of which can influence and shape strategy over time. There is no sharp distinction between formulation and implementation from this perspective. 'Strategizing' is a blend of individual interactions and the organizational context over time and not necessarily in a strict (or seemingly logical) sequence.

Running in parallel to the strategy as practice approach, Heracleous (2003) also questions the traditional approaches to strategy and argues for a more situated and more micro perspective. He argues that strategy is best understood as a performative art, represented both by what managers do (practice) and by what/how they communicate (discourse). Strategy is a creative art form, argues Heracleous, which can be best understood by looking at the language managers use and the activities in which they engage. Language matters at all levels. For example, drawing on the work of Dru and Lemberg (1997), Heracleous shows how simple language changes (brand descriptions) can successfully reposition a product and its perception in the market. He cites IBM moving from 'Selling Computers' to 'Providing solutions for a small planet' and Oil of Ulay moving from 'selling youth, beauty is about looking younger' to 'selling a lifetime of beauty, beauty is about looking beautiful at any age'. Both repositionings via language were successful.

Such language changes can achieve significant changes in market/consumer perceptions of a product and a company, but they do not require significant changes internally in the organization. However, Heracleous reminds us that most strategic decisions are not so neutral in terms of demanding significant changes in an organization and that language plays an important part in determining whether or not a strategy will be successful or not when fundamental changes need to be made. He reminds us that verbal and text-based communications in organizations are predominantly 'local'. That is, each organization will have its own modes of expression and communication which effectively represent social and organizational reality. Such discourses are causally related to ways of thinking and acting in organizations. Values and beliefs are reinforced and created in this way; actions are taken and structures are created; relationships are created and reinforced and organizational culture is sustained. Changing the discourse is likely to achieve significant change in what managers do, how they do it and how they perceive the world of the organization around them. As Heracleous (2003, p. 117) argues, such communications and language are 'the central avenue by which it (the organization) can be influenced' and hence changed. We examine the question of strategic change in Chapter 13 of this book.

10.6 Summary

Organization theorists and strategic management scholars converge in their thinking about strategy, although the two subject disciplines developed somewhat separately. They share a common root in the work of the Carnegie-Mellon pioneers such as Cyert, March and Simon who championed the cause of organization, especially its limitations with respect to optimal solutions and processes. The limits of organization (and its individuals) provided a firm foundation for both behavioural and processual theories of strategy. Below are listed some key concepts introduced in this chapter with some brief explanations:

Organizational perspectives: Strategy is shaped and influenced by features of organizations such as their people, structure and culture (see below).

Behavioural perspectives: Individuals exhibit behaviours which do not conform to the assumptions of 'economic man'. Individuals do not always seek to maximize profit; they have a limited grasp of available alternatives and possible solutions (imperfect knowledge). Individuals also exhibit political behaviours where they fight for scarce resources or try to influence decisions in a way that benefits their interests. Markets also exhibit behavioural characteristics. In particular, the fit (or alignment) of an organization with its environment is key to performance and survival. Strategy, from this perspective, is about ensuring as close an alignment as possible between an organization and its operating environment.

Process perspectives: Strategy happens and unfolds over time. To understand strategy from this perspective means being able to characterize how strategy and time are related. In particular, the process perspective raises two key questions. First, it questions whether strategy can ever be planned in advance, arguing that most of the time it simply emerges from a cluster of activities (including decision making) and what emerges is what we call strategy. Secondly, this perspective questions whether the process of thinking, deciding and acting (implementing) occurs in a strict (or linear) sequence over time. Process scholars argue that all these 'phases' of strategy often happen simultaneously, or that implementation may occur in advance of thinking (or deciding), for example.

Structural perspectives: These approaches show how the structure of an organization is related to strategy and argue that strategy and structure should not be treated independently. One key relationship is that organizational structure follows strategy. Made famous as almost a truism by Alfred Chandler in the 1960s, he showed that successful organizations adapted and changed their structures to suit the strategy they were adopting. Subsequently, other scholars have questioned the sequencing of this relationship, arguing with equal strength and evidence that strategy follows structure or that there is a reciprocal relationship between them (see Chapter 12). Either way, this perspective shows how strategy can only be understood by also taking organizational structure into account.

Cultural perspectives: These approaches argue that the 'softer' sides of an organization have a strong influence on strategy. Norms, beliefs, value and even dress codes can influence how strategy unfolds and on what criteria (and values) decisions are made. The cultural approach also took a wider lens by examining the cultures of nation states, arguing that different countries in the world exhibit different combinations of features such as tolerance of ambiguity, the exercise of power and collective or individual behaviours. Most famous amongst these scholars is the Dutchman Geert Hofstede who classified 50 different countries by these characteristics and argued that it was these factors which impacted most upon strategy. He argued that this was because different countries exhibit different degrees of mental programming (such as Austrians will wait at a red pedestrian light even when there is no traffic, but a Dutch person will cross the road). These 'programmed' differences heavily influence strategy.

Practice perspectives: Essentially, this is a micro focus on strategy, examining what managers actually do when they engage in creating and implementing strategy. It examines actions, narratives (how actions are described and communicated) and the contexts in which these actions take place. This perspective argues that what matters most is seeing how managers use (or do not use) strategy tools and concepts in their work. It also argues that strategy can be viewed as how managers perform, in particular what they say and how they communicate key messages around the organization. Such practices create and reinforce beliefs, values and norms which, in turn, influence organizational strategy.

In the following chapters of this book, we examine the major aspects of such organizational approaches. We examine how risk (and its perception) can be modelled mathematically in search of some form of optimum probability, but that it is also a highly behavioural concept where perceptions of risk matter as much as probabilities. We examine in greater detail how strategic decisions are made and which factors shape and influence both the processes and the outcomes of strategic decision making. Finally, the remaining chapters examine the impact of strategy on organizations both in terms of knowledge and learning and the inevitable requirement to manage change in the light of decisions made.

Key terms

Recap questions and assignments

1 Think of a recent strategic decision in which you have been involved (or are familiar with).

2 Look at how it was made and examine how these characteristics match against Mintzberg's ten schools of thought.

3 Which of the many faces of strategy do you think best describes how decisions are really made in organizations? Why do you think this?

Case study 10.1: **The cash-register guy**

After his first year, Mark Hurd is putting Hewlett-Packard back on course. On his desk, atop a small pile of papers, sit some shiny brass knuckles of the sort used by street fighters. The gleaming metal weapon seems incongruous in the otherwise bland office of Mark Hurd, Hewlett-Packard's prim-and-proper boss. Is the lethal object intended for inquisitive Wall Street analysts or pernickety journalists? Perhaps it is to remind him of the battles he faces as he tries to turn around a sprawling, $90 billion technology company, following years of lacklustre performance.

One year after he took the job, following the forced departure of the flashy but flawed Carly Fiorina, Mr Hurd has started to revive the fortunes of a legendary Silicon Valley firm. He has slashed costs (and 10% of the workforce), focused the firm's strategy around a few core areas, and separated product divisions. He has hired top managers from outside the famously insular firm. These are the sort of routine aspects of business that rarely generate headlines – and because of that, precisely what HP needs.

The new chief executive is an understated operations geek, the type of manager that excels at HP, the epitome of an engineering-driven company. 'Vision without execution is nothing,' he says. 'Whenever anyone asks me about vision, I get very nervous. You've got to be able to tie it back to strategy; you've got to tie accountability to things.' Mr Hurd prefers to stand when he talks rather than sit; he wears crisply knotted ties while his managers are allowed open-collared shirts. At 49 years old, his hair is cropped short and every strand is perfectly in place, as one might expect from a man who spent the past 25 years ascending the ranks of a century-old business in Dayton, Ohio called NCR – originally National Cash Register.

When Mr Hurd took charge of HP, it was reeling from the aftershock of a controversial merger in 2002 with Compaq, a struggling computer-maker. The idea had been to attain greater economies of scale in the low-margin PC business, rather than be reliant on the firm's core money-makers: printers and ink cartridges. Ms Fiorina staked her job on the Compaq deal – which was only just approved, by 51% of shareholders, despite the opposition of the Hewlett and Packard families. Yet her penchant for self-promotion estranged her from the company's rank and file – and she failed to get quick results. Wall Street wearied of her. In such a climate, Mr Hurd was called in to set things right.

What he found was a firm spread thin with many units losing money and propped up by the sales of printer-ink cartridges. Its activities spanned both the consumer and business market, selling everything from high-end software to flat-panel television screens. Yet instead of shedding business units, Mr Hurd has decided to (in his words) 'double down' on his bets, and simply do more of the same, but better.

Over the past year he has reorganised HP into three main divisions: enterprise computing and services; general tech hardware (such as PCs, handheld devices and the like); and imaging and printing. The company hopes to capitalise on trends such as computing on the move, and the growing demand for printing, including sophisticated commercial printing.

Some of the reforms are starting to bear fruit. For instance, in 2003 following the Compaq merger, the printing and imaging business alone represented around three-quarters of the company's overall profits; today this has dropped to slightly more than half. Every division now makes money. By making managers and the sales force more accountable and by encouraging cross-selling, the firm has increased the amount of extra products it sells alongside its hardware. Even the commodity business of PC sales is showing signs of life, making margins of around 3%, while printing and services units are forecast to have margins upwards of 15%. People inside and outside HP say Mr Hurd has re-energised the troops.

No surgery needed

How did a 'cash-register guy' arriving from the Midwest manage to achieve all this at a Silicon Valley information-technology firm? Mr Hurd learned some valuable lessons at NCR. He made his mark there by scrutinising the firm's operational data the better to understand its performance, and uncover inefficiencies. That is what he has in effect done in his first year at HP. His time at NCR also gave Mr Hurd a crash course in the 'do's and don'ts' of handling a merger. In 1991 AT&T purchased NCR (then, the fifth-largest computer-maker) as a way to get into the computing business, but after poor integration, AT&T ended up shedding it in 1996 for $4 billion less than it paid. Asked if there are any parallels to be drawn with HP, Mr Hurd firmly says not. (It is the orthodoxy at HP to speak favourably of Ms Fiorina, just as it is only to chirp the praises of the Compaq merger.)

Mr Hurd has ruled out selling bits of the company for the moment – although many analysts argue that the PC division should be jettisoned – as well as making big acquisitions. Smaller buys are being made, however. In the past 18 months, HP has bought a score of firms to boost its software, services and printing divisions. Ultimately, the strategy must be to carve out a distinct identity for HP – so that the firm is no longer constantly measured against the pole stars of Dell for PCs and IBM for software and services.

Yet if this sounds like a coherent, well-reasoned plan, of course it is not. HP is only in all these businesses by an accident of its evolution, and its focus is opportunistic. HP managers gush about the inherent synergies among the units – such as bundling software on PCs, or selling both servers and the devices that access them. But the rationales sound slightly contrived. Mr Hurd is simply playing the cards he has been dealt. In time, if HP is successful in the areas it is emphasising, the differences among the businesses will only increase. Would proud HP be willing to be broken up? Mr Hurd's brass knuckles may yet come in handy.

Source: 'The Cash-Register Guy', *The Economist*, 18 March 2006

Questions

1 Explain how Mr Hurd has managed to bring success to HP.

2 How do his approaches to strategy differ from his predecessor (Ms Fiorina) and what effects did this have? Why was this the case?

3 What challenges face Mr Hurd in his continuation of the HP strategy outlined in the case?

References

Alchian, A.A. (1950) Uncertainty, evolution and economic theory. *Journal of Political Economy*, **58**, 211–21.

Aldrich, H. (1979) *Organizations and Environments*, Prentice-Hall, Englewood Cliffs, NJ.

Allison, G.T. (1969) Conceptual models and the Cuban missiles crisis. *American Political Science Review*, LXIII, **3**, 689–718.

Allison, G.T. (1971) *Essence of Decision*, Little, Brown, Boston, MA.

Bloor, G. and Dawson, P. (1994) Understanding professional culture in organizational context. *Organization Studies*, **15**, 275–95.

Braybrooke, D. and Lindblom, C. (1963) *A Strategy of Decision*, Free Press, New York.

Carroll, G.R. (1985) Concentration and specialization: dynamics of niche width in populations of organizations. *American Journal of Sociology*, **90**, 1262–83.

Chandler, A.D. (1962) *Strategy and Structure: Chapters in the History of the American Industrial Enterprise*, MIT Press, Cambridge, MA.

Clegg, S., Hardy, C., Lawrence, T. and Nord, W. (eds) (2006) *The Sage Handbook of Organization Studies*, 2nd edn, Sage, London.

Crozier, M. (1964) *The Bureaucratic Phenomenon*, Tavistock, London.

Crozier, M. (1976) Comparing structures and comparing games. In G. Hofstede and M. Sami Kassem (eds) *European Contributions to Organization Theory*, Van Goreum, Amsterdam, 193–207.

Cyert, R.M. and March, J.G. (1963) *A Behavioral Theory of the Firm*, Prentice-Hall, Englewood Cliffs, NJ.

Deal, T.E. and Kennedy, A.A. (1982) *Corporate Culture: The Rites and Rituals of Corporate Life*, Addison-Wesley, Reading, MA.

Dru, J-M. and Lemberg, R. (1997) Disrupt your business. *Journal of Business Strategy*, May–June, 24–9.

French, J.R.P., Jr and Raven, B. (1960) The bases of social power. In D. Cartwright and A.F. Zander (eds) *Group Dynamics*, Row Peterson, Evanston IL.

Grey, C. (2005) *A Very Short, Fairly Interesting and Reasonably Cheap Book about Studying Organizations*, Sage, London.

Goffman, E. (1968) *Stigma: Notes on the Management of Spoiled Identity*, Penguin, Harmondsworth.

Hamel, G. and Prahalad, C.K. (2005) Strategic intent. *Harvard Business Review*, **83**, 7, 148–61.

Hannan, M.T. and Freeman, J. (1977) The population ecology of organizations. *Sociology*, **82**, 929–64.

Harrigan, K. (1985) *Strategies for Vertical Integration*, Lexington Books, New York.

Heracleous, L. (2003) *Strategy and Organization: Realizing Strategic Management*, Cambridge University Press, Cambridge.

Hickson, D.J., Butler, R.J., Cray, D., Mallory, G.R. and Wilson, D.C. (1986) *Top Decisions: Strategic Decision Making in Organizations*, Jossey-Bass, San Francisco, CA.

Hickson, D.J., Hinings, C.R., Lee, C.A., Schneck, R.E. and Pennings, J.M. (1971) A strategic contingencies theory of intraorganizational power. *Administrative Science Quarterly*, **16**, 2, 216–29.

Hinings, C.R., Hickson, D.J., Pennings, J.M. and Schneck, R.E. (1974) Structural conditions of intra-organizational power. *Administrative Science Quarterly*, **19**, 1, 22–44.

Hofstede, G. (1980) *Culture's Consequences*, Sage, London.

Jarzabkowski, P. (2005) *Strategy as Practice: An Activity-Based Approach*, Sage, London.

Jarzabkowski, P. and Wilson, D.C. (2006) Actionable strategy knowledge: a practice perspective. *European Management Journal*, **24**, 5, 348–67.

Kotter, J. and Heskett, J. (1992) *Corporate Culture and Performance*, Free Press, New York.

Lomi, A. and Larsen, E.R. (1996) Interacting locally and evolving globally: a computational approach to the dynamics of organizational populations. *American Management Journal*, **39**, 4, 1287–321.

March, J.G. and Simon, H.A. (1958) *Organizations*, Wiley, New York.

Martin, J. (1992) *Cultures in Organizations: Three Perspectives*, Oxford University Press, New York.

Martin, J. and Siehl, C. (1983) Organizational culture and counterculture: an uneasy symbiosis. *Organizational Dynamics*, **122**, 52–65.

McGee, J. and Thomas, H. (1986) Strategic groups: theory, research and taxonomy. *Strategic Management Journal*, **7**, 2, 141–60.

Miller, S., Hickson, D.J. and Wilson, D.C. (2004) Beyond planning: strategies for successfully implementing strategic decisions. *Long Range Planning*, **37**, 3, 201–18.

Mintzberg, H. (1979) *The Structuring of Organizations*, Prentice-Hall, New York.

Mintzberg, H. (1994) *The Rise and Fall of Strategic Planning*, Prentice-Hall, Hemel Hempstead.

Mintzberg, H., Raisinghani, D. and Theoret, A. (1976) The structure of 'unstructured' decision processes. *Administrative Science Quarterly*, **21**, 246–75.

Mintzberg, H., Ahlstrand, B. and Lampel, J. (2002) *A Strategy Safari: A Guided Tour Through the Wilds of Strategic Management*, Prentice-Hall, London.

Morgan, G. (1981) The schismatic metaphor and its implications for organizational analysis. *Organization Studies*, **2**, 1, 23–44.

Nelson, R.R. and Winter, S.G. (1982) *An Evolutionary Theory of Economic Change*, Harvard University Press, Cambridge, MA.

Pascale, R. and Athos, A. (1982) *The Art of Japanese Management*, Penguin, London.

Peters, T. and Waterman, R. (1982) *In Search of Excellence*, Harper & Row, New York.

Pettigrew, A.M. (1992) The character and significance of strategy process research. *Academy of Management Review*, **13**, 5–16.

Pettigrew, A.M. (2003) Strategy as process, power and change. In S. Cummings and D.C. Wilson (eds) *Images of Strategy*, Blackwell, Oxford.

Porter, M. (1980) *Competitive Strategy*, Free Press, New York.

Prahalad, C.K. and Hamel, G. (1994) Strategy as a field of study: why search for a new paradigm? *Strategic Management Journal*, **15**, 5–16.

Quinn, J.B. (1980) *Strategies for Change: Logical Incrementalism*, Irwin, Homewood, IL.

Rosenfeld, R. and Wilson, D.C. (1999) *Managing Organizations: Text, Readings and Cases*, McGraw-Hill. Maidenhead.

Schein, E. (1992) *Organizational Culture and Leadership*, 2nd edn, Jossey-Bass, San Francisco, CA.

Sillince, J.A. (2006) The effect of rhetoric on comparative advantage: knowledge, rhetoric and resource-based theory. In S. Clegg, C. Hardy, T. Lawrence and W. Nord (eds) *The Sage Handbook of Organization Studies*, 2nd edn, Sage, London.

Simon, H.A. (1945) *Administrative Behavior*, 2nd edn, Free Press, New York.

Simon, H.A. (1960) *The New Science of Management Decision*, Harper & Row, New York.

Thompson, J.D. (1967) *Organizations in Action*, McGraw-Hill, New York.

Whittington, R. (2001) *What is Strategy and Does it Matter?* 2nd edn, Thomson Learning, London.

Wilson, D.C. (1999) *A Strategy of Change*, International Thomson, London.

Wolfgang, M.E. and Ferracuti, F. (1970) Subculture of violence: an integrated conceptualization. In D. O. Arnold (ed.) *The Sociology of Subcultures*, The Glendessary Press, Berkeley, CA, 135–49.

Zellner, W.W. (1995) *Countercultures: A Sociological Analysis*, St. Martin's Press, New York.

Further reading

Bazerman, M. and Chugh, D. (2006) Decisions without blinders. *Harvard Business Review* **84, 1**, 88–98.

Bower, J.L. and Gilbert, C.C. (2007) How managers' everyday decisions create or destroy your company's strategy. *Harvard Business Review*, Feb, 72–9.

Bromiley, P. (2005) *The Behavioural Foundations of Strategic Management*, Blackwell, Oxford.

Grant, R.M. (2008) The future of management: where is Gary Hamel leading us? *Long Range Planning* **41, 5**, 469–83.

Hamel, G. and Brean, B. (2007) *The Future of Management*, Harvard Business School Press, Boston, MA.

Johnson, G.N. and Yip, G. (2009) Transforming strategy. *Business Strategy Review* **18, 1**, 11–16.

Pfeffer, J. and Sutton, R.I. (2006) Evidence-based management. *Harvard Business Review*, **84, 1**, 62–76.

Schoemaker, P.J.H. and Day, G.S. (2009) How to make sense of weak signals. *Sloan Management Review*, **50, 3**, 81–9.

Chapter 11

Risk, uncertainty and strategy

Chapter contents

Introduction

All strategic decisions are taken in the context of both uncertainty (which is unquantifiable) and risk. Decisions involve predictions of future states of affairs and are based on incomplete information. They also commit resources which could otherwise be used elsewhere in organizations, hence there is a large degree of opportunity cost. Putting resources into one project therefore carries with it varying degrees of risk. It might be a poor choice and jeopardize the chances of taking an alternative course of action which may have yielded better results. On the other hand, the decision itself may turn out to be poor, yielding poor results or, for example, in the extreme, financial disaster for the organization.

The concepts of risk and uncertainty are, however, difficult to define precisely. This is made even more difficult because many authors define one aspect (risk) in terms of the other (uncertainty).

For example, Hertz and Thomas (1983, p. 9) note that many authors define risk as 'degrees of variability or uncertainty'. This does not help distinguish the key elements of risk and uncertainty. To do this, we need to add more precision to the definitions of each concept. Uncertainty is relatively easier to define. In this chapter, we take **uncertainty** to mean the unpredictability of and the extent of knowledge about a particular subject or event.

For decision makers, uncertainty has many meanings. Phrases they associate with uncertainty include 'it is likely' or 'the chances are' or, in the case of little uncertainty, decision makers may say 'it is quite certain that'. All of these phrases, while themselves imprecise, cluster around the notion of probabilities. Another way of understanding uncertainty, therefore, is to describe uncertainty as:

> *the subjective interpretations of probability by decision makers and analysts of problems in organizations (i.e. about the 'unknown unknowns').* (adapted from Knight, 1921)

Risk is harder to define. There are key components of risk in a decision-making situation; exposure to loss, chance of potential loss and the magnitude of potential loss.

It is clear that dictionaries typically describe risk in terms of the exposure to the possibility of destruction, loss or damage. In business organizations, however, risk also takes on other characteristics. For example, insurance companies categorize risk into at least two distinct types: 'pure' risk and 'speculative' risk. An example of a pure risk is the likelihood of damage to assets and liabilities through fraud or criminal acts. It either will happen or it will not. However, speculative risks are characterized by the likelihood of gains *and* losses from which decision makers hope profit will eventually accrue (Hertz and Thomas, 1983). Risk and reward are the essence of business. Investment in marketing, production and financial underpinning for a project are all risks undertaken by decision makers – and are risks from which they eventually hope to make some profit. Knight (1921) argues:

> *The only 'risk' which leads to a profit is a unique uncertainty . . . profits arise out of the inherent, absolute unpredictability of things.*

This takes us nearer to understanding risk. It is about the *degree and type of unpredictability* (rather than the notion that unpredictability exists, which is closer to describing uncertainty). Risk is therefore associated, in strategic contexts, with lack of time, lack of information and lack of control. We may say, then, that risk can be defined generically as:

> *The assessment, severity, amount and nature of losses which an action may incur, whether such actions are generated within an organization (such as a decision,) or are imposed upon it (such as a natural disaster). Risk is the measurable consequence of uncertainty for an organization.* (Authors' broad definition)

Thinking about risks and taking risks appears fundamental to human behaviour in social groups. In the 1960s social psychologists such as Stoner (1968) showed that individuals will accept higher levels of risk when taking decisions in groups. He found that there was tendency for groups to go for risky and high pay-off decisions, while individuals favour relatively safe decisions with moderate pay-offs. Groups do not represent the 'average' risk of their members. Stoner referred to this tendency for higher risk taking in groups as 'risky shift' decision making.

Since organizations comprise many groups, the likelihood of many examples of risky-shift decision making increases. In addition, degrees of risk will vary from sector to sector and from decision to decision. We explore these aspects of risk in the next sections. First, we need to explore the many different images and origins of risk.

11.1 Different images of risk

For instance, from one perspective, risks faced by organizations can be viewed (and defined) as a set of wholly exogenous influences or shocks which they have to face. These could include changes in the natural environment or macroeconomic instability. Natural disasters such as hurricanes, earthquakes or tornados would fall into this category, as would disruptive technological changes which force decision makers to make choices not of their own making (technologies may be invented outside the organization, forcing decision makers in the organization to respond reactively). However, few analysts of risk maintain that uncertainties due to these exogenous shocks are wholly crucial to understanding how organizations both create and deal with risk. A noticeable movement has taken place over the past 20 or so years towards viewing risk as 'man-made' (Turner, 1978) or manufactured (Beck, 1992). Both these authors argue that these organizationally created risks influence the social and natural environments. Furthermore, they may also influence national and global economic systems. The number of completely exogenous shocks to organizations is very small indeed, according to these theorists.

Events which seem to be 'natural' are argued to have an organizational origin. For example, the current global credit crunch had its origin in poor bank lending practices and 'unsustainable' housing bubbles. Further, the risks posed by earthquakes have been argued to have an organizational component, namely poor or disregarded building regulations. However, the possible occurrence of the earthquake itself is undeniably an exogenous risk. Technological failures, such as the Bhopal disaster, or the *Challenger* space shuttle (Starbuck and Farjoun, 2005), are argued to be determined by organizational processes. Perrow (1984) argued that one common factor in disasters that places people at risk is the mismatch between organizational structure and its technology in use. The explosion in the Union Carbide plant in Bhopal, India, was argued to be a result of the firm growing in size but not adapting to new technologies. When a fault occurred in the plant, it was not immediately noticed since the specialization of roles together with the remoteness of the manufacturing process (relying on arm's-length safety checks) did not accommodate inter-role communication, which would have been needed to avert disaster. When a switch was thrown (accidentally), giving a false 'all systems OK' message, role specialization meant there was no possibility of checking this, despite it being obvious that something was wrong. By the time the problem was recognized it was too late. No individual had the capacity to stop the inevitable explosion which caused long-term damage to human and plant life.

Alexander (1996) accounts for the bursting of a gas pipeline in New Jersey in March 1994 as being attributable to the structure of the Texas Eastern Transmission Company, which was traditional, centralized and inflexible, and wholly unable to cope with the demands of gas transmission. Greening and Johnson (1996) argue that highly interactive, tightly coupled and high-risk technologies can lead to high risk in an organizational structure which is bureaucratic and inflexible. They argued that one of the problems of such organizations is the inability of top-level managers to cope with (or to prevent) disasters. This was seemingly prophetic, given the economic disasters which were to follow as a result of top-level failures (such as Enron; see Chapter 15). The events of 11 September 2001 and the subsequent invasion of Iraq have also been blamed on organizational failures, in this case the paucity of information exchange between security agencies worldwide. Therefore, we can view risk as being something organizations create, as well as have to manage when external events (such as natural disasters) are imposed directly upon them.

To try to bring some order to understanding risk in an organizational context, it is useful to break down risk into subcategories that correspond to organizational activities. This allows decision makers to assess risks which are internal to the organization and those which are external to it. Table 11.1 gives some examples of how this might be done and highlights risk management tools (discussed in this book and chapter) which can help to assess risks.

Table 11.1 Categories of risks facing organizations

Risk category	Examples	Endogenous/exogenous to the organization
Strategy	Changing patterns of demand	Mostly exogenous
	Competitor actions	Mostly exogenous
	Changing markets	Mostly exogenous
	Business/government relationships	Endogenous and exogenous
	New disruptive technologies introduced	Exogenous
Operations	Manufacturing/process systems	Endogenous
	Financial/accounting controls	Endogenous
	Regulators	Exogenous
Economic	Poor cash flow	Mostly exogenous
	Changes in interest rates	Exogenous
	Currency exchange	Exogenous
	Poor credit	Exogenous and endogenous
Hazards	Natural disasters such as earthquakes or volcanoes	Exogenous
	Terrorist attacks	Exogenous
	Criminal activity	Exogenous and endogenous
	IT failure	Exogenous

Table 11.1 is not intended to be exhaustive. There are many more risks than those illustrated here, but breaking down risks into these (or similar) categories allows decision makers to assess what would happen in the worst case if one or more of these were to occur. In that way, decision makers can rate each risk for severity and potential loss. In total, such a rating can produce an overall risk assessment score for an organization.

It is difficult for many of these risks to label them either as endogenous or as exogenous. In the majority of cases, they are a combination of both. For example, new technologies and scientific developments (such as genetic engineering or gene therapy) have been described as the 'new' risks by a number of commentators (Jorian, 2000). Mostly these are seen as exogenous risks to organizations (and to individuals in society). Nuclear power and biotechnology are developed 'out there' and provide sources of cheap energy or improved crop production for organizations. But they are considered risky since the 'downsides' of each are well known. Yet, decision makers inside organizations can actually increase (or multiply) these risks. For example, decision makers in Monsanto ignored public anxieties about the testing of gene technologies and it incurred heavy financial losses as a result. What began as an external risk was badly managed internally and resulted in Monsanto facing even greater levels of risk.

However, even narrowing down risk to categories and origin (endogenous or exogenous) is not without its problems. Several strands of research have emphasized different attributes of, and meanings to, risk. The main difficulties stem from the difficulties in disentangling *organizational* risk from *managerial* risk. We explore this difficulty in the next section.

11.1.1 Organizational risk and managerial risk

Many authors have grappled with the many different definitions and descriptions of risk. Baird and Thomas (1990) argue that risk is multidimensional and that it is important to distinguish between *managerial* and *organizational* risk. *Managerial risk* taking is where managers make choices associated with uncertain outcomes. *Organizational risk* is where organizations face volatile income streams which are associated with turbulent and unpredictable environments. It is important not to confuse the two. If, for example, we use organizational risk as a substitute term for managerial risk, we make the unwarranted assumption that managerial risk taking leads to variations in organizational performance. This may not be the case. There is little empirical evidence on the relationships (if any) between organizational and managerial risk. Miller and Bromiley (1990) found that risk loaded on three separate factors (managerial, firm performance, market performance) but their study concluded little about the possible interrelationship of these factors.

Despite the relative lack of empirical evidence and the theoretical confusion, Palmer and Wiseman (1999) provide some clear and concise definitions of risk at the managerial and organizational levels. These are summarized in Table 11.2.

Differentiating between these two levels of analysis (organizational and managerial) allows decision makers a clearer evaluation of both the location and source of risks. Hazards that are clearly identified as being at the organizational level help decision makers focus on (say) environmental characteristics and help avoid needless and perhaps pointless examination of managerial processes (such as the composition of top teams). Clarity, not only over the source of risk (Table 11.1) but also its levels of analysis (Table 11.2), helps decision makers begin the process of *assessing risk*.

However, the interrelationships (if any) between organizational risk and managerial risk are much more in dispute. Some authors (for example, Fiegenbaum and Thomas, 1988) assume managerial risk taking to be congruent with organizational risk. The one and the other are essentially the same. Others (for example, Palmer and Wiseman, 1999) argue that decisions which have high levels of uncertainty (such as R&D investments) provide only a partial explanation of organizational risk. There is presently too little empirical evidence to support one view or the other. It is clear that there are some interrelationships between managerial and organizational risk, but the extent of that relationship is, as yet, unknown.

11.1.2 Prospect theory and risk

Fiegenbaum and Thomas (1988) utilize 'prospect theory' to reach their conclusions. Prospect theory is a modification of expected utility theory. It helps explain choice behaviours which do not fit with expected *utility theory*. For example, decision makers can be observed to persist in committing resources to risky and uncertain projects in an attempt to try to recover prior sunk costs which were invested earlier in the decision process. This behaviour considers *sunk costs to be relevant* to future decision trajectories, but it is in violation of the assumptions of expected utility theory which argue that *sunk costs should be ignored* in risky decision making. *Prospect theory* holds that decision makers make choices between risky alternatives influenced by both the magnitude and the probabilities of outcomes. Outcomes are evaluated as gains or losses (positive or negative deviations) from a neutral reference point. Gains and losses are evaluated using an S-shaped value function which illustrates that (say) the disappointment at losing a lot of money is greater than the pleasure associated with winning the same amount. It also implies that decision makers will tend to prefer a sure gain over a probable gain of expected equal value. This means that a sure chance of winning 20,000 euros is preferred to a 50% chance of winning 40,000 euros, but a 50% chance of losing 40,000 euros is preferred to a sure chance of losing 20,000 euros.

Table 11.2 Organizational and managerial risks

Organizational risk factors	Characteristics
Complex–simple environments	The more complex the environment, the greater the degree of organizational risk. Complexity corresponds to industry size as well as the number and heterogeneity of competitors. Simple environments, such as oligopolies, have institutional rules of behaviour. Complexity is likely to lead to blind spots, making it difficult for organizations to calculate risk or prepare for the responses of rivals since not all are understood or even known.
Scarcity–munificence	Munificence refers to the abundance of resources, which include human, financial and capital. Abundance provides a context in which greater risk can be tolerated more easily. For example, mergers are tolerated to a greater extent in periods of growth rather than periods of economic closure. The reverse is true of scarcity, when firms face less risk as they all look inward to tighten controls and to reduce costs.
Dynamism	Dynamism refers to the stochastic characteristics of the environment. These include, for example, discontinuities caused by the introduction of new technologies or novel products from competitor organizations.

Managerial risk	Characteristics
Aspirations and expectations	Aspirations are used to judge the quality of actual performance. Expectations indicate the level of anticipated future performance. Higher aspirations induce higher risks. Higher expectations mean better performance is more likely and this will induce lower levels of risk taking. The framing of a situation as either a gain or a loss may also influence propensity to take risk. For example, when managers/decision makers are faced with the likelihood of failing to meet their objectives, they are likely to accept greater levels of risk in order to try to reach their objectives and to avoid losses. When managers/decision makers are faced with the likelihood that they will achieve objectives, they are likely to favour safer options and avoid risk.
Top-team characteristics	High levels of heterogeneity in top teams are likely to promote greater risk taking. Managers with varied backgrounds (educational, international, other companies) will bring different perspectives and interpretive schema to bear upon decisions. Such groups are more likely to consider and take action on more risky, uncertain and non-routine decisions. High levels of homogeneity will induce a greater tendency to preserve the status quo and only take action on less risky decisions.
Ownership	Managers/decision makers who do not hold an equity stake in their organizations are less likely to take risky decisions than managers/decision makers who do hold a stake. Equity ownership prompts owner-managers to make decisions which are in line with shareholder goals through carefully calculated risk taking. Other things being equal, equity ownership mitigates the risk aversion of managers who hold risk-neutral preferences held by diversified shareholders. Non-owner-managers may feel that taking risks puts their employment at risk, because gambles which do not succeed can result in them being fired or, in the extreme, firm bankruptcy. They also have a less strong interest in the outcomes of successful risky decisions.
Slack	Slack means an organization has spare resources which can buffer it against fluctuations in environmental conditions. It acts to absorb shocks which could otherwise harm performance. Slack allows managers/decision makers to avoid risky decisions and major strategic changes. Low levels of slack induce more risky decisions. This 'hunger-driven' view of risk taking is shared by some authors and not by others. For example, Wiseman and Bromiley (1996) provide evidence that supports the argument. On the other hand, Singh (1986) found a positive relationship between slack and risk taking by managers. Firms do not necessarily have to be hungry for managers to take risks in this perspective. Palmer and Wiseman (1999), however, found evidence in favour of the hunger-driven view of risk taking, showing that organizations which have greater levels of slack take fewer risks.

Source: adapted from Palmer and Wiseman (1999)

One critical aspect of prospect theory is that gains and losses are assessed relative to a neutral (or reference) point. However, this point is not really neutral. Options can be framed or presented in a highly positive way, thus affecting the placement of the supposedly neutral point (Kahneman and Tversky, 1973). A set of prospects presented as likely losses will induce risk taking, whereas a set of prospects presented in terms of gains will induce less risky decision making.

However, prospect theory appears to explain many decisions one can observe in organizations. Organizations with returns which are above target level are characterized by having managers who are risk averse. Organizations which have returns below target levels are characterized by managers who are risk-seeking in their decision making. Prospect theory also helps explain what may seem, at first sight, to be odd behaviour. This is because individual managers are likely to set different levels of aspiration. For example, one manager may have set his or her aspirations very high (say for a new product). These may be aspirations about brand strength, for example. The new product may indeed reach the aspirations of one manager in terms of brand strength, but may actually perform less well in the market. Few people buy the new product. A second manager whose aspirations centred around sales would likely argue against further investment and take the sunk costs as something to write off. The first manager, however, is much more likely to commit more money to advertising and promotion of this product which (by another's criteria) is failing. So prospect theory helps us untangle the relativism which pervades individual choice processes. Gains or losses are subjectively constructed and a so-called neutral point from which potential gains and losses are calculated is rarely neutral. Finally, this begs the question of whether the reference point is individually or organizationally constructed. Organizations, as well as individuals, have goals and objectives. Organizational goals can mask what appear to be behaviours at solely managerial levels and vice versa.

11.2 Uncertainty

Uncertainty is the principle that there is a limit to the precision and the extent of knowledge about a subject or an event. Uncertainty creates risk for strategic decision makers. Uncertainty arises because we cannot know everything:

> We do not perceive the present as it is, and in its totality, nor do we infer the future from the present with any high degree of dependability, nor yet do we accurately know the consequences of our actions. In addition… we do not execute our actions in the precise form in which they are imagined and willed. (Knight, 1921, p. 203)

Such uncertainties vary in themselves, with some strategies being taken in response to a relatively predictable future, while others are taken in the face of highly unpredictable and sometimes unknowable futures. This may be seen as a scale of uncertainty, ranging from *predictable uncertainty* at one end to *uncertain uncertainty* at the other ('unknown unknowns'), (Luhmann, 1993). An example of a relatively predictable uncertainty would be world demographics. An uncertain uncertainty might be trying to predict technologies which have not yet been invented or developed.

As far as demographics are concerned, we already know, for example, that the worldwide population is estimated to grow by 29% by 2021 (a rise of 1.79 billion people). In the UK, estimates are for a 4% population increase in the same period (2.5 million people). The number of 16–34-year-olds will decline by 15% (1995–2021) and the number of 55–64-year-olds will have increased 40% in the same time period (source: Office for National Statistics). The question for the strategic decision maker is what effects will such knowable futures have on business and what strategic decisions might be taken now in anticipation of these changes? Table 11.3 lists some of the factors a clothes

> **Table 11.3** Some typical effects of demographic changes on clothing retailers
>
> - Larger market for clothes in the late-middle-aged group of the population
> - More opportunities for design and style in this market (feeding the 'Jeans Generation' which comprises this segment of the population)
> - A declining number of high-spending fashion-conscious 15 – 24-year-olds (and 25 – 34-year-olds)
> - A greater number of more affluent 'grannies' (who may spend more money on clothes for the fewer babies that will be around)

retailer might take into consideration to inform future strategies in relation to the relatively predictable uncertainties of demographics.

Uncertainties also stem from not being able to anticipate changes in the macro or competitive context or not being able to predict the consequences these might have for the firm. Uncertainties also stem from the nature of the business you are in. An example of trying to reduce uncertainties can be seen in the music industry (see Case box 11.1).

Case box 11.1: The Muzak effect of reducing uncertainty and risk

The music industry is risky. Radio programming for music is a notoriously risky business. If you get it wrong, people switch programmes and do not listen any more. Many radio stations looked to the way the Muzak company researched tastes in music to reduce their risk exposure. Muzak began as a way of streaming music of different styles and tempos to hotels and restaurants. The music was designed to fit in with the context of the restaurant (for example) and was rarely heard, although in quiet places such as lifts it could be heard a little louder than intended (and was dubbed 'elevator music').

But Muzak had an interesting attitude to risk reduction and it was one picked up by many radio programmes. Muzak found that when programming music for a whole group, risk can be reduced by choosing music that all people in the group will tolerate, instead of music that individuals in the group are passionate about.

Individual tastes in music are much more varied than the collective agreement within any typical consumer target market. And, much music that some fans are positively passionate about often prompts more negative passions in others, while music that is merely tolerable has a greater chance of being tolerable to others.

Take even just ten quasi-random people, all of a similar age, gender, income and geographical location – the marketing business calls these similar demographics. You'll generally find that they have rather widely diverging tastes in music.

Try to find music that all ten can tolerate well enough in a radio programme not to switch the station. You'll find they agree on only a small sub-set, out of all the music that they individually like. And, if you ask them how much they like the music they all agree on, it turns out it usually isn't all that much. They tolerate it, but their personal favourites are generally not included.

Conversely, if you ask them about what their most favourite music is, it's very unlikely that all nine others would also like it. Maybe a few others in the group might like it, but usually not all. And even if they don't dislike it, it's usually not their favourite music.

Music is personal. Mass media are impersonal. At the end of the day, it's a bad fit.

This means the more successfully a radio programme satisfies a large group of people enough for them not to switch the channel, the less likely the programme includes music that any individual listeners are passionate about, aside from the most peer-driven target markets (you guessed it: the kids). The great success of mass music carries with it the inevitable failure of music that many individual fans call their favourites.

When people talk about popular music culture being broken (as opposed to the music business being broken), this is usually what they are talking about, whether they know it or not. The music market is currently structured in a way that does not serve individual music fans with their passions, but simply gets them not to turn off the programme.

And then fans make their purchase selections mostly from those choices. In business terms, there is no measurable difference between mere tolerance and real positive passion. As long as the listener is still listening, the ads have ears and the radio station is making money. And, the record labels are getting promotion for their products.

But Muzak was relatively short lived. Anecdotal evidence from the grass roots suggests many active fans don't listen to music radio regularly or even at all. They just can't stand it any more – the hits don't work, with them.

And as a group their tastes are fragmented enough that they don't add up to big enough chunks for group-wise programming to be profitable, either for radio ad revenue or for record promotion. So they are simply lost to the mass media marketplace, entirely. And without a strong alternative to the mass market, they are increasingly lost to the recorded music business overall.

Once they fall out of the recorded music market, the industry ignores them. Labels and stations are looking for market share, not expecting to grow the market. But some people think revenues from recorded music could as much as double if the complete untapped market were reached.

Muzak filed for bankruptcy at the end of 2009 with an accumulated debt rumoured to be around 500 million US dollars. It's a risky business.

Source: based on material originally at www.musicunbound.com

The music industry is notoriously a risky and fickle sector. Yet decision makers in most industries are always surrounded by uncertainties. What techniques have they developed over time to cope with and to reduce uncertainty and risk?

One well-known tool for this assessment is the PEST analysis (see Chapter 1). This will be familiar to many readers and includes:

- **Political/Legal**: legislation (e.g. monopolies), environmental protection, taxation and foreign trade regulations, employment law, government stability.
- **Economic**: business cycles, interest rates, inflation, income and GNP trends, market share and price/volume relationships.
- **Socio-cultural**: demographics, income distribution, lifestyle changes, levels of education, attitudes to work and leisure and social mobility.
- **Technological**: levels of research spend (government and industry), rates of obsolescence and innovation, speed of technology transfer, e-commerce and the impact of digital technologies more broadly.

However, such macro-changes also need to be assessed alongside the more micro-changes which organizations face (such as industry structure, the influence of suppliers, competitors and customers). Although complex, Miller (1992) provides an example of combining macro and micro influences. These are shown in Table 11.4.

Some factors (such as product/market) in Table 11.4 span both industry- and firm-level uncertainties. Hence they can appear 'between columns'. Complicated though Miller's list is, it nevertheless allows the strategist to consider simultaneously both macro- and micro-level factors. It also presents

Table 11.4 Macro- and micro-level influences

Environmental uncertainties	Industry uncertainties	Firm uncertainties
Political War Revolution Coup d'état Other political turmoil Raw materials shortages	**Input market** Quality uncertainty Shifts in market supply Changes in quantity used	**Operating** Labour uncertainties Labour unrest Employee safety Input supply
Governmental policy Fiscal and monetary Price controls Trade restrictions Nationalization Government regulation Barriers to earnings Inadequate provision of public services Repatriation	**Product/market** Quality changes Changes in consumer tastes Spare parts restrictions Availability of substitutes Production uncertainties Scarcity of complementary goods Machine failure	
Macroeconomic Inflation Changes in relative price Exchange rates Foreign exchange rates Interest rates	**Competitive** Rivalry among competition New entrants Technological uncertainty Innovation	**Liability** Product liability Emission of pollutants
R&D Terms of trade Uncertain results of R&D	**Credit** Problems with collectibles	
Social Social unrest Riots Changing social concerns Demonstrations Small-scale terrorist movements		
Natural uncertainties Variations in rainfall Hurricanes Earthquakes Other natural disasters		

Source: adapted from Miller (1992)

the strategist with the problem of both measuring and analysing these factors. Many of them are difficult to measure with any level of precision or probability. We examine techniques to assess probabilities in the next sections of this chapter.

11.3 Risk analysis and assessment techniques

A variety of methods have been proposed to assess the level of risk associated with pursuing a particular strategy in the face of uncertainty. These range in complexity from observation (taking action and seeing what happens) through to quantification via Delphi techniques and multivariate analyses such as econometric and computer models.

Risk analysis provides a set of techniques for assessing the effects of uncertainty on decision making, especially capital investment decisions (Hertz and Thomas, 1983). There are a number of variations in a set of different techniques, but they tend to be variations on a theme. The theme is that:

> *the assessment of whether or not the decision is 'worth' making is achieved by taking into account the varying degrees of uncertainty surrounding the input variables to a decision.*

There are a number of commonly used measures of worth, such as *net present value* (NPV) and *internal rate of return* (IRR). The decision maker first has to define the input variables to a decision and then has to make subjective assessments of the likelihood of each. Typically, the uncertain variables are costs, prices and economic factors, and these can be identified and quantified.

For example, decision makers may be considering an investment decision in a research and development (R&D) project. In a totally certain world, decision makers would know the cash flow pattern that would occur over the life cycle of the project and a definite value could be calculated for NPV. Uncertainty, however, means that there will be unpredictability in the various factors which comprise the cash flow pattern for the project. Risk analysis provides a technique whereby the decision maker can assess and characterize the impact of these uncertainties on NPV. The probability distribution for the NPV measure is derived from the input variables and the expected value of NPV can be mapped out and evaluated. The basic steps in such a risk analysis comprise:

- Identify the main factors of the decision which are uncertain (e.g. raw material costs, selling price of final product, likely level of sales).

- Estimate the range of values within which each variable is expected to fall and assess the likelihood of occurrence. For example, raw material costs may be expected to lie within a range of 20–45 euros per tonne. Decision makers, however, might assign a probability of 0.5 that the cost will be 40 euros and 0.1 that it will be 20 euros. Each variable in the decision can thus be assessed. However, some variables may be interdependent (raw material costs will influence selling price) and the decision maker must estimate the strength of the correlations between them in assessing subjective possibilities. This can be done by a series of probability distributions in a specified range of values.

- Select at random from the distribution of values for each factor one particular value. Then, combine the values for all the factors and compute the rate of return (IRR) from that combination. For example, the lowest in the range of prices might be combined with the highest in the range of growth rates.

- Conduct the previous stage many times to define and evaluate the odds of occurrence of each possible rate of return (IRR). There are, of course, potentially many thousands of possible combinations of values. Therefore, we need to work out the likelihood that various specific returns on the investment will occur. This whole procedure has been referred to as the simulation method or the Monte Carlo method and is performed typically using a computer simulation. The distribution of NPVs thus obtained can be explained and measures of mean and variance calculated. Further, the probability of loss (negative NPV) or gain (positive NPV) can be assessed.

Figure 11.1 shows some possible shapes for NPV distributions derived from the risk analysis approved for alternative investment prospects A, B and C. Faced with these data, decision makers would want to know:

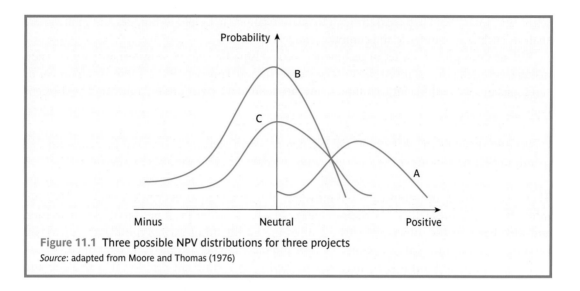

Figure 11.1 Three possible NPV distributions for three projects
Source: adapted from Moore and Thomas (1976)

- What is the probability of making a loss? (NPV < neutral)
- What is the average (or mean) NPV?
- What is the probability of making a gain greater than some pre-specified level?
- How risky is the project? Is the variability or spread (variance) of the NPV distribution large in relation to the mean?

With reference to Figure 11.1, we can see that project C has about a 50:50 chance of an NPV exceeding zero. Project B has about a 75% chance of an NPV below zero. Project C is highly risky (it has a large spread in relation to the mean) and project B is unlikely to yield a positive NPV. Project A always yields a positive NPV and this is low risk. Based on this analysis, decision makers probably would choose project A.

Knowing the shapes of possible NPV distributions helps decision makers assess the expected NPV. Of course, the shape of the distribution depends for its validity on the degree of accuracy with which subjective probabilities of the key variables in the decision or project are assessed. In addition, the decision eventually arrived at by using this technique does not take into account later decisions which may be dependent on the original decision. Risk analysis only considers the levels of risk of one decision at a time. Decision makers, however, want more than just knowing the level of risk as assessed by probabilities; they also want to make choices. In making choices, decision makers build up multiple and interrelated patterns of decisions. They rarely just make one stand-alone decision (see Chapter 13). To consider risk in multiple related decisions, we need to combine risk analysis with techniques such as **decision trees** (Thomas, 1984).

11.3.1 Decision trees and risk analysis

Hespos and Strassmann (1965) developed the stochastic decision tree method as a way of representing and analysing a series of decisions over time. It puts together classic decision tree analysis (where individual decisions are built up over time) with risk analysis techniques such as those described in the previous section. This technique is designed to handle situations of sequential investment decision making (e.g. new product launches, downsizing or internationalization) and assess risk across a series of related decisions.

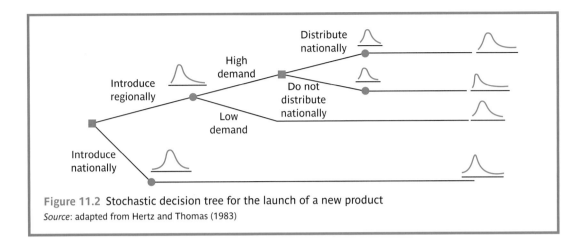

Figure 11.2 Stochastic decision tree for the launch of a new product
Source: adapted from Hertz and Thomas (1983)

According to Hespos and Strassman (1965), such stochastic decision trees assume that:

- All quantities and factors, including chance events, can be represented by continuous, empirical probability distributions.
- The information about the results from any, or all, possible combinations of decisions made at sequential points in time can be obtained in a probabilistic form.
- The probability distribution of possible results from any particular combination of decisions can be analysed using the concepts of utility and risk.

Hertz and Thomas (1983) give an example of structuring an investment decision (in this instance a new product decision) using this technique. First the decision team identifies the range of alternative options and assesses the chance events which might occur along the way. They also examine potential ways of measuring performance and outcomes. Then they can begin to structure the decision tree, as in Figure 11.2.

Figure 11.2 shows that the initial decision is whether or not to market the product nationally or regionally. If the decision is to market regionally, the firm can later expand nationally or can remain regional. Once the decision to launch the new product has been made, uncertain cash flows can be associated with each branch and represented by individual probability distributions by employing a Monte Carlo simulation. The process is repeated and the net cash flows resulting are accumulated to give separate frequency distributions for each of the four possible final net cash flows in the tree.

It should be noted that Figure 11.2 represents an unusually simple set of strategic decisions. In practice, decision makers are faced with more complex situations (each with associated risks) and the decision tree becomes more complicated with a large number of branches. A variety of option-reduction techniques can be employed to 'prune' the branches of the decision tree. These can involve working backwards through the tree, using expected monetary value (EMV) as an outcome. Where a branch has a lower EMV and higher variance than another branch it would be eliminated. This process would be reiterated until the decision tree was in a more simplified form and decision makers could begin working forwards again through the probabilities in the branches. Computer simulations can also have a similar effect. Setting up decision rules before any simulation will reduce the number of branches. For example, one rule could be to abandon branches where chance events exceed some previously specified value; then that option would not be considered and the branch of the decision tree would be removed.

In summary, the purpose of such a decision tree approach is to encourage a policy dialogue (Thomas, 1984) amongst decision makers about the decision problem before choosing a particular option.

11.3.2 Limitations of risk analysis techniques

This would typically involve discussion about the assumptions and limitations of the analytical model but, more importantly, add other insights about the problem drawn from further information and the viewpoints of the senior management team. However, as with any analytical approach, decision makers must be fully aware of the limitations of the approach. They are outlined below:

- They can easily be interpreted as falsely precise (since they are numerically complex). Complex numbers give the impression of more certainty than perhaps is the case.

- When carrying out decision analysis, it is crucial that the decision-structuring phase has been carried out with sufficient thought and attention to detail. This includes the specifying of key variables and assessing probabilities thoroughly.

- Models can be over-reliant on past relationships between variables which may not hold true for the current or future situations.

- Models may exclude important variables and parameters.

- Another limitation is the difficulty of incorporating 'soft' factors, such as cultural and social differences, which may be critical to success or failure of decisions (see Chapter 12).

- Finally, such models rarely take into account the nature of the decision, or the characteristics of the firm making the decision (although the risk attitude of the firm might be assessed by utility/prospect theory). Models cannot easily measure the degree of 'perceived' risk which individuals may feel. Such perceptions may vary widely (such as people's perceived risk in eating genetically modified foods, for example).

11.4 Risk indices

There are a range of published risk indicators, such as those from Business Environment Risk Index (BERI) or the Economic Intelligence Unit (EIU), which allow firms to use data based on expert opinions. These indices tend to select a range of variables covering a range of political, economic and financial or operational aspects of the country. The variables will be weighted. Not all may be of equal importance, so some may be given a higher weighting than others. In the BERI system, weights range between 0.5 and 3.0. The weighting makes some variables count more strongly in measuring overall attractiveness than others.

For example, in foreign market entry decisions, an expert panel gives each country a score for each variable. Scoring systems vary. In the BERI index, scores range between 0 (unacceptable risk) and 4 (superior conditions). The score and its weight are multiplied for each variable to reach a total 'risk' score for each country. The maximum country score is 100. Broadly speaking, a score of over 70 is very attractive and less than 55 unattractive. The scale is banded:

- 100–71: a stable country with a good business climate;
- 70–56: a moderate-risk country with some difficulties in the business climate;
- 55–41: a high-risk country with a poor business climate for foreign investors;
- 0–40: unacceptable levels of risk for these countries.

In 2006, the scoring was:

US (75 points)

Switzerland (74)

Belgium (73)

Japan (72)

Netherlands (66)

Germany (61)

Portugal (58)

Austria (57)

Turkey (56)

Czech Republic (55)

Hungary (55)

Poland (52)

China (46)

Other systems may use letters, A = very attractive ... E = unattractive, or a range from 'hot' or attractive countries, through to 'cold' or unattractive (Goodnow and Hansz, 1972; Litvak and Banting, 1968). Such scores are liable to significant fluctuations as economic, social and political conditions change and as new entrants appear on the list (for example, Taiwan was rated 5th on this list in 2009).

11.4.1 Limitations of risk indices

- *Risk indices* may give initial insights but are macro-level and cannot be easily tailored to inform specific decisions.

- It is possible that a country rating as unattractive may be the best choice for a particular firm depending on its circumstances. If, for example, a multinational corporation already operates in a large number of countries, it may be choosing between remaining investment targets that are all high risk.

- Similarly, markets which appear attractive may be subject to intense international competition, whereas in a market with difficult conditions, a firm that masters these may achieve high levels of success.

- Indices assume we can say something about the future based on what has happened in the past. This assumption may not be true in rapidly changing market conditions – known as discontinuous change (high uncertainty). If the future is uncertain, can history help us predict what might happen?

11.5 Using scenarios to help reduce risk and uncertainty

Alternative techniques for understanding and trying to reduce both risks and uncertainty use more qualitative approaches. One dominant approach of this type is the use of scenarios.

According to Bain & Co. (www.bain.com):

Scenario planning is not about predicting the future. Rather it attempts to describe what is possible. The result of a scenario analysis is a group of distinct futures, all of which are plausible. The challenge then is how to deal with each of the possible scenarios.

In Shell's words (www.shell.com):

> *Scenarios are carefully crafted stories about the future embodying a wide range of ideas and integrating them in a way that is communicable and useful. They help us link the uncertainties we hold about the future to the decisions we make today. When we reflect on situations, we see the world through our own frames of reference. The purpose of scenario work is to uncover what these frames are, respecting differences rather than aiming for a consensus that puts them to one side.*

These definitions remain broadly unchallenged. More recent approaches use language such as 'visualizing alternative futures' so that we can design 'flexible options for strategy' to cope with the 'diversity within these futures'.

In practice, scenarios are:

- Attempts to look into the future by bundling together plausible and logically consistent factors.
- Together, these factors help tell a story about the future influences in an organization and give it key characteristics (no matter how apparently wild these seem today).
- Such characteristics are key to helping strategists plan and effect changes to meet the anticipated futures.

11.5.1 Which organizations should use scenarios?

In theory, all organizations can use scenarios, but it is clearly important for large, capital-intensive firms (such as oil companies) to get the future context as right as possible. Sunk costs and opportunity costs are very high in these industries and getting it wrong can have disastrous consequences. Equally, pharmaceutical firms have very high R&D levels and manufacturing costs. Getting the future wrong can be a disastrous problem in such contexts and is also a problem for venture capitalists in assessing the futures of their investment portfolio.

- Scenarios can be projections of up to (and beyond) ten years into the future. The advantage of this is that strategies for change can be formulated which are relatively independent of business and economic cycles.
- Organizations which need to use scenarios are especially those which are unable to react quickly and effectively to changing events as they occur.
- Organizations which can react quickly and maintain high levels of flexibility have the option of pursuing a 'trading' strategy involving rapid changes and quick fixes. So long as this capability lasts, such organizations need not necessarily concern themselves with longer-term scenarios.
- In hypercompetitive environments classified by high levels of ambiguity and uncertainty – which includes a wide range of industries such as media, publishing, electronics – scenarios are essential. With respect to this point, see Chapter 7 which looks at organizations and competition in the new economy.

11.5.2 Scenarios and scenario thinking

Earlier in this book we considered the difficulties of planning over time scales that fall beyond the limits of competitive strategy. In particular, we noted that most companies have difficulty in quantifying any factors beyond two product life cycles. Yet strategic thinking cannot be neglected. It was Alvin Toffler who said:

> There is a slightly odd notion in business today that things are moving so fast that strategy becomes an obsolete idea. That all you need is to be flexible or adaptable or, as the current vocabulary puts it, 'agile'. This is a mistake. You cannot substitute agility for strategy. If you do not develop a strategy of your own you become a part of someone else's strategy. You, in fact, become reactive to external circumstances. The absence of strategy is fine, if you don't care where you're going.
> (*Source*: Bain & Co. website, www.bain.com)

We suggested in earlier chapters an adaptation of competitive advantage thinking that would in a qualitative way enable strategic thinking to be taken beyond two product life cycles. In this section we look at scenario planning, a method of longer-run thinking that has become very well known and adopted in many diverse situations. A search on the internet through Google reveals over 50 pages of sites whose prime descriptor is scenario planning. It is said to have its roots in military strategy studies and notably through Herman Kahn, who was famous for his work related to the possible scenarios associated with thermonuclear war ('thinking the unthinkable'). It was transformed into a business tool in the late 1960s and early 1970s at Royal Dutch Shell, firstly through Pierre Wack, Kees van der Heijden and Peter Schwartz. At a time of very low oil prices Shell's use of scenario planning enabled it to be better prepared for the oil shocks of the 1970s, the oil crisis followed by the oil glut. Indeed the subsequent success of the method owes much to Shell's success in predicting the first oil price shock in 1973. High-profile users in the US include the White House, the Pentagon and the Economic Planning Agency.

11.5.3 How useful are scenarios?

A scenario is useful in assessing the long-term ramifications of a firm's overall strategy. Analysis of multiple scenarios enables the assessment of the implications of different futures for alternative strategies and the uncertainties and risks associated with them. According to Shell (again, from their website):

> Scenarios are particularly useful in situations where there is a desire to put challenges on the agenda proactively (for example when there are leadership changes and major impending decisions) and where changes in the global business environment are recognised but not well understood (such as major political changes and emerging technologies).

A well-constructed scenario enables the ordering of one's perceptions about alternative future environments in a manner in which it is likely that one's decisions might be played out.

Therefore, there are two key characteristics of a good 'story'. The first is that it results from the subjective assessments of a wide range of informed individuals or groups. A valid story has to be built on facts and assumptions that can be validated and supported. This requires that the process of scenario development should be objective and replicable and not rest simply on guesswork, however inspired. Second, it recognizes that decision makers have some influence on future development. The simple assumption is that decision makers are in a position to react to the dimensions of the story as it unfolds. The stronger view is that the unfolding story allows for the dynamic interaction of the decision makers with the environment.

11.5.4 Writing a scenario

A scenario starts with the focal issue or decision. A generic worry about, for example, the implications of new technologies will lead in myriad directions. The issue for the firm must revolve around key dilemmas or challenges that are on the horizon (or just over) but for which there is little early guidance. The purpose of the scenario is to provide a frame within which some guidance for major commitments can be developed. Nevertheless, the focal issue can be described in quite broad terms (e.g. what will be the future for technology in banking?). Or they could be quite specific (what are the implications of new technologies for traditional banking organizations?). The longer the time frame, the broader will be the focal issue. The shorter the time frame, the easier it is to collapse scenario thinking into detailed forecasting and planning.

The second stage is to identify the primary driving forces of the future. This is usually based on the PEST analysis. Because the scope of PEST includes politics, economics, technology and social dynamics, this encompasses most of the forces that are likely to be relevant.

You are now ready to construct your story of the future (Schoemaker, 2002). A structured view of the *scenario planning* process might look as follows:

1 Identify the focal issue(s).

2 Specify the scope of the planning and its time frame.

3 Establish the broad background that includes the organization within its 'deep' structure (PEST characteristics).

4 Identify the driving forces that link the focal issues with the long-term future: these are events that are predetermined and virtually certain to occur.

5 Identify the critical uncertainties in the environment. At this point macroeconometric forecasting will be useful.

6 Combine the driving forces with the uncertainties to create alternative futures (the scenarios). These are the 'stories' of the scenarios in words.

7 Validate the alternative futures (e.g. by Delphi-style processes or by qualitatively assessing their likelihood of occurrence).

8 Analyse the scenarios for similarities, differences and sources of difference, mutual dependence.

9 Quantify the effect of each scenario on the firm (impact) and formulate appropriate strategies. Again the impact on the firm has to be assessed qualitatively since quantitative assessments would not be viable for time horizons of 10 to 15 years.

10 Develop strategy options and criteria for future choices and paths.

Although some of the above may seem similar to the probabilities and assessments made in risk analyses described earlier in this chapter, there are two main differences with respect to scenarios. First, the time horizon considered is significantly longer. Scenarios typically look 10 or 15 years into the future. Second, the specificity of the analysis is far broader and, of necessity, less precise.

The processes around points 3, 4, 5, 6, 7 and 8 may take place typically in workshop settings where executives, technical experts and policy analysts bring together a wide range of experience and expertise in order both to identify and to validate the key assumptions about the driving forces and the uncertainties, and how they interact to create the basic scenarios. Figure 11.3 shows the basic drivers of two scenarios distilled into three sets of variables, some common to both scenarios and some exclusive to one or the other.

	Common variables	Variable one	Variable two
Scenario one	Yes	Yes	No
Scenario two	Yes	No	Yes

Figure 11.3 Distinguishing the drivers of scenarios

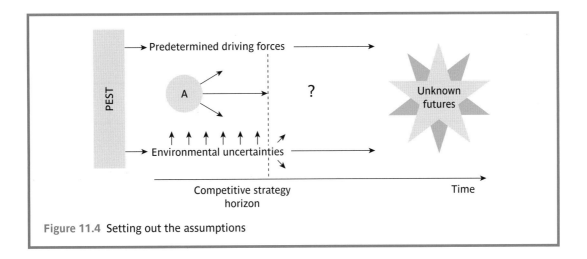

Figure 11.4 Setting out the assumptions

The analysis methods at points 8 and 9 involve testing each scenario in two ways. The first is a cross-impact analysis to establish the extent to which scenarios have common drivers and different drivers. And the second is to relate each scenario to a short list of the key variables to test for sensitivity/robustness.

Figure 11.4 shows the early stages of the analysis in which the PEST environment is determined and the competitive strategy horizon for the firm is established, leading to a specification of the focal issues. The futures are unknown and even the points of arrival on the competitive strategy horizon are uncertain.

Figure 11.5 shows the establishment of the basic stories, here characterized as 'optimistic' and 'pessimistic'. They depend on the specification of the assumptions from the first figure and the way in which the drivers and the uncertainties interact. A difficult part of this is initially to keep the stories distinct since it is all too easy to end up with minor variants on a common theme. The second problem is to restrict the number of stories to a manageable number, typically two or three. Here the need is to sacrifice complexity for the tractability of analysis. This is why at this stage it is important to restrict the key drivers and uncertainties to only what are considered the most important. Hence you can appreciate the need to consult opinion from far and wide so as to avoid our normal perceptual filters.

Figure 11.6 articulates the strategies, the options, and the paths. The paths illustrate the potential complexities. First, the starting point at the competitive strategy horizon may not be clear; points a, b and c are possible, but are broadly similar. However, point d is quite different (i.e. the current competitive strategy has failed to deliver). Second, common paths are possible and choices might be deferred until the situation becomes clearer. Thus, points e, f and g represent choices to be made along the top path. Point f leads unambiguously (as far as we can see now) towards the 'optimistic'

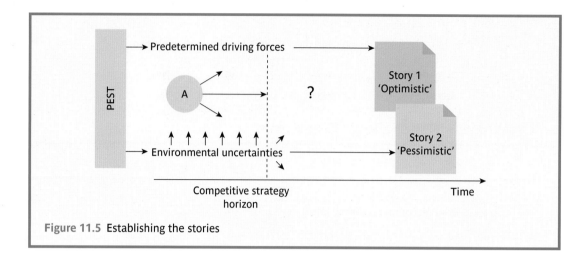

Figure 11.5 Establishing the stories

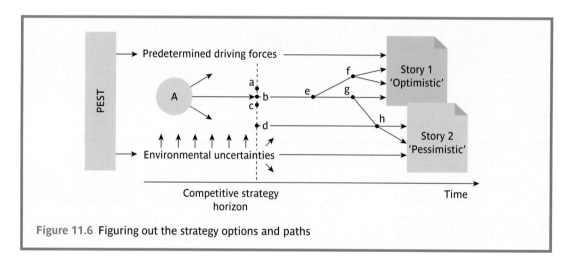

Figure 11.6 Figuring out the strategy options and paths

story with the possibility of two paths onward, one being more optimistic than the other. Point g represents a more difficult choice where either story is possible but a commitment must be made. Point h is a point along the low path to the 'pessimistic' story, the main question being how pessimistic?

Figure 11.6 in many ways mirrors the same kind of analysis as we found in decision trees (see earlier in this chapter). Reinforcing this point, Thomas (1984) argues that decision trees (and the logic of thinking through them) are vehicles for policy dialogue in a similar way to scenarios.

The process of scenario planning seeks to achieve a set of options with assessments of potential pay-offs and risks that can be unfolded over time, taking account of events as they emerge, correcting errors and acknowledging expert opinion as it changes (which it will do). Scenarios are not intended or expected to be 'right' in the sense that forecasts are intended to anticipate the correct outcome. They are intended to:

1 explore the long term beyond conventional planning horizons;

2 build on a wide set of assumptions;

3 explore a wide range of outcomes;

4 meld assumption–outcome sets to derive ranges of possible futures;

5 explore paths required to move from the present to these futures.

In doing this we need to keep our mindset very strategic. Look for common paths. Watch out for forks in the road (divergences). Identify the key risks. Find common paths where possible. Do not commit too early. Avoid the avoidable commitments. But, in the end, the commitments have to be made against the risk. If scenario planning achieves anything (and it is not a panacea) it helps to *assess risk* over the longer term and identify strategic options for the organization. It should be emphasized that organizations are unlikely to survive by scenarios alone.

Note that, in the short and medium terms, decision and risk analysis, alongside the risk/return trade-offs introduced earlier in this chapter, are more useful and immediate ways of formulating strategies and engaging in appropriate policy dialogue.

Case box 11.2, from a real situation, shows how scenario analysis can be used.

Case box 11.2: Strategic considerations for a European business in a global economy

This case is taken from a study conducted on the implications for European-based firms of a more global economy and greater economic integration within Europe. It demonstrates three levels of analysis, the world economy, Europe, and (European) companies. It also shows the distinctive variables established at each level of analysis. These then were taken to be distinctive factors that shaped each level, although recognizing that there were other actors common across the levels.

Two scenarios were established – 'pessimistic' and 'optimistic'. For the world economy this elicited the following comparison:

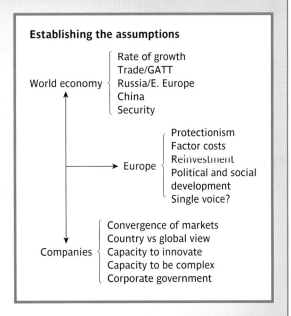

Establishing the assumptions

World economy
- Rate of growth
- Trade/GATT
- Russia/E. Europe
- China
- Security

Europe
- Protectionism
- Factor costs
- Reinvestment
- Political and social development
- Single voice?

Companies
- Convergence of markets
- Country vs global view
- Capacity to innovate
- Capacity to be complex
- Corporate government

Pessimistic	Optimistic
Low growth	Sustained growth
Inability of LDCs to grow	LDC and ex-communist growth
Protracted difficulties in China and Russia	Islam and Christian rapprochement
Inability to balance budgets: welfare costs and macro policy problems	Welfare reforms
The 1990s bubble remains burst	Radical Right makes a breakthrough?
	New surge of innovation

For Europe, there is a similar dichotomy:

Pessimistic	Optimistic
Regulation and protection increases	Political voice
Divergence from rest of world	Major trading bloc
Politically inchoate	Thrives on variety and innovation
High cost	Good home base for global companies
Low innovation	Transformation of labour markets

In staying with a dichotomy the distinction is probably too sharp and a third possibility should be explored, a simple middle of the road. The dichotomy for companies is also sharp:

Pessimistic	Optimistic
Country managers remain	Strong global market growth
Global view restrained	New federal organizations
MNEs do not evolve into more complex federal forms	Innovation becomes central to profitability
Efficiency concerns outweigh innovation challenges	Service and financial companies have v. high growth
Country–company difficulties	Emergence of new breed of MNEs from China, Russia and East Asia

The simple interaction between the pessimistic columns produces the overall 'pessimistic' scenario, and likewise for the 'optimistic' columns.

Pessimistic scenario

1 Failure to resolve the current set of dilemmas against a background of stagnation, insecurity (anarchy?) and weakening of political control and influence. There is continued failure of macroeconomic policy to resolve excessive government spending. Consumer pessimism continues to hold back aggregate demand.

2 Growth will be around 'polar' points rather than uniformly spread. World increasingly has different speeds.

3 Companies seek national or regional patronage from host countries. Trade becomes politicized; politico-economic trade-offs become the norm; trade fortresses re-emerge.

4 Power of existing MNEs is likely to be reinforced because of lack of effective competition.

Optimistic scenario

1 Marked by prosperity and high growth across the world. Multiplier effect of major investments enhanced by rapid learning in newer economies. Emergence of major new markets plus increased innovation and opportunity for development of large, new corporations.

2 Corporate environment is competitive but highly dynamic. Political influence focused primarily on investing and opening up rather than on protection.

3 Companies are able to change through growth. They are able to develop transnational and federal character but against a background which is not dominated by the largest players. Look for emergence of Chinese and Russian MNEs.

The scenarios in the case box lead to the development of two possible strategies for an organization. Companies either seek to become expert at politico-economic trade-offs, or they seek to grow transnationally and become expert on innovation and segmentation and seek to establish new organizational structures to support the federal approach. So far, so good. But as Schoemaker (2002) points out, strategy formulation is only one (important) part of the story. Should the firm pursue such strategies, there will need to be a careful assessment of the extent to which the organization is capable and able to implement these chosen strategies.

11.6 Back to the organization: identifying gaps

The above examples (and the use of scenarios in general) show that it can be easy to treat scenarios as ends in themselves. That is, the question of whether or not the organization *is capable* of implementing the future strategies informed by the scenario is either not addressed or is overlooked. Scenarios are simply tools which help reduce uncertainty and risk. They also help identify one or two future strategic directions which the organization might take, but they cannot help determine to what extent such strategies are capable of being implemented, or what changes would need to occur to make such strategies a realistic proposition for the organization concerned. The same holds true for strategies identified by risk and decision analyses. Our mythical firm in Figure 11.2 may decide to market the new product nationally rather than regionally. But the key question is, to what extent it can do this effectively?

Fahey and Randall (1998) suggest that, following the identification of future strategies, decision makers should:

■ Reflect the formulated strategy back against the organization. What gaps are there (if any) in key factors such as capabilities, capacities, competences and structures?

■ Identify what changes may need to be made to the organization in the light of the above 'gap' analysis.

■ Identify and select key indicators and signposts which will help monitor and assess the implementation and the performance of the chosen strategies. This will involve careful selection and imaginative choice as well. Using current performance indicators may not be appropriate.

There are a number of ways of doing the above, but most revolve around some form of *gap analysis*. This is where core competences of the organization are assessed against future strategies that have been crafted following the scenario analysis.

Table 11.5 shows a typical gap analysis. This is based on defining an organization's core competences and then assessing to what extent each competence contributes towards (supports) the chosen strategy. This can be done simply by using plus, minus or neutral signs. Plus signs indicate where a *core competence* supports the strategy. Neutral is where the core competence provides little or no support and minus signs indicate where a current competence actually detracts from a future strategy. Core competences are difficult to define, as we have seen earlier in this book, but they can be thought of as distinctive capabilities of the organization which:

■ create value in terms of economic rent;

■ are difficult to imitate (why can't competitors do that?);

■ are 'implicit' as part of an organization's history, routines and social capital.

Table 11.5 Gap analysis: future strategies and core competences: an example

Core competences (examples)	Current strategy	Future strategy one (e.g. expand product range incrementally; retain existing technologies)	Future strategy two (e.g. adopt new technologies and develop new product ranges to meet anticipated future)
Product advantages (lighter, smaller, cheaper)	+	+	0
Time to market (faster)	+	+	0
Ability to innovate (high)	0	0	+
Proprietary knowledge	+	0	+
Flexible structures	0	0	+

In our mythical example organization in Table 11.5, we can see that two future strategies had been crafted, each based on a particular scenario. One strategy (based on an optimistic scenario that there will still be demand for these types of products) is to retain the existing technology base, but to compete on the strength of expanding the existing product range. A second strategy (based on a pessimistic scenario that new products will be needed as well as new technologies to produce them) is to develop an entirely new product range and to invest in new or emerging technologies. The table also records the firm's current strategy.

The existing core competences of the organization had been identified as ranging from product advantages (lighter, smaller and cheaper) to flexible organizational structures. For each competence, its utility in each strategy has been assessed on a scale ranging from minus, through zero to plus. In the example there are no core competences which actually detract (or work against) any strategies, but there are core competences which vary from neutral to positive.

For example, having a flexible organizational structure does not positively support either the current or future strategy one. It is needed and will be a positive support under strategy two, when R&D and innovation will need to be communicated and processed effectively and swiftly around the organization. Having proprietary knowledge is a core competence now, but under strategy one its potency will become eroded as other organizations compete using the same or similar products. Under strategy two, where R&D will be crucial, proprietary knowledge again becomes key. Other competences, such as time to market and product advantages, are eroded under strategy two (presuming new advantages will be needed and that time to market may not be a key aspect of competition).

The utility of doing this gap analysis (which can be carried out by a small focus group) is that it shows how the constellation of competences shifts depending on the strategy adopted. The gap analysis may also reveal much longer-lasting capabilities in the organization, its distinctive long-lived assets. Finally, it may show where new competences are needed in the future and where existing competences may be abandoned. For example, under strategy two in Table 11.5, the organization may be advised to switch resources into additional competences such as high investment in R&D and a greater emphasis on environmental scanning and benchmarking as well as ensuring the selection and recruitment of the 'best and the brightest' staff to grow the firm's intellectual capital, or what March (1999) terms 'organizational intelligence' (see Chapters 12 and 14).

11.7 Summary

All organizations and all managers face uncertainties. The effects are to increase the degree of risk faced by strategic decision makers. Most techniques of strategic decision making under uncertainty (e.g. risk analyses) assume that the returns from a decision are arranged on a probability distribution conditional on the choices made. In general, decision makers are assumed to have a preference for alternatives which have higher expected values, but at the same time, they consider the riskiness of other alternatives. Decision makers seek an appropriate trade-off between risk (variance) and return (expected value).

Risk itself is a variable concept. In the consideration of alternatives, risk taking is correlated to the risk takers' changing fortunes (March and Shapira, 1999). For example, if risk is perceived to be life-threatening, then individuals, it seems, will either take highly risky decisions or will be traumatized to take very risk-averse decisions and play safe. We currently know these are the polarized choices decision makers may take, but we do not yet know enough to predict when and under what circumstances they will opt for high risk or will play safe.

Higher levels of organizational slack seem to encourage experimentation and innovation and encourage risk taking (probably because of a relaxation of controls). Lower levels of organizational slack (or when slack becomes negative) mean tighter controls, and efforts to improve efficiencies and procedures encourage lower levels of risk taking. Decision makers' aspiration levels are also not fixed. Over time they will vary, often considerably, and therefore the degree of perceived risk will vary depending on where the aspiration level is fixed. This is because risk-averse behaviour will be defined as being below the aspiration threshold and risky behaviour will be defined as being above it. Equally, individuals' self-confidence changes over time. Past successes can breed confidence (and sometimes overconfidence) in taking risky decisions. Overconfidence can occur when decision makers wrongly assume they were wholly responsible for past successes (and do not attribute success to exogenous factors, such as errors by competitors or a munificent macroeconomy where resources are easily available).

Risk itself is subject to varying interpretations and definitions. Risk can be viewed as something totally exogenous to organizations and therefore out of managers' control. Equally, risk can be seen as wholly endogenous. Even seemingly external events and threats (such as terrorist attacks) can be attributed ultimately to the actions, or inactions, of individuals and groups. From this perspective, all risk is argued to be ultimately man-made. Typically, decision makers will face some level of uncertainty between these polarized views. There will always be earthquakes, flooding and volcanoes and there will always be man-made disasters.

A key question for strategists is how to manage risk and how to craft strategic decisions in the face of risk. Stulz (2007) argues that risk managers routinely make six fundamental mistakes:

1 relying on historical data;
2 focusing on narrow measures;
3 overlooking knowable risks;
4 overlooking concentrated risks;
5 failing to communicate;
6 not managing in real time.

Many empirical models of risk have been developed and some of the main ones have been mentioned in this chapter. The limitation of all these approaches is that they are essentially short to medium term in their time horizons. In order to build in a longer-term time dynamic, scenario analysis can be beneficial to strategists, enabling them to plan future decisions based on a contingent view of what a plausible future (or set of futures) may be. This chapter has described in some detail one

▶ way of dealing with scenarios, both to develop strategies and to help make decisions in the face of uncertainties. Finally, the chapter returns to the level of analysis of the organization, since the ability to implement such strategies depends very much on the capacities and capabilities built into the organization's infrastructure. In particular, we have highlighted the role of core competences, effective governance and ensuring the organization can undertake strategic change and continue to learn. Each of these topics and its influence on strategy implementation is developed in the following chapters.

Key terms

assessing risk	363	organizational risk	363
core competence	381	prospect theory	363
decision trees	370	risk	360
gap analysis	381	risk indices	372
internal rate of return	369	scenario planning	373
managerial risk	363	uncertainty	360
net present value	369	utility theory	363

Recap questions and assignments

1 Build three scenarios for an organization with which you are familiar. Name them and provide a thumbnail sketch of their key characteristics.

2 Choose the scenario you consider to be most likely and assess the impact of this on organizational factors such as customer demand, costs, levels of competition, changes in technology etc.

3 From the story told in (2) above, suggest one or two strategies the organization might adopt now to prepare for the future you have outlined.

4 Assess the organization's capabilities in implementing your identified strategies. What additional core competencies will be needed (if any) and which current competences may become redundant?

Case study 11.1: Svante Arrenhius, climate change and global warming: what's the risk?

In the 19th century, a Swedish electrochemist suggested that burning fossil fuels would release carbon dioxide into the atmosphere and that this, in turn, was likely to change the climate on Earth. His name was Svante Arrenhius. The problem was less to do with his electrochemistry and more to do with the certainty (or not) that such a change would take place and over what time frame. He asked the question 'is the mean temperature of the ground in any way influenced by the presence of the heat-absorbing gases in the atmosphere?' He examined what would be the likely effect of doubling the earth's carbon dioxide (atmospheric CO_2) on global climate and what would be the extent of the change. He later won the Nobel Prize for Chemistry in 1903. Despite this groundbreaking work, Arrenhius was unable to be precise about the level of risk involved nor the time frame in which changes would (or would not) occur. Today, we face the same questions and it seems that science has failed to clarify the uncertainty – and the levels of risk – surrounding global warming. It is arguable that such is the proliferation of recent scientific studies that we are more uncertain about the global warming debates rather than have greater certainty over what the changes and risks are likely to be.

To an extent this is because scientists (and their spokespersons in the media and in politics) have divided into at least two distinct camps. There are those who suggest (with claims of 90% accuracy) that CO_2 levels and other greenhouse gases are having a marked effect on climate change. There are also those who claim that such science is spurious and that there are few, if any, significant relationships between greenhouse gas levels and climate change. In addition, the debate has been widely exposed and debated in the media and in political circles, with perhaps the most public face of the former camp being represented by Al Gore of the US – arguing strongly for the climate change effect (predicting floods and other disasters). The latter camp (popularly known as 'sceptics') often draw upon the work of two Danish scientists, Professor Eigil Friis-Christensen, Director of the Danish National Space Centre, and Henrik Svensmark, who researches in the same Centre. These two scientists have presented the rationale for believing that global warming is more related to natural variations in the cycle of sunspots on the solar surface than to man-made emissions of CO_2. The use of the term 'sceptics' has been extensively employed in the media. Although the science of the sceptics may be as valid and reliable as that from whom (amongst others) Al Gore draws his research, their presentation and description in the media as 'sceptical' arguably detract a little from their scientific credibility.

On 2 February 2007 it seemed the debate was over. At least that was the message from a report released in Paris by the Intergovernmental Panel on Climate Change (IPCC), the UN body of leading researchers charged with analysing climate science and producing the final word on what is happening and what will happen to global climatic conditions. IPCC scientists declared that it is 'very likely' that global warming is (in the main) driven by the build-up of CO_2 and other greenhouse gases caused by human activity, and that dangerous levels of warming and sea rise are on the way.

This report was the product of 2,500 scientists, 130 nations and six years of work. The major change from the report of the same panel in 2001 was that the likelihood of climate change was now 90% as opposed to an assessment of around 65% in 2001. Robert Watson, Chief Scientist at the World Bank and a former chair of the IPCC, argued that substantial action is needed now (and quickly). The IPCC estimated that should the concentration of carbon dioxide reach twice the pre-industrial level of 280 parts per million, temperatures could rise between 3.2 and 7.1 degrees Fahrenheit, with a more than 10% chance of even greater warming. Sea levels could rise between 7 and 23 inches. Heat waves and droughts will become more intense and longer-lived. The 2007 IPCC assessment doesn't go into the social impacts of climate change, but the implications are that such changes will have a widespread effect on human life on the planet.

The 2009 IPCC report (18–20 March) mostly builds upon and confirms what was contained in the 2007 report. It then goes on to consider more detailed and other ways of measuring CO_2 levels – the absorption of heat by the oceans, the development of 100-year scenarios – and argues that more sophisticated and accurate probability functions can be developed to support the scenarios. The 2009 report does acknowledge that there needs to be better communication between the science community and society generally and that messages can get lost or confused (increasing uncertainties). For example, there is a plea for better information to support risk management decisions at the local (regional) levels. There is also an acknowledgement that there are barriers to assessing risks not least in incomplete information; different information needs and capacities in different regional contexts; different languages of audiences receiving the information; multiple sources of information with conflicting messages and other important issues which compete for time and attention. But the overall assumption of this and previous reports is

▶ that the science is right – it just needs communicating better. Much of this communication is taking the form of scenarios, based upon a range of studies with high confidence limits, and suggests, for example, that we should plan for a 4 degree Centigrade rise in temperature (over pre-industrial times) rather than the predicted 2 degree rise by the 2060s or 2070s. Such scenarios are sophisticated, but ultimately rely on individual research studies ranging from measures of CO_2 emissions and feedback loops in the carbon cycle, to the tendency in many countries to political inertia to act to reduce emissions (for example).

The sceptics maintain that the case for alarm (and supposed scientific consensus) regarding climate change is grossly overstated. For example, the sceptics argue that surface temperature changes over the past century have been episodic and modest. They argue that there has been no net global warming for over a decade since 1989. They argue that if you control for population growth and increasing property values, there has been no increase in the extent and cost of damage from severe weather-related events. Finally, they suggest that the computer models forecasting rapid temperature change virtually all fail to explain recent climate behaviour. It is not just the scientific disputes which rage long and hard. Uncertainties are also increased by the politicization of these risk debates. For example, many sceptics have been criticized for their politics. Climate change deniers tend to be relatively conservative and some have been said to occupy the extreme ends of right-wing thinking. More problematic from a political perspective is that they have also been accused of being linked to right-wing think tanks (such as the Carbon Sense Coalition) which have variously been alleged to have received multi-million-dollar donations from rich oil families and corporations (Exxon has been named in a number of reports). Yet there is a large scientific community of respected scholars worldwide who have produced strong arguments which deny climate change and present credible evidence for their claims.

From the point of view of scenario creation, this schism between climate change believers and deniers presents a fundamental problem even if it does allow for the creation at least of two extreme 'pessimistic' and 'optimistic' scenarios. The scientific basis of the assumptions which have to be made to support any scenario are arguably questionable enough to allow damaging criticism of most, if not all, climate change scenarios, although some recent data do seem to support creating a pessimistic scenario. For example, this has been the hottest decade since 1850 (according to British meteorologists) and it seems we are already living with some degree of global warming. Recent floods and high seas also seem to increase the probabilities of warming, although deniers argue that recent building on the flood plains of rivers has meant that flood water now has nowhere else to go except to flood the cities in its path. And they argue we have always had tropical storms and tsunamis. The schism between believers and deniers is filled by those who believe that even if global warming is increasing at the rate claimed, more energy-efficient technologies will slow the rise in temperature. Enough to keep a scenario analyst busy for some years to come.

One feature of these conflicting positions is that a global version of game theory has begun to unfold. Although, logically, all countries in the world should cooperate on actions that would seem to be in all their interests, this has been far from the case (as witnessed at the recent Copenhagen summit in December 2009). China (which may supplant the US as the world's largest emitter of carbon in 2010) plays a game with the US. In return for allowing greater scrutiny and verifiability of its carbon emissions, China argues the case for having less stringent emission targets than other developed economies (such as the US). Large, well-developed economies have the most to lose. They will bear the brunt of lowering emissions. Developing economies argue that in order to develop they must have less stringent targets and so the game continues. The Copenhagen Accord, as it was named in December 2009, refers to the need to keep temperature rises to no more than 2 degrees Centigrade and says that rich countries will commit to cutting greenhouse gases and developing nations will take steps to limit the growth of their emissions, but it sets no targets for them. The first moves in the game are seemingly won by the developing nations. This is not least because there is no time scale (as yet) in which any targets become legally binding agreements between countries. Many countries also decided not to play the game, including Venezuela, Bolivia, Ecuador and Cuba, and so will not be part of any game theoretic modelling in the near future.

For those left in the game, one can begin to calculate the probability that countries would get what they wanted if they chose one course of action (for example, extend negotiations) or another (such as refusing to accept limits), weighting the probabilities by an estimate of how much the decision makers valued winning, losing, or intermediate compromise outcomes. Of course, in true game theory style, countries would have to work out how others might respond to the choices they made. The end result may be that negotiations actually result in the game achieving the lowest common denominator rather than the optimum agreement since countries are unlikely to sign up for anything that changes their behaviour (and actions) much from what they are already doing.

Thomas Schelling (Nobel Prizewinner in Economics in 2005) is more optimistic. He argues that this is the first time that virtually all nations in the world have tried to cooperate. He also argues that, because the discussions are not single issues, discussion and agreement will be the eventual outcome. The talks are not just about emissions, argues Schelling. They are about creating low-carbon energy infrastructures, deciding on new ways of reducing deforestation, and initiating new funding to help the poorer countries adapt to likely climate changes. Whatever the outcome, it is certain that the debate will continue for some time to come and that decisions on climate change represent one of the key examples of risk management in the world.

Source: compiled by D.C. Wilson, Warwick Business School

Questions

1 Which tools and techniques of risk analysis used in business strategy might best be applied to the analysis of climate change and its associated risks?

2 Try to construct a scenario based on available evidence and scientific results (plenty of these are available on various websites and are continually updated).

3 Using game theory, examine what you think the likely outcome of global negotiations on climate change is likely to be.

References

Alexander, C.B. (1996) Planning for disaster. *American Gas*, **78**, **2**, 24–7.

Baird, I.S. and Thomas, H. (1990) What is risk anyway? Using and measuring risk in strategic management. In R.A. Bettis and H. Thomas (eds) *Risk, Strategy and Management*, JAI Press, Greenwich, CT, pp. 21–52.

Beck, U. (1992) *Risk Society: Towards a New Modernity*, Sage, London.

Fahey, L. and Randall, R. (1998) *Learning from the Future: Competitive Foresight Scenarios*, John Wiley & Sons, New York.

Fiegenbaum, A. and Thomas, H. (1988) Attitudes toward risk and the risk-return paradox: prospect theory explanations. *Academy of Management Journal*, **31**, 85–106.

Goodnow, J.D. and Hansz, J.E. (1972) Environmental determinants of overseas entry strategies. *Journal of International Business Studies*, **3**, 33–50.

Greening, D.W. and Johnson, R.A. (1996) Do managers and strategies matter? A study in crisis. *Journal of Management Studies*, **33**, **1**, 25–51.

Hertz, D. and Thomas, H. (1983) *Risk Analysis and its Applications*, Wiley, New York.

Hespos, R.F. and Strassmann, P.A. (1965) Stochastic decision trees for the analysis of investment decisions. *Management Science*, **11**, **10**, 244–59.

Jorian, P. (2000) Value, risk and control: the call for integration. *The Financial Times*, 16 May.

Kahneman, D. and Tversky, A. (1973) Judgement under uncertainty. In G.M. Kaufman and H. Thomas (eds) *Modern Decision Analysis*, Penguin, Harmondsworth.

Knight, F.H. (1921) *Risk, Uncertainty and Profit*, University of Chicago Press, Chicago, IL.

Litvak, I.A. and Banting, P.M. (1968) A conceptual framework for international business arrangements. In R.L. King (ed.) *Marketing and the New Science of Planning*, AMA Fall Conference Proceedings, American Marketing Association, Chicago, IL.

Luhmann, N. (1993) *Risk: A Sociological Theory*, Aldine de Gruyter, Berlin.

March, J.G. (1999) *The Pursuit of Organizational Intelligence*, Blackwell, Oxford.

March, J.G. and Shapira, Z. (1999) Variable risk preferences and the focus of attention. In J.G. March (ed.) *The Pursuit of Organizational Intelligence*, Blackwell, Oxford.

Miller, K.D. (1992) Framework for integrated risk management. *Journal of International Business*, Summer, 311–31.

Miller, K.D. and Bromiley, P. (1990) Strategic risk and corporate performance: an analysis of alternative risk measures. *Academy of Management Journal*, **39**, 91–122.

Moore, P.G. and Thomas, H. (1976) *The Anatomy of Decisions*, Penguin, Harmondsworth.

Palmer, T.B. and Wiseman, R.M. (1999) Decoupling risk from income stream uncertainty: a holistic model of risk. *Strategic Management Journal*, **20**, 1037–62.

Perrow, C. (1984) *Normal Accidents: Living with High Risk Technologies*, Basic Books, New York.

Schoemaker, P.J.H. (2002) *Profiting from Uncertainty: Strategies for Succeeding No Matter What the Future Brings*, Free Press, New York.

Singh, J.V. (1986) Performance risk and slack taking in organizational decision making. *Academy of Management Journal*, **29**, 562–85.

Starbuck, W. and Farjoun, M. (eds) (2005) *The Limits of Organization*, Blackwell, Oxford.

Stoner, J. (1968) Risky and cautious shifts in group decision: the influence of widely held values. *Journal of Experimental Social Psychology*, **4**, 442–59.

Stultz, R.M. (2007) *Risk Management and Derivatives*, Thomson Business, London.

Thomas, H. (1984) Strategic decision analysis: applied decision analysis and its role in the strategic management process. *Strategic Management Journal*, **5**, 139–56.

Turner, B. (1978) *Man-Made Disasters*, Wykeham, London.

Wiseman, R.M. and Bromiley, P. (1996) Toward a model of risk in declining organizations: an empirical examination of risk, performance and decline. *Organizational Science*, **7**, 524–43.

Further reading

Scenarios and scenario-based planning

Peter Schwartz (1991) *The Art of the Long View – Planning for the Future in an Uncertain World*, Doubleday, 258pp; ISBN 0-385-26731-2; paperback 1996, ISBN 0-385-26732-0
This is one of the best starting books describing the fundamentals of scenario planning. Peter Schwartz is a futurist and a founder of the *Global Business Network* (GBN) but has also worked at Stanford Research Institute (SRI) and Shell.

Kees van der Heijden (1996) *Scenarios – The Art of Strategic Conversation*, Wiley, 305pp; ISBN 0-471-96639-8
This an excellent book about scenario planning in a business context because it connects to strategy and its practice in a strategic context. The author Kees van der Heijden is one of the founders of GBN and has also a history as head of the Scenario Planning group at Shell.

Gill Ringland (1998) *Scenario Planning – Managing for the Future*, Wiley, 401pp; ISBN 0-471-97790-X
This is mainly focused on providing experiences from a number of scenario planning projects in different companies. Gill Ringland works for ICL and the book reflects scenario projects within ICL, but there are also examples from a number of other projects in other contexts.

Liam Fahey and Robert M. Randall (1998) *Learning from the Future*, Wiley, 446pp; ISBN 0-471-30352-6
This contains a number of articles focusing on different application areas or aspects of scenario planning.

Art Kleiner (1996) *The Age of Heretics*, Doubleday, 414pp; ISBN 0-385-41576-1
This book relates stories about the heretics who challenged the prevailing views at companies like Royal Dutch/Shell. By using scenario planning they saw possible future events which management didn't see at all. Art Kleiner, among other interests, teaches a scenario class focusing on the future for telecommunication infrastructure at New York University.

Wilkinson, Lawrence (1996) How to build scenarios. *Scenarios: Special Wired Edition*, January: 74–81.

Ghemawat, P. (2009). The risk of investing in a recession. *Sloan Management Review*, **50**(3): 31–39.

McGrath, R.G., MacMillan, I.C. (2009) How to rethink your business during uncertainty. *Sloan Management Review*, **50**(3): 25–30.

Useful websites

www.library.nijenrode.nl/library/publications/nijrep/1997-01/1997-01.html
Scenarios, strategy and the strategy process
Interesting paper by Kees van der Heijden, a strategic planning veteran from Shell who is also a member of GBN. Scenario planning is treated as a strategic tool that can be used to develop a business idea by testing it in several futures and getting a more powerful and more robust strategy.

www2.shell.com
Current Royal Dutch/Shell scenarios and introductory texts
Shell provides both introductory information about scenario planning as well as several downloadable scenarios.

www.innovation.gov.uk/projects/converging_techn/summary/html
Converging technologies – consequences for the new knowledge-driven economy
A UK government initiative on innovation has produced a number of scenarios on the effects of technology on an economy.

Strategic decision making: process analyses

Introduction[1]

James March and Herbert Simon suggested in 1958 that managing organizations (developing a strategy; achieving growth) and decision making were virtually synonymous. The dynamics of strategy development require a deep understanding of decision making. As organizations grow and become more complex, decision making becomes a central activity. Managers are expected to make choices among often uncertain alternatives and to choose wisely in order to benefit both the organization and its key stakeholders. Researchers, therefore, have tried to identify the characteristics of decision processes to understand its characteristics and to suggest ways in which decisions might be improved.

---

[1] This introduction section is adapted from Wilson (2007).

The study of decision making covers many levels of analysis (from individual cognition to the cultural characteristics of nation states) and many disciplines inform such studies (from mathematics to behavioural theories). The term *strategic* decision making is usually used to indicate important or key decisions made in organizations of all types. The term organization includes any collective social, economic or political activity involving a plurality of human effort. **Strategic decisions** emphasize the social practice of decision making as it is carried out among and between a group of such individuals. It is both the organizing of decision activity as a collective phenomenon and the cognitive processes of individual choice makers that take centre stage in analysing decision making.

Strategic decision making is more than an exercise involving computation for judgement and choice. Various branches of mathematical statistics and economics can inform us about risk, options, game theory and choice. All have their value in understanding choice processes, but are less useful when considering how organizations full of people make decisions in practice. As an example, consider a two-person game as a variant of **game theory**. This is often called the prisoners' dilemma game where two criminals are in separate cells and have to decide whether or not to betray each other (having agreed not to betray in advance of the game). The greatest pay-offs come from both prisoners sticking to their agreement, but most betray each other and the pay-offs are significantly reduced. The clear lesson is that computational mathematics and choice theory can help the players maximize their returns. This is just part of the strategic decision-making story. What happens in practice (betrayal) does not match the predictions of choice theory and various decision-making studies try to explain why this is the case. We, therefore, explore some of the main approaches and findings in this chapter.

12.1 What are strategic decisions?

A view popularized by Minzberg et al. (1976) is that strategic decisions are large, expensive, and precedent-setting as well as having high levels of ambiguity (uncertainty) often. No one (in this organization) has faced this kind of situation before. Once implemented, strategic decisions set the course of many operational (everyday) decisions that follow in their wake. A further characteristic of strategic decisions is they are difficult to reverse once resources (human and financial) have been committed to their cause. A more complete list of the characteristics of strategic decisions would include the following:

- They are difficult to define precisely (the nature of the problem is elusive).
- Understanding the problem is also part of understanding what is a viable solution.
- There is rarely one best solution, but a series of possible solutions.
- Each solution is associated with different trade-offs and priorities.
- They are difficult to assess in terms of benefits (performance), since they tend to continue through the organization without a clear final end point against which performance can be judged.
- They are highly interconnected with other problems in the organization.
- They have high levels of ambiguity and uncertainty associated with them.
- They require decision makers to accept fairly high degrees of risk.
- They are likely to be discontinuous and political, with different competing interests trying to influence the outcome in line with their preferences.

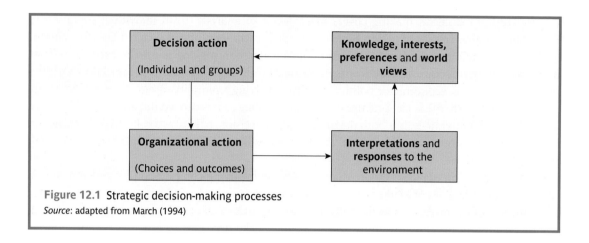

Figure 12.1 Strategic decision-making processes
Source: adapted from March (1994)

12.1.1 The decision process

At its simplest, strategic decision making may be considered an instantaneous action, a **choice** between two or more known alternatives. However, this 'point of decision' approach is unable to capture the richness and complexity of:

■ the processes that lead up to the point of decision;

■ the influences that impact on uncovering problems and putting the decision into action;

■ assessing the ultimate benefits of that decision.

Decision making from this simple perspective also assumes that managers have full control over decisions. But many times they may have very limited discretion to make decisions or choose amongst alternatives. This could be the case, for example, where strategic decisions in organizations are heavily constrained by interventionist government policies (such as privatization or deregulation) where all strategic decisions are framed and shaped by this wider **context**. Nevertheless, managers still have some degree of strategic choice even if the wider context (e.g. privatization) is firmly set in place. Managers can still make strategic decisions, for example, concerning such key topics as organizational design, choice of suppliers, choice and sophistication of information systems and general product or service portfolios.

The overall steps in the process of strategic decision making have been summarized by James March and are depicted in Figure 12.1.

The major contribution of this simple flow diagram is twofold. The processes it identifies underpin the centrality of decision making in strategic management. Secondly, its very simplicity can be very misleading. The cycle can be broken or can malfunction at each stage of the process and between stages. James March taught us to beware assumptions of rationality both in individuals and in organizations. Actions can be taken for a variety of reasons which correspond to the ways in which organizations are structured (each specialized function developing its own view on what should happen, for example). At its most extreme, this could be characterized as what a sales department thinks is crazy, a production department may think makes perfect sense. Production can produce 1,000 units per hour (so they do). But sales (who know the market) say they can sell a maximum of 100 units per week! This idea of organizations comprising multiple rationalities (and not just one) entered the vocabulary of organizational decision making as the concept of 'local rationality' (Cyert and March, 1963).

12.1.2 Different perspectives on the nature of decision making

Like many theories of how we organize, plan and act, decision making has multiple lenses through which we might try to understand its complexity. We examine some of these lenses here. For example, Mintzberg et al. (1998) identify five different (and sometimes mutually exclusive) frameworks for strategic decision making:

1 Decision making as a *plan*: the decision is a consciously intended course of action. In the same way that you might intend to catch an aeroplane to a specific destination at a particular time, decision making is a process which is carried out in advance of the action which follows and is developed with a clear purpose.

2 Decision making as a *ploy*: a decision from this perspective is a set of actions designed to outwit the competition and may not necessarily be the 'obvious' content of the decision. For example, a decision to build a new building in order to expand may not be the overt strategy, but is more concerned with increasing barriers to entry for potential competitors. There are obvious connections here with game theory (Von Neumann and Morgenstern, 1944), which examines the choices players make in every possible situation. Forcing one's opponent to move (to achieve a short-term win), so that this puts them at a longer-term disadvantage, is an example of such a ploy. Equally, there are connections with strategy as conceived in its military roots, where the plans of campaigns may have similar intentions to the game analogy (Von Clausewitz, 1976).

3 Decision making as a *pattern*: decisions are not necessarily taken with a planned purpose and decision makers do not always have access to the range of knowledge required to plan wholly in advance. What happens is that multiple decisions taken over time form a pattern. It is this pattern of resulting (emergent) behaviour that we call the strategy of the firm. Strategy is therefore characterized as a pattern which emerges from a stream of decisions.

4 Decision making as a *position*: decisions are less about the dynamics of planning or gamesmanship and more about trying to achieve a match between the organization and its environment (Hofer and Schendel, 1978). This position can be one of alignment, so that the organization matches its environment (for example, choosing highly decentralized structures to match a turbulent and unpredictable environment) or one of trying to secure competitive advantage (where the organization achieves a unique position in the market for some time). Positions, of course, can be planned, emerge or be a combination of both emergent and planned processes. The key point is that successful positioning of the firm is likely to be a result of a number of strategic decisions, each aimed at creating (or refining) a position of competitive advantage and/or greater alignment with its environment.

5 Decision making as a *perspective*: decisions here are characterized as a reflection of how strategists in an organization see and perceive the world and their organization (often termed strategic vision). For example, the strategic perspective of Nokia is one of continuous and sometimes radical change (Nokia began as a paper and pulp company, as can be seen from the following case box).

Case box 12.1: **Nokia**

Nokia's new chief wants to lead the mobile-phone giant into new markets
The story of Nokia's transformation from an obscure Finnish conglomerate into the world's largest maker of mobile phones is an object lesson in the virtue of specialisation. A sprawling business that once made everything from tyres to toilet paper to televisions, Nokia switched its focus to mobile phones in

the 1990s under its visionary chief executive, Jorma Ollila. Under his leadership, the company overtook Motorola, its American rival, to become the world's largest handset-maker – a position it has clung to ever since. As Mr Ollila steps down on June 1st, however, he hands his successor, Olli-Pekka Kallasvuo, the difficult task of leading Nokia into new markets as the distinction between mobile phones and other consumer-electronics devices becomes increasingly blurred.

Mr Kallasvuo, a member of the tight-knit group that has run Nokia since the early 1990s, will inherit a company in excellent shape. Nokia has a renewed spring in its step, having recovered from a stumble in early 2004, when a lacklustre product line-up caused its market share to drop below 30% for the first time in years. A pioneer in design, Nokia lost its edge when it failed to anticipate the popularity of slim 'clam-shell' phones. It fought back, first by cutting prices and then by revamping its designs. Its market share is now at around 35%. The mood at the company is buoyant: in addition to the satisfaction of having bounced back so convincingly, Nokia's strong financial performance meant big bonuses for many employees. 'If you look at the portfolio, I think we have regained leadership,' says Mr Kallasvuo. 'The foundation is there, so that we can concentrate on what is next.'

And what is that? As the leader in mobile phones, Nokia now has to take a broader view of the market, he believes. 'Comparison with our own industry is not adequate any more,' he says. 'We need to look at this in a much wider way.' The rise of the camera-phone means that Nokia now sells more cameras than anyone else does, for example, and advanced handsets often also include music-playing, video-recording and computing (including e-mail). Mr Kallasvuo does not mention names, but his drift is clear: rather than just comparing itself with rival handset-makers such as Motorola or Samsung, Nokia now considers its competitors to be Apple, Sony, Canon and other consumer-electronics firms. 'The convergence of internet and media content is happening in the way everyone predicted four or five years ago,' he says. 'We are more and more competing against other people, against new types of competitors. We are all converging.'

Nokia has responded by launching a range of advanced handsets, called the Nseries, which focus on specific features in addition to being phones. The N73 camera-phone, for example, is aimed at people who maintain photo blogs, and includes software for uploading images to Flickr, a popular image-sharing website. Similarly, the N91 phone doubles as an iPod-style music player with a built-in hard disk; the N92 is a mobile television; and the N93 is a video camera. Perhaps most surprising, however, is Nokia's 770 Internet Tablet, a hand-held computer that does not contain a mobile phone at all. Instead, it supports web-browsing, e-mail and voice-over-internet calls (using Google Talk software) via short-range Wi-Fi technology. 'It is the best possible illustration of convergence,' says Mr Kallasvuo. It also highlights Nokia's willingness to step outside its usual market.

That sounds a pretty ambitious expansion strategy. But Mr Kallasvuo also wants more from traditional markets. Nokia may strive to emulate Apple with its most expensive phones, but the core of its business, with its efficient logistics and huge volumes, has more in common with Dell. (Of the 900m mobile phones that will be sold this year, 320m of them will be made by Nokia.) Around 70% of the industry's growth this year will come in the developing economies, and Nokia's cheapest handsets are doing well in China, India and Latin America. Some critics argue that Nokia ought to focus solely on high-margin products such as the Nseries, but Mr Kallasvuo disagrees. 'With our volumes, our economies of scale, we want to be in all of these markets,' he says. Even Nokia's cheapest handsets are profitable, he points out. And if your first handset is a Nokia, you are more likely to stay with the brand when moving upmarket – 'so being strong at the low end has strategic importance.'

Opportunity in complexity

One market in which Nokia could plainly do better is North America. It has been weak there, because many networks use a different wireless standard (called CDMA) rather than the GSM technology used in Europe. Nokia has devoted a lot of effort to raising its profile in North America in the past two years and has recently formed a joint venture with Sanyo of Japan to produce fancy CDMA handsets. Tellingly, Mr Kallsvuo plans to spend one week a month in America, which is important not just as a big market but also because it is where trendsetting products, such as Apple's iPod, often appear first.

The breadth of Mr Kallasvuo's ambition – more convergence, more China, more America, more everything – looks potentially overwhelming, particularly as Nokia moves into a new and fiercely competitive market – consumer electronics. Managing the complexity of converged devices is difficult, Mr Kallasvuo concedes, but it also provides scope for differentiation, 'and overall that's an opportunity.' Another danger is that Nokia may alienate wireless operators, its main customers, by helping consumers get round their proprietary networks and instead supporting open, internet-based services such as Google Talk in its devices. But the rise of internet standards means the industry's old rules no longer apply. 'We will need to be agnostic enough to make pragmatic decisions,' says Mr Kallasvuo. 'Natural evolution is happening in the marketplace, and we need to act accordingly.'

Source: 'More, More, More', *The Economist*, 27 May 2006.

Strategic decisions favour change, innovation and new markets. IBM favours a dominant marketing perspective, and its strategic decisions reflect this marketing bias, while Hewlett-Packard favours an engineering excellence perspective with its key decisions focusing on the operational excellence of products, processes and machines. More widely, we can see the effects of this embedded view of decision making by observing that organizations in similar industries often choose similar strategic decisions. They become institutionalized. For example, universities tend to follow broadly similar strategies, as do large retailers or service organizations.

Bowman et al. (2001) remind us that not only can we identify different perspectives on decision making, but the past 40 or 50 years has also seen radical changes in the ways in which links between strategic decisions and corporate strategy have been established. For example, the 1950s/1960s saw an emphasis on the planning approach to decision making. The focus was on tools and techniques to help managers make informed decisions about future business directions. Such tools included industry structure analyses and portfolio matrices (for example, the Ansoff matrix or the Boston Box). Decision making was mostly about planning. The late 1970s and 1980s onwards saw a changed emphasis. Decisions were now supposed to emphasize the pay-offs to organizations that may accrue if they pursued different strategic directions. Typical options were diversification decisions, but this was also the era of innovation (R&D), acquisition, joint venture and internationalization decisions.

The late 1980s and 1990s saw a move away from examining the content of strategic decisions (that is, what they were about) to examining them more as processes. The question now became whether we could map the progress of a strategic decision and make any inferences about why such processes might occur. Hickson et al. (1986) characterized such processes as sporadic (discontinuous), fluid (continuous and smooth) or constricted (restricted to a small group of stakeholders). Mintzberg et al. (1976) had also identified a number of specific process types in a similar vein. Pettigrew (1986) underscored the importance of such processes since they underpinned the recognition amongst managers for strategic change. Here Pettigrew established a clear link between strategic decision making and change (a theme which will be described in greater detail in Chapter 13). The late 1990s and 2000s were characterized by the adoption of decentralized organizational structures. In these structures, strategic business units (SBUs) would often operate as profit centres, with the SBU managers having a great deal of influence over strategic decision making both in their own unit and in the firm overall. As some organizations become more networked and less formally structured, the influence of key decision makers in local or decentralized units becomes a key factor in understanding the strategic decision-making process. Hence, recent research in decision making has seen a continuing interest in unfolding the characteristics of decision processes, but the emphasis has changed to focus on whether or not there are any links between decision-making activity and performance (did the decision succeed or fail?). And did decisions made in different parts of a decentralized organization (for example) lead to success or failure of the SBU and/or the firm overall? We examine aspects of decision making and performance later in this chapter.

12.2 Choice selection and strategic decision making

The question of how individuals make decisions is deceptively simple. Deeper analysis reveals that trying to explain the *how* of decision making, even if limited to trying to explain how managers make decisions in organizations (rather than, say, the cognitive processes of individuals generally), is still very complex indeed. One of the enduring features of complex organizations is that they operationally codify the knowledge and experience of individuals. As managers take decisions, the rules of thumb they may use become standardized as procedures and activities for *planning* and *evaluating* – standardized operating procedures or SOPs as March and Simon described them. This allows a degree of *strategic programming* to take place. Resource allocation, schedules and priorities can be planned, evaluated and assessed by such metrics and they become embodied in the formal planning system of the organization.

The links between planning and forecasting metrics and strategy vary depending upon how strategy is viewed. If the classic Chandler (1962, p. 13) perspective is taken – strategy is 'the determination of the long-term goals of an enterprise' – then tools such as scenario planning and macroeconomic forecasting are appropriate metrics. These help assess complex environments often over long time horizons (25 years is not unusual in scenario analysis, for example) from the perspective of the organization–environment interaction. We describe these techniques in more detail in Chapter 8 of this book. Alternatively, if we define strategy as the sum of its parts – a pattern amongst a handful of decisions – then we need metrics which are finer grained. Once the level of analysis becomes the decision itself, managers need more specific tools and techniques to help them in option selection from a range of alternatives. Table 12.1 summarizes some typical planning and forecasting techniques.

12.2.1 Game theories

Game theories help decision makers by providing a thinking framework about the actions of others. By posing choice amongst alternatives in the form of different games, decision makers can judge to what extent their assumptions about others' rationality are valid. Typically portrayed as a matrix

Table 12.1 Planning and forecasting techniques and strategy

Strategy is viewed as...	The remit of strategists	Typical techniques
The long-term alignment of an organization with its economic, social and political environment	Long-term, wide-span control of organizational affairs	■ Scenario building ■ Macroeconomic analysis and forecasting
The handful of strategic decisions which drive and shape the fortunes of an organization and which characterize its strategy	The management of shorter-term decisions which involve the disposition of limited resources	■ Game theory ■ Sensitivity analysis ■ Options ■ Decision analysis

Company B	Invest in process	Invest in quality	Make no investment
		Company A	
	50 : 50	30 : 70	85 : 15
	60 : 40	45 : 55	80 : 20
	25 : 75	20 : 80	30 : 30

Invest in process

Invest in quality

Make no investment

Figure 12.2 A simple example of game theory
Source: adapted from Powell (2003)

between two 'players', game theory examines what is likely to happen when two players make choices and what are the best outcomes or pay-offs. Powell (2003, p. 392) gives an example, using two firms facing investment opportunities in an existing market. Each firm can invest in process or quality, or can make no investment. Investment in process should reduce price and investment in quality should improve differentiation. Figure 12.2 shows the pay-offs.

First, the rules of the simple game depicted above are that Company A chooses first which column to play. In the cells of the table are the pay-offs in percentages to Company B and Company A (in that order). The pay-offs are not symmetrical since each company has different capabilities. If both companies choose not to invest, then it will be easier for new entrants to come into the market, hence both Company A and Company B will receive only 60%.

Company A logically chooses the least bad case. This is a decision to invest in quality where, whatever the choice of Company B, Company A will receive at least 55% pay-off. Company B would also reason similarly. The least worse choice is to invest in quality where Company B would receive at least 45%. The game assumes that these decisions are made at the same time, although even if they were made in sequence, the inbuilt time lags in the market would reduce immediate effects of the investment.

Now, if the game is played deliberately in sequence making the assumption that Company B moves first and immediately sees the choices of Company A, then Company B has the following decision choices. Investing in process would be likely to make A choose quality (this would yield a pay-off of 70%). Investing in quality would persuade A to choose quality as well, since the pay-off will be larger for them (55%) than B. If B were to choose not to invest then A would invest in quality to gain an 80% return. The best case is, therefore, for B to invest in quality and gain 45%, with A gaining 55%.

From a decision-making perspective, these type of games may vary depending upon whether the game is played more than once with the same 'players'. If both parties know that they will be playing the same game again under the same rules, then the evidence suggests that they will be more predisposed to cooperate and trust each other than if the game were only played once.

Of course, these simple heuristics make some heroic assumptions. For example, players are assumed to be perfectly rational in their behaviours and choices. They are also assumed to have perfect knowledge of the rules (shared equally between them) and will always want to maximize their returns. However, they improve understanding because they do show clearly some of the choices and returns which may happen, should managers make best use of the resources and knowledge at their disposal.

12.2.2 Sensitivity analysis

In many respects, this thinking framework is similar conceptually to the broader models of risk or decision analysis (see Chapter 11), but it operates at a much more operational level. It is a technique for investigating what happens if some of the assumptions underlying a strategic decision are questioned and changed. For example, a strategic decision may be taken to launch a new product, but there is uncertainty about the prices that could be charged over a five-year horizon. Even small changes in price might yield large changes in volumes sold, therefore managers need to know what will happen if they make even slight changes to product price. Sensitivity analysis allows the manager to build in varying assumptions about price for each year over the five-year horizon and then assess through a risk analysis simulation the effects of varying price on the financial performance of the new product.

It should be clear that sensitivity analysis can be performed in a wide range of business contexts, e.g. insurance, capital investment etc., in order to identify the financial performance effects of critical uncertainties such as pricing in the case of insurance or construction costs in capital investment. Thus, the most sensible strategy options in insurance and capital investment can be more clearly identified.

12.2.3 Options analysis

Options analysis helps managers to more formally address the range of strategic options and then make key decisions about future business activities. From a decision-making perspective, the word options can be misleading in that it can be taken to refer to the micro-detail of operations (costs, sales volumes and so on) so that forecasts can be 'exact'. In fact, options techniques are relatively macro in their focus. They rely on two related dimensions: the identification of the key additional or alternative organizational capabilities which might be needed to meet product or service needs in the future; and the identification of potential future markets and/or new customer behaviours. In order to assemble an accurate set of options, decision makers need to assess both of these dimensions. For example, in the mobile telephony industry, customer needs might be predicted to change towards using the mobile telephone as the major way of accessing internet and telephony needs. Thus the mobile telephone becomes the key focus in terms of an organization's capabilities to deliver such technologies. Bandwidth and voice over internet protocols will all be capabilities which will have to be developed and honed in order to meet market demands. Figure 12.3 illustrates how the need to address both capabilities and develop a knowledge of new potential markets is important for decision makers.

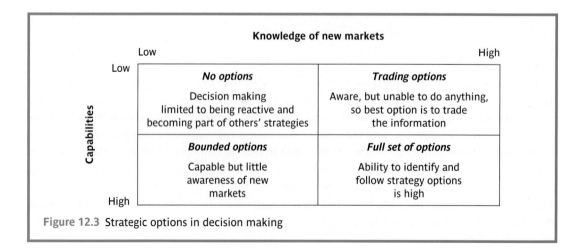

Figure 12.3 Strategic options in decision making

Figure 12.3 simply outlines the options available to organizations which fall into the various cells of the matrix. While this is a useful analysis, it tells decision makers little about actions – or the type of actions they may take. For example, decision makers may have identified two or three options but then may choose to retain these as ideas which might be explored sometime in the future. Just holding these options as ideas is fairly cost free, but is obviously low on action. Decisions involving options and implementation often require significant analysis and investment. Choosing between options is necessary since pursuing all identified options would be prohibitively expensive. Then decisions have to be made about how to implement the chosen option or options. We explore these processes of strategic decision making in the following sections.

12.3 The processes of strategic decision making

Before reading this section, go back to Chapter 2 and re-read the introductory section on strategic decision making and the characterization of decision processes (Chapter 2: Figure 2.5). Also re-read Chapter 10, where many of the behavioural and political aspects of decision making were introduced.

You will recall that decisions can be planned or can be chaotic, with almost no planning involved. And decisions may be substantially aimed at solving problems with the whole organization working together, or may instead be characterized by different parts of the organization fighting to influence the decision process in ways which will bring perceived benefits to themselves.

This leaves us with the large task of trying to see if there are any common characteristics at all in decision making and whether these characteristics matter (and, if so, in which ways) to such factors as speed, accuracy and performance of the decision. We explore these aspects in the following sections.

12.3.1 Characterizing the decision process

From the large-scale empirical studies of Hickson et al. (1986) (based upon a sample of 155 decisions from a range of organizations) we know that strategic decision-making processes can be classified into three distinct types:

Sporadic: the decision process is subject to delays and recycles. Mainly this is because information used is uneven in its quality and usefulness and comes from a wide range of sources which are not easily comparable. Negotiation between different factions in the organization is the norm. Decisions can take a long time as a result.

Fluid: almost the opposite of the above sporadic characterization. Much less interaction, with more formal meetings and fewer delays and recycles. The flow of the decision is therefore smoother and duration is shorter.

Constricted: in between fluid and sporadic in terms of decision flow (they may recycle but to a lesser extent than sporadic processes), but these processes are mainly characterized by revolving around a central senior figure (for example, a CEO or a finance or production director) who involves only a small number of other senior participants before the decision is made.

The sample was drawn from private and public sector organizations, large and small. It is impossible, however, to predict which decisions will follow a particular trajectory. Will all new product decisions be smooth and fluid, for example? Do organizations differ in the kind of decision processes?

In fact, there appear to be few organizational influences. Apart from a very slight tendency for public sector (and some manufacturing) organizations to show a bias towards sporadic processes, each process type is found in all organizations. From a practical point of view, it seems it does not matter what kind of organization you work in, strategic decision processes will be a mix of similar characteristics. The type of organization is certainly not the strongest determinant of the type of decision process.

The key **influences** that determine which process type a decision follows are a combination of two factors – the *political* nature of the decision and the *complexity* inherent in the decision itself.

Politicality: This refers to the degree of influence which is brought to bear on a decision by various stakeholders (internal and external to the organization) and how this influence is distributed across and within organizations (some decisions may be almost totally externally influenced, for example, perhaps by regulatory authorities or government agencies).

Complexity: This refers to the nature and range of the problems which making the decision involves. For example, some decisions are more novel than others (this may be the first time an organization has taken a decision on this topic); or they may need to gather more information from diverse sources; or they may differ in how widespread and serious the consequences may be in making a decision. Finally, decisions differ in the extent to which they are comprehensible and understood throughout the organization.

It is important to note that this way of characterizing decisions is different from the topic of the decision. Topics are the familiar way we describe decisions by classifying them by what they are about (e.g. a new product or service or a structural reorganization). But all new product or reorganization decisions are not the same across different organizations because they differ in the number of stakeholders they may involve (politicality) and differ in their levels of complexity. It is the particular combinations of politicality and complexity in a decision which shapes the decision process and not the topic for decision. These combinations of politicality and complexity are not straight-forward, but some clear patterns emerge from the Hickson et al. (1986) study.[2] These are shown in Table 12.2.

Understanding the above perspectives and linking them to the nature of the decision problem is clearly an important and difficult task. However, 'mapping' the decision topic with its degree of complexity and politicality may enable strategic decision makers to understand the potential configuration of the decision in their own organization. If the mapping is done effectively, a decision maker may be able to predict the evolution of the decision-making process and even influence what is likely to happen before it takes place.

To understand strategic decision making in greater depth means examining at least three further aspects. These are:

1 decision-specific characteristics;

2 the organizational context;

3 relationships between decision making and performance.

---

[2] This empirical study was the first large-scale study into the characteristics of strategic decisions and, along with many other publications on decision making, is among those often known as the 'Bradford Studies' (David Hickson and his colleagues were then researching at the Bradford Management Centre in the UK).

Table 12.2 Three modes of decision-making process			
Nature of decision topic	**Degree of complexity**	**Degree of politicality**	**Process characteristic of the decision**
Normal and recurrent Important but familiar (such as some budgeting decisions over a fixed term)	**Least complex** Not novel with limited and non-precursive consequences	**Less political** In particular influenced mostly by a small number of internal stakeholders	**Constricted** Fairly smooth and quick process with only a few senior managers involved
Novel but non-controversial These decisions are new to the organization in question but are perceived to have rather less important consequences should they go wrong (such as a new service or changing a supplier)	**Less complex** Rare, but does not involve diverse stakeholders; consequences are diffuse but can set precedents for later decisions	**Least political** Evenly influenced and relatively non-contentious amongst stakeholders	**Fluid** A smooth and linear decision (few recycles and interrupts)
Important and controversial These are decisions which the organization may have experienced before, but which have very important consequences should they go wrong (such as a change of CEO, growth or contraction of business)	**Complex** Involve a diverse range of stakeholders; consequences are serious for the organization	**Political** Highly contentious with stakeholders taking diverse positions and perspectives. In many cases, can involve dominant stakeholders who are external to the organization	**Sporadic** Relatively lengthy decision processes which tend to recycle, get delayed and go round many times before a final decision is made

Source: adapted from Hickson et al. (1986, p. 175)

12.3.2 Decision-specific characteristics

We can categorize decision-specific characteristics into two broad areas:

1 the interpretation of a problem or problems by decision makers;
2 the characteristics of the decision or problem to be solved.

The same internal or external stimuli may be interpreted differently by managers across different organizations, or sometimes even within the same organization. Therefore, relying on the stimulus itself is unlikely to tell us much about what follows in terms of strategic decision making (Nutt and Wilson, 2010).

It is also clear that the ways in which managers categorize decisions strongly influence the ways in which subsequent processes happen. For example, decisions may be perceived as an opportunity by some managers and as a crisis by others. Where managers perceive decisions to be more of a crisis than an opportunity, the process is characterized by the overarching threat of the crisis. The search for alternatives becomes wider and the collection of information and intelligence relevant to the decision becomes greater. Overall, the decision-making activity becomes more comprehensive in scale and in scope (since it tends to involve more participants). It will become more complex and political (and is therefore likely to be sporadic in its process).

Such complex and political decisions have been studied by other researchers. For example, problems have been characterized as 'wicked' or 'tame' (de Wit and Meyer, 1999). Wicked problems are not evil, but are complex and political. They are permeated with uncertainty caused either by the technical nature of the decision or by the politics and intrigue it engenders amongst decision participants.

Recall that complex decisions are those which are unprecedented, carry high levels of uncertainty and may have fundamental precedent-setting consequences for subsequent decisions. They may also require information of a different type and from a different source to be gathered and interpreted. Political decisions are those which draw in a specific set of stakeholders (inside and outside the organization). The more interests that are represented in the decision (multiple and conflicting voices), the more political is the strategic decision (see Table 12.2).

Decisions which are complex and political share some or all of the following characteristics, as noted in the section 'What are strategic decisions?' in this chapter:

- They are difficult to define precisely (the nature of the problem is elusive).
- Understanding the problem is also part of understanding the solution.
- There is rarely one best solution, but a series of possible solutions.
- Each solution is associated with different trade-offs and priorities.
- They are difficult to assess in terms of performance, since they tend to continue through the organization without a clear final end point against which performance can be judged.
- They are highly interconnected with other problems in the organization.
- They have high levels of uncertainty associated with them.
- They require strategists to accept fairly high degrees of risk in making decisions.
- Once made, they are difficult to reverse.
- They are likely to be discontinuous and political, with different competing interests trying to influence the outcome in line with their preferences.

Simple (or tame) decisions reflect the opposite characteristics to those listed. The research of Hickson et al. (1986) would indicate that in most organizations, at least a third of strategic decisions will be complex (wicked) decisions. Since most organizations at any one point in time are likely to have around six or seven strategic decisions being considered (Hickson et al., 1986; de Wit and Meyer, 1999), two or three of these are likely to be wicked and complex.

12.4 The organizational context

Before reading this section, go back to Chapter 10 and refresh your memory about the main influences of organizational characteristics such as structure, culture and institutionalization on strategy. What follows here is an expansion of these factors with specific regard to decision making.

There are many ways of defining the organizational context, but a number of major influences which impact upon decision making are:

- Systems;
- Structure;
- Ownership and control;
- Cultures.

Internal *systems*, such as information or formal planning processes, both influence the flow of information across the organization and to some extent determine the nature and context of human interaction. It is not surprising, then, that they have a strong influence over strategic decision making and its practice. Control systems and measurement and reward systems also prescribe what is given priority and therefore what decision makers focus most of their attention upon. In decision making, such systems will set parameters around trade-offs and what levels of risk are tolerable, for example:

- The more regulated the formal systems, the more strategic decision making tends to be routine and predictable and the more it will have to accommodate a large number of specialist functions.

- The more complex the system, the more decision making becomes reliant on knowledge experts and information-gathering and synthesis.

- The more automated systems become, the more flexibility and space there is for strategic decision making which relies upon expertise (or the intellectual capital of the organization). The obsession with control tends to be reduced, since controlled systems do not require watching over. (When they go wrong, however, they can cause havoc!)

- The greater the scope of the system, the greater the reliance on expertise and intellectual capital. This is true of e-commerce and e-business, for example, where the scope of information goes beyond the single organizational unit.

The *structure* of an organization also has an impact on strategic decision making. The most obvious example of the interrelationship between strategy and structure is the debate (which still rages) about whether structure follows strategy or vice versa. Chandler (1962) argued that structure follows strategy, yet others (see Hall and Saias, 1980; Rumelt, 1974) have argued that strategy follows structure. Rasche (2007) shows how the strategy–structure debate can be seen as reciprocal over time, in that today's current strategy influences the ways in which the scanning mechanisms of managers work (it can limit them, for example). In turn, this scanning influences the set of decisions that make up tomorrow's strategy which, in turn, determines the shape of tomorrow's organizational structure. Here, we take the view that strategy and structure are like two legs. You need both to walk, but whether you lead with the left or the right leg is fairly arbitrary. One may be said to follow or to lead the other. No matter, you are still walking. Decisions both *create* structures and are also *influenced* by them.

It is clear that a set of relationships between strategic decision making and structure can be identified in a number of aspects of management. In relation to strategic decision making, some of the key influences are listed below:

- Formalized structures are associated mainly with older organizations. Decision making becomes formalized and has a tendency to become more predictable. This is especially so in the 'seen it all before' attitudes that may prevail, and repeating what was done in the past as solutions to today's problems.

- Larger organizations formalize processes more, even if they are structured into smaller business units. Strategic decision making becomes more about rule-following than rule-bending (or breaking) practice.

- Decentralized structures may appear to avoid the above, but decision making can become dominated by trying to ensure coordination and communication across the decentralized organization (rather than producing new products and services, for example). Decentralized structures often require more rather than less hands-on management before they can become effective and efficient.

Organizational structures reflect the age of the industry from its founding date. Industries which pre-date the Industrial Revolution (for example, the church, universities or the military) are characterized by centralized and formal structures (whatever the age of the organization in the industry). In terms of organizational size, the main effect on strategic decision making appears to be formalization rather than size itself. Hickson et al. (1986) found no differences in strategic decision-making processes which could be attributed to organizational size. One implication of this finding is that large organizations which manage to retain less formal structures may not necessarily exhibit the rule-following strategic decision-making processes which are likely to be followed by their more formalized counterparts. Formalization, not size, matters when looking at decision making.

Ownership and control exert separate influences over strategic decision making. In family-owned firms, for example, the overlap between the two social systems of the family and the firm creates decision processes in which personal stakes are high and delegation may be rare, since decision-making authority and the strategic direction of the firm are controlled by the owners. Interestingly, there is strong evidence to show that public versus private ownership seems to make little difference to the ways in which strategic decision making occurs (at least in the UK).

Public sector organizations:

- Take no longer than privately owned organisations to make strategic decisions.
- Do not have more committees involved in the decision-making process.
- Do not have more stakeholders than private sector organisations (but the type of stakeholder may differ, with government agencies such as the Treasury prevailing).

Source: Hickson et al. (1986)

It is still debatable whether national ownership exerts much influence on strategic decision making. There is some evidence to show that patterns of national cultural stereotypes permeate the practice of decision making. For example, North American organizations decide quicker than UK firms and both are significantly faster than Swedish organizations. But the results are far from conclusive.

12.4.1 The paradox of 'strong' organizational cultures

We know from Chapter 10 that organizational culture can exert a strong influence over a range of processes which, unsurprisingly, include decision making. Collins and Porras (1994) and Barney et al. (2001) argued that 'strong' organizational cultures are an important source of competitive advantage because strong (unitary) cultures exert a stabilizing force on organizations by encouraging cohesion, organizational commitment, and desirable work behaviours among members (see, for example, Deal and Kennedy, 1982; Nemeth and Staw, 1989; O'Reilly and Chatman, 1986, 1996). This stability generates cultural clarity and consistency among members. Because this strong culture can be aligned to the strategic goals of the organization, decision making becomes less complex and less political, encouraging smooth and fluid decision processes, thereby enhancing organizational performance and increasing competitive advantage (e.g. O'Reilly, 1989; Kotter and Heskett, 1992). Collins and Porras (1994) argued that successful companies were those where strategic decisions were influenced by timeless guiding principles (a result of strong cultures) which require no external justification. This cherished core ideology represents the key values of the organization and is the cultural 'glue' which holds it together in the face of other changes. So long as key decisions are taken in line with these cherished principles, then outstanding performance over a sustained period is the result.

The paradox, however, is that organizations can also become trapped by their strong cultures into routines which impair the development of new and different strategies (an example might be the strong culture operating in General Motors and the organization's difficulty in accepting the innovatory ideas of John DeLorean for reinventing the company, see Chapter 10). The practice of strategic decision making, therefore, becomes trapped rather than enhanced by the organizational culture. Decision makers can only think along the rigid lines demarcated by the strong culture. Innovation and creative thinking are precluded and invoking learning in the organization becomes very difficult, since the culture resists new ideas.

Decision makers, therefore, have to be very clear whether the culture of the organization is working for its success, or is actually constraining choice activities. Spotting the difference can be very difficult since the choice-enhancing factors identified by Collins and Porras (1994) very closely resemble the 'mindguards' that can detract from innovative thinking. Mindguards constrain strong-culture organizations from initiating or reacting to change, a necessary capability for optimizing performance (Lawrence and Lorsch, 1967). Strong cultures can provide organizations with significant advantages. However, when growth and survival rest on an organization's ability to change and adapt, a strong culture can be a liability since it constrains innovative decision making by narrowing down acceptable alternatives.

Some researchers (e.g. Flynn and Chatman, 2001) have proposed that one way that strong-culture organizations can avoid being constrained in strategic thinking without losing their basis of strength is by allowing sub-cultures to be created. Such sub-cultures arguably allow decision makers to remain responsive to dynamic environments. Sub-cultures can permit an organization to generate varied responses to the environment without necessarily destroying its internal coherence. Sub-cultures may provide the flexibility and responsiveness that a unitary culture may preclude. However, a strong organizational culture has a strong tendency to preclude the emergence of subcultures (O'Reilly, 1989; Saffold, 1988; Martin, 1992). For example, sub-cultures may theoretically strengthen an organization's overall organizational culture so long as they are not sufficiently dominant as to threaten the overall organizational culture. In addition, sub-cultures may emerge in response to changing demands and can serve as an outlet for members to express conflict and dissent arising during turbulent times.

These ideas of constraint versus innovation in decision making (as a direct result of strong organizational cultures) raise a number of questions about the ability of organizations to be agile and to be able to change. We address these questions in Chapter 13 when we specifically examine the question of organizational change. No less important, however, are questions about performance. Do strong cultures have any relationship with successful decisions, for example? Conversely, do weak or fragmented cultures lead to rather less successful decision making? And if culture seems not to be a strong influence on decision performance, then which factors are influential? We examine these questions in the next section of this chapter.

12.5 Strategic decision making and performance

What are the relationships between decision processes and their outcomes? Does it matter what managers do in the strategic decision-making process? What difference, if any, do managerial actions make to both processes and outcomes?

For nearly 30 years, practitioners and scholars alike have argued about what brings success. So complex have some of these arguments become that there is virtually a whole industry of analysts devoted to arguing whether planned or emergent strategies (for example) capture the essence of strategy, or whether the effective positioning of the organization in its industry and value chain leads to greater or lesser **performance**. Sub-industries have also sprung up, including, for example, focusing on whether organizations could learn better from failures than successes and whether key technological advancements (for example, killer applications) render any form of strategic planning redundant. Other analysts focused on the levels of uncertainty facing decision makers, arguing that when faced with extreme uncertainties, success was more probable if managers took action (leaps of faith in the dark) rather than no action at all. Of course, this rich analysis has not only provided a large number of industry overviews and industry shake-outs (for example, in the telecommunications industry) but has also provided many case studies and war stories for others to pick over and make sense of.

Focusing on strategic decisions rather than sectors (for example) allows us to examine the many slips that can occur 'between cup and lip' (that is, between decision processes and outcomes). Spotting decision 'failures' is easy after the event. They can take the organization into decline or, in extreme cases, can seal the demise of the organization. Typical decision failure characteristics include:

■ failure to address the original (or the real) problem;

■ the decision made the problem worse rather than better;

■ the decision becomes irreversible when things begin to go wrong and decision makers get deeper and deeper into crisis.

So where do things go wrong in this process view of decision making? If we knew in advance that decision pathways were going to result in failure, then we would not waste our time on them and would choose other alternatives. However, such is the level of uncertainty surrounding strategic decisions that this predictive dimension is almost impossible to identify, especially at the early stages of decision making. For example, it can be in the implementation stages of decision making that things can go wrong, despite what may have seemed like good ideas during formulation. Of course, there is a critical temporal element here. Before implementation, it is extremely difficult to differentiate what will be an effective strategy from one that ultimately fails. Despite all the attempts to assess the degree of future risk (through techniques such as risk analysis), strategic decisions seemingly succeed or fail independently of such criteria.

Research is beginning to identify patterns of implementation which indicate the key factors associated with higher-achieving decisions (Hickson et al., 2003; Miller et al., 2004). These factors are a combination of organizational features, such as structures and the receptiveness of organizational culture to the decision; features of what actions managers take during the process, such as how far they can specify what must be done in advance or whether the required expertise can be accessed inside the organization; and features of the decision process itself, such as its duration. We examine the issue of duration in the next section.

12.5.1 The duration and decision success

Hickson et al. (1986) produced an empirical classification of strategic decision processes up to the point of authorization. One aspect of process was duration. They found that from first mention to the point of authorization, the bulk of decisions take between 4 and 24 months to process. The mean for 155 cases was 12.4 months. Implementation, however, covers a far greater range of time, with some decisions taking only a few months to put into practice and others taking many years.

Implementation is defined here as the time taken from the point of authorization to when the decision was put into practice (for example, the new building was built or the reorganization put in place). Duration of implementation is not associated directly with success. Short, fast decisions are no more successful than longer processes. It seems that the time taken to make and implement strategic decisions matters little in terms of decision performance. Long, drawn-out processes can be associated with very successful decisions, while faster decision times are no guarantee of success. The following two vignettes show examples of these temporal extremes, one decision taking four years, the other nine months.

Example 12.1: Long implementation time (successful)

Organization:　　　　　Glass manufacturer

Strategic decision:　　Build a new manufacturing plant

Implementation time:　4 years

Achievement:　　　　　Highly successful

This organization has always enjoyed a worldwide reputation for technical excellence in process and product innovation, especially in the revolutionary float-glass process it pioneered. However, first-mover advantage in float glass was soon eroded and market share reduced considerably, as competitors moved to float-glass technology. Benchmarking revealed that the glass division in general was becoming increasingly inefficient compared to competitors producing similar products with similar technology. Competition was hotting up, especially after the expiry of its manufacturing process licences.

The senior planning team assessed the situation and set up a lengthy process of working parties and committees to consider whether to increase dramatically the production of float glass by building a new plant. The decision was made even more dramatic since it would signal this organization's possibly complete move into float-glass technology. Parallel production processes of other types of glass might have to be abandoned.

Fortunately, the necessary technical expertise was in-house. A very strong R&D team provided up-to-the minute technical information to the planning team, assisted by very strong design information from the engineering department. The decision was by no means clear to the planning team and a further two years were spent deliberating the costs and benefits associated with the investment. During this time, the business environment was becoming increasingly competitive, but the planning team chose to consult widely across the organization, so that managers and workers could absorb the need for change and could become its supporters once the decision had been put into practice.

The new site was built following this two-year deliberation and consultation period. It subsequently became the most successful plant of its type worldwide and a role model for change internally in the organization, spreading out to other divisions such as insulation and opthalmics.

Example 12.2: Short implementation time (unsuccessful)

Organization:　　　　　Paint and model manufacturer

Strategic decision:　　Expand capacity

Implementation time:　9 months

Achievement:　　　　　Unsuccessful

This highly successful international organization had developed a very profitable business, manufacturing and supplying plastic model kits of planes, cars, ships and so forth. They also had a successful business manufacturing and selling the specialized paints model builders needed to decorate their plastic models. All was going well in the market and a possible joint venture with a French company was being considered. Such a move would make this the largest plastic model manufacturer in the world.

The operations manager, who was associated with a number of successes in the plastic kit businesses, had been looking at alternative materials for model kit-building. In this case he was assessing the potential for balsa wood kits as an alternative to plastic construction. Margin on balsa wood kits was, however, not attractive, since the supply of balsa wood around the world was virtually a price monopoly. However, the managing director located another supplier in Chile who was prepared to undercut the balsa monopoly. A hastily convened meeting between the managing director and the operations director ended with the realization that if they were to enter the balsa kit market on any scale, they would have to invest in a new production line in a new factory to accommodate it.

Coincidentally, a new site for the new factory became available. A government grant was available with the only proviso that an extra 20 people were employed. Neither manager thought this to be a problem and the investment was made. Almost immediately, the first shipment of balsa wood became a problem. It was full of dead insects and other debris, which made it unsuitable for building model kits. While trying to negotiate with the balsa wood suppliers, the joint venture with the French plastic kit manufacturer was abandoned (the French company pulled out of negotiations). It now became even more crucial to get good quality supplies of balsa wood.

The French company introduced a range of innovative plastic kits which were an immediate success. Demand for balsa wood kits plummeted worldwide. The organization was left with a supply contract for material they did not now need, a factory with rent to pay and a workforce to lay off. It took five years to recover financially from this strategic decision.

From the previous two examples, it can be seen that success and the speed at which implementation occurs seem to be unrelated. Indeed, over the whole sample of 155 (Hickson et al., 1986) strategic decisions studied, duration had very little association with decision success. So which factors do seem to be associated with success? We explore these next.

12.5.2 Performance of decisions

There have been relatively few studies at the level of strategic decisions which focus upon the performance of the decision. Recent research (Hickson et al., 2003; Miller et al., 2004) has summarized this work, relating characteristics of how a strategic decision was made to how successful the decision was in practice.

Using achievement as a surrogate measure of performance (to what extent did the decision achieve stated objectives), two key factors emerge:

1 the knowledge base of managers;
2 the receptivity of the organizational context to the strategic decision being implemented.

The knowledge base of managers: The key factors with respect to performance are concerned with *how familiar* managers are with the problem to be addressed. Where managers are clear about the parameters of the problem and what information is needed to address it, they can begin to take action towards implementation. Two other processes are associated with this knowledge base. They are the *ability to plan* and *to resource* strategic decisions. Knowledge facilitates planning and helps argue a good case for resourcing. Strategic decisions do not succeed on knowledge alone; they need resources to back them up.

The receptivity of the organizational context: The key factor here is how ready the organization is to adopt the changes required by the strategic decision. The greater is the readiness in the organization's culture to undertake the change, the easier it is for managers to take action and to begin to prioritize their various strategic decisions.

However, even a high state of cultural readiness can be blocked by organizational structures which are overly formal or bureaucratic. Hence, both organizational culture and structure have to be co-aligned, if higher levels of performance are to be expected from the strategic decision-making process. Putting these factors together, we can see that the best decision performance (achievement of stated objectives) arises when both knowledge base and receptivity are high. Figure 12.4 summarizes the situation.

Figure 12.4 reveals some key findings:

- The highest-performing decisions occur where knowledge base and organizational receptivity are high. These are rare, however. Only 6% (11 decisions) of the sample were located in the top right-hand cell.
- The least well-performing decisions occur where knowledge base and organizational receptivity are low.
- In terms of decision performance, there are better pay-offs from a high knowledge base than a receptive organizational context.

The research also reveals that there are very few organizational effects:

- No single organization had all its strategic decisions in one cell of Figure 12.4.
- This underscores the value of the decision level of analysis, since there is considerable variation within organizations about where strategic decisions are located on Figure 12.4.

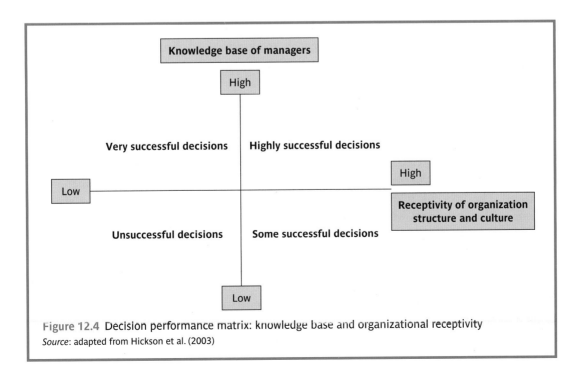

Figure 12.4 Decision performance matrix: knowledge base and organizational receptivity
Source: adapted from Hickson et al. (2003)

- Getting more decisions in the top right (or, failing that, top left) cell is likely to result in better organizational performance overall (since a relatively greater number of decisions in the organization will be successful).

- There were no differences between public, private, manufacturing and service organizations in the disposition of their strategic decisions on the matrix. Performance in all organizations, therefore, depends on managers knowing what they are doing and how far the organization is receptive to their decisions.

In many ways, this empirical study reinforces the earlier works of Chandler (1962) and Rumelt (1974) who argued that strategy and structure need to be aligned in order to contribute towards high performance. However, it adds the dimension of the knowledge base of managers to this alignment. This knowledge resource would seem important in determining the success or otherwise of strategic decisions because it examines to what extent managers are familiar with what they are doing and whether they can assess tasks to be done clearly and precisely, enabling them to allocate (prioritize) resource allocation to supporting the decision made and ensuring it is implemented. These findings resonate with the work on knowledge and innovation, viewing knowledge as a key resource in the firm (see, for example, Nonaka and Takeuchi, 1995). We examine knowledge as a strategic resource in Chapter 14 of this book.

12.6 Putting decisions into practice: implementation

Studies of strategic decision making are many (as we have seen in the chapter), but the majority of these studies have concentrated on what can be termed the **formulation** of a decision rather than putting the decision into practice (implementation). In brief, most research looks at how decisions are made (the negotiations, the fights, the people, the process) rather than how they are put into practice (the new product is launched or the new building is built). Yet the study of implementation has revealed some interesting insights, not least in terms of decision performance (see previous section) but also in giving a much fuller picture of the whole decision process and how its constituent parts (formulation and implementation) are interlinked. In particular, the empirical work of Miller et al. (2008) reveals which managers and functions are centrally involved in strategic decision making and contribute to its performance. We examine these aspects briefly in the following sections.

12.6.1 Linking formulation and implementation

Miller and Wilson (2004) examined how (and if) formulation and implementation were linked. On a sub-set (55 decisions) of the original 155 UK strategic decisions examined over a period of up to 20 years, there appear to be three ways in which formulation and implementation are connected. The first link is through *anticipation.* This linkage explains how thinking ahead to implementation influences what happens in the deciding phase (formulation). The thought of what implementation might involve and what is likely to be faced later affects the ways in which the decision is perceived and dealt with at the formulation stage. This is the one association with the duration of decision. Where decision makers anticipate a difficult implementation (for example, if a large number of intricate tasks have to be brought together), then formulation (planning, discussing, deciding to take action) takes significantly longer than the mean decision time (taking 23 months rather than the mean of 12.4 months). Successful decisions with intricate implementation processes take longer. Rushing the process can have disastrous consequences (quite literally) as the example below illustrates.

Example 12.3: **A disastrous decision**

The Columbia space shuttle disaster: an intricate decision which was rushed
On February 1, 2003, the shuttle *Columbia* disintegrated over the USA (Texas) with the loss of all seven crew members. Foam insulation 'strikes' (NASA terminology) caused damage to the shuttle, causing it to break up on re-entry killing all on board.

The foam insulation struck the left wing, damaging the shuttle's thermal protection system which prevents the shuttle burning up on re-entry. NASA's shuttle safety regulations stated that external tank foam shedding and subsequent debris strikes upon the shuttle itself were safety issues that needed to be resolved before a launch was cleared.

However, launches were often given the go-ahead because none of the engineers could agree on how this could be prevented, nor how risky shedding such debris might be.

Source: Starbuck and Farjoun (2005)

There has been much analysis of the above disaster from many perspectives. Woods (2005) gives a decision perspective which clearly shows the launch decision was rushed without knowing sufficient information in advance. Woods shows how intense time pressures (to launch on time) meant information from engineers was often ignored. In fact, engineers had been ignored in previous flights which had encountered no problems. So here was the second problem: taking past successes as indications of future performance. Secondly, in NASA there was poor communication and information sharing between different parts of the organization (many reports talk of working in silos), so the bringing together of intricate tasks into a coherent implementation was extremely difficult. Finally, Woods noted that there was a failure in NASA to revise estimates/actions as new evidence accumulated and the decision to launch just went ahead anyway.

A second link between formulation and implementation can be termed a *political* connection. This is because high levels of political activity during formulation (lots of different stakeholders fighting it out; constant disagreements and failure to compromise) make implementation problematic because key information is not available (political activity distracts from getting key or accurate information or knowing when to buy it in) and because political disagreements continue into the implementation phase. This is a classic case of a low knowledge base and low receptivity decision, very likely to fail (see Figure 12.3). The only thing that seems to 'save' such decisions from always being failures is where decision makers can see the seriousness of the consequences if things were to go wrong. If this can be brought to the attention of decision makers (either through their own interpretations or via other senior managers in the organization), then implementation can proceed relatively smoothly and successfully.

The third and final link between deciding and implementing is perhaps the most obvious. Who (or which functions) are *involved*? Are they involved throughout formulation and implementation and which have the greatest influence over decision making?

12.6.2 Involvement and influence in strategic decision making

Miller et al. (2008) have identified the key functions involved. Table 12.3 summarizes. From the columns labelled 'Decision making' and 'Implementation' it can be seen that (omitting the CEO whom we discuss later) there are four key stakeholders who are most involved in both making strategic decisions and implementing them. These are Production and Service Delivery (P/SD), Finance, Suppliers and Marketing (with sales). A line is drawn in Table 12.3 at the first major change

Table 12.3 Involvement in decision making and implementation (number of decision cases from a maximum 55 in which stakeholders are involved)

Stakeholders	Decision making (formulation)			Implementation			Continuity of involvement (number of cases in which the stakeholders appear in both formulation and implementation stages)
	No.	%	Rank	No.	%	Rank	
(I) CEO	44	80	1	44	80	1	25
(I) Production/service delivery	39	71	2	35	64	2	28
(I) Finance	38	69	3	24	44	3	19
(E) Suppliers	32	58	4	22	40	4	17
(I) Marketing and sales	26	47	5	20	36	5	17
(E) Shareholders, auditors	20	36	6	9	16	6	6
(I) Personnel, maintenance	18	33	7	7	13	7	5
(E) Trade unions	18	33	8	6	11	10	2
(E) Customers	16	29	9	7	13	7	7
(I) R&D	12	22	10	7	13	7	4
(I) Liaison	9	16	11	2	4	13	2
(E) Govt, Inspectorates	7	13	12	5	9	12	3
(E) Competitors	6	11	13	1	2	14	1
(I) Purchasing	4	7	14	6	11	10	4

(I) Internal to the organization
(E) External to the organization
Source: adapted from Miller et al. (2008)

in continuity from deciding through implementation. There is a marked gap between fourth and fifth places, between Marketing and Shareholders/Auditors, showing a big drop in involvement from 36% to 16%. Above the line there is greater continuity throughout the process with, for example, P/SD being involved in 39 out of the 55 cases (71%) of decision making and in 64% of cases of implementation.

P/SD, Finance and Marketing are involved most frequently in creating and implementing the decisions that shape the strategic direction (and success) of an organization. They play a central and sustained role at the heart of the organization. Suppliers are the only external interest to feature so often in both phases. Their role is one of providing inputs, so they are involved in helping to think through alternative decision choices and in providing resources to ensure that what is agreed can go ahead. Overall, analysis reveals that P/SD was concerned with either decision making or implementation, or both, in 84% of the cases; Finance in 78%, Suppliers in 65% and Marketing in 53%.

Table 12.3 also shows the widespread involvement of the CEO. He (without exception all CEOs were male in this study) was involved at some stage in 80% of all cases (44 out of 55 decisions and the same proportion of implementations). There is no evidence here that chief executives steer strategic decisions through and then cease any interest in their implementation. That may be so on more operational decisions but not where strategic decisions are concerned. They remain centrally involved throughout in most organizations.

Table 12.4 Internal and external stakeholder influence in decision making and implementation (ordered first by rank in the decision-making stage)

Stakeholder/function	Decision making (formulation) Mean influence score	Rank	Implementation Mean influence score	Rank
(I) CEO	4.3	1	4.2	1
(I) Purchasing	3.5	2	3.1	11
(I) Marketing and sales	3.3	3	3.8	5
(I) R&D	3.1	4	4.0	2
(I) Finance	2.9	5	3.4	7
(E) Shareholders, auditors	2.8	6	3.4	7
(I) Production/service delivery	2.7	7	3.7	6
(E) Suppliers	2.7	7	2.8	14
(E) Customers	2.6	9	3.3	9
(I) Liaison	2.6	9	4.0	2
(I) Personnel, Maintenance	2.3	11	3.3	9
(E) Govt, Inspectorates	2.1	12	3.1	11
(E) Competitors	2.0	13	4.0	2
(E) Trade unions	1.6	14	3.0	13

(I) Internal to the organization
(E) External to the organization
Source: adapted from Miller et al. (2008)

How far is any **involvement** in decision making sustained through into implementation? The final column labelled 'Continuity of involvement' in Table 12.3 shows that these key players do connect deciding with implementing. Of the 35 cases where they were involved in implementation, P/SD were also involved in decision making in 28 of them. Similarly, Finance were involved in 24 implementations, 19 of which they helped to decide.

While involvement suggests having a voice in what goes on, it does not specify whose voice is louder. To understand this requires an examination of *influence*. Influence between stakeholders was compared (on a 5-point scale where 5 = high) by aggregating **influence** scores for all stakeholders in every case to arrive at a mean influence score for each. Table 12.4 summarizes the results for decision making and for implementation.

In decision making (formulation), the four key most involved functions (Marketing, Finance, P/SD and Suppliers), plus the CEO, again feature towards the top half of the table. Centrally involved and crucially influential in shaping the strategic agenda, they are joined by Purchasing, R&D and Shareholders/Auditors who, though not involved as frequently, have an influential voice in decision making when called in.

In implementation, R&D remains influential, as do Marketing, P/SD and Finance. Suppliers, however, drop to the bottom, as might be expected when the details of implementation become the responsibility of other functions inside the organization. The influence of Purchasing disappears almost completely when it comes to implementation. It is relegated to the sidelines during implementation.

Those who are less involved tend to have lower influence. Local and national government (inspectorates and the like), trade unions and personnel are left out of most decision making and have little muscle when they are represented. The lack of union influence reflects the national picture of waning union power in the UK and elsewhere globally.

Although there are fewer stakeholders/functions involved in implementation, the weight of influence of each increases during the implementation phase. One explanation may be that it takes more pressure to get things done than to decide they should be done. Bringing together the findings on involvement and influence, it can be seen that there are heavyweights and lightweights in this arena. Of each group, some are core, central to most decision-making activity that goes on in organizations (CEO, Finance, Marketing, Production, R&D), while others generally remain on the periphery of the action.

12.7 Summary

To look at strategy through the lens of decision making is a complex activity. Decisions can focus on choices made, or on how managers make decisions. The focus can also concentrate on the characteristics of the decision process itself and recent work has begun to establish some relationships between these process characteristics and decision performance.

Key features of these decision-making processes are knowledge, planning, resourcing and specifying. Stakeholders must also be broadly aligned to be supportive of the decision. Organizational culture should be open to the changes the decision will bring about, and organizational structure should not impede the process of implementation by being too formal or cumbersome and a barrier to change.

Some functions appear core to decision-making processes and, along with the CEO, powerful and influential functions include Finance, Production, R&D and Marketing. Other functions and stakeholders may be involved, but seem to exert less influence on the decision and its implementation.

Key terms

choice	392	involvement	413
context	392	options	398
formulation	410	performance	405
game theory	391	processes	395
implementation	406	strategic decisions	391
influence	400		

Recap questions and assignments

1 Pick a strategic decision with which you are familiar, or in which you were a participant. How would you describe its key process features?

2 Using the same example (or you can choose another strategic decision), describe what was done and by whom during the process.

3 What, in your view, were the major influences on the decision and its final outcome?

Case study 12.1: **Magic restored**

Under its new boss Disney has staged an impressive creative turnaround – and is making synergy work

In 'Ratatouille', the most recent animated film from Pixar, a film studio owned by Disney, a talented cook named Remy, who happens to be a rat, finds his way into the kitchen of a once-great restaurant. Its head chef has given up on creativity and instead plans to churn out ready meals branded with the name of the restaurant's revered founder, Auguste Gusteau. Eventually the chef loses control of the restaurant, the frozen meals are tossed out and Remy's cooking helps it regain its reputation and inventive flair.

Something similar appears to have happened at Disney. Four years ago it was in turmoil, with its then chief executive, Michael Eisner, under siege from shareholders who accused him of stifling the firm's creative culture. Today under Bob Iger, who took over as chief executive in 2005, Disney is enjoying a remarkable and profitable run of hit TV programmes and films. 'Disney's creative momentum is so strong now that there's no comparison between it and other big media companies,' says Lawrence Haverty, a fund manager at Gabelli Asset Management.

In the past Disney concentrated mainly on the very young, but in recent years it has found a new audience among 'tweens', or nine- to 14-year-olds. In 2006 the Disney Channel in America started showing 'Hannah Montana', a TV series about an ordinary girl with a double life as a rock star, and broadcast 'High School Musical', a television film about a romance between two pupils from different cliques at school. Both turned into huge hits with staying power: in fiscal 2006 and 2007 combined, Disney made over $100m of operating profit from 'High School Musical' and various spin-off products. Coming soon is 'Camp Rock', a Disney Channel film starring the Jonas Brothers, a wholesome boy-band which has already sold over a million CDs for Hollywood Records, Disney's recorded-music label.

At the same time Disney's broadcast-TV network, ABC, is benefiting from a number of hits, such as 'Desperate Housewives', 'Lost' and 'Ugly Betty'. Disney has also improved the fortunes of its film business, which earned $1.2 billion in operating profit last year, up from $200m in 2005. Some of the increase came from the firm's acquisition of Pixar for $7.4 billion in 2006, but the performance of Disney's live-action films, such as 'Enchanted', drove most of the improvement. On April 8th Disney laid out ambitious plans for ten new animated films in the next four years.

What accounts for this renaissance? Mr Iger's management style is said by many to have unlocked Disney's creativity. 'There was already creativity inside Disney, but Bob removed the barriers to it,' says Peter Chernin, chief operating officer of News Corporation, a rival media group. 'Michael Eisner was all about his own creativity,' says Stanley Gold, a former Disney board director who led a campaign to oust Mr Eisner in 2004, referring to the way in which the former boss meddled in the detail of Disney's parks and movies. In contrast, he says, 'Bob pushes creative decisions to the people below him.'

In addition, Mr Iger's acquisition of Pixar, a studio that insists on creative originality, has sent a signal to people inside and outside Disney. 'A few years ago we weren't necessarily seen by the creative community as the place to be,' says Tom Staggs, Disney's chief financial officer, 'but now that has changed and people want to work here.' Mr Iger immediately put Pixar's top people in charge of Disney's animation business, and last year he put an end to the practice of making cheap direct-to-video sequels of old favourites, such as 'Cinderella II: Dreams Come True' – Disney's equivalent of frozen food.

Before Mr Iger took over, Disney had a factory-like process for animation in which a business-development team came up with ideas and allocated directors to them. 'With the arrival of the Pixar leadership, Disney has adopted the director-driven development and production approach that Pixar has used so successfully,' says Mr Staggs. The full proof of Pixar's impact on Disney's animation will be seen in November when the firm releases 'Bolt', the first film developed entirely under the new bosses. To be sure, Mr Iger paid a high price for Pixar, and box-office revenue in America for the studio's films has declined with each release since 'Finding Nemo' in 2003, points out Ben Swinburne of Morgan Stanley. Pixar's next film is 'WALL-E', about the adventures of a robot in the year 2700, which will open in American cinemas in July.

One former Mouseketeer argues that Mr Iger cannot take much credit for Disney's recent string of hits. 'All the great new shows from Disney were developed, and many of them launched, when Michael Eisner was leading the company,' says David Hulbert, a former president of Walt Disney Television International. 'The TV and studio creative cycle lasts several years, so we will have to wait some time yet to see what Bob Iger's cautious, centralised and consensual management style produces,' he adds. Disney executives counter that Mr Eisner had made Mr Iger responsible for ABC, the Disney Channel and ESPN, its sports network.

What is certain is that under Mr Iger, Disney has perfected the art of media synergy. The firm has turned 'High School Musical', for instance, into a live concert tour, a stage musical, a show on ice, and a series of books and video games. Pixar's 'Cars' may have slightly disappointed at the box office, but Disney sold 100m model vehicles on the back of it, plans to build a 'Cars Land' attraction in its California Adventure theme park and is developing an online virtual world tie-in.

Synergy in action
Disney's revenues (*operating income*) 2007, $bn

Broadcast and cable television 15.0 (*4.3*)

Theme parks and resorts 10.6 (*1.7*)

Consumer products 2.3 (*0.6*)

Films 7.5 (*1.2*)

Source: Company reports

Disney now has ten 'franchises' that it treats in this way, from Mickey Mouse to Disney Fairies. Every media conglomerate pursued synergy some years ago, but Disney is the only one to have made it work consistently across the whole company. It helps, of course, that so many of its customers are children, who tend to be more receptive to spin-off products than adults.

Mr Eisner certainly pushed synergy hard, but Mr Iger's collaborative management style is better suited to it, insiders say. In Britain, says a Disney executive based in London, the firm's programme-sales group worked hard to sell 'High School Musical' to the BBC, even though it contributed relatively little to their own division's bottom line, because exposure on free-to-air TV then bolstered sales of 'High School Musical' DVDs, pencil cases and other products. 'A few years ago they wouldn't have bothered,' says the executive, 'but now the key properties are so drummed into us that everyone is behind them.'

Not everything is perfect in the Magic Kingdom. Investors worry about the impact of a recession on Disney's theme parks, which accounted for just over a quarter of the firm's revenues in the first fiscal quarter of this year. Mainly for that reason, the firm's share price has fallen by 14% in the past year. Disney says that its American parks are more resilient during slowdowns than those of its rivals. Like its peers, Disney still earns most money from traditional media, and needs to expand its businesses on-line. But its creative momentum and proven ability to extract value from its hits means it can afford to feel more optimistic about the future than most big media firms.

Source: 'Magic Restored', *The Economist*, 17 April 2008
© The Economist Newspaper Limited, London 2008. All rights reserved.

Questions

1 How has Bob Iger used the knowledge base of the organization to good effect?

2 What links can you see between Iger's management style and the knowledge base of Disney?

3 What does this case tell us about the relationships between strategy and structure?

References

Barney, J., Wright, M. and Ketchen, D.J. (2001) The resource based view of the firm: ten years after 1991. *Journal of Management*, **27**, **6**, 625–41.

Bowman, E.H., Singh, H. and Thomas, H. (2001) The domain of strategic management. In A.M. Pettigrew, H. Thomas and R. Whittington (eds) *Handbook of Strategy and Management*, Sage, London.

Chandler, A.E. Jr (1962) *Strategy and Structure: Chapters in the History of the American Industrial Enterprise*, MIT Press, Cambridge, MA.

Collins, J.C. and Porras, J.I. (1994) *Built to Last*, Century Books, New York.

Cyert, R.M. and March, J.G. (1963) *A Behavioral Theory of the Firm*, Prentice-Hall, Englewood Cliffs, NJ.

De Wit, B. and Meyer, R. (1999) *A Strategy Synthesis*, International Thomson Press, London.

Deal, T. and Kennedy, A. (1982) *Corporate Cultures*, Addison-Wesley, Reading, MA.

Flynn, F. and Chatman, J.A. (2001) Strong cultures and innovation: oxymoron or opportunity? In S. Cartwright et al. (eds) *International Handbook of Organizational Culture and Climate*, Wiley, Chichester, pp. 263–87.

Hall, D.J. and Saias, M.A. (1980) Strategy follows structure! *Strategic Management Journal*, **1**, 149–63.

Hickson, D., Butler, R., Cray, D., Mallory, G. and Wilson, D. (1986) *Top Decisions: Strategic Decision Making in Organizations*, Jossey-Bass, San Francisco, CA.

Hickson, D., Miller, S. and Wilson, D. (2003) Planned or prioritized? Two options in managing the implementation of strategic decisions. *Journal of Management Studies*, **40**, **7**, 1803–36.

Hofer, C.W. and Schendel, D. (1978) *Strategy Formulation: Analytical Concepts*, West, New York.

Kotter, J.P. and Heskett, J.L. (1992) *Corporate Culture and Performance*, Free Press, New York.

Lawrence, P.R. and Lorsch, J.W. (1967) *Organization and Environment*, Harvard University Press, Cambridge, MA.

March, J.G. (1994) *A Primer on Decision Making. How Decisions Happen*, Free Press, New York.

March, J.G. and Simon, H.A. (1958) *Organizations*, Wiley, New York.

Martin, J. (1992) *Cultures in Organizations: Three Perspectives*, Oxford University Press, New York.

Miller, S. and Wilson, D.C. (2004) *Actioning Strategic Decisions: Connecting Deciding and Implementing*. Paper presented at the Academy of Management Conference, New Orleans.

Miller, S., Wilson, D. and Hickson, D. (2004) Beyond planning: strategies for successfully implementing strategic decisions. *Long Range Planning*, **37**, **3**, 201–18.

Miller, S., Hickson, D.J. and Wilson, D.C. (2008) From strategy to action: involvement and influence in top level decisions. *Long Range Planning*, **41**, 606–28.

Mintzberg, H., Raisinghani, D. and Theoret, A. (1976) The structure of 'unstructured' decision processes. *Administrative Science Quarterly*, **21**, 246–75.

Mintzberg, H., Quinn, J.B. and Ghoshal, S. (1998) *The Strategy Process*, Prentice Hall, New York.

Nemeth, C.J. and Staw, B. (1989) The tradeoffs of social control and innovation in groups and organization. In L. Berkowitz (ed.) *Advances in Experimental Social Psychology*, **Vol. 22**, Academic Press, San Diego, CA, pp. 175–210.

Nonaka, I. and Takeuchi, H. (1995) *The Knowledge-creating Company: How Japanese Companies Create the Dynamics of Innovation*, Oxford University Press, New York.

Nutt, P.C. and Wilson D.C. (2010) *Handbook of Decision Making*, Wiley, New York.

O'Reilly, C. (1989) Corporations, culture, and commitment: motivation and social control in organizations. *California Management Review*, **314**, 9–25.

O'Reilly, C. and Chatman, J. (1986) Organizational commitment and psychological attachment: the effects of compliance, identification and internalization on prosocial behavior. *Journal of Applied Psychology*, **71**, 492–9.

O'Reilly, C. and Chatman, J. (1996) Culture as social control: corporations, cults, and commitment. In B.M. Staw and L. Cummings (eds) *Research in Organizational Behavior*, **Vol. 18**, JAI Press, Stanford, CT, pp. 287–365.

Pettigrew, A.M. (1986) *The Awakening Giant: Continuity and Change in ICI*, Blackwell, Oxford.

Powell, J.H. (2003) Game theory in strategy. In D. Faulkner and A. Campbell (eds) *The Oxford Handbook of Strategy*, Oxford University Press, Oxford.

Rasche, A. (2007) *The Paradoxical Foundation of Strategic Management*, Physica-Verlag, Berlin.

Rumelt, R. (1974) *Strategy, Structure and Economic Performance.* Division of Research, Harvard Business School, Boston, MA.

Saffold, G.S. (1988) Culture traits, strength, and organizational performance: moving beyond 'strong' culture. *Academy of Management Review*, **13**, 546–58.

Starbuck, W. and Farjoun, M. (eds) (2005) *Organization at the Limit: Lessons from the Columbia Disaster*, Blackwell, Oxford.

Von Clausewitz, C. (1976) *On War* (translated by M. Howard and P. Paret), Princeton University Press, Princeton, NJ.

Von Neumann, J. and Morgenstern, O. (1944) *Theory of Games and Economic Behaviour*, Princeton University Press, Princeton, NJ.

Wilson, D.C. (2007) Strategic decisions. In G. Ritzer (ed.) *Blackwell Encyclopedia of Sociology*, Blackwell, Oxford, pp. 4784–9.

Woods, D.D. (2005) Creating foresight: lessons for enhancing resilience from Columbia. In W. Starbuck and M. Farjoun (eds) *Organisation at the limit*, Blackwell, Oxford.

Further reading

Cummings, S. and Daellenbach, U. (2009) A guide to the future of strategy? The history of long range planning. *Long Range Planning*, **42**, **2**, 234–63.

Whittington, R. (2007) Strategy practice and strategy process: family differences and the sociological eye. *Organization Studies*, **28**, **10**, 1574–86.

Strategic decision making: managing strategic change

Chapter contents

Introduction

As de Wit and Meyer (1999) point out, thinking and acting strategically will, of necessity, involve an organization in some degree of strategic change. Such changes can be to structures, processes, technologies, markets, products and services, ownership and so forth. Change processes themselves can also be characterized, for example, as relatively continuous (that is, piecemeal and evolutionary) or discontinuous (that is, dramatic and revolutionary). The story of strategy implementation is also the story of strategic change.

It is obviously important to understand the change process, since no matter how sophisticated strategic thinking is, a poorly managed implementation is likely to result in a more difficult or complex set of strategic changes, or no change at all. This chapter examines change in organizations as it relates to strategic management.

In this chapter our primary focus will be the following:

- analysing and understanding the characteristics and dimensions of change processes;
- their relationship to organizational strategies;
- what we know about relatively more and less successful change strategies.

13.1 The characteristics and dimensions of change processes

The examination of change requires intention and anticipation to be fully explored (Wensley, 2003). Organizations and individuals exhibit dual aspects of *intention* – the purpose or the goal of an action and *anticipation* – the action of looking forward to something however ill-defined. A profit-making organization, for example, may state in its strategic reports that it *intends* to increase market share by 5% in one year. A public service organization may have a statement about making the world a better place or *anticipating* a future where (for example) education is somehow 'better' and more accessible to individuals.

Analysing such strategy statements is difficult because the antecedents to change are to be found in a wide range of disciplines ranging from philosophy and the understanding of human nature, through psychology and the analysis of motives, personality, to the socio-cultural aspects of organizing and organization. For example, economists provide convincing rationales for change. These range from those generated within *microeconomics*, which examines markets and the behaviours of organizations and individuals; those that arise in *macroeconomics*, which examines national income and growth; and theories of *international economics*, which examine international trade based upon the exchange of goods and services by people in different national economies. Each approach has a distinctive account of drivers for, and explanations of, change (see Wilson, 2009). For example, microeconomists argue that individuals will seek to maximize the utility profile of various situations. They will assess what they gain and lose from a situation or a change, and make a rational choice to embrace the option or the outcome which most closely maximizes individual gain, elevating self-interest to a priority. Macroeconomists and international economists argue that the drivers of change can be found in the economic and competitive infrastructure of national economies (see Porter, 1986, 1998) where the exploitation of inequalities such as the costs of production or raw materials provide a stimulus for organizational changes. In this way, economists provide an explanation for the apparent paradox that some countries will import goods that, domestically, they are demonstrably capable of producing for themselves (e.g. textiles, coal).

Thus, the drivers of change become resources, cost minimization and profit maximization. Porter's concept of 'clusters', or groups of interconnected firms, suppliers, related industries and institutions that arise in particular locations, became a strong argument for companies and governments to think about economies, to assess the competitive advantage of locations and, as a result, often instigate changes in private and public sector policies to support or discourage domestic production.

Understanding change covers a wide range of levels of analysis, from the macro socio-economic to the subjectively constructed world of the individual. Table 13.1 outlines the range of levels of analysis and describes their key features, disciplines and orientations.

Table 13.1 Key orientations towards organization change		
Level of analysis	**Key features (examples)**	**Key disciplines**
Socio-Cultural	■ Examines changes in the nature, the social institutions, the social behaviour or the social relations of a society, community of people, or other social structures ■ Includes any events or actions that affect a group of individuals that have shared values or characteristics ■ Acts of advocacy for the cause of changing society in a normative way	History, Politics, Anthropology and Sociology
Socio-Economic	■ Examines the economic bases of societies and the changes produced as a result ■ Includes world trade, capital transfers, foreign direct investment and the economic role of the multinational enterprise ■ Advocacy for the globalization of goods and services and striving for national advantage	Macroeconomics and International Business
Socio-Organizational	■ Examines the socio-cultural aspects of organizations and groups ■ Includes culture, structure, power, conflict and social theories of decision making ■ Examines organizations as social groups where the understanding of social behaviours can underpin and inform an understanding of change	Organization Theory, Sociology of Organization, Strategy
Economic Organizational	■ Examines the competitive or efficiency bases of organization ■ Includes resources, the economic power of suppliers, customers, competitors and the impact and influence of government regulations ■ Market-based models of organization (e.g. apply economic yardsticks of performance to all organizations, including voluntary and public sector to effect change); or views economic booms and slumps as drivers of change	Economics, Politics (especially government regulation) and Political History
Individual	■ Examines the psychological characteristics and/or the subjective interpretative world of the individual ■ Includes personality, identity, values, and norms ■ Focuses on individual interpretations and accounts of change	Psychology, Sociology of Social Construction, Discourse Analysis and Sense-Making

13.2 Theoretical approaches to change

The first issue concerns to what extent change can be viewed as a *planned* or an *emergent* process and the second question the extent to which change might be seen as a *voluntaristic* or *determined* activity.

■ **Planned change** describes a sequence of steps or phases which prescribe what managers should do and has been summarized by Pettigrew and Whipp (1991) as 'leading change'. Briefly this means a process by which managers develop concerns (creating an agenda to change); foster an understanding of the problem throughout the organization; plan, act and eventually stabilize the change, locking it into place in the organization.

- **Emergent perspectives** view change as a process which emanates from a host of organizational and individual activities. These processes are visible as patterns in streams of decisions and actions (Mintzberg and Waters, 1985). Change, therefore, can only be characterized after it has happened.

- **Voluntarism** and **determinism** are also opposite ends of the dimension of social action (Parsons, 1937). The term voluntarism is applied to those theories of change that are based upon the intentions or motives of actors who are assumed to act 'voluntarily' and not as 'determined' by social or organizational structures.

These dimensions help map some of the key theoretical approaches to change. As Van de Ven and Poole (1995) observed, there are over one million articles published on the subject of change in pure and social science disciplines. Since that research (conducted in 1994) the number is now closer to two million articles. Nevertheless, the ideal-type classification system used by Van de Ven and Poole (1995, p. 514) helps begin to make sense of the major approaches which shape how strategists may view and understand change. Van de Ven and Poole identified four main approaches: life-cycle, teleological, dialectic and evolutionary.

1 **Life-cycle theories:** conceptualize change as a process which follows the 'natural' life-cycle of entities such as products, projects and organizations themselves from birth through maturity to old age and death. The key underlying premise of such approaches is that of deterministic development. That is, change has a logic to it which can be examined by reference to the present state. Thus, youth will progress to maturity and old age and the change process will begin and end deterministically, withstanding environmental changes and even shocks. Change is a pre-programmed series of events or phases.

2 **Teleological theories:** conceptualize change as planned, or as emanating from purpose, and these theories have found considerable support in many management theories, including Lewin's (1947) force field analogy in which planned change progresses through three stages which he termed unfreezing (from the old state), moving and refreezing (to the new state). These three simple phases or steps provided the foundations for a whole raft of approaches describing and advising steps to be taken by those leading change. These include approaches by Judson (1991), Kotter (1996) and Armenakis et al. (1999).

3 **Dialectic theories:** conceptualize change as a process of conflicting interests which struggle against one another to try to influence both the processes and the outcomes of change. Change depends upon, and is shaped by, clashes of contradictory interests (individual, organizational or societal) and the outcome represents a synthesis of these conflicting struggles. This theory of change is based on elements of dialectical enquiry, i.e. thesis, antithesis and synthesis (see Hegel, 1937; Kolakowski, 1978), and the resultant change emanates from innate political tensions in organization and organizing (Wilson, 1999).

4 **Evolutionary theories:** conceptualize change as cumulative processes that occur at the level of populations of organizations, communities or societies. Derived from biological metaphors concerning the survival and development of species, typical theories would include the population ecology approach in organization theory (Hannan and Freeman, 1977). Organizations, like biological species, survive only if they can adapt to environmental shocks or stimuli which can be unforeseen (Aldrich, 1979). These shocks create variation in an otherwise stable system. Survival depends on an organization's ability to compete for scarce resources and to adapt to new circumstances.

These different approaches to change reveal significant variation in how the change process might be conceptualized by strategists, but they tell us little about the characteristics of the process itself. This is developed in the next section.

Table 13.2 Levels and degrees of operational and strategic change		
Degree of change	Level of change	Characteristics
Status quo	Can be both operational and strategic	No change in current practices. A decision *not* to do something can be strategic as well as operational
Expanded reproduction	Mainly operational	Change involves producing 'more of the same' (for example, goods and services)
Evolutionary transition	Mainly strategic	Sometimes radical changes occur but they do so within the existing parameters of the organization (for example, existing structures or technologies are retained)
Revolutionary transition	Predominantly strategic	Change involves shifting or redefining existing parameters. Structures, processes and/or technologies likely to change

Source: Wilson (1999, p. 20)

13.3 Levels of change

Change is called strategic (rather than operational) when it involves relatively high-level and pervasive changes to the structures, processes and core businesses of the organization. Such changes are usually novel to the organization in question (although not necessarily novel in themselves). They are changes which set precedents for subsequent strategic decisions made in the organization, and they are difficult to reverse once in motion and tend to be capital hungry (in terms of both human and financial capital). Table 13.2 summarizes one way of viewing change along a scale which moves from status quo to revolutionary change, at the same time distinguishing between strategic and operational changes.

The Case box below illustrates the difficulties inherent in the process of strategic change in the context of Apple and its strategic growth.

Case box 13.1: Where 'Think different' is taking Apple

Rather than accept being a niche PC maker, Steve Jobs is transforming his baby into a high-end consumer-electronics and services company
From the word go nearly two years ago, sales of Apple Computer's iPod MP3 player have been music to the PC maker's ears. Never has that been more true than on July 16, when Steve Jobs & Co. stunned analysts by announcing they had sold 304,000 players in the company's third quarter, nearly four times most analysts' expectations. The reason: Customer demand soared in May after Apple launched its third-generation iPod, which stores 7,500 songs in a player that's lighter than two CDs – and is compatible with Microsoft's Windows operating system. Apple's flagship retail store in New York City's Soho section stayed open until 11 p.m. the day of the launch just to meet the demand.

'It's a paradigm shift at the company,' says Charles Wolf, an analyst at investment firm Needham & Co. and a longtime Apple watcher (who owns shares of Apple stock). 'They are redefining what kind of company they are.' Indeed, the release of iPod for Windows last August established the demarcation line in an extraordinary strategic change for Apple, a company that over the past two decades has steadfastly refused to loosen its control over the creation, manufacturing, or distribution of its products.

BEYOND THE MAC. Years after Apple launched its advertising campaign admonishing customers to 'Think Different,' CEO Steve Jobs appears to be taking his own advice. Instead of resigning himself to the idea that Apple will never be more than a niche PC supplier, Jobs is slowly transforming it into a high-end consumer-electronics and services company à la Sony (SNE) – one that he hopes ultimately will be less dependent on sales of the Macintosh PC, which now account for about 80% of revenues.

Apple's transformation has been gradual. It started in October of 1999, when the company introduced iMovie, a video-editing program for the Mac that brought professional-quality digital editing to the masses. iTunes software for playing and managing digital music files came next, in January of 2001. Then just 10 months later, Apple launched the first iPod.

Though iPod got rave reviews, it soon became clear that most people weren't going to abandon their Windows PC just for the chance to use what arguably was the best MP3 player on the market. So in August of 2002, Apple introduced an iPod for Windows. By Christmas, it plans to launch more new Windows-compatible products, such as the wildly successful music-download service, the iTunes Music Store, originally just for Macs.

'That represents a shift in strategy, whether they realized it at first or not,' says Wolf. 'The iPod was the first product that wasn't tethered to the Mac.' Apple executives decline to comment on the company's strategy.

'CADILLAC OPERATION.' Nonetheless, a look at Apple's balance sheet reveals why it's so anxious to broaden its audience beyond the Mac's niche audience. In its third quarter, which ended June 30, Apple earned $428 million in gross profit, a 27.7% margin on sales of $1.55 billion, but it spent $419 million on operating expenses, leaving it with an operating margin of just 0.6%.

'Apple's gross margins are the envy of the industry,' says IDC analyst Roger Kay. 'But below the line, they give it all back. They pour money into R&D and [selling, general, and administrative expenses]. They have expensive retail locations and high-end advertising. It's a Cadillac operation.'

Wall Street hasn't punished the stock, however. Apple shares are trading at a 52-week high of about $21. But to rise further, Apple has to do one of two things: Increase revenues and profits – or cut staff and development and marketing costs. Jobs has clearly stated that his aim is to do the former. When the Net bubble burst in 2000, he promised his staff that there would be no layoffs. Instead, he said, Apple would 'innovate through the downturn.'

SKYROCKET POTENTIAL? The iPod was the first step. According to an analysis by Needham's Wolf, at the current wholesale price of $360, a Windows version of iPod should have been able to capture close to a 10% share of the 2002 MP3 market – about 900,000 units, worth about $325 million in revenue.

At a lower price point, sales could skyrocket. Wolf figures that at a wholesale price of $315, Apple would still earn more than 20% gross margins and sell 1.25 million players. That's $400 million in revenues. Couple that potential with market researcher IDC's prediction that the MP3 market will nearly triple over the next three years, and it's possible that by 2006 Apple could generate $600 million in annual sales on the iPod for Windows – boosting its total revenues by about 10%. 'The iPod is the first step. It should not be the last,' says Wolf.

Morphing into a consumer-electronics company also capitalizes on a hip brand – the cult of cool – that Apple has spent billions building. Take the iTunes Music Store, which launched with much hoopla in April. Apple was the first player in that business to persuade the five major music labels to sign on to a pure à la carte download service, where music aficionados could buy individual tracks for 99 cents and burn them to a CD or transfer them to an MP3 player.

STREET CRED. Until iTunes, customers' only legal option had been the more complex subscription services hawked by the label-backed services, Pressplay and MusicNet (see BW Online, 4/30/03, 'Steve Jobs, the Pied Piper of Online Music', and 4/22/03, 'Web Music Gets Its Act Together'). On its first day, Apple sold a million downloads. By the end of July, it had sold about 7.5 million tracks.

Media reports at the time credited Jobs's street credibility in Hollywood as key to getting the service off the ground. (Jobs personally called individual artists, including Eagles lead singer Don Henley, to persuade them to make their music available on the service.) But insiders say it was more Apple's popularity with elite style influencers that helped persuade gun-shy music execs to grant the licenses required to create a less restrictive service.

Says one label exec: 'Until Apple, it wasn't cool to buy digital music. This was about getting to that pivotal group of people – the people who buy the cool sneakers and wear the right clothes – and showing them that legally downloading music could be cooler than stealing it.'

Source: Reprinted from 30 April 2003 issue of Bloomberg BusinessWeek by special permission © 2010 by Bloomberg L. P.

Since the launch of the iPod, Apple has used the change (and innovation) platform created in the company to launch the iPad in 2010. The iPad is not the first tablet released in the world, but its release is likely to focus attention on tablets across the sector. Apple's success means changes for others in the sector. Not least, these changes are predicted to be large, with some analysts forecasting changes from 4 million tablet shipments annually in 2010 to over 50 million in 2015. Intense media coverage surrounding Apple's iPad has generated renewed interest in the tablet sector across the globe. In this respect, Apple has created an advantage for all other tablet producers by raising the public profile of the media tablet.

13.4 Analysing and understanding change from a strategy perspective

Researchers and practitioners in strategic management have proposed various ways in which we might understand strategic change and, more importantly, which perspectives will yield the most useful results in making changes work successfully. Nutt et al. (2000) provide a useful summary of the main approaches taken. They argue that there are five predominant ways to craft a strategy in the face of strategic change issues. These are:

1 analytical approaches;

2 stakeholder approaches;

3 adaptive approaches;

4 gap analyses;

5 systems-based analysis of strategic 'tensions'.

In brief, *analytical approaches* examine the strategic portfolio of the organization (services and products) to see how well its portfolio of activities fits with its commitment to find resources to change the mix to improve performance. Strategic change, therefore, is a constant process of aligning and shifting the mix of products and services, clients, funding sources, skills and image (for example, brand strength).

Stakeholder approaches argue that strategies are crafted in line with those stakeholders who are in a position to be influential over strategic decision making or who can place heavy demands on the organization. Thus, strategic changes are designed to satisfy stakeholder interests.

Adaptive approaches take the view that strategic change is more a process of alignment of an organization's activities, structures and cultures with the characteristics of the external operating environment it faces. Classic contingency studies of organizations fit into this category (for example, the proposition that decentralized structures outperform centralized structures in turbulent environments).

Gap analyses focus on assessing the current core competences of the organization and seeing where there are 'gaps' in competences to provide a changed future portfolio of products and services. This current versus future thinking, and the requirements in terms of organizational resources (human and financial), is the essence of gap analysis.

The *strategic tensions* approach attempts to move beyond position-based bargaining (as may characterize the stakeholder perspective, for example). Such a perspective also accords with that taken by Pettigrew and Whipp (1991) who argue that change can only be understood in terms of its content (what the change is about); its processes (how organizations craft strategies to get from state *a* to state *b*); and its context (the wider environment of infrastructure, culture, sector, nation etc.). This approach relies on managers being able to identify as accurately as possible the various tensions in the wider system. Easy to say, but difficult to do! However, the approach argues that even a partial identification of the set of tensions is better than a fuller analysis of more focused and local issues (but which ignore context).

Examples of some common strategic tensions are illustrated in Table 13.3.

Nutt et al. (2000) argue that the systemic tensions perspective gives a better chance of success in crafting change strategies than any of the other approaches. They cite examples from the public and private sectors, showing that context (in the organization or the wider system) is crucial for facilitating win–win situations among competing interests. Like Pettigrew and Whipp (1991), Nutt

---

Table 13.3 Examples of strategic tensions and their main characteristics

Examples of strategic tensions	Characterized by
Equity–Equity	Clashes between different interests (e.g. between clients, suppliers) all of whom call for a different set of actions to be taken. The key question is whose interests will be served?
Transition–Transition	Where several competing plans for what should change are in conflict. The usual characteristic of these tensions is where there are disputes over diagnostics (that is, 'my data are better than yours' and/or having to choose between several plans for change.
Preservation–Preservation	Difficulties in maintaining the status quo when it is unclear what the organization should be doing and what is appropriate for it to be doing.
Preservation–Innovation	Where there are disputes over anticipated pay-offs from strategic changes. The tensions are about who gets what out of the change, once implemented. The key danger here is that of inertia (nothing happens other than conflict).
Expansion–Contraction	Where departments (for example) are expected to produce more with fewer resources. This can happen to organizations, to sectors and to national economies.
Innovation–Tradition	The tension here is between values. There are those who argue that current practices are to be preserved and that what is being proposed violates central norms and values in the organization.
Change–Ethics	The urgency is to try to reconcile changes with ethical considerations such as commitment to environmental principles or to humanizing the workplace.

Source: adapted from Nutt et al. (2000) and Wilson (1999)

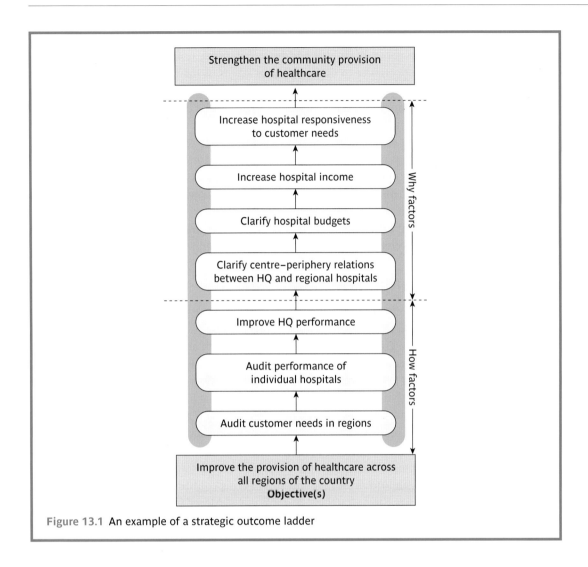

Figure 13.1 An example of a strategic outcome ladder

and his colleagues argue that a cooperative organizational culture (context) will create commitment and support for actions to be taken, since competing interests will always see something of value to them in the change.

Practical steps for managers crafting such change strategies would be to 'widen the arena' of the issues discussed (and hence of the change process). One way of achieving this is to communicate both the *how* and the *why* of change. Various techniques can be used for this, the most popular being a simple laddering exercise. At the bottom of the ladder are placed the *how* factors of strategies and then in logical ascending order the *why* factors are listed. A simple example of such a ladder is given in Figure 13.1.

In Figure 13.1, the objective of the change is to improve the standard and provision of healthcare over all the regions of a country. The ladder begins at the bottom with three sets of actions (the how factors) and then ascends through a series of why factors to complete the loop, since the last why factor very closely resembles the first objective.

The reason for using the laddering technique is to create a context in which the likelihood of 'buy-in' to the change is increased. Buy-in is a much misunderstood idea. Many senior managers ask how they can achieve 'buy-in' as if there were some kind of magic formula which they could apply to the organization after the fact, to win the hearts and minds of all individuals. The problem is that strategic changes are about meanings and interpretations, not simply process maps; and meaning grows from the opportunity to engage at early stages in the formulation and discussion processes. Newsletters, corporate social events, prizes and vision statements communicate facts and can provide a route map of the change, but they can never communicate behaviours or help individuals make sense of what is happening in the change process. Therefore, even a broad understanding of the wider context is only part of the answer to implementing change. We also have to understand the role of individuals in the process, both change initiators and those who are recipients of the process and the outcome. A contextual assessment of what happens when strategy meets organization has been outlined in Chapter 2 of this book. In the current chapter, we therefore examine some specific issues of what happens when strategic changes happen in an organization. We will consider both the role and influence of organization as well as the impact and influence of individuals on change. First, we examine the change–organization interrelationships.

13.5 Strategic change and organization

The basic question which surrounds *change and organization* is in the tension between the continuity and discontinuity and the size, scale and scope of the change (Greiner, 1972; Gersick, 1991). *Continuous change* assumes a gradual evolution of changes which arise out of the current state of affairs in the organization. Change is thus incremental, taken in small steps, and each change effort continuously builds upon the previous phase of change activity. Strategy implementation is therefore concerned with ensuring that current strategies 'fit' with existing practice, either by not deviating too far from the existing script, or by adding incrementally to what is already in place. Key examples of this approach can be found in the process improvement approaches in manufacturing industries.

We deal in more depth with process and quality issues later in this book (see Chapters 10 and 16), but this model of continuous change embraces a business model which goes far beyond manufacturing improvements. Its philosophy is that only by ensuring continuity in strategic changes will organizations be able to realize their strategies. As de Wit and Meyer (1999, p. 144) point out, the tortoise of Aesop's fable keeps moving slowly, but surely and continuously. It wins the race. The hare, on the other hand, shows off its ability to sprint and take great leaps forward, but eventually loses the race. Diligent tortoises, it seems, win the day. Endurance, persistence and small, but significant, improvements to the ways in which we organize help ensure survival and growth for firms.

Advocates of continuous change cluster around three basic principles:

1 continuous improvement;
2 continuous learning;
3 constant adaptation to changing conditions.

Continuous improvement means that all individuals in an organization should always be driven to change, which is rooted in their dissatisfaction with the status quo. This attitude needs to be constructive so that changes can be suggested, designed and put in place. The overall philosophy is that things can always be done better (Stacey, 1993).

Continuous learning means that all individuals in an organization should continually update or increase their knowledge base. This means acquiring new knowledge and techniques as well as acquiring knowledge sufficient for decision makers to say 'no' to what might seem reasonable proposals at first sight and to be able to challenge taken-for-granted behaviours and attitudes in the organization. Crises need to be avoided as far as possible since they inhibit longer-term thinking and promote short-term reactions and decisions (Senge, 1990).

Constant adaptation to changing conditions means that organizational design must be such that it avoids becoming inflexible and hence a barrier to further change. Flexible structures and systems, coupled with open and change-receptive cultures, provide sufficient motivation, security and curiosity for individuals to tolerate the inevitable uncertainty and insecurity associated with change (Kagono et al., 1985).

On the other hand, many scholars and practitioners argue that continuous change is a false friend in terms of trying to plan change (intention) and in terms of accurately describing what happens in practice. This is the argument for understanding change as a *discontinuous* process. Discontinuity is derived from the principle that both organizations and individuals resist change. This is not resistance for its own sake but is a function of the organizing process whereby most organizations develop routines over time (accepted and settled ways of working) and individuals feel comfortable in such rather predictable structures. Indeed, this is one of the ways that can bring about the demise of many organizations (Miller, 1990). Success can breed the seeds of its own destruction since it further embeds and reinforces routines and practices in organizations which create inertia, run deep and are resistant to change.

Organizations are very effective at creating stabilities which act as strong barriers to change. These stabilities can be found in formal and informal systems, standard operating procedures, the distribution of power and the strong ties of organizational culture. They can also be found in factors such as long-term contracts and commitments, fixed investments and inflexible financial and accounting procedures (Arthur, 1996; Ghemawat, 1991). As a result, long terms of stability occur in organizations, held together by these multi-ingredients of the corporate glue. If significant change is to happen then crises (real or constructed) need to be created. The organization becomes jolted into action. This kick-start effect is known as the punctuated equilibrium view of change (Gersick, 1991). Change happens in bursts of activity (followed by further periods of consolidation). These discontinuities can be analysed at different levels of analysis. At the individual level, reluctance to change and settled ways of doing things make individuals predisposed to maintain the status quo and only embark upon change when things become too tough to remain as they are. Groups (social or work) will exhibit the same behaviours. Organizations will have structural and cultural – institutional – arrangements which act as barriers to change unless significant and threatening events spur action. Industries, too, will exhibit inertia until a crisis point means the equilibrium is punctured and radical change occurs. The airline industry is a good example of discontinuous change at this level of analysis.

Seven of America's biggest airlines had combined losses of $5.9 billion in the second quarter of 2008, but there was optimism since crude-oil prices fell sharply. Morgan Stanley predicted that much of the airline industry could return to profit in 2009. When crude-oil futures reached nearly $150 a barrel in July 2008, the airlines seemed doomed to continue to get deeper in crisis. However, oil futures fell, reaching $112.31 on 12 August. The drop in fuel costs has given airlines breathing space, even if demand weakens. Lower fuel prices, together with the measures the airlines were already taking to cut capacity (by grounding older planes) and raise revenue (by charging for services that used to be free), may be enough to return Delta, Continental and United to profit.

The airline industry seems to have avoided its crisis 'trigger' point for discontinuous change once again. How long this will last is another question over which many analysts disagree. Some are optimistic that the industry has avoided a crisis (and hence the need for major change). Others argue that capacity is still growing faster than demand (capacity rising by 5.5%; passenger growth is 3.8% – IATA data, June 2008). In addition, some 40% of the fuel used by the world's airlines is still hedged at $75–85 a barrel. When those hedges expire, it will be another possible equilibrium-puncturing event and radical change will again loom on the horizon.

Current responses amongst airlines have been to favour a strategy of consolidation to create fewer, but larger, airline companies which can carve up the global routes between them and survive. Such moves will depend on regulators and anti-trust legislation but, if allowed, could herald a turn-around in the fortunes of the surviving few – the global mega-airlines. If not, then the surviving airlines will yet again face a crisis which will require discontinuous and substantial change.

Discontinuous change can also occur as a result of perhaps risky, rash or ill-informed decisions which can trigger a series of unplanned and unanticipated events (see also Chapter 11). These strategic decisions can lead the organization into a series of bad moves which, in the worst case, can seal the demise of the firm. Another example from the airline industry (European) illustrates this process clearly (see the Sabena case box).

Case box 13.2: **Bankruptcy at Sabena**

The Belgian airline Sabena became bankrupt in 2001. There were many explanations for the bankruptcy, but a report to the Belgian government in 2003 revealed that the organization undertook a series of key strategic decisions which together led to Sabena's demise. The final of these 'fateful' decisions was made when McKinsey were called in to advise Sabena on future strategy. Just as they had with Swissair (which controlled Sabena), McKinsey recommended the airline embark upon a high-risk growth strategy. Swissair went bankrupt trying to follow the same strategy in 2001.

McKinsey's strategy for growth, however, was based on some flimsy foundations in the airline. In 1996, Sabena's then Swiss boss, Paul Reutlinger, took a series of strategic decisions which embarked Sabena upon a era of deal making with Virgin Express (part of the Branson airlines). The first of these was a one-year deal on Sabena's London–Brussels route. Virgin's planes and crew flew the route using Sabena's Heathrow slots. Sabena paid Virgin Express for 85 seats whether or not they were filled. This decision was quite normal in the airline industry and was a way of reducing competition. However, Reutlinger followed up this decision with another two similar deals signed later the same day (29 October 1996). These were eight-year deals with Virgin for flights to Rome and Barcelona. During these decisions, the London–Brussels deal was also extended from one to eight years. These deals became a huge cash drain in Sabena, costing over 30 million euros a year. Virgin were kept well afloat financially by these deals while Sabena haemorrhaged. Moreover, over 80% of passenger complaints to Sabena originated in these Virgin flights. In March 1997, Reutlinger sold Sabena's slots at Heathrow to Virgin Atlantic Airways for $8 million. The report to the Belgian government alleges that these decisions were taken without full consultation and ratification by the Sabena board. When McKinsey was called in and recommended a strategy of growth, the strategy was in effect built upon a financial house of cards. It failed and the airline went bankrupt.

The Sabena example vividly illustrates discontinuous changes which were prompted by the strategic decisions of one individual (or a small group of individuals) and the perhaps misplaced external advice from McKinsey to embark upon a high-risk growth strategy, which proved fatal to both Swissair and Sabena.

In addition to examining the continuity or discontinuity of change processes, the size, scale and scope of change relates both to organization and to the likelihood of success in implementing the change. There is relatively little empirical work in these areas, but work by Hannan et al. (2003) uncovered some revealing (if mathematically complex) relationships. Using the collapse of Barings Brothers (a British bank) in 1995 as an example, these authors argue that reorganization in the bank had created an infrastructure (organizational architecture) which allowed Nicholas Leeson (the so-called 'rogue trader') to operate in a way that sealed the demise of the bank. Without letting Leeson off the hook for rogue trading activities, the authors explain that the organizational conditions under which these activities took place allowed his actions to go undetected. In a different firm with a different architecture, Leeson would have been identified early on in the process and prevented from trading.

In brief, the context of Barings allowed a number of activities to take place which amounted to significant changes in its size, scale, scope and eventual disaster for the organization. According to Hannan et al. (2003, p. 428):

■ The structure of the organization was porous, with no clear lines of responsibility and accountability. This allowed Leeson to operate undetected for at least two years.

■ Confusion of the reporting lines in the organization could be traced to the recent reorganization of the bank.

■ The matrix structure which resulted from the reorganization failed to work in practice. It was never clear who Leeson's product managers were (a common problem of ambiguous responsibility in matrix structures) and they had little knowledge of his trading activities.

■ Leeson was in charge of both the front and back office functions of the bank and was therefore in a position to override any internal controls.

■ The organizational sub-units (departments) which dealt with Leeson's activities were very poor at communicating with one another and this allowed Leeson to trade in the now infamous account 88888, of which senior managers of the Baring Group claimed they had no knowledge.

The conclusion drawn from the above example is that changes can go badly wrong when organizations change their architectures. The new design of the organization can allow large changes to sweep through the organization, with often few or no controls to keep them in check. These authors derive two concepts from their mathematical model. These are:

1 Opacity: low opacity occurs when there is limited foresight about how different units in the organization are interconnected and work together. The lower the opacity, the higher the likelihood of changes becoming out of control and beyond the capacity of the organization to deal with them when things go wrong.

2 Asperity: high asperity indicates an organizational culture (see Chapter 2) which will not readily accept changes and which will cling to the 'old' ways of working. The higher the asperity, the greater the likelihood that changes will fail.

Key explanations for failure lie in the scale and scope aspects of change processes. For example, high opacity leads to individuals underestimating the time a reorganization will take as well as the associated costs of change, thereby prompting them to undertake changes with adverse consequences. Put simply, complex, opaque organizations which have a high level of cultural asperity will tend to get themselves into trouble by implementing changes that cost far more than was foreseen. In the worst cases, these can be costs that cannot be covered by whatever new organizational form or circumstances the change has brought about. Like Barings, the organization may well go bankrupt.

The Barings and the Sabena examples also illustrate the impact that one person, or a small group, can have on the fortunes of an organization and the speed with which change (mostly discontinuous) can occur. We examine these aspects of change in the next section.

13.6 Change, individuals and strategic leadership

Popular literature (both management and non-management) is replete with the contribution that individuals can make to the success (or otherwise) of the processes and outcomes of change. Much of the literature focuses on the contribution of individuals through the process of leadership, although a sizeable proportion of work also examines the contribution of, for example, creative or innovative individuals to drive change in organizations. To cover the field of leadership is beyond the scope of this chapter. Instead, we focus on what has become termed 'strategic leadership' (Senge, 1990). This term describes how individuals may lead changes in ways which are non-individualistic and are not necessarily related to the charisma or power of the individual concerned. Strategic leadership is concerned with teaching, learning, stewardship and the ability to challenge prevailing modes of thought in the organization.

Whatever their position in the organizational hierarchy, strategic leaders are strongly associated with the strategic changes which occur in their organizations. In some cases this may mean that other individuals (who may be more senior in the hierarchy) defer to these strategic leaders since their abilities or their reputation ensures they have credibility and support. In other cases, strategic leadership may be more systemically rooted. For example, the founders of a family firm or the owners of a small business will almost certainly assume a strategic leadership role since they are the 'owners' of the business idea as well as the business philosophy. Another way in which strategic leadership may be systemically rooted is through organizational history. For example, an individual chief executive may have implemented very successful strategies in the past, or may have saved the company from decline. Such a history endows this individual with a position of strategic leadership since he or she embodies, or personifies, the organization, its development and its success. An example of an individual leader effecting large-scale change in the banking world is Gail Kelly who is credited with the turnaround of St George Bank in Australia, Australia's fifth largest bank (see Case box 13.3).

Case box 13.3: **Leadership at St George Bank, Australia**

Ms Gail Kelly joined St George Bank in January 2002, just in time for the removal of the bank's restrictive articles, leaving it open for a takeover. But despite expectations the bank would be snapped up by one of its bigger rivals, Ms Kelly has overseen an almost $3 billion increase in its market capitalization as the bank outperformed its suitors. 'The bank has performed extremely well ever since she joined,' said Brett Le Mesurier, banking analyst at Wilson HTM. 'It's had the highest earnings per share growth among the larger banks by some margin.' And the bank is keen to keep Ms Kelly. Shareholders will be asked to approve the granting of 57,600 shares and 500,000 options as a long-term incentive, on top of her pay rise, at the annual meeting on December 17 2006. 'Her leadership has benefited greatly the bank's shareholders as evidenced by the very strong financial results of the last few years,' chairman Frank Conroy said in a statement. Listening to her talk about banking is to hear a veteran of 10,001 PowerPoint presentations. She speaks quickly, eyes blaze brightly, remnants of her South African accent clip the words along and her speech is sprinkled with anecdotes. 'I've got lots of energy,' she says. 'My whole model is based around gathering the best people you can around you and creating an environment where people can do their best work, and creating a team and powering a team that has fun, and a team that likes working together, and a team that delivers . . . I'm not driven by money, ego, power or any of those things. I like to achieve – I like to achieve quality outcomes.' But there are some personal traits that have especially fitted Kelly for success. For instance, she is a quick reader. 'I don't sleep a whole lot – four hours a night – I'm very quick as well. I'm not talking about intellectually quick.

Everything I do is quick. I'm fairly impatient.' There's some element of stress in that, but you also just get things done. 'I don't waste time. I move. I finish things. I don't try and do things to the nth degree. I know what's important and what's not. I've really learned that. That's a judgement I've learned, what really matters.' Kelly believes personal contact is the key to successful banking. But when she arrived in Australia she worked with a bank that was taking flak for closing rural branches and was just about to embark on another public relations disaster, to close city branches. She believes the banking future is about re-engagement. St George, in particular, has a natural advantage in that it came out of the building society environment in which engaging with customers was a part of its culture. 'There's a very simple strategy that we're running here that really says if you seek to engage people, people are willing, people are positive,' she says. Kelly values 'people who like people, people who care, people who are energetic, people who want to try, people who aren't cynical, who aren't arrogant, who aren't self-serving'. She says: 'I sometimes use my Latin (teaching) background here when I talk about satisfaction. Satisfaction isn't enough. Satisfaction comes from the Latin word *satis*, meaning enough, and *facio*, which means to do or make. Well, we're about doing more. We're about delighting. We're not about satisfaction.' Kelly's office is on the 15th floor of St George's George Street branch in Sydney. It's standard issue corporate decor, big desk, conference table, a view of Sydney Cove and the Harbour Bridge and the quiet hush of big money being made. Kelly says there is one reason alone that she has been able to do what she has done. 'It is Allan. He is a most fantastic husband, fantastic support, clearly a professional in his own right...very generous, very hard working, great sense of humour, just a lovely person.' The Kellys took out Australian citizenship soon after arrival in Sydney and have established a sort of family compound on the North Shore, with her own triplets, her mother and brother and his parents living nearby. 'I try to make a point about how you need to do work that you love.'

Source: Business Lunch Interview, Sydney, Australia, May 2007. Author unknown

Kelly's characteristics (impatient, only a few hours asleep, prioritizing what matters and surrounding herself with good people) are those traditionally associated in the leadership literature with good and effective leaders. She also demonstrates that the context in which individual leaders operate also matters greatly. A supportive family, equally driven work colleagues and a 'can do' organizational culture contribute in no small part to her undoubted success. However, individual leaders with whom great successes and changes are associated face inevitable problems of continuity and sustaining both the pace and the direction of strategic change.

In particular, family firms seem to suffer from this lack of continuity. Some powerful individuals can both drive change and act as effective barriers to further change. The offspring of founding fathers are prime examples of individual leadership that can prevent an organization thinking and acting strategically and effecting change.

Just as there are polarized views on whether or not strategy is planned or emerges as a pattern in a stream of decisions, strategic leadership can be viewed from the same, mutually exclusive perspectives. Assuming that strategic leadership is planned means that we view leaders as:

- predominantly people who plan a path forward by thinking analytically;
- predominantly people who bring past experience to bear on the present situation (the change worked successfully last time, so it should work again in the new situation);
- appointable chiefly through their demonstrable analytical ability and foresight and their ability to think systematically through a problem and come up with an implementation plan.

On the other hand, we may take the position that strategic leadership emerges in organizations rather than it being planned. This perspective means we would view strategic leadership as:

- Less associated with individuals in key positions, but something which emerges from new and sometimes competing ideas from all parts of the organization. Capturing such ideas is a key activity and it may be that this is the key role of individual leaders.

- A role in which highly intuitive individuals who have demonstrable vision should be favoured in any appointment process. These individuals can see what others cannot and are happy to embrace new ways of seeing the organization or undertake new ways of working.

The small amount of empirical evidence so far produced on this topic suggests that both approaches can bring performance benefits and can enhance change processes. Peters and Waterman (1982) argued that strategic leadership was about an individual being able to take a highly abstract and perhaps intuitive view as well as being able to handle the operational detail involved in change implementation. Leavy and Wilson (1994) demonstrated how these abilities may be time dependent. In some circumstances, change requires hands-on detail; in others, change requires abstract and perhaps lateral thinking, leaving the processes of implementation to others in the organization. Debates as to whether any of the above approaches are connected to the personality of individual leaders are many, but inconclusive. We just do not know whether or not personality makes a key difference to a leader's ability to handle or manage change (see Farkas and Wetlaufer, 1996).

13.6.1 Creative individuals and change

Once we shift our focus from key 'leadership' positions in an organization, we may see that individuals who can see beyond the self-evident, and often in quite creative ways, can be the drivers of organizational change wherever they are in the organizational hierarchy. For example, writers and artists (such as Baudelaire or Picasso) challenged established beliefs with new ideas, which in turn transformed our understanding and appreciation of art and literature. Political leaders (such as Gandhi or Luther) were individuals who were also able to effect such transformations. In business organizations, people such as Sloan, Carnegie, Packard, Welch (GE), Barnevik (ABB) and Branson (Virgin) are commonly cited as those who questioned received wisdom about organizational designs and manufacturing procedures. They said the unsayable and thought the unthinkable.

In change strategies, the temptation is to seek individuals who have this special insight and foresight. However, they are remarkably rare. As March (1999) reminds us:

> *most current leaders seem to be competent and analytical rather than imaginative and visionary . . . they seek to refine the establishment rather than challenge or transform it.* (March, 1999, p. 226)

This may be a product of modern times and organization, or it may simply be that we have learned to distrust creativity alone as a guide for strategic change.

> *The difference between visionary genius and delusional madness is much clearer in history books than in experience.* (March, 1999, p. 226)

The problem lies in identifying which novel ideas will turn out to be successful and which will turn out to be little more than crackpot visions. The ratio of successful creative ideas (in practice) to ones which turn out unsuccessful is not good. Most new ideas will not pay off, so we usually retreat into what is knowable, familiar and doable. The paradox here is that without a heavy reliance on conventional thinking, highly creative leadership is in more danger of failing than it is of succeeding.

At the same time, organizations need to have stimuli which prevent complacency and encourage new ideas and new ways of thinking and acting strategically. Such leadership (which can come from any part of the organization, not just senior executives) is commonly termed 'transformational' in the management literature. Such leadership seems to centre upon:

■ Successfully coping with, and developing the intellectual challenge of, new ideas (for example, a new or unique competitive position in an evolving environment). Many 'dot.com' companies are founded on such expertise and yet many fail because individuals cannot successfully continue to differentiate their companies from other dot.coms.

■ Meeting the social and political challenges of keeping dialogue and communication going when different stakeholders view the same world through very different lenses.

■ Having a design in mind which will align the activities, structures and processes in organizations with the strategic intentions. This involves being able to synthesize a great many ideas which may come from all parts of the organization.

■ Being able to live with the results of the change in terms of both ethics and performance.

Such a list of factors is a tall order. Individuals are notoriously poor at achieving even one of the above factors, never mind all of them. In relation to strategic management, we can identify a number of reasons why this is so.

Managing change by individual foresight is only possible if environmental signals are seen clearly and in time to act. This is a conundrum which has beset organizations from the very beginning. As Arie de Geus, strategy analyst with Shell, pointed out:

You cannot see what your mind has not experienced before.

Case box 13.4: Mind traps: locked in our own worlds of experience

We are all familiar with the example of explorers who stumble upon a tribe of natives isolated from the outside world. Their chief is highly intelligent and has a rich and deep understanding of the world from the tribe's perspective. The explorers begin to explain the modern world. They take the chief to a large city and show him what is going on. He is exposed to thousands of signals from a new environment. However, when the explorers ask him what he has learned, he mentions only one thing. He has seen a market trader pushing a cart full of vegetables, more vegetables than he has ever seen before. This is what he wants to bring back to the tribe from his experiences, more vegetables. All other signals had been discarded as irrelevant to the chief's needs!

Source: adapted from de Geus (1997)

Individuals with different backgrounds pick up different signals. Yet even long-standing and highly experienced companies miss important and relevant signals. Why?

One explanation lies in the ways in which individuals relate to knowledge and the future independently of their prior experience. We are all familiar with the adage that experienced managers utilize more knowledge from the past than the present and future. The path, looking backward, is relatively clear. Looking forward, the path is full of uncertainty and ambiguity. However, even in looking forward, strategists can become locked into what de Geus terms the 'memory of the future'.

He argues that managers are constantly looking at potential futures and making plans and programmes for these futures. These plans become organized in an almost sequential way so that they create time paths into the future. The variable nature of this activity lies only in how many alternative paths are created (de Geus argues that this is dependent upon how healthy is the brain, with more healthy brains seeing more alternative time paths). However, all brains store and code these alternative future paths and commit them to memory. Paradoxically, therefore, strategists can create a memory of the future! The implication of this way of thinking is that individuals will tend to pick up only those signals which are relevant to a future they have already worked out. The rest are likely to be missed.

13.6.2 Subjectivity: emotion and organizational change

An emerging perspective on individuals, organizations and change is that strategic change is a complicated and highly emotional psycho-social drama (O'Donnell, 2000). The ability to trust your own and others' emotions is argued to be at least as important as viewing intelligence or creativity as a set of cognitive attributes which a person 'has'. The ability to be aware of one's own mental processes lies at the heart of understanding change as an emotional activity. It is key to understanding change as a *subjective* phenomenon (Sparrow, 2000). This ability has become known as *emotional intelligence* (Goleman, 2001). It is argued that managers who display emotional intelligence are able to use meta-abilities or meta-cognitions to understand both how they act and how their actions are interpreted by others, and they are able to develop better information networks, generate higher levels of trust and have greater levels of influence in implementing change. Although much work on emotional intelligence has been conducted outside formal work organizations, its attributes can easily be seen. According to Sparrow (2000, p. 26), emotional intelligence:

■ emphasizes pre-conscious thought and shares many common neurological processes with creativity and intuition;

■ is a strong source of energy (feelings and personal drive) which can sustain individuals through a change process and can guide individuals to see unexpected or previously unseen possibilities;

■ helps individuals cope with change since it emphasizes self-awareness, empathy, personal style and communications.

A key difficulty is one of assessing or measuring emotional intelligence. Many of its reflections (such as high levels of trust or effective communication and empathy with opposing viewpoints) are best assessed through the eyes of others (Steiner, 1997). Dulewicz and Herbert (1998) assessed emotional intelligence as:

■ sensitivity;

■ resilience;

■ influence and adaptability;

■ decisiveness and adaptability;

■ energy and leadership.

They found that managerial advancement was positively related to the 'possession' of emotional intelligence (36% of managerial advancements could be traced to emotional intelligence). This finding should be put in the context of other findings from the same study: 27% of promotions could be traced to rational and intellectual analysis (such as judgement, planning and organizing) and only 16% to management process effectiveness (such as business sense, initiative and independence). Although we are not yet at a stage where we can clearly demarcate emotional intelligence as a valid construct with a set of valid measures, it nevertheless seems to have a beneficial influence both on smoothing change processes and on advancing the careers of managers who display higher levels of it.

Emotional intelligence would also seem to be vital to underpinning Beer and Eisenstat's (1996) principles of the relatively more successful implementation of strategic change:

- Change should be systemic: the focus of the change should accommodate and recognize the complex system that is the organization. Such factors include strategy, structure, behaviours, analysis and emotions.
- Change should allow the discussion of barriers: people cannot develop realistic and implementable plans for change unless all impediments are taken into account.
- Change should involve a partnership between all stakeholders in the process.

Argyris (1992) suggests that individuals mostly operate on the basis of what he terms 'defensive routines' and hence never engage with the emotional desiderata listed above. He suggests that individuals:

1 bypass embarrassment or threat wherever possible;
2 act as if they were not bypassing them;
3 refuse to discuss bypassing behaviour or actions as above;
4 don't discuss the undiscussability of the undiscussable.

It remains to be seen whether or not emotional intelligence develops into a valid construct and stops being potentially perceived as yet another management fad and fashion. Nevertheless, Argyris's four principles, above, apply to virtually all change processes and can act as significant barriers to the implementation of strategic change.

13.6.3 Using outsiders to implement change

The 'external' aspects of change are rather less well covered in the literature than the 'internal' features of structures, cultures and individuals. Outsiders can take a number of forms. They can include, for example, bringing in a new chief executive from a related industry where he or she has had demonstrable success. Or, a significant influx of new managers to an organization (especially over a short time period) can also help break down high-asperity cultures (strong cultures which are change resistant). The old guard can be swept away effectively by these newcomers. Taking a stakeholder perspective, there are likely to be a large number of strong influences from outside the organization which have an impact on the change process. These can include suppliers, customers, investors and government agencies.

By far the most obvious of external *change agents*, however, are management consultants. The role of the vast majority of consultants (both individual consultants and consultancy firms) is that of providing expert advice. It is hardly surprising, therefore, that the majority of large consulting firms (e.g. McKinsey, PricewaterhouseCoopers) become involved with the execution of strategic changes in organizations. These processes are complex, take time and (perhaps cynically) can create the opportunity for new or continuing relationships between consultant and organization.

Different consulting firms become involved in different phases of the change process. For example, McKinsey have a reputation as being excellent at the analytical and planning phases of strategic change, but are rather less well involved in the implementation phases (putting idea into practice). KPMG are the reverse. These consultancies are centrally involved in the performance aspects of implementation (such as standardized solutions for cost reduction, or the application of programmatic 'solutions' to change such as business process re-engineering). Technical and functional expertise (for example, human resource management) can be found in consulting firms such as Hay or PA Consulting. Given the longevity of change as an organizational problem, some consulting firms (such as Cap Gemini) have specialized in producing customized change models (such as the 'transformation' model of Gemini) and these have become major products in their own right. The Gemini model is described briefly in the case box below.

Case box 13.5: **The Gemini model of corporate transformation**

The high failure rate of business process re-engineering (BPR) projects has led to the development of a more subtle approach which has been called a biological model of corporate transformation, identifying the corporation as essentially an organic evolving entity. The model consists of four broad categories of activity leading to transformation and, as developed by Gemini Consulting, corporate transformation is defined as 'the orchestrated redesign of the genetic architecture of the corporation, achieved by working simultaneously – although at different speeds – along the four dimensions of Reframing, Restructuring, Revitalization and Renewal'. These four dimensions are seen as a biological process as follows:

1 *Reframing* is seen as shifting the company's perception of what it is and what it can achieve and is designed to open the corporation's mindset and allow it to refocus.

2 *Restructuring* deals with the body of the corporation and addresses competitive fitness. This activity is most akin to the BPR approach and involves similar techniques.

3 *Revitalization* endeavours to link the revised corporate body to its environment, and is considered to be the factor which most clearly differentiates transformation from the harshness perceived of re-engineering. The intention is not to obliterate activities but, rather, to change them positively to encourage revitalized performance.

4 *Renewal* is concerned with the 'people' side of transformation and with the spirit of the company. It is concerned with investment in skills and purpose to allow the company to self-regenerate with new confidence and enthusiasm rather than the often morale-sapping impact of re-engineering projects, which are a major cause of failure. This activity is perhaps the most difficult to achieve, and is seen by many critics of re-engineering change to be the point at which many consultants, brought in as change agents, leave their clients.

Gemini believes that 12 corporate 'chromosomes' comprise the biocorporate genome, three for each of the four Rs. While each chromosome can be considered independently they are all integrated into a total system. The chief executive officer and the executive leadership are seen as the genetic architects of the corporation and are thus not expected to be involved in operational detail.

The reframing chromosomes

1 *Achieve mobilization*. This activity is the process of bringing together the mental energy required to initiate the transformation process, and involves moving motivation and commitment from the individual to the team and ultimately to the total corporation.

2 *Create the vision*. The development of a corporate vision is essential to provide a shared mental framework which stretches the future dimensions of the corporation and in human terms provides

a common sense of purpose which people can identify with. The role of the CEO in establishing such a vision is crucial.

3 *Building a measurement system*. Once the corporation is mobilized and provided with a vision, new measurement systems which allow management to monitor progress towards the future will usually be required. While often quantified, such measures will usually emphasize the strategic progress rather than the financial history. In human terms, the system should also create an identifiable sense of commitment; see Chapter 5 on the balanced scorecard.

The restructuring chromosomes

4 *Construct an economic model*. This involves the systematic top-down disaggregation of a corporation in financial terms from shareholder value-based planning to activity-based costing and service level assessment. It provides a detailed view of how and where value is created or cost allowed in the bio-analogy of the cardiovascular system for resources to be deployed where they are needed, and redistributed from where they are not needed.

5 *Align the physical infrastructure*. This element is analogous to the corporate skeletal system and consists of the appropriate alignment of the resources of the corporation's assets, such as plants, warehouses, transportation, equipment and the like. While these are relatively fixed, there is also a need for continuous monitoring and, on occasion, change as when a bone is fractured, to allow for strategic healing.

6 *Redesign the work architecture.* The work of the corporation is achieved via a complex network of processes which is identified as the work architecture. These need to be correctly configured and aligned and this process can be linked to re-engineering.

The revitalization systems

7 *Achieve a market focus*. To Gemini, revitalization implies growth. To achieve this, customer focus provides the starting point, as developing new and perhaps undiscovered benefits that the corporation can offer to its customers leads to business growth. For the corporation, market focus provides the senses in the biological analogy.

8 *Invent new business.* Growth can also occur as the result of the development of new businesses. These can emerge from the cross-fertilization of capabilities from within the corporation or by the introduction of activities from outside via mergers and acquisitions, strategic alliances, joint ventures and the like. The biological analogy of this concept can be seen as the reproductive system.

9 *Change the rules through information technology*. The strategic use of information technology can produce new ways to compete by redefining the rules of the game in many traditional industries. Biologically, the use of such technology is analogous to the nervous system.

The renewal systems

10 *Create a reward structure.* An appropriate reward structure is seen as a major motivating force on human behaviour. When the motivation system is wrongly aligned with desired behaviour it can also act as a serious demotivator and encourage undesired behaviour.

11 *Build individual learning.* Corporate transformation can only successfully take place when the skills and learning of many individuals are also transformed. Individual learning promotes self-actualization of the people who constitute the corporation.

12 *Develop the organization.* Corporations are seen as needing to organize for continuous learning, enabling them to constantly adapt to an ever-changing environment in which the pace of change is often accelerating. Organizational development thus allows the corporation to evolve and fosters a sense of community among individuals.

Conclusion

The corporate transformation process has been applied in many corporations around the world. Such transformations often involve modifying the behaviour of many thousands of people, often on a global basis. Such transformations take time, often involving a number of years, but the end result is expected to produce transformed corporations capable of continuous adaptation to permit successful evolution.

Source: McGee, J. and Channon, D. (eds) (2005) *Encyclopedic Dictionary of Strategic Management*, 2nd edition, Blackwell, Oxford

Whether or not consulting firms help or hinder organizational change processes (or are relatively neutral in their influence) is an open question to which there is insufficient evidence to present any firm conclusions. On the positive side, there are arguments that consultants learn from academics and from their client organizations. In these ways, consultants both codify often abstract and complex academic thinking (mostly from business schools) and also develop their own knowledge base from clients so that effective knowledge can progress from one client to another, ideally from leaders to laggards (Abrahamson, 1991).

On the more negative side, some authors argue that consultants 'borrow your watch to tell you the time' (they are simply symbolic agents, often engaged to fulfil a political motive of driving a change through an organization which would have been more difficult if solely an internal process) or they overgeneralize their solutions so that one size fits all (Alvesson, 1993).

13.7 Creative organizational contexts

If creative foresight and heretical, off-the-wall ideas are so elusive (and likely to be just as dangerous as they are useful), then how can organizations be designed and arranged to encourage strategic thinking to enable the strategic change process? This is an approach to strategic change which relies less on the creativity of individuals and more upon designing the creative organizational contexts in which strategies for change can be crafted.

Kanter (1999) argues that such creative contexts are formed and sustained by three major elements:

1 *Concepts*: These are ideas and technologies which are driven by innovative thinking and the innovations produced by other organizations.

2 *Competences*: These are the repertoires of skills and abilities of individuals in the organization. They also involve the ability to use such skills in the organization. Many individuals who work in organizations have useful skills which they only use in hobbies (for example) away from the workplace. The trick is to engage these competences in the workplace.

3 *Connections*: These are the important strategic relationships which individuals, teams and organizations create (such as networks). They are nurtured by collaboration rather than competition and can be extended and reconfigured as new ideas emerge.

Chapter 14 explores some of these organizational themes in more detail in the context of assessing how organizations might remain innovative and how they might continue to learn.

13.8 Summary

This chapter has examined the issues of, and widely differing approaches to, strategic change. Since the implementation of virtually any strategy will involve an organization and its members in a degree of change, understanding its processes and its problems can be an advantage.

The chapter has highlighted variation in both the degree of change (radical to incremental) and the extent to which change is discontinuous or is smoother and more continuous. It has also shown how we can examine change from a multitude of levels of analysis.

There are important links in this chapter to the themes and debates of other chapters in this book. In particular, readers should work through this chapter in conjunction with the material in Chapters 2, 12 and 14.

Key terms

asperity	431	emotional intelligence	436
change agents	437	mind traps	435
change and organization	428	opacity	431
continuous change	428	strategic tensions	426
discontinuous change	429		

Recap questions and assignments

1 Identify an *unsuccessful* strategic change with which you are familiar. You may wish to choose an example from the business press, a case example you have studied, or you may draw on experience of a strategic change in which you were involved in an organization. What were the key characteristics that contributed to this being an unsuccessful change process?

2 Identify a *successful* strategic change and identify its key characteristics as above.

3 What aspects would you introduce in your organization to improve the implementation of strategic change and why?

Case study 13.1: The education of Andy Grove

A Harvard historian explains how Intel's legendary chief became the best model we have for leading a business in the 21st century

In 1991, an instructor at Stanford's Graduate School of Business presented his class with a case study. It went like this: A CEO was scheduled to address a major industry gathering, and he could give one of three speeches. The first would publicly commit his company to incorporating a sexy, sophisticated new technology in its products. The second speech would reaffirm the company's commitment to developing its existing technology. The third speech would do neither, leaving the decision to 'the market.' The stakes were enormous: A wrong decision could well ruin the business. What should the CEO do? The question was more than academic, because the CEO described in the case was also the man at the front of the classroom. Dr. Andrew S. Grove, like professor Indiana Jones, was better known for his exploits as 'Andy,' the famous leader of Intel Corp. But unlike Indy, Grove wasn't simply biding time here between adventures.

His question was meant not just to challenge students' thinking but to advance his own. That big speech was three weeks away, and Grove had yet to make up his mind. He didn't know the answer.

It's not common for any CEO to stand before an audience and say, 'I don't know what to do. What do you think?' It's even less common for that CEO to listen to the responses and take them seriously. But Grove, 69, has never lost track of the truth: that Intel has always been one wrong answer away from disaster – and that a closed mind is a trap door to the abyss.

Grove and Intel are now embedded so deeply inside our minds, our computers, and our culture – the man has been on 77 magazine covers, by one count – that with hindsight, their success seems foreordained. But the opposite is the case: By all odds, Intel should have failed. It should have been destroyed by the same brutal international competition that has killed apparel companies, tire companies, and television companies, or fallen into obscurity like Zilog and other successful chipmakers. Intel, too, should have stumbled on the terrifying treadmill of Moore's Law, which requires betting billions upon billions of dollars on ever more costly factories to make chips you're still developing for customers who've yet to demand them. It should have been eclipsed by an upstart competitor with a better mousetrap. Intel's success should never have happened – it was an anomaly, an outlier, a freak.

That's why Grove had chosen himself as the day's case study in the class he was teaching with Professor Robert Burgelman, his longtime collaborator and the author of *Strategy Is Destiny*. In business you often don't see the cliff until you've already walked over it. Visibility on the ground is bad, and the roadmap – well, that can't be trusted either. To spot the next cliff, Andy Grove was willing to let go of his instincts – since they could be wrong – and view himself as a student might: from outside, peering down with the wide-angle, disinterested perspective of the observer. Did the man below seem aware of his surroundings? Was he choosing the correct path? Was there a 1,000-foot drop ahead?

Normally, our society observes a division of labor. Musicians don't critique, and critics don't compose. Quarterbacks decide on Sunday, and fans deride on Monday. It is the singular ability to inhabit both roles at once – subject and object, actor and audience, master and student – that sets Grove apart. And it's why, for everything that has been written by and about him, we have yet to appreciate his biggest legacy. Andy Grove is America's greatest student and teacher of business.

By analyzing the decisions he made on the road to becoming a great leader, you can learn to hone your own leadership skills. Because there's no gain in being able to recruit great employees, handle a board, dazzle Wall Street, or rally your cavalry for a glorious charge at dawn's early light if you haven't figured out which way to point the horses.

Grove's output as a teacher of management has been prodigious. He has taught from the lectern, in the op-ed pages, in his famous (sometimes feared) one-on-one sessions, and with his books, including 1983's *High Output Management* and 1996's *Only the Paranoid Survive*, whose title entered the lexicon along with its phrase 'strategic inflection point,' which Grove defines as 'a time in the life of a business when its fundamentals are about to change.' His teaching would have been an impressive career in itself. Yet it is one thing to search for truth in the ivory tower and quite another to take those lessons, however wrenching, and apply them to a living, breathing business like Intel. Grove's most powerful lessons have been in the doing.

What can others learn from Grove's odyssey? As we face a future where change is not only constant but accelerating, reality will transform itself more swiftly than most humans – or most companies – are hard-wired to handle. Even startups that overturn one reality are easily overturned by the next big change. Grove has escaped natural selection by doing the evolving himself. Forcibly adapting himself to a succession of new realities, he has left a trail of discarded assumptions in his wake. When reality has changed, he has found the will to let go and embrace the new.

It's a performance as remarkable as his life story. There will not be another CEO who survived both the Nazis and the communists before becoming a naturalized capitalist. And yet Grove is the best model we've got for doing business in the 21st century. If you hope to thrive in an environment of rapid change, it is this outlier – his strengths forged in a distant and vanished world – that you should follow. Begin your lesson in leadership the same way Andy Grove attacks a problem: by setting aside everything you know.

As a historian whose subjects have been, until now, no longer living, I found it a jolt to face a very alive Andy Grove. When he gets to a particularly intense point in a conversation, Grove leans forward and fixes you directly with his eyes, which are a startling blue. 'That is not the right question,' he will say, briefly taking over the duties of the interviewer. It's not personal. It's about an invisible third party: the truth. The truth is so precious and so hard to coax into view – surrounded by its bodyguard of politics and half-truths – that there is simply no time for fuzzy thinking. There are moments when you can almost experience firsthand the flow of self that went into Intel. And Grove's state-of-the-art memory can transport you from the deck of his home – where a commanding view of Silicon Valley spreads out at his feet – to vivid places in time. Like the day not long after the Stanford case study when Intel executives Craig Kinnie and Dennis Carter arrived in his cubicle to confront him.

In the run-up to the speech about technology choices, Grove had uncharacteristically wavered. He'd told Stanford's Burgelman that he was inclined to stick with Intel's mainstay chip technology known as CISC (for complex instruction set computing – don't ask). But when Intel published its annual report, the cover included a new, fashion-forward RISC chip (for reduced instruction set computing). Engineers across the industry were enamored of RISC because of its elegance: It required fewer transistors to accomplish most computing tasks. Grove had even appeared in an Intel rap video to promote RISC.

But Kinnie and Carter had trained at the Grove school of management – Grove's MO as a leader has always been to depend on 'helpful Cassandras' to make sure that he doesn't win an argument he ought to lose. The two were blunt. 'Andy, you can't do this,' Carter said. Abandoning CISC for RISC, they argued, would truncate one of the most profitable franchises in business history for . . . what? Leveling the playing field for Intel's competition? When the discussion ended, Kinnie and Carter had achieved a feat of monumental difficulty. They'd won an argument with Andy Grove.

Grove has been grateful to them ever since. He looks back at this episode with anger – at himself. 'We almost wrecked the company,' he told me. 'We had established our technology as the industry standard. This franchise was worth millions, billions. We . . . I . . . almost walked away from it because the elegance of a new product seduced me into taking my eye off the market.' The sun is shining, the view is stunning, and Andy Grove is berating himself for a mistake he didn't make a decade and a half ago. It's a measure of the demanding life he has lived – a life that, at critical junctures, has hung on Grove's ability to transform himself, to move from role to role as the moment required.

The early adapter

To be born a Hungarian Jew in 1936 was to be born on the wrong side of history. Grove was forced to adapt to a succession of threatening realities from the very beginning.

Transformations were the story of Grove's young life. When the Nazis invaded Hungary in 1944, his mother changed his name from Andras Grof to the Slavic Andras Malesevics. When the communists arrived the following year, he once again became Andras Grof. As a young man, he switched from journalism to chemistry after publishers started rejecting his articles for political reasons.

Communism nauseated him. One of his most vivid recollections is the May Day parade of 1950. Cheering was broadcast from loudspeakers around Budapest. But when Andy and his schoolmates arrived at Heroes' Square, they discovered there was no crowd at all: The cheering was recorded. Six years later, when the Hungarian Revolution caused the border with Austria to be open for a brief period, Grove faced an immediate and unanticipated decision. He had never been outside Hungary. An only child, he would be leaving parents he might never see again. He had little idea of what he'd be running to. If ever there was a plunge into the unknown, that was it.

He arrived in the U.S. on Jan. 7, 1957 – the same day that Time's 'Man of the Year' issue featured **THE HUNGARIAN FREEDOM FIGHTER** on its cover. Soon he would change his name for a third and final time. At the City College of New York, where he enrolled, Andras Istvan Grof was struck from the transcript and above it was written Andrew Stephen Grove. He had left behind his home, and he needed a name people could pronounce.

The self-made manager

By the late 1960s Grove had earned a Ph.D. in chemical engineering at the University of California at Berkeley and joined Fairchild Semiconductor, birthplace of the integrated circuit. When colleagues Robert Noyce and Gordon Moore quit to start Intel, Grove declared he was coming too. In 1968 they put their 32-year-old protégé in charge of operations. That forced Grove into an unfamiliar role: having to lead people.

Quite suddenly Grove found himself on the shop floor of a manufacturing startup. There the human dynamics proved far more complex than the fluid dynamics he'd studied at Berkeley. The job, he quickly recognized, required something he knew nothing about: It required management. What was that, anyway? Grove decided he had to figure it out.

On July 4, 1969, he opened a school notebook and pasted in a clipping from a story in *Time* magazine about movie directors. 'Vision to Inspire,' it read. 'Any director must master formidable complexity. He must be adept at sound and camera work, a soother of egos, a cajoler of the artistic talent. A great director has something more: the vision and force to make all these disparate elements fuse into an inspired whole.' Above the clipping, Grove wrote with a red pen: 'My job description?'

So began the self-education of Andy Grove, manager. It was a quest in which he immersed himself. His classroom would be a remarkable set of journals that he kept for years – and that have never, until now, been revealed. They're a window into the mind of an engineer grappling with the challenge of managing people. How did a company's growth rate, for instance, relate to its employees' ability to grow? In an entry from the early 1970s, Grove noted, 'Three groups of people can be identified: (A) don't belong in their jobs in the first place. These are 'defective choices,' nothing to do with growth. (B) These are the previously discussed cases, people who can't grow with their jobs. (C) This is everybody else, including those that have demonstrated all kinds of growth capability before.

'The point is, there is a growth rate at which everybody fails and the whole situation results in a chaos. I feel it is my most important function (as being the highest-level manager who still has a way to judge the impending failure) to identify the maximum growth rate at which this wholesale failure phenomenon begins.'

Grove succeeded where others didn't, in part, by approaching management as a discipline unto itself. There's real urgency in his efforts to school himself: He never lost his Hungarian refugee's apprehension of the risk of imminent failure.

The change agent

By 1983, when Grove distilled much of his thinking in his book *High Output Management* (still a worthwhile read), he was president of a fast-growing $1.1-billion-a-year corporation, a leading maker of memory chips, whose CEO was Gordon Moore. Could Grove and Moore save the company from an industry that was filled with ferocious competitors?

In many ways change was in Intel's DNA. It was Moore who had famously observed that the number of transistors you could cram onto a chip tended to double every couple of years (later refined to 18 months). What Moore's Law did not and could not predict was that Japanese firms, too, might master this process and turn memory chips into a commodity. That was change of a different order, and not even Intel was prepared for it.

The company's top executives simply could not believe the growing evidence that they were being outcompeted in a market they had created. Intel was the memory company, period. Its chips were in many of the best minicomputers and also in the new breed of machine that was then taking off, the personal computer. In the early 1980s profits from other products helped to sustain the delusion that memories were a viable future.

Intel kept denying the cliff ahead until its profits went over the edge, plummeting from $198 million in 1984 to less than $2 million in 1985. It was in the middle of this crisis, when many managers would have obsessed about specifics, that Grove stepped outside himself. He and Moore had been agonizing over their dilemma for weeks, he recounts in *Only the Paranoid Survive*, when something happened: 'I looked out the window at the Ferris wheel of the Great America amusement park revolving in the distance when I turned back to Gordon, and I asked, "If we got kicked out and the board brought in a new CEO, what do you think he would do?" Gordon answered without hesitation, "He would get us out of memories." I stared at him, numb, then said, "Why shouldn't you and I walk out the door, come back, and do it ourselves?"'

The words 'I stared at him, numb' suggest that in the crucial moment, Andy ceased to be Andy. Instead he was Dr. Grove the engineer, the teacher, looking down at his own case study. And from this realm of pure reason he could see that Intel's present course had an obvious ending: disaster. It was a cognitive tour de force, yet within moments Andy Grove the executive returned – and was dismayed by what Andy Grove the teacher had concluded. Professors overturn ideas, but they don't upend lives. 'To be completely honest about it,' Grove wrote, 'as I started to discuss the possibility of getting out of the memory chip business, I had a hard time getting the words out of my mouth without equivocation.' One of his managers even persuaded him 'to continue R&D for a product that he and I both knew we had no plans to sell.' Grove's devotion to reason did not mean that he was a machine. Far from it. What he found in the end was the will to do what was painful, the will to let go.

'Welcome to the new Intel,' Grove said in a speech not long afterward, to rally the troops behind the decision to exit memories. Intel the memory company was dead, he explained, but there was another product on which it could stake its future: the microprocessor. Invented at Intel in 1971, it had spent the 1970s timing traffic lights and helping bacon packers slice their bacon into even strips. Not all that exciting. But once IBM chose Intel's microprocessor to be the chip at the heart of its PCs, demand began to explode. Even so, the shift from memory chips was brutally hard – in 1986, Intel fired some 8,000 people and lost more than $180 million on $1.3 billion in sales – the only loss the company has ever posted since its early days as a startup.

The reality shifter

Grove and Moore had no way of knowing that Intel was on the verge of a remarkable ten-year run. They did know they were betting the company – and that to make the shift they had to risk angering IBM. The $60-billion-a-year giant was not only Intel's biggest customer but also its biggest shareholder – it had bought a large stake in the company to shore up its shaky supplier.

Intel did not set out to dominate the computer industry any more than humans set out to dominate the planet. In both cases the main concern was survival. Humans were so vulnerable to being eaten by larger, faster creatures that their only hope of survival was to control their environment. The 'new Intel,' too, was subject to forces beyond its control. Grove would later use a graphic that depicted Intel as a castle with the 386 chip in the center. The castle was under siege by rival chipmakers Sun Microsystems, Harris, Motorola, and NEC, not to mention RISC. But in the mid-1980s, before the graphic was ever made, Intel faced a more basic challenge: It was not so much a kingdom as a vassal state. Its dominant customer, IBM, had long insisted that Intel license its microprocessor designs to other chipmakers so that Big Blue could always be certain of a ready supply of chips at a pleasant price.

Grove decided that had to change. 'Finally, we had a real winner of a device,' Grove says of the 386 chip. But if Intel wanted a more secure future, 'we not only had to win; we had to win our way.' The 386 marked a genuine milestone of computer engineering. As Microsoft and other software developers figured out how to make full use of the new chip, Grove knew, the PC market would probably grow even hotter. Yet as long as Intel had to share its designs with other chipmakers, it would always face the anonymous and uncertain life of a parts supplier, subject to the whim of a customer 60 times its size.

To become its own kingdom, Grove realized, Intel had to make itself effectively the sole source of microprocessors. Getting IBM to buy the idea posed a challenge – he had no way of knowing how his giant partner would react – but he knew the status quo did not give Intel the freedom it needed to grow. So Intel moved unilaterally: In 1985, when it launched the 386, it declared the technology would not be licensed to other producers. IBM at first did not build 386s into its machines. But as archrival Compaq picked up the chip, IBM came around, cutting a deal with Intel to make some of the 386s it expected to use in its own chip factories. The gamble had paid off. 'To insist on our way meant we might lose,' Grove says. 'But to me, that is better than losing by compromising your advantages away.'

The fallible human

During Grove's 11-year tenure as CEO, Intel grew at a compound annual growth rate of nearly 30%. Together with Microsoft, Intel supplanted IBM as the dominant standard in computing. In 1992, Intel's profits topped $1 billion for the first time – on $5.8 billion of sales. What made such extraordinary growth possible under Grove's leadership was his continuing ability to adapt to shifting realities – but even Mr Strategic Inflection Point could stumble.

The 386 caught on, and sure enough, Microsoft used it to transform computing – its smash-hit Windows 3.0 operating system, which debuted in 1990, was designed to work on 386-based machines. Grove's breakthrough about changing the rules of the game opened the door to an epiphany about branding and marketing. In 1990 marketing chief Dennis Carter – the same Dennis Carter who had badgered Grove on RISC – came to him with a scheme to launch a large-scale consumer marketing campaign around the slogan 'Intel Inside.' It is hard to recapture how foreign the concept of branding was at an engineering company like Intel. According to Carter, when he pitched the idea to a roomful of Intel senior executives, 'most of them thought it was nuts. But not Andy. He said, "It's brilliant. Go make it happen."' Improbably, it turned an internal component into one of the most recognized brands in the world. Grove so loved the idea of marketing to consumers that he selected the name Pentium himself.

There's a rate of growth, though, at which everybody fails, including Andy Grove. His biggest tumble from the learning curve began in 1994. That fall Thomas Nicely, a mathematician at Lynchburg College in Virginia, spotted 'inconsistencies' in the way Intel's latest Pentium chip performed a rare, complex scientific calculation.

Intel engineers knew about the bug but deemed it too insignificant to report. By their calculations, a spreadsheet user would encounter it once every 27,000 years of spreadsheet use. But when Nicely's findings were posted on an Internet newsgroup, the discussion became a tempest, then burst into public view. Soon IBM announced it was suspending shipments of its Pentium-based computers.

It was a moment when Grove should have switched into observer mode and asked, 'What has changed here?' Instead, he kept thinking like an engineer and waded into the online mob himself, as though it were purely a technical debate. The uproar grew, though, until Grove was forced to adopt a no-questions-asked replacement policy and to apologize to customers. The apology was not very gracious. 'What we view as a minor technical problem has taken on a life of its own,' he declared. 'We apologize. We were motivated by a belief that replacement is simply unnecessary for most people. We still feel that way.' In effect he was telling consumers that they wanted something they did not need, but Intel had decided to indulge their irrationality.

A customer replied on the Internet with a poem:

When in the future we wish to deride
A CEO whose disastrous pride
Causes spokesmen to lie and sales streams to dry
We'll say he's got Intel Inside

For a man who strives to grasp objective reality, Grove had missed a fundamental shift in the nature of his business. Intel had become a marketing company. And while a chip is built in a factory, a brand is co-created with the customer. This required a rethinking of the meaning of 'objectivity.' In branding, a customer's subjective reality, even if confused, becomes your objective reality. The learning experience was more expensive than most: The Pentium recall required a $475 million writedown that marred Intel's year.

The data-driven patient

A few months later Grove faced crisis again: He was diagnosed with prostate cancer. In the intense period that followed, he remained on the job for all but two-and-a-half days. He handled the decision about his treatment the same way he handled decision-making at Intel: as if life depended on it.

Grove had never been one to rely on others' interpretations of reality. Hungary, in this regard, served as How-Not-To-Do-It University. Reality there was shaped by one's position in the system. At Intel he fostered a culture in which 'knowledge power' would trump 'position power.' Anyone could challenge anyone else's idea, so long as it was about the idea and not the person – and so long as you were ready for the demand 'Prove it.' That required data. Without data, an idea was only a story – a representation of reality and thus subject to distortion. Hungary had been a grotesque funhouse mirror. The slim man looked fat, and the fat man slim. But when he was diagnosed with prostate cancer in 1995, Grove found himself in the position of most patients: frightened, disoriented, and entirely reliant on the advice of doctors. Their advice was straightforward: Surgery was the best option, and that was pretty much all there was to it.

Was it, though? It took very little to discover that there was much, much more to it. There were alternatives to surgery. No surgeon advised him to take them seriously. But the expert opinions, Grove soon determined, were just that – opinions, based on little if any hard data. Data did exist. What Grove found most shocking is that no one had done the hard work of pulling it together. Plainly, Grove would have to do it himself.

The patient, in effect, became his own doctor. It was a massive research undertaking whose details Grove chronicled in a 1996 story for *FORTUNE*. One is left with the image of Grove, awake late at night, plotting and cross-plotting the data in his own methodically constructed charts. What did the data tell him? That he would be better off with an alternative procedure known as radiation seeding. That was the treatment he selected.

What Grove found most appalling, in the end, was the utter fixity of belief among doctors who failed to separate knowledge from conventional wisdom. Even the doctor who carried out Grove's procedure was captive to it. 'If you had what I have, what would you do?' Grove asked him at one point. The doctor said he'd probably have surgery. Confounded, Grove later asked why. The doctor thought about it. 'You know,' Grove remembers him saying, 'all through medical training, they drummed into us that the gold standard for prostate cancer is surgery. I guess that still shapes my thinking.'

'Let's think for ourselves'

Grove stepped down as CEO in spring 1998 to become Intel's chairman. The betting at Intel was that he'd never really let go of the reins, but Andy surprised everyone. He dug into his new assignment as he has every other – setting out to examine and improve the way the board governed Intel and thereby to set an example for corporate boards everywhere (see 'Inside Andy Grove's Latest Crusade' on fortune.com).

Last May, when Paul Otellini succeeded Craig Barrett as CEO, Grove officially became 'senior advisor' to the company. The title didn't matter. Grove was still teaching.

On a Monday last month, Grove stood before 400 or so Intel employees, the advance troops of the company's health-care initiative. (Intel wants to make its chips the basic building blocks of 21st-century health-care and medical technology.)

Many had never seen Grove in person before, and he got a standing ovation before he said a word. His speech was a strong statement about strategy. Understanding comes from action. So 'be quick and dirty,' he said. 'Engage and then plan. And get it better. Revolutions in our industry in our lifetime have taken place using exactly this formula. The best example is the IBM PC – created on the fly by a team in Boca Raton.'

Then he took questions. A European software engineer stood up with microphone in hand. He asked about handling health-care information. 'How can we address the problem of privacy protection and data protection?'

'Stay with me for a minute,' Grove said quickly. 'Can I ask you a question? Why do you care?'

'Because health-care information might find its way to insurance companies and might result in higher insurance rates,' the engineer replied.

'Explain to me why,' said Grove, almost before the engineer could finish speaking.

'Many people have said it would be a bad thing if insurers knew all about the health history of everyone in the population,' he replied.

Intel's senior advisor sized up the engineer's comments this way: 'I think we have a tendency toward adding imaginary complexities to a problem which is already unimaginably complicated.' He added, 'Let's think for ourselves. Let's not repeat mindlessly . . . excuse me, automatically . . . suppositions that are true merely because somebody else says they are.'

Did the engineer care about having been cross-examined and momentarily called mindless in the presence of 400 co-workers by his legendarily blunt leader? He smiled at Grove's choice of words. 'Go ahead,' he told Grove. 'I was prepared.'

Source: Richard Tedlow, *Fortune*, 12 December 2005

Questions

1 What are the key features of Grove's change strategies? What are the hallmarks of his strategic thinking and acting?

2 Why are his change strategies successful?

3 To which theories of change does Grove subscribe?

References

Abrahamson, E. (1991) Managerial fads and fashions: the diffusion and rejection of innovations. *Academy of Management Review*, **16**, 586–612.

Aldrich, H. (1979) *Organizations and Environments*, Prentice-Hall, Englewood Cliffs, NJ.

Alvesson, M. (1993) Organizations as rhetoric: knowledge intensive firms and the struggle with ambiguity. *Journal of Management Studies*, **30**, **6**, 997–1016.

Argyris, C. (1992) *Organizational Learning*, Blackwell, Oxford.

Armenakis, A.A., Harris, S. and Field, H. (1999) Paradigms in organizational change: change agent and change target perspectives. In R. Golembiewski (ed.) *Handbook of Organizational Behaviour*, Marcel Dekker, New York.

Arthur, W.B. (1996) Increasing returns and the new world of business. *Harvard Business Review*, July/August, 100–9.

Beer, M. and Eisenstat, R.A. (1996) Developing an organization capable of implementing strategy and learing. *Human Relations*, **48**, **2**, 97–126.

De Geus, A. (1997) *The Living Company: Habits for Survival in a Turbulent Business Environment*, Booz, Allen and Hamilton, London.

De Wit, B. and Meyer, R. (1999) *Strategy Synthesis: Resolving Strategy Paradoxes to Create Competitive Advantage*, International Thomson Press, London.

Dulewicz, V. and Herbert, P.J. (1998) Predicting advancement to senior management from competencies and personality data: a seven year follow-up study. *British Journal of Management*, **10**, **1**, 13–23.

Farkas, C.M. and Wetlaufer, S. (1996) The ways chief executive officers lead. *Harvard Business Review*, May–June, 110–12.

Gersick, C.J.G. (1991) Revolutionary change theories: a multi level exploration of the punctuated equilibrium paradigm. *Academy of Management Review*, **6**, 10–36.

Ghemawat, P. (1991) *Commitment: The Dynamics of Strategy*, Free Press, New York.

Goleman, D. (2001) *The Emotionally Intelligent Workplace*, Jossey-Bass, San Francisco, CA.

Greiner, L.E. (1972) Evolution and revolution as organizations grow. *Harvard Business Review*, July/August, 37–46.

Hannan, M.T. and Freeman, F. (1977) The population ecology of organizations. *American Journal of Sociology*, **82**, 929–64 .

Hannan, M., Polos, L. and Carroll, G.R. (2003) Fog of change. *Administrative Science Quarterly*, **48**, **3**, 399–432.

Hegel, G.W.F. (1937) *The Philosophy of History*, Dover, New York.

Judson, A. (1991) *Changing Behaviour in Organizations: Minimizing Resistance to Change*, Blackwell, Cambridge, MA.

Kagono, T., Nonaka, I., Sakakibara, K. and Okumara, A. (1985) *Strategic versus Evolutionary Management: A US-Japan Comparison of Strategy and Organization*, North Holland Press, Amsterdam.

Kanter, R.M. (1999) Change in everyone's job: managing the extended enterprise in a globally extended world. *Organizational Dynamics*, **28**, **1**, 7–23.

Kolakowski, L. (1978) *Main Currents of Marxism, Volume 1*, Oxford University Press, Oxford.

Kotter, J. (1996) Leading change: why transformation efforts fail. *Harvard Business Review*, **73**, **2**, 59–67.

Leavy, B. and Wilson, D.C. (1994) *Strategy and Leadership*, Routledge, London.

Lewin, K. (1947) Frontiers in group dynamics. *Human Relations*, **1**, 5–41.

March, J.G. (1999) *The Pursuit of Organizational Intelligence*, Blackwell, Oxford.

Miller, D. (1990) *The Icarus Paradox: How Excellent Companies Bring about Their Own Downfall*, Harper Business, New York.

Mintzberg, H. and Waters, J.A. (1985) Of strategies, deliberate and emergent. *Strategic Management Journal*, July/Sept, 257–72.

Nutt, P., Backoff, R. and Hogan, M. (2000) Managing the paradoxes of strategic change. *Journal of Applied Management Studies*, **9**, **1**, 5–31.

O'Donnell, D. (2000) The emotional world of strategy implementation. In P. Flood, T. Dromgoole, S. Carroll and L. Gorman (eds) *Managing Strategy Implementation*, Blackwell, Oxford.

Parsons, T. (1937) *The Structure of Social Action*, McGraw-Hill, New York.

Peters, T. and Waterman, R. (1982) *In Search of Excellence: Lessons from America's Best Run Companies*, Harper & Row, New York.

Pettigrew, A. and Whipp, R. (1991) *Managing Change for Competitive Success*, Blackwell, Oxford.

Porter, M.E. (1986) *Competition in Global Industries*, Harvard Business School Press, Boston, MA.

Porter, M.E. (1998) *The Competitive Advantage of Nations*, Free Press, New York.

Senge, P. (1990) The leader's new work: building learning organizations. *Sloan Management Review*, Fall, 7–23.

Sparrow, P. (2000) A world turned upside down. In P. Flood, T. Dromgoole, S. Carroll and L. Gorman (eds) *Managing Strategy Implementation*, Blackwell, Oxford.

Stacey, R. (1993) Strategy as order emerging from chaos. *Long Range Planning*, **26**, **1**, 10–17.

Steiner, C. (1997) *Achieving Emotional Illiteracy*, Bloomsbury, London.

Van de Ven, A.H. and Poole, M.S. (1995) Explaining development and change in organizations. *Academy of Management Review*, **20**, **3**, 510–40.

Wensley, R. (2003) Strategy as intention and anticipation. In S. Cummings and D.C. Wilson (eds) *Images of Strategy*, Blackwell, Oxford.

Wilson, D. (1999) *A Strategy of Change: Concepts and Controversies in the Management of Change*, International Thomson Press, London.

Wilson, D. (2009) Organizational change management. In C. Cooper and S. Clegg (eds) *Handbook of Macro-Organizational Behaviour*, Sage, London.

Further reading

Buckingham, M. (2005) What great managers do. *Harvard Business Review*, **83**, **3**, 1–10.

Campbell, A., Whitehead, J. and Finkelstein, S. (2009) Why good leaders make bad decisions. *Harvard Business Review*, Feb, 60–7.

Charan, R. (2006) Conquering the culture of indecision. *Harvard Business Review*, **84**, **1**, 109–17.

Garvin, D.A., Edmondson, A.C. and Ginx, F. (2008) Is yours a learning organisation? *Harvard Business Review*, **86**, **3**, 109–17.

Hamel, G. (1996) Strategy as revolution. *Harvard Business Review*, **74**, July, 70–82.

Jarzabkowski, P. and Spee, A.P. (2009) Strategy as practice: a review and future directions for the field. *International Journal of Management Reviews*, **11**, **1**, 69–77.

Lovallo, D.P. and Sibony, O. (2006) Distortions and deceptions in strategic decisions. *McKinsey Quarterly*, **1**, 18–29.

Martin, R. (2007) How successful leaders think. *Harvard Business Review*, **85**, **6**, 60–8.

Ocasio, W. and Joseph, J. (2008) Rise and fall or transformation? The evolution of strategic planning at the General Electric Company, 1940–2006. *Long Range Planning*, **41**, **3**, 248–72.

Sminia, H. (2009) Process research in strategy formation: theory, methodology and relevance. *International Journal of Management Reviews*, **11**, **1**, 97–125.

Chapter **14**

Strategy as knowledge:
innovation and learning

Chapter contents

Introduction

In earlier chapters in this section of the book we have seen the importance of knowledge as a key organizational resource. We have seen how knowledge can act as a source of competitive advantage and we have seen how knowledge is a key factor in ensuring successful strategic decisions. In this chapter, we examine in greater depth some key aspects of knowledge by linking these with innovation and learning. New areas of strategy and organizational science such as knowledge management (Nonaka, 1994), organizational learning (Senge, 1990) and the knowledge-based view of strategy

(Grant, 1996; Spender, 1996) have grown rapidly and have, in turn, posed critical questions about processes of *innovation* and the meaning of knowledge. We explore these here.

In this chapter we begin by discussing the literature on innovation and technological change and introduce a number of competing concepts including 'disruptive innovations and the innovator's dilemma' (Christensen, 1997), 'innovation as revolution' (Hamel, 2000), and 'value innovation' (Kim and Mauborgne, 1999). We try to define key terms such as knowledge, technology, innovation and core competences as a basis for examining four different perspectives on knowledge: knowledge as assets, knowledge through innovation, knowledge embedded in routines, and knowledge through learning. We then try to present the elements of the knowledge-based view of strategy and provide insights about how to foster organizational commitment to innovation and to structure the organization to achieve growth through learning.

14.1 Concepts of knowledge and innovation

Nonaka and Takeuchi (1995) argued that the *systemic knowledge* ingrained in the firm, its processes and its people are the single most important resources for the firm. This systemic knowledge is slowly developed, is distinctive and unique to the firm, is not easily transferable to others and may be protected by intellectual property regulations or other competitive barriers. The ease with which the knowledge is capitalized by the firm depends in part on how the knowledge is managed internally in the firm and transferred and replicated easily throughout the organization. For instance, Wal-Mart's inventory management and replenishment systems and McDonald's knowledge transfer of restaurant technology throughout its restaurant systems are prime examples of knowledge management and transfer in successful organizations. We define knowledge management as follows:

> *The process of identifying, extracting and managing the information, intellectual property and accumulated knowledge that exists within a company and the minds of its employees.*

An important characteristic of knowledge is that it increases the ability to embrace technology and innovation. For example, Cooper and Schendel (1976) examine the nature of strategic responses to technological threats and indicate that incremental technological changes (competence-enhancing changes) reinforce the competitive positions of established firms in the industry, whereas more radical technological innovations (competence-destroying changes) may put pressure on existing incumbent firms to develop new competences, skills and capabilities. Dussage et al. (1996, p. 14) point out clearly the distinction between 'incremental' innovations (refining and improving existing products or processes) and 'radical' innovations (introducing totally new concepts). Note that innovation may involve the development of new technologies, such as bio-engineering and genetic engineering which define new industries, or the application of existing technologies to create new products, such as PCs, or to enhance existing products, such as digital cameras versus 35mm cameras. Generally, new products such as the CT scanner or the PC are new product configurations which link existing technologies and components in a new way. In these cases of new innovations (arising from *inventions* that create new products from new knowledge or distinctive combinations of existing knowledge) the product innovator is often not the eventual product winner. For example, Table 14.1 shows a range of innovative products for which the innovator is not the product winner. From a British viewpoint Sir Geoffrey Household of EMI won the Nobel Prize for the CT scanner yet the innovation was capitalized by GE. As a counter-example, however, Pilkington Glass of the UK was the innovator for float glass and also the winner in the marketplace despite US competition from Corning.

Table 14.1 Product innovators and winners

Product	Innovator	Product winner (follower)
Jet plane	British Aerospace: Comet	Boeing (707)
CT scanner	EMI	GE
Video-cassette recorder	Ampex	Sony/Matsushita
Video games	Atari	Nintendo/Sega
Photocopier	Xerox	Canon
Office P/C	Xerox	IBM

Source: Teece (1987); Anderson and Tushman (1990)

14.1.1 Disruptive technologies

Christensen (1997) examined what he calls the innovators' dilemma in confronting different innovation types. He distinguishes between *sustaining technologies*, which foster improved product performance among existing firms, and *disruptive technologies*, which result in worse short-term product performance and which initiate the leading firm's failure. The dilemma for incumbent leading firms is that any adoption of disruptive breakthrough technologies requires cannibalization of purchases of existing products by current mainstream customers. This loss of revenue can lead these firms to go slow on implementing breakthrough technologies.

Their mainstream customer focus, and associated market research, can then prevent leading firms from new product development, new markets and new customers in the future. This strategic weakness can allow entrepreneurial firms to exploit the new product pathway left open by the inertia and resistance to change of incumbent, leading firms.

Table 14.2 shows a list of the impacts of such disruptive innovations on the economic performance of leading incumbent firms.

14.1.2 Value innovation

Writers such as Kim and Mauborgne (1999) extend the concept of technological innovation to value innovation. They point out that while an innovator such as Ampex failed to capture the rents from inventing the VCR, its inventions nevertheless benefited the economy because later value innovators such as Sony and Matsushita made a success of the Ampex innovation. Value innovation places emphasis on the buyer as the centre of strategic thinking. To *value innovate*, companies must ask two questions:

1 Are we offering customers radically superior value?
2 Is our price level accessible to the mass of buyers in our target market?

In essence, the major inputs for value innovation are knowledge and ideas, new product concepts etc., which reject competitive strategies based on imitation but do not necessarily require new technology in order to succeed.

Table 14.3 shows a range of examples of value innovation given by Kim and Mauborgne (1999). It is instructive to note that in virtually all the cases given, the innovation shown is generally not a

Table 14.2 Examples of disruptive technologies (innovations)

Company	Disruptive innovation	Firms disrupted	Prior industry leader
DEC (Digital Equipment Corporation)	Minicomputer	Mainframe computer manufacturers	IBM
HMOs e.g. Kaiser Permanente	Health maintenance organizations	Conventional health insurance	Blue Cross/Blue Shield
Compaq	Personal computer CPC	Minicomputer manufacturers	IBM, DEC
Dell	Direct order, customized PCs	Retail stores	Compaq
Charles Schwab	Discount trading/broking	Investment banks	Merrill Lynch
Ford	Model T	Specialized car makers	Many
Toyota	Small cars and lean manufacturing	Large-volume car manufacturers	GM, Ford
Canon	Desk top photocopiers	High-speed photo-copying manufacturers (IBM, Kodak, Xerox)	Xerox
Wal-Mart	Discount retailing	Department stores	Macy's
Sony	Portable radios, TVs	Vacuum tube-based electronic products	RCA, Zenith

Source: Christensen, 1997

Table 14.3 Examples of value innovations

Company	Innovation
Callaway Golf – 'Big Bertha'	– made playing golf less difficult and more fun
SWATCH	– a price-competitive watch as a fashion accessory
Starbucks	– good coffee in a 'coffee bar'
Wal-Mart	– discount retailing
Charles Schwab	– investment and brokerage account management
CNN	– innovation in news broadcasting (24-hour news)
IKEA	– fashion home products and furniture retailing
SAP	– business applications software
Barnes & Noble	– book retailing
Southwest Airlines	– short-haul air travel
Body Shop	– organic cosmetic retailing
Home Depot (B&Q)	– home improvement retail
Virgin Atlantic	– 'upper class' – first-class service at a business-class price

Note: In virtually all these cases, with perhaps the exception of SAP, the concept is not a patentable innovation, i.e. a scientifically excludable innovation
Source: Kim and Mauborgne (1999)

new 'technology' of a technical kind, but really a new product concept or a new way of developing a business opportunity using existing technologies and knowledge.

14.1.3 Revolutionary innovators

Hamel (2000) also stresses the importance of innovation as the engine to sustain corporate growth. Like Kim and Mauborgne, he believes that imitative strategies based on competitive strategy analysis have no basis in today's marketplace. He believes that the time has passed for strategies based on efficiency models (e.g. productive efficiency or benchmarking 'best practices' in competitors or the best-run companies). Senior managers must recognize the clear differences between innovation and imitation. Imitative approaches to the market mean that companies act reactively and try to emulate existing competitive strategies. In so doing, they misunderstand the customer demands and buyer needs in emerging mass markets.

Table 14.4 gives a few examples of companies seen as revolutionary innovators by Hamel.

Note that many of the viewpoints here rely on creative, innovatory ideas and product concepts, and creative reconfigurations of existing technologies. New economy strategies are different and are discussed in Chapter 7.

The chapter now examines a number of perspectives or viewpoints about knowledge which can influence strategic decision making. They involve:

1 *economic concepts* discussed earlier (for example, the resource-based view of the firm);

2 *alternative definitions of innovation* (for example, radical, incremental, disruptive or value-based);

3 *organizational approaches* based on organizational evolution, routines and organization learning.

The traditional economic approach treats knowledge as an entity which affects the nature of the economic equilibrium, like so many other variables, but does not feature as a central element, with predictable effects on the competitive outcome. As we move towards placing knowledge at the centre of strategy theory we argue that there are four distinct approaches to how knowledge works. The first is the resource-based view (RBV) that provides us with the 'knowledge as asset' metaphor. A second view is Schumpeterian (Schumpeter, 1934) in origin, picturing knowledge as innovation and as an essential element in the general theme of creative destruction of existing technological/knowledge bases. Third, evolutionary economics[1] moves away from a decision orientation towards a focus on the internal organization of the firm and the role of organizational routines in the

Table 14.4 Hamel's revolutionary innovators	
Company	**Innovatory idea**
SWATCH	Small objects of desire – combines Swiss watchmaking with Lego plastics
easyJet/Ryanair	Reinvented basic economics of airline business – real value to customers
Dell	Reinvented product cycle and cost structure of PCs
Nokia	Understood youth culture and its linkage to mobile phones
Source: Hamel (2000)	

---

[1] Nelson and Winter (1982) are most commonly identified with evolutionary economics. But the roots run deeper: *see* Veblen, 1898, on cumulative change; Marshall, 1920, on 'economic biology' and his well-known appreciation of dynamic analysis; and Alchian, 1950, 1953, on the implications of selection for the economic system.

acquisition of organizational knowledge. The use of a Darwinian natural selection process coupled with adaptive feedback mechanisms explains the nature of organizational routines in large organizations. Such routines and their adaptation over time require embedded knowledge, acquisition of knowledge, and transfer and integration of knowledge within organizations. Finally, the Teece et al. (1997) approach to dynamic capabilities adds the elements of learning and other dynamics to the RBV and suggests paths by which both RBV and evolutionary approaches can take place in practice, creating genuine cross-cutting and forward-looking capabilities as the organization evolves and grows. The writers of these approaches and perspectives did not place knowledge explicitly at the centre of their writing. Therefore, to a large degree, what follows is a reinterpretation of existing theory in terms of our view of knowledge and the role of knowledge in the processes of competitive strategy formulation and strategy development.

Case box 14.1: What do we know about the knowledge economy?

The science of describing, understanding, and measuring knowledge will always be an imperfect one. The knowledge identified in this forum turned out to be capricious: sometimes sticky, often slippery, rarely tangible, frequently tacit, and extremely heterogeneous. (Report of the Centre for Educational Research and Innovation (CERI) Washington Forum, June 1999)

Economic success is increasingly based on the effective utilisation of intangible assets such as knowledge, skills and innovative potential as the key resource for competitive advantage. The term 'knowledge economy' is used to describe this emerging economic structure. (Economic and Social Research Council (ESRC), 2005)

There was much hype about the knowledge economy in the 1990s where the view was taken that the ICT revolution allowed firms to exploit scientific and technical knowledge bases providing them with a distinct competitive advantage by reducing transaction and processing costs. This new knowledge economy would give rise to new organisational forms within and between companies and would create more knowledge workers as portfolio workers, freelancers, or as self-employed individuals. Following the dot com collapse which followed this promise of a brave new world, the questions came thick and fast about whether and to what extent a new knowledge economy existed at all. Was not all innovation driven by knowledge and new technologies and had that not always been the case? Why were we bothering to name this apparent new phenomenon the knowledge economy when it had always been with us?

There is, however, some evidence that investment in knowledge can be measured and is increasing steadily in some regions. The OECD has produced a composite indicator of 'investment in knowledge' which comprises investment in R&D, investment in higher education, and investment in IT software. Using this input measure, Brinkley (2006) identified three groups of economies:

1 High knowledge investment economies (Sweden, USA, Finland, Korea, Denmark, Japan, Canada), investing around 6 per cent of GDP.

2 Middle knowledge investment economies (Australia, Germany, Belgium, Netherlands, France, UK, Austria) investing between 3 and 4 per cent of GDP.

3 Low investment economies (Spain, New Zealand, Ireland, Italy, Greece, Portugal) investing between 2 and 3 per cent of GDP.

Most high investment economies stepped up their knowledge investment by between 1 and 2 percentage points of GDP between 1996 and 2004 while the middle and low investment economies showed relatively little change over the same period.

So it looks as if there are some significant changes at least in investment in knowledge as defined by the OECD. The challenge lies in identifying the benefits of this investment. Other forms of investment (e.g. physical investment) seem to pay off more than knowledge investment according to a recent OECD report (2006). It may be that ICT makes the world smaller, with production of goods in lower cost economies with design, marketing and perhaps service provided by Europe or the USA (design, marketing and service being more 'knowledge based').

But the key questions remain. Is there something tangible and different called the knowledge economy and does it ultimately make any difference (and if so to what)? And does investment in R&D tell us anything about a company's performance? Apple, for example, spends only a small fraction on R&D spend, compared to its larger competitors such as Sony or Microsoft. In 2008 Apple revenue was 47% of Microsoft's revenue. In 2009 it was 76% and increasing (see also the Apple case box in this chapter on the iPod). Defining the knowledge economy is not going to be easy.

Source: *Defining the Knowledge Economy: Knowledge Economy Programme Report* (2006), Ian Brinkley, The Work Foundation, London

14.2 Knowledge as assets

Figure 14.1 portrays the market-based view commonly found in economic models in resource-based terms. The internals of the firm are explained in terms of resources and capabilities, the conventional description that permits discrimination between assets based on knowing and skills based on experience and actions. We do not summarize the key elements of the resource-based view here. They are familiar enough (see Wernerfelt, 1984; Barney, 1991; Grant, 1991) and presented in depth in Chapter 6. Instead we suggest some conclusions in the language of *core competences*.

First, core competences can have a very significant impact by their effect on firm scope (boundaries), and by the (long) time scales over which they exist and change. They arise typically through collective learning – very much in the economics tradition of *objectified knowledge* (Spender, 1996). Also, their impact is to create a framework through which we can view competition. In this framework competition involves the acquisition of distinctive skills in which competition in product markets is a 'superficial expression' of the more fundamental competition about competences. Therefore, the dynamics of the strategic theory of the firm focuses on the process of core competence acquisition and collective learning because it occurs logically prior to product market evolution.

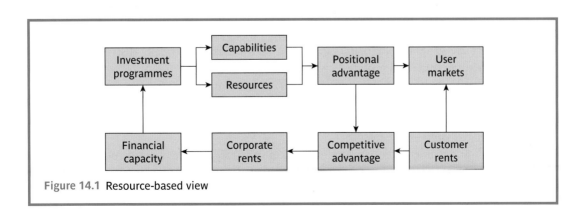

Figure 14.1 Resource-based view

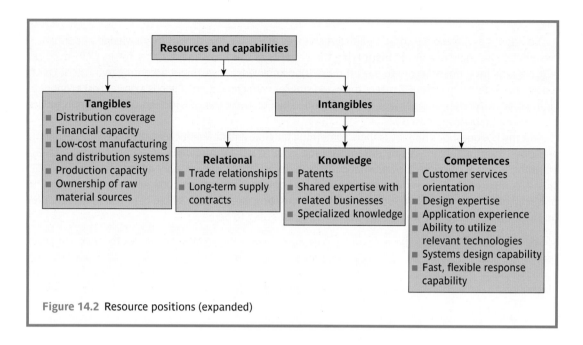

Figure 14.2 Resource positions (expanded)

Figure 14.2 is a simple expansion of the range and nature of asset positions that are implied in Figure 14.1.[2] The broad categories of tangible and intangible assets give some idea of the differing demands on internal processes and on the challenge for integration of these different positions through the organization, acting as some form of *corporate glue*, which integrates and binds these diverse asset positions for corporate value maximization. Many authors have provided classifications and explanations of the language of resources, assets, capabilities and competences. Grant (1991), for example, distinguishes between resources and capabilities, viewing resources as inputs and capabilities as those intermediate processes derived within the production function that are the main source of competitive advantage (refer back to the discussion in Chapter 7). Both are hard to define objectively and indeed Grant goes as far as to say that capabilities are organizational routines. Amit and Schoemaker (1993) (first discussed in Chapter 7) also deploy the language of resources and capabilities but seek to draw links with the industry analysis framework. From their perspective, resources are intermediate goods (in contrast to Grant), and capabilities are '*based on developing, caring and exchanging information through the firm's human capital*'. They are built by combining physical, human and technological resources at the corporate level. The link with industry (or product-market) arises when certain resources and capabilities become the prime determinant of economic rents and value. This can only occur if these resources and capabilities are subject to market failure and their possession can therefore be firm-specific. Amit and Schoemaker refer to these as 'strategic assets'. This enables a distinction to be drawn between those resources and capabilities that are generally attainable and those that are asymmetrically distributed between firms, and difficult to trade and imitate.

Prahalad and Hamel (1990) (see also Chapter 6) have made famous the language of core competence and avoid using the language of resources and capabilities. For them, '*core competences are the collective learning in the organization, especially how to coordinate diverse production skills and integrate multiple streams of technologies*'.

Just as Amit and Schoemaker extend their notion of strategic assets towards product-markets with a concept of strategic industry factors, so also do Prahalad and Hamel in making core

---

[2] See the teaching notes in De Wit and Meyer (1994) for a practical illustration. Also see Barney (1991) and Grant (1991) for similar deconstructions of resources.

competences the foundation for core products. For them the insight is not what is a core competence and how to build one, but a view of the strategic architecture of the firm, by which they mean '*a road map of the future that identifies which core competences to build and their constituent technologies*'. For these and other authors writing in the same vein, the common characteristic is the appeal to economic reasoning in the form of asymmetric distribution of assets to support economic rents and value. But the critical contribution of firm-specific resources can lie anywhere between inputs and outputs, with alternative scenarios about the contributory roles of organization structure and process, and managerial culture.

Our own approach, focusing on intangible and tangible assets, in Figure 14.2 is more modest in intent. We seek only to distinguish between some categories of resources and capabilities so that we can see more clearly the different roles that knowledge can play in gaining competitive advantage. The distinction between tangible and intangible assets is important and occurs prior to any distinction between resources and capabilities. We divide intangibles into three parts.

1 The first outlines those assets that are relational in character and involve the relationship of the organization with the outside world.
2 The second is more explicitly concerned with knowledge and know-how. Although some entries under this heading suggest explicit knowledge (such as patents), they are surrounded by or produced by know-how that is essentially tacit.
3 In the third part, our term competences can be used interchangeably with capabilities, some of which are explicit in their design but many are likely to display characteristics of organizational routines. They promote the competitive architecture for new product generation.

14.3 Knowledge as innovation

The resource-based view (see Figure 14.2) provides a theory of protection and sustainability of competitive advantage, once determined. For an understanding of the initial formation of advantage we have to turn elsewhere, particularly to theories of dynamic innovation. The Schumpeterian approach (Schumpeter, 1934) offers innovation as the medium through which creative destruction of existing technologies and knowledge bases takes place (see Case box 8.1). The element of destruction depicts intuitively and vividly, but also convincingly, how the old is replaced by the new. But it also sets these mechanisms in waves and floods of change, suggesting that a calculation of the benefits of change and innovation is overwhelmed by the magnitude of the opportunities on offer. Thus, Schumpeter suggested there were patterns of change and ferment (radical innovation) interspersed with stability (incremental innovation). In this way Schumpeter emphasized dynamic efficiency above static efficiency. Some recent writings clearly have their origins in Schumpeter. See, for example, d'Aveni's (1994) approach to hypercompetition, where he argues that the sources of competitive advantage are being created and destroyed at an increasingly rapid rate. Hamel and Prahalad (1993) use the language of dominance to assert a doctrine of strategic intent and define the gap between ambition and resources as strategic stretch. But the Schumpeterian world of enormous opportunity is not the only context for innovation. Firms may wish to create their own shocks or, more modestly, may seek to internally generate finer pieces of sustainable advantage, through processes of strategic stretch.

14.3.1 Innovation competition

But who innovates? Economists such as Kenneth Arrow have formulated models to explain whether new entrants have advantages over incumbents, whether monopoly players can innovate more readily than those in competitive markets, and whether potential entrants can outwit monopolists.

Of course, the answers depend on the situation but there is good reason for thinking that incomers often provide the wellspring of innovation – eventually. The behaviour to be explained is not that of the innovator who rationally examines the balance between costs and revenues in the light of prevailing competition and makes innovations when the return–risk ratio looks promising. The more difficult behaviour to explain is the reluctance and inertia of incumbents to innovate in the light of expected innovation from new entrants (see also Christensen, 1997).

The two common economic explanations for this are the *sunk cost effect* and the *replacement effect*. The former arises when the incumbent assesses his existing technology by comparing its contribution margin to no new costs of investment beyond that of simple replacement. By contrast, a new technology has a stiffer hurdle because the contribution margin (assuming for simplicity the same revenue stream from both technologies) has to cover new investment as well (see Besanko et al., 2000, pp. 488–9).

The replacement effect was first formulated by Arrow (1962) in considering who has the greater propensity to invest, the monopolist or the new entrant. The incentive for the monopolist to invest in a radical new technology requires a comparison of the new stream of monopoly profits with the existing stream. However, for the new entrant who, if successful, will become the new monopolist, the incentive is simply the new stream of monopoly profits. Through innovation an entrant can replace a monopolist but a monopolist can only replace itself, hence this is called the replacement effect. Thus, established firms under this thinking are less willing to stretch themselves to innovate.

However, if the monopolist anticipates that new competitive entry is likely, then the incentives reverse in favour of the monopolist. The incentive for the monopolist to innovate in the teeth of potential competitive intrusion is that of retaining monopoly profits from successful innovation versus sharing the market with a new entrant as a duopoly within which prices will be lower due to competition. This is greater than that of the new entrant who, expecting the monopolist to defend by innovation, can only anticipate the profit streams from sharing a competitive duopoly. Arrow referred to this as the *efficiency effect*. The balance between these three effects depends on the probability of successful innovation by potential entrants. Where this is low, the sunk cost and replacement cost effects will dominate and the monopolists will prefer to maintain their existing cash flows. Where the probability is high then the efficiency motives will dominate and monopolists will seek to maintain their market position even if it is less favourable in absolute terms.

Case box 14.2: **Outsource your innovations**

When Frito-Lay added a little curl to its snacks, the company's sales improved. Of such seemingly modest innovations are great fortunes made. Next month Gillette will launch the successor to its sensationally successful Mach3 razor. Much as the company would like it to be as revolutionary as the Mach3 was in its day, the battery-operated vibrating beard-remover is unlikely to be more than evolutionary. That may not, however, prevent it from making a sizeable contribution to Gillette's profits.

Big firms still aspire to make truly great breakthrough inventions – products that will underwrite their profits for at least a decade. They are, however, coming up with such inventions less and less often, even though many industries, notably pharmaceuticals, continue to spend vast sums trying. Indeed, for most of industrial history, small firms have been responsible for the bulk of breakthrough products. America's Small Business Administration claims that the pacemaker, the personal computer, the Polaroid camera and pre-stressed concrete all emerged from small entrepreneurial outfits, and those are taken only from the list of items beginning with the letter P.

Big firms are better at less eye-catching forms of innovation – for example, Frito-Lay adding a little curl to its snacks, the clever twist allowing consumers to scoop up their guacamole or salsa dip and place relatively more of it in their mouths and less on their rugs, and generally improving the ways in which products invented elsewhere are manufactured, marketed and continually enhanced. Henry Ford did not invent the automobile. He 'merely' invented a far superior way to manufacture it – namely, the mass-production assembly line. And on that was built an industrial empire that has thrived for almost a century. Likewise, in the past few decades most of the companies that have created truly extraordinary amounts of wealth have done so by inventing great processes, not great products. Dell, Toyota and Wal-Mart, for example, have risen to the top of their respective industries by coming up with amazingly efficient ways of getting quite ordinary products into the hands of consumers more cheaply than their rivals.

Does this mean that big firms should sack all their scientists and leave inventing to others? In practice, more and more are doing just that. For some time, the computer industry has, in effect, relied for much of its research and development on small firms backed by venture capital, and the telecoms industry is outsourcing more and more research to smaller firms in India and elsewhere. Without their own in-house labs, however, big firms fear that they will be taken by surprise by what a Harvard Professor, Clayton Christensen, famously described as a 'disruptive technology', an innovation so revolutionary that it will enable an upstart outsider to crush them, much as the PC did to the mainframe-computer business.

But, as history has shown time and time again, a bevy of in-house scientists gives no guarantee that their output will protect their employer from technological change. Xerox, AT&T and IBM spent billions on research but all failed to exploit much of what came out of their labs, and all ended up being caught out by new technologies. It is far better if big firms' managers keep their binoculars well trained on the outside world and their minds open to any new ideas they spot there. They can then buy them and do what they do best: find innovative ways to bring them to market.

Source: 'Less glamour, more profit', *The Economist*, 22 April 2004

Questions

1 If in-house R&D is so risky, what are the arguments for doing it?

2 What are the arguments for outsourcing R&D?

14.3.2 Technology races

This analysis of innovation competition focuses on the pay-offs to innovation. There is also a literature on choosing the right levels of R&D under market uncertainty and under uncertainty about the response of rivals. The analysis of first-mover advantage is well known. It asserts that the first mover gains advantage by establishing explicit knowledge protected by patents and trademarks and goes on to build advantages of scale, experience and scope so that later movers can never erode the early advantage (see the discussion in Chapter 6 of Ghemawat's 1997 analysis of Du Pont in titanium dioxide). There is also an interesting empirical literature on technology races and patent races (Gottinger, 2003). These races describe the battles between firms to complete a successful R&D programme and to be the first to market with an innovation, with all the benefits of first-mover advantage. A race is an interactive pattern of competition characterized by firms constantly trying to get ahead of their rivals, or trying not to fall too far behind. Like the **dominant design** literature,[3]

---

[3] Dominant design can be defined as 'after a technological innovation and a subsequent era of ferment in an industry, a basic architecture of product or process that becomes the accepted market standard', from Abernathy and Utterback 1978, cited by Anderson and Tushman 1990. Dominant designs may not be better than alternatives, nor innovative. They have the benchmark features to which subsequent designs are compared.

Examples include the IBM 360 computer series and Ford's Model T automobile, and the IBM PC.

racing behaviour is also a dynamic story of how technology unfolds in an industry recognizing the fundamental importance of strategic interactions between competing firms.

A simple race between two firms might involve the following. The leader may consider further investment to outdistance its rival and get to the winning post first. But it is aware of the diminishing marginal productivity of research for itself and the uncertainty of innovation for its rival. It therefore has to balance the risks and expenditures associated with pressing on with the benefits of delay in terms of consolidating its own knowledge and the difficulty for its rival of catching up. By contrast, the follower is faced with the need to catch up, but has the same concerns about the productivity of research, offset to some degree by at least some knowledge about the successful path followed by its rival. The leader has considerable incentives to be cautious, whereas the follower might be more inclined to plunge ahead. Clearly the variables are many and imponderable given the uncertainty of success in R&D and the difficulty of predicting the responses of rivals. Gottinger summarizes the implications:

> At one level, racing behaviour has implications for understanding technology strategy at the level of the individual firm and for understanding the impact of policies that aim to spur technological innovation. At another level, racing behaviour embodies both traditions that previous writings have attempted to synthesize: the 'demand-pull' side emphasized by economic theorists and the 'technology-push' emphasized by the autonomous technological innovation school. (Gottinger, 2003, pp. 37–8)

Gottinger observes from his research on the telecommunications and computer industries the apparent inability of technology-oriented companies to maintain leadership in fields that they pioneered (op. cit., p. 51). These failures might be due to agency problems or other suboptimal managerial behaviour. But of more interest here is the existence of market asymmetries that affect racing behaviour: (i) risk-driven and (ii) resource-driven asymmetries. The latter are clearly linked to the replacement effect (above). All this literature (Abramowitz, 1986; Gottinger, 1998, 2001; Lerner, 1997; Scherer, 1991) carries implications for knowledge in terms of its creation, how it is accessed, transferred and integrated, and who has the incentives for these activities.

Case box 14.3: **Does IT matter?**

Nicholas Carr has foisted an existentialist debate on the mighty information-technology industry
His argument is simple, powerful and yet also subtle. He is not, in fact, denying that IT has the potential to transform entire societies and economies. On the contrary, his argument is based on the assumption that IT resembles the steam engine, the railway, the electricity grid, the telegraph, the telephone, the highway system and other technologies that proved revolutionary in the past. For commerce as a whole, Mr Carr is insistent, IT matters very much indeed.

But this often has highly ironic implications for individual companies, thinks Mr Carr. Electricity, for instance, became revolutionary for society only when it ceased to be a proprietary technology, owned or used by one or two factories here and there, and instead became an infrastructure – ubiquitous, and shared by all. Only in the early days, and only for the few firms that found proprietary uses for it, was electricity a source of strategic – i.e., more or less lasting – advantage. Once it became available to all firms, however, it became a commodity, a factor of production just like office supplies or raw materials, a cost to be managed rather than an edge over rivals, a risk (during black-outs) rather than an opportunity.

Computer hardware and software, Mr Carr argues, have been following the same progression from proprietary technology to infrastructure. In the past, American Airlines, for example, gained a strategic advantage for a decade or two after it rolled out a proprietary computerised reservation system in 1962, called Sabre. In time, however, its rivals replicated the system, or even leap-frogged to better ones. Today, the edge that a computer system can give a firm is fleeting at best. IT, in other words, has now joined history's other revolutionary technologies by becoming an infrastructure, not a differentiator. In that sense, and from the point of view of individual firms, 'IT no longer matters.'

And what's IT all about?

Surely though, Mr Carr's critics counter, IT is different from electricity or steam engines. Even if hardware tends to become a commodity over time, software seems, like music or poetry, to have infinite potential for innovation and malleability. True, it may have, answers Mr Carr, but what matters is not whether a nifty programmer can still come up with new and cool code, but how quickly any such program can be replicated by rival companies. Besides, today's reality in the software industry has nothing to do with poetry or music. Many companies are furious about the bug-ridden, pricey and over-engineered systems that they bought during the bubble era and are doing their best to switch to simple, off-the-shelf software, offered in 'enterprise-resource planning' packages and the like. If there is any customisation at all, it tends to be done by outside consultants, who are likely to share their favours with other clients.

But surely Mr Carr does not appreciate the impressive pipeline of new technologies that is about to hit the market – the wireless gadgets, the billions of tiny radio-frequency identity tags that will turn Aspirin bottles, shirt collars, refrigerator doors and almost everything else into smart machines, and so on? Those are impressive indeed, says Mr Carr. But again, the issue is whether they will be proprietary technologies or open infrastructures. And everything points to the latter.

This is not a debate for the ivory tower. Since IT can no longer be a source of strategic advantage, Mr Carr urges CIOs to spend less on their data-centres, to opt for cheaper commodity equipment wherever possible, to follow their rivals rather than trying to outdo them with fancy new systems, and to focus more on IT's vulnerabilities, from viruses to data theft, than on its opportunities. As it happens, CIOs have been taking exactly this approach for the past three years, and their bosses like it that way.

Source: 'Does IT matter?', *The Economist*, 1 April 2004

Questions

1 If all innovations are destined to become commodities, what is the incentive to innovate?

2 What is it about knowledge that makes it 'strategic' for the economy and for society but a mere commodity for firms?

3 How might a firm resist the move towards commoditization of its intellectual property?

14.4 Knowledge embedded in routines[4]

Routines are the organizational processes that form the basis for a firm's strategy (Teece et al., 1997; Eisenhardt and Martin, 2000). They encompass the routines, competences and capabilities of the firm that shape its development in the long run. This approach shifts the focus of attention from the market-positioning view to a more micro-analytic approach that aims to go even deeper than the resource-based view, aiming to understand the way in which competitive advantage is actually developed (Johnson and Bowman, 1999). Our interest here is in the routinized elements of strategy

---

[4] The approach adopted in this section owes much to Menuhin (2001) and Menuhin and McGee (2003).

making. This is well grounded in the literature (March and Simon, 1958; Nelson and Winter, 1982; Cyert and March, 1963; and Teece et al., 1997).

Less well known and certainly less commonly cited is the long-standing preoccupation of economists with evolution.[5] Veblen (1898, p. 397) talks about *the process of cumulative change*. Marshall used the term *economic biology* and argued that '*the key-note is that of dynamics rather than statics*' (Marshall, 1920, p. xiv). These represent early arguments about economic evolution. Although economists have spent considerable time developing the neoclassical theory of the firm (a poorly chosen term for a theory of markets), the notion of *evolutionary economics* has gained considerable momentum. Some of the impetus for this derived from the long controversies about *marginalism*.[6] This led to the breaking open of the black box that was the firm in traditional micro-economics and the onset of the new theory of the firm. The essence of this is to throw light on the internal organization of the firm. Whereas the traditional theory is concerned with prices and output, the new theory is interested in how transactions are organized. The intellectual progress of this strand of economics is marked by Coase's (1937, 1988) path-breaking paper on the nature of the firm, new approaches to understanding the nature of ownership bringing in property rights (Alchian and Demsetz, 1972) and agency costs (Jensen and Meckling, 1976), and Williamson's transaction cost economics (1985, 1987). Coase anticipated all of this, pointing out that the essential differentiating feature of intrafirm transactions, as opposed to interfirm transactions, is authority and hierarchy. This stream of thinking does reinforce the idea of 'efficiency management' – Williamson expressed it as the strategy of *economizing* (1981), and this has strong resonance with the idea of cost minimization from neoclassical theory. But, more important than this, it opens the door to ideas about the evolution of efficient organizational forms. Vronen (1995, p. 2) maintains that evolutionary economics is inspired by the new institutional economics. This examines processes through which institutions evolve (Langlois, 1986). Similarly, the sociologist Granovetter (1985, p. 488) argues that:

> *social institutions and arrangements previously thought to be the adventitious result of legal, historical, social or political forces are better viewed as the efficient solution to certain economic problems.*

Competitive pressures force firms to evolve towards the most efficient organizational forms. Although there are considerable debates about the precise forms and implications of this process, the selection argument is at the centre of evolutionary theory. Evolution is a form of organizational ecology where firms engage in behaviour that is routine rather than purposive. Adaptation takes place by mimicking the survivors, which may be accidentally well adapted. Managers get little credit in this view. Quinn (1978) describes this as *logical incrementalism* in which minor changes in strategy take place as a response to changes in the external environment in an evolutionary and adaptive manner.

Nelson and Winter's (1982) approach (drawing heavily on Winter, 1964) argues that selection is not an ad hoc or involuntary response, but is systematic and purposeful firm behaviour. They advocate collections of routines based on *tacit knowledge* supplemented by organized search behaviour for modifications or substitutes. This allowed for the evolution of economic thinking (over many decades) to map on to the newer thinking from management theorists attempting to understand and map organizational processes. The essential link is the purposive behaviour of

---

[5] This is described and analysed in great detail by Vronen (1995).

[6] See, for example, the anti-marginalist critique exemplified by the Oxford Research Group in the 1930s, especially Hall and Hitch (1939) and the American economist Lester (1946).

managers and we shall argue that this is characterized by asset and knowledge accumulation and by learning processes that allow knowledge to be transformed from a tacit to an explicit form (Nonaka and Takeuchi, 1995). Thus we see Burgelman (1983) arguing that the intellectual basis for activist and explicit roles for top managers is based on complex organizations that are subject to both evolutionary and planned processes. Nelson and Winter introduced us to evolutionary economics but much is owed to Simon (1955, 1959) with his seminal concepts of *satisficing* and *bounded rationality* and Penrose's (1959) theory of the growth of the firm. Although Nelson and Winter's tone is somewhat hostile to traditional economics, their approach can be seen as a rehabilitation of the theory of the firm by providing (far more) realistic assumptions. They shift attention to the firm's internal organization where organizational routines regularly and automatically make 'decisions' based on the knowledge and best practice embedded in those routines. The argument for routines that make 'good decisions' is based on two points: one, a Darwinian natural selection process at an organizational level that ensures that only the 'best' routines are kept in operation and, two, on an adaptive feedback mechanism at the individual level that permits new knowledge to be accessed and then diffused through the organization to be eventually embedded in routines. Routines are thus embodiments of organizational memory – better called organizational genetics.

The evolutionary approach is saved from ecological sterility by the learning process (based on Simon). Through this we can see the essential elements and characteristics of a **knowledge-based view** (KBV) starting to take shape: tacit versus explicit knowledge; relative roles of individuals, groups and organizations; sourcing and accessing of knowledge; transfer and integration of knowledge (note the classic formulation by Nonaka and Takeuchi, 1995).

14.5 A knowledge-based view (KBV)

At this point, we have reviewed three different perspectives on knowledge in strategy and in strategy making: knowledge as assets for protection, knowledge through innovation and knowledge embedded in routines. We examine the concept of knowledge through learning later on in this chapter. The KBV approach argues that knowledge is embedded in individuals and through complex organizational processes is socialized and reintegrated into the organization at large. The key questions to be addressed are the following:

- Do these various perspectives on knowledge enable us to articulate a *knowledge-based view of strategy* whose implications allow us to draw inferences about strategy and strategy making that are either absent from other theories or in contradiction to them?
- What are the essential ingredients of the knowledge-based view?

14.5.1 Organizational knowledge and the theory of the firm

Grant (1996) and Spender (1996) see the firm as an institution for integrating knowledge, where knowledge is individually held and is typically tacit. The organization's role is to access, transfer and integrate that tacit knowledge within and throughout the organization. This approach is similar to that of Nonaka and Takeuchi (1995). The firm is viewed as a coordinating mechanism, with implications for organizational design and for the nature of organizational process. Spender sees knowledge as too contentious a concept to easily bear the weight of a theory. The biggest problem, he sees, is the multitude of types and definitions. He therefore argues (as Grant does implicitly) for a pluralistic viewpoint and advances the idea of interplay between explicit and tacit knowledge, and between different units within the organization (from individuals through to collectives). This leads to a set of ideal types (see Figure 14.3). He moves from this to knowledge as activity and argues

	Individual	Social
Explicit	Conscious	Objectified
Implicit	Automatic	Collective

Figure 14.3 Different types of organizational knowledge
Source: Spencer (1996)

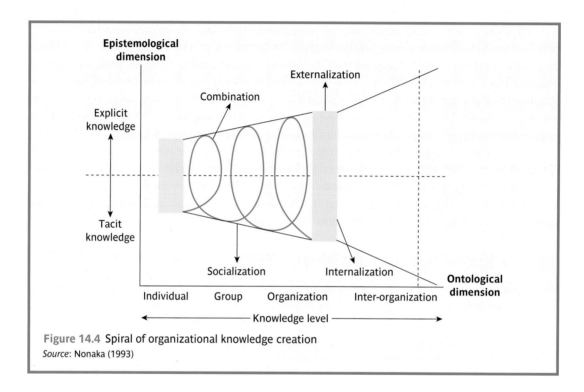

Figure 14.4 Spiral of organizational knowledge creation
Source: Nonaka (1993)

eventually for a Penrosian view – a historical, path-dependent process in which the individual rather than organizational machine bureaucracies are the important strategists. It is useful to start with Spender's view that our concepts of knowledge are highly varied and in many ways inconsistent or incapable of being interrelated:

> *Knowledge is a highly contentious concept, far too problematic to bear the weight of a useful theory of the firm without a clear statement of the epistemology which gives it meaning.* (Spender, 1996, p. 48)

He then proceeds by making three points:

1 Knowledge is the interplay between the *tacit/implicit* and the *explicit*, the vertical dimension in Figure 14.4.

2 This distinction allows for several different *adaptation mechanisms* – for example, Nelson and Winter's own use of adaptive feedback mechanisms where the interplay between tacit and explicit takes place through individual choices that are eventually embedded in organizational routines ('organizational genetics').

3 Many theorists, starting with Polanyi (1966) and Nonaka and Takeuchi (1995), see the origin of all knowledge in individual intuition. So the third element is the transformation and communication of what is known tacitly by individuals into collective or social knowledge. Hence the second, horizontal dimension in Figure 14.4.

Therefore, Spender advances four ideal types connected by an adaptation mechanism. He observes that the organizational intent is to transform tacit, individual knowledge into collectively owned, objectifiable knowledge – this is the world of standards, procedures, practices, patents, science, training, but still recognizably a world that remains dependent on the knowledge held by individuals, although, in this diagram, the adaptation mechanisms of transformation and conversion process are ignored. Given different types of knowledge, Spender questions whether there are different types of knowledge-based theory. For example, a theory of *conscious* knowledge would have to solve agency problems – how can inventors be persuaded to pass on their codified knowledge to an organization? A theory based on *automatic* knowledge also has agency problems, where the brilliant man must be persuaded to stay with the firm (perhaps through work-out clauses for entrepreneurs when they sell their businesses). A theory of *objectified* knowledge raises problems of imitability in a world where knowledge is explicit. A theory based on inherently immobile *collective* knowledge (the preferred end-point of Nonaka and Takeuchi's and Nelson and Winter's theories) leads to a conclusion that this is the most secure and strategically significant kind of organizational knowledge.

Nonaka and Takeuchi's knowledge spiral (Figure 14.4) pre-dates Spender's model by some three years. Their arena (matrix) has become a standard framework of its kind. Their focus is on a *knowledge spiral*, an adaptation mechanism through which knowledge is converted and then transferred between the tacit and the explicit (it can go either way) and among individuals, groups and the whole organization.

- *Socialization* is the sharing of experiences so that tacit knowledge is shared between individuals, from individuals to the organization through the development of culture and shared mental models, and from the organization to individuals.
- *Externalization* is the conversion of tacit into explicit knowledge through its articulation and systematization within the organization.
- *Combination* involves the conversion of explicit knowledge held by individuals and groups into explicit knowledge at the organizational level, and subsequent conversion of organizational knowledge back to the individual in a different form. This is the key role of information systems within the firm.
- *Internalization* is conversion of explicit knowledge back into tacit knowledge in the form of individual know-how and organizational routines.

The *knowledge spiral* is, therefore, the dynamic process by which knowledge is translated through separate but related stages, through socialization to combination and externalization, and back to internalization. Thus, individual creativity can be linked to the growth of collective knowledge.[7] Spender's contribution relates to the different types of organizational knowledge whereas Takeuchi and Nonaka use the same intellectual space to portray the adaptation mechanisms that organizations can use to convert and transfer various kinds of knowledge to inimitable and therefore rent-earning organizational knowledge.

---

[7] We are indebted to Rob Grant for this articulation of Nonaka and Takeuchi's model.

14.5.2 From value chain to value web

The value chain, popular for its simple and robust character, can be restated firstly in the language of core competences and the RBV but more fundamentally in this language of knowledge. This characterization restates the linear chain of activities as a similar chain of core competences. The activities of the value chain might be dispersed across different owners but in any event they are controlled in economic terms through the operation of core competences. Thus economic power is operated through the conjunction and interaction of core competences. However, the linearity of the chain metaphor is uncomfortable where the empirical record suggests that knowledge is multifaceted and capable of being attached to other pieces of knowledge in a variety of expected and unexpected ways, particularly as interface standards are developed and 'knowledge as Lego' becomes more and more possible.

The notion of a web is intuitively appealing (Figure 14.5). At the centre is the *corporate glue* (McGee, 2003), that is, the organizationally held tacit knowledge that cannot readily be imitated – the *collective knowledge* according to Spender, and the *knowledge architecture* according to Henderson and Clark (1990). This is characteristically a collective concept but also a tacit and sticky concept, meaning that the organization can be readily and sustainably differentiated by it. This corporate glue supports and is supported by a set of core competences within which elements of objectifiable knowledge may be evident.[8] These are reinforced by closely held partnerships with other organizations where the ability to control the agency costs becomes really important. More remotely managed are the subcontract relationships where market contracting suffices. The value of the web is a framework within which the *activity sets* formerly given pride of place in the value chain are now replaced by *knowledge concepts*.

Inherent in a knowledge-based view of strategy (and also in an economist's concept of a knowledge production function) are three key linkages between:

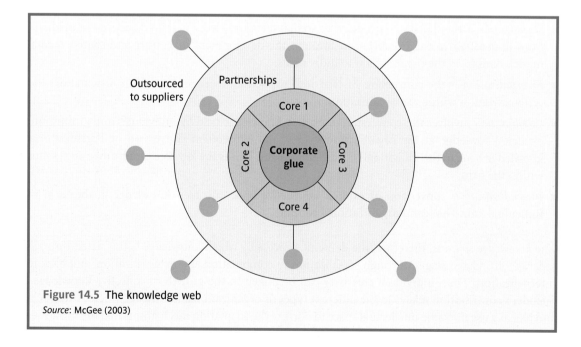

Figure 14.5 The knowledge web
Source: McGee (2003)

---

[8] An alternative description would be to describe the corporate glue as supported by elements of objectifiable knowledge and the conjunction of the two being core competence. This has the merit of defining core competence explicitly in terms of knowledge concepts.

1 knowledge as assets;

2 knowledge embedded in processes; and

3 the pathways to competitive advantage.

According to the Teece et al. (1997) discussion of dynamic capabilities, there are four knowledge processes:

1 entrepreneurial (creative);

2 coordinative and integrative (static);

3 learning (dynamic); and

4 reconfigurational (transformational).

In asset or resource terms we see knowledge as embedded in many different classes of assets such as technology, complementary, financial, reputational, structural, institutional, and market structure. For example, Amit and Schoemaker (1993) provide an excellent description (see Chapter 6) of strategic assets and their linkage to organizational rent (competitive advantage). Following but not replicating Teece et al. (1997), we express the linkages to competitive advantage in terms of *dynamic pathways*. Whereas Amit and Schoemaker (1993) and Peteraf (1993) only assert that assets create profit possibilities, in this approach the dynamic pathways are defined in terms of path dependency (which allows us to call on an evolutionary perspective) and technological opportunities (which allows for returns to scale,[9] first/early-mover advantage, and oligopolistic gaming). The strength of this approach lies in its organizational inclusivity, ranging from internal process to asset positions, linked over time through management of the pathways. Empirical evidence here is patchy but attracting increasing research interest. In summary, this approach includes entrepreneurial (creative) processes and a more explicit characterization of linkages of knowledge to competitive advantage as dynamic pathways.

14.5.3 A knowledge-based view of strategy?

This approach enables us to see that there are elements of knowledge that can be related to sustainable competitive advantage. These knowledge concepts lie deeply embedded behind the well-known notions of strategic positioning and the resource-based view and are powerful in that they, in a fundamental sense, are the drivers behind core competences and competitive advantage. So, is it possible to draw this thinking together into a perspective that we might call the knowledge-based view of strategy? Our approach is to suggest three categories (Figure 14.6) called specific knowledge, organizational knowledge, and the knowledge web.[10]

Specific knowledge (Figure 14.7) relates to the knowledge production function and draws links between knowledge, production, access to knowledge, knowledge diffusion, connections between elements of knowledge, and knowledge renewal (including the discarding of knowledge). The foundations of this are highly dispersed throughout the academic literature. There is a considerable economic literature on innovation competition and on R&D. There is a considerable scientific and social science literature on innovation processes. There is also some considerable mystery about creativity, usually captured under the heading of serendipity.

---

[9] Especially network externalities where 'winner takes all' strategies are possible; McGee and Sammut Bonnici (2002a, 2002b), summarized in Chapter 12.

[10] Alternatively knowledge in action.

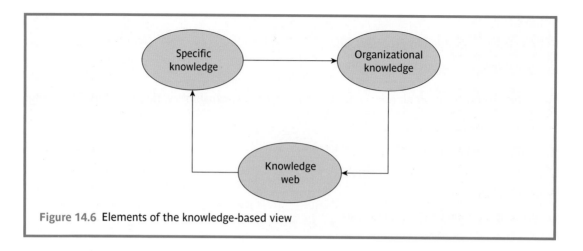

Figure 14.6 Elements of the knowledge-based view

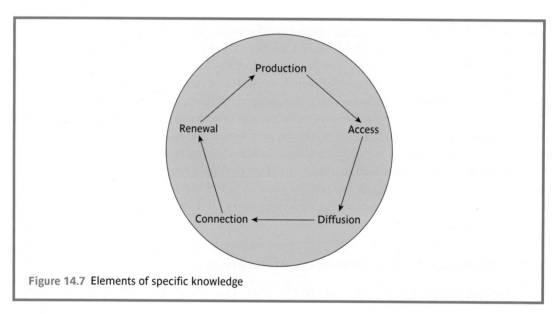

Figure 14.7 Elements of specific knowledge

Organizational knowledge (Figure 14.8) is the process by which various elements of specific knowledge are taken into the organization, transformed into social/collective knowledge and, through dynamic pathways, linked into other organizational activities. The key elements are characterized as types of organization knowledge, the knowledge creation process, and dynamic pathways. The inheritance from such writers as Spender, Takeuchi and Nonaka, and Teece et al. is self-evident.

The knowledge web (see Figure 14.5) represents the way in which specific knowledge and organizational knowledge are captured into value-creating activities within the firm (discussed above) (see also Winter, 1987 for an earlier exposition of this point). Both specific and organizational knowledge feed into the knowledge web. The notion of corporate glue or knowledge architecture stems directly from the conjunction of tacit and social knowledge. But specific knowledge is also evident from its role within core competences and within the core competences of strategic partners. The knowledge web is also dynamic in that incentives to innovate and to create new linkages between knowledge components are created here and therefore provide the link back to the knowledge production function that is captured within the category of specific knowledge.

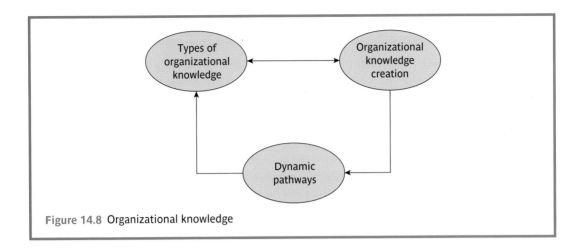

Figure 14.8 Organizational knowledge

This approach allows us to connect three strands. The first concerns the ways in which knowledge is produced, accessed, diffused, renewed and discarded. The second concerns the notion of organizational knowledge as an essentially invisible asset fostered and conditioned by visible and defined organizational routines and ad hoc processes. The third is a strategic theory of the firm in which positioning and resource-based approaches are recast in the form of knowledge.[11] Again, knowledge is the invisible asset but captured here in the form of specific activities on which management focuses attention.

Our treatment of the knowledge-based view raises some additional interesting and important questions. We suggest the following list.

1 *How is knowledge produced and accessed?* This includes the imponderable of 'knowledge creation' as well as 'knowledge conversion' (a word used by Grant, 1996 and by Nonaka, 1994 and has a parallel to the economists' idea of a production function). We know more about the processes of innovation and we also know quite a lot about the economic analysis of new technology decisions.

2 *How does knowledge fit into supply chain and value chain thinking?* In other words, how does it link and coordinate with the other activities of the firm to produce competitive advantage? The knowledge web is a useful framework but much needs to be done to identify the specifics in actual cases and applications.

3 *How do pieces of knowledge connect up?* How do they change the nature of the corporate 'glue' – the integrative strategic architecture? The burgeoning function of knowledge management within knowledge-intensive organizations perhaps reflects these considerations.

4 *What difference does any of this make for the analysis of strategic decisions such as diversification and acquisition?* Does this have anything to contribute to economists' thinking about increasing returns industries where the 'new economy' appears to be challenging basic assumptions behind traditional thinking (see McGee and Sammut-Bonnici, 2002a, 2002b, and the discussion in Chapter 7)? These are not simply criteria for shaping and assessing a theory but they are also conjectures. They are conjectures about the nature of knowledge itself, whether such a multifaceted concept can be marshalled into the constraints inherent in a normative, organizationally focused theory.

---

[11] A link here could be made with Rumelt (1984) by developing the argument that our use of knowledge as corporate glue is directly analogous to his use of isolating mechanisms.

Case box 14.4: **Innovation at Apple: the iPod**

Innovation is about much more than new products. It is about reinventing business processes and building entirely new markets that meet untapped customer needs. As the internet and globalization widen the pool of new ideas, innovation is about selecting and executing the right ideas and bringing them to market in record time.

About 10 years ago music was becoming digitally accessible to the masses and there was a company (Napster) that allowed free downloads, but Apple had no jukebox software for managing digital music. To catch up with this revolution, Apple licensed the SoundJam MP music player from a small company and hired its programmer, Jeff Robbin. Robbin spent several months revamping SoundJam to create iTunes. While Robbin was working on iTunes, Jobs and his team started looking for gadget opportunities which could play music. Existing digital music players were either too large or small and useless (slow, limited storage with short battery life). Most were based on fairly small memory chips, either 32 or 64 MB, which stored only a few dozen songs, which was similar to the existing portable CD player.

Apple's team were convinced they could solve most of the problems of the Nomad (the best digital music player on the market at the time). The Nomad 'Jukebox' was manufactured in Singapore. Its FireWire connector could transfer songs from the computer to player quickly (a CD in a few seconds or a library of MP3s in minutes). In addition, because of the rapidly growing cell phone industry, new batteries and displays were constantly coming to market.

In February 2001 Rubinstein visited Toshiba, Apple's supplier of hard drives, where he was shown a tiny drive the company had just developed. The drive was 1.8 inches in diameter (most others were 2.5-inch and larger) but Toshiba didn't have any clear ideas what its application might be other than thinking of perhaps putting it in a small notebook. This was what Rubinstein needed. Rubinstein said to Steve Jobs that he now knew how to build a music player. He had all the parts. The iPod was now ready to be designed.

Its impact on the world was significant. People previously used to read, sleep and talk to each other. All of that changed with the iPod. At eight ounces you could carry around all of your music in a box less than half the size of a CD player. Headphones became commonplace in virtually all public spaces. In particular, trains, buses and aeroplanes were suddenly full of people listening to music. Earphones were more common than books or newspapers on commuter runs. The iPod was a dramatic success. Building on the success and technology of the iPod, Apple then came out with the iPhone and people then had most of the capability of a computer in a piece of plastic which would easily slip into their pocket. The iPhone provides music, a camera, pictures, phone, texting, internet, weather, GPS-enabled maps, and there is more to come.

To launch the iPod, Apple had to network (create a novel agreement among music companies to sell their songs online via iTunes), to create a new business model (songs sold very cheaply online), to create strong branding (the iPod became an almost instant icon) and to integrate different technologies into one product. People love the iPod, but it is often overlooked that the iTunes software platform turned an otherwise novel MP3 player into a huge innovation success. The combination of these two factors created significant success for the iPod. The success of the iMac, iPod and iTunes has revived the company's reputation for product innovation among investors, resulting in the company's rapid stock increase (from $16/share in 2003 to $68/share in 2005 to $210/share in 2010). One lesson is that if you hope to turn a company around, focus first on making quality products and then the rest will be easier to manage.

Source: compiled by David C. Wilson

Questions

1 How would you describe Apple's approach to innovation?

2 Why did the iPod succeed so well?

3 How is Apple an example of a knowledge web?

14.6 Routines and learning

We now turn to an examination of how an organization can achieve growth through learning and through knowledge absorption. In this section we move from the previous theoretical perspectives on knowledge, to learning and the accumulation of knowledge organizationally. Nelson and Winter's second set of routines are those that determine the long-run changes in the firm's stock of capital – hence they are called *strategizing routines*. Attention has been paid to the contribution of planning and budgeting processes to the accumulation of fixed assets over time. But more central to our argument are the product and technology development processes. For example, Henderson and Clark (1990) developed the concept of *architectural knowledge* explaining how the dominant organizational design '*incorporates a range of choices about the design that are not revisited in every subsequent design*' (1990, p. 15). They go on to link this architectural knowledge to the development of innovation processes.

Strategizing routines contribute to strategy and strategy making as they store the firm's experience in such a way that it can be used in a new context (for example, consultants such as McKinsey and Bain discuss how they develop experience libraries of problems and problem solutions through their ongoing consulting activities). They channel the structure of decision-making processes into the type of behaviour that has brought success in the past. But such routines have a negative side.

However, over time as the environment changes, new forms of organization become appropriate and gaps emerge between environmental requirements and existing capabilities. These gaps cause routines to become dysfunctional (Teece et al., 1997; Leonard-Barton, 1992) and inhibit future development of the firm (Levitt and March, 1988; Henderson and Clark, 1990; Leonard-Barton, 1992; Teece et al., 1997; Collinson and Wilson, 2006). Creating new routines requires organizations to learn.

Case box 14.5: Inertia in organizations through routines

Japanese organizations, previously held to be the foundations of innovation, change and flexibility, can equally contain significant barriers to change, innovation and adaptation in turbulent economic environments. In a study of two leading Japanese firms, these firms displayed specific weaknesses in the ways in which they integrate and bundle knowledge, in particular around their research and development (R&D) functions. Despite the adoption of strategies of technological innovation and internationalization, the pursuit of both strategies was beset by barriers of inertia. Embedded internal network connections and knowledge-sharing routines between central R&D and other divisions were inappropriate for the revised strategy. Existing external connections, with preferred suppliers and customers within *keiretsu* structures, and close relationships with existing R&D partners retarded these firms' strategic flexibility. Because these organizations had a limited variety of latent routines, knowledge, capabilities and agency to draw on when needed, they had limited levels of organizational responsiveness and high levels of path-dependency and inertia. Routines became dysfunctional. Knowledge transfer by routines must balance utilizing current knowledge with developing new knowledge (learning) or the firm will ossify.

Source: adapted from Collinson and Wilson (2006)

14.6.1 Organizational learning

Garvin (1993) defines a learning organization as one able to create, acquire and transfer knowledge and to change its behaviour to reflect new knowledge. Organizational learning involves experimentation, creative moments, learning from experience as well as best practice and transferring knowledge quickly and efficiently throughout the organization. However, as Senge (1990, p. 285) argues:

> *Human beings are designed for learning ... children come fully equipped with an insatiable drive to explore and experiment. Unfortunately, the primary institutions of our society are oriented predominantly toward controlling rather than learning, rewarding individuals for performing for others rather than for cultivating their natural curiosity and impulse to learn.*

Here, Senge is pointing out two important aspects of learning:

- Learning can be viewed from different levels of analysis, ranging from individual learning to organizational learning.
- Organizations appear rather less adept at learning than individuals.

Senge (1990) suggests that learning is both an *adaptive* process and a *generative* process:

- *Adaptive learning* describes the processes whereby an organization can adapt to its environment and to accelerating or decelerating rates of change. Adaptive learning can thus best be described as the processes organizations engage in to cope with changing external conditions. But the learning process is much deeper than a desire to respond and adapt to external changes. Such responses may render an organization more efficient or effective in the short term, but cannot generate increased or new capabilities – the bedrock of innovation and creativity. Only generative learning can provide this.
- *Generative learning* requires new ways of looking at the world, whether this involves making sense of the external environment or in understanding how to manage internal business processes better. Such learning is important for the visionary aspects of strategy formulation. To achieve new ideas, an organization needs to develop its capacity for strategic thinking, which is the generative (or creative) learning to which Senge refers. However, in order to understand an organization's capacity to implement strategy as well as to formulate it (thinking and acting strategically) it is necessary to engage and develop both adaptive and generative learning.

These two types of learning originate from what Argyris and Schön (1987) termed single and double-loop learning. This has been variously referred to in the literature as first- and second-order learning, exploitation and exploration, or convergence and reorientation (see Table 14.5). When learning enables the organization to carry out its present activities and goals without disturbing existing cultural values and norms, it is termed *single-loop learning*. Single-loop learning is important for increasing effectiveness in implementing strategy because it ensures that the organization is becoming better at undertaking its existing strategies. In the terminology of Peters and Waterman (1982), this form of learning helps an organization to 'stick to the knitting'. Single-loop learning is embodied in the experience curve of an organization. The more experience a firm has of an activity, the greater its efficiency and effectiveness become *in that activity*.

Single-loop learning does not expose an organization to new activities or new ways of conceptualizing old activities. When learning involves modification of an organization's underlying cultural values, assumptions and norms, it is termed *double-loop learning*. In terms of complexity, single-loop learning is relatively simple to achieve while double-loop learning is far more complex. This is because individuals are constrained by their mental models to identify familiar patterns for solving problems. As existing patterns are within the managerial 'comfort zone' of tacit knowledge and experience, this occurs even when the problem is significantly different and requires new solutions. The longer an organization has been using an existing set of practices, the harder it is to

Table 14.5 Theories and approaches to organizational learning

Learning type (key authors)	Definitions/key words	Advantages	Disadvantages
Adaptive (Senge, 1990) Single loop (Argyris and Schön, 1987) First order (Lant and Mezias, 1992) Exploitation (March, 1991) Convergence (Tushman and Romanelli, 1985)	Increases effectiveness Incremental adaptation Refinement Efficiency Implementation Execution Stability Routine Conservative	Increases familiarity with existing strategy and routines Improves short-run effectiveness Improves capacity to make decisions and act Enhances strategy implementation	Provides a barrier to conceptualizing new ways of evaluating strategies Becomes rigid and resistant to change May result in performance downturn in the long term
Generative (Senge, 1990) Double loop (Argyris and Schön, 1987) Second order (Lant and Mezias, 1992) Exploration (March, 1991) Reorientation (Tushman and Romanelli, 1985)	Expanding capabilities New paradigms Reflexivity Exploring alternatives Discontinuity Risk taking Experimentation Flexibility Discovery Innovation	Encourages creative thinking Improves flexibility and speed in changed environments Associated with innovation and redefining products/markets Prevents long-run myopia	Risky, new ventures have potential to fail Difficult to 'manage' In excess, can lead to dilution of distinctive competences

Source: adapted from Jarzabowski (2004)

conceptualize new ways of doing things. Thus, paradoxically, single-loop learning, which involves existing mental models, is necessary for improving efficiency and effectiveness in existing strategic practices, but poses a barrier to developing new ways of learning.

Double-loop learning may occur when a change in strategy is so difficult to implement that it exposes the problems in existing practices, causing fundamental changes in the way the organization approaches strategic problems. Senge (1990) provides a classic example of this at Shell. Realizing 'that they had failed to change behaviour in much of the Shell organization', Group Planning set about altering the mental models of managers. They developed tools, such as scenario planning, to encourage managers to envision alternative futures. In this way, managers learned flexibility in their current practices. Using scenarios, they could work backwards from a series of anticipated futures to change the practices in the current organization. The capacity to learn enabled Shell to be more responsive than its competitors to changes in the political environment, such as the development of OPEC.

However, for many organizations, the gap between efficient current practices, which involve single-loop learning, and the capacity to double-loop learn, that is, to create viable futures, is exposed only during a performance downturn. An organization needs to engage in both types of learning; single-loop learning to improve familiarity with existing practices, aiding strategy implementation, and double-loop learning to encourage exploration of new opportunities. A firm that can manage to encompass both has the capacity for continuous learning, thus potentially improving performance and avoiding crisis.

14.6.2 Learning and communities of practice

Learning in organizations is argued to occur continuously in individuals and in the groups in which those individuals interact. Such groups are called *communities of practice* because they involve people participating in the actual practices of work (Brown and Duguid, 1991). The practice of work may not mirror the formally documented rules and regulations by which work is supposed to occur. In practice, people innovate and experiment with ways of getting the job done more easily or more efficiently, or may improvise because the existing rules (organizationally codified procedures) fail to provide them with sufficient information to get the task done. The immediate work community provides a learning context because people tell each other stories about work and they share information and concepts through the social processes of the group.

Such learning is occurring at the peripheries of the organization all the time and may be extremely valuable to the firm. However, its value and its occurrence can easily be overlooked in the wider organizational context for two reasons. First, it occurs at the margins or peripheries where the specific task is located; therefore, it is not within the 'mainstream' of organizational activities. Second, since such practices do not always mirror the formal descriptions of how to act, they may be suppressed in discussion with supervisors or senior managers. Indeed, the community may not see itself as a valuable learning resource, simply regarding itself as a group of people who help each other.

Wenger and Snyder (2000) suggest that communities of practice are a means of helping to drive the emergent properties of strategy and help to surface organizational innovation. Members of a community learn through participation in tasks together, transferring practices, ideas and concepts about the work process. As they do so, the individuals in the group increase their own knowledge and skill base, creating a virtuous circle of enlarging knowledge at the individual and group level. Such communities provide particular benefit where they bring together individuals with different skills and backgrounds. Wenger and Snyder (2000) argue that communities of practice can be cultivated by providing a fertile environment. They suggest that managers can:

- identify potential communities of practice that will enhance the company's strategic capabilities;
- provide the infrastructure that will support such communities and enable them to apply their expertise effectively;
- use non-traditional methods to assess the value of a community of practice.

In order to bring the work of communities from the periphery into the mainstream of organizational information flows, they need to be given legitimacy. Communities need to be given resources, such as IT support and reward structures that create incentives for collaboration, if they are to be recognized as important to the strategic development of the company. American Management Systems (AMS) has managed this through a formalized system of sponsoring communities. Recognizing that they were losing their capacity to leverage knowledge due to their rapid growth during a period of global development, AMS encouraged business units to nominate 'thought leaders'. The company paid for up to three weeks of the leaders' time each year to be devoted to developing communities of practice in strategic areas. Community membership is seen as a privilege for people recognized as experts by their business units. The communities are actively involved in developing knowledge-creating projects for which they are funded. An annual conference brings together all the communities of practice to share knowledge across the organization. In this way, communities of practice are recognized, given resources and perceived as prestigious because their work is important to the company. Many companies do not have such formal processes for developing and recognizing communities, but they may, nonetheless, provide senior management support for informal groups that arise.

One company that does have formal processes for developing communities of practice is 3M, illustrated in Case box 14.6. Over 50 years ago, 3M's CEO William McKnight argued that, 'As our business grows, it becomes increasingly necessary to delegate responsibility and to encourage men and women to exercise their initiative. Mistakes will be made, but if a person is essentially right, the mistakes he or she makes are not as serious in the long run as the mistakes management will make if it is dictatorial and undertakes to tell those under its authority exactly how they must do their jobs.' 3M's response to this was the establishment of independent R&D efforts known as 'skunkworks'.[12] Time and resources could be appropriated from the company in order to experiment and try out new products. The development of the 'Post-It' Note was an example of a product which resulted from such experimentation. The glue initially developed for another application did not stick. It failed all the sheer and adhesion tests which 3M applied to judge the quality of an adhesive. Yet the skunk team (a community of practice) saw an application for this 'poor' adhesive and produced the 'Post-It' Note which became one of 3M's most successful products.

Case box 14.6: 3M's seven pillars of innovation

3M may be 104 years old, but the company churns out cutting-edge products like a brash new startup. Here are the secrets of its success. After more than a century in business, it would be understandable for a company to run out of fresh ideas. But 3M is still at it, at age 104. The manufacturing conglomerate, an abrasives maker that broke out by inventing masking tape in 1925, is introducing new products as if it were a startup.

The latest: Post-it Picture Paper. Rolled out nationally this spring, the product marries the adhesives of 3M's iconic sticky notes with photo paper so consumers can print digital snapshots at home and slap them up on the fridge or any other flat surface. Moreover, the company already is testing its next Post-It extension: stickable index cards. 'The innovation machine remains strong,' observes analyst Mark Gulley of Soleil Securities Group in New Canaan, Conn.

Indeed, 3M is third in this year's *BusinessWeek* ranking of the world's most innovative companies, based on a global survey of top executives. It finished second in 2005.

BREAKING IT DOWN. So how does an old company stay so inventive? Larry Wendling, vice-president of 3M's corporate research labs at its St. Paul (Minn.) campus, thinks he knows. In fact, Wendling, an engineer who joined 3M right out of graduate school in 1977, has boiled it down to a seven-point list. You might call it 'The Seven Habits of Highly Innovative Corporations.'

1 From the chief executive on down, the company must be committed to innovation. One sure way to show that is with money. In 2005, 3M spent $1.24 billion on research and development, or 6% of its $21.2 billion in revenue. That's an unusually high amount for an industrial manufacturer. And of that R&D outlay, a fifth went to basic research or pursuits that have no immediate practicality. 'If you're going to be an innovative company,' Wendling says, 'organic growth and new products have to be what drives the company.'

2 The corporate culture must be actively maintained. Though 3M has had a new CEO every five years on average over the past 40 years, the philosophy of William L. McKnight, its inspirational leader from 1929 to 1966, is passed along by old-timers like Wendling to every new scientist or engineer. In a nutshell: 'Hire good people and let them do their job in their own ways. And tolerate mistakes.' Newcomers also quickly learn the stories of how 3M developed the first audio tapes, for instance, or Scotchgard. Tribes and peoples keep their cultures alive through oral histories; so does 3M.

---

[12] The term skunk works originated in a satirical American comic strip 'Li'l Abner' in the 1950s. Li'l Abner Yokum was a hillbilly who lived in the mountains. In the mountains there was one man who ran the 'skunk works' skinning dead skunks Both he and his 'skunk works' were avoided because of the terrible smells. In the late 1950s, at the height of the Cold War, Lockheed set up a small group of highly skilled engineers to work on very secret projects. The head of this group named this group the 'Skunk Works' to describe their small size and their distance from the main body of engineering. They became famous for developing some of Lockheed's most radical and successful designs more quickly than anyone else in aeronautical history. Today, the term 'skunk works' is usually used for a small group of developers who are physically separated from the rest of the organization to work on special projects (in the hope of producing new and innovative products and services).

3 Innovation is impossible without a broad base of technology. For instance, 3M claims to have leading know-how in 42 diverse technologies. That allows researchers to take an idea from one realm and apply it to another. For example, 3M scientists have used a technology behind layered plastic lenses to make more durable abrasives, more reflective highway signs, and golf gloves that allow you to get a tighter grip without squeezing as hard. Companies that remained 'unidimensional,' as Wendling puts it, typically run out of ideas after their first success.

4 Talk, talk, talk. Management at 3M has long encouraged networking – formal and informal – among its researchers. Wendling calls this 3M's secret weapon. The scientists themselves formed an organization called the Technical Forum in 1951. It invites all of the company's 9,700 R&D personnel to an annual symposium, where everyone can see what everyone else is working on. Labs also host their own conferences and Webcasts and elect representatives to a governing body to set policy. The formal structure enables researchers to get to know one another informally, as well, so they know whom to call for advice or to team up with on a project.

5 Set individual expectations and reward employees for outstanding work. The folks who call themselves 3Mers take pride in discoveries that lead to real-world products. Management reinforces this by fostering a dual-career ladder so veteran researchers can continue to move up without becoming managers. It also honors hundreds of employees – nominated and selected by their peers – for scientific achievements every year. And it gives the top 20 overachievers and their spouses a four-day holiday at 3M's corporate retreat in Park Rapids, Minn.

6 Quantify efforts. 3M tallies how much of its revenue comes from products introduced in the past four years to judge whether its R&D money is being spent wisely. That way management can assess which lab is hitting its mark and which may be falling short. After reviewing its data, the company centralized basic research from 14 centers around the world to its headquarters campus in 2003.

7 Research must be tied to the customer. Employees spend a lot of time with customers to understand what their needs are so they can go back to the labs to come up with valuable products. The Post-It Photo Paper came out of such research. While digital photography is easy, 3M researchers learned that most people store their images on a computer, which means they might have to scroll through them all to find a particular shot. And if consumers do print out their favorites, they often stuff them in a drawer, where they're just as hard to find. The solution: Photos that are as easy to display as a Post-It Note.

Of course, results will vary. Still, Wendling says his points have made the difference at 3M. 'We do think innovation is more than an accident,' he says, 'and that you can create the environment for innovation by paying attention to these seven things.'

Source: Reprinted from 10 May 2006 issue of Bloomberg BusinessWeek by special permission, copyright © 2010 by Bloomberg L. P.

Questions

1 Review and understand 3M's approach to creating and developing innovation.

2 Is the Post-It Note the only example of creative innovation at 3M?

It is difficult to assess the value of a community of practice in terms of wider value of the organization. First, the outcome of a community of practice may not occur in a measurable way within the community itself, but in the work of the business units that surround the community. Second, since communities have informal processes, it is difficult to know whether innovative ideas are a result of the community or whether they may have occurred anyway. It is complex to evaluate the motivational, knowledge-sharing opportunities and outcomes that communities provide. Wenger and Snyder (2000) suggest that senior managers need to listen to the *stories* arising from communities of practice to understand how such communities provide value. They note that AMS, which has formal processes for developing and recognizing communities, conducts an annual 'audit' of such stories. An analysis of a sample of stories revealed that the communities had saved the company between $2 million and $5 million and increased revenue by more than $13 million in one year. Other companies, such as Shell, recognize the value of communities' stories as learning resources for the wider organization, publishing them in internal newsletters and reports.

14.6.3 Learning and all that jazz

The jazz metaphor has gained considerable ground over the last decade. The metaphor has been used to help describe the processes by which organizations learn. Improvisation (spontaneous composition) is an essential element of jazz music. Jazz employs in a sense a retrospective method. This means allowing for errors, haphazard elements, and some degree of formlessness (Gioia, 1998). Jazz improvisation also has a sense of looking forward. Berliner (1994, p. 362) quotes the musician Lee Konitz:

> *I want to relate to the bass player and the piano player and the drummer . . . the goal is always to relate as fully as possible to every sound that everyone is making . . . but whew! It's very difficult for me to achieve.*

Improvisation is a form of knowledge transfer which involves learning by looking backward and forward. Projecting into the future, however, relies on retrospective sense making:

> *The improviser may be unable to look ahead at what he is going to play, but he can look behind at what he has just played; thus each new musical phrase can be shaped with relation to what has gone before. He creates his form retrospectively.* (Gioia, 1998, p. 61)

The demands on organizations are for them to be flexible, adaptable to change, to be networked and to learn. Hence the jazz metaphor has a degree of appropriateness for analysing learning in networks, temporary alliances and partnerships which characterize much of modern organizational life. The basic idea is that interrelating all organizational activities at once, especially in strategic decision making, is impossible, so adopting the techniques of improvisation may help since these involve retaining some elements of structural stability (the melody, for example) with experimental flexibility as improvisation takes place (Weick, 1989; Eisenhardt, 1997; Crossan, 1998; Hatch, 1998, 1999; Hatch and Weick, 1998; Kamoche and Cunha, 2001; Kamoche et al., 2002).

Other relevant aspects from the jazz metaphor include the eclectic pool of knowledge from which jazz musicians draw (ranging from classical to blues music) and the often surprising results which emerge from connections made across this spectrum. There are obvious links to innovation here. There is also learning as new harmonies, melodic structures and rhythms are created. Jazz deliberately creates spaces for innovation and change in what may at first seem to be established structures. Finally, the jazz metaphor allows the exploration of diversified roles which individuals can adopt in teams, in particular knowing when to lead (solo) and when to take a back seat and play a supporting role.

14.7 Summary

Knowledge is a central element of the resource-based view. Dynamic theories of the firm cannot operate without some clear and operational concepts of knowledge. However, knowledge is a highly contentious concept. For example: know-how versus know-what; explicit versus implicit; individual versus collective; knowledge as knowing, as learning, as activity all serve to make precise definitions elusive. Nevertheless, the applicability of knowledge as a significant explanatory variable may be supported empirically; for example, see the wide range of citations in Eisenhardt and Santos (2002). The writing on organizational knowledge has shown it as the lynchpin between internal organizational structures and processes and the capture of economic rents. More controversially, there is a case for an evolutionary theory incorporating dynamic pathways as the external manifestation of organizational knowledge.

The approach in this chapter has not been to attempt to provide 'a unified theory of absolutely everything'.[13] Rather, we have attempted to find a way of incorporating knowledge variables into the explanation of the long-run performance of firms, their long-run sustainable competitive advantages. To do this we offer a simple categorization that links three types of literature: on specific knowledge (a dispersed literature), on organizational knowledge (which made considerable progress in the 1990s), and on organizational learning. In many ways, this approach mirrors the 'holographic design' model of Morgan (1997, p. 100) where the qualities of the whole are enfolded in all the constituent parts. In this way, the organization can be seen as a system or web in which it can self-organize, learn and regenerate on a continuous basis. Figure 14.9 summarizes this approach to the learning organization.

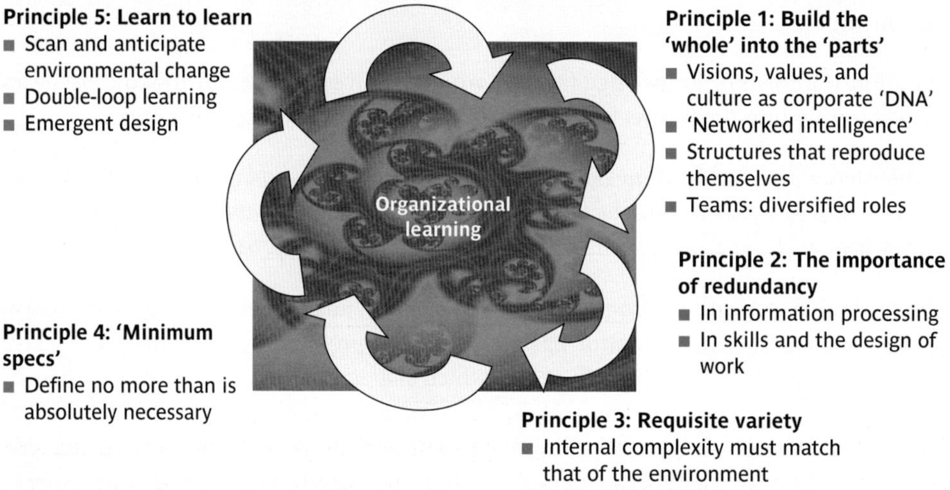

Principle 5: Learn to learn
- Scan and anticipate environmental change
- Double-loop learning
- Emergent design

Principle 4: 'Minimum specs'
- Define no more than is absolutely necessary

Organizational learning

Principle 1: Build the 'whole' into the 'parts'
- Visions, values, and culture as corporate 'DNA'
- 'Networked intelligence'
- Structures that reproduce themselves
- Teams: diversified roles

Principle 2: The importance of redundancy
- In information processing
- In skills and the design of work

Principle 3: Requisite variety
- Internal complexity must match that of the environment

Figure 14.9 A systemic view of organizational knowledge and learning
Source: adapted from Morgan (1997)

These strands, we suggest, are mutually reinforcing and interconnected. In particular, from a managerial perspective we can see how knowledge issues have a very direct economic content via the knowledge production/diffusion function, and a very organizational and individual element through the analysis of organizational knowledge. These do not stand, however, as separable issues, although elements of the problem can be treated in isolation. Rather, the system-wide characteristics of knowledge are evident, particularly in the knowledge web through which value creation activities are composed.

Finally, the knowledge web and the systemic frameworks allow firms to monitor threats. They prompt managers to question the adequacy of existing business models and to analyse the unconventional responses that new entrants and innovators may be 'cooking up' to attack the entrenched positions of leading firms. Many leading firms fail to innovate because they act like hierarchies, not markets. They allocate resources for bureaucratic, political but not economic reasons. Too few of them make their organizational processes and routines receptive to idea and value innovation. Unfortunately, they do not see innovation, learning and knowledge acquisition as key elements of the corporate DNA.

---

[13] See the debates that have taken place in theoretical physics on just this issue.

Key terms

disruptive technologies	453	objectified knowledge	457
dominant design	461	replacement effect	460
efficiency effect	460	sunk cost effect	460
innovation	452	sustaining technologies	453
knowledge-based view	464	tacit knowledge	464
knowledge web	469	value innovation	453

Recap questions and assignments

1 Compare the discussion of the knowledge economy in this chapter with the discussion of the new economy in Chapter 7. Identify the common elements and their effect on strategic discussions.

2 Consider also the discussion of risk in Chapter 11. What does a knowledge-based view of strategy imply for strategic risk and strategic decision-making?

3 Compare the action of disruptive technologies in this chapter with Schumpeter's 'Creative destruction'. What role does tacit knowledge play in these ideas?

Case study 14.1: Don't laugh at gilded butterflies

The Gillette company's website flashes out a message to the e-visitor: 'Innovation is Gillette', it claims. There are few big companies that would not like to make a similar claim; for they think innovation is a bit like Botox – inject it in the right corporate places and improvements are bound to follow. But too many companies want one massive injection, one huge blockbuster, to last them for the foreseeable future. Unfortunately, successful innovation is rarely like that.

The latest manifestation of Gillette's innovative skill will appear in stores in North America next month. The global leader in men's 'grooming products' is rolling out a successor to its popular three-bladed Mach3 range. It will not, as comedians had long anticipated, be a four-bladed version (Schick-Wilkinson Sword reached that landmark first, in September 2003, and Gillette has taken it to court for its pains). Rather, it will be the world's first vibrating 'wet shave' blade. The battery-powered M3Power is designed to bounce around on your skin to give (yes, you guessed it) 'a smoother, more comfortable shave'.

For a company that claims to embody innovation, this is less than earth-shattering. On the innovation scale it falls closer to Brooks Brothers' new stain-proof tie than to the video-cassette recorder or the digital camera – especially since there is a suspicion that Gillette may be keener to create synergy between its razor and its batteries division (it owns the Duracell brand) than it is to usher in a genuinely new male-grooming experience.

But the launch is symptomatic of an important business trend: blockbuster new products are harder and harder to come by, and big companies can do much better if they focus on making lots of small things better. Adrian Slywotzky of Mercer Management Consulting says that, 'in most industries, truly differentiating new-product breakthroughs are becoming increasingly rare.' He claims, for example, that there has not been a single new dyestuff invented since 1956.

Even in relatively zippy businesses like pharmaceuticals, genuinely new products are fewer and further between. Spending on pharmaceutical R&D has doubled over the past decade, but the number of new drugs approved each year by America's Food and Drug Administration (the industry's key regulatory hurdle) has halved. Drug companies still live in the hope of finding a big winner that will keep their shareholders happy for a long time. But this focus means that many unglamorous, but potentially interesting, compounds may be bottled up in their laboratories.

Big companies have a big problem with innovation. This was most vividly described by Clayton Christensen, a Harvard Business School professor, in his book, *The Innovator's Dilemma* (Harvard Business School Press, 1997). Few conversations about innovation take place without reference to this influential work.

The Oxford English Dictionary defines innovation as 'making changes to something established'. Invention, by contrast, is the act of 'coming upon or finding: discovery'. Whereas inventors stumble across or make new things, 'innovators try to change the status quo,' says Bhaskar Chakravorti of the Monitor Group, another consulting firm, 'which is why markets resist them.' Innovations frequently disrupt the way that companies do things (and may have been doing them for years).

It is not just markets that resist innovation. Michael Hammer, co-author of another important business book ('*Re-engineering the Corporation*', HarperCollins) quotes the example of a PC-maker that set out to imitate Dell's famous 'Build-to-Order' system of computer assembly. The company found that its attempts were frustrated not just by its head of manufacturing (who feared it would lead to most of his demesne, including his job, being outsourced), but also by the head of marketing, who did not want to upset his existing retail outlets. So the innovative proposal got nowhere. Dell continued to dominate the business.

Mr Christensen described how 'disruptive innovation' – simpler, cheaper and more convenient products that seriously upset the status quo – can herald the rapid downfall of well-established and successful businesses. This, he argues, is because most organisations are designed to grow through 'sustaining innovations' – the sort, like Gillette's vibrating razor, that do no more than improve on existing products for existing markets.

When they are hit by a disruptive innovation – as IBM was by the invention of the personal computer and as numerous national airlines have been by low-cost carriers – they are in danger of being blasted out of their market. This message found a ready audience, coming as it did just as giant businesses from banking to retailing, and from insurance to auction houses, were being told that some as-yet-unformed dotcom was about to knock them off their pedestal.

William Baumol, a professor at New York University, argues that big companies have been learning important lessons from the history of innovation. Consider, for example, that in general they have both cut back and redirected their R&D spending in recent years. Gone are the droves of white-coated scientists surrounded by managers in suits anxiously awaiting the next cry of 'eureka'. Microsoft is a rare exception, one of the few big companies still spending big bucks on employing top scientists in the way pioneered by firms such as AT&T (with its Bell Laboratories) and Xerox (with its Palo Alto Research Centre, the legendary PARC).

This will prove to be a wise investment by Microsoft only if its scientists' output can be turned into profitable products or services. AT&T and Xerox, when in their heyday, managed to invent the transistor and the computer mouse (respectively); but they never made a penny out of them. Indeed, says Mr Baumol, the record shows that small companies have dominated the introduction of new inventions and radical innovations – independent inventors come up with most of tomorrow's clever gizmos, often creating their own commercial ventures in the process.

But big companies have shifted their efforts. Mr Baumol reckons they have been forced by competition to focus on innovation as part of normal corporate activity. Rather than trying to make money from science, companies have turned R&D into an 'internal, bureaucratically driven process'. Innovation by big companies has become a matter of incremental improvements within the processes that constitute daily operations.

In some industries, cutbacks in R&D reflect changes in the way that new products travel down the 'invention pipeline'. During the late 1990s, for example, Cisco Systems kept itself at the cutting edge of its fast-moving high-tech business (making internet routers) by buying a long string of creative start-ups financed originally by venture capital. The company's R&D was, as it were, outsourced to California's venture capitalists, who brought together the marketing savvy of a big corporation and the innovative flair of a small one – functions that were famously divorced at AT&T and Xerox.

These days there is less money going into venture capital, and a new method of outsourcing R&D is on the increase. More and more of it is being shifted to cheaper locations 'offshore' – in India and Russia, for example. One Indian firm, Wipro, employs 6,500 people in and around Bangalore doing R&D for others – including nine out of ten of the world's top telecom-equipment manufacturers.

Pharmaceutical giants continue to get their hands on new science by buying small innovative firms, particularly in biotech. Toby Stuart, a professor at the Columbia Business School in New York, thinks that this shows another change in the supply chain of invention. He says that many of the biotech firms are merely intermediating between the universities and 'Big Pharma', the distributors and marketers of the fruits of academia's invention. Universities used to license their inventions to these firms direct, but small biotech companies make the process more efficient. They are well networked with the universities, in whose 'business parks' they frequently locate their offices. They may not, of themselves, be very innovative.

Companies need to resist the feeling that it is not worth getting out of bed for anything other than a potential blockbuster. Product cycles are getting shorter and shorter across the board because innovations are more rapidly copied by competitors, pushing down margins and transforming today's consumer sensation into tomorrow's commonplace commodity. Firms have to innovate continuously and incrementally these days to lift products out of the slough of commoditisation. After it used innovation to create a commoditised market for fast food, McDonald's struggled before recently managing to reinvigorate its flow of innovations.

Another factor to take into account is the fragmentation of markets. Once-uniform mass markets are breaking up into countless niches in which everything has to be customised for a small group of consumers. Looking for blockbusters in such a world is a daunting task. Vijay Vishwanath, a marketing specialist with Bain, a consulting firm, says that Gillette's bouncy blade may yet end up as no more than a niche product – fine if it is profitable.

Mr Chakravorti believes that the problem lies with the marketing of new innovations. It has not, he says, caught up with the way that consumers behave today. 'Executives need to rethink the way they bring innovations to market.' Too many are still stuck with the strategies used to sell Kodak's first cameras almost 120 years ago, when the product was so revolutionary that the company could forget about competition for at least a decade. Today, no innovation is an island. Each needs to take account of the network of products into which it is launched.

Companies that fail to come up with big new headline-hitting blockbusters should not despair. There are plenty of other, albeit less glamorous, areas where innovation can take place. Management thinkers have identified at least three. Erik Brynjolfsson of the MIT Sloan School of Management, says that the roots of America's productivity surge lie in a 'genuine revolution in how American companies are using information technology'. Good companies are using IT 'to reinvent their business processes from top to bottom'.

Reinventing, or simply trying to improve, business processes can offer surprising benefits to firms that do it well. The software that runs many business processes has become an important competitive weapon. Some business processes have even been awarded patents. These are controversial and, because they may stifle rather than encourage the spread of new ideas, are probably not in the wider public interest. Yet Amazon obviously views its patent for one-click internet purchasing as valuable, and there are plenty of other examples, particularly in the financial-services industry.

Nevertheless, there is no doubt that, patented or not, what Mr Hammer calls 'operational innovation' can add to shareholder value. In an article in the April issue of the *Harvard Business Review*, he asks why so few companies have followed the examples of Dell, Toyota and Wal-Mart, three of the greatest creators of value in recent times. None of them has come up with a string of revolutionary new products. Where they have been creative is in their business processes.

While superficially mundane, Wal-Mart's pioneering system of 'cross-docking' – shifting goods off trucks from suppliers and straight on to trucks heading for the company's stores, without them ever hitting the ground at a distribution centre – has been fundamental to the company's ability to offer lower prices, the platform for its outstanding success. Is it not over the top, though, to glorify such a common-sense change with the title 'innovation'? For sure, it does not call for a higher degree in one of the obscurer corners of science. But Wal-Mart did something no competitor had ever dreamed was feasible and that was highly innovative.

Mr Hammer, who was once a professor of computer science at MIT, believes that the best qualification for innovation is a basic training in engineering. Crucially, he says, engineers are taught that design matters; that most things are part of a system in which everything interacts; that their job is to worry about trade-offs; and that they must continually be measuring the robustness of the systems they set up. Such a frame of mind, he believes, fosters innovation. It may be no coincidence that many of the greatest corporate leaders in America, Europe and Japan, past and present, trained first as engineers.

Companies are being encouraged to embrace other forms of innovation too. In a recent issue of the MIT Sloan Management Review, Christopher Trimble and Vijay Govindarajan, two academics from Dartmouth College's Tuck School of Business, recommend that they try a little 'strategic innovation'. The authors point to examples such as Southwest Airlines, a low-cost American regional carrier, and Tetra Pak, a Swedish company whose packaging products are handled at least once a day by most citizens of the western world. Such companies succeed, they say, 'through innovative strategies alone, without much innovation in either the underlying technologies or the products and services sold to customers.'

Tetra Pak's strategic innovation involved moving from the production of packages for its customers to the design of packaging solutions for them. Instead of delivering ready-made containers, the company increasingly provides the machinery for its customers to make their own packages: the fishing rod, not the fish.

But customers can then use only Tetra Pak's own aseptic materials to make their containers. This strips out all sorts of transport and inventory costs from the production process, for both Tetra Pak and its customer. It also makes it very difficult for the customer to switch suppliers.

Southwest's innovative strategies include its bold decision to increase capacity in the immediate aftermath of September 11th 2001, and its carefully timed rolling out this May of competitively priced routes focused on Philadelphia, an important hub for the ailing US Airways, an airline lumbered with an expensive legacy (such as highly paid crews). The low-cost carrier 'is coming to kill us,' said US Airways chief executive David Siegel shortly before his recent resignation. And he was not exaggerating.

In his recent book, *How to Grow When Markets Don't* (Warner Books, 2003), Mr Slywotzky and his co-author Richard Wise recommended another form of innovation. 'A handful of far-sighted companies', they claim, have shifted their focus from product innovation to what they call 'demand innovation'. They cite examples such as Air Liquide and Johnson Controls, which have earned profits not by meeting existing demand in a new way but 'by discovering new forms of demand' and adapting to meet them.

The French company Air Liquide, for example, was a market leader in the supply of industrial gases. But by the early 1990s gas had become a commodity, with only price differentiating one supplier from another. As its operating income plunged, Air Liquide tried to behave like a far-sighted company: it almost doubled its R&D expenditure. However, it reaped few fruits. An ozone-based alternative to the company's environmentally unfriendly bleach for paper and pulp, for example, required customers to undertake prohibitively expensive redesigns of their mills.

The company's saviour came serendipitously in the form of a new system for manufacturing gases at small plants erected on its customers' sites. This brought it into closer contact with its customers, and led it to realise that it could sell them skills it had gained over years – in handling hazardous materials and maximising energy efficiency, for example.

After exclusively selling gas for decades, Air Liquide became a provider of chemical- and gas-management services as well. In 1991, services accounted for 7% of its revenues; today they are close to 30%. And because service margins are higher, they account for an even bigger share of profits. An ozone-based bleach could never have done half so well.

In his latest book, *The Innovator's Solution*, published late last year, Mr Christensen argued that established companies should try to become disruptive innovators themselves. He cites, for example, Charles Schwab, which turned itself from a traditional stockbroker into a leading online broker, and Intel, which reclaimed the low end of the semiconductor market with the launch of its Celeron chip.

There are, says Mr Christensen, things that managers can do to make such innovations more likely to happen within their organisations. For example, projects with potential should be rapidly hived off into independent business units, away from the smothering influence of the status quo. The ultimate outcome of any one disruptive innovation may still be unpredictable; the process from which it emerges is not.

In the end, though, 'no single innovation conveys lasting advantage,' says Mr Hammer. In the toys and games business today, up to 40% of all products on the market are less than one year old. Other sectors are only a little less pressured. Innovation and, yes, invention too, have to take place continually and systematically.

Source: 'Don't Laugh at Gilded Butterflies', *The Economist*, 24 April 2004

Questions

1 Discuss the proposition that rather than chasing wonder new products or services, big companies should focus on making lots of small improvements.

2 Is it correct to say that successful innovation comes from predominantly thinking like an engineer (as Hammer suggests)?

3 What roles do routines, controls, knowledge and learning play in Gillette's innovation strategy?

References

Abramowitz, M. (1986) Catching up, forging ahead, and falling behind. *Journal of Economic History*, **66**, 385–406.

Alchian, A.A. (1950) Uncertainty, evolution and economic theory. *Journal of Political Economy*, **58**, 211–21.

Alchian, A.A. (1953) Biological analogues in the theory of the firm: comment. *American Economic Review*, **43**, 600–3.

Alchian, A.A. and Demsetz, H. (1972) Production, information costs, and economic organisation. *American Economic Review*, **62**, 777–95.

Amit, R. and Schoemaker, P.J. (1993) Strategic assets and organisational rent. *Strategic Management Journal*, **14**, 33–46.

Anderson, P. and Tushman, M.L. (1990) Technological discontinuities and dominant designs. *Administrative Science Quarterly*, **35**, 604–33.

Argyris, C. and Schön, D.A. (1987) *Organizational Learning: A Theory of Action Perspective*, Addison-Wesley, Reading, MA.

Arrow, K. (1962) Economic welfare and the allocation of resources for inventions. In R.R. Nelson (ed.) *The Rate and Direction of Economic Activity*, Princeton University Press, Princeton, NJ.

Barney, J. (1991) Firm resources and sustained competitive advantage. *Journal of Management*, **17**, 99–120.

Berliner, P. (1994) *Thinking in Jazz: The Infinite Art of Improvisation*, University of Chicago Press, Chicago, IL.

Besanko, D., Dranove, D. and Shanley, M. (2000) *Economics of Strategy*, 2nd edn, John Wiley & Sons, New York.

Brown, J.S. and Duguid, P. (1991) Organizational learning and communities of practice: toward a unified view of working, learning, and innovation. *Organization Science*, **2**, **1**, 40–57.

Burgelman, R.A. (1983) A model of the interaction of strategic behaviour, corporate context, and the concept of strategy. *The Academy of Management Review*, **8**, **1**, 61–70.

Christensen, C.M. (1997) *The Innovator's Dilemma*, Harvard Business School Press, Boston, MA.

Coase, R. (1937) The nature of the firm. *Economica*, **4**, 386–405.

Coase, R. (1988) Lecture on the nature of the firm, III. *Journal of Law, Economics and Organisation*, **4**, 33–47.

Collinson, S. and Wilson, D.C. (2006) Inertia in Japanese organizations: knowledge management routines and failure to innovate. *Organization Studies*, **27**, **9**, 1359–87.

Cooper, A.C. and Schendel, D.E. (1976) Strategic response to technological threats. *Business Horizons*, **19**.

Crossan, M.M. (1998) Improvisation in action. *Organization Science*, **9**, **5**, 593–9.

Cyert, R.M. and March, J.G. (1963) *A Behavioral Theory of the Firm*, Prentice-Hall, Englewood Cliffs, NJ.

D'Aveni, R.A. (1994) *Hypercompetition: Managing the Dynamics of Strategic Manoeuvring*, Free Press, New York.

De Wit, R. and Meyer, R. (1994) *Strategy: Process, Context, and Content*, West, St Paul, MN.

Dussage, P., Hart, S. and Ramanantsoa, B. (1996) *Strategic Technology Management*, Wiley, New York.

Eisenhardt, K.M. (1997) Strategic decisions and all that jazz. *Business Strategy Review*, **8**, **3**, 1–3.

Eisenhardt, K.M. and Martin, J.A. (2000) Dynamic capabilities: what are they? *Strategic Management Journal*, Special issue, 1105–21.

Eisenhardt, K.M. and Santos, F.M. (2002) Knowledge-based view: a new theory of strategy? In A.M. Pettigrew, H. Thomas and R. Whittington (eds) *The Handbook of Strategy and Management*, Sage, London.

Garvin, D.A. (1993) Building a learning organization. *Harvard Business Review*, July–August, 78–91.

Ghemawat, P. (1997) *Strategy and the Business Landscape*, Addison-Wesley, Reading, MA.

Gioia, T. (1998) *The Imperfect art: Reflections on Jazz and Modern Culture*, Portable Book Series, Stanford, CA.

Gottinger, H-W. (1998) Technological races. *Annual Review of Economics* (Japan), **38**, 1–9.

Gottinger, H-W. (2001) Stochastic innovation races. *Technological Forecasting and Social Change*, **68**, 1–18.

Gottinger, H-W. (2003) *Economics of Network Industries*, Routledge, London.

Granovetter, M. (1985) Economic action and social structures. *American Journal of Sociology*, **91**, 481–510.

Grant, R.M. (1991) The resource based theory of competitive advantage: implications for strategy formulation. *California Management Review*, Spring, 119–45.

Grant, R.M. (1996) Toward a knowledge-based theory of the firm. *Strategic Management Journal*, **17** (Winter Special Issue), 109–22.

Hall, R.L. and Hitch, C.J. (1939) Price theory and business behaviour. *Oxford Economic Papers*, 2, reprinted in T. Wilson and P.W.S. Andrews (eds) (1951) *Oxford Studies in the Price Mechanism*, Clarendon Press, Oxford.

Hamel, G. (2000) *Leading the Revolution*, Harvard Business School Press, Boston, MA.

Hamel, G. and Prahalad, C.K. (1993) Strategy as stretch and leverage. *Harvard Business Review*, March/April.

Hatch, M.J. (1998) Jazz as a metaphor for organizing in the 21st century. *Organization Science*, **9**, **5**, 556–7.

Hatch, M.J. (1999) Exploring the empty spaces of organizing: how improvisational jazz helps redescribe organizational structure. *Organization Studies*, **20**, **1**, 75–100.

Hatch, M.J. and Weick, K.E. (1998) Critical resistance to the jazz metaphor. *Organization Science*, **9**, 600–4.

Henderson, R.M. and Clark, K.B. (1990) Architectural innovation: the reconfiguration of existing technologies and the failure of established firms. *Administrative Science Quarterly*, **35**, **1**, 9–30.

Jarzabowski, P. (2004) Recursiveness and adaptive strategic practices in use. *Organization Studies*, **25**, **5**, 412–25.

Jensen, M.C. and Meckling, W. (1976) Theory of the firm: managerial behaviour, agency costs, and ownership structure. *Journal of Financial Economics*, **3**, 305–60.

Johnson, G. and Bowman, C. (1999) *Strategy and Everyday Reality: The Case for Study of Micro-strategy*. Working paper, 15th EGOS Colloquium.

Kamoche, K. and Cunha, M.P. (2001) Minimal structures: from jazz improvisation to product innovation. *Organization Studies*, **22**, **5**, 733–64.

Kamoche, K.N., Cunha, M.P. and Cunha, J.V. (eds) (2002) *Organizational Improvisation*, Routledge, London.

Kim, W.C. and Mauborgne, R. (1999) Strategy, value innovation and the knowledge economy. *Sloan Management Review*, **40**, **3**, Spring, 41–54.

Langlois, R.N. (1986) Rationality, institutions, and explanation. In R.N. Langlois (ed.) *Economics as a Process: Essays in the New Institutional Economics*, Cambridge University Press, Cambridge, 225–55.

Lant, T.K. and Mezias, S.J. (1992) An organizational learning model of convergence and reorientation, *Organization Science*, **3**, **1**, 47–71.

Leonard-Barton, D. (1992) Core capabilities and core rigidities: a paradox in managing new product development. *Strategic Management Journal*, **13** (Special Issue), 111–26.

Lerner, J. (1997) An empirical exploration of a technology race. *The Rand Journal of Economics*, **28**, **2**, 228–34.

Lester, R.A. (1946) Shortcomings of marginal analysis for wage-employment problems. *American Economic Review*, **36**, 63–82.

Levitt, B. and March, J.G. (1988) Organisational learning. *Annual Review of Sociology*, **14**, 319–40.

March, J.G. (1991) Exploration and exploitation in organizational learning. *Organization Science*, **2**, **1**, 71–87.

March, J.G. and Simon, H.A. (1958) *Organisations*, John Wiley, New York.

Marshall, A. (1920) *Principles of Economics*, 8th edn, Macmillan Press, London.

McGee, J. (2003) Strategy as orchestrating knowledge. In D. Wilson and S. Cummings (eds) *Images of Strategy*, Blackwell, Oxford.

McGee, J. and Sammut-Bonnici, T. (2002a) Network industries in the new economy. *European Business Journal*, **14**, **3**, September, 116–32.

McGee, J. and Sammut-Bonnici, T. (2002b) Network strategies for the new economy: emerging strategies for new industry structures. *European Business Journal*, **14**, **4**, December, 174–85.

Menuhin, J. (2001) *Strategising Routines: The Emergence of Strategic Initiatives*, unpublished PhD thesis, University of Warwick.

Menuhin, J. and McGee, J. (2003) *Strategising Routines in HSBC (UK)*, unpublished working paper, University of Warwick, Warwick Business School.

Morgan, G. (1997) *Images of Organization,* 2nd edn, Sage, London.

Nelson, R.R. and Winter, S.G. (1982) *An Evolutionary Theory of Economic Change,* Belknap Press, Cambridge, MA.

Nonaka, I. (1993) *On a Knowledge Creating Organization.* Paper presented at AIF National Congress, Posma, October.

Nonaka, I. (1994) A dynamic theory of knowledge creation. *Organization Science,* **5,** 14–37.

Nonaka, I. and Takeuchi, H. (1995) *The Knowledge-creating Company: How Japanese Companies Create the Dynamics of Innovation,* Oxford University Press, New York.

Penrose, K.T. (1959) *The Theory of the Growth of the Firm,* Basil Blackwell, Oxford.

Peteraf, M.A. (1993) The cornerstones of competitive advantage: a resource-based view. *Strategic Management Journal,* **14, 3,** 179–91.

Peters, T. and Waterman, R. (1982) *In Search of Excellence,* Harper Row, London.

Polanyi, M. (1966) *The Tacit Dimension,* Anchor Day Books, New York.

Prahalad, C.K. and Hamel, G. (1990) The core competence of the corporation. *Harvard Business Review,* May/June, 79–81.

Quinn, J.B. (1978) Strategic change: logical incrementalism. *Sloan Management Review,* Fall.

Rumelt, R.P. (1984) Towards a strategic theory of the firm. In R. Boyden Lamb (ed.) *Competitive Strategic Management,* Prentice-Hall, Englewood Cliffs, NJ.

Scherer, F. (1991) International R&D races: theory and evidence. In L-G. Mattsson and B. Stymme (eds) *Corporate and Industry Strategies for Europe,* Elsevier Science, New York.

Schumpeter, J. (1934) *The Theory of Economic Development,* Harvard University Press, Cambridge, MA (first published in 1911, republished 1968).

Senge, P. (1990) The leader's new work: building learning organizations. *Sloan Management Review,* Fall.

Simon, H.A. (1955) A behavioural model of rational choice. *Quarterly Journal of Economics,* **69,** 99–118.

Simon, H.A. (1959) Theories of decision-making in economics and behavioural science. *American Economic Review,* **49,** 253–83.

Spender, J-C. (1996) Making knowledge the basis of a dynamic theory of the firm. *Strategic Management Journal,* **17,** Winter Special Issue, 45–62.

Teece, D.J. (ed.) (1987) *The Competitive Challenge: Strategies for Industrial Innovation and Renewal,* Ballinger, Cambridge, MA.

Teece, D.J., Pisano, G. and Shuen, A. (1997) Dynamic capabilities and strategic management. *Strategic Management Journal,* **18, 7,** 509–33.

Tushman, M.L. and Romanelli, E. (1985) Organizational evolution: a metamorphosis model of convergence and reorientation. In L.L. Cummings and B.M. Staw (eds) *Research in Organizational Behaviour,* 7th edn, JAI Press, Greenwich, CT, 171–222.

Veblen, T. (1898) Why economics is evolutionary science. *Quarterly Journal of Economics,* **12,** 373–97.

Vronen, J. (1995) *Economic Evolution,* Routledge, London.

Weick, K.E. (1989) Organized improvisation: 20 years of organizing. *Communication Studies,* **40, 4,** 241–8.

Wenger, E.C. and Snyder, W.M. (2000) Communities of practice: the organizational frontier. *Harvard Business Review,* Jan/Feb, 139–45.

Wernerfelt, B. (1984) A resource-based view of the firm. *Strategic Management Journal,* **5, 2,** 171–80.

Williamson, O.E. (1981) Strategizing, economizing, and economic organization. *Strategic Management Journal,* **12,** Winter Special Issue, 75–94.

Williamson, O.E. (1985) *The Economic Institutions of Capitalism,* Free Press, New York.

Williamson, O.E. (1987) Transactions costs economics. *Journal of Economic Behaviour and Organisation,* **8,** 617–25.

Winter, S.G. (1964) Economic 'natural selection' and the theory of the firm. *Yale Economic Essays*, **4**, 225–72.

Winter, S.G. (1987) Knowledge and competence as strategic assets. In D.J. Teece (ed.) *Competitive Challenge – Strategies for Industrial Innovation and Renewal*, Ballinger, Cambridge, MA.

Further reading

Barsh, J., Capozzi, M. and Davidson, J. (2008) Leadership and innovation. *McKinsey Quarterly*, **1**, 37–47.

Bhide, A. (2009) Where innovation creates value. *McKinsey Quarterly*, **2**, 119–26.

Birkenshaw, J. and Mol, M.J. (2006) How management innovation happens. *Sloan Management Review*, **47**, 4, 81–8.

Christensen, C.M., Kaufman, S.P. and Shih, W.C. (2008) Innovation killers: how financial tools destroy your capacity to do new things. *Harvard Business Review*, **86**, 1, 98–105.

Hamel, G. (2006) The why, what and how of management innovation. *Harvard Business Review*, **84**, 2, 72–84.

Hamel, G. (2009) Moon shots for management. *Harvard Business Review*, Feb, 91–9.

Helgesen, S. (2008) The practical wisdom of Ikujiro Nonaka. *Strategy + Business*, **33**, Winter, 80–9.

Mol, M.J. and Birkinshaw, J. (2007) *Giant Steps in Management – Key Management Innovations*, FT/Prentice Hall, London.

Rao, H. (2009) Market rebels and radical innovation. *McKinsey Quarterly*, **2**, 126–33.

Strategy and corporate governance[1]

Chapter contents

Introduction

The strategic **performance** of an organization is highly dependent upon its ability to make effective strategic decisions, remain flexible enough to change as environmental conditions fluctuate and always be open to new knowledge and to learning. Somewhat surprisingly, the importance of the governing body in organizational decision making has been under-represented in research in strategic

---

[1] Contributions to this chapter were made by Dr Derek Condon, Warwick Business School.

management and organization. However, in recent years there has been an increasing effort by analysts to describe and understand the central role of corporate governance and the influence of the board (or its equivalent) in organizational strategy.

Research may have been relatively limited, but concerns over effective governance have a long history, particularly among scholars of industrial sociology. It is not without a strong sense of irony (writing this chapter in the early stages of a global financial crisis) that one can revisit the work of sociologists such as Veblen (1904) who were concerned about the **power** of businesses and their owners and the effects of their actions in wider society.

> *Ownership is not all-pervading and all-dominant, but it pervades and dominates the affairs of civilized peoples more freely and widely than any other single ground of action, and more than it has ever done before. It follows . . . that under these circumstances the men who have the management of such an industrial enterprise, capitalized and quotable on the market, will be able to induce the putative and actual earning-capacity, by expedients well known and approved for the purpose, partial information, as well as misinformation, sagaciously given out at a critical juncture, will go far toward producing a favorable temporary discrepancy of this kind, and so enabling the managers to buy and sell securities of the concern with advantage to themselves.*
> (Veblen, 1904, Chapter 4 on Business Principles)

Veblen, along with many sociologists of the time, was concerned about the power and the (lack of) accountability of those who owned corporations and who could manipulate both capital and information to their own advantage and to the disadvantage of society at large. Veblen presaged aspects of the current (2008/2009) financial crisis when he argued that:

> *Business depression and exaltation are, at least in their first incidence, of the nature of psychological fact, just as price movements are a psychological phenomenon.* (Veblen, 1904, p. 128)

Our recent experience of arguably poor governance on the part of financial institutions has pointed out the relevance of both of these aspects of self-interest and psychology in creating and perpetuating a crisis. Financial institutions and governments have been criticized (Taylor, 2009) for talking up property prices, taking extremely big risks on unsecured loans and feathering the nests of senior managers through large bonuses based on hype rather than fact. Further, Taylor (2009) notes that a marked lack of regulation over the actions of boards may also have contributed to their self-interested actions.

Perhaps we should not be surprised. Veblen argued that there was no reason why the interest of corporate managers and the interests of the organization or wider society should coincide. He argued that management self-interest and the broader community interests in efficiently produced output would (logically) seldom coincide. Their respective values and expectations were very different. Managers were interested in the manipulation of the stock price of the company (its value) and rather less in the production and sale of products. Manipulations of the value of stock carried a risk to the company but little risk to the managers who governed the organization.

Periodically, Veblen's financial theories resurface, especially after times of financial and market instability. In the middle of the 20th century, Veblen's critique was used to review the financial reforms of the 1930s. After the crash of 1987, his critique was used to examine the 1980s financial markets. It is no surprise, therefore to begin this chapter, as another recession looms and financial markets are in crisis, by revisiting Veblen. His arguments force us to focus on the governing body or an organization (usually the board of directors) and their responsibilities to **stakeholders** and to wider society.

Cadbury (2000) and Cassidy (2000) offer accounts of the rise and rise of corporate governance as an issue in the US and Europe since the 1980s. Central to their argument about why this issue has risen so far up the policy agenda have been:

■ a succession of corporate scandals;

■ performance weaknesses of many firms which could be attributed at least in part to poor governance and leadership;

■ lack of congruence between the compensation of CEOs and executive directors and the financial performance of the companies they are managing (Conyon and Murphy, 2000).

There also are a common set of *endogenous* pressures and questions which revolve around the purposes, responsibilities, control, leadership and power of boards. These questions include:

■ How is oversight to be exercised over those delegated to the executive management of the firm?

■ How are owner's interests to be protected?

■ How are the interests of the other stakeholders such as consumers, employees and local communities to be protected?

■ Who sets the purpose and direction of the organization and ensures its accountability?

■ How is power over the organization legitimized and to whom is an organization accountable and responsible?

Although Veblen was pessimistic, writing in 1904, he argues that boards of directors would always act in their own interest and they would deliberately talk up (or talk down) prices, value and corporate performance as it suited their needs.

15.1 What is corporate governance?

There is no single model of good governance. However, the OECD (2004) has identified corporate governance as one of the key elements in improving economic efficiency and growth as well as enhancing investor confidence. The OECD (2004) describes corporate governance as:

> ... involving a set of relationships between a company's management, its board, its shareholders and other stakeholders. Corporate governance also provides the structure through which the objectives of the company are set, and the means of attaining those objectives and monitoring performance are determined. Good corporate governance should provide proper incentives for the board and management to pursue objectives that are in the interests of the company and its shareholders and should facilitate effective monitoring.

The OECD's Principles of Corporate Governance go on to say that:

> Corporate governance is only part of the larger economic context in which firms operate that includes, for example, macroeconomic policies and the degree of competition in product and factor markets. The corporate governance framework also depends on the legal, regulatory and institutional environment. In addition, factors such as business ethics and corporate awareness of the environment and societal interests of the communities in which a company operates can also have an impact on its reputation and its long-term success.

15.1.1 Why does corporate governance matter?

The value of corporate governance practices is also frequently questioned during periods of economic expansion (as well as in recession) as companies and shareholders concentrate on wealth generation rather than ensuring that governance mechanisms are working appropriately for the retention of wealth, and its future use (Clarke, 2004, p. 153). During times of growth, companies and investors can become complacent about corporate governance. Corporate governance mechanisms are frequently regarded as unnecessary 'red tape', reducing a company's ability to act quickly as well as being costly both financially and in time spent. However, at times of economic contraction and, especially, corporate collapse, pressure frequently builds up for a re-evaluation of governance and the viability of regulatory systems. This has led to the tendency for interest in corporate governance issues to be cyclical (Clarke, 2004, p. 153). The Asian Development Bank (ADB) (2000, p. 3) noted that during the years of high growth that had preceded the 1997 Asian economic crisis investors appeared to pay *'inadequate attention to corporate governance as long as investments were profitable and the return on investment adequate'* and *'cared little about the excessive long-term risks that some projects were exposed to'*. However, failures in corporate governance, resulting in tens of billions of pounds worth of losses to shareholders, commencing with the Asian economic crisis of 1997, followed by the high-profile collapses in the US that included Enron, WorldCom, Tyco and Global Crossing and the later failures of corporate governance in Europe that included Parmalat and Shell, led to a resurgence of interest in corporate governance. More recently, the corporate governance failures in RBS and Home Depot (see case examples below) have focused further debate on issues of corporate governance.

Case box 15.1: **Goodwin stands firm on £16m RBS pension**

Sir Fred Goodwin's pension arrangements were at the centre of a war of words on Thursday as the former chief executive of Royal Bank of Scotland traded allegations over the terms of his departure from the ailing bank with Lord Myners, the City minister.

The two men exchanged terse letters in public after it emerged that Sir Fred, who was forced out of RBS last October without a payoff, had started collecting a £693,000-a-year pension.

Gordon Brown, the prime minister, on Thursday demanded action on the issue, arguing that the pension payment for Sir Fred could not be justified. However, in a letter to Lord Myners, Sir Fred said he was not giving up the pension and alleged that the minister had been involved in discussions with members of the RBS board about his pension arrangements when he was negotiating his departure.

Last night Lord Myners fired back. In a letter to Sir Fred he described the decision as 'unfortunate and unacceptable'. He also claimed to have only recently become aware that the decision to allow Sir Fred to claim a pension was discretionary rather than a contractual arrangement. 'It was only last week that the Government became aware that the decision of the previous Board of RBS may have been a discretionary choice,' he wrote.

Sir Fred's letter

The row comes against the backdrop of the government's decision to insure £325bn of RBS assets in an effort to stabilise the ailing bank and kick-start lending to the economy.

The dispute centres on negotiations between Sir Fred, the RBS board and the government last October, when the government injected £20bn in fresh capital into the bank. At the time Sir Tom McKillop, then chairman of RBS, and Bob Scott, the director who was chairman of the board's remuneration committee, led negotiations with Sir Fred over the terms of his departure. According to people familiar with the matter, Mr Scott had regular conversations with Lord Myners to keep him informed about the discussions.

The result of the negotiations was that Sir Fred agreed to give up his contractual entitlement to a year's salary, worth around £1.3m, and – following further pressure from the government – also gave up the right to share options worth another three months' salary. However, he insisted on holding on to his pension, which would allow him to start drawing an annual payment almost immediately. 'I believed that these "gestures" were appropriate in the circumstances, and sufficient, and revisiting the position today, I believe that they remain so,' Sir Fred wrote.

Sir Fred's early departure effectively doubled the value of his total pension from around £8m to more than £16m. According to people involved in the talks, Mr Scott told Lord Myners that he estimated Sir Fred's pension pot had increased in value.

On Thursday it emerged that the RBS board could have denied Sir Fred his early pension if it had dismissed him as chief executive rather than allowing him to depart as a so-called 'good leaver'. However, people with knowledge of the matter said such a move would have been likely to have triggered a legal challenge by Sir Fred, opening the bank to greater liabilities.

Gordon Brown, prime minister, and Alistair Darling, chancellor, insisted they only became aware of Sir Fred's £693,000 annual pension settlement in the past few days. Lord Myners' letter last night says the government only learned last week that the pension deal with RBS was discretionary.

Mr Brown had said earlier he would explore all legal avenues to try to claw some of the pension back. And in his letter Lord Myners goes on to say: 'UK Financial Investments [the state's bank holding company] has, on behalf of the Government, been vigorously pursuing with the new Group Chairman whether there is any scope for clawing back some or all of your pension and whether, at the point the Board made their decision, it was made clear to the then remuneration committee and Board that the scale of the pension payment was discretionary, as it now proves to be.'

Mr Darling's call came amid increasing political pressure on ministers over the 'eye-watering' pension that Sir Fred, aged 50, is now drawing from the bank that he ran until it needed a multibillion-pound taxpayer bailout.

'You cannot justify these excesses,' Mr Darling stated earlier in the day. The chancellor said he had asked Lord Myners, the City minister, to speak to Sir Fred on Wednesday and 'put it to him quite simply – "look, in the circumstances in which this bank is now in, do you not think it right that you should forgo this?"'

'I am very clear that we will do whatever we can. That's why we have the lawyers looking at this,' Mr Darling told the BBC. 'But I do think that, on a voluntary basis, Sir Fred could resolve this problem and he could do it quite quickly.'

Source: Financial Times, 27 February 2009
© The Financial Times Ltd 2010

Putting in place and implementing corporate governance codes of conduct involve extra costs to companies and their owners. The costs resulted in an initial reluctance by companies to adopt the Sarbanes–Oxley Act[2] in the US following the Enron collapse, because (companies argued) the value of this expenditure is hard to quantify. Whereas it is possible to calculate the value of preventing a building collapse, it is much more difficult to evaluate the benefit of changing the behaviour and conduct of directors. Therefore it is not surprising that some owners and managers believe that corporate governance codes of conduct place more of a burden than a potential gain upon a company and the 'market' is the best regulator of a company and its managers' behaviour.

[2] The Sarbanes–Oxley Act of 2002 dramatically changed corporate governance in the US, including the responsibilities of directors and officers, the regulation of accounting firms that audit public companies, corporate reporting, and enforcement in US listed companies (Lander, 2004, p. 1).

They argue that the market will reward well-managed companies and punish poor ones through the allocation of resources and that this is the most effective form of regulation. Although this argument is plausible, it is perhaps more difficult to convince Enron investors who lost $80 billion when the company collapsed. It is also impossible for companies in the US to avoid compliance with Sarbanes–Oxley since non-compliance invokes strong legal repercussions on companies and individual directors.

15.2 Corporate governance theories

Beyond codes of conduct, there are a number of theoretical approaches to corporate governance which are important to examine. They include a range of what are known as agency theories and stakeholder theories. We cover these in the following sections of the chapter.

15.2.1 Agency theory

The agency approach can be traced to the work of Berle and Means (1932) who were the first to explore the structural and strategic implications of the growing separation of power between the executive management of major public companies in the US[3] and their increasingly diverse and remote shareholders (Cadbury, 2000, p. 5; Clarke, 2004, p. 154; Condon, 2007, p. 635).

Berle and Means (1932) identified what has become known as the 'agency problem' and led to the development of the principal–agent model which is underpinned by agency theory.[4] In this, the principals are the shareholders and the agents are corporate managers. The principals have no assurances that the agents will take actions and make decisions which are in the principals' interests.

The principal–agent model assumes that the sole purpose of the firm is to maximize shareholder value (Kirkbride and Letza, 2003, p. 464) and is concerned with the relationship between the principal and the agent, and the management of the company, which the shareholder has engaged to run the company on his or her behalf. Agency theory assumes that all social relations in economic interaction can be reduced to sets of contracts between principals and agents.

As outlined above, a key assumption of agency theory is that the goals of the principal and the agent conflict. The agency problem arises when agents make decisions that are not necessarily in the best interests of the principals. It is possible that managers may act in an opportunist fashion where they benefit to the detriment of the long-term interests of shareholders. Managers may also be tempted to supplement their salaries by awarding themselves generous perks such as expense accounts that permit costly non-essential expenditure, long holidays, inflated pension schemes and high termination payments. In addition, they could act in a fashion designed to fulfil needs at the expense of shareholders' interests, for example by expanding the company and increasing the agents' perceived importance, instead of increasing returns to the company's shareholders.

To ensure that shareholders' and managers' interests are aligned, a mechanism needs to be put in place that will allow this to happen. This has been described by Jensen and Meckling (1976) as a 'nexus of contracts', both explicit and implicit, between the principal and agent.

Such a contract argues that an effective board of directors, which is appointed by the shareholders, will identify with shareholders' interests and be responsible for ensuring that there is an adequate control framework for the company. This includes monitoring the performance of managers and putting in place the necessary mechanisms and contracts that will bring managers' interests into

---

[3] Prias (1976) showed that a similar structure of ownership and control operated in the UK.

[4] It can be argued that the agency problem was initially identified by Adam Smith who noted that the directors in a joint stock company could not be expected to be as careful with other people's money as they were with their own (Letza et al., 2004, p. 248).

line with shareholders'. If they are to carry out their task effectively the company will need to be structured in a way that provides the board with the information that it needs to undertake its role. This is achieved through the corporate governance system adopted by the company, which, in addition to giving the directors the power to set the company's aims and objectives and how they are to be achieved, enables them to use their experience in decision making and control to reduce any self-interested tendencies of corporate management through the adoption of what they determine to be the most efficient type of contract (behaviour or outcome oriented) to govern the principal–agent relationship. In addition, it provides the directors with the authority to question financial reports and information provided by managers, appoint senior management and determine their remuneration, and recommend new directors.

15.2.2 Multiple and double agency

These are relationships which are commonly found in large and complex organizations. It describes the situation where a principal has to rely upon more than one set of agency relationships to get their voice heard and their interests served. Let's consider double agency first. The first principal–agency relationship is the one described above where the shareholders expect corporate management to 'do the right thing' in running the company. The second (double) agency relationship is that between top management and the rest of the organization to ensure that there is a close alignment between objectives and effective implementation. However, we know from Chapter 12 on strategic decision making that such an alignment is rare. There are many cases where production and service providers in organizations behave and perform in ways which are not aligned with the wishes and the interests of top management. These agents, although located at lower levels in the organizational hierarchy, can have a powerful influence over what happens in practice and this can effectively destroy the first (or primary) principal–agent relationship between shareholders and corporate management.

There are many behavioural and structural reasons why relationships between subordinate managers and corporate (senior) managers are often mis-aligned. One is political in nature. Subordinate managers want to preserve autonomy and not be wholly controlled by senior managers. Once control has broken down, the double agency problem emerges. Another is hierarchical in nature. Subordinate managers may be looking to be promoted to senior levels. They therefore act in ways which enhance their prospects of promotion rather than effective strategy execution. Such behaviours include redefining strategic goals and communicating these to their own departments and juniors as well as filtering information sent upwards to senior managers to make the subordinates appear to be performing well in the eyes of the board.

Any organization theorist would recognize the above behaviours as well known and perhaps obvious. It is important, however, to recognize that the majority of governance theories (including the normative codes of conduct we shall discuss later) assume an unproblematic set of relationships between senior managers and subordinates. Put simply, most theories of governance assume perfect control of a company by its most senior managers.

Multiple agency occurs when, for example, a firm enters into a joint venture or subcontracts to another firm (or firms) to get the job done. Not only is the principal interacting with the focal firm's principals, he or she is also (albeit at arm's length) interacting with principals from other companies with which the original agents have agreed to do business. Another form of multiple agency occurs because of the likelihood that any form of joint management will have multiple owners, each of which will act as a principal (each will have its own reasons for entering into a relationship and will want specific things out of it). The managers of the joint venture will act as agents for the owners (with all the potential problems of double agency occurring, as outlined above).

15.2.3 Stakeholder theory

An alternative, and contrasting, view to agency theory is provided by stakeholder theory. Agency theory's underlying assumption is that profit maximization is the main objective to be pursued by the firm. Stakeholder theory, instead, stresses the importance of all parties who are affected by a firm's operations. Blair (1995) argued that 'what is optimal for shareholders often is not optimal for the rest of society'. Parties having a 'stake' in the firm include shareholders and directors, but also other actors such as employees, government, customers, suppliers, bankers and local communities. Stakeholder theory reveals that not only shareholders risk their capital in the company. Employees, for instance, risk their human capital when they work for a firm and, unlike shareholders, they are not in the position to be able to reduce their risk through diversification.

However, stakeholder theory is not free of ambiguity. Jensen (2001) argues that 'because stakeholder theory provides no definition of "better", it leaves managers and directors unaccountable for their stewardship of the firm's resources. With no criteria for performance, managers cannot be managed in a principled way.' In Jensen's view, this unproductive expansion of the power of managers increases agency costs in the economic system. However, Jensen emphasizes that a firm cannot maximize its value if it ignores the interests of stakeholders.

15.3 Corporate governance in the UK

Modern UK corporate governance regulations began with the Cadbury Report (1992), which reviewed the financial aspects of corporate governance and led to the publication of the Code of Best Practice. This was followed by the Greenbury Committee (1995), which reviewed directors' remuneration, while the Hampel Committee on Corporate Governance (established in 1995 and reporting in 1998) had a broader remit that built on Cadbury and Greenbury, essentially picking up new issues that had arisen from both reports. Following the report of the Hampel Committee, the first edition of the Combined Code was published by the London Stock Exchange (LSE) Committee on Corporate Governance and was added as an appendix to the LSE Listing Rules. The code superseded all previous codes for UK-listed companies and was derived from Cadbury, Greenbury, Hampel and the LSE's Listing Rules. The principles behind the code were those of market and self-regulation. The code was not legally enforceable, but a company was required to explain how the principles of the code had been followed and to disclose when and why they did not follow the code.

Since the publication of the first edition of the Combined Code, three other important reports have been published to date. These are the Turnbull Report, which provides guidelines for directors on how to meet the Code's provisions on internal control; the Smith Report, which relates to the provisions on audit committees and auditors; and the Higgs Report, which was a review of the role and effectiveness of non-executive directors. The findings of these reports have been incorporated into the latest edition of the Combined Code (building on Higgs, 2003). It represents something of a 'capstone' to the previous reports and it has had a significant impact on the structures and processes of boards in the UK. Like all previous codes, the Combined Code seeks to influence board structure and conduct by means of codes of practice and not through legislation. Boards are expected to *comply or explain* why they have not complied in their reporting mechanisms. The key requirements of the combined code are summarized in Table 15.1.

The reasons for not choosing a legal requirement for disclosure and relying on codes of practice lies, on the one hand, in the less than adequate provision of the legal structure in the UK to ensure good practice and, on the other, to encourage the spirit of self-regulation. This is in contrast to the Sarbanes–Oxley code in the US which we introduced in the beginning of this chapter. Sarbanes–Oxley is rooted in legal (rather than voluntary) requirements and those who transgress (for example, the directors of Enron) can be prosecuted and jailed.

> Table 15.1 Key elements of the Combined Code

The main disclosures required are:
- A statement of how the board operates and which types of decisions are taken by the board and which are delegated to management.
- Number of meetings of the board and its committees including a list of annual attendance by directors.
- A description of how performance evaluation of the board, its committees and its directors is conducted.
- What steps have been taken to ensure that members of the board, especially non-executive directors, understand the views of major shareholders about their organisation.
- A description of how the nomination committee works and why open advertising or an external search agency have not been used in the appointments of either a chairman or a non-executive director.
- A description of the processes and activities of the remuneration and audit committees.

The main principles of the Code are:
- Every company should be headed by an effective board which is collectively responsible for the success of the organisation.
- A clear division of responsibilities. The roles of chairman and chief executive should not be exercised by the same individual and no one individual should have unfettered powers of decision. It is worth noting here that almost ten percent of UK listed companies have a joint chairman/chief executive (Hemscott, 2003).
- The board should include a balance of executive and independent non-executive directors.
- Transparency of all procedures.
- The board should undertake a formal and rigorous evaluation of its own performance and that of its committees and individual directors.
- All directors should be submitted for re-election at regular intervals subject to continued satisfactory performance. Refreshing the board with new members should be planned and implemented.
- Levels of remuneration should be sufficient to attract, retain and motivate directors but this should not include paying more than is necessary for this purpose. There should be a transparent policy on remuneration.
- Financial reporting should be understandable and transparent and subject to strict internal controls.

UK law rests on the principle that the owners (shareholders) appoint agents (directors) to run the business, and the directors report annually on their stewardship. In practice, in public limited companies (of which there are around 2,000 in the UK), there is a two-link chain of accountability. Management is accountable to directors, and directors are accountable to shareholders. PLCs registered after 1 November 1929 are legally required to have at least two directors. There is no distinction between classes of directors; for instance, between executive (inside or full-time) directors and non-executive (outside and part-time) directors. The law refers only obscurely to chairmen and barely mentions boards. This legal minimalism leads Charkham (1999) to conclude that

> the superstructure as we know it: boards, board committees, chairmen, non-executive directors – are pragmatic adaptations. In law none is essential; to this day ICI could legally be run by two directors, like the consulate of the Roman Republic. (Charkham, 1999, p. 62)

Many UK boards divide the chairman and chief executive officer (CEO) roles, and the position of chairman is often part time. Chairmen have major responsibilities in determining the size, balance, composition and agenda of the board. They can also play a significant part in handling external relationships with key stakeholders such as government, institutional investors, regulators and banks. Chairmen are normally appointed by non-executive directors. Non-executive directors play an increasingly important role in influencing board processes, heading up important committees of the board such as the audit or remuneration committees. Audit and remuneration committees comprise only non-executive directors and nomination committees are headed by a non-executive director or the chairman who must meet the independence criteria laid out in the Combined Code.

Compliance with codes, however, does not mean that the board is working efficiently or effectively. At the extreme, compliance with any code could merely be a process of 'box ticking', indicating little of how the board really operates. We examine these questions in the next sections of this chapter.

15.4 The role of the board

O'Neal and Thomas (1996, p. 314) outline the three basic functions of the board:

1 advising and counselling top management;

2 monitoring and controlling top management;

3 developing corporate strategy.

These are echoed by Nadler et al. (2006) and a whole range of Harvard Business School authors and executive training courses aimed at building better boards. Most include a focus on engaging the board with corporate strategy, the role of the board in corporate crises and effective leadership of the board.

Conger et al. (2001), Ward (2000) and the OECD (2004) all offer principles against which board effectiveness might be judged. In particular, these authors emphasize that the board should be able to exercise judgement in decision making and corporate affairs generally, independently of other influences, particularly the voices of management. Since boards should appoint non-executive directors to exercise independent judgement over key areas such as financial reporting, nomination and remuneration, the board ought to be able to exercise independent and informed judgement away from the day-to-day managerial concerns of the organization. In addition, these authors emphasize the importance of boards being able to access and be supplied with accurate, timely and relevant information in order to carry out their strategic decision-making roles effectively. Finally, the role of accountability is emphasized, not only compliance with the law and acting on good faith, but also in the interests of all shareholders and the social responsibilities of the organization. These issues are summarized in the next sections.

15.4.1 The board as a team

Surprisingly, the board as an organizational team has been relatively neglected in empirical study. While there are plenty of studies on teams (and top teams) in organizations (see Katzenbach and Smith, 1992; Hambrick et al., 1998), there are very few studies of boards using the key variables identified from these team studies. Applying the empirical knowledge of team processes and performance to boards would emphasize a number of key aspects.

First, the board is an odd 'team' since on most occasions directors turn up for a board meeting individually, have a discussion and then leave, not meeting again until the next meeting. This sporadic process does not build a particularly effective team. Many boards suffer (lack of) attendance problems where directors are absent from board meetings and hence lose all possibilities of contributing to the discussions. Many boards have begun to establish attendance requirements for all directors as a result. Secondly, appropriate composition of the board is important since the expertise in the team needs to match and be able to support strategy. This will mean assessing such factors as industry experience, international experience, functional experience and prior board

Table 15.2 Key team roles of a company board	
Team characteristics	**Team roles in the board**
Specialised knowledge/abilities	Ability to think and act strategically Key functional expertise needs to be represented
Process of team meetings	Sporadic. Board meetings are unlike other top team meetings (which are continuous and frequent). Board meetings are discontinuous and relatively infrequent
Key relationships in the team	CEO with the Chair CEO with the Board Executive and Non-Executive Directors

experience. Specific expertise may be required where the board may need specialized knowledge about foreign markets or complex information technologies.

Table 15.2 summarises the key team roles of a company board.

Thirdly, the board needs to build in maintenance and learning functions to its operations and processes. The board's role as the key strategic decision-making body calls for a high level of commitment of all members as well as the ability of those members to learn from experience and apply that learning to decisions and judgements they are required to take. Training and development (e.g. perhaps an induction programme for newly appointed directors) should also be beneficial, as should specific training in the key areas of decision making (see Chapter 12) such as strategy, risk and evaluating performance. Like all groups in organizations, some assessment of their own performance as a team and as individuals in that team should ensure greater effectiveness. We look at board effectiveness later in this chapter.

15.4.2 The board and strategic decision making

As the key group in strategic decision-making processes, the board needs both to understand how decisions are made (on what basis and with what stated objectives, for example) and how they go about decision making as a team. This is another aspect of the interface between organization and strategy (see Chapter 2). In making strategic decisions, the board stamps its mark on the organization and, in turn, the organization becomes a distinctive entity with its own structure, culture and philosophy. A resource-based view of the organization would imply that a key role of the board is to ensure precisely what is the core business or purpose of the organization and to ensure that organizational competences and resources are in place to support that core purpose. This is akin to creating and preserving that 'cherished core ideology' that Collins and Porras (2000) argue is the vital constant of successful organizations when all else around them is subject to change. In essence, the board represents and needs to preserve the glue which holds the organization together and which is the guiding principles by which key decisions are made.

The board also has the responsibility not only of overseeing its own internal processes in this respect, but also of ensuring that this 'strategy with values' is disseminated effectively throughout the organization and that processes, rewards and organizational structures are aligned with the strategy. Opinions differ about the level of involvement that is both possible and desirable for boards in the strategy process. Some argue that boards should have a proactive or initiating role of shaping strategy. Others contend that the board should challenge, question and eventually approve strategic ideas and decisions formulated below the board in the executive team. McNulty and Pettigrew (1999) have examined the contribution to strategy by chairmen and non-executive

Table 15.3 Board member involvement in strategy

	Taking strategic decisions	Shaping strategic decisions	Shaping the content, context and conduct of strategy
Definition	Influence is exerted inside the boardroom at the end of the capital investment decision process.	Influence occurs early in the decision process as part-time board members shape the preparation of capital investment proposal by executives.	Influence is continuous and not confined to decision episodes.
Board behaviour	Inside the boardroom, boards take decisions to accept, reject or refer capital investment proposals.	Consultation with part-time board members by the executive, either formally or informally, while a capital investment proposal is being prepared enables board members to test ideas, raise issues, question assumptions, advise caution, and offer encouragement. Executives 'sieve' capital investment proposals in anticipation of the need for board approval.	The board develops the context for strategic debate, establishes a methodology for strategy development, monitors strategy content and alters the conduct of the executive in relation to strategy.
Board involvement	All boards take strategic decisions.	Some boards shape strategic decisions.	A minority of boards shape the context, content and conduct of strategy.

Source: adapted from McNulty and Pettigrew (1999)

directors of large UK companies. The collective label of part-time board member was used to refer to individuals performing these two roles (although a limited number of chairmen in the UK have executive and virtually full-time positions). Table 15.3 summarizes the involvement of the board directors in strategic decision making.

Most non-executives claimed they were much more influential in stopping initiatives than in starting them (McNulty and Pettigrew, 1999). The executives interviewed claimed that around 80% of the strategic decisions they took to the boardroom were approved or confirmed by the whole board.

Shaping strategic decisions entails a higher degree of non-executive board member influence. If the non-executives are consulted and involved earlier in the strategy process they can shape the assumptions, alternatives and actual choices in the process. Shaping also occurs when executives restrict the range of their own proposals (knowing that certain alternatives will not be accepted at board level).

The ultimate way for a board to shape strategy is to fire the CEO and other executive directors. This is happening with increasing frequency in UK boardrooms. The new generation of CEOs entering UK boardrooms are likely to be younger, to have had experience in more than one company and industry, and to have a shorter tenure in post than their predecessors of the 1980s and early 1990s.

15.5 Board effectiveness

There are many measures of board effectiveness, some initiated internally in a board review process (or in a review of the CEO's performance), while others are judged more externally, such as the extent to which the board has ensured compliance with codes of ethics, high standards of behaviour, effective decision making and social responsibility. We examine these in the following sections.

15.5.1 Board effectiveness and corporate social responsibility

A question of increasing importance to all organzations is to what extent the board has ensured that strategic decisions incorporate ethical, socially responsible and sustainable factors. It is the duty of a diligent board to assess and to take into consideration issues of a sustainable environment. In many respects, corporate social responsibility (CSR) is not a separate issue but is one which permeates all board activities (in particular, decision making and **risk** assessment).

An organization operating in a manner contrary to CSR faces the risk of poor market ratings and adverse publicity. Those facing large ethical concerns also face the results of poor and adverse publicity. A well-known example of this is the case of BP-Amoco which suffered greatly as a result of its exploration activities in Colombia. Eventually accused of working for a corrupt government, BP Amoco suffered bad publicity, a drop in market value and a drastic drop in reputation. Few boards would want to ignore CSR. They would do so at their peril.

Two aspects of formalizing CSR have now become the remit of boards worldwide. The first is known as the 'triple bottom line'. This means that, alongside financial and other hard measures of performance, a measure of CSR (the third measure) should be included alongside them as an equal arbiter of performance. The second is known as the 'global compact', resulting from a meeting of the World Economic Forum in 1999. The then UN Secretary-General, Kofi Annan, set out nine principles on human rights, labour and the environment that organizations need to address (and be judged against). Table 15.4 summarizes the nine core principles of the global compact.

A study by Contardo and Wilson (2001) revealed a patchy take-up of these nine principles by the boards of 20 organizations. These 20 organizations were drawn from ten different nations in order to see if country of origin had any significant impact on the implementation of the nine principles. The results revealed that country of origin had no impact at all. The data from this study revealed that boards were experiencing some difficulties in implementing the nine principles, especially in older organizations. Boards in older organizations experienced difficulties in assessing the relative priority of these principles in relation to other, externally determined standards (such as International Standards or Health and Safety). In general, the boards of older organizations were making progress in networking with stakeholders in order to try to establish partnerships and had often set up new

Table 15.4 The nine principles of the global compact	
Human rights	Businesses should: ■ Support and respect the protection of international human rights within their sphere of influence ■ Ensure their own corporations are not involved in human rights abuses (implicitly or explicitly)
Labour	■ Recognize the right of labour to collective bargaining and freedom of association ■ Eliminate forced and compulsory labour ■ Abolish child labour ■ Eliminate discrimination in terms of employment and occupation
Environment	■ Take a precautionary approach to environmental challenges ■ Promote greater environmental responsibility ■ Encourage the development and diffusion of environmentally friendly technologies

functions in the organization to deal with CSR issues. For example, Unilever had created a special department addressing CSR issues and had engaged with many stakeholders (including strong critics of the organization) in order to weave environmental consciousness throughout their business. Shell Brazil has introduced a clause in its contracts with distillers forbidding the use of child labour. Shell Brazil was awarded the title 'Child Friendly Company' for its work in discouraging the use of child labour in the production of sugar cane alcohol, which it is legally obliged to sell on its forecourts and include in its gasoline. BASF has established a sustainability council at board level to try to make sustainability a part of everyday processes in the company and Starbucks has committed to being a deeply responsible company (see Case box 15.2). Overall, however, the data from Contardo and Wilson (2001) point to a very patchy worldwide take-up of the nine principles by a wide range of organizations, with boards in particular finding it difficult to add these responsibilities to their existing portfolio of activities.

Case box 15.2: Starbucks' CSR statement

Our commitment to being a deeply responsible company

Contributing positively to our communities and environment is so important to Starbucks that it's one of the six guiding principles of our mission statement. We work together on a daily basis with partners (employees), suppliers, farmers and others to help create a more sustainable approach to high-quality coffee production, to help build stronger local communities, to minimize our environmental footprint, to create a great workplace, to promote diversity and to be responsive to our customers' health and wellness needs.

To inspire and nurture the human spirit – one person, one cup, and one neighbourhood at a time. Here are the principles of how we live that every day:

Our Coffee

It has always been, and will always be, about quality. We're passionate about ethically sourcing the finest coffee beans, roasting them with great care, and improving the lives of people who grow them. We care deeply about all of this; our work is never done.

Our Partners

We're called partners, because it's not just a job, it's our passion. Together, we embrace diversity to create a place where each of us can be ourselves. We always treat each other with respect and dignity. And we hold each other to that standard.

Our Customers

When we are fully engaged, we connect with, laugh with, and uplift the lives of our customers – even if just for a few moments. Sure, it starts with the promise of a perfectly made beverage, but our work goes far beyond that. It's really about human connection.

Our Stores

When our customers feel this sense of belonging, our stores become a haven, a break from the worries outside, a place where you can meet with friends. It's about enjoyment at the speed of life – sometimes slow and savored, sometimes faster. Always full of humanity.

Our Neighbourhood

Every store is part of a community, and we take our responsibility to be good neighbors seriously. We want to be invited in wherever we do business. We can be a force for positive action – bringing

▶ together our partners, customers, and the community to contribute every day. Now we see that our responsibility – and our potential for good – is even larger. The world is looking to Starbucks to set the new standard, yet again. We will lead.

Our Shareholders

We know that as we deliver in each of these areas, we enjoy the kind of success that rewards our shareholders. We are fully accountable to get each of these elements right so that Starbucks – and everyone it touches – can endure and thrive.

Onward.

Environmental mission statement

Starbucks is committed to a role of environmental leadership in all facets of our business.

We fulfil this mission by a commitment to:
Understanding of environmental issues and sharing information with our partners.
Developing innovative and flexible solutions to bring about change.
Striving to buy, sell and use environmentally friendly products.
Recognizing that fiscal responsibility is essential to our environmental future.
Instilling environmental responsibility as a corporate value.
Measuring and monitoring our progress for each project.
Encouraging all partners to share in our mission.

Source: www.starbucks.com/mission

15.5.2 Board effectiveness and strategy

The board has two major strategic purposes:

1 to exercise *control* (by overseeing the performance of the organization and those who lead it);
2 to provide *strategic leadership* (by shaping the values, identity and strategic decisions of the organization).

Many have argued that the former has taken precedence over the latter over the last decade or so – box-ticking the requirements of the Combined Code, for example, rather than engaging in strategic thinking. The board needs to be strategic, oversightful and operate in a way which cross-cuts the organization in terms of decisions and communication. This may mean a change in the ways many boards operate, for example by not spending the bulk of board time ploughing through reports by executive directors, but by delegating such work to the next line of senior management down from the board. In practice, this process could operate very similarly to a two-tier board (like those found in continental Europe) without necessarily adopting the two-tier structure.

In securing strategic leadership, the board stamps its mark upon the organization and, in turn, the organization becomes a distinctive entity with its own unique structure, culture and identity. A key role of the board strategically is to ensure precisely what is the 'core business' of the firm and to ensure that competences and resources are in place to support that core purpose. This 'cherished core' is the vital constant of successful organizations when all else around them is changing.

15.5.3 Board effectiveness and strategic decision making

Research has revealed that one of the key roles in successful strategic decision making is the CEO (see Chapter 12). Where the CEO is not involved (and not influential) in both the formulation and implementation stages of a decision, performance suffers (Miller et al., 2008). The CEO does not work alone, of course. There is a small group (well defined) who work with the CEO to increase the chances of success in strategic decision making. The points below summarize:

- Production/Service Delivery (P/SD), Marketing and the CEO are both the most frequently involved and the most influential through both the deciding and the implementation of strategic decisions, with Finance and Suppliers the next most influential. The CEO is crucial in orchestrating this relatively small core team.
- This core team *oversees* some of the most important areas of an organization's activity, *deciding its future strategic direction* and *shaping* how this is made a reality.
- Other players such as Purchasing, Research and Development, and Human Resources are usually on the sidelines, and thus have only a limited influence in shaping strategic decisions.

How the board itself works has been studied by Business School researchers. In particular, McNulty and Pettigrew (1999) have produced the following classification of effective and ineffective boards. One of the key factors underpinning a successful board is a good and clearly defined working relationship between the chair and the CEO. There are many autobiographical accounts by practitioners of board effectiveness but few independently conducted analyses of board conduct and performance. Recently a study conducted by Pettigrew and McNulty has generated first-hand data on board conduct, power relationships and strategy processes (Pettigrew and McNulty, 1995, 1998; McNulty and Pettigrew, 1999.) This study used a multi-method approach combining a survey of the chairmen, CEOs and non-executive directors of the top 500 PLCs with personal interviews with 65 part time and 43 full time board members and the analysis of publicly available documentary material.

Ineffective boards can be characterized by:

- poor chairing;
- cliques and politicking;
- marginalizing the non-executives;
- fixation on a narrow set of issues, short-term agendas;
- failure to encourage open discussion and allow 'issue spotting';
- closed process of recruitment to the board.

Effective boards can be characterized by:

- non-executive directors allowed into strategic decision-making processes;
- non-executive directors allowed to roam outside the boardroom;
- possibly needing to remove the 'old' power system embodied in the CEO and the chair;
- high levels of trust and openness (allows challenge, discussion and enhances confidence and innovation);
- ensuring that the relative balance of power between the chair and the CEO is clear.

15.6 International corporate governance

Aguilera and Cuervo-Cazurra (2004, p. 419) concluded that there were 72 codes of good governance by the end of 1999 spread across 24 industrialized and developing countries. Table 15.5 summarizes:

Table 15.5 Numbers of codes of governance worldwide (to end 1999)	
Country	**Total number of codes**
English-origin legal system	
Australia	4
Canada	4
Hong Kong	4
India	2
Ireland	2
Malaysia	1
Singapore	1
South Africa	1
Thailand	1
UK	11
USA	17
French-origin legal system	
Belgium	4
Brazil	1
France	4
Greece	1
Italy	2
Mexico	1
Netherlands	2
Portugal	1
Spain	2
German-origin legal system	
Germany	1
Japan	2
Korea	1
Scandinavian-origin legal system	
Sweden	2
Total countries 24	**Total codes 72**

Source: adapted from Aguilera and Cuervo-Cazurra (2004, p. 423)

The codes produced under different legal systems have often been customized to particular national settings and this has reinforced the governance differences identified by Charkham (1999). However, institutions such as the World Bank and OECD are calling for common principles and common governance structures and processes, at least to a minimum level. *Exogenous* forces are influencing the adoption of reasonably common codes. As organizations become more a part of the global economy, for example, the transmission of common practices becomes easier and, some would say, necessary. Government liberalization and the increasing influence of foreign institutional investors also force the pace for common codes and standards. In this way, exogenous pressures force countries to show that their codes of corporate governance are 'legitimate' in the global economy.

15.6.1 Corporate governance and the multinational enterprise

Corporate governance can play an important role in the operations of an MNE in a number of ways. An effective system of corporate governance will consist of practices and procedures that will protect a company's assets and the interests of its shareholders and other key stakeholders. Internal control systems will enable the company's senior management to monitor the performance of its managers and subsidiaries on a global basis. While a strong independent board of directors will be able to challenge the decisions of management and oversee strategy at the macro level, one of its key roles is to ensure that all shareholders (not just majority shareholders) are treated equally.

However, the board will need effective reporting mechanisms to increase the level of transparency of the operations of the company not only for management but also for existing or potential shareholders. Effective control will enable headquarters-based managers to monitor and where necessary question the actions of local managers, ensuring that their behaviour is consistent with the interests of the company as a whole. Effective communication will also make it easier to grow the business internationally in a coordinated fashion, allowing for the effective allocation of resources into the highest-yielding opportunities. Furthermore, by effectively monitoring the behaviour of its subsidiaries a company will be able to reduce the likelihood of behaviour that could damage the reputation of the company, which could negatively affect it both by redirecting management efforts away from more profitable activities and by reducing the share price as institutional investors choose to disassociate themselves from the company.

Effective corporate governance should also increase a company's ability to raise capital for growth (domestic or international). An Economist Intelligence Unit survey (2003, p.18) indicates that 70% of 310 international executives surveyed believe the perception of good governance standards has a positive impact on stock prices while 79% believe a negative impact will occur if the perception is poor (Mintz, 2005, p. 583). Furthermore, as a result of recent corporate governance scandals, banks are far more likely to take into consideration a company's standard of corporate governance when making a decision whether to provide it with capital. In short, investors demand transparency and accountability in return for their capital (Monks and Minow, 2004, p. 297).

15.6.2 Corporate governance models: country differences

The system of corporate governance in a country is determined by both internal and external factors. Internal factors include corporate ownership structure, the state of the economy, the legal system (see Table 15.5), government policies, culture and history. External factors include the extent of capital inflows from abroad, the global economic climate and cross-border institutional investment (Solomon and Solomon, 2004, p. 147). Each system of corporate governance is unique to that country, making it very difficult to categorize a country's corporate governance system. However, as corporate governance operates differently in two broadly distinct worlds (Buck and

Shahrim, 2005, p. 42), a broad categorization of corporate governance systems is possible using the 'insider/outsider' approach suggested by Short et al. (1998, p. 154) or the voice/market-exit approach proposed by Hirschman (1984, p. 89) and Nooteboom (1999, p. 846). Most systems of corporate governance fall somewhere between these two approaches, sharing some of each other's characteristics (Solomon and Solomon, 2004, p. 148).

The outsider/market-exit approach, often referred to as the Anglo-Saxon system of corporate governance, emphasizes the rights of one group of stakeholders in a company – shareholders (outsiders) – and the mechanisms to maximize their investment in a company. The firm is conceived as a combination of managerial directors operating for the benefit of shareholders, or as an instrument for the creation of shareholder wealth (Weimer and Pape, 1999, p. 154). Managers' decisions can be influenced by shareholders adopting a 'market-exit' approach. If shareholders are dissatisfied with the behaviour and performance of the company's managers they could decide to sell or reduce their investment in the company, thereby depressing the company's share price and penalizing managers whose rewards are determined in some way by the company's share price, e.g. through stock options. In addition, a reduction in the share price may leave the company vulnerable to a hostile[5] takeover which could result in substantial job losses among the company's existing managers. This approach, which has been adopted in the UK, depends upon high levels of information disclosure by listed companies and laws[6] that protect minority shareholders (La Porta et al., 2000). High levels of information allow investors to decide whether to buy or sell the shares of a company and provide them with the knowledge needed when they exercise their rights as shareholders, e.g. voting at shareholders' meetings. Protection of minority shareholders prevents expropriation of minority shareholders by the controlling shareholders.

The second approach – insider/voice – refers to the means by which any of the firm's stakeholders (not just shareholders) may control managers' decisions (Buck and Shahrim, 2005, p. 43). Managers are influenced mainly by the 'voice' of stakeholders (insiders) who are highly committed to the firm, closely connected, and are prepared to contribute formally to its governance and not by potential or actual movements in share prices. In this alternative, relational world of governance, different groups of stakeholders may dominate in individual countries (Buck and Shahrim, 2005, p. 43). They could be banks, other companies with cross-holdings in the company, controlling shareholders, customers and employees. This relational approach, which is commonplace in the stakeholder model of corporate governance, is characterized by low levels of transparency and information disclosure to outsiders and limited protection for minority shareholders. Given that shareholdings are generally concentrated in the hands of a small number of investors, it is easier for a company to resist a hostile takeover attempt. It is also possible for managers to adopt a more relaxed approach to short-term fluctuations in their company's stock price as it is less likely to play a role in their remuneration package and career advancement.

15.6.3 Differences in corporate governance systems: a comparison of the United Kingdom, Germany and Japan

This section will consider differences in national corporate governance systems relating to the separation between ownership and control; board structure and responsibility; shareholder rights; and the market for corporate control. The three countries under consideration – UK, Germany and

---

[5] Takeovers are termed 'hostile' when the management of the target firm opposes them (Franks and Mayer, 1990).

[6] Relevant legislation includes the Companies Act 1985, the Financial Services and Markets Act 2000 (the FSMA) and the insider dealing provisions of the Criminal Justice Act 1993. UK and EU competition legislation and the UK Financial Services Authority's Listing, Prospectus and Disclosure Rules may also apply. The cornerstone of these regulations and a number of regulations governing substantial acquisition of a number of shares is that shareholders should be 'fairly' treated (Weimer and Pape, 1999, p. 163).

Japan – are chosen to represent the outsider/market-exit shareholder approach and two variants of the insider/voice stakeholder approach respectively.

15.6.4 Separation between ownership and control

All three countries are characterized by concentrated control of outstanding shares. However, in the UK shares are normally controlled by financial institutions whose involvement in the management of companies is far less commonplace than is the case with major shareholders in Germany and Japan. In both of these countries the most influential shareholders are financial (primarily banks through direct and indirect holdings[7]) and non-financial (significant cross-holdings between companies). This means that when analysing control in German and Japanese companies, one needs to look at the links between companies (Mallin, 2007, p. 163). Representatives of these shareholders frequently sit on company boards and cross-directorships are commonplace with directors directly linked to one company often sitting on the boards of another company in whom their company has a shareholding. In turn, that company will often own shares in their company and have representation on their board of directors.

Pyramidal/chain ownership structures are common in both Germany and Japan, with one company, often a bank, playing the dominant role. Such structures can lead to agency problems arising from large deviations between control and cash flow rights. When this occurs a company at the top of the chain is able to exert control over a company further down the pyramid, even though it has a relatively small shareholding in the company. Example 15.1 shows Company A having 100% control over Company F while having an effective interest in the company of only 3.5%.

In recent times shareholder activism has increased in all three countries. In the UK this is a reflection of growing concentration of shareholdings in the hands of institutional investors that makes it difficult for them to adopt an 'exit' approach[8] and the recommendations included in the Combined Code on Corporate Governance.[9] In Japan and Germany major shareholders are under greater pressure from their own shareholders to justify large shareholdings in other companies.

The role of non-shareholding groups in the control of a company also differs across the three countries. In the UK, companies are managed to maximize shareholders' returns and the level of government intervention in their operations is normally limited.[10] In Germany and Japan, the interests of other stakeholders (e.g. employees, government, suppliers, etc) are usually considered, although this can vary greatly from one stakeholder to another.

15.6.5 Board structure and responsibility

Companies in the UK and Japan are controlled by a single unitary board elected by shareholders. In Germany the corporate governance system is based around a dual board system comprising a management and a supervisory board. The management board, whose members are appointed by the supervisory board, consists of employees and is responsible for managing the company, while

---

[7]   In Japan, although banks are limited to a 5% ownership in a company, the degree of influence they have is often far greater than would be expected by such a small shareholding, due to the other services they provide for the company such as playing the role of lead bank in raising debt finance.

[8]   The popularity of index funds with investors that are required to hold all of the shares in a certain index, e.g. FTSE 100, means that institutions have no option but to hold shares in a company. In this case they are forced to adopt a 'voice' approach to influence the actions of company management.

[9]   The UK Combined Code of Corporate Governance (2006) Principle E.1 says: '*Institutional shareholders should enter into a dialogue with companies based on mutual understanding of objectives.*'

[10] The government may become involved if a company achieved a position of market dominance that was deemed detrimental to the economy as a whole.

Example 15.1: **Chain/Pyramid ownership structures and control**

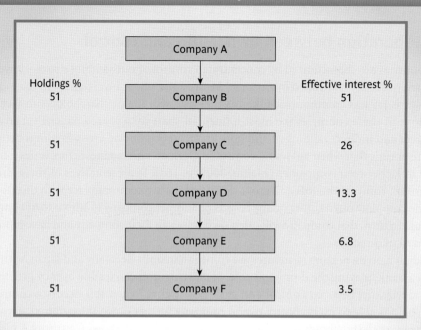

Holdings %		Effective interest %
	Company A	
51	Company B	51
51	Company C	26
51	Company D	13.3
51	Company E	6.8
51	Company F	3.5

This is achieved through Company A's 51% shareholding in Company B that gives it 100% control over Company B. Company B's 51% shareholding in Company C gives it 100% control and so on down to the last company in the chain – Company F – which is 51% owned and 100% controlled by Company E. As Company A controls Company B who controls Company C who controls Company D who controls Company E who controls Company F, Company A controls Company F. However, due to the 51% stake held by each company in the following company, .51 × .51 × .51 × .51 × .51 gives Company A an effective interest of 3.5% in Company F and subsequently, despite 100% control of the company, a claim on only 3.5% of the company's income. This creates a potential agency problem, with a small shareholder being in a position to exert control over the entire company.

the supervisory board controls the direction of the business. Members of the supervisory board are either elected by the shareholders or appointed by employee groups. In companies with between 500 and 2,000 employees, one-third of the supervisory board consists of employee representatives, a number that increases to half of the supervisory board in companies with over 2,000 employees. Both sets of directors are equally obliged to act in the enterprise's best interests.

In the UK, the majority of directors are non-executive and independent.[11] In Japan, the number of directors classified as outsiders is steadily increasing but is still very low, with data prepared by J-IRIS Research in 2004 (Charkham, 2005, p. 135) showing the average number of outside directors at 0.6 per company. Furthermore, the degree to which they are independent can be hard to determine. In Germany, partly as a result of employee representatives, the number of independent directors on the supervisory board is likely to be less than 25% of the total.

The boards of UK companies are, on average, the smallest of the three countries, averaging around 8.5 members (PIRC, 2003). In Japan, the number has been steadily decreasing, following criticisms of unwieldy boards that were unable to engage effectively in the management of the

---

[11] What is meant by independence is clearly explained in the UK Combined Code of Corporate Governance (Code Provision A3.1).

company, and in 2004 averaged 10.5 (Charkham, 2005, p. 135). In 2003, German supervisory boards on average numbered 16 members (Korn/Ferry, 2003).

If the board comprises a large number of non-independent directors, their interests may not be in line with other stakeholders', especially those that do not have a long-term relationship with the company. This may lead the company to take decisions that are not necessarily in the best interests of all of its shareholders. In the cases of both Germany and Japan this has often been reflected in a criticism that companies are more concerned with the long term, often at the cost of failing to maximize returns for shareholders in the short term. Up until the 1990s this was often lauded as a positive, but a period of poor returns for investors (especially in Japan) has led to a significant change in attitudes.

15.6.6 Shareholder rights

Corporate governance in the UK emphasizes the rights of shareholders whose interests are protected in law. Companies demonstrate high levels of transparency in their operations, with the Combined Code on Corporate Governance (2006) Principle C.1 stating that '*The board should present a balanced and understandable assessment of the company's position and prospects*'. Without a high degree of transparency there cannot be effective accountability (Charkham, 2005, p. 330). Through the annual report and other announcements made by the company, shareholders will, among other things, be made aware of the company's audited financial condition, key operational developments, the remuneration of directors, their involvement in the company and how they were appointed.

Despite the pre-eminence of shareholders, UK companies are demonstrating an increasing awareness of the importance of other key stakeholders, frequently including in their annual report a statement on corporate and social responsibility that discusses how they engage with non-shareholding key stakeholders. This is, in part, recognition by companies that in order to maximize shareholder returns they also need to protect the interests of other stakeholder groups.

In Japan and Germany, shareholder rights, levels of legal protection and transparency are less than those of the UK. This is not surprising given the stakeholder orientation of their corporate governance systems. Charkham (2005, p. 108) describes the three main concepts that influence Japanese attitudes to corporate governance as obligation, family and consensus. The first refers to obligation to the company; the second refers to the strong need to be part of a family (company); and the third, consensus, means an emphasis on agreement rather than antagonism (Mallin, 2007, p. 221). The corporation is a social entity, with the survival of the firm and life-long employment the main goals. Historically this has been reflected by the emphasis Japanese companies have placed on market share rather than shareholder return. The commitment to other stakeholders in Germany has already been discussed in Section 15.6.3.

15.6.7 Market for corporate control

The market for corporate control refers to the opportunities available to a company to acquire or merge with another company. This is relevant to MNEs in two respects: First, is the local corporate governance regime supportive of takeovers, especially 'hostile' takeovers?[12] Second, should an MNE successfully acquire a local company, will it be able to successfully transfer the corporate governance practices expected by its listing authority, given differences between the operating environments in each country?

The market for corporate control in the UK is highly developed and active, with mergers and acquisitions commonplace among both local and foreign companies establishing or increasing

---

[12] Takeovers are termed 'hostile' when the management of the target firm opposes them (Franks and Mayer, 1990).

their presence in the UK. Government intervention is only likely to occur if the government is concerned that the 'new' company will be in a monopolistic position or the takeover has failed to follow the provisions of the Takeover Panel's code,[13] e.g. a failure to treat all shareholders of the same class equally.

In Germany (and particularly in Japan), the market for corporate control is far less developed, with hostile takeovers by foreign companies uncommon. In Germany, the large shareholdings held by banks that have a relationship with the target company make the likelihood of a successful bid less likely. Furthermore, local and national government also tend to apply political pressure supporting local ownership. One notable exception to this was the acquisition of Mannesmann by the UK's Vodafone, at the time the largest takeover in history. In this case the key to Vodafone's success was that two-thirds of Mannesmann was held by non-German investors.

Mergers between willing companies have long been a feature of the Japanese industrial scene (Charkham, 2005, p. 146). Hostile bids were, and are, still largely unknown, regarded as culturally unacceptable and very difficult given the degree of cross-shareholding. Furthermore, takeover attempts by foreign companies are likely to be opposed by politicians, who frequently have close relationships with private sector companies.

15.7 Summary

This chapter has examined some key aspects of boards and their role in strategic decision making. The board has a strategic and public responsibility to provide direct returns for shareholders, employees and suppliers and has a responsibility towards the communities in which they operate. In the wake of recent corporate scandals and collapses, governments worldwide have been reviewing the role and the processes of governance.

Because the board is in place to lead and control the organization, it should have a clearly defined set of responsibilities and codes of operation. This chapter has outlined the main features of those responsibilities and some of the major features of the emerging guidelines.

Although board structures differ from country to country, most countries have a common set of principles of governance, namely that no individual director has unrestrained power to control and direct the organization and that there should be a countervailing influence to insiders on the board from outside directors who act as the guardians of board conduct and decision-making processes. Case box 15.3 shows, in the case of Coca-Cola in Nigeria, the importance of corporate governance in less stable economic environments.

Future research into boards continues. Warwick Business School has set up a research agenda with the boards of some of the FTSE top 350 companies which, amongst other topics, will examine key under-researched areas such as:

- The pivotal role of the non-executive directors and the difficulty of recruiting new ones.

- The need to develop and identify accurate and robust key performance indicators so that the board can effectively provide strategic leadership.

- The importance of maintaining good media relations.

- The importance of the board being quorate and non-executive directors and executive directors interacting effectively. The extent to which informal interaction is key to (or the glue in) successful boards.

- Effectively balancing risk and control in rapidly changing contexts.

---

[13] The Takeover Panel, established in 1968, is a non-statutory body whose main functions are to issue and administer the City Code on Takeover and Mergers and to supervise and regulate takeovers and other matters to which the code applies.

Case box 15.3: **In Nigeria: Coke is it?**

The Nigerian government welcomes Coca-Cola's new investment, but critics are wary

Multinational soft drink giant Coca-Cola has announced a fresh investment of $150 million into the Nigerian economy, the largest single foreign investment in the country in recent years, a move widely interpreted by analysts as an indication of growing investor confidence in Nigeria. The Nigerian government is hailing this as a great boon for the country and a sign the economy is on the mend after years of mismanagement and corruption.

'We are indeed most delighted with the Coca-Cola Company's consistent investment in Nigeria... This is how multinationals should operate,' president Olusegun Obasanjo said.

Despite this vote of confidence by the officials, anti-Coca-Cola campaigners are suspicious that the new investment may worsen the water crisis in areas where new bottling plants will be commissioned.

This, of course, is in addition to the perennial charge that Coca-Cola is helping to erode dietary habits in the third world and making young people addicted to an unwholesome drink.

Coca-Cola, smarting from recent troubles in Kerala, India, over the vexed issue of water sourcing, is sensitive to such charges, and says its Nigeria operation will largely depend on existing water sources and is environmentally sustainable.

Pollution

Sam Olukoya, a Nigerian journalist who writes on environmental issues, told Ethical Corporation Coca-Cola has over the years enjoyed good relations with local communities in Nigeria, unlike the major oil companies operating in the Niger Delta, and has largely escaped blame for environmental pollution except for a brief episode some years ago when a bottling plant was accused of polluting a local river.

But those campaigning for good corporate governance and social responsibility in Nigeria disagree and say the new investments will further increase environmental pollution, and worsen Coca-Cola's alleged 'detestable' labour practices like 'casualisation' – the practice of keeping workers on casual contracts for years – which means they are not entitled to pension and medical cover.

'Nigeria faces a siege of environmental pollution and water sourcing threats from the increased investment activities of Coca-Cola,' Asolo Adeyeye Adewole, the executive secretary of the West African Network on Business Ethics, told Ethical Corporation.

Reformist government

Coca-Cola Nigeria officials say most of the new funds will go into the setting up of more bottling plants and facilities to manufacture aluminium cans and fruit concentrates.

Alex Cummings, group president of Coca-Cola Africa, says the new investment demonstrates Coca-Cola's 'continuing commitment' to support Obasanjo's reformist government, which is keen to attract foreign investment, create more jobs and wean the country off its dependence on oil.

Obasanjo's administration is riding a wave of international goodwill amid his spirited fight against corruption. The Paris Club of creditors recently wrote off $18 billion of debt, signalling a shift of attitude towards Nigeria.

Analysts say foreign investors are once again eyeing the potentially lucrative Nigerian market and the government, desperate to clinch a deal, may at times disregard some ethical and environmental concerns.

Troubled history

Critics of Coca-Cola question the soft drink giant's commitment to corporate social responsibility, human rights and good governance in Nigeria.

They say Coca-Cola has for decades ignored the injustices and human rights abuses committed by successive military dictatorships in Nigeria and even suggest its investments helped prop up the brutal regime of General Sani Abacha, one of the most vicious tyrants to have ruled the country.

Indeed, Coca-Cola has been one of the favourite targets of pro-democracy groups in Nigeria and abroad with numerous campus protests in the US in the spring of 1998, backed by Amnesty International, calling on Coca-Cola to disinvest from the country.

Although Coca-Cola executives have always stated that the company's presence in Nigeria in no way indicated its support for the government of the day, it is difficult for them to continue to claim that the company is a 'good corporate citizen' while turning a blind eye when things go wrong in a society in which it operates.

Goodwill

To its credit, Coca-Cola was one of the first multinationals to respond positively to the growing HIV/Aids pandemic in Nigeria, rolling out an expensive treatment programme to its staff infected with the virus, a move widely hailed across Africa.

This has won the soft drink giant a great deal of support and goodwill in the country, but as any corporation knows, this can easily be lost if the old attitude of insensitivity to public concerns and a 'we are here to do business' approach prevails.

Source: Ethical Corporation (2005), www.ethicalcorp.com
© Ethical Corporation 2009

Key terms

agency	495	principals	495
control	497	regulation	495
interests	495	risk	502
performance	490	stakeholders	491
power	491		

Recap questions and assignments

1 Why are governance processes and structures important to our understanding of strategy?

2 With regard to an organization you know well (or is in the public domain), what would you assess as its good and less good features in terms of governance structures and processes?

3 What do you see as the key changes and challenges for the future for corporate governance?

Case study 15.1: **Too many turkeys: executive pay**

Are bosses overpaid? Executive pay is on the rise again – and so are complaints that ordinary performance is attracting extraordinary rewards

America's top executives had plenty to celebrate as they tucked into their turkey this Thanksgiving – a resurgent stock market, record profits and, above all, their own ever-expanding pay packets. In the years immediately after the bursting of the dotcom bubble and the scandals at Enron and the like, executive pay fell – at least by some measures. But that, it is now clear, was but a blip, mostly reflecting managers' reluctance to cash in share options in what was then an unattractive stock market.

Executive compensation in America – already far ahead of the rest of the world, despite the best efforts of overseas managers to catch up – is now rising inexorably again. In fiscal year 2004 the total compensation of the median American company boss rose in every industry, by between 9.7% in commercial banking and 46.1% in energy, according to a new report by the Conference Board, a research organisation. In the big companies that comprise the S&P 500 index, median total chief-executive compensation increased by 30.2% last year, to $6m, compared with a 15% rise in 2003, according to a study published last month by the Corporate Library, a firm that tracks corporate-governance data.

Recent higher profits are part of the explanation for higher pay. But there is a longer-term trend at work. In 2004 the ratio of chief executives' compensation to the pay of the average production worker jumped to 431 to one from 301 to one in 2003, according to 'Executive Excess', a recent study of 367 big American firms by the left-leaning Institute for Policy Studies. That is not quite a record: in 2000 the ratio reached 525 to one. In 1990 the ratio was 107 to one and in 1982 a mere 42 to one. This year's numbers seem certain to show the gap widening still further.

But while unionists and left-leaning politicians are worried about social equity, investors typically have a different sort of concern. They are happy to pay for exceptional performance; but less delighted when mediocre managers get lavishly rewarded. The contrasting cases of James Kilts and Michael Eisner make the point.

Mr Kilts, the boss of Gillette, has publicly accused critics of the $165m bonus he got for selling his firm to Procter & Gamble for $53 billion of 'unsubstantiated, inaccurate and irresponsible criticism' and of treating him like a 'piñata' – a sweet container that American children bash at parties. Piñata Jim may have a point. He did a lot to restructure Gillette – allowing it to be sold for a fancy price, to the huge benefit of its shareholders. It is when vast payments are the reward for poor performance that it is time to cry foul. Michael Eisner was an outstanding manager during the first part of his more than 20 years at the top of the Walt Disney Corporation. But as Leo Hindery points out in a new book ('It Takes a CEO'), he was also paid $800m over a 13-year-period during which the company's shareholders would have done better by investing in Treasury bonds.

The populist end of the debate has led to some action in Congress. Barney Frank, a left-wing Democrat, has just introduced legislation intended to tackle the 'problem of runaway executive compensation'. Wisely, he is mostly seeking to improve disclosure, rather than actually to cap pay at a specific level, which experience suggests would encourage creative ways around the cap.

A 1994 reform that limited tax deductibility of executive pay to $1m merely turned the $1m maximum into the de facto norm, and inspired the rapid growth of share options as an alternative form of tax-favoured compensation. Some experts now blame the peculiar risk-taking incentives created by share options for many subsequent corporate scandals. Although Mr Frank's legislation is not expected to become law, it is adding to the pressure on the Securities and Exchange Commission to make better use of its powers to demand full disclosure.

Even some businessmen are now calling for restraint. Edgar Wollard, a former boss of DuPont, recently proposed that a chief executive's compensation should be indexed to the pay of the senior vice-presidents that head his firm's divisions. At DuPont, he was limited to 150% of the average pay of those other top executives. Mr Hindery, a serial CEO in the telecoms and media businesses, says he has published his book partly because greed in corporate America is now damaging capitalism.

Many experts see the continuing rise of executive compensation – and the continuing lack of a demonstrable link to performance – as a symptom of a massive failure of corporate governance. Greater pressure from shareholders is generally regarded as the only real antidote. But critics of perceived executive excess have been frustrated by shareholder passivity, which is sometimes blamed on the short time horizons of many investors.

So is there a cure? Certainly, fuller disclosure would help, argues Lucian Bebchuk of Harvard Law School and co-author of a recent book, 'Pay Without Performance: The Unfulfilled Promise of Executive Compensation'. If there were proper disclosure of forms of executive pay such as pensions, supplementary pensions and deferred compensation, then it would be easier for shareholders to see whether chief executives are being rewarded for genuinely good work.

It is the issue of aligning incentives and rewards – rather than the absolute level of pay – that tends to concern professional investors most. 'There is no right or wrong number', says Bob Pozen, chairman of MFS Investment Management, which has $160 billion under management. It is hard to judge the merits of a package without looking carefully at the details, he says, which is why he has little time for Mr Frank's proposal for shareholders to vote each year on the executive compensation package. In Britain, where shareholders now get a non-binding vote on compensation, it has had no real impact, he reckons.

Mr Pozen reserves his fiercest ire for the kind of executive pay package that rewards bosses generously even if they fail. And he is extremely critical of the role of compensation consultants. They, he says, tend to be chosen by the chief executive, and to drive up pay by recommending that the top man should be paid more than his peers, having chosen a group of peers whose pay errs on the high side.

Ira Kay, an executive-compensation consultant at Watson Wyatt, strongly disagrees, pointing out that the compensation committee of the board increasingly hires the consultant – a change he regards as 'revolutionary'. Moreover, in the past few years many American firms have changed their approach to executive pay, he says, improving disclosure and changing the composition of pay packages so that they provide stronger incentives to manage for the long run. In particular, share-option grants have fallen sharply, while there are more grants of restricted stock (that pay out only over time or when a performance target is hit).

Even so, a survey Mr Kay is working on suggests that there is now as 'large a gap as I have seen between what institutional investors and boards think about executive compensation'. Boards think they are doing a good, shareholder-friendly job; institutional investors do not. Mr Kay fears that if the institutions do grow more militant about executive pay, there is a 'risk of a return to the 1970s', with bosses paid like bureaucrats and talented managers seeking more rewarding work elsewhere.

That would indeed be a bad thing. But judging by recent trends – and the continuing failure to reform board elections to make it easy for shareholders to vote out directors who are too friendly to management – hell is more likely to freeze than bosses' pay.

Source: 'Too Many Turkeys', *The Economist*, 26 November 2005

Questions

1 Discuss whether or not executive compensation should be linked to performance – and performance of what, the individual, the organization or some other indicator.

2 Outline the problems and advantages of using compensation consultants to decide on executive compensation.

3 What roles do institutional investors play in the question of executive compensation?

4 What should, in your view, happen to executive compensation during financial crises such as the 2009 global recession?

References

Aguilera, R.V. and Cuervo-Cazurra, A. (2004) Codes of good governance worldwide: what is the trigger? *Organization Studies*, **25**, **3**, 415–43.

Asian Development Bank (2000) *Corporate Governance and Finance in East Asian, Vol. 1*, Asian Development Bank, Manila.

Berle, A.A. and Means, G.C. (1932) *The Modern Corporation and Private Property*, Macmillan, New York.

Blair, M.M. (1995) *Ownership and Control: Rethinking Corporate Governance for the Twenty-first Century*, Brookings Institution, Washington, DC.

Buck, T. and Shahrim, A. (2005) The translation of corporate governance changes across national cultures: the case of Germany. *Journal of International Business Studies*, **36**, 42–61.

Cadbury, A. (2000) The corporate governance agenda. *Corporate Governance: An International Review*, **8**, **1**, 7–15.

Cadbury Report (1992) Committee on the Financial Aspects of Corporate Governance, London.

Cassidy, D.P. (2000) Whither corporate governance in the 21st century? *Corporate Governance: An International Review*, **8**, **4**, 297–302.

Charkham, J.P. (1999) *Keeping Good Company: A Study of Corporate Governance in Five Countries*, 2nd edn, Oxford University Press, Oxford.

Charkham, J. (2005) *Keeping Good Company: Corporate Governance Ten Years On.* Oxford University Press, Oxford.

Clarke, T. (2004) Cycle of crisis and regulation: the enduring agency and stewardship problem of corporate governance. *Corporate Governance: An International Review*, **12**, **2**, 153–61.

Collins, J.C. and Porras, J.I. (2000) *Built to Last: Successful Habits of Visionary Companies*, Random House, New York.

Combined Code on Corporate Governance (2006) Financial Reporting Council, London.

Condon, D. (2007) *The Role of the Turnbull Guidelines and the Management and Identification of Risk in UK Multi-National Companies*, PhD Dissertation, Warwick Business School, UK.

Conger, J.A., Lawler, E., III and Finegold, D.L. (2001) *Corporate Boards: Strategy for Adding Value at the Top*, Jossey-Bass, San Francisco, CA.

Contardo, I. and Wilson, D.C. (2001) *The United Nations' Global Compact: A Report on Case Study Evidence*, Global Compact, London, and Research Paper, Warwick Business School.

Conyon, M.J. and Murphy, K.J. (2000) The prince and the pauper? CEO pay in the US and UK. *The Economic Journal*, **110**, F640–F671.

Economist Intelligence Unit (2003) *Corporate Governance: Business under Scrutiny*, London.

Franks, J.R. and Mayer, C. (1990) Capital markets and corporate control: a study of France, Germany and the UK. *Economic Policy*, 191–231.

Greenbury, R. (1995) *Directors' Remuneration: Report of a Study Group Chaired by Sir Richard Greenbury*, Gee Publishing, London.

Hambrick, D.C., Nadler, D.A. and Tushman, M.L. (eds) (1998) *Navigating Change: How CEOs, Top Teams and Boards Steer Transformation*, Harvard University Press, Boston, MA.

Hampel, R. (1998) *Committee on Corporate Governance: Final Report*, Gee Publishing, London.

Hemscott (2003) *The Current Population of Non-executive Directors.* Hemscott Group Limited, London.

Higgs, D. (2003) *Review of the Role and Effectiveness of Non-Executive Directors*, Department of Trade and Industry, London.

Hirschman, A.O. (1984) Against parsimony: three easy ways of complicating some categories of economic discourse. *American Economic Review*, **74**, **2**, 89–96.

Jensen, M.C. (2001) Value minimisation, stakeholder theory and the corporate objective function. *European Financial Management*, **7**, **3**, 297–317.

Jensen, M.C. and Meckling, W.H. (1976) Theory of the firm: managerial behaviour, agency costs, and ownership structures. *Journal of Financial Economics*, **3**, **4**, 305–60.

Katzenbach, J.R. and Smith, D.K. (1992) *The Wisdom of Teams: Creating the High Performance Organization*, Harvard Business School Press, Boston, MA.

Kirkbride, J. and Letza, S. (2003) Establishing the boundaries of regulation in corporate governance: Is the UK moving toward a process of collaboration? *Business and Society Review*, **108**, **4**, 463–85.

Korn/Ferry International (2003) *World Study on Corporate Governance*, Los Angeles, CA.

La Porta, R., Lopez-de-Silanes, F., Shleifer, A. and Vishny, R. (2000) Investor protection and corporate governance. *Journal of Financial Economics*, **58**, **1–2**, 3–334.

Lander, G.P. (2004) *What is Sarbanes-Oxley?* McGraw-Hill, New York.

Letza, S., Sun, X. and Kirkbride, J. (2004) Shareholding verses stakeholding: a critical review of corporate governance. *Corporate Governance: An International Review*, **12**, **3**, 242–61.

Mallin, C.A. (2007) *Corporate Governance*, 2nd edn, Oxford University Press, Oxford.

McNulty, T. and Pettigrew, A.M. (1999) Strategists on the board. *Organization Studies*, **20**, **1**, 47–74.

Miller, S., Hichson, D.J. and Wibon, D.C. (2008) From strategy to action: involvement and influence in top level decisions. *Long Range Planning*, **41**, **6**, 606–28.

Mintz, S.M. (2005) Corporate governance in an international context: legal systems, financing patterns and cultural variables. *Corporate Governance: An International Review*, **13**, **5**, 582–97.

Monks, R.A.G. and Minow, N. (1992) *Power and Accountability: Restoring Balance of Power Between Corporations, Owners and Societies*, Harper Business, New York.

Monks, R.A.G. and Minow, N. (2004) *Corporate Governance*, 3rd edn, Blackwell, Malden, MA.

Nadler, D., Behan, B. and Nadler, M.B. (2006) *Building Better Boards: A Blueprint for Effective Governance*, Mercal Delta Consulting, Harvard, MA.

Nooteboom, B. (1999) Voice- and exit-forms of corporate control: Anglo-American, European, and Japanese. *Journal of Economic Issues*, **33**, **4**, 845–60.

OECD (2004) *Principles of Corporate Governance*, available at www.OECD.org

O'Neal, D. and Thomas, H. (1996) Developing the strategic board. *Long Range Planning*, **29**, 314–30.

Pettigrew, A.M. and McNulty, T. (1995) Power and influence in and around the boardroom. *Human Relations*, **48**, **8**, 845–73.

Pettigrew, A.M. and McNulty, T. (1998) Sources and uses of power in the boardroom. *European Journal of Work and Organizational Psychology*, **7**, **2**, 197–214.

PIRC (2003) *Corporate Governance Annual Review*, London.

Prias, S. (1976) *The Evaluation of Grant Firms in Britain: A Study of Concentration in British Manufacturing in Britain 1909–1970*, Cambridge University Press, Cambridge.

Short, H., Keasey, K., Hull, A. and Wright, M. (1998) Corporate governance, accountability and enterprise. *Corporate Governance: An International Review*, **6**, **3**, 135–212.

Solomon, J.F. and Solomon, A. (2004) *Corporate Governance and Accountability*, John Wiley & Sons, Chichester.

Taylor, M. (2009) The global financial crisis: four key issues on the research agenda. *Economy Opinion*, ESRC, London, p. 44.

Veblen, T. (1904) *The Theories of Business Enterprise*, Scribners, New York.

Ward, R.D. (2000) *The Boardroom Insider Guidebook*, Wiley, New York.

Weimer, J. and Pape, J.C. (1999) A taxonomy of systems of corporate governance. *Corporate Governance: An International Review*, **27**, **3**, 152–66.

Further reading

Bank of England (1998) Composition of company boards. *Bank of England Quarterly Bulletin*, May, 242–45.

Bernstein, P.L. (1996*) Against the Gods: The Remarkable Story of Risk*, Wiley, New York.

Bostock, R. (1995) Company responses to Cadbury. *Corporate Governance: An International Review*, **3**, **2**, April, 72–7.

CADS (1995) *The Financial Aspects of Corporate Governance: Compliance with the Code of Best Practice*, May, Stock Exchange, London.

Conyon, M.J. (1994) Corporate governance changes in UK companies between 1988 and 1993. *Corporate Governance: An International Review*, **2**, **2**, 97–109.

Conyon, M.J. (1995) *Cadbury in the Boardroom*, in Arthur Anderson Corporate Register, Hemmington Scott, London.

Conyon, M.J. and Mallin, C. (1997) Women in the boardroom: evidence from large UK companies. *Corporate Governance: An International Review*, **5**, **3**, 112–17.

Hutton, W. (1996) *The State We're In*, Vintage Press, London.

Institute of Chartered Accountants (1999) *Internal Control: Guidance for Directors on the Combined Code*, ICA, London.

Institute of Chartered Accountants (1999) *Implementing Turnbull: A Boardroom Brief*, ICA Centre for Business Performance, London.

Keasey, K., Thompson, S. and Wright, M. (eds) (1997) *Corporate Governance: Economic Management and Financial Issues*, Oxford University Press, Oxford.

Lorsch, J.W. and Clark, R.C. (2008) Leading from the boardroom. *Harvard Business Review*, **86**, **4**, 104–41.

Mellahi, K. (2005) The dynamics of boards of directors in failing organisations. *Long Range Planning*, **38**, **3**, 261–81.

Stybel, L.J. and Peabody, M. (2005) How should board directors evaluate themselves? *Sloan Management Review*, **47**, **1**, 67–72.

Analysing and measuring strategic performance

Chapter contents

While the principle that the fundamental objective of the business corporation is to increase the value of its shareholders' investment is widely accepted, there is substantially less agreement about how this is accomplished. (Rappaport, 1986, p. 1)

Introduction

The concept of strategic performance and its measurement is a central issue in the field of strategic management. In earlier chapters of this book, performance constructs such as a strategic 'business model', managing a business for value and the 'balanced scorecard' illustrate the fundamental importance of analysing the performance and health of the firm. Our organizing framework – the systemic model (see Chapter 2) – shows that performance feedback provides important information to enable organizational renewal and strategic reorientation to take place.

In this chapter, we note that firms have a range of targets or goals with profit maximization or shareholder value maximization often stated as one of the key strategic objectives. We will also discuss the following issues about performance metrics:

- the idea of multiple measures of performances, e.g. accounting-based, market-based, etc;
- the concepts of economic value and, in particular, 'shareholder value' and 'economic value-added';
- an examination of the 'value-based' management approach;
- an analysis of the 'balanced scorecard' approach to performance measurement, with its focus on key performance indicators to address the multiple goals and foci of the business (e.g. financial, marketing, internal process and learning goals).

In summary, organizations and managers must link their choice of critical success factors (CSFs), performance measures and key performance indicators with the overall strategy and any likely adjustment and re-evaluation of strategic priorities. Appropriate and robust performance metrics allow managers to evaluate strategic success and 'fine tune' the 'business model' to achieve corporate goals and targets.

16.1 The domain of business performance

Venkatraman and Ramanujam (1986) present a very useful conceptualization to explain the domain of business performance. This is shown in Figure 16.1. We shall use this as an organizing structure for this chapter.

In this diagram, three perspectives of performance are offered, namely, financial performance, operations performance and organizational effectiveness. We will discuss each briefly in turn:

Financial measures of performance: The narrowest view of performance (represented by the inner circle) focuses on financial performance and argues that well-crafted strategy pursues primarily profitability goals, well examined in the accounting literature, such as return on investment, return on equity or earnings per share. This approach assumes the dominance of financial goals and associated measures, whether they are accounting-based or financial market-based.

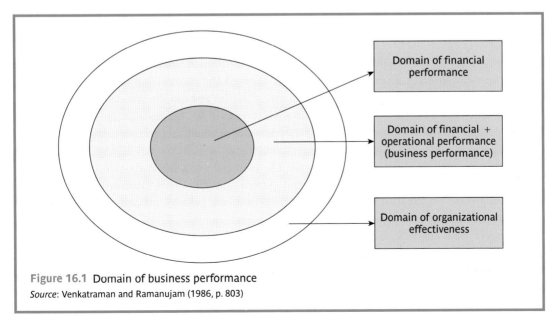

Figure 16.1 Domain of business performance
Source: Venkatraman and Ramanujam (1986, p. 803)

Operational measures of performance: Operational performance indicators (see the middle ring of the diagram) examine a range of internal performance factors which might lead to success for the company and its set of businesses. These include market position indicators such as the absolute level or growth rate of sales, market-share (as a percentage of sales) and the rate of new product introductions. Other measures might involve a focus on efficiency and include value-added in manufacturing, product quality and other indicators of technological efficiency (e.g. potential economies of scale and scope).

Measures of organizational effectiveness: Beyond economic and operational performance fundamentals, the selection of performance factors that should be monitored and benchmarked must reflect the strategic goals of the entire firm (the outer ring of the figure), and their often multiple and conflicting nature (Cameron and Whetten, 1983). Management's challenge, therefore, is to build relationships with all stakeholders and constituents of the firm, from shareholders, suppliers and employees through to consumers, in order to build value throughout the organization. For example, they might measure critical success factors such as corporate image/reputation and examine supply-chain relationships in order to build and create long-term strategic knowledge for the organization.

In summary, value creation in performance terms is clearly the central task and purpose of senior management. It means that managing performance outputs as well as resource inputs is an imperative and requires a perspective that encompasses a systemic and dynamic understanding of performance. In other words, if performance is sound, then it can be assumed that there is a clear 'fit' between the elements of strategy (e.g. competition, capabilities, etc.) and organizational success. If, on the other hand, there is evidence of performance weaknesses, these may indicate that there are problems in the strategic framework, involving perhaps a weak competitive strategy or a short-fall in organizational core competences and capabilities.

What is critical in managing performance is the existence of well-chosen and robust performance metrics, which enable managers to predict economic performance and identify necessary changes in strategic and operational positioning.

16.2 Concepts of value and performance management

16.2.1 Accounting-based performance metrics

In their search for efficiency, managerial thinkers such as Alfred P. Sloan of General Motors (1963) and his financial director, Donaldson Brown, put forward the proposition that the fundamental aim of a business is to earn a satisfactory return on capital (or the money invested in the business). Financial efficiency as measured by return on investment (ROI = net income/capital investment) became perhaps the most commonly used of the measures of financial position alongside return on equity (ROE = net income/shareholders' equity), return on sales (ROS = net income/sales revenue) and return on assets (ROA = net income/assets). The financial press and corporate analysts' reports also placed great emphasis on measures of earnings per share (EPS = net income/number of shares outstanding) and price/earnings ratios (P/E = ratio of stock price/net income) as indicators of corporate performance.

Managers and analysts use accounting earnings and accounting profits as a benchmark because financial accounts are readily available and the measures, themselves, are easy to calculate. Yet, according to Doyle (2000, pp. 26–7), the measurement of accounting earnings can be arbitrary, subjective and easily manipulated by management (see also Smith, 1992). Accounting profits also exclude investments, ignore the time value of money (see Rappaport, 1986) and produce a focus on short-term results. Indeed, many of these criticisms imply that managers may uncritically focus on accounting numbers without recognizing the judgements, conventions and realities involved in the construction of those numbers.

Writers such as Rappaport (1986), in particular, demonstrate the detailed shortcomings of accounting numbers and advance the concept of shareholder value creation as the new standard for business performance. Indeed, Rappaport points out that research confirms that satisfactory earnings growth (for example, growth in EPS) does not necessarily lead to a concomitant increase in the market value of the company's shares.

Hayes and Abernathy (1980) also point out the shortcomings of management who wrongly assume that, by improving ROI, ROE etc., consequent improvements in share price must necessarily follow. Indeed, they criticize ROI for helping to hasten the process of 'managing our way to economic decline'. They point out that ROE, with its short-term emphasis, can lead to a decline in investments of a long-term character such as those in innovations which provide the impetus for the growth paths and long-term strategic direction for many organizations.

Quite apart from the accounting judgements necessary to measure accounting earnings, there is a similar set of problems in measuring assets. Typically, financial accounts recognize and measure physical assets but ignore the intangible assets increasingly developed by knowledge-based companies, e.g. patents, R&D, new technologies, brands and customer loyalty. With the wide growth of knowledge-based companies in IT, biotechnology, pharmaceuticals, etc., measures of ROA will be over-recorded with such companies, since knowledge assets will be under-recorded. There will also probably be similar over-recording for mature manufacturing companies who have gradually depreciated their assets over time, making the book value of the assets quite small in the denominator of the ROA measure. Such anomalies in the measurement of ROA, therefore, suggest that comparing the financial performance of companies in the FTSE listing (*Financial Times* and the London Stock Exchange), for example, using ROA would provide a very questionable measure of comparative performance. Indeed, there may be an inverse relationship between ROA performance and improvements in share price performance.

In summary, writers such as Rappaport and others hastened the value creation trend in measures of financial performance.

16.2.2 Economic value added (EVA) and financial performance

Consultants such as Stern Stewart (1996) promoted the movement from a focus on accounting profit to economic profit, or economic rent as exemplified in our earlier discussion of the resource-based view (RBV) (see Chapter 6). Indeed, Kay (1993) defines added value as the difference between the value of a firm's output and the cost of the firm's inputs. Stern Stewart (1996) define an essentially similar concept, which they call economic value-added (EVA). They define EVA as (EVA = net operating profit after tax (as a percentage) – weighted average cost of capital). The resulting value of EVA can then be interpreted as a measure of the strategic value of the business and a useful metric for judging ongoing performance. In essence, the EVA approach argues that a firm and its set of businesses are creating value when they earn returns in excess of the firm's weighted average cost of capital – a position which is consistent with an objective of maximizing shareholder value. However, EVA links value creation to current operating performance, i.e. it is a single-period measure of value creation, developed from balance sheet measures, and provides a tight financial lens through which a company can address whether it is adding value for shareholders.

It is important to recognize that measures such as 'economic profit' or EVA help firms identify a value for the business. However, the main problem with the 'economic profit' metrics is that they do not help to address the issues associated with future investments such as new product development, whose time period, future earnings and capital requirements are somewhat uncertain and unpredictable. In this situation, the shareholder value approach (SVA), with the emphasis on discounted cash flow, and the shareholder value principle popularized by Rappaport (1986) are the more appropriate methodology. This is discussed in more detail in the next section.

16.2.3 The shareholder value (SVA) approach

The clear operating principle underlying the SVA approach is that the company's dominant strategic goal is to maximize its shareholder wealth. In essence, this means that corporate and business strategies should focus on the economic gains they produce for shareholders, i.e. in terms of maximizing the value of their shares through dividend policies and share price rises.

Rappaport (1986) then addresses the issue of how to value the company's shares and advances the view that share prices should be calculated by evaluating expectations of the cash flows that will arise from the company's corporate and business strategies over time. SVA then measures the total value of the corporate strategy by discounting these cash flow predictions to allow for the time value of money and risk. Any introductory textbook (e.g. Brealey and Myers) explains clearly the discounted cash flow (DCF) approach and it has been widely used for many years in practice, for example to evaluate the worth of alternative capital projects or capital investments (see also Chapter 3 in this book). However, it is only over the past 15 years or so, through Rappaport's influence, that the focus of DCF has switched to shareholder value and the evaluation of strategic planning and management strategies. Ultimately, the SVA approach calculates a net present value (NPV) for each alternative strategy option available to the company, using the company's weighted average cost of capital as the discount rate. The strategy which has the highest NPV of all the options is generally selected as the preferred alternative.

It is important to stress that SVA is not simply a financial approach or a financial technique. It requires all of the corporate knowledge, core capabilities and strategy development processes that have been discussed in this book for the senior managers to outline a viable series of strategic options before putting them under the 'financial' microscope of the SVA approach.

First and foremost, therefore, the senior managers must develop their own *business model* (see the discussion in Chapters 5 and 8 and particularly Yip, 2004), which is essentially a 'theory' about how their particular business system (i.e. the total corporate set of businesses) operates. Such a model is a set of assumptions about the processes and structures necessary for the business to achieve competitive success. It involves a clear outline of how the whole business system will work and provides full detail about the economic and business relationships that must be in place for the corporate strategy to work in the competitive marketplace. As such, it will include many of the strategic system features (see figures in Chapter 2) already discussed in this book: an environmental and competitive model; a capability (core competence) framework; a marketing/consumer model; an operations model; and an overall organizational structure and systems model, which links people, incentive systems, vision, leadership, etc. with the economic relationships necessary for effective strategy implementation. In practice, a business model can be articulated in terms of detailed plans and budgets that provide guidance to managers relating to their operational responsibilities. The logic that drives plans and budgets lies within the business model. The business model itself is the mechanism through which a business intends to generate revenue and profits.

Yip (2004, p. 20) identifies the following elements in his conceptualization of a 'business model' as shown in Figure 16.2 (see also Chapter 5 where this business model is also discussed):

- value proposition (i.e. the strategic concept);
- nature of inputs;

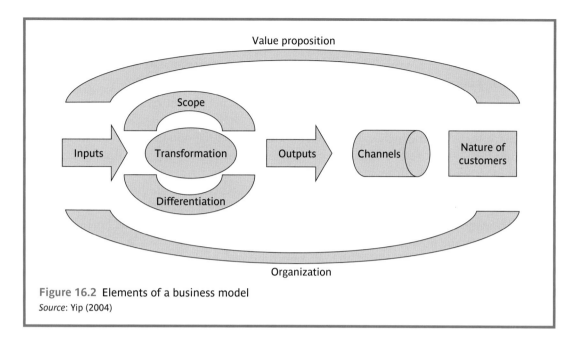

Figure 16.2 Elements of a business model
Source: Yip (2004)

- how to transform inputs (including technology);
- nature of outputs;
- vertical scope;
- horizontal scope;
- geographic scope;
- nature of customers;
- how to organize.

Yip's business model explains the logic of the intended strategy in terms of the key strategic choices and the specific operations that have to take place. With this detailed plan, the consequences for cash flows can be determined and the link between (intended) strategy and (expected) performance can be established. In many ways this is simply a restyled value chain – an activity map onto which can be placed assets, revenues and costs. The value chain reflects the firm's strategic choices – the business model goes one step further in making the link to cash flows.

Yip demonstrates the application of his business model using a range of examples, including easyGroup's core value proposition of bringing cheap and efficient services (airlines, car rental etc.) to the mass market. Further examples from other sectors are given in this chapter.

Assuming, then, that a sound 'business model' is developed, the elements and steps involved in the SVA approach for valuing strategies are:

1 Clear identification of the 'business model', including the organization strategic value drivers (e.g. capabilities), operational drivers (including supply chain management), marketing drivers (including brands, image, loyalty etc.) and financial drivers (including cash flows, financial strength, risk profile etc.).

2 Derivation from the 'business model' of the set of viable strategic options for the company in the competitive marketplace.

3 Evaluation and estimation of the cash flow profiles associated with each strategic option.

4 Estimation of the company's cost of capital (weighted average cost of capital) in view of the company's current and future projected investments (e.g. debt and loan structure implications).

5 Discounting the cash flow profiles for each strategic option (using the weighted average cost of capital) and calculating a net present value for each option.

6 Choosing the strategic option/alternative with the highest net present value.

In summary, therefore, the highest NPV strategy ensures that the option chosen maximizes firm value from the perspective of shareholders and provides the positive net cash flow to satisfy the claims of other stakeholders/constituents in the business system.

However, as with all such 'financially oriented' approaches, there are limitations and issues involved in its application. First, an objective of shareholder value maximization is not always understood by employees and senior managers who feel that it is too short-term and financial market oriented, may ignore options for growth and neglect important issues associated with managing the long-term future strategic direction and competitiveness of the firm. Second, as indicated in our chapter on risk (see Chapter 11), estimating and forecasting future cash flows must rely on the quality of judgements about such factors as market evolution, technological change, competition etc. Typically, most companies are used to making range or probabilistic forecasts (and scenarios) over a five-year planning horizon and, as a consequence, knowledge and learning about forecasting capabilities are being accumulated in organizations over time, leading to improvements in forecasting performance. Third, as indicated above, SVA techniques do not allow for the consideration of long-term strategic decisions, particularly with regard to 'option-type' investments. For example, pharmaceutical and biotechnology companies regularly invest in new research programmes which, at the outset, do not necessarily have clear goals. However, they do allow firms an option to exploit the results of R&D obtained at a later date for the future development of new products. Option pricing models in finance such as the Black–Scholes model (see Brealey and Myers, 2009) provide a basis for attacking this problem and writers in the strategy field such as Bowman and Hurry (1993) have suggested adaptations to strategy valuation processes using option-type models.

Overall, therefore, the evolution of performance measurement techniques based on economic profit such as EVA and more systemic value-based management techniques such as SVA has usefully linked strategy to the finance literature and provided vehicles for companies to both understand the business models and drivers underlying shareholder value and develop the capability to identify further strategic options and alternatives to create value for the business.

The balanced scorecard approach below is a logical development of EVA and SVA techniques, and provides a broader perspective and framework for managers to use in determining which key critical success factors and performance indicators should be used to monitor and, subsequently, drive organizational strategy. First, however, look at Case boxes 16.1 and 16.2 and see how the Freeserve and Punch Taverns business models can be mapped against the Yip framework.

Case box 16.1: **Freeserve's business model**

Freeserve described their mission in their flotation prospectus as being: 'to become the UK's preferred internet portal by delivering both free internet access and an integrated offering of UK focused content, e-commerce and community.'[1]

Freeserve believed when they launched that they could improve on the fundamental internet business model with their 'free access' approach. In their presentation to investors at the time of flotation they describe the traditional business model with the diagram below:

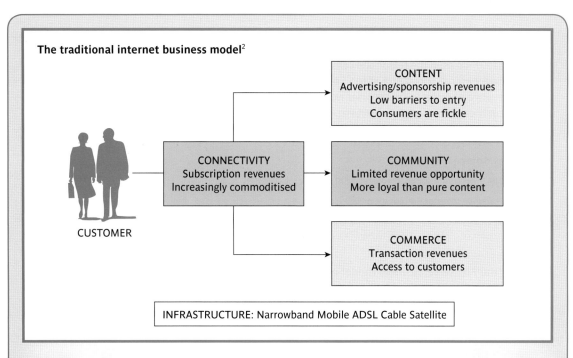

The traditional internet business model[2]

They recognized income as being gained either as an ISP through subscriptions or as a portal through advertising, sponsorship and commission from commerce.

They positioned themselves to provide their customers with both of these services:

- a dial-up mechanism to access the internet, in which they compete with other ISPs such as AOL and BT, and

- an internet portal which offers content, tailored web services and a virtual marketplace for consumers to buy and sell products or services, in which they compete with the likes of AOL, Yahoo, Microsoft, Lycos etc.

They proposed to change the business model described above profoundly by not charging users for connect time to their ISP. They went on, in the same presentation to investors, to describe their business model with the diagram below:

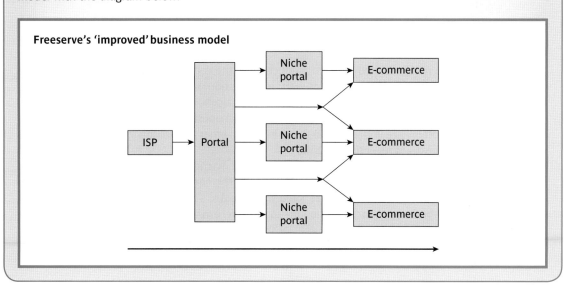

Freeserve's 'improved' business model

▶ Their belief was that by offering free access to the internet they would corner the market in people dialling-up to get online. Some income would be generated by agreements with the telephone companies to split the revenue from the telephone call charges, but more importantly, those people would, by default, come to the Freeserve portal first. If the Freeserve portal was good enough, offering sufficient flexibility and a wide range of niche areas, the user would stay with Freeserve, access the internet through its pages and its search engine, read its adverts and buy goods through its sponsors. In that way, the free ISP would be a loss leader to get people into the portal, which would generate the income.

References/Source:

[1]Freeserve. The Freeserve Solution. Freeserve Mini Prospectus (12/7/99): p. 4

[2]Freeserve. Freeserve Investor Presentation (1999) URL:

http://www.aboutfreeserve.com/investor/presentations/index.html

Questions

1 Rewrite the Freeserve business model using the Yip framework in Figure 16.2. What, if anything, is missing from Freeserve's model?

2 Can you describe how Freeserve proposes to generate cash flows? Profits?

3 What risks does its business model identify?

Case box 16.2: **Punch Taverns**

Punch Taverns is a public limited company which owns about 7400 pubs across the UK
The company has agreements with retailers, who are self-employed and operate a retail business within our pub. The company does not directly manage the retail business in the pubs.

The agreements are generally leases (10- to 25-year agreements assignable after two years and with full repairing liability), or tenancies (non-assignable, non-repairing agreements of up to 6 years). Lease agreements generally apply in bigger outlets. The primary lease offer currently is the Punch Growth Lease (PGL). Other short-term agreements exist for temporary situations (notably the tenancy at will – TAW). We also have a legacy of older agreements.

Under all agreements the retailer pays a rent based on a share of the estimated fair maintainable profitability of the pub. The rent is usually index linked and subject to upward-only rent reviews (after 5 years in leased pubs).

The retailer is also required to buy certain products from the company ('the tie'). In general, the tie covers all beer and lager products (sometimes with the exception of one guest ale). Depending on the agreement it may also cover cider, soft drinks, and flavoured alcoholic beverages.

The gross price charged for products is the brewer's or manufacturer's national wholesale price. Discounts are offered off invoice in the Growth Lease. In certain other agreements we offer a retrospective volume-target-based discount incentive scheme.

In some agreements the company agrees to manage the machine income opportunity in the pub and shares the net income, usually 50:50, with the retailer. The company also receives a rebate from machine suppliers where their machines are sited in our pubs. The agreement provides a low-cost entry into running a business with professional support. We expect adherence to the terms of the agreement, but we are prepared to consider special situations. The key operational output is business planning, with the objective of helping the retailer to build a better business. The main activities that drive success are:

- recruiting and training the right retailer;
- agreeing the right business lease, and ensuring adherence to this lease;
- developing the pub to give the right consumer offer, often using shared investment with the retailer.

Fundamentally, the two key company objectives are to maximize the profitability of each pub, and to optimize the company's share of that profit.

The company has organized support functions to assist the retailer build his business. Support activities range from essential processes (order taking, debt collection), through care and maintenance (business manager support, customer administration) to development (estate management and investment). In addition, the company maintains an infrastructure covering finance, systems, purchasing, HR etc.

A third key company objective is to expand the estate by acquiring more pubs. This can be successful as the company is able to add value to a pub through its purchasing power and support services, thereby earning a good return on investment.

The profitability of the company is driven by two main income streams of beer margin and rent. Machine income and non-beer margin are important growth areas, but of smaller scale. Overhead costs are relatively low and with fairly stable income streams the company has very low operational gearing risk, and is very cash generative.

The company is financed by debt and equity, having floated on the London Stock Exchange in May 2002, and ranked within the UK FTSE 250. Debt comprises some 70% of enterprise value, relatively high but secure due to the nature of the income model. The main debt is securitized in two pub groupings, known as security nets, with further debt capacity for new acquisitions. The business is asset rich, with pub values being comparable to the enterprise value of the company.

Questions

1 Rewrite Punch Taverns' business model using the Yip framework in Figure 16.2. What, if anything, is missing from Punch Taverns' model?

2 Can you describe how Punch Taverns proposes to generate cash flows? Profits?

3 What risks does its business model identify?

4 Compare the Freeserve and Punch Taverns approaches to describing and presenting their business models. Which do you prefer? Why?

16.2.4 The balanced scorecard concept: managing for value

We introduced the idea of the balanced scorecard in Chapters 1 and 2 and showed an example in Figure 5.18. The context for this was to show how progress against objectives might be assessed and how the scorecard approach enables managers to relate progress to the concepts of competitive strategy and to the content of a strategic plan (see Chapter 5, Figure 5.18).

The balanced scorecard concept developed by Kaplan and Norton (1992) is a clear example of how value-based management approaches have become much more than a toolkit of financial techniques to apply to critical business issues. The scorecard concept provides insight into the linkages between the strategic value drivers, e.g. operational efficiency at Toyota, high-quality production engineering and engine design at Honda, and strategic outcomes and forces senior managers to question both the soundness of the overall corporate strategy and the potential need to reorient the strategy towards an alternative set of strategic priorities.

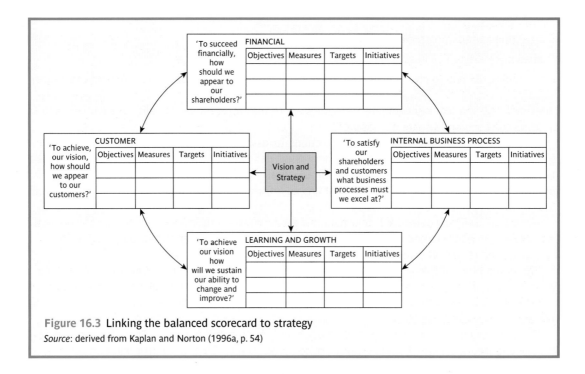

Figure 16.3 Linking the balanced scorecard to strategy
Source: derived from Kaplan and Norton (1996a, p. 54)

The balanced scorecard allows managers to examine each business and the overall corporate vision and strategy through four perspectives or lenses: financial, customer, internal and innovation and learning. Figure 16.3 shows the logic of the approach.

What the basic concept of a balanced scorecard provides is a disciplined framework through which to impose a series of questions (Kaplan and Norton, 1992, p. 22) that should be addressed by the company and its senior managers:

■ *How do we look to shareholders?* [The financial lens]: Metrics in this area encompass the SVA and EVA approaches, as well as accounting-based measures of performance.

■ *How do customers see us?* [The customer lens]: Metrics in this area include market-share, brand image and customer satisfaction.

■ *What must we excel at?* [The internal lens]: The issues in this area involve the internal business processes necessary to develop a successful strategy. Metrics would include supply-chain processes, quality etc.

■ *How can we continue to improve and create value?* [The innovation and learning lens]: Metrics in this area address the firm's ability to innovate and develop new capabilities through new product growth and development and improved R&D processes.

Doyle (2000, pp. 152–4) provides a basic and more extended checklist of potential measures or key performance indicators (KPI) for each of these lenses. Broadly, these comprise:

■ **Financial lens measures**
  – Return on capital employed
  – Operating margins
  – Economic value added
  – Cash flow
  – Sales growth

- **Consumer lens measures**
  - Market share
  - Brand image and awareness
  - Customer satisfaction
  - Customer relations
  - Customer acquisition
- **Internal lens measures**
  - Percentage of sales from new products
  - Manufacturing cost
  - Manufacturing cycle time
  - Inventory management
  - Quality indices
  - Supply-chain management processes
- **Innovation and learning lens measures**
  - New product development capabilities
  - R&D core competences
  - Technological capabilities
  - Human resource development and capabilities
  - Improved manufacturing and business processes
  - Improved sales methods and techniques

Checklists of measures, however, beg the question of what the best set of measures or key performance indicators (KPIs) for any company are. Fundamentally, we argue that important critical success factors and KPIs must link to the company's strategy and vision and track/monitor the key elements of that strategy. They must also take account of any changes in the broader economic and technological environment the company faces. In essence, the KPIs chosen should be regarded as a future-oriented set of metrics that will allow the company to benchmark and monitor the economic and competitive outcomes and examine the stability of the firm's strategy (the long-term perspective) and operations (the short-term perspective).

These KPIs relate back to the discussions in earlier chapters. Whereas KPIs are a manifestation of performance that we seek to measure, the drivers of KPIs (the critical success factors) are deep within the firm and within the logic of the strategy analysis in Chapter 6, Section 6.4 (see Figures 6.12 and 6.13). Performance analysis and the analysis of progress against strategic milestones were introduced in Chapters 1 and 2. The idea of rents and 'superprofits' as goals for strategy making stems from the economic analysis of markets that was introduced in Chapter 2. Imperfections were discussed explicitly in Chapter 3. These discussions provide essential background for the very financially oriented KPI measures in the financial lens measures. The trade-off between long- and short-term profits (the time horizon problem) is unresolved by any of these measures. The correct way to account for long-lived assets is captured to some degree by EVA measures.

The customer lens relates to the ideas that were germinated in Chapters 1 and 3 and discussed explicitly in Chapter 5. Key or critical success factors (KSFs) and KPIs can be confused. KSFs are often portrayed as intuitive in their conception but Chapter 5 shows how they derive from what customers want (analysis of demand). Chapter 5 provides a detailed discussion of this and how to beat competitors (analysis of competition). Thus, KSFs are manifestations of strategic choice and should reflect the intended competitive advantages. They should therefore be drivers of KPIs, and high scores on KPIs would be an indication that the KSFs are in place as intended. Furthermore, Chapter 5 shows a framework for analysing value (see Figure 5.19). This captures elements of customer value and shows some examples of KPIs of customer value. It also captures elements of costs and efficiency inherent in the strategy (the internal lens measures). Chapter 5 also has sections on differentiation advantage and on strategic market segments that are relevant to these aspects. Note that the internal process characteristics of the firm in terms of total quality management and supply-chain management also contribute to the internal lens.

The innovation and learning lens presents many problems, largely because the issues involved are process-sensitive and are both subtle and complex. The usual KPIs are relatively crude and often do not do justice to the underlying strategic choices. Chapter 14 introduced learning as an organizational phenomenon. Here the idea of the learning spiral and its four levels of activity (from individual, to one-to-one, to group, to organization) in Figure 14.5 and the framework for organizational learning in Figure 14.6 provide important perspectives that allow general managers and strategists to 'unpack' the KPIs shown in this lens. Chapter 14 takes further the discussion on knowledge and learning. This is driven from the resource-based view (Chapter 6) and provides a strong albeit subjective framework for generating useful KSFs and KPIs for the innovation and learning lens.

The strength of the balanced scorecard approach is its inclusivity of the range of strategy concepts and the way of linking them together in a single map (Figure 16.4). There is strength also in the way in which measurable KPIs are used to ground the map in reality and to make it an operational tool for managers. But this is also its weakness. Not all elements of competitive strategy are easy to measure, although many firms have strategic planning processes that make an heroic attempt to do this. More difficult is the area of management process which, as we have discussed earlier in this section of the book (e.g. Chapter 10), provides an essential grounding for strategy analysis decisions. Without good or appropriate process, good decisions cannot be made. However, the balanced scorecard is relatively silent on matters of process. The balanced scorecard should really be seen as a designed set of KPIs that provide early warning indicators rather than as a diagnostic

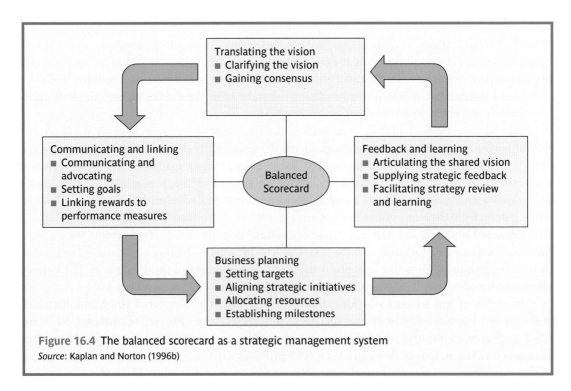

Figure 16.4 The balanced scorecard as a strategic management system
Source: Kaplan and Norton (1996b)

system that indicates the nature of problems and the sources of them. This is a controversial area that will benefit from progress on two fronts: (i) better conception and measurement of KPIs, and (ii) better linkage of strategy process elements to strategic decisions. The management process issues have been the subject of much attention and are discussed below.

As Kaplan and Nolan note (1996b, p. 75), the earlier version of the balanced scorecard as a balanced multi-perspective performance measurement system has evolved to a new strategic management system, linking long-term strategic objectives with short-term actions (see Figure 16.4), following the usage and experience gained from applying the original scorecard concept in a wide range of 100 or so organizations. Each of those organizations found that the balanced scorecard approach supplied a structure and a framework for such critical management processes as goal-setting, business planning, capital allocations, strategic initiatives and feedback and learning that facilitated strategic thinking and stimulated the analysis of alternative policy options for the organization.

The new strategic management system involves a set of four management processes which interact to enable the management of the strategic balance between short-term productivity objectives and long-term growth perspectives. The first of these processes is that involved in the *translation of the vision and strategy statements* using the model shown in Figure 16.3, so that they form a clear and well-understood set of objectives and measures that are agreed and endorsed by all senior managers.

This vision/strategy facilitates the framing of the strategy map and identification of the long-term drivers, whether marketing, organization or financial, that will determine the long-term success of the company. Ultimately, a well-structured vision and strategy statement builds organizational commitment.

The second of these processes – *communicating and linking* – requires managers to discuss and communicate their strategy as the corporate vision throughout the company and link that strategy to departmental and individual objectives. Thus, the scorecard provides a vehicle for debate and undertakes a strategic role in ensuring that the organizational strategy is understood by all organizational levels and, more importantly, that both departmental and individual objectives are linked and closely aligned to the strategy.

The third of these processes – *business planning* – provides a basis for the integration of business and financial plans. Since the balanced scorecard links strategy to performance measures (KPIs), managers can use the scorecard measures and associated goals to allocate resources and set priorities to achieve long-term strategic objectives at the business unit level. In other words, business unit scorecards are designed to link with the corporate scorecards.

The fourth of these processes – *feedback and learning* – allows the company to use feedback from the balanced scorecard and benchmarking processes to provide an insight into, and evaluation of, existing strategy at business unit and corporate levels. Thus, strategies can be changed, or reoriented, to take account of the real-time learning and feedback achieved by the company and its employees. Thus, corporate and business unit scorecards can be reviewed and updated. As Kaplan and Norton point out (2001, p. 97), the balanced scorecard in this context can be viewed as a systems dynamics model that provides a comprehensive, quantified model of a business's value creation process and enables the corporate strategy and vision to be continually refined and reviewed.

Kaplan and Norton also argue that the strategic plan should ultimately describe how the company intends to maximize shareholder value and continually create and sustain that shareholder value over time. By focusing on value, the strategic scorecard approach breaks the organizational effectiveness value equation into at least three main elements: namely, operational effectiveness (improving the efficiency of core business processes), customer management (understanding and leveraging customer relationships better) and product innovation (developing new products, markets and relationships to sustain future growth). Operational effectiveness strategies have a relatively short-term focus, customer management strategies have a more medium-term focus and product innovation strategies are much longer term in orientation. In each case, management must set 'stretch' objectives/targets for each of the KPIs and benchmark them on a regular basis. It is important to note that corporate strategy may be modified as economic and other conditions change (for example, in recessionary environments) with, in some cases, shorter-term productivity and operational strategies taking precedence over more innovative, longer-term product strategies.

16.3 How does the strategic management system work in practice?

The vision and strategy element of the balanced scorecard process in Figure 16.4 is the core process owned by the senior management team. It leads to a strategy map such as that shown in Figure 16.5.

This strategy map unfolds the four lenses of the balanced scorecard (the core process) and builds them systematically from workforce and operational issues to a customer value proposition that leads to improved shareholder value. The important KPIs are outlined in the diagram.

Once the vision and strategy have been identified through the strategy map, different senior managers must take responsibility for managing the four strategy processes shown in Figure 16.4, with the balanced scorecard activity as the 'hub' and organizing framework of the process. It is

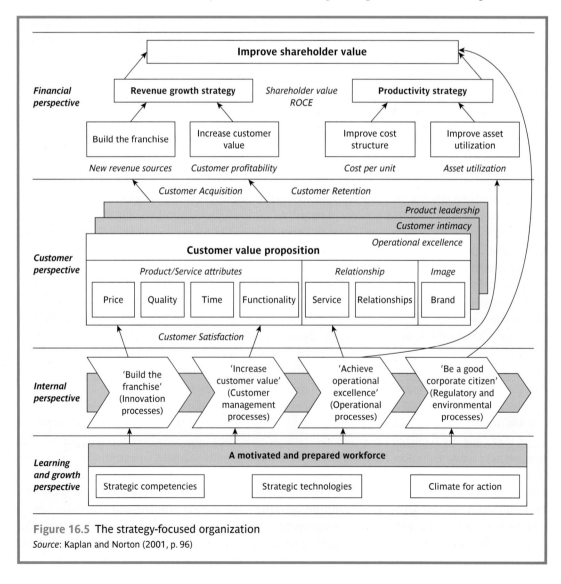

Figure 16.5 The strategy-focused organization

Source: Kaplan and Norton (2001, p. 96)

likely that the director of strategic planning or a very senior executive officer will manage the strategic planning process to clarify and translate the vision and strategy exemplified in the strategy map. Normally, the CFO (Chief Financial Officer) has responsibility for annual planning and budgeting and can be assigned the management of the business planning process, including target-setting and resource allocation. The process of strategic feedback and learning may be given to a chief information officer, or a strategic planning director. He or she would have clear responsibility for competitive intelligence benchmarking and the management of strategic databases/management information systems. The important role of communicating and linking should probably be the function of the Director of Human Resources, who would manage the goal-setting, incentive and reward systems in the organization.

A number of points are of critical importance in implementing the scorecard as a strategic management system. First, it is critical that the CEO and the senior management team responsible for the scorecard system should meet and exchange dialogue about system performance on a regular basis. Second, the role of managerial intuition and judgement throughout the organization will be important in drawing conclusions from system feedback and the wide range of KPIs offered by the scorecard (often 25 or so in Kaplan/Norton's framework). The underlying logic of how to interpret this data relies critically on the creativity, openness and rapport among members of the senior management team. At the heart of the process is the capability to translate KPIs into a 'bottom-line' performance view of the business and the willingness to continually amend, craft and evolve the emergent strategy of the business.

16.3.1 An example of the scorecard in practice: integration with the human resource (HR) process

Kaplan and Norton (1996b, p. 81) ask the following question: 'Should compensation systems be linked to the balance scorecard measures?' Clearly, the attractiveness of linking financial compensation rewards to performance is a powerful motivator discussed at length in the literature of strategic human resource management (e.g. Devanna et al., 1984).

The main potential pitfalls are whether the performance reward process involves too many risks in implementation. For example, are the right measures on the scorecard? Are valid and reliable data available for each of the selected measures? Other questions could clearly be posed here. To illustrate the dilemma, we offer an example from Kaplan and Norton (2001, pp. 242–3) based on the experience of Winterthur International, a major insurance company, who tried to link the balanced scorecard to a performance management model for the HR function. The diagram shown in Figure 16.6 presents a new HR management structure that Winterthur executives designed and which specifies job families and defines KPIs, skills and knowledge/competencies associated with each job family.

The company's experience was that many of the skills and competencies were difficult to measure, e.g. conceptual thinking, relationship building etc. However, the exercise of proposing the measures and identifying the organization's strategic themes made clear to many employees how they could contribute to achieving the strategic objectives of the organization. This alone made them more motivated employees. It should be noted from this evidence that the eventual goal may be to spend more time on the HR processes of translating organizational and business scorecards and associated KPIs into personal development scorecards, which employees can use with HR personnel to review and monitor performance. This may, in turn, lead to subsequent design of rewards/incentive systems as a longer-term goal.

Case box 16.3 gives an example of a business for sale. You can assess its business model and its performance using some of the concepts we have just introduced. Case box 16.4 examines the case of business schools as an example of the balanced scorecard approach.

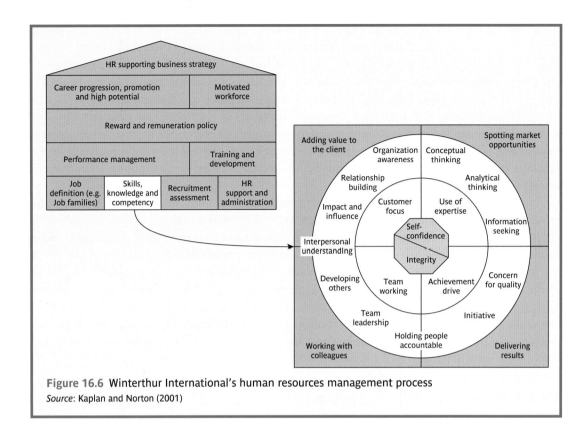

Figure 16.6 Winterthur International's human resources management process
Source: Kaplan and Norton (2001)

Case box 16.3: **Sales memorandum**

Confidentially offered for sale

The National Model Agency
Profits available to the owners
Exceed £176,000 per annum
Asking Price £800,000

Business profile

This model and promotional agency provides more services for clients and models than either the high-profile London-based agencies, which act for a limited number of big-name professional models, or the provincial agents who serve small local communities. The difference being that none of these traditional agencies have the number of models or geographical coverage that this successful national agency has to offer, by way of choice and a full United Kingdom wide promotion campaign.

The National agency represents professional and amateur models regardless of race, gender, ethnic or national origins, marital status, sexuality, education, age, physical impairment, religion or belief, language, appearance or class. The agency offers access to the world of fashion, film, television and photography.

Several thousand prospective models approach the agency each month. Online use of the unique bespoke software enables their national database of more than eighteen thousand contracted models to be searched precisely and accurately for clients, requirements producing for them comprehensive data including instant photographic images.

Clients who employ the agency can call for a choice of models at very short notice, for various work fields including advertising, promotions, television, film, fashion, photographic, catalogue, and media, and see a national selection immediately downloaded from their PC.

Commercial photographic shoots, television commercials, and magazine layouts that are being shot every day used to expect expensive, time-consuming postal portfolios to be sent by small inefficient agencies. Now these same clients, casting directors, and magazine editors can look at the models' portfolio on the web from the computer on their desk and find the model they require in minutes, versus several days or weeks! The agency avoids so-called glamour work. The length of management contract between each model and this agency is one to three years.

Ancillary services to models include photographic shoots, training courses, videos, books and merchandise together with access to over 400 professional United Kingdom Master photographers.

As a 'Client focused' agency the agency has achieved excellence in understanding and responding to the demands of new and existing clients, thus generating maximum satisfaction and profitability.

This agency has a strong ability to identify trends and establish itself in new markets thereby exploiting the most profitable opportunities. This has led to heavy investment in a sophisticated computer structure and an increasing focus in establishing a significant Internet presence. The ten thousand quarterly newsletters and merchandising range provide a potentially strong marketing platform.

The agency is now poised for global development with a licensed franchised system ability to encompass European and Intercontinental business.

Types of clients

Clients represent a wide variety of organizations:

- Retailers
- Restaurants
- Hospitals
- Religious organizations
- Universities
- Manufacturing firms
- Film & Video producers
- Television Companies
- Racecourses
- Motor Racing Groups
- Luxury Hotel Groups
- Hairdressers

- Drinks Companies
- Dairy Companies
- Newspapers
- Car Rental
- Theatres
- Publishing Houses
- Car Manufacturers
- Building Societies
- Hospitals
- Brewers
- City Councils
- …and others.

Financial information

The business and property are being offered for sale on a going concern basis.

All financial discussions will take place directly between the vendors and interested party.

Market and competitors

There is no known direct national competitor.

Management and staff

The operation is fully managed with guidance provided by the principals.

Future prospects

The media requirement for the human image for advertising and promotion remains almost insatiable.

The business model could grow to a worldwide operation should the new owners have the drive and ability to manage an operation of this size.

Reason for sale

The owners feel the business is reaching the optimum size for their management ability.

Source: Turner & Co, http://www.turnerandco.com/model_agency_businessforsale.html

Questions

The above is a notice advertising the sale of the National Model Agency.

1 From the content of this notice for sale, identify the business model that is in place.

2 Also, how would you assess the performance of the National Model Agency from this data?

3 If you were selling a company of this kind, how much information would you give about the underlying business model and the historic performance of the company?

Case box 16.4: Business school strategy and the metrics for success

Business schools have gained strong recognition over the last 100 years. Despite the fact that US schools continue to dominate the global business school landscape, formidable competitors sensitive to local market needs now exist in Europe, Asia and Latin America.

However, with recent increasing competition in the business school environment, there has been a parallel and quite critical discussion about the nature, value and relevance of business schools.

Critics have simultaneously accused the business schools, inter alia, of:

- doing irrelevant research
- being too market-driven and pandering to the ratings
- failing to ask important questions
- pursuing curricular fads
- 'dumbing down' course content
- focusing more on specialist, analytical rather than professional managerial skills.

Given this increased criticism and competition, it is important for business schools, and their deans, to be clear about their strategy, strategic positioning and alignment to the competitive environment.

The strategy map

The strategy map is a framework both for thinking about policy and strategy and as a vehicle for carrying out a dialogue about strategic options in any business school context.

This map is a system model and a thinking framework that ranges from the setting of a business school's overarching direction and the design of its strategies and programmes to the processes of learning, feedback and strategic renewal. Each stage in the diagram encompasses a set of issues and, typically, invites a specific question from overarching direction (where do we want to be as a business school?) to measures of performance (how do we check business school performance relative to the set of school goals?).

Given the importance of organisational performance in the strategic systems perspective, the next section focuses on potential measures of business school performance.

Measures of business school performance

In the literature on organisational performance three broad categories are typically identified:

- financial performance
- operational performance
- organisational effectiveness.

Examples of each of the performance categories in a business school context are:

- financial measures – profitability, financial surplus, level of endowment funding
- operational measures – faculty quality, student quality, research quality, teaching quality, programme efficiency, measures of market positioning
- organisational effectiveness – league table rankings, reputation, student satisfaction, employer satisfaction, accreditation.

Clearly, a high level of financial performance creates funds for a business school dean to invest in strategic investments such as new faculty, software development and research activity. Also, the severe reduction of government funding in higher education worldwide has made the generation of these financial surpluses an important management issue, not only for business school deans but also for university vice-chancellors and presidents.

Increasingly, business schools have also recognised the need to generate strategic funds through external fundraising in order to build endowments for research, teaching and faculty support activities.

Currently, American business schools have been much more successful at this and the increased money made available has allowed certain elite American schools that have built endowment 'mountains' (for example, Harvard and Wharton) to further increase their academic quality, branding and competitive positioning in the marketplace.

Business schools constantly examine the efficiency and effectiveness of their operations. Faculty recruitment and retention in an environment where there is a shortage of suitably qualified doctoral faculty is an important issue for many schools. The quality of faculty is also a critical element for attracting high-quality students who can, in turn, stretch the faculty in their teaching and research activities.

In many countries research and teaching performance are monitored and reviewed by government agencies. Such government-produced ratings are widely examined by potential students and evidence of excellence is trumpeted on business school websites. League table rankings of business schools routinely provided by publications such as *Business Week*, *The Economist*, *Financial Times* and *Wall Street Journal* are another important measure of customer satisfaction.

Attestation of school quality for external constituencies (such as employers and students) is further provided by accreditation agencies such as the Association to Advance Collegiate Schools of Business (AACSB International), the European Quality Improvement System (EQUIS) of the EFMD and the Association of MBAs (AMBA).

The key management question with the strategy map, therefore, is how to translate the strategic framework into a financial, operational and organisational measurement scheme that links strategy to organisational goals.

The balanced scorecard framework offers an appropriate model for 'piloting' the strategy of an organisation across a range of indicators of organisational performance and adjusting its 'flight-path' in order to improve future performance.

The balanced scorecard framework and business schools

The balanced scorecard allows managers to examine each area of the organisation and the overall corporate vision and strategy through four perspectives or lenses: financial; customer; internal; and innovation and learning.

What the basic concept of a balanced scorecard provides is a disciplined framework through which to impose a series of questions that should be addressed by the business school:

- How do we look to stakeholders, particularly university presidents or vice-chancellors? (the financial lens): metrics in this area include accounting-based measures of profitability and surplus generation.
- How do customers see us? (the customer lens): metrics in this area include market-share, brand image, and student, alumni and employer satisfaction.
- What must we excel at? (the internal lens): the issues in this area involve the internal business processes necessary to develop a successful strategy: metrics would include supply-chain processes, research quality, teaching quality and so on.
- How can we continue to improve and create value? (the innovation and learning lens): metrics in this area address a school's ability to innovate and develop new capabilities through research, new product growth and development, and improved funding opportunities.

Source: H. Thomas, EFMD Global Focus Magazine, Vol 3, 1, 2009

Questions

1 Checklists of measures, however, beg the question of what the best set of measures or key performance indicators (KPIs) are for any specific business school. Identify appropriate measures for a business school with which you are familiar.

2 How can the balanced scorecard link to the strategic planning process?

3 How can performance weakness influence the processes of strategic dynamics and change?

16.4 Summary

The underlying theme of this chapter has been that the performance feedback loop is critical in terms of both assessing and making strategic choices. Taking purely a planning approach to strategy (for example) is rather a one-eyed perspective, since it ignores the value of the feedback from actual (or expected) performance. Curiously, much of the field of strategic management has paid relatively scant attention to analysing and measuring performance as it relates to the strategy process. This chapter has attempted to fill that gap. The importance of the performance feedback loop cannot be over-stressed. It enables strategists to assess strategic decisions, of course, but more importantly, it facilitates the generation of new ideas, allows human resource managers to assess appropriate rewards, and underpins organizational as well as individual learning.

In this chapter we have discussed the evolution of concepts of performance measurement and their linkage to the strategy process. Given a goal of shareholder value maximization, we have presented a range of performance measures, including accounting-based measures of performance, economic value-added (EVA) metrics based on concepts of 'economic profit' and shareholder value approaches (SVA) based upon discounted cash flow concepts from finance. We concluded with a discussion of a set of more holistic value-based management techniques called the balanced scorecard approach. We believe that this approach has considerable value as a strategic management tool, particularly in its linkage to strategy and a range of KPIs.

Key terms

accounting	521	growth	523
balanced scorecard	526	indicators	522
effectiveness	521	planning	533
efficiency	522	shareholders	522
feedback	533	stakeholders	522

Recap questions and assignments

1 Why is the balanced scorecard arguably a significant advance on other performance measures?

2 What would you say are the key weaknesses or drawbacks of the balanced scorecard approach?

Case study 16.1: **The Continental Household Mortgage Company**

The Continental Household Mortgage Company (known internally simply as 'The Company') is a US-based financial services company specializing traditionally in household mortgages and latterly in personal savings products. Tom Howlett is a newly appointed strategic planner with a remit to review the planning and performance assessment processes.

The Company's strategic planning process uses a balanced scorecard approach for assessing progress against its objectives and for assessing the relevance and the sense of its competitive strategy.

It describes its strategy as follows:

1 Scale is central to all its products and services.

2 All business units are required to make accounting profits.

3 Customer relationships are central to business retention and development of new products.

4 Product development relies on the core product (mortgage services) being able to attract customers and then to generate interest in other products.

Its approach to assessing its strategy is captured in the Strategy Map (Figure 1). In this the four lenses of the balanced scorecard are used to identify the key management processes that will 'deliver' the strategy. For example, the learning and growth lens identifies the need for in-depth product knowledge and customer service skills (and other elements as well). From a customer perspective there is a need for the company's agents to be 'trusted'. The strategy map provides a linkage between key processes and financial measures relating to sales growth and productivity.

Behind the strategy map is another document that provides a strategy perspective (Figure 2). This shows how the four lenses of the balanced scorecard are reflected in 'Vision' statements. The financial vision is about profitability. The customer vision is about access to professional advice. The internal perspective concerns the nature of the customer contact experience. Finally, the learning and growth vision is about how these customer relationships will evolve and be developed in the future.

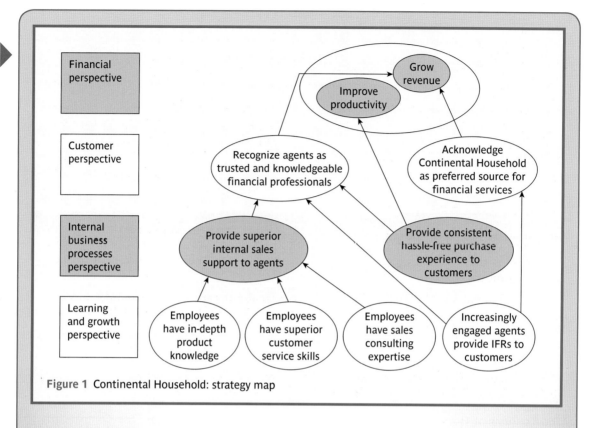

Figure 1 Continental Household: strategy map

Purpose
To help people manage the risks of everyday life, recover from the unexpected, and realize their dreams. By offering a comprehensive portfolio of financial products to help customers secure their financial future, agents can deepen their existing customer relationships and strengthen the long-term retention of customers.

Financial perspective
Each business unit will become self-sustaining and profitable, contributing to top-line revenue growth and bottom-line results.

Customer perspective
Every client will have access to a knowledgeable, friendly professional who is able to conduct a personalized financial review (IFR) and offer a range of financial products that help clients achieve their financial goals.

Internal perspective
Agents and customers will have a consistent, friendly, responsive and hassle-free experience across all contact points. Integrated back-office operations will focus on providing superior service so that agents and customers want to do business with us.

Learning and growth perspective
Agents will move to a relationship-oriented approach to customers. Agents will establish a new pattern of interaction with customers by focusing on proactively understanding customers' financial goals and needs, and marketing an expanded set of products. Employees will focus on helping the agent have successful client relationships by providing timely assistance, friendly support, and knowledgeable guidance.

Figure 2 Continental Household: strategy perspective

Strategic position

To become the provider of choice for customers who want help securing their financial future, we must offer financial products that are perceived by customers as better value than those offered by our competitors. At the same time, our offering has to be matched by a cost structure that is capable of delivering an acceptable rate of return on investment.

Financial perspective

At least three of our four business units will be profitable. Regardless of profitability, all business units will contribute significantly to top-line revenue growth and meet expense management targets.

Internal perspective

The application process for core, high-volume financial services will be integrated and simplified so that our customers' purchase experience is consistent and hassle-free. Agents will be receiving superior internal sales support for core financial products from an integrated contact and support system.

Customer perspective

The Company's reputation and brand will extend to all financial services so that our existing customer base readily acknowledges The Company as a preferred source for quality financial products. In addition more customers than ever will recognise their agent as a knowledgeable and trusted financial professional capable of delivering personalised, high quality service and meeting their needs with a full line of financial products.

Learning and growth perspective

More than half of our agents will be increasingly engaged in marketing and selling products that meet the broad financial goals of our customers by providing a personalised financial review (IFR) to interested customers. These engaged agents, with the support of their staff, will be achieving sales success that meets or exceeds scorecard levels of production. While employees in every business unit will be providing superior customer service to agents and customers, those employees in support roles will also possess in-depth product knowledge and sales consulting skills so that they can help agents build deeper relationships with clients.

Figure 3 Continental Household: strategy objectives

This perspective is supplemented by strategy objectives that identify specific business objectives so as to make measurable progress towards company goals. These are expressed through each lens of the balanced scorecard (see Figure 3).

The strategy is then elaborated in terms of product scope, market scope, market segmentation and key target markets, capped by a clear value proposition. This is phrased in terms of quality products, simple transactions, skilled and friendly staff, convenient and consistent customer service, and a professional approach to sales.

In the strategic plan there are entries for each of the balanced scorecard lenses. Each of them contains the following headings: Business Goal and its Measure, Action Plan, and Major Initiative. The principal measures are:

Balanced scorecard lens	Business goal	Measures (KPIs)
Financial	1. Increase sales revenue 2. Improve productivity	1. % revenue growth (12%pa 2004–6) 2. Expense ratio (21% falling to 16%, 2004–6)
Customer	1. Wide recognition by customers of Company products 2. Customer recognition of sales agent as financial professional	1. % households with a Company product (20% to 25% 2004–6) and # Company products per Company customer (1.8 to 2.25 2004–6) 2. % Company agents fully participating in the product line
Internal	1. Customer-facing business processes integrated and simplified 2. Company agents receive superior sales support from integrated contact and support system	1. % agents satisfied with the application process (increase over 2003 of 0% in '04, and 10% by '06) 2. % agents satisfied with internal support (increase over 2003 baseline of 5% in '04, 10% in '05 and 15% in '06
Learning and growth	1. More agents providing a personal financial review to actual and potential customers 2. Employees in internal sales support possess in-depth product knowledge, sales consulting expertise and superior customer service skills	1. % agents fully participating in marketing Company product line 2a. % agents very satisfied with employee product knowledge (increase over 2003 of 5% in each year to '06) 2b. ditto with customer service 2c. ditto with sales consulting skills

Note that sales agents are self-employed typically marketing financial services products from a range of providers.

Questions

Tom Howlett is worried about a number of things which underpin the four case questions below.

1 Is the strategy described properly?
2 What are the key success factors?
3 Do these relate to the key performance indicators?
4 What initial steps should he take to improve the process?

References

Bowman, E.H. and Hurry, D. (1993) Strategy through the option lens: an integrated view of resource investments and the incremental choice process. *Academy of Management Review*, **15**, 4, 760–82.

Brealey, R.A. and Myers, S.C. (2009) *Principles of Corporate Finance* (8th edn), McGraw-Hill, New York.

Cameron, K.S. and Whetten, D.A. (1983) (eds) *Organisational Effectiveness: A Comparison of Multiple Methods*, Academic Press, New York.

Devanna, M.A., Fombrun, C.J. and Tichy, N.M. (1984) A framework for strategic human resource management. In C.J. Fombrun, N.M. Tichy and M.A. Devanna (eds), *Strategic Human Resource Management*, John Wiley & Sons, New York, chapter 3, pp. 33–56.

Doyle, P. (2000) *Value-based Marketing*, John Wiley & Sons, Chichester.

Hayes, R.L. and Abernathy, W. (1980) Managing our way to economic decline. *Harvard Business Review*, July–August, 66–67.

Kaplan, R.S. and Norton, D.P. (1992) The balanced scorecard – measures that drive performance. *Harvard Business Review*, Jan–Feb, 71–9.

Kaplan, R.S. and Norton, D.P. (1996a) Linking the balanced scorecard to strategy. *California Management Review*, **39**, **1**, Fall, 53–79.

Kaplan, R.S. and Norton, D.P. (1996b) Using the balanced scorecard as a strategic management system. *Harvard Business Review*, Jan–Feb, 75–85.

Kaplan, R.S. and Norton, D.P. (2001) *The Strategy-focused Organisation*, Harvard Business School Press, Cambridge, MA.

Kay, J. (1993) *Foundations of Corporate Success: How Corporate Strategies Add Value*, Oxford University Press, Oxford.

Rappaport, A. (1986) *Creating Shareholder Value: The New Standard for Business Performance*, Free Press, New York.

Sloan, A.P. (1963) *My Years with General Motors*, MIT Press, Cambridge, MA.

Smith, T. (1992) *Accounting for Growth*, Century Business Books, London.

Stern Stewart (1996) *The Stern Stewart Performance 1000: A Ranking of America's Most Value-adding companies*, Stern Stewart, New York.

Venkatraman, N. and Ramanujam, V. (1986) Measurement of business performance in strategy research: a comparison of approaches. *Academy of Management Review*, **11**, **4**, 801–14.

Yip, G. (2004) Using strategy to change your business model. *Business Strategy Review*, **15**, **2**, 17–24.

Further reading

Crouch, C. (2006) Modelling the firm in its market and organisational environment: methodologies for studying corporate social responsibility. *Organisation Studies*, **27**, **10**, 1533–51.

Kaplan, R.S. and Norton, D.P. (2008) Mastering the management system. *Harvard Business Review*, **86**, **1**, 62–77.

Case Study Section

Table of Contents

A guide to using case studies

The main text of our book contains fifty-four case boxes within the chapters and sixteen short case studies at the end of the chapters. These have been chosen to exemplify and enlarge upon the concepts and issues raised in each chapter. They are practical examples of how strategy concepts and ideas are manifested in the real world of making strategic decisions. Together with the Recap Questions at the end of each chapter these represent a practical study content, that is further developed in the Online Learning Centre that accompanies this book at www.mcgraw-hill.co.uk/textbooks/mcgee.

The case studies that appear in this section take your learning onto a different level. These case studies are written around real, practical problems but in using them you should recognize that they are not intended as illustrations of either effective or ineffective management practice. In reading the previous chapters we hope to have persuaded you that the world of strategy and practice is messy and complicated. It follows usually that it is not easy or indeed sensible to attempt to categorize management practice as good or bad. These case studies are intended to provide a basis for analyzing and discussing a range of different situations in which the decisions to be taken are either not obvious or their implementation carries risks and complexities. These cases are typically quite long and contain considerable detail. Whereas the earlier case boxes and end of chapter cases are designed to be short so as to highlight the learning of concepts, the case studies in this section show the application of strategy theory and concepts in the real world of complex detail that is characteristic of companies and other organizations. The learning objective of analyzing long case studies is to bring together your ability to think conceptually with your ability to collect, select, analyze and interpret considerable amounts of data. Taken together, these abilities are the basis for being able to understand and make strategic decisions.

This general and overarching objective can be broken down into specific learning experiences.

1 The first step is to gain practice in identifying key problems. The strategist's usual questions are: Where are we going? How are we going to get there? How do we expect to be able to succeed? These questions need to be fully articulated so that the context of the case is properly captured in the questions. For example, it is not enough to simply make a distinction between a growth strategy and

a share retention strategy. The alternatives have to be expressed in terms of the detail of the situation so that the nature of the required judgements can be understood.

2 The cases are also designed to give practice in specifying what is meant by key concepts such as competitive advantage and core competence in real terms. As intellectual constructs these are powerful ideas but only gain real meaning when placed within the specific context of the individual company.

3 Case studies also allow the analyst to gain practice in how to shape an implementation plan. This should be expressed in terms of the business model, the key functional strategies and tactics, the key decisions to be taken and the risks involved.

4 The complexity of the real worlds of these cases allows you to explore larger issues such as mergers and acquisitions, technical innovation and R&D, performance assessment, corporate governance, and ethics and social responsibility. These represent significant 'strategic issues' that have concepts and content of their own and attract significant debate and controversy.

The summary table that follows displays how the cases relate to the chapters. There is an indication of the main focus of each case and also an indication of the minor focus. Each case may apply to more than one chapter and may cover a variety of concepts. The country location of each case is also shown so that you can choose to focus or diversify your use of cases as you wish.

In using cases you should be aware that before going on to the main theme of the case you will need to carry out a strategy analysis such as that shown in Chapters 5 and 6 (where the basic idea of competitive strategy is explained). Thus, a question posed in the case might be: 'Should Unilever buy cosmetics company X?'. In order to address this question properly it is first necessary to undertake a preliminary strategy analysis in order to understand the major strategic objectives, the nature of the competitive advantage and the degree of success of the implementation of the current strategy. This places the 'buy/not buy' decision in proper context.

A guide to the main focus of the cases

Page	Companies/Industries featured	Chapter 1: What is strategy? Concepts and practices	Chapter 2: A systemic analysis of strategy and practice	Chapter 3: Industry analysis and competitive advantage	Chapter 4: The macroeconomics of strategy	Chapter 5: Competitive strategy: the analysis of strategic position	Chapter 6: Competitive strategy: the analysis of strategic capability	Chapter 7: Strategy for the digital economy	Chapter 8: Corporate strategy: adding value in multi-business firms	Chapter 9: Global strategies and international advantage	Chapter 10: Organisational models and strategy	Chapter 11: Risk, uncertainty and strategy	Chapter 12: Strategic decision making: process analyses	Chapter 13: Strategic decision making: managing strategic change	Chapter 14: Strategy as knowledge: innovation and learning	Chapter 15: Strategy and corporate governance	Chapter 16: Analysing and measuring strategic performance	Country location of case study
550	**Canon**			★		★★	★★		★									Japan
568	**Southwest Airlines**			★★		★★				★	★★		★	★			★	USA
584	**Honda (A)**	★★	★	★	★	★★					★							Japan/USA
593	**Honda (B)**	★★	★	★	★	★★					★							Japan/USA
601	**Low-Cost Airlines**	★	★	★★		★★	★								★		★★	UK/Europe
636	**Renault-Nissan**	★	★	★★						★★	★			★★	★		★★	Europe/Japan
649	**Apple**	★	★★			★★	★	★						★★	★★	★	★	USA
663	**Vanke**			★		★★			★★			★		★★				Europe/China
673	**Citigroup**				★	★★			★★	★	★★			★			★	USA

Key: ★ = major focus

★ / ★ = important subsidiary focus

CASE 1: Canon: Competing on Capabilities

INSEAD

In 1961, following the runaway success of the company's model 914 office copier, Joseph C. Wilson, President of Xerox Corporation, was reported to have said, 'I keep asking myself, when am I going to wake up? Things just aren't this good in life'. Indeed, the following decade turned out to be better than anything Wilson could have dreamed. Between 1960 and 1970, Xerox increased its sales 40 percent per year from $40 million to $1.7 billion and raised its after-tax profits from $2.6 million to $187.7 million. In 1970, with 93 percent market share world-wide and a brand name that was synonymous with copying, Xerox appeared as invincible in its industry as any company ever could.

When Canon, 'the camera company from Japan', jumped into the business in the late 1960s, most observers were sceptical. Less than a tenth the size of Xerox, Canon had no direct sales or service organiz-ation to reach the corporate market for copiers, nor did it have a process technology to by-pass the 500 patents that guarded Xerox's Plain Paper Copier (PPC) process. Reacting to the spate of recent entries in the business including Canon, Arthur D. Little predicted in 1969 that no company would be able to challenge Xerox's monopoly in PPC's in the 1970s because its patents presented an insurmountable barrier.

Yet, over the next two decades, Canon rewrote the rule book on how copiers were supposed to be produced and sold as it built up $5 billion in revenues in the business, emerging as the second largest global player in terms of sales and surpassing Xerox in the number of units sold. According to the Canon Handbook, the company's formula for success as displayed initially in the copier business is 'synergistic management of the total technological capabilities of the company, combining the full measure of Canon's know how in fine optics, precision mechanics, electronics and fine chemicals'. Canon continues to grow and diversify using this strategy. Its vision, as described in 1991 by Ryuzaburo Kaku, President of the company, is 'to become a premier global company of the size of IBM combined with Matsushita'.

Industry Background

The photocopying machine has often been compared with the typewriter as one of the few triggers that have fundamentally changed the ways of office work. But, while a mechanical Memograph machine for copying had been introduced by the A.B. Dick company of Chicago as far back as 1887, it was only in the second half of this century that the copier market exploded with Xerox's commercialisation of the 'electrophotography' process invented by Chester Carlson.

Xerox

Carlson's invention used an electrostatic process to transfer images from one sheet of paper to another. Licensed to Xerox in 1948, this invention led to two different photocopying technologies.

This case was prepared by Mary Ackenhusen, Research Associate, under the supervision of Sumantra Ghoshal, Associate Professor at INSEAD. It is intended to be used as a basis for class discussion rather than to illustrate either effective or ineffective handling of an administrative situation.

The Coated Paper Copying (CPC) technology transferred the reflection of an image from the original directly to specialized zinc-oxide coated paper, while the Plain Paper Copying (PPC) technology transferred the image indirectly to ordinary paper through a rotating drum coated with charged particles. While either dry or liquid toner could be used to develop the image, the dry toner was generally preferable in both technologies. A large number of companies entered the CPC market in the 1950s and 1960s based on technology licensed from Xerox or RCA (to whom Xerox had earlier licensed this technology). However, PPC remained a Xerox monopoly since the company had refused to license any technology remotely connected to the PPC process and had protected the technology with over 500 patents.

Because of the need for specialized coated paper, the cost per copy was higher for CPC. Also, this process could produce only one copy at a time, and the copies tended to fade when exposed to heat or light. PPC, on the other hand, produced copies at a lower operating cost that were also indistinguishable from the original. The PPC machines were much more expensive, however, and were much larger in size. Therefore, they required a central location in the user's office. The smaller and less expensive CPC machines, in contrast, could be placed on individual desks. Over time, the cost and quality advantages of PPC, together with its ability to make multiple copies at high speed, made it the dominant technology and, with it, Xerox's model of centralized copying, the industry norm.

This business concept of centralized copying required a set of capabilities that Xerox developed and which, in turn, served as its major strengths and as key barriers to entry to the business. Given the advantages of volume and speed, all large companies found centralized copying highly attractive and they became the key customers for photocopying machines. In order to support this corporate customer base, Xerox's product designs and upgrades emphasized economies of higher volume copying. To market the product effectively to these customers, Xerox also built up an extensive direct sales and service organization of over 12,000 sales representatives and 15,000 service people. Forty percent of the sales reps' time was spent 'hand holding' to prevent even minor dissatisfaction. Service reps, dressed in suits and carrying their tools in briefcases, performed preventative maintenance and prided themselves on reducing the average time between breakdown and repair to a few hours.

Further, with the high cost of each machine and the fast rate of model introductions, Xerox developed a strategy of leasing rather than selling machines to customers. Various options were available, but typically the customers paid a monthly charge on the number of copies made. The charge covered not only machine costs but also those of the paper and toner that Xerox supplied and the service visits. This lease strategy, together with the carefully cultivated service image, served as key safeguards from competition, as they tied the customers into Xerox and significantly raised their switching costs.

Unlike some other American corporations, Xerox had an international orientation right from the beginning. Even before it had a successful commercial copier, Xerox built up an international presence through joint ventures which allowed the company to minimize its capital investment abroad. In 1956, it ventured with the Rank Organization Ltd. in the U.K. to form Rank Xerox. In 1962, Rank Xerox became a 50 percent partner with Fuji Photo to form Fuji Xerox which sold copiers in Japan. Through these joint ventures, Xerox built up sales and service capabilities in these key markets similar to those it had in the United States. There were some 5,000 sales people in Europe, 3,000 in Japan and over 7,000 and 3,000 service reps, respectively. Xerox also built limited design capabilities in both the joint ventures for local market customization, which developed into significant research establishments in their own rights in later years.

Simultaneously, Xerox maintained high levels of investment in both technology and manufacturing to support its growing market. It continued to spend over $100 million a year in R&D, exceeding the total revenues from the copier business that any of its competitors were earning in the early 70s, and also invested heavily in large-size plants not only in the U.S., but also in the U.K. and Japan.

Competition in the 1970s

Xerox's PPC patents began to expire in the 1970s, heralding a storm of new entrants. In 1970, IBM offered the first PPC copier not sold by Xerox, which resulted in Xerox suing IBM for patent infringement and violation of trade secrets. Canon marketed a PPC copier the same year through the development of an independent PPC technology which they licensed selectively to others. By 1973, competition had expanded to include players from the office equipment industry (IBM, SCM, Litton, Pitney Bowes), the electronics industry (Toshiba, Sharp), the reprographics industry (Ricoh, Mita, Copyer, 3M, AB Dick, Addressograph/Multigraph), the photographic equipment industry (Canon, Kodak, Minolta, Konishiroku) and the suppliers of copy paper (Nashua, Dennison, Saxon).

By the 1980s many of these new entrants, including IBM, had lost large amounts of money and exited the business. A few of the newcomers managed to achieve a high level of success, however, and copiers became a major business for them. Specifically, copiers were generating 40 percent of Canon's revenues by 1990.

Canon

Canon was founded in 1933 with the ambition to produce a sophisticated 35mm camera to rival that of Germany's world-class Leica model. In only two years' time, it had emerged as Japan's leading producer of high-class cameras. During the war, Canon utilized its optics expertise to produce an X-ray machine which was adopted by the Japanese military. After the war, Canon was able to successfully market its high-end camera, and by the mid-1950s it was the largest camera manufacturer in Japan. Building off its optics technology, Canon then expanded its product line to include a mid-range camera, an 8mm video camera, television lenses and micrographic equipment. It also began developing markets for its products outside of Japan, mainly in the U.S. and Canada.

Diversification was always very important to Canon in order to further its growth, and a new products R&D section was established in 1962 to explore the fields of copy machines, auto-focusing cameras, strobe-integrated cameras, home VCRs and electronic calculators. A separate, special operating unit was also established to introduce new non-camera products resulting from the diversification effort.

The first product to be targeted was the electronic calculator. This product was challenging because it required Canon engineers to develop new expertise in microelectronics in order to incorporate thousands of transistors and diodes in a compact, desk model machine. Tekeshi Mitarai, President of Canon at that time, was against developing the product because it was seen to be too difficult and risky. Nevertheless, a dedicated group of engineers believed in the challenge and developed the calculator in secrecy. Over a year later, top management gave their support to the project. In 1964, the result of the development effort was introduced as the Canola 130, the world's first 10-key numeric pad calculator. With this product line, Canon dominated the Japanese electronic calculator market in the 1960s.

Not every diversification effort was a success, however. In 1956, Canon began development of the synchroreader, a device for writing and reading with a sheet of paper coated with magnetic material. When introduced in 1959, the product received high praise for its technology. But, because the design was not patented, another firm introduced a similar product at half the price. There was no market for the high priced and incredibly heavy Canon product. Ultimately, the firm was forced to disassemble the finished inventories and sell off the usable parts in the 'once-used' components market.

Move into Copiers

Canon began research into copier technology in 1959, and, in 1962, it formed a research group dedicated to developing a plain paper copier (PPC) technology. The only known PPC process was protected by hundreds of Xerox patents, but Canon felt that only this technology promised sufficient quality, speed, economy and ease of maintenance to successfully capture a large portion of the market. Therefore, corporate management challenged the researchers to develop a new PPC process which would not violate the Xerox patents.

In the meantime, the company entered the copier business by licensing the 'inferior' CPC technology in 1965 from RCA. Canon decided not to put the name of the company on this product and marketed it under the brand name Confax 1000 in Japan only. Three years later, Canon licensed a liquid toner technology from an Australian company and combined this with the RCA technology to introduce the CanAll Series. To sell the copier in Japan, Canon formed a separate company, International Image Industry. The copier was sold as an OEM to Scott Paper in the U.S. who sold it under its own brand name.

Canon's research aiming at developing a PPC technical alternative to xerography paid off with the announcement of the 'New Process' (NP) in 1968. This successful research effort not only produced an alternative process but also taught Canon the importance of patent law: how not to violate patents and how to protect new technology. The NP process was soon protected by close to 500 patents.

The first machine with the NP technology, the NP1100, was introduced in Japan in 1970. It was the first copier sold by Canon to carry the Canon brand name. It produced 10 copies per minute and utilized dry toner. As was the standard in the Japanese market, the copier line was sold outright to customers from the beginning. After two years of experience in the domestic market, Canon entered the overseas market, except North America, with this machine.

The second generation of the NP system was introduced in Japan in 1972 as the NPL7. It was a marked improvement because it eliminated a complex fusing technology, simplified developing and cleaning, and made toner supply easier through a new system developed to use liquid toner. Compared with the Xerox equivalent, it was more economical, more compact, more reliable and still had the same or better quality of copies.

With the NP system, Canon began a sideline which was to become quite profitable: licensing. The first generation NP system was licensed to AM, and Canon also provided it with machines on an OEM basis. The second generation was again licensed to AM as well as to Saxon, Ricoh, and Copyer. Canon accumulated an estimated $32 million in license fees between 1975 and 1982.

Canon continued its product introductions with a stream of state-of-the-art technological innovations throughout the seventies. In 1973 it added colour to the NP system; in 1975, it added laser beam printing technology. Its first entry into high volume copiers took place in 1978 with a model which was targeted at the Xerox 9200. The NP200 was introduced in 1979 and went on to win a gold medal at the Leipzig Fair for being the most economical and productive copier available. By 1982, copiers had surpassed cameras as the company's largest revenue generator (see Exhibits 1 and 2 for Canon's financials and sales by product line).

The Personal Copier

In the late 1970s, top management began searching for a new market for the PPC copier. They had recently experienced a huge success with the introduction of the AE-1 camera in 1976 and wanted a similar success in copiers. The AE-1 was a very compact single-lens reflex camera, the first camera that used a microprocessor to control electronically functions of exposure, film rewind and strobe. The product had been developed through a focused, cross-functional project team effort which had resulted in a substantial reduction in the number of components, as well as in automated assembly and the use of unitized parts. Because of these improvements, the AE-1 enjoyed a 20 percent cost advantage over competitive models in the same class.

After studying the distribution of offices in Japan by size (see Exhibit 3), Canon decided to focus on a latent segment that Xerox had ignored. This was the segment comprised of small offices (segment E) who could benefit from the functionality offered by photocopiers but did not require the high speed machines available in the market. Canon management believed that a low volume 'value for money' machine could generate a large demand in this segment. From this analysis emerged the business concept of a 'personal side desk' machine which could not only create a new market in small offices, but potentially also induce decentralization of the copy function in large offices. Over time, the machine might even create demand for a personal copier for home use. This would be a copier that up to now no one had thought possible. Canon felt that, to be successful in this market, the product had to cost half the price of a conventional copier (target price $1,000), be maintenance free, and provide ten times more reliability.

Top management took their 'dream' to the engineers, who, after careful consideration, took on the challenge. The machine would build off their previous expertise in microelectronics but would go much further in terms of material, functional component, design and production engineering technologies.

Exhibit 1 Canon, Inc. – Ten-Year Financial Summary (Millions of yen expect par share amounts)

	1990	1989	1988	1987	1986	1985	1984	1983	1982	1981
Net sales:										
Domestic ¥	508,747	413,854	348,462	290,382	274,174	272,966	240,656	198,577	168,178	144,898
Overseas	1,219,201	937,063	757,548	686,329	615,043	682,814	589,732	458,748	412,322	326,364
Total	1,727,948	1,350,917	1,106,010	976,711	889,217	955,780	830,388	657,325	580,500	471,262
Percentage to previous year	127.9%	122.1	113.2	109.8	93.0	115.1	126.3	113.2	123.2	112.5
Net income	61,408	38,293	37,100	13,244	10,728	37,056	35,029	28,420	22,358	16,216
Percentage to sales	3.6%	2.8	3.4	1.4	1.2	3.9	4.2	4.3	3.9	3.4
Advertising expense	72,234	54,394	41,509	38,280	37,362	50,080	51,318	41,902	37,532	23,555
Research and development	86,008	75,566	65,522	57,085	55,330	49,461	38,256	28,526	23,554	14,491
Depreciation	78,351	64,861	57,627	57,153	55,391	47,440	39,995	30,744	27,865	22,732
Capital expenditure	137,298	107,290	83,069	63,497	81,273	91,763	75,894	53,411	46,208	54,532
Long-term debt	262,886	277,556	206,083	222,784	166,722	134,366	99,490	60,636	53,210	39,301
Stockholders' equity	617,566	550,841	416,465	371,198	336,456	333,148	304,310	264,629	235,026	168,735
Total assets	1,827,945	1,636,380	1,299,843	1,133,881	1,009,504	1,001,044	916,651	731,642	606,101	505,169

Exhibit 1 *Continued*

	1990	1989	1988	1987	1986	1985	1984	1983	1982	1981
Per share data:										
Net income:										
Common and common equivalent share	78.29	50.16	51.27	19.65	16.67	53.38	53.63	46.31	41.17	34.04
Assuming full dilution	78.12	49.31	51.26	19.64	16.67	53.25	53.37	45.02	38.89	33.35
Cash dividends declared	12.50	11.93	11.36	9.09	11.36	11.36	9.88	9.43	8.23	7.84
Stock price:										
High	1,940	2,040	1,536	1,282	1,109	1,364	1,336	1,294	934	1,248
Low	1,220	1,236	823	620	791	800	830	755	417	513
Average number of common and common equivalent shares in thousands	788,765	780,546	747,059	747,053	746,108	727,257	675,153	645,473	564,349	515,593
Number of employees	54,381	44,401	40,740	37,521	35,498	34,129	30,302	27,266	25,607	24,300
Average exchange rate ($1 =)	143	129	127	143	167	235	239	238	248	222

Source: Canon 1990 Annual Report

Exhibit 2 Canon – Sales by Product (Millions of Yen)

Year	Cameras	Copiers	Other Business Machines	Optical & Other Products	Total
1981	201,635	175,389	52,798	40,222	470,044
1982	224,619	242,161	67,815	45,905	580,500
1983	219,443	291,805	97,412	48,665	657,325
1984	226,645	349,986	180,661	73,096	830,388
1985	197,284	410,840	271,190	76,466	955,780
1986	159,106	368,558	290,630	70,923	889,217
1987	177,729	393,581	342,895	62,506	976,711
1988	159,151	436,924	434,634	75,301	1,106,010
1989	177,597	533,115	547,170	93,035	1,350,917
1990	250,494	686,077	676,095	115,282	1,727,948

Source: Canon Annual Report, 1981–1990

Exhibit 3 Office Size Distribution, Japan 1979

Copier Market Segment	Number of Office Workers	Number of Offices	Working Population
A	300+	200,000	9,300,000
B	100–299	30,000	4,800,000
C	30–99	170,000	8,300,000
D	5–29	1,820,000	15,400,000
E	1–4	4,110,000	8,700,000

Source: Breakthrough: The Development of the Canon Personal Copier, Teruo Yamanouchi, Long Range Planning, Vol. 22, October 1989, p. 4

The team's slogan was 'Let's make the AE-1 of copiers!', expressing the necessity of know-how transfer between the camera and copier divisions as well as their desire for a similar type of success. The effort was led by the director of the Reprographic Production Development Center. His cross-functional team of 200 was the second largest ever assembled at Canon (the largest had been that of the AE-1 camera).

During the development effort, a major issue arose concerning the paper size that the new copier would accept. Canon Sales (the sales organization for Japan) wanted the machine to use a larger-than-letter-size paper which accounted for 60 percent of the Japanese market. This size was not necessary for sales outside of Japan and would add 20–30 percent to the machine's cost as well as make the copier more difficult to service. After much debate worldwide, the decision was made to forego the ability to utilize the larger paper size in the interest of better serving the global market.

Three years later the concept was a reality. The new PC (personal copier) employed a new-cartridge based technology which allowed the user to replace the photoreceptive drum, charging device, toner assembly and cleaner with a cartridge every 2,000 copies, thus eliminating the need to maintain the copier regularly. This enabled Canon engineers to meet the cost and reliability targets. The revolutionary product was the smallest, lightest copier ever sold, and created a large market which had previously not existed. Large offices adjusted their copying strategies to include decentralized copying, and many small offices and even homes could now afford a personal copier. Again, Canon's patent knowledge was utilized to protect this research, and the cartridge technology was not licensed to other manufacturers. Canon has maintained its leadership in personal copiers into the 1990s.

Building Capabilities

Canon is admired for its technical innovations, marketing expertise, and low-cost quality manufacturing. These are the result of a long-term strategy to become a premier company. Canon has frequently acquired outside expertise so that it could better focus internal investments on skills of strategic importance. This approach of extensive outsourcing and focused internal development has required consistent direction from top management and the patience to allow the company to become well grounded in one skill area before tasking the organization with the next objective.

Technology

Canon's many innovative products, which enabled the company to grow quickly in the seventies and eighties are in large part the result of a carefully orchestrated use of technology and the capacity for managing rapid technological change. Attesting to its prolific output of original research is the fact that Canon has been among the leaders in number of patents issued world-wide throughout the eighties.

These successes have been achieved in an organization that has firmly pursued a strategy of decentralized R&D. Most of Canon's R&D personnel are employed by the product divisions where 80–90 percent of the company's patentable inventions originate. Each product division has its own development centre which is tasked with short- to medium-term product design and improvement of production systems. Most product development is performed by cross-functional teams. The work of the development groups is coordinated by an R&D headquarters group.

The Corporate Technical Planning and Operation centre is responsible for long-term strategic R&D planning. Canon also has a main research centre which supports state-of-the-art research in optics, electronics, new materials and information technology. There are three other corporate research centres which apply this state-of-the-art research to product development.

Canon acknowledges that it has neither the resources nor the time to develop all necessary technologies and has therefore often traded or bought specific technologies from a variety of external partners. Furthermore, it has used joint ventures and technology transfers as a strategic tool for mitigating foreign trade tensions in Europe and the United States. For example, Canon had two purposes in mind when it made an equity participation in CPF Deutsch, an office equipment marketing firm in Germany. Primarily, it believed that this move would help develop the German market for its copiers; but it did not go unnoticed among top management that CPF owned Tetras, a copier maker who at that time was pressing dumping charges against Japanese copier makers. Canon also used Burroughs as an OEM for office automation equipment in order to acquire Burroughs software and know-how and participated in joint development agreements with Eastman Kodak and Texas Instruments. Exhibit 4 provides a list of the company's major joint ventures.

Canon also recognizes that its continued market success depends on its ability to exploit new research into marketable products quickly. It has worked hard to reduce the new product introduction cycle through a cross-functional programme called TS 1/2 whose purpose is to cut development time by 50 percent on a continuous basis. The main thrust of this programme is the classification of development projects by total time required and the critical human resources needed so that these two parameters can be optimized for each product depending on its importance for Canon's corporate strategy. This allows product teams to be formed around several classifications of product development priorities of which 'best sellers' will receive the most emphasis. These are the products aimed at new markets or segments with large potential demands. Other classifications include products necessary to

Exhibit 4 Canon's Major International Joint Ventures		
CATEGORY	**PARTNER**	**DESCRIPTION**
Office Equipment	Eastman Kodak (U.S.)	Distributes Kodak medical equipment in Japan; exports copiers to Kodak
	CPF Germany	Equity participation in CPF which markets Canon copiers
	Olivetti (Italy) Lotte (Korea)	Joint venture for manufacture of copier
Computers	Hewlett-Packard (U.S.)	Receives OEM mini-computer from HP; supplies laser printer to HP
	Apple Computer (U.S.)	Distributes Apple computers in Japan; supplies laser printer to Apple
	Next, Inc. (U.S.)	Equity participation; Canon has marketing rights for Asia
Semiconductors	National Semiconductor (U.S.)	Joint development of MPU & software for Canon office equipment
	Intel (U.S.)	Joint development of LSI for Canon copier, manufactured by Intel
Telecommunications	Siemens (Germany)	Development of ISDN interface for Canon facsimile; Siemens supplies Canon with digital PBX
	DHL (U.S.)	Equity participation; Canon supplies terminals to DHL
Camera	Kinsei Seimitsu (Korea)	Canon licenses technology on 35 mm Camera
Other	ECD (U.S.)	Equity participation because Canon values its research on amorphous materials
Source: Canon Asia, Nomura Management School		

catch up with competitive offerings, product refinements intended to enhance customer satisfaction, and long-run marathon products which will take considerable time to develop. In all development classifications, Canon emphasizes three factors to reduce time to market: the fostering of engineering ability, efficient technical support systems, and careful reviews of product development at all stages.

Canon is also working to divert its traditional product focus into more of a market focus. To this end, Canon R&D personnel participate in international product strategy meetings, carry out consumer research, join in marketing activities, and attend meetings in the field at both domestic and foreign sales subsidiaries.

Marketing

Canon's effective marketing is the result of step-by-step, calculated introduction strategies. Normally, the product is first introduced and perfected in the home market before being sold internationally. Canon has learned how to capture learning from the Japanese market quickly so that the time span between introduction in Japan and abroad is as short as a few months. Furthermore, the company will not simultaneously launch a new product through a new distribution channel – its strategy is to minimize risk by introducing a new product through known channels first. New channels will only be created, if necessary, after the product has proven to be successful.

The launch of the NP copier exemplifies this strategy. Canon initially sold these copiers in Japan by direct sales through its Business Machines Sales organization, which had been set up in 1968 to sell the calculator product line. This sales organization was merged with the camera sales organization in 1971 to form Canon Sales. By 1972, after three years of experience in producing the NP product line, the company entered into a new distribution channel, that of dealers, to supplement direct selling.

The NP copier line was not marketed in the U.S. until 1974, after production and distribution were running smoothly in Japan. The U.S. distribution system was similar to that used in Japan, with seven sales subsidiaries for direct selling and a network of independent dealers.

By the late 1970s, Canon had built up a strong dealer network in the U.S. which supported both sales and service of the copiers. The dealer channel was responsible for rapid growth in copier sales, and, by the early 1980s, Canon copiers were sold almost exclusively through this channel. Canon enthusiastically supported the dealers with attractive sales incentive programmes, management training and social outings. Dealers were certified to sell copiers only after completing a course in service training. The company felt that a close relationship with its dealers was a vital asset that allowed it to understand and react to customers' needs and problems in a timely manner. At the same time, Canon also maintained a direct selling mechanism through wholly owned sales subsidiaries in Japan, the U.S. and Europe in order to target large customers and government accounts.

The introduction of its low-end personal copier in 1983 was similarly planned to minimize risk. Initially, Canon's NP dealers in Japan were not interested in the product due to its low maintenance needs and inability to utilize large paper sizes. Thus, PCs were distributed through the firm's office supply stores who were already selling its personal calculators. After seeing the success of the PC, the NP dealers began to carry the copier.

In the U.S., the PC was initially sold only through existing dealers and direct sales channels due to limited availability of the product. Later, it was sold through competitors' dealers and office supply stores, and, eventually, the distribution channels were extended to include mass merchandisers. Canon already had considerable experience in mass merchandising from its camera business.

Advertising has always been an integral part of Canon's marketing strategy. President Kaku believes that Canon must have a corporate brand name which is outstanding to succeed in its diversification effort. 'Customers must prefer products because they bear the name Canon', he says. As described by the company's finance director, 'If a brand name is unknown, and there is no advertising, you have to sell it cheap. It's not our policy to buy share with a low price. We establish our brand with advertising at a reasonably high price'.

Therefore, when the NP-200 was introduced in 1980, 10 percent of the selling price was spent on advertising; for the launch of the personal copier, advertising expenditure was estimated to be 20 percent of the selling price. Canon has also sponsored various sporting events including World Cup football, the Williams motor racing team, and the ice dancers Torvill and Dean.

The company expects its current expansion into the home automation market to be greatly enhanced by the brand image it has built in office equipment (see Exhibit 1 for Canon's advertising expenditures through 1990.)

Manufacturing

Canon's goal in manufacturing is to produce the best quality at the lowest cost with the best delivery. To drive down costs, a key philosophy of the production system is to organize the manufacture of each product so that the minimum amount of time, energy and resources are required. Canon therefore places strong emphasis on tight inventory management through a stable production planning process, careful material planning, close supplier relationships, and adherence to the **kanban** system of inventory movement. Additionally, a formal waste elimination programme saved Canon 177 billion yen between 1976 and 1985. Overall, Canon accomplished a 30 percent increase in productivity per year from 1976 to 1982 and over 10 percent thereafter through automation and innovative process improvements.

The workforce is held in high regard at Canon. A philosophy of 'stop and fix it' empowers any worker to stop the production line if he or she is not able to perform a task properly or observes a quality problem. Workers are responsible for their own machine maintenance governed by rules which stress prevention. Targets for quality and production and other critical data are presented to the workers with on-line feedback. Most workers also participate in voluntary 'small group activity' for problem solving. The result of these systems is a workforce that feels individually responsible for the success of the products it manufactures.

Canon sponsors a highly regarded suggestion programme for its workers in order to directly involve those most familiar with the work processes in improving the business. The programme was originally initiated in 1952 with only limited success, but in the early 1980s, participation soared with more than seventy suggestions per employee per year. All suggestions are reviewed by a hierarchy of committees with monetary prizes awarded monthly and yearly depending on the importance of the suggestion. The quality and effectiveness of the process are demonstrated by a 90 percent implementation rate of the suggestions offered and corporate savings of $202 million in 1985 (against a total expenditure of $2 million in running the programme, over 90 percent of it in prize money).

Canon chooses to backward integrate only on parts with unique technologies. For other components, the company prefers to develop long-term relationships with its suppliers and it retains two sources for most parts. In 1990, over 80 percent of Canon's copiers were assembled from purchased parts, with only the drums and toner being manufactured in-house. The company also maintains its own in-house capability for doing pilot production of all parts so as to understand better the technology and the vendors' costs.

Another key to Canon's high quality and low cost is the attention given to parts commonality between models. Between some adjacent copier models, the commonality is as high as 60 percent.

Copier manufacture was primarily located in Toride, Japan, in the early years but then spread to Germany, California and Virginia in the U.S., France, Italy and Korea. In order to mitigate trade and investment friction, Canon is working to increase the local content of parts as it expands globally. In Europe it exceeds the EC standard by 5 percent. It is also adding R&D capability to some of its overseas operations. Mr Kaku emphasizes the importance of friendly trading partners:

> 'Frictions cannot be erased by merely transferring our manufacturing facilities overseas. The earnings after tax must be reinvested in the country; we must transfer our technology to the country. This is the only way our overseas expansion will be welcomed.'

Leveraging Expertise

Canon places critical importance on continued growth through diversification into new product fields. Mr Kaku observed,

> 'Whenever Canon introduced a new product, profits surged forward. Whenever innovation lagged, on the other hand, so did the earnings...In order to survive in the coming era of extreme competition, Canon must possess at least a dozen proprietary state-of-the-art technologies that will enable it to develop unique products.'

While an avid supporter of diversification, Mr Kaku was cautious.

> 'In order to ensure the enduring survival of Canon, we have to continue diversifying in order to adapt to environmental changes. However, we must be wise in choosing ways toward diversification. In other words, we must minimize the risks. Entering a new business which requires either a technology unrelated to Canon's current expertise or a different marketing channel than Canon currently uses incurs a 50 percent risk. If Canon attempts to enter a new business which requires both a new technology and a new marketing channel which are unfamiliar to Canon, the risk entailed in such ventures would be 100 percent. There are two prerequisites that have to be satisfied before launching such new ventures. First, our operation must be debt-free; second, we will have to secure the personnel capable of competently undertaking such ventures. I feel we shall have to wait until the twenty-first century before we are ready.'

Combining Capabilities

Through its R&D strategy, Canon has worked to build up specialized expertise in several areas and then link them to offer innovative, state-of-the-art products. Through the fifties and sixties, Canon focused on products related to its main business and expertise, cameras. This prompted the introduction of the 8 mm movie camera and the Canon range of mid-market cameras. There was minimal risk because the optics technology was the same and the marketing outlet, camera shops, remained the same.

Entrance into the calculator market pushed Canon into developing expertise in the field of micro-electronics, which it later innovatively combined with its optics capability to introduce one of its most successful products, the personal copier. From copiers, Canon utilized the replaceable cartridge system to introduce a successful desktop laser printer.

In the early seventies, Canon entered the business of marketing micro-chip semiconductor production equipment. In 1980, the company entered into the development and manufacture of unique proprietary ICs in order to strengthen further its expertise in electronics technology. This development effort was expanded in the late eighties to focus on opto-electronic ICs. According to Mr Kaku:

'We are now seriously committed to R&D in ICs because our vision for the future foresees the arrival of the opto-electronic era. When the time arrives for the opto-electronic IC to replace the current ultra-LSI, we intend to go into making large-scale computers. Presently we cannot compete with the IBMs and NECs using the ultra-LSIs. When the era of the opto-electronic IC arrives, the technology of designing the computer will be radically transformed; that will be our chance for making entry into the field of the large-scale computer.'

Creative Destruction

In 1975 Canon produced the first laser printer. Over the next fifteen years, laser printers evolved as a highly successful product line under the Canon brand name. The company also provides the 'engine' as an OEM to Hewlett Packard and other laser printer manufacturers which when added to its own branded sales supports a total of 84 percent of world-wide demand.

The biggest threat to the laser printer industry is substitution by the newly developed bubble jet printer. With a new technology which squirts out thin streams of ink under heat, a high-quality silent printer can be produced at half the price of the laser printer. The technology was invented accidentally in the Canon research labs. It keys on a print head which has up to 400 fine nozzles per inch, each with its own heater to warm the ink until it shoots out tiny ink droplets. This invention utilizes Canon's competencies in fine chemicals for producing the ink and its expertise in semiconductors, materials, and electronics for manufacturing the print heads. Canon is moving full steam forward to develop the bubble jet technology, even though it might destroy a business that the company dominates. The new product is even more closely tied to the company's core capabilities, and management believes that successful development of this business will help broaden further its expertise in semiconductors.

Challenge of the 1990s

Canon sees the office automation business as its key growth opportunity for the nineties. It already has a well-established brand name in home and office automation products through its offerings of copiers, facsimiles, electronic typewriters, laser printers, word processing equipment and personal computers. The next challenge for the company is to link these discrete products into a multifunctional system which will perform the tasks of a copier, facsimile, printer, and scanner and interface with a computer so that all the functions can be performed from one keyboard. In 1988, with this target, Canon introduced a personal computer which incorporated a PC, a fax, a telephone and a word processor. Canon has also introduced a colour laser copier which hooks up to a computer to serve as a colour printer. A series of additional integrated OA offerings are scheduled for introduction in 1992, and the company expects these products to serve as its growth engine in the first half of the 1990s.

Managing the Process

Undergirding this impressive history of continuously building new corporate capabilities and of exploiting those capabilities to create a fountain of innovative new products lies a rather unique management process. Canon has institutionalized corporate entrepreneurship through its highly autonomous and market focused business unit structure. A set of powerful functional committees provide the bridge between the entrepreneurial business units and the company's core capabilities in technology, manufacturing and marketing. Finally, an extraordinarily high level of corporate ambition drives this innovation engine, which is fuelled by the creativity of its people and by top management's continuous striving for ever higher levels of performance.

Driving Entrepreneurship: The Business Units

Mr Kaku had promoted the concept of the entrepreneurial business unit from his earliest days with Canon, but it was not until the company had suffered significant losses in 1975 that his voice was heard. His plan was implemented shortly before he became president of the company.

Mr Kaku believed that Canon's diversification strategy could only succeed if the business units were empowered to act on their own, free of central controls. Therefore, two independent operating units were formed in 1978, one for cameras and one for office equipment, to be managed as business units. Optical Instruments, the third business unit, had always been separate. Since that time, an additional three business units have been spun off. The original three business units were then given clear profitability targets, as well as highly ambitious growth objectives, and were allowed the freedom to devise their own ways to achieve these goals. One immediate result of this decentralization was the recognition that Canon's past practice of mixing production of different products in the same manufacturing facility would no longer work. Manufacturing was reorganized so that no plant produced more than one type of product.

Mr Kaku describes the head of each unit as a surrogate of the CEO empowered to make quick decisions. This allows him, as president of Canon, to devote himself exclusively to his main task of creating and implementing the long-term corporate strategy. In explaining the benefits of the system, he said:

> 'Previously, the president was in exclusive charge of all decision making; his subordinates had to form a queue to await their turn in presenting their problems to him. This kind of system hinders the development of the young managers' potential for decision-making.

> 'Furthermore, take the case of the desktop calculator. Whereas, I can devote only about two hours each day on problems concerning the calculator, the CEO of Casio Calculator could devote 24 hours to the calculator…In the fiercely competitive market, we lost out because our then CEO was slow in coping with the problem.'

In contrast to the Western philosophy of stand-alone SBUs encompassing all functions including engineering, sales, marketing and production, Canon has chosen to separate its product divisions from its sales and marketing arm. This separation allows for a clear focus on the challenges that Canon faces in selling products on a global scale. Through a five-year plan initiated in 1977, Seiichi Takigawa, the president of Canon Sales (the sales organization for Japan), stressed the need to 'make sales a science'. After proving the profitability of this approach, Canon Sales took on the responsibility for world-wide marketing, sales and service. In 1981, Canon Sales was listed on the Tokyo stock exchange, reaffirming its independence.

Canon also allows its overseas subsidiaries free rein, though it holds the majority of stock. The philosophy is to create the maximum operational leeway for each subsidiary to act on its own initiative. Kaku describes the philosophy through an analogy:

'Canon's system of managing subsidiaries is similar to the policy of the Tokugawa government, which established secure hegemony over the warlords, who were granted autonomy in their territory. I am "shogun" [head of the Tokugawa regime] and the subsidiaries' presidents are the "daimyo" [warlords]. The difference between Canon and the Tokugawa government is that the latter was a zero-sum society; its policy was repressive. On the other hand, Canon's objective is to enhance the prosperity of all subsidiaries through efficient mutual collaboration.'

Canon has also promoted the growth of intrapreneurial ventures within the company by spinning these ventures off as wholly owned subsidiaries. The first venture to be spun off was Canon Components, which produces electronic components and devices, in 1984.

Building Integration: Functional Committees

As Canon continues to grow and diversify, it becomes increasingly difficult but also ever more important to link its product divisions in order to realize the benefits possible only in a large multiproduct corporation. The basis of Canon's integration is a three dimensional management approach in which the first dimension is the independent business unit, the second a network of functional committees, and the third the regional companies focused on geographic markets (see Exhibit 5).

Kaku feels there are four basic requirements for the success of a diversified business: 1) a level of competence in research and development; 2) quality, low-cost manufacturing technology; 3) superior marketing strength; and 4) an outstanding corporate identity, culture and brand name. Therefore, he has established separate functional committees to address the first three requirements of development, production and marketing, while the fourth task has been kept as a direct responsibility of corporate management. The three functional committees, in turn, have been made responsible for company-wide administration of three key management systems:

— The Canon Development System (CDS) whose objectives are to foster the research and creation of new products and technologies by studying and continuously improving the development process;

— The Canon Production System (CPS) whose goal is to achieve optimum quality by minimizing waste in all areas of manufacturing;

— The Canon Marketing System (CMS), later renamed the Canon International Marketing System (CIMS), which is tasked to expand and strengthen Canon's independent domestic and overseas sales networks by building a high quality service and sales force.

Separate offices have been created at headquarters for each of these critical committees, and over time their role has broadened to encompass general improvement of the processes used to support their functions. The chairpersons of the committees are members of Canon's management committee, which gives them the ability to ensure consistency and communicate process improvements throughout the multiproduct, multinational corporation.

Using information technology to integrate its world-wide operations, Canon began development of the Global Information System for Harmonious Growth Administration (GINGA) in 1987. The system will consist of a high-speed digital communications network to interconnect all parts of Canon into a global database and allow for the timely flow of information among managers in any location of the company's world-wide organization. GINGA is planned to include separate but integrated systems for computer integrated manufacturing, global marketing and distribution, R&D and product design, financial reporting, and personnel database tracking, as well as some advances in intelligent office automation. As described by Mr Kaku, the main objective of this system is to supplement Canon's efficient vertical communications structure with a lateral one that will facilitate direct information exchange among managers across businesses, countries, and functions on all operational matters concerning the company. The system is being developed at a total cost of 20 billion yen and it is targeted for completion in 1992.

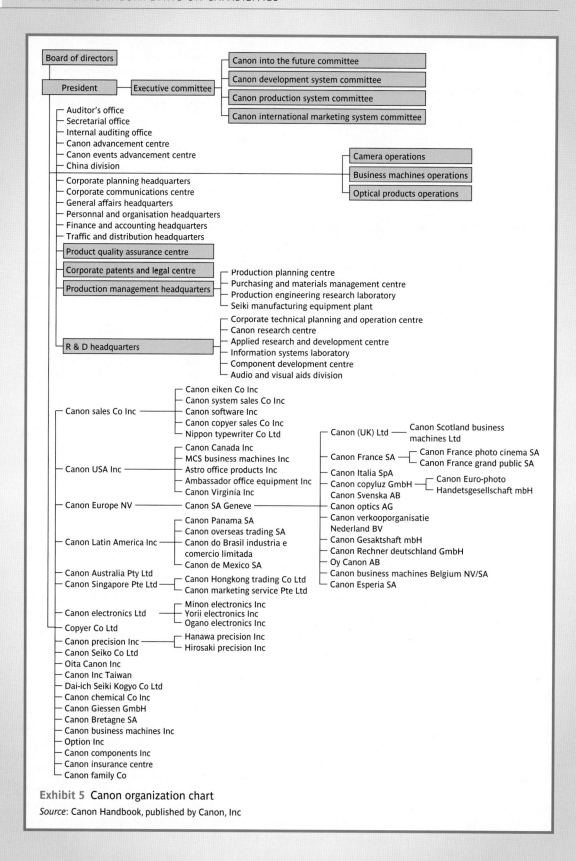

Exhibit 5 Canon organization chart

Source: Canon Handbook, published by Canon, Inc

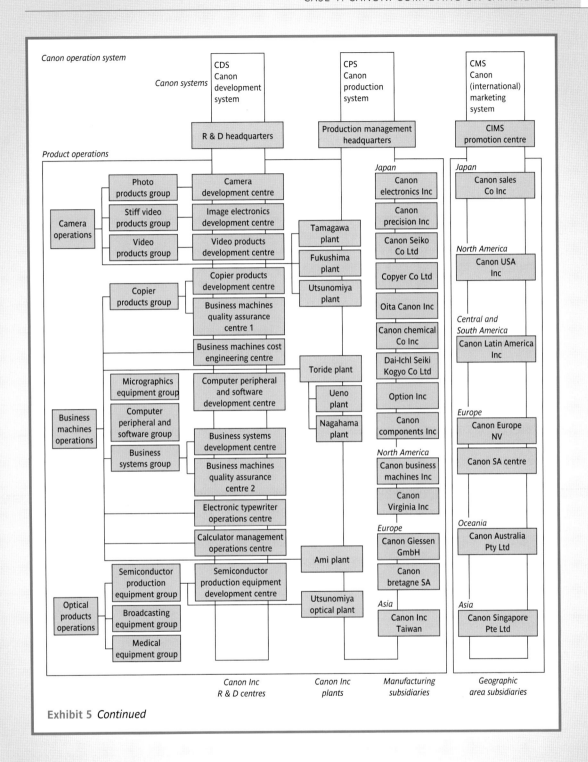

Exhibit 5 *Continued*

Managing Renewal: Challenges and Change

Mr Kaku was very forthright about some of the management weaknesses of Canon prior to 1975:

> 'In short, our skill in management – the software of our enterprise – was weak. Management policy must be guided by a soundly created software on management; if the software is weak, the firm will lack clearly defined ideals and objectives. In the beginning we had a clearly defined objective, to overtake West Germany's Leica. Since then our management policy has been changing like the colours of a chameleon.

> 'In the past our management would order employees to reach the peak of Mount Fuji, and then before the vanguard of climbers had barely started climbing, they would be ordered to climb Mount Tsukuba far to the north. Then the order would again be suddenly changed to climb Mount Yatsugatake to the west. After experiencing these kind of shifts in policy, the smarter employees would opt to take things easy by taking naps on the bank of the river Tamagawa. As a result, vitality would be sapped from our work force – a situation that should have been forestalled by all means.'

Mr Kaku's first action as President of Canon was to start the firm on the path to global leadership through establishing the first 'premier company plan', a six-year plan designed to make Canon a top company in Japan. The plan outlined a policy for diversification and required consistently recurring profits exceeding 10 percent on sales.

> 'The aim of any Japanese corporation is ensuring its perpetual survival. Unlike the venture businesses and U.S. corporations, our greatest objective is not to maximize short-term profits. Our vital objective is to continually earn profits on a stable basis for ensuring survival. To implement this goal, we must diversify.'

By the time the original six-year plan expired in 1981, Canon had become a highly respected company in Japan. The plan was then renewed through 1986 and then again into the 1990s. The challenge was to become a premier global company, defined as having recurring profits exceeding 15 percent of sales. R&D spending was gradually increased from 6 percent of sales in 1980 to 9 percent in 1985 as a prerequisite for global excellence. As described by Mr Kaku:

> 'By implementing our first plan for becoming a premier company we have succeeded in attaining the allegorical top of Mount Fuji. Our next objective is the Everest. With a firm determination, we could have climbed Fuji wearing sandals. However, sandals are highly inappropriate for climbing Everest; it may cause our death.'

According to Mr Kaku, such ambitions also require a company to build up the ability to absorb temporary reversals without panic; ambition without stability makes the corporate ship lose its way. To illustrate, he described the situation at Canon during the time the yen depreciated from 236 to the dollar in 1985 to 168 to the dollar in 1986. With 74 percent of Canon's Japanese production going to export markets, this sudden change caused earnings to fall to 4.6 billion yen, one tenth of the previous year. Some board members at Canon sought drastic action such as a major restructuring of the company and cutting the R&D budget. Mr Kaku had successfully argued the opposite:

> 'What I did was calm them down. If a person gets lost in climbing a high mountain, he must avoid excessive use of his energy; otherwise his predicament will deepen…Our ongoing strategy for becoming the premier company remains the best, even under this crisis; there is no need to panic. Even if we have to forego dividends for two or three times, we shall surely overcome this crisis.'

While celebrating the company's past successes, Mr Kaku also constantly reminds his colleagues that no organizational form or process holds the eternal truth. The need to change with a changing world is inevitable. For example, despite being the creator of the product division-marketing company split, he was considering rejoining these two in the nineties:

> 'In the future, our major efforts in marketing must be concentrated on clearly defining and differentiating the markets of the respective products and creating appropriate marketing systems for them. In order to make this feasible, we may have to recombine our sales subsidiaries with the parent company and restructure their functions to fully meet the market's needs.'

While constantly aware of the need to change, Kaku also recognizes the difficulties managers face in changing the very approaches and strategies that have led to past successes:

> 'In order for a company to survive forever, the company must have the courage to be able to deny at one point what it has been doing in the past; the biological concept of "ecdysis" – casting off the skin to emerge to new form. But it is difficult for human beings to deny and destruct what they have been building up. But if they cannot do that, it is certain that the firm cannot survive forever. Speaking about myself, it is difficult to deny what I've done in the past. So when such time comes that I have to deny the past, I inevitably would have to step down.'

Please note that INSEAD does not distribute its case studies directly.
INSEAD cases are distributed world-wide by three centres, the details of which are listed below:

The European Case Clearing House (ECCH)   **Centrale des Cas et de Médias Pédagogiques**

The European Case Clearing House   ECCH at Babson Ltd.   C.C.M.P.
Cranfield University   Babson College   49 rue de Tocqueville
Wharley End   Babson Park   75017 Paris
Bedford MK43 0JR   Wellesley MA 02457   France
ENGLAND   USA

CASE 2: Creating the Future at Southwest Airlines

MARY B. TEAGARDEN

Our essential difference is minds, hearts, spirits, and souls.
Herb Kelleher

Gary Kelly had reason for pause as he assumed the role of president and chairman of Southwest Airlines in the summer of 2008. To begin with, he was filling the shoes of legendary and larger-than-life Southwest co-founder Herb Kelleher. The company was celebrating an astounding 35 consecutive years of profitability. Kelly had filled many other roles at Southwest, including controller, CFO, vice president of finance, and CEO. In fact, Kelly had just been named one of the best CEOs in America by *Institutional Investor* magazine. Southwest was known for innovation in both its business model and strategic human resource practices. Under Kelleher's leadership, Southwest introduced innovative responses in the face of difficult industry conditions, not just once but several times. These innovations resulted in industry consolidation, ongoing profitability for the company, and Southwest was even credited with creating the discount airline industry segment. Kelly faced many challenges at a time when the airline industry was experiencing the worst environment in its history. Would Southwest's cost advantage erode in the face of spiraling fuel costs, costly labor concessions, and the ever-increasing efficiency of rivals? As he contemplated the next moves in this increasingly turbulent environment, Kelly grappled with the most fundamental issues. What would he have to do to keep Southwest's innovativeness alive? More importantly, was it time to reinvent the 40-year old Southwest Airlines?

The Birth of Southwest

The story of Southwest Airlines' founding is legendary – the company got started in a bar. Herb Kelleher, a lawyer in San Antonio, and his client, Rollin King, a Texas banker, founded the company over drinks at a local bar in 1966. They had a simple vision: 'If you get your passengers to their destinations when they want to get there, on time, at the lowest possible fares, and make darn sure they have a good time doing it, people will fly your airline.'[1] Kelleher invested $10,000 of his own money to launch the business – an investment now worth more than $200 million. Their idea was revolutionary: a cut-rate airline that would fly between San Antonio, Dallas, and Houston – the three big cities in Texas. Kelleher admits that he was not sure that the idea would work. Not only did the idea work, this bold move was the start of the discount airline industry, and is considered the principal driving force for transformation of the airline industry.

The major airlines, Southwest's competitors, were determined to make sure Southwest failed by launching fights to block the company's every move. For the first decade of their existence, Kelleher's lawyer skills came in handy. He spent most of his time in court defending against lawsuits from incumbents. Kelleher reflected:

> I love battles. I think it's part of the Irish in me. It's like what Patton said, 'War is hell, and I love it so.' That's how I feel. I've never gotten tired of fighting. For the past 35 years, my job has been helping Southwest Airlines get through one battle after another. We've been like the French Foreign Legion – they had a firefight about every two days. That's like us. Even before our first airplane got off the ground, we were fighting…There were already several big carriers in Texas. But then I really looked into it and realized it was feasible. Of course, I also realized it was going to mean Armageddon. I knew the incumbents – Braniff, Texas International, Continental – were going to fight us tooth and nail.[2]

And fight tooth and nail they did. Three-and-a-half years of continual litigation later – including a rejection from the Texas Supreme Court to hear competitors' petitions – Southwest found itself two days away from their first scheduled fight when an Austin, Texas, trial judge enjoined them from starting service. Kelleher recalled:

> I was very angry. The constant proceedings had gradually come to enrage me. There was no merit to our competitors' legal assertions. They were simply trying to use their superior economic power to squeeze us dry so we would collapse before we ever got into business. I was bound and determined to show that Southwest Airlines was going to survive and was going into operation. If it didn't, then something was very wrong about our whole system, about our whole society…So I headed back to the Texas Supreme Court to get the injunction lifted. I told Lamar Muse – who was CEO of Southwest Airlines at the time – to go ahead with our scheduled flight no matter what. Lamar said, 'Gee, Herb, what do I do? Suppose the sheriff shows up and tries to prevent the flight? So I said, 'Leave tire tracks on his shirt. We're going, come hell or high water.'…And we did. We went into service the next day as scheduled. That's how the first Southwest airplane got off the ground.[3]

The colorful Kelleher, well known for pranks, stunts, and outrageous behavior, became chairman of Southwest in 1978. Ron Kirk, mayor of Dallas, described Kelleher's genius and over-the-top behavior:

> One more cigarette, and he'd go up in flames…When I first met Herb, to be honest with you, I thought the guy would just spontaneously combust. I just didn't see how anybody – certainly not anyone that much older than me – could play as hard, work as hard, drink as hard, smoke as much as Herb Kelleher. I just knew one more drop of Wild Turkey or one more cigarette, and he'd go up in flames. But the man is inexhaustible. If you want to understand Herb and Southwest, you have to spend Halloween there. They shut down the whole corporate office for a day. It is the most insightful, outrageous, fun-filled eight hours anybody could spend…When your standard-bearer is Herb Kelleher, you can't be outrageous enough. Every department gets this huge budget – they plan this for months – and every department is transformed into some theme. That's when I really understood the genius behind what Herb does. I found out how much he loves the company, and how much everyone in that company loves him.[4]

Kelleher's learning curve was steep when he assumed the role of CEO in 1982. He had thoroughly enjoyed the outside role he had played as the Southwest legal representative. More importantly, he had no experience running a company. Nevertheless, he took over the reins at a most challenging time. He commented:

> In my first year as CEO…I had to learn how to run a company – in a big hurry. Wow, that was some year: Twelve thousand air-traffic controllers were on strike – they had all walked out on the same day. It was a huge crisis. Whether or not you got the right to fly your new airplanes was determined by a lottery in Washington…We had new airplanes coming in, and airplanes don't do very

well if you just put them against a fence and plant geraniums in them. I came back from Washington and thought, 'Man, this is an emergency.'[5]

When Herb took over, the airline had 27 planes, $270 million in revenues, and 2,100 employees. They flew to 14 cities, and, as a small start-up, an underdog, they had to fight hard. Kelleher commented, 'We didn't make much for a while…It was like being the tallest guy in a tribe of dwarfs.'[6] In response to the lottery, in characteristic Southwest fashion, Herb used a bold approach to gain advantage. They had an inoperative subsidiary called Midway Southwest Airlines. Even though it was not operating, it was considered a new airline, and new airlines got preference in the lottery on drawing for flight slots. Southwest used Midway to get flight slots, which they then transferred to Southwest. Kelleher commented:

It wasn't against the rules, but people started getting very angry about it. The FAA summoned me to Washington, and they said what we were doing was not what was intended. I said, 'Well, I don't care what was intended. The rules permit you to do it.' They said, 'Well, you have to be an operating carrier to participate in the slot lottery.' So I sold Midwest Southwest to a guy who operated one Lear jet, and that made it into an operating carrier. He would get the slots and then transfer them to us. After we started doing that, I got summoned to Washington by Lynn Helms, the administrator of the FAA. When I walked into his office, he said, 'Close the door.' So I closed the door. He said, 'Herb, I think this is the funniest thing I've ever seen. You've completely taken advantage of the rules!' And he started laughing. He thought the whole thing was funny as hell. But he told me that the general counsel's office was really peeved, and he was supposed to be telling me off. 'When you walk out of here, I want you to look like I've really given you a good hiding, that I have just cleaned your clock,' he told me. So I left this office, walking along with my shoulders slumped like I'd just gotten caned.[7]

Getting Southwest up and running was just the tip of the iceberg. The bold challenge to the FAA was followed by a brutal fare war with Braniff Airlines. At one point, Braniff cut the price of one-way fares from Houston to Dallas from $26 to $13. Kelleher credits Lamar Muse with a brilliant way to match this price cut. 'We'd offer customers a choice: They could pay $13 – or they could pay $26 and we'd throw in a free bottle of whiskey. That made us the largest liquor distributor in Texas for a couple of months.'[8] The head-to-head battle escalated, and Keller recalled:

The fare war turned into a real war. I mean a physical war. We were the barroom brawlers of the American airline industry. One time, some Braniff people went up to the roof of the terminal in Houston and hung a sign over the edge to advertise their service to Dallas. Our station manager went up there and tried to cut it down with a knife. He ended up getting into a tussle with their people right there on the top of the terminal. Another time, Braniff didn't have enough room to move one of its planes away from the terminal. They asked us to move our airplane. We said no. So they tried to power it out using all their engines and blew two of them out. That was a great day. Finally, the FAA told us, 'Guys, unless you two quit this, we're going to throw you both out of here.' Still, those early battles were the basis of Southwest's warrior spirit. They bred a consciousness that life can be very short – even in business – very precarious. And that's how we learned to endure and survive.[9]

The ability to think out of the box and the willingness to consistently push the limits paid off for the Southwest warriors. With 35 consecutive years of profitability, the most productive workforce in the industry, and the best customer service ratings in the business, Southwest dominated the low-fare, high-frequency, short-haul, point-to-point market. From their humble beginnings, they grew to more than 34,000 employees and flew to 64 cities throughout the U.S. Southwest's market capitalization, $11 billion, was more than twice that of American Airlines, United Airlines, and Continental combined. When Southwest came into a market, they lowered fares by 30 to 50 percent. Braniff, the early nemesis with whom they had brutal fare wars, is no longer in business. Southwest's extraordinary success made it difficult to maintain the original 'underdog' value among employees, but the 'warrior spirit' remained alive and well.

Southwest Operations and the Copycats

Southwest gave birth to the discount airline industry. They pioneered the point-to-point operating model, no-frills service, generally fewer amenities, fewer restrictions on low fares, and more leniency with itinerary changes. No frills meant that expensive meals were not served, there were no seat reservations, and baggage was not transferred to other airlines, which all made fast aircraft turnarounds a reality. Faster turnarounds resulted in higher airport gate utilization, a major cost saving. It was claimed that the discount airlines successfully reduced customer expectations by offering fewer amenities, which resulted in fewer disappointed customers.[10]

The airline industry relied on two significantly different operating models – the 'point-to-point' model, pioneered by Southwest, and the 'hub-and-spoke' model. The hub-and-spoke operating model, used by most airlines in the airline industry, was designed to maximize traffic through the hubs in which many airlines were 'headquartered.' The cost of establishing a major hub in a city like Chicago or Atlanta required an investment of as much as $150 million for gate acquisition and terminal construction.[11] The spokes fed customers into the hub where they transferred and flew to their final destination. This model's flight schedules were constructed to attract high volumes of low-yield connecting flights, resulting in airport congestion, slow aircraft turnaround, and thus an inefficient use of equipment (planes), facilities (gates), and people (air and ground staff).

In contrast, the point-to-point discount airline operating model was designed to maximize traffic on a route. The airports used in point-to-point flights were often smaller and less congested than those used by the majors. This lean operating approach did not require the variety of aircraft used by the majors. Southwest flew more than 500 Boeing 737 aircraft between 64 cities (the top ten are shown below). In the early 1990s, discount airline routes overlapped the majors by only 15 percent. In 2003, Southwest's success and the proliferation of Southwest imitators resulted in a 55 percent overlap of majors' routes by discount carriers.

Southwest Airlines Top Ten Airports				
City	Daily Departures	Number of Gates	Nonstop Cities Served	Service Established
Las Vegas	243	21	55	1982
Chicago-Midway	228	29	47	1985
Phoenix	205	24	43	1982
Baltimore/Washington	168	26	38	1993
Houston-Hobby	148	17	29	1971
Dallas-Love Field	144	14	16	1971
Oakland	134	13	21	1989
Los Angeles (LAX)	128	11	19	1982
Orlando	114	14	37	1996
San Diego	110	10	19	1982

Source: Southwest Airlines Fact Sheet; http://www.southwest.com/about_swa/press/factsheet.html#About%20the%20 Company

While competitors relied on large hubs, Southwest flew point-to-point. Unlike competitors who flew a variety of aircraft, Southwest used one type of plane, the Boeing 737, for all of its routes, which meant less expensive maintenance; smaller parts inventories; fewer, focused crew training facilities; and a more flexible workforce. This, in turn, resulted in overall lower operating costs. They were the largest single operator of the Boeing 737 in the world. They did not assign seats or transfer baggage to other airlines. They were the pioneer of online ticket purchase, thus cutting out the middleman. Instead of 'airplane food,' Southwest served passengers peanuts and beverages by flight attendants wearing polo shirts and shorts, not uniforms like the competition. Kelleher consistently maintained the discipline to keep Southwest focused on what it did well. This low-cost, low-fare, no-frills operating strategy reduced maintenance costs, training and inventory costs, and operating costs. It also increased safety and flexibility. Southwest had the best safety record in the industry and more flexibility for crew and flight schedules.

In response to the discount airlines, some majors launched their own low-cost imitators – the airline within an airline approach. TED by United, which replaced United Shuttle, was an example. Continental's CALite and Delta's Song, other examples, are no longer operating. Southwest's business model was repeated many times around the world. Europe's easyJet and Ryanair were two of the best-known airlines to follow Southwest's business strategy on that continent. Other international imitators included Canada's WestJet, Malaysia's AirAsia, Qantas' Jetstar, and Thailand's Nok Air.

Many companies tried to replicate Southwest's operating strategy, one that appeared relatively transparent and easy to understand. Unfortunately, most misunderstood the extraordinary power of Southwest's unique culture and the extent to which the culture supported the operating strategy. The Southwest culture emphasized team effort, flexibility, family orientation, fun, and outrageous customer service. Its 'people first' philosophy contributed to its distinction as one of *Fortune* magazine's best places to work in America. Herb Kelleher always believed that people – including himself – should not 'check their personalities at the door' when they came to work. He expected employees to think and act like owners of the business.

Crisis or Key Inflection Point?

Do you know how to make millions in the airline industry? Start with billions.

Richard Branson, Virgin Air.

The domestic U.S. majors – American, Continental, United, Delta and Northwest (soon to merge) – flew a variety of long, short, low-traffic, and high volume routes. This approach required a variety of aircraft types that resulted in more expensive maintenance, large and expensive spare parts inventories, redundant crew training facilities, and highly specialized, and thus inflexible, employees. It was common practice among the majors to impose costly fare increases on customers for last-minute itinerary and upgrade changes.[12] Cost increases in fuel, equipment, or labor were passed on to customers and, historically, there was little price competition among the majors. By the end of 2000, the weaknesses of this model were becoming apparent. The economy was slipping as a result of the dotcom bust, and a general economic downturn had begun. Travelers were seeking lower fares, fuel costs were increasing, and there were fewer travelers. To make matters worse, the high labor cost concessions that had been granted to keep peace with the unions had trapped the majors in money-losing competitive positions.

The terrorist attacks of September 11, 2001, further exacerbated the industry's woes since it further decreased passenger traffic. The excessive expenses of the hub-and-spoke model, plus the other challenges, were taking a toll on the largest airlines. American, Delta, and United accounted for 60 percent of the industry's revenue, but their collective net loss of $2.14 billion during the third quarter of 2002 represented 95 percent of the industry's losses. United lost $47 for every passenger that boarded one of its planes, and burned through an average of $7 million each day, while rival American burned through $4 million to $5 million per day. American planned to park 42 of its 800 aircraft in the desert in 2003, and Delta planned to idle many planes and lay off 8,000 employees.[13] The situation was desperate for the major competitors.

Discount airlines – Air Tran, ATA, Frontier, JetBlue, and Spirit – stood in sharp contrast to the majors, and all were trying to emulate Southwest's low-cost model. The discount airlines offered lower fares, resulting in increased demand for air travel. Most of the growth in the airline industry was from leisure travelers for whom point-to-point flights were an alternative to other means of transportation, such as buses and personal automobiles. In the 20-year period 1975–1995, domestic air travel increased from 200 million travelers to 500 million travelers. The economic downturn that threatened the majors gave a boost to the discount airlines, which now flew 32 percent of domestic passengers.[14] In 2005, Southwest once again was identified as one of the top 10 most admired companies in the prestigious ranking by *Fortune*.[15]

Herb's Style and Strategy

Herb Kelleher was characterized as the 'airline industry's jokemeister, the High Priest of Ha-Ha, a man who had appeared in public dressed as Elvis and the Easter Bunny, who had carved an antic public persona out of his affection for cigarettes, bourbon, and bawdy stories.'[16] *Fortune* described his antics as a guest speaker while he was chairman of Southwest:

> *Members of a professional aviation society called the Wings Club are gathered for a speech by Herbert D. Kelleher, the 63-year-old chairman of Southwest Airlines, and many are already chuckling to themselves…A fair percentage of the crowd has been up late swapping lies with Herb a time or two, and now they are waiting for him to say something…outrageous…Herb does not disappoint. A lean man just a shade over six feet, with a weathered face and thinning white hair, he glides to the microphone, Merit Ultra Lite in hand, and begins speaking in a honeyed baritone. 'You know,' he says, 'a fellow introduced me on the podium the other day, and he said that if I were proud of anything I had accomplished that I should probably go ahead and talk about that. Well, I'm here to tell you that I am proud of a couple of things.' He pauses and rocks back and forth – teasing the faces in the crowd, letting them know the good stuff is coming. 'First,' he says, 'I am very good at projectile vomiting.' Another pause as a great hoot of laughter erupts throughout the ballroom. 'Second, I've never had a really serious venereal disease.' The laughter is sustained this time…Kelleher owns this crowd, as he would any gathering even faintly familiar with the U.S. airline industry.[17]*

Behind Kelleher's antics, called lunacy by some, lurked a formidable leader. His credo was to take the business, not himself, seriously. Herb was relentless in controlling the financials. One of Herb Kelleher's most significant contributions to Southwest was his ability to manage trade-offs and maintain differences. These trade-offs resulted in a powerful and enduring business model.

Like the operating model, Herb Kelleher's management philosophy was fairly simple, resting on three pillars – preparation, action, and an unswerving focus on people, customers, and employees. His first pillar was **preparation for every scenario**. In a 2001 interview with *Fortune*, Kelleher reflected:

> *The way I've approached things is to be prepared for all possible scenarios of what might happen. I usually come up with four or five different scenarios. I do this all the time. I do it in the shower. I do it when I'm out drinking. Right now I'm thinking through the scenarios of the possibility of United Airlines and American dividing US Airways, the scenarios of American's acquiring TWA. You have to think, 'Okay, American's bought TWA: How's it going to integrate it? What is its emphasis going to be?' You have to do that sort of thing so you're prepared to go one way or the other way depending on what American does. You have to think that way all of the time.[18]*

A second pillar of his philosophy was a **bias for quick action**. He again reflected:

> *The way you have to be in the airline business is 'ready, fire, aim,' because if you take too much time aiming, you never get to fire. You have to strike quickly with blinding speed. When US*

Airways announced it was pulling out of six cities in California, I got on the phone and I said, 'Get out there, get extra airplanes, get extra gates.' I called our properties department to get busy getting those gates lickety-split because they'd only be available for a nanosecond. I called finance and said we'd probably need five or six extra airplanes just as soon as we could get them – scour the market and get some as soon as you can. We've got to move. If you don't do it, someone else is going to.[19]

Kelleher was identified as the kind of leader who would 'stay out with a mechanic in some bar until four o'clock in the morning to find out what is going on. Then he will fix whatever is wrong.'[20] Employees were encouraged to generate ideas and then to try them. The third pillar of the Kelleher philosophy of management was to **listen to your customers and employees**. Kelleher continued reflecting:

Reading letters from customers is extremely valuable. Customers have given us some tremendous ideas. Employees have given us tremendous ideas as well. So the rule at Southwest is, if somebody has an idea, you read it quickly, and you respond instantaneously. You may say no, but you give a lot of reasons why you're saying no, or you may say we're going to experiment with it in the field, see if it works. But I think showing respect for people's ideas is very, very important because as soon as you stop doing that, you stop getting ideas. We tell people that if you need a suggestion box, then you're not doing what you should be doing. You shouldn't have to interpose the box between you and your people with ideas. You ought to be talking to them on a regular basis. You ought to be with your people enough that they are comfortable to just pop on in and give you their ideas.[21]

Herb stayed relentlessly focused on the future. When asked about his typical day, Kelleher responded, 'I never look back, really I don't…When people ask me what I did yesterday, I can't answer them. I'm not faking it. I try to remain directed forward.' 'Besides,' he chuckled, 'it's convenient to forget about all the mistakes I've made.'[22] Herb surrounded himself with people he trusted and to whom he happily delegated:

Why get bogged down in the details of scheduling when there are mechanics to chat up, government panels to sit on, new markets to shake up, and competitors to poke fun at. Herb has executive vice president Colleen Barrett construct his day. Barrett started out as his legal secretary before Southwest took off, so she knows exactly what meetings, trips, and interviews will make Kelleher tick. Make no mistake: her control is pretty complete. When Barrett slaps a jacket on his back, Kelleher says, he feels like asking, 'Am I cold, or am I going somewhere?' And any Southwest employee knows she takes this job quite seriously. A few years back, Barrett realized that Kelleher was blowing appointments by sneaking off to hobnob with employees. Solution: She had the door between his office and the hallway sealed.…Kelleher admits that left to his own devices, he would probably ignore most matters that just don't seem important or fun. So he arrives in the office each day to find a list prepared by Barrett that contains two categories: things that must absolutely get done and things that can be postponed until no later than the following morning. 'It's a magical thing,' says Kelleher, who disregards the list now and then 'just to be contrary.'[23]

Southwest's Culture and Commitment

Herb Kelleher built commitment the 'old-fashioned' way by building loyalty between employees and the company. Veteran airline analyst Michael Derchin commented, 'To an extreme degree, Herb has been able to make working in this business an adventure for his people.'[24] The bond between Southwest and its employees was cult-like. In response to the cult comparison, Kelleher commented, 'I feel that you have to be with your employees through all their difficulties – that you have to be interested in them personally. They may be disappointed in their country. Even their family might not be working out for them way they would wish it would. But I want them to know that Southwest will always be there for them.'[25] Kelleher was the glue that bound this culture, the 'Maximum Leader' of Southwest:

> Kelleher reigns over his band of 12,000 loyalists like some sort of manic father figure. He is often at the center of the festivities that break out frequently on the headquarters party deck overlooking the flat Texas countryside. Whatever the occasion – a holiday, someone's retirement, Friday – Kelleher can be found in the middle of a worshipful crowd, drink and cigarette ever at hand. The Southwest chief works his way through the five packs of smokes a day, and only after he lost his voice a while back did doctors persuade him to move to the lower-tar variety.[26]

Kelleher said that from the beginning he tried to instill 'an insouciance, an effervescence' in employees. One result was that Southwest employees went out of their way to amuse, surprise, or somehow entertain customers. For example:

> During delays at the gate, ticket agents will award prizes to the passenger with the largest hole in his or her sock. Flight attendants have been known to hide in the overhead luggage bins and then pop out when passengers start filing onboard. Veteran Southwest fliers looking for a few yuks have learned to listen up to announcements over the intercom. A recent effort: 'Good morning, ladies and gentlemen. Those of you who wish to smoke will please file out to our lounge on the wing, where you can enjoy our feature film, Gone with the Wind.' On that same flight, an attendant later made this announcement: 'Please pass all plastic cups to the center aisle so we can wash them out and use them for the next group of passengers.'[27]

Many companies tried to replicate Southwest's operating strategy without understanding the power of its unique culture. Kelleher commented, 'Our *esprit de corps* is the core of our success. That's the most difficult for competitors to imitate. They can [buy] all the physical things. The thing you can't buy is dedication, devotion, loyalty – feeling you are participating in a cause or a crusade.'[28] At Southwest, culture was by design: It was not an accident, as can be seen below from an internal communication with Southwest employees:

To Our Employees

> We are committed to provide our Employees a stable work environment with equal opportunity for learning and personal growth. Creativity and innovation are encouraged for improving the effectiveness of Southwest Airlines. Above all, Employees will be provided the same concern, respect, and caring attitude within the organization that they are expected to share externally with every Southwest Customer.[29]

Warrior Spirit	Servant's Heart	Fun-LUVing Attitude
■ Work Hard	■ Follow the Golden Rule	■ Have FUN
■ Desire to be the Best	■ Adhere to the Basic Principles	■ Don't Take Yourself Too Seriously
■ Be Courageous	■ Treat Others with Respect	■ Maintain Perspective (Balance)
■ Display a Sense of Urgency	■ Put Others First	■ Celebrate Successes
■ Persevere	■ Be Egalitarian	■ Enjoy Your Work
■ Innovate	■ Demonstrate Proactive Customer Service	■ Be a Passionate Team Player
■ Embrace the SWA Family		

Source: Southwest.com/about_swa/southwest_cares/our_people.html

Recruiting and Selection

Southwest hired for attitude and trained for skill. Kelleher said, 'We draft great attitudes. If you don't have a good attitude, we don't want you, no matter how skilled you are. We can change skill levels through training. We can't change attitude.'[30] In 2007, they received 329,200 resumes and from these filled 4,200 jobs.[31] The primary selection criteria were attitude and cultural fit. The interview process, like the company, could be unconventional, as a finance executive discovered as noted in the example cited below:

> Mary Ann Adams, 44, recently landed a job as a finance executive at Southwest Airlines...She had to prove she knew her weighted average cost of capital, but then the interviewing got really tough: She had to prove she had a sense of humor. Adams met the company's levity test by recounting a practical joke in which she turned an unflattering picture of her boss into a computer screensaver for her department. 'I get results, but I like to have fun, too,' she says...A sense of humor is a very serious requirement. If a candidate seems particularly taciturn, the interviewer may go for the jugular, demanding, 'Tell me a joke.' Even candidates in such mirth-deficient disciplines as finance and infotech are required to mesh with the company's famously jocular culture.[32]

Despite the very high rejection rate, Southwest remained sensitive to the possibility that it was rejecting potential customers. 'The recruiting process is designed not to make applicants feel inferior or rejected.'[33] Ann Rhodes, former head of Southwest's People Department, claimed '...that some people have told her they had a better experience being rejected by Southwest than they did being hired by other companies.'[34] The emphasis on selecting for attitude and fit and the importance of culture naturally led to a very important role for training at Southwest.

Training and Development

Southwest's University for People provided professional and personal training for its entire workforce. The University for People was an umbrella department of Southwest's highly decentralized training department. All new employees participated in the 'New Hire Celebration' – a course designed to get new employees enthused and excited.

> New flight attendants go through four weeks of classes, typically with less than five percent attrition. Much of this training is oriented towards customer service – 'the care and feeding of customers.' Customer expectations about service are high, and these are communicated to both new and experienced employees. All new hires are exposed to the history, principles, values, mission, and culture of the company. They are also told how the company views leadership and management. In all training, there is an emphasis on teamwork and team building, all in good humor.'[35]

Coordination and Control

Hiring, training, and development practices were designed to enhance coordination and control at Southwest. Their coordination and control mechanisms were embedded in their strategic human resource management practices. For example, many customer service failures were based on problems between two or three different employee groups. American Airlines held the specific function involved accountable. According to one American employee, if a delay occurred, managers on duty were responsible for figuring out which function caused it. Referring to Robert Crandall, former CEO and chairman, he asserted, 'Crandall wants to see the corpse. It is management by intimidation.'[36] On the other hand, Southwest used a 'team delay' concept to point out problems between two or three different employee groups working together. Performance management was less precise at Southwest, but the benefit was increased problem-solving and enhanced productivity. At American Airlines, conflict resolution was designed to address grievances that employees filed against managers. Their managers were not rewarded for supporting good work relationships. At Southwest, there was a proactive approach to conflict resolution. Conflict was seen as inevitable and there were processes to attempt to resolve it at the source, and emphasize understanding the other person's perspective.

The following table highlights differences between approaches to coordination and control taken by American and Southwest.

Element	American	Southwest
Accountability of Front-Line Employees	Functional Accountability	Cross-Functional Accountability
Accountability of Field Managers	Focus on Measurement	Focus on Learning
Supervision	Large Supervisory Spans of Control (30–40)	Small Supervisory Spans of Control
Employee Selection	No Regard for Teamwork	Selection for Team Fit
Conflict Resolution	Minimal	Proactive

Source: Adapted from *Paradox of Coordination and Control*

Labor Relations

Michael E. Levine, former dean of Yale's School of Organization and Management and executive vice president for marketing at Northwest Airlines, commented, 'Herb is an extremely gifted labor-relations talent, especially when you consider he has somehow managed to get union people to identify personally with this company.'[37] Like the rest of the airline industry, nearly 90 percent of Southwest's workforce was organized into nine unions. The pilots and three small technician unions were independent organizations. The flight attendants and ramp workers were members of the Transportation Workers Unions (TWU), the customer service and reservation agents were represented by the International Association of Machinists (IAM), and the mechanics and cleaners were represented by the Teamsters (IBT).[38]

Southwest enjoyed peaceful labor relations from its beginning. Its founders had a collaborative philosophy, and were not opposed to unions and invited them into the organization. Southwest's management worked hard to ensure that the unions maintained the same objectives as the company. Unlike many companies that had cumbersome formal structures and processes for consultation and representation, Southwest only had negotiation and grievance procedures. Southwest did, however, keep the union representatives informed of new developments. None of Southwest's achievements would have been possible without its unusually good labor-management relations, attributed to Kelleher's hands-on efforts, as exemplified by the following anecdote:

> A Wall Street analyst recalls having lunch one day in the company cafeteria when Kelleher, seated at a table across the room with several female employees, suddenly leapt to his feet, kissed one of the women with gusto, and began leading the entire crowd in a series of cheers. When the analyst asked what was going on, one of the executives at his table explained that Kelleher had at that moment negotiated a new contract with Southwest's flight attendants.[39]

Developing and maintaining empathy is part of the skill of good labor-management relations. At one point, tensions broke out between flight attendants and their schedulers – the ones with the sorry job of telling flight attendants they have to work on a day off – because the flight attendants believed the schedulers were overworking them. The schedulers claimed the flight attendants were hostile and uncooperative. The solution was very Southwest: both sides had to switch jobs for a day and see how difficult the other side had it. The solution eased the tension and developed empathy between flight attendants and schedulers.

Colleen Barrett, who was credited with masterminding the Southwest culture, believed that competitors did not enjoy Southwest's success, 'Because they don't get it…What we do is simple, but it's not simplistic. We really do everything with a passion. We scream at each other and we hug each other.'[40] This zany environment in which Barrett was so comfortable was described by an analyst:

> To truly understand why this company continues to be such a hit with customers, you have to go behind the wall and take a look. Pay a visit to Southwest's headquarters just off Love Field in Dallas, and you'll probably think you've wandered onto the set of Pee-wee's Playhouse. The walls are festooned with more than ten thousand picture frames – no exaggeration – containing photos of employees' pets, of Herb dressed as Elvis or in drag, of stewardesses in miniskirts, of Southwest planes gnawing on competitors' aircraft. Then there are teddy bears, and jars of pickled hot peppers, and pink flamingos. There is cigarette smoking, and lots of chuckling, and nary a necktie to be seen.[41]

Southwest's pep-rally culture was not just window dressing, according to an industry analyst:

> Southwest employees are more productive than most others in the industry…so maintaining morale is critical…While Southwest has tweaked its formula over the years – adding more long-distance flights, for instance – it's still mainly a point-to-point, short-hop airline that uses one aircraft type to simplify training and maintenance.[42]

Herb and His Successors

'Herb is going to be very hard to replace,' sighed board member June Morris in an extraordinary understatement. Nevertheless, Herb Kelleher announced his intention to retire in 2000, and stepped down as president and CEO in 2001. He commented:

> I had an agreement with the board that when I got to be 70, we ought to do something about succession. I guess the board just thought it might be embarrassing to have a chairman and president and CEO who was 70. You should never become infatuated with power. If you have any common sense, you know the time will come when you have to let go.[43]

Kelleher said he thought about his successor very seriously for quite a long time. He said, 'My biggest concern was that I wanted someone who would be respectful of Southwest's culture and would be the sort of person who was altruistic in nature.'[44] He decided that Jim Parker, Southwest's general counsel and Herb's friend since 1979, and Colleen Barrett, who had been with Herb since the beginning of Southwest and had risen through the ranks, fit the criteria. Parker was selected to fill the CEO position and serve as vice-chairman of the board, and Barrett was selected to be president and COO – the first man-and-woman team to run an airline. Although controversial, Herb remained as chairman with responsibility for managing strategy and government relations. Jim and Colleen assumed their new responsibilities the day Southwest turned 30.

Soft-spoken and bespectacled James Parker, who joined Southwest in 1986 after seven years as a partner at Kelleher's law firm, commented, 'I told Herb I had put too much of my life into Southwest Airlines to walk away from a chance to try and move ahead.'[45] He was a thoughtful University of Texas-trained lawyer who looked like he would be more comfortable writing wills in a country town than running an airline. Parker was a stark contrast to Herb. Nevertheless, Kelleher sang Parker's praises and wryly observed, 'Parker is exactly the kind of leader Southwest needs…[Although] I think we have different personalities…' Some noted that it was not likely that Parker would engage in Kelleher's attention-getting antics, such as dressing up like the King of Rock and Roll. 'He is more English professor than Elvis impersonator,' contended one long-time industry observer.[46] In his self-effacing style, Parker observed, 'I'm not Herb. Colleen's not Herb…So we are just going to have to be ourselves.'[47]

Parker planned to continue the Southwest business model by keeping the low-cost, low-fare, no-frills airline it had always been. Kelleher contended, 'There will be no change in our core philosophy and basic business model…'[48] The Southwest model was one that Parker helped refine and reinforce during his tenure at Southwest, often in a very hands-on way. For example, prior to taking the CEO role, he negotiated a ten-year contract with Southwest pilots that significantly controlled costs. It was typical for airlines to lock in labor costs for a three- or four-year period only. In addition, Parker was the champion of Southwest's move to sell tickets on the Internet. These online sales later accounted for more that $1 billion in revenues.

Colleen Barrett began her career as Kelleher's secretary in his San Antonio law firm. She followed Herb to Southwest, and was at his side every step of the way. She was considered an unsung hero at Southwest, and was selected to replace Kelleher as president. This made her the highest ranking woman in the U.S. airline industry. She described herself as a passionate and emotional communicator, and said, 'Some CEOs will still introduce me as Herb's secretary.'[49] She did not care when people mistook her for Kelleher's secretary. Reflecting on her considerable accomplishments, she said, 'Actually, I just laugh at it…I loved being a secretary.'[50]

Prior to taking over the role of president and COO, Barrett oversaw Southwest's marketing, advertising, customer service, and human resources activities. She was also considered chief guardian of Southwest's *esprit de corps*. According to Glenn Engle of Goldman Sachs, 'She built the infrastructure on which Southwest's culture is based.'[51] Some identified her as Herb's alter ego. Kelleher once commented, 'One of our strengths is that we are so complementary.'[52] Once Kelleher and Barrett took the Myers-Briggs personality assessment, and scored at opposite extremes. Barrett elaborated:

> Herb could have a dream in the middle of the night and say, 'Okay, this is what I want to do.' But he wouldn't have a clue, God love him, what steps have to be taken to get there…I'm not the most brilliant person in the whole world, but I can see systematically from A to Z, and I know what has to be done.[53]

Jim Parker had taken on probably the toughest job in business, replacing Herb Kelleher, just as the airline industry was facing the most severe economic downturn in years. When someone asked Parker how he was going to handle succeeding Herb, he quipped, 'Well, Colleen's going to handle the smoking, and I'm going to handle the drinking.'[54] Later, he commented, 'Nobody can replace Herb. I'd never try to. Actually, I'm fairly boring. I'm not as zany as Herb is – no Elvis suits or anything. When I moved into Herb's office, they had to totally detoxify it. They pulled out the carpet, took out the wall cover, took out the ceiling tiles to get all that cigarette smoke out of there. Fortunately, our people have been very accepting of the fact that I'm just trying to be myself.'[55]

Then the terrorist attacks of September 11, 2001, happened. Parker was able to call on Herb for backup. He commented:

> I felt no pressure in becoming CEO after Herb because this was not exactly a turnaround situation. My biggest challenge was to maintain direction and focus of the company. Still, it's been a uniquely stressful year in the airline industry, and one of the things I am grateful for is the fact that Herb has been a total failure at retirement. He continues to be actively involved as our chairman of the board. It was very comforting to me that he was here after September 11. After all, if you had a chance to get advice or guidance from any living human being about the airline industry, who would you seek out? I can't think of anyone better than Herb Kelleher.[56]

Running Southwest Airlines was not as easy as Herb made it look. A year after Jim and Colleen assumed their new responsibilities, an analyst commented:

> Southwest Airlines is rapidly approaching middle age. While it may once have been the little guy, the upstart who had to try harder, today the eternal underdog is a national institution which

passed its 30th birthday last year. Not only has it outlasted old giants such as Pan-Am and TWA, but its post-September 11 market capitalization at $17 billion exceeds American, Delta, and United combined. With age has come maturity, and with maturity a move away from reliance on the founder Herb Kelleher and his legendary charisma. In his place come executives who have grown up within the airline, and who have the very clear duties of institutionalizing the two things that have served Southwest so well: its business model, and its corporate culture.[57]

Cracks in the Façade?

Southwest was now 37 years old. As the fifth largest airline in the U.S. by revenue, it had lost its credibility as an underdog. Additionally, this giant's no-frills flights were starting to look 'chintzy,' as competitors like JetBlue matched low fares while adding frills like satellite TVs and assigned seating.

As long as Kelleher was around, employees would go the extra mile in the name of Herb. Prior to his retirement in 2001, 'he was able to implement Southwest's unique cost structure and work rules,' says an executive of another airline. 'If you were a union leader, you couldn't badmouth Kelleher: he was an icon. But anybody new was going to be just another corporate executive.'[58]

The problem with being the one profitable major airline post 9/11 was that airline workers got greedy. Concessions by unions at the six major carriers stood in sharp contrast to the big wage and salary demands by employees of Southwest. The pilots of its 737s had the highest compensation in the industry, 'making $190,000 in salary and profit sharing, plus up to another $100,000 in stock option grants.'[59] Southwest had also seen its stranglehold on low-cost, young labor erode. Kelleher was pressed back into service to help end the stalemated, embittered flight attendant negotiations. He got the deal done, but at a significant cost. An industry analyst observed:

When Southwest Airlines flight attendants gathered for the camera this summer, it was the antithesis of the warm-and-fuzzy photo ops on which the low-cost carrier built its image. Instead, the attendants were showing off a banner calling for 'Discount Fares – Not Discounted Employees and Families.'…Its attendants' contract resulted in 31 percent average wage hikes, so that within three years they will be the best paid in the sky, earning up to $56,350 annually. In one fell swoop, its labor cost, at 3.2 cents to fly one seat mile, soared above the 3.0 cents at Texas rival Continental…Under the new wage scale, Southwest's overall cost to fly a seat one mile jumped from 7.6 cents to 8.1 cents…[60]

A Morgan Stanley analyst commented, 'It's worth asking whether Southwest is finally facing the same issues and challenges that legacy carriers have experienced for some time.' He continued, 'We believe there is a risk that as a generational change occurs and the oldest Southwest employees retire (who remember the early years of struggle), the company's low-cost culture will change.'[61] Another analyst commented:

From 20 percent to 25 percent annual growth in the mid-1990s, earnings have fallen an average of two percent annually the past five years. The market may be catching on. Southwest's stock is down 30 percent the past year to a recent $13.80. Even so, its lofty $10.9 billion market value is more than that of the nation's ten other largest airlines combined.[62]

Southwest had weathered a dizzying series of events since 2001. Parker and Barrett were grappling with important strategic decisions in the face of major industry setbacks – terrorism, spiraling fuel prices, and labor unrest. They were trying to figure out how to respond to increasing, credible competition. Then, in September 2004, CEO James Parker suddenly resigned.

Reorganizing for the Future?

Parker's resignation was followed by reorganization at the low-cost carrier in which CFO Gary Kelly, who had devised Southwest's fuel-hedging strategy which insulated it from fuel cost shock, stepped into the role of CEO. Kelly's first job at Southwest had been to bring the accounting and information management systems into the computer age. He had an uphill battle convincing the waste-averse, penny-conscious, skeptical Kelleher that investment in technology could lead to cost-cutting, revenue-generating innovations. Kelly was characterized as a demanding 'born leader' with character, a straight-forward and honest communication style, integrity, and a track record of treating people right. Kelly's nurturing style made his followers 'willing to run through walls for him.'[63]

Kelly commented that costs 'are rising much faster than the overall rate of inflation and our own revenue growth.'[64] Kelly had been with Southwest for 19 years, and had seen all of the easy growth opportunities exploited. Upon taking the reins, he observed, 'Growth opportunities have become more precious.'[65] But the balance sheet was a financial manager's dream. According to Tammy Romo, Southwest's VP and treasurer, 'We ended the year with $1.3 billion in cash, and our leverage...is well under 40 percent.'

Despite the financial strength, Kelly commented, 'There is a lot of competition. There is a weakened air traffic demand environment. And that's before you even get to the cost side of the equation.'[66] The commercial aviation environment had changed dramatically in the last eighteen months. The larger legacy rivals – the majors – had achieved considerable labor restructuring agreements, which eroded Southwest's 'once considerable' wage advantage. Overcapacity was putting pressure on passenger yields, pushing them lower than Southwest would prefer. Other low-cost carrier rivals like JetBlue, AirTran, and Spirit were establishing niches that eroded opportunity for Southwest in the 'underserved and overpriced markets' at the core of their niche.

Southwest had seen three chief executives in four years, compared to the twenty years that Kelleher filled the role. Parker had been in the post for what were characterized as the three worst years in the history of aviation. Barrett remained president until the summer of 2008, and retained her title and role as chief morale officer. Less than a year into the new job, Kelly gave the annual 'Message to the Field' speech to the employees, where he told the crowd, 'The Southwest brand is under attack. These next years are going to be some of the hardest the airline has ever had. Be prepared for some sacrifices.' The crowd got very quiet.[67] Kelly believed, 'The issue right now is that there is a glut of seats, there is an energy-price crisis for our industry, and it's time to get through as opposed to making a lot of bets on what customers do or don't want.'[68]

Kelly's foresight into the energy-price crisis could not have been more accurate, and his response more strategic. The price of fuel skyrocketed in the spring of 2008, and rising fuel costs hit airlines hard. Industry-wide fuel expenses were expected to total $61 billion in 2008, compared to $41 billion in 2007, according to the Air Transport Association. Southwest benefited from Kelly's fuel price-hedging strategy, and had been able to hold down its fuel costs while competitors struggled to cope as the price of crude spiraled ever higher. In 2007, Southwest locked in the price it would pay for fuel in 2008 based on a crude oil price of $51 per barrel, far less that the $162 per barrel that crude reached in July 2008. With this huge cost advantage, Southwest did not have to increase fares as much as other airlines or follow other carriers in imposing new baggage or beverage service fees and cutting flights by as much as 15 percent. Southwest had four modest fare increases in 2008, compared to more than twenty by other major airlines. Kelly commented, 'Right now, it comes as a sweet advantage, and we are trying to take advantage of it. Reservation agents tell me the first question they get when customers call right now is, 'Do you charge for the first bag?' I believe deeply we are gaining passengers because of our approach.'[69] This advantage would not continue. Southwest was not able to hedge as much as it wanted for fuel it would need in 2009 and 2010, and faced the very real possibility of having to raise airfares significantly.

Kelly had many issues to weigh as he continued to pursue the conservative management and aggressive expansion that built Southwest Airlines and kept it profitable for 35 of the last 37 years. Could Southwest preserve the Herb-centric culture now that Kelleher had turned operations over to successors? Was the Southwest culture critical to their continued success, especially as they were becoming more like the majors they once mocked? Would Southwest lose its leadership position to copycat competitors? Would they have to copy the copycats to meet customer expectations for things like assigned seats, baggage transfer, and personal entertainment systems? Would their cost advantage erode in the face of spiraling fuel costs, costly labor concessions, and the ever-increasing efficiency of rivals? Should they provide service to those routes being abandoned by the majors? As he contemplated the next moves in this increasingly turbulent environment, Kelly grappled with the most fundamental issues. Were minds, hearts, spirits, and souls sufficient to continue to differentiate Southwest? Was it time to reinvent the 40-year-old Southwest Airlines?

Endnotes

[1] http://southwest.com/about_swa/airborne.html.

[2] K. Brooker, 'The Chairman of the Board Looks Back as Herb Kelleher Hands Over the Controls,' *Fortune*, May 28, 2001.

[3] Ibid.

[4] Ibid.

[5] Ibid.

[6] K. Labich and A. Hadjian, 'Is Herb Kelleher America's Best CEO?' *Fortune*, Volume 129, Issue 9, 1994.

[7] Brooker, 'The Chairman of the Board Looks Back as Herb Kelleher Hands Over the Controls.'

[8] Ibid.

[9] Ibid.

[10] J. Clark, 'Low-Cost Airlines Get a Lift in Fiscally Turbulent Times,' *USA Today,* April 18, 2003, pp. 1D, 2D.

[11] A. Inkpen, 'Southwest Airlines 2002,' Thunderbird Case, #A07-02-0009, 2002, p. 3.

[12] T. Hansson, J. Ringbeck, and M. Franke, 'Flight for Survival: A New Operating Model for Airlines, *Strategy + Business*, December 9, 2002.

[13] S. McCartnery, 'Big Three Airlines Face Tough Tasks,' *The Wall Street Journal*, October 24, 2002, p. D5.

[14] Ibid.

[15] J. Useem, 'America's Most Admired Companies,' *Fortune*, Vol. 151, Issue 5, 2005, pp. 66–70.

[16] Ibid.

[17] Ibid.

[18] Brooker, 'The Chairman of the Board Looks Back as Herb Kelleher Hands Over the Controls.'

[19] Ibid.

[20] Labich and Hadjian, 'Is Herb Kelleher America's Best CEO?'

[21] Brooker, 'The Chairman of the Board Looks Back as Herb Kelleher Hands Over the Controls.'

[22] S. Branch, 'So Much Work, So Little Time,' *Fortune*, Volume 135, Issue 2, 1997.

[23] Ibid.

[24] Labich and Hadjian, 'Is Herb Kelleher America's Best CEO?'

[25] Ibid.

[26] Ibid.

[27] Ibid.

[28] K. Brooker, 'Can Anyone Replace Herb?' *Fortune*, Volume 141, Issue 8, 2000.

[29] http://southwest.com/about_swa/southwest_cares/our_people.html.

[30] S. Chakravaty, 'Hit 'em Hardest with the Mostest,' *Forbes*, September 16, 1991.

[31] http://www.southwest.com/about_swa/press/factsheet.html#About%20the%20Company.

[32] Ibid.

[33] C. O'Reilly and J. Pfeffer, 'Southwest Airlines; Using Human Resources for Competitive Advantage (A),' Graduate School of Business, Stanford University, 1994.

[34] Ibid.

[35] Ibid.

[36] Jody Hoffer Gittell, 'Paradox of Coordination and Control,' *California Management Review*, 42 (3), 2000, pp. 101–117.

[37] Labich and Hadjian, 'Is Herb Kelleher America's Best CEO?'

[38] T.A. Kochan, 'Southwest Airlines,' Working Paper #WP09, May 1, 1999.

[39] Labich and Hadjian, 'Is Herb Kelleher America's Best CEO?'

[40] A. Serwer, 'The Hottest Thing in the Sky,' *Fortune*, Volume 149, Issue 5, 2004, p. 86.

[41] Ibid.

[42] W. Zellner, 'Southwest: After Kelleher, More Blue Skies,' *Business Week*, Volume 45, Issue 3726, 2001.

[43] Brooker, 'Can Anyone Replace Herb?'

[44] Ibid.

[45] D. Fisher, 'Is There Such a Thing as Nonstop Growth?' *Forbes*, Volume 170, Issue 01, 2002.

[46] Ibid.

[47] Ibid.

[48] Ibid.

[49] Brooker, 'The Chairman of the Board Looks Back as Herb Kelleher Hands Over the Controls.'

[50] Ibid.

[51] Ibid.

[52] Ibid.

[53] Ibid.

[54] Ibid.

[55] J. Parker, 'Replacing a Legend,' *Fortune* (Europe), Volume 146, Issue 9, 2002, p. 36.

[56] Ibid.

[57] D. Field, 'Southwest Succession,' *Airline Business*, Volume 18, Issue 4, 2002.

[58] J. Helyar, 'Southwest Finds Trouble in the Air,' *Fortune* (Europe), Volume 150, Issue 3, 2004, p. 15.

[59] M. Tatge and N. Weinberg, 'What Goes Up…,' *Forbes*, Volume 174, Issue 8, 2004, p. 116, 3p, 4c.

[60] Ibid.

[61] Helyar, 'Southwest Finds Trouble in the Air.'

[62] B. Gimbel, 'Southwest's New Flight Plan,' *Fortune*, Volume 151, Issue 10, May 16, 2005.

[63] D. Reed, 'Southwest CEO Puts Emphasis on Character,' *USA Today*, September 26, 2004.

[64] Ibid.

[65] 'Kelly Becomes CEO at Southwest,' *AirFinance Journal*, Issue 273, September 2004, p. 7.

[66] Ibid.

[67] Ibid.

[68] Ibid.

[69] P. Pae, 'Southwest Airlines Will Soon Be No. 1 at Four of Five Area Airports,' *Los Angeles Times*, July 25, 2008.

CASE 3: Honda (A)

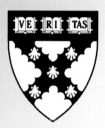

The two decades from 1960 to 1980 witnessed a strategic reversal in the world motorcycle industry. By the end of that period, previously well-financed American competitors with seemingly impregnable market positions were faced with extinction. Although most consumers had an initial preference to purchase from them, these U.S. manufacturers had been dislodged by Japanese competitors and lost position despite technological shifts that could have been emulated as competition intensified.

The Japanese invasion of the world motorcycle market was spearheaded by the Honda Motor Company. Its founder, Sochiro Honda, a visionary inventor and industrialist, had been involved peripherally in the automotive industry prior to World War II. However, Japan's postwar devastation resulted in the downsizing of Honda's ambitions; motorcycles were a more technologically manageable and economically affordable product for the average Japanese. Reflecting Honda's commitment to a technologically based strategy, the Honda Technical Research Institute was established in 1946. This institute, dedicated to improvements in internal combustion engines, represented Honda's opening move in the motorcycle field. In 1947, Honda introduced its first A-type, 2-stroke engine.

As of 1948, Honda's Japanese competition consisted of 247 Japanese participants in a loosely defined motorcycle industry. Most competitors operated in ill-equipped job shops, adapting clip-on engines for bicycles. A few larger manufacturers endeavored to copy European motorcycles but were hampered by inferior technology and materials that resulted in unreliable products.

Honda expanded its presence in the fall of 1949, introducing a lightweight 50cc, 2-stroke, D-type motorcycle. Honda's engine at 3 hp was more reliable than most of its contemporaries' engines and had a superior stamped metal frame. This introduction coincided closely, however, with the introduction of a 4-stroke engine by several larger competitors. These engines were both quieter and more powerful than Honda's. Responding to this threat, Honda followed in 1951 with a superior 4-stroke design that doubled horsepower with no additional weight. Embarking on a bold campaign to exploit this advantage, Honda acquired a plant, and over the next two years it developed enough manufacturing expertise to become a fully integrated producer of engines, frames, chains, sprockets, and other ancillary parts crucial to motorcycle performance.

Motorcycle manufacturers in the Japanese industry tended to minimize risk by investing in one winning design and milking that product until it became technologically obsolescent. Beginning in the 1950s, Honda began to depart from this pattern – seeking simultaneously to (1) offer a multiproduct line, (2) take leadership in product innovation, and (3) exploit opportunities for economies of mass production by gearing designs to production objectives. Most notably, in 1958 Honda's market research

Dr. Richard T. Pascale of Stanford Graduate School of Business prepared this case with the collaboration of Professor E. Tatum Christiansen of Harvard Business School as a basis for class discussion rather than to illustrate either effective or ineffective handling of an administrative situation.

Note: This case is based largely on the Harvard Business School's 'Note on the Motorcycle Industry – 1975' (No. 9-587-210) and on a published report of the Boston Consulting Group ('Strategy Alternatives for the British Motorcycle Industry'), 1975.

identified a large, untapped market segment seeking a small, unintimidating motorcycle that could be used by small-motorcycle businesses for local deliveries. Honda designed a product specifically for this application: a step-through frame, automatic transmission, and one-hand controls that enabled drivers to handle the machine with one hand while carrying a package in the other. The 50cc Honda was an explosive success. Unit sales reached 3,000 per month after six months on the market. Deciding to make this the product of the future, Honda gambled, investing in a highly automated 30,000-unit-per-month manufacturing plant – a capacity 10 times in excess of demand at the time of construction.

Honda's bold moves set the stage for a yet bolder decision – to invade the U.S. market. The following section depicts the sequence of events as taken from a Harvard Business School case on the motorcycle industry.[1]

In 1959…Honda Motor Company…entered the American market. The Japanese motorcycle industry had expanded rapidly since World War II to meet the need for cheap transportation. In 1959, Honda, Suzuki, Yamaha, and Kawasaki together produced some 450,000 motorcycles. With sales of $55 million in that year, Honda was already the world's largest motorcycle producer…

In contrast to other foreign producers who relied on distributors, Honda established a U.S. subsidiary, American Honda Motor Company, and began its push in the U.S. market by offering very small lightweight motorcycles. The Honda machine had a three-speed transmission, an automatic clutch, five horsepower (compared with two and a half for the lightweight motorcycle then sold by Sears, Roebuck), an electric starter, and a step-through frame for female riders. Generally superior to the Sears lightweight and easier to handle, the Honda machines sold for less than $250 retail, compared with $1,000 – $1,500 for the bigger American or British machines.

Honda followed a policy of developing the market region by region, beginning on the West Coast and moving eastward over a period of four to five years. In 1961 it lined up 125 dealers and spent $150,000 on regional advertising. Honda advertising represented a concerted effort to overcome the unsavory image of motorcyclists that had developed since the 1940s, given special prominence by the 1953 movie *The Wild Ones*, which starred Marlon Brando as the surly, destructive leader of a motorcycle gang. In contrast, Honda addressed its appeal primarily to middle-class consumers and claimed, 'You meet the nicest people on a Honda.' This marketing effort was backed by heavy advertising, and the other Japanese exporters also invested substantial sums: $1.5 million for Yamaha and $0.7 million for Suzuki.

Honda's strategy was phenomenally successful. Its U.S. sales rose from $500,000 in 1960 to $77 million in 1965. By 1966, Honda, Yamaha, and Suzuki together had 85% of the U.S. market. From a negligible position in 1960, lightweight motorcycles had come to dominate the market.

The transformation and expansion of the motorcycle market during the early 1960s benefited British and American producers as well as the Japanese. British exports doubled between 1960 and 1966, while Harley-Davidson's sales increased from $16.6 million in 1959 to $29.6 million in 1965. Two press reports of the mid 1960s illustrate these traditional manufacturers' interpretation of the Japanese success:

> 'The success of Honda, Suzuki, and Yamaha in the States has been jolly good for us,' Eric Turner, chairman of the board of BSA Ltd., told Advertising Age. 'People here start out by buying one of the low-priced Japanese jobs. They get to enjoy the fun and exhilaration of the open road and frequently end up buying one of our more powerful and expensive machines.' The British insist that they're not really in competition with the Japanese (they're on the lighter end). The Japanese have other ideas. Just two months ago Honda introduced a 444cc model to compete, at a lower price, with the Triumph 500cc. [Advertising Age, December 27, 1965]

> 'Basically we do not believe in the lightweight market,' says William H. Davidson, son of one of the founders and currently president of the company (Harley-Davidson). 'We believe that motorcycles

---

[1] D. Purkayastha and R. Buzzell, 'Note on the Motorcycle Industry – 1975,' HBS No. 9-578-210, pp. 5 – 7.

are sports vehicles, not transportation vehicles. Even if a man says he bought a motorcycle for transportation, it's generally for leisure time use. The lightweight motorcycle is only supplemental. Back around World War I, a number of companies came out with lightweight bikes. We came out with one ourselves. We came out with another one in 1947 and it just did not go anywhere. We have seen what happens to these small sizes.' [Forbes, September 15,1966]

Meanwhile, the Japanese producers continued to grow in other export markets. In 1965, domestic sales represented only 59% of Honda's total of $316 million, down from 98% in 1959. Over the same period, production volume had increased almost fivefold, from 285,000 to 1.4 million units. In Europe, where the Japanese did not begin their thrust until the late 1960s, they had captured a commanding share of key markets by 1974.

In short, by the mid-1970s the Japanese producers had come to dominate a market shared by European and American producers 20 years earlier...

It was often said that Honda created the market for the recreational uses of motorcycles through its extensive advertising and promotional effort.

The company achieved a significant product advantage through a heavy commitment to R&D and advanced manufacturing techniques. Honda used its productivity-based cost advantage and R&D capability to introduce new models at prices below those of competitive machines. New products could be brought to market very quickly; the interval between conception and production was estimated to be only 18 months. Honda was also reported to have a 'cold storage' of designs that could be introduced if the market developed....

Since 1960, Honda had consistently outspent its competitors in advertising. It had also established the largest dealership network in the U.S. On average, Honda dealers were larger than their competitors. In new markets, Honda had been willing to take short-term losses in order to build up an adequate selling and distribution network.

In 1975, the Boston Consulting Group was retained by the British government to diagnose the British motorcycle industry and the factors contributing to its decline. The remainder of this case, reflecting on Honda's strategy, consists of excerpts from that report:[2]

The market approach of [Honda] has certain common features which, taken together, may be described as a 'marketing philosophy.' The fundamental feature of this philosophy is the emphasis it places on market share and sales volume. Objectives set in these terms are regarded as critical, and defended at all costs.

The whole thrust of the marketing program...is towards maintaining or improving market share position....We have seen some ways in which this goal is pursued. It is worth adding, as an example of how pervasive this objective is...that in an interview with a Honda personnel director, we were told that the first question a prospective Honda dealer is asked is the level of his market share in his local area. 'I don't know why, but this company places an awful lot of emphasis on market share' was the comment....We shall return to the reasons why market shares are critical for commercial success in the industry.

We were also told by representatives of [Honda] that their primary objectives are set in terms of sales volume rather than short-term profitability. Annual sales targets – based on market share penetration assumptions and market growth prospects – are set, and the main task of the sales company is to achieve these targets. The essence of this strategy is to grow sales volume at least as fast or faster than any of your competitors.

A number of more specific policies follow from this general philosophy, and our descriptions of each of the Japanese competitors provide ample examples of these policies:

---

[2] Boston Consulting Group, 'Strategy Alternatives for the British Motorcycle Industry,' Her Majesty's Stationery Office, London, 30 July 1975, pp. 16 – 17, 23, 39 – 43, 54 – 55.

1 Products are updated or redesigned whenever a market threat or opportunity is perceived.

2 Prices are set at levels designed to achieve market share targets and will be cut if necessary.

3 Effective marketing systems are set up in all markets where serious competition is intended, regardless of short-term cost.

4 Plans and objectives look to long-term payoff.

The results of these policies for the Japanese competitors have, of course, been spectacularly successful. Over the last fifteen years, the rates of growth of the four major Japanese companies have been as shown in [**Table A**].

Table A Growth of Japanese Production			
	Production in 1959 (000 units)	**Production in 1974 (000 units)**	**Average Annual Growth Rate (% p.a.)**
Honda	285	2,133	14
Yamaha	64	1,165	21
Kawasaki	10	355	27
Suzuki	96	840	16

Source: Japan Automobile Industry Association

Selling and distribution systems. We have so far discussed market share as a function of the product features and prices of particular models. Market share across all cc classes is also influenced by what we shall call the selling and distribution system (s and d system). Within the s and d system we include all the activities of the marketing companies (or importers) in each national market:

■ Sales representation at the dealer level
■ Physical distribution of parts and machines
■ Warranty and service support
■ Dealer support
■ Advertising and promotion
■ Market planning and control.

We also include the effects of the dealer network established by the marketing companies:

■ Numbers and quality of dealers
■ Floor space devoted to the manufacturers' products
■ Sales support by dealers.

The s and d system supports sales of the manufacturer across the whole model range, and its quality affects market shares in each cc class where the manufacturer is represented. **Table B** compares the s and d systems of the four full-line Japanese manufacturers in the USA, and shows that high market shares both overall *and* in each cc class go with high levels of expenditure on s and d and with extensive dealer networks.

The interaction between product-related variables and s- and d-related variables is complex. The better the product range in terms of comprehensiveness, features, and price, and the more sophisticated the s and d system of the sales company, the easier it will be to attract good dealers. This is because

Table B The Selling and Distribution Systems of Japanese Companies in the U.S.A.

	Estimated Total S&D Expenditure by Sales Company 1974 ($m)	Advertising Expenditure 1972 ($m)	Dealers 1974 Numbers	Units Sold per Dealer	1974 % Share of Total Market (units)	Lowest % Share of any cc Class	Highest % Share of any cc Class
Honda	90–100	8.1	1,974	220	43	34	61
Yamaha	40–45	4.2	1,515	135	20	4	34
Kawasaki	30–35	2.2	1,018	127	13	9	19
Suzuki	25–30	3.0	1,103	98	11	5	16

Source: R.L. Rolk, Motorcycle Dealer News, Ziff-Davis Market Research Dept., BCG estimates

good products, which are well supported at the marketing company level, lead to good retail sales. Equally, good dealers themselves improve retail sales, and active competition between dealers can lead to retail discounting which acts as a volume-boosting price cut to the public. The manufacturers' products and s and d system therefore influence sales both directly, at retail, and proximately, through their effect on the dealer network.

In particular cc categories, each manufacturer's position is substantially influenced by its specific product offerings. For example, Kawasaki are strong in the 750cc- and over class due to the Z-1, and Yamaha have been weak due to its poor 750cc model. Outstanding products obtain market shares that are unusually high for a manufacturer, and weak products lead to atypically low market shares. For products of average attraction, however, market shares seem to move towards some equilibrium level. For each manufacturer, this level in the USA appears to be:

Honda   40–50%

Yamaha   15–25%

Kawasaki   10–15%

Suzuki   9–12%

As overall market leaders, the Japanese have dominated pricing in the motorcycle industry. It is therefore appropriate to begin this analysis by examining the extent to which the experience curve concept appears to explain the performance of the Japanese. Unfortunately, it is impossible directly to determine unit cost performance data for competitors, since the data are not publicly available. Sources can be found, however, for unit price and production volume data. Over the long term, price behavior is a useful guide to movements in the underlying costs, and so an experience curve analysis on prices can be extremely revealing.

Japanese price performance. In **Figure A**, price experience curves are drawn for the Japanese motorcycle industry as a whole, based on aggregate data collected by MITI. These curves show price reduction performance of a consistent nature for each of the size ranges of motorcycle considered, the rate of price reduction being most rapid of all in the largest range, 126–250cc, which is following an experience curve slope of 76%. The other slopes are more shallow, at 81% and 88%, but there is no mistaking the fact that real prices are descending smoothly over time. These experience-based price reductions clearly go a long way towards explaining the historical competitive effectiveness of the Japanese in the marketplace in small and medium motorcycles.

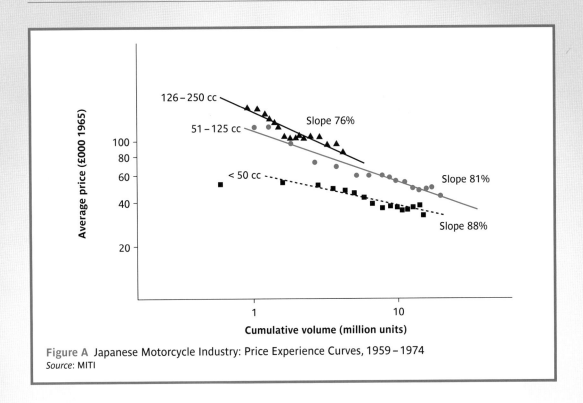

Figure A Japanese Motorcycle Industry: Price Experience Curves, 1959–1974
Source: MITI

For the purposes of strategy development…it is [helpful] to look more closely at price performance in the larger bike models. The Honda CB 750 has been the pacesetter in superbikes in terms of both market penetration and pricing. In **Figure B**, price experience curves are plotted for this product and for two other large Honda bikes. The prices of other Japanese manufacturers have been broadly comparable to Honda's in the equivalent size range (they usually tend if anything to price at a slight premium relative to Honda), so that we may use Honda as a good 'benchmark' for the Japanese competition in big bikes in general.

It is clear from **Figure B** that price performance in the large bikes has been consistent with that in small: real prices have declined along experience curve slopes in the region of 85%–87%. This has also been true of the price in the United States, when converted into yen terms.

An interesting feature of the curves is that the prices in the United States are so much higher than [those] of the same products in Japan. As shown in **Table C**, the premiums are high across almost the entire range of bikes and are far larger than seems necessary, even allowing for the extra costs incurred for duty, freight, and packing in shipping bikes from Japan to the United States. This certainly suggests that there is no possibility that the Japanese are 'dumping' their products in the U.S. market: quite the reverse. Furthermore, it may well indicate that competitive though the Japanese have been in the United States, based on the downward trends in their real price levels over time, there may well be plenty of scope for them to be even more competitive in the future if seriously challenged in that market. They could simply reduce their margins on exports to the United States to levels more in line with those enjoyed in their domestic business.

Japanese cost performance. The implication of the downward trends in real prices for the Japanese is, of course, that there have been underlying experience-based cost reductions: that the decline has not been accounted for simply by a reduction in margins.…However, the major Japanese manufacturers have been continuously profitable, and this suggests that cost reductions have indeed taken place in parallel with real price reductions. On the other hand, all the Japanese motorcycle manufacturers also make a significant proportion of products other than motorcycles (in 1974 about 35% of Honda's turnover, and about 40% of Suzuki's, was accounted for by cars; of Yamaha Motor's turnover about 40%

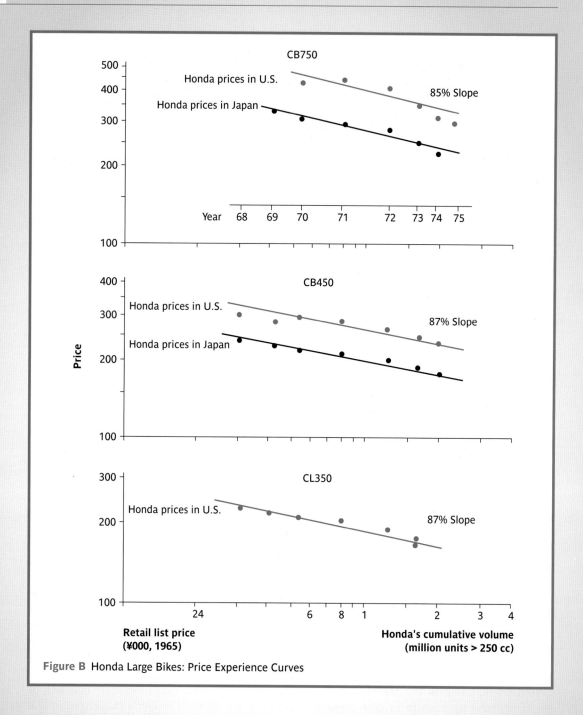

Figure B Honda Large Bikes: Price Experience Curves

was in products such as boats and snowmobiles). It is, perhaps, reasonable to question whether these products are sufficiently profitable to 'subsidize' the motorcycle business.

...It seems clear that...none of [the three major Japanese] manufacturers is subsidizing the motorcycle business from other businesses. Indeed, Honda was actually losing money in its car business in 1974, which suggests that their motorcycle business that year may have shown returns of the order of 20% (BIT) compared with the 12.4% return earned by the company overall. The overall inference from this profit performance must be that each manufacturer has indeed achieved an experience curve effect on costs in parallel with those achieved on price. The existence of this experience curve effect in the motorcycle industry has important strategy implications.

Table C Honda price premium, USA vs Japan

Premium on retail list prices, 1974

Model	Japan Price ¥000	$ Equiv.	U.S. Price ($)	Premium
CB 750	395	1411	2024	43%
CB 550	355	1268	1732	37%
CB 450	303	1082	1471	36%
CB 360	253	904	1150	26%
CB 350	275	982	1363	39%
MT 250	218	779	965	24%
MT 125	158	564	743	32%
CB 125	166	593	640	8%

Premium allowing for freight, duty and packing

CB 750, U.S. retail price 1975 = $2112
- Price to dealer — $1584 (75% of 2112)
- Price to distributor — $1373 (65%)
- Japan list price — ¥440,000 or $1517 (equivalent)
- Price to distributor — $986 (65%)
- Ocean freight to LA — 60
- Duty — 63 (3% U.S. Retail Price)
- Packaging costs — 40
  - $163

Thus, indicated price to U.S. distributor for equal manufacturer's margin to that on bikes sold in Japan
= $986 + 163
= $1149

Thus, premium in U.S.A. even after allowing for freight, duty and packing
= (1373/1149 − 1) × 100
= 20%

Note: The versions of the smaller bike models shipped to the States may be slightly more expensive than their Japanese equivalents (extra lighting, etc.). The versions of the larger bikes are, however, reported to be identical in both markets.

Competitive Strategy Implications

As we have discussed, failure to achieve a cost position – and hence cost reductions over time – equivalent to your competitors' will result in commercial vulnerability. At some point your competitors will start setting prices which you cannot match profitably, and losses will ensue. The strategic importance of the experience curve is that it explains clearly the two possible long-term causes of uncompetitive costs:

- Relative growth: failure to grow as rapidly as competitors, thereby progressing more slowly than them along the experience curve.
- Relative slopes: failure to bring costs down the characteristic experience curve slope achieved by competitors....

Summary

From the perspective of the writers of the BCG study, a fundamental cause for the Japanese success was their high productivity. The motorcycle industry was exhibiting the effects that differences in growth rates, volume, and level of capital investment among competitors can have on relative costs. The high rates of growth and levels of production achieved by the Japanese manufacturers resulted in their superior productivity. In terms of value added per employee, Honda outperformed Western competitors by as much as four times. Even the smaller Japanese competitors were able to outperform their Western counterparts by a factor of two or three.

The BCG report also countered the common argument that the relatively inexpensive Japanese labor was the primary source of competitive advantage. The Japanese competitors in fact had higher labor costs than companies in the West. Their relative high growth and scale caused total costs to drop quickly enough to support regular pay increases and price decreases at the same time.

Essentially the argument presented by BCG was that the Japanese emphasis on market share as the primary objective led to high production volume, improved productivity, low costs, and in the long term to higher profitability than their competitors.

CASE 4: Honda (B)

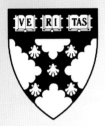

Sochiro Honda, an inventive genius with a legendary ego, founded the Honda Motor Co., Ltd., in 1948. His exploits have received wide coverage in the Japanese press. Known for his mercurial temperament and bouts of 'philandering,'[1] he is variously reported to have tossed a geisha out a second-story window,[2] climbed inside a septic tank to retrieve a visiting supplier's false teeth (and subsequently placed the teeth in his own mouth),[3] appeared inebriated and in costume before a formal presentation to Honda's bankers requesting financing vital to the firm's survival (the loan was denied),[4] hit a worker on the head with a wrench,[5] and stripped naked before his engineers to assemble a motorcycle engine.[6]

Company Background

Postwar Japan was in desperate need of transportation. Motorcycle manufacturers proliferated, producing clip-on engines that converted bicycles into makeshift 'mopeds.' Sochiro Honda was among these, but his prior experience as an automotive repairman provided neither the financial, managerial, nor technical basis for a viable enterprise.

Sochiro Honda viewed 'technology' as the vehicle through which Japanese society could be restored and the world made a better place in which to live. Reflecting the intensity of this commitment, he established the Honda Technical Research Institute in 1946. The term institute was somewhat misleading, since the organization was composed of himself and a few associates and had no practical means of support. Under this organizational umbrella, he began to tinker, and, as a means of livelihood, he purchased 500 war surplus engines and retrofitted them for bicycle use. Lacking marketing know-how, he entered into an exclusive arrangement with a distributor, who packaged a motorcycle conversion kit for bicycles. The Honda Motor Company was formed. Further tinkering led, in turn, to the introduction of the 'A-design' – a 2-stroke, 50cc engine. The engine had numerous defects, and sales did not materialize. Scraping by on occasional orders, the company lost money in 1947 and grossed $55,000 in 1948.

---

[1] Sakiya, Tetsuo. 'The Story of Honda's Founders,' *Asahi Evening News,* June 1–August 29, 1979, Series #2 and #3.

[2] Interviews with Honda executives, Tokyo, Japan, July 1980.

[3] Sakiya, Tetsuo. *Honda Motor: The Men, The Management, The Machines,* Kadonsha International. Tokyo, Japan, 1982, p 69; also Sakiya, 'Honda's Founders,' Series #4.

[4] Sakiya, 'Honda's Founders,' Series #7 and #8.

[5] Sakiya, *Honda Motor,* p. 72.

[6] Sakiya, 'Honda's Founders,' Series #2.

Dr. Richard T. Pascale of Stanford Graduate School of Business wrote this case with the collaboration of Professor E. Tatum Christiansen of Harvard Business School as the basis for class discussion rather than to illustrate either effective or ineffective handling of an administrative situation. It is based largely on internal Honda sources and interviews with founders of Honda Motor Co., Ltd., and the Japanese management team that founded Honda of America.

In 1949, Sochiro Honda turned to friends. Raising $3,800, he developed and introduced the 2-stroke, D-type engine. This engine, generating 3 hp, was more reliable than most on the market and enjoyed a brief spurt of popularity. Recruiting a work force of 70 employees, Honda produced engines one at a time and approached an annualized production rate of 100 units per month by the end of 1949.

Success was short-lived, however. Honda's exclusive distributor elected to artificially limit sales to 80 units per month in order to maintain high margins. Sochiro Honda was irate and vowed to avoid such dependencies in the future. In late 1949 he set out to raise additional financing but suffered a second setback when competitors leapfrogged the 2-stroke design and introduced quieter and more powerful 4-stroke engines.

A classic dilemma now faced the struggling enterprise. Honda's engine was obsolete, and his distribution system held him at ransom. Without additional financing he could not correct these deficiencies, and banks and investors did not regard him as a sound management risk.

In late 1949, an intermediary urged him to accept a partner – Takeo Fujisawa. Fujisawa was prepared to invest 2 million yen (about $7,500). More important, Fujisawa brought financial expertise and marketing strengths.

Despite Fujisawa's presence, the firm continued to falter. No further capital could be raised in 1950. Fujisawa pressed his partner to quit tinkering with his noisy 2-stroke engine and join the industry leaders with a 4-stroke design, since it was clear that competition had threatened Honda with extinction. At first too proud to accept this counsel, in 1951 he unexpectedly unveiled a breakthrough design that doubled horsepower over competitive 4-stroke engines. With this innovation, the firm was off and putting, and by 1952 demand was brisk.[7]

Honda's superior 4-stroke engine enabled Fujisawa to raise $88,000 in 1952. With these funds, Fujisawa committed to reduce dependency on suppliers and distributors by becoming a full-scale motorcycle manufacturer. To forestall technological obsolescence, he encouraged Honda to stay abreast of technological developments. He also sought more flexible channels of distribution. Unfortunately, Honda was a relatively late entrant; the best Fujisawa could do was to arrange for several distributors to carry Honda as a secondary line. He compensated for weak product positioning by going directly to the consumer with advertising.

In late 1952 a sewing machine plant was purchased and converted to a crude motorcycle factory. Neither partner had managerial or manufacturing experience, and there was no real plan other than to work as long as necessary each day to keep up with orders. Honda's more powerful engine and superior stamped motorcycle frame created considerable interest, and demand remained strong. Employment leaped from 150 in 1951 to 1,337 by the end of 1952. Honda integrated into the production of chains, sprockets, and motorcycle frames. Altogether, these factors greatly complicated the management task. There were no standardized drawings, procedures, or tools. For several years the plant was, in effect, a collection of semi-independent 'activities' sharing the same roof. Nonetheless, by the beginning of 1959 Honda had become a significant participant in the industry, with 23% market share (see *Exhibit 1*).

Honda's successful 4-stroke engine eased the pressures on Fujisawa by increasing sales and providing easier access to financing. For Sochiro Honda, the higher-horsepower engine opened the possibility of pursuing one of his central ambitions in life: to build and to race a high-performance, special-purpose motorcycle – and win. Winning provided the ultimate confirmation of his design abilities. Racing success in Japan came quickly. As a result, in 1959 he raised his sights to the international arena and committed the firm to winning at Great Britain's Isle of Man – the 'Olympics' of motorcycle racing.[8] Again, Honda's inventive genius was called into play. Shifting most of the firm's resources into this racing effort, he embarked on studies of combustion that resulted in a new configuration of the combustion chamber, which doubled horsepower and halved weight. Honda leapfrogged past European and American competitors – winning in one class, then another, winning the Isle of Man manufacturer's prize in 1959, and sweeping the first five positions by 1961.[9]

---

[7] Sakiya, *Honda Motor,* pp. 71 – 72.

[8] Sakiya, 'Honda's Founders,' Series #11.

[9] Ibid.

Exhibit 1 Motorcycle Production in Japan by Japanese Makers

Calendar Year	Honda	Yamaha	Suzuki	Kawasaki	Other	Total
1950	531	–	–	–	6,960	7,491
1951	2,380	–	–	–	21,773	24,153
1952	9,659	–	–	–	69,586	79,245
1953	29,797	–	–	–	131,632	161,429
1954	30,344	–	–	200	133,929	164,473
1955	42,557	2,272	9,079	–	205,487	259,395
1956	55,031	8,743	18,444	5,083	245,459	332,760
1957	77,509	15,811	29,132	6,793	280,819	410,064
1958	117,375	27,184	66,363	7,018	283,392	501,332
1959	285,218	63,657	95,862	10,104	425,788	880,629
1960	649,243	138,153	155,445	9,261	520,982	1,473,084
1961	935,859	129,079	186,392	22,038	531,003	1,804,371
1962	1,009,787	117,908	173,121	31,718	342,391	1,674,925
1963	1,224,695	167,370	271,438	34,954	229,513	1,927,970
1964	1,353,594	221,655	373,871	33,040	128,175	2,110,335
1965	1,465,762	244,058	341,367	48,745	112,852	2,212,784
1966	1,422,949	389,756	448,128	67,959	118,599	2,447,391
1967	1,276,226	406,579	402,438	79,194	77,410	2,241,847
1968	1,349,896	423,039	365,330	78,124	34,946	2,251,335
1969	1,534,882	519,710	398,784	102,406	21,091	2,576,873
1970	1,795,828	574,100	407,538	149,480	20,726	2,947,672
1971	1,927,186	750,510	491,064	208,904	22,838	3,400,502
1972	1,873,893	853,317	594,922	218,058	25,056	3,565,246
1973	1,835,527	1,012,810	641,779	250,099	22,912	3,763,127
1974	2,132,902	1,164,886	839,741	354,615	17,276	4,509,420
1975	1,782,448	1,030,541	686,666	274,022	28,870	3,802,547
1976	1,928,576	1,169,175	831,941	284,478	20,942	4,235,112
1977	2,378,867	1,824,152	1,031,753	335,112	7,475	5,577,359
1978	2,639,588	1,887,311	1,144,488	326,317	2,225	5,999,929
1979	2,437,057	1,653,891	1,100,778	308,191	79	5,499,996
1980	3,087,471	2,241,959	1,551,127	521,846	–	7,402,403
1981	3,587,957	2,792,817	1,764,120	521,333	–	8,666,227

Source: Japan Automobile Manufacturers Association, Inc.
Note: KD sets and scooters are included.

Throughout the 1950s, Fujisawa sought to turn his partner's attention from enthusiasm with racing to the more mundane requirements of running an enterprise. By 1956, as the innovations gained from racing had begun to pay off in vastly more efficient engines, Fujisawa pressed Honda to adapt this technology for a commercial motorcycle.[10] He had a particular segment in mind. Most motorcyclists in Japan were male, and the machines were used primarily as an alternative form of transportation to trains and buses. However, a vast number of small commercial establishments in Japan still delivered goods and ran errands on bicycles. Trains and buses were inconvenient for these activities. The purse strings of these small enterprises were controlled by the Japanese wife – who resisted buying conventional motorcycles because they were expensive, dangerous, and hard to handle. Fujisawa challenged his partner: Can you use what you've learned from racing to come up with an inexpensive, safe-looking motorcycle that can be driven with one hand (to enable carrying packages)?[11]

The First Breakthrough

In 1958 the Honda 50cc Supercub was introduced – with an automatic clutch, 3-speed transmission, automatic starter, and the safe, friendly look of a bicycle (without the stigma of the outmoded mopeds). As a rule of thumb, a 50cc engine is 50% cheaper to make than a 100cc engine. Achieving high horse-power with a small engine thereby reaps automatic cost savings – making the new bike affordable. Innovative design provided a cost advantage without requiring Honda to manufacture more efficiently than its competitors. (This was fortunate since the firm, having expanded into three plants in the 1950s, had still not achieved a well-integrated production process.)

Overnight, Honda was overwhelmed with Supercub orders. Demand was met through makeshift, high-cost, company-owned assembly and farmed-out assembly through subcontractors.[12] By the end of 1959 Honda had skyrocketed into first place among Japanese motorcycle manufacturers. Of its total sales that year of 285,000 units, 168,000 were Supercubs.[13] The time seemed appropriate to build an automated plant with a 30,000-unit-per-month capacity. 'It wasn't a speculative investment,' recalls one executive. 'We had the proprietary technology, we had the market, and the demand was enormous.'[14] The plant was completed in mid-1960.

Distribution Channels

Fujisawa utilized the Supercub to restructure Honda's channels of distribution. For many years, Honda had rankled under the two-tier distribution system that prevailed in the industry. As noted earlier, these problems had been exacerbated by Honda's being carried as a secondary line by distributors whose loyalties lay with older, established manufacturers. Further weakening Honda's leverage, all manufacturer sales were on a consignment basis.

Fujisawa had characterized the Supercub to Honda's distributors as 'something much more like a bicycle than a motorcycle.' The traditional channels, to their later regret, agreed. Under amicable terms, Fujisawa began selling the Supercub directly to retailers – and primarily through bicycle shops. Since these shops were small and numerous (approximately 12,000 in Japan), sales on consignment were unthinkable. A cash-on-delivery system was installed – giving Honda significantly more leverage over its dealerships than the other motorcycle manufacturers enjoyed.[15]

---

[10] Ibid., Series #13; also Sakiya, *Honda Motor,* p. 117.

[11] Sakiya, 'Honda's Founders,' Series #11.

[12] Pascale, Richard T., Interviews with Honda executives, Tokyo, Japan, September 10, 1982.

[13] Data provided by Honda Motor Company.

[14] Pascale interviews.

[15] Ibid.

Honda Enters U.S. Market

Sochiro Honda's racing conquests in the late 1950s had given substance to his convictions about his abilities. Success fueled his appetite for new and different challenges. Explosive sales of the Supercub in Japan provided the financial base for new quests. The stage was now set for the exploration of the U.S. market.

From the Japanese vantage point, the American market was vast, untapped, and affluent. 'We turned toward the United States by a process of deduction,' states one executive. 'Our experiments with local Southeast Asian markets in 1957 and 1958 had little success. With little disposable income and poor roads, total Asian exports had reached a meager 1,000 units in 1958.[16] The European market, while larger, was heavily dominated by its own name-brand manufacturers, and the popular mopeds dominated the low-price, low-horsepower end.'

Two Honda executives – the designated president of American Honda Motor Company, Kihachiro Kawashima, and his assistant – arrived in the United States in late 1958. Their itinerary: San Francisco, Los Angeles, Dallas, New York, and Columbus. Kihachiro Kawashima recounts his impressions:[17]

My first reaction after traveling across the United States was 'How could we have been so stupid to start a war with such a vast and wealthy country!' My second reaction was discomfort. I spoke poor English. We dropped in on motorcycle dealers who treated us discourteously and, in addition, gave the general impression of being motorcycle enthusiasts who, secondarily, were in business. There were only 3,000 motorcycle dealers in the United States at the time, and only 1,000 of them were open five days a week. The remainder were open on nights and on weekends. Inventory was poor, manufacturers sold motorcycles to dealers on consignment, the retailers provided consumer financing, and after-sale service was poor. It was discouraging.

My other impression was that everyone in the United States drove an automobile – making it doubtful that motorcycles could ever do very well in the market. However, with 450,000 motorcycle registrations in the United States and 60,000 motorcycles imported from Europe each year it didn't seem unreasonable to shoot for 10% of the import market. I returned to Japan with that report.

In truth, we had no strategy other than the idea of seeing if we could sell something in the United States. It was a new frontier, a new challenge, and it fit the 'success against all odds' culture that Mr Honda had cultivated: I reported my impressions to Fujisawa – including the seat-of-the-pants target of trying, over several years, to attain a 10% share of the U.S. imports. He didn't probe that target quantitatively. We did not discuss profits or deadlines for breakeven. Fujisawa told me if anyone could succeed, I could, and authorized $1 million for the venture.

The next hurdle was to obtain a currency allocation from the Ministry of Finance. They were extraordinarily skeptical. Toyota had launched the Toyopet in the United States in 1958 and had failed miserably. 'How could Honda succeed?' they asked. Months went by. We put the project on hold. Suddenly, five months after our application, we were given the go-ahead – but at only a fraction of our expected level of commitment. 'You can invest $250,000 in the U.S. market,' they said, 'but only $110,000 in cash.' The remainder of our assets had to be in parts and motorcycle inventory.

We moved into frantic activity as the government, hoping we would give up on the idea, continued to hold us to the July 1959 start-up timetable. Our focus, as mentioned earlier, was to compete with the European exports. We knew our products at the time were good, but not far superior. Mr. Honda was especially confident of the 250cc and the 305cc machines. The shape of the handlebar on

---

[16] Ibid.

[17] Ibid.

these larger machines looked like the eyebrow of Buddha, which he felt was a strong selling point. Thus, after some discussion and with no compelling criteria for selection, we configured our start-up inventory with 25% of each of our four products – the 50cc Supercub and the 125cc, 250cc, and 305cc machines. In dollar-value terms, of course, the inventory was heavily weighted toward the larger bikes.

The stringent monetary controls of the Japanese government together with the unfriendly reception we had received during our 1958 visit caused us to start small. We chose Los Angeles where there was a large second- and third-generation Japanese community, a climate suitable for motorcycle use, and a growing population. We were so strapped for cash that the three of us shared a furnished apartment that rented for $80 per month. Two of us slept on the floor. We obtained a warehouse in a run-down section of the city and waited for the ship to arrive. Not daring to spare our funds for equipment, the three of us stacked the motorcycle crates three-high, by hand; swept the floor; and built and maintained the parts bin.

We were entirely in the dark the first year. We were not aware that the motorcycle business in the United States occurs during a seasonable April-to-August window – and that our timing coincided with the closing of the 1959 season. Our hard-learned experiences with distributorship in Japan convinced us to try to go to the retailers direct. We ran ads in the motorcycle trade magazine for dealers. A few responded. By spring 1960, we had 40 dealers and some of our inventory in their stores – mostly larger bikes. A few of the 250cc and 305cc bikes began to sell. Then disaster struck.

By the first week of April 1960, reports were coming in that our machines were leaking oil and encountering clutch failure. This was our lowest moment. Honda's fragile reputation was being destroyed before it could be established. As it turned out, motorcycles in the United States are driven much farther and much faster than in Japan. We dug deeply into our precious cash reserves to air freight our motorcycles to the Honda testing lab in Japan. Throughout the dark month of April, Pan Am was the only enterprise in the United States that was nice to us. Our testing lab worked 24-hour days bench testing the bikes to try to replicate the failure. Within a month, a redesigned head gasket and clutch spring solved the problem. In the meantime, events had taken a surprising turn.

Throughout our first eight months, following Mr Honda's and our own instincts, we had not attempted to move the 50cc Supercubs. While they were a smash success in Japan (and manufacturing couldn't keep up with demand there), they seemed wholly unsuitable for the U.S. market where everything was bigger and more luxurious. As a clincher, we had our sights on the import market – and the Europeans, like the American manufacturers, emphasized the larger machines.

We used the Honda 50s ourselves to ride around Los Angeles on errands. They attracted a lot of attention. One day we had a call from a Sears buyer. While persisting in our refusal to sell through an intermediary, we took note of Sears's interest. But we still hesitated to push the 50cc bikes out of fear they might harm our image in a heavily macho market. But when the larger bikes started breaking, we had no choice. We let the 50cc bikes move. And surprisingly, the retailers who wanted to sell them weren't motorcycle dealers; they were sporting goods stores.

The excitement created by Honda Supercub began to gain momentum. Under restrictions from the Japanese government, we were still on a cash basis. Working with our initial cash and inventory, we sold machines, reinvested in inventory, and sunk the profits into additional inventory and advertising. Our advertising tried to straddle the market. While retailers continued to inform us that our Supercub customers were normal everyday Americans, we hesitated to target toward this segment out of fear of alienating the high-margin end of our business – sold through the traditional motorcycle dealers to a more traditional 'black leather jacket' customer.

Exhibit 2 Honda's Financial Performance and U.S. Motorcycle Sales

Calendar Year	Gross Sales (million yen)	Honda U.S. Motorcycle Sales (units)	Outside Financing (million yen)	Employees
1948	14.3	–	1	20
1949	34.6	–	2	70
1950	82.8	–	–	90
1951	330.3	–	–	150
1952	2,438	–	15	1,337
1953	7,729	–	60	2,185
1954	5,979	–	–	2,494
1955	5,525	–	120	2,459
1956	7,882	–	–	2,377
1957	9,786	–	360	2,438
1958	14,188	–	720	2,705
1959	26,165	–	1,440	3,355
1960	49,128	1,315	4,320	4,053
1961	57,912	6,052	8,640	5,406
1962	64,552	27,840	9,090	5,798
1963	83,206	65,869	–	6,816
1964	97,936	110,470	–	7,696
1965	123,746	227,308	–	8,481
1966	106,845	272,900	–	9,069
1967	141,179	181,200	–	11,283
1968	193,871	174,706	18,180	13,165
1969	244,895	272,600	–	16,614
1970	316,331	441,200	–	17,511
1971	332,931	656,800	–	18,079
1972	327,702	707,800	–	18,297
1973	366,777	556,300	19,480	18,287
1974	519,897	628,500	24,350	18,455
1975	563,805	343,900	–	18,505
1976	668,677	444,624	25,500	19,069
1977	849,635	439,822	29,600	19,968
1978	922,280	401,114	–	21,316

Note: Above figures are related solely to Honda Motor Co.. Ltd., and are not consolidated with those of its subsidiaries.

An Advertising Twist

As late as 1963, Honda was still working with its original Los Angeles advertising agency, its ad campaigns straddling all customers so as not to antagonize one market in pursuit of another.

In the spring of 1963, while fulfilling a routine class assignment, an undergraduate advertising major at UCLA submitted an ad campaign for Honda. Its theme was 'You Meet the Nicest People On a Honda.' Encouraged by his instructor, the student passed his work on to a friend at Grey Advertising. Grey had been soliciting the Honda account – which, with a $5-million-a-year budget, was becoming an attractive potential client. Grey purchased the student's idea – on a tightly kept nondisclosure basis. Grey attempted to sell the idea to Honda.[18]

Interestingly, the Honda management team, which by 1963 had grown to five Japanese executives, was badly split on this advertising decision. The president and treasurer favored another proposal from another agency. The director of sales, however, felt strongly that the Nicest People campaign was the right one – and his commitment eventually held sway. Thus, in 1963, Honda adopted a strategy that directly identified and targeted that large, untapped segment of the marketplace that was to become inseparable from the Honda legend.[19]

The Nicest People campaign drove Honda's U.S. sales at an even greater rate. By 1964 nearly one out of every two motorcycles sold was a Honda. As a result of the influx of medium-income leisure-class consumers, banks and other consumer credit companies began to finance motorcycles – shifting away from dealer credit, which had been the traditional purchasing mechanism available. Honda, seizing the opportunity of soaring demand for its products, took a courageous and seemingly risky position. Late in 1964 it announced that thereafter, it would cease to ship on a consignment basis but would require cash on delivery. Honda braced itself for a revolt that never materialized. While nearly every dealer questioned, appealed, or complained, none relinquished the Honda franchise. In one fell swoop, Honda shifted the power relationship from the dealer to the manufacturer. Within three years, C.O.D. sales would become the pattern for the industry.[20]

Honda's growth on several dimensions is shown in *Exhibit 2*. Automobiles were introduced into the product line in 1963, shifting resources and management attention heavily in that direction in the ensuing years.

25 Years Later

In late 1972, anticipating the company's twenty-fifth anniversary, Fujisawa, 62, raised the issue of retirement. 'We are strong dominating individuals,' he said. 'I must step aside and let the younger men lead our company.' Sochiro Honda, 66, also conceded to retire. In September 1973, the two stepped down. States one source: 'Fujisawa retired early to provide Mr. Honda with an opportunity to retire, also. It is a reflection of Fujisawa's genuine personal friendship with Mr Honda.'[21]

[18] Ibid.
[19] Ibid.
[20] Ibid.
[21] Sakiya, Tetsuo. 'The Story of Honda's Founders,' *Asahi Evening News,* August 29, 1979.

CASE 5: The Low-Cost Airlines Industry in Europe 2007

1 Background

1.1 Early Airline History

The world's first passenger airline, DELAG, flying Zeppelin airships, was formed in Frankfurt Germany in 1909. The airline industry really got underway in Europe after the development of military air transport during World War One. Being a new era, industry firsts were being recorded all the time. For example on 25th August 1919 the world's first 'civil international scheduled airline passenger' was carried, in a converted de Havilland 4A WWI bomber, on the daily two-hour London to Paris flight.

An early indication of the financial turbulence associated with airline industry was in the early 1920s. By February 1921 all UK airlines had stopped international, i.e. cross-Channel, services due to financial difficulties caused by subsidised foreign services. Faced with this stoppage the UK government started giving airlines financial support. Finally the government decided to set up a single UK international airline by the forced merger of four airlines and in April 1924 Imperial Airways was formed. Imperial was the first flag-carrier. Imperial was to develop UK commercial air transport in the empire; maintaining

Philip Winters prepared this case under the supervision of Professor John McGee as a basis for class discussion rather than to illustrate either effective or ineffective handling of a business situation. This case study is based on an earlier case study prepared by Andrew Hodge at Warwick Business School.

air routes, pioneered by the RAF, to the colonies. After the start of World War Two Imperial was nationalised to form part of the war effort and after the war it became part of British Overseas Airways Corporation.

1.2 Regulation and Deregulation

The airline industry has always been subject to assorted regulation within countries and by treaties between countries, or airline/country agreements. A primary area of regulation was to establish which airlines could fly on which routes and the fare scheme, to be imposed.

In 1940 in the United States, the Civil Aeronautics Board (CAB) was set up to promote and develop the airline industry, allied with economic and other legal powers; the US had similarly regulated the railways in the 1880s after years of competition issues.

The CAB would use its power to decide who could enter and exit markets, and any route subsidies, plus regulate the fares charged. It typically allowed only one or two airlines to fly a particular route. A symbiotic relationship existed between the airlines and regulator, customers' priorities not taking precedence. As airline costs rose the CAB allowed fares to rise. The airlines' only real form of competition took the form of the level of customer service. During the 1960s the consumers who could afford to fly were labelled the 'jet set', i.e. rich people. Due to the regulation the airlines industry operated under, airline costs and fares were high. The airlines didn't particularly consider cost efficiency, which would turn into a problem many years later.

In 1958 the CAB's legal remit changed; it continued economic regulation of airlines that flew across state lines, however airlines that only flew within a state were not economically regulated, good news if someone wanted to offer low fares. The real seismic shift in the US airline industry happened with the 1978 Airline Deregulation Act, and 1980 Air Transportation Competition Act. The 1978 Act phased out the CAB's economic regulation of the airlines. However the infrastructure, airports and air traffic control were still regulated.[1] By late 1984 the CAB had ceased operation, its non-economic regulatory powers being passed to other bodies.

With deregulation the US domestic airlines market would be subject to market forces; regulators would not determine route entry and price competition. By 1982 the environment for dynamic airline competition existed, and since deregulation fares have fallen by half in real terms.[2]

The major airlines had fought against deregulation; they now found themselves in the position of having businesses with high cost structures that included expensive labour with uneconomic planes and infrastructure. Among the assumptions behind regulation had been that demand for air travel was inelastic, i.e. insensitive to price change.

The UK government moved towards domestic deregulation and bilateral deregulation with some EU states in 1984. Ireland and the UK bilaterally deregulated in 1986 and in 1987 the UK government privatised British Airways (BA).

Deregulation in the EU domestic airline market occurred with three legislation packages in 1987, 1990 and 1992. With the 1992 package, coming into force in January 1993, airlines had the freedom to set air fares. Deregulation was completed by 1997, with freestanding cabotage, when airlines from one EU state could operate scheduled domestic flights within another EU state.[3] EU deregulation now also applies to various degrees in Iceland, Norway, Liechtenstein and Switzerland.

Deregulation triggered the rise of low-cost airline industries in the US and EU, and the demise of more than a few of the traditional full-service airlines. The low-cost airline industry founder is credited to Southwest Airlines with their low-cost strategy and policy of low fares.

As of today there are more islands of deregulation, also called liberalisation, with Australia, the Middle and Far East deregulating to various degrees.

---

[1] Airline Deregulation: The Unfinished Revolution; Robert W. Poole, Jr. and Viggo Butler Mar 1999.
[2] The Economist (London): In the land of free flight; Jun 16, 2007. Vol.383, Iss. 8533; p6.
[3] Boeing website; The Economic Impact of Air Service Liberalization; 2006.

From late March 2008 the US–EU 'open skies' bilateral agreement comes into force. Open skies allows any US airline to fly into any EU airport and from there, anywhere within the EU or on to anywhere in the rest of the world. EU carriers do not get onward access after landing in the US, denying them access to the US domestic market. Before open-skies London Heathrow was the primary gateway into Europe from the US. Also the agreement allows US and EU airlines to buy into each other; however the US has ensured that US airline boards are controlled by US nationals.

1.3 Airline Terminology

The low-cost airlines are also called low cost carriers (LCC), budget airlines, or no-frills carriers. The legacy airlines are the traditional full-service carriers that operated prior to deregulation. The network airlines, national airlines and flag-carriers also belong to the legacy airline group.

Low-cost does not necessarily translate into low-fares, as fares tend to rise the closer to departure date; airlines use yield management systems which use 'price discrimination' to set fares (see appendix 6). The low-cost airlines activities feature: ticket-less travel; sales primarily forced over the internet; only one fare is available at one time; they earn additional revenue by selling travel related services over the internet; minimal infrastructure (offices etc.); no frequent flyer programmes; no free food or drink; no in-flight magazines; no airport lounges; no pre-assigned seating; flying to less popular secondary or regional airports often further from the city than the principal airport; no transfer or network services; sell single non-return tickets; tickets non-refundable; flights under two hours; stand-alone operations; and no cargo.

Another low-cost airlines signature is that they operate in the short-haul, i.e. within Europe, market flying either the Boeing 737 or Airbus A320 family of aircraft (see appendix 10). The regional airlines are a variant of the low-cost airline, e.g. Flybe. They fly smaller, capacity under 100 seats, regional jets (RJ). The regional airlines can function over 'thin' routes where passenger traffic would not support the standard low-cost airlines.

In order to operate from a busy airport an airline has to acquire 'slots'. These are the rights to land and take-off at a particular time. Slots are 'grandfathered' to the incumbent user. At primary airports such as Heathrow these slots are difficult to obtain as the airport is operating at near capacity, hence the knock-on problems with processing passengers at the airport. Depending on how busy the airports are, secondary and regional airports do not necessarily operate with landing and take-off slots. Secondary airports are the less attractive airports that serve the city of the primary airport, e.g. for London the primary airport is Heathrow and the secondary airports are Stansted and Gatwick.

'Hub' airports are where network airline passengers are concentrated in order to fill connecting flights to other hub airports, and then on to their final destination. The hub's destinations can be seen as the spokes of a wheel, hence the hub-and-spoke system. Primary airports are attractive to the lucrative business traveller market. The network airlines tend to dominate the hub airport and hence exclude the competition. The low-cost airlines tend to fly point-to-point networks flying directly to the passenger's final destination airport.

Codesharing agreements are primarily legacy airline alliances that allow airlines to expand networks without adding new services. The partnership allows an airline to sell tickets under its own name for travel that occurs within both partners' networks.

A common term used in evaluating an airlines performance is load factor. The primary one is the passenger load factor, how full the airlines flights are. Passenger load factor is RPK divided by ASK (as %); RPK 'revenue passenger kilometres' is the number of revenue passengers carried, multiplied by the distance flown; ASK 'available seat kilometres' is the number of seats available for sale, multiplied by the distance flown. The annual ASK figure is also used as a statistic for comparing airline performance and capacity, although the statistic may not be as transparent as it seems when it comes to comparing airlines.

2 The Low-Cost Airline Industry

2.1 Industry Characteristics

The aviation supply chain is made up of the aircraft manufacturers; aircraft leasing companies; airports; airlines; computer reservation system companies; travel agents; cargo companies and aviation services inc. catering, aircraft maintenance, ground handling and fuelling.

> 'Air transport is critical to the global economy. Airlines are the US$450 billion heart of a value chain. That supports US$2.9 trillion in economic activity. In Europe this brings employment to 7 million. And adds US$1 trillion to the European GDP.'
>
> Giovanni Bisignani, Director General & CEO IATA; 28 September 2006

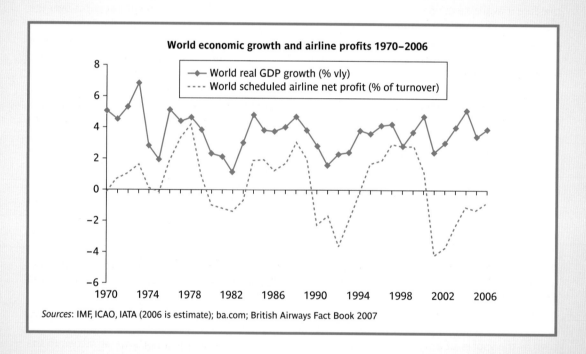

World economic growth and airline profits 1970–2006

Legend:
- World real GDP growth (% vly)
- World scheduled airline net profit (% of turnover)

Sources: IMF, ICAO, IATA (2006 is estimate); ba.com; British Airways Fact Book 2007

Economic activity and increasing wealth are the main drivers of increased demand for air travel. However substantial portions of consumer spend on airline travel is discretionary, accounting for consumer spending effects on airline industry profits.

Recession

Passenger demand for the airlines is notoriously cyclical. There are the normal seasonal swings in the number of passengers carried, and then there is the economic cycle effect to overlay onto passenger numbers. Passenger numbers can also suddenly fluctuate with world events such as disease, e.g. bird-flu; terrorism, e.g. 9/11 or politics, e.g. conflicts in the Middle East. In the early 2000s all the above negative influences were visited on the airline industry together with the rise of the low-cost airlines.

The recession after 2001, plus the events of 9/11, triggered cost cutting in the worldwide airline industry. In Europe several legacy airlines got into financial difficulties; Swissair failed in late 2001, became Swiss, which was taken over by Lufthansa in 2005; Sabena failed in November 2001; KLM was taken over by Air France in 2004.

The recession forced the legacy airlines to face up to the need for long-overdue change, individual airlines not wanting to be the one who blinks first and cuts capacity. The airlines embarked on programmes of severe cost cutting, productivity improvements, operational changes, and fleet and route rationalisation, as they struggled to survive in adverse conditions. While doing this they faced the strong short-haul competition from the low-cost carriers. The major low-cost airlines coped very well financially during the 2001–2005 economic downturn in the airline industry. By getting the cost and productivity equation right a low-cost airline can remain profitable while competitors get into financial trouble – the low-cost strategy gaining from simple organization, product design and service delivery. By April 2007 IATA reported that the low-cost sector represented 13% of global operations by ASK.

The new dilemma for the industry is what should the strategy be to deal with the record rises in the cost of fuel and the likelihood that higher prices are here to stay. All the airlines are moving to more fuel efficient aircraft with some adding winglets to reduce fuel consumption.

Structure

The industry is labour intensive with high fixed costs, i.e. wages and aircraft capital/lease costs, and low profit margins. It is also highly regulated and has to meet regulations on such things as security, aircraft noise and maximum total duty times for aircraft crew.

The low-cost airlines work their assets hard; for instance BA's pilots typically fly fewer hours than their low-cost peers. Captains are legally limited to 900 hours a year. Captains on low-cost airlines normally get near this limit. Captains at BA typically clock up between 600 and 650 hours a year.[4]

On the more mundane side of the industry: extreme weather is a problem for airlines, for example fog at Heathrow airport in December 2006 grounded flights for several days. After weather or even strike events it takes airlines days to resume normal services because crews and aircraft are in the wrong places. Also airlines have to deal with the daily delays attributed to air-traffic control; due to the increasing volume of traffic the bandwidth cannot cope.

Passenger traffic

Not all passengers who fly with low-cost airlines have defected from legacy airlines. Rather, low fares and factoring in time savings and other utility factors encourage people to fly when they would otherwise have gone by road, sea, rail, or not even travelled. Ryanair initially tapped into this latent demand for travel in Ireland, with a population that was accustomed to travelling abroad.

The charter airline companies, with their consumers shifting away from package holidays to self-booked holidays, have ready-made infrastructures to convert from charter-airline companies into low-cost airline hybrids, e.g. MyTravel Lite, Thomson Fly, Monarch and Air Berlin.

In 2004, it was estimated, there were 54[5] European airlines offering versions of the low-cost formula; compare that to the flag-carriers that ran to about one airline per European country.

During 2006 the low-cost airlines had the following shares of the airline industry:

2006	Total flights	Total available seats	Low-cost share of flights	Low-cost share of seats
Within Europe	6,606,508	752,950,569	17%	24%
Within US	9,730,962	899,427,282	18%	27%
Source: OAG				

---

[4] Daily Telegraph; Walsh is losing any goodwill he had; 20 Jan 2007.

[5] The Times; European dogfight for budget airlines; 9 May 2004.

The European low-cost airlines' share of seats during summer 2006 is split as follows:[6]

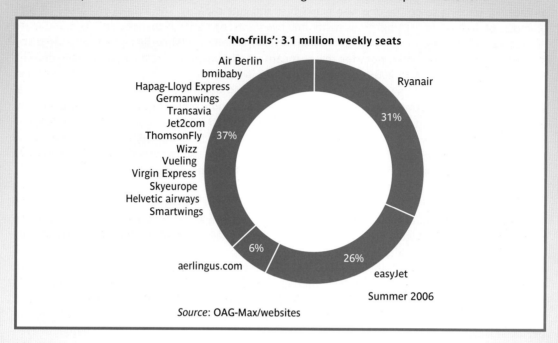

'No-frills': 3.1 million weekly seats

Air Berlin
bmibaby
Hapag-Lloyd Express
Germanwings
Transavia
Jet2com
ThomsonFly
Wizz
Vueling
Virgin Express
Skyeurope
Helvetic airways
Smartwings

Ryanair 31%

37%

6%

26%

aerlingus.com

easyJet

Summer 2006

Source: OAG-Max/websites

The RPK growth rate is set to grow from 4.8%, for 1986–2006, to 5% to 2026:

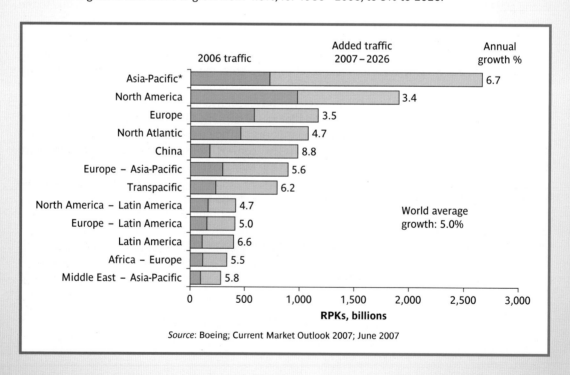

	2006 traffic	Added traffic 2007–2026	Annual growth %
Asia-Pacific*			6.7
North America			3.4
Europe			3.5
North Atlantic			4.7
China			8.8
Europe – Asia-Pacific			5.6
Transpacific			6.2
North America – Latin America			4.7
Europe – Latin America			5.0
Latin America			6.6
Africa – Europe			5.5
Middle East – Asia-Pacific			5.8

World average growth: 5.0%

RPKs, billions (0, 500, 1,000, 1,500, 2,000, 2,500, 3,000)

Source: Boeing; Current Market Outlook 2007; June 2007

[6] AEA (Association of European Airlines) Yearbook 2006; p10.

2.2 Southwest Airlines: the Low-Cost Benchmark

Southwest was born in the pre-internet age. Southwest's first customer flight was in June 1971. Using three Boeing 737s it served three Texas cities, the 'Texas Triangle' destinations. By only flying within Texas Southwest was able to offer unregulated low fares, outside the remit of the CAB. Low-fare airlines also operated within California. Southwest's philosophy has always been low fares, keeping costs low so that flying could be affordable instead of a luxury for the few.

Deregulation allowed Southwest to fly across state lines and continue charging low fares. In 1979 with deregulation, American Airlines moved its HQ from New York to the newly built primary airport at Dallas/Fort Worth, where it controls 80% of the gates, with Southwest staying at its home base in downtown Dallas at the (now) secondary airport Love Field.[7] Southwest pioneered the low-cost airline activity model (see appendix 3) which became the basis for the rise of low-cost airline industry around the world.

In 2003 for the first time in aviation history the low-cost airline Southwest became market leader. By December 2006 Southwest posted its 34th consecutive year of profits (see appendix 1). The success of Southwest is also creating a new breed of low-cost airlines that varies the characteristics of the low-cost activity model such as adding superior in-flight service.

Now the legacy airline industry has restructured to reduce its cost difference relative to Southwest, Southwest is having to look to increase its revenues to maintain profits. CEO Gary Kelly has indicated that Southwest is looking at international flights, and the airline is considering assigned seating as part of trying to encourage the more demanding business traveller.[8]

The key attributes of Southwest's success

Southwest was the first airline to consider going back-to-basics with air-travel. It determined that a basic product offering could strip away unnecessary operating expenses. First to be discarded was the assignment of seats and the provision of in-flight meals. Not only did this save on catering and cleaning costs, but it also allowed for an alternative cabin configuration that eliminated the on-board galley, thus freeing up space for more seats to generate more revenue.

Southwest offers a low-fare, high-frequency, point-to-point no-frills service that is in marked contrast to the established market offering from the US legacy carriers who provide a hub-based network, meaning that customers will often stop and wait at an intermediate point in order to reach their destination, which incurs greater costs and results in higher fares for passengers. In the US the low-cost airlines now account for 27% of all domestic passenger seats.

Operational efficiency is achieved via the utilisation of a single aircraft type: Southwest fixed on the Boeing 737. This simplifies scheduling and flight operations, reduces maintenance cost by decreasing spare parts inventory and rationalizes training of both engineers and crew. Another critical benefit of operating a single aircraft type is the potential to negotiate favourable terms with the aircraft manufacturer. Moreover, Southwest quickly realised that aircraft make no money when they are sitting on the ground, so it pioneered the concept of a quick turnaround. By using less congested secondary airports the average amount of time spent at the gate is 25 minutes. For an industry characterized by high fixed cost, high asset utilization is the key to success; by reducing the time aircraft spend on the ground Southwest is able to offer more services with fewer aircraft. Southwest's fleet are in the air for an average of 11 hours 34 minutes a day, more than any other major airline.[9]

Further efficiency is achieved through employee productivity, employees performing multiple roles. The US airline industry has a long history of having poor labour relations. However, Southwest's employees are considered an integral part of its success; the pilots fly 80 hours per month in comparison to 50 hours at United Airlines whilst flight attendants work 150 hours per month compared to

---

[7] In 1979 the Wright Amendment was passed which limited (Southwest) flight operations from Love Field.

[8] Wall Street Journal; As Competition Rebounds, Southwest Faces Squeeze; 27 Jun 2007.

[9] Southwest Annual Report 2006.

80 hours at many rival airlines. Herb Kelleher, Southwest's charismatic founder, is quoted as saying 'We are not a company of planes; we are company of people'.[10]

Employee productivity has been achieved without sacrificing service to customers. The unique culture instilled by Herb Kelleher has had a large part to play in the employee and customer relations. 'If the employees are happy, satisfied, dedicated, and energetic, they'll take good care of the customers.' 'When the customers are happy, they come back. And that makes the shareholders happy.'[11]

Another key facet of Southwest's business strategy is to operate from less congested secondary airports, thus facilitating quick aircraft turnaround times. Southwest targets airports with large consumer markets, which are underserved by competitors in terms of flight frequency or high fares. Choosing to compete in these markets attacks the markets of the legacy carriers. Consequently it is common for fares to drop by much as 70% when Southwest enters the market.

Over time the differentials in cost structures between legacy and low-cost airlines have significantly diminished. This has led to more intense competition in the airline industry. The re-emerging legacy airline competitiveness has put pressure on low-cost airlines. However Southwest has continued to maintain its cost advantage, improve employee productivity and pursue growth[12] though Southwest didn't renegotiate its labour contracts during the recent downturn and its labour cost advantage has narrowed. Southwest is still the largest domestic internal passenger carrier in the US.

Southwest introduced limited codesharing in 2005. Southwest has a frequent flyer programme based on trips flown and the use of Southwest partners products, e.g. car rentals, hotels, phones and credit cards. The amount of free travel in 2006 was 6.4% of revenue passengers carried.

The rising cost of fuel is the bête noire of the airline industry becoming a major cost element in their operations. Fuel replaced labour as the largest single cost item for the US airline industry in 2006. Southwest's average cost of jet fuel, net of hedging gains and excluding taxes, was:

Year	Jet Fuel Cost (millions)	Average Cost per US Gallon	% of Operating Expenses
2002	$762	$0.68	14.7%
2003	$830	$0.72	14.9%
2004	$1,000	$0.83	16.3%
2005	$1,341	$1.03	19.6%
2006	$2,138	$1.53	26.2%
Source: Southwest Annual Report 2006			

In six of the 16 fiscal quarters since April 2003, Southwest would have reported operating losses if it weren't for hedging. Without hedging Southwest would have recorded an $85 million full-year operating loss in 2005.[13] Southwest began its fuel hedging strategies in 2003, to protect against the risk of rising fuel costs. See Appendix 1 for details of Southwest's future hedging; in forward fuel derivative contracts, the principal commodities used in hedging are crude oil, heating oil, and unleaded gasoline.

Because of the competitive nature of the low-cost airline industry, airlines cannot always pass on fuel cost increases to the customer. The legacy airlines have no such qualms with fuel surcharges; take for example the BA/Virgin fuel surcharge cartel where Virgin eventually blew the whistle and BA was fined for collusion by both the British and American regulators.

---

[10] Southwest Annual Report 2003.

[11] Jon Magratta 'What Management is: How it works and why it's everyone's business', The Free Press 2002, p199.

[12] Southwest Annual Report 2006.

[13] Aviation Daily; Southwest Could Feel Cost Pinch As Hedging Benefits Wane; 21 May 2007; p3.

3 EU Low-Cost Start-Ups

The success of the low-cost airlines has signalled others to followed suit, attracted by new market opportunities. However, most ventures have proved to be short-lived. Of the 80 carriers that began operations after 1992, 60 were bankrupt by 1996.[14] Of the starts-ups born in the 1990s two airlines successfully exploited market opportunities: Ryanair and easyJet. Due to the UK and Ireland deregulating early, both Ryanair and easyJet were first into the European low-cost market. Later entrants have had difficulty in matching the cost base, providing sufficient low fares, establishing a route network, building brand recognition and building up traffic. In the early 2000s Air Berlin relaunched as a low-cost airline and is now the third largest European low-cost airline. By 2005 the rivals Ryanair and easyJet were carrying up to three-quarters of all EU low-cost passenger traffic.[15]

The European low-cost segment accumulated losses of almost $300m between 1996 and 2001.[16] Casualties of these losses included Debonair, AB Airlines and ColorAir. Ryanair and easyJet have seen off potential competitors and grown through acquisition: easyJet purchased GO, BA's low-cost airline, in 2002, whilst Ryanair acquired Buzz, KLM's low-cost airline in 2003. Appendix 9 provides a comparison between Air Berlin, Ryanair and easyJet.

Photo: Low-cost rivalry in 2006
source: skyscrapercity.com/showthread.php?p12170933

Barriers to Free Market Entry in EU

In theory, liberalisation allowed EU-based airlines to operate on routes between any EU airports, but in practice this proved difficult to execute; in order to fly into a busy airport an airline needs to hold landing and take-off slots. For historical reasons the incumbent national flag carriers control a large percentage of the slots at the principal hub airports: London Heathrow, BA 41%; Paris Charles De Gaulle, Air France-KLM 59%; Amsterdam Schiphol, Air France-KLM 54%; Frankfurt, Lufthansa 63%[17]; thus creating

---

[14] Thomas C Lawton; Cleared for Take-Off; Ashgate Publishing; 2002.
[15] Mintel; No-frills/Low-cost Airlines UK; Feb 2005.
[16] Thomas C Lawton; Cleared for Take-Off; Ashgate Publishing; 2002.
[17] Financial Times; BA buys extra slots at Heathrow; 31 Mar 2007; p21.

a barrier to entry at key airports. Increasingly, the legacy carriers are realising the value of these slots and a grey market in slot trading has now opened up – in 2003 BA paid SN Brussels, the airline created from the bankruptcy of Sabena, £30m for eight daily slot pairs.[18] There are about 9,000 slots a week at Heathrow; the going price for a pair of peak-period slots is more than £10m.[19]

3.1 Ryanair

Ryanair is an Irish airline that began operating in 1985 with one aircraft. In 1986 they used the newly deregulated Dublin to London Luton route to launch a fare war. Ryanair charged £99 return, less than half the price of the BA-Aer Lingus lowest return fare. Both BA and Aer Lingus slashed their prices in response to Ryanair.

By 1990 Ryanair was serving 26 city pairs and carrying 700,000 passengers but rapid growth in aircraft, routes and the intense price competition caused it to accumulate IR£20m in losses. The reincarnation of Ryanair began when Ryanair director Michael O'Leary was sent to Texas to examine Southwest's operations. The Ryanair business strategy became a clone of Southwest's. The airline was relaunched in 1991 under new management as Europe's first low fare no-frills airline and O'Leary became CEO in January 1994.

> 'For all his marketing skill, O'Leary doesn't know where to draw the line, as we saw last month when a disabled passenger took Ryanair to court (and won) because the airline insisted on charging him extra for the use of a wheelchair. Being pitiless saves money, but it's awful to watch.'
>
> *The Telegraph; Don't like Ryanair, hate the way it's been treated; 8 Feb 2004*

In 1994 Ryanair started replacing its outdated BAC1-11 jets with a fleet of eight used Boeing 737 aircraft, as per Southwest's standardisation strategy, which grew to eleven 737s during 1995. During 1995 Ryanair began its first UK-to-UK domestic flights, followed in 1997 by UK-EU flights. In May 1997 Ryanair completed its IPO and by mid 2002 Ryanair had a market capitalisation of €4.9 billion, some 45% larger than BA, Ryanair flying 44 aircraft verses the BA group with 360 aircraft.

O'Leary has many traits in common with Southwest's Herb Kelleher. He is a fiercely competitive, outspoken character who relishes a fight and has spurred Ryanair on to become Europe's most successful, most profitable and highly valued airline.

> O'Leary likes to be underestimated: 'I'm not a thinker'. He'd have us believe that he got lucky by making it up as he goes along: 'a long-term plan is a waste of time'.
>
> *Telegraph; How O'Leary flies high on his unique form of alchemy; 30 Aug 2007*

Ryanair grew by acquisition in April 2003 when it bought the low-cost airline Buzz for €20.1m. Buzz came with 110 out of 500 staff, the leases for six Boeing 737-300s, returned in October 2004, four BAe146-200s, returned in March 2004, and 12 routes plus a substantial number of slots at Buzz's London Stansted base.

Ryanair's growth has been based on actively stimulating the market for low-cost travel. Low fare routes have provided an alternative to travelling with the legacy carriers. Moreover, Ryanair has provided consumers with an alternative transport method to road or rail. By making air travel affordable Ryanair has fuelled its own growth: as passenger numbers increase it is able to benefit from operating

---

[18] Financial Times; Swiss Slots; 24 Sept 2003; p20.

[19] Telegraph.co.uk; BA buys bmi's Heathrow slots; 31 Mar 2007.

efficiencies, thus creating a multiplier effect, decreasing costs and fares, to a point. However, at the same time, profits have continued to be one of the highest in the airline industry. Appendix 4 contains more detailed information on Ryanair's financial performance.

Table 1 provides a comparison between Ryanair and other European airlines 'operating costs per ASK', after adjusting for differences in stage lengths. The comparison figures are against the operating costs for legacy airlines of €11.53 per ASK.

Table 1 Breakdown of Ryanair's Cost Advantage v Average of the Top Three European Legacy Airlines in 2005 (in € cents)

Cost item	Ryanair's advantage over legacy airlines	Ryanair's cost lead per ASK [easyJet]
Aircraft ownership, operations and fuel costs	Ryanair in particular used the cyclical downturn after 2001 to order new more fuel efficient aircraft at discount prices, helping to lower both average fleet age, and maintenance requirements.	1.2 [0.8]
Infrastructure	Ryanair uses secondary or regional airports to lower its infrastructure costs. Lower airport fees, passenger and aircraft handling, and ground handling charges	2.2 [0.8]
Sales and distribution costs, Passenger services, General administrative	A significant amount of these additional costs reflect the different quality of service offered by the legacy airlines	2.4 [2.0]
Labour costs	Reflects differences in labour productivity	0.5 [0.3]
Seat density	The lower seat density used by legacy airlines is equivalent to adding 1.1 cents to total unit costs. (LCCs typically have 18% more seats on equivalent aircraft)	1.1 [1.1]
Total		7.4 [5.0]

legacy airlines = €11.53 per ASK
Ryanair   = €4.13 per ASK
easyJet   = €6.51 per ASK

EU legacy airlines were Air France, Lufthansa and BA – European legacy airlines have a larger cost gap to their low-cost competitors than in the US.

Source: Adapted from IATA Economics Briefing, Airline Cost Performance; March 2007

The legacy airlines' ticket price includes cost items that the low-cost airlines have unbundled from their ticket price, the unbundled items becoming specific revenue generating items for the low-cost operators.

'The judge concurred with the plaintiff's claims that in refusing to honour the promise, O'Leary had been "hostile, bullying and aggressive". It's a sentiment shared by many in the airline industry. It seems that nobody has told him about being nice to people when you're on the way up because you meet the same faces on the way down.'

The Telegraph; Ryanair is heading for a nose dive; 22 Jun 2002

As the table above indicates, a part of Ryanair's cost advantage comes from the way that O'Leary has been true to and exploited the Southwest low-cost strategy, and his suppliers. Away from the congested primary airports there is a vast amount of spare capacity in secondary and regional airports across Europe. O'Leary took advantage of this by exploiting local regeneration efforts in Charleroi, Belgium. Ryanair received €15m as a sweetener from the regional government. However, in February 2004 the EU Commission ruled that this amounted to state aid, even though the regional government provided the funds as a spur for economic regeneration. Ryanair was forced to pay back €4m of the subsidy. Without the subsidy it is likely that some of Ryanair's thin routes will be cancelled. Furthermore, it also sends a signal to airports competing for Ryanair's business that the balance of bargaining power may shift back in their favour.

Areas that Ryanair has conspicuously chosen not to copy Southwest in are employee relations and customer care. Ryanair staff have to buy their own uniforms and were banned from charging their own mobile phones at work.[20] On customer care O'Leary's mantra is low fares, not customer service. In contrast to Herb Kelleher, O'Leary views the two as being mutually exclusive. Customer service is seen as an additional expense and a barrier to keeping fares low. One of O'Leary's politer quotes regarding customers is 'What part of no refund don't they understand?'[21] His mission is to re-educate customers that flying should be akin 'to taking a bus' and that low fares can only be achieved through cutting costs across the board. In February 2005 the EU stepped in with a law to compensate passengers for denied boarding, delayed flights, or flights cancelled less than 14 days from departure. The penalties operate unless an airline can show the problems were caused by 'unavoidable, extraordinary circumstances' – which is how airlines circumvent the law.

O'Leary's sound bites:

'An airplane is nothing more than a bus with wings on'

'I never wanted to be a pilot like those other platoons of goons who populate the air industry'

'Our strategy is like Wal-Mart: We pile it high and sell it cheap'

BBC News website; From no-frills to flag carrier; 5 Oct 2006

3.2 easyJet

easyJet was the UK's first low-cost airline. Around the same time that Ryanair were copying the Southwest strategy, Stelios Haki-Ioannou, who likes to be known as just Stelios, was developing his own version of a low-cost airline, based out of London's Luton airport. Stelios is the son of a Greek shipping magnate and persuaded his father to invest £5 million in his start-up airline. Stelios started operations at the end of 1995 with two leased 737s and in order to keep costs down acted as a virtual airline by contracting-in everything required from pilots and check-in staff to an airline operating certificate.

easyJet's inaugural flights were from Luton to Edinburgh and Glasgow, which were promoted via innovative advertising on the side of the aircraft 'Fly to Scotland for the price of a pair of Jeans'. In the early days easyJet used aggressive marketing techniques in order to build up brand recognition and attack the competitors. easyJet has probably been the most successful low-cost airline at attacking the market space traditionally occupied by the full-service airlines.

Stelios became famous for high profile media battles with competitors, this type of entrepreneurial behaviour having the added benefit of inciting employee loyalty and getting valuable publicity. For example, when BA launched its own low-cost subsidiary GO, Stelios booked himself on the inaugural

---

[20] BBC web news; From no-frills to flag carrier; 5 Oct 2006.

[21] Financial Times; Ryanair talks of disaster, but the low-cost revolution flies on; 7 Feb 2004.

flight and set a high profile media battle in motion. Ironically GO was purchased by easyJet in 2002. GO operated 27 leased 737s on 36 routes.

All of the media stunts had the by-product of educating the general public on the true costs of air travel and promoting the benefits of low fare airlines. The spin-off was that customers saw that there was a real benefit to flying on a low fare carrier, whilst companies with large travel budgets also recognised that low fare provided a real alternative to legacy airlines fares.

A part of easyJet's success is attributed to the unique working culture, 'orange culture', that Stelios instilled in the airline; the objective was to instil a sense of pride in the staff, which would enable superior customer service. The confidence that Stelios had in his staff was revealed in January 1999 when he allowed ITV to film a fly on the wall documentary of life for both the passengers and staff at easyJet. The program is still being produced in 2007. For easyJet it provided priceless publicity. However, without a strong culture of customer service this venture could have proved to be a spectacular own goal. But in contrast to O'Leary, Stelios took customer satisfaction extremely seriously, often taking easyJet flights in order to interact with the passengers. Stelios believed that this was the best form of market research possible.

> 'If you create the right expectations and you meet or exceed those expectations, then you will have happy customers.'
>
> *Stelios Haki-Ioannou – IMD Case Study easyJet 'The Web's Favourite Airline'*

easyJet quickly started to attract business travellers eager to find cost effective travel solutions. On some routes business travellers soon accounted for 50% of the passengers. In contrast to Ryanair's use of secondary airports, easyJet's expansion has been based around operations from Europe's principal cities: easyJet now has bases in London (Luton and Gatwick), Geneva, Paris and Berlin. In this context easyJet has drifted away from the original low-cost strategy of operations to secondary airports. Appendix 2 contains financial data for easyJet. easyJet even allows passengers to pay for entry into third party business lounges at selected airports.

easyJet's IPO was in 2000, its 'easyBrand' trade mark and livery being under licence from easyGroup company, controlled by Stelios. The licence imposes duties on easyJet and restricts easyJet to its core business. The easyBrand currently operates in more than a dozen industries.

As part of getting the best deal from its aircraft suppliers there was a head-to-head battle between Boeing and Airbus. Although having a Boeing fleet easyJet announced in October 2002 its intention to appoint Airbus as its preferred aircraft supplier and placed a firm order for 120 Airbus A319 aircraft. Appendix 10 contains data on the number of seats by aircraft type. easyJet has taken delivery of 1 new A319 every 12 working days since September 2003.[22]

While converting the fleet to Airbus, easyJet has lost the efficiencies in training, maintenance and the lower operating costs that are associated with single fleet operations. Despite the additional complexities of operating another type of aircraft easyJet maintains that the financial benefits of the deal far outweigh the migration costs. Sir Colin Chandler, easyJet's then Chairman, stated that the Airbus deal was 'significantly better value than the offer made by Boeing'.[23]

As the low-cost industry matures, easyJet's culture has also been evolving. In 2003 Stelios stepped down as Chairman, a sure sign that the entrepreneurial spirit required to set up the airline was less relevant in the running of a maturing business. However in May 2005 Stelios, still the largest shareholder at 16%, rejoined the Board as a non-executive director and was knighted in June 2006 for services to entrepreneurship.

In May 2007 easyJet chief executive Andy Harrison, said 'that for the busy summer months from April to September, when the group generates all of its profits, it had reduced many of its lead-in fares and

---

[22] easyJet; 2007 Interim Results; 9 May 2007.

[23] easyjet.com; easyJet letter to shareholders; 24 Feb 2003.

had increased its promotional activities in order to fill its aircraft'. 'Costs are being driven down thanks to lower maintenance expenses and aircraft ownership costs, as easyJet replaces its older Boeing aircraft with new jets from Airbus, and also due to lower charges and handling costs at some airports' plus 'easyJet was aiming to double in size in five years with a planned increase of 15 percent a year'.[24]

3.3 Air Berlin

Air Berlin was founded in 1978 as a charter airline, it became a scheduled IATA carrier in 1997 and in the early 2000s it converted to a low-cost strategy. With 19.7m passengers in 2006 Air Berlin is Germany's second largest airline after Lufthansa, and Europe's third largest low-cost carrier. Its IPO was in May 2006.

In 2005 Air Berlin operated from eighteen German airports to 56, mainly tourist, airports outside Germany with hubs at Nuremberg, Majorca and London Stansted plus a major presence at Vienna and Zurich. It also operates to tourist destinations outside Europe in North Africa.

Its charter origins are still given away by its Majorca shuttle that in 2006 operated daily flights from 17 German, plus 3 non German, airports to its prime hub destination of Majorca and then on to destinations in Spain, the Balearic Islands and Portugal.

Air Berlin operates a low-fare with premium service, i.e. no-frills plus. It is attempting to differentiate itself by occupying the gap between the pure low-cost and legacy airlines. Air Berlin still operates in the charter market where seats are sold, by the tour operators, six to nine months before departure. See appendix 12 for Air Berlin data.

3.4 Low-Cost Route Networks[25]

In 2005 the low-cost carriers, dominated by Ryanair and easyJet, accounted for 49% of total UK domestic traffic and 52% of UK-EU scheduled traffic.[26] As Ryanair expands its network the contribution from its Ireland-UK routes is decreasing.

Across the EU as a whole the low-cost industry growth figures are:

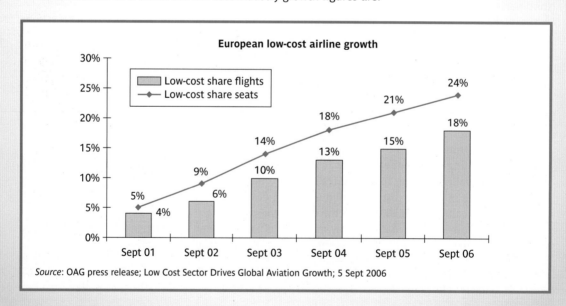

Source: OAG press release; Low Cost Sector Drives Global Aviation Growth; 5 Sept 2006

---

[24] Financial Times; easyJet halves its seasonal losses; 10 May 2007.

[25] EU; DG TREN – Analysis Of The European Air Transport Industry; various 2001–2007; http://ec.europa.eu/transport/air_portal/.

[26] Financial Times; No-Frills Airlines Had 'Little Impact On Growth'; 16 Nov 2006; p6.

The growth of the low-cost airlines has generated high volatility in the EU airline route networks. The airline industry makes more of its operating income in the spring and summer months. Summer and winter schedule changes account for a lot of the variation, plus low-cost airlines taking advantage of the ease with which they can enter routes or exit routes. In winter it may be cheaper for an airline to park-up some aircraft for the season.

Ryanair and easyJet are expanding their networks setting up European airport 'bases', or nodes where they keep a number of aircraft and operate a network of local point-to-point routes. Using bases gives the low-cost airlines additional bargaining power at airports that may help them to keep costs down. New routes to secondary or regional airports, being underutilised, cheap to operate from, and not always requiring slots, are relatively easy to initiate, the operators welcoming the business. Low-cost airlines can axe their unprofitable routes easily as they don't need to consider the overall network effects as legacy airlines do. See appendix 16 for details of Ryanair and easyJet bases and appendix 13 for easyJet's route network.

At June 2005 70% of European schedule airline services were single-carrier routes. About 20% of routes are two-carrier routes, and the other 10% of routes are three or more carrier routes, double the percentage compared to 1994. The routes with three or more carriers are the routes serving large markets. The single-carrier routes have very 'thin' capacity. The number and type of competitors on a route may dictate the fare strategy used by a low-cost airline.

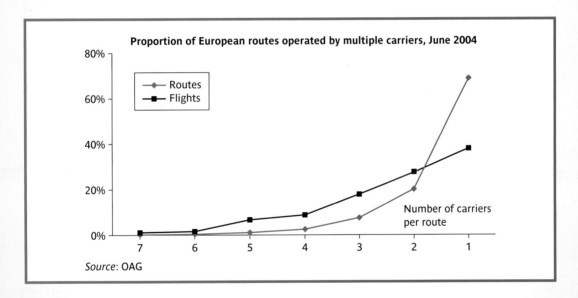

Proportion of European routes operated by multiple carriers, June 2004

Source: OAG

The reason for the large number of single-carrier routes is likely to be low-cost airlines' point-to-point networks. Many of these routes have 'thin' passenger traffic and therefore unlikely to attract competition. Ryanair tends to choose single-carrier routes therefore dominating a large number of small markets. Ryanair's initial tactic on entering a market is to offer very low fares along with plenty of promotional activity. easyJet's network offers business and leisure travellers an alternative to the legacy airline product, operating on fewer large routes with greater frequency than Ryanair. The Barclaycard Business Travel Survey 2004/05 shows that 71% of UK business travellers had flown on low-cost airlines and that 96% were very satisfied and would use one again.[27] easyJet's route strategy puts them in competition with two or more other carriers on the same route, to a far higher degree than Ryanair.

---

[27] OAG; European Low-Cost Carriers White Paper; March 2006.

3.5 Innovation – Unbundling

By definition the low-cost airlines have a low cost base and by the law of diminishing returns this means their options for reducing costs at constant fares to generate further profit are limited as time progresses. In order to increase profit the low-cost airlines are unbundling their offerings, although they don't sell it that way. Unbundling means that the services traditionally included in the airfare are broken into their constituent parts and then paid for individually. So are you still getting that low fare? Unbundling makes price transparency difficult, transparency being one of the drivers behind consumers being able to make the informed choice that helped create the low-cost market.

Ryanair in 2006 introduced charges for checked baggage, presented as a revenue-neutral cost-cutting exercise, but this has since been acknowledged as a significant revenue source.[28] Ryanair's 'ancillary revenues' from sources other than ticket sales contributed €362m to its 2007 profit before tax of €451m. Other examples of low-cost unbundling are assigned seating and priority boarding.

The low-cost airlines are unbundling the traditional baggage allowance:

Hold Baggage Prices (economy class) July 2007	Pre-paid	Pay at Airport	Paid for Hold Baggage kg	Excess Baggage per kg	Hand Baggage Allowance kg (n.b. size limits)
Ryanair	£5	£10	15	£5.50	10
bmibaby	£3.99	£10	20	£6	32
easyJet (from Oct 07)	£2	£5	20	£6	10
Flybe	£4	£7	23	£5.50	10
Air Berlin	free	free	20	€5	6

Source: Company websites

Also the number of baggage items can incur a charge; even BA is following this low-cost trend. These charges not only generate revenue but are designed to reduce the airlines' costs by reducing the charge for airport baggage handling and making aircraft lighter thereby saving fuel.

4 The Legacy Airline Response

4.1 British Airways

British Airways has worldwide reach. Based on its RTK figures where RTK equals one tonne of revenue traffic transported per one km, its scheduled RTK per region in 2006 was: North Atlantic 39.7%; Far East 27.0%; Europe 13.4%; Africa 11.2%; Latin America 4.6%; Middle East 4.1%.[29]

With the advent of the low-cost airlines BA's short-haul operations didn't break even for over ten years until 2006.[30] BA was one of the first to realise that the market for short-haul traffic was undergoing a structural change as a result of the low-cost airlines. BA set up its own low-cost airline GO, based at Stansted airport, in 1998. However three years later in June 2001 BA sold GO in a management buy-out backed by venture capitalists. At the time of the sale BA's CEO was quoted as saying that the £110m BA received for GO represented a good return on the initial investment of £25m.[31] Subsequently in August 2002 easyJet acquired GO for £374m, making easyJet Europe's then largest low-cost airline, and a good profit for the venture capitalists. See appendix 5 for BA's financial figures.

---

[28] AEA (Association of European Airlines) Yearbook 2006; p10.

[29] AEA Yearbook 2007.

[30] BA Annual Report 2006.

[31] BA press release 14 June 2001, available on www.britishairways.com.

The rationale for the sale of GO was that operating a no-frills service alongside a full-service strategy was not sustainable in the long term, cannibalising the market. More specifically BA was finding it difficult to justify a substantial price premium for its full-service offerings; effectively it was eating into its own profits. As Willie Walsh then of Aer Lingus pointed out, the size of the premium charged for additional service features had shrunk forever.

In 2001, when 85% of BA's passengers travelled economy[32] BA began to de-hub Gatwick operations, copying the low-cost airlines, concentrating on point-to-point short-haul rather than on long-haul network operations from the airport. In April 2002 BA rolled out its continuing strategy response to compete against the low-cost airlines. It introduced year-round cheaper fares on its short-haul routes, along with a new internet booking system, scrapped its traditional restrictions on tickets, and reduced travel agency commissions in the UK, all backed by a simpler business strategy. By July 2003 BA was facing low cost competition on 58 of its European routes, representing 69%, up from 34% in July 1998, of the airline's European capacity.[33]

Table 2 How The Legacy Airlines' Cost-Cutting Response has been Matched by the Low-Cost Carriers (LCCs)

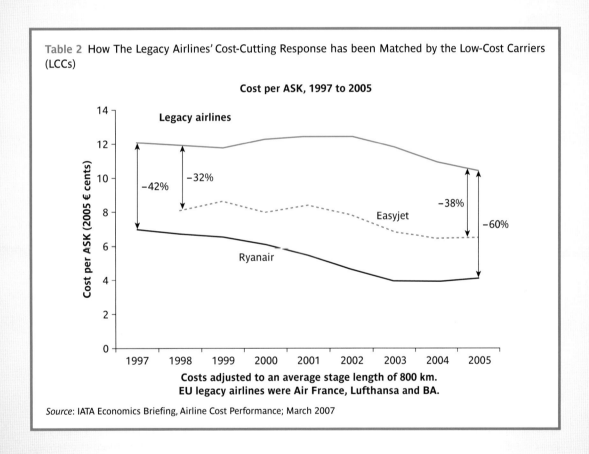

Cost per ASK, 1997 to 2005

Costs adjusted to an average stage length of 800 km.
EU legacy airlines were Air France, Lufthansa and BA.

Source: IATA Economics Briefing, Airline Cost Performance; March 2007

Table 2 indicates that even though the legacy airlines have recently been cutting costs at a higher rate than the low-cost airlines, the low-cost airlines are still maintaining significant differentials. The low-cost airlines' costs appear to be near rock bottom, flattening out, unless they can find new cost cutting avenues.

BA's strategy changes have focused on continued cost reductions mainly from manpower reductions, restructuring operations, removing complexity from the businesses, and applying elements of

---

[32] BA Annual Report 2001.
[33] EU; DG TREN – Analysis of The European Air Transport Industry 2003; January 2005.

low-cost business strategy to the airline. One of the main strategy goals is to achieve a 10% operating margin, a goal BA has never achieved in its history.[34]

BA's regional arm, BA Connect, was sold in early 2007, after making losses of £20m in 2006 on top of £27m in 2005. Analysts report that more than 50% of BA's profits come from its transatlantic routes, primarily on first-class travel between London and New York.[35]

As a result of adjusting their marketing, legacy airlines are now able to sell the alternative benefits to pure no-frills travel. For customers that value convenience, that is being flown directly to their destination, as opposed to a satellite airport up to 100km away. Plus having the level of service associated with a traditional airline including assigned seating and onboard meals, the established airlines have started to sell an alternative to the no-frills carriers. Indeed much of BA's current advertising is explicit in promoting the benefits of travel with a full-service airline.

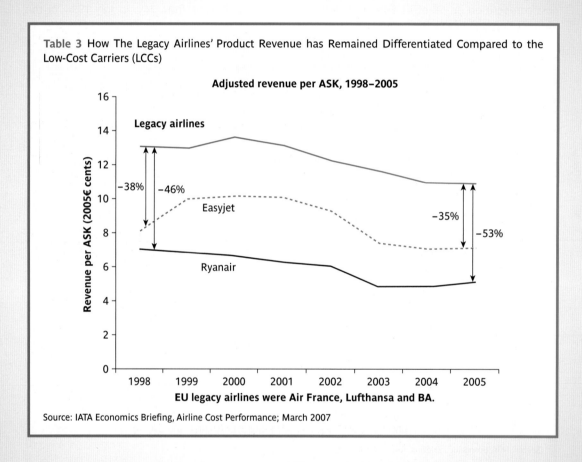

Table 3 How The Legacy Airlines' Product Revenue has Remained Differentiated Compared to the Low-Cost Carriers (LCCs)

Source: IATA Economics Briefing, Airline Cost Performance; March 2007

Table 3 indicates that even though revenues, per ASK, are reducing across the industry the legacy airlines have been able to maintain the differentiation between their and the low-cost product offerings, i.e. the legacy airlines can still charge a premium for their product.

BA announced the 'Fit for 5' programme, in February 2005, a once in a generation opportunity to make significant strategy changes by reforming operations at Heathrow, in preparation for the airlines move to Terminal 5 in 2008. BA has a history of staff unrest; for example in the summer of 2005 many unionised BA staff walked out in sympathy with striking employees of Gate Gourmet, the airline catering company, in an action that led to the cancellation of hundreds of flights and cost the airline more than £70m. In this environment the move to Terminal 5 needs special handling.

---

[34] BA Annual Report 2004.

[35] The Telegraph; Walsh bullish about transatlantic competition; 10 Mar 2007.

In October 2005 Willie Walsh became BA's CEO. Walsh had been CEO of the ailing Aer Lingus where he had a track record of cost cutting along with lowering fares and expanding networks in order to drive up passenger numbers and load factors.

Walsh underlined his commitment to maintaining BA's two-class operations on short-haul routes. He says BA had rejected a proposal to begin single-class operations with paid-for in-flight food and drink at Gatwick.[36]

After putting in place plans to tackle its pension fund deficit and sorting out its short-haul operations, BA is now focusing on long-haul operations. In March 2007 it announced four firm orders for Boeing 777-200ERs for delivery in 2009, along with plans to cut manpower by a further 2,000, to 40,000 employees by March 2008. In September 2007 BA confirmed firm orders for 12 Airbus A380s and 24 Boeing 787s, for delivery from 2010 as part of its programme to expand capacity and replace older aircraft.

4.2 bmi

As the UK's second largest full-service airline after BA, bmi has proved vulnerable to the growth of low-cost carriers. bmi's main base is at London Heathrow, where it holds 11.5% of the landing/takeoff slots, operating 19 short-haul routes. The Heathrow slots are a valuable asset with Virgin Atlantic holding takeover talks with bmi in 2003, and BA also reported as being interested. bmi operates around 1650 flights per week with a fleet of 42 aircraft. See appendix 8 for data on bmi.

After continuing losses in 2003, bmi initiated a 'Blue Sky' programme aimed at reducing operating costs. These cuts have reduced short-haul capacity by a quarter over the past three years.[37] In late 2005 bmi made changes to its domestic and European services at Heathrow with the introduction of a single-class service, simpler fares, internet check-in and quicker processes at airports. However on routes with significant business travellers bmi has retained separate economy and business class.

bmi's response to the threat posed by the low-cost airlines was to start its own low-cost subsidiary bmibaby in 2002. bmibaby now has five bases in the UK. bmi is running a full-service and a low-cost airline in tandem by keeping the route networks separate.

bmibaby is always seeking to saving money transporting each of its 5m passengers each year, a 1p saving translating to an additional £50,000 profit over a year. Along with other low-cost airlines it maximises bookings over the internet and does not issue tickets. It also tries to make sure the plane is as light as possible by carrying just enough fuel, plus reserve, to get to its destination. It encourages passengers to carry less and lighter items of baggage hence saving fuel. bmibaby charges for hold baggage with the intention of reducing ground handling and turnaround times. The cabin crew is encouraged to maximise onboard sales of food and drink to passengers.

bmibaby has a fleet of 21 planes with 207 pilots at July 2007. A pilot's longest flight is the 3-hour journey to Spain. When on duty pilots work a 10 to 11 hour day, flying up to 4 flights around Europe.

Its Birmingham airport base has eight 737 aircraft serving 21 destinations. The airline does 25-minute turnarounds and all aircraft return to Birmingham each evening so that the airline saves on crew hotel costs. In the future they are looking to introduce lightweight seats, saving fuel.[38]

In February 2007 bmi paid £30m to acquire the airline British Mediterranean giving it access to Middle Eastern routes. bmi's primary focus has been on domestic and short-haul travel; it now plans to expand its medium and long-haul operations. bmi announced an order for 10 new Airbus aircraft to expand its long-haul fleet, the first A330 being due for delivery in Spring 2008.[39] As a medium-sized carrier with a relatively high fixed operating cost base at Heathrow bmi has lost market share to easyJet and Ryanair's short-haul operations hence the focus on medium and long-haul.

[36] Financial Times; BA's new pilot is calm and focused; 04 Oct 2005; p26.
[37] Travel Trade Gazette, UK and Ireland; bmi to axe short haul routes from Heathrow; 4 May 2007.
[38] Source; http://news.bbc.co.uk/media/avdb/regions/west_midlands/video; July 2007.
[39] Telegraph.co.uk; bmi plans $750m fleet expansion; 11 July 2007.

5 Challenges Facing Low Cost Airlines

5.1 Immediate Challenges

In regions of Europe the high-speed rail networks provide greater competition for the airlines. The European high-speed rail networks are rapidly extending with more than 3,000 miles of track linking the networks of Germany, France, the Netherlands, Austria, Switzerland and Belgium and this figure is expected to triple by 2020. However the high capital railway infrastructure costs are borne by the taxpayer, unlike the airlines where landing fees finance airport infrastructure. Air France has its own railway carriages that it uses for passengers travelling between Paris and Brussels instead of flying them. The rail companies involved in the European alliance want to attract at least 25m passengers annually by 2012, an increase of 10m in the next five years. Continental rail travel is also getting cheaper. Return fares from London to Paris start at £59, while connections from Paris to Frankfurt start at £62 one-way.[40] The EU is due to deregulate the railways in 2010 allowing different companies to operate on the same track, which should bring rail fares down. In the UK, taking a non-London centric view, the airline Flybe's regional routes are targeted at passengers where train journey time is more than two and a half hours.

The low-cost airlines are susceptible to cost pressure from their suppliers, especially the airports. The low-cost airlines need to keep costs low by negotiating good deals for the use of airport facilities, ground handling and landing fees. Most low-cost airlines contest airport charges, and are prepared to move their operations if the price is not right. The low-cost airlines argue that they do not use many airport facilities, and therefore they should be charged less. In 1999 Manchester airport wanted to increase its charges so Ryanair transferred its Manchester flights to Leeds/Bradford, raising the airport's market share. Finally Manchester agreed to reduced airport charges and Ryanair returned to Manchester. In November 2004, easyJet ceased all flights to Zurich, which it said was 'the most costly airport in its network'. According to easyJet, Zurich had more than doubled its passenger fees over the previous two years, thus making its routes unprofitable. Ryanair currently has issues with increased landing fees at Stansted, Dublin and Cork airports.

> 'Any fool can grow in the airline industry whilst losing money and we are surrounded by many fine examples of this in Europe at present. The difference with Ryanair is that we achieve consistent growth, but deliver equally consistent profit growth at high margins despite offering the lowest air fares in Europe. The challenge facing us over the coming years will be to maintain our growth, whilst improving customer service, upgrading the fleet with the new 737s, but continuing to lower our unit costs and maintaining industry leading margins.'
>
> *Michael O'Leary – Ryanair Annual Report 2003*

5.2 Long Run Prospects

As the EU market for short-haul low fare travel in Western Europe becomes more saturated fewer new routes become viable. As a consequence the low-cost airlines have turned their attention towards Eastern Europe and North Africa in order to provide growth.

With the number of aircraft orders placed by the low-cost operators, overcapacity in the low-cost sector is on the horizon followed by an industry shakeout. In the long run the low-cost airlines will have to compete head to head for increased market share to fully utilise their fleets. In 2005 the low-cost airlines were in direct competition on just 4% of their routes, thus minimising competition costs on their revenues,[41] although the catchment areas they serve overlap to a greater extent. To add to the future industry woes there is the habitual industry cyclical recession.

---

[40] Telegraph.co.uk; Airport delays drive tourists on to the rails; 07 July 2007.
[41] McKinsey Quarterly; The Battle For Europe's Low Fare Flyers; Aug 2005.

With the US-EU open skies agreement creating new markets, the legacy and newly established long-haul low-cost airlines will compete to get their share in these new markets, along with fighting over the traditional long-haul market. However the short-haul low-cost strategy is a formula based on flights that last about two hours allowing multiple flights per day and subsequent high aircraft utilisations. The new markets will necessitate new innovative strategies for the long-haul low-cost airlines and new or counter responses from the legacy airlines.

Ryanair has stated it will enter the long-haul transatlantic market by 2011. The current transatlantic long-haul low-cost airlines are Zoom and three business-class only airlines: Silverjet, EOS and Maxjet, all offering London-New York routes. See appendix 15 on factors influencing airline choice.

On open skies:

'We don't need governments to determine markets. Passenger demand should decide.'

'But I am optimistic: First because it makes good business sense. It could add US$5 billion to our bottom line.'

'Moreover, an agreement would allow us to start looking at ownership. Lufthansa and Swiss demonstrated that cross-border ownership is possible. Airlines are businesses. But the flag on the aircraft tail is so heavy that it is sinking the industry. Liberalisation within the European banking industry saw a 26% decline in numbers. But an enormous increase in their competitiveness.'

'We need to run our business as a business. No subsidies or handouts. In most cases airlines are free to go out of business. Merging across borders should also be an option. Governments must give airlines the same commercial freedoms that other industries take for granted.'

Giovanni Bisignani, Director General and CEO IATA; 28 September 2006

The short-haul low fare market now belongs to the low-cost airlines even though the legacy airlines have shown they can respond to the low-cost airlines by providing viable consumer products on short-haul routes. The short-haul low-cost strategy has over a thirty year heritage; in Southwest's case the strategy has provided sustainable competitive advantage. There is no reason that the low-cost, cost leadership strategy should not continue to work in the long term for a select number of firms, such as Ryanair and easyJet, although there are not enough market opportunities for every would-be low-cost player.

The airline industry is expanding, predicted to double in capacity by 2030 and triple by 2050. Along with expansion will come a forecast four-fold increase in aircraft emissions by 2050. Will fares increase to such an extent to ration air travel in order to limit carbon emissions?

Appendix 1 Southwest Airlines Load Factor and Financial Data

	2000	2001	2002	2003	2004	2005	2006
Turnover $m.	5,650	5,555	5,522	5,937	6,530	7,584	9,086
Pre-tax profit $m	1,018	828	317	604	339	779	790
Pre-tax profit margin	18.0%	14.9%	5.7%	10.2%	5.2%	10.3%	8.7%
Passengers m.	63.7	64.4	63.0	65.7	70.9	77.7	83.8
Load Factor	70.5%	68.1%	65.9%	66.8%	69.5%	70.7%	73.1%
Aircraft Utilisation (hh:mm per day)	11:18	11:10	11:12	11:09	11:20	11:25	11:34

Financial year-end 31 December.

Southwest Airlines aircraft fleet 481 (of which 93 are leased):

Aircraft	Number in fleet	Seating
Boeing 737-300	194	137
Boeing 737-500	25	122
Boeing 737-700	262	137

- Firm aircraft orders 115 (Boeing 737-700)

Southwest fuel derivative contracts (Annual Report 2006):

Year	% of jet fuel needs US$ per barrel
2006	70% at $36
2007	95% at $50
2008	65% at $49
2009	50% at $51
2010	25% at $63
2011	15% at $64
2012	15% at $63

1 barrel = 42 US gallons (= 158.99 litres).

Source: Company Reports

Appendix 2 easyJet Load Factor and Financial Data

	2000	2001	2002	2003	2004	2005	2006
Turnover £m	263.7	356.9	551.8	931.8	1,091.0	1,341.3	1,619.7
Pre-tax profit £m	22.1	40.1	71.6	51.5	62.2	67.9	129.2
Pre-tax profit margin	8.4%	11.2%	13.0%	5.5%	5.7%	5.1%	8.0%
Passengers m.	5.6	7.1	11.4	20.3	24.3	29.6	33.0
Load Factor	80.8%	83.0%	84.8%	84.1%	84.5%	85.2%	84.8%

Financial year-end 30 September. Note: easyJet's financial data is published in £.

■ In October 2007 easyJet took over GB Airways based at Gatwick. GB Airways operates to 31 destinations across southern Europe and North Africa with a fleet of 15 A320 aircraft. It has 39 routes of which 28 are from Gatwick

easyJet aircraft fleet 122 (of which an average of 86 are leased):

Aircraft	Number in fleet	Seating
Boeing 737-300	3	148
Boeing 737-700	32	149
Airbus A319	87	156

Source: Company Reports

Appendix 3 Southwest Airlines Activity System[42]

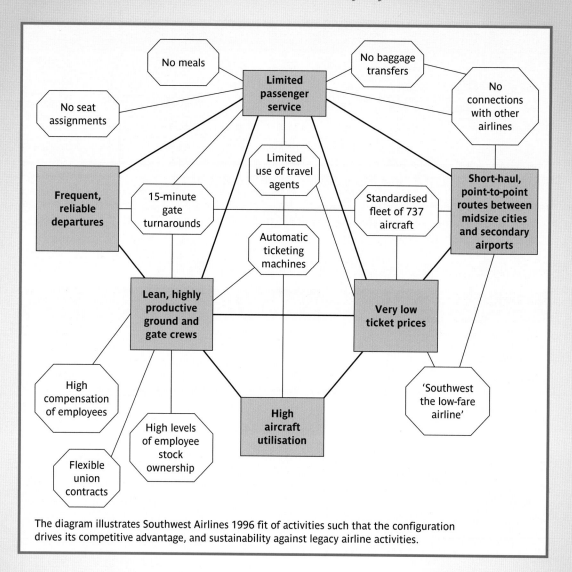

The diagram illustrates Southwest Airlines 1996 fit of activities such that the configuration drives its competitive advantage, and sustainability against legacy airline activities.

[42] What Is Strategy?; Harvard Business Review, Nov – Dec 1996; Michael E Porter.

Appendix 4 Ryanair Load Factor and Financial Data

	2001	2002	2003	2004	2005	2006	2007
Turnover €m	487.4	624.1	842.5	1,074.2	1,336.6	1,692.5	2,236.9
Pre-tax profit €m	123.4	172.4	264.6	228.5	295.9	338.9	451.0
Pre-tax profit margin	25.3%	27.6%	31.4%	21.3%	22.1%	20.0%	20.2%
Passengers m.	8.1	11.1	15.7	23.1	27.6	34.8	42.5
Load Factor – booked	77%	81%	85%	81%	84%	83%	82%
Load Factor flown	70%	74%	78%	74%	78%	77%	76%

Financial year-end 31 March.
Note: Ryanair's financial data are published in €, easyJet in £.

■ Ryanair purchased 25.2% of Aer Lingus after its IPO in 2006 and made a takeover bid that was vetoed by the EU. After this rejection there have been rumours Ryanair is interested in acquiring Air Berlin, affecting its share price.[43]

Ryanair aircraft fleet 133 (of which 21 are leased):

Aircraft	Number in fleet	Seating
Boeing 737-800	133	189

Appendix 5 British Airways Load Factor and Financial Data

	2001	2002	2003	2004	2005	2006	2007
Turnover £m	9,278	8,340	7,688	7,560	7,813	8,515	8,492
Pre-tax profit (loss) £m	150	(200)	135	230	415	620	611
Pre-tax profit (loss) margin	1.6%	(2.4%)	1.8%	3.0%	5.3%	7.3%	7.2%
Passengers m.	44.4	40.0	38.0	36.1	35.7	32.4	33.1
Load Factor	71.7%	70.4%	71.9%	73.0%	74.8%	76.1%	76.1%
Aircraft Utilisation (hours per day)	8.79	8.32	8.91	9.21	9.83	10.29	10.82

Financial year-end 31 March (figures for BA Group inc. BA and BA CityFlyer).

■ BA aircraft fleet 233, BA CityFlyer aircraft fleet 9 (regional jets)
■ In March 2007 BA sold its subsidiary BA Connect to Flybe. As part of the transaction BA received a 15% shareholding in Flybe; BA retained the Manchester to New York service; and a new BA subsidiary BA CityFlyer took over the BA Connect London City airport operations and aircraft

Source: Company Reports

---

[43] Airwise News (Reuters); Air Berlin Up On Talk Of Ryanair Interest; 5 July 2007.

Appendix 6 easyJet Yield Management

Customer fare proposition:

- Early bookers pay low fares
- Higher prices protect seat availability for late bookers (target load factor 85%)

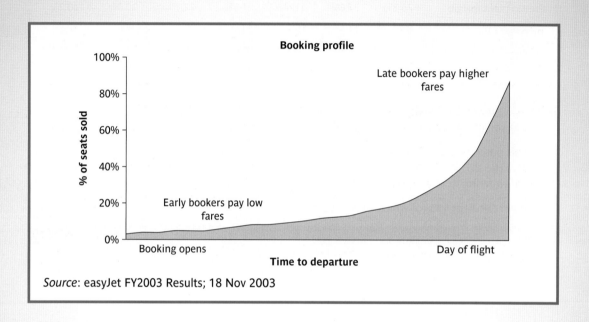

Booking profile

Source: easyJet FY2003 Results; 18 Nov 2003

Appendix 7 American Airlines (AA) Load Factor and Financial Data

	2000	2001	2002	2003	2004	2005	2006
Turnover $m	18,117	17,484	15,992	17,403	18,608	20,657	22,490
Pre-tax profit (loss) $m	1,282	(2,449)	(3,669)	(1,409)	(821)	(892)	164
Pre-tax profit (loss) margin	7.1%	(14.0%)	(22.9%)	(8.1%)	(4.4%)	(4.3%)	0.7%
Passengers m.	na	na	94.1	88.8	91.6	98.0	98.1
Load Factor	72.4%	69.0%	70.7%	72.8%	74.8%	78.6%	80.1%

Financial year-end 31 December.

- American Airlines' aircraft fleet 697
- American Airlines is part of the AMR Corporation, which also owns American Eagle (aircraft fleet 306 regional jets) and American Connection (whose flights are subcontracted out)
- In April 2001, American Airlines took over Trans World Airlines (TWA, then the eighth largest US carrier) making American the largest scheduled passenger airline in the world

Source: Company Reports

Appendix 8 bmi Selected Statistics (inc bmibaby and bmi regional)

	2000	2001	2002	2003	2004	2005	2006
Turnover £m	739.2	756.9	723.8	772	830	869	905
Pre-tax profit (loss) £m	8.2	12.4	(19.6)	(9.8)	2.6	10.0	29.7
Pre-tax profit margin	1.1%	1.6%	(2.7%)	(1.3%)	0.3%	1.2%	3.3%
Passengers m.	7.1	6.7	7.5	9.4	10.5	10.5	10.5

Financial year-end 31 December.

- bmi aircraft fleet 28, bmi regional aircraft fleet 14 (regional jets), bmibaby aircraft fleet 21
- bmibaby fly older Boeing 737s however these aircraft are not declared on bmi's website, bmibaby being a separate entity
- bmi acquired the airline British Mediterranean (BMED) for £30m in February 2007, acquiring 17 Middle East destinations
- bmi regional are based in Aberdeen and serve niche regional routes with the 14 regional jets
- bmibaby carried almost 40% of bmi's 10.5m passengers in 2006[44]
- bmi has 83 daily slot pairs (take-off and landing) at Heathrow (11.4%), the second largest after BA at 41.4%. Lufthansa is third with 4.3% and Virgin Atlantic has 3.4%.[45]

Source: www.flybmi.com

---

[44] The Daily Telegraph, Business section p83; 3 May 2007.
[45] BA buys extra slots at Heathrow; Financial Times (London); 31 Mar 2007; p21.

Appendix 9 Low-Cost Airlines Comparison Summary

Data from annual reports issued closest to 31 December 2006

	easyJet	Ryanair	Air Berlin inc dba	British Airways inc Cityflyer
Turnover €m	€2,381.0	€2,236.9	€1,575.4	€12,483.2
Profit before tax €m	€189.9	€451.0	€45.1	€898.2
Pre-tax profit margin	8.0%	20.2%	2.9%	7.2%
Passengers	33.0 m.	42.5 m.	19.7 m.	33.1 m
Load Factor	84.8%	82%	75.3%	76.1%
Destinations	74	136	97	147
Aircraft				
B737 family	35	133	56	33
A320 family	87		15	66
Other 737 equivalents				13
Regional jets			17	9
Twin aisle jets				121
Total	122	133	88	242
Confirmed aircraft orders	105	175[46]	134	18

Results in £ have been converted to € using an exchange rate £1 = €1.47 (Mar 2007).

■ IATA estimate the average cost of capital of 7.5% for the airline industry

Source: Company Reports

Appendix 10 Low-Cost Aircraft Type and Seat Numbers

The low-cost airlines favourite planes are single-aisle, twin-engine jets, with typically 100 – 200 seats and maximum ranges of 5,000 – 7,000 km (average Ryanair/easyJet sector (flight/stage/haul) length in 2006 was about 975 km).

Current production Airbus A320 and Boeing 737 Next-Generation (NG) aircraft:

Airbus A320 family	Maximum Number of Seats single-class (manufacturer typical)		Boeing 737 family
A318	117	132	737-600
A319	134	149	737-700
A320	164	189	737-800
A321	199	215	737-900ER

Source: Company websites

---

[46] Source Boeing website 'Ryanair Orders' May 2007.

Each family of aircraft has a common cockpit thereby making it cheaper to certify pilots on the aircraft family and also easier to schedule pilots when more than one family variant is operated.

■ The remnants of the world's commercial airline manufacturing industry fall into two groups, one containing Boeing and Airbus who make jet aircraft with greater than 100 seats, the other containing Embraer and Bombardier who make regional jet (RJ) aircraft (roughly defined as aircraft with less than 100 seats)

■ The aero engine makers are down to three main players General Electric (GE Aircraft Engines), Pratt & Whitney and Rolls-Royce, with joint ventures and consortiums being formed between themselves and other manufactures to produce engines

■ easyJet was the launch customer for the A319 in a single class cabin configuration. The number of seats on its aircraft is 156, the extra 22 seats were achieved by easyJet's requirement to reduce the space for galleys, lavatories and storage

■ JetBlue first flew in February 2000 and now operates the world's largest fleet of A320s. Its 100th A320 was delivered in March 2007, with 78 additional A320s on firm order. The airline also operates 25 Embraer 190 regional jets with 76 additional 190s on firm order (March 2007)

■ Both Ryanair and Air Berlin operate the B737-800, however, Ryanair squeezes an additional 3 seats into its version (189 v 186)

■ The first delivery of a 737 NG (a 737-700) to an airline was in December 1997

■ Boeing (June 2002) reported: 'The Boeing 737 makes up more than 90% of the combined fleets of the low-fare carriers around the world'

■ Boeing (May 2007) reported: 'As of April 30, Boeing had received orders for more than 3,800 Next-Generation 737s, and has unfilled orders exceeding 1,500 airplanes, worth over $100 billion at current list prices'

■ Boeing has the production facilities to produce 28 737s each month, planned to increase to 31 during 2008[47]

■ Boeing[48] forecasts the number of jet airliners required by the airline industry increasing from 18,230 in 2006 to 36,420 by 2026. Of the 36,420 the new build breakdown is: 10,400 to replacements, 18,200 to growth (average 1,400 per year). The breakdown in aircraft types is:

a/c type	New build numbers 2006-2026	
747 and larger jets	960	(3%)
Twin-aisle jets	6,290	(22%)
Single-aisle jets	17,650	(62%)
Regional jets	3,700	(13%)

■ Airbus' 2006 forecast, which excludes regional jets, is that 21,860 new passenger aircraft (1,093 per year) are required by 2025,[49] 30% of the 15,330 new single-aisle aircraft going to LDCs.

[47] Boeing Reinvents its Supply Chain; Leslie Wayne, Neil Shister. World Trade. Apr 2007. Vol.20, Iss. 4; p36.
[48] Boeing; Current Market Outlook 2007; June 2007.
[49] Airbus; Global Market Forecast 2006 – 2025; Nov 2006; p56 (p64).

Appendix 11 Ryanair and easyJet Share Prices

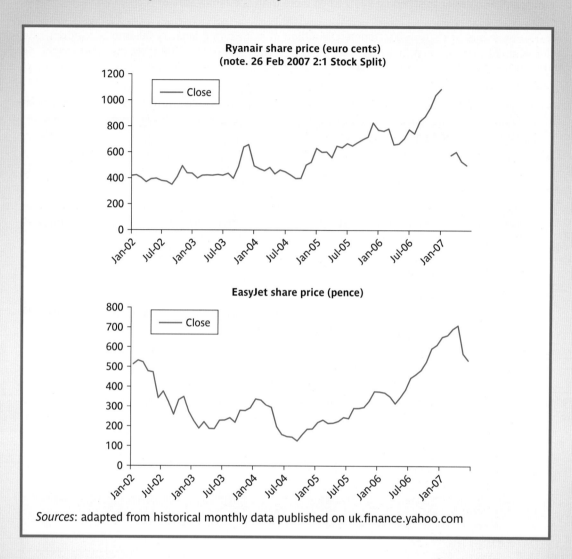

Ryanair share price (euro cents)
(note. 26 Feb 2007 2:1 Stock Split)

EasyJet share price (pence)

Sources: adapted from historical monthly data published on uk.finance.yahoo.com

Appendix 12 Air Berlin Load Factor and Financial Data

	2003	2004	2005	2006
Turnover €m	863.2	1,033.9	1,215.2	1,575.4
Pre-tax profit (loss) €m	44.8	16.9	(70.9)	45.1
Pre-tax profit (loss) margin	5.2%	1.6%	(5.8%)	2.9%
Passengers m.	10.0	12.1	13.5	19.7
Load Factor	76.7%	79.5%	78.6%	75.3%
Aircraft Utilisation (hrs per day)	11.17	11.52	11.47	na

Financial year-end 31 December.

- Air Berlin IPO May 2006; acquisition of dba airline (originally Deutsche BA) in August 2006
- Acquisition of German long-haul charter carrier LTU in March 2007 (given competition approval in August 2007), LTU operates 27 planes and employs about 2,800 people. LTU flew 5.75 million passengers in 2006 with an 82.1% load factor

Air Berlin aircraft fleet 88 (of which 26 are leased):

Aircraft	Number in fleet	Seating
Boeing 737-300	14	144
Boeing 737-500	1	112
Boeing 737-700	6	144
Boeing 737-800	35	186
Airbus A319	4	144
Airbus A320	11	174
Fokker 100	17	100

Source: Company Reports

Appendix 13 easyJet's route network

A diagram indicating the concentration of easyJet's route network. Although this map is not very clear it is apparent how many routes easyJet covers.

Source: easyJet Annual Report 2006

Appendix 14 How Low-Cost Airlines Reduce Unit Costs[50]

Cost Category	Cost Item	Levers for Reducing Costs
Aircraft Ownership Costs	■ Ownership Structure ■ Fleet Structure ■ Aircraft Utilisation	■ Anti-cyclical purchasing ■ Optimise owned/leased mix ■ Fleet harmonisation ■ Optimise mix of older and new aircraft ■ Reduce turnaround times ■ Reduce maintenance downtime
Fuel Costs	■ Route Efficiency ■ Purchasing Costs ■ Weight Reduction	■ Shorter en-route and approach times ■ Reduce delays, use smaller airports ■ Reduction in service fees ■ Use of fuel hedging strategy ■ Calculation of "no show" passengers ■ Through product innovation, e.g. seats
Maintenance Costs	■ Fleet ■ Service Costs	■ Fleet harmonisation ■ Reduce average fleet age ■ Optimise maintenance activities ■ Joint purchasing of some work
Crew Costs	■ Productivity ■ Wage-related Costs ■ Crew Costs	■ Improved planning of crew logistics ■ Lower block hour restrictions ■ Fewer and/or less senior cabin crew ■ Reduction of extra-wage allowances ■ Reduce need for overnight stays ■ Reduce allowances for overnight stays
Handling Costs	■ Service Level ■ Insourcing ■ Reduce Handling Fees	■ Standardisation of SLAs ■ Revise SLA components ■ Pre-cleaning activities by cabin crew ■ Loading/unloading support from crew ■ Global contracts with key suppliers ■ Off-peak pricing
Catering Costs	■ Reduce unit costs ■ Reduce volumes	■ Simplification of meal choice ■ Reduce logistics costs for delivery ■ Monitor passengers v available meals ■ Improve waste management
Distribution	■ Ticketing ■ Sales Channels ■ Sales Commissions	■ Development of E-ticketing ■ Self-service check-ins ■ Divert customers to on-line channels ■ Efficient customer service call centre ■ Target-driven contracts with agents ■ Reduce commissions

All IATA airlines are committed to 100% e-ticketing by Jan 2008 reducing industry costs by US$3 billion. It also has plans for 'radio frequency identification' RFID baggage tags to improve the US$90 per bag, lost baggage problem.[51]

■ Another area for cost cutting – air quality? During flights, aircraft cabins are generally maintained at a pressure equivalent to an altitude between 7,000 and 8,000 feet.[52] Also the oxygen content of the ambient air is reduced by 25% relative to sea level (in line with the standards first issued in 1957). The air-conditioning systems also cause passenger dehydration

---

[50] IATA; Airline Cost Performance, Briefing No 5; July 2006; table 7.1.
[51] IATA Annual Report 2007.
[52] House of Commons Transport Committee; Passengers' Experiences of Air Travel Vol 2 (HC 435-II); Jul 2007.

Appendix 15 Factors Influencing Airline Choice

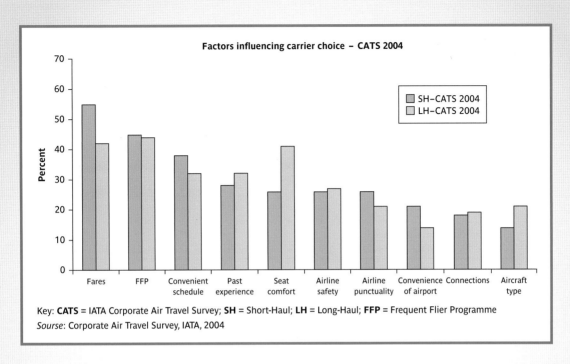

Factors influencing carrier choice – CATS 2004

Key: **CATS** = IATA Corporate Air Travel Survey; **SH** = Short-Haul; **LH** = Long-Haul; **FFP** = Frequent Flier Programme
Source: Corporate Air Travel Survey, IATA, 2004

■ The 2004 survey indicates that price is the main factor for short-haul carrier choice whereas for long-haul, seat comfort; frequent flier and price are 'equally' important in the choice of carrier. The 1999 survey is shown below.

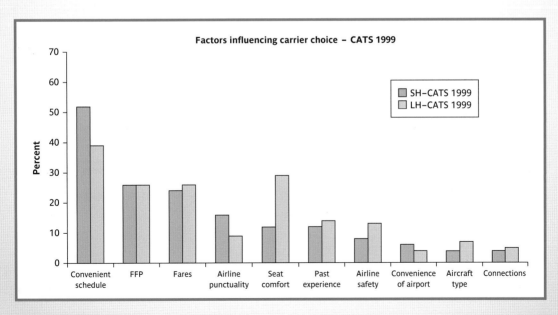

Factors influencing carrier choice – CATS 1999

Source: EU; Analysis of The EU Air Transport Industry; Final Report 2004[53]

---

[53] Available from http://ec.europa.eu/transport/air_portal/.

Appendix 16 Breakdown of Ryanair and easyJet Bases

Sept 2006	Routes	Aircraft	Airports served	Countries	Bases	Scheduled flights per year
easyJet	262	122	74	21	16	253,548
Ryanair	305	107	115	19	15	250,000 (estimate)

Sept 2006	Ryanair bases (15)	Routes	a/c	EasyJet bases (16)	a/c
Ireland	Dublin	52	15		
	Shannon	25	3		
	Cork	4	1		
UK	London (Stansted)	92	39	London (Stansted)	13
	Nottingham E Mids	15	2	Nottingham E Mids	3
	Liverpool	32	5	Liverpool	8
	Glasgow (Prestwick)	23	4	Glasgow	4
	London (Luton)	12	4	London (Luton)	17
				London (Gatwick)	18
				Belfast	5
				Bristol	9
				Edinburgh	3
				Newcastle	6
Italy	Milan (Bergamo)	20	4	Milan (Malpensa)	3
	Pisa	17	2		
	Rome (Ciampino)	21	5		
Germany	Frankfurt (Hahn)	41	7	Berlin	8
				Dortmund	4
Switzerland				Geneva	6
				Basel	4
Other	Barcelona (Girona)	22	3	Paris (Orly)	5
	Brussels (Charleroi)	17	4		
	Stockholm (Skavsta)	13	4		
	Tactical aircraft		5		6
	Total unique routes	305	107		122

Source: Company reports

Key a/c = aircraft

■ Ryanair cancelled 13 routes, launching 90 new routes and 3 bases in the 12 months to September 2006

■ By March 2007 Ryanair had a total of 20 bases and 487 routes

easyJet's choice of base/airport

easyJet has a dedicated airport negotiation team tasked with reducing unit costs at existing airports. They offer volume commitments in return for discounts. easyJet has withdrawn from high cost airports in the past.

easyJet new airport selection criteria:

■ Efficient infrastructure and processes suitable for easyJet

■ Convenient access to large catchment area (for high frequency services)

■ Partnerships through sustainable deals

■ Airport charges maintain low cost base

Source: easyJet FY2003 Results; 18 Nov 2003

CASE 6: Renault-Nissan: The Challenge of Sustaining Strategic Change

KANNAN RAMASWAMY

Twenty-six years! Twenty-six years of decline! I was amazed. In a company where you have 26 years of decline of the market, you have a lot of things to do first to stop, then reverse, the trend. It's not that in a couple of months you are going to fix this problem. We know it will require new products that we are bringing [out], higher brand power, more marketing, promotion, [and] advertising skills.

Mr. Carlos Ghosn in conversation with *BusinessWeek*, April 19, 2000.

So, is it time to write off Mr. Ghosn as a gifted turnaround artist who began to believe his own publicity and overreached himself when he took on the running of Renault as well as Nissan in 2005? And is the much-touted alliance between the two companies really superior, as he claims, to the car industry's usual approach of mergers, which often go wrong and destroy value?

The Economist, September 15, 2007.

Eight years had flown by since Renault and Nissan had announced their historic alliance in 1999. Nissan, at that time, seemed to have exhausted all avenues to revive itself. Saddled by a huge debt burden, a bloated supply chain structure, declining global market share, and dim prospects for the future, Nissan had turned to Renault as its partner of last resort. Renault had sized up the realities of the emerging shakeout in the global marketplace, and appeared to be determined to reshape itself so that it could engage in the intense rivalry that was emerging globally.

Louis Schweitzer, then CEO of Renault, signed an alliance deal with Nissan, invested $5.4 billion in the company, and chose Carlos Ghosn to take charge of the Nissan turnaround. In just three years, Ghosn had managed to dramatically turn the company around, a feat that successive CEOs at Nissan had been unable to engineer even over a couple of decades. However, Nissan's performance path after the crisis years seemed to have become increasingly rocky. A softening of demand in key markets, along with a resettling of the internal crisis within the company, appeared to have depleted its store of resolve and its will to continue striving. Renault itself was in deep trouble and struggling with an aging product line, strong unions, and lingering questions about its continued profitability. By early 2008, many questions had emerged about Ghosn's ability to maintain the momentum for change at both Nissan and Renault. Anything short of spectacular performance threatened to sully his meteoric rise in the world of global business. (Appendix 1 provides historical performance data for Renault and Nissan.)

The Global Automotive Industry in 1999

The late 1990s promised to reshape the evolution of the automotive industry in fundamental ways. Mergers and acquisitions dominated the landscape with $71.4 billion worth of deals announced in 1999 alone.[1] Fuelled by declining returns to shareholders and an intense competition for new customers, most automotive manufactures faced formidable odds against their success. Western Europe and North America comprised the two most important markets for the industry, accounting for roughly 65% of global product sales. Japan and the rest of Asia accounted for 21%, giving the industry a tripartite power structure. Although growth in key regions such as the United States was driven by the overall health of the economy, incentives that eased the customer price had become the rule of the game. Dealer and customer incentives ranged between 11% and 15%, depending on the size of the car and the dealer structure involved. This 'pay to sell' approach had begun to drain the economic health of the major companies and only served to continue the illusion of acceptable performance.

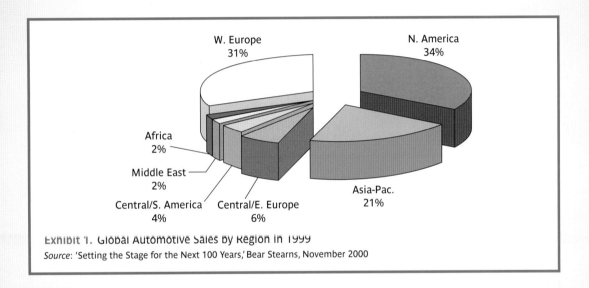

Exhibit 1. Global Automotive Sales by Region in 1999
Source: 'Setting the Stage for the Next 100 Years,' Bear Stearns, November 2000

Customers had become a central driving force in the business. Characterized by a general reluctance to pay ever-increasing prices, they had begun to assert their power by delaying purchases and demanding more features for the money they were paying. They were no longer content with the usual six-year model cycles complemented by annual incremental facelifts and makeovers. Platform consolidation, the process of combining multiple product lines into a smaller set of chassis and drive train combinations, promised requisite efficiencies that would allow manufacturers to offer more variety while at the same time holding down manufacturing costs. They had relied on value engineering, supply chain rationalization, and careful planning of product lines to reduce operating costs while offering a better value proposition to customers. Many leading companies had been able to reduce costs significantly, especially in replacement models, selling cars for several thousands of dollars lower than earlier versions in the same model line. Often, these later models were much better equipped, even at the base trim levels, and presented a winning value proposition to customers, especially when packaged with monetary incentives such as '0' down or 0% interest. For the manufacturers, these cost and innovation pressures had a direct impact on the bottom line. This spending pattern was expected to grow significantly with the advent of new technologies, more stringent emission standards, and the demands for greater fuel efficiency.

The entire supply chain felt the shift toward cost reduction and value focus. Many of the auto parts manufacturers faced the very same downward costs and margin pressures that the automakers were facing. Seeking to build efficiency through scale, many of the bigger players had bought out the smaller players, thus thinning the ranks of auto parts companies worldwide. By the turn of the century, six automotive groups controlled 82% of the industry and, remarkably, none of the six groups had existed in their current form even two years earlier.[2] Analysts believed that automakers had to move aggressively into new and emerging markets, purely as a matter of survival. Bear Stearns analysts had observed, 'With the largest markets being most mature, it is essential for the current players to seek growth in emerging markets....foreign assets in a region where an automaker does not have a local presence can be extremely valuable if they are accompanied with a developed distribution system that can be leveraged to bring other products to the market.'[3]

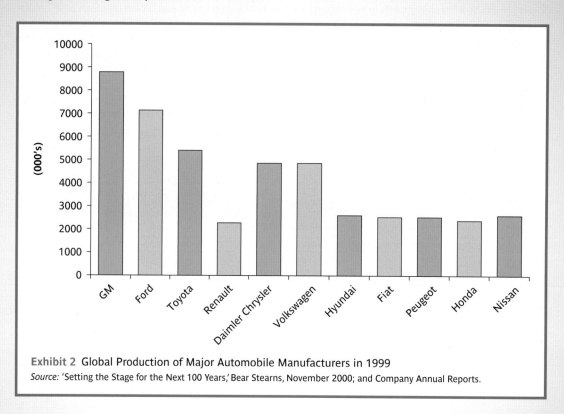

Exhibit 2 Global Production of Major Automobile Manufacturers in 1999
Source: 'Setting the Stage for the Next 100 Years,' Bear Stearns, November 2000; and Company Annual Reports.

The Renault-Nissan Alliance

It's a marriage of desperation for both parties. In the global consolidation race sweeping the industry, neither was the pick of the pack. Other big Japanese outfits rejected Renault's advances, while Nissan's attempts to cuddle up to both DaimlerChrysler and Ford Motor Co. flopped. But each of the two perennial wallflowers has something the other needs.

'Dangerous Liaison: It Could Take 10 Years for Renault-Nissan to Yield a Return,'
BusinessWeek, March 29, 1999.

Renault and Nissan were both jilted partners in the automotive world of the mid '90s. Although they each had their own unique desires for the pursuit of partnerships, they had been unable to attract any viable suitors. Renault had been quite a profitable company, with profits jumping a massive 63% in 1999. It had been very successful in launching a new line of cars reflecting the design savvy that it had come to be known for in Europe. The Megane line of cars and the Scenic minivan had become hot sellers for the company. The company had undergone a major restructuring process resulting in a compact supply chain and prudent cost control systems, although productivity and quality seemed to hold back the company from growing quickly. Many analysts believed that Renault lacked the engineering and productivity skills needed to further trim its cost structure to meet global benchmarks.

Renault's product line had limited appeal outside the immediate Western European market. Its early foray into the U.S. marketplace was met with stiff customer resistance. Finding the cars quite small, underpowered, and poorly appointed, American buyers had not embraced the brand. The bland styling and poor product quality proved insurmountable, leading to Renault's exit from the U.S. in 1986. It sold off its holdings in American Motor Company (AMC) and returned to its home markets. The decade of the 1990s had been one of regeneration for the company. It had established many design partnership programs to create a flair for its products, a critical missing ingredient when it retreated from the U.S. It had also embarked on a major realignment program that saw plant closings, layoffs, and cost-cutting measures implemented across the board. By 1999, the company seemed to be poised to seize the next major opportunity.

The first such opportunity emerged when Renault bid for the Swedish carmaker Volvo, a deal that would have consolidated its position in Europe. The deal, however, failed to materialize. Cultural incompatibilities were one of the many reasons that were blamed for the outcome. Renault did not have much of a global footprint like many of the bigger European and American counterparts in the business, however. It sold four of every five cars it manufactured within the Western European market, mostly France. Its emphasis on small cars and smaller engines meant that it did not have the broad portfolio needed to confidently enter the global marketplace in locations such as the U.S. where minivans, SUVs, and light trucks were the rage. In an increasingly globalized industry, with the global consolidation race well under way worldwide, Renault's future remained uncertain.

Nissan, on the other hand, had been teetering on the brink of collapse. It had been losing market share globally for eight years in a row, and had seen home-based rivals chipping away at its market position in Japan. It had lost market share in its home market for 26 years straight with no end in sight. Over the years, the benevolent banking system in Japan had given Nissan a wide berth by extending significant loans that helped it tide over its misfortunes. In the face of widespread economic stagnation in the country, even the friendly banks, however, decided to call in the loans and pressured the company to find a partner willing to bail it out. The automotive debt burden for Nissan had risen to $20 billion by that time, while overall debt exceeded $38 billion dollars – four times the company's market capitalization.

The reasons for the dramatic failure were manifold. Nissan was viewed as a bureaucratic company, run much like a state-owned enterprise, complete with multiple layers of decision making, lax control, and a weak performance culture. It had fairly complex supply chains encompassing more than 3,000 suppliers supporting 25 different platforms. Only four of its 43 models were profitable,[4] and it had an excess capacity of roughly 50% – a production network it had built in the heyday of the luxury business when the company had attempted to double its sales to 1.5 million units in a short time. The projected demand never materialized, and the company had nothing to show for its investments but an annual interest bill that totaled $1 billion in 1998. Three successive CEOs had tried to stem the decline by launching transformation programs. Yukata Kume, the CEO in 1992, made the first attempt to save the sinking ship by launching a program that called for plant closings, rationalization of models and supply chains, and overall cost reductions. However, his plan did not achieve much traction, and the situation continued to deteriorate when Yoshifumi Tsuji took over in 1993. Tsuji drafted another transformation program that was quite similar to the one established by his predecessor. However, by 1996 there were still no signs of a real turnaround. Yoshikazu Hanawa took over the reins of the company at that time and was blessed with a fortuitous decline in the Japanese yen, which helped lift the company's exports, placing Nissan in second position behind Honda in Japan. This blessing was short lived because the underinvestment in its plants caught up with the company, forcing it to extend model years and cut R&D expenditure. Hanawa launched another transformation effort in 1998 following disappointing losses, and started the quest for partners.

Renault and Nissan initiated talks in July 1998, and began to seriously explore the potential for a deal over the next six to eight months. This period of due diligence was characterized by intense cooperation between the two companies, and involved a fairly large group of top leaders as well as middle managers.[5] Three sets of people simultaneously examined the potential benefits of the deal. They included the two leaders of the companies, Louis Schweitzer and Y. Hanawa, five lead negotiators for Renault, and four lead negotiators for Nissan, representing functions ranging from finance to legal and corporate planning functions, and about a hundred engineers and specialists from each side.[6] Twenty-one joint study teams were formed to examine each distinct element of the operations of both companies. The study teams offered personnel from both groups the opportunity to understand organizational priorities, organizational culture practices, and to build trust across the firms even before the deal was signed. The negotiations stalled at a critical juncture when the legalities of establishing a joint venture structure threatened to get in the way of the deal. Schweitzer sought counsel from his trusted adviser Carlos Ghosn, who was not directly involved in the process of negotiations or due diligence. Ghosn advised Schweitzer to drop the joint venture approach and pursue an alliance instead. This proved to be a critical rallying point during the process and helped the teams overcome the legal wrangling and smooth out their differences.

In March 1999, Schweitzer and Hanawa signed an alliance agreement allowing Renault to buy 36.8% of Nissan for $5.4 billion. Renault was also given the right to increase its holding to 44.4% from May 2001 if it so desired. Nissan took a 10% stake in Renault. The deal was promoted as an alliance. The main distinction was that both firms would keep their identities separate and would be run by separate management teams. However, they would leverage common synergies through custombuilt processes spanning a range of functions from design to engineering, and product development to distribution. This organizational design caused further consternation among industry watchers who had already discounted the potential for the deal. The deal was variously described as an alliance of the weak, and a marriage of the poor.[7] One European CEO summed up the prospects by observing, 'Two mules don't make a race horse.' Bob Lutz, then CEO of Chrysler, remarked that investing $5 billion in Nissan would be tantamount to putting the money in a container and sinking it in the ocean.

Implementing the Deal: Carlos Ghosn Comes to Tokyo

...for a recently turned-around Renault, the Nissan link is a dangerous liaison. Auto-industry experts figure it could be 8 to 10 years before Renault saw a real return on its investment, if all goes well. Meantime, potential conflicts over everything from management control to cost-cutting loom large – even though Renault's 35% stake would enable it to veto decisions it doesn't like. And if Nissan's makeover fails, the wasted investment could kill Renault's chances of remaining independent.

'Dangerous Liaison: It Could Take 10 Years for Renault-Nissan to Yield a Return,'
BusinessWeek, March 29, 1999.

Having signed the alliance agreement, Louis Schweitzer called on Carlos Ghosn to head to Japan to oversee the Nissan turnaround. Although Ghosn himself rated the probability of his success at 50%, Schweitzer had much greater confidence in his abilities, and was convinced that he had a very good shot at achieving success.[8] Schweitzer had seen Ghosn in action when they had to shut down a plant and make some tough decisions in Viloorde, Belgium. Ghosn had displayed remarkable skill in cutting costs, restructuring operations, and maintaining employee morale all through the layoffs. The complexities involved in turning Nissan around were undeniably greater. Colored by a very strong business culture, a proud automotive heritage, and a deeply ingrained sense of process, restructuring Nissan would prove to be a formidable challenge.

Carlos Ghosn: Credentials to Get the Job Done*

Carlos Ghosn was born in Porto Bello, Brazil, to parents of Lebanese origin. After a period of schooling at a Jesuit institution, Ghosn was accepted to the famous *École Polytechnique* in Paris. He was fluent in English, French, Arabic, and Portuguese. After completing studies at the *Polytechnique*, Ghosn continued his education at another *grande école, L'École des Mines*. Michelin recruited him even before his graduation to oversee construction of a new tire plant in Brazil. After stints in corporate R&D, he rose to become the COO of Michelin's South American operations at the young age of 30. In Brazil, he learned the skills to manage under extreme uncertainty, given poor economic conditions that prevailed with hyperinflation. His success was soon rewarded with a transfer to the U.S. as COO of North American operations in 1989. The assignment centered on integrating the operations of Uniroyal Goodrich, a company that Michelin had acquired. Ghosn was caught between two completely different corporate cultures, ownership philosophies, and working styles. Being a family-owned company, Michelin emphasized long-term growth, while Uniroyal focused on short-term earnings. During the U.S. recession at the time, Michelin sought predictable sales volumes that were guaranteed by OEM (original equipment manufacturers) contracts with leading car companies. Uniroyal, however, focused on the replacement market, where margins were much higher. This was reflective of the fundamental differences that Ghosn had to blend into a successful operation. He quickly realized the neither the French approach nor the U.S. approach to management was ideal, and for best results he had to merge the best elements of both while minimizing the unique downsides that each brought. He crafted a new governance structure built on cross-functional teams (CFTs) to meet those ends. After the recession in 1994, Michelin reported its first sizable profits in the U.S., and Ghosn attributed the results partly to the CFTs that helped rally different functional interests toward achieving organizational objectives. In 1996, Renault extended him an offer to join them in Paris as their new EVP of Operations, spanning functions such as manufacturing, engineering, product development, purchasing, and cost control. The company had just reported losses of $1 billion that year.

Ghosn wasted no time in drafting plans for cost reductions of $2.4 billion over three years. The central themes of his initiative encompassed elimination of excess production capacity, improving the speed and agility of the product development and engineering process, rationalizing car platforms, and shrinking the supplier network. In helping create the momentum for these significant changes, he introduced the CFT concept that had worked so well in Michelin, Brazil. By 1998, Renault had become a healthy, profitable car company.

The Nissan Challenge

In a sense, Ghosn was expecting to be called upon to lead the Nissan turnaround. 'I suppose I was a natural candidate for the job, as I had contributed to the turnaround at Renault....I had been in challenging situations before then as well,' he observed.[9] Despite the professional excitement surrounding the assignment, Ghosn had to tackle some organizational issues before deciding to go to Japan. He realized that the job would require a great deal of latitude from Renault headquarters, and that he would not have the time to wait for approval on critical decisions. He discussed his reservations with the company and obtained top leadership approval to make decisions locally in Japan without reverting to Paris. He also reserved the right to pick his own team.

He assembled a small group of executives that included many Renault veterans and other potential high fliers. Only one member spoke Japanese, and none had worked in Japan before. Ghosn was more concerned about the innate abilities of his team to make dramatic changes and act as catalysts of change in a fairly staid and stodgy environment. Prior to his departure for Tokyo, the group met for a three-day briefing on 'do's and don'ts' but, more importantly, to focus on the key messages that Ghosn wanted them to fully embrace. He wanted them to know that they were not going to Japan as missionaries of social change, preaching new ideas about the role of women in society, or the merits of a performance culture vs. a hierarchy based on seniority. Instead, he wanted them to focus on fixing Nissan exclusively without getting mired in social debates about prevailing business custom and practice in the country.

He was officially appointed as the COO of Nissan in June 1999, with Hanawa continuing in the role of president of the company. Ghosn, along with two other Renault executives, Patrick Pelata and Thierry Moulonguet, was nominated to the board of Nissan. Hanawa was looking to Ghosn for some guidance

---

* Much of this section is drawn from Carlos Ghosn's 2004 autobiography, *Shift: Inside Nissan's Historic Revival*, Currency Books.

about board appointees from Nissan, but Ghosn demurred, emphasizing that Hanawa should have the final say and pick executives he thought would complement Ghosn well. In the spirit of forging close links between the two companies, Tsumoto Sawada, the former EVP of Manufacturing and Engineering at Nissan, was appointed as an adviser to Schweitzer. This helped Renault gain a vantage position to help transfer technologies across the companies, especially in the areas of engineering.

Structural Changes

Ghosn believed in maintaining an open mind during all stages of the transformation process. He observed, 'You must start with a clean sheet of paper, because the worst thing you can have is pre-fabricated solutions....you have to start with a zero base of thinking, cleaning everything out of your mind. You have to have the approach of a scientist. [A scientist] has a lot of knowledge, but his knowledge is only a tool. Observation of fact brings him the solution.'[10] In keeping with this belief, he did not have a well-hewn plan to turn Nissan around when he arrived in Japan. He did hit the ground running, however. Traveling to all of Nissan's plants, he engaged in conversation with the entire cadre of the company, ranging from shop floor employees to executives. Aided by translators, he was curious to hear from the shop floor workers about their views on what ailed Nissan and what they thought needed fixing. He also showed the same curiosity in conversations with Nissan dealers, primarily focusing on issues such as product design and appeal, possible new offerings, and the key impediments in the marketplace. These conversations were characterized by respect and trust, the twin qualities that Ghosn believed were essential in cementing interorganizational relationships.

Taking a page from his previous management experience at Michelin and Renault, Ghosn created a structure around Cross-Company Teams (CCTs) and Cross-Functional Teams (CFTs). The eleven CCTs were organized around 'synergy' areas such as purchasing, manufacturing, product platforms, and technology. Staffed by 10 members each, almost exclusively from middle management ranks, the CCTs were the key drivers for generating the revival plan for the company. Appointments to the CCTs were made solely on the basis of merit. Smaller teams that lent specialized expertise in focus areas such as capacity planning and investments supported the CCTs. The work of the CCTs was complemented by the CFTs within each of the companies. As Ghosn saw it, 'The cross-company teams and the cross-functional teams working separately inside Nissan and Renault have complementary roles: the company CFTs serve as guardians of each company's revival plan, while the CCTs feed the alliance.'[11]

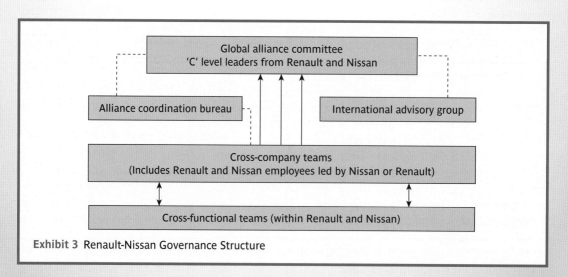

Exhibit 3 Renault-Nissan Governance Structure

Ghosn used the team selection process as a vehicle to convey the gravity of the situation as well as his intent to rely on middle management expertise. To this end, he asked that 1,500 profiles of leading Nissan candidates for these assignments, both from Japanese as well as international operations, be posted at headquarters so that choices could be made on the basis of merit. He was personally interested in this important task, and shaped choice assignments himself. As one executive observed, 'Ghosn brought a lot of mavericks with him. He has shown those are the kinds of people he likes.'[12] The teams were given 90 days to prepare actionable plans for the turnaround. There were no sacred cows, and everything was on the table for discussion and change. As the teams began the hard work to draft specific plans, Ghosn was priming the employees for change. He unfailingly mentioned the fact that Nissan had just ceded the #2 spot in the market to Honda, and that the revival plan that the teams were working on represented the last hope for Nissan. Very visible on plant floors across the Nissan network, Ghosn engaged in conversations with the rank and file to elicit their ideas and impressions. His instincts, sharpened while at Michelin and Renault, proved right. The workers on the shop floor did have important insights about the problems that plagued the company and possible solutions that could fix them.

English was chosen as the common language of communication for all official exchanges under the alliance. English language courses were offered to both Nissan and Renault employees, while Ghosn himself was taking Japanese conversation courses. He took the additional step of creating a dictionary of sorts, because he realized that some key English terms such as commitment, targets, and transparency had different meanings in Japan and France. He urged his top management team to be transparent in thought, word, and action. 'What we think, what we say, and what we do must be the same. We have to be impeccable in ensuring that our words correspond to our actions. If there are discrepancies between what we profess and how we behave, that will spell disaster.'[13] In a break with tradition, Ghosn insisted that the press be invited to the first annual meeting. Ghosn started his address in Japanese and switched to English, outlining the challenges that lay ahead. He told the audience, 'I have not come to Japan for Renault, but for Nissan. I will do everything in my power to bring Nissan back to profitability at the earliest date possible and revive it as a highly attractive company.'[14]

The Nissan Revival Plan was ready for launch in October 1999, three months after the new governance structure had been implemented. On the eve of the annual Tokyo Motor Show, Ghosn presented the restructuring plan to a wide audience of journalists and car enthusiasts worldwide. This was the first time most Nissan employees themselves heard about the plan and its projections. He made the case for change rather succinctly by recalling the abysmal performance history of the company, declining market share, enormous debt burden, lack of profitable exciting new models, and a culture that seemed to take poor performance in its stride. He then proceeded to identify the key milestones for the transformation. Purchasing costs that had ballooned on the backs of multiple platforms, bloated supply chains, and a benevolent keiretsu system would be reined in by 20% over three years. Manufacturing capacity, which was estimated at 53% excess, would be cut by 30% through plant closures and platform consolidation. Nissan's shareholding in nonstrategic keiretsu networks would be liquidated to fund the transformation plan and pay down Nissan debt. For example, Nissan had an investment of $216 million in Fuji Heavy Industries, a company that made Subaru cars, Nissan's competitor. Central to this major transformation would be a rekindling of the innovative spirit of design and product excellence within the company. Toward that end, Ghosn announced that Nissan would be reviving the 'Z', an icon of design and engineering prowess that had been discontinued due to a lack of funding.

In his closing remarks, Ghosn acknowledged that if the revival plan succeeded, it would have many fathers, but if it failed, it would have only one – himself. He summarized his objectives in three areas: (1) a return to profitable operations by 2000, (2) operating margin of at least 4.5% by 2002, and (3) decrease Nissan's outstanding debt to $6.3 billion by 2002. The top management would be personally accountable for meeting these objectives, he added. 'The big risk is that if you announce ambitious goals, people will not believe you. They'll say, 'He said 100%, but if he gets 50% he will be happy'....Well, we want 100 and we're going to get 100. If we don't get it next year, that's it: we will resign...'[15]

Delivering on the Promise

'What people see is what we execute. Part of my Latin surroundings is an ability to talk too much and not implement. I've seen it in many places – Brazil, France, and Italy – where people tend

to think about a problem and talk about it without doing anything about it. The temptation to talk is so big. I consider it pleasant on a personal level; extremely unpleasant in business.'
D. Magee, *Turnaround: How Carlos Ghosn Rescued Nissan*, Harper Collins: NY, 2003.

Ghosn focused his energies almost exclusively within the company to keep the employees motivated and driven to succeed. Realizing that massive changes usually bring forth significant uncertainty, he assured all employees that everyone would have a role in Nissan, provided they were willing to abide by the new performance expectations and keep the best interests of the company in mind. Although plant closings would result in a reduction of the workforce by 21,000 jobs over three years, there would be no layoffs. Instead, the company would use attritions, early retirements, and relocations to ease the pain of plant closings.

The message was clearly one of positive engagement and implementation of revival plans under very tight deadlines. The governance structure originally created to develop the revival plans was continued because it seemed to offer a good approach to bringing the best of both companies together. It was apparent that a change in mindset was crucial to achieving a successful transformation. Ghosn consistently told employees that they should spend 95% of their time on implementation and only 5% of their time in planning, contrary to the tradition at Nissan and Renault. The cultures on both sides had to become more receptive to new ideas, new ways of looking at existing obstacles, and creative approaches to leveraging new opportunities that were emerging.

The exchange of ideas across companies was fostered through several mechanisms in addition to the CCTs that were in place. Teams of Renault engineers and production employees visited Nissan and vice versa to share their expertise. Those on deputation were explicitly told that they should not think of themselves as Nissan employees working at Renault or Renault employees working at Nissan. Instead, they were to consider themselves as working for the alliance. Nissan's production supervisors, adept at controlling operating and engineering processes, were quite visible on plant floors in Renault plants. The Asian *Wall Street Journal* reported a scene where a Japanese shop floor supervisor was demonstrating to a group of French workers the right way to hold a wrench while performing a particular process and how the workers seemed to be listening with rapt attention despite the apparent cultural differences between them and the Japanese demonstrator.[16]

On the Nissan side of the equation, Patrick Pelata, who was overseeing some of the key marketing functions, learned that the brand identity for Nissan was quite a confusing mix of messages that differed significantly across key markets. In forging a common identity, Nissan's design team was relocated from the engineering group to the marketing group. Some of the top executives were stationed in major markets such as the U.S. as opposed to Tokyo as had been the usual practice. A global marketing team was created to coordinate Nissan's activities across the globe, offering much higher levels of clarity and transparency. Regional presidencies in Europe and North America were folded down and replaced by a committee structure with both area and function VPs jointly deciding on geographic strategies. This had the beneficial impact of reducing miscommunication and again emphasized clear strategic direction and responsibility traceable to the very top of the organization. By mid-2002, 30% of all purchasing was jointly done between Renault and Nissan. This required some deft handling of sensitivities across the two companies, since both parties felt that they had more exacting standards than the other. Within the purchasing organization, there was a new structure in place with a general manager overseeing each of the major input areas, namely power trains, vehicle parts, and materials and services. Under each of the general managers, there were Global Supplier Account Managers (GSAMs) who negotiated with large suppliers worldwide. Deputy GSAMs assisted the GSAMs. When the GSAM was a Renault employee, the DGSAM was a Nissan employee, and vice versa. This 'mirror-effect' helped immensely since the decision-makers were talking to counterparts who shared similar concerns and perspectives on the other side. They spoke the same language of the function, i.e., purchasing. Global structures were established for managing finance, manufacturing, IT, and R&D functions. Similar changes (see Exhibit 4) were introduced to seek synergies in a range of areas spanning product design and manufacturing to managing dealerships.

Exhibit 4 Alliance Actions and Benefits

Action	Remarks	Benefits
Joint Purchasing	By 2007, 82% of purchasing was done jointly. The companies share 64% of the same suppliers.	Input costs account for 70% of a car's value. The Alliance has been able to gain a 4% price reduction each year.
Common Platforms	The Alliance has seven common platforms. Nissan has also reduced its platforms from 25 to about 15.	Platform synergies include sharing common parts, design specifications, and manufacturing processes.
Joint R&D	The Alliance has pooled resources to pursue fuel cell technologies and new designs for more fuel-efficient engines.	Economies of scale and scope are realized. Knowledge-sharing benefits can magnify research potential.
Common Manufacturing	The Alliance shares factories in Brazil, Spain, South Africa, and Mexico	Savings in CAPEX, economies of scale, increased capacity utilization.
Joint Distribution	Nissan merged its admin. operations with Renault in Europe and obtained greater access to South America through Renault. Renault entered Australia, Taiwan, and Indonesia	Market access and economies of scope. Costs benefits in overhead cost reduction through shared facilities.

Changing Mindsets

Management of talent and human resources was an integral part of the change effort. Ghosn saw that his plans would only be successful if he could replace key elements of the administrative heritage of Nissan, and that obviously called for radical changes in managing people. There were three key dimensions that warranted further examination; namely, (1) the seniority system of career growth and advancement, (2) a culture of blame, and (3) lack of clear motivation and rewards.

Like most Japanese companies, managers were promoted from within on the basis of seniority; hence, the longer they stayed in the firm, the more power and monetary rewards they were able to garner independent of their performance. Having risen in rank, they had little incentive to adopt new methods, or radically new ideas, choosing instead to maintain the consensus-driven status quo. Although this proved to be a major impediment in the transformation, Ghosn did not want to challenge the system directly. Instead, he made sure that all nominations for promotions and compensation rewards would be based entirely on performance. He created and headed a team called the Nomination Advisory Committee to review promotion recommendations in the company. It was mandated that within a year, every promotion had to be ratified by this committee solely on performance considerations before it could take effect. In so doing, he was able to elevate a younger cadre of high-performing managers through the ranks at a pace that would have been impossible in the traditional company. Two VPs who were in their early 40s were promoted to Senior VP rank, an unheard-of progression in the company. However, he made sure that they did not discriminate against managers solely on the basis of their age. In fact, most of the senior VPs the committee nominated during the first two years were long-serving veterans who had delivered results.

Performance bonuses were instituted with much tighter definitions as to what constituted superior performance. In the past, most employees received a bonus independent of their performance levels. The high performers were only marginally better compensated than others. This extended all the way to top management. Using a stock options program, Ghosn spearheaded a more individualized system that set targets and commitments, almost completely new terms in the Nissan lexicon. Performance outcomes were closely monitored and rewarded almost immediately. Cash incentives, spot promotions, and other motivational devices were introduced. Ghosn appeared willing to take a chance on younger managers who demonstrated performance although they did not have a long track record.

The performance-oriented culture required clear delineation of responsibilities and expectations at all levels, something that was absent at Nissan. This critical lapse had led to departmental battles where one department would blame the other for missed targets or other performance shortfalls. Designers would blame engineering, who would in turn blame manufacturing, who would then blame finance, and so on. In a clear departure from the past, even the most senior leaders were held accountable, and there were indeed some who were let go. Cross-functional teams, global functions, and periodic personnel rotations fostered a climate where people began gaining a clearer picture of their interconnected roles.

Emerging Victorious

In May 2001, when the first full-year results after the transformation began were announced, there was reason for at least cautious celebration. Sales had grown by 1.9% to nearly $50 billion and debt had shrunk nearly 50%. Operating margins had tripled to 4.75%. In many ways, Ghosn had not only fulfilled some of the key promises he made when unveiling the revival plan, but in fact delivered the promises in a much shorter time frame than had been expected. For the first time in 26 years, Nissan seemed to have found the right road to prosperity. At the Tokyo Auto Show later that year, the first-half results for 2001 were revealed to be more promising. Nissan's operating margin had reached 6.8%, and 18 of its 38 models were now profitable. Ghosn's colleagues and industry analysts waxed poetic at this miraculous turnaround. Executive VP and Board member Norio Matsumura observed, 'His greatest performance is that he was able to restructure people's mindsets.'[17] A shareholder commented, 'Japanese managers couldn't have done what he has done. They'd have felt too many obligations. They wouldn't have been able to take bold measures'[18]

> *No matter how promising your resources, you will never be able to turn them into gold unless you get the corporate culture right. A good corporate culture taps into the productive aspects of a country's culture, and in Nissan's case we have been able to exploit the uniquely Japanese combination of keen competitiveness and sense of community that has driven the likes of Sony and Toyota – and Nissan itself in earlier times…people have to believe that they can speak the truth and that they can trust what they hear from others…*
>
> C. Ghosn, 'Saving the Business without Losing the Company,' *Harvard Business Review*, January 2002.

New Responsibilities and New Challenges

Louis Schweitzer announced his retirement from Renault in the summer of 2005. While Nissan had shown promising signs of rebirth and revival, Renault had taken a turn for the worse. Profitability had declined precipitously, and the products it had to offer were too old and stodgy for a dynamic marketplace. It had also been unable to profitably enter new emerging markets and still depended on Europe for 72% of its revenues. The competition at home was getting tougher. Toyota had joined hands with French rival Citroën to boost its market share in France. Renault, in the meantime, still encountered quality and productivity problems. Nissan proved to be a great portfolio investment for Renault in retrospect, because its 44.4% stake in that company yielded 50% of its entire profitability in 2004. Although not as dire as Nissan's situation in 1999, Carlos Ghosn was tapped once again to take over the reins from Schweitzer, and arrived in Paris in May 2005.

He set out a revival plan dubbed Commitment 2009, which called for an increase in sales of about 800,000 vehicles, an increase in operating profit of 6% from 3.2%, and an increase in dividends per share from 1.80 to 4.50. No mass manufacturer other than BMW had achieved a margin of 6% in Europe. By 2007, the news was far from good. One of the key projects, a luxury car named Vel Setis, failed due to poor styling and other performance considerations. Operating margins hovered around

2.5%. Forays into markets such as Russia had proven to be expensive with an initial run of negative double-digit operating margins.

Since taking over as CEO of Renault, Ghosn was the first leader to run two major automobile companies in tandem. This had begun to take its toll. There were critical setbacks in the U.S. market for Nissan. The plant in Canton, Ohio, was just coming up to speed, having fixed many of the quality problems that had plagued it since its inception. In February of 2007, Nissan issued its first profit warning since the turnaround, and reported its first annual loss immediately after. The company had indicated that it would miss its sales target of 4.2 million vehicles in 2009. Operating margins had declined by 11%, and sales in its home market were not promising either. Nissan had dropped its market share from 18.4% to 16.6% in its home market, and the overall industry itself was in the grip of a 20-year low in Japan.

Many were beginning to question whether Ghosn would be able to manage a comeback for Nissan in view of the ominous signs on the horizon. Combined with a faltering Renault that was just barely beginning to show signs of resurgence, would he be able to manage the monumental task of making a course correction for both companies? Some believed that Ghosn had driven a bit too hard at Nissan, and continuing the pace of transformation would be quite difficult now that the crisis had passed. As The Economist observed, 'Much will depend on his ability to rekindle the sense of urgency that helped bring Nissan back from the brink eight years ago. In today's less dramatic circumstances, it will not be easy.'[19]

Notes

[1] 'Megamergers Accelerating Strong Trends That Are Reshaping the Global Automotive Industry's Approach to the Car Buyer,' *Business Wire*, May 16, 2000.

[2] 'Global Auto Consolidation,' CommerzBank, 14 September 2000.

[3] 'Setting the Stage for the Next 100 Years,' Bear Stearns, November 2000.

[4] 'Renissant?' *The Economist*, March 20, 1999, pp. 65–66.

[5] S. Miller, 'Renault Steers Forward. After a Failed Marriage to Volvo, Schweitzer Gets It Right with Nissan,' *The Wall Street Journal*, February 15, 2001.

[6] Pierre-Yves Gomez, H. Korine, and O. Masclef, 'Generating Cooperative Behavior Between the Unacquainted: A Case Study of the Renault/Nissan Alliance Formation Process,' Working Paper, EM Lyon and London Business School, 2002.

[7] Y. Ono, 'Lesson for Today: When in Japan, Bow to Shareholders,' *The Asian Wall Street Journal*, June 21, 2000.

[8] G. Edmondson, 'How Renault Jump-Started Nissan, *BusinessWeek*, October 1, 2004.

[9] C. Ghosn, 'Saving the Business without Losing the Company,' *Harvard Business Review*, January 2002, pp. 3–11.

[10] D. Magee, *Turnaround: How Carlos Ghosn Rescued Nissan*, Harper Collins: NY, 2003.

[11] Ghosn, 'Saving the Business without Losing the Company.'

[12] T. Burt, and A. Harney, 'Le Cost Killer Makes His Move,' *Financial Times*, November 9, 1999.

[13] V. Emerson, 'An Interview with Carlos Ghosn,' *Journal of World Business*, Spring 2001, pp. 3–11.

[14] S. Strom, 'In a Change, Nissan Opens Annual Meeting to Press,' *New York Times*, June 26, 1999.

[15] T. Peterson, 'Nissan's Carlos Ghosn: No If's, No And's, No But's,' *BusinessWeek*, January 18, 2000.

[16] S. Miller, and T. Zaun, 'Nissan Intends to Return a Favor to a French Ally,' *The Asian Wall Street Journal*, April 5–7, 2002.

[17] A. Taylor, 'Nissan's U-Turn to Profits,' *Fortune*, February 18, 2002.

[18] I. Williams, 'Japan's New Superstar,' *Sunday Telegraph*, July 1, 2001.

[19] 'Tough Ghosn; Face Value,' *The Economist*, September 15, 2007.

Appendix

	1999	2000	2001	2002	2003	2004	2005	2006
Historical Performance Trends for Renault (Thousands of Euros)								
Sales Revenues	36278	38583	34617	34586	35658	38772	39978	40097
Cost of Goods Sold	28264	30214	28240	28178	29273	31162	32137	32499
Operating Income	2205	2022	473	1483	1402	2418	1323	1063
Operating Margin %	6.08	5.24	1.37	4.29	3.93	6.24	3.31	2.65
Income from Nissan	−330	56	497	1335	1705	1767	2275	1871
EPS	2.23	4.5	4.38	7.53	9.32	13.35	13.19	11.17
Shares Outstanding	239798	239798	239998	259560	265960	265960	255177	256994
Historical Performance Trends for Nissan (Millions of Yen)								
Sales revenues	5977075	6089620	6196241	6828588	7429219	8576277	9428292	10468583
Cost of Sales	4568233	4633780	4546526	4872324	5310172	6351269	7040987	8027186
Operating Income	82565	290314	489215	737230	824855	861160	871841	776939
Operating Margin %	1.38	4.77	7.90	10.80	11.10	10.04	9.25	7.42
EPS	−179.98	83.53	92.61	117.75	122.02	125.16	126.94	112.33
Employees	141526	133833	125099	127625	123748	183607*	183356	186336

*Increase in employees due to growth activity and acquisitions in China and elsewhere.
Source: Company annual reports.

CASE 7: Strategic Leadership and Innovation at Apple Inc[1]

WARWICK
BUSINESS SCHOOL

'Stop and look at Apple for a second, since it's an odd company....While most high-tech firms focus on one or two sectors, Apple does all of them at once...Apple is essentially operating its own closed miniature techno-economy....If you follow conventional wisdom, Apple is doing it all wrong. And yet...this is the company that gave us three of the signature technological innovations of the past 30 years: the Apple II, the Macintosh and the iPod' (Grossman, 2005).

Apple's Fall and Rise

Voted as the most innovative company for three consecutive years during 2006–2008 and as America's number 1 most Admired Company (McGregor, 2008), Apple seemed to have it all: innovative products that have redefined their markets (such as the iMac and the iPod), a consumer base as loyal as a fun club, and a business model characterized by vertical integration and synergies that no competitor could easily imitate. The Apple brand had transcended the barriers of the computer industry to traverse the consumer electronics, record, movie, and the video and music production industries (see Figure 1 for an outline of Apple's product and service portfolio). In 2008 the Apple brand was listed as the 24th most valuable global brand (up from 33rd place the previous year), valued at $13.7bn (Interbrand, 2008).

After a lacklustre period during 1989–1997 when Apple was nearly written off, its dynamic comeback was impressive. Between 2003 and 2008 Apple's sales tripled to $24 billion and profits increased to $3.5 billion, up from a mere $24 million (see Table 1 for an outline of Apple's financial performance during 2006–8). Apple topped Fortune 500 companies for total return to shareholders both over 2003–2008 (94% return) as well as over 1998–2008 (51% return) (Morris, 2008: 68), a remarkable achievement.

But things haven't always been that rosy for the company once known as the underdog of the computer industry. During the time when Steve Jobs was not part of the organization (1985–1997) Apple progressively degenerated to the point of struggling for survival. Apple charged premium prices and operated through a closed proprietary system, at a time when more economical, IBM-compatible PCs gained mass appeal. Its cost base was high compared with its major competitors. This combination of factors led to shrinking market share and lower profitability. Apple lost momentum in the PC industry, despite the effort of three different CEOs to reverse the downfall (see Table 2 for a timeline of Apple's CEO tenures).

This case was written by Professor Loizos Heracleous and Angeliki Papachroni, Warwick Business School. It is intended to be used as the basis for class discussion rather than to illustrate either effective or ineffective handling of a management situation. The case was compiled from published sources.

[1] This case was prepared by Professor Loizos Heracleous and Angeliki Papachroni for the purposes of class discussion and is not meant to illustrate effective or ineffective handling of administrative situations. Warwick Business School, loizos.heracleous@wbs.ac.uk, January 2009.

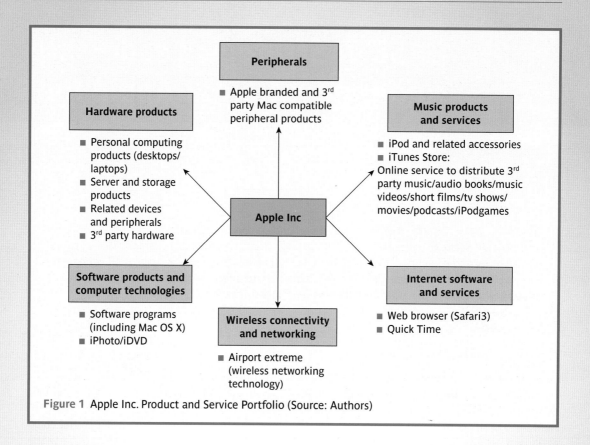

Figure 1 Apple Inc. Product and Service Portfolio (Source: Authors)

John Sculley attempted to gain market share (at the time around 7%) by introducing lower priced products that still had a technological edge, forged alliances with IBM to work on a joint operating system and multimedia applications, and outsourced much of manufacturing to subcontractors to cut costs. A joint alliance was also formed with Novell and Intel to reconfigure Apple's OS to run on Intel chips. By the end of Sculley's tenure in 1993 however, market share was at around 8%, and Apple's gross profits reduced from around 50% to 34% (Yoffie & Slind, 2008).

During Spindler's tenure, the alliances with Intel and Novell, as well as with IBM, were exited, and a decision was taken to license Apple's OS to companies that would make Mac clones (a decision reversed by Jobs in 1997). There was focus on international growth, and more cost-cutting efforts. With performance remaining flat, Spindler was replaced by Gil Amelio. In 1996, under Amelio, Apple went through three successive restructurings and further cost cutting. At the same time, Amelio aimed to return Apple to its premium price, differentiation strategy (Yoffie & Slind, 2008). The biggest challenge at the time was the release of Apple's new generation operating system in response to the release of Microsoft's Windows 95, which had received great attention upon its release one year earlier. Apple's OS system named Copland, on the other hand, was so behind schedule that the company decided to turn to external help. Ironically, Apple turned to NeXT, a software company founded by Steve Jobs after his departure from Apple in 1985. Meanwhile, Apple's market share fell to 3% and Amelio was forced out by the board of directors.

After NeXT's help with the new version of Apple's operating system, Apple's executive board resolved to buy the company. A year later, in July 1997, Jobs was offered the title of Apple's CEO, after spending a few months as a consultant at Apple. This was a crucial time in the company's history. Apple's stock had sunk to $3.30 and the company reported a net loss of $708 million in its second quarter that year, flirting with bankruptcy. At the same time competitors like Dell and Microsoft were thriving, following the tech boom of the late 1990's. Jobs took on the role of Interim CEO in 1997 and then became CEO during 2000.

Table 1 Selected Apple Financial Data

	2008	Change	2007	Change	2006
Net Sales by Operating Segment:					
Americas net sales	$ 14,573	26%	$ 11,596	23%	$ 9,415
Europe net sales	7,622	40%	5,460	33%	4,096
Japan net sales	1,509	39%	1,082	(11)%	1,211
Retail net sales	6,315	53%	4,115	27%	3,246
Other Segments net sales (a)	2,460	40%	1,753	30%	1,347
Total net sales	$ 32,479	35%	$ 24,006	24%	$ 19,315
Unit Sales by Operating Segment:					
Americas Mac unit sales	3,980	32%	3,019	24%	2,432
Europe Mac unit sales	2,519	39%	1,816	35%	1,346
Japan Mac unit sales	389	29%	302	(1)%	304
Retail Mac unit sales	2,034	47%	1,386	56%	886
Other Segments Mac unit sales (a)	793	50%	528	58%	335
Total Mac unit sales	9,715	38%	7,051	33%	5,303
Net Sales by Product:					
Desktops (b)	$ 5,603	39%	$ 4,020	21%	$ 3,319
Portables (c)	8,673	38%	6,294	55%	4,056
Total Mac net sales	14,276	38%	10,314	40%	7,375
iPod	9,153	10%	8,305	8%	7,676
Other music related products and services (d)	3,340	34%	2,496	32%	1,885
iPhone and related products and services (e)	1,844	NM	123	NM	–
Peripherals and other hardware (f)	1,659	32%	1,260	15%	1,100
Software, service, and other sales (g)	2,207	46%	1,508	18%	1,279
Total net sales	$ 32,479	35%	$ 24,006	24%	$ 19,315
Unit Sales by Product:					
Desktops (b)	3,712	37%	2,714	12%	2,434
Portables (c)	6,003	38%	4,337	51%	2,869
Total Mac unit sales	9,715	38%	7,051	33%	5,303
Net sales per Mac unit sold (h)	$ 1,469	– %	$ 1,463	5%	$ 1,391
iPod unit sales	54,828	6%	51,603	31%	39,409
Net sales per iPod unit sold (i)	$ 167	4%	$ 161	(17)%	$ 195
iPod unit sales	11,627	NM	1,389	NM	–

(a) Other Segments include Asia Pacific and FileMaker.

(b) Includes iMac, Mac mini, Mac Pro, Power Mac, and Xserve product lines.

(c) Includes MacBook, iBook, MacBook Air, MacBook Pro, and PowerBook product lines.

(d) Consists of iTunes Store sales, iPod services, and Apple-branded and third-party iPod accessories.

(e) Derived from handset sales, carrier agreements, and Apple-brand and third-party iPhone accessories.

(f) Includes sales of Apple-brand and third-party displays, wireless connectivity and networking solutions, and other hardware accessories.

(g) Includes sales of Apple-branded operating system and application software, third-party software. AppleCare, and Internet services.

(h) Derived by dividing total Mac net sales by Mac unit salts.

(i) Derived by dividing total iPod net sales total iPod unit sales.

NM = Not Meaningful

Source: Apple Inc. Annual Report, 2008

Table 2 Timeline of Apple's Chief Executive Officers	
1977–1981	Michael Scott
1981–1985	Mike Markkula
1985–1993	John Sculley
1993–1996	Michael Spindler
1996–1997	Gil Amelio
1997–2000	Steve Jobs (Interim CEO)
2000–2009	Steve Jobs
Source: Authors	

The Competitive Landscape

The giants: IBM and Microsoft

By 2009, the computer technology industry had undergone some profound changes that shaped the competitive context within which Apple operated. IBM, the once undisputed leader in PC manufacturing, had moved away from its traditional territory of computer hardware and with a focus on computer technology, research and service consulting became a very different company from what it used to be in the 1990s. In 2009 IBM was the world's second largest software company after Microsoft, and its acquisition of PwC Consulting in 2002 marked IBM's serious entry to the business services sector (Doz & Kosonen, 2008: 38). After selling its PC and laptop business to Chinese company Lenovo in 2005 (a segment it had itself created) to allow more strategic focus on services, and higher end servers, IBM's strategy also moved to encompass open business approaches. IBM was a significant contributor to open source movements such as Linux by investing in the program's development, growth and distribution (Linux is supported on all modern IBM Systems) and in 2005 the company gave away approximately 500 software patents (valued over $10 million) so as to enhance global innovation and profit from newly created business opportunities. Through these actions, IBM aimed to enlarge the global market for IT products and services and to benefit by responding to this demand. IBM made over 50 acquisitions during 2002–2007, building a portfolio around 'networked, modularized and embedded technologies, including service-oriented architecture (SOA), information on demand, virtualization and open, modular systems for businesses of all sizes' (IBM Annual Report, 2007: 2). With IBM exiting the PC manufacturing industry the competitive environment in this front included HP, Dell, Acer and Lenovo, which together accounted for more than 50% of worldwide PC shipments in 2007 (Yoffie & Slind, 2008).

Following the launch of the IBM PC, Microsoft dominated the PC operating system market mostly because it offered an open standard that multiple PC makers could incorporate into their products. Windows OS became the standard operating system in the industry with more than 85% of all PCs in the world running on some Windows version (Yoffie & Slind, 2008). Microsoft's revenue reached $60.4 billion in fiscal year 2008, an increase of 18 percent over the previous year (Microsoft Annual Report, 2008). By 2009 Microsoft faced increased competition in the software front from Apple, HP, IBM and Sun Microsystems, as well as Linux OS derived from UNIX. Microsoft's portfolio also included the online search and advertising business (MSN portals, Live Search etc) in which the company sought to invest further. This was indicated by Microsoft's interest in acquiring Yahoo, a deal which by the end of 2008 had not reached agreement. The failing of initial talks led to calls for the resignation of Yahoo's CEO, who indicated that he would resign as soon as a successor was found. In late 2008 Microsoft's interest in Yahoo was rekindled, but only in its search business. Microsoft's position in the entertainment industry was holding strong with the Xbox 360 console selling more than 19 million units and Xbox Live having more than 12 million members (Microsoft Annual Report, 2008).

The computer vendors: Hewlett-Packard and Dell

After the acquisition of Compaq in 2002 that brought significant scale in its desktop and laptop product lines, HP became the world's largest PC vendor, surpassing rival Dell in 2007 with a 3.9% market share lead. In 2007 the company's reported revenue was $104 billion, making it the first IT company in history to exceed revenues of $100 billion, and the world's largest technology company in terms of sales after IBM. HP's portfolio included personal computing, imaging and printing-related products and services, and enterprise information technology infrastructure, including enterprise storage and servers, technology support and maintenance, consulting and integration and outsourcing services (HP Annual Report, 2007).

Dell Inc. offered a range of product categories including desktop personal computers, servers and networking products, storage, mobility products, software and peripherals, and services. It was the first computer company to sell customized PCs directly to consumers without using intermediaries. Once the leading PC vendor in terms of both profitability and market share, Dell faced increased competition in the desktop and notebook business that made it difficult to sustain its earlier growth and profitability rates. Although Dell had based its success in its distinctive business model of direct sales and built to order manufacturing, in 2007 the company initiated a strategic change program that included investment in the design and release of consumer friendly products through retail distribution.

Gaining scale from significant acquisitions, Acer became the 3rd largest PC vendor in the world. Acer focused on the consumer market and in particular in the production of notebook PCs. Lastly China-based Lenovo became the 4th biggest PC vendor after acquiring IBM's PC business for $1.75 billion. Lenovo had a strong position in the Chinese market where it held 35% market share.

Microprocessors: Intel

In the microprocessors front Intel was the undisputed leader accounting for more than 80% share in the market of PC Central Processing Units. AMD was Intel's closest competitor in terms of market share. Intel's portfolio additionally included wired and wireless Internet connectivity products and communications infrastructure products. The company was effective in guiding the co-evolution of its offerings with those of its customers, and had relentlessly driven the evolution of computing power down a predictable trajectory of semiconductor density increase, cost reduction and performance improvement (Doz & Kosonen, 2008). As a result the 2007 fiscal year ended with an 8% revenue increase, at $38.3 billion, with net income of $7 billion, up by 38% over 2006. By 2007 Intel was investing in new product areas such as mobile internet devices and ultra-mobile PCs that leveraged on its micro-processor architecture and manufacturing technology (Intel Annual Report, 2007).

Apple 1997–2009: Turnaround and Re-building an Innovative Organization Jobs' *turnaround*

The return of Steve Jobs to Apple in 1997 marked the beginning of a new era for the company. Jobs worked for a salary of $1 per year for 30 months, leading Apple's successful turnaround. His priority was to revitalize Apple's innovation capability. '*Apple had forgotten who Apple was*', as he noted in an interview (Burrows, 2004), stressing that it was time for Apple to return to its core values and build on them. At the time, Michael Dell was asked at an investor conference what Jobs should do with Apple. He replied 'I'd shut it down and give the money back to the shareholders' (Burrows & Grover, 2006).

According to a former Apple executive who participated in Jobs' first meeting with the top brass on his return to Apple, Jobs went in with shorts, sneakers, and a few days' of beard, sat on a swivel chair, spun slowly, and asked them what was wrong with Apple. Jobs then exclaimed that it was the products, and that there was no sex in them anymore (Burrows & Grover, 2006). Upon taking charge, Jobs announced that Microsoft would invest $150m in Apple, reaffirming its commitment to producing Microsoft Office and other products for the Mac, and soon scrapped the Mac OS licensing program, that he believed was cannibalizing Mac sales (Yoffie & Slind, 2008). He axed 70% of new products in development, kept 30% that he believed were 'gems', and added some new projects that could offer breakthrough potential. He also revamped the marketing message to take advantage of the maverick, creative Apple brand, and re-priced stock options to retain talent (and pushed for the resignation of board members who did not agree with the repricing) (Booth, 1997).

In January 2000, when Apple became profitable with a healthy share price, Apple announced that it would buy Jobs a Gulfstream V jet, at a cost of $88m, fulfilling Jobs' request for an aeroplane so he could take his family on vacation to Hawaii and fly to the East coast. Larry Ellison, Oracle CEO and a board member at Apple, said at the time, 'with what he's done, we ought to give him five airplanes!' (Elkind, 2008).

Innovation at Apple

Long before it was voted as the world's most innovative company, Apple had placed its trademark on a long list of technological breakthroughs including the mouse, the graphical user interface, color graphics, built-in sound, networking and wireless LAN, FireWire and many more. Apple's approach over the years had been to make use of a personal computer as easy and intuitive as possible through developing a highly responsive operating system, establishing standard specifications to which all applications software packages were expected to conform, strict control of outside developers, and delivering computers that did what they promised (Cruikshank, 2006).

Apple's innovations enhanced the consistency across applications, which translated to ease of use, an attribute that helped to explain to some extent Apple's loyal consumer base. Another significant characteristic of Apple's approach to innovation was the diffusion of innovation across the value chain (Cruikshank, 2006) with both high end and low end products that appealed to a much wider audience ranging from amateurs to professionals (see Figure 2 for an outline of Apple's key product innovations). According to Jobs, *'Apple's DNA has always been to try to democratize technology. If you make something great then everybody will want to use it'* (quoted in Morris, 2008: 69).

Many of the disruptive innovations Apple has introduced are based on what employees call *'deep collaboration'*, *'cross pollination'* or *'concurrent engineering'*. This refers to products not developed in discrete stages but by *'all departments at once – design, hardware, software – in endless rounds of interdisciplinary design reviews'* (Grossman, 2005). In an interview about how innovation is fostered in the company, Jobs noted that the system for innovation is that there is no system: *'The reason a lot of us are at Apple is to make the best computers in the world and make the best software in the world. We know that we've got some stuff that (is) the best right now. But it can be so much better....That's what driving us...And we'll sleep well when we do that'* (quoted in Cruikshank, 2006: 25).

Although Apple has been envied for its ability to catch the wave in new technology fronts earlier than competitors (such as in the case of iTunes and the iPhone) Jobs describes it as a rather slow process: *'Things happen fairly slowly, you know. They do. These waves of technology, you can see them way before they happen, and you just have to choose wisely which ones you are going to surf. If you choose unwisely, then you can waste a lot of energy, but if you choose wisely, it actually unfolds fairly slowly'* (Jobs, quoted in Morris, 2008: 70).

Redefining the PC industry

Loyal to the value of user friendliness, Steve Jobs led the launch of the first iMac in 1998, his first project after his return to the company. The iMac, or *'the computer for the rest of us,'* its slogan when it was launched, revolutionized desktop computing by combining technological advancements and unique design. The combination of a CPU, a CD ROM drive and a modem all packed in a translucent case, that could support all 'plug and play' peripherals that were designed for Windows based machines, for the compelling price of $1,299, marked Apple's dynamic comeback.

Even though the iMac was the fastest selling Macintosh model ever, Apple refused to rest on its laurels, continually updating its hardware and operating system, and launching updated models and software almost every 4 months. Most importantly the iMac was the first Apple product with wide

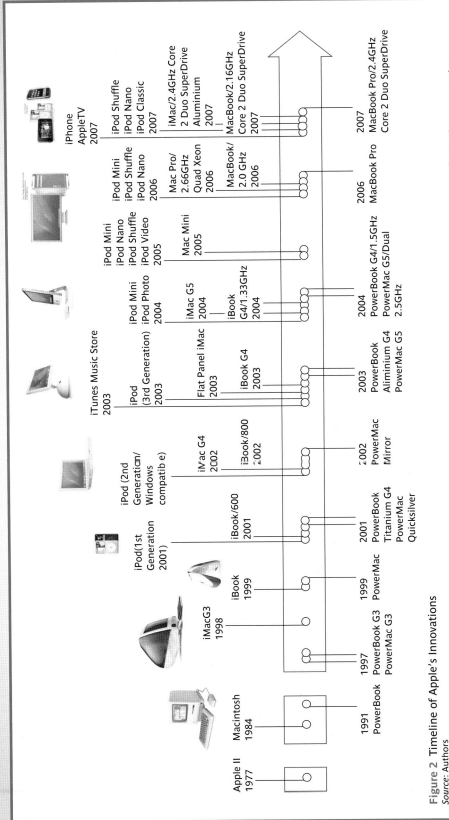

Figure 2 Timeline of Apple's Innovations

Source: Authors

Notes: Figure shows selected product offerings that are indicative of their categories. Consumer segment products are shown *above* the timeline, and professional segment products are shown *below* the timeline.

consumer acceptance, since 70% of sales were adding to the Macs already in use, helping Apple double its worldwide market share to 6% by the end of 1998 (Linzmayer, 2004).

In parallel Steve Jobs proceeded to simplify Apple's product mix in terms of four lines of desktop and portable computers designed for both the professional and consumer markets. Following the iMac's success, the iBook was launched in 1999. This consumer portable computer featured an optional AirPort wireless networking hub that allowed up to ten Macs to share an Internet connection. Just six weeks after the iBook's unveiling, Apple had received more than 140,000 advance orders, making it a success equal to the iMac (Linzmayer, 2004).

After the introduction of the iMac and the iBook, Apple's figures looked a lot healthier. In October 1999 Apple announced its eighth consecutive profitable quarter and closed that fiscal year with revenues of $6.1 billion and net earnings of $601 million. Whereas most of Apple's innovations led to an even more closed Apple archipelagos (software and hardware integration), at the same time Jobs decided to loosen control in other areas, for example the use of standard interfaces, such as the USB port. This change made the Mac a more open system since users of a Mac Mini for example could use a non-Mac keyboard (Yoffie & Slind, 2008). In the years to follow, a variety of innovative proprietary applications, developed in-house, supported the Macintosh product lines. These include programs such as those in the iLife package (iDVD, iMovie, iPhoto) that offered editing and creative opportunities to users as well as Apple's own Web browser, Safari, developed in 2003.

Breakthrough innovation in consumer electronics and entertainment industries

In 2001 Apple introduced its first iPod, launching a new era for the company as it entered the consumer electronics industry. Capitalizing on the emerging trend of MP3 music, Apple introduced a breakthrough product that soon became synonymous with the MP3 music player category. With impeccable design and easy to use menu, the iPod could load 1000 songs in just 10 minutes and play music for 10 hours. The integration with the iTunes 2.0 software also made synchronizing music libraries a matter of a few seconds. A year later, in 2002 Apple released more capacious iPods that could also work with Windows, a move that helped to skyrocket iPod sales. By the end of 2003 more than one million iPods were sold marking the first substantial stream of revenues apart from the Macintosh. Since then the iPod product range has been renewed every 3 to 5 months and the company announced in 2007 that it sold the 100 millionth iPod. These numbers made the iPod the fastest selling music player in history (Apple, 2007).

Arguably, one the most important innovations for Apple has been the launch of the iTunes Music store in 2003, a revolutionary service through which consumers could access and purchase online music for only $0.99 per song. The iTunes Music Store was compatible with all iPods (running both in Macs as well as Windows based computers) and served as Apple's Trojan horse to what Jobs has envisioned as the digital hub where digital content and Apple devices would be seamlessly interconnected. The downloaded songs had royalty protection and could only be played by iPods, bringing the interoperability between Apple's hardware, software and content to a new level and creating higher barriers to entry in this ecosystem.

Apple's next big innovation was the iPhone, a device combining a phone, a music player and a personal computer that was expected to redefine the mobile phone industry in the same way iPod and iTunes revolutionized the music industry. According to Jobs, '*It was a great challenge: Let's make a great phone that we fall in love with. Nobody had thought about putting operating systems as sophisticated as an OS X inside a phone, so that was a real question*' (quoted in Morris, 2008: 69). iPhone's success is attributed not only to its technological capacity but also to its design: '*We had a different enclosure design for this iPhone until way too close to the introduction to ever change it. And it came one Monday morning and I said: I just don't love it. And we pushed the reset button. That happens more than you think because it is not just engineering and science. There is art too.*' (Jobs quoted in Morris, 2008: 70). According to Burrows & Grover (2006), 'Jobs' true secret weapon is his ability to meld technical vision with a gut feel of what regular consumers want and then market it in ways that make regular consumers want to be part of tech's cool club'.

Playing by Different Rules: Sticking with a Proprietary Ecosystem

Apple's innovations have redefined existing product categories such as music players, and helped the company successfully enter hotly contested new markets such as the entertainment industry. Key to these achievements have been the focus on design, the consumer experience, and the seamless integration of hardware and software (such as in the case of the iPod and iTunes).

The tight integration of its own operating system, hardware and applications, has been a strategy followed diligently by Apple. As Steve Jobs says: *'One of our biggest insights [years ago] was that we didn't want to get into any business we didn't own or control the primary technology, because you'll get your head handed to you. We realized that for almost all future consumer electronics, the primary technology was going to be software. And we were pretty good at software'* (Morris, 2008: 70).

Apple is nearly unique among contemporary technology companies in doing all of its own design in-house, at its Cupertino campus. Other companies have outsourced most or all of their product design function, relying on outsourced design manufacturers (ODMs) to develop the products that with minor adaptations will fit into their product lines. Apple however believes that having all the experts in one place – the mechanical, electrical, software, and industrial engineers, as well as the product designers, leads to a more holistic perspective on product development; and that a critical mass of talent makes existing products better and opens the door to entirely new products. According to Jobs, *'...you can't do what you can do at Apple anywhere else. The engineering is long gone in the PC companies. In the consumer electronics companies they don't understand the software parts of it. There's no other company that could make a MacBook Air and the reason is that not only do we control the hardware, but we control the operating system. And it is the intimate interaction between the operating system and the hardware that allows us to do that. There is no intimate interaction between Windows and a Dell computer'* (quoted in Morris, 2008).

The company's tightly knit proprietary system has been frequently seen as the reason for Apple's loss of initial momentum in the PC industry and increasing isolation until the mid 90's. According to Kahney, *'When Jobs returned to Apple in 1997, he ignored everyone's advice and tied his company's proprietary software to its proprietary hardware'* (Kahney, 2008: 142). He has persisted in following this strategy over the years even when all other Silicon Valley firms turned towards openness and interoperability. Tony Fadell, Vice President of engineering in the iPod division, notes that Apple aims to develop a self-reinforcing, synergistic system of products rather than a series of individual products: *'The product now is the iTunes Music Store and iTunes and the iPod and the software that goes on the iPod. A lot of companies don't really have control, or they can't really work in a collaborative way to truly make a system. We're really about a system'* (quoted in Grossman, 2005).

Over the years, there have been some notable exceptions to this proprietary approach. In order to reach a broader consumer base, in late 2003 Apple offered a Windows compatible version of iTunes allowing not only Windows users to use the iPod but more importantly to familiarize them with Apple products. Another milestone came with the company's switch from PowerPC processors made by IBM to Intel chips, a decision announced in mid-2005. This decision allowed Macs to run Windows software, implied lower switching costs for new Mac consumers and also allowed software developers to adapt more easily their programs for Apple. A previous alliance with Microsoft occurred in 1997 when Microsoft agreed to invest $150 million in Apple, reaffirming its commitment to develop core products such as Microsoft Office for the Mac.

Apple has developed a series of strategic alliances in the course of its efforts to become the center of the digital hub, where digital content would be easily created and transferred to any Apple device. Development of the iPod, iTunes and iPhone have necessitated these alliances, since entry in the entertainment and consumer electronics markets would not have been possible without some key strategic partners (for example the big record labels for iTunes such as EMI, Sony BMG, Universal and Warner Brothers, or YouTube for the iPhone). In this process of building systems, Apple has been very selective about its partners. Rather than aiming for the most partners, Apple focuses on engaging with the best companies for a specific purpose (for example Apple has partnered with Google, in developing mapping and video applications for the iPhone).

At the same time Apple has proceeded with a number of acquisitions intended to strengthen its core competencies. For example, in 2002 Apple acquired the German specialist in music software, Emagic, as well as Prismo Graphics, Silicon Grail and Nothing Real, three small companies involved in professional level video creation and production. In April 2008 Apple also announced the acquisition of the boutique microprocessor company PA Semi, known for its highly sophisticated and low priced chips. With that acquisition Apple is said to be moving towards bringing its chip design in-house, building an ever more tightly knit ecosystem that helps to prevent copycat designs from rivals and to design chips for supporting specific new products or applications. According to COO Tim Cook: *'One traditional management philosophy that's taught in many business schools is diversification. Well, that's not us. We are the antibusiness school'* (Burrows, 2007).

In 2001, Apple created a retail division to enable it to sell its products directly to the public. By mid-2008 there were 215 retail stores, most of them in the US, accounting for almost 20% of total revenues. In 2006 Apple entered into an alliance with Best Buy, and by the end of 2007 Apple products could be purchased in over 270 Best Buy stores (Yoffie & Slind, 2008).

Corporate Culture and Human Capital

According to Apple's COO Tim Cook, Apple *'is not for the faint of heart'* (Morris, 2008: 69). Apple's culture is all about intense work and perfectionism but in a casual environment. Jobs stimulates thinking out of the box and encourages his employees to experiment and share with others 'the coolest new thing' they have thought of. It may not be accidental that Apple's emblem of corporate culture is a pirate flag with an Apple rainbow colored eye patch, designed after a famous Jobs quote: *'It's better to be a pirate than join the navy'*. This flag was hanging over the Macintosh building as Apple's team was working on the first iMac, to act as a reminder of their mission. *'Processes lead according to Jobs to efficiency, not innovation nor new ideas. These come from people meeting up in the hallways, calling each other in the middle of the night to share a new idea or the solution to a long thought as unsolved problem'* (Grossman, 2005).

Along with the rebel spirit that Jobs wants to maintain, Apple has a tradition of long working hours and relentless pursuit of perfection. Each manufacturing and software detail is worked and reworked until a product is considered perfect, thus providing a seamless integration of software and hardware. Apple's engineers spend so much time on each and every product that they are able to foresee and respond to any possible difficulties a consumer might encounter when using it. *'It's because when you buy our products, and three months later you get stuck on something, you quickly figure out [how to get past it]. And you think, 'Wow, someone over there at Apple actually thought of this!' And then six months later it happens again. There's almost no product in the world that you have that experience with, but you have it with a Mac. And you have it with an iPod'* (Jobs, quoted in Burrows, 2004).

Apple's employees are not paid astronomically. They are not pampered, nor do they enjoy unique privileges beyond what most large companies offer. They are talented people with passion for excellence, proud to be part of the Apple community. Moreover they want to be part of a company that believes that the best way to predict the future is to invent it. This pride stems from a corporate culture that fosters innovation and a sense of Apple's superiority against competitors. Apple recruits talent of the highest caliber, and Jobs is known for approaching people who are known as the best in what they do and recruiting them to Apple. According to Gus Mueller, founder of a software development firm that develops software for Apple, *'Apple only hires top-notch folks. I know a number of people there, and they are all super smart and creative. I don't know a single person who shouldn't be there'* (Guardian, 2008). As Steve Jobs said: *'We may not be the richest guy in the graveyard at the end of the day, but we're the best at what we do. And Apple is doing the best work in its history'* (quoted in Burrows, 2004).

Steve Jobs' Leadership

When Jobs returned to Apple in 1997 after an absence of 12 years, he arrived with much historical baggage. He was Apple's co-founder at the age of 21, and was worth $200 million by the age of 25. He was then forced to resign by the age of 30, in 1985, after a battle over control with CEO John Sculley which ended in Jobs losing all operational responsibilities. Jobs (who had been executive VP and General Manager of the Macintosh division) was considered a threat to the company, accused of trying to 'play manager' and control areas over which he had no jurisdiction. He was considered 'a temperamental micromanager whose insistence on total control and stylish innovation had doomed his company to irrelevance' (Burrows & Grover, 2006).

Twenty-two years later however Jobs was voted as one of the greatest entrepreneurs of all time by *Business Week* (Tozzi, 2007). His personality left a mark on Apple in a way that only a few leaders had achieved, making his name synonymous with the company and its remarkable turnaround. Described by his colleagues as brilliant, powerful and charismatic, he could also be a demanding and impulsive perfectionist. As Jobs puts it: *'My job is not to be easy on people. My job is to take these great people we have and to push them and make them even better. How? Just by coming up with more aggressive visions of how it could be'* (quoted in Morris, 2008: 70).

Many believe that Jobs' achievement of being regarded as one of the greatest technology entrepreneurs is not based so much on his knowledge of technology (he is not an engineer or a programmer, neither does he have an MBA or college degree) but on his innate instinct for design, the ability to choose the most talented team and *'the willingness to be a pain in the neck for what matters for him most'* (Grossman, 2005).

With regard to the iMac, for example, a product concept he and Jonathan Ive, Head of design had envisioned, the engineers were initially sceptical: *'Sure enough, when we took it to the engineers, they said, "Oh." And they came up with 38 reasons. And I said, "No, no, we're doing this." And they said, "Well, why?" And I said, "Because I'm the CEO, and I think it can be done." And so they kind of begrudgingly did it. But then it was a big hit'* (Grossman, 2005). Jobs has cited himself as 'co-inventor' on 103 separate Apple patents (Elkind, 2008).

Jobs could be both inspirational but also experienced as scary. According to Guy Kawasaki, former head of developers, *'Working for Steve was a terrifying and addictive experience. He would tell you that your work, your ideas, and sometimes your existence were worthless right to your face, right in front of everyone. Watching him crucify someone scared you into working incredibly long hours…Working for Steve was also ecstasy. Once in a while he would tell you that you were great and that made it all worth it'* (Cruikshank, 2006: 147). Apart from displaying such behaviors as parking his car in handicapped places and publicly losing his temper, Jobs often made his employees burst into tears through direct and personal criticism. Robert Sutton, management professor at Stanford, discussed Steve Jobs in his book 'The no asshole rule' in the chapter on the virtues of assholes (Sutton, 2007). Sutton then reflected further on his discussion of Steve Jobs in his blog, suggesting that Jobs may be mellowing as he gets older (Sutton, 2008). Yet, according to Palo Alto venture capitalist Jean-Louis Gasse, a former Apple executive who once worked with Jobs, *'Democracies don't make great products. You need a competent tyrant'* (Gasse, quoted in Elkind, 2008).

The high praise as well as high criticism made people try harder, jump higher and work later into the night. Jobs is credited with imposing discipline on Apple, a quality that the company had lacked for years. The company that used to be known as the 'ship that leaks from the top' (Linzmayer, 2004) due to its relaxed management style and corporate culture was soon transformed into a tightly controlled and integrated machine after Jobs' arrival. At Pixar, things were seen differently than at Apple however. Reportedly Jobs spent less than a day per week there, and was hands off, particularly on the creative front. According to a Pixar employee, 'Steve doesn't tell us what to do…Steve's our benevolent benefactor' (quoted in Burrows & Grover, 2006).

Jobs' charisma is depicted in the way he briefed his team concerning a new product: *'Even though Steve didn't draw any of the lines, his ideas and inspiration made the design what it is. To be honest, we didn't know what it meant for a computer to be "friendly" until Jobs told us'* (Terry Oyama, quoted in Cruikshank, 2006, p. 30). As author Scott Kelby put it: *'There is one thing I am certain of: Steve's the right man to lead Apple. There's never been anyone at Apple who has had the impact that Steve has since his return. He may be a tyrant, demanding, unforgiving and the worst boss ever. But he is also a visionary. A genius. A man who gets things done. And the man who kept Apple afloat when a host of other nice guys couldn't'* (Cruikshank, 2006, p. 175).

Jobs brought his own brand of strategic thinking to Apple: '*The clearest example was when we were pressured for years to do a PDA, and I realized one day that 90% of the people who use a PDA only take information out of it on the road. Pretty soon cell phones are going to do that so the PDA market's going to get reduced to a fraction of its current size. So we decided not to get into it. If we had gotten into it we wouldn't have the resources to do the iPod*' (quoted in Morris, 2008: 69). Jobs has often said 'I'm as proud of what we don't do as I am of what we do' (quoted in Burrows & Grover, 2006).

Challenges on Steve Jobs' watch

In October 2003 Jobs was diagnosed with pancreatic cancer. Whereas this disease is fatal, his case was a rare but treatable form, if operated on. Jobs, a vegetarian and Buddhist, decided not to get operated but to follow a special diet and to seek alternative medical approaches that he believed would cure him. Apple's board of directors was aware of his condition, but a decision was made to not disclose it to investors. The board of Pixar, the other public company where Jobs was CEO, was not aware of his condition. In July 2004, after a scan revealed a growth in the tumor, Jobs finally had the surgery. The next day his employees and the media found out about his situation, through an email he sent his employees that was released to the press. On the day of the announcement Apple's shares dropped by 2.4%, a relatively low figure, bearing in mind the severity of the situation. Assuring everyone that he was cured, Jobs returned to his duties a few months later (Elkind, 2008).

Jobs' recent tenure has also been marred by other issues. In 2006, after a series of articles in the *Wall Street Journal* about options backdating, Apple set up a board committee to examine whether it had engaged in this practice, and the committee concluded that it had done so between 1997 and 2001 with regard to 6,428 option grants (around a sixth of the total). There were no backdating issues before Jobs took over as CEO. Disney also investigated option grants at Pixar during Jobs' CEO tenure and found irregularities as well. However, Steve Jobs did not personally benefit from the options backdating, and Apple has been extremely co-operative with the SEC investigation on the issue. The SEC filed charges against Apple's former general counsel and CFO for organising the backdated option grants and falsifying relevant documentation. In a public statement, the CFO said that he had made Jobs aware of the accounting implications of the backdated options (Elkind, 2008).

When Jobs took over at Apple in 1997, he re-structured the board of directors to create a new board with six members, two of which remained from the earlier board. The new members included Oracle CEO Larry Ellison, a close friend of Jobs, as well as Intuit CEO Bill Campbell, a former employee of Apple and Jobs' neighbour. Former SEC chairman Arthur Levitt was surprised to be first invited by Jobs to join the new board, and then 'dis-invited', after Jobs had read one of Levitt's speeches on corporate governance and concluded that the issues Levitt mentioned in that speech were not applicable to Apple.

This tight relationship between Jobs and Apple along with his health status that some perceive as fragile, have given room for speculation about his replacement, should that be necessary. Fortune magazine named Tim Cook, Apple's COO as the most probable candidate for the position (Lashinsky, 2008). Cook's role in Apple's operations since 1998 has given him a prominent position next to Jobs, as he is the only person to have a vast area of responsibility apart from Jobs himself and the one who replaced him while he was recovering from his pancreatic operation. In any case Jobs' plans regarding his future successor remain veiled. Jobs' immense influence on Apple has given pause for scepticism regarding Apple's future without him. As Fortune's editor Elkind notes: '*In the 26 years that Fortune has been ranking America's Most Admired Companies never has the corporation at the head of the list so closely resembled a one-man show*' (Elkind, 2008).

Looking to the Future

In January 2007, Apple Computer changed its name to Apple Inc. (Yahoo finance, 2008), signifying a shift away from its computer vendor roots. Since 2006, revenues from desktop and portable computers were accounting for less than half of Apple's total revenues. By early 2009, Apple had come a long way: it had produced the world's fastest personal computer, introduced a series of attractive new Macintosh models with a reliable, competitive operating system known for its astonishing backward compatibility, created a cult following of iPod users, and begun its inroads into the mobile phone industry with the iPhone.

Despite Apple's impressive comeback, its share in the worldwide PC industry hovered below 3%, and the growth prospects of the iPod and iPhone were far from guaranteed. The company was faced with the threat of commoditization as the iPod market in developed countries showed some signs of maturity and music over mobile phones was becoming increasingly popular. Apple's competitors were introducing alternative products and some were attempting to copy Apple's approach to doing business. Sony for example, hired one of Apple's former executives, Tim Schaaff, as the company's new senior vice president for software development, and set the goal of imitating Apple's interoperability amongst products (Edwards, Hall & Grover, 2008). In September 2008 T-Mobile, a mobile operator owned by Germany's Deutsche Telekom, presented its new phone, the G1, made by HTC, a Taiwanese manufacturer. The device was the first to be based on the Android software (Google's open-source operating system), while Samsung, HTC, LG Electronics, and Motorola were among the companies that said they would also produce phones that ran on Android.

E-giant Amazon set up its own online music store in September 2007 to provide music compatible with both Windows Media Player, iTunes and any MP3 player device. Half of the tracks available through Amazon MP3 store were priced at $0.89 compared to Apple iTunes' price at the time of $1.29 (Amazon, 2007). Finally MySpace, the world's largest social network, announced in April 2008 its cooperation with Sony, Universal and Warner to form Myspace Music, a one stop shop where visitors could communicate, share and buy music (WMG press release, 2008).

Some analysts believed that Apple's closed system might once again hold the company back from its potential mass appeal (as in the 80's with the Mac OS) and recommended that Apple's future should be more based on openness and partnerships (Guardian, 2008).

In January 2009, Jobs announced that he was taking leave of absence from Apple until June, due to health issues relating to a 'hormone imbalance'. COO Tim Cook would handle day to day operations, and Jobs would stay involved in major strategic decisions. Commentators disagreed on the degree of impact Jobs' absence would have. Some said that the new products Apple would introduce over the following 18 months had already been developed under Jobs' leadership, and that Cook would manage Apple effectively in Jobs' absence. Others, however, believed that Jobs' motivational role, negotiation skills and creative vision were crucial for Apple (Macworld, 2009).

Meanwhile, a week later Apple announced that its performance for the last quarter of 2008 beat expectations, with a net profit of $1.61bn. By that time, it also emerged that the Securities and Exchange Commission were carrying out an investigation to ensure that Jobs' health related disclosures did not mislead investors (BBC, 2009; Bloomberg, 2009).

By early 2009, Apple was faced with some critical decisions regarding its strategy for the future. Was its competitive advantage becoming eroded through product imitation, and attempts by other companies to duplicate Apple's key competencies? Should Apple focus more on the consumer electronics or the computer markets? Was it time for Apple to re-think its closed proprietary ecosystem? What would happen to Apple if it lost Steve Jobs for good? Was Apple still on the rollercoaster that characterized its history, at risk of heading downwards, after its upward climb?

References

Amazon, 2007. Amazon.com launches public beta of Amazon MP3, 25 September, http://phx.corporate-ir. net/phoenix.zhtml?c=176060&p=irol-newsArticle&ID=1055054&highlight=Amazon.com%20 Launches%20Public%20Beta%20 of%20Amazon%20MP3, press release accessed on 1 December 2008.

Apple Inc. Annual Report, 2007–8, 95 pp.

Apple Inc. 2008. Apple reports first quarter results, 22 January, http://www.apple.com/pr/library/ 2008/01/22results.html, accessed on 1 December 2008.

Apple Inc. 2007. 100 million ipods sold. http://www.apple.com/pr/library/2007/04/09ipod.html, accessed on 23 December 2008.

BBC, 2009. Apple posts best quarterly profit. January 21. http://news.bbc.co.uk/1/hi/business/7843769.stm, accessed on 24 January 2009.

Bloomberg, 2009. Apple soars as record sales ease concerns about Jobs. http://www.bloomberg.com/apps/news?pid=20601087&sid=alPjQDdwDFnc&refer=home, accessed on 24 January 2009.

Booth, C. 1997. Steve's job: Restart Apple. *Time*, 18 August, http://www.time.com/time/magazine/article/0,9171,986849,00.html, accessed on 23 December 2008.

Burrows, P. 2004. The seed of Apple's innovation, Interview with Steve Jobs, *Business Week*, 12 October, http://www.businessweek.com/bwdaily/dnflash/oct2004/nf20041012_4018_db083.htm, accessed on 1 December 2008.

Burrows, P. & Grover, R. 2006. Steve Jobs' magic kingdom. *Business Week*, 6 February. http://www.business-week.com/magazine/content/06_06/b3970001.htm, accessed on 23 December 2008.

Cruikshank, J. 2006. *The Apple Way*, McGraw Hill: New York.

Dell Annual Report, 2007, 105 pp.

Doz, Y. & Kosonen, M. 2008. *Fast Strategy*, Wharton School Publishing, Pearson Education, Harlow.

Edwards, C., Hall, K. & Grover, R. 2008. Sony chases Apple's magic, *Business Week*, October 30, http://www.businessweek.com/magazine/content/08_45/b4107048234222.htm, accessed on 1 December 2008.

Elkind, P. 2008. The trouble with Steve Jobs, *Fortune*, March 5, http://money.cnn.com/2008/03/02/news/companies/elkind_jobs.fortune/index.htm, accessed on 1 December 2008.

Grossman, L. 2005. How Apple does it, *Time*, October 16, http://www.time.com/time/magazine/article/0,9171,1118384,00.html, accessed on 1 December 2008.

Guardian, 2008. Reading the runes for Apple, January 10, http://www.guardian.co.uk/technology/2008/jan/10/apple.steve.jobs, accessed on 11 December 2008.

HP Annual Report, 2007, 162 pp.

IBM Annual Report, 2007, 124pp.

Intel Annual Report, 2007, 115pp.

Interbrand, 2008, Best Global Brands Rankings, http://www.interbrand.com/best_global_brands.aspx, accessed on 23 December 2008.

Kahney, L. 2008. How Apple got everything right by doing everything wrong, *Wired Magazine*, April, pp. 137–142.

Linzmayer, O.W. 2004. *Apple Confidential 2.0: The Definitive History of the World's Most Colorful Company*. San Francisco: No Starch Press.

Macworld, 2009. Jobs to take leave of absence until June. January 14. http://www.macworld.com/article/138215/2009/01/jobs.html?t=201, accessed on 24 January 2009.

Microsoft Annual Report, 2008, 71pp.

McGregor, J. 2008. The world's most innovative companies. *Business Week*, April 17. http://www.businessweek.com/magazine/content/08_17/b4081061866744.htm?chan=ma gazine+channel_special+report, accessed on 23 December 2008.

Morris, B. *What Makes Apple Golden*, *Fortune*, 17 March 2008 157(5), pp. 68–71.

Sutton, R.I. 2008. Fortune story on the trouble with Steve Jobs: Asshole, genius, or both? March 6. http://bobsutton.typepad.com/my_weblog/2008/03/fortune-story-o.html, accessed on 23 December 2008.

Sutton, R.I. 2007. *The no asshole rule: Building a civilized workplace and surviving one that isn't*. Business Plus.

Tozzi, J. *The Greatest Entrepreneurs of All Time*, *Business Week*, 27 June 2007, http://www.businessweek.com/smallbiz/content/jun2007/sb20070627_564139.htm, accessed on 1/12/2008.

WMG Press Release, 2008. MySpace, Sony BMG Music Entertainment, Universal Music Group and Warner Music Group partner In landmark joint venture: 'MySpace Music. April 3rd, http://www.wmg.com/news/article/ ?id=8a0af81218f1a369011914f426661bb4, accessed on 1 December 2008.

Yahoo Finance, 2008. Apple Inc. profile. http://finance.yahoo.com/q/pr?s=AAPL, accessed on 23 December 2008.

Yoffie, D.B. & Slind, M. 2008. *Apple Inc., 2008*. Harvard Business School Case 9-708-480, 32pp.

CASE 8: Vanke (a): Transforming from a diversified conglomerate to a focused property company

In early 2008 Wang Shi, chairman of China Vanke Co., one of the largest residential property developers in China in terms of market value, faced a dilemma. Should the company lower its prices or not?

Towards the end of 2007, Wang and his management team had observed that income per capita was not increasing in line with the increase in house prices, and that new housing constructions were well above the number of units sold nationwide, which meant there was too much inventory in the market. As a result, they expected that China's residential market would experience a downturn.

So, as an experiment, in the fourth quarter, Vanke had sold five new residential communities at prices lower than the market rate. This was an unusual move in China, where companies tended to charge the highest prices that the market would bear. Vanke's reduction was well received by buyers, who flocked to buy the apartments.

At a press conference at the end of 2007 Wang said that China's residential market was at a turning point. Yet there were no obvious signs of this in the economy. Indeed, several competitors had just bought land at record prices. His words led to heated debates among competitors, house buyers and the media.

Now in the new year, Vanke needed to decide whether or not it should lower prices on a broader scale. Given its competitors' seeming confidence, would it needlessly be losing out on profits? But if the market did decline, as Wang and his management team expected, would the company be left with huge amounts of costly inventory, which would impact the cash flow that was critical to a developer's survival?

Background

A Brief History of Vanke

The precursor of Vanke was founded in Shenzhen in 1984. It was a state-owned company whose major business was the import of equipment such as video cameras and recorders, projectors, photocopiers and the like. Wang was general manager of the company. Due to waves of office equipment upgrades at local government agencies business was booming.

But in 1985, the Chinese government introduced a policy of macro-regulation and control, imposing quotas and strictly limiting the import of electronic devices. To make things worse, the Renminbi/US dollar exchange rate was devalued from RMB 2.8 to the dollar to RMB 3.2 to the dollar in 1985 and was further devalued to RMB 3.7 to the dollar in 1986. Reflecting Wang's management style of finding opportunities in any situation, the company adapted to the changed market. It set up a joint venture

Research Associate Lily Zhang prepared this case under the supervision of Professor Winter Nie as a basis for class discussion rather than to illustrate either effective or ineffective handling of a business situation.

with a local watch factory and a Hong Kong company to produce watches, as well as jointly exporting iron with an iron and steel factory in Shanxi Province.

In 1987 the government changed its policy to allow only the import of components for electronic devices, rather than the finished product. This meant that foreign manufacturers had to export components to China and have them assembled there.[1] The company maneuvered to become a distributor for Sony and JVC. It imported components from the two Japanese manufacturers and sent them to three local plants for assembly before selling them to customers. The company also set up a maintenance center with authorization from Sony.

In 1988 the Chinese government promulgated a policy that allowed the transfer of land use rights from the state to companies, beginning a period of reform in the real estate market. The company entered the real estate industry that year. Wang recalled:

We made two judgments at that time. One was that the real estate industry would have very bright prospects. The other was that the industry was so new that there were no state-owned monopoly companies in it, which meant a low barrier to entry for us.

In November 1988 the company changed its name to Vanke. A month later, Vanke launched an initial public offering (IPO) on the Shenzhen Stock Exchange. As a result, the Shenzhen government's shareholding in the company decreased from 60% to 30%.[2]

In 1991 Vanke decided to copy the business model of the Japanese GTC (General Trading Company), building a diversified empire which covered opportunistic businesses ranging from commerce, manufacturing and real estate to entertainment and advertising.[3] It established its first Vanguard department store in Shenzhen, and within two years, Vanguard was present in nine cities. But all the stores failed because Vanke had little experience and expertise in the retail business. Wang and his management team went to the US to learn from Wal-Mart. At the beginning of 1994, Vanke shut down all its stores in other cities to focus on those in Shenzhen. In July it opened a revamped Vanguard store on North Huaqiang Road. It was the largest warehouse store in China at the time, with a shopping area of 5,000 square meters. The unique retail store combined the size and price advantages of a warehouse with the ambiance and product variety of a department store. The new Vanguard was a blockbuster, with a turnover of more than RMB 80 million in only half a year.[4]

The Housing Market in China

Until 1988, when the transfer of land use rights was permitted for the first time, all land in China belonged to the state. Housing was provided by the companies (mostly state-owned) that people worked for. The standard was pretty basic, uniform and functional.

In 1998 China abandoned the welfare-oriented public housing distribution system and the housing market was reformed. For the next decade, China's real estate market – especially the residential market – went through exceptional growth, fueled by the fast urbanization process. Real estate development was a totally new industry with no existing developers. Many companies like Vanke entered the market, buying land and building residential communities for sale. Typically a residential community consisted of several to dozens of blocks of apartments. Generally the developers provided the 'shell' of an apartment and the owners were responsible for fitting out the interior. The developer usually also acted as the property management company. The owners paid a monthly service fee to the company for providing garbage disposal, lighting of the common parts and overall maintenance. As the market developed, a few of the high-end residential communities offered better design and began selling apartments that

---

[1] Wang Shi, autobiography. *The Path and the Dream*. China CITIC Press, 2006, p. 45.

[2] In 2001 China Resource Land bought the Shenzhen government's remaining Vanke shares.

[3] Vanke had about two dozen subsidiaries scattered in 12 cities at the peak of its diversification.

[4] By 1997, North Huaqiang Road had become one of Shenzhen's two main business centers thanks to the initial stream of customers attracted by Vanguard.

were fully fitted out inside, instead of just a shell. There might also be other amenities, such as a swimming pool or tennis courts. Because there was a strong culture of saving in China, most buyers paid the down payment – normally 20% to 30% of the total – with their savings or by borrowing from family, and took out a bank loan for the remaining 70% to 80%.

According to Sun Jia, a Harvard graduate and former McKinsey consultant who was the general manager of Vanke's strategy & investment management department, the average growth rate of China's residential market from 1998 to 2008 was between 20% and 30%. This was two to three times the growth rate of China's gross domestic product (GDP). Sales of residential properties nationwide amounted to RMB 1.7 trillion in 2006 and reached RMB 2.5 trillion in 2007, accounting for 10% of China's GDP that year.

Within such a fast-growing industry, it was easy to make quick money. All a developer needed to do was to buy land, build houses and sell them at high prices. But was this kind of growth sustainable?

Becoming More Focused

In 1993 China implemented a new round of macro-adjustment policies including the tightening of credit and other measures aimed at curbing an overheated economy. Vanke rethought its diversification strategy to focus on real estate development, which had higher margins, and on retailing since it had more potential relative to other businesses because it was a new area. But this process of refocusing was harder to implement than it was to conceptualize, and it took a long time.

Divesting the Non-core Businesses

From 1995 onward, Vanke began to sell all its manufacturing, entertainment and advertising businesses as well as other non-core businesses. Vanke had observed and tried to follow the model of Sun Hung Kai Properties – one of the leading property developers in Hong Kong which developed commercial properties, office buildings, hotels and residential properties. According to Wang, more than half of Sun Hung Kai's revenue came from the rental income of the properties it owned. He realized that it would be impossible to imitate Sun Hung Kai's success by taking the same approach:

> In about 1995, we compared our size to that of Sun Hung Kai. We were only one-sixtieth the size of Sun Hung Kai. Moreover, though we were listed, the mainland stock market was much smaller in size and far less efficient than the Hong Kong market, which meant if we continued to follow Sun Hung Kai's model, we would inevitably face a problem with capital turnover.[5]

Focusing on residential property development was a way to circumvent the issue of capital turnover if the developer was able to sell the residential properties quickly. 'But there was a disadvantage in this solution,' said Wang, 'in that the residential property market was easily affected by economic cycles.'

Nevertheless, Vanke decided that the advantages outweighed the risks, and it converted all the office buildings, hotels, shopping malls and factory buildings it had developed to residential properties. The change was extremely difficult, both technically and psychologically. Many project managers were reluctant to accept the change. Wang issued a tough order that all executives and managers who were unwilling to accept the change would be fired.

And Then There Were Two

By 2001, Vanke had two businesses left – residential property development and retailing. The net profit from the residential property business grew by an annual rate of 28.3% in 1999 and grew another

---

[5] Capital turnover is a measure indicating how effectively capital is used to produce revenues; it is expressed as a ratio of annual sales to invested capital. When a developer owns many commercial properties, more capital will be tied up and less revenue will be produced, thus capital turnover will slow down.

31.5% in 2000.[6] At the same time, Vanguard, Vanke's retail store chain, was ranked No. 1 in Guangdong province, where Vanke was based, and No. 14 nationwide, in terms of scale of operation.

Wang faced the hard choice of whether or not to give up the retail business. After much deliberation, he decided to sell Vanguard because it would not be possible to grow both sides of the business simultaneously. He recalled:

> We looked at our resource allocation and found that we had allocated about 90% of our financial resources and 95% of human resources on residential property, only 10% of financial resources and 5% of human resources on retailing. Though both businesses had good prospects and we were in favorable positions in both, we would face huge risks by keeping retailing as we would have a serious shortage of talent if we wanted to grow. We believed that it would be better to focus on one rather than splitting resources between the two. For these reasons, I really heaved a sign of relief when we finally sold Vanguard.

Developing the Residential Property Business

Vanke's headquarters were located in Shenzhen, and it set up subsidiaries – for both real estate development and property management – in other provinces and cities when the opportunity arose. Vanke would bid to buy land with residential construction rights in suitable locations all over the country when the government put it up for sale. It would then decide on what type of community to build – luxury or basic – depending on the location of the land and the price it had paid. It worked with small internal teams in each subsidiary, but hired architects and construction companies for the implementation. Monitoring costs and quality was the primary responsibility of Vanke staff. By 2007 the company had operations in 29 cities throughout China.

Learning from Experience and from Other Companies

Vanke as a company was open to learning. The top management team were always willing to learn from past experience and from benchmarking other companies.

Learning from Past Experience

Wang had a familiar saying: 'Vanke will not be involved in businesses that have a profit margin of over 25%.' This was a lesson learned from Vanke's past experience as an exporter of many different products, depending on what seemed most profitable at the time. According to Wang, in the 1980s the profit margin on exporting electronic devices was once as high as 200%, which resulted in so many companies entering the business that profit margins began to come down again and eventually became negative. Wang said:

> When we exited the export business, we had a review of the financial results and found that, athough we had made huge profits, we had even bigger losses overall. The market is fair. It will force you to return the excessive profit you have made.

Learning from Benchmark Companies

By looking at successful companies both locally and internationally, Wang and his management team were able to apply best practice principles to Vanke.

---

[6] Securities Daily. February 21, 2001.

Sony

When it acted as a distributor for Sony in the early years, Vanke learned the concept of after-sale services, with which most Chinese business people were not familiar at the time. According to traditional Chinese thinking, only products of poor quality needed a warranty. Sony's products were of very high quality, and yet it provided high quality after-sales service as well. When Vanke began to develop residential properties later, it was a trendsetter in applying this concept to property management.

Sun Hung Kai

Vanke's first role model in the real estate industry was Sun Hung Kai. It learned the real estate development process, customer relationship management and the concept that quality was a precondition for obtaining lifetime customers. Following Sun Hung Kai's example, Vanke set up the Vanke Customer Club to maintain customer relationships and provide value-added services (*see below*).

Pulte Homes

Another benchmark in the real estate industry was the US company Pulte Homes.[7] Vanke's research on Pulte, mainly based on public information, revealed that Pulte had remained profitable for more than 50 years with an average annual return on equity of over 16%. Vanke identified several business strategies that had contributed to Pulte's success and were worth closer examination: outstanding customer service, customer segmentation and branding.

Toyota/Toyota Housing

Wang often said that Vanke's future lay in the industrialization of residential development, which meant 'building houses in the way the cars are manufactured.' The idea was borrowed from Toyota/Toyota Housing.[8] Vanke even hired a senior R&D expert from Toyota Housing to lead its own R&D center.

Differentiating Itself from Competitors

Vanke was something of an oddity in China's real estate industry. Most real estate developers had both a commercial and a residential property business, but since 1995 Vanke had focused only on the latter. In the past decade, the Chinese real estate market had gone through such rapid expansion that property was selling fast. Most developers were busy buying land, developing properties and delaying the sale of new apartments until prices went up further. But Vanke did not delay sales; instead it sold at the current market price. Furthermore, it differentiated itself from its competitors.

Property Services

At the core of Vanke's property services was the concept of after-sales service, which it learned from Sony. Vanke was the first developer in China to establish customer clubs and management committees of property owners. It was also the first property management company to pass ISO9902 international quality management certification.

Vanke had a set of operational performance standards which was updated every year and aimed at guiding the operations and services of all its 27 property management subsidiaries. It set the internal standards higher than the 'excellence' criteria set by the state. Every subsidiary would be evaluated based on the operational performance standards each year and 'Property Management Stars' would be selected based on the evaluations.

---

[7] Pulte was ranked among the 'Forbes 400 Best Big Companies' for five consecutive years since 2003.

[8] Not only is Toyota a successful car manufacturer, but it has also used the auto industry as a model for the mass-production of houses.

In all Vanke residential communities, customer service representatives could be reached 24 hours a day through customer service hotlines or via the internet. Property owners could also meet with the head of customer service to communicate their opinions and suggestions directly.

Besides the standard services, Vanke tried to provide value-added services to cater for the owners' special needs. For example, the '4:30 school service' met the needs of working families with children who needed to be taken care of after school, before their parents returned from work.

Vanke's customer service representatives would also visit property owners and have meetings with the management committees to get to know the owners' thoughts better. Once every three months, Vanke property management companies would conduct customer satisfaction surveys and display the service reports in the residential communities. Once a year they would submit an annual service report to the management committees of property owners as well as conducting an annual customer satisfaction survey through an independent third party.

Vanke renamed all its property management companies property service companies in 2007 to better reflect their functions and emphasize the relationship with customers.

All of Vanke's residential quarters in 29 cities were rated as 'Excellent Property Management Quarters' in their respective cities, and 20 of the residential quarters were rated as excellent at the national level by the Ministry of Housing and Urban-Rural Development.

Building Brand Loyalty

Learning from Pulte, Vanke positioned itself to create value along the customers' whole lifecycle. This meant it had to build its brand as well as brand loyalty from the very beginning when customers bought their first apartment from them.

Quality was the cornerstone of Vanke's brand. As early as 1995, when Vanke decided to focus on residential development, Wang wrote an article called 'Quality is Vanke's Lifeline.' In 2000 Vanke implemented the 'Pirate Program,' attracting architecture experts from competitors and famous architecture institutions. In 2001 the company launched the 'Alloy Program' which combined the best practices in residential development of all Vanke subsidiaries to create written standards. In 2003 Vanke started the 'Rock Program' which mapped out a five-year engineering management plan aimed at improving the quality of its residential properties. Using this as the base, Vanke put forward several other programs with the aim of improving quality in the following years. Thanks to these series of programs and measures, many residential properties developed by Vanke won awards, including first prize for architectural design awarded by the Ministry of Housing and Urban-Rural Development, Luban Award – the highest award for architectural quality in China.

Vanke also built its brand through continuous communication of the core values of its brand to the public. In 2001, Vanke introduced the core value: Construct an unlimited life. A Vanke speaker explained at the press conference, 'Just as people's lives present unlimited choices, there are unlimited choices when it comes to buildings and lifestyles; we hope to construct an unlimited life with our customers.' Based on this core value, Vanke put forward different slogans each year to further promote and strengthen its brand image (refer to **Exhibit 1**).

Vanke invited Gallup to conduct annual customer satisfaction surveys since 2002. The 2007 survey showed that customer satisfaction was 89%, 2 percentage points higher than 2006. According to the survey, by the end of 2007, on average each current Vanke customer recommended Vanke property to 7.11 other people.

Customer Segmentation

To lock in lifetime customers, Vanke had to develop customer lifecycle management (CLM), which was the foundation of customer segmentation. This was another lesson learned from Pulte.

Customers were divided along two dimensions. One was the different life stages they were at. There were four groups here: (1) 'first-time buyers,' who were getting married and wanted to buy their first

Exhibit 1	Brand Building: Construct an Unlimited Life	
Year	**Slogan**	**Interpretation**
2002	Constructing your life begins with understanding your life.	Vanke is your close friend who understands you, cares about you and, with its refined taste and creativity, helps you create an ideal life.
2003	An unlimited life is constructed with hearts.	Vanke is a doer of deeds that represents superior quality for both your house and your life. (2003 was the year Vanke started a series of plans aimed at improving quality.)
2004	Achievements, life and dreams.	Vanke is focused and professional. 2004 marked Vanke's 20th anniversary. The company hosted activities such as 'The Same Dream' essay competition and '10 most…employees & 10 most…customers in 20 years' rating, which aimed to enhance the sense of belonging and pride among employees and customers.
2005/2006	Construct an unlimited life.	Vanke managed to return to the essence of residential buildings while the Chinese real estate market grew at exceptional speed in 2005 and 2006.
2007	Complement life with architecture.	Vanke is a pilgrim of life and human beings. The essence of architecture is to serve human beings. Vanke reveres life through its great architecture.

Source: Company information

home; (2) 'first-time upgraders,' married couples who needed more space now that their first child had been born; (3) 'second upgraders,' middle-aged people who had achieved financial success; and (4) 'retired buyers,' who decided to live separately from their grown-up children.

The second dimension was customers' sensitivity to price and functionality of the apartments. For example, first-time buyers tended to be more sensitive to the overall price tag, which was directly linked to the down payment, than to the price per square meter. These customers were young and their means were limited. First-time upgraders, although sensitive to the total price, tended to pay more attention to the layout and function of the apartments. They might not care whether the total area was 120 square meters or 140 square meters – what was most important for them might be an additional room for their newborn babies.

Corresponding to customer segmentation, Vanke also segmented the land reserve. Vanke divided its land reserves into three major categories. The first category was known as the G-area. In Beijing, this included land between the Third Ring Road and Fourth Ring Road.[9] This category mainly targeted the two 'upgrader' customer groups. The second category was C, which tended to be roomy and well supported with facilities and was mainly located in the suburbs. This category would target several different customer groups. The third category was T, which was in satellite towns.[10] Vanke had no residential quarters in this category yet.

Customer segmentation and land category were combined to form different products (residential properties) catering for different clienteles. For example, land reserves labeled C might be more suitable for building apartments for first-time buyers, with relatively small surface areas (less than 90 square meters) so that the total price would be more affordable. Land category C could also be suitable for building houses for first-time upgraders, with larger areas and typically three rooms (one bedroom, one

---

[9] The land between the Third and Fourth Ring Roads is nice, but not the best location in Beijing.

[10] Further out than the suburbs.

study and one child's room[11]). In addition, it usually had supporting facilities such as kindergartens, catering to the needs of this segment.

Innovation: Industrialization of Residential Development

When Vanke began to focus only on the residential property business, Wang set a long-term goal to become the largest residential developer in China. This meant that Vanke had to have the capability to build a large number of residential properties of high quality. To this end, industrialization was a solution. Industrialization meant manufacturing all the housing components in factories and then assembling them on site.

Vanke began researching the industrialization process in 2003 by establishing its own R&D center and experimental bases. By the end of 2008, the R&D center owned about 30 patents for residential development industrialization.

According to Wang, the greatest advantage of industrialization was that it shortened the construction cycle while maintaining high quality. The resulting cost increase (initial investment and set-up cost) would be partially offset if the construction reached a certain scale.

Should Vanke Lower the Price or Not?

By 2007, Vanke's market share was 2.1%, covering 29 cities in the Yangtze River Delta, Pearl River Delta, and the Bo Hai Bay area. The company sold about 48,000 residential property units in 2007, placing it at No. 1 in the world.[12] Vanke's revenue and net profit were RMB 33.49 billion and RMB 4.84 billion, respectively, up by 98.1% and 110.8% from the previous year (*refer to **Exhibit 2***). Vanke's compound annual growth rate in revenue for the previous three years was 93.5%, compared with 33.7% for China's commercial housing sales revenue growth.[13]

Now, in early 2008, Wang was considering whether or not to lower the price of Vanke's units. The experiment in 2007 had been greeted with enthusiasm by potential buyers, but other stakeholders had been less sure. As the first to lower prices, Vanke would enjoy the benefits of clearing out inventory. As the bellwether of the real estate industry in China, Vanke's every move was surely going to be scrutinized by its customers, competitors and local governments. Should Vanke proceed to lower prices?

---

[11] A living room and dining room are considered essential and not included in the number of rooms.

[12] AWSJ.

[13] Vanke's 2007 annual report.

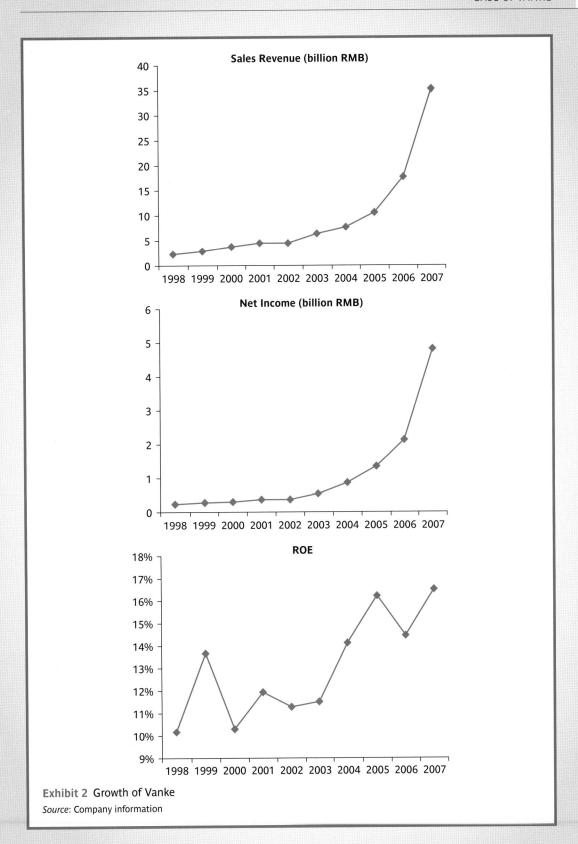

Exhibit 2 Growth of Vanke

Source: Company information

Exhibit 3 Major Competitors

	Vanke	Poly*	China Overseas*	SOHO
Business	Residential property development	Residential & commercial property development	Residential & commercial property development	High-end commercial property development
Cities covered	29 cities	11 cities	20 cities	Beijing
Sales volume (billion RMB)	47.87	15.11	26.66	7.73
Net income (RMB)	4.03 billion	2.24 billion	4.46 billion**	399 million
Debt ratio	67.44%	70.8%	61%	45.82%
ROE	12.65%	15.9%	15.20%	2.85%
Cash (billion RMB)	19.98	5.47	7.95**	9.91
Total assets (billion RMB)	119.24	53.63	75.51**	26.07

* Both Poly and China Overseas are state-owned companies.

** Original amounts are quoted in Hong Kong dollars in the annual report. An exchange rate of RMB 1 = HK$1.13 has been used.

Source: 2008 annual reports of Vanke, Poly, SOHO and China Overseas

CASE 9: What Happened at Citigroup?

CLAYTON ROSE, ALDO SESIA

What we are doing is creating a model of the financial services company of the future.[1]

– Sandy Weill, April 1998

In 1998, the Travelers Group (Travelers) and Citicorp merged to create Citigroup Inc., considered the first true global 'financial supermarket,' and a business model to be envied, feared and emulated. At year-end 2006 the firm had a market capitalization of $274 billion, with $1.9 trillion in assets and $24.6 billion in earnings. Ten years after the merger it ended in tears. In July of 2009, the firm was effectively nationalized, with billions of dollars in bailout money converted into a 34% ownership stake for the U.S. government. Citigroup was worth less than $16 billion, having lost more than $250 billion in value from its peak. (See **Exhibit 1** for Citigroup's year-end market value, 1999–2008.)

What went wrong?

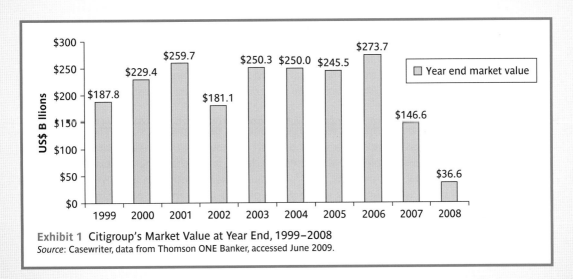

Exhibit 1 Citigroup's Market Value at Year End, 1999–2008
Source: Casewriter, data from Thomson ONE Banker, accessed June 2009.

The First Financial Supermarket

The October 8, 1998 merger of Travelers and Citicorp formed, at the time, the largest financial services firm in the world with a market value of $155 billion and with assets of over $400 billion. Travelers was run by Sandy Weill, a legendary Wall Street figure, who after being ousted from American Express, bought

Senior Lecturer Clayton Rose and Senior Researcher Aldo Sesia of the Global Research Group prepared this case. This case was developed from published sources. HBS cases are developed solely as the basis for class discussion. Cases are not intended to serve as endorsements, sources of primary data, or illustrations of effective or ineffective management.

a troubled Baltimore firm, Commercial Credit, in 1986 and in a series of well timed and well negotiated acquisitions bought the brokerage firm Smith Barney (1987), the investment bank Salomon Brothers (1997) and the insurance companies Primerica (1988) Travelers (1993), and Aetna Casualty and Surety (1996) to cobble together a firm with a market capitalization of approximately $15 billion at the end of 1997. Citicorp was one of the pillars of global banking, with a dominant share of the corporate lending market and an innovative retail banking system; John Reed, Citicorp's CEO at the merger, was responsible for developing the ATM. But Citicorp had a near death experience in the early 1990s, as a result, in large part, to having too many bad loans in the commercial real estate sector. Its stock traded below $9 per share in 1991, and operated for a period with the active oversight of the Federal Reserve.

The merger of Travelers and Citicorp was the brainchild of Weill, and was driven by his strong and long held belief in the potential of 'cross-selling' – offering to customers a range of products under the same roof.[2] If viable, the economics of the idea were compelling – little incremental cost to selling an additional product to a client. The merger created a company that provided an array of financial services including commercial and investment banking, retail banking and consumer finance (e.g., credit card lending), investments (e.g., mutual funds), securities brokerage, and insurance. Consistent with Weill's reputation as a savvy dealmaker, at the time of the merger it was illegal for a single firm to be in both the banking and insurance businesses. The deal was struck assuming that the law would be changed, and if it could not be changed the new firm agreed it would divest its property and casualty insurance business.[a]

The new company operated in 52 countries, though it did not offer all of its products and services in all countries. Citigroup's 250,000 staff, for example, provided mortgages in Manhattan, loans in Malaysia, credit cards in Bahrain, and bond underwriting in Guatemala.[3] Weill and Reed released the following statement in 1998:

> Citicorp and Travelers Group bring together some of the best people in the financial services business, creating a resource for customers like no other – a diversified global consumer financial services company, a premier global bank, a leading global asset management company, a preeminent global investment banking and trading firm, and a broad-based insurance capability. Our ability to serve consumers, corporations, institutions, and government agencies, domestic and foreign, will be without parallel.[4]

The merits of a financial supermarket were, at the time, not universally accepted. There were many doubters within the business and academic communities.[5] Citigroup, after all, was not the first company to aspire to be a large cross-selling financial services firm. In the late 1970s, American Express had been intent on becoming a global conglomerate, with huge, multifaceted businesses and diversified income streams that could protect the company in the event of hard times in one of its core businesses.[6] American Express made several large acquisitions including Shearson Loeb Rhoades, First Data Resources, Trade Development Bank, Lehman Brothers Kuhn Loeb, and Investors Diversified Services.[7] The synergies between the subsidiaries did not, however, come to pass. By 1985, American Express had revised its strategy: It shifted its focus to developing its core businesses while shedding its non-core activities.[8]

For Weill building a 'financial supermarket in which cross-selling would make the whole more profitable than the sum of its parts' had been a driving ambition of his since the early 1980s when he was the second-in-command at American Express.[9] Both Weill and Reed said the combined companies expected to generate substantial incremental earnings from the significant cross-selling opportunities that would be created as well as cost savings that would be realized.[10] In the retail space, cross-selling included plans to market investment products to its banking, insurance, and brokerage customers; and selling banking products to its brokerage and insurance customers. In the wholesale space, Citigroup envisioned cross-selling commercial insurance lines, investment banking, lending, and 401(k) products to its corporate customer base.[11] Shortly after the merger, Sallie Krawcheck, an analyst at Sanford Bernstein who later became Citigroup's CFO, argued that the potential for cross-selling synergies was significant, and resided primarily in the retail areas and in Europe, where the 'universal bank' model had been present

---

[a] The Bank Holding Act of 1965 (which required the separation of banking and insurance activities) was repealed in 1999 as a direct result of the Citicorp/Travelers deal.

for years.[12] Others were more skeptical. One analyst said, 'no-one at Citigroup has ever been able to prove to me how these synergies (between banking and insurance) will positively affect return on equity.'[13]

In addition to cross-selling, the primary benefits of the merger were said to be diversification and cost savings. The merger was intended to create a global financial services company where weakness in one division or region could be balanced by out-performance in another.[14] In a July 2002 interview, Weill argued that Citigroup's combination of consumer and investment services had particular merit as the bank expanded overseas. For example, by using local deposits to fund other activities, he maintained, it could avoid the kind of cross-border exposures that had upended other lenders.[15] One analyst estimated that in the first year of the deal, the firm was able to cut $2 billion of cost, with another $1 billion of savings in the second year.[16]

Leadership

Initially, Citigroup was led by co-CEOs Reed and Weill. They were joined in 1999 by former U.S. Treasury Secretary and former Goldman Sachs CEO Robert Rubin, and the three formed an 'Office of the Chairman.' Rubin had agreed to join the firm under the condition that he act as an advisor and have no operational responsibilities. He would later describe his role as one where he was, 'an experienced senior person with no axe to grind.'[17] Weill and Reed had different management styles and those styles had informed the cultures of the two organizations they led prior to the merger. Reed was known as a remote, hands-off leader.[18] Weill, on the other hand, was volatile and loved the spotlight.[19] Travelers' managers were lean and mean and willing to get their hands dirty; Citicorp managers preferred a think-tank atmosphere free of constant bottom-line pressures.[20] The merger brought change to the company's leadership below Reed and Weill. Nearly 80% of Citicorp's most senior executives and 60% of Travelers' top managers left within one year of the merger.[21]

By February 2000, Reed and Weill conceded to the board that operating the company under a dual-CEO arrangement was not working. Reed wanted both men to retire together and a new CEO brought in. The board saw it differently and named Weill as the sole CEO, effective in April 2000.

Weill at the Controls

The merger of Travelers and Citicorp had been considered the crown jewel of Weill's long and successful career on Wall Street and sealed his reputation as one of the greatest deal makers of his generation.

Early under Weill's leadership, Citigroup seemed to be proving the merger logic right. In a 2001 report, Putnam Lovell Securities stated that, 'The benefit of diversity, clearly evident in Citigroup's second quarter earnings, allowed the company to grow earnings 14% from a year ago compared to an average 15% drop among its large financial services peers.'[22] At that point in the company's history, cross-selling of financial products was already said to comprise up to 15% of total revenue.[23] According to a 2002 *Money* magazine article:

> *Despite gale-force winds battering the financial services industry – bear market, recession, Sept. 11, Enron, Argentina – Citi has grown earnings at a 17% annual clip over the past three years. More important, the company has rewarded shareholders with a 163% total return since the merger became official, trouncing Standard & Poor's 500 as well as Citi's biggest rivals in banking, brokerage and insurance.*[24]

In March 2002, however, Weill spun off Travelers' property and casualty (P&C) division via an IPO. To some observers this was an indication that banking and insurance (specifically property/casualty insurance) was not a good fit. An *American Banker* article stated, 'Several financial services analysts say they see no compelling rationale for banking and property/casualty insurance to be gathered under one corporate umbrella. And Citigroup's decision last month to spin off its Travelers property/casualty unit truncated the only real-world financial supermarket, though Citigroup kept its life insurance operation.'[25]

Weill had concluded that the P&C business would simply be more valuable on its own. 'We drive our company to achieve, on average, double-digit earnings growth,' he said at the time. 'We didn't feel

[Travelers' P&C business] had the potential for top-line growth over a long period of time.' Plus when Citigroup attempted to cross-sell home and auto insurance to its retail bank and brokerage customers, the strategy backfired. 'The people who ended up taking our insurance policies were those with the greatest risks,' Weill explained. 'We ended up losing a lot of money.'[26] 'We think that our shareholders end up better in having the companies split apart. And we think that when you would look at Citigroup, you would see higher returns on equity and higher growth rates than what we've seen over the last three years with the inclusion of [Travelers' P&C business].'[27] The property/casualty business had proven an earnings laggard, generating annual returns on equity of 15%, compared with 22% for Citigroup as a whole.[28] Weill said, 'The spin-off netted Citi a $1 billion gain while also giving shareholders a better, more focused exposure to the P&C business.'[29]

While there was success in cross-selling lending and investment banking products to corporate and institutional clients, gains in the retail areas were more difficult. Some suggested that this was due to the flawed nature of the strategy; customers did not want to buy all financial products from a single source. Others attributed the problems to poor execution by Citigroup, in particular a lack of proper incentives for the various retail sales forces. In 2000, Weill asked both Charles Prince, the firm's general counsel and co-chief operating officer, and Todd Thompson, the CFO, to jump start the cross-selling effort in the retail areas, although neither of them had any formal authority over the relevant lines of business.[30] And Weill dismissed the need for proper incentives, suggesting that people should, 'think about doing the business first, and worry about who gets the credit second.'[31]

While the cross-selling efforts were meeting with mixed success, Weill's acquisition strategy was firing on all cylinders. Industry watchers found the company's acquisition process to be a 'core competency' for Citigroup as a whole and major engine of its growth.[32] For example, he worked a 2000 deal to acquire the UK investment bank Schroder's PLC, and in 2001 acquired the second largest bank in Mexico, Grupo Financiero Banamex-Accival, for $12.5 billion. With each new deal, the firm was able to generate incremental earnings from some combination of reducing the acquired firm's cost of capital (by using Citigroup's cheaper funding), cutting costs and adding clients. In early 2001, Reed, who was no longer with the firm, gave a speech where he questioned the wisdom of continuing growth by acquisition, 'I'll tell you that Citigroup is right at the edge of how big things can be and be managed.'[33]

The firm under Weill had not developed a distinct and common culture. Prince would later say, 'I used to joke that we don't have a good culture – we have five or six good cultures.'[34] Weill was well known for his derisive view of the importance of culture, suggesting that it 'sounds like you're talking about yogurt.'[35] Weill's management style evolved, at least to some extent, during this period. He had always been a 'hands-on' manager who relied little on organization charts and had a strong aversion to meetings. At Rubin's urging he began to bring a somewhat more structured process to working with his subordinates, and to gathering and sharing information.[36] He was also well known for his aversion to the risks that came from large trading operations, especially those that were proprietary and not geared towards serving clients. He preferred business that generated stable and steady fees.[37]

By 2002, Citigroup had become embroiled in controversy surrounding its financing of Enron and its analysis of WorldCom – both involving Salomon Smith Barney (SSB). The U.S. government had launched an investigation into SSB's business practices. In December 2002, Citigroup received a fine of $400 million for conflicts of interest between its research department and investment bank. (Two years later the company settled a class-action suit brought by WorldCom's shareholders for $2.7 billion.) In June of 2003, the corporate governance research group, The Corporate Library (TCL), rated Citi's board as the least effective of the 1,700 US companies it reviewed. The poor rating was driven in large part by TCL's view that the board lacked independence from Weill as demonstrated by his compensation (estimated at $14.5 million) in spite of significant ethical lapses. TCL also noted, and praised Reuben Mark, a Citi director and the CEO of Colgate-Palmolive, for not standing for reelection because of his concerns about a lack of adequate succession planning.[38]

By the end of 2003, Citigroup was generating $77 billion of revenues, up from $66 billion in 1999, $17.8 billion of earnings (from $11.2 billion in 1999), had $1.3 trillion of assets on its balance sheet (from $902 billion) and a market capitalization of $250 billion (from $188 billion). (See **Exhibits 2** and **3** for Citigroup's Income Statement and Balance Sheet for 1999–2000, and **Exhibit 4** for key metrics.)

Exhibit 2 Citigroup Income Statement, 1999–2008 (US$ millions, except per share amounts)

Year Ended December 31	2008	2007	2006	2005	2004	2003	2002	2001	2000	1999
Revenues										
Interest revenue	$106,655	$121,429	$93,611	$75,916	$63,631	$ –	$ –	$ –	$111,826	$94,396
Interest expense	52,963	76,051	55,683	36,676	22,004	17,271	21,248	4,463	36,638	28,674
Net interest revenue	53,692	45,378	37,928	39,240	41,617					
Commissions and fees	11,227	20,706	18,850	3,132	2,726	16,314	15,258	15,593	16,363	13,229
Principal transactions	(22,188)	(12,086)	7,990	17,143	15,981	5,120	4,513	5,544	5,981	5,160
Administration and other fiduciary fees	8,560	9,132	6,903	6,443	3,716	5,665	5,146	5,389	5,338	4,164
Realized gains (losses) from sales of investments	(2,061)	1,168	1,791	6,119	5,524	510	(485)	237	806	541
Insurance premiums	3,221	3,062	2,769	1,962	833	3,749	3,410	3,450	12,429	11,504
Other revenue	342	11,135	10,096	9,603	9,238	6,308	5,775	4,463	–	–
Total non-interest revenues	(899)	33,117	48,399	44,402	38,018					
Total revenues, net of interest expense	52,793	78,495	86,327	83,642	79,635	77,442	71,308	67,367	75,188	65,722
Provisions for credit losses and for benefits and claims										
Provision for loan losses	33,674	16,832	6,320	7,929	6,233	8,046	9,995	6,800	5,339	4,760
Policyholder benefits and claims	1,403	935	967	867	864	3,895	3,478	3,520	10,147	9,120
Provision for unfunded lending commitments	(363)	150	250	250	–	–	–	–	–	–
Total provision for credit losses and for benefits and claims	34,714	17,917	7,537	9,046	7,117	11,941	13,473	10,320	15,486	13,880
Operating expenses										
Compensation and benefits	32,440	33,892	29,752	25,772	22,934	21,288	18,650	19,449	18,663	16,169
Net occupancy	7,125	6,648	5,794	5,141	4,791	4,280	4,005	3,735	–	–
Technology/communication	4,897	4,511	3,741	3,524	3,518	3,414	3,139	3,068	–	–
Advertising and marketing	2,292	2,803	2,471	2,533	2,653	–	–	–	–	–
Insurance underwriting, acquisition, operation	–	–	–	–	–	1,063	992	1,115	3,643	3,765
Restructuring	1,766	1,528	–	–	–	(46)	(15)	454	759	(53)
Other operating	22,614	10,420	8,543	8,193	15,886	9,169	10,527	8,707	15,524	13,810
Total operating expenses	71,134	59,802	50,301	45,163	49,782	39,168	37,298	36,528	38,559	33,691

Exhibit 2 *Continued*

Year Ended December 31	2008	2007	2006	2005	2004	2003	2002	2001	2000	1999
Income (loss) from continuing operations before income taxes and minority interest	(53,055)	776	28,489	29,433	22,736	26,333	20,537	20,519	21,143	18,151
Provision (benefit) for income taxes	(20,612)	(2,498)	7,749	9,078	6,464	8,195	6,998	7,203	7,525	6,530
Minority interest, net of taxes	(349)	285	289	549	218	285	91	87	99	251
Income (loss) from continuing operations	(32,094)	2,989	20,451	19,806	16,054	17,853	13,448	13,229	13,519	11,370
Discontinued operations										
Income from discontinued operations	1,478	925	1,177	908	1,446	–	965	1,378	–	–
Gain on sale	3,139	–	219	6,790	–	–	1,270	–	–	–
Provision (benefit) for income taxes and minority interest, net of taxes	207	297	309	2,866	454	–	360	323	–	–
Income from discontinued operations, net of taxes	4,410	628	1,087	4,832	992	–	1,875	1,055	–	–
Net income (loss)	($27,684)	$3,617	$21,538	$24,589	$17,046	$17,853	$15,276	$14,126	$13,519	$11,243
Basic earnings per share[a]										
Income (loss) from continuing operations	(6.42)	$0.60	$4.17	$3.90	$3.13	$3.49	$2.63	$2.61	$2.69	$2.26
Income from discontinued operations, net of taxes	0.83	0.13	0.22	0.95	0.19	–	0.37	0.21	–	–
Net income (loss) per share[a]	($5.59)	$0.73	$4.39	$4.84	$3.32	$3.49	$2.99	$2.79	$2.69	$2.23
Weighted average common shares outstanding	5,265.4	4,905.8	4,887.3	5,067.6	5,107.2	5,093.3	5,078.0	5,03.7	4,977.0	4,979.2
Diluted earnings per share[b]										
Income (loss) from continuing operations	($6.42)	$.059	$4.09	$3.82	$3.07	$3.42	$2.59	$2.55	$2.62	$2.19
Income from discontinued operations, net of taxes	0.83	0.13	0.22	0.94	0.19	–	0.36	0.20	–	–
Net income (loss) per share[a]	($5.59)	$0.72	$4.31	$4.75	$3.26	$3.42	$2.94	$2.79	$2.62	$2.17
Adjusted weighted average common shares outstanding	5,795.1	4,995.3	4,986.1	5,160.4	5,207.4	5,193.6	5,166.2	5,147.0	5,122.2	5,127.8

[a] Includes the effects of accounting changes.

[b] Diluted shares used in the diluted EPS calculation represent basic shares for 2008 due to the net loss. Using actual diluted shares would result in anti-dilution.

Source: Adapted from Citigroup's 2008 10-K report, p. 116; 2006 10-K report, p. 104; 2004 10-K report, p. 106; 2003 10-K report, p. 102; 2001 10-K report, p. 80.

Exhibit 3 Citigroup Balance Sheet 2000–2008 (US$ millions, except shares)

December 31	2008	2007	2006	2005	2004	2003	2002	2001	2000
Assets									
Cash and due from banks (including segregated cash and other deposits)	$29,253	$38,206	$26,514	$23,632	$23,556	$21,149	$17,326	$18,515	$14,621
Deposits with banks	170,331	69,366	42,522	31,645	23,889	19,777	16,382	19,216	16,164
Federal funds sold and securities borrowed or purchased under agreements to resell, at fair value	184,133	274,066	282,817	217,464	200,739	172,174	139,946	134,809	105,877
Brokerage receivables	44,278	57,359	44,445	42,823	39,273	26,476	25,358	35,155	25,696
Trading account assets	377,635	538,984	393,925	295,820	280,167	235,319	155,208	144,904	132,513
Investments	256,020	215,008	273,591	180,597	213,243	182,892	169,513	160,837	120,122
Loans, net of unearned income									
Consumer	519,673	592,307	512,921	454,620	435,226	379,932	337,681	244,159	228,879
Corporate	174,543	185,686	166,271	128,883	113,603	98,074	110,124	147,774	138,143
Loans, net of unearned income	694,16	777,993	679,192	583,503	548,829	478,006	447,805	391,933	367,022
Allowance for loan losses	(29,616)	(16,117)	(8,940)	(9,782)	(11,269)	(12,643)	(11,101)	(10,088)	(8,961)
Total loans, net	664,600	761,876	670,252	573,721	537,560	465,363	436,704	381,845	358,061
Goodwill	27,132	41,053	33,415	33,130	31,992	27,581	26,961		
Intangible assets (other than MSRs)	14,159	14,307	15,901	14,749	15,271	13,881	8,509		
Reinsurance receivables					4,783	4,577	4,356	12,373	10,716
Separate and variable accounts					32,264	27,473	22,118	25,569	24,947
Mortgage servicing rights (MSRs), at fair value	5,657	8,380							
Other assets, at fair value	165,272	168,875	100,936	80,456	81,364	67,370	75,209	118,227	93,493
Total assets	**1,938,470**	**2,187,480**	**1,884,318**	**1,494,037**	**1,484,101**	**1,264,032**	**1,097,590**	**1,051,450**	**902,210**

Exhibit 3 *Continued*

December 31	2008	2007	2006	2005	2004	2003	2002	2001	2000
Liabilities									
Non-interest-bearing deposits in U.S. offices	60,070	40,859	38,615	36,638	31,533	30,074	29,545	23,054	21,694
Interest-bearing deposits in U.S. offices, at fair value	229,906	225,198	195,002	169,277	161,113	146,675	141,787	110,388	58,913
Non-interest-bearing deposits in offices outside the U.S.	37,412	43,335	3,519	32,614	28,379	22,940	21,422	18,779	13,811
Interest-bearing deposits in offices outside the U.S., at fair value	446,797	516,838	443,275	353,299	341,056	274,326	238,141	222,304	206,168
Total deposits	774,185	826,230	712,041	591,828	562,081	474,015	430,895	374,525	300,586
Federal funds purchased and securities loaned or sold under agreements to repurchase, at fair value	205,293	304,243	349,235	242,392	209,555	181,156	162,643	153,511	110,625
Brokerage payables	70,916	84,951	85,119	70,994	50,208	37,330	22,024	32,891	15,882
Trading account liabilities	167,478	182,082	145,887	121,108	135,487	121,869	91,426	80,543	85,107
Contractholder funds and separate and variable accounts					68,801	58,402	49,331	48,932	44,884
Insurance policy and claims reserves					19,177	17,478	16,350	49,294	44,666
Investment banking and brokerage borrowings					25,799	22,442	21,353	14,804	18,227
Short-term borrowings, at fair value	126,691	146,488	100,833	66,930	30,968	36,187	30,629	24,461	51,675
Long-term debt, at fair value	359,593	427,112	288,494	217,499	207,910	162,702	126,927	121,61	111,778
Other liabilities, at fair value	92,684	102,927	82,926	70,749	64,824	48,380	53,142	62,486	47,654

Citigroup or subsidiary-obligated mandatorily redeemable securities of subsidiary trusts holding solely junior subordinated debt securities of									
– Parent					–	5,217	4,657	4,850	2,300
– Subsidiary					–	840	1,495	2,275	2,620
Total liabilities	1,796,840	2,074,033	1,764,535	1,381,500	1,374,810	1,264,032	1,166,018	970,203	836,004
Stockholders' equity									
Preferred stock ($1.00 par value; authorized shares: 30 million), at aggregate liquidation value	70,664	–	1,000	1,125	1,125	1,125	1,400	1,525	1,745
Common stock ($0.01 par value; authorized shares: 15 billion)	57	55	55	55	55	55	55	55	54
Amount paid-in capital	19,165	18,007	18,253	17,483	18,851	17,531	17,381	23,196	16,504
Retained earnings[a]	86,521	121,769	129,267	117,555	102,154	93,483	81,403	69,803	58,862
Treasury stock, at cost	(9,582)	(21,724)	(25,092)	(21,149)	(10,644)	(11,524)	(11,637)	(11,099)	(10,213)
Accumulated other comprehensive inccme (loss)	(25,195)	(4,660)	(3,700)	(2,532)	(304)	(806)	(193)	(844)	123
Unearned compensation					(1,946)	(1,850)	(1,691)	(1,389)	(869)
Total stockholders' equity	141,630	113,447	119,783	112,537	109,291	98,014	86,718	81,247	66,206
Total liabilities and stockholders' equity	$1,938,470	$2,187,480	$1,884,318	$1,494,037	$1,484,101	$1,264,032	$1,097,590	$1,051,450	$902,210

[a] Citigroup's opening *Retained Earnings* balance was reduced by $151 million to reflect a prior period adjustment to *Goodwill*. This reduction adjusted *Goodwill* to reflect a portion of the losses incurred in January 2002, related to the sale of an Argentinean subsidiary of Banamex that was recorded as an adjustment to the purchase price of Banamex. There was no tax benefit and no income statement impact from this adjustment.

Source: Adapted from Citigroup's 2008 10-K report, p. 117; 2006 10-K report, p. 105; 2004 10-K report, p. 107; 2003 10-K report, p. 103; 2001 10-K report, p. 81.

Exhibit 4 Citigroup Key Metrics, 1999–2008

	2008	2007	2006	2005	2004	2003	2002	2001	2000	1999
Average deposits (US$ billions)	$288	$276	$237	$232	$214	$349	$348	$298	$249	$215
No. of Branches	7,730	8,247	7,826	7,237	6,690	3,050	3,125	NA	NA	NA
Allowance for loan losses	4.27%	2.07%	1.32%	1.68%	2.05%	2.64%	2.48%	2.48%	2.33%	1.87%
Value at Risk (VAR) (US$ millions)	$292	$142	$99	$109	$101	$80	$66	$63	$52	NA
Tier 1 capital	11.92%	7.12%	8.59%	8.79%	8.74%	8.91%	8.47%	8.42%	8.38%	8.87%
Total capital	15.70%	10.70%	11.65%	12.02%	11.85%	12.04%	11.25%	10.92%	11.23%	11.32%
Leverage	16.45X	24.81X	19.38X	18.69X	19.23X	17.99X	17.64X	17.73X	16.75X	15.13X
Tangible Common Equity (TCE)/Tangible Assets (TA)	1.56%	2.72%	3.79%	4.39%	4.24%	4.53%	4.69%	7.58%	7.14%	NA
Approximate number of employees at year end	323,000	375,000	327,000	296,000	283,000	253,000	255,000	272,000	242,000	180,000

Source: Adapted from Citigroup's 1999-2004, 2006, and 2008 10-K reports and Citigroup Financial Snapshot at http://www.citigroup.com/citi/fin/data/snapshot0903.pdf?ieNocache=902, accessed July 9, 2009.

Prince Succeeds Weill

In July 2003, Weill recommended to the board that Chuck Prince succeed him as CEO. The recommendation of Prince – then CEO of Citigroup's Global corporate and investment bank – surprised many. Prince, a lawyer by training, began working with Weill in 1986 and eventually became his 'right hand man' in executing mergers and acquisitions. Weill also named Robert Willumstad, head of the consumer bank and long time loyal lieutenant, to be chief operating officer. In effect, Weill was naming Willumstad the pseudo co-CEO because of his operational experience, which Prince lacked and which was considered by many to be Prince's chief handicap.[39] Both men would earn the same salary and compensation.

Prince, described as a 'quiet man and consummate insider,'[40] took over the top job in October 2003. At the time Weill planned to stay on as chairman for two more years. Some suspected that Weill chose Prince because of the regulatory issues and lawsuits facing the company while others expected that Weill would continue to wield the true power within Citigroup. Weill had come under pressure to retire both due to his age (70) and the recent Wall Street scandals. An article in *The Economist* stated, 'In naming Mr. Prince as his successor, Mr. Weill essentially put his lawyer in his place, which is what people often do to resolve a transient problem.'[41] A *Financial Times* article said: 'No matter how forbidding the circumstances or how onerous or menial the task, Mr. Prince's job has been to make trouble go away for Mr. Weill.'[42] New York Attorney General Eliot Spitzer acknowledged that Prince played a pivotal and powerful role in negotiating a $1.4 billion settlement with 10 brokerages (including Citigroup) that had been accused of misleading clients with faulty stock research.[43]

Upon taking the helm, Prince clearly stated that one of his main goals was to keep Citigroup out of the headlines. But a series of controversial business decisions at ground level in Japan, Europe, and again in the U.S. kept the company in the spotlight. (See **Exhibit 5** for a list of Citigroup's troubles with regulators under Prince's watch.) According to a *Euroweek* article written in October 2004:

Exhibit 5 Regulatory Troubles under Prince's Reign

Date	Geography	Charges	Outcome
2003	Japan	Japan FSA[a] investigates Citigroup's private bank for complaints of 'gouging'	Investigation turned up many issues: failures to disclose risk, unfair transactions, and unauthorized sales, making loans used by customers for stock manipulation, helping customers misrepresent their profits, and failing to perform criminal background checks on new clients.[102]
2004	Japan	Issues with both private banking and accusations against Nikko Salomon Smith Barney, a Citigroup joint venture, of manipulating stock prices.	Japan's FSA revoked the private bank's license and it was closed down.
2004	Europe	Citigroup's European government bond trading desk earned about $18.2 million in profits when its traders sold euro zone bonds at artificially high prices created by the traders.[16]	Investigations in the U.K, Germany, Italy, France, Spain, Portugal, Greece, and Belgium. Results: penalty payment of $7.3 million in the U.K., case dismissed for lack of evidence in Germany, Eurex (the Europe Exchange) disciplinary committee cleared Citigroup but instituted a small fine, MTS[b] appeals board ruled that Citigroup breached a number of rules. Citigroup had to return the profits generated by the trade.
2004	Italy	Parmalat scandal included allegations of corporate fraud.	Charge to fourth-quarter earnings stemmed from $689 million of total exposure to Parmalat.

[a] Japan's Financial Services Agency (FSA) was responsible for ensuring the stability of Japan's financial system, and protection of depositors, insurance policyholders and securities investors.

[b] MTS was the largest market in Europe selling fixed income investments.

Source: Casewriter.

Citigroup may like to boast that the sun never sets on its sprawling global empire – and, indeed, this is true up to a point. However, the problem is that while the God-fearing and law-abiding Mr. Prince and his top New York managers are asleep, some Citigroup employees in a different time zone are up to all sorts of mischief.[44]

At the time Prince became CEO, the company operated in 100 countries on six continents with 275,000 employees.[45] The organization continued to focus on its diversification by both product and geographic region. In its annual report for 2003, Citigroup stated that it received a record $15.5 billion in revenue from its cross-marketing initiatives (20% of the total).

Still some of Weill's own team members came to doubt the financial supermarket strategy. A former executive reflected: 'We came to realize that instead of a financial supermarket we should think of Citi more like a financial mall. Different sets of customers would come to buy different products from a variety of outlets under the same overall umbrella.'[46] In February of 2005, the firm sold much of its life insurance business, Travelers Life & Annuity, to Metropolitan Life.

Prince stated his intention to move the company away from growth through acquisition and focus on internal, organic growth. Organic growth, however, would require much improved product innovation as well as continued cost cutting. Moving the company away from acquisitions was a striking change in direction for Citigroup. Prince felt that financial institutions had become too expensive, making them a poor growth strategy. 'We don't need to transform who we are,' said Chief Financial Officer Todd Thomson, 'We just have to think how to build out what we have.'[47] Prince joked that Citigroup was already so large that, 'The only way we could do a transformational acquisition would be to buy Canada.'[48]

In the spring of 2005, Prince had laid out his four broad goals for the firm: 1) make Citigroup the world's most respected financial firm; 2) grow the consumer business, 3) grow the international business; and 4) make the corporate and investment bank best in class.[49] (See **Exhibits 6a** and **6b** for Citigroup's net income by business segment and geography, 2001–2008, and **Exhibit 7** for the company's competitive position in certain lines of business, 1999–2008.) Prince aimed to increase Citigroup's net income from international business to 50% in the future, up from 38% in 2002, and much of this was expected to come from consumer financial services outside of the U.S. Citigroup believed the number of 'bankable' households with a disposable income of more than $10,000 a year was expected to grow from 112 million to 122 million in the U.S. by 2008, while, internationally, the number of bankable households was expected to grow from 349 million to 415 million in the same period. 'You get a chance like this once in a generation,' a Citigroup official told analysts.[50] Prince stated publicly he expected the company's annual earnings to grow earnings by 10% or more.[51]

In late 2004 Prince and Willumstad started to reshape the company's senior management and its organization structure. They fired Thomas Jones, who ran asset management; Deryck Maughan, the former Salomon CEO who headed international operations; and Peter Scaturro, CEO of the private banking group – all casualties of the company's problems with regulators in Japan. At one point Weill had considered both Jones and Maughan for the CEO job.[52] Prince named Sallie Krawcheck as chief financial officer and moved former CFO Todd Thomson to run Smith Barney.

Citigroup's 2004 profit came in at $17 billion, which was a 5% drop from the prior year. The chief culprit was a $4.95 billion charge to settle litigation over Citigroup's role in touting WorldCom's stock and to increase reserves for cases involving its role in financing Enron and other companies in the dotcom bubble era. The company also took a $242 million charge for credit and trading losses connected to the collapse of Italy's Parmalat. By 2004, Citigroup had paid or set aside in excess of $9 billion for these settlements, more than wiping out its investment banking profits over the prior two years.

Citigroup's share price dipped 10% in 2004. That compared with a 2% slip in the value of JP Morgan Chase & Co. shares and the 5% gain posted by Bank of America Corp. At these prices, Citigroup's stock traded at 10 times expected earnings, half the multiple that the shares fetched in the first few years after Citicorp and Travelers Group merged.

In 2005, as part of an effort to boost earnings, Prince began to significantly increase Citigroup's risk profile, which was apparently done in consultation with Rubin, who was reported to have said,

Exhibit 6a Citigroup Net Income by Business Segment, 1999–2008 (US$ millions)

Business Segment	2008	2007	2006	2005	2004	2003	2002	2001	2000	1999
Global Cards	$166	$4,674	$4,978							
Consumer Banking	(12,280)	2,157	6,073							
Total Global Consumer	(12,114)	6,831	10,051	$10,897	$11,987	$9,648	$8,252	$6,813	$6,004	$4,975
Institutional Clients Group	(20,117)	(4,155)	8,611	6,895	2,042	5,387	3,159	6,166	6,166	5,138
Global Wealth Management	1,091	1,974	1,443	1,244	1,209	2,322	1,523	2,414	1,445	1,219
Corporate/Other	(954)	(1,661)	(654)	(667)	48	(56)	(706)	(615)	(858)	(637)
Income (loss) from continuing operations	(32,094)	2,989	20,451	19,806	16,054	17,853	14,569	13,229	14,140	11,345
Net income (loss)	**($27,684)**	**$3,617**	**$21,538**	**$24,589**	**$17,046**	**$17,853**	**$15,276**	**$14,126**	**$13,519**	**$11,243**

Source: Casewriter estimation from Citigroup's 10-K reports, years: 2008, 2006, 2003, and 2001.

Exhibit 6b Citigroup Net Income by Geography, 2000–2008 (US$ millions)

Geography	2008	2007	2006	2005	2004	2003	2002	2001	2000
North America	($29,035)	($1,825)	$12,631	$11,951	$6,718[a]	$11,272	8,409	8,753	7,290
Europe, Middle East, Africa	(1,741)	(1,713)	2,159	1,373	2,331	1,607	1,429	1,435	1,520
Latin America	(1,983)	3,595	2,815	2,789	2,841	1,855	911	953	890
Asia	1,619	4,593	3,500	3,776	2,603	2,587	2,742	2,478	2,241
Total Regions	(31,140)	4,650	21,105	17,914	14,493	17,321	13,448	13,619	10,896
Corporate/Other	(954)	(1,661)	(654)	(668)	48	166	7	(615)	(1,050)
Inccme (loss) from continuing operations	(32,094)	2,989	20,451	19,221	16,054	17,853	13,448	13,229	12,231
Net income (loss)	**($27,684)**	**$3,617**	**$21,538**	**$24,589**	**$17,046**	**$17,853**	**$15,276**	**$14,126**	**$13,519**

[a]Includes a $4.95 billion after-tax charge for the WorldCom and litigation reserve charge.

Note: Mexico included in Latin America region.

Source: Casewriter estimation from Citigroup's 10-K reports, years: 2008, 2007 2006, 2004, 2003, and 2002.

Exhibit 7 Citigroup's Competitive Position

Criteria		2008	2007	2006	2005	2004	2003	2002	2001	2000	1999
Industry Ranking											
Deposits (U.S.)[a]	Volume of time deposits	#3	#4	#4	#4	#3	#3	NA	NA	NA	NA
Credit Cards (U.S.)[b]	Volume of outstanding debt	#3	#3	#3	#3	#2	#1	#1	#1	#1	#1
Merger & Acquisitions[c]	Volume based on deal value	#4	#3	#3	#2	#4	#4	#4	#4	#5	#7
Market Share											
Debt and equity underwriting[c]	Global Proceeds	6.1%	8.0%	8.0%	8.3%	8.6%	9.3%	9.6%	10.1%	8.4%	9.0%

[a] Nilson Reports vols: 732,756, 780, 803, 826, 849, 872, 895, 919, 2001.
[b] Business Ranking Annual 2000–2009.
[c] Thomson Financial, SDC (based on full year business).
Source: Casewriter estimates

'You have to take more risk if you want to earn more.'[53] Rubin was also said to have warned that the increased risk-taking required robust controls and oversight.[54] An important area of growth was in the creation, management, and sale of securitized instruments related to home mortgages, in particular collateralized debt obligations (CDOs).[b] Notwithstanding Rubin's admonitions, risk controls at Citigroup appeared to be seriously inadequate. There was insufficient investment in systems, incorrect assumptions were built into the risk models, and there was inappropriate segregation of duties between those charged with overseeing risk and those who had revenue responsibility and took the risk in the fixed income division.[55] Lynn Turner, the former chief accountant for the Securities and Exchange Commission said, 'If you're an entity of this size, if you don't have controls, if you don't have the right culture and you don't have people accountable for the risk that they are taking, you're Citigroup.'[56]

The lack of proper controls extended beyond the trading room. In March of 2005, the U.S. Federal Reserve prohibited Citigroup from making further acquisitions until management demonstrated that it could properly manage the firm. The Fed said, in part;

> *Given the size, scope, and complexity of Citigroup's global operations, successfully addressing the deficiencies in compliance risk management that has given rise to a series of adverse compliance events in recent years will require significant attention over a period of time by Citigroup's senior management and board of directors. The (Federal Reserve) Board expects that management at all levels will devote the necessary attention to implementing its plan fully and effectively and will not undertake significant expansion during the implementation period. The Board believes it is important that management's attention not be diverted from these efforts by the demands that mergers and acquisitions place on management resources.*[57]

At the same time, on March 1, 2005, Prince launched his 'Five Point Plan,' which included new standards for training, development, compensation, and annual reviews, all designed to inspire and monitor ethical behavior. Citigroup created a DVD sent to employees and journalists around the globe. Within two months, Prince personally addressed some 45,000 employees in 11 town hall meetings in 10 countries.[58]

At the end of July 2005, Willumstad left to become CEO of American International Group (AIG). A *Fortune* article attributed the move to Willumstad concluding that Prince was poor at both partnering and managing.[59] Other top executives also left the company. For example, Marge Magner, chairwoman and CEO of the Global Consumer Group, left the company in October 2005 to pursue a career change. On the exodus of talent, Prince said at conference that 'half the people who used to work for Citi are at JPMorgan now.'[60] Prince did, however, bring in some new high-profile individuals. For example, in November 2005 he hired James Wolfensohn, the former head of the World Bank, to advise senior management on global strategy and on international matters.

Citigroup earnings surged to $24.6 billion in 2005, a 37.7% jump over 2003. However, its stock continued to hover at $50 per share reflecting lack of investor confidence due largely to upwardly spiraling operating expenses, which had increased 15.3% from 2003 to 2005.

In early 2006, Prince formed a 14-member business heads committee, a 34-member operating committee, and a management committee of nearly 100 members, all to create greater oversight and a more cohesive corporate culture (including a company-wide code of ethics). Others felt that the committees slowed decision making and hampered innovation. Many industry observers felt Prince was making necessary changes but the results would take time to bear fruit – time that Wall Street might not allow. One analyst gave Prince 'points for making decisions that depress current results for

---

[b] These securities were created when mortgage-backed securities were pooled into a special purpose company, and 'tranches' (or slices) of obligations were created that were backed by the mortgages. Each tranche was designed to appeal to a different type of investor. The most senior tranche had the first call on the pool's cash flows, was rated AAA (the highest credit rating available), and carried the lowest risk and return. Progressively lower rated, higher return, and higher risk tranches were also created, including an equity tranche. The risk in each of the tranches and the rating that each obtained from the rating agencies was determined in part by the assumed default rate of the underlying mortgages, which was based on the historical experience of similar pools of underlying assets.

the benefit of long-term growth potential' but at the same time the analyst downgraded the stock from 'buy' to 'neutral.'[61] To Weill's dismay, Prince had leaned very little on the chairman.[62]

By mid-2006, Prince's strategies were showing mixed results. The Fed saw enough 'significant progress' in Citigroup's internal controls to lift its ban on acquisitions.[63] In the second quarter of 2006, revenues were up 9%, but expenses rose 15%. And only 2% of the cost increase was due to new investments, such as building retail branches.[64] Saudi Prince Alwaleed bin Talal, the largest individual investor with a 4.3% stake in Citigroup worth more than $10 billion, told the *Financial Times* that the company's costs were out of control and that 'draconian' measures would be required to curb expenses. He declared his confidence in Prince but he warned: 'I'm patient but enough is enough.'[65]

In response, Prince sent a memo to employees announcing that he had asked business heads to evaluate every line item and squeeze out 'business-as-usual' costs for items as small as newspaper subscriptions. But he was vehement about not cutting investments to shortchange the future.[66] Much of these future investments took the form of expanding retail banking outlets in locations where customers of the company's Smith Barney brokerage lived, hoping to sell them banking products.

In December 2006, Prince replaced Willumstad. He named Robert Druskin as chief operating officer and put him in charge of a comprehensive cost-cutting plan and told him to streamline computer systems and management groups, and move back offices to lower-cost areas of the U.S., Europe and Asia.[67] Druskin, president and chief executive of Citigroup's Corporate and Investment Banking unit at the time, had decades of operational experience in the industry. Druskin said that in the late 1990s and in the first part of the new decade, the company had 'over-earned and underinvested.'[68] One analyst said, 'He (Prince) inherited a gobbelgook of companies that were never integrated, and it was never a priority of the company to invest. The businesses didn't communicate with each other. There were dozens of technology systems and dozens of financial ledgers.'[69]

Citigroup's 2006 revenues grew nearly 8% over 2005, but its net income fell 12% year-over-year. Expenses were up 12% in 2006 as the company invested aggressively in its organic growth objectives for the year, including opening an average of three bank branches each day.[70] Despite the drop, Citigroup's net income was $21.5 billion – the second highest annual earnings in its history.

In the spring of 2007, Citigroup announced 15,000 job cuts (5% of its 327,000 employees) and further cost cutting that industry analysts predicted would mean $2 billion in cost savings. Prince said that the company was pruning its core business portfolios to improve overall returns, but there were no plans to either sell or spin-off the businesses.[71] In addition, Prince said the company was rethinking its investment strategy in international markets. While Citigroup had no plans to pull out of the 100 or so countries where it operated, it would begin to concentrate on a smaller number of countries to build market share.[72] Prince also unveiled an effort to unify the disparate cultures, and to rationalize the brand, under an internal 'one Citi' campaign – an effort to use only the Citi name externally where possible, and the abandonment of the red umbrella logo that came from Travelers at the merger in 1998.[73]

The first two quarters of 2007 were the company's best under Prince's leadership. Net income for the second quarter was up 18%. However, in the second half of 2007, Prince struggled to cut costs and generate new revenue. He continued investing in the expansion of retail outlets, but many industry observers felt that the actions were too late in an already oversaturated market.

In April of 2007, Citigroup bought the hedge fund Old Lane Partners (Old Lane), and brought into the firm's management the fund's CEO, Vikram Pandit. Pandit had been head of the institutional business at Morgan Stanley, and had been mentioned as a candidate for Morgan Stanley's CEO position. He left in 2005 after a messy and public battle with the former CEO, Philip Purcell. Old Lane was founded by Pandit and another former Morgan Stanley executive, John Havens (who also joined Citigroup), in 2006. Citigroup paid $800 million for the year old firm, which had $4.5 billion of assets. It was widely acknowledged that the deal was more about obtaining the services of Pandit than buying another newly minted hedge fund. Pandit reportedly received in excess of $165 million from the sale, of which $100 million was to be reinvested in the hedge fund until 2011. Pandit, who grew up in Mumbai, India, came to the U.S. as a teenager, and held a doctoral degree in finance from Columbia University. He was named to run Citigroup's Alternative Investment unit.[74]

By the spring of 2007 the realities of a declining housing market had finally caught up with the broader financial markets. In August 2007, two hedge funds managed by Bear Stearns that invested in mortgage related securities failed. This began a precipitous decline in the value of mortgage related securities, which had a profound effect on the profitability of Wall Street firms that held significant amounts of these securities in inventory, and it marked the start of the historic crisis that would grip the financial markets and global economy.

On October 1, 2007 Citigroup took the unusual step of pre-announcing third quarter earnings two weeks early. Citigroup warned investors that because of the mortgage crisis and its effects on the quality of credit and value of securities more broadly in the third quarter, it would write-down approximately $1.4 billion on highly leveraged financing commitments, and $1.3 billion in subprime mortgage holdings, as well as take a charge of $2.6 billion for future losses in consumer credit. Amid some discussion about Prince's future as CEO, Rubin said, 'I think Chuck's going to be here for a lot of years.'[75] (See **Exhibit 8** for Citigroup's Significant Risk Exposures, 2007–2008.)

On October 15, Citigroup reported a profit of $2.2 billion for the third quarter, down 58% from a year earlier. The significant write-downs and losses were much in line with what was announced on October 1st. Citigroup also noted that expenses for the quarter had increased by 22%. As part of a reorganization to spark revenue growth, Prince announced that Citigroup's Investment Bank and Alternative Investments units would be merged and headed by Pandit, and be called the Institutional Client Group.[76]

On November 4, 2007 Citigroup announced Prince was stepping down as chairman, and the firm would take an additional $8 billion to $11 billion in write-downs in the fourth quarter. Prince resigned, saying in a memo to employees, 'I am responsible for the conduct of our businesses.' He continued, 'The size of these charges makes stepping down the only honorable course for me to take as chief executive officer.'[77] He resigned five days after Merrill Lynch & Co. ousted CEO Stanley O'Neal following

Exhibit 8 Securities and Banking Significant Risk Exposure, 2007–2009 (US$ billions)

	Risk exposure		
	March 31	December 31	
As of	2009	2008	2007
Sub-prime related direct exposure[a]	$10.0	$14.1	$37.3
Highly leveraged loans and financing commitments[b]	1.1	10.0	43.2
Alt-A mortgage securities[c]	1.9	12.6	22.0
Auction Rate Securities	2.9	8.8	8.0
Commercial Real Estate[d]	5.7	37.5	53.7
Structured Investment Vehicles	0.1	16.6	46.4
Private Equity and Equity Investments	7.5	–	–
Total significant revenue items	$29.2	$99.6	$210.6

[a] Net of impact from hedges against direct subprime asset-backed securities collateralized debt obligation super senior positions.

[b] Net of underwriting fees.

[c] Net of hedges.

[d] Excluded positions that were included in the structured investment vehicles portfolio.

Source: Citigroup 2008 10-K report and March 2009 Earnings Call document.

Exhibit 9 CDO league tables, 2002–2008

2008 rank	Name	2007 rank	2002–2008 cumulative rank	2008 Number of issues	2008 Amount (US$ billions)	2008 Percent of total
1	Deutsche Bank AG	2	4	48	$11.1	8.8%
2	JP Morgan	3	2	28	6.2	6.8
3	Morgan Stanley	10	6	10	6.0	5.6
4	Bank of America Merrill Lynch	1	1	29	5.4	4.5
5	Goldman Sachs & Co.	6	9	6	5.4	4.3
6	**Citigroup**	2	3	21	5.4	3.7
7	Lehman Bros.	19	19	6	4.9	3.6
8	Barclay's Capital	5	5	13	3.2	3.5
9	Credit Suisse	7	7	8	3.2	3.4
10	CITC	NA	NA	3	2.1	2.6
	Others			53	14.6	53.2
	Total Market			**225**	**$61.5**	**100.0%**

Source: Casewriter, data from Thomson Financial, accessed July 2009.

an $8.4 billion write-down that was more than 50% greater than the bank had forecasted.[78] The Securities and Exchange Commission also opened an investigation into Citigroup's accounting practices related to those losses.

The mortgage crisis, and its effects on asset values and the availability of credit, had created two significant problems for Citigroup, both stemming from the trading areas within its investment banking business. First, as a market leader in the issuance of CDOs, Citi held substantial subprime and mortgage related positions on its balance sheet, creating the potential for substantial losses as the markets for mortgage related securities collapsed. (See **Exhibit 9** for CDO league tables.) On its third quarter earnings call with analysts, Citigroup reported that its exposure to subprime assets in its CDO positions was less than $13 billion. On November 5, the company reported that its subprime exposure through CDOs was $55 billion. The higher number included $43 billion of 'super senior' CDO exposure, which had as its underlying assets subprime residential mortgaged-backed securities.[c] Citigroup apparently had believed that the 'super senior' ranking of its portion of these CDOs insulated the company from the decline in the subprime market, and therefore management had not included them in their earlier subprime exposure estimates. As the rating agencies downgraded many of the mortgaged backed securities and CDOs in October, the securities' values declined, resulting in the additional estimated loss to Citigroup of between $8 and $11 billion. (See **Exhibit 10** for Citigroup's exposure to subprime mortgages, Q3 2007–Q4 2008.)

In addition, Citigroup's substantial involvement with structured investment vehicles (SIVs) was presenting the firm with major challenges. As described in Citigroup's September 2007 10-Q:

---

[c] Gary Crittenden, Citigroup's CFO, explained on November 5 that $25 billion of this exposure to subprime came in the form of 'liquidity puts' that Citigroup wrote to clients that bought the 'super senior' tranches of these CDOs. Because the puts would be used by the clients to sell back these securities when the value of underlying subprime mortgages fell, Citigroup had the same economic exposure to the subprime market as if it had owned the CDOs.

Exhibit 10 Citigroup's Exposure to Subprime, Q3 2007 to Q4 2008 (US$ billions)

	Sept. 30, 2007 exposures	Q4 2007 write-downs	Q4 2007 sales, transfers, etc.	Dec. 31, 2007 exposures	Q1 2008 write-downs	Q1 2008 sales, transfers, etc.	Mar. 31, 2008 exposures	Q2 2008 write-downs	Q2 2008 sales, transfers, etc.
CDO Super Senior									
Total gross exposures	$53.4			$39.8			$33.2		
Hedged exposures	10.5			10.5			10.5		
Net exposures									
ABCP/CDO[a]	24.9	(4.3)	0.0	20.6	(3.1)	(0.7)	16.8	(2.0)	(0.4)
High grade[b]	9.5	(4.9)	0.3	4.9	(1.0)	(0.1)	3.8	(1.3)	(0.5)
Mezzanine[b]	8.3	(5.2)	0.5	3.6	(1.5)	(0.1)	2.0	0.1	(0.5)
ABS CDO-squared	0.2	0.1	0.0	0.2	(0.1)	(0.0)	0.1	0.0	(0.0)
Total net exposures	**42.9**	**(14.3)**	**0.8**	**29.3**	**(5.7)**	**(0.9)**	**22.7**	**(3.2)**	**(1.5)**
Lending and Structuring									
CDO warehousing/unsold tranches of ABS CDOs	$2.7	($2.6)	$0.0	$0.2	(0.1)	0.1	0.2	(0.0)	(0.1)
Subprime loans purchased for sale or securitization	4.2	(0.2)	0.0	4.0	(0.2)	(0.2)	3.6	(0.3)	(0.6)
Financing transactions secured by subprime[b]	4.8	(0.1)	(0.9)	3.8	(0.0)	(1.1)	2.6	(0.1)	(1.0)
Total lending and structuring exposures	**11.7**	**(2.9)**	**(0.9)**	**8.0**	**(0.3)**	**(1.2)**	**6.4**	**(0.3)**	**(1.7)**
Total net exposures[c]	**$54.6**	**($17.2)**	**($0.1)**	**$37.3**	**($6.0)**	**($2.2)**	**$29.1**	**($3.5)**	**($3.2)**
Reserve (credit adj.) on hedge counterparty exposure		(0.9)			(1.5)			(2.4)	
Total net write-downs		**($18.1)**			**($7.5)**			**($5.9)**	

Exhibit 10 *Continued*

	June 30, 2008 exposures	Q3 2008 write-downs[a]	Q3 2008 sales, transfers, etc.	Sept. 30, 2008 exposures	Q4 2008 write-downs[a]	Q4 2008 sales, transfers, etc.	Dec. 31, 2008 exposures
CDO SUPER SENIOR							
Total gross exposures	$27.9			$25.7			$18.9
Hedged exposures	9.8			9.4			6.9
Net exposures							
ABCP/CDO[a]	*14.4*	*(0.8)*	*(0.3)*	*13.3*	*(3.1)*	*(0.3)*	*9.9*
High grade[b]	*2.0*	*0.2*	*(1.1)*	*1.1*	*(0.4)*	*0.1*	*0.8*
Mezzanine[b]	*1.6*	*0.3*	*(0.2)*	*1.7*	*(0.3)*	*(0.2)*	*1.3*
ABS CDO-squared	*0.2*	*(0.0)*	*(0.0)*	*0.1*	*(0.1)*	*(0.0)*	*0.0*
Total net exposures	**18.1**	**(0.3)**	**(1.5)**	**16.3**	**(3.9)**	**(0.3)**	**12.0**
LENDING AND STRUCTURING							
CDO warehousing/unsold tranches of ABS CDOs	*0.1*	*(0.0)*	*(0.0)*	*0.1*	*(0.0)*	*(0.0)*	*0.0*
Subprime loans purchased for sale or securitization	*2.8*	*(0.3)*	*(0.4)*	*2.1*	*(0.5)*	*(0.2)*	*1.3*
Financing transactions secured by subprime[b]	*1.5*	*(0.2)*	*(0.2)*	*1.1*	*(0.1)*	*(0.3)*	*0.7*
Total lending and structuring exposures	**4.3**	**(0.5)**	**(0.6)**	**3.3**	**(0.7)**	**(0.5)**	**2.0**
Total net exposures[c]	**$22.5**	**($0.8)**	**($2.1)**	**$19.6**	**($4.6)**	**($0.9)**	**$14.1**
Reserve (credit adj.) on hedge counterparty exposure		(0.9)			(0.9)		
Total net write-downs		**($1.7)**			**($5.6)**		

[a] Primarily consists of high grade ABS CDOs.

[b] Includes credit costs.

[c] Comprised of net CDO super senior exposures and lending and structuring exposures.

Note: Quarterly write-downs in 2008 include profits/losses associated with liquidations.

Source: Adapted from Citigroup 2008 10-K Report, p. 48; 2008 Q1 10-Q Report, p. 22; 2008 Q2 10-Q Report, p. 30; 2008 Q3 10-Q Report, p. 34; and Casewriter estimates.

SIVs are special purpose investment companies that seek to generate attractive risk-adjusted floating rate returns through the use of financial leverage and credit management skills, while hedging interest rate and currency risks and managing credit, liquidity and operational risks. The basic investment strategy is to earn a spread between relatively inexpensive short-term funding (commercial paper and medium-term notes) and high quality portfolios with medium term duration, with the leverage effect providing attractive returns to junior note holders, who are third party investors and who provide the capital to the SIVs.

Citigroup has no contractual obligation to provide liquidity facilities or guarantees to any of the Citi-advised SIVs and does not own an equity position in the SIVs.

At the end of the third quarter, the total asset value of Citi-managed SIVs was $83 billion across seven entities, down from $100 billion at mid-year. Only a tiny fraction of the SIV assets were related to subprime mortgages; the problem lay with the funding arrangement. As the crisis caused the credit markets to freeze, the SIVs faced significant difficulty refinancing the commercial paper funding, raising the specter of having to repay the commercial paper lenders. Because the markets were in crisis, investors were not buying many assets, leaving Citigroup potentially unable to sell enough SIV assets to repay the commercial paper lenders. While not under a legal obligation to fund the SIVs (which would have required Citigroup to put the assets and liabilities on its balance sheet, detrimentally affecting the firm's capital position), Citigroup was faced with some implicit obligation to assist clients that had purchased the SIV assets, as well as the potential for affecting the broader financial system if it tried to force the sale of significant amounts of assets at a difficult moment.[79]

Prince's departure hastened calls to break up the company. Citigroup shares fell 32% in 2007, and had declined by 17% since Prince became CEO in October 2003. Rubin, who had chaired Citigroup's executive committee, was named chairman. Sir Win Bischoff, who ran Citigroup's European operations, was named acting CEO while a board committee sought a new leader for the firm.

Pandit Replaces Prince

In December 2007, Citigroup's board appointed Pandit to succeed Prince as the company's CEO and named Bischoff as chairman. Rubin described Pandit as the 'best athlete' among the candidates for the job.[80] Some major shareholders wanted Willumstad to return as the new CEO. Willumstad was interested and made a presentation to the search committee. Willumstad argued that Citigroup's consumer and corporate businesses did little for each other. 'The stock market,' he remarked, 'has been saying for years that it doesn't like Citi's business model. If you were interested in me for this job, you would have to tell me you would seriously consider breaking this company up.' Willumstad believed he shocked the committee.[81]

On December 13, just two days after Pandit assumed the CEO role, Citigroup announced that it was placing the assets and liabilities of seven SIVs, valued at $49 billion, on its balance sheet. The assets in the SIVs had been reduced from $87 billion in August through sales, and the firm said that almost none of the remaining assets were related to subprime mortgages. This action provided an explicit acknowledgement that Citigroup would be providing the funding for the structures to prevent the SIVs forced liquidation at potentially draconian values. The action followed a failed attempt by the U.S. Treasury to create an industry wide 'super SIV' that would take assets from such entities at a number of firms, and also the decision by other banks to bring similar vehicles onto their balance sheets.[82]

Citigroup reported a loss of $9.83 billion for the fourth quarter of 2007, including $18 billion of subprime related write-downs, and $4.1 billion in increased credit costs. For the full year, the firm generated $3.6 billion in earnings, down 83% from $21.5 billion in 2006. It had $37.3 billion in subprime related assets on its balance sheet, and $133.4 billion in Level 3 assets. Its Tier 1 capital ratio was 7.12%, while its TCE/TA ratio stood at 2.72%. (See **Exhibit 11** for Citigroup's mark-to-market asset values under FAS 157 for year end 2007 and 2008.)

Exhibit 11 Citigroup's Mark-to-Market Asset Values (FAS 157) at Year End 2007 and 2008 (US$ millions)

At December 31, 2007	Level 1	Level 2	Level 3	Gross Inventory	Netting[a]	Net Balance
Assets						
Federal funds sold and securities borrowed or purchased under agreements to resell	$ –	$132,383	$16	$132,399	$(48,094)	$84,305
Trading account assets						
Trading securities and loans	151,684	234,846	75,573	462,103	–	462,103
Derivatives	7,204	438,779	31,226	467,209	(390,328)	76,881
Investments	64,375	125,282	17,060	206,717	–	206,717
Loans[b]	–	3,718	9	3,727	–	3,727
Mortgage servicing rights	–	–	8,380	8,380	–	8,380
Other financial assets measured on a recurring basis	–	13,570	1,171	14,741	(4,939)	9,802
Total assets	**$223,263**	**$938,578**	**$133,435**	**$1,295,276**	**($443,361)**	**$851,915**
	17.2%	72.5%	10.3%	100.0%		

At December 31, 2008	Level 1	Level 2	Level 3	Gross Inventory	Netting[a]	Net Balance
Assets						
Federal funds sold and securities borrowed or purchased under agreements to resell	$ –	$96,524	$ –	$96,524	($26,219)	$70,305
Trading account assets						
Trading securities and loans	90,530	121,043	50,773	262,346	–	262,346
Derivatives	9,675	1,102,252	60,725	1,172,652	(1,057,363)	115,289
Investments	44,342	111,836	28,273	184,451	–	184,451
Loans[b]	–	2,572	160	2,732	–	2,732
Mortgage servicing rights	–	–	5,657	5,657	–	5,657
Other financial assets measured on a recurring basis	–	9,890	359	10,249	(4,527)	5,722
Total assets	**$144,547**	**$1,444,117**	**$145,947**	**$1,734,611**	**($1,088,109)**	**$646,502**
	8.3%	83.3%	8.4%	100.0%		

[a]Represents netting of: (i) the amounts due under securities purchased under agreements to resell and the amounts owed under securities sold under agreements to repurchase in accordance with FIN 41, and (ii) derivative exposures covered by a qualifying master netting agreement in accordance with FIN 39, cash collateral and the market value adjustment.

[b]There was no allowance for loan losses recorded for loans reported at fair value.

Source: Adapted from Citigroup's 2008 10-K report, pp. 197–198.

Industry analysts largely felt that although Pandit was well equipped to tackle Citigroup's investment banking problems, his inexperience in consumer banking 'could be a disadvantage as banks stand at the doorstep of a credit cycle, and given that the Global Consumer businesses contribute 50% to 60% of Citigroup's consolidated net income.'[83] Upon accepting his new position, Pandit expressed his intent to focus Citigroup on identifying and investing in the best growth opportunities, and he committed to conducting 'an objective and dispassionate' review of the bank's businesses. Many took the latter comment to indicate openness to splitting Citigroup into smaller units. According to the same analyst, 'We would not be surprised if following his review certain businesses were either sold or restructured. A sale of businesses could also serve as a much needed source of capital.'[84]

Reflecting on all that had happened to Citigroup, Reed described the merger as a 'mistake' and implied that the business model was to blame.[85] Weill responded that poor execution drove the poor results. 'And,' he said, 'I get an F for succession planning.'[86] Ken Lewis, the CEO of Bank of America, said in an interview that, 'Citi's problem (in US and international retail banking) was being unimportant in many places.'[87]

Looking forward Pandit described three key steps he deemed critical to stabilizing Citigroup. First was the need to raise capital. In the first half of 2008 Citigroup raised over $33 billion in capital. In addition, Pandit slashed the dividend by 41%. Second, he wanted to make sure that the firm retained its key employees, and arranged for the bonuses for 2007 work (paid in early 2008) to be determined as if the firm had not had losses. Finally, he said he needed to protect the firm from the adverse effects of the remaining toxic assets on the balance sheet, saying 'We've got to ring fence these assets. We've been completely focused on bringing these down and managing them as well as we can for our shareholders.'[88]

By May 2008, Pandit had decided he would not split Citigroup, but instead would retain the universal bank model, based on four key global products: credit cards, wealth management, corporate banking, and investment banking.[89] He would also focus on significantly reduce Citigroup's expenses.

During the first half of 2008, the firm lost $8 billion, with write-downs on mortgage related assets totaling about $16.5 billion, and increased credit costs for the derivatives book of $7.6 billion. Citigroup had reduced headcount by 11,000, and had sold some small pieces of the firm. Some would later suggest that Pandit's cerebral, low-key management style and uninspiring public speaking had failed to lift morale among Citigroup's 350,000 employees, while his propensity to rely on an inner circle of aides from Morgan Stanley, his former employer, had alienated many long-time Citigroup executives.[90]

In September, the crisis in the financial markets came to a boil. Mortgage giants Fannie Mae and Freddie Mac were put under government conservatorship, Lehman Brothers filed for bankruptcy (the largest in U.S. history), Merrill Lynch sold itself to Bank of America to avoid Lehman's fate, Goldman Sachs and Morgan Stanley became bank holding companies, and AIG effectively sold 80% of itself to the U.S. government to prevent its failure. The Reserve Fund, the nation's oldest money market fund, 'broke the buck' because it owned significant amounts of worthless Lehman Brothers commercial paper, causing significant concern about the risk of a 'run' on other money market funds. Similar problems were occurring overseas.

On September 29, Citigroup bid $2.2 billion, or $1 per share, for the banking assets of Wachovia Corporation, which was about to fail. The Federal Deposit Insurance Corporation (FDIC) had determined that the failure of Wachovia would represent a risk to the broader financial system; to forestall this event the agency initially encouraged Wachovia to accept Citigroup's offer, which it did. For Citigroup, it was a transaction that would both demonstrate its viability and significantly expand its U.S. retail footprint. While it would have to take a loss from writing down Wachovia's assets, and would need to raise at least $10 billion in new capital, Citigroup would receive assistance from the FDIC to protect the value of Wachovia's asset. Wells Fargo had initially expressed interest in Wachovia, but then dropped out of the discussions. However, within a few days of the agreement, while Citigroup and Wachovia were negotiating the details of the transaction, Wells returned with a $7 per share bid for the entire company, which it could acquire without FDIC assistance. Over Citigroup's protest (and later lawsuits), and apparently with some encouragement from the FDIC, Wachovia accepted Wells Fargo's offer.[91]

With an appetite among global market participants for cash and liquidity that was virtually insatiable, and fears that assets of every type were worth far less than their stated values, the credit markets froze in October. Financial firms were unwilling to lend to one another at almost any price. In an effort to restore some confidence in the financial system, the U.S. government implemented the Troubled Asset Relief Program (TARP). TARP allowed the U.S. Treasury to purchase up to $700 billion of bank capital, in the form of preferred stock.[d] On October 13, the CEOs of the nine largest U.S. financial firms, including Pandit, were called to the U.S. Treasury and told that they had to accept the government's money. Citigroup received a $25 billion investment. In late November, after the government reviewed Citigroup's books, another $20 billion was invested, and the government provided guarantees on $301 billion (after a first loss of $29 billion) of Citigroup's $2 trillion in assets. Citigroup issued another $7 billion in preferred stock, as well as warrants, to compensate the U.S. Treasury and FDIC for the guarantee. The dividend was virtually eliminated. One money manager said, 'This is chemo. They need this capital to stay alive.'[92] Some laid the necessity for the government bailout squarely at Pandit's feet. 'He didn't go into crisis mode early enough, or at least it wasn't obvious,' said one academic. 'It should have been a more aggressive reduction of risk 11 months ago.'[93]

In the fourth quarter of 2008, the firm lost $8.3 billion. Over the full year, it lost $18.7 billion. In the final quarter, Citigroup took write-downs on mortgage related assets of $5.6 billion, increased credit costs for derivatives by $6.1 billion (following a $4.9 billion increase in the third quarter) and allocated an additional $6 billion to its allowance for loan losses (following a $3.9 billion allocation in the third quarter). (See **Exhibit 12** for Citigroup's derivative exposures 2005-2008.) At the end of the quarter Citigroup restated its earnings, taking an additional charge of $9.9 billion on an impairment to goodwill from the declining value of Nikko Asset management. Headcount had been cut by 52,000 since the beginning of 2008, and the expense run-rate had been reduced by 14%. Tier 1 capital stood at 11.92% and TCE/TA was 1.56%.

In January 2009, both board chairman Bischoff and Rubin retired. According to some industry watchers, '(Rubin's) tenure at Citi has tarnished the reputation he built as a talented, nimble leader at the head of Goldman Sachs and as Secretary of the Treasury for the Clinton administration.' In his resignation letter, Rubin wrote '[my] great regret is that I and so many of us who have been involved in this industry for so long did not recognize the serious possibility of the extreme circumstances that the financial system faces today.'[94]

As a result of the shake-up of Citigroup's board, Richard Parsons, the former CEO of Time Warner, became chairman. Pressure on Pandit to turn around the company intensified. In mid-January, Pandit announced plans to split Citigroup into two units – effectively breaking up the 'supermarket' model it had been trying to make work over the past decade.[95] Reports in the *Wall Street Journal* indicated that Citigroup planned to reduce the size of the company by one-third. As part of this initiative, Citigroup announced on January 14, 2009 plans to split off its Smith Barney retail brokerage into a joint venture with Morgan Stanley.[96] This deal provided Citigroup with $2.7 billion of badly needed cash. As this news emerged, Citigroup shares fell to $5.08.[97] 'For Citi, the joint venture provides significant synergies and scale, substantially reduces our expenses and enables us to retain a significant stake in a company that immediately becomes the industry leader with real growth opportunities,' said Pandit.[98]

In February 2009, Pandit responded to ongoing criticism from investors, Congress and the general public by vowing to accept only $1 in salary with no bonuses until Citigroup returned to profitability. Considerable anger stemmed from the company's purchase of a $50 million jet after accepting federal bail-out funds. 'We hold ourselves accountable and that starts with me,' Pandit told the House Financial Services Committee. 'We did not adjust quickly enough to this new world,' he added. 'I get the new reality and I will make sure Citi gets it as well.'[99]

In the first quarter of 2009 the firm generated $1.6 billion of earnings on $24.8 billion in revenues. The Institutional Clients Group business was the key contributor to earnings, with $2.3 billion in net income, while the Consumer Group lost $1.2 billion. Since the beginning of 2008, Citigroup had reduced

---

[d] The government used preferred stock to avoid taking direct ownership in the firms and creating the impression that the banks were being nationalized.

Exhibit 12 Derivative Exposure, 2005–2008
EXPOSURE BY NOTIONAL AMOUNT[a] (US$ billions)

As of December 31	Trading derivatives[b,c]				Nontrading derivatives[d]				Asset/Liability management hedges[e]	
	2008	2007	2006	2005	2008	2007	2006	2005	2006	2005
Total interest rate contract notionals	$23,747.0	$25,362.9	$22,028.7	$18,352.1	$945.7	$881.8	$684.9	$481.0		
Total foreign exchange contract notionals	4,069.9	5,155.7	3,612.2	2,575.5	107.1	123.3	98.4	92.0		
Total equity contract notionals	1,094.6	1,361.7	884.3	491.3	–	–	–	–		
Total commodity and other contact notionals	168.9	153.5	81.9	53.4	–	–	–	–		
Total credit derivatives	3,033.5	3,674.8	1,945.0	1,030.7	–	–	–	–		
Total derivative notionals	$32,113.9	$35,708.6	$28,552.2	$22,503,012	$1,052.8	$1,005.1	$783.3	$573.1		

[a] Includes the notional amounts for long- and short-derivative positions.
[b] Trading Derivatives includes proprietary and market-making activities where the changes in market value were recorded to trading assets or trading liabilities.
[c] Trading Derivatives include proprietary position, as well as certain hedging derivatives instruments that qualified for hedge accounting in accordance with SFAS No. 133, *Accounting for Derivative Instruments and Hedging Activities* (SFAS 133).
[d] Nontrading derivatives include only those end-user derivative instruments where the changes in market value were recorded in *Other Assets* or *Other Liabilities.*
[e] Asset/Liability Management Hedges include only those end-user derivative instruments where the changes in market value were recorded to other assets or other liabilities.

Exhibit 12 *Continued*
EXPOSURE BY MARK-TO-MARKET (MTM) AMOUNT, (US$ billions)

As of December 31	Derivatives receivables – MTM				Derivatives payable – MTM			
	2008	2007	2006	2005	2008	2007	2006	2005
Trading derivatives[b]								
Interest rate contracts	$667.6	$237.7	$167.5	$192.8	$654.2	$237.9	$166.1	$188.2
Foreign exchange contracts	153.2	77.9	52.3	42.7	160.6	72.0	47.5	41.5
Equity contracts	35.7	27.4	26.9	18.6	57.3	66.9	53.0	32.3
Commodity and other contracts	23.9	8.5	5.4	7.3	22.5	8.9	5.8	7.0
Credit derivatives[f (2007, 2008)]			14.1	8.1			15.1	9.3
Citigroup as the Guarantor	5.9	5.0			198.2	73.1		
Citigroup as the Beneficiary	222.5	78.4			5.5	11.2		
Cash collateral paid/received[g (2007, 2008)]	63.9	32.2			65.0	19.4		
Total	$1,172.7	$467.2	$266.2	$269.6	$1,163.3	$489.4	$287.4	$278.2
Less: Netting agreements, cash Collateral and market value adjustments	(1,057.4)	(390.3)	(216.6)	(222.2)	(1,046.5)	(385.9)	(212.6)	(216.9)
Net receivables/payables	$115.3	$76.9	$49.5	$47.4	$116.8	$103.5	$74.8	$61.3
Net receivables/payables[e (2007, 2008)]								
Asset/liability management hedges[e (2005, 2006)]								
Interest rate contracts	$14.8	$8.5	$1.8	$3.8	$7.7	$7.2	$3.3	$1.6
Foreign exchange contracts	2.4	1.6	3.7	1.4	3.7	1.0	1.0	1.1
Total	$17.2	$10.2	$5.5	$5.2	$11.5	$8.1	$4.3	$2.8

[b] Trading Derivatives includes proprietary and market-making activities where the changes in market value were recorded to trading assets or trading liabilities.

[e] Asset/Liability Management Hedges include only those end-user derivative instruments where the changes in market value were recorded to other assets or other liabilities.

[f] Credit derivatives were arrangements designed to allow one party (the 'beneficiary') to transfer the credit risk of a 'reference asset' to another party (the 'guarantor'). These arrangements allowed a guarantor to assume the credit risk associated with the reference asset without directly purchasing it. The Company entered into credit derivatives positions for purposes such as risk management, yield enhancement, reduction of credit concentrations and diversification of overall risk.

[g] In addition to the cash collateral paid or received, as of December 31, 2008 the Company provided $7.9 billion and received $6.8 billion of marketable securities as collateral under derivative contracts.

Source: Adapted from Citigroup's 2008 10-K report, pp. 90–91 and 2006 10-K report, p. 69.

its exposure to toxic assets by 47%, to $101.5 billion, had decreased its expense run rate by 23%, and downsized its headcount by 16% to 309,000.[100]

On June 10, 2009 Citigroup announced that it would convert and swap $58 billion of preferred shares for common stock in an effort agreed upon with U.S. regulators to bolster the firm's tangible capital. As a result of the action, the U.S. government would own 34% of the firm. On the same day, the chairman of the FDIC, Sheila Barr, reportedly told Citigroup's board that she remained concerned about Pandit's lack of lending and commercial banking experience. The Administration of U.S. President Barack Obama appointed a 'compensation czar' with broad powers to oversee the executive compensation at seven firms that required extraordinary government assistance, including Citigroup.[101]

Endnotes

[1] Jan Hopkins, Charles Molineaux, Citicorp/Travelers Merger CNNfn: Street Sweep 6 April 1998, via Factiva, accessed January 8, 2009.

[2] 'Citigroup's confused chemistry,' *Euromoney on the Web*, January 1, 2000, http://www.euromoney.com, accessed June 2009; Carolo J. Loomis, 'CitiCorp: Sandy Weill's Monster,' *Fortune*, April 16, 2001, http://www.fortune.com, accessed June 2009; 'King of Capital, Part 1,' BusinessWeek, June 25, 2002, http://www.businessweek.com, accessed June 2009.

[3] David Wighton, *Financial Times*, London Ed.1, October 6, 2004, p. 17, at http://w4.stern.nyu.edu/news/nsews.cfm?doc_id=3193, accessed January 7, 2009.

[4] 'Citicorp, Travelers to merge,' *Reuters News*, April 6, 1998, via Factiva, accessed January 8, 2009.

[5] 'Citigroup's confused chemistry,' *Euromoney on the Web*, January 1, 2000, http://www.euromoney.com, accessed June 2009.

[6] http://home3.americanexpress.com/corp/os/history.asp, accessed January 7, 2009.

[7] Ibid.

[8] Ibid.

[9] Bill Stoneman, 'Cross-Selling Proves to Be a Hard Sell at Citigroup,' American Banker, Vol. 167, No. 199, October 17, 2001, p. 8A, via Factiva, accessed January 8, 2009.

[10] 'Citicorp,Travelers to merge,' *Reuters News*, April 6, 1998, via Factiva, accessed January 8, 2009.

[11] Putnam Lovell Securities, 'Citigroup Inc.: A Truly Diverse Player' Commercial Banking Report, June 2001.

[12] Sanford C. Bernstein & Co, Inc, 'Citigroup: Not Your Father's Cross-Selling Synergies,' Bernstein Research, April 17, 1998.

[13] 'Citigroup's confused chemistry,' *Euromoney on the Web*, January 1, 2000, http://www.euromoney.com, accessed June 2009.

[14] Duncan Hughes, Citigroup faces a tough new reality where big is not necessarily beautiful, The Business, 15 September 2002, via Factiva, accessed January 8, 2009.

[15] Ibid.

[16] 'Citigroup's confused chemistry,' *Euromoney on the Web*, January 1, 2000, http://www.euromoney.com, accessed June 2009.

[17] John Gapper, 'Time to give something back, Bob,' *Financial Times on the Web*, December 3, 2008, http://www.us.ft.com, accessed June 2009.

[18] Monica Langley, *Tearing Down the Walls* (New York, NY: Simon & Schuster, 2003) p. 279.

[19] Ibid, p. 279.

[20] Ibid, p. 302.

[21] Ibid, p. 349.

[22] Putnam Lovell Securities, 'Citigroup Inc.: A Truly Diverse Player,' Commercial Banking Report, June 2001.

[23] Putnam Lovell Securities, 'Citigroup Inc.: A Truly Diverse Player,' Commercial Banking Report, June 2001.

[24] Jon Birger; With Nick Pachetti, 'Leader Of The Pack; SANDY WEILL HAS BUILT CITIGROUP INTO A FINANCIAL SERVICES EMPIRE. IS HIS FORMULA FOR SUCCESS A BLUEPRINT FOR THE REST OF THE INDUSTRY?' *Money Magazine*, June 2002.

[25] David Reich-Hale, 'Trimming the Financial Supermarket Down to Size', American Banker Vol. 167, No. 9, January 14, 2002.

[26] Jon Birger; With Nick Pachetti, 'Leader Of The Pack; SANDY WEILL HAS BUILT CITIGROUP INTO A FINANCIAL SERVICES EMPIRE. IS HIS FORMULA FOR SUCCESS A BLUEPRINT FOR THE REST OF THE INDUSTRY?' *Money Magazine*, Vol. 31, Issue. 6, June 1 2002, via Factiva, accessed January 8, 2009.

[27] David Boraks, 'Citi Cites Cross-Sell Woe in Spinoff,' American Banker, Vol. 167, No. 243, December 20,2001, via Factiva, accessed January 8, 2009.

[28] David Reich-Hale, 'Trimming the Financial Supermarket Down to Size', American Banker Vol. 167, No. 9, January 14, 2002.

[29] Jon Birger; With Nick Pachetti, 'Leader Of The Pack; SANDY WEILL HAS BUILT CITIGROUP INTO A FINANCIAL SERVICES EMPIRE. IS HIS FORMULA FOR SUCCESS A BLUEPRINT FOR THE REST OF THE INDUSTRY?' *Money Magazine*, June 2002.

[30] Carol J. Loomis, 'CitiCorp: Sandy Weill's Monster,' *Fortune*, April 16, 2001, http://www.fortune.com, accessed June 2009.

[31] Ibid.

[32] Putnam Lovell Securities, 'Citigroup Inc.: A Truly Diverse Player,' Commercial Banking Report, June 2001.

[33] Carol J. Loomis, 'CitiCorp: Sandy Weill's Monster,' *Fortune*, April 16, 2001, http://www.fortune.com, accessed June 2009.

[34] Joseph N. DiStefano, 'Prince tears up Weil playbook, forfeits shareholder returns,' *Bloomberg.com*, October 4, 2007, http://www.bloomberg.com, accessed June 2009.

[35] Tearing Down the Walls, p. 258.

[36] Carol J. Loomis, 'CitiCorp: Sandy Weill's Monster,' *Fortune*, April 16, 2001, http://www.fortune.com, accessed June 2009.

[37] Ibid; Peter Truell, 'Salmon set to end group on arbitrage,' *New York Times on the Web*, July 7, 1998, http://www.nytimes.com, accessed June 2009; Justin Baer, 'Maheras, Citigroup's high roller, sheds caution in profit quest,' *Bloomberg.com*, September 5, 2006, http://www.blommberg.com, accessed June 2009.

[38] 'Citigroup has Highest Risk Board in the US According to The Corporate Library's new rating of Corporate Directors,' *PR Newswire*, June 9, 2003, via Factiva, accessed July 6, 2009.

[39] Eric Dash and Landon Thomas Jr., 'The Man in Citi's Hot Seat,' *New York Times*, Late Ed., p. 1, October 7, 2007, via Factiva, accessed February 6, 2009.

[40] Daniel Kadlec, Daren Fonda and Jyoti Thottam, 'Citi Gets A New Prince', *Time*, July 2003.

[41] 'Prince for a Weill – The Challenges Facing the New Boss of Citigroup,' *The Economist*, January 1, 2004, via Factiva, accessed July 20, 2009.

[42] Gary Silverman, 'The Citi state's next ruler – MAN IN THE NEWS – CHARLES PRINCE', *Financial Times*, July 19, 2003.

[43] Mara Der Hovanesian, 'Rewiring Chuck Prince; Citi's Chief Hasn't Just Stepped Out of Sandy Weill's Shadow – He's Stepped Out of His Own as He Strives to Make Himself into a Leader with Vision,' *Business Week*, February 20, 2006, via Factiva, accessed July 20, 2009.

[44] 'Forget Sympathy-Citigroup Needs a Clean Up,' EuroWeek, October 8, 2004, via Factiva, accessed July 20, 2009.

[45] Citigroup 2003 Annual Report, page 2.

[46] Greg Farrell, Gary Silverman, Francesco Guerrera, 'Universal Model Fades as Bank Goes Back to Basics,' *Financial Times*, London Ed2, January 14, 2009, p. 22, via Factiva, accessed February 5, 2009.

[47] Aaron Elstein, 'Citi switches to slow lane; Shuns acquisitions, gets outscored on branches; investors jump ship. Changing Banks,' Crain's New York Business, July 19, 2004.

[48] Marcia Vickers, Doris Burke, 'The Unlikely Revolutionary Critics are sniping and the stock is lagging, but Citigroup's Chuck Prince keeps charging ahead, blowing up business practices put in place by his famed mentor, Sandy Weill,' *Fortune*, March 2006.

[49] Peter Lee, 'What Citigroup needs to do next,' *Euromoney on the Web*, July 1, 2005, http://www.euromoney.com, accessed June 2009.

[50] Stephen Timewell, 'Bring Me Your Consumers, Your Unbanked Masses…' The Banker, June 1, 2006, via Factiva, accessed January 14, 2009.

[51] Andrew Bary, 'Citigroup is booming, but its shares aren't: Sandy Weill not pleased,' *Barron's,* March 17, 2004.

[52] Marcia Vickers, Doris Burke, 'The Unlikely Revolutionary Critics are sniping and the stock is lagging, but Citigroup's Chuck Prince keeps charging ahead, blowing up business practices put in place by his famed mentor, Sandy Weill,' *Fortune*, March 2006.

[53] Eric Dash and Julie Creswell, 'Citigroup saw no red flags even as it made bolder bets,' *New York Times on the Web*, November 23, 2008, http://www.nytimes.com, accessed June 2009.

[54] Eric Dash and Julie Creswell, 'Citigroup saw no red flags even as it made bolder bets,' *New York Times on the Web*, November 23, 2008, http://www.nytimes.com, accessed June 2009; Eric Dash and Louise Story, 'Rubin leaving Citigroup; Smith Barney for sale,' *New York Times on the Web*, January 10, 2009, http://www.nytimes.com, accessed June 2009.

[55] Ibid.

[56] Eric Dash and Julie Creswell, 'Citigroup saw no red flags even as it made bolder bets,' *New York Times on the Web*, November 23, 2008, http://www.nytimes.com, accessed June 2009.

[57] Peter Lee, 'What Citigroup needs to do next,' *Euromoney on the Web*, July 1, 2005, http://www.euromoney.com, accessed June 2009.

[58] 'Rewiring Chuck Prince,' *Business Week*, February 20, 2006 at http://www.businessweek.com/magazine/content/06_08/b3972105.ht, accessed March 12, 2009.

[59] Carol Loomis, 'Can Anyone Run Citigroup?' *Fortune*, May 5, 2008, p. 80, via Factiva, accessed March 6, 2009.

[60] 'Rewiring Chuck Prince,' *Business Week*, February 20, 2006 at http://www.businessweek.com/magazine/content/06_08/b3972105.ht, accessed March 12, 2009.

[61] Marcia Vickers and Doris Burke, 'The Unlikely Revolutionary,' *Fortune*, March 2006.

[62] Carol Loomis, 'Can Anyone Run Citigroup?' *Fortune*, May 5, 2008, p. 80, via Factiva, accessed March 6, 2009.

[63] Peter Thal Larsen and David Wighton, 'Under fire,' *Financial Times*, October 9, 2006.

[64] Mara Der Hovanesian and Maria Bartiromo, 'CLEANED UP BUT FALLING BEHIND,' *BusinessWeek*, October 2006.

[65] Peter Thal Larsen and David Wighton, 'Under fire,' *Financial Times*, October 9, 2006.

[66] Mara Der Hovanesian and Maria Bartiromo, 'CLEANED UP BUT FALLING BEHIND,' *BusinessWeek*, October 16, 2006.

[67] 'Citigroup Earnings Decline,' *Financial Mirror*, April 18, 2007, via Factiva, accessed March 11, 2009.

[68] Joseph N. DiStefano, 'Prince Tears up Weil playbook, forfeits shareholder returns,' *Bloomberg.com*, October 4, 2007, http://www.bloomberg.com, accessed June 2009.

[69] Eric Dash and Julie Creswell, 'Citigroup saw no red flags even as it made bolder bets,' *New York Times on the Web*, November 23, 2008, http://www.nytimes.com, accessed June 2009.

[70] Citigroup 2007 Annual Report, p. 5.

[71] Eric Dash, 'Is the Dance Over? Citigroup is Upbeat,' August 3, 2007, at http://www.nytimes.com/2007/08/03/business/03citi.html?_r=1&th&emc=th&oref=slogin, accessed February 6, 2009.

[72] Ibid.

[73] 'Citigroup's management window dressing,' *Euromoney on the Web*, January 1, 2007, http://www.euromoney.com, accessed June 2009; Joseph N. DiStefano, 'Prince tears up Weil playbook, forfeits shareholder returns,' *Bloomberg.com*, October 4, 2007, http://www.bloomberg.com, accessed June 2009.

[74] Eric Dash, 'Investors flee chief's fund at Citigroup,' *New York Times on the Web*, May 3, 2008, http://www.nytimes.com, accessed June 2009; Carolo J. Loomis, 'Can anyone run Citigroup,' *Fortune*, May 5, 2008, http://www.fortune.com, accessed June 2009.

[75] Duff McDonald, 'The hanger-on,' *New York Magazine*, October 15, 2007, http://www.nymag.com, accessed June 2009.

[76] Landon Thomas Jr. and Eric Dash, 'Big Shake-Up as Citigroup Combines Two Key Units,' *New York Times*, Late Ed., p. 1, October 12, 2007, via Factiva, accessed February 6, 2009.

[77] Jonathan Stempel and Dan Wilchins, 'Citigroup May Face $11 Billion Writeoff,' *Reuters News*, November 5, 2007, at http://www.reuters.com/article/topNews/idUSWEN234820071105, accessed July 9, 2009.

[78] Ibid.

[79] JPMorgan, *Citigroup Inc., SIV concerns overdone, current steps expandable*, October 25, 2007; 'Citigroup Inc. to Discuss Recent Announcements – Conference Call,' Thompson StreetEvents, November 5, 2007; 'Q3 2007 Citigroup Inc. Earnings Conference Call,' Thompson StreetEvents, October 15, 2007; Citigroup, 2007 Q3 10Q (New York: Citigroup. 2007).

[80] Carol Loomis, 'Can Anyone Run Citigroup?' *Fortune*, May 5, 2008, p. 80, via Factiva, accessed March 6, 2009.

[81] Ibid.

[82] Christian Plumb and Dan Wilchins, 'Citi to take $49 bln in SIVs into balance sheet,' *Reuters*, December 13, 2007, http://www.reuters.com, accessed June 2009; 'Citigroup makes $49bn SIV rescue,' BBC News on the Web, December 14, 2007, http://www.bbc.co.uk, accessed June 2009.

[83] Greg Morcroft & Alistair Barr, 'Citi names Pandit CEO; Bischoff is chairman,' MarketWatch, December 11, 2007.

[84] Ibid.

[85] Carol Loomis, 'Can Anyone Run Citigroup?' *Fortune*, May 5, 2008, p. 80, via Factiva, accessed March 6, 2009.

[86] Ibid.

[87] Shawn Tully, 'Say Goodbye To the Big Citi,' *Fortune*, January 15, 2009, http://money.cnn.com/2009/01/14/magazines/fortune/investing/citi_future.fortune/index.htm.

[88] Carol Loomis, 'Can Anyone Run Citigroup?' *Fortune*, May 5, 2008, p. 80, via Factiva, accessed March 6, 2009.

[89] Ibid.

[90] Francesco Guerrera, 'Flawed conception,' *Financial Times*, Asia Ed1, January 17, 2009, p. 8, via Factiva, accessed February 5, 2009.

[91] Eric Dash and Andrew Sorkin, 'Citigroup buys bank operations of Wachovia,' *New York Times on the Web*, September 30, 2008, htpp://www.nytimes.com, accessed June 2009; David Mildenberg and Bradley Keoun, 'Wells Farfo's $12 billion bid beats Citi to Wachovia,' *Bloomberg.com*, October 10, 2008, htpp://www.bloomberg.com, accessed June 2009.

[92] Mara Der Hovanesian, 'Citigroup's uneasy victory,' *BusinessWeek.com*, November 25, 2008, accessed via Factiva, June 2009.

[93] 'Citigroup CEO Pandit gets emergency help,' *Reuters*, November 24, 2008.

[94] David Enrich, 'Rubin Departs Citi on a Low Note,' *The Wall Street Journal*, January 10, 2009.

[95] Chicago Tribune Wire Reports, 'Richard Parsons, former Time Warner CEO, to replace Win Bischoff as chairman of Citigroup,' January 21, 2009.

[96] 'Citigroup Ready to Shrink Itself by a Third,' Wall Street Journal Online, January 14, 2009.

[97] Madlen Reed and Sara Lepro, 'Citigroup Breaks Up: Financial Supermarket Model Dead,' *AP*, January 14, 2009.

[98] Diana Golobay, 'Citigroup Confirms Brokerage Spinoff Plans', HousingWire, January 13, 2009.

[99] Paul Tharp, 'CITI'S PANDIT VOWS TO TAKE $1 SALARY AND NO BONUS,' *New York Post*, February 12, 2009.

[100] Citigroup, First Quarter 2009 Earnings Review, April 17, 2009.

[101] Stephan Labaton, 'Treasury to set top pay at 7 ailing firms,' *New York Times on the Web*, June 10, 2009, http://www.nytimes.com, accessed June 2009.

[102] 'Administrative Actions on Citibank, N.A., Japan Branch,' Financial Services Agency, Government of Japan, September 17, 2004 (provisional translation by the FSA).

Index